D1130063

UNEMPLOYMENT
OLD AGE AND SOCIAL INSURANCE

HEARINGS

BEFORE A

SUBCOMMITTEE OF THE
COMMITTEE ON LABOR
HOUSE OF REPRESENTATIVES

SEVENTY-FOURTH CONGRESS

FIRST SESSION

ON

H. R. 2827

A BILL TO PROVIDE FOR THE ESTABLISHMENT
OF UNEMPLOYMENT, OLD AGE AND SOCIAL
INSURANCE AND FOR OTHER PURPOSES;

H. R. 2859

A BILL TO PROVIDE FOR THE ESTABLISHMENT OF
UNEMPLOYMENT AND SOCIAL INSURANCE
AND FOR OTHER PURPOSES;

H. R. 185

A BILL TO PROVIDE FOR THE ESTABLISHMENT OF
A SYSTEM OF UNEMPLOYMENT INSURANCE
AND FOR OTHER PURPOSES; AND

H. R. 10

A BILL TO PROVIDE FOR THE ESTABLISHMENT OF
UNEMPLOYMENT AND SOCIAL INSURANCE
AND FOR OTHER PURPOSES

FEBRUARY 4, 5, 6, 7, 8, 11, 12, 13, 14, and 15, 1935

INDEXED

UNITED STATES
GOVERNMENT PRINTING OFFICE
WASHINGTON : 1935

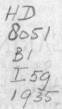

COMMITTEE ON LABOR

HOUSE OF REPRESENTATIVES

SEVENTY-FOURTH CONGRESS, FIRST SESSION

WILLIAM P. CONNERY, Jr., Massachusetts, *Chairman*

MARY T. NORTON, New Jersey
ROBERT RAMSPECK, Georgia
GLENN GRISWOLD, Indiana
KENT E. KELLER, Illinois
MATTHEW A. DUNN, Pennsylvania
REUBEN T. WOOD, Missouri
JENNINGS RANDOLPH, West Virginia
JOHN LESINSKI, Michigan
JOE H. EAGLE, Texas
CHARLES V. TRUAX, Ohio
MARCELLUS H. EVANS, New York
JAMES H. GILDEA, Pennsylvania
AUBERT C. DUNN, Mississippi
ERNEST LUNDEEN, Minnesota
GEORGE J. SCHNEIDER, Wisconsin

RICHARD J. WELCH, California
FRED A. HARTLEY, Jr., New Jersey
W. P. LAMBERTSON, Kansas
CLIFFORD R. HOPE, Kansas
VITO MARCANTONIO, New York

MARY B. CRONIN, *Clerk*

SUBCOMMITTEE

MATTHEW A. DUNN, Pennsylvania, *Chairman*

REUBEN T. WOOD, Missouri
JOHN LESINSKI, Michigan
ERNEST LUNDEEN, Minnesota
GEORGE J. SCHNEIDER, Wisconsin

RICHARD J. WELCH, California
FRED A. HARTLEY, Jr., New Jersey

II

CONTENTS

ECONOMISTS REPRESENTED

FOREWORD

This record of the hearings on the workers' unemployment, old-age, and social insurance bill (H. R. 2827) introduced by Congressman Lundeen, of Minnesota, heard before the subcommittee on unemployment, old-age, and social insurance of the Committee on Labor of the House of Representatives, contains the testimony of 80 witnesses. These witnesses came from 14 different States and the District of Columbia. Among them were represented a wide variety of occupational groups, experts, organizations, and such representatives as may be said to speak for the masses of the American people. There were 12 representatives of American Federation of Labor locals who, in most instances, had been delegated by district committees of American Federation of Labor local unions, in some cases representing a hundred or more locals in their vicinity. Farmers' organizations, veterans' groups, unemployed councils and leagues, youth organizations, transient workers, Negro organizations, fraternal societies, a small home and land owners' federation were all represented by spokesmen before the Labor Subcommittee.

The wide-spread effects of the depression on all groups of workers was made emphatic by the testimony of professional workers representing, broadly, the entire range of the professions. Testimony was heard from such professional workers as writers, teachers, physicians, architects, engineers, chemists, technicians, dentists, and others.

Expert testimony which was heard before the subcommittee may be said to have encompassed the major economic questions confronting the American people with reference to unemployment and its consequent destitution, as well as the social problems similarly involved.

Seven noted economists from universities, foundations, and related institutions testified on the economic problems involved in H. R. 2827. Mary van Kleeck of the Russell Sage Foundation, New York City, presented the general scope of the problem involved in unemployment and social insurance. Dr. Joseph Gillman of the College of the City of New York (1) estimated the extent of unemployment at the present time; (2) suggested methods of raising funds to cover the costs involved in carrying out the provisions of H. R. 2827; (3) estimated the cost of the various aspects of social insurance embraced by this bill. Maxwell Stewart, economist and associate editor of the Nation, examined the problem of what "Recovery" has meant to the working class. Mildred Fairchild, associate professor of social economy at Bryn Mawr College, dealt with women in industry and unemployment. Dorothy Douglas, professor of economics at Smith College, showed the inadequacy of non-Federal plans for insurance as revealed by similar attempts abroad, particularly in England and Germany. Broadus Mitchell, professor of economics at Johns Hopkins University, and Horace B. Davis, economist and author of studies of labor conditions, examined economic problems in general and the need for genuine unemployment and social insurance. Harry Lurie, social worker and chairman of the committee to formulate a national social-welfare program of the American Association of Social Workers, showed the inadequacy of present relief measures and the need for such an insurance measure as H. R. 2827. Leo Linder, New York lawyer and member of the International Juridical Association, examined at considerable length and in exhaustive fashion, the constitutionality of H. R. 2827. Reuben Young, physician, revealed the need for maternity insurance, such as is provided by this bill. T. Arnold Hill, social worker and executive secretary of the National Urban League, testified on conditions prevailing among the Negro people.

It will be clearly seen that this record contains a comprehensive survey and picture of the problems facing the people of our country and of the way in which these problems can be met. The material presented here is substantial and comprehensive and constitutes an adequate basis for action by the Congress.

MATTHEW A. DUNN of Pennsylvania,
Chairman Subcommittee on Unemployment, Old-Age,
and Social Insurance of the Committee on Labor.

MARCH 5, 1935.

UNEMPLOYMENT, OLD AGE, AND SOCIAL INSURANCE

MONDAY, FEBRUARY 4, 1935

House of Representatives,
Subcommittee of the Committee on Labor,
Washington, D. C.

The subcommittee met at 10 o'clock a. m., in the caucus room, House Office Building, Hon. Matthew A. Dunn of Pennsylvania (chairman) presiding.

Mr. Dunn. The subcommittee will please come to order. We have before us for consideration at this time H. R. 2827, known as "The Workers' Unemployment, Old Age, and Social Insurance Act", introduced in the House of Representatives, January 3, 1935, by Congressman Ernest Lundeen.

(H. R. 2827 is as follows:)

[H. R. 2827, Seventy-fourth Cong., First Sess.]

A BILL To provide for the establishment of unemployment, old age, and social insurance, and for other purposes

Be it enacted by the Senate and House of Representatives of the United States of America in Congress assembled, That this Act shall be known by the title "The Workers' Unemployment, Old Age, and Social Insurance Act."

SEC. 2. The Secretary of Labor is hereby authorized and directed to provide for the immediate establishment of a system of unemployment insurance for the purpose of providing compensation for all workers and farmers above eighteen years of age, unemployed through no fault of their own. Such compensation shall be equal to average local wages, but shall in no case be less than $10 per week plus $3 for each dependent. Workers willing and able to do full-time work but unable to secure full-time employment shall be entitled to receive the difference between their earnings and the average local wages for full-time employment. The minimum compensation guaranteed by this Act shall be increased in conformity with rises in the cost of living. Such unemployment insurance shall be administered and controlled, and the minimum compensation shall be adjusted by workers and farmers under rules and regulations which shall be prescribed by the Secretary of Labor in conformity with the purposes and provisions of this Act through unemployment insurance commissions directly elected by members of workers' and farmers' organizations.

SEC. 3. The Secretary of Labor is hereby further authorized and directed to provide for the immediate establishment of other forms of social insurance for the purpose of providing compensation for all workers and farmers who are unable to work because of sickness, old age, maternity, industrial injury, or any other disability. Such compensation shall be the same as provided by section 2 of this Act for unemployment insurance and shall be administered in like manner. Compensation for disability because of maternity shall be paid to women during the period of eight weeks previous and eight weeks following childbirth.

SEC. 4. All moneys necessary to pay compensation guaranteed by this Act and the cost of establishing and maintaining the administration of this Act shall be paid by the Government of the United States. All such moneys are hereby appropriated out of all funds in the Treasury of the United States not

1

otherwise appropriated. Further taxation necessary to provide funds for the purposes of this Act shall be levied on inheritances, gifts, and individual and corporation incomes of $5,000 a year and over. The benefits of this Act shall be extended to workers, whether they be industrial, agricultural, domestic, office, or professional workers, and to farmers, without discrimination because of age, sex, race, color, religious or political opinion or affiliation. No worker or farmer shall be disqualified from receiving the compensation guaranteed by this Act because of past participation in strikes, or refusal to work in place of strikers, or at less than average local or trade-union wages, or under unsafe or unsanitary conditions, or where hours are longer than the prevailing union standards of a particular trade or locality, or at an unreasonable distance from home.

The committee also had under consideration the following bills:

[H. R. 10, Seventy-fourth Cong., First sess.]

A BILL To provide for the establishment of unemployment and social insurance, and for other purposes

Be it enacted by the Senate and House of Representatives of the United States of America in Congress assembled, That this Act shall be known by the title "The Worker's Unemployment and Social Insurance Act."

SEC. 2. The Secretary of Labor is hereby authorized and directed to provide for the immediate establishment of a system of unemployment and social insurance for the purpose of providing insurance for all workers and farmers unemployed through no fault of their own in amounts equal to average local wages. Such insurance shall be administered by workers and farmers and controlled by them under rules and regulations prescribed by the Secretary of Labor in conformity with the purposes and provisions of this Act, through unemployment insurance commissions composed of the rank-and-file members of workers' and farmers' organizations. Funds for such insurance shall hereafter be provided at the expense of the Government and of employers, and it is the sense of Congress that funds to be raised by the Government shall be secured by taxing inheritance and gifts, and by taxing individual and corporation incomes of $5,000 per year and over. No tax or contribution in any form shall be levied on workers for the purposes of this Act. In no case shall the unemployment insurance be less than $10 per week plus $3 for each dependent.

SEC. 3. The Secretary of Labor is further authorized and directed to provide for the establishment of other forms of social insurance in like amounts and governed by the conditions set forth in section 1 of this Act for the purpose of paying workers and farmers insurance for loss of wages because of part-time work, sickness, accident, old age, or maternity.

SEC. 4. The benefits of this Act shall be extended to workers and farmers without discrimination because of age, sex, race, or color, religious or political opinion, or affiliation, whether they be industrial, agricultural, domestic, or professional workers, for all time lost. No worker shall be disqualified for the benefits of this Act because of refusal to work in place of strikers, at less than normal or trade-union rates, under unsafe or unsanitary conditions, or where hours are longer than the prevailing union standards at the particular trade and locality, or at any unreasonable distance from home.

[H. R. 185, Seventy-fourth Cong., First sess.]

A BILL To provide for the establishment of a system of unemployment insurance, and for other purposes

Be it enacted by the Senate and House of Representatives of the United States of America in Congress assembled, That this Act may be cited as the "Workers' Unemployment Insurance Act."

SEC. 2. The Secretary of Labor is hereby authorized and directed to provide for the immediate establishment of a system of unemployment insurance for the purpose of providing insurance for all workers unemployed through no fault of their own in amounts equal to 50 per centum of average local wages: Provided, That such amounts shall not exceed $15 per week, and no payment shall be made until a worker has been unemployed for a period of four weeks. Such administration shall be administered and controlled by workers under rules and regulations prescribed by the Secretary of Labor in conformity with the purposes and provisions of this Act, through unemployment insurance committees composed of the rank-and-file members of workers' organizations.

SEC. 3. Reserve funds for the payment of such insurance shall be set aside by each employer and shall be obtained (1) through employees' contributions of 1 per centum of their total salary, and (2) through employers' contributions of 2 per centum of their total pay roll, but employees' contributions shall cease when the total amount contributed by them shall equal $100 per eligible employee.

SEC. 4. The benefits of this Act shall be extended to employees of more than six months' service, without discrimination because of age, sex, race, or color, religious or political opinion or affiliation, whether they be industrial or professional workers, for all time lost, including part-time workers, except that benefits to such workers shall be governed by the difference, if any, between their actual earnings and 50 per centum of their average earnings when working full time.

SEC. 5. The term "employer" means any person, partnership, association, corporation, or the legal representative, trustee in bankruptcy, receiver, or trustee thereof, or the legal representative of a deceased person, who or whose agent or predecessor in interest has, within each twenty or more calendar weeks in the taxable year, employed at least ten persons entitled to the benefits of this Act; except that the term "employer" shall not include the Federal Government, the governments of the several States, municipal corporations, or other governmental instrumentalities. The term "employee" means any employed person in an industry or profession who is covered by a State law and/or may become eligible for the benefits of this Act.

SEC. 6. The benefits provided under this Act shall be extended to an eligible employee for not more than thirteen full weeks in any one calendar year.

SEC. 7. The reserve funds created by this Act may be invested in short-term Government or municipal bonds in such manner as the Secretary of Labor may by regulations prescribe. Employees and employers shall be permitted to claim exemption from taxation of the full amount of their contributions to the fund. The disposition of any balance in the reserve fund credited to an employee upon cessation of his employment shall be (1) paid to the employee, (2) paid to his duly appointed beneficiary, or (3) transferred to reserve fund of another employer, such disposition to be optional with the employee.

SEC. 8. The benefits of this Act shall not become payable until it has been in operation two years.

SEC. 9. The employer's liability, as created by this Act, shall be limited to the amount of his reserve fund, and benefits shall cease when such fund is exhausted and until additional contributions have been made.

SEC. 10. Every employer affected by this Act shall make a statement under oath within one month after the close of the year with respect to total amounts contributed to such unemployment insurance fund and disposition of same. Such statement shall be sent to the Secretary of Labor and shall contain such information and be made in such manner as the Secretary of Labor may by regulations prescribe.

SEC. 11. No worker shall be disqualified for the benefits of this Act because of refusal to work in place of strikers, or under unsafe or unsanitary conditions, but the benefits of the Act shall not extend to workers who refuse to accept bona fide employment when offered in good faith.

[H. R. 2859, Seventy-fourth Cong., First sess.]

A BILL To provide for the establishment of unemployment and social insurance, and for other purposes

Be it enacted by the Senate and House of Representatives of the United States of America in Congress assembled, That this Act shall be known by the title "The Workers' Unemployment and Social Insurance Act."

SEC. 2. The Secretary of Labor is hereby authorized and directed to provide for the immediate establishment of a system of unemployment and social insurance for the purpose of providing insurance for all workers unemployed through no fault of their own. Such insurance shall be administered by workers controlled by them under rules and regulations prescribed by the Secretary of Labor in conformity with the purposes and provisions of this Act, through unemployment insurance commissions composed of the rank and file members of workers' organizations. Funds for such insurance shall hereafter be provided at the expense of the Government and of employers, and it is the sense of Congress that funds to be raised by the Government shall be secured by taxing inheritance and gifts, and by taxing individual and corporation incomes of $5,000 per year and over.

SEC. 3. The Secretary of Labor is further authorized and directed to provide for the establishment of other forms of social insurance in like amounts and governed by the conditions set forth in section 1 of this Act for the purpose of paying workers insurance for loss of wages because of part-time work, sickness, accident, old age, or maternity.

SEC. 4. The benefits of this Act shall be extended to workers without discrimination because of age, sex, race, or color, religious or political opinion, or affiliation, whether they be industrial, agricultural, domestic, or professional workers, for all time lost. No worker shall be disqualified for the benefits of this Act because of refusal to work in place of strikers, at less than normal or trade-union rates, under unsafe or unsanitary conditions, or where hours are longer than the prevailing union standards at the particular trade and locality, or at any unreasonable distance from home.

Mr. DUNN. There have also been referred to this subcommittee three other bills of similar nature, H. R. 2859, H. R. 10, and H. R. 185. While the requests for appearance before us thus far have been only with reference to H. R. 2827, I desire to state on behalf of the subcommittee that we shall be prepared to hear testimony also in connection with the other three bills mentioned, and testimony touching this general subject matter.

STATEMENT OF ERNEST LUNDEEN

Mr. LUNDEEN. Mr. Chairman, at the opening of the hearings, I would like to make a brief statement as to the purpose and plan of this bill.

These are times that call for vision, planning, and statesmanship. " Where there is no vision, the people perish." The times call for candor and plain speaking.

I might discuss in these brief minutes the blunders that plunged us onward into this great disaster—and I protested in Congress and on the public platform for years, every un-American and foreign-minded step we took into costly foreign investments and foreign entanglements.

We now have a permanent army of unemployed somewhere between five and ten million American citizens willing to work.

At the present time, this army exceeds 10 million, but under the most hopeful predictions for the future, we will still have a permanent army of about 5 million unemployed. We can no longer hope that some miracle will be performed which will suddenly solve our problems and dispel our fears. Something more substantial than that must be in the picture.

American men and women cannot do their best and are not at their best when they face the fear of old age without financial security which rightfully belongs to them, after years of toil and struggle to build up this mighty America of ours. They must be given security and a feeling of confidence in the future. We must lift the terrible pall of fear which grips at the hearts of millions.

PART-TIME WORKERS MUST BE PROTECTED

When we turn to the problem of unemployment, we must not forget part-time employment. We hear a great deal of unemployment insurance, but we never hear about part-time employment insurance. An American citizen working 1 day a week and out of work the balance of the week, or working a few days or a week per month cannot bring sufficient food and shelter to his family. He must be protected along with the millions of wholly unemployed.

SOCIAL INSURANCE A NATIONAL PROBLEM

We need thorough-going planning. Piecemeal, inadequate legislation only brings us into trouble and casts doubt upon the methods and means adopted—injuring the vital, underlying principles of recovery. American business should remember, and professional men should remember, that every dollar thrown into unemployment insurance, part-time employment insurance, and old age pensions will immediately seek its level in the channels of business, stimulating American trade. This money will immediately flow into the channels of trade, because the future of our people is secure, and the money will be expended in the absolute confidence that the morrow is safe, and that the home and the fireside is safe.

We are all tremendously interested in health problems. Already millions of children are receiving dental and medical inspection in our schools; our great hospitals and a corps of health workers throughout America are efficient and willing to serve their fellow men. But here again we need better planning, more thought to the methods and means of preventing disease and epidemics, and we certainly must make health service available to those who are unable to afford that service; and if there are those among us who are selfish in that matter, they must realize that any citizen suffering from disease is a source of contagion and danger to us all. Health service is a matter of national concern for our entire American people.

Recently I have been gathering the most appalling statistics of accidents, industrial and automobile. This unlimited, increasing slaughter must be stopped. Here is a field for planning sound, adequate legislation.

Numerous American states have already enacted laws giving maternity and mothers' pension benefits. Many States and business firms have entered upon old age pensions and there has been some attempt to move along unemployment insurance lines. But, my fellow-citizens, these are national problems. They cannot be solved by the State of Minnesota, the State of New York, or the State of California. They must be solved by the American people, the entire American Nation.

States can do a certain amount of experimenting which is very valuable. Many States like Wisconsin, North Dakota, and Minnesota have given us great governmental laboratories, and we have learned valuable lessons from them.

We must move forward along new lines. There are those who are greatly agitated about a new deal and who indulge in throwing stones at anything that would change the old order. Calling names will not accomplish anything. Constructive and progressive legislation is needed. If our old parties cannot meet the situation, they will be thrown aside like old and outworn garments. That has happened before in our history and it may happen again.

ADHERE TO AMERICAN PRINCIPLES

There is no necessity to strike down any great principles that have been laid down in our Declaration of Independence and in our Constitution. There is no necessity for hauling down the American flag and flying any other banner in our American skies. If we adhere to the fundamental principles laid down by Washington, Jefferson, Jackson, and Lincoln, and work along the lines laid down by our Revolutionary fathers and those who builded and saved the Nation, there is no limit to the progress we can make. Our Constitution is flexible, and our form of government is flexible, and our Supreme Court has shown that it is willing to adjust itself to the times, as shown in the Minnesota moratorium decision on mortgage foreclosures, recognizing then as that great Court does, our State and National emergencies.

The complacent, the self-satisfied, the smug and reactionary who refuse to move, would sit here in the midst of destitution and poverty, surrounded with an ocean of plenty—a spectacle of misery and lack of vision and planning to the outside world. There is no necessity for all this misery. America has solved every problem we have ever faced in all our history. We have never failed, and we are not going to fail now!

To those who say, " Where is the money coming from? " I say, the reports of our National Treasury show every bond issue many times oversubscribed. Billionaire fortunes exist, and millionaire salaries are still being paid in America today.

For years we have thrown huge sums into the laps of kings and emperors of Europe, and those of us who protested were brushed aside. I think we will somewhat delay our future expeditions and ventures to save the world. " He who will not first take care of his own is worse than an infidel."

When we return to the Americanism of Washington, Jefferson, Jackson, and Lincoln, we will conserve our immense financial reservoirs, and with vision, store food and finances for the evil day. Remember Joseph and the 7 fat years and the 7 lean years.

From now on, we are going to be just plain Americans. We have learned our lesson. We have drained the bitter cup. From now on, we have no time for those who want Uncle Sam to change to a European Santa Claus. From now on we are looking to red-blooded Americans who think in terms of America first.

SOCIAL SECURITY MEANS GOVERNMENT SECURITY

A crusading spirit is growing in America, and men and women are willing to sacrifice time, energy, and money for intelligent national planning. Many good citizens fear that some great storm will sweep over our country and shatter our National Constitution and the principles laid down in the Declaration of Independence, and tear the American flag out of our skies. If you want to make sure that this will not happen, write legislation along social-insurance lines, so that every man shall be safe and secure in his home and in his bread. For every citizen who desires to labor has an inalienable right to the bread and fireside which his wage will earn for him. When great armies of unemployed march in America, intelligent planning will put these men and women to work upon great national projects.

HISTORY OF LUNDEEN BILL

You will remember that during the Seventy-third Congress, March 4, 1933, to January 3, 1935, I introduced on February 2, 1934, an unemployment, old-age pension, and social insurance bill, H. R. 7598. This bill received the endorsement of a number of State federations of labor, thousands of labor unions and fraternal and professional organizations. It had more endorsements than any other bill that came before the Seventy-third Congress.

The Labor Committee to which the bill was referred did not report the bill out for consideration on the floor of the House. The chairman of the Labor Committee, Mr. William P. Connery of Massachusetts, a very able, liberal, and progressive Democrat, and the committee members, held hearings, however, and citizens appeared before the committee and urged their views in favor of unemployment insurance, old-age pensions, and social insurance in general. Their statements appear in the committee hearings of the House Labor Committee of the Seventy-third Congress.

After 30 days during which the Labor Committee failed to report the bill out, I filed a motion on the first possible day, to withdraw the bill from the committee and place it on the Speaker's desk for consideration. That motion received the signatures of some 30 Congressmen.

That is a general résumé of what happened to the most widely discussed social insurance bill of the Seventy-third Congress. The bill was generally denominated radical and bitterly opposed by conservatives.

Just before adjournment of the Seventy-third Congress, the President sent a message stating that although nothing had been done about social insurance in the Seventy-third Congress, action would be taken in the Seventy-fourth Congress. We who were out in front battling for social insurance, felt that something had been accomplished since the President took notice of the situation. In the interim, commissions were appointed by the President and by various organizations and a great deal of work was done along these lines.

Now the Congress is blossoming out with scores of social insurance bills, from the Townsend plan down to the most obscure bill. The Lundeen Bill, once considered radical, now represents the golden mean between the extreme measures that have since been proposed, and the meagre allowances proposed by the administration plan. I have again introducd the same social insurance measure that I introduced in the last session under the title now of H. R. 2827.

CHAIRMAN CONNERY ENDORSES LUNDEEN BILL

A most splendid thing happened on January 7, 1935, when a large delegation of leather workers and shoe workers appeared in conference with Chairman Connery of the Labor Committee and secured his endorsement of the Ernest Lundeen Social Insurance Bill, H. R. 2827. Chairman Connery endorsed the bill in a letter to Mr. Benjamin E. Waite, of the Lynn Sponsoring Committee for unemployment and social insurance at Lynn, Mass. Congressman Connery's letter states:

DEAR MR. WAITE: In response to your inquiry as to whether I will support H. R. 2827, Seventy-fourth Congress (a bill providing for the establishment of unemployment, old age, and social insurance, and for other purposes), introduced by Mr. Lundeen of Minnesota, may I say that I will be glad to call hearings on this bill which has been referred to the Committee on Labor, and I will be glad to support this bill in committee and on the floor of the House.

With all personal good wishes, I am,
Sincerely yours,

WM. P. CONNERY.

This certainly was a body blow to the opposition to our bill. The strongest and most prominent Democratic labor leader in Congress had endorsed the Lundeen Bill, H. R. 2827, and a prominent statement of that endorsement appeared in the Washington Post, a leading newspaper in Washington, D. C. on the morning of January 8, 1935. Headlines in this paper stated: "Lundeen Bill gets support of Labor Committee head in House."

The Post's article stated in part: Representative William P. Connery, chairman of the House Labor Committee, yesterday announced he would support the Lundeen Unemployment and Social Insurance Bill advocated by labor and professional groups which last evening ended a 3-day Congress at the Washington Auditorium.

An editorial in The Nation for January 16, 1935, says with reference to the Lundeen Bill,

Pressure for its adoption on the part of labor and professional groups should materially strengthen the hands of those seeking to liberalize the Administration's program.

TERMS OF WORKERS' BILL

This bill is generally referred to as the Lundeen Workers' Unemployment, Old Age, and Social Insurance Bill, and provides that unemployed, part-time employed, aged persons, and persons unable to work because of sickness, accident, or maternity, shall be paid a sum equal to the difference between their earnings and the average local wage in the community in which they reside, the average local wage to be determined by the Labor Department at Washnigton, a department which has available all statistics and information necessary to determine the average local wage. There may be communities in the United States where the standard of living is very low and where the average local wage would be inadequate to take care of the unemployed and old-age pensioners. For that reason, the Lundeen Bill provides a minimum of $10 per week for each person and $3 per week for each dependent. That is, however, only the minimum and not the maximum, although some newspapers have reported this figure as the maximum. The maximum is the average local wage of the community in which the person resides, and $10 per week for each person with $3 per week for each dependent is the minimum amount.

The bill goes into effect at once, without any waiting period, and we do not wait a year or two or three to build up a reserve because the amount is paid out of the Federal treasury by means of taxation levied upon inheritances, private, and corporation incomes above five thousand and gift taxes, and other funds available in the Federal treasury.

This bill has been generally endorsed by numerous organizations in the State of Minnesota and throughout the Nation, and endorsements are rolling into Washington every day in ever-increasing numbers. We have received thousands upon thousands of post cards and letters endorsing H. R. 7598, and the flood of endorsements for H. R. 2827 is just beginning.

LUNDEEN BILL APPROVED BY LABOR

The thing that pleases me about this bill is that it is generally accepted by labor throughout the country. I have the honor to represent the greatest labor district in the State of Minnesota and in the Northwest—the third congressional district—and I am exceedingly interested in the viewpoint of labor in these matters.

No plan for social security up to the present time which has been advanced by the administration, recognizes that human beings who are unemployed, must be fed; must be taken care of. In others words, the proposed administration measure is discriminatory. It eliminates professional workers; it eliminates white-collared workers; it proposes an administration which would make possible denying certain groups in any community the benefits of social security.

If this panic can do nothing more at this stage, than to show that all human beings who are willing to work must be considered as a part of the picture—it has served a significant purpose. For the first time in America's history, the white-collared worker is willing to stand with the man in overalls and demand recognition with him. Hunger has united the farm worker, the industrial worker, and the office worker.

This measure will overcome the great menace which confronts our Nation—uprisings, revolts—and in that spirit I appeal to you, my colleagues, to help save our country by serving it. The hungry man has nothing to lose. His wife and family are starving.

The man and woman who have served their country honestly and faithfully in peace time and in war time are the ones who are made to bear the brunt of the break-down, and that constitutes the soul and the spirit of America.

LABOR OPPOSES ADMINISTRATION BILL

Labor is not satisfied with the administration's social security program now being heard before the Ways and Means Committee and the Senate Finance Committee, and by the way, the administration bill, in my opinion, should have been referred to the labor committee and hearings held by this committee. In support of my statement that labor is not satisfied with the administration bill, I offer the statement of Wm. Green, president of the American Federation of Labor, the largest and most powerful labor organization in the Western Hemisphere. The president of this large organization states positively that the administration program is pitiably and utterly inadequate and will not solve the problem. Mr. Green's statement is quoted in part, and comments are made on it in Labor, Washington, D. C., for February 5, 1935. I ask permission to have inserted at this point, in the record of the hearings, excerpts from the paper Labor of February 5, 1935, containing the statement of Wm. Green, president of the American Federation of Labor, on the administration's social security program, and comments thereon.

Mr. DUNN. If there is no objection, your request will be granted.

(The statement submitted by Mr. Lundeen is as follows:)

LABOR STATES POSITION ON SOCIAL SECURITY; "F. D.'s" PLAN TOO MODEST, DECLARES GREEN

A. F. L. CHIEFTAIN CALLS ON ADMINISTRATION TO TAKE BOLD STAND; SAYS TRAIL IS TOO WELL BLAZED TO JUSTIFY HALTING AND TIMID EXPERIMENTATION

By Charles M. Kelley

Organized labor is far from being satisfied with President Roosevelt's social security program. It regards it as halting and timid, and some of its provisions as containing grave danger to the labor movement.

This was made clear this week when President William Green of the American Federation of Labor sharply criticized the Wagner-Lewis bill, which embodies the administration's recommendations, before the Senate Finance Committee.

The labor chieftain pleaded with Congress to take a bold stand and follow a trail well blazed by pioneers in social security.

The labor chieftain emphasized at the outset that he was heartily in favor of action by Congress, his contention being that the question has been too long neglected. This country, he pointed out, is the last great industrial nation to give serious consideration to unemployment insurance and assistance to the aged, and he said he regretted that it was proposed to take a " hesitant, faltering step."

MILLIONS LIVE IN FEAR

" The lives of millions of our people ", the committee was told, " are governed by fear of losing their jobs. Economic security is our greatest national problem. Our belief that it will take care of itself has been rudely shattered by the bitter experiences of the past 5 years."

This point was driven home with figures showing that more than 11,000,000 people are still looking for work, and that more than 19,000,000 are dependent on Uncle Sam's bread. Yet, Green contended, the depression has merely aggravated a situation that is always present, in proof of which he cited the fact that in 1928 more than one-third of the total population was in poverty— millions existing below the barest subsistence level.

UNEMPLOYMENT CHRONIC

A fact that has been lost sight of, Green said, is that unemployment is by no means confined to periods of depression. For example, he recalled that in 1923—when unemployment was at its lowest point—more than 1,500,000 wage earners were jobless.

These appalling statistics were recited by the labor chieftain to show the need of adequate job insurance and old age pensions, and he stressed the danger of approving plans that might reduce a large part of the people to a condition of chronic beggary.

" The primary object of unemployment insurance," Green said, " is to secure the worker and his family against privation and suffering and to help them preserve some standard of health and decency.

" But the program of unemployment insurance we are considering now will not solve the problems."

Conceding that no system could be devised that would be a " cure-all," nevertheless, Green insisted, the right kind of a program would be a great help in bringing about a more equitable distribution of income. He added:

" We should seek to obtain the best possible plan in order to save ourselves the necessity of making sweeping changes later. It is wise now to initiate the type of plan which we wish to continue. There is a world of experience to guide us in the right direction."

LABOR REPRESENTATION NEEDED

Green insisted that one of the things that should be done to inspire confidence among workers is to include labor representation on the Social Insurance Board which is to have charge of security plans. He was amazed, he said, that Congress should be asked to establish an agency dealing with the lives of wage earners without giving them a voice in its administration.

While the committee listened attentively, the labor spokesman dealt in forceful manner with the outstanding provisions of the job insurance proposal.

He asserted that labor was in violent disagreement with the recommendation to establish State systems.

FAVORS FEDERAL SUBSIDIES

" Labor," he declared, " favors a national unemployment insurance measure, because it would establish fair and equalized conditions in so far as costs and benefits are concerned. It would establish a uniformity of standards which could be achieved in no other way."

If constitutional objections are raised to a national system, Green asserted, they could be successfully met through Federal subsidies. This plan, he emphasized, could readily be converted into a national system when constitutional barriers are later removed.

"Our unemployment problem is not a state problem," Green said. "Industries extend beyond State lines, reaching across whole sections of the country, and even across the entire continent.

"There is no reason why we should go through a long period of experimentation in the States. We have the experience of other countries and the advice of our own experts to guide us. We do not want 48 different types of insurance.

WILL BREED INJUSTICES

"Wide variations in types of fund, in length of waiting period, in amount of benefits and length of time during which payments are made would be highly objectionable to labor and disastrous to the President's professed aims.

"These variations will give rise to great inequalities and injustices. Uniform standards can be established only by the Federal Government. The proposed bill fails to establish any standards whatever for State laws. It does not prohibit compulsory employee contributions, leaving the State free to experiment in any way it chooses.

"I strongly urge that standards be written into the bill to be met by any State which secures a subsidy from a Federal fund."

Labor's vigorous opposition to employee contributions, as the legislation permits, is that wages are so low for the vast majority of wage earners that they simply will not permit even very small contributions. Green continued:

TAXING BREAD AND BUTTER

"Employee contributions would literally come out of the bread and butter of the workers.

"How can workers be asked to reduce their expenditures for living still further, in order to finance insurance against a hazard for which they are in no way responsible, and towards the elimination of which they can do nothing?

"The cost of unemployment is a legitimate charge on the cost of production. Unemployment is just as much an accompaniment of our present system of production as is any other overhead cost."

Green pointed out that contributions by employees would ultimately be passed on to the consumer, while the contributions of the workers would come out of slender earnings and could not be shifted. As consumers, Green showed, workers would pay the employer's contribution as well as their own.

"Workers have borne the entire cost of unemployment in the past", the labor chieftain asserted. "They will continue to bear at least 50 percent of the cost, when they receive only 50 percent of their wages when unemployed. On top of that, it is unfair to ask them to pay the employers' share.

"It is my urgent request that any unemployment insurance measures enacted shall contain a provision that State laws must provide that the entire cost shall be borne by the employer."

Green contended that the proposed 3 percent tax on pay rolls is "entirely inadequate" and demanded that it be boosted to 5 percent.

The standards possible under the lower tax were declared to be so low as to be wholly unacceptable.

Green recommended that benefits be increased from a maximum of $15 to $25, with $15 the minimum, and that the period of payment be increased from 16 to 25 weeks.

DREADS PUBLIC RELIEF

"I see no reason", he said, "why, in the richest country in the world, a worker who qualifies for pensions should be forced to depend upon public relief at the end of 16 weeks of unemployment.

"This period is pitiably inadequate. The benefit period should be extended in simple justice to the workers."

A waiting period of 4 weeks before benefits are paid was declared to be unreasonably long. Green recalled that the British system provides a waiting period of only 6 days, and said he knew of no reason why we should not follow that example.

The most serious objection raised by Green was a "deadly menace" to labor organizations in a provision permitting companies to establish their own insurance reserves in lieu of paying the pay roll tax.

DANGER IS REAL

"I cannot be too emphatic in regard to this danger", he declared. "Such reserves will be of benefit only to those employers whose risks are low and will be taken advantage of only by those employers.

"Company or industry reserves are not unemployment insurance. There is a serious menace to organized labor in the individual company reserve. Employers who are strongly opposed to the free and independent organization of trade unions will be able to use their reserves as a weapon in their fight against organization of their employees.

"They may offer slightly higher benefits upon the understanding that their employees remain unorganized, or they could use their reserves around which to build a 'company union' and thus prevent the growth of bona fide unions.

"Speaking for the American Federation of Labor, and the millions of workers who are members of the Federation, I protest emphatically against any provision which permits a State to set up reserves on the basis of company or of industry."

Responding to a question by Senator James Couzens (Rep., Mich.), Green said that the American Federation of Labor membership is between five and six millions. He also declared that these unionists had expended more than $60,000,000 during the last year in taking care of their unemployed.

Painting a picture of "darkness and misery" during 5 years of depression, President Green passed on to old age pensions, which he contended are long overdue. He said that, out of a total of 6,500,000 persons 65 years or over, 2,700,000. were supported wholly or partly by others in 1930, and that the number of needy had since increased enormously.

LIVING STANDARDS LOW

"The present low standard of living of the average worker's family", he declared, "makes it impossible for the wage-earning class to assure old age security to its members."

Pensions are vastly better than any form of poorhouse, Green said, but he insisted that the administration's proposal falls short of what the aged have a right to expect.

Instead of a maximum payment of $30 a month, he suggested that $50 should be the minimum, and

DREADS PUBLIC RELIEF

"I see no reason," he said, "why, in the richest country in the world, a worker who qualifies for pensions should be forced to depend upon public relief at the end of 16 weeks of unemployment.

"The Wagner-Lewis bill is pitiably inadequate. The benefit period should be extended in simple justice to the workers."

A waiting period of 4 weeks before benefits are paid was declared to be unreasonably long. Green recalled that payments should be available at 60 years, instead of 65, as has been proposed.

"We are building on a new foundation of social justice", Green continued, "and provision for the aged must get at the root of the problem. Economic requirements of our day will not admit of half measures.

SAFEGUARD MEANINGLESS

"There is no minimum established in the bill, other than a broad statement that a 'reasonable subsistence' must be provided. This safeguard is meaningless and is utterly inadequate. In some States the payments have been as low as $5 a month."

The national system of contributory old-age insurance also came in for some lusty wallops from the labor chieftain. His main objection was that it is being launched on too low a scale. Instead of starting with a tax of 1 percent on pay rolls and increasing until 5 percent is reached in 1957, Green advocated an immediate levy of 3 percent and increasing it to 5 percent in 1947.

The only reason for this "over-modest beginning", Green declared, is that "no large immediate burden should be put upon industry."

Annuities should begin at 60 years and larger pension should be available to lower-paid workers, Green insisted.

Mr. DUNN. The first witness to appear before our subcommittee is Mr. F. Elmer Brown, chairman of the National Congress for Unemployment and Social Insurance, of New York City.

STATEMENT OF F. ELMER BROWN, CHAIRMAN OF THE NATIONAL CONGRESS FOR UNEMPLOYMENT AND SOCIAL INSURANCE; MEMBER OF TYPOGRAPHICAL UNION NO. 6, NEW YORK CITY

Mr. DUNN. Mr. Brown, in order that the record may be clear on the matter, will you please state whom you represent?

Mr. BROWN. I am here as chairman of the National Action Committee in support of Federal unemployment and social insurance, also as national secretary of the Amalgamation Party for the International Typographical Union, of the American Federation of Labor.

Mr. SCHNEIDER. Mr. Brown, just what is that organization?

Mr. BROWN. It is an organization of those workers in the printing industry, members of the American Federation of Labor, who are attempting to amalgamate the various printing crafts into a printing union.

Mr. SCHNEIDER. Does the organization have the approval of the International Typographical Union?

Mr. BROWN. It has a legal standing within the International Typographical Union, but if you care for evidence, I have evidence from the union, addressed to me in care of the Amalgamation Party of the International Typographical Union, on official stationery.

Mr. SCHNEIDER. Does the International Typographical Union endorse this bill?

Mr. BROWN. The national body has not, but various local bodies have. The local body of which I am a member, local no. 6, being the largest local body, has endorsed it.

Mr. LUNDEEN. What was it you stated about its being the largest body?

Mr. BROWN. It is the largest local body within the International Typographical Union.

Mr. LUNDEEN. That is what I wanted to know.

Mr. DUNN. How many members belong to the organization you represent?

Mr. BROWN. The Amalgamation Party has over 5,000.

Mr. DUNN. Thank you.

Mr. BROWN. Typographical Union No. 6, of which I am also a member, has endorsed the principles outlined in this bill.

Mr. DUNN. You are speaking of the Lundeen bill, H. R. 2827?

Mr. BROWN. Yes. Typographical Union No. 6 has a membership of some 10,000, on which I will submit a statement later.

Mr. WELCH. Local No. 6 is a New York local, is it not?

Mr. BROWN. Correct.

Mr. SCHNEIDER. But you are not here representing the International Typographical Union, as such?

Mr. BROWN. I am only representing a body within the International Typographical Union. I present at this time a letter dated January 30, 1934, from the New York Typographical Union No. 6.

Mr. LUNDEEN. Is that your authorization for being here?

Mr. BROWN. It could be taken as an authorization, because it is from the secretary, giving me certain information to submit to this body.

Mr. LUNDEEN. Do you want the letter placed in the record?

Mr. BROWN. I do not think it is necessary for the record, because there is so much extraneous matter in it.

Mr. DUNN. Very well. At this time we will omit it from the record. Proceed.

Mr. BROWN. On behalf of the National Action Committee, I submit the following statement:

Answering a call of representatives of national organizations, deeply concerned with the plight of the millions of unemployed workers in America, more than 2,500 elected delegates, representing many millions of workers, assembled in this city on January 5, 6, and 7, 1935, to formulate a system of Federal unemployment and social insurance, which would meet the needs of the millions of destitute Americans.

Represented in this congress for unemployment and social insurance, were:

Six delegates from the State of Alabama; Arkansas, 9; Colorado, 6; California, 6; Connecticut, 54; Florida, 12; Georgia, 1; Indiana, 8; Illinois, 112; Iowa, 8; Kansas, 1; Kentucky, 7; Louisiana, 6; Maine, 5; Maryland, 7; Massachusetts, 89; Michigan, 48; Minnesota, 19; Mississippi, 4; Missouri, 4; Montana, 1; Nebraska, 1; New Hampshire, 7; New Jersey, 145; New Mexico, 3; New York, 904; North Carolina, 10; North Dakota, 2; Ohio, 217; Oklahoma, 1; Oregon, 1; Pennsylvania, 554; Rhode Island, 11; South Carolina, 1; Tennessee, 1; Texas, 6; Vermont, 6; Virginia, 38; Washington, 2; West Virginia, 15; Wyoming, 1; Wisconsin, 35; District of Columbia, 61; and Canada, 1.

Seven hundred and forty-two of the delegates were members of the American Federation of Labor, out of whom 338 were elected by their unions to officially represent the union at the congress. Two hundred and twenty-one delegates represented independent, or unions not affiliated with the American Federation of Labor. Two hundred and seven were T. U. U. L. Unions, and 145 represented independent unions of professional workers. Thirty-seven came from shop organizations, 517 from unemployed organizations, 578 from fraternal organizations and lodges, and 463 from church, Negro, women's, youth, veterans', and other national organizations.

These delegates, coming from 40 States, with credentials authorizing them to speak for trade unions, fraternal, professional, farmer, Negro, women's, youth, veterans', and many other organizations, representing every shade of political, religious, and social opinion, formed the broadest and most representative congress of the American people ever held in the United States.

These representatives of the American toilers, at tremendous personal sacrifices and hardships, came to this Congress because they know and feel the wants and sufferings of their fellow countrymen.

After having discharged their task of formulating the kind of unemployment and social insurance system they need and want, they left the congress more determined than ever to broaden and strengthen the movement and to continue the fight until it had been enacted into law and they and their fellow toilers were assured by their Government that they would not suffer hunger because they had produced too much food; nor suffer cold and exposure because they had produced too much clothing and built too many fine houses.

It is in behalf of the January 5, 6, and 7, 1935, Congress for Unemployment and Social Insurance that I appear before the House subcommittee of the Labor Committee of the Seventy-fourth United States Congress to urge the enactment of H. R. 2827.

H. R. 2827 has the endorsement of the millions who were represented at the January Congress. It is the only bill yet proposed which even approaches the needs of the American masses who are denied the right to work.

It is the only bill which places the responsibility for unemployment where it belongs—upon the Federal Government and the owners of the tools and natural resources of the country.

The American workers are willing and able to produce enough to properly feed, clothe, and house every American. There are enough natural resources to provide all the materials needed. There are enough factories, farms, and mines to supply all the needs. There are enough railroads, steamships, automobiles, and airplanes to transport and distribute the necessities of life to every citizen. There are enough houses to shelter everyone. Under the circumstances it is the immediate duty of the Federal Government to provide compensation to every worker who is willing, but unable to find employment.

It is not enough for the Government to promise aid through reserves. The millions of unemployed and short-time workers are unable and unwilling to be taxed for unemployed and old-age reserves. The Federal Government cannot escape its responsibility to provide adequate protection against hunger and exposure by shifting the burden of unemployment from one shoulder of the worker to the other.

In the January 5, 6, and 7 Congress, the broadest and most important congress ever held in the United States, not only did the delegated representatives of the many million workers throughout the country endorse H. R. 2827, but they decided to bring to the attention of their Government the wide sufferings and needs of the millions of aged, youth, and unemployed workers and their families. During the course of these hearings, we will bring before the committee not only experts who will testify, but also many workers direct from the farm, mine, mill, office, and factory. Also domestic, Negro, women, youth, and other workers who will not come here as professional sociologists to give an academic thesis on old age or unemployment, but they will come from every section of the United States to give personal testimony as to the conditions under which they are compelled to live. They will testify as to the needs for an unemployment and social insurance system such as is contained in H. R. 2827.

This testimony will be important, because perhaps for the first time in American history it will represent the voice of the vast majority of the American workers who are the vast majority of the American people. I do not need to remind you that wise rulers heed the voice of their people.

Every day new sections of workers are being informed about the actions of the National Congress for Unemployment and Social Insurance, and they are adding their endorsement and support. The national committee elected from this January Congress will continue to enlist the support of the American workers until they compel their Congressmen and Senators to write H. R. 2827 upon the law books of the country.

We hold that the American workers have every right to expect, and should demand that the Federal Government immediately provide compensation sufficient to permit every worker and his family to live in decency, whether he has a job or not. Moreover, we insist that full compensation be paid to all those workers who are unable to find employment.

We vigorously oppose the various reserve and part-time partial payments for loss of compensation such as suggested in the Wagner bill (S. 1130). We insist that workers should under no circumstances be denied full compensation for all time lost because of unemployment or because of lockouts or strikes.

We shall resist every attempt to reduce the already inadequate relief now given to unemployed workers. We strongly condemn the suggestion that the unemployed and aged be taken care of by eleemosynary institutions.

In behalf of the more than 2,000 delegates who participated in the January Congress for Unemployment and Social Insurance, and the many millions of American workers represented by them—and in behalf of the millions who have since endorsed the actions of the Congress, I call upon this committee and the Seventy-fourth United States Congress to immediately enact H. R. 2827.

I now desire to submit a statement dealing with the printing trades, some of the information upon which it is based having been gained from official sources, and the figures contained in the statement are certified to by a certified public accountant.

Compensation due to unemployment because of old age, sickness, or other reasons for which the worker is not responsible is not something new to the 150,000 organized workers in the printing industry. For many years the printing-trades unions have administered unemployment relief, sick benefits, and old-age pensions to their members. Funds for these social features have been collected from the membership. However, technological development, in which the workers shared but little, with other maladjustments inherent in our social system, has compelled these organizations to either abandon the practices or curtail them to such a degree as to render them almost of no value.

The printing-trades unions hesitated to enter the broad movement for a Federal system of unemployment and social insurance until they had almost exhausted all their resources. Typographical Union No. 6, the largest local within the International Typographical Union, while endorsing the principles contained in H. R. 2827, more than two years ago, did not actively participate in the movement for a Federal law until the National Congress for Unemployment and Social Insurance met in Washington January 5, 6, and 7, 1935. This organization, with 10,000 members, and one of the oldest in the American Federation of Labor, was officially represented at the Congress.

Another reason why the printing-trades unions have until now refrained from joining in the movement for a genuine Federal unemployment and social-insurance system was because of the many promises made by the N. R. A. and amplified by officials of the American Federation of Labor. However, the rank-and-file workers in the printing industry are now awake and are ready to join with the millions of agricultural, domestic, professional, and industrial workers in this broad and all-important fight for a Federal law establishing a genuine unemployment and social insurance system such as H. R. 2827.

The fight for the enactment of H. R. 2827 now becomes a necessary part of the program of the printing-trades unions. Typographical Union No. 6 of New York City will serve as an example of the tremendous burden which has been placed upon the workers in the printing industry as a result of the economic crisis. Since 1928 this orgainzation of printing workers has spent:

For pensions for the aged	$2,767,071.05
For unemployment relief	5,128,121.90
For other emergency relief	242,804.48
Total	8,137,997.43

These staggering figures represent only what one organization of printing workers has done. Thousands of other organizations of printing workers have a like record. With more than half of the workers in the industry unemployed, with the many additional demands upon the pocketbooks of those still working, it has come to pass that these workers can no longer shoulder a burden of caring for the unemployed workers in the industry. They are now joining with the millions of toilers throughout the United States and demanding that the Federal Government accept its responsibility of providing the necessary unemployment and social insurance, not at the expense of low-paid workers, but at the expense of profit takers.

The workers in the printing industry see in H. R. 2827 the correct principle of unemployment and social insurance. They will insist that H. R. 2827 be enacted and the burden of unemployment and social insurance placed where it belongs—upon the Government and owners of industry.

The bitter experience with the N. R. A. and its codes has taught the rank-and-file workers in the printing industry not to accept promises, even if the promises come from the high places and have the personal recommendations of the officials of the American Federation of Labor. The kind of unemployment and social insurance they will accept must be genuine. Counterfeit bills will be exposed and rejected. So far, the only bill brought forward which approaches genuine unemployment and social insurance is H. R. 2827.

Mr. DUNN. At this time, gentlemen, Mr. Brown is willing to answer questions. Mr. Schneider, you may proceed to interrogate the witness, if you desire to do so.

Mr. SCHNEIDER. I have no questions.

Mr. LESINSKI. And I have no questions.

Mr. DUNN. Do you have any questions, Congressman Lundeen?

Mr. LUNDEEN. Yes. Are the figures which you gave, about the millions of dollars expended, taken from your official record?

Mr. BROWN. They are taken from the official record; yes.

Mr. LUNDEEN. Of the union?

Mr. BROWN. Yes. Would you care to have an elucidation of them?

Mr. LUNDEEN. I would like to know that they are authoritative and not based merely on rumor.

Mr. BROWN. Then, for the record I will submit this letter, signed by the secretary of the union.

Mr. LUNDEEN. Will that clear up the point?

Mr. BROWN. This contains the figures.

Mr. LUNDEEN. That will clear up that point?

Mr. BROWN. Yes.

Mr. LUNDEEN. Very well.

Mr. BROWN. And as I said at the beginning, the figures up to a year ago have been certified by a certified public accountant, because those figures were secured through an accounting agency for the purpose of the code hearings of the printing industry, and since then the figures have been certified by the secretary of Typographical Union No. 6, whose signature appears on this letter, which I now submit.

(The witness thereupon presented for the record a letter dated January 30, 1935, from the New York Typographical Union No. 6, addressed to Mr. Elmer Brown, care of the Amalgamation Party, New York City. The letter is as follows:)

NEW YORK TYPOGRAPHICAL UNION No. 6,
January 30, 1935.

Mr. ELMER BROWN,
 % *Amalgamation Party, International Typographical Union,*
New York City.

DEAR MR. BROWN: In your letter of January 24 you requested additional material to amplify the code committee briefs for your hearing before the congressional Committee on Labor, in connection with the movement for unemployment and social insurance.

The amounts expended by Typographical Union No. 6 contained in this letter are the figures for the fiscal year from June 1933 to May 1934. If the amounts herewith are added to those in the briefs which you have from the code committee hearing, you will get a pretty comprehensive picture of the situation. At the present time Typographical Union No. 6 approximates a membership of 9,700. Of this amount 775 are on the old-age pension roll. These members received during this period from the local old-age pension fund $78,634.66. From the additional local fund $217,042.34. From the pension and mortuary of the International Typographical Union $155,956.92. These payments make a grand total of old-age pension payments amounting to $451,633.

Funeral expenses during this period amounted to $17,300. There was paid to members under the constitutional provision of $3 per day for hospitalization, reimbursements in the amount of $14,142.99. The special emergency cases coming under the jurisdiction of the benefit board received from the appeals fund $7,752. This makes a total expenditure for these purposes of $39,194.99. In the copy of the code committee report which we have at headquarters, we notice the account has included the unemployment relief disbursements up to July 31, 1933. During the month of August there was expended in direct payment for unemployed relief, the sum of $42,733, and for September, when the payments ceased, the amount of $15,752, making a total of $58,485. The grand total of all the expenditures innumerated here amounts to $549,313.91. These figures itemized individually are as follows:

Local old-age pension	$78,634.66
International Typographical Union pension and mortuary	155,956.92
Additional International Typographical Union and local	217,042.34
Funeral expenses	17,300.00
Hospitalization	14,142.99
Appeals	7,752.00
Relief (for the months of August and September 1933 only)	58,485.00
Total	549,313.91

The unemployment figures up to the time of cessation of relief are as follows: Up to and including July 1933 there was disbursed in unemployment benefits $2,569,636.90. A close estimate puts the day off per week under the 5-day work-week law at 250,000 days. This approximates $2,500,000 and, added to the above sum of $2,569,636.90, totals $5,069,636.90 toward unemployment relief. When the August and September 1933 expenditures are added No. 6 spent for unemployment relief alone, since January 1, 1928, approximately $5,128,121.90.

As you requested in your letter, we have given you the disbursements for those activities which could be classed as of a benevolent nature, and which would come under the classification of work done in connection with unemployed and social insurance.

Trusting this will help you materially before the congressional committee, and extending to you a wish for success, I remain,

Fraternally yours,   JAMES J. McGRATH,
                                              Secretary-Treasurer.

Mr. LUNDEEN. I would like to ask you another question or two. You referred to millions of people who were represented by delegates. How do you arrive at those figures?

Mr. BROWN. The credentials committee of the congress gave a report in which they estimated that somewhere between three and four million people were represented by the delegates who appeared at the congress.

Mr. LUNDEEN. You mean that a certain delegate was selected by a union having a certain number of members?

Mr. BROWN. Having 10,000 members, for instance. We calculate that the delegate represents the members of that organization.

Mr. LUNDEEN. For instance, certain of the delegates came from Lynn, Mass. I met them at Mr. Connery's office. They presented credentials showing that they represented so many members of so many unions. That is the way you arrived at the figure?

Mr. BROWN. That is the only way that we could arrive at it, yes.

Mr. LUNDEEN. You believe, then, that the figures stated by you are accurate?

Mr. BROWN. The credentials would state how many members were in the organization which had sent the delegate to the congress.

Mr. LUNDEEN. You believe, yourself, that the figures are accurate, do you?

Mr. BROWN. I believe they are as accurate as could possibly be secured, and I think that the number would be a conservative figure, because there are many unorganized workers who are in sympathy with and will support the bill, but who were not represented, because they have no organizations which permit them to elect delegates.

Mr. LUNDEEN. Do you know, offhand, how many of the delegates were members of the American Federation of Labor? I believe you have it in your statement, there.

Mr. BROWN. Yes; 742, I believe.

Mr. LUNDEEN. And you mentioned some 300?

Mr. BROWN. Three hundred and thirty-eight were officially elected by American Federation of Labor unions. The other members of the American Federation of Labor, who were there as delegates, were delegates from fraternal organizations, church organizations, and so forth.

Mr. LUNDEEN. Who were not chosen by American Federation of Labor units?

Mr. BROWN. No; but they were members of the American Federation of Labor who were chosen by our organizations, other than their union.

Mr. LUNDEEN. And what was the number—338?

Mr. Brown. Three hundred and thirty-eight were officially elected by American Federation of Labor bodies.

Mr. Lundeen. Affiliated with the American Federation of Labor?

Mr. Brown. Affiliated with the American Federation of Labor, which, I might add, in my opinion comes nearer to representing the American Federation of Labor than would an American Federation of Labor convention.

Mr. Lundeen. By that, you mean they are more from the rank and file?

Mr. Brown. Yes.

Mr. Lundeen. But the delegates to the national convention of the American Federation of Labor are also selected by the rank and file, are they not?

Mr. Brown. Yes; but the legislation and the resolutions which they adopt can be adopted by 11 organizations, or 11 individuals can control the American Federation of Labor convention, while in the January Congress the 338 delegates there, who were officially representing the American Federation of Labor, only represented their organization, and had an equal vote, which is not true in the American Federation of Labor conventions, where 11 organizations, or the heads of 11 organizations, can control all the votes in the convention.

Mr. Lundeen. That is all.

Mr. Lesinski. I have no question.

Mr. Dunn. Have you read the Wagner-Lewis bill-

Mr. Brown. Yes.

Mr. Dunn. Then you are convinced beyond any doubt that that bill will not take care of the unemployment situation?

Mr. Brown. Yes; beyond a doubt I am convinced that it is inadequate and will not take care of the situation.

Mr. Dunn. But you believe that H. R. 2827, introduced by Congressman Lundeen, of Minnesota, is the bill to take care of the unemployed of the United States?

Mr. Brown. I do.

Mr. Dunn. I have no further questions, Mr. Brown.

Mr. Wood. I did not hear all of your statement, but you said a while ago that the American Federation of Labor had never sponsored, or was maybe somewhat opposed to unemployment insurance—referring to the officialdom of the American Federation of Labor—until your group, whatever it is, representing as you call it, the " rank and file ", had created so much sentiment that you compelled the American Federation of Labor to take official action.

Mr. Brown. No; that was not the statement, Congressman Wood.

Mr. Wood. What was the statement?

Mr. Brown. The statement was that in the Congress for Unemployment Insurance, held January 5, 6, and 7, there were 338——

Mr. Wood. No, no; before that statement, you said that the American Federation of Labor had not taken any interest in the unemployment insurance until the rank-and-file organization had dissemiated information and created the enthusiasm among the membership, which had caused the American Federation of Labor, now, to take action.

Mr. Brown. You perhaps refer to the statement I made of Typographical Union No. 6. I said that while it endorsed the principles contained in H. R. 2827, which were in the bill introduced by Mr. Lundeen——

Mr. Wood. Let us refer back to the record and see just what your statement was regarding Typographical Union No. 6. I think this is it. I do not know (reading):

> Another reason why the printing trades unions have until now refrained from joining in the movement for a genuine Federal unemployment and social insurance system, was because of the many promises made by the N. R. A., and amplified by officials of the American Federation of Labor. However, the rank-and-file workers in the printing industry are now awake and are ready to join with the millions of agricultural, domestic, professional, and industrial workers in this broad and all-important fight for a Federal law establishing a genuine unemployment and social insurance system, such as H. R. 2827.

Whose bill is that?

Mr. Brown. That is Congressman Lundeen's bill.

Mr. Wood (continuing reading):

> The fight for the enactment of H. R. 2827 now becomes a necessary part of the program of the printing trades unions. Typographical Union No. 6 of New York City will serve as an example of the tremendous burden which has been placed upon the workers in the printing industry.

That leaves the inference that this " rank-and-file " organization of yours had created the interest in that unemployment insurance, in the face of some fabulous promise made by the American Federation of Labor. What do you mean by that?

Mr. Brown. If you will read the first part of the statement, you will see it refers to promises made by the N. R. A.

Mr. Wood. Yes, " and amplified by officials of the American Federation of Labor."

Mr. Brown. Yes; amplified by the officials of the American Federation of Labor.

Mr. Wood. What promises were they? I want to get some light on that.

Mr. Brown. The promises made by the N. R. A. were many— that purchasing power would be increased, for one thing, hours would be shortened, and when the codes were signed, they would provide for shorter hours for workers. Those promises, so far as the printing workers were concerned, meant nothing, because the codes were signed with hours longer than the established hours in the printing industry.

Mr. Wood. What has that to do with promises of the American Federation of Labor? You are telling me, or giving as the reason why this social insurance legislation has not been brought out sooner, promises made by the N. R. A., and amplified by officials of the American Federation of Labor. In other words, you leave the inference that the American Federation of Labor officials had promised the workers something in order to keep them from advancing the principle of out-of-work insurance, which is not true. That leaves an inference.

Mr. Brown. Perhaps I would have to disagree with you that it was not true. The N. R. A. came forward with certain promises of increasing the purchasing power and reducing the hours of labor. These promises were repeated to the workers of the American Federation of Labor by the officials of the American Federation of Labor.

Mr. Wood. Certainly.

Mr. Brown. They came forward and said that it was a "New Magna Charta for labor", and since then we do not have to argue with the workers in the printing industry to convince them that it was not a "Magna Charta" for printing labor. It did not increase purchasing power, so far as these workers were concerned. It did not reduce the hours of labor.

Mr. Wood. Of course, while the N. R. A. has not reached the point or the goal we were striving to reach, no one will deny that it has put a million and a half or two million people to work, by shortening hours, not in one industry but in a great number of industries. It is a good adage to "give the devil his dues", and I am giving the N. R. A. its dues, although it has not gone nearly as far as we all contemplated. You cannot get away from the fact that hours have been reduced and people have been put to work as the result of the N. R. A.; but that has nothing to do with this social insurance. The fact of the matter is, that the American Federation of Labor went on record for social insurance in 1931, officially, and in 1932 they made a report to the convention as to the type of unemployment insurance they favored. Since 1931 the American Federation of Labor has been out, open and above board, and has taken the lead for not only unemployment insurance, but old-age pensions and social legislation.

Mr. Brown. Well, that is certainly a debatable question so far as I am concerned. They have come out for certain reserves.

Mr. Wood. They are not just coming out for the type of legislation that you think ought to be enacted?

Mr. Brown. Furthermore, so far as the N. R. A. was concerned, their promises were not made good.

Mr. Wood. Do you not know, as a matter of fact, that there is not a man in this country, who is an authority on unemployment insurance? That is, as to what sort of plan would be best to apply in this country? Do you claim that you are an authority on that?

Mr. Brown. I claim it does not take a high order of intelligence for a worker to know whether or not a bill such as H. R. 2827 is a bill that would provide him with what he needs.

Mr. Wood. It is not a question of intelligence, it is a question of information. I favor Mr. Lundeen's bill. You understand that. I favor any kind of unemployment insurance we can get that is feasible, but you are contending that because the American Federation of Labor has advocated a certain type of unemployment insurance, they do not favor it. You should be broad enough to give every man an opportunity to think for himself and to advocate whatever type of insurance he believes to be the best. It is not the type of insurance that is standing in the way so much. It is the question of getting everybody, or a great majority of the people of this country, the majority of its officialdom, all in favor of unemployment insurance, and getting them to realize it is an absolute necessity. That is the main thing, and then afterward the mechanics of it can be worked out in detail.

Mr. Brown. I do not take from anyone the right to have an opinion or to promote any legislation that he thinks is good for him, but I reserve the right to expose the weaknesses of their proposals, and to disagree with them.

Mr. Wood. That is all right, but not to insinuate that they are opposing out-of-work insurance. I have heard the American Federation of Labor maligned so many times in these hearings that I am getting tired of it.

Mr. Brown. I am not maligning the American Federation of Labor.

Mr. Wood. In fact, we would not have any social legislation in this country but for the American Federation of Labor. It has been the vanguard in all types of social legislation, remedial legislation in the interests of the workers. There has not been an organization in this country that has done more consistent and persistent battling before Congress and all the legislatures of this Nation for all types of legislation in the interests of the workers—shortening of hours, women's legislation, child labor, compulsory school attendance by children, and free textbooks, a movement that was led by the American Federation of Labor; all types of safety legislation in mills and mines and factories; every conceivable type of legislation in the interest of the workers, irrespective of whether they belong to one class or another. The American Federation of Labor has been the leader, and now, at this late date, after 35 or 40 years of battle, I do not like to see some new organization step into the breach here, and try to leave the impression that the American Federation of Labor, through some sinister influences working among its officials, is inducing people to oppose some type of social legislation.

Everybody knows that the representatives of the American Federation of Labor wrote section 7 (a) of the National Recovery Act. They wrote section 7 of the Transportation Act, and many other things I could mention, just in the last three sessions of the Congress, measures that the representatives of the four train-service brotherhoods and the American Federation of Labor have sponsored.

What legislation have they sponsored that was not in the interest of the people? I want somebody to tell me that. When the American Federation of Labor has been the only organization, the really large moving force that has been the bulwark standing between organized capital and the people, for someone at this late day to try to impugn the motives of the American Federation of Labor is absurd. How long has your organization been established?

Mr. Brown. The Typographical Union?

Mr. Wood. No; this National Joint Action Committee.

Mr. Brown. The National Joint Action Committee was selected from the congress held on January 5, 6, and 7, in this city.

Mr. Wood. When?

Mr. Brown. January 5, 6, and 7 of this year. It was elected from that congress.

Mr. Wood. And you come in to take credit for all the laws the American labor movement has been attempting to secure in the last 50 years, and claiming to know more about it, this morning, than they do?

Mr. Brown. I think you are attempting to put words into my mouth. I have not impugned the motives of the American Federation of Labor. I am a member of the American Federation of Labor, if you please, and I applaud every move made by the officials of the American Federation of Labor which is in the interest of the workers, but I contend that they do not go far enough.

Mr. Wood. Now, awhile ago you made a statement on the record that your committee came nearer to representing the American Federation of Labor than the American Federation of Labor, itself.

Mr. Brown. I said, the American Federation of Labor delegates at this Congress, in my opinion, came nearer to representing the sentiment of the American Federation of Labor than did the delegates at the last convention of the American Federation of Labor, because there were 338 delegates representing unions at this national Congress, and in the American Federation of Labor they have fewer delegates than that.

Mr. Wood. What do you give as your reason for that statement?

Mr. Brown. Because of the fact of my personal contact and observation within the American Federation of Labor unions, in which I work as a worker.

Mr. Wood. Wherein does this committee represent the rank and file more than the American Federation of Labor, and to a larger degree? In what respect?

Mr. Brown. Because in this congress there were 742 members of the American Federation of Labor who expressed themselves as favoring the principles laid down in H. R. 2827.

Mr. Wood. You had 742 delegates? The reason for that statement is that you had 742 people in this convention?

Mr. Brown. And what they represented.

Mr. Wood. You say there were more individuals represented in that convention than the American Federation of Labor had represented in its last convention?

Mr. Brown. I pointed out that eleven individuals control the American Federation of Labor conventions, and that was not true in the congress.

Mr. Wood. Eleven individuals?

Mr. Brown. Yes.

Mr. Wood. Can you name those individuals?

Mr. Brown. Not offhand, I cannot.

Mr. Wood. I know something about the American Federation of Labor, having been in it for the last 30 years, and I have attended a number of American Federation of Labor conventions.

Mr. Brown. Then perhaps you know that it is true?

Mr. Wood. I would like to know where you could find ground for the statement that 11 members control the convention?

Mr. Brown. Eleven organizations can control the American Federation of Labor. I do not recall offhand who they are.

Mr. Wood. In what manner do they control the convention?

Mr. Brown. Because of the voting. They vote on their per capita paid in to the secretary of the American Federation of Labor.

Mr. Wood. Because 11 organizations have a larger vote, you say they control the American Feideration of Labor; is that your statement?

Mr. Brown. That is correct.

Mr. Wood. In other words, your contention is, those 11 organizations are always together and voting together, and they form a little ring that operates the American Federation of Labor convention. Is that your contention?

Mr. Brown. Well, I do not say that they necessarily do that, but I said the possibility was that 11 could control.

Mr. Wood. When have they done so on any question? Can you point out any question on which these 11 organizations you are speaking about have done that?

Mr. Brown. I do not recall any instance where they were divided in just that manner.

Mr. Wood. No, you cannot recall that?

Mr. Lesinski. Mr. Chairman, I do not believe this debate is germane to the bill. I believe we have had ample time on it. I think we should proceed. I admire Mr. Wood's stand in backing the American Federation of Labor, but it has nothing to do with this bill, just at this time.

Mr. Brown. Mr. Chairman, I would like to continue, since the gentleman asked his questions and made the inferences, at least, that I am not in sympathy with the American Federation of Labor.

Mr. Dunn. Proceed.

Mr. Brown. I want to say that I am a member of the American Federation of Labor, and I intend to remain a member. I intend to work as hard as I possibly can, within and without the American Federation of Labor, to make it a better organization. Because I disagree with some of the leadership of the American Federation of Labor, that does not mean that I am not in step with that organization.

Mr. Wood. Is that the way you are going to make it better, by saying here before this committee that the great labor movement of this country is controlled by 11 men or 11 organizations? Is that the way you are going to help it?

Mr. Brown. Well, to make it possible to control it by referendum votes, if necessary.

Mr. Wood. I would like for you to tell me of some vote where 11 organizations of the American Federation of Labor, out of the 114, controlled a convention, and tell me on what measure.

Mr. Brown. I said I did not recall any instance where they were divided in that way.

Mr. Dunn. Are there further questions?

Mr. Schneider. I would like to ask Mr. Brown if he is familiar with the unemployment compensation legislation in Wisconsin.

Mr. Brown. Not an authority on it. I have read the Wisconsin act.

Mr. Schneider. For your own information and for the record, then, I wish to state that in 1920 the convention of the Wisconsin State Federation of Labor, affiliated with the American Federation of Labor, ordered a bill introduced in the legislature, providing for unemployment insurance, which was introduced for the first time in the legislature of 1921, and in 1931 it was enacted into law, and is now in effect.

Mr. Brown. But as I understand the Wisconsin act, it does not provide unemployment insurance except for a certain period. It is not continuous compensation for unemployment.

Mr. Schneider. That is true, but the point I wish to make is that it established the principle in legislation, in fact, of unemployment compensation.

Mr. Lundeen. Mr. Brown, in view of the fact that so much was said about the American Federation of Labor, I would like to call your attention to an article in Labor, which we all know is an excellent magazine, where a statement concerning social insurance is made by the president of the American Federation of Labor. I think it is in this week's issue. President William Green states that the administration bill is pitiably inadequate.

Mr. DUNN. Are there any further questions?

Mr. WOOD. I should like to ask the gentleman who organized his association?

Mr. BROWN. The Congress was organized, as the beginning of the prepared statement said.

Mr. WOOD. I mean the National Joint Action Committee.

Mr. BROWN. As I said, the National Joint Action Committee was elected from this Congress, and as I said at the beginning of the testimony here, the sponsoring committee for that Congress was organized by heads of national organizations throughout the country. I do not have a list.

Mr. WOOD. What heads are they?

Mr. BROWN. I can perhaps name some of them offhand. There was Mary Van Kleeck, of the Interprofessional Association, chairman of the Interprofessional Association, at that time.

Mr. WOOD. That is not an organization affiliated with the American Federation of Labor?

Mr. BROWN. It includes members of the American Federation of Labor. It is an interprofessional organization.

Mr. WOOD. What labor organization, or what national organizations participated in this? Did any official of the International Union, or any officials of your organization help start it?

Mr. BROWN. None of the International officials.

Mr. WOOD. National organizations?

Mr. BROWN. The Actors Equity, I believe also had representatives

Mr. WOOD. The national organization, or just the rank-and-file members?

Mr. BROWN. The American Federation of Labor organization.

Mr. WOOD. What I am trying to ascertain is whether any national organization of the American Federation of Labor sponsored this or helped organize your committee?

Mr. BROWN. No national officials of the American Federation of Labor that I recall now, at this time.

Mr. WOOD. How many local unions or local organizations of the American Federation of Labor have endorsed this bill?

Mr. BROWN. Approximately three thousand.

Mr. WOOD. Three thousand?

Mr. BROWN. Yes. They have endorsed the principles, but not H. R. 2827. They have endorsed the previous bill, which contained practically the same thing.

Mr. WOOD. Of course, they have adopted the principle, and so has the American Federation of Labor. The labor movement has endorsed it for the past 4 years.

Mr. BROWN. No; I am talking about the principles contained in H. R. 2827, the bill introduced by Mr. Lundeen in the last Congress, which is described here.

Mr. WOOD. I am not talking about a bill. All the members of the American Federation of Labor give whole-hearted endorsement to the out-of-work insurance plan. Now, there are more than 3,000 local unions that have done that. They all endorsed it, not

ay particular plan, but they are all for out-of-work insurance, or
ocial insurance. There is no disagreement among the locals at
l.

Mr. BROWN. I refer to a particular bill that more than 3,000
adorsed.

Mr. LUNDEEN. Do you mean that they gave the number of the
ll in their resolution?

Mr. BROWN. Yes.

Mr. LUNDEEN. H. R. 7598, Seventy-third Congress?

Mr. BROWN. 7598.

Mr. LUNDEEN. That is the same bill, with two or three minor
anges?

Mr. BROWN. Yes. That is what I mean.

Mr. LUNDEEN. And did they name the bill in their resolutions?

Mr. BROWN. Yes. They referred to it by number, I believe in most
ses, and sometimes it was referred to as the "Lundeen bill."

Mr. LUNDEEN. Have you a list of those unions?

Mr. BROWN. I do not have a list with me. There is a list of them.

Mr. LUNDEEN. Will you furnish one for the record?

Mr. BROWN. I will submit one later if I can secure it in time.

Mr. LUNDEEN. As long as it is in issue, we might as well find out
ho they are.

Mr. BROWN. Other witnesses will appear, and I will see that they
urnish it.

Mr. LUNDEEN. I would like to find out exactly.

Mr. SCHNEIDER. Mr. Chairman, I do not regard that as important.
am not criticizing Mr. Lundeen. This proposition is nearly as
opealing as is the Townsend plan, and if read before a local union,
course, there is always somebody there to make a motion that
be endorsed, and it is endorsed; but nobody understands what
is, nor anybody who knows anything about it. or what the posi-
on of the American Federation of Labor is on it. It is endorsed,
d thereafter it is thrown into the basket as one of the thousands
ho have endorsed it. I might say that the State Federation of
abor convention last year had this bill before it, and it was before
very strong committee in the convention. It was not endorsed.

Mr. DUNN. Pardon me, Mr. Schneider. That was the State Fed-
ation of Labor of what State?

Mr. SCHNEIDER. Of Wisconsin. It was not endorsed. The prin-
ple of unemployment insurance, of course, was endorsed, as well
old-age pensions. The latter is in effect in Wisconsin.

Mr. DUNN. Do you mean they did not endorse the Lundeen bill?

Mr. SCHNEIDER. They did not endorse the Lundeen bill.

Mr. LUNDEEN. Would you care to state their reason for not doing
?

Mr. SCHNEIDER. No.

Mr. WOOD. I could say as much for the Missouri State Federa-
on of Labor. On numerous occasions during the past 8 or 10 years
ey have endorsed out-of-work insurance. We have had a bill
fore our legislature the past four or five sessions that provided
r social insurance, but they have never endorsed any particular
ll.

Mr. LUNDEEN. Mr. Chairman, I think that any bill which speaks
$200 a month, or thereabouts, is a very different bill from one

which speaks of the average local wage. There is a great difference between those figures. I think the gentleman will concede that.

Mr. Brown. It has been my experience where the bill has been brought up, that it has been debated by all the members. I know in the case of Typographical Union No. 6, which endorsed it, it was debated and subsituted for the Wagner-Lewis bill at that time. A motion was brought forward to endorse the Wagner-Lewis bill, and the Lundeen bill was substituted for the Wagner-Lewis bill, and the members there thoroughly understood what they were doing. I would hate to see you underestimate the intelligence of the workers in these trade unions. I believe they know what they are doing when they endorse the bill.

Mr. Wood. How can they know what they are doing until they examine the bill? Can you tell me that?

Mr. Brown. Well, I think most of them have examined it, or had plenty of opportunity to do so.

Mr. Wood. How can the members of your organization examine the bill in all of its details?

Mr. Brown. Because the Lundeen bill has been printed and millions of copies distributed to the workers in all industries.

Mr. Wood. Do you really believe that all members of organized labor in these local unions examine a bill before they vote on out-of-work insurance?

Mr. Brown. Not all, but I believe the vast majority do.

Mr. Wood. The fact of the matter is, that when the question of out-of-work insurance comes before a local organization, the natural reaction is that the individuals are for it, and they vote for it because it says it is out-of-work insurance. They know what that means. They know it means they get paid when they are laid off, a certain portion, and there is no disagreement among the workers on that, none whatever. So far as the mechanics of the thing are concerned, that is an entirely different proposition.

Mr. Brown. I wish that were altogether true, because sometimes there is disagreement on it. I wish that it were true that they were always in agreement on those things.

Mr. Wood. In agreement on out-of-work insurance?

Mr. Brown. Yes.

Mr. Wood. Do you mean to tell me there are any workers in this country who have any degree of intelligence who are not in favor of an out-of-work bill?

Mr. Brown. Well, I do not know anything about the degree of intelligence, but I know that there are workers who are still " rugged individualists."

Mr. Wood. You are the first man I have ever heard say that. I have my first man to ever say he is opposed to out-of-work insurance.

Mr. Brown. I attend some four or five union meetings every month.

Mr. Dunn. Pardon me, Mr. Wood, may I make a statement? I have heard over the radio certain individuals who were supposed to have intelligence oppose unemployment insurance, old-age pensions, and other kinds of social legislation. In fact, the statement was made—that this kind of legislation was nothing more than communism.

Mr. Wood. But, Mr. Chairman, he had a motive. I am talking about the rank-and-file of labor.

Mr. Dunn. I see.

Mr. Wood. I am not talking about some man that makes a radio speech for the purpose of confusing the people's minds.

Mr. Dunn. I mean, as individuals.

Mr. Wood. That is, as to what this legislation means. I know here are people making speeches over the radio against all social legislation, but I am talking about the membership of the American Federation of Labor, the average worker, the man in the street who works for wages. I have never seen one yet in my life that had ever opposed out-of-work insurance, or that would be so foolish as to oppose legislation of that type, meritorious legislation. I say it is the most meritorious legislation that has ever been presented to any legislative body. Certainly, plenty of people make radio speeches against the old-age pension, out-of-work insurance, the 8-hour day, the 6-hour day. Plenty of them have made speeches against all types of remedial legislation and relief legislation, but these people that are the recipients of them, who would be the workers, I have never yet seen one that said he opposed receiving compensation when he was discharged. I would not belittle the intelligence of the average American workingman, to even think or even suspicion that he would oppose legislation of that type.

Mr. Dunn. Mr. Wood, do you have any more questions?

Mr. Wood. No.

Mr. Lundeen. Would it not be well for you to insert a copy of the bill in the record preceding your remarks?

Mr. Brown. Yes. I referred to it, and I would like to insert the bill referred to in the statement, in the record, H. R. 2827, of course.

Mr. Dunn. The bill, H. R. 2827, will be inserted at the beginning of this record.

Mr. Wood. I would just like to make this observation before we close, Mr. Chairman. What I had in mind in questioning this gentleman was the fact that the sentiment of the people, for the past 2 years, have been very well established, for not only out-of-work insurance, but old-age pensions. There is no question in my mind or in the mind of anyone else who has given the matter any attention, for the past 3 or 4 years, but what the sentiment in this country of the rank and file of the people is very decidedly in favor of old-age pensions, social insurance, including out-of-work insurance, and I have noted in the past that when a certain piece of legislation gets to a point where it is popular, where it has attracted the favorable attention of a great portion of the people, many organizations arise for the purpose of floating on the wave of enthusiasm. We had an experience in the last two sessions of Congress. Dr. Pope, with his one-man pension organization, led a great many thousands of people to believe that he was doing a great deal; in other words, that he was blazing the trail for old-age pensions. He was simply riding upon the wave, and a great many of these new organizations come in for the purpose of getting themselves ensconced because they attack the older organizations. Some of these organizations are a detriment to social legislation. I know nothing about the organization this gentlemen represents, but I know that there are organizations formed for no other purpose than to ride upon the wave of popular sentiment and enthusiasm, for motive best known to themselves. Very frequently, they are a very great detriment to the progress of the legislation.

I just want to state that I certainly have been in favor of out-of-work insurance for a number of years, that I have introduced in the Missouri Legislature for the past 15 years an old-age pension law. We introduced a bill 4 years ago to amend the constitution of the State, to make an old-age pension lawful and constitutional. We passed the bill in the last session of the legislature. The mechanics of it were postponed for 2 years because of the lack of finances, and I am sure that some sort of an old-age pension bill will be passed by the Missouri Legislature at its present session. I am intensely in favor of all this legislation, and what I may say to any representative of any organization or association coming before this committee cannot be construed in anywise to indicate that I am opposed to any of this legislation. I think that those who know me best know that that has been my function for the past 22 years, to appear before the Missouri Legislature to advocate labor legislation, legislation in behalf of the worker, both organized and unorganized.

Mr. DUNN. Mr. Wood, you are, I believe, the president of the Federation of Labor in the State of Missouri?

Mr. WOOD. Yes, I am still the president of it.

Mr. LESINSKI. Mr. Chairman, I believe we ought to organize a little bit, here; first, before we go on. I believe every member should be allowed 5 minutes for questioning the witness, and then by unanimous consent additional time may be given, if necessary; otherwise we will be rambling along and will not hear the witnesses.

Mr. WOOD. Mr. Chairman, I heartily agree with that suggestion.

Mr. DUNN. I wanted to make this what might be called a really democratic meeting. That does not mean, however, a meeting for Democrats. It refers to men of all political parties. Do you wish to make a motion to that effect, Mr. Lesinski?

Mr. LESINSKI. I move that, yes; that every member of the committee be allowed 5 minutes to question a witness.

Mr. DUNN. And that, by unanimous consent, he may have more time? Do I hear a second to that?

Mr. LUNDEEN. I second that.

Mr. WOOD. Mr. Chairman, before you put that, I am going to vote for the motion, after having taken up 15 or 20 minutes here. It appeared that no one else wanted to question the witness, and I just wanted to bring out a few things.

Mr. DUNN. That is why we allowed you to take the time.

Mr. WOOD. I am in favor of the 5-minute rule. From experience I know it is best. I am going to vote for it, but I do not want to have it appear, after I have taken 15 or 20 minutes of the witness' time, that I want to cut off everybody else with 5 minutes. I think that rule should prevail after this hearing.

Mr. DUNN. We have had an excellent meeting this morning.

Mr. SCHNEIDER. Mr. Chairman, I am in favor of that motion, except I think that every witness who comes before the committee should be required to qualify; that is, he should be required to state his qualifications for being here, and should state positively whom he represents and how he represents them.

Mr. DUNN. Surely. It will not be necessary to put that into the motion.

Mr. SCHNEIDER. No; but sometimes it takes 5 minutes of a member's time in order to get from the witness whom he really represents.

Mr. DUNN. We will get that information before he starts his address.

(The motion was agreed to.)

Mr. DUNN. Mr. Brown, we thank you very, very much, and appreciate what you have told the committee. On behalf of the committee, thank you.

Mr. BROWN. I thank the committee for their courtesy and consideration.

Mr. DUNN. Miss McChesney, my secretary, will read the names of the witnesses who wish to appear this afternoon.

Miss McCHESNEY. For the afternoon session, beginning at 2 o'clock, the first witness is Prof. Broadus Mitchell, of Johns Hopkins University, economist; former candidate for Governor of Maryland on the Socialist ticket, and member of the Interprofessional Association.

The second witness this afternoon will be Dr. Joseph M. Gillman, statistician, economist, staff of the department of economics of the College of the City of New York; general chairman of the research committee of the Interprofessional Association.

The third witness will be Lewis C. Bentzley, executive committee, Farmers National Committee for Action.

Mr. LESINSKI. What is this Interprofessional Association? Whom does it represent, and what is it? I have heard the name referred to here very often today.

Mr. LUNDEEN. I think, Mr. Chairman, Miss Mary van Kleeck will be here in a day or two, and she is really the chairman of that association. Miss van Kleeck is with the Russell Sage Foundation, and can give us much-needed information.

Mr. WELCH. What is the title of the last witness referred to, who will appear this afternoon?

Miss McCHESNEY. The last one will be Lewis Bentzley, of the executive committee of the Farmers National Committee for Action, of Pennsylvania.

(The hour of 11:20 a. m., having arrived, the subcommittee took a recess until 2 p. m. this afternoon.)

AFTERNOON SESSION

(The recess having expired, the subcommittee reconvened at 2 p. m., and was called to order by Mr. Dunn, as chairman of the subcommittee.)

Mr. DUNN. Dr. Mitchell, will you please come forward.

STATEMENT OF DR. BROADUS MITCHELL, ASSOCIATE PROFESSOR OF POLITICAL ECONOMY, JOHNS HOPKINS UNIVERSITY, BALTIMORE, MARYLAND, MEMBER OF THE GOVERNOR'S COMMITTEE ON UNEMPLOYMENT INSURANCE AND RELIEF, OF THE STATE OF MARYLAND

Mr. DUNN. Doctor, you may proceed.

Mr. MITCHELL. I would like, Mr. Chairman, and members of the committee, to make a general statement intended to orient the committee, as far as I see it, as to the problem before it.

Mr. DUNN. You have that privilege. Proceed.

Mr. MITCHELL. You cannot talk about this workers' bill, or Lundeen bill, it seems to me, without talking also about the administration's measure by contrast; and I speak of that only on account of my wish to draw that contrast. We have to understand, it seems to me, the situation in which the country finds itself, and the situation into which it is rapidly going.

I do not blame the framers of the administration measure for any thing except lack of insight and understanding. I am sure they have acted in the best faith, that they consider themselves conscientious and generous-minded people. What they do not understand, it seems to me, is that you cannot provide for security in the kind of economic system that we have, with grudging, small benefits granted after a long waiting period and extending over a short time. We have entered a period of abundance. It is a totally new economy. The administration's measure is framed in the spirit of our old economy of scarcity. It is dictated by fear, the fear of want. Now what we are confronted with is not too little but too much. Any social-security measure must consider first, then, it seems to me, the fundamentals of the economic system. You cannot have any social security in an essentially unstable economy. Now, they speak of the administration bill as a "first line of defense." Why should we in the richest country on earth, with a Government engaged systematically in destroying goods and limiting services, content ourselves with a "first line of defense"? When will we ever be in a better position to guarantee real security to the American people? It is important in an economy of plenty to have sustained purchasing power, obviously. The administration measure, which allows small benefits, will have the effect, it seems to me, of damming up goods and providing no sluice gates to protect the dam, itself. This Lundeen bill, on the contrary, provides ample outlet in comparison with the administration measure. What we need in this country is, of course, not conservation but destruction. What we need is not more production but ampler consumption. This bill assists that.

In saying that, I want to indicate my sincerity and the accuracy of my statement, by saying that it is contrary to my wishes. I do not want to see this economic system preserved. If you want to preserve it, do not pass the administration measure but pass the Lundeen bill. Back of that, the Lundeen bill looks forward to an economic reorganization, because it draws the funds not from workers, not from purchasers, but from large incomes. It accomplishes, then, or tends to accomplish, a redistribution of economic power in the country. It tends toward a socialization of our productive resources. The difficulty now, as I see it, is that with the ownership of the sources of wealth in a few hands, we are unable to distribute the goods which our enormous productive equipment turns out. If we can socialize the source of wealth, it seems to me we will be getting on toward economic stability.

I should think that a sense of humor alone would deter the Congress from looking with favor upon the administration bill. It is grudging, fearful, inspired as I have said by old inhibitions of an economy of too little. It is necessarily said, I suppose, that the Lundeen bill is too radical. My conservative friends tell me they would approve of it but it is a dream only, we cannot accomplish such an about-face in our national policy as this bill represents. Well, in thinking of that my mind goes back, if you will permit me a moment, to a situation in our country 150 years ago, about, when the Articles of Confederation had broken down, when the States were jealous of one another, when we were on the verge of national bankruptcy, when we had no respect abroad or peace at home. In that situation, many of the best accredited thinkers counseled caution. They said, "Let us amend the Articles of Confederation. Let us patch and tinker and fix." But a man like Alexander Hamilton, and General Washington with him, had the courage and the wisdom as it seems to me to say, "No; this thing has failed. There is no use talking about it. We have got to have a new, fundamental instrument of Government. We have come to throw sovereignty to the central power and sink the States into relative insignificance. We have got then to grasp political sovereignty for the central Government." Now, our situation today, it seems to me, is very similar, except that what is involved now is economic relationships primarily, rather than political ones. We have got similarly a great business depression. We have got economic anarchy. We have got jealousies and confusions and international turmoil. In that situation, it seems to me we need another Hamilton who will say, " We need a new charter of economic liberties. We need to grasp economic power for the central authority."

The administration bill, on the contrary, leaves the settlement of important particulars in the hands of the State. The central Government is to have oversight rather than responsibility, except by inference. We are turning our backs, it seems to me, in the administration measure, on the whole development of our country up to this time. We all have our State loyalties. I am perfectly content for them to remain, so long as they are largely sentimental. Mine are sentimental. But when it comes to the critical matter of propping the American people against industrial hazard, we cannot revert, it seems to me, to reliance on the States. They are all now pensioners of the Federal Government, the State themselves. The real governor of Maryland today is the Federal Relief Administrator. I am very sorry that the counsels of those on the Security Committee who wanted a national bill did not prevail.

Now, the Lundeen bill provides that. It is modern in its political economic thinking. Mr. Chairman, that is all I intended to say, sir.

Mr. DUNN. Doctor, I appreciate what you said, and it was very interesting.

Now, gentlemen, do you desire to ask questions? Mr. Lesinski, you have 5 minutes in which to interrogate the doctor.

Mr. LESINSKI. Mr. Chairman, I have not heard the testimony, and I have no questions at this time.

Mr. DUNN. Congressman Lundeen?

Mr. LUNDEEN. When you speak of criticism of the administration measure, no less a person than William Green, himself, has criticized it, now, as shown in the article published in the weekly magazine called " Labor ", and covering about an entire page. I referred to that this morning. In that article, he describes the administration bill as being " inadequate ", and he uses other terms along that line.

Probably all of you noted in yesterday morning's papers the conflict between the Federation of Labor and the administration on these very points, on these questions that we are discussing here, so you are not alone in that, as you well know, Dr. Mitchell. Speaking of preserving our present system of government, I understood you to say that passing the Lundeen bill would tend to preserve our present economic system of government.

Mr. MITCHELL. Our present economic system, I meant.

Mr. LUNDEEN. Yes; that is what I meant, the economic system; but, if you want to endanger that system, just pass the administration measure?

Mr. MITCHELL. Yes; the administration measure.

Mr. LUNDEEN. Because that is a pitiably inadequate approach to a vital question, is it not?

Mr. MITCHELL. Exactly.

Mr. LUNDEEN. I was very much struck by what you said about a new charter of economic liberty. That might be worthy of thinking about. I can bear that out from what knowledge I have—I am not familiar with all the States, of course, or their statistics—but the States with which I am familiar are certainly beginning to be pensioners of the Federal Government; and how they are going to carry their end of the administration measure, carrying half the load—is not that the purport of it?——

Mr. MITCHELL (interposing). Yes.

Mr. LUNDEEN (continuing).—when they, themselves, must come down here, the Governors and administrators, by airplane, every day, begging the Federal Government to furnish more funds, is beyond me. They just cannot do it, and the press reported here the other day that four or five States had announced in advance that they would be unable to carry out the administration's proposal of meeting one-half of the Federal amount. Whether that statement is correct or not, I do not know, but it was reported in the press.

Mr. MITCHELL. Certainly, judged by their performance in the matter of relief and by the number of bankruptcies and tax sales in certain of our States, it would be very difficult for them, I should think, to bear their part.

Mr. LUNDEEN. I think that is all.

Mr. DUNN. Congressman Wood, do you desire to interrogate the doctor?

Mr. WOOD. Mr. Chairman, I did not hear the doctor.

Mr. DUNN. I can tell you briefly what he said. He maintains the administration measure is inadequate, and that in his opinion the Lundeen bill goes a great deal further, and, may I say, Doctor, meets the situation at the present time.

Mr. MITCHELL. I think it is a much closer approximation to it. I tried to indicate, Mr. Chairman, that I thought it would be impossible to have social security by any legislative means in the kind of economic system that we have, because it is fundamentally unstable, but I think this bill would go much further toward stabilizing our economic order, by giving larger benefits in sustaining the purchasing power than would the administration measure.

Mr. WOOD. I agree with you there, heartily.

Mr. LUNDEEN. May I ask you if you deem the bill practical and feasible?

Mr. DUNN. Do you mean the Lundeen bill?

Mr. LUNDEEN. Yes. Can you carry it out? Have you made any search along that line?

Mr. MITCHELL. I have made no research; no, sir; of that kind. My feeling would be that it would involve considerable assumption of authority; it would involve considerable responsibility for industrial life by the Government; that recruiting the needed funds through taxes on great wealth would probably bear so hard on private enterprise that the Government would have to extend itself into actual industrial operations at many points. Of course, we need not be shocked at that, because the Government is doing that, every hour, now, of course.

Mr. LUNDEEN. With the T. V. A., and all that?

Mr. MITCHELL. If it were not for the Government's support of private enterprise, none of us can even faintly imagine where our country would be today.

Mr. LUNDEEN. But may I ask if this bill would be practical and feasible, and workable, if the Federal Government backed up the taxation system proposed here?

Mr. MITCHELL. Yes, sir.

Mr. LUNDEEN. You would say that, as an economist?

Mr. MITCHELL. Yes, sir.

Mr. LESINSKI. Dr. Mitchell, do you propose to raise all of this money through taxation of industry? I mean, on the profits of industry.

Mr. MITCHELL. Yes; using the term "industry" broadly. It would include land as well as industry, of course.

Mr. LESINSKI. If, for instance, you take the years of 1930 and 1931, when there was practically no industry that made money, where would you then raise the money?

Mr. MITCHELL. As a matter of fact, of course, there were income-taxes paid in the worst years of the depression, and from reasons that we can understand, dividends continued long after wages disappeared. We have seen, just in the last year, a spectacular increase in the income payments, so that I do not think we need to be alarmed on that score.

Mr. LESINSKI. I happen to know personally a good many large industries have lost 40 or 50 or 60 million dollars a year, while the same industries, in good years, made maybe $100,000 or $150,000.

Mr. MITCHELL. Yes; there has been a great decline, there is no question of that.

Mr. LESINSKI. I realize the utilities have made money, most of them, but industrial concerns have not; and most of your income would be from industry. Then what would we do? Have you given that any thought?

Mr. MITCHELL. Yes; I have just tried to indicate that where employers are unable to discharge their responsibilities to their employees, the Government would have to step in and socialize that industry.

Mr. LESINSKI. Isn't it a fact that at the present time our largest trouble in industry is our speed-up system, to which we have not given any thought?

Mr. MITCHELL. You mean, sir, the speed-up, in the sense of better equipment and technological improvement?

Mr. LESINSKI. No.

Mr. MITCHELL. Or you mean in the narrow sense of the "stretch out?"

Mr. LESINSKI. The stretch service.

Mr. MITCHELL. That has had much to do with it, undoubtedly, si

Mr. LESINSKI. It has?

Mr. MITCHELL. New inventions, and getting more out of the em ployees that are continued in their jobs.

Mr. LESINSKI. Isn't it first logical to investigate the speed-up sys tems, so that in the course of years they would cut the speed dow and employ more men, and would help improve the conditions i the country, and would also improve the employment, and besides would take care of a lot of this unemployment we have today?

Mr. MITCHELL. I know exactly what is in your mind, sir, but think you are falling into the same fallacy that the "new deal" ha encountered at many points, and as illustrated. That is, they tr to solve their problem by running away from it. They conduc what amounts to an elaborate sabotage on progress.

Mr. LUNDEEN. Sabotage on progress?

Mr. MITCHELL. Trying to slow down our operation, to hobbl our ingenuity, to thwart science. By and large, you cannot do that That is a perfectly useless undertaking. American ingenuity an the drive for production, I think, in the opinion of all of us, wil break out of any confines in which you try to restrict it. If w could have planned leisure, which would be one interpretation o what you have suggested; if we could have shorter work hours o the part of everybody, according to a deliberate system which woul maintain the standard of living, or improve it, and at the same tim give greater leisure, I, and I think every sensible man, would be i favor of that. I am afraid that the form in which the suggestio is now made, however, would lead to simply a slowing down, numbing of our industrial operations.

Mr. LESINSKI. I do not mean it that way. I mean it this way Where, in 1929, 1 man operated a machine, the same machine that i used today, making 13 articles on that particular machine; on Feb ruary 1, 1934, the same man was operating 3 machines and making 17 articles. Has not that helped more to create unemployment, jus on that account?

Mr. MITCHELL. Oh, certainly, sir.

Mr. LESINSKI. Eliminating two men and speeding the machine up

Mr. MITCHELL. Certainly, sir, and there have been a great many other forces operating in exactly the same direction—new invention greater economies in business management, saving in overhead, an so on. I come from the Southern States where we have the stretch out in our industrial mills, and that has been a principal complaint of course, of the workers. They are trying to think in terms of ou broad economic problem in the country, and I think we ought t guard against any national policy which would have the purpose of using labor instead of machinery. What we want to do is t make machinery do our work and let laborers get the benefit.

Mr. LESINSKI. Correct.

Mr. MITCHELL. That is our point. We do not want to rely or sweat, but on steam, if I may put it that way.

Mr. LESINSKI. Well, unless the speed-up makes one man operate three machines, and we are getting the sweat out of him instead of the machine operating for the man.

Mr. MITCHELL. Right.

Mr. LESINSKI. What would you say about every plant recognizing seniority rights in its establishment?

Mr. MITCHELL. I shall have to ask you to elaborate a little bit.

Mr. LESINSKI. You will find that many plants keep turning over their labor, for the purpose of speed-up systems.

Mr. MITCHELL. And keeping on the old employees?

Mr. LESINSKI. If the seniority right were established in each plant, and after establishing this seniority right every employee would have the right to employment, providing the plant were operating. If there were unemployment it would be up to this plant to provide for that employee with funds put aside every year for the purpose.

Mr. MITCHELL. Of course, there are two difficulties with that, sir, in my judgment. One is that this plan of which you speak, neglects the insurance principle altogether. That is simply a savings account. It is what we term a "reserve", do we not, rather than an insurance pool at all? It does not distribute risk, therefore, and as a consequence of that the second point, that the abilities of the particular plant depend upon its own individual management, depend upon economic conditions in part outside the control of the management of the plant, so that I think these funds would be often exhausted. I think they would give very little protection to their workers. That is the difficulty with the Wisconsin scheme, which is held to by an important faction of those interested in social insurance. It seems to me their idea that it would regularize employment is altogether misconceived. The average employer, in a period of business depression, certainly cannot do anything about it. He is just as much a victim as are his employees. He can iron out certain seasonal unemployment, but the great cyclical dip that we are all concerned with is entirely outside his compass.

Mr. LESINSKI. If these funds were controlled through State control, under Government supervision, would not that solve it?

Mr. MITCHELL. No, sir. I think that would complicate it, because you have the problem of investing the funds, in the first instance, and the liquidating of them, in the second instance, and it is hard to tell which is more vexatious. You are building up these enormous funds in periods of prosperity, of rising prices. They would be invested, let us say, in public securities mainly, in order to provide safety and liquidity. This would release further funds for private industry. More would flow into capital equipment. Product would be added to. At the same time, the means of the workers of purchasing this product is not augmented. You would accentuate the steepness of the upcurve, it seems to me. The reverse would be true in the period of liquidation. You have got to realize on the securities, whether public or private. You are going to have to buy them at a high price and sell them at a low price; and liquidating such an enormous fund, it seems to me, would necessarily have a disastrous effect on business. It strikes me that only the Federal Government can meet that problem; that these great reserves built up, have got to be put in—I started to say, into Federal securities. It seems to

me they have got to be treated, in the last analysis, as practically th
same as currency; that it has got to be made the basis of currency i
some way. I cannot see any other method of liquidating them.

Mr. Wood. Doctor, you said awhile ago, I believe, that the levi
provided in this bill—on inheritances and gifts and individual an
corporation income—you felt would not be sufficient to maintain th
legislation?

Mr. Mitchell. No, sir; it is altogether a relative matter as to ho
deep you cut.

Mr. Wood. Isn't it significant that last year there were 85,000 le
individuals that paid taxes on incomes of $5,000 or less; and in tl
extremely higher brackets, in some instances, there were more ind
viduals paid income taxes on their incomes?

Mr. Mitchell. Yes, sir; right.

Mr. Wood. That indicates that the whole structure is topheavy
that is to say, that while those who were drawing smaller incomes i
the lean years were greatly inconvenienced by the depression, to tl
extent in 1933 that 85,000 less paid taxes on incomes of $5,000 (
less, on the other hand, in some of the extremely high brackets, the
were more people that paid incomes on taxes, as enumerated in th
bracket?

Mr. Mitchell. Yes, sir.

Mr. Wood. That indicates to me that those who were drawir
fabulous salaries have not been hurt by this depression; that is, a
indicated in the year 1933. I think your statement was that if v
would attempt to burden those who are paying incomes in the high
brackets, and those who receive inheritances and gifts, it would ter
to retard industry. It occurs to me that while industry was retarde
these gentlemen who are drawing fabulous salaries have been i
creased in number; so it would not indicate to me that if they we
taxed heavily on their income it would have a thing in the wor
to do with the rise and fall of the activity of industry. The fact (
the matter is that England pays two or three times more taxes th
we do, in the higher brackets. If we had the taxation of England, v
could pay all these benefits, old-age pensions, out-of-work securit
and a good many others. Then, if that be the case—if that were n
sufficient to bear the burden—where would be the next taxes y(
would levy?

Mr. Mitchell. I am afraid you misunderstood me, sir.

Mr. Wood. Would you levy it on industry, or what?

Mr. Mitchell. I am afraid you misunderstood what I tried to sa
Maybe I was very awkward about it.

Mr. Wood. I just took your language literally.

Mr. Mitchell. I do not think that these would tend to reta
industry. What I tried to say was that in certain instances, undoul
edly, individuals, firms, or industries even, if they were in a depress
state, might be unable to meet their share of the expense of the soci
insurance; that in that case it seems to me there is nothing for
except for the Government to step in and socialize those industri(
I think, on the contrary, if you will excuse me——

Mr. Wood. What reason is there for their not being able to me
the requirements?

Mr. Mitchell. Well, that is due to the instability of our econon
system.

Mr. Wood. But it does not show any instability in their system, because they are getting more. Those paying income taxes in the higher brackets have been receiving more.

Mr. Mitchell. I understand, sir. I am talking about the particular industries and employers that would not be able to pay in excess-profits taxes, in income taxes. There are many of those. Now, I think we would get back a large share of the " predatory wealth ", as I will describe it, without slowing down industry at all. I think we could get rid of many of the individuals that receive this income, without injuring our productive capacity. On the other hand, I think if you took those funds and gave them to the workers and permitted them to spend them, it would help industry.

Mr. Dunn. Pardon me, Mr. Wood. Five minutes have elapsed.

Mr. Wood. Is my 5 minutes up, already?

Mr. Mitchell. I was enjoying the conversation.

Mr. Dunn. There is no objection. Proceed, Mr. Wood.

Mr. Wood. I just want to get this point. Since the war, this Government has given back to industry nearly four billions of dollars to the Rockefellers, the Morgans, and that aggregation of industrial pirates. They have given back nearly four billions of dollars of what they term were income taxes that were collected.

Mr. Lundeen. Refunded.

Mr. Mitchell. Refunded.

Mr. Wood. That is, in excess of that authorized by law. Now, what effect has that had on industry? We have given back nearly four billions of dollars, and right after that came the depression. Did that encourage those gentlemen who got back their billions of dollars to reinvest it and make business good, or what has happened?

Mr. Mitchell. It encouraged them to reinvest it and make business worse. This is the kind of business which is strangled by its own methods. That is really the question—we are poor because we are so rich.

Mr. Wood. No; but you talk about reinvestment. What sort of reinvestment do you mean? In Cities Service stock?

Mr. Mitchell. I think the public utilities—as suggested by Congressman Lundeen, I think—have been more stable than some of the others. There has been comparatively little capital investment in the last years of the depression, of course.

Mr. Wood. Oh, yes.

Mr. Mitchell. Comparatively little; but what there is has been to the injury of our economic system—of this economic system.

Mr. Wood. What mode of taxes would you suggest, then, in addition to those enumerated here?

Mr. Lundeen. Pardon me, Congressman Wood, may I interrupt there, one moment, with your permission? Your statement regarding the $4,000,000,000 is very interesting. I have before me here the Washington Post of this morning, stating, in confirmation of your statement, in which I am very much interested, " U. S. refunds $48,664,202 in 1934 income taxes."

Mr. Wood. Yes.

Mr. Lundeen. And that is $10,000,000 less than they refunded in 1933; so there was 'way in excess of $100,000,000 refunded in income taxes in just 2 years, which go to make up part of that $4,000,000,000, or whatever the figure was that you mentioned.

Mr. Wood. And that is a very small portion, of course.

Mr. Lundeen. Yes.

Mr. Wood. That is a very small portion in comparison to the amount refunded in the 4 or 5 years prior to that.

Mr. Lundeen. Yes; surely.

Mr. Dunn. Are there any more questions, Congressman Wood?

Mr. Wood. I just wanted to get from the doctor his notions about what other mode of taxation he would suggest.

Mr. Mitchell. You mentioned a sales tax. I think that is the worst mode, of course.

Mr. Wood. I agree with you heartily.

Mr. Mitchell. Because that is a tax on poverty. That is trying to make the people who are already bearing the brunt of economic insecurity, bear it doubly. "A sales tax", Professor Seligman, of Columbia, has said, " is the last resort of Government." We have not reached that point yet, as long as we have these income and inheritance taxes about which the Congressman speaks.

Mr. Wood. The sales tax does not remedy anything.

Mr. Lundeen. What institution is Professor Seligman with?

Mr. Mitchell. Columbia University.

Mr. Dunn. Are there any further questions, Mr. Wood?

Mr. Wood. No.

Mr. Dunn. Mr. Lundeen?

Mr. Lesinski. I have none.

Mr. Lundeen. I have some questions, here. This morning, Congressman Schneider, of Wisconsin, mentioned, in questioning a witness here, the Wisconsin system, and you happened to use the phrase, " The trouble with the Wisconsin system." I wonder if you could just state in a few sentences what you think of that system, because it is apt to come up again, and we would like to have your opinion on that.

Mr. Mitchell. Thank you, sir. My feeling is simply that by partitioning off our resources and confining them to particular industries, or even firms, we are in the position of a city that tries to protect itself against fires by having a tank on every citizen's roof; that we would do much better, of course, by estimating our probable needs, with an ample allowance over, and pooling our resources in a central reservoir; that this accomplishes a great saving of water, and also a saving of homes, protecting them against fire.

Mr. Lundeen. What is the central method of the Wisconsin plan?

Mr. Mitchell. There is no central plan, no central pool in the Wisconsin plan.

Mr. Lundeen. That is the trouble, is it not?

Mr. Mitchell. That is like the tank on every person's roof.

Mr. Lundeen. You mean each plant acts independently?

Mr. Mitchell. In each plant, right; and when that gives out they get unemployment for a definite period, or that business may fail, as far as that is concerned.

Mr. Lundeen. If I were employed in a solvent business, I would be all right perhaps, but if you were employed in a plant that goes " haywire " in a depression, then you are out?

Mr. Mitchell. I am out. If, on the other hand, all plants contribute to a central pool, the plants that continue to operate will be supporting the plants which, due mainly to social causes—that is, causes ouside their control—therefore, are unable to operate.

Mr. LUNDEEN. Is there a State contribution, too, in addition to that?

Mr. MITCHELL. No, sir. In the Wisconsin plan, I believe it all comes from the employers, not even from the employees.

Mr. LUNDEEN. It is a tax on the pay roll?

Mr. MITCHELL. Right.

Mr. LUNDEEN. Now, there is another question. The English rate of taxation, of which Congresman Wood spoke, is much higher than ours on incomes and inheritances. That is my recollection.

Mr. WOOD. It is more than double, in the higher brackets.

Mr. LUNDEEN. Of course, I have not the figures in mind.

Mr. MITCHELL. No.

Mr. LUNDEEN. But if we adopted the rate here that they have on great inheritances and incomes, that certainly would help some in taking care of the aged and unemployed?

Mr. MITCHELL. It would certainly help tremendously. I am unable to say whether it would be adequate, sir.

Mr. LUNDEEN. Certainly England is getting along pretty well these days.

Mr. MITCHELL. Better than we are.

Mr. LUNDEEN. Yes; better than we are. They have less unemployment. They have only 2 million plus unemployed in the British Isles, according to their published statement. Perhaps their taxation shock might not kill us after all.

Mr. DUNN. The population of the British Isles amounts to but about 46,000,000.

Mr. MITCHELL. He means the proportion is much less, and that they have had an absolute reduction in the last year.

Mr. LUNDEEN. Their unemployment is only two million and some hundred thousands, which would be equal to about six or seven million here, would it not, at that rate, or something like that?

Mr. DUNN. Yes; it would be just that.

I presume there are no more questions, Doctor. We appreciate what you have said was very interesting. We have learned a great deal.

Mr. LUNDEEN. I would like to ask if you have any statement you would like to insert in the record?

Mr. MITCHELL. I should like very much to see inserted in the record, Congressman Lundeen, the list of endorsers of the Lundeen bill.

Mr. LUNDEEN. Mr. Chairman, I ask that that be inserted.

Mr. DUNN. Is there an objection? No objection.

(The list of endorsers of the Lundeen bill, H. R. 2827, is as follows:)

CITY COUNCILS, COUNTY AND MUNICIPAL BODIES

Connecticut, city council, Bridgeport.
Idaho, city council, Coeur D'Alene.
Illinois, city councils, Belleville, Benald, Casey, Caseyville, Collinsville, Tarvey, Midlothian, Norwood Oak, Rockford, Thayer, Virden, and Ziegler.
Iowa, county board of Des Moines.
Kentucky, county board, Covington.
Maine, county board supervisors, St. George.

Michigan, city councils, Caspian, Platt, Sault Ste. Marie; board of supervisors, Baraga County; advisory board district council of Detroit City Commission, Sault Ste. Marie.

Minnesota, city councils, Eveleth, Hibbing, Minneapolis, Rochester, and White; city fire department, Eveleth.

Missouri, city council, St. Louis.

Montana, city council, Great Falls.

Nebraska, Douglas County Board, Omaha.

New Jersey, city councils, Bayonne, Clifton, Garfield, Linden.

New York, city council, Buffalo.

Ohio, city councils, Bedford, Brooklyn Village, Canton, Landale, and Toledo.

Oklahoma, Montgomery County commissioners; city council, Cushing.

Oregon, city councils, Klamath Falls and Portland.

Pennsylvania, town councils, Freedom Boro, Sonway, Defiance, Dudely Longandale; city councils, Allentown, Arnold, and Conway Dickson City, Forest Hills, Glassport, Swissvale, and Wilkensburg; school board of Challfont Boro.

Washington, city councils, Aberdeen, Tacoma.

Wisconsin, city councils, Cudahy, Racine, Milwaukee, Superior, West Allis, Lake.

VETERANS' ORGANIZATIONS

Italian Ex-Servicemen's League, Bridgeport, Conn.; Veterans' National Rank and File Committee, District of Columbia; American Legion Post, Chicago, Ill.; 3 American Legion Posts, Schenectady; 4 American Legion Posts, Long Island; Big Six Post, Veterans of Foreign Wars, New York; Workers Ex-Servicemen's League, New York; Daily News American Legion Post; United States War Veterans, Manhattan Camp 1; United States War Veterans, George R. Tilly Camp 66; United States War Veterans, Roosevelt Camp 10; United States War Veterans; Abraham Lincoln Auxiliary 54, New York City, N. Y.; American Legion Post, Glassport, Pa.; American Legion posts, West Virginia.

INTERNATIONAL UNIONS

Iron, Steel, and Tin Workers, Amalgamated Association.
Mine, Mill, and Smelter Workers, International Union.
American Federation of Full Fashioned Hosiery Workers.
Moulders' Union of North America.
Textile Workers of America, United.

STATE FEDERATION OF LABOR

Arkansas, Colorado, Iowa, Montana, Nebraska, Rhode Island.

CENTRAL LABOR UNIONS

San Diego Federated Trades and Labor Council, San Diego, Calif.
Central Labor Union, Danbury, Conn.
Central Labor Union, Gibson County, Ind.
Trades Labor Assembly, Sioux City, Iowa.
Federation of Labor, Kalamazoo, Mich.
Central Labor Union, Minneapolis, Minn.
Central Labor Union, St. Louis, Mo.
Building Trades Council, Great Falls, Mont.
Cascade Trades and Labor Assembly, Great Falls, Mont.
Central Labor Union, Grand Island, Nebr.
Central Labor Union, Lincoln, Nebr.
Central Labor Body, Atlantic City.
Central Labor Union, Newark.
Essex Trades Councils, Newark, Essex, N. J.
Central Labor Union, Albuquerque, N. Mex.
Central Labor Union, Jamestown, N. Y.
District Council of Queens and Nassau Counties, N. Y.
Trades Assembly, Schenectady, N. Y.
Bradford Trades Assembly, Bradford, Pa.
Federation of Labor, Hazelwood, Pa.
Central Labor Council, Pittsburgh, District of Pennsylvania.
Central Labor Union of Jeanette, Pa.

Central Labor Union of New Kensington.
Federated Trades Council, Reading, Pa.
Federated Labor Union, Providence, R. I.
Building Trades Council, Providence, R. I.
Federation of Labor; Salt Lake City, Utah.
Central Labor Union, Spokane, Wash.
Trades Labor Council, Racine, Wis.

LOCAL UNIONS

Asbestos Workers, International Association of Heat and Frost Insulators. Local 31, Providence, R. I.

Barbers' International Union, Journeymen: Locals, 175 Danbury, 72 Norwalk, Conn.; Belleville, Ill.; 182 Boston, Mass.; 913 Brooklyn, N. Y.; 2 Philadelphia, Pa.; Salt Lake City, Utah.

Bakery and Confectionery Workers' International Union of America: Locals, 125 Berkeley, 43 Fresno, 24 San Francisco, Calif.; 62, 237, 2, 49, Chicago, Ill.; 190 Metuchen, N. J.; 79, 164 New York City, 14 Rochester, N. Y.; 39, 334 Cleveland, 177 Youngstown, Ohio; 45 Boston, Mass.; 204 Pittsburgh, Pa.; 122 Providence, R. I.; 473 Bellingham, Wash.

Bill Posters and Billers of America, International Alliance of: Local 49 Seattle, Wash.

Blacksmiths, Drop Forgers and Helpers, International Brotherhood of: Locals, 303 Butte, Mont.; 77 Milwaukee, Wis.

Boiler Makers, Iron Ship Builders and Helpers of America, International Brotherhood of: Locals, 244 Sioux City, Iowa; 81 Readville, Mass.; 104 Seattle, Wash.; 249 Huntingdon, W. Va.

Brewery, Flour, Cereal, and Soft Drink Workers of America, International Union: Locals, Butte, Great Falls, Mont.; Tacoma, Wash.; Newark, N. J.

Bricklayers, Mason and Plasterers International Union of America: Locals, Baltimore, Md.; 2 Detroit, Mich.; 19 St. Louis, Mo.; Brooklyn, 3 locals in New York, N. Y.; 18 Cincinnati, Ohio; 3 Philadelphia, Pa.; Providence, R. I.; 2 locals, Oshkosh, Wis.; 8 Milwaukee, Wis.; 5 Huntingdon, W. Va.

Building Service Employee's International Union: Locals, 1077 New York. N. Y.; 125 Providence, R. I.

Bridge and Structural Iron Workers International Association: Locals, 420 Reading, Pa.; 2416 Portland, Oreg.; 350 Atlantic City, N. J.

Carmen of America, Brotherhood Railway: Locals, 227 Chicago, Ill. and 210; 23 Princeton, Ind.; 2031, 266 Sioux City, Iowa; 56 Atchison, Kans.; 431 Bay City, 1054 Detroit, 641 Port Huron, Mich.; 299 Minneapolis, Minn.; 628 Providence, R. I.; 823, 1085 New York, N. Y.; 698 Spokane, Wash.

Carvers' Association of North America, International Wood. Locals. Philadelphia, Pa.; Chicago, Ill.; New York, N. Y.

Clerks, National Federation of Post Office: Local, 10 New York, N. Y.

Clerks International Protective Association, Retail: Local 753 Philadelphia, Pa.; Butte, Mont.

Cigarmakers International Union of America: Locals, 225 Salt Lake City, Utah; 14 Chicago, Ill.

Coopers' International Union of North America: Local, 9 Philadelphia. Pa.; 54 Detroit, Mich.

Carpenters and Joiners of America, United Brotherhood of, District Councils—Carpenters District Council, Kansas City, Mo. 29th Annual Convention, New Jersey State Council of Carpenters, Newark, N. J.: Locals, 1687 Montgomery, Ala.; 1089 Phoenix, Ariz.; 891 Hot Springs, Ark.; 210 Stamford, Conn.; 132 District of Columbia; 352 Anderson, 1953 Greencastle, 487 Linton, Ind.; 523 Keokuk, 948 Sioux City, Iowa; 1784, 416, 419, 13, 58, 62, 181, 504 Chicago, 896 Crystal Lake, 1366 Quincy, 16 Belleville-Springfield, Ill.; 720 Auburn, 11. 56, 157 Boston, 296 Brockton, Mass.; 116 Bay City, 337 Detroit, 1299 Iron River, 1199 Pontiac, Mich.; 361 Duluth, 7, 1865 Minneapolis, 87 St. Paul, Minn.; 1329 Independence, Mo.; 286 Great Falls, Mont.; 2237 Bayonne, 349 East Orange, 119, 1782 Newark, 299 Union City, N. J.; 2717 Brooklyn, 2372 Garnersville, 66 Jamestown, 2090, 2163 New York City, 163 Peekskill, 1115 Pleasantville, 203 Poughkeepsie, 1660 Raymondsville, 188 Yonkers, N. Y.; 224 Cincinnati, 1180, 2159 Cleveland, 735 Mansfield, 186 Steubenville, Ohio; 226 2218, 2154 Portland, 1065 Salem, Oreg.; 2008 Ponca City, Okla.; 59 Lancaster, 207 Chester, 122, 277, 1050, 1051. 1073. 1856, 2194 Philadelphia, Pa.; 1695 Cranston, 810 Kingston, R. I.; 2016 Eastland, 1666 Kingsville, Tex.; 1984 Magna, Utah; 317 Aberdeen,

562 Everett, 1184, 1335 Seattle, 84, 98 Spokane, Tacoma, Wash.; 161 Kenosha, 2244 Little Chuta, 849 Manitowoc, 1053, 2073 Milwaukee, 460 Wausau, Wis.; 1620 Rocksprings, 1241 Thermopolis, Wyo.

Clothing Workers of America, Amalgamated: Joint Council St. Louis, Mo.; Joint Board of Philadelphia, Pa.: Locals, 1 Boston, Mass.; 4 New York, N. Y.; 75 Philadelphia, Pa.; 38 Chicago, Ill.

Draftsmen's Union, International Federation of Technical Engineers, Architects: Local 54 Milwaukee, Wis.

Electrical Workers of America, International Brotherhood of: Locals, 82 Los Angeles, Calif.; 122 Great Falls, Mont.; 292 Minneapolis, Minn.; 31 Brooklyn, N. Y.; 623 New York, N. Y.; 65 Butte, Mont.; 48 Sioux City, Iowa.

Engineers International Union of Operating: Locals, Sioux City, Iowa; 5 Detroit, Mich.; 34 Minneapolis, Minn.; 48 Los Angeles, Calif.; 3 Brooklyn, N. Y.; 506, 506a, 835 Philadelphia, Pa.; 37 Providence, R. I.; 83 Spokane, Wash.

Engravers Union of North America, International: Local 5 Chicago, Ill.

Federal Union: Locals, Ice and Cold Storage Workers, 16918, Centralia, Wash.; Casket Makers, 19306 Chicago, Ill.; Automobile Workers, United, Federal Labor, 18677 Detroit, Ternsted Local of United Auto Workers Union, Detroit, Buick Local A. F. of L., Flint, Mich.; Federal Local 19253 Great Falls, Mont.; Dental Laboratory Technicians, 18405 St. Louis, Mo.; Federal Labor Union, 19128 Lincoln, Nebr.; Aeronautical Workers, Federal Labor, 18286 Buffalo, N. Y.; Midvale Steel Federal Union, Philadelphia, Brass Bobbin Winders, 14659 Philadelphia, Brass Bobbin Winders, Philadelphia, Radio Workers, Federal Labor, 18832 Philadelphia, Pa.; Automobile Workers, United Federal Labor, 18614 Cleveland, Ohio; Federal Labor, Providence, R. I.; Federal Labor Union, 19155 Breckenridge, Tex.; Sawmill, 19515 Huntington, Chemical Workers, 18634 Huntington, W. Va.; Federal Labor (Vincent McCall), 18846 Kenosha, Simmons Bed Federated Union, 18456 Kenosha, Federal Labor, 18546 Milwaukee, Wis.

Fire Fighters, International Association of: Locals, 37 Chicago, Ill.; 301 Burlington, Iowa; 96 Butte, Mont.; 287 Long Beach, L. I., N. Y.

Firemen and Oilers, International Brotherhood of: Locals, 32 Detroit, Mich.; 13 Spokane, Wash.

Fur Workers' Union of United States & Canada, International: Local 3 Brooklyn, N. Y.

Garment Workers' Union, International Ladies': Locals, 65, 64 Los Angeles, Calif.; 64 Chicago, Ill.; 20, 22, 66 New York, N. Y.

Garment Workers of America, United: Local 75 Philadelphia, Pa.; 27 Minneapolis, Minn.

Glass Cutters' League of America, Window: Local 528 New York, N. Y.

Glass Workers' Union, American Flint, Locals, 93 Chicago, Ill.; 2 Glassport, Pa.

Glove Workers' Unions of America, International: Local 69 Gloversville, N. Y.

Granite Cutters' International Association of America: Locals, Concord, Peacock, N. H.; Barre, Vt.

Hatters, Cap and Millinery Workers International Union, United: Locals, 10 Danbury, Conn.; 8 New York, N. Y.; 6 Philadelphia, Pa.

Hod Carriers, Building & Common Laborers' Union of America, International: Locals, 591 Santa Barbara, 270 San Jose, Calif.; Bridgeport, Conn.; 455 New Haven, 524 Norwich, 499 Stamford, Conn.; Belleville, Centralia, Zeigler, Ill.; Princeton, Ind.; Waltham, 210 Worcester, Mass.; 563 Minneapolis, Minn.; 150 Butte, 278 Great Falls, 187 Missoula, Mont.; 680 Newark, 31 Union City, N. J.; 141 Portchester, 435 Rochester, N. Y.; 173 Pittsburgh, Pa.; 271 Providence, R. I.; 242 Seattle, Spokane, Wash.

Hotel and Restaurant Employees and Beverage Dispensers' International Alliance: Locals, 94 San Francisco, 271 Petaluna, Calif.; 781 Washington, D. C.; 733 Detroit, Mich.; 34 Minneapolis, Minn.; 109 Newark, 508 Atlantic City, N. J.; 325, 2 Brooklyn, N. Y.; 72 Cincinnati, Ohio; 659 Dallas, Tex.

Iron, Steel, and Tin Workers, Amalgamated Association of: Locals, 709 New Britain, Conn.; 184 Sioux City, Iowa; Sparrows Point, Md.; 410 Great Falls, Mont.; 149 Clairton, Pa.; Ellwood City, 169 Ellwood City, 68, 67 Johnstown, Pa.; 37 Providence, R. I.; 1 Follansbee, W. Va.

Jewelry Workers Union, International: Locals, 2 Newark, N. J.; 1, 21 New York.

Lathers', International Union of Wood, Wire, and Metal: Locals, 305 Great Falls, Mont.; 113 Sioux Falls, Iowa; 455 Lake Worth, Fla.

Laundry Workers' International Union: Local 108 St. Louis, Mo.

Leather Workers, United International Union: Locals, New York, N. Y.; Chelsea, Mass.; 52 Philadelphia, Pa.

Lithographers' International Protective and Beneficial Association of the United States and Canada: Local 5 St. Louis, Mo.

Longshoremen's International Association Pacific Coast Convention: Locals, 38, 12 Seattle, Wash.

Machinists, International Association of, Convention of International Association of All Machinists of New England, Boston, Mass.: Locals, 84 Berwyn, 234, 83, 337, 915 Chicago, 390 Park Ridge, Ill.; 178 Sioux City, Iowa; 404 Baltimore, Md.; 64 Massachusetts; 1122 Detroit, Mich.; 459 St. Paul, Minne.; Concord, N. H.; 816 Hoboken, N. J.; 447, 402, 226 New York, 417 Staten Island, N. Y.; 162, 729 Cincinnati, 439 Cleveland, 203 Akron, 404 Youngstown, Ohio; 187 Sharpsville, Pa.; 119 Newport, 110 Newport, R. I.; 79 Seattle, Wash.; 57 Huntington, W. Va.; 116 Milwaukee, Wis.

Marble, Slate and Stone Polishers, Rubbers and Sawyers, Tile and Marble Setters, Helpers and Terrazzo Helpers, International Association of: Locals, 62 Philadelphia, Pa.; 8 Providence, R. I.; 47 Milwaukee, Wis.

Meat Cutters & Butcher Workmen of North America, Amalgamated: Locals, 333 Butte, Mont.; 545 St. Louis, Mo.; 18, 174 New York, N. Y.; 110 Philadelphia, Pa.

Maintenance of Way Employees, Brotherhood of: Locals, 1077 New York, N. Y.; Sioux City, Iowa.

Metal Workers' International Association, Sheet: Locals 2 Stockton, Calif.; 615 Buffalo, 137 New York, N. Y.; 329 Salisbury, N. C.; 37 Providence, R. I.; 446 Great Falls, Mont.

Mine, Mill, Smelter Workers, International Union of: Local, Bessemer, Ala.; Eveleth, Minn.; 3 Bingham, Utah; Spelter, W. Va.; 125 Iron River, Mich.; 1636 Kansas City, Mo.; Salt Lake City, Utah.

Mine Workers of America, United: Locals, 3664 Auburn, 3543 Benton, 52, 1397 Centralia, Glen Ridge, 3464 Gillespie, 2840 Middlegrove, 2109 Nashville, 721 Pana, 2403 Springfield, 720 Staunton, 691 Troy, 5599 Westville, Ill.; 6303 Bicknell, 5584 Princeton, Ind.; 13 Des Moines, 916 Hitema, Iowa; 191 South Hibbling, Minn.; 1 Butte, Mont.; 4472 Glen Robins, 5497 Powhatan, Ohio; 1451 Connerton, 2399 Dairytown, 4439 Fayette, 494 Homer City, 1560 Lost Creek, 807 Maple Hill, 2587 Raven Tun 1545 Torty Fort, 5383, 3506 Renton, 1398 Shaft, 2611, 113, 2346, 1509, 1414, 1443, 1685, 6109, 1467 Shenandoah, Three Locals Westmoreland, Six Mile Run, 4439 South Brownsville, 458 Swoyersville, Pa.; 6147 Besoco, 6107 Killarney, 6106 Meade, 2980 Pimberton, W. Va.; Ladies Auxiliary 920, Pittsburgh, Ladies Auxiliary 762 Pittsburgh, Pa.

Molder's Union of North America, International: Locals, 161 Stamford, Conn.; 182 Belleville, 275 Chicago, 153 Hazelcrest, Ill.; 24 Baltimore, Md.; 388 Kalamazoo, Mich.; Anaconda, Mont.; 84 Buffalo, 78 Watertown, N. Y.; 27 Cleveland, Ohio; Cheltersham, Philadelphia, 111 Philadelphia, 348 Reading, Pa.; 171 Port Orchard, 158 Seattle, 338 Spokane, Wash.

Musicians, American Federation of: Locals, 403 Willimantic, Conn.; 219 Stanton, Ill.; 24 Akron, Ohio, 362 Huntington, W. Va.

Oil Field, Gas Well and Refinery Workers of America: Chemical and Oil Workers Union, Oakland, Calif.; Local 210 Hammond, Ind.

Painters, Paperhangers, and Decorators of America, Brotherhood of: District councils: Painters District Council 46, Los Angeles; Painters District Council, San Francisco, Calif.; District Council-Advisory Board Painters Brotherhood, Detroit; Semiannual Conference Michigan State Painters, Lansing, Mich.; Painters District Council, Kansas City, Mo.; Painters District Council, Newark, N. J.; Painters District Council 21, Philadelphia: Locals, 713, 449 Glendale, 235, 5 Hollywood, 1346 Inglewood, 256 Long Beach, 1065, 92, 1345, 1348, 51, 202, 1345, 51, 831, 792, 644, 511, 636, 202, 1348, 1063 Los Angeles, 92 Montrose, 1147 Roseville, 315 San Jose, 821 Venice, 441 Whittier, 949 Wilmington, Calif.; 930 Denver, Colo.; 190 Bridgeport, 1276 Westport, Conn.; 368 Washington, D. C.; 1088 Daytona Beach, 1321 Clearwater, 1175 Coral Gables, Fla.; 193 Atlanta, Ga.; Belleville, 627, 275, 294, 637 Chicago, 863 Lake Forest, 460 Hammond, Ill.; 1215 Boone, Iowa; 277 Atlantic City, 653 East Rutherford, 997, 426 Haddon Heights, 705 Irvington, 777 Newark, 174, 140 Passaic 144 Perth Amboy, N. J.; 201 Albany, 442 Brooklyn, 504 Flushing, Long Island, 822 Glen Cove, 721 Islip, 498 Jamestown, 121 Long Island City, 848, 892, 499, 997, 1101, 905, 261 New York City, 707 Oneida, 1035 Richmond Hill, Long Island, 795 Rockaway Beach, Long Island, 1134 Rockville Center, N. Y.;

229 Kansas City, Kansas; 1244 New Orleans, La.; 623 Chelsea, 258 Boston, Mass.; 675 Dearborn, 42, 357, 591, 37, 552 Detroit, Mich.; 9 Kansas City, Mo.; 1086, 386 Minneapolis, 681 Rochester, 540 Winona, Minn.; 720 Butte, 260 Great Falls, Mont.; 50, 308, 866, 531 Cincinnati, 765, 867, 128 Cleveland, 1103 Mentor, 546 Toledo, Ohio; 443 Okmulgee, 935 Tulsa, Okla.; 788 Sandusky, 438 Steubenville, 476, Youngstown, Ohio; 751 Gibsonia, 1114 Danesville, 380 Lancaster, 887 Oil City, 306, 997, 703, 632 Philadelphia, 479, 282, 6, 84 Pittsburgh, Pa.; 15 Central Falls, 195, 692 Providence, R. I.; 586 Spartanburg, S. C.; 965 Jackson City, Tenn.; 123 Gilman, Vt.; 743 Olympia, 1220 Tacoma, 1114 Janesville, Wash.

Pattern Makers League: Local, Detroit, Mich.

Paper Plate and Bag Makers: Local, 107 New York City, N. Y.

Paving Cutters Union of the United States of America and Canada: Locals, Clark Island, 108 Tenants Harbor, 9 Thomaston, Maine; 43 Woodstock, Md.; 53 Rockport, Mass.; Concord, N. H.

Plasterers International Association of the United States and Canada United: Locals, 87 Montgomery, Ala.; 346 Long Beach, 460 San Francisco, Calif.; 32 Denver, Colo.; Bloomington, Ill.; 155 Baltimore, Md.; 65 Minneapolis, Minn.; Omaha, Nebr.; 60 New York, N. Y.; 1 Cincinnati, 7 Toledo, 179 Youngstown, 214 Hamilton, Ohio; 40 Providence, 182 Franklin, R. I.; 31 Pittsburgh, Pa.; 746 Mount Vernon, 77 Seattle, Wash.; 110 Great Falls, Mont.; 428 Racine, Wis.; 352 Ovel, Wyo.

Plumbers and Steam Fitters of the United States and Canada, United Association of: Locals, 230 San Diego, Calif.; 18 Sioux City, Iowa; 64 Northampton, Mass.; 98 Detroit, Mich.; 41 Butte, 139 Great Falls, Mont.; 1 Brooklyn, 206 Elmira, N. Y.; 98 Cleveland, 108 Hamilton, Ohio; 42 Reading, Pa.; 476, 29 Providence, R. I.; 504 Beaumont, Tex.; 608 West Allis, Wis.

Polishers, Metal, International Union: Locals, 6, 277 Chicago, Ill.

Printing Pressmen's and Assistants' Union of North America: Locals, 140 San Diego, Calif.; 147 Wichita, Kans.; 3, 4 Chicago, Ill.; 196 New Brunswick, N. J.; 23 New York City, N. Y.

Pulp, Sulphite, and Paper Mill Workers of the United States and Canada International Brotherhood of: Locals, 37 East Millinocket, 27 Woodland, Maine.

Plush Weave—Textile Workers' of America, United: Local, 471 Philadelphia, Pa.

Quarry Workers, International Union of North America: Locals, 82 Rockport, 81 Lanesville, Mass.

Railway Brotherhood, Order of Railway Conductors of America: Local, 55 Port Jervis, N. Y.

Brotherhood of Railroad Trainmen: Local, Milwaukee, Wis.

Brotherhood of Locomotive Engineers: Delegates from 150 Divisions of Locomotive Engineers, Kansas City, Mo.; Locals: 405 Milwaukee, Wis.; West Virginia.

Brotherhood of Locomotive Firemen and Enginemen: Locals, 23 Jersey City, N. J.; 183 Cleveland, Ohio; Montivedo, Minn.; 1 Port Jervis, N. Y.

Order of Railway Conductors of America: Locals, 69 El Paso, Tex.; 1 Oak Park, Ill.; 698 Chicago, 227 Chicago, Ill.

Roofers, Dam and Waterproof Workers' Association United Slate, Tile and Composition: Locals, 80 Great Falls, Mont.; 4 Newark, N. J.

Stage Employes and Moving Picture Machine Operators of the United States and Canada, International Alliance of Theatrical: Locals, 130 Altoona, Pa.; 361 Kenosha, Wis.; 475 Eau Clair, Wis.; 598 Marion, Ohio; 644 New York, N. Y.; 3 Sioux City, Iowa; 150 Los Angeles, Calif.; 306 New York, N. Y.; 223 Providence, R. I.; 460 Racine, Wis.; International Alliance of Projectionists New York, N. Y.

Stereotypers' and Electrotypers' Union of North America, International: Locals, 8 East St. Louis, Ill.; 114, 15 Dayton, Ohio.

Stonecutters' Association of North America, Journeymen: Locals, Akron, Ohio; Concord, N. H.

Switchmen's Union of North America: Locals, 240 Libera, Kans.; 291 Padeah, Ky.

Typographical Union, International: Locals, 231 San Jose, 899 Whittier, 221-21 San Diego, Calif.; 41 Atlanta, Ga.; 491 Pocatello, 241 Turvi Falls, Idaho; 330 Berwyn, 215 Decatur, 306 Alton, Ill.; 292 Cedar Rapids, Iowa; 590 Hobart, 10 Indianapolis, Ind.; 727 Hibbing, Minn.; 131 Elmhurst, L. I., 6 New York, N. Y.; 499 Okmulgee, Okla.; 62 Toledo, 2 in Toledo, Ohio; 242 York, Pa.; 43 Charleston, S. C.; 202 Seattle, Wash.; Daily News Chapel, New York City, N. Y.

Tailors' Union of America, Journeymen: Locals, Youngstown, Ohio; 46 Buffalo, N. Y.; 131 Pittsburgh, 323 Bethlehem, Pa.; 106 Spokane, Wash.; 86 Milwaukee, 282 Green Bay. Wis.

Teachers, American Federation of: Local 256, Grand Rapids, Mich.

Teamsters, Chauffeurs, Stablemen, and Helpers of America, International Brotherhood of: Locals, 429 Reading, Pa.; Los Angeles, Calif.; Atlantic City, N. J.; Duluth, Minn.; 156 Philadelphia, Pa.

United Textile Workers of America, United Textile Workers Convention; District Council of American Federation of Full Fashion Hosiery Workers of New Jersey; District Council of American Federation of Full Fashion Hosiery Workers of New York, New York City, N. Y.; Convention of American Federation of Hosiery Workers, Reading, Pa.: Locals, New Orleans, La.; 31 Northampton, Mass.; 1733 Paterson, 2052 Union City, N. J.; 5 New York, N. Y.; Allentown, 4 Langhorn, 1750, 702, 1589, 1526, 706, Philadelphia, Pa.

Upholsterers' International Union of North America: Locals, 75 Baltimore, Md.; 77 Philadelphia, Pa.

INDEPENDENT UNIONS

California: Agricultural and Cannery Workers Industrial Union.

Connecticut: Shoe Makers Association of New Haven.

Illinois: Progressive Miners of America of Cuba, Taylor Springs and Springfield, Workers Alliance Union of Staunton.

Massachusetts: Weavers Progressive Association of Fall River, Workers Protective Union of Lowell, National Textile Workers Union.

Michigan: Registered Pharmacists Association of Detroit, Sheet Metal Workers of Detroit, Auto Workers Union of Detroit, International Society of Detroit, United Workers of Dental Co. of Escanaba.

Minnesota: Packinghouse Workers Industrial Union.

New York City: Association of Laboratory Technicians, American Newspaper Guild, Alteration Painters, Drygoods Workers' Union, Food Workers Industrial Union, Furniture Workers Industrial Union, Glass and China Decorators Industrial Union, Laundry Workers Industrial Union, Marine Workers Industrial Union, Needletrades Workers Industrial Union, Tobacco Workers Industrial Union, Steel and Metal Workers Industrial Union, Soft and Bristle Hairdressers Union, Toy Workers Industrial Union, Photographic Workers Industrial Union.

Ohio: Mechanics Educational Society, Cleveland.

Pennsylvania: Union of Beaver County of Rochester, National Miners Union of Pittsburgh, United Ribbon Workers Association of Allentown, Independent Coal Operators Association of Shamokin, Independent Union of the Columbia Steel and Shaft Co. of Carnegie.

Rhode Island: American Independent Textile Workers Union of Pawtucket.

Texas: Laborers Association of Breckenridge, Associacion de Domesticos, Associacion de Jornaleros.

Washington: Fisherman and Cannery Workers Industrial Union of Seattle, National Lumber Workers Union of Seattle.

CLUBS

Connecticut: New Britain Association of Lithuanian Workers Inc. Branch 108, Lithuanians' Citizens Independent Club, Polish Workers, Scandinavian Entertainers, Scandinavian Workers, First Polish, Slovak Political.

Illinois: Polish Democratic Club, Chicago, Progressive Workers of Brookside Township, Polish-American Citizens, Chicago Heights, Hunters Protective Club.

Michigan: Chippewa County Workingmen's of Sault Ste. Marie, Slovak American Citizens Club.

New York City: Associated Workers Club, Moshulu Progressive, Pelham Parkway Workers, New Youth Group, Fordham Progressive, Tremont Progressive, Midas Youth, Ridgewood Youth, Utica Center, Canarsie Workers, New Youth, Progressive Workers, Social Youth, Progressive Community Center, American Youth, Taxpayers Civic, Ann's of Maspeth, Inc., Italian American Progressive, New Group, Pequoits Ladies Social, Tamacqua Social, Unionport Political, Yorkville Workers, A. C., Oceana Social, Boro Park Culture, New Group, New Culture, Rugby Youth, Red Sparks, Cli Grand, West Side, W. C., New Youth Center, Hollis Circle Democratic Club, Elmhurst, Crematorial Society Bremer

Ladies, James W. Husted Fellowcraft, National John Reed Clubs, Italian American Progressive Club.

New Jersey: American Slovak Citizens' Club.

Ohio: Julian Marchlewski Polish Club, Doumanian Democratic Social Club.

Pennsylvania: Polish Club, Carnegie, Workers Educational Club, Monessen, Polish Workers Club, Fairhope Rod and Gun Clubs.

FRATERNAL ORGANIZATIONS

California: Workermen's Sick and Death Benefit fund of United States of America.

Connecticut: Italian Fraternal Association, St. Stanislaus Society, 102, Polish Union of America; Daughters of Mary; St. Vincent Society; L. D. S., Youth Branch 143; Modern Woodman of America, Camp 10431; Grand Duke Withold; Ladies Evangelical Congregational Circle; National Slovak Society; Slovak Evangelical Union A. C. of America; Hungarian Aid Association of America; Education Zirgvoikis Benefit Society; International Workers Order; St. George Benefit Society; St. Andrews Benefit Society; St. Joseph Benefit Society; St. Kasimer Benefit Society, Lithuanian; Russian Mutual Aid Society of America; Sons and Daughters Benefit Society; Towarzystwo Swietego Krzyza.

Illinois: Russian National Mutual Aid Society, Mutual Protective Association Inland Steel Local, Scandinavian Unity Conference, Italo-American National Union, Aido Chorus, Slovak Evangelical Union A. C. of America.

Indiana: Slovak Evangelical Union A. C. of America.

Iowa: Slovak Evangelical Union A. C. of America.

Louisiana: Knights of Peter Claver.

Montana: Slovak Evangelical Union A. C. of America, International Workers Order.

Maryland: Polish American Citizens League.

Massachusetts: Polish District Chamber of Labor, Tadeusz Kosciusko, S. B. Liasve's Chorus.

Minnesota: Slovak Evangelical Union A. C. of America.

Missouri: Slovak Evangelical Union A. C. of America, International Workers Order.

West Virginia: Slovak Evangelical Union A. C. of America.

Michigan: Lithuanian Art Chorus; United Ukrainian Toilers; Italian Lodge; Czechoslovak Baptist Church; Evangelical Slovak Women's Union; National Slovak Society; Slov. Ev. Av. Confession Union; All Saints Society; Slovak Evangelical Union A. C. of America; United Sausage Distributors Union, local 122; Slovak Gim U Sokol.

New Jersey: International Workers Order; Association of Lithuanian Workers; Russian National Mutual Aid Society; Slovak Evangelical Union A. C. of America; Russian National Mutual Aid Society; Elso Newarki Magyi Garoby Gaspar B. S. E.; Rakocsi Hungarian Sick Benefit Association; Verhovay Aid Association; Czechoslovak Society of America, Lodge 236, Dunellen, N. J.; Bohemian Workers Sick and Death Society; Hungarian Workers Home and Amateur Society; Joseph Poniatowski Beneficial Association, Inc.; Carteret Workers Association; Slovak Gymnastic Union, Sokol, lodge 220; Slovak National Society; National Slovak Society; First Catholic Slovak Union.

New York City: Independent Order of Odd Fellows: Thomas Jefferson Lodge 441, Pannonia Lodge 185. Knights of Columbus: Brendan Council 306, Vincentian Council. Foresters of America: Grand Court State of New York, Court 16, 200, 211, 349, 439, 453. Independent Sons of Italy: Supreme Lodge. Sons of Italy Grand Lodge: Loggia Cesare Battisti 583, Loggia Uguaglianza 83. Workmen's Circle: Branches 35, 38, 396, 405, 407, 417, 515, 554, 956. Workmen's Sick and Death Benefit Fund: National Committee; Manhattan Agitation Committee, branches 1, 6, 23, 24, 25, 28, 70, 103, 157, 158, 180, 224; Biellese Workers Mutual Society. Geisen Sick Benevolent Society: Ind. Ostrolenker Y. M. B. A.; Adolph Ullman Aid Society; Radnick Chorus; Slovak Evangelical Union A. C. of America, branch 28. International Workers Order: 1,100 branches. International Workers Order, youth section, 450 branches: Independent Tomashpoler Society; Prager Warschauer Y. M. A. S. Russian National Mutual Aid Society: Branches 45, 47, 65, 66, 69, 86, 88, 104; Slovak Catholic Sokol Society; Woodman of the World, Liberty Camp 279; Workmen's Benevolent and Benefit Society; Loggia B. Cellini; First Dimerer Progressive Society; Sun Ray Democratic Association; Fraternal Federation for Social Insurance; Bershader Benevolent Society; Catholic Sokol; Fathers Club of the

Lavanburg Homes; Societá Campobello di Mazzara; Societá Cittadini di
Favara; Societá Concordia Partanna; Societá Cor Bonum Corigliarrere;
Societa' Progressiva Italiana; Ribera Mutual Aid Society; Sant'Agata Militello
Rosmarino; S. M. S. Sauteramio in Colle; Unita' Adornese di M. S., Inc.; So-
cieta' Mutuo Soccorso Furnarese; Association of Lithuanian Workers, Inc.,
branches 13, 14, 15; Association of Lithuanian Workers, Youth Branch; Lithuan-
ian St. George's Society; Roumanian Christian Society; Roumanian Society
Avram Iancu; Ukranian Benefit Society "Bukowina"; Ukranian Free Alliance;
Vereinigte Arbeiter Kranken und Sterbe Kasse, of N. A. Branch 6; Arod and
Vicinity Sick and Benevolent Association; First Stepiner Benevolent Association; Warschauer Brotherly Love Benevolent Society; First Orgayever Benevolent Association; Maramaros Young Men's Society of Brooklyn; First Stepiner
Benevolent Society; Lomzer Young Men's B. A.; Independent Forest Odessa S.
Ben. Association; Polonker Society; Odesser Young Ladies Benevolent Associa-
tion.

New York State: Independent Sons of Italy in America; Workmen's Sick and
Death Benefit Fund, branches 211, 28; Russian National Mutual Aid Society;
Association of Lithuanian Workers; Slovak Evangelical Union A. C. of Amer-
ica; Bohemian Citizens Benevolent Association; Workmen's Circle, branch 221.

Ohio: Slovak Evangelical Union A. C. of America, Societa' di Mutuo Soccorso,
San Nicola Savoia di San Polo Matese.

Pennsylvania: Superior Order of Lithuanian, local 3; Pennsylvania Slovak
Union; Croatian Benefit and Education Society; Croatian Fraternal Union 94;
Slovanian National Benefit Union 505; Dante Alighieri Society, Inc.; Fraternal
Order of Eagles of Pitcairn; Polish Beneficial Association of St. John; Canitus;
American Slavic Benevolent Association; Italian Sons and Daughters of Amer-
ica; Polish Workers Aid Fund N-107; Ukranian Women's League; Lemko As-
sociation, chapter 8; A. L. D. L. D., branch 399; National Slovak Society; Slovak
Evangelical Union A. C. of America.

Rhode Island: Swedish Workingmen's Association.

Wisconsin: Italian-American Society, Blue Bird Lodge 116, W. A. Gardner
Lodge 191, Polish National Alliance, Slovak Evangelical A. C. of America.

Women's Organizations: Lithuanian Girls and Ladies Benefit Society, New
Britain, International Women's Council, New Haven, Conn.; P. M. A. Women's
Auxiliary, Belleville, Ill.; Ukranian United Toilers Women's Section, branch 4,
Detroit, Mich.; United Council Working Class Women, New York; Ladies Aux-
iliary to United Mine Workers of America 762, South Brownsville, Pa.; Women's
Auxiliary International Association of Machinists Local, Milwaukee, Wis.

UNEMPLOYED AND RELIEF WORKERS' ORGANIZATIONS

California—California Workers Association.
Colorado—Workers Unemployed Council of Nucla.
Connecticut—Unemployment Protective Association of New Haven.
Florida—Florida State Federation of Workers League, Tampa.
Kansas—American Workers Union.
Illinois—Chicago Workers Committee, Illinois Workers Alliance.
Indiana—Fort Wayne Unemployed League.
Massachusetts—Springfield Unemployed League.
Michigan—Single Men's Club of Gaspian, Iron River.
Minnesota—Central Council of Workers of Minneapolis, Roosevelt C. W. A.
Club of Eveleth.
Montana—Butte Workingmens Union 12985 of Butte.
New Mexico—Clayton Unemployed Council.
New York—South Shore Unemployment Association of Elmont, L. I., Eastern
Federation of Unemployed and Emergency Workers, Unemployed Hatters Union
8, Workers Unemployed Union, County Unempioyed and Relief Workers Union
of Schenectady.
Ohio—National Unemployed League, Columbus.
Pennsylvania—Unemployed Ribbon Workers Association of Allentown, Unem-
ployed Citizens League of Allegheny County, Workers Relief Protective Associ-
ation of Erie, Roosevelt New Deal Federation of Monessen, Druggist Unem-
ployed of Philadelphia, Unemployed Teachers Council of Philadelphia.
South Dakota—United Workers League of Sioux Falls.
Washington—Relief Workers Association of Port Angeles.
West Virginia—West Virginia Unemployed League District 2 (22 locals) of
Huntington, Brotherhood of Locomotive Engineers Unemployed Union, West
Virginia Unemployed Leagues.

Wisconsin—Wisconsin Federation of Workers Committees of Racine.
COMMUNIST PARTY OF AMERICA.
FARMER LABOR FEDERATION, MINNESOTA.
SOCIALIST PARTY OF UNITED STATES OF AMERICA.
      (See statement at end of hearings, p. 716.)
YOUNG COMMUNIST LEAGUE.
YOUNG PEOPLE'S SOCIALIST LEAGUE, WASHINGTON, D. C.
Scandinavian Workers League, New Britain; A. M. E. Zion Methodist Church;
Inter-Racial Protective League, Chicago, Ill.; A. M. E. Zion Methodist Church,
Baltimore, Md.; Conference of Jewish Social Service, Atlantic City, N. J.;
League of Struggle for Negro Rights, American Youth Congress; Brighton
Beach Parent Teachers Society, Class Room Teachers Groups, Social Workers
Discussion Club, Interprofessional Association for Social Insurance, Federation
of Architects, Engineers, Chemists, and Technicians, Associated Office and Pro-
fessional Emergency Employees, League Against War and Fascism, International
Labor Defense, Daily News Subs' Club, New York City, N. Y.; Church of As-
sembly of God, Cushing, Okla.; Young Bay Coop Diary, Astoria, Oreg.; Farmers
National Committee of Action, Pa.; A. M. E. Zion Methodist Church, Philadelphia, Pa.

STATEMENT OF DR. JOSEPH M. GILLMAN [1]

Mr. GILLMAN. Mr. Chairman, and members of the committee: I
am an economist, a university professor by experience, by training,
and by interest. I am at present connected with the College of the
City of New York in the Economics Department. I came here this
afternoon as the general chairman of the research committees of the
Interprofessional Association, also as an economist who has been
studying the question of insecurity and the various legislative
proposals.

Mr. LESINSKI. May I ask, what is the Interprofessional Association?

Mr. GILLMAN. The Interprofessional Association is an organization of representatives of professional groups, nurses, physicians,
actors, teachers, groups of engineers, architects, and so on, and they
have organized themselves for the sole purpose—in fact, if the chairman wishes me to, I can read the purpose of our own constitution.
It is a small phrase.

Mr. DUNN. Is there very much to it?

Mr. GILLMAN. No; just two lines.

Mr. DUNN. Proceed.

Mr. GILLMAN. " The purpose is to cooperate with industrial workers in promoting unemployment insurance and other social insurance." We, as an organization, are supporting the Lundeen bill.
The task assigned to me by the association was to make a study of
the extent of unemployment, of the probable cost of the Lundeen
bill, and the sources of funds.

Mr. LUNDEEN. They gave you quite a job, there, didn't they?

Mr. GILLMAN. My committee worked, and my group of committees, and I am the chairman of the various committees, as I said.

This afternoon, I have with me a carefully prepared estimate of
the extent of unemployment and of the sources of funds. It is our
hope that before the hearings are over we may present a detailed

[1] Ph. D. Columbia University, in economics; statistician for the Council for National
Defense; statistician for the Emergency Fleet Corporation, Great Lakes District; Senior
Examiner for Shipping Board; chairman of Department of Business Statistics and
director of the Bureau of Business Research at the University of Pittsburgh; private
economist; College of the City of New York economics staff; general chairman of the
Research Committee of the Interprofessional Association for Social Insurance.

statement also of the cost. We were not able to get that ready in the detail by now as we wished, because of the tremendous complications of that particular problem. I may want to say a word on the complications, later; for one thing, perhaps—and I am mindful of that question now because it was discussed with the preceding gentleman—namely, that in order to estimate the cost we have to arrive at some kind of an estimate of the number that might likely be reemployed. At the same time, we must make provision for the fact that, under the present extent of technological advance, millions of people now unemployed will remain unemployed, and that is a very highly technical question, and, as the gentlemen know, that number has been estimated at anywhere from 5 to 7½ million. So it is our hope, as I said, in the next few days, to have those calculations also in a shape to present to the committee, and we will be glad to forward it, of course, to you.

First, I will address myself to the question of the total number of unemployed. As you undoubtedly know, we have no official estimates or official figures of the extent of unemployment in America. This, in spite of the fact that we have now been going through, for a period of 5 years, a most extensive unemployment, and in spite of the fact that on almost every other conceivable economic fact we have statistics. If some of you may have followed the stock market, for instance, we know for every moment of the 6 hours that the Stock Exchange is open the changes within a cent of the price of a thousand different kinds of stocks, yet we do not know within millions the extent of unemployment which represents these miseries of so many millions, except by guess. On the other hand, the economic statistician must make out with any and all possible information he can pick up. We have in the first place, a periodic report by the Labor Department on the number of employed, an estimate of the employed, indexes of employed in the various industries. If we can estimate the number of employed in one year, and again the number of employed another year, we can deduct one from the other as a matter of arithmetic. Unfortunately, during these past 5 years there have been so many shifts in occupational distributions that if we start from any beginning, let us say the census of 1930, we become constantly involved in extremely hazardous guesses. But this, it seems to me, is very important. A year ago, under a request of the United States Senate, the Department of Commerce made a very exhaustive study of the national income, and in that study an estimate had to be made of the extent of unemployment and the average number of unemployed for the year 1932, arrived at in that study, was 14,400,000, nearly 14½ million unemployed for the average of 1932.

Now, the two gentlemen who headed that particular study happen to be thorough-going scientists, Dr. Willard Thorp and Dr. Simon Kuznets. I have the utmost respect for their integrity, sincerity, and ability, and it is by their methods of procedure that I have attempted to bring down to date estimates of the number of unemployed in the United States. The study, as you know, is called "National Income, 1929-32." Following that procedure, I have prepared a table which gives me, first, the average number of employed in the specific industries that are at all measurable, for the years 1929, 1932, 1933, and 1934.

Mr. LUNDEEN. Why do you leave out 1930 and 1931?

Mr. GILLMAN. Merely for the purpose of condensing it into one sheet. It is not necessary to give further detail.

Mr. LUNDEEN. No; perhaps not.

Mr. GILLMAN. Because, after all, I am concerned with getting the latest possible estimates, and then, simply by comparison, showing the earlier year is 1929, 1932, and then again 1933 and 1934.

In this estimate, we find there has been during this period a drop in the total number of employed of something like 9,000,000 people, but at the beginning of the period, over 2,000,000 people were already unemployed, and since that time over 3,500,000 have become available for employment; so that, following these figures, we arrived at a total number of unemployed, averaged for the year 1934, for 10 months or 11 months, depending on how many were available up to the time I made my calculations, of slightly over 14,000,000 unemployed.

When I arrived at that figure it struck me very forcibly that if, in 1932, our total number of unemployed was 14½ million, roughly, and if now we had only 500,000 fewer unemployed, it simply means that, while there has been an increase of the number of people on the pay rolls of about 2,000,000, there has been at the same time an increase of the availables of one million and a half; so that the sum total of additions, due to all our administrative efforts of the past 2 years, has resulted in an increase of not more than 500,000 people to the pay rolls of private industry in America.

Of this grand total, I have very little doubt as to the accuracy. Of course, as you know, estimates have been made wildly, anyway, running from 3,000,000 up to about 10,000,000. The highest figure that is usually presented is that of the American Federation of Labor, as you know, and they differ by considerable amounts, something like 3,000,000, and, if we think of the 1932 estimates of the National Income Senate Committee report, we find that at that time the American Federation of Labor estimate was something like 2,000,000 less, so that we come out fairly accurately with respect to the calculations.

When it comes to making estimates as to the amount of unemployment among the several industries, we are a little bit less certain, because you remember we start out with over 2,000,000 unemployed in 1929, and we have to add over 3,000,000 new employables. The estimate is, basing ourselves on the United States census, that there are something like 710,000 human employables being added each year. Multiplying by the 4 or 5 years we get that total.

When it comes to making estimates of the number of unemployed among individual industries, we are faced with the problem of allocating that additional 5,000,000, and inasmuch, as I said, as there has been such a terrific shift in industrial occupational distribution of the population, we have to become more or less—well, shall we say?—" shrewd guessers ", having only our integrity and sincerity as economists, as statisticians, as our guides. Having this, then, before us, I might mention a few instances of the extent of unemployment among specific industries. I have this table, too, and, of course, Mr. Chairman, this will be presented to the secretary. For instance, for manufacturing industries as a whole, the average number of unemployed in 1934 was almost 29 percent, and in the construction industry 70 percent; in domestic service 39 percent; an average for all of them of 28 percent. Transportation, for instance, was 40 percent, communication 41 percent, and so on. If any of the gentlemen wish to know any more of those, I will be glad to repeat.

This, then, is a statement of the extent of the unemployed, the average for the year 1934. We turn next to an estimate of the possible sources of funds, and I was glad, as I was sitting in the audience and listening to the conversations here before, that question already has been raised, and it seems to me it is quite appropriate that I have these figures.

Following the Lundeen bill, we look for sources of funds to meet the social-insurance program from existing wealth, from taxes on current income and existing wealth, and at this point perhaps it is desirable to draw a contrast between the Lundeen bill and the present administration bill.

It was not my purpose to discuss the administration bill at all this afternoon, because other people that will follow me will probably discuss that bill, but the question was raised before, and it seems to me at this particular juncture we could make this contrast.

The administration bill, and all bills that follow that general type, would place the burden of unemployment insurance on the workers whom it intends to help, because there you place a tax on pay rolls. Whether only on pay rolls or on pay rolls plus contributions by the employees, you automatically make the worker bear the burden of his own presumed benefit, because if the worker has to make a contribution, naturally you have already automatically deducted from his current wages, low as they are; you are simply lowering his standard of living. A tax on pay rolls, as every elementary student in public finance knows, is immediately either directly deducted from the wages themselves or placed into the cost of operation, and goes down into the market as additional cost and price, and the worker, who represents the majority of the consumers, pays these increases in prices.

I am making this statement more or less, by the way, simply to show the contrast between the Lundeen bill and all these other bills. Under that bill the proposal is to collect the funds to meet these benefits from existing wealth, where the others would simply increase the burden on the workers themselves.

Now, following the provisions of the bill, the first source of income naturally is a tax on individual incomes of $5,000 a year and over, and while we are not at all presuming to suggest the exact tax rate that Congress may wish to place on individual incomes, it is quite pertinent to show that if we were to apply the rate now prevailing in England, and in some brackets, these are not the highest—in France and in Germany, the rates in some brackets are even higher—if we were to apply the British tax rate to individual income, for instance in 1928, the Federal Government would have enjoyed an income of over 5¾ billions dollars, as against only slightly over 1 billion dollars; in other words, over five times as much.

In 1932, to come down to a very low year of income—and 1933 was higher—we would have collected, on the same basis, $1,128,000,-000, as against the actual collection of $324,000,000; again something like four times as much.

In 1933 the relationship is about the same. This, then, I submit as one possible way of raising funds for the bill before you for consideration.

Another source is a corporation tax. Our corporation tax rate is extremely low compared to those of other countries, and in order not to go into too great detail, I have taken for the corporation incomes of $5,000 and over a flat 25 percent. I did not graduate it. Instead of raising it higher and higher, I simply got a flat 25 percent, so as to get a calculation, and I find on that basis, in 1928, we would have raised $2,600,000,000, as against not quite $1,200,000,000; more than twice as much.

In 1932 we would have had a similar result, and this is also true of 1933. In 1933 the total income from corporations was only about $353,000,000, while we could have raised it to about $750,000,000.

A third source of income is inheritance or estates, and here, frankly, in my own studies, familiar as I am with these figures, when I came to these computations I was shocked. We practically neglect in America the tax on estates. For instance, in 1928, on a total declared gross estate of 3½ billion dollars, the total amount collected in the Federal taxes was only $42,000,000, or just a little over 1 percent.

Mr. DUNN. That is 1928?

Mr. GILLMAN. It was less than 1 percent in 1932. It was higher in 1933. That is on the gross. On the net it is higher, because there is a deduction of almost 50 percent. " right off the reel ", so that the net tax in 1928 was 2.1 percent.

I have submitted here three columns. Taking both the gross estate and the net estate as reported for 1928, 1932, and 1933, I have applied an average of 25 percent, 50 percent and 75 percent, merely to show comparable figures. And even on the base of a 25-percent flat average tax, we would have got in 1928, $888,000,000 as against $42,000,000, and on 50 percent, of course, double.

You finally come to a source which is very seldom mentioned, but it seems to me a very important source. Now incidentally, I am not saying anything about taxing, raising revenue from taxation on tax-exempt securities, which at present amount to, well, we do not know. The last amount I have is something like $15,000,000,000. That was for 1932. Since that time the Government has issued tremendous sums of bonds.

The CHAIRMAN. Bringing it up to about $28,000,000,000?

Mr. GILLMAN. Tremendous sums of tax-exempt securities, which, if Congress saw fit to tax income on them, it would be a new source. I should not say a " new source ", because at one time there were no tax-exempt securities. It would be an additional source of revenue, but one source which I want to emphasize at this moment, in addition to the others, is an imposition of a tax on corporate surplus and undivided profits.

I would like to call the gentlemen's attention to the fact that the net corporate surplus in 1928 amounted to over $47,000,000,000, and even in 1932, after 3 years of losses, the total corporate surplus amounted to over $36,000,000,000. As you all know—I need not emphasize that—a corporate surplus simply represents the accumulation by the corporations of funds which had not been distributed beforehand to the workers and to capital.

Now, it is obvious to any common-sense reasoning that those accumulations were made possible by the cooperation of labor and capital. Then, the use of the surplus, however, has been set aside entirely to meet capital claims in times of exigencies, and none at all for workers. In other words, if you take, for instance, the report of the national income account—and here I am looking at the survey of current business, of January 1934, reporting the national income for 1933—we find, for instance, that, as regards interest charges and funded debt, there has been practically no change in the amount that had been paid out in 1929, 1930, 1931, 1932, and 1933. Even in 1933 it was only 5 percent less than in 1929, whereas at the same time the amount that has gone to labor, in 1933, was only 41 percent of what it was in 1929. Labor has lost 60 percent of its earnings. Capital is still drawing the same earnings as before, but is drawing those earnings from two sources, current income plus these accumulations, and it strikes me, and it seems to me it would strike any common-sense justice, that labor has a claim on a certain portion of these funds, which labor has helped to accumulate, has helped to produce.

The position we take is that modern production, the modern manufacturing-industrial system, is as Adam Smith, 150 years ago, stated, a "collective undertaking." No one is nowadays, or few of us are, self-sufficient economically. We can operate, we can work only when others work, and to that extent we become socially organized, desiring to produce wealth, and this socially produced wealth naturally must meet the claims of labor as well as of capital. The position presents this more or less in a logical fashion. When the machinery remains idle, because of a depression period, the machine keeps on drawing a return; but when the man, the worker, becomes idle, because the machine becomes idle, he is completely disregarded, as regards a return from the very wealth which he, together with the machine, has produced in the past; so that, gentlemen, these are in general the conclusions which I draw from the figures. I naturally will present these tables to you, and if you care to have any more sustaining data, I have those prepared, but not yet typewritten, which I shall be glad to send to you, and I only need to be asked to do so.

Mr. LUNDEEN. Mr. Chairman, I ask that the additional figures be inserted in the record.

Mr. GILLMAN. I will be glad to do that.

Mr. DUNN. There is no objection.

Mr. GILLMAN. I only reiterate that in the making of these estimates, I have followed the procedure that had been devised, and obviously to my mind very accurately followed by the two gentlemen who did this study for the Department of Commerce in 1932–33, which published it in this document, Senate Document 124, of the Seventy-third Congress, second session. In this study, the exact procedure is explained in the appendixes.

In my own studies, I have naturally built up my results by carefully following and summarizing the procedure, and at the request of Congressman Lundeen, I shall submit those.

Mr. LUNDEEN. For what committee was that document compiled?

Mr. GILLMAN. In response to Senate Resolution 220.

Mr. LUNDEEN. Oh, it is a resolution?

Mr. GILLMAN. It is Resolution 220, a report on national income. I beg your pardon, here it is, "Referred to the Committee on Finance."

Mr. LUNDEEN. All right.

Mr. GILLMAN. I think, gentlemen, this is all I want to say in the general manner, but I shall be glad to answer questions.

Mr. DUNN. Thank you, Doctor.

Mr. LESINSKI. Dr. Gillman, you are not ready to give figures on what the cost would be under the enactment of the Lundeen bill?

Mr. GILLMAN. No, sir; I am sorry, for the reasons I explained to you, before.

Mr. LESINSKI. Yes, I see, Doctor.

Mr. GILLMAN. The complications there are terrific, and I would much rather be safe than have to retract, for after all I take this to be a very important representative body of Congress, and I do not want to present to you any figures which we may want to modify afterwards, so I would rather be safe on that.

Mr. LESINSKI. In your statement, you stated that there are approximately 14½ million out of employment.

Mr. GILLMAN. About 14,000,000—14,021,000.

Mr. LESINSKI. And let us take an average of a very low wage, say $20 a week, it would take from 15 to 16 billion dollars to take care of that amount of unemployment?

Mr. GILLMAN. Possibly, but we have to remember that in the first place—that is the question I raised before—the moment we begin paying anything like benefits, the reemployment procedure starts and reduces the total number eligible for unemployment insurance, but at the same time, there are other considerations. Mr. Lundeen's bill provides not only for unemployment insurance but for old-age pensions. Now, when, for instance, we take out of the total number available for benefits, those who have become available for old-age pensions, we have again decreased the total number of unemployed, and in that case the totals that are supposed to be provided for are not the same, the averages are not the same as for the unemployed, and that requires some calculation and working out.

Mr. LESINSKI. Speaking of the old-age pension, under the so-called "Townsend proposition", it would take $20,000,000,000 to take care of the old people. Where would that money come from?

Mr. GILLMAN. I am not speaking of the Townsend plan, gentlemen. I am speaking of the Lundeen bill.

Mr. LESINSKI. In your unemployment, does not the unemployment mostly consist of people of the age of 40 and over? Industry at the present time attempts to employ only youth and younger men in the country, and has shoved aside the older people, people who own real estate, who own their homes, and who have raised their families. Isn't that where it occurs, more than anywhere else?

Mr. GILLMAN. Unfortunately, we have no figures by which we can make any, even the slightest guess as to the age distribution of the unemployed, and I should venture no figure at all. We know from experience and from reports that the older folk are losing out, and that is why I take it that the Lundeen bill provides for old-age pensions as an integral part of a total social-security program. We can no longer talk of various kinds of social-insurance programs. It must be an integrated system, and I presume—that is my feeling—that is why we have such a proposal in this bill.

Mr. LESINSKI. Has not industry a reason for doing that, in that a younger man can work faster on a machine than an older person who might be reliable but yet he cannot keep up with the speed of production as the younger man can?

Mr. GILLMAN. As an economist, I should say that is probably a consideration, though most of the work that is carried on in manufacturing industries precisely is running a machine, and anyone from 25 to 55 can push the same button at the same rate. The thing runs by itself, but after all we must not forget that there are all sorts of occupations where people over 40 and 50, and under 25, can be employed. I mean, we do not have just one kind of a job where only certain men or certain women of a certain age can be employed, and it seems to me perfectly reasonable if you had anything like a system of rational organization, anyone who is willing to work and able to work ought to find a job, if the system would provide for it.

Mr. LUNDEEN. If the Congressman will permit, I want to say, I think you referred to just what I saw, for instance, in our folding room down here. I went down to see the boys insert letters in envelops, and there was a young man there, very skilled, who was inserting them, 1, 2, 3. There was an aged man there who was going 1, 2, 3, much slower.

Mr. LESINSKI. Exactly. That is what I mean.

Mr. GILLMAN. The aged man, perhaps, should not be folding envelops.

Mr. LUNDEEN. No.

Mr. GILLMAN. There are other occupations in which he can more easily fall in line.

Mr. LUNDEEN. But as you say, of course, where they push a button on a machine, that is different.

Mr. LESINSKI. That is a different story. There are not enough buttons to go around.

Mr. GILLMAN. That is the problem.

Mr. LESINSKI. Now, in your statement, you were giving the percentages of unemployment in different crafts. You said the largest unemployment is in the building trades?

Mr. GILLMAN. Yes. The largest unemployment is in the construction industries, 70 percent.

Mr. LESINSKI. If the construction industry were boosted up, the other unemployment will cease, because the heavy goods industry would move then?

Mr. GILLMAN. There is no doubt, if we had a comprehensive housing program, not only would we reemploy a good many of those unemployed in the construction industry, but as you suggest, through increasing demand for the operations of other industries that employ others, of course, employment would increase.

Mr. LESINSKI. In bringing about taxation for this purpose, you have made the statements regarding 25 to 75 percent on incomes. If we levied a 75-percent tax on a million dollars or over, would that produce a large sum of money?

Mr. GILLMAN. I have the exact estimates, if you care to have me give them to you.

Mr. DUNN. Pardon me, Doctor. Five minutes is up Mr. Lesinski, but I do not think anybody will object, if you desire to continue.

Mr. LUNDEEN. I certainly will not.

Mr. DUNN. No objection? All right, proceed.

Mr. GILLMAN. I will simply say that for over a million—that is, for 1928—we would have gotten as much as $831,000,000.

Mr. LESINSKI. That would be quite a sum, at that.

Mr. GILLMAN. Yes; for the group of a million up to 5,000,000, 75 percent of it.

Mr. LESINSKI. And if we were to add to that a tax on the tax-exempt securities?

Mr. GILLMAN. I have not calculated the tax-exempt amounts of securities, for the reason, in the first place, we do not know what the existing tax-exempt securities are.

Mr. LESINSKI. Except the Government?

Mr. GILLMAN. Except the Government, you see, but Congress could easily find out. I mean, we have difficulty getting information of that sort. We must go to Congress and to the congressional reports to get those figures; and such figures at this moment are not available.

Mr. LESINSKI. In your statement you were talking about corporate surpluses.

Mr. GILLMAN. Yes, sir.

Mr. LESINSKI. Most of the corporate surpluses are not in cash in a bank. A corporation probably starts with $100,000, and it keeps earning money and putting the money back into the plant and rebuilding its plant, and it probably puts most of the surplus back into building plants. That is already a taxable portion of the corporation.

Mr. GILLMAN. Yes.

Mr. LESINSKI. I would not rely very much on corporate surplus. I happen to know that most of the corporate surpluses are reinvested in plants and machinery. In other words, instead of enlarging the capital of the corporation, it is in the surplus.

Mr. GILLMAN. Yes.

Mr. LESINSKI. So that most of that portion is always taxable by local taxation.

Mr. GILLMAN. I doubt whether we agree on that. This net surplus which I have is not in tangibles, but most of it is in intangibles, in securities and other things, rather than in tangibles. Now, there is, of course, a return on these investments. Some of them may be exactly in tax-exempts, but what I had in mind, and what I thought I emphasized was, it was from this total, from this net surplus, as a liquid fund, that dividends and interest charges are made in times of depression when current income is not so very high; and my claim is that precisely the same procedure should be followed in paying some of this liquid fund money to the unemployed, to the workers who have been thrown out of work at the same time that the machines have stopped operating.

They do not raise any questions as to how they have invested their funds, but they paid, as I pointed out, even in 1933, only 5 percent less on interest charges than in 1929, but the workers are getting 60 percent less. It seems to me there is a common fund, to the upbuilding of which both capital and labor have contributed portions. If we take only 25 percent of that, we could meet Mr. Lundeen's bill, very nearly.

Mr. LESINSKI. Speaking again of surpluses, I happen to have seen a statement of a utility corporation that, in 1900 or thereabouts, had a capital stock of about $8,000,000. In 1934 the capital stock was something around $380,000,000, including surplus. The surplus in that corporation does not show that it is in cash or in bonds or in moneys that would be laid aside as a surplus and reinvested. It shows that most of that amount is in the plants and in extensions made to the plant. I am bringing that up because you spoke to the effect that corporate surpluses could be used in taxation here.

Mr. GILLMAN. Yes.

Mr. LESINSKI. That kind of a surplus could not be utilized for taxation, because when you jump up, in the period 1900 to 1934, from $8,000,000 to $380,000,000, it is a big jump, and still that money is not available, and it is not in securities of any kind, because it is invested in plants and extensions.

Mr. GILLMAN. There again, in my mind, there is a question whether the accounting system would call that "surplus." It is the "surplus" before it is plowed under that concerns me.

Mr. LESINSKI. It is capital and surplus.

Mr. GILLMAN. Capital and surplus.

Mr. LESINSKI. I happened at one time to own a corporation myself that only had $100,000 capital, and it had about $400,000 surplus, but that was all reinvested in the plant.

Mr. GILLMAN. I should say about 25 percent, I think, of the net surplus is in cash.

Mr. LESINSKI. Well, I would say yes; you might be right, but you could not say 100 percent.

Mr. GILLMAN. I would not; no.

Mr. LESINSKI. You could not.

Mr. GILLMAN. Oh, no. I do not think I would say that.

Mr. LESINSKI. Of course, there are banks that carry surpluses they have made. They reinvest that cash, that is true.

Mr. GILLMAN. You are raising a very important question as to the whole method of reporting income and profits and surplus. Congress knows something about that. They learned something about that during the inquiry, about a year ago, relative to the exemptions that some gentlemen claimed, and in the end did not pay anything. Some of our great millionaires had nothing on which to pay. Now, of course, that is another question. If Congress could only get at some of those sums, there would be sources of income.

Mr. LESINSKI. That will be all, Mr. Chairman.

Mr. DUNN. Mr. Lundeen?

Mr. LUNDEEN. I understand that you propose to raise the revenue. That is, you list all sources of revenue, individual income taxes, corporation income taxes, inheritance and gift taxes, and so forth?

Mr. GILLMAN. Yes.

Mr. LUNDEEN. Corporation income tax?

Mr. GILLMAN. That is right.

Mr. LUNDEEN. Inheritance taxes?

Mr. GILLMAN. That is right.

Mr. LUNDEEN. Taxes on tax-exempt securities?

Mr. GILLMAN. Yes.

Mr. LUNDEEN. We have not all the information there, and I might say, by the way, we had a resolution on that today in the Congress. We just attended roll call on it, and the resolution was defeated by 106 to about 250.

Mr. DUNN. And you were on the side that was defeated, and so was I.

Mr. LUNDEEN. That was calling for the same information, and, of course, we know that it runs into many billions of dollars.

Mr. GILLMAN. Many billions.

Mr. LUNDEEN. How many billions, of course, we do not know exactly.

Now, we talk a good deal about gift taxes, because inheritances might escape the tax.

Mr. GILLMAN. True.

Mr. LUNDEEN. Would you tell us something about that? Have you made any studies of the possibilities of gift taxes and the methods of stop-gapping the loss of inheritance taxes through gifts.

Mr. GILLMAN. There is no way of stopping it, except by some kind of a congressional law that would tax gifts made, let us say, within a certain number of years before the death of the decedent.

Mr. LUNDEEN. Would that stop it?

Mr. GILLMAN. Well, some people will escape any kind of a law, of course, but it seems to me that would be one way of stopping it.

Mr. LUNDEEN. If you said all gifts within so many years, during that period you would catch them, anyway.

Mr. GILLMAN. Yes. You see, Mr. Lundeen, you have even on the reported income, let alone the gifts, only the magnificent total sum amounting to 1 percent in taxes. It seems to me right there, and without going further than the actual amount reported, you have a source of revenue. Questions of deductions must be redefined by Congress. What is a deductible sum?

Mr. LESINSKI. Mr. Lundeen, speaking about gifts, for instance, one of our wealthy Senators donates $1,000,000 to the welfare fund, would you tax that?

Mr. LUNDEEN. I do not think so.

Mr. LESINSKI. It is a gift?

Mr. LUNDEEN. Well, there could be an exception made. I suppose you have in mind Senator Couzens' million-dollar gift to the community of Detroit, and I do not think we ought to tax that.

Mr. LESINSKI. I would not say that. I would not say that.

Mr. GILLMAN. We economists, when we talk about "gifts", have in mind the passing of a fortune from the father, or whoever owns it, to his children, in anticipation of death, so it will escape a tax, and those are tremendous sums.

Mr. LUNDEEN. I think that can be handled by legislation, anyway. Now, as I understand it, the Committee on Finance got out a Senate document, during the Seventy-third Congress entitled a "Report on National Income", and it is Senate Document 124?

Mr. GILLMAN. Yes, sir.

Mr. LUNDEEN. And that gives a great deal of this information?

Mr. GILLMAN. It gives the information which I followed, bringing the material up to date in 1934.

Mr. LUNDEEN. That is in one volume?

Mr. GILLMAN. It is in one volume.

Mr. LUNDEEN. It is in pamphlet form?

Mr. GILLMAN. It is a very heavy pamphlet. There was a tremendous amount of work done on it. I am told that these two gentlemen had several hundred clerks working on these things during a period of months, because it was really an original piece of work.

Mr. LUNDEEN. It is a singularly valuable work.

Mr. GILLMAN. It is a tremendously valuable piece of work.

Mr. LUNDEEN. We can depend on it as our authority.

Mr. GILLMAN. You can depend on that.

Mr. LUNDEEN. Now, I am impressed with the difference in figures. The American Federation of Labor gives an unemployment figure of about, I think, 10,600,000.

Mr. GILLMAN. Ten or eleven million, about.

Mr. LUNDEEN. It is close to 11,000,000?

Mr. GILLMAN. For November, it was close to 11,000,000; yes.

Mr. DUNN. November of what year?

Mr. GILLMAN. November of this last year.

Mr. DUNN. 1934?

Mr. LESINSKI. That did not include people on F. E. R. A. work?

Mr. LUNDEEN. Is that where you got the other millions?

Mr. GILLMAN. No.

Mr. LUNDEEN. Where did you get those?

Mr. GILLMAN. In the first place, it does not include farm labor.

Mr. LUNDEEN. It did not include farm labor?

Mr. GILLMAN. Farm laborers.

Mr. LUNDEEN. That is, the hired man on the farm?

Mr. GILLMAN. That is right.

Mr. LUNDEEN. He is not included?

Mr. GILLMAN. That is right. The American Federation of Labor estimates are essentially a trade-union figure.

Mr. LUNDEEN. Do they include domestics?

Mr. GILLMAN. I doubt it very much. Unless domestics had a trade-union organization, they would not be caught very well in the estimates.

Mr. LUNDEEN. Perhaps the American Federation of Labor figures are correct for what they are trying to do.

Mr. GILLMAN. I do not question their sincerity.

Mr. LUNDEEN. But there must be many more.

Mr. GILLMAN. Many more, not included in their estimates. For instance, there are professional workers, particularly self-employed professional workers, who are not included there. Any number of categories are not sufficiently provided in their estimates.

Mr. LUNDEEN. Now, how long will it be before you can furnish these supplementary figures?

Mr. GILLMAN. I have them all calculated but not typewritten.

Mr. LUNDEEN. How long will that be?

Mr. GILLMAN. Two or three days.

Mr. LUNDEEN. Then, you will have them sent in here?

Mr. GILLMAN. I shall mail them to the committee.

Mr. DUNN. Doctor, I desire to ask a question or two. You said the figure you had given of the unemployed was about how many?

Mr. GILLMAN. Fourteen million average for 1934.

Mr. DUNN. I would like to get this information, Doctor. Do you include men and women who are physically incapacitated?

Mr. GILLMAN. They are included in the total figure; yes, sir.

Mr. DUNN. That is what I wanted to find out.

Mr. GILLMAN. Incidentally, that is why those figures fit in with the Lundeen bill, because our social insurance program, as contemplated by this committee, provides for the handicapped.

Mr. DUNN. Are there any more questions, gentlemen?

Mr. LESINSKI. That will be all.

Mr. LUNDEEN. I want you to know, Doctor, we have an open-minded committee here, and a good committee of members who seek information. We have an able, open-minded chairman, Congressman Matthew A. Dunn who is fearless and is going right into this thing. In Congressman Connery, Chairman of the Labor Committee, and Congressman Dunn, chairman of our subcommittee, we have the two best chairmen in the House of Representatives.

Mr. GILLMAN. Mr. Lundeen, that is my feeling. I feel that I have been received properly, and I have no complaints to make. I hope that I have given you some information. Naturally, there may be a great many more ideas in your mind, in which I have not participated, of course.

Mr. DUNN. Doctor, I want to say you have given me a great deal of valuable information.

Mr. GILLMAN. I am glad I did.

Mr. DUNN. We appreciate the figures you have given us—in fact, everything you have said.

Mr. GILLMAN. Thank you.

(The material prepared under the direction of Dr. Gillman on the costs of the bill is contained in the testimony of Albion A. Hartwell, given on Feb. 14, 1935. See pp. 581–590.)

The statements presented by Dr. Gillman for the record are as follows:

TABLE 1.—*Estimates of the average number employed in specified years by given industry*

[Thousands of persons]

Industry	1929 [1]				1932 [1]	1933				1934			
	Wage earners	Salary earners	Entre-preneurs	Total	Total	Wage earners	Salary earners	Entre-preneurs	Total	Wage earners	Salary earners	Entre-preneurs	Total
Agriculture (excluding family labor)	2,027	70	5,495	7,592	7,288	1,432	82	5,700	7,214	1,317	82	5,700	7,099
Mines and quarries	955	99	14	1,068	644	574	68	14	656	663	72	14	749
Electric light and power and manufactured gas		[2]336		336	283		[2]268		268		[2]285		285
Manufacturing	8,387	1,503	133	10,023	6,257	5,788	891	75	6,754	6,609	938	75	7,622
Construction (excluding P. W. A.)	1,205	155	168	1,528	673	360	60	100	520	333	56	100	489
Transportation	[2]2,905		168	3,073	2,140	[2]1,853		161	2,014	[2]1,919		161	2,080
Communication		[2]533		533	402		[2]358		358		[2]358		358
Wholesale and retail trade (adjusted for part-time employment)		[2]5,562	1,601	7,163	5,619		4,050	1,654	5,704		4,300	1,654	5,954
Finance		[2]1,422		1,422	1,135		1,158		1,158		1,183		1,183
Government					3,122								
(a) Excluding public education		[2]1,935		1,935			1,924		1,924		1,914		1,914
(b) Public education		[2]1,069		1,069			1,139		1,139		1,089		1,089
Service					4,283								
(a) Recreational		[2]407	48	455			[2]283	33	316		[2]312	37	349
(b) Personal		[2]1,072	40	1,112			[2]817	29	846		[2]891	30	921
(c) Domestic		[2]2,760	545	3,305			[2]1,560	560	2,120		[2]1,762	560	2,322
(d) Professional		[2]309	45	354			[2]738	33	771		[2]740	33	773
(e) Miscellaneous		[2]309		309			[2]322		322		[2]322		322
Miscellaneous industries	[2]2,255		692	2,947	2,285	[2]1,566		680	2,246	[2]1,729		680	2,409
Total	[2]17,734	[2]17,541	8,949	44,224	34,131	[2]11,573	[2]13,718	9,039	34,330	[2]12,570	[2]14,304	9,044	35,918

[1] Figures for 1929 and 1932 from National Income, 1929-32.

[2] Wage and salaried combined.

NOTE.—According to National Income, 1929-32, there were 2,200,000 unemployed in 1929. Adding the increase in employables from 1929 to 1934 (703,000 per annum. See National Income, 1929-32, p. 18) of 3,515,000 and the decrease in employment from 1929 to 1934 of 8,300,000 (approximately), we arrive at an average amount of unemployment in 1934 of 14,000,000 (approximately). In order to arrive at a distribution by industry of the employables and the unemployed it is necessary to distribute the total of 5,715,000 among the various industries. This is done in supplement to table I., p. 73.

TABLE 2.—*Estimates of the average number of unemployed in 1934*

[Thousands of persons]

Industry	Wage earners	Salary earners	Entrepreneurs	Total unemployed	Total employables	Percent unemployed
Agriculture (excluding family labor)	(1,137) / 710	(12) / −12	(205) / −205	1,847	8,946	20.6
Mines and quarries	(−61) / 292	(−9) / 27	--------	249	998	24.9
Electric light and power and manufactured gas	--------	[1] (22) / [1] 51	--------	73	358	20.4
Manufacturing	(567) / 1,778	(78) / 565	58	3,046	10,668	28.6
Construction	(87) / 872	(9) / 99	68	1,135	1,624	69.9
Transportation	[1] (423) / [1] 986		7	1,416	3,496	40.5
Communication	--------	[1] (78) / [1] 175	--------	253	611	41.4
Wholesale and retail trade (part time employment reduced to full time)		(938) / 1,262	−53	2,147	8,101	26.5
Finance		(188) / 239	--------	427	1,610	26.5
Government:						
(a) Excluding public education		(78) / 21		99	2,013	4.9
(b) Public education		(205) / −20		185	1,274	14.5
Service:						
(a) Recreation		[1] (113) / [1] 95	11	219	568	38.6
(b) Personal		[1] (279) / [1] 181	10	470	1,391	33.8
(c) Domestic		[1] (576) / [1] 547	--------	1,123	2,885	38.9
(d) Professional		[1] (353) / [1] 20	−15	358	1,658	21.6
(e) Miscellaneous		[1] (92) / [1] 13	12	91	446	20.4
Miscellaneous industries	[1] (345) / [1] 526	--------	12	883	3,292	26.8
Totals	(2,498) / 5,164	[1] (3,012) / [1] 3,237	[1] (205) / [1] −95	14,021	49,939	28.1

[1] Wage and salary earners combined.

NOTE.—Figures in parentheses represent the allocation of aditional availables (5,715,000).

TABLE 3.—*Estimates of funds available for unemployment and social insurance*

[All figures in 1,000's]

Source	1933	1932	1928
I. Individual income [1]	$1,129,277	$1,127,773	$5,787,068
Estate tax, 50 percent of gross	1,030,478	1,415,194	1,777,135
Corporate tax, net income 25 percent [2]	626,520	538,278	2,615,273
Corporate tax, net surplus, 25 percent [3]		9,019,881	11,789,046
Expenditures on war preparations	[4] 750,000		
Total		12,101,126	21,968,522
II. Individual income [1]	1,129,277	1,127,773	5,787,068
Estate tax, 75 percent of gross	1,545,717	2,122,791	2,665,701
Corporate tax, net income, 25 percent [2]	626,520	538,278	2,615,273
Corporate tax, net surplus, 25 percent [3]		10,823,858	14,146,855
Expenditures on war preparations	750,000		
Total		14,612,700	25,214,897

[1] Estimated on graduated scale approximating British tax rate but higher than the British rate for incomes from $500,000 to $5,000,000.
[2] This should be a graduated tax averaging 25 percent.
[3] Surplus and undivided profits less deficit: 1932, 36,079 millions; 1928, 47,156 millions.
[4] As of Aug. 1, 1934.

TABLE 3.—*Estimates of funds available for unemployment and social insurance*—Continued

TAX INCOME, 1928

	Total net income reported	Tax rate	Revenue available
I. INDIVIDUAL RETURNS		*Percent*	
Income classes:			
$5,000–$10,000	$4, 282, 520, 000	16	$685, 203, 000
$10,000–$15,000	1, 953, 395, 000	22	429, 747, 000
$15,000–$20,000	1, 218, 787, 000	24	292, 509, 000
$20,000–$25,000	865, 670, 000	30	259, 701, 000
$25,000–$50,000	2, 326, 503, 000	35	814, 276, 000
$50,000–$100,000	1, 857, 878, 000	40	743, 151, 000
$100,000–$250,000	1, 745, 403, 000	45	785, 431, 000
$250,000–$500,000	926, 079, 000	55	509, 343, 000
$500,000–$1,000,000	670, 861, 000	65	436, 060, 000
$1,000,000–$5,000,000 and over	1, 108, 863, 000	75	831, 647, 000
Total available			5, 787, 068, 000
Tax collected			1, 164, 254, 000
Additional revenue			4, 622, 814, 000
II. CORPORATION RETURNS			
Income classes:			
Under $1,000–$2,999	181, 420, 000	10	18, 142, 000
$3,000–$4,999	119, 482, 000	15	17, 922, 000
$5,000–$9,999	211, 525, 000	25	52, 881, 000
$10,000–$24,999	467, 605, 000	25	116, 901, 000
$25,000–$99,999	1, 055, 074, 000	25	263, 768, 000
$100,000–$499,999	1, 753, 943, 000	25	438, 485, 000
$500,000 under $1,000,000	898, 405, 000	25	224, 601, 000
$100,000 under $5,000,000	2, 119, 926, 000	25	529, 981, 000
$5,000,000 and over	3, 810, 359, 000	25	952, 589, 000
Total			2, 615, 273, 000
Tax collected			1, 184, 000, 000
Additional returns			1, 431, 273, 000

Returns of corporations submitting balance sheets, 1928 (all returns):[1]

Tax-exempt securities _____ $10, 116, 160, 404
Surplus _____ 52, 069, 292, 140
Net surplus (after deduction of deficit) _____ 47, 156, 183, 422

[1] Statistics of Income, 1928, p. 32.

TAX INCOME, 1932

	Total net income reported	Tax rate	Revenue available
I. INDIVIDUAL RETURNS		*Percent*	
Income classes:			
$5,000–$10,000	$1, 677, 039, 000	16	$268, 326, 000
$10,000–$15,000	595, 573, 000	22	131, 026, 000
$15,000–$20,000	329, 512, 000	24	79, 083, 000
$20,000–$25,000	235, 312, 000	30	70, 594, 000
$25,000–$50,000	629, 638, 000	35	220, 373, 000
$50,000–$100,000	393, 206, 000	40	157, 282, 000
$100,000–$250,000	216, 625, 000	45	97, 481, 000
$250,000–$500,000	73, 747, 000	55	39, 561, 000
$500,000–$1,000,000	57, 874, 000	65	37, 618, 000
$1,000,000–$5,000,000 and over	35, 239, 000	75	26, 429, 000
Total available			1, 127, 773, 000
Income tax collected			324, 745, 000
Additional revenue			803, 028, 000

TABLE 3.—*Estimates of funds available for unemployment and social insurance—Continued*

II. CORPORATE RETURNS (TAX INCOME, 1932)

1. Returns of corporations submitting balance sheets for 1932 (all returns) :[2]

Cash (in till or deposits in bank)	$15,917,202,000
Investments, tax-exempt	11,916,864,000
Investments other than tax exempt	75,630,257,000
Surplus and undivided profits	45,663,746,000
Net surplus (less deficit of $9,584,221,000)	36,079,525,000

2. Returns of corporations showing net lincome (1932):

Total gross income	[3] $31,707,963,000
Total net income	[3] 2,153,113,000
Income tax	[4] 245,689,000
Available revenue at flat 25 per cent rate	538,278,000

[2] Statistics of Income, 1932, p. 160.
[3] Statistics of Income, 1932.
[4] Revised figure as given in Statistics of Income, 1933, preliminary report.

TAX INCOME, 1933

	Total net income reported	Tax rate	Revenue available
I. INDIVIDUAL RETURNS			
Income classes:		*Percent*	
$5,000–$10,000	$1,477,827,000	16	$236,452,000
$10,000–$15,000	559,850,000	22	123,167,000
$15,000–$20,000	310,246,000	24	74,459,000
$20,000–$25,000	226,778,000	30	68,033,000
$25,000–$50,000	621,182,000	35	217,414,000
$50,000–$100,000	394,766,000	40	157,906,000
$100,000–$250,000	240,681,000	45	108,306,000
$250,000–$500,000	81,253,000	55	44,689,000
$500,000–$1,000,000	59,511,000	65	37,682,000
$1,000,000–$5,000,000 and over	81,559,000	75	61,169,000
Total			1,129,277,000
Tax collected			372,968,000
Additional revenue			756,309,000

II. CORPORATION RETURNS (TAX INCOME, 1933)

Total net income reported	$2,506,078,279
Income tax	347,649,990
Excess profits tax	6,266,721
Total	[5] 353,916,261
Available revenue at flat 25 per cent rate	626,520,000

[5] 14.1 percent.

ESTATE TAX

	Jan. 1–Dec. 31, 1928	Jan. 1–Dec. 31, 1932	Jan. 1–Dec. 31, 1933
Gross estate	$3,554,270,000	$2,830,388,000	$2,060,956,000
Tax paid	$41,959,000	$23,674,000	$61,415,000
Percent to gross	1.1	0.8	2.9
Net estate	$1,992,503,000	$1,423,437,000	$828,302,000
Tax paid	$41,959,000	$23,674,000	$61,415,000
Percent to net	2.1	1.7	7.4

REVENUE AVAILABLE

	Average 25 percent	Average 50 percent	Average 75 percent
Gross estate:			
1928	$888,567,000	$1,777,135,000	$2,665,701,000
1932	707,597,000	1,415,194,000	2,122,791,000
1933	515,239,000	1,030,478,000	1,545,717,000
Net estate:			
1928	498,126,000	996,252,000	1,494,378,000
1932	355,859,000	711,718,000	1,067,577,000
1933	207,075,000	407,150,000	621,225,000

TABLE 4.—*Comparison of income tax (married person, no dependents, all income from salary)*

[Conversion units: 1 pound=$4.86; France, 1 franc=$0. 0392; Germany, 1 mark=$0. 2382]

	Percent of tax to net income			
	United States	Britain	France	Germany
$1,000	0	0. 88	3. 38	7. 90
$2,000	0	5. 57	8. 51	15. 84
$3,000	0. 07	10. 38	12. 20	18. 11
$5,000	2. 0	14. 22	17. 15	21. 59
$7,500	3. 4	16. 29	22. 02	26. 02
$10,000	4. 8	18. 62	25. 25	29. 89
$15,000	6. 8	22. 95	31. 26	34. 46
$25,000	10. 08	29. 47	38. 04	39. 78
$50,000	17. 20	39. 30	47. 43	45. 13
$100,000	30. 01	48. 10	53. 65	47. 44
$500,000	52. 72	61. 58	53. 93	49. 49
$1,000,000	57. 11	63. 91	53. 97	49. 74

Source: New Republic, Jan. 24, 1934.

TABLE 5.—*Comparison of death taxes in the United States and Great Britain (entire estate to widow)*

[Source: Preliminary report of Subcommittee on the Committee of Ways and Means, relative to Federal and State taxation and duplication therein (1933), p. 237.]

	United States	Britain
$1,000	0	1
$5,000	0	3
$10,000	0	3
$15,000	0	3
$25,000	0	4
$50,000	0	5
$100,000	1. 5	9
$150,000	3. 33	12
$200,000	4. 75	14
$300,000	6. 50	17
$400,000	7. 62	19
$500,000	8. 50	21
$600,000	9. 25	23
$800,000	10. 56	25
$1,000,000	11. 75	27
$2,000,000	15. 77	33
$3,000,000	18. 45	37
$5,000,000	22. 99	41
$10,000,000	30. 94	51

Conversion: £1=$4.86.

SUPPLEMENT TO TABLES 1 AND 2, SHOWING METHODS OF ESTIMATING 1933 AND 1934 EMPLOYMENT AND UNEMPLOYMENT FIGURES

[Figures from National Income 1929-32, a report issued by the United States Department of Commerce in January 1933]

Agriculture

Year	Farm population	Farmers, owners and tenants	Farmers, equivalent full time [1]
1931	30, 913, 000	[2] 6, 009, 000	[2] 5, 622, 000
1932	31, 742, 000	[2] 6, 031, 000	[2] 5, 722, 000
1933	32, 370, 000	6, 048, 000	[3] 5, 700, 000
1934	32, 500, 000	6, 052, 000	[3] 5, 700, 000

[1] Balance of time is supposed to be spent in other occupations.
[2] From National Income, 1929-32.
[3] Estimated.

Increase in farm population 1932 over 1931 ... 800, 000
Increase in number of farms 1932 over 1931 ... 22, 000

1933 and 1934 estimates, same proportion.
See Department of Agriculture, "Agricultural Situation", April 1934.

Agriculture—Continued

Year	Gainfully oc-cupied [4]	Unpaid fami-ly labor	Employable farm labor
1931	[2] 10, 669, 000	[2] 1, 729, 000	[2] 2, 853, 000
1932	[2] 10, 955, 000	[2] 1, 828, 000	[2] 3, 014, 000
1933	11, 171, 000	1, 902, 000	3, 139, 000
1934	11, 216, 000	1, 918, 000	3, 164, 000

[4] A deduction of the amount of time farmers spend in other occupations should be made to derive "Gain fully occupied in agriculture."

Basis: Ratio gainfully occupied to population 1930 Census.

Year	Hired farm labor (equiv-alent full time	Managers and other salaried employees
1931	[2] 1, 748, 000	[2] 78, 000
1932	[2] 1, 484, 000	[2] 82, 000
1933	[6] 1, 432, 000	[3] 82, 000
1934	[7] 1, 317, 000	[3] 82, 000

[6] August 1934, Crops and Markets: Cash wages, 1933, $341,000,000; 86 (farm wage index, 1932); cash wages, 1932, $380,000,000; 80 (farm wage index, 1933). Ratio 0.9647×1,484×1432.
[7] Survey Current Business: Average hired labor per 100 farms, 1933, −87, median; 1934, −80, median; $\frac{80}{87}$×1,432,000=1,317,000.

NOTE.—Under national income methods increase in farm population is divided into gainfully and non-gainfully occupied on basis of 1930 census. After deducting from the former 1. Farmers and 2. Managers and other salaried employees (estimated on the basis of Department of Agriculture data) the balance is divided into family and hired labor on the basis of the 1930 census.

Unemployed, 1929=667,000. (See National Income 1929–32, p. 49, table 31, line 6 and 7).
Employables, 1929; Lines 4, 5, and 6, 8,259,000.
Employees, 1934; 5,700,000, farmers; 3,164,000, farm labor; 82,000, managers, isolated employees; total 8,946,000.
Increase in employables, 1929–34, 687,000; total 1,354,000.

Mines, quarries, oil and gas

WAGE EARNERS

Year	Anthra-cite	Bitumi-nous	Metal	Nonmet-al	Oil and Gas
1931 [1]	118, 015	382, 880	70, 781	65, 021	83, 830
1932 [1]	91, 627	310, 169	43, 714	47, 271	69, 476
1933 [2]	98, 761	312, 500	41, 400	43, 300	78, 100
11 months average, 1934	113, 467	54, 337	[3] 49, 223	[3] 47, 850	[3] 97, 400

[1] National income.
[2] Pa. Rep. on Prod. Ind. 1933.   All other Estimates, Basis Bl. S Indices.
[3] 10 months.

Year	Wage earners	Salaried workers	Entre-preneurs	Total
1931 [1]	720, 527	83, 903	14, 109	818, 539
1932 [1]	562, 257	67, 882	14, 109	644, 248
1933	574, 061	[2] 68, 000	14, 100	656, 161
10 months average	662, 000	[3] 72, 000		748, 000
11 months average			14, 000	

[1] National income.
[2] Pa. Report Prod. Industries 1932 and 1933 shows practically no change in number of salaried workers, 1932, 10109; 1933, 10,160.
[3] Ratio used manufacturing industries, 68,000×1.053.

Electric light and power and manufactured gas; communiciations industry

Year	Power and manufactured gas	Year	Communications
1931	[1] 322, 024	1931	[1] 448, 622
1932 [2]	[1] 282, 504	1932 [3]	[1] 402, 433
1933	268, 000	1933	358, 200
11 months average 1934	285, 000	11 months average 1934	358, 000

[1] National income.
[2] Census Electrical Industries, 1932; and American Gas Associations, 1933 and 1934, B. L. S. Indexes.
[3] Census Electrical Industries, Telephones 1932, 1933, and 1934, B. L. S. Indexes, Telephone and Telegraph.

Manufacturing industries

[Definition: See National Income Report, 1929–32. Base: Census of Manufactures 1929, 1931, and 1933]

Year	Wage earners	Salaried employees	Entrepreneurs	Total
1931 [1]	6, 152, 340	1, 321, 489	92, 365	7, 566, 194
1932 [1]	5, 107, 900	1, 084, 033	64, 693	6, 256, 626
1933	[2] 5, 787, 611	121, 000 [2] 770, 162	[3] 75, 200	6, 753, 973
1934, 11 months average	6, 609, 000	938, 000	75, 000	7, 622, 452

[1] National income.
[2] Census manual, 1933. Release dated Jan. 23, 1935; 770,162 from Census; 121,000 is estimate of central administrative office employees based on ratio in 1929 Census Manual.
[3] Census 1933, number of establishments $\frac{141,776}{174,225} \times 92,365 = 75,200$.
Census 1931, number of establishments

1934 estimate, wage earners, basis B. L. S. indexes.
Salaried employees: New York State Act 1934 $\frac{37,182}{35,311} \times 891,162 = 938,000$.
New York State Act 1933

Ratio $\frac{37,182}{35,311} = 1,053$, also used on p. 4.

Construction: Employees of private construction firms, excluding workers on P. W. A. jobs

Year	Wage earners	Salaried employees	Entrepreneurs	Total
1931 [1]	766, 930	119, 181	167, 811	1, 053, 992
1932	432, 566	72, 584	167, 811	672, 961
1933	360, 000	[2] 60, 000	[2] 110, 000	530, 000
1934	333, 000	[2] 56, 000	[2] 100, 000	489, 000

[1] National income.
[2] Estimated on basis of trends of wage earners.

[Engineering News Record index, 1932]

Wage earners: Value of construction contracts, Dodge, 1933, $\frac{1,256}{1,351} \times \frac{156.5}{175.2}$ 1933.
1933 construction contracts, 1932,
Engineering News Record index of construction costs, ratio, $0.8302 \times 432,566 = 360,000$.
1934 Dodge reports, all classes, $1,537,000,000; deduct, $225,000,000, account P. W. A., total, $1,312,000,000.
Public Works contracts: 1932, $514,700,000; 1933, $499,518,000; 1934, $728,000,000. 1934, increase over 1933 and 1932 average: $225,000,000.

1934 estimate, $\frac{1,312 \ (1934)}{1,351 \ (1932)} \times \frac{156.5}{197.8}$ $770 \times 432,566 = 333,000$.

Transportation (includes railroad repair shops)

WAGE AND SALARIED WORKERS

[Base: Statistics of Railways, I. C. C. Statistics of Common Carriers, 1929–32, and various sources]

Year	Steam railroads [1]	Motor transportation and street railroads [2]	Water transportation and miscellaneous [3]	Entrepreneur motor and other trucks	Total
1931 [4]	1,401,463	653,422	265,221	172,764	2,492,870
1932 [4]	1,151,386	596,478	230,968	161,130	2,139,962
1933	1,083,700	553,000	216,000	161,000	2,013,700
1934, 10 months average	1,149,000	546,000	224,000	161,000	2,080,000

[1] Steam railroads, 1933–34 (checked with Interstate Commerce Commission figures).
[2] Motor and street railroads, B. L. S. indexes.
[3] Water transportation and miscellaneous, same percent change as above, steam railroads and motor trucks.
[4] National income.

Wholesale and retail trade (adjusted for full- and part-time unemployment)

[Base: Census 1929, 1933; 1934 estimates based B. L. S. Indices]

Year	Wholesale		Retail		Total
	Employees	Entrepreneur	Employees	Entrepreneur	
1931 [1]	1,400,484	83,000	3,563,046	1,130,000	6,176,530
1932 [1]	1,264,649	80,000	3,224,373	1,050,000	5,619,022
1933 [2]	[2] 1,098,000	80,000	[2] 2,952,000	[2] 1,574,341	5,704,000
10 months, 1934	1,185,000	80,000	3,115,000	1,575,000	5,954,000

[1] National income.
[2] Census of Wholesale and Retail Trade (except Wholesale Entrepreneur).

Wholesale, 1933 census: All employees' salaries ____ $1,645,539,000
            =1,098,000
      Average full-time salary ____ 1,499—
Retail census: All employees, salaries ____ $2,910,445,000
            =2,952,000
      Average full-time salary ____ 986—

Finance

SALARIED WORKERS

[Base: Various]

Year	Banking	Insurance	Real estate
1929 [1]	386,104	455,831	579,903
1930 [1]	374,666	463,578	549,303
1931 [1]	341,525	455,644	477,524
1932 [1]	309,781	437,713	387,386
1933	312,000	446,000	400,000
10 months, 1934 [2]	313,000	455,000	415,000
Total, October 1, 1934		1,183,000	

[1] National income.
[2] B. L. S. shows following percentage increases, October 1934 over October 1933: Banks, 0.4 percent; Insurance, +1.9 percent; real estate, +3.4 percent. Assume 10 months of 1934 over average 1932: Banks, 1 percent; insurance, 4 percent; real estate, 7 percent.

Government

EMPLOYEES

	Federal	State and County	City	Public education	Total
1929 [1]	933, 040	351, 450	650, 158	1, 068, 624	3, 033, 272
1930 [1]	955, 821	363, 262	710, 703	1, 126, 585	3, 156, 371
1931 [1]	964, 490	364, 631	624, 046	1, 174, 118	3, 127, 285
1932 [1]	952, 419	388, 809	591, 505	1, 189, 188	3, 121, 921
1933	954, 000	390, 000	580, 000	1, 139, 000	3, 063, 000
1934	[2] 957, 000	390, 000	567, 000	[3] 1, 089, 000	3, 003, 000

[1] 1929–32 figures are national income 1929–32; all other estimates except Federal 1934, no supporting data available.
[2] Reported in B. L. S. September 1934.)
[3] N. E. A. estimate; Hopkins' estimate; etc.

Recreation and amusement

	Employees	Entrepreneurs	Total
1929	407, 105	48, 089	[1] 455, 194
1930	399, 115	43, 247	[1] 442, 362
1931	333, 055	36, 652	[1] 369, 707
1932	295, 691	34, 201	[1] 329, 892
1933	283, 000	33, 000	[2] 316, 000
10 months, 1934	312, 000	37, 000	[2] 349, 000

[1] National incomes follows trend of employees in manufacturing and wholesaling and retailing.
[2] Both employees and entrepreneurs.

1933 $\frac{10,729}{15,452} \times 407 \times 48$

1934 $\frac{11,847}{15,452} \times 407 \times 48$

Personal service

[Combined index B. L. S. hotels, dyeing and cleaning, power laundries for employees, according to 1932 distribution of national income]

	Employees	Entrepreneurs	Total
1929	1, 072, 477	39, 743	[1] 1, 112, 220
1930	1, 041, 430	36, 069	[1] 1, 077, 499
1931	970, 807	31, 214	[1] 1, 002, 021
1932	860, 772	29, 109	[1] 889, 881
1933	817, 000	29, 000	846, 000
1934	891, 000	30, 000	921, 000

[1] National income.

Percent

1932	80. 0
1933	76. 4
10 months, 1934	83. 3

Domestic service

1929	[1] 2, 309, 480
1930	[1] 2, 078, 555
1931	[1] 1, 766, 315
1932	[1] 1, 412, 878
1933	1, 560, 000
11 months, 1934	1, 762, 000

[1] National income figures follows same trend as manufacturing industry (wage and salary).

Manufacturing industry

WAGE AND SALARY EMPLOYEES

[Census of Manufactures]

1929	9, 890, 000
11 months, 1934	7, 547, 000

$$\frac{7,547}{9,890} \times 2,309 = 1,762$$

Professional service [1]

	Employees	Entrepreneurs	Total
1929 [2]	759, 789	544, 629	1, 034, 418
1930 [2]	772, 891	559, 645	1, 332, 536
1931 [1]	761, 343	559, 645	1, 320, 998
1932 [2]	736, 127	559, 645	1, 295, 772
	738, 127	560, 000	1, 298, 000
1934	740, 000	560, 000	1, 300, 000

[1] Medical (private practice or private hospitals), dental, legal, engineering, nurses, private educators. All employees of public institutions or Government excluded; includes about two-thirds of all professionals.
[2] National income.

Miscellaneous services

(Y. M. C. A., SOCIAL SERVICES, BUSINESS SERVICES, UNDERTAKING, ETC.)

	Employees	Entrepreneurs	Total		Employees	Entrepreneurs	Total
1929	309, 029	44, 929	353, 958	1932	322, 079	32, 797	354, 876
1930	304, 238	40, 725	344, 963	1933	322, 000	33, 000	355, 000
1931	316, 255	34, 673	350, 928	1934	322, 000	33, 000	355, 000

Miscellaneous industries (fishing, forestry, brokerage, taxicabs, architects, authors, miscellaneous professions, hand trades, industry not specified in census)

	Employees	Entrepreneurs	Total		Employees	Entrepreneurs	Total
1929 [1]	2, 255, 292	692, 395	2, 947, 687	1932 [1]	1, 605, 103	679, 834	2, 284, 937
1930 [1]	2, 076, 715	689, 045	2, 765, 760	1933	1, 566, 000	680, 000	2, 246, 000
1931 [1]	1, 832, 640	681, 870	2, 514, 510	1934 [2]	1, 729, 000	680, 000	2, 409, 000

[1] National income.
[2] 10 months.

Follows trend of (manufacturing and wholesale and retail) all employees:

$$1933 = \frac{10729}{15452} \times 2255$$

$$1934 = \frac{11847}{15452} \times 2255$$

SUPPLEMENT TO TABLE 1.—*Allocation of additional employables*

Unemployed 1929 (National Income 1929–32)	2, 200, 000
Increase in employables 1929–34 (National Income 1929–32, p. 18)	3, 515, 000
Total	5, 715, 000
Allocated to agriculture	1, 354, 000
Total	4, 361, 000

The above was distributed to the various industries in proportion to the increase between 1920 and 1930 of gainfully occupied.

U. S. Census classification	Increase 1930 over 1920 (in thousands)	Percentage of total increase	Allocation to National Income classification of industries
Forestry and Fish	−20	−0. 004	To miscellaneous industries.
Extraction of minerals	−106	−. 014	To mining and quarrying.
Manufacturing and mechanical	1, 279	+. 173	To manufacturing electrical construction and ½ miscellaneous.
Transportation and commerce	747	+. 101	To transportation and commerce.
Trade	1, 823	+. 246	To wholesale and retail, finance, ¼ miscellaneous.
Pulbic service	117	+. 016	To Government.
Professional:			
Teachers	300	+. 041	To public education.
All others	782	+. 106	To ⅔ professional ⅓ miscellaneous.
Domestic and personal	1, 572	. 212	To recreational personnel, domestic, and miscellaneous.
Clerical	913	. 123	To all industries.
Total	7, 607	1, 000	

NOTE.—Allocated to above in proportion to 1929 employables.

Percentage of increase, 4,361,000 allocated

	Wage	Salary	All employees
Mining and quarrying	−0. 014	−0. 002	−0. 016
Electrical and manufactured gas			+. 005
Manufacturing	. 130	. 018	+. 148
Construction	. 020	. 002	+. 022
Transportation			+. 097
Communication			+. 018
Whlosale and retail trade			+. 215
Finance			+. 043
Government (excluding public education)			+. 018
Public education			+. 047
Service:			
Recreational			+. 026
Personal			+. 064
Domestic			+. 132
Professional			+. 081
Miscellaneous			+. 021
Miscellaneous industries			+. 079
Total			1. 000

STATEMENT OF LEWIS C. BENTZLEY, REPRESENTING THE EXECUTIVE COMMITTEE OF THE FARMERS NATIONAL COMMITTEE FOR ACTION

Mr. DUNN. Mr. Bentzley, for the purpose of informing the committee, will you please tell us whom you represent?

Mr. BENTZLEY. I represent the executive committee of the Farmers National Committee for Action. This is a committee that was set up 2 years ago in Washington by farm delegates that met here and sent committees around to the Congressmen.

Mr. LUNDEEN. And what were they advocating?

Mr. BENTZLEY. They had a militant farm program.

Mr. LUNDEEN. Was it the Frazier-Lemke bill, and bills like that?

Mr. BENTZLEY. No; not the Frazier-Lemke bill. Then, they had another conference in Washington this last year, on the 15th of November, and this is a committee elected by those delegates to carry on the work of those organizations that were affiliated with it. We have a membership of 110,000.

Mr. DUNN. That is, 110,000 throughout the United States?

Mr. BENTZLEY. Yes.

Mr. LUNDEEN. What farm bill are you supporting? That is, your organization. What is the number of the bill?

Mr. BENTZLEY. What is the number of the farm bill we are supporting?

Mr. LUNDEEN. Yes.

Mr. BENTZLEY. We are supporting the Lundeen bill here.

Mr. LUNDEEN. I know; but is there not some farm bill?

Mr. BENTZLEY. Yes. I will speak of that farm bill later.

Mr. LUNDEEN. This Farmers National Committee for Action is interested in this bill here?

Mr. BENTZLEY. Absolutely.

Mr. LUNDEEN. And will you state the reason why?

Mr. BENTZLEY. Absolutely.

Mr. DUNN. All right, proceed.

Mr. BENTZLEY. I am speaking for the Farmers National Committee for Action, with offices in Philadelphia and Sioux Falls, S. Dak. Our interest is in the millions of poor farmers who suffer under the lash of farm debt and evictions, to whom the so-called " blessings " of the drought and the " new deal " are sheer mockery. Our work is in the interest of the 2,000,000 drought-stricken farm families in the Middle West, who have been forced to reduce their herds and cattle by 10,000,000 and 7,000,000 head of hogs. Many of these farmers are now on relief. In the West and North Central part of our country there are many counties where 80 percent of the farm families receive relief of some sort. Official relief reports tell us that over 40 percent of the entire State of South Dakota is on relief.

Poor farmers, whether hit by drought or the " surplus " milk racket, are interested in unemployment. One-crop farmers have unemployment periods of their own, which lower their net incomes. Subsistence standards of living, set by relief, doles, charity, and bread lines, means an almost total disappearance of our markets.

Take the dairy industry, for example. The Department of Agriculture experts investigated the profits of the milk distributors and found that they were making as high as 30 percent during the period of the depression. Although these findings were made public over a year ago, nothing has been done to cut down on this immense profit. In fact, the price of milk has jumped from 11 to 12 cents a quart in Philadelphia during this past year, and the spread between producer and consumer has increased. The result is to drive thousands of farmers off the land into unemployment. Is there any good reason why industry, which is making paupers of these unemployed people, should not be forced to keep them?

The F. E. R. A., in one of its November bulletins, stated that Maine's destitute may be doubled before January because potatoes are down to 40 cents a barrel; the 40,000,000 bushels which Aroostock County expects to ship will not pay for the fertilizer, spraying, gas, oil, and wear and tear on machinery. Not taking payment for labor into consideration, to a farmer and his family that rents, this would mean starvation and eviction, not because he did not work, but because he followed the teachings of the United States Department of Agriculture and produced 315 bushels of potatoes per acre. For this achievement he is pauperized.

The boasted increase in farm income of $1,000,000,000 from the low point of 1932 has been very unevenly distributed. For instance, in 1930, in so-called "prosperity", 40 percent of the farmers received only 14 percent of the farm income, and during the depression this section of poor farmers has undoubtedly increased.

The increase in income in the form of benefit payments was given as farmer relief, but turned out to be banker and insurance company relief. A study made in Iowa of corn-hog checks shows that only 6 cents on every dollar actually went to the average farmer. In many counties, the county treasurer takes in the check as the farmer comes up the stairs after he has received it from the corn-hog committee man. Those farmers who still hold a large equity in their property got the benefit payments without deductions. The 1935 Agricultural Outlook report states that " In the areas severely affected by the drought, cash income for 1933 will be extremely low."

It is common knowledge that the average net income per farm family for the last few years has been below $350. The 1933 and 1934 income is only about one-half what it was in 1929. The increase in 1934 has been largely eaten up by increase of prices of the necessities of life.

There are no complete and adequate figures to show how many farmers are unemployed, but we do know that in 1932 and 1933, half a million farmers lost their homes through forced sales, and that in spite of moratoria on farm foreclosures for tax delinquencies or failure to make payments on the mortgage, the same thing has been happening in 1934 all over the country—except where they have been prevented by the organized resistance of farmers. In my home county of Bucks County, Pa., 6,000 pieces of real property were advertised for auction on August 6, 1934, for failure to pay taxes for the years 1931 and 1932. The resistance that the farmers put up forced the commissioners to adjourn the sales for the 1932 taxes. But 1,500 pieces of property were sold for the 1931 taxes.

We also know that in the South and other sections where tenancy is high, the acreage reduction program has forced thousands of farmers and their families off the land. Landlords refused to renew their contracts. An authority on the South recently stated that there were from 200,000 to 500,000 floating families in the South, displaced by the reduction in cotton and tobacco acreages and the cold-blooded dismissal of former tenants and share-croppers by plantation owners. I am sure that the agricultural workers will be represented at these hearings, and will tell you how many of them have been made unemployed by the reduction programs of the Agricultural Adjustment Act.

Not only are farmers being evicted or being deprived of their farms through the operations of an economy of scarcity, but many—around 3,000,000—of those farmers who remain on the land are unable to make a decent living. Their modern motor machinery lies rusting around the farmhouses, while the patched and primitive muscle types take their place in the fields. Farmers are loaded with debt; their credit is exhausted. According to the report of the Secretary of Agriculture for 1934 the farm debt is now about $12,000,000,000, and this is no doubt a conservative estimate. Many of these farmers for whom I speak have been reduced to a subsistence level of farming, where all they can do is produce a little of their own food. They have to work on relief for the feed needed to keep their few remaining animals alive.

Altogether, the program of the Government aims to remove 2,000,000 farm families—and presumably a million agricultural wage workers—15,000,000 people from agricultural production. I quote from a speech of Assistant Secretary Tugwell, made on August 4, 1933:

We must study and classify American soil, taking out of production not just one part of a field or farm, but whole farms; whole ridges; perhaps whole regions. * * * It has been estimated that when lands now unfit to till are removed from cultivation, something around 2,000,000 persons who now farm will have to be absorbed by other occupations.

With all these facts showing where the farmer is headed, it is clear that he as well as the city worker must be interested in unemployment and social insurance which will provide a minimum of health and decency to farm families, and markets for his products.

In looking over the administration's program for unemployment insurance and old-age pensions—the bill known as " S. 1130 "—I can see no definite minimum set for the unemployed. The only part that seemed definite was the setting up of big salaries for the administrators, in amounts ranging from $60,000 down. This bill makes no provision for those unemployed at the present time, or for the millions of farmers who are being driven off their farms. Furthermore, the minimum depends on the " generosity " of individual States, and we have good samples of that in the past.

Mr. LUNDEEN. Pardon me. Are you speaking of the Wagner-Lewis bill, now?

Mr. BENTZLEY. No; not the Wagner bill. It is the "administration bill ", as it is now called.

Mr. LUNDEEN. You mean the administration bill?

Mr. BENTZLEY. Yes.

Mr. DUNN. He is making a comparison.

Mr. BENTZLEY. And we have good samples of this generosity in the past.

We are here today to deal with our interests in country-wide unemployment of millions of workers and farmers, who would be affected by this bill.

For these millions of our population, the Lundeen bill—H. R. 2827—offers the only security which we can find in any of the so-called " social-insurance bills." It provides that farmers living on the land, as well as dispossessed farmers, shall receive " compensation for all workers and farmers above 18 years of age, unemployed through no fault of their own." It also takes care of all workers of the soil who are only employed part time, giving them the difference between what they earn and the "average local wages for full-time employment."

Besides this minimum of security against unemployment, under H. R. 2827, the farmer can be sure that he will be taken care of during other periods of crisis, such as sickness, old age, maternity, industrial injury, or other disability, and that the workers' standards, being increased, will by the same token increase demand for agricultural products.

Above all, I wish to emphasize that while this bill does not provide an adequate standard—one that the country is capable of sustaining—but only a minimum standard of living for the farming population, nevertheless, it offers the only adequate minimum for health and decency. Present relief under which these people are living is totally inadequate to preserve health and live decently. The Wagner social-insurance bill, S. 1130, is likewise totally inadequate. The same type of insurance has been tried out in England and proved a failure. Relief only averaged $24 a month in the countryside, scarcely enough to provide the minimum food budget—if it could all have been used for food—of the Department of Agriculture, without considering at all the other necessities of life.

We feel that placing the distribution of these funds in the hands of workers and farmers is wise—for who has a better understanding of those needing relief than neighbors—the people that administer relief today never had to live under the conditions of those needing relief; they are, therefore, bad judges of their needs; they condescend to us with pity and sympathy, then proceed to cut the already miserable relief levels that they had.

The Lundeen bill is designed to put purchasing power in the hands of the masses of the people, at least 40,000,000 of whom are destitute. This, in itself, will broaden the market for farm products; placing money in their hands so they can make those badly needed repairs to buildings and machinery, as well as buy clothes and other necessities. This, in turn, would put thousands of workers back to work. There would be no need of this trickling from the top, through the R. F. C. and P. W. A., which was tried, and we on the bottom know it never trickled through.

The compensation provided in the Lundeen bill will broaden the market far more than that provided in the Wagner bill. This is shown by the minimum pay provided for unemployment and other forms of disability in the Lundeen bill—in this bill the minimum of $10 per week for the unemployed or old persons, $3 for every dependent, which comes to about $80 per month. Contrast this with the average of $24 now provided for those on relief. And this is a real increase in "purchasing power" and will not be frozen in the vaults of our creditor's bank.

The Lundeen bill furthermore provides for average local wages for unemployed, full or part time, during the entire period of unemployment. The Wagner bill, when the amount is definitely established, will come to far less than this. It gives security for only 16 weeks in the year; and the funds under the Wagner bill are not available until 1936, while the need is right now.

The comparison on the old-age provisions of the two bills shows the same complete inadequacy of compensation under the administration-sponsored bill, which provides only $15 a month for people now 65 years of age or over. In the Lundeen bill an old person is simply an unemployed person receiving the benefits listed above, namely, $80 a month.

The Wagner bill is another example of bootstrap economics. In order to receive benefits for old age, the worker must have paid in, out of his own low standard of living, up to 2½ percent of his wages—half the reserves built up. The Lundeen bill, on the other hand, places the responsibility squarely where it belongs, on the backs of rich corporations and individuals, with incomes above $5,000, who can well afford to take the responsibility for the wear and tear on human lives devoted to the building up of their profits and society.

The Lundeen bill was discussed and endorsed by the farmers in their local meetings. In all cases it was practically 100 percent. The President and Congressmen know from the postcards and letters the widespread approval of this bill.

Because the workers'-unemployment, old-age, and social-insurance act includes farmers and agricultural workers, as well as industrial workers; because it provides sufficient for the minimum health and decency standard of living; and because it leaves no gaps in the security of workers and farmers from the age they start to work until they die, the organization I represent favors the immediate enactment of Lundeen bill, H. R. 2827.

Mr. LESINSKI. Mr. Bentzley, with your statement made now, and adding to the 14½ million unemployed, that would make nearly 20 million people unemployed, if you include all the farmers and the farm hands, would it not?

Mr. BENTZLEY. It would come close.

Mr. LESINSKI. Or that proportion? It would come pretty close to that?

Mr. BENTZLEY. It would come pretty close to that.

Mr. LESINIKI. I do not see where we can discuss the question of the price of the farm product, and so on. That would have nothing to do with this bill. I personally am a believer in N. R. A. and controlled prices, and that is what the farmers would want—those that have farms and are producing their milk, grain, and so forth—but to discuss it here in the Lundeen bill, I think is out of place. The only thing we could discuss would be the farm hands and that portion of farmers who have lost everything. I doubt that beyond that we could have any discussion of any kind.

Mr. BENTZLEY. Will you let me answer that?

Mr. LESINSKI. Yes.

Mr. DUNN. Yes; you may answer it.

Mr. BENTZLEY. My only reason for illustrating that was to show you that although the Secretary of Agriculture investigated the enormous profits of the milk distributors, instead of decreasing it and giving the producer of milk the benefit, it was really increased, and it was this enormous profit that was driving those farmers into the ranks of the unemployed and into the special lines. That is my purpose, and only my purpose, in showing the decreasing price.

Mr. LESINSKI. That is why I made the statement. I am a great believer in N. R. A. and controlled prices. If the big milk dealers are making big profits and paying a small price for the milk to the farmers, I doubt if that is right. I think that the farmers are entitled to their share—they should be—and the only way you can accomplish that is by controlled prices. I still also realize that the administration has not fulfilled that portion of it that it has promised. I know that in different types of codes the same thing has happened; and into that same category you could put the small business man, and if you are going to add the small business man into the same category, you are going to raise unemployment to 25,000,000; or taking 4 people to each family, would be 100,000,000, with the rest of them working, with most of the country out of employment; so it would be a pretty hard thing to do, and I do not think we will reach that far; but I realize that there has to be something done for the farm hand, because he is unemployed on account of the farmer not being able to pay him.

Mr. DUNN. Pardon me, what is it you say we cannot reach? How far do you say we can go?

Mr. LESINSKI. I say, we cannot include in all of our work up here, and the testimony, the question of controlled prices, and the question that the gentleman has brought up in his statement here. Of course, that has nothing to do with the Lundeen bill. He has only presented it as he has stated, to show what is the farmers' trouble.

Mr. DUNN. But we can accept his figures.

Mr. LESINSKI. Oh, surely.

Mr. DUNN. And agreed with him that it is absolutely necessary and essential for the Federal Government to do something for these unemployed farmers. That is what we can do.

Mr. LESINSKI. The farmer himself is not unemployed.

Mr. DUNN. Yes; he is unemployed.

Mr. LESINSKI. But he is not getting sufficient money for his product to give him an American standard of living. He is just starving on his farm.

Mr. BENTZLEY. No. Just let me give you an example. For instance, suppose you are a farmer and have lost your farm. Your next step is to have the farm offered back for you to rent. Rather than move, you think you can get enough out of your crop the following year to pay the rent for that farm. Suppose you were on a potato farm up in Maine, and you had specialized in potatoes, and had raised 315 bushels of potatoes on this farm, and after you have got your crop, you find out that you do not have enough to pay for your fertilizer, your spraying, your gas and oil, and the wear and tear of your equipment. Where are you going to get the money for your man? What happens to you? Do you go into the unemployed class, or do you still remain on the farm and try to take another chance next year? You see, that is the way the farmer is affected directly, and not only the farm hand. There are lots of those people.

Mr. LESINSKI. The farmer himself should get a sufficient price for his product so that he can enjoy the American standard of living.

Mr. BENTZLEY. Yes.

Mr. Lesinski. The only way he can get it is by getting a price for his potatoes.

Mr. Bentzley. Yes.

Mr. Lesinski. Now, if he gets 40 cents a barrel, I realize that he just cannot make an existence on it, and cannot pay anything to anyone.

Mr. Bentzley. But suppose it is milk, the same thing applies.

Mr. Lesinski. If he gets a small price for that, he is entitled to more money. That would be a question, on our present set-up in N. R. A., of a controlled price which should be in existence, although I realize everybody is against it. Personally, I am for it.

Mr. Bentzley. Does not this bill make provisions for that? Does not the Lundeen bill place the purchasing power at the bottom, where it will be possible for those people who are denying themselves the right to buy milk, or who are now denying themselves the proper amount of potatoes and our products to eat—would it not place the purchasing power, there, so that they could buy them, and thereby broaden their market so we would be able to get a decent price for our stuff?

Mr. Lesinski. I doubt if this bill is that broad in its scope.

Mr. Bentzley. It is much broader than the other bills are.

Mr. Lesinski. Oh, I realize that. It is much a better bill than we have ever had up here. I am for the bill, personally, but what I am trying to bring up is, it is necessary in this country to get everybody back to where he belongs, and get back to the American standard of living instead of starving.

Mr. Bentzley. That is why I am here. Now, to answer Mr. Lundeen, if you will pardon me——

Mr. Dunn. Are you through, Mr. Lesinski?

Mr. Lesinski. I am through.

Mr. Bentzley. To answer your question, Mr. Lundeen, I did not have a chance before. We have got a farmers' emergency relief bill introduced into Congress by Congressman Burdick.

Mr. Lundeen. Congressman Burdick of North Dakota.

Mr. Bentzley. Yes.

Mr. Lundeen. Have you the number?

Mr. Bentzley. I cannot give you the number.

Mr. Lundeen. But he introduced the bill?

Mr. Bentzley. You will find he introduced it.

Mr. Lundeen. That is the farm bill you are sponsoring?

Mr. Bentzley. That is the farm bill we are supporting and sponsoring.

Mr. Lundeen. Does that give you a price control, or what?

Mr. Bentzley. Well, I could not go into the discussion of that bill right now.

Mr. Dunn. Are there any more questions, Mr. Lundeen?

Mr. Lundeen. I think not.

Mr. Dunn. Are there any more questions, Mr. Lesinski?

Mr. Lesinski. No; that is all.

Mr. Dunn. Mr. Bentzley, I presume nobody else desires to interrogate you, and I want to thank you personally in behalf of the committee for your wonderful address, and we will do the best we can for the poor unfortunate farmer.

Mr. BENTZLEY. I thank you.

Mr. DUNN. We are very glad to have had you come before the committee.

Mr. LESINSKI. I move we adjourn until tomorrow at 10 o'clock.

Mr. DUNN. Why not recess?

Mr. LESINSKI. All right, we will recess until tomorrow morning.

Mr. LUNDEEN. All right. I will second that motion.

(The motion was agreed to; accordingly, at 5 p. m., the subcommittee recessed until tomorrow, Tuesday, Feb. 5, 1935, at 10 a. m.)

UNEMPLOYMENT, OLD AGE, AND SOCIAL INSURANCE

TUESDAY, FEBRUARY 5, 1935

House of Representatives,
Subcommitte of the Committee on Labor,
Washington, D. C.

The subcommittee of the Committee on Labor met at 10 a. m., in the caucus room, House Office Building, Hon. Matthew A. Dunn (chairman) presiding.

(The subcommittee had under consideration H. R. 2827, H. R. 2859, H. R. 10, and H. R. 185.)

Mr. Dunn. The subcommittee will be in order. The first witness today will be Miss Mary van Kleeck, chairman of the Interprofessional Association for Social Insurance.

STATEMENT OF MISS MARY VAN KLEECK [1]

Miss van Kleeck. Congressman Dunn and members of the committee: This subject of the workers' bill is, of course, very far-reaching, and it is difficult to know exactly what material to bring forward. I have tried, in the prepared statement which follows, to cover the main subjects that are related directly to the bill, and I suggest that, at the close of the hearings, if additional material be needed on any of these subjects, we are entirely willing to document the record.

Mr. Lundeen. Pardon me.

Mr. Chairman, I wish Miss van Kleeck would state her connections in beginning her testimony.

Miss van Kleeck. Very gladly. I have made a note here for the record, of the work which bears directly on this testimony. In it, I mention that I am the author of "Miners and Management" which was published by the Russell Sage Foundation in 1934. That study deals particularly with the problems of irregularity of employment in relation to excess capacity in the bituminous coal industry; as a natural resource, that industry illustrates some of our problems of unemployment. I also mention that for the period from 1922 to

---

[1] Chairman of the Interprofessional Association for Social Insurance; Economist. New York; Director of Industrial Studies, Russell Sage Foundation; testifying as national chairman of the Interprofessional Association for Social Insurance; author, "Miners and Management," published by Russell Sage Foundation, 1934 (a study dealing particularly with the problems of irregularity of employment in relation to excess capacity in the bituminous coal industry); member of President's Conference on Unemployment, 1921, and of committee on unemployment and business cycles appointed by the Secretary of Commerce, Herbert Hoover, to carry forward the work of the President's Conference; chairman, 1922–33, committee on governmental labor statistics of the American Statistical Association; vice president, American Statistical Association; member, 1915–16, of Mayor Mitchel's committee on unemployment, New York City; chairman of program committee of world social economic congress, Amsterdam, Holland, 1931, under whose direction studies were made of fluctuations in employment in various countries of the world, published under the title "International Unemployment."

83

1933, I was chairman of the committee on governmental labor statistics of the American Statistical Association, which was developing the statistics on employment and unemployment, in the Federal Government and in the various States, and in that connection I made a special study in 1930 of the census of unemployment and its shortcomings and advantages. I think the statement regarding my experience covers all that I can confess to in this field. The fact that we have the worst unemployment crisis in history is perhaps a reflection on the past efforts of many groups.

Mr. DUNN. What you have just informed the Committee demonstrates that you are qualified to speak before this Committee.

Mr. LUNDEEN. I would say, Mr. Chairman, it is a very distinguished record.

Mr. DUNN. Yes; I agree with you.

Miss VAN KLEECK. And a record of failure to deal with the problems of unemployment, on which I am glad to testify today.

Security for all who work for their living in the United States is the primary and all-important obligation on which the Seventy-fourth Congress is called upon to act. The Interprofessional Association for Social Insurance, on whose behalf the present witness speaks, supports H. R. 2827, the Workers' Unemployment and Social Insurance bill, because it undertakes to provide compensation for insecurity for the masses of the unemployed and, as such, is the first step in the comprehensive program which the establishment of security for the American people will require in the next few years.

The Interprofessional Association for Social Insurance, which includes individual members from all the recognized professions and is just now beginning to serve also as a center for the professional organizations in a program for the security of professional workers, was organized to express the demand of professional workers that they be included in legislation for social insurance. Recognizing the identity of interest of professional workers with industrial workers and farmers in the need for economic security, the Interprofessional Association does not develop its own program but undertakes to cooperate with all other workers and with trade unions in support of inclusive legislation.

The specific reasons for support of H. R. 2827 by the Interprofessional Association for Social Insurance are as follows:

(1) The continuance of extensive mass unemployment demands comprehensive action to provide insurance for all workers, in lieu of income from earnings.

(2) Professional workers are suffering gravely from the extent of unemployment, but in most professions they are not covered by any other legislative proposal, and can be protected only in such an inclusive bill as H. R. 2827.

(3) The great and vital need of the unemployed for means with which to buy the necessities of life for themselves and their families is not and cannot be met by the uncertain and inadequate provision for relief.

(4) This mass unemployment is not an unusual emergency, but has recurred at regular and frequent intervals in this country, so that the time has come for the definite recognition of the obligation of

Government and the economic system to insure continuity of income.

(5) Technicians and scientists agree that the productive capacity of the United States is equal to a far greater measure of security and to higher standards of living than have yet been established; and science and invention promise to expand this productivity to a higher level, if the productive system can be freed from the recurrent burdens of industrial depressions.

(6) As a continuing problem, mass unemployment requires Congressional action because of the mandate laid upon Congress by the Constitution to provide for the general welfare.

It is because the general welfare is undermined at all points by unemployment that this bill is important, not only in itself but because of the setting in which it has to be placed in relation to the whole economic policy of the Government as established by Congress; and I look upon this bill as establishing a new policy, looking in a new direction of responsibility for unemployment on the part of the nation as a whole.

These reasons are amplified with supporting data in the following statements.

The most recent report of the Bureau of Labor Statistics as to trends in factory employment and pay rolls showed an increase in employment in December as compared with November; but the factory employment index stood at the alarmingly low level of 78.1 and the pay roll index at 63.2, as compared with the 3-year average of 1923–25, which is taken as 100. Thus for every 100 employed in 1923–25 only 78 were at work in December of last year—that is, 2 months ago—and of every dollar paid to workers in 1923–25 only 63.2 cents went into workers' income in December 1934. Not only is this indicative of a very serious decline in income for factory workers, but the fact that employment has increased somewhat more rapidly than pay rolls is a sign of the lowering of individual incomes.

These statistics, which are part of a series covering also other industries, in which, however, the factory index is the most significant figure, show trends in employment and earnings but do not measure unemployment. The only way to determine the number of the unemployed is to make estimates based on data from a number of sources, including these statistics of trends of employment. In that connection, I wish to call attention to figures published by the National Industrial Conference Board, December 10, 1934, in the Conference Board Bulletin, which gives an index of manufacturing industries, based also upon 1923–25 as 100, and it agrees virtually with these figures that have just been read. It gives an index of employment of 78.6, pay rolls, 60.7; output per worker, 92.9; and output per man-hour, 129.5.

You see that during this period we have already enormously increased our output per man-hour, which indicates a very serious situation; in fact, that we shall now begin to get along without workers that would otherwise have been employed; that during this period of unemployment we are increasing our output per man-hour, which is a clear indication of more unemployment to be expected.

In this connection, on the present trends in employment, I have here some very detailed statistical material which I wish to put into the record in the form of an appendix to what I have to say. I asked the Commissioner of the New York State Department of Labor to designate the statistician, D. E. Varley, to give us the analysis, at this time. It happens that New York State industries as a composite, constitute, generally speaking, a fair index of the country. Except for Massachusetts, New York has the oldest of the series—somewhat older than that of the Federal Bureau of Labor Statistics. I referred to the fact that I was a member of Mayor Mitchel's committee on unemployment in 1915–16, and it was a sub-committee of that committee which worked out this series, both for the Federal Bureau and for the New York State Department of Labor. It is a series which measures the number on the pay rolls and the total pay rolls, month by month. We have here for the record the indexes of employment in New York State during the whole period from 1915 to 1934.

There is a table here which is very interesting in showing the great constrasts between the different localities. In other words, a general summary, such as is published monthly by the Federal Bureau, tends to iron out differences. A group of textile workers in Massachusetts who are laid off tend to balance in the general index a group who may be taken on in Detroit in the automobile industry, but it does not help the textile workers in Massachusetts to have some automobile workers taken on in Detroit, although it helps the general situation in the country. We must always remember the differences between different localities; for example, here is Albany and Schenectady and Troy which had an index of 62 in 1934 as compared with 1925–27, which is taken as 100 for the index in New York State; compared to 71 for the State as a whole, and 118 in Binghamton. Apparently they had increased employment in the shoe industry in Binghamton.

These figures go into details for such important industries as metals, which were way down to 60 in December, 2 months ago, in New York State. An index of only 60 in the metals industry, which is an important key industry, indicates a rather serious condition.

This analysis contains material not only about New York State, but here is information also about Massachusetts. Massachusetts takes the manufacturing census for the United States Government, and therefore it has quite a complete record. There is a table here which shows the difference between the high point and the low point in 1920 and 1921, and in 1929 and 1932, and in intervening cycles. From the high point of January 1920 to the low point of January 1921, employment went down 29.8 percent, and that was considered a very serious depression, you will remember, in 1921; but from the high point in September 1929 the decline by June 1932 was 48.2 percent in the manufacturing industries in Massachusetts.

Massachusetts took a census of unemployment on January 2, 1934, which was a year ago, of course, but that, I believe, is the most recent State-wide census that has been taken. At that time 19.1 percent were wholly unemployed; temporarily employed on Government projects, 5.6; temporarily employed on private work, 0.2; and employed part time, 9.6; which means that the total who were unemployed, or not fully employed, was 34.5 percent, which of course is alarmingly high. Figures are appended, also, for the State of Pennsylvania, based on an unemployment survey there, which show correspondingly high percentages.

A table computed from the census shows labor's share in the value added by manufacture in New York State a declining share. The index in 1919 was 111.7, with 1929 as 100; and 97.3 in 1931. The percentage of value added by manufacture in 1919 was 37.1 but declined to 32.3 in 1931. That decline has to be looked at, not as a question of whether that is a fair share for labor, but as a question of whether you can possibly sustain purchasing power if wages steadily decline in proportion to the added value of the product.

The committee will have before it, in the testimony of other witnesses, various estimates of unemployment. These vary widely, from 10,000,000 to 17,000,000, but all estimates agree in showing that the present extent of unemployment is extremely hazardous not only for the unemployed but for all workers and for the general welfare of the Nation. This unemployment represents a curtailment of the distribution of the necessities of life, and this in turn will create more unemployment unless the trends can be reversed by some such effective policy as is represented in House Resolution 2827.

In connection with all the estimates that have been given, it should be stated that no provision has been made by the Federal Government to count the number of unemployed since the census of 1930. It is necessary to use data gathered in several Government departments and to make estimates on the basis of these statistics. In some occupations, notably the professions, domestic service, and agriculture, there is little or no basis even for an estimate. It must be said at once, therefore, that one of the important tasks of the Seventy-fourth Congress is immediately to pass a resolution calling for a complete census of the unemployed, to be taken under the direction of the Bureau of the Census; or at least a careful sample of various occupations and regions which would provide Congress with the necessary basis for action to meet the needs of the unemployed. Moreover, the occasion should be taken also to improve greatly the current statistics of employment and earnings gathered by the Bureau of Labor Statistics and particularly to provide for regular reporting on the extent of employment and unemployment in the professions. Moreover, careful current studies of standards of living should be made in order that the country may be currently informed concerning the number of workers in the various occupations whose earnings are insufficient to provide for the minimum standard of living required for health and decency. We ought to have these studies of the lowest standards of living, just as the health departments report the rates of diseases. It is extremely important that the welfare of the people should be shown, not in general statistics, but that we should know currently how many families in this country are falling below the level of the necessities of life; and that knowledge ought to compel us to take some action to relieve that situation.

The duration of unemployment is of great importance in connection with proposals for unemployment insurance. The administration's bill (H. R. 4142) implies a severe limitation which would probably be less than 15 weeks. No comprehensive data exist regarding the length of unemployment of those who are now without jobs, but there are several studies, one of which may be quoted here. It happens to be Congressman Lundeen's State. The University of Minnesota made a study of 500 unemployed, published under the title "Social Consequences of Prolonged Unemployment" (Aug. 1933). It was found that only 22.9 percent had been unemployed less than 1 year, and 45 percent had been unemployed 2 years and over. Compensation for 15 weeks' unemployment you see, would have been long ago forgotten by those who were still unemployed after 2 years.

This is a clear indication of the fact that to provide funds for so limited a period as 15 weeks or even 6 months in a year is merely to postpone dealing with the problem of compensation for unemployment, since when funds are exhausted the need for some definite provision of income again arises.

This same study gives facts about the resources of the unemployed, which doubtless could be matched in other parts of the country. In the Minnesota study it was found that in 16 percent of the cases families had doubled up to reduce expenses; among those having at least one member employed, expenses had been reduced to a minimum below the level of safety for family welfare; in some cases women became the sole wage earners, the husbands sometimes taking over the household duties; cash savings of course were rapidly exhausted; homes were lost; insurance policies were cashed; and debts were incurred either with individuals or with tradespeople. It is clear that the burdens of unemployment have constituted an increasing weight upon the standard of living of the American people.

Though the present industrial depression is marked by great intensity as well as by its duration and its extent in the different countries of the world, it should not be regarded merely as an emergency, and least of all as due primarily to the war and therefore calling merely for patience and "cooperation" in the expectation that recovery will come of itself. Students of the business cycle have shown that between 1780 and 1925 the United States had 32 business cycles with an average length of 4 years from panic to panic, or from recession to recession. This is a study made by the National Bureau of Economic Research, Business Annals of the United States, England, France, and 14 Other Countries, by Willard Long Thorp, with an introductory chapter by Wesley C. Mitchell, who is one of the leading economists of the country. It was published in New York in 1926. Stated differently, it was found by these economists that in the period from 1790 to 1925 the United States had only a year and a half of prosperity for every year of depression.

Thus it appears that this Nation must face recurrent unemployment as a continuing characteristic of its business, industry, and finance, and must work out a program designed to prevent the undermining of the general welfare by this insecurity which is ever present, since years of prosperity are always followed by years of depression. That this is not inevitable is beginning to dawn on the minds of many who realize that a country of such great resources and with such a high degree of technological development can and must find the way to establish social and economic security.

Mr. DUNN. Pardon me a moment. There were how many "business cycles" between 1780 and 1925?

Miss VAN KLEECK. Thirty-two.

Mr. DUNN. And for every year of depression we had a year and a half of prosperity. Is that correct?

Miss VAN KLEECK. That is correct.

Mr. SCHNEIDER. I would like to ask, right at this point: Have those who made the compilation of those depressions occurring in our country and in the world made any recommendations for the curing of that condition?

Miss VAN KLEECK. Not very thorough-going recommendations. Dr. Wesley C. Mitchell has been active in the public service in relation to these questions. He is a member of the National Resources Board in the Department of Interior now. That National Resources Board has just put in a report. It recommends a planning board for the country, but the difficulty about this recommendation is that it is not clear how planning can be carried out under these conditions which Dr. Mitchell himself discovers in the study of business cycles.

This is to be said for these studies: They are objective scientific studies which reveal what happens in industrial depressions. On the whole they stop at that point. The conclusions have to be drawn by others.

Here it is necessary only to refer briefly to the fact that the productive capacity of the United States is equal to the maintenance of a standard of living far higher than has yet been attained. It is also important to point out that this productive capacity, through technological invention, is under present circumstances actually causing an increase in unemployment—" The richer we are, the poorer we are." Competition in industry leads to the introduction of new machines in the hope of reducing the cost of production, and this in turn means that labor is permanently displaced. And unless provision be made for income, the general welfare is permanently undermined.

In a paper read before the International Industrial Relations Institute in New York, November 24, 1934, the Commissioner of Labor Statistics, Isador Lubin, declared:

If employment in the manufacturing industries alone of the country is to return to the level of 1929, jobs must be provided for approximately 2,000,000 workers. Four hundred thousand of these jobs must be provided by the consumer-goods industries, where employment is now at about 90 percent of the average for the peak year, 1929. * * * In the durable-goods industries, such as those producing iron and steel, machinery, transportation equipment, and metals, employment must be increased by 50 percent if the predepression level is to be attained. For every thousand workers on the pay rolls of these industries in 1929 only 633 are today employed.

Commissioner Lubin went on to say that reabsorption of workers in manufacturing will by no means solve the problem. Referring to the service and transportation industries, he said:

It is doubtful whether these industries could immediately reemploy the 2,000,000 of their former employees who are no longer on their pay rolls. Nor is there a prospect of private construction of sufficient magnitude to expect the building industry to take on the 1½ million unemployed construction workers.

Thus we have accounted already for 5½ million, for whom he says there is not very much hope of reemployment. He continues:

We must bear in mind also that there are hundreds of thousands of unemployed agricultural workers whose chances of getting back their former jobs are not so very bright. Then again it is estimated that something approaching a half million small business men, forced to the wall by the depression, must also be considered as part of the unemployed wage-earning population.

These figures all indicate the necessity for just such an inclusive program as is proposed in H. R. 2827. And it is also clear that a way must be found to utilize the productive capacity of the Nation so that unemployment will be eliminated. Meanwhile unemployment compensation is essential for the general welfare.

I want to call attention at this point to the burden of unemployment and its effect on the small business man. In our relief programs, which declare that there must be a "means test", a person must prove he has to have relief. That is, he must prove that he cannot get any more credit from the small business man, and that he cannot get any more relatives or friends to give or lend him money. Virtually that is what the "means test" is. It asks "Have you relatives working, or can you get some money from some other source?" The extent to which the small business man has borne the burden of this depression is something that statistics do not reveal, but we must be perfectly clear that the payment of unemployment insurance to the workers would sustain many of the small business men who now go to the wall through the fact that they must pay the costs of unemployment, over which they have themselves no more control than have the workers. And of course the greatest burden is borne by the working class as a whole, as revealed by those figures, which show the fact that the pay rolls represent 63.1 percent, and those people who are earning those lower wages are at the same time taking care of that 22.1 percent plus of the unemployed; so that we are resting the burden of this thing upon the workers, with a lowered standard of living, with all of its menacing results for the welfare of the people. A contributory insurance system and a contributory old-age-pension system, such as is proposed in the Wagner-Lewis bill, the administration bill, would increase the burden for those workers who are already carrying the unemployed, because the Federal Government is not giving anything like adequate relief.

It is basic in the workers' bill that the sources of funds come from general taxation and from income taxes and taxes on inheritance and gifts. Testimony by others takes up the details of the cost of this bill. Reference here is rather to the general principles involved. It is a sound principle to undertake this redistribution of the national income in a period of crisis to meet mass unemployment by tax on profits and higher incomes. Other proposals, which call for the withholding of part of the wages of workers and a tax on pay rolls, which is inevitably passed on to the consumer, tend merely to rearrange workers' income, decreasing current earnings in the interest of building up reserve funds against future unemployment. These funds enter into channels of investment, which really constitute increase in the debt burden of American industry and still further throw out of gear the purchasing power of the people in relation to productive capacity. Attention ought to be called, I think, to the Federal Reserve System's reports for 1934, as described in the New York Times, which showed large reserves for which the banks were "seeking employment."

A specific illustration could be given of the coal industry, to indicate the basic problems involved. Their solution cannot be brought about by any system of social insurance. Any such system is merely compensation for the existence of insecurity. But the national policy which undertakes through social insurance to compensate for insecurity must also be molded in the direction of preventing the lowering of standards of living by such restrictions on production as are characteristic of the present economic program of the Federal administration.

This bill is not a simple thing, as I am sure those of you who are working on it in this committee know. It is not simply a question of providing compensation for the unemployed. It virtually commits the Federal Government to a reversal of its policies which at present are restricting production of goods and even of food which the people need, in order to increase prices. This bill calls for a reversal of that policy in the direction of undertaking to maintain and raise the standards of living of the people, and that means very many fundamentally related measures in addition to the compensation for insecurity.

In the last analysis the sources of funds must be in the productivity of industry. But in the present these funds must be taken out of past productivity, namely, out of income and profits, in such a way as to prevent the increase of the burdens upon those now employed.

It is worth while to point out at this point that in 1933 Senator Wagner made a statement before the American Federation of Labor, in which he described the distribution of the national income. He pointed out that in 1929 the value of goods produced in factories in the United States was $10,000,000,000 more than in 1922. Of this increase, 6 percent went into wages, 8 percent into salaries, 38 percent into raw materials, and 48 percent into profits and other costs; and Senator Wagner goes on to say:

Is it any wonder that during the heyday of our vaunted prosperity, less than one-tenth of the population received one-third of the national income, while three-fourths of the people lived below the standards of comfort set by the United States Bureau of Labor Statistics? Wage improvements under the " new deal " should not be simply enough to keep factories going. Wages must be fixed with reference to a social program which intends to insure everyone a comfortable living standard, and labor its just share of the national wealth.

But unfortunately, Senator Wagner's present " Economic Security " bill would not tend in that direction, but H. R. 2827 would, to the extent of using some of these past profits, so to speak, for the overdue current compensation of labor, instead of attempting to establish a so-called " Security Act ", which takes from labor in the present part of its already meager earnings, to take care of unemployment in the future.

Mr. LUNDEEN. Pardon me. Senator Wagner's statement there is a pretty good statement in favor of our bill, is it not?

Miss VAN KLEECK. I think it is an excellent statement in favor of our bill. I am going to have the pleasure of reading it into the record this afternoon before the Committee on Ways and Means. It is not fair to say that the 48 percent mentioned by Senator Wagner is all profits. It is profits and other costs, but it is a wholly disproportionate amount.

On the subject of changes in the buying power of the dollar, the workers' bill has a section which declares that the minimum compensation guaranteed by this act shall be increased in conformity with rises in the cost of living.

Some comment must be made on this point. The bill will fail o its purpose if nothing be said about the necessity for stability ii the dollar paid to workers either in wages or salaries or in in surance. We are talking here about stability of the worker's dollars not stability of the banker's dollar. Stability of the worker's dolla implies the possibility of purchasing always a suitable quantity o the necessities of life. And whether the dollar be measured in th value of a metal or in terms of a commodity, both farmers and in dustrial workers must be able to count upon the stability of thei income on the one hand and, on the other hand, on the stability o the elements of the standards of living which this country make possible. The Nation must sooner or later develop a " workers index " which will currently inform all who work for their living a to the efficiency of the instrument of exchange which money repre sents. The insurance dollar must be kept stable by some sucl workers' index.

I think, Mr. Chairman, that is all I have to say.

Mr. DUNN. That was a very interesting address.

Congressman Welch, do you wish to interrogate Miss Van Kleeck

Mr. WELCH. I came in late, Mr. Chairman. I had to appear befor the Rules Committee this morning; I am sorry.

Mr. DUNN. We will ask Mr. Schneider. Do you have any question to ask, Mr. Schneider?

Mr. SCHNEIDER. I have no question in particular. I was in hope the witness would present some solution for this whole problem, witl reference to the cost of administration of a bill of this kind.

Miss VAN KLEECK. I have not taken up that question specifically because I think that other witnesses will bring out more material I have, however, made some study of it, and of course, as I said ii this statement, I believe that the first source should be, as this bil provides, general taxation; that this should be a primary claim The necessity for paying compensation—that is, for assuring con tinuity of income of those who work for their living—should, o course, be prior to war preparations. There is the first source o funds. Instead of putting money into preparations for war, tha money should be made available for the current costs of unemploy ment.

Secondly, general taxation should include higher income taxe for individuals and for corporations. I have here some interestinp comparisons of the income tax as between Great Britain and th United States. I have the impression that Dr. Gillman yesterda afternoon went into more detail on this point, and so I do not thinl it is necessary for me to deal with what might be the higher income tax rate. It is my opinion that the Treasury Department ought t be asked to do some figuring on this. After all, those of us who ar outside the Government are not able to have access to all the mate rial that is in it. I think the Treasury Department ought to b charged with making a thoroughgoing study of our taxation systen and the utilization of the money; but it is perfectly clear that th income tax is higher in Great Britain, which has been held up more or less recently as a country of greater stability, shall I say, or nearer to prosperity than the United States itself. Great Britain collects much more from its income taxes than do we, and at all the different levels it is a higher income tax. There is no point at which it is not higher. For example, whereas for incomes of $50,000 to $100,000, Great Britain collects 39 percent, we collect 17 percent, and so all the way along the line, we compare with France and Great Britain as collecting very much less from income taxes. When it comes to inheritances and estates, again, we collect very much less than do these foreign countries.

We could get more out of those sources and out of such a distribution of purchasing power would of course come some increase in employment. I am unwilling to suggest this as the ultimate solution, because we cannot solve this problem of recurrent depressions in our unplanned system, and we cannot establish security without planning; but we can compensate for insecurity.

Mr. SCHNEIDER. Can we plan sufficiently nationally, and in a world-wide way, under the present capitalistic profit system?

Miss VAN KLEECK. No. I think capitalism and economic planning for expansion are mutually incompatible. We are engaged in planning for restriction. If we look over the world today, we see that there are two kinds of planning. There is planning for restriction and there is planning for expansion. The system which runs into an economic crisis such as our own turns at once to an effort to increase prices and sustain profits by restriction on production, and what we are doing under N. R. A. codes is to restrict production in the effort to raise prices, and that means restricting the output of industry. Of course America does not like the idea of planning for restriction. We always want business to be " bigger and better." We want bigger and better standards of living than we have had in the past, but I believe it is being proved that we cannot plan for expansion.

Mr. DUNN. Have you any further question, Mr. Schneider?

Mr. SCHNEIDER. No.

Mr. DUNN. Mr. Welch, do you have any questions?

Mr. WELCH. No questions.

Mr. DUNN. Mr. Lundeen?

Mr. LUNDEEN. Miss van Kleeck, you spoke of the Treasury Department, and you spoke of some figures there. Just yesterday we tried to make available the names of those who are worth over $100,000 in tax-exempt securities, but we could only muster 106 votes, and yet we are fresh from the people last November.

Mr. DUNN. I was one of the 106.

Miss VAN KLEECK. Of course I need not point out that we have a conflict of interests here, which is one reason for the very great importance of maintaining our civil liberties, and maintaining the rights of workers to organize; this has a very close bearing on this whole issue, because as the national income declines, the pressure, the conflict over its distribution becomes all the greater.

Mr. LUNDEEN. I would like to say to Congressman Schneider that Mr. Gillman yesterday took up sources of revenue and it will be found in yesterday's testimony, the point that we were speaking of there.   He went into it quite thoroughly.   I do not believe you were here at the time.

Miss VAN KLEECK. The study presented by Dr. Gillman was made on behalf of the Research Committee of the Interprofessional Association for Social Insurance.

Mr. LUNDEEN. I want to thank you for your very able and spendid statement. So far as I am concerned, I enjoyed it very much, and I know the country will enjoy reading it.

Miss VAN KLEECK. Thank you very much.

Mr. DUNN. Congressman Hartley, do you wish to ask Miss van Kleeck any questions?

Mr. HARTLEY. I am sorry. I have no questions, not having heard her remarks.

Mr. DUNN. Mr. Lesinski?

Mr. LESINSKI. I have no questions.

(The witness Van Kleeck submitted for the record the following data:)

STATEMENT OF D. V. VARLEY, STATISTICIAN OF DIVISION OF STATISTICS, NEW YORK STATE DEPARTMENT OF LABOR

In order to have a clear picture of the extent of unemployment, it is not sufficient to consider the total number of unemployed in the country. Additional factors to be considered are fluctuations in employment and severity of unemployment by different trades and industries as well as by different localities, total unemployment in different areas, duration of unemployment, and relative earning positions of different groups of workers. Only then should the extent of unemployment in the country as a whole be considered.

The New York State Department of Labor has been collecting statistical data on employment for a period of years and its indexes of employment in manufacturing industries are widely accepted as reliable indicators of employment. Table I shows changes in employment for New York State as a whole and for selected districts of the State for the period 1915-34. Observation of the data brings out clearly the wide difference in levels of employment in different cities of the State as compared with the employment in the State as a whole. Employment indexes thus indirectly indicate the extent of unemployment in different localities at the same period of time.

TABLE I.—*Employment in New York State, by different localities, 1915–34*

[1925-27=100]

Year	All State	New York City	Albany, Schenectady, Troy	Binghamton	Rochester	Utica
1915	100	118	94	63	77	107
1916	117	126	116	82	93	133
1917	122	128	123	90	96	130
1918	124	128	122	85	98	152
1919	116	124	110	88	105	111
1920	120	125	118	95	110	117
1921	94	106	88	81	92	84
1922	101	110	98	92	90	100
1923	112	114	117	102	102	112
1924	102	105	107	98	96	100
1925	101	103	102	103	96	100
1926	101	101	104	97	102	101
1927	97	97	94	101	102	98
1928	93	90	93	99	99	94
1929	98	92	110	110	105	95
1930	86	83	91	113	97	82
1931	73	72	76	109	82	70
1932	59	59	54	105	67	55
1933	61	62	52	107	65	63
1934	71	73	62	118	73	69

Source: Division of Statistics, New York State Department of Labor.

When various industries are considered separately (tables II, III, and IV) the same factor is brought out—i. e., various levels at which employment stood in different industries for the corresponding dates.

Table V, based on the United States Census of Manufactures, shows employment for different manufacturing groups for 1919 to 1931. It shows not only a sharp decline from 1929 to 1931 for industry as a whole but varying differences in the several industries. While one industry shows a decline of only 6.5 percent from 1929 to 1931, another industry shows a decline of 44.6 percent. The table also reveals the instability of unemployment and wide fluctuations for the entire period of 1919–31. That this situation is not confined to New York State alone is demonstrated by the fact that New York State, as far as manufacuring industries are concerned, occupied the same position in relation to the country as a whole throughout the entire period.

TABLE II.—*Employment. Metals and machinery, New York State, 1921–34*

[1925–27 = 100. 0]

Month	1921	1922	1923	1924	1925	1926	1927
January	99.3	78.1	110.1	109.3	100.1	105.2	97.7
February	94.0	81.2	111.4	109.3	101.4	105.9	99.0
March	91.0	82.8	115.2	109.8	102.1	107.0	100.1
April	85.7	33.8	115.5	106.4	100.1	105.7	99.3
May	81.8	87.3	115.0	101.0	98.9	104.2	98.3
June	75.9	90.4	114.1	96.7	96.6	103.7	97.3
July	72.2	87.7	113.0	92.1	94.8	101.4	95.0
August	71.8	91.8	112.4	92.4	94.6	101.7	95.4
September	73.8	94.3	110.9	94.2	96.9	103.1	95.7
October	76.6	101.6	112.3	96.0	100.9	103.8	95.4
November	78.4	106.1	111.4	98.0	104.0	101.5	94.2
December	80.0	109.0	110.4	100.4	105.6	100.9	92.3

Month	1928	1929	1930	1931	1932	1933	1934
January	89.7	98.9	94.8	72.4	56.1	41.5	54.3
February	91.1	102.5	93.5	72.6	56.1	41.2	57.3
March	91.4	104.6	92.3	72.3	55.2	38.6	60.5
April	92.2	106.0	91.7	71.3	52.6	39.9	63.7
May	92.6	106.4	90.6	70.4	47.6	40.3	63.5
June	92.9	105.9	88.1	68.2	44.5	45.9	62.1
July	91.3	105.6	82.0	64.7	40.8	48.6	60.5
August	92.4	104.4	80.7	60.8	40.1	52.1	59.1
September	93.7	104.7	79.4	61.7	41.7	55.6	59.2
October	96.4	104.3	77.9	59.8	43.3	54.9	58.5
November	97.4	101.6	76.3	59.8	44.7	54.6	58.5
December	97.1	97.2	74.2	59.4	42.9	54.7	59.7

Source: Division of Statistics, New York State Department of Labor.

TABLE III.—*Employment. Food and tobacco, New York State, 1921–34*

[1925–27 = 100]

Month	1921	1922	1923	1924	1925	1926	1927
January	102.0	106.4	108.3	106.1	101.5	97.6	90.8
February	105.9	110.0	112.0	110.2	103.4	98.8	90.7
March	108.7	113.2	114.9	111.2	104.0	99.5	90.7
April	107.4	107.8	110.1	107.2	99.7	97.2	90.7
May	106.9	109.4	110.1	107.0	100.2	96.4	92.4
June	111.6	113.5	113.1	111.0	105.1	99.9	97.0
July	113.8	121.7	118.7	113.4	106.9	103.8	99.4
August	116.6	121.7	113.8	111.8	106.4	100.4	97.1
September	119.3	122.0	117.6	117.0	111.4	102.7	102.2
October	119.7	118.6	120.6	115.9	111.2	102.9	103.3
November	115.2	119.8	118.4	111.5	107.9	100.1	98.0
December	109.6	115.3	111.8	105.9	103.4	94.4	92.8

TABLE III.—*Employment. Food and tobacco, New York State, 1921–34*—Contd.

[1925–27 = 100]

Month	1928	1929	1930	1931	1932	1933	1934
January	88.1	90.5	83.0	70.4	68.3	65.0	73.1
February	89.4	91.7	82.2	73.4	67.9	64.8	77.1
March	91.4	91.7	82.0	73.7	68.6	63.0	78.6
April	90.2	90.0	79.9	72.4	67.6	65.4	78.1
May	89.5	90.7	80.1	72.1	65.9	67.7	79.1
June	91.9	93.1	83.0	74.5	68.0	70.1	80.5
July	96.7	93.8	93.4	77.4	69.8	73.8	83.9
August	93.0	93.8	84.4	76.7	68.6	73.8	83.0
September	101.6	97.4	92.2	85.5	75.2	85.2	93.0
October	102.4	97.6	85.1	77.3	70.5	83.3	88.0
November	98.0	92.8	80.6	74.7	68.3	79.2	84.3
December	94.5	85.6	74.4	73.3	68.5	77.8	81.8

Source: Division of Statistics, New York State Department of Labor.

TABLE IV.—*Employment. Clothing and millinery, New York State, 1921–34*

[1925–27 = 100]

Month	1921	1922	1923	1924	1925	1926	1927
January	88.5	109.1	119.0	110.6	101.2	106.3	99.5
February	100.6	116.8	121.0	113.4	107.4	109.4	103.8
March	107.6	117.2	124.6	113.7	111.2	108.7	104.0
April	109.0	111.9	122.7	107.9	105.9	103.6	97.2
May	108.4	106.6	118.3	99.4	100.3	97.8	91.6
June	106.0	106.0	113.8	99.0	101.4	96.7	92.0
July	105.8	105.7	111.0	94.1	100.3	90.8	90.4
August	100.1	108.8	111.5	97.0	101.4	90.7	92.3
September	113.2	112.7	114.5	103.8	106.2	97.6	97.0
October	114.7	115.1	117.7	104.1	106.1	100.1	97.9
November	109.1	113.9	109.7	100.2	104.3	98.2	93.2
December	109.0	116.0	108.7	100.4	104.0	98.7	93.2

Month	1928	1929	1930	1931	1932	1933	1934
January	94.4	89.7	90.3	75.3	64.9	60.6	69.0
February	97.7	95.2	91.5	79.4	68.3	65.8	76.5
March	98.2	100.4	93.3	84.7	70.6	64.0	80.6
April	91.3	93.8	88.1	83.4	66.4	65.3	78.5
May	86.5	88.1	82.5	77.4	58.3	60.7	70.9
June	86.9	90.4	78.9	71.6	54.0	61.3	68.9
July	85.8	87.6	75.0	69.9	48.1	62.1	66.0
August	87.7	91.9	79.9	75.1	58.2	66.8	75.7
September	92.9	96.8	87.4	81.2	67.4	75.0	81.6
October	92.8	96.8	85.9	77.1	70.0	76.7	81.0
November	90.3	93.0	79.2	68.0	65.1	70.9	77.7
December	90.8	89.1	75.8	66.5	60.4	65.5	[1] 76.2

Source: Division of Statistics, New York State Department of Labor.

TABLE V.—*Employment in New York State manufacturing industries, 1919–31*

[1929 = 100.0]

Year	Total	Food preparations	Textiles	Forest products	Paper and allied products	Printing and publishing	Chemicals	Petroleum and coal products	Rubber goods
1919	110.5	108.5	110.7	107.0	108.2	91.1	102.3	72.6	102.8
1921	90.5	96.7	101.3	95.5	92.5	86.5	70.5	89.4	74.2
1923	104.1	102.6	106.5	110.0	104.2	92.4	92.3	93.7	91.4
1925	96.4	93.7	95.6	107.7	99.3	90.3	92.7	98.4	119.9
1927	97.0	94.0	98.2	102.5	96.6	93.8	101.2	115.1	83.6
1929	100.0	100.0	100.0	100.0	100.0	100.0	100.0	100.0	100.0
1931	76.9	88.8	79.7	70.3	83.5	89.0	84.3	93.5	71.6

TABLE V.—*Employment in New York State manufacturing industries, 1919–31—*
Continued

[1929 = 100.0]

Year	Leather and its manufac- tures	Stone, clay, and glass	Iron and steel	Nonfer- rous metals and their products	Machin- ery, not including trans- portation equip- ment	Trans- portation equip- ment	Railroad repair shops	Miscella- neous
1919	94.9	91.2	117.0	109.0	98.8	144.6	121.5	148.0
1921	88.7	89.7	70.6	83.0	71.7	71.4	95.1	112.0
1923	105.1	111.1	103.4	113.4	92.7	93.2	125.4	120.9
1925	98.0	119.2	95.8	96.8	89.0	82.3	109.7	106.8
1927	98.3	122.1	97.0	93.0	89.3	82.7	104.7	102.0
1929	100.0	100.0	100.0	100.0	100.0	100.0	100.0	100.0
1931	88.7	77.5	63.4	64.1	61.8	55.4	80.6	78.5

Source: Computed from United States Census of Manufactures.

Fluctuations in employment during comparatively short periods of time were also brought out by the Massachusetts Special Commission on Stabilization of Employment. Table VI shows, for instance, that employment in Massachusetts manufacturing industries declined from March 1923 to July 1924 by 23.0 percent. This decline amounted in actual figures to 159,600 persons. From March 1926 to July 1928, 114,000 persons lost employment in the manufacturing industries, the decline amounting to 18.3 percent. It should be noted that this particular period is regarded as a fairly normal one in the economic life of the country. The largest decline occurred during the period of September 1929 to June 1932 in which 276,400 persons lost employment; that is a decline of 48.2 percent from September 1929.

TABLE VI.—*Highs and lows of the average number of wage earners employed in Massachusetts manufacturing industries, 1920–32*

Date	Number employed	Change	
		Number	Percent
High, Jan. 1920	757,100	−225,600	−29.8
Low, Jan. 1921	531,500	−225,600	−29.8
High, Mar. 1923	693,700	+162,200	+30.5
Low, July 1924	534,100	−159,600	−23.0
High, Mar. 1926	623,700	+89,600	+16.7
Low, July 1928	509,700	−114,000	−18.3
High, Sept. 1929	572,900	+63,200	+12.4
Low, June 1932	296,500	−276,400	−48.2

Source: Final report of the Massachusetts Special Commission on Stabilization of Employment. Dec. 1932, p. 85.

Although no unemployment surveys have been taken for the country as a whole since April 1930, there has been a number of local surveys of unemployment which demonstrate its rapid increase since 1929. Table VII shows unemployment in Buffalo, N. Y., to have increased from 6.2 percent of all persons able and willing to work to 28.2 percent in 1933, that is, out of every 100 persons able and willing to work more than 28 persons unemployed.

TABLE VII.—*Unemployment in Buffalo, 1929–33*

Number of unemployed as percentage of all persons able and willing to work

1929	6. 2
1930	17. 2
1931	24. 3
1932	32. 6
1933	28. 2

Source: Buffalo unemployment studies, based on selected areas of Buffalo as of November of each year. Division of Statistics, New York State Department of Labor.

A state-wide census of unemployment was taken in Massachusetts in January 1934. The number of employable persons who were wholly unemployed stood at 346,021 or 19.1 percent of the total number of employables; in addition to that, 5.8 percent were temporarily employed on governmental and private projects and 9.6 percent were working part time bringing the number of wholly unemployed or not fully employed up to 624,526.

TABLE VIII.—*Unemployment in Massachusetts as of Jan. 2, 1934*

Employment status	Number			Percent, based on number of employable persons		
	Males	Females	Total	Males	Females	Total
Unemployed, wholly	243, 480	102, 541	346, 021	18. 9	19. 6	19. 1
Temporarily employed on Government projects	94, 724	7, 217	101, 941	7. 3	1. 4	5. 6
Temporarily employed on private work	2, 144	749	2, 893	. 2	. 1	. 2
Employed, part time	119, 381	54, 290	173, 671	9. 3	10. 4	9. 6
Total wholly unemployed or not fully employed	459, 729	164, 797	624, 526	35. 7	31. 5	34. 5

Source: Massachusetts Unemployment Census, 1934.

The Pennsylvania Department of Labor publishes monthly estimates of unemployment which are given in table IX. Inspection of this table shows clearly what a large part of the working population of Pennsylvania was wholly unemployed.

TABLE IX.—*Estimated number of totally unemployed persons and percent of working population in Pennsylvania, 1932–34*

Month	1932		1933		1934	
	Estimated number totally unemployed	Percent of working population	Estimated number totally unemployed	Percent of working population	Estimated number totally unemployed	Percent of working population
January	1, 017, 730	27. 3	1, 309, 850	35. 2	1, 028, 563	27. 6
February	1, 013, 642	27. 2	1, 321, 842	35. 5	980, 467	26. 3
March	1, 059, 793	28. 5	1, 379, 351	37. 1	890, 505	23. 9
April	1, 072, 937	28. 8	1, 346, 549	36. 2	906, 832	24. 4
May	1, 144, 627	30. 7	1, 314, 835	35. 3	873, 269	23. 5
June	1, 191, 331	32. 0	1, 259, 987	33. 8	878, 479	23. 6
July	1, 281, 562	34. 4	1, 147, 179	30. 8	935, 649	25. 1
August	1, 291, 167	34. 7	1, 037, 606	27. 9	962, 029	25. 8
September	1, 234, 836	33. 2	909, 363	24. 4	968, 260	26. 0
October	1, 138, 966	30. 6	906, 787	24. 4	915, 080	24. 6
November	1, 152, 209	31. 0	893, 337	24. 0		
December	1, 160, 354	31. 2	867, 022	23. 3		
Average for year	1, 146, 596	30. 8	1, 141, 143	30. 7		

Source: Pennsylvania Department of Labor and Industry.

The two following tables (tables X and XI) deal with the duration of unemployment. The table of duration of unemployment of males in Buffalo, N. Y., shows that those who lose their jobs remain unemployed. Thus, there is a steady increase in the percentage of unemployed who have been out of work for 52 weeks and over. In 1933, 68.2 percent of unemployed were in this group. The table also shows high percentage of unemployed in the group unemployed from 4 to 10 weeks and from 10 to 20 weeks.

TABLE X—*Duration of unemployment of all males able and willing to work but unable to find jobs, in Buffalo, N. Y., 1929–33*

Duration of unemployment	1933	1932	1931	1930	1929
	Percent	*Percent*	*Percent*	*Percent*	*Percent*
Under 2 weeks	2.7	1.4	2.6	4.3	15.8
2 and under 4 weeks	5.2	2.7	5.0	7.9	22.2
4 and under 10 weeks	10.1	6.3	12.7	21.0	30.4
10 and under 20 weeks	5.7	7.8	13.4	17.9	12.3
20 and under 30 weeks	4.4	10.7	11.7	14.3	6.2
30 and under 40 weeks	2.3	5.9	6.4	7.9	3.1
40 and under 52 weeks	1.4	5.1	5.2	5.6	0.7
52 weeks and over	68.2	60.1	43.0	21.1	9.3
Total	100.0	100.0	100.0	100.0	100.0

Source: Buffalo Unemployment Studies, Division of Statistics, New York State Department of Labor.

TABLE XI.—*Duration of unemployment of those wholly unemployed in Massachusetts as of Jan. 2, 1934*

Duration	Male	Female	Total
Less than 1 month	6,619	3,593	10,212
1 month, less than 2 months	8,814	4,184	12,998
2 months, less than 3 months	11,499	5,388	16,887
3 months, less than 4 months	29,131	13,074	42,205
6 months, less than 12 months	33,588	19,023	52,611
12 months, less than 24 months	42,241	20,241	62,482
24 months, less than 36 months	48,378	17,389	65,767
36 months, less than 48 months	33,247	9,374	42,621
48 months and over	26,767	8,577	35,344
Not reported	3,196	1,698	4,894
Total	243,480	102,541	346,021

Source: Massachusetts Unemployment Census.

The table on duration of unemployment in Massachusetts confirms the Buffalo finding; i. e., heavy concentration of unemployed in groups with duration of 12 months or more.

Another factor to be considered in studying unemployment is the relative position of what may be called the upper strata of workers and the great mass of workers. Table XII gives real wages in the United States by cycles from 1897 to 1933. When real wages for the entire duration of cycles are compared, a truer picture of the actual standards of living of labor is revealed. This study made by J. Kuczinski shows that since 1897 real wages of the great masses of workers have risen only a little and that during the last decade they have suffered a decline.

TABLE XII. *Real wages in United States* (*cycle averages*)

[1897–1908=100]

Cycle	Upper strata of workers	Great mass of workers
1897–1908	100	100
1908–14	102	102
1915–21	103	108
1922–33	127	105

Source: Jurgen Kuczinski, Die Entwicklung der Lage der Arbiiterschaft in Europa und America 1870–1933. Basel, 1934, p. 36.

It should be noted that while declining real wages definitely show that conditions of labor grow worse; increasing real wages may not necessarily mean improvement in the conditions of labor. Growing intensity of labor, declining span of working life, increasing accidents, greater distance from places of work, centralization with resulting bad-health conditions of city life—all these cannot be measured by real wages.

Perhaps an increasing share of the value of products produced could compensate labor for the negative effect of the aforementioned factors. Yet, as table XIII shows for New York State, labor's share in value added by manufacture has been steadily declining from 1921 through 1931.

TABLE XIII.—*Labor's share in value added by manufacture in New York State, 1919–31*

Year	Percent	Index (1929=100)
1919	37.1	111.7
1921	39.8	119.9
1923	37.7	113.6
1925	36.0	108.4
1927	34.9	105.0
1929	33.2	100.0
1931	32.3	97.3

Source: Computed from United States Census of Manufactures.

As it was demonstrated above, the extent of unemployment varies by industries and by localities. The question may arise whether or not decline in number of persons employed is especially severe in larger firms. My studies based on New York State firms reporting employment data lead me to the conclusion that a decline in employment caused by an industrial depression is just as severe, or more so, in smaller firms than in larger ones. While it is true that firms with a large number of employees may drastically decrease their force, smaller firms go out of business entirely. This factor, in my opinion, is the chief reason why fluctuations in employment in smaller firms are as severe, or more severe, than in the larger ones. This point is of especial importance, because a number of unemployment-insurance bills exclude establishments having only a few employees.

Although a number of local unemployment surveys have been made during recent years, no count of unemployed was undertaken on a national scale since April 1930. While the extent of unemployment can be judged indirectly through the use of employment indexes, one must depend on estimates in arriving at the figure giving total number of unemployed in the country.

There are various estimates of unemployment prepared by different research institutions and other organizations. They differ widely as to their totals. Both of the two best-known estimates, i. e., one made by the American Federation of Labor and the other by the National Industrial Conference Board, underestimate unemployment. American Federation of Labor estimate errs in underestimating an increase in the number of those seeking gainful employment as a result of natural increase in population. This estimate also counts as employed those living with relatives on farms, since they have food and shelter, a procedure which definitely minimizes the extent of unemployment. The chief defect of the National Industrial Conference Board estimate is the exclusion of the decline of employment in a number of groups since 1930. These groups include agriculture and professional service. It also understates a natural increase of those seeking gainful employment.

My investigation of various estimates on unemployment has brought me to the conclusion that the estimate prepared by the Labor Research Association is more reliable and nearer to actual conditions than the others. Table XIV presents this estimate in detail. Total number of unemployed in November 1934 is given as 17,157,000. Corresponding figures for 1932 and 1933 are 16,-320,000 and 16,886,000. The figures indicate that at the end of 1934 unemployment increased by 837,000, as compared with 1933, and surpassed the number of unemployed in 1932. However, as the table indicates, close to 3,000,000 people were engaged on relief projects financed by Government funds.

TABLE XIV.—*Estimate of unemployment in November 1934 (preliminary)* [1]

Occupation	Wage earners	Salaried employees, independents, owners	Total
Agriculture	719, 000	[2] 1, 070, 000	1, 789, 000
Forestry and fishing	81, 000	4, 000	85, 000
Extraction of minerals:			
Coal	165, 000	4, 000	169, 000
Metal mining	85, 000	} 9, 000	139, 000
Quarries and nonmetal	45, 000	{	
Oil and gas wells	30, 000	7, 000	37, 000
Manufacturing and mechanical:			
Building			2, 041, 000
Manufacturing [3]	2, 629, 000	631, 000	3, 260, 000
Transportation and communication:			
Railroads (steam)			621, 000
Telephone, telegraph			182, 000
Postal service			34, 000
All other			612, 000
Trade:			
Wholesale, retail [4]			903, 000
All other			427, 000
Professional service			852, 000
Domestic and personal service:			
Laundries, cleaning, dyeing, etc			60, 000
Hotels, restaurants, etc			276, 000
All other			868, 000
Public service			132, 000
Industry not specified			643, 000
Increase in number of gainful workers since 1930			3, 227, 000
Deficiency in unemployment census, etc			800, 000
Total			17, 157, 000

[1] Part-time workers are considered as employed. Persons working on Government relief projects are considered as unemployed. These workers on special Government funds were counted by U. S. Bureau of Labor Statistics for October 1934, as follows:

On construction projects financed by Public Works Administration	508, 000
Emergency work program	1, 950, 000
Emergency conservation work	392, 000
Total	2, 850, 000

[2] Includes unemployed family labor and farmers.
[3] Includes auto repair, railroad repair shops, and independent hand trades.
[4] Includes automotive agencies.

Source: Labor Research Association, Economic Notes, February 1935.

The above estimate shows that over three million people were added since 1930 to those gainfully occupied or seeking gainful occupation as a result of natural increase in population. This is an important factor, since it shows that any drastic curtailment of unemployment should bring employment to a level higher than that of any of the previous years.

Mr. DUNN. We will now hear from Mr. Elmer Rice.

STATEMENT OF ELMER RICE, REPRESENTING THE AUTHORS LEAGUE OF AMERICA

Mr. DUNN. Mr. Rice, will you please tell the committee whom you represent?

Mr. RICE. I am here officially representing the Authors League of America. For purposes of identification I will state that I have been a practicing playwright for about 20 years or more. I am a member of the executive council of the Authors League of America, and one of the honorary vice presidents of the Authors League of America, also a member of the executive council of the Dramatists Guild. I also helped to organize the Screenwriters Guild, about

12 years ago, and for a time was on their governing body. Although this may not be particularly relevant, I am also a member of the British Society of Authors, and a member of the newly formed League of British Dramatists. I am on their executive council, and am also a member of the French Authors Society, and also, although I am not actively engaged in the practice of law, I am a member of the New York bar, having been admitted in New York State in 1913.

As I say, I am here officially representing the Authors League of America, which recently, at a meeting of its executive body, unanimously endorsed this bill, H. R. 2827. In speaking for the authors, naturally I speak only for the Authors League officially, but I think the problem of the author is in general the problem of the professional man throughout the country, doctor, lawyer, engineer, technician, nurse, and so on, anyone who is engaged in the practice of a profession.

The Authors League has a membership of some 4,000. It is a nonpartisan, nonpolitical organization, and is nonsectional. Its members, as you may well imagine, reside in all parts of the country and are drawn from almost every shade of religious belief, political opinion, and social and economic class, and so on.

The Authors League consists of three guilds, the Screenwriters Guild, which of course has its headquarters in Hollywood, the Dramatists Guild, which in the main is concentrated in New York, and what is called the Authors Guild, which includes novelists, writers, feature writers, and so on, which has a very diversified membership spread throughout the country.

Although the actual membership of the Authors League is only about 4,000, it actually is the only official organization in the United States which represents authors in their professional capacity, and it may readily be said that practically every author in the United State, of whom there are of course many, many thousands, many thousands of whom cannot even afford the rather moderate annual dues of $25; and that, of course, is the point that I want to make, the rather low economic status of most authors; that the Authors League speaks officially for practically all the authors in the country. In addition, we are in very close touch with the recently formed American Newspaper Guild, which as you know is a rapidly growing organization that at the present time has a membership of something like 18,000, I believe, and is rapidly increasing, and represents newspaper men throughout the country, and which at this moment is very seriously considering an affiliation with the Authors League. So that I may say that I speak more or less officially for practically all the people in the United States who earn their living by writing.

While their numerical strength is not great compared, let us say, to the numerical strength of industrial workers, obviously their importance is great, because of course we all recognize the tremendous power of the stage and of the screen and of the published word, whether in books or in magazines or elsewhere, so that I think in speaking for authors, I speak for a very important and very influential section of our community.

The reason that the Authors League—and I may say parenthetically that I think that you gentlemen, in your many years of legislative experience, will agree that you have not been besieged very much by professional people. I mean, of the various groups who appear before you, I am sure that the professions badger you very little and bother you very little, and the reason for that is that on the whole, professional people have a kind of pride and a kind of dignity and a kind of self-respect, which makes it difficult for them to go and ask favors, and to impose themselves upon others and to seek relief, whether legislative or any other sort. On the whole, they are not an aggressive or an acquisitive group, and I speak now not only for authors but for professional people in general. And so that very often they are left out of account in situations where other groups, who are more aggressive, who are more militant, let us say, come and seek relief and even get it.

The Authors League favors this bill, of course. So far as we know, it is the only bill which makes any provision for the professional worker. The professional has learned to his bitter experience that whatever dignity and glory may attach to his profession as such, whatever honors fortunate individuals in his profession may receive, that, taking that by and large, the professional worker has much the same status that the industrial worker has. He is subject to the same fluctuations, the same uncertainties in the practice of his profession, that the industrial worker is subject to. He is in the grip of the same economic forces which control the destinies of the industrial worker, and he has no more control over that situation than the industrial worker has. So that the need for relief for professional workers is a very grave and serious one indeed. In the course of my professional and social life, I come in contact with people in numerous professions. Among my friends and acquaintances, and the people with whom I work in the course of my daily work, I meet actors, doctors, lawyers, teachers, university professors, engineers, and so on, and I find that the condition among the professionals is rather pitiable. When we think of doctors or lawyers or writers we usually think of some conspicuous or outstanding member of the profession who has a large income and who is among the leaders in our community, and we forget that the conditions among the rank and file of the practitioners of any profession in this country are pitiable.

Now, I am to speak specifically about authors, because I represent them, but what I say about authors, by inference, applies to all professional workers. The authors are divided roughly into two groups. There is a group, notably the screenwriters, who have the status of salaried employees. That is, they sell their services for hire, just as any other white-collared worker or industrial worker might do, so that they really are in the class of wage earners.

The majority of authors, however, are dependent for their livelihood upon the sale of the product of their creative labor, either by an outright sale of their material to a publisher, or the owner of a magazine, or for the most part income derived from royalties under Federal copyright.

The profession of writing is probably without exception the most hazardous profession that there is anywhere. There is no certainty about it. There is no security. There is no continuity about it. The author is dependent from year to year upon the salability of his particular product for the given year. He has no security. He has nothing that he can rely upon, nothing that he can depend upon. When we think of authors, we think, perhaps, of such glittering successes as Sinclair Lewis or Mary Roberts Rinehart, or Zane Grey, or Booth Tarkington, or somebody of that sort, but those eminently successful people are a very small minority of the number of authors in this country.

I have no figures here to give you of the average earnings of the rank and file of the authors in this country, but I assure you that it is not much higher than that of the average industrial worker. The successes are few and far between, and while undoubtedly the authors who succeed are talented authors, we know from our experience in other professions that there is not always a direct relationship between talent and reward, that very often the most talented people are not the most highly rewarded, and that very often success is due to fortuitous circumstances that have very little to do with the abilities of the individuals, so that we cannot say that success and talent are synonymous, and we know very well that there are many talented authors who have great difficulties in making a living.

During the depression, authors have been hit particularly hard for the reason that their product, while we all would agree that it is a social necessity, in one sense, is in an individual sense more or less of a luxury or a marginal activity. As you know from the experience among your own friends, when they are hard up, when their income shrinks, the first thing that they cut out is going to theaters, going to the movies, buying books, buying magazines, and so on, so that instantly there is a contraction either of the author's source of income, which has nothing whatever to do with the qualities of his work or with the amount of his work, so that he is peculiarly vulnerable in an economic crisis, and subject to these very sharp contractions of income.

Furthermore, with the falling off of the volume of business, there is also a falling off, naturally, of the volume of advertising in magazines, for example, which means that the magazines contract in bulk, and also contract in the amount of money which they spend for their materials, so that the author is subject to these terrific uncertainties and hazards and conditions in the writing profession in the last few years have been really pitiable.

If I could divulge professional confidences I could tell you the names of people that are familiar to you as writers of ability, who have been made literally destitute during the last few years, and through no fault of their own, and with no provision whatever for any amelioration of their condition.

Now, while I know that this committee is not concerned with questions of income tax, I want to point out to you the inequitable operation of the provisions of the income-tax law with relation to authors. The author's income, as I have said, is a fluctuating one. All authors, even successful authors, have a wide range of fluctuation in their income. If they happen one year to write a successful book or a successful play, the income for that year is liable to be a very large one. Now, they may go along for 3 or 4 or 5 years before they strike another success, with a very rapid dwindling of income. The operations of the income-tax law take no account of that at all. In other words, the author who happens to have a good year and make a large income in that particular year, is not permitted under the operation of the income-tax law to set aside any reserve which he can rely upon in the lean years that follow, because he immediately runs into the higher surtax brackets, and so large a proportion of his income is taken from him that he has no opportunity to set aside a reserve. No adjustment is made for all the lean years in which very probably his expenditures exceed his income.

For example, suppose an author takes 2 or 3 years in the preparation of a book, which he could very well do. During that time he is probably living upon advance royalties which he receives from his publisher. The book is published and it is a success and he has a fairly large income in that year. He has to pay back, naturally, to his publisher, the advances before he receives any income whatever, but his income is all bulked, as in that particular year, so that although it has been spread as far as he is concerned over a period of years, the income tax calculations are on the specific year in which the income is earned.

Now, that is a most inequitable system. In other countries, notably in England, the hazardous earnings and the fluctuational earnings of authors are recognized, and an adjustment is made in taking the average income over a period of years, and the income tax calculations are based upon that.

Furthermore, under the extraordinary rulings of the Treasury Department, an author's earnings, unless he is a salaried employee, from his writings, are not considered earned income. In other words, the product of his creative labor and of his talents and of his brain are not regarded as earned income, and he is allowed no credit for earned income, on the theory that his income is not earned but is derived through a Federal grant or copyright, which obviously is a very strained interpretation of the situation, since of course what he writes is the product of his labor.

Furthermore, he has none of the advantages, and this applies not only to authors but it applies to doctors, it applies to engineers, it applies to lawyers, it applies to all professionals who have to undergo such a long and arduous course of training before they become equipped to practice their profession. No allowance is made for the expenditure of time and money which is involved in becoming qualified to practice a profession. A business man is allowed to consider his capital investment in a business with relation to his income. The professional man is allowed no credit whatever. Although he is told that he is not a wage earner and has no credit for his income as earned income, at the same time he does not have the status of a business man and is not allowed to capitalize himself and regard his time and labor as a capital investment; so that he gets the thing both coming and going, so to speak.

There is no provision in any of these bills for the professional worker, and for the author specifically, or for the professional worker in general. The burden of providing for the destitute authors in the last few years has fallen upon a private charity called the "Authors League Fund", to which the handful of successful authors have voluntarily taxed themselves, in order to provide partial support, partial relief for their needy fellow artists.

Obviously, that is an unjust and inequitable system, because not only is the author subject, at the very maximum, to the income tax provisions whereby he is taxed in general for the relief of industrial workers, in which benefits he does not participate at all, but in addition he imposes a self-taxation upon himself to keep many of his fellow practitioners in the writing profession literally from starvation.

Many of you are professional men yourselves. You have professional men among your friends, and you know how difficult it is for a professional man to apply for charity, to apply for relief, to submit himself to the kind of scrutiny which the applicant for relief is subjected to in order to obtain the relief that he needs; so that you have this burden put upon the authors, providing for themselves, and of course it is wholly inadquate. Even the Authors League Funds, despite the generous contributions of successful authors, is wholly inadequate to care for the authors.

Now, being a worker in the theater, being a dramatist, I happen to know that the same situation is true of actors, of whom there are many, many thousands in this country. The situation among actors is pitiable. Theaters are closing right and left. Plays run less and less frequently, so that the average income of an actor is so small that you would not believe the figures if they were presented to you. There, again, they have the status of the professional worker and not of the industrial worker. For that reason, feeling that the professional worker—the writer, specifically, the professional worker in general—plays an important function in the community, that he serves a useful social purpose, and that without him what we call culture, civilization and progress cannot be carried on, we feel that it is the obligation and the duty of the community in general to make provision for the professional worker, and at least to guarantee him some meager security, some sense of a feeling that starvation is not around the corner, and that he at least has the price of a meal and of a room, so that he can continue his activities. We feel that that is a duty of the community, and that any bill which recognizes only industrial workers and does not recognize professional workers is an unjust and an inadequate bill.

We ask nothing more than that we receive the same treatment that is accorded to industrial workers. So far as we know, this is the only bill which makes such provision. For that reason, despite the fact that the Authors League is a nonpartisan organization and a nonpolitical organization, which has never taken any part in any political activity, which as I have said ranks in its membership persons of every shade of political belief, we have unanimously endorsed this bill, and strongly urge upon you gentleman to endeavor to secure its passage, for the reason that we see no other way at present of getting even this very small minimum of security for those who work in our profession.

I thank you.

Mr. DUNN. Mr. Rice, I want to substantiate many of the statements you have made. Many professional men and women came to my office in Pittsburgh seeking employment.

Mr. RICE. Thank you very much.

Mr. DUNN. Now, I am going to call upon the other members of the Committee to interrogate you. You do not mind being interrogated?

Mr. RICE. No; I would be very glad to answer questions.

Mr. DUNN. Congressman Wood, this is Mr. Rice, representing the Authors League of America. He has just delivered a wonderful address.

Mr. WOOD. I am sorry I could not have been here. I have been up at the Pension Committee hearings until just a few minutes ago.

Mr. RICE. We have made an abstract, here.

Mr. DUNN. You will be able to read it in the record.

Mr. LESINSKI. I have no questions.

Mr. DUNN. Mr. Schneider?

Mr. SCHNEIDER. I agree with everything the witness has said. While I do not know much about the authors, it is true that most of the professional men he mentioned secure their income from the struggling masses of the working people in America, and they have lent little support to this struggle in the past. They have held themselves above the workers in America and have, in the main, been opposed to the attempts of labor to get a little more wages and a better lot in life, but they are now meeting the same struggle that labor has met.

Mr. RICE. Yes.

Mr. SCHNEIDER. I hope they will throw their support to the working class of America and the farm people who are trying to improve their conditions.

Mr. RICE. I think that is very true. I think that is a very fair criticism of the professional class, with this reservation which I should like to make, and that is, that the professions, on the whole, have been articulate mostly through their professional organizations, rather than as individuals. Those professional organizations as a whole have been in the hands of the more successful members. For example, the bar associations have been more or less in the hands of the corporation lawyers. The medical association has been more or less in the hands of the fashionable and highly paid specialists, and so on.

I think you would find that among the rank and file of the professionals, there has always been a good deal of sympathy with workers in general, with industrial workers, and with other workers, and that the rather hostile or apathetic attitude which you have indicated, has evidenced itself in the expressions of these professional organizations, many of which are in the hands of the more well to do.

I agree with you that there has been in the last few years, due entirely to economic pressure, a clearer realization among professional workers, that they must identify themselves with those who are obliged to work for their living, and that economically they have no superior status to that of any other worker; and I think that what you might call the " snobbish " attitude is beginning to break down, and there is a much greater cooperation now among professional workers, white-collar workers, and industrial workers. It is certainly true of such groups as teachers, for example. I mean, I do not think that there is any doubt that it is true, and among my own friends I find many lawyers and doctors and authors, and so on, many of whom have been very hard hit by the depression, and the economic situation has been brought into focus for them in a way that it never was before, and they realize the necessity of taking a stand on these economic questions. I think that is undoubtedly true, and I think it is a rather healthy sign, myself. Nevertheless, the situation of the people in these professions is for the most of them pitiable. I have not the figures. I am not a statistician. I have not Miss Van Kleeck's ability to present figures, but I should say that at least 50 percent of the workers in every profession are below a subsistence level at this moment, with very little prospect of improving their condition.

Mr. LUNDEEN. You say they are below a subsistence level?

Mr. RICE. I should say they are below; yes. I should say so. I mean, I know actors of whom that is true.

For example, to give you an illustration of how the thing works, I was talking to a very well-known actress the other day, who is a personal friend of mine, whose salary when she works is $350 a week. "Well", we immediately say, "she is a plutocrat, she gets $350 a week." In the last 2 years she has had 2 weeks' pay. She has had 2 weeks' employment, so that her aggregate income for 2 years has been $700. You can readily see what her condition is. I mean, I do not know what she lives on—borrowing from friends, perhaps, charity, or perhaps a little money that she managed to save during good years, or something, but that is not an uncommon thing, even among people who are highly paid when they work.

The profession is a hazardous one, and as a matter of fact, as we know, even lawyers and doctors who are busy cannot collect their fees. I am sure every one of us has among his friends many doctors, lawyers, and so forth, who are simply working, and they are rendering useful services to their clients and to their community, but they cannot collect their fees. Nevertheless, their fees and expenses go on. Their living expenses go on. A doctor or a lawyer cannot be down at the heels. He has to maintain a standard of appearance, a certain standard of professional dignity, and so on, and yet his income is curtailed, and he has nothing on which he can rely at all. It is a very grave situation.

Mr. SCHNEIDER. May I ask another question?

Mr. DUNN. Yes.

Mr. SCHNEIDER. Is it not true that the actors particularly are the victim of a great evolution in the theatrical business, the talking movies, and the like, including everything that goes with it?

Mr. RICE. Yes, yes.

Mr. SCHNEIDER. And particularly the vicious concentration of that industry into the hands of a few people?

Mr. RICE. Oh, quite; yes. Oh, yes; of course. That is undoubtedly true. There is no question about that. The conditions among actors are really indescribable. I mean, the insecurity among actors. Of course, I am not here officially to speak for the actors, other than simply as a dramatist and as a person who is constantly working with actors, and who has hundreds of actors among his personal friends. I happen to know very, very closely what the condition is among actors, and I know that they are getting jobs in Woolworth's and Child's restaurants, and anywhere that they can get a job that will give them the price of a meal, they will work.

Mr. LUNDEEN. If they can get a job?

Mr. RICE. If they can get it; exactly. There is scarcely a day that goes by that I do not receive from some restaurant or shop or department store or something, a form saying, " So-and-so, who worked on one of your plays, has applied for a job as a waiter or as a salesman, or what not. Will you say a few words of recommendation for him? "

Mr. DUNN. Mr. Wood, do you want to ask Mr. Rice a question?

Mr. WOOD. No; I do not. I have enjoyed his testimony, Mr. Chairman, that that I have heard of it. I did not hear his entire testimony, but I would just like to submit for the record, Mr. Chairman, a report of the executive council of the American Federation of Labor, the fifty-seventh convention, held on November 21 to December 1, 1932, on unemployment insurance. This report was accepted by unanimous vote of the American Federation of Labor convention. The reason why I submit this is because the statement was made yesterday by Mr. F. Elmer Brown, who represented the national joint action committee, that some of these rank-and-file organizations had taken the matter up; and consciously or unconsciously, he left the impression that the officials of the American Federation of Labor had been forced into acceptance of the principle of unemployment insurance. For that reason, I want to submit the report of the executive council, to be made a part of the record, for the American Federation of Labor.

Mr. DUNN. Is there any objection? There being none, it is so ordered.

(The report submitted by Mr. Wood is as follows:)

UNEMPLOYMENT INSURANCE

REPORT OF THE EXECUTIVE COUNCIL ADOPTED BY THE FIFTY-SECOND ANNUAL CONVENTION OF THE AMERICAN FEDERATION OF LABOR, CINCINNATI, OHIO, NOVEMBER 21 TO DECEMBER 2, 1932

Because local conditions of each State vary to such a marked degree that it is imposible to frame a single model bill to be enacted in every State, the report contains basic principles which are recommended for the guidance of our State federations of labor in framing unemployment insurance measures. The report follows in full.

In reporting to the last convention of the American Federation of Labor which was held at Vancouver, British Columbia, beginning October 5, a year ago, the executive council in dealing with the subject of unemployment insurance stated:

"There are just two approaches to this problem—prevention and relief. Either we must make employment secure or provide an income for the unemployed."

In another section of its report to the Vancouver convention the executive council made the following direct and positive reference to this social justice problem:

"Working men have arrived at the point where they are firmly of the belief that they are as much entitled to work security, to enjoy the opportunity to work, as the owners of capital are to returns from their investments. Labor demands that these principles be recognized and accepted by the employers of labor. Obviously, the owners and management of industry must decide as to whether working men and women shall enjoy the opportunity to work, or, whether as a result of the denial of this opportunity to work, industry shall have fastened upon it compulsory unemployment insurance legislation. It must be work or unemployment insurance.] Working people must be privileged to earn a living or be acorded relief. If compulsory unemployment insurance is fastened upon our industrial, political, and economic life it will be because

industrial ownership and management have failed to provide and preserve
work opportunities for working men and women."

The experience which working men and women have been forced to face
and undergo during the past year, has been most bitter and disappointing.
They cannot be expected to maintain faith in an economic order which has
failed them so completely. They charge industrial management with failure
to stabilize employment. The facts are that the management of industry has
not provided work security or created work opportunities for those who are
able, willing, and eager to work. Unemployment has increased; there are
more workers idle now than there were 1 year ago; approximately 11,000,000
are out of work, seeking employment, unable to find it.

The American Federation of Labor has always emphasized both the necessity
and importance of supplying work for all. Working people and their families
depend upon wages earned for a livelihood. Life and living, in the full meaning
of that term, are inseparably associated with employment, wages, work security,
the possession of a job, and the exercise of the right to work.

The executive council has given most careful, painstaking, and serious
consideration to the problem of unemployment and to the application of the
principle of unemployment insurance. The council would much prefer that
working people be privileged to work and be accorded job security than to
see them forced to accept relief because of unemployment. The extension
and enjoyment of the opportunity to work at decent wages, so that working
men and women may earn a decent living, is the real objective of the American
Federation of Labor. The executive council urges work first and relief second,
but it must be clear that working people must be permitted to earn a living
or be supplied relief. They must earn their living or be supported. They
cannot earn their living unless jobs are provided and work opportunities accorded them.

Obviously, the owners and management of industry have failed to provide
work for all and thus make it possible for all to earn a livelihood. Their
failure is reflected in the fact that during the past 3 years unemployment has
steadily increased and that at the present time about 11,000,000 people are
idle. The executive council believe that the owners of industry and industrial
management must have known that the creation of an army of 11,000,000
unemployed, forced to shift for themselves, to become dependent upon local,
State, and Federal relief agencies, would create an intolerable economic
situation fraught with most serious consequences.

The economic facts arising out of the unemployment situation, the continued
displacement of millions of working men through the mechanization of industry,
and the substitution of power for human service, make it absolutely necessary
in the opinion of the executive council, to develop and put into operation through
the enactment of appropriate legislation, an unemployment insurance plan which
will provide for the payment of weekly benefits to working men and women
who are forced to suffer from unemployment.

The council holds that because the ownership and management of industry
have failed to provide and maintain work opportunities for working men and
women, unemployment insurance legislation is made imperatively necessary.
The responsibility for this state of affairs rests squarely upon industry and
industrial management. They control industry; consequently, they control
jobs. Labor cannot wait longer; it must now act. Industry must be compelled
to do what it has thus far failed to do. Work or relief must be provided.
If industrial management fails to provide work, it must be compelled to
assume the burden of supplying relief.

Having all these facts in mind, the executive council at a meeting held
July 12–22, 1932, directed the president of the American Federation of Labor
to draft and present to a subsequent meeting a plan of unemployment insurance
legislation. These instructions were complied with. As a result of a detailed
survey and careful study of the subject the president of the American Federation of Labor submitted to a meeting of the executive council held October
18–27, 1932, a report which embodied within it a plan of unemployment insurance legislation.

The executive council has always endeavored to guard jealously the organization structure of the American Federation of Labor. For that reason the
council was apprehensive over the effect which compulsory unemployment
insurance legislation might have upon the exercise of the right of working
men and women not only to join but to maintain membership in trade unions.

In the drafting of an unemployment insurance measure, the council has constantly kept three very distinct fundamental principles in mind:

First. It has endeavored to provide in the plan which it submits to the convention a full measure of protection to the membership of the American Federation of Labor, and the preservation of the right to become a member and to continue membership in a trade union.

Second. That the payment of relief shall be made a fixed charge upon industry. Relief funds should be created out of the earnings of industry. The council does not believe it is fair or just that any part of the money out of which relief would be paid during periods of unemployment should be collected from employees.

Third. That unemployment insurance should be compulsory and that the execution and administration of unemployment insurance laws should come wholly within the control and administration of Federal and State governments.

The executive council submits the following plan for the consideration and approval of the convention. This plan embodies within it the fundamental principles just enunciated and represents the best thought and judgment of the members of the executive council and of the trained experts upon social justice legislation who rendered valuable assistance in the preparation of the plan. The council recommends this plan of unemployment insurance legislation for the favorable consideration and acceptance of the officers and members in attendance at the convention.

Principles recommended for unemployment insurance measures.—It would be desirable, were it possible, to press for the enactment of one uniform measure for unemployment insurance applicable throughout the United States. But, due to the provisions and limitations of the United States Constitution, as interpreted by the courts, since the regulation of manufacture and industry lies primarily within the province of State rather than Federal activity, it is practically impossible to enact constitutional Federal legislation adequately providing for unemployment insurance covering employees engaged in work in the different States. The American Federation of Labor, therefore, advocates the passage of unemployment insurance legislation in each separate State, and the supplementing of such State legislation by Federal enactments; such, for instance, as bills covering employees engaged in interstate commerce, or employed in the District of Columbia or in Federal Territories, or such as the bill recently introduced into Congress by Senator Wagner, allowing corporations substantial income-tax credit on their Federal income taxes for such payments as they have made under State laws toward the creation of unemployment reserves.

It is evident that the local conditions of each State vary to such a marked degree that it would be unwise, even were it possible at the present time, to frame a single model bill to be enacted in every State. It is possible, nevertheless, to set forth certain general fundamental principles and standards to which such State legislation should conform. The American Federation of Labor, after mature consideration and discussion, has formulated the following principles which should guide in the framing of State unemployment insurance bills:

1. *Protection of union standards.*—Every unemployment-insurance act should contain specific provisions to protect union members from being obliged to accept work contrary to the rules and regulations of their organizations or employment under conditions such as tend to depress wages or working conditions.

2. *Underlying object of unemployment insurance.*—Unemployment-insurance legislation in this country should be carefully devised to promote its two primary objectives: (a) The stimulation of more regular employment, insofar as possible, and (b) the payment of unemployment compensation to those who are temporarily out of work through industry's failure to provide steady employment for its working forces.

3. *Voluntary v. compulsory schemes of insurance.*—The American Federation of Labor advocates a scheme of unemployment compensation made compulsory by law. Voluntary schemes are unlikely to pervade industry generally and are frequently open to other serious objections. Only by compulsory legislation can workers be adequately protected.

4. *How and from whom contributions should be made.*—Since unemployment is, to a certain extent, one of the inevitable incidents of production and must, therefore, be regarded as part of the inescapable cost of industry, it, like other

costs of industry should be paid by industry itself. It, therefore, follows that, as a matter of principle, no part of the contributions to support unemployment insurance should be paid out of the wages of labor, but the whole should be paid by management as part of the cost of production. The necessary funds should be raised as a charge on industry.

The amount of such contribution must depend upon the local conditions in each State. A minimum contribution must be required sufficient to cover (a) the building up of adequate reserves, (b) the cost of the benefits to be paid under the act, and (c) the costs of administration. To cover these costs the American Federation of Labor believes that the contribution rate should be not less than 3 percent of the total pay roll. The exact percentage, however, must vary in different States, and will come to depend upon various actuarial data, which must be carefully collected as a basis for such determination from the experience gained both before and after the passage of the act. The absence of complete data should not, however, prevent the passage of a law, since the liability of the fund is limited to the amount of the income provided by law. As experience is accumulated it will be possible to determine the income necessary to provide the benefits decided upon in the law.

5. *Reserve v. insurance systems.*—At this time the American Federation of Labor deems it inadvisable to take an irrevocable stand as between the plant reserves system or unemployment insurance embodied in the Wisconsin law and an insurance system such as is under consideration in Ohio and in operation in many European countries. Whatever plan is adopted, whether based on plant reserves or on a broader basis, we believe that it should be administered by the State and all reserve funds held and invested by the State. We are unalterably opposed to company-controlled unemployment reserves and believe that without State administration plant reserves will prove but another " company union " device. We are also of the opinion that, at least at the outset, it is advisable to have but a single unemployment insurance fund (with, if a plant reserves system is adopted, separate accounts for separate employers) and a flat rate of contributions by employers regardless of the industry in which they may be engaged. Later on, after more accurate data are obtained, the contributions in each industry, occupation, or enterprise may be scaled according to the hazard of unemployment, but sufficient data are not now available to warrant such classifications at this time.

6. *Exclusion of private insurance companies.*—Sound public policy requires that no insurance company in this country be allowed to invade this new field of unemployment compensation. No insurance company is allowed under present State laws to write this class of insurance. The federation believes that this policy is wise and should in no case be abandoned.

7. *Investment of funds.*—All funds should be invested in Federal securities or in the bonds of State or municipalities such as have never defaulted in the payment of principal or interest.

8. *Eligibility for benefits.*—Insurance in general should cover temporary and involuntary unemployment. Unemployment means the conditions caused by the inability of an employee who is capable of and available for employment to obtain work in his usual employment or in another for which he is reasonably fitted. Nothing in the unemployment compensation act should require an employee to accept employment, nor should any employee forfeit his right to benefits under the act by refusing to accept employment under any or all of the following conditions:

(a) In a situation vacant directly in consequence of a stoppage of work due to a trade dispute;

(b) If the wages, hours, and conditions offered are less favorable to the employee than those prevailing for similar work in the locality, or are such as tend to depress wages and working conditions;

(c) If acceptance of such employment would abridge or limit the right of the employee either (1) to refrain from joining a labor organization or association of workmen, or (2) to retain membership in and observe the rules of any such organization or association.

(d) Workers who quit work without good cause or who are discharged for misconduct shall not thereby forfeit benefits beyond a reasonable period.

9. *Scope or coverage.*—The coverage should be as wide as possible. It should include clerical as well as manual workers. There are, however, certain classes of employment which it may be necessary to exclude from the general operation of the act, and these classes will vary according to local condi-

tions. It would seem that the legislation should approximate, insofar as practicable, the coverage of State workmen's compensation acts. As time goes on the scope or coverage of the act may well be broadened.

10. *Payment of benefits.*—The claim of employees to receive unemployment compensation as provided under the act should be clearly recognized as a legal right earned by previous employment within the State. Receipt of unemployment benefits shall in no way entail loss of suffrage or other civil rights. Persons not legal residents of the State and those not citizens of the United States shall not by reason of that fact be disqualified from receiving benefits.

The amount of benefits to be paid and the number of weeks during which they shall be paid must depend upon the local conditions in each State and upon the amount of contributions paid into the fund. We are informed, for instance, that under the conditions prevailing in Ohio, a contribution of 3 percent of the total pay roll makes it possible after a waiting period of 3 weeks per year to pay benefits for a maximum period of 16 weeks in a year based upon 50 percent of the normal weekly wages, but not to exceed $15 a week.

It seems advisable to restrict the payment of benefits to unemployment occurring after a specified waiting period. The length of this waiting period will materially affect the amount of the benefits which can be paid and the length of time during which they can be paid.

Workers who are partially unemployed should receive unemployment compensation at a reduced rate. The exact amount of the reduction will presumably vary in different States. We suggest that a fair principle would be to pay for partial unemployment the amount of the benefit which would be payable in case of total unemployment reduced by subtracting one-half of the amount of the wages actually received.

11. *Administration*—(*a*) Nature of Commission.

The administration of the scheme of unemployment compensation and the responsibility for the keeping and investment of the unemployment funds should be in the hands of a State commission. This should be either a special commission created for the specific purpose, or an already existing State commission or department of labor.

(*b*) Both labor and management should have a voice in the administration of unemployment insurance. Advisory committees composed of an equal number of representatives of labor and management will prove very useful and, in some States, local appeal boards similarly constituted will be found desirable. It should be recognized, however, that workingmen can have genuine representation only through labor organizations. Unless labor can, in effect, through its organization select its own representatives, pretended representation is but a farce.

(*c*) Cost of administration.

The cost of the administration of unemployment compensation should be met out of the unemployment fund itself.

(*d*) Employment exchanges.

The operation of employment exchanges is closely and vitally connected with the administration of unemployment insurance. The commission should take over, supervise and expand public employment exchanges in States where these already exist, or in States where none exists should create and operate such exchanges.

(*e*) Procedure for obtaining benefits.

The administration regulating the payment of benefits should be decentralized as far as possible. Payments should be made upon claims presented through local agencies, established and supervised by the commission and acting in close cooperation with the public employment offices. Appeals should be allowed to a central authority.

12. *Regularization of employment.*—The whole scheme should be so construed as to induce and stimulate so far as possible the regularization and stabilization of employment. This may be affected in various possible ways; as for instance, by basing the amount of contributions payable upon some merit-rating scheme, or in States not adopting an exclusive State fund, by the establishment of separate industry or separate plant funds.

This statement embodies within it certain standards and principles that we believe should be incorporated in unemployment insurance legislation. We suggest, however, that a flexible policy be pursued in all the States, and that unemployment insurance legislation be secured which will maintain the above standards, so far as possible, and yet which will accommodate itself to the varying circumstances and conditions in each State. It is essential that the protection of the rights of citizenship and of union membership be maintained in all acts.

Pending the adoption of compulsory State insurance, voluntary unemployment compensation schemes should be subject to state regulation. We, therefore, believe it vital that suitable legislation be enacted to provide for State supervision of all such plans, including as a minimum the deposit of benefit funds in separate trust accounts, whether or not such funds include payments made from employees.

Mr. Dunn. Congressman Hartley, do you wish to ask the witness any questions?

Mr. Hartley. Yes; I do, Mr. Chairman; and I want to preface my questions by saying that I am personally in favor of a more liberal unemployment insurance bill than another committee in the House is planning to submit to Congress, but there are certain questions that I would like to clear up with reference to this bill, and I would like to ask Mr. Rice, as an attorney, if he has given any study or consideration to the constitutionality of this particular bill. The reason I ask that question is that the Supreme Court has been handing down some decisions lately, and certainly if we are going to write an unemployment insurance bill, we want one that is going to stand up later, and my question is based on the feeling that we want to write a bill that is going to stand up, and as liberal a bill as we possibly can.

Have you given any thought to that situation?

Mr. Rice. As I understand it, Congress has the power both to tax and to appropriate money, and it seems to me that the machinery of this bill is simply that. It simply provides for the appropriations of money, to be raised by taxation. The income tax already exists. I mean, it is an amendment, a part of the Constitution. It has been upheld by all the courts. There is nothing to prevent a change in the case of the income tax. I mean, that is certainly well within the limits of constitutionality. I do not believe that any limits have been imposed upon the rates of taxation. That is a differential. As we know, the income-tax schedule of rates fluctuates from year to year, so it seems to me that that is entirely within the realm of constitutionality, and I think also the right of Congress to appropriate money for relief, which does it on a rather large scale.

Mr. Hartley. I agree with you that we have the right to tax, but have we the right to set up a Federal bureau and use those funds for the purpose of providing unemployment insurance? As you probably know, the Wagner-Lewis bill, which is the bill I referred to before, and which I do not think is liberal enough, has tried to get around that question, in the first instance, by imposing an excise tax on payrolls, to coerce the States into writing unemployment insurance. Can we, as this bill suggests, set up a Federal agency, use the funds that are raised by taxation, and then set up machinery to provide this unemployment insurance?

Mr. Rice. I am not a constitutional lawyer, and I do not think my opinion on that would be valuable. I mean, I am really not a lawyer at all. I am a member of the bar, but I am not engaged in active practice, and I would not presume even to suggest to this body of men here an opinion on constitutional questions. It would seem to me that if Congress has the power to tax and has the power to appropriate money, in order for the money to be appropriated and spent, obviously some machinery for the disbursement of that money must be set up. Now, just what the constitutional technicalities of that machinery would be, I do no feel at all qualified to say.

Mr. LUNDEEN. I was just going to say to Congressman Hartley, we will have an attorney here who has made an extensive study of the constitutional question, and he will present that phase of it to this committee.

Mr. HARTLEY. I would be glad to listen to that, Mr. Chairman.

There is another question I wanted to ask, too. Have you given any thought to the most effective machinery to put such an act into operation? That is, do you believe that the Federal Government, by setting up agencies throughout the country, which of course would be necessary, can handle this problem more effectively, or do you feel that putting it under the control of the States, or even going right down to the very municipality in which the man receiving unemployment insurance is to receive it, that they can handle it best? Which agency do you think can handle it most effectively?

Mr. RICE. Personally, I feel that if you put the thing in the control of the States, you would have a terrific fluctuation and inequities in working it out. It seems to me that if the principle of the thing is acceptable, it should have a universal, national application, and not be subjected to the variations in its administration which might occur in the States. As I understand the provisions of this bill, the actual administration would be by the workers in a given industry or profession; that is to say, the standards of administration would be set up by the workers themselves. I may be wrong about that, but that is my understanding of the bill. Am I correct about that, Mr. Lundeen?

Mr. LUNDEEN. They are in there, with their committees, and so on.

Mr. RICE. Exactly, and I feel that after all this is a national problem. We are nationally an economic unit, and while I am not arguing against States' rights, the rather arbitrary division in the geographical units and into States certainly does not give you a picture of the economic situation. I mean, the economic situation cuts across State lines, and this certainly is a national problem and a national condition. We are economically a national entity. We do not fit into 48 little geographical subdivisions with varying populations, varying areas, and so on, and therefore it seems to me that the only way it could be equitably and nationally administered is on a national basis.

Mr. HARTLEY. Do you feel that the raising of these funds by taxation rather than by contributions on the part of employers and employees is better?

Mr. RICE. I do, for this reason: The effect of this bill would be to give immediate relief to the people who are at present unemployed. I mean, as I understand these other unemployment insurance schemes, they are on an actuarial basis; that is to say, the man must first have a job.

Mr. HARTLEY. That is right.

Mr. Rice. And then contribute something, and then become unemployed, before he is subject to relief. Now, what about the millions who cannot find jobs? I mean, there is no provision made for them at all. This would apply immediate, not relief but social security, and of course I believe, while I am not an economist or a statistician, the amount involved, the amount of purchasing power which would be released by this immediate redistribution of income, the aggregate purchasing power which would be released would be so great that a stimulation of industry would be bound to follow, and unemployment itself would be reduced as a logical consequence of that, because obviously the fellow who is getting whatever the provisions of this bill are, $10 a week and $3 for each dependent, if you assume a man with a wife and two children, who would be getting $19 a week, it is very unlikely that he would be hoarding that money or putting it into securities. He would be spending it for shoes and clothing and groceries, and the aggregate purchasing power would certainly be an immediate stimulus to industry and result in an increase in employment, which would at once result in a decrease of the amount of money necessary for the administration of the bill. It seems to me it would inevitably work out that way.

Mr. Hartley. Thank you.

Mr. Dunn. Congressman Lundeen?

Mr. Lundeen. In connection with the questions of Congressman Hartley, it occurs to me that the papers published—of course, we do not know how correct the statement is—but the papers published recently that some 4 or 5 States had already announced that they would be unable to meet the requirements of the administration bill. As meager as it is, they cannot meet it. That is all the more reason why there should be a national bill, but I feel we should probably have some more testimony as to the machinery of administering it, about which I think Congressman Hartley is concerned.

Mr. Hartley. Yes.

Mr. Lundeen. And I think we will have it, before we get through.

Mr. Dunn. Congressman Wood, have you any questions?

Mr. Wood. No.

Mr. Dunn. Does any other member of the committee have a question?

Mr. Wood. The only thing that disturbs me about the Lundeen bill is as to what is the necessary appropriation to make this law effective immediately.

Mr. Lundeen. We are going to take that up in detail here before we get through our hearings, and we will have some statistics on it. There are some statistics being prepared now.

Mr. Wood. I am in favor of the bill. We ought to be clear upon that point, as to just how much it will require to start the administration of the law. the first 6 months or the first year.

Mr. Lundeen. I think we can give you something about that, Congressman Wood.

Mr. Wood. Upon the theory that both those employed now and those unemployed now will be the recipients of the legislation.

Mr. Lundeen. We have hearings now, scheduled ahead for more than a week, have we not?

Mr. Dunn. Oh, yes.

Mr. Lundeen. About 2 weeks? So we will cover that point.

Mr. Dunn. The hearings will continue all of this week and probably longer.

Mr. Wood. I did not know whether you had made any arrangements for developing what the cost would be.

Mr. Lundeen. Yes; we have information on the cost and the source of the funds. We are going into both those points, both the cost of the bill and the source of the funds.

Mr. Wood. You will have to do that, necessarily.

Mr. Lundeen. Yes; we will do that.

Mr. Hartley. Mr. Chairman, I would like to make a statement. I am sincerely interested in this bill, and in getting as liberal an unemployment insurance measure out of this House as we possibly can, but we must be guided by the experience of other countries that have tried similar propositions. Great Britain, as an example, studied the question of their dole, which is practically the same as what we are proposing, for 20 years, and then found that the statistics that had been compiled did not begin to cover the situation. If Congressman Lundeen has some figures available, I would like to see them so that we can examine them and possibly make some suggestions. It is not for the purpose of criticizing that I want them. I would like to get them so that if we have criticism, we can make it constructively, so that we can properly cooperate in getting out a good bill. Certainly there is no committee in the House that is going to give more decent consideration to a measure of this kind than this committee, and it will probably give it more consideration than some other committees that are considering this type of legislation.

Mr. Wood. Mr. Chairman, that is the reason I asked the question.

Mr. Lundeen. The point that you are mentioning now is comparative statistics with other countries?

Mr. Wood. Yes.

Mr. Hartley. I would like to get, if possible, the amount of money that it is estimated will be required to put this bill into operation.

Mr. Lundeen. We will have that.

Mr. Hartley. And also, if possible, to get figures as to the increase on income taxes over $5,000.

Mr. Lundeen. The source of the funds?

Mr. Hartley. Yes, sir; that is right; so we can give it some study.

Mr. Lundeen. And do you want something on the comparison with other countries, on what they have done?

Mr. Hartley. Yes; if you have that. I have a good many figures on that, myself, but if you have anything, I should like to have it.

Mr. Lundeen. We would like to have your figures. The committee would like to have whatever data you may have on the subject that you would care to present.

Mr. Hartley. I have got material on that which I will be glad to give you.

Mr. Dunn. Mr. Rice, we have taken up your valuable time.

Mr. Rice. It has been very kind of you to give me so much time.

Mr. Lundeen. I move we recess until 2 o'clock.

(The motion was agreed to; accordingly, the hour of 12:15 p. m. having arrived, the subcommittee took a recess until 2 o'clock this afternoon.)

The subcommittee reconvened at 2 p. m.

STATEMENT OF JOSEPH MURRAY

Mr. DUNN. Mr. Murray, will you tell the committee what organization you represent, and so forth?

Mr. MURRAY. Gentlemen, I am a representative of 1,600 transients in the District of Columbia, unemployed transients in Washington.

Mr. SCHNEIDER. How do you represent them?

Mr. MURRAY. Well, as chairman of their committee, the rank and file committee of unemployed transients.

Mr. LUNDEEN. Have you had a meeting and elected delegates.

Mr. MURRAY. Yes, sir. We have a committee at the Transient Bureau. I am chairman.

Mr. LUNDEEN. What percentage of the 1,600 is represented?

Mr. MURRAY. Well, there are 500 men that are permanent transients——

Mr. SCHNEIDER. You say "permanent transients"?

Mr. MURRAY. Yes, sir.

Mr. LUNDEEN. I did not know there was any such thing as a "permanent transient."

Mr. MURRAY. Well, these men linger on at the Transient Bureau. Some men stay on an average of 2 or 3 days, or a week, and then they leave the city. But there are 500 that always remain.

Mr. LUNDEEN. You call them "permanent transients"?

Mr. MURRAY. Yes, sir. There are men that have been here since the establishment of the Transient Bureau, which was about a year ago.

Mr. LUNDEEN. I understand.

Mr. MURRAY. As a representative for the transients of the Washington Transient Bureau in the District of Columbia, permit me to present in brief the demands and conditions that exist in the Washington Transient Bureau.

On January 27, 1935, the transients, assembled in a meeting at the Boys' Lodge, at which 450 were present, adopted and endorsed the Lundeen unemployment and social insurance bill, H. R. 2827.

Mr. LUNDEEN. May I interrupt there? Did you put in the address or location of your headquarters—where your office is located.

Mr. MURRAY. That is it.

Mr. LUNDEEN. I want to look that up and find out something about it.

Mr. MURRAY. Well, I can explain that to you, Congressman Lundeen. The Transient Bureau has five lodges: No. 220 Express Court is what they call the "Boys' Lodge." That is the lodge in which they have an auditorium—where we hold our meetings.

Mr. LUNDEEN. You mean the big auditorium?

Mr. MURRAY. Well, it holds, I believe around 450 men.

Mr. LUNDEEN. That is your auditorium?

Mr. MURRAY. Yes, sir. We have our entertainments there.

Mr. SCHNEIDER. You are a transient?

Mr. MURRAY. Yes, sir.

Mr. LUNDEEN. Where is that headquarters located?

Mr. MURRAY. No. 220 Express Court.

Mr. LUNDEEN. Express Court?

Mr. MURRAY. Yes, sir.

Mr. LUNDEEN. Is there a phone there?

Mr. MURRAY. I believe there is.

Mr. SCHNEIDER. You are a transient?

Mr. MURRAY. Yes, sir.

Mr. SCHNEIDER. Where do you come from?

Mr. MURRAY. I come from New York City.

Mr. SCHNEIDER. How long have you been here?

Mr. MURRAY. I have been here close on to five months.

Mr. SCHNEIDER. Does that constitute you a transient, since you have been here 5 months?

Mr. MURRAY. Yes, sir. I live at the Transient Bureau, which I will explain later here, how I came to be a transient. Well, I need not take up my case personally, what caused me to become a transient. But I am here, a transient; that is the reason I am here. I migrated into the city. Therefore, I went up to the Transient Bureau in the District of Columbia, and I live at the present time in the Transient Bureau.

Mr. LUNDEEN. Where is this Express Court? How do you get there?

Mr. MURRAY. It is on Third Street.

Mr. LUNDEEN. Near Pennsylvania Avenue?

Mr. MURRAY. It is one block above Pennsylvania Avenue.

Mr. LUNDEEN. Northwest?

Mr. MURRAY. Yes, sir.

Mr. LUNDEEN. I see. I think I know where it is.

Mr. MURRAY. But the office of the Transient Bureau is 220 John Marshall Place.

Mr. LUNDEEN. And where is that?

Mr. MURRAY. John Marshall Place; 220.

Mr. LUNDEEN. Is that anywhere near 220 Express Court?

Mr. MURRAY. Yes, sir; two blocks away.

Mr. LUNDEEN. I have it located now. I want to go down and see the men—how they are taken care of.

Mr. MURRAY. We would appreciate it if you would come down.

Mr. DUNN. Congressman, men have come into my office for assistance, and I have given them letters and sent them to this place that the gentleman is speaking of. No doubt you have had the same experience.

Mr. LUNDEEN. Then you are familiar with this service, too, Mr. Chairman?

Mr. DUNN. Oh, yes. You will find they have a telephone. I have given them letters, and they are taken care of. Have you had that experience?

Mr. LUNDEEN. I have had some people come in, but I did not know where they came from; they have come in and presented their difficulties.

Mr. DUNN. My secretary can tell you more about it. I have instructed her, and the other secretary, to take care of everybody that comes into the office.

Mr. LUNDEEN. Is that Bureau under the District of Columbia, or under some Federal bureau?

Mr. MURRAY. It is under the District of Columbia. Commissioner Allen has charge of it.

Mr. DUNN. There is an appropriation made for its maintenance. I do not know whether it is a District of Columbia or a regular congressional appropriation.

Mr. MURRAY. This Transient Bureau comes under the jurisdiction of Commissioner Allen's office. I am told it is under the F. E. R. A.

Mr. SCHNEIDER. Do women also have access to relief from that program?

Mr. MURRAY. Yes, sir. At the present time I believe there are 200 women receiving aid through the Transient Bureau.

Mr. LUNDEEN. Is there a gentleman down there who has anything to do with it by the name of David Linden?

Mr. MURRAY. Yes. sir.

Mr. LUNDEEN. Is he at your John Marshall Place office?

Mr. MURRAY. Yes, sir. He is one of Mr. Gebhart's assistants.

Mr. LUNDEEN. He came to my office one day, and talked with me about transient service.

Mr. MURRAY. I had a conversation with him on Saturday morning in his office, and he seemed interested in this Lundeen bill.

Mr. LUNDEEN. You understand we just want to locate the service and find out where you are.

Mr. MURRAY. Yes, sir.

Mr. LUNDEEN. So we can learn more about its activity.

Mr. MURRAY. As I say, transients adopted and endorsed this bill. The transients realize that this is the only bill that will take them out of the flophouses and bread lines.

The Wagner-Lewis bill does not provide for the 16 million unemployed who are unemployed at the present time through no fault of their own.

We have the right, as American citizens, to demand that adequate relief be provided from the Government for us to live as human beings, and not to lead the miserable and unsettled vagrant life of the transients today.

So far the Roosevelt administration has not made any successful efforts to better our present condition in the transient camps. The present Wagner-Lewis bill does not attempt to help the unemployed, who today have no honest prospects of employment under present economic conditions. Most of the transients come within this class. We realize, therefore, that the Lundeen bill for workers unemployment and social insurance, H. R. 2827, is the only bill that can benefit the unemployed.

Transients represent sections of all the unemployed class, such as mechanics, professionals, and laborers, who being unable, through the deep unemployment and crisis which is now affecting the whole country, to properly provide for themselves at home, are forced to leave and seek employment elsewhere.

The conditions that exist in the transient camps relative to sanitation, housing, and sustenance, are such as to keep the transients migrating from city to city, seeking employment and decent living conditions, which they never find.

At a conference recently held by officials of the Federal Emergency Relief Administration, Mr. Plunkett, representing Mr. Hopkins, stated that transients' camps were the best means of keeping transients employed, at the wage rate of $1 a week, consisting of 30 hours work. Such a sum is considered sufficient, by the officials, for the rehabilitation of the transients.

Mr. LUNDEEN. Did I understand you to say a dollar a week?

Mr. MURRAY. Yes, sir.

Mr. MURRAY. That is what 1,600 men receive, $1 a week.

Mr. LUNDEEN. No human being can live on that. Don't they get any work outside of that?

Mr. MURRAY. They do 24 hours work at the Transient Bureau, for which they receive $1 a week.

Mr. DUNN. That 24 hours is divided into how many days?

Mr. MURRAY. Six days, 4 hours a day.

Mr. DUNN. That is what they call "real union wages", is it?

Mr. MURRAY. Yes; apparently.

Mr. LUNDEEN. I did not know that there was any such rate as that paid.

Mr. LUNDEEN. There must be some other source of income which these men have.

Mr. SCHNEIDER. The District gives them shelter and food, does it not?

Mr. MURRAY. Yes, sir; they receive shelter and food.

Mr. LUNDEEN. Well, that is what we want to know, because otherwise I would think that the $1 is all they get.

Mr. SCHNEIDER. The dollar that you get is given to you? It is not particularly for this work that you do, is it? It is given to you to buy some tobacco with, and so forth?

Mr. MURRAY. Yes, sir.

Mr. SCHNEIDER. Or anything else that is urgently needed by the average fellow that is in one of these institutions?

Mr. MURRAY. Well, the dollar that a man receives is for laundry, and in the event a man likes to keep his suit pressed, he pays for that out of his dollar, and his tobacco money.

Mr. SCHNEIDER. Do you have a laundry in your institution?

Mr. MURRAY. No, sir.

Mr. SCHNEIDER. What do you do during that 24 hours that you are working?

Mr. MURRAY. Well, take my case for instance. I am considered what they call a watchman. I watch a door to see that no one comes in or out that does not belong in the house, in one of the lodges. The other men work in the kitchen, peeling potatoes; some do porter work; some work in the wood yard. There are 500 of the men working in the wood yard; the majority are working there.

Mr. SCHNEIDER. They do not have a laundry?

Mr. MURRAY. There is no laundry in the five lodges that are operated under the Transient Bureau.

Mr. SCHNEIDER. Have you any facilities for doing your own laundry work?

Mr. MURRAY. There are these wash bowls that the men use for washing their faces. They use them for washing their shirts, underwear, and socks. I send my shirts out to the laundry. Quite a number of the other men do.

Mr. LUNDEEN. You pay regular rates?

Mr. MURRAY. Well, I pay 10 cents for a shirt.

Mr. DUNN. With that dollar you cannot get any permanent wave or take any turkish bath?

Mr. MURRAY. No, sir. We challenge the officials who declare that the wage of $1 a week will bring back prosperity, which President Roosevelt has been trying for the past 2 years to do.

Now, what is life in a transient camp like?

The camps are unsanitary, overcrowded, improperly heated and ventilated; no hot water is provided, and bathing facilities are bad; the medical service is not nearly adequate to take care of the poor health of the men. There is not enough food to go around. The menu is monotonous, and the quality is poor, often not fit for human consumption. Such conditions actually exist in the Washington Transient Bureau today.

On several occasions the transients of Washington have demanded of the District and the F. E. R. A. officials to pay transients at the prevailing union wage rate of 50 cents per hour for laborers in Washington; also that 24 hours per week be guaranteed to each transient. This demand has not been granted, or even considered by the various officials. Therefore we, the transients, can see no solution of our problems and difficulties through the efforts of officials of the present administration.

Therefore we transients of the Washington Transient Bureau turn to the Lundeen unemployment and social insurance bill, H. R. 2827, as a partial solution of our problems, by giving us the opportunity to live independently at an American standard.

In conclusion, we, the transients, hereupon demand the immediate passage of the Lundeen bill, H. R. 2827; and in the period pending the passage of the above mentioned bill, H. R. 2827, we demand that the transients be provided for as indicated above.

I present that to you as chairman of the Transient Rank and File Committee.

Mr. DUNN. Gentlemen, Mr. Murray is ready to be interrogated.

Mr. LUNDEEN. You say you are 1,600 in number?

Mr. MURRAY. Yes, sir.

Mr. LUNDEEN. Men and women?

Mr. MURRAY. No, sir; the women have outside maintenance; they have private rooms.

Mr. LUNDEEN. You are not here to represent them at all?

Mr. MURRAY. Well, I believe so.

Mr. LUNDEEN. They are included in the 1,600?

Mr. MURRAY. No; there are 1,600 men.

Mr. LUNDEEN. How many women?

Mr. MURRAY. I believe 200; somewhere around that.

Mr. LUNDEEN. If anybody becomes seriously ill there, what hospital facilities are given?

Mr. MURRAY. They have a lodge over here at Fifth Street, I believe it is, where they send these men. It is called an " infirmary."

At this infirmary they have no doctor. They have a man representing himself as a doctor, who has no degree. This has been taken up with the District officials and with the F. E. R. A.

Mr. LUNDEEN. But he has hospital training, has he not?

Mr. MURRAY. Well, there is one man who is over there claiming that he was an orderly in a hospital. Two weeks ago one of the transients down at the lodge at Canal Street was taken sick; I believe at the time he had a hemorrhage; and they had no one there to attend him.

Mr. LUNDEEN. What became of this man?

Mr. MURRAY. So they took this man over to the hospital, and he did not receive proper medical attention; and I believe 2 days later he died.

Mr. LUNDEEN. When you say " hospital ", what do you mean?

Mr. MURRAY. Infirmary.

Mr. LUNDEEN. That is the only hospital you have?

Mr. MURRAY. That is the only hospital.

Mr. LUNDEEN. If you become seriously ill, that is where you are sent?

Mr. MURRAY. Yes, sir.

Mr. LUNDEEN. That is where you remain, or die?

Mr. MURRAY. The Bureau officials admit that they cannot send a transient to an outside hospital.

Mr. LUNDEEN. I take it that the infirmary is more or less a first-aid affair?

Mr. MURRAY. That is all it is.

Mr. LUNDEEN. That is all the hospital facilities you have?

Mr. MURRAY. Yes; that is all.

Mr. LUNDEEN. I think we ought to take this up with some of the departments and get hospital aid for these men.

Mr. DUNN. I agree with you.

Mr. SCHNEIDER. Is a doctor called in when anyone is taken ill in the institution?

Mr. MURRAY. No, sir. There was a case 2 weeks ago in my room at 638 D Street, right in the room with me, which houses six men, a very small room. A man was taken sick at 11 o'clock at night. The result was that the man had to get up out of bed——he had pneumonia——and dress himself and walk over to the infirmary and they failed to admit him. The place was overcrowded; they had 20 men in beds over there.

Mr. LUNDEEN. What became of that man?

Mr. MURRAY. The man came back, came up to the room, told us what happened, and two more of us put on our clothes and went over and demanded that they take him in; and they finally admitted him to the hospital, to this infirmary.

Mr. LUNDEEN. You say he had pneumonia. How do you know he had pneumonia?

Mr. MURRAY. When they took his temperature, they found out he had 103 temperature.

Mr. SCHNEIDER. I wanted to get a more clear picture of the institution. You say that these 1,600 are all housed in this one building?

Mr. MURRAY. No, sir. There are five lodges in which they are housed.

Mr. SCHNEIDER. Five different buildings in which they are housed?

Mr. MURRAY. Yes, sir.

Mr. SCHNEIDER. I presume they are all rented by the Government or by the F. E. R. A.?

Mr. MURRAY. I believe the District has control of the buildings.

Mr. SCHNEIDER. How many employees are paid, outside of you folks, those you represent? How many officials are employed in the administration of your affairs?

Mr. MURRAY. Approximately, in the Bureau itself, I should judge, 300.

Mr. SCHNEIDER. Approximately 300 people are employed?

Mr. MURRAY. Yes, sir.

Mr. SCHNEIDER. There is someone at the head of the institution?

Mr. MURRAY. Yes, sir.

Mr. SCHNEIDER. And then they have many underlings, all the way down?

Mr. MURRAY. Yes, sir.

Mr. SCHNEIDER. What do they all do.

Mr. MURRAY. Well, in the Bureau itself, in the general office, they have what they call an " administrative staff." These men are advisers to the director or assistant director of this Transient Bureau. Then we have what they call " caseworkers." Each transient at the transient bureau has a caseworker. In the event that a man needs relief, he goes to this caseworker, and tells the caseworker just what he needs; and if the caseworker sees fit to give it to him, he will make out a requisition for him; and if he does not, the man can keep moving. We have at least 30 of them. These people are not transients.

Mr. SCHNEIDER. A good deal of the work in connection with taking care of these people is done by those you represent, themselves?

Mr. MURRAY. Yes, sir.

Mr. SCHNEIDER. That is, cooking?

Mr. MURRAY. Yes, sir.

Mr. SCHNEIDER. And cleaning, and taking care of the institution; that is largely done by you folks. And then, as you state, there are about 300 governmental employees who are on the pay roll, paid for the purpose of checking up, case work, and so on?

Mr. MURRAY. Yes, sir.

Mr. DUNN. Do you have an age limit?

Mr. MURRAY. No, sir.

Mr. DUNN. Do you know how many of the men are married?

Mr. MURRAY. Quite a number.

Mr. DUNN. Do they have families?

Mr. MURRAY. Yes, sir. In their home towns from which they come.

Mr. DUNN. How long is a man permitted to stay there?

Mr. MURRAY. As long as he cares to stay.

Mr. DUNN. As long as he cares to stay?

Mr. MURRAY. Providing he keeps up the rules and regulations of the institution.

Mr. DUNN. Are there many men over 60 in your institution?

Mr. MURRAY. I could not say off-hand how many there are there but there are quite a few.

Mr. Dunn. What is the youngest?

Mr. Murray. The youngest is 16.

Mr. Dunn. Sixteen? Do they take them that young?

Mr. Murray. Yes, sir.

Mr. Dunn. And all these men that stay at this institution, are they given a dollar a week?

Mr. Murray. Yes, sir.

Mr. Dunn. But they must work for it?

Mr. Murray. Yes, sir.

Mr. Dunn. Thank you.

Mr. Schneider. When transients come to town, they check them over; and what constitutes ordering a man to move on?

Mr. Murray. Do you mind if I outline to you just what a transient goes through at the time of registration?

Mr. Schneider. Yes; that is what we want.

Mr. Murray. When a transient arrives at the Transient Bureau he gives his name, address where he comes from, age, religion, occupation, and so on. That is put down on the record, but as far as the Transient Bureau officials are concerned, it is never looked up. It is just put on the papers and put in the file, and that is the end of it.

Mr. Schneider. Then can he remain here as long as he wants to?

Mr. Murray. Yes; as long as he cares to.

Mr. Schneider. Is that the condition all through the country?

Mr. Murray. Yes, sir.

Mr. Schneider. Is is not true that in some cities they make them move on; they have a lodging over night, and the next day they must move on?

Mr. Murray. I understand in Baltimore they keep you one night, and then you move on.

Mr. Schneider. But here in Washington, under these rules, they are more liberal?

Mr. Murray. It is permanent here in Washington.

Mr. Dunn. For your information, Congressman Schneider—if you will excuse me, Mr. Murray?

Mr. Murray. Yes, sir.

Mr. Dunn. May I say that I believe there is an organization in this town that takes care of men just for a day or two. In fact, I have contacted that department. Am I right, Miss McChesney?

Miss McChesney. Yes; I understand they take care of them for 2 or 3 days at the most, and then they move on.

Mr. Dunn. I know there is an organization in this town that takes care of people for 2 or 3 days. In fact, I know it is true, because a man came to my office right before we adjourned last year, and stated that he would like to have me call the department and get permission for him to remain for another day or two; and I did, and they took care of him. Whether they have abolished that since last June, I do not know.

Mr. Murray. Well, the only place that I know of is the Central Union Mission. That is a mission. That place will put a man up for 3 days, I believe, and then he has to move on.

Miss McChesney. Was not the place you have reference to an institution for ex-service men?

Mr. MURRAY. Oh, it might be a soldiers' home.

Mr. DUNN. I believe that is it.

Mr. SCHNEIDER. Mr. Chairman, I do not want the record to indicate that I am in favor of making them move on, but believe there should be a permanent place for these folks to remain——

Mr. DUNN. I know you would not want to do that, because you are too humane.

Mr. DUNN. Now, do you mean to tell me that this institution will take every person in that comes to them for assistance?

Mr. MURRAY. Yes, sir.

Mr. DUNN. No matter where they come from?

Mr. MURRAY. Yes, sir.

Mr. DUNN. All they have to do is come there and give their name and address?

Mr. MURRAY. Yes, sir.

Mr. DUNN. And they will take care of them?

Mr. MURRAY. Yes, sir.

Mr. DUNN. And they may stay at this institution as long as they want?

Mr. MURRAY. Yes, sir.

Mr. DUNN. As long as they abide by the rules and regulations?

Mr. MURRAY. Yes, sir.

Mr. DUNN. For instance, you come up before this committee to testify, and we appreciate that you have done this. But are you not afraid that the officials of the institution will get after you for it?

Mr. MURRAY. No; I am not afraid of that.

Mr. DUNN. You are not afraid of being deprived of that big dollar a week?

Mr. MURRAY. No, sir.

Mr. LUNDEEN. Was there any objection made to your coming here?

Mr. MURRAY. I would like to tell you an incident that happened, I believe it was 10 minutes of 1. We put a sign up outside the mess hall, telling of the committee coming up here before this subcommittee; and we requested, or at least we urged, all transients to come up and attend these sessions. The result was that the police officer came out of the mess hall and told the men to move on. Well, one man did not move fast enough for him and he went to kick him—that is, the officer did; he made a kick at one of the transients, and the result was—well, we moved on.

But as far as the officials are concerned, they do not like the idea of this; but I believe we have the privilege of coming up here.

Mr. DUNN. You have that right, and we are glad to get this information; it is valuable.

Mr. LUNDEEN. Congressmen are supposed to be your representatives and your servants.

Mr. SCHNEIDER. Mr. Chairman, I suggest that you invite one of the officials down there to come before the committee.

Mr. DUNN. It is a very good suggestion.

Mr. LUNDEEN. I was going to ask in that connection, who is the head of the institution; what is his name?

Mr. MURRAY.. Mr. Richard Gebhart.

Mr. LUNDEEN. Does he live down there?

Mr. MURRAY. No, sir.

Mr. LUNDEEN. Or does he just come to the office?

Mr. MURRAY. Just comes to the office.   Now, Mr. Chairman, may I say a word in regard to Mr. Gebhart?

Mr. DUNN. Proceed.

Mr. MURRAY. Two months ago there was an investigation started of the Transient Bureau by Mr. Hopkins.   Mr. Hopkins brought in a man from Chicago by the name of Mr. Sands, to start investigation of the Transient Bureau.   Well, when the investigation was half way through, Mr. Sands resigned and left for Chicago.   With that, Mr. Gebhart came along to complete the investigation; and he is the present director of the Transient Bureau.   The investigation was completed, but there was never any report given out in regard to the investigation.

Mr. LUNDEEN. Is that Mr. Harry L. Hopkins that you refer to?

Mr. MURRAY. Yes, sir.   The present director completed the investigation of the Transient Bureau, but there has never been a report given out.

Mr. DUNN. What is this gentlemen's name who is supervisor or superintendent of the institution?

Mr. MURRAY. Mr. Richard Gebhart.

Miss MCCHESNEY. Would his address be Third Street Northwest, or 220 John Marshall Place?

Mr. MURRAY. 220 John Marshall Place.

Mr. SCHNEIDER. I would like to say that so far the witness has presented to the committee such information as the committee desires to secure, in my estimation.

Mr. DUNN. Yes; I agree with you, Mr. Schneider.   I think the treatment these men are receiving should be stopped.

Mr. LUNDEEN. I would like to ask about the statement that Mr Murray made here, about six men in one room, the small room.

Mr. MURRAY. Yes, sir.

Mr. LUNDEEN. In the Army I have slept six or seven in a tent, and we were pretty much packed in there.   Now, do you sleep on the floor?

Mr. MURRAY. No, sir.

Mr. LUNDEEN. What kind of beds do you have?

Mr. MURRAY. We have cots similar to Army cots.

Mr. LUNDEEN. There would be six individual cots in the room?

Mr. MURRAY. Yes, sir.   And the Bureau pays $2.45 a week to the people that operate this private house.   At the present time there are over 75 men in this house.   There are other men living in hotels that the Bureau pays for.   Some men eat in restaurants that the Bureau pays for.   And we, the majority, have to eat in the mess hall for all the transients, while the rest can go out and eat in restaurants, and the Bureau pays for it.

Mr. LUNDEEN. Do you know anything about that long line of men that you see at certain times, right off Pennsylvania Avenue, near the Standard Oil Building?

Mr. MURRAY. I have seen them.

Mr. LUNDEEN. What is that line?

Mr. MURRAY. That is at the Volunteers of America.

Mr. LUNDEEN. That has nothing to do with your institution?

Mr. MURRAY. No, sir. But there are quite a number of the men in the line that are members of the Transient Bureau, for the simple reason that they do not receive enough to eat there.

Mr. LUNDEEN. That is what I was wondering about. You are right nearby there?

Mr. MURRAY. Yes, sir. We do not receive enough to eat at the Transient Bureau. For instance, today at dinner we received a tablespoonful of spinach, a tablespoonful of salmon—you could not call it salmon; it was more like soup; a tablespoonful of potatoes; three pieces of bread; and all the coffee you can drink.

Mr. DUNN. Mr. Murray, they never give you castor oil for dessert?

Mr. MURRAY. No, sir.

Mr. LUNDEEN. How about the 300 that you spoke of there? Are they included in the 1,600?

Mr. MURRAY. The 300?

Mr. LUNDEEN. You spoke of 300 employees.

Mr. MURRAY. Oh, no, sir.

Mr. LUNDEEN. What is that?

Mr. MURRAY. That is part of the administrative staff. They are outsiders.

Mr. LUNDEEN. They do not belong to the 1,600?

Mr. MURRAY. No, sir.

Mr. LUNDEEN. In other words, the 300 take care of the 1,600?

Mr. MURRAY. Yes, sir.

Mr. LUNDEEN. One thousand six hundred men and two hundred women?

Mr. MURRAY. Yes, sir.

Mr. LUNDEEN. That would be 1,800 people?

Mr. MURRAY. Yes, sir.

Mr. LUNDEEN. There is a staff of 300 to take care of them?

Mr. MURRAY. Yes, sir.

Mr. LUNDEEN. That is one for every 6?

Mr. DUNN. Are they salaried people?

Mr. MURRAY. Yes, sir.

Mr. LUNDEEN. Do you know anything about their salaries?

Mr. MURRAY. Well, some receive $25 a week, some $35, and others receive $10. They range in all different ways. I believe the House of Representatives, the Senate, is practically represented every day by the transients. That is all you can hear down there: "Well, if I can't get a pair of socks, or receive a shirt, I will go up to see my Senator, or I will go up to see my Congressman."

That is all you hear down there. All kinds of letters coming in from these officials. I know I had to go to Senator Wagner to get a pair of overalls.

Mr. LUNDEEN. Don't you get any supplies at all by requisition?

Mr. MURRAY. Well, as I explained before, Congressman, they have a case worker there. You go in to the case worker and you tell the case worker just what you need.

Mr. LUNDEEN. By the case worker, you mean one of those 300?

Mr. MURRAY. If he sees fit to give you what you ask, you receive it. It is up to him to give it to you. If he does not care to give it to you, you have no recourse. Therefore you have to go up to your Senator or Congressman and get a letter off of him to the Director of the Bureau. I have a letter in my possession right now from Senator Wagner, when I requested the Senator to write this letter asking for overalls in order to save my suit, working in the wood yard.

Mr. LUNDEEN. And you got the overalls?

Mr. MURRAY. Yes, sir; I went up and requested overalls, and they told me I was not there long enough. At the time I was there 2 weeks. So I went up to Senator Wagner and explained the situation to him. I told him this was the only suit I had and I would like to have a pair of overalls, which the Bureau could give me in the event he gave me a letter, which he did; and I still have the letter.

Mr. LUNDEEN. That is all, Mr. Murray.

Mr. DUNN. Thank you, Mr. Murray

STATEMENT OF MRS. ELLA REEVE BLOOR

Mr. DUNN. We will be glad to hear you, Mrs. Bloor.

Mrs. BLOOR. I am sorry I have not a statement prepared, as I did not expect to talk this afternoon. I understood the committee was scheduled to hear other witnesses just at this point.

But while we are waiting, I would like to say something about the woman's part of this bill.

Mr. DUNN. Will you tell us whom you represent?

Mrs. BLOOR. I represent the farm women. I am a member of the national executive committee of the Farmers' National Committee for Action, with headquarters in Philadelphia, 720 Locust Street. I was elected at one of their big conventions in Chicago to this executive committee. Naturally, my work has been quite a lot with the farm women in North Dakota, Nebraska, Iowa, and most of the Middle West, some in Colorado. Now I am located in Philadelphia. I have not been there long enough to study the condition of the farm women of Pennsylvania, only in a limited area around Philadelphia—towns around there.

Now, why do I speak of the farm women in connection with this bill? I think very few of us who are in the cities realize the poverty that the women are suffering, especially the young women in the farm districts, on account of not only the drought and the usual conditions there, but especially the fact of maternity in these isolated places. I want to call your attention especially to the maternity clause in this bill. We found in the women's section of the unemployed congress which took place in Washington recently, when I met with those women two or three times, that they were especially interested in this part of the bill, about maternity: "Compensation for disability because of maternity shall be paid to women during the period of 8 weeks previous and 8 weeks following childbirth."

Now, I do not think that you can realize what that would mean to the women who suffer so long in these isolated regions. Many of them give birth to children without doctors. They have no means of studying birth control. It is considered a sin in most States to teach women, mothers, birth control. And so we found that this bill would be of great service to these women, not only the farm women, but working women everywhere. At this caucus of women in connection with the Congress, several single women spoke, and they said they felt that we must have a bill such as this, which makes no distinction between men and women in its benefits. In other clauses of the bill it just says "workers" and "farmers"; it never says "male workers." It never makes any distinction, and they liked the bill on that account, because in much of our work we have been overlooking the single woman. One woman spoke at the women's caucus at the congress, and spoke very frequently about the condition of single unemployed girls and women who come to her in the Young Women's Christian Association. She said it seems almost impossible to make people realize the condition of these single women.

I think perhaps with the last witness you had some idea of the condition of the single men. You can imagine what it means for women.

I am sorry I did not know I was going to speak, and I have not all the facts with me. But there are facts and figures dealing with the number of single women unemployed. I think there will be one woman here who has made a special study of the number of unemployed single women. It is alarming. This was brought up by the women in the congress, and they are for this bill.

Mr. LUNDEEN. You say there will be such a woman here?

Mrs. BLOOR. I think so, if I can get hold of her.

Mr. LUNDEEN. We hear very little on that subject, and I think it would be very helpful.

Mrs. BLOOR. Yes, sir; it is a very important part of the subject, because the increase of prostitution in many cities flows directly from the tremendous suffering of these single women. So I feel that this will be of great service to them.

I have talked with many of them in cities, and the women that are employed, part-time employed, in the farming districts, would surprise you, too. For instance, in Nebraska, the farm girls have nothing to do on the farm now; nothing, because there are no crops. They used to do canning, sewing, and things of that kind. But now they go to the villages and towns near by and try to get jobs. The most natural thing is that they get jobs, if possible, in the processing of food; for instance, in the dairies, such as the Fairmont Creameries, and the big trust factories of that kind, picking chickens and doing all kinds of work of that kind. Well, now they are out of employment there. Many of them are out of employment on account of the fact that the purchasing power has so decreased that the farmers cannot get the price for their chickens, because the unemployed in the cities cannot buy their chickens. You would be surprised to know what an industry the chicken-picking industry was before, for the unemployed farm women.

I think it would be a great help in raising the standard of living of the great mass of farmers' daughters as well as farmers' wives, because I would not want to speak alone for the farmers' wives. The farmers' sons and daughters cannot get jobs at all now. So I believe that this bill would raise the standard of living among farmers tremendously, and raise the purchasing power of the people liv-

ing in the villages and towns; and in that way better the condition
of the unemployed all over, as well as the workers who are employed.

I feel very strongly about the maternity clause of this bill, and I
hope that when you speak of it in Congress you will emphasize
that. You must not forget the woman's part of this bill.

Mr. DUNN. I agree with you that we should take care of them.
We have a Miss Dorothy Douglas, of Smith College, as a speaker
for Thursday.

Mrs. BLOOR. She will cover some of the facts and figures about
unemployed women.

Mrs. BLOOR. I think Dorothy Douglas will cover that.

Then there is another special woman who has gotten facts and
figures about the number of unemployed single women. She has
been devoting her whole life to it, especially in the last year; and I
will try to get hold of her. I do not know her address. I think I
will be able to find her in New York.

Mr. LUNDEEN. Miss Dorothy Douglas is a very able woman.

Mr. DUNN. Yes, sir. She will be here Thursday.

Mr. LUNDEEN. I would like to say for your information, with the
chairman's permission, that in 1911 Minnesota, among other States,
enacted a mother's pension law. I was a young member of the legislature at the time and, of course, I voted for it. Ever since that
time I have been very strong for these mateurnity benefits and mothers' pensions. I cannot conceive of anything more important to the
State than motherhood and the care of women—mothers. We went
into this thoroughly at that time, and it made a very deep impression
on me. Certainly if there is any human being in this world whose
struggles against hardship should be lessened, it is the mother; and
she should be taken care of first.

Mrs. BLOOR. It seems so to me. I have had 40 years' experience
working with women and men, among the workers and farmers; and
in the last 5 years among the farmers' homes. I feel very strongly,
more so than I ever did before, not only as a mother but as a citizen.
I have six children of my own, and I know what a mother has to
suffer. When it comes to conditions that they are suffering today,
not only on the farm but in the villages near the farm, I think it
would be of tremendous advantage if we could have such a statement
in connection with this bill, showing the actual conditions which
exist among the farm women. If you will permit me, I will try to
write such a statement and send it to you.

Mr. DUNN. We will put it in the record. Now, Mrs. Bloor, I
want to say this about the unfortunate women. The Federal Government, the State governments, and the municipal governments
are spending tremendous sums of money trying to reduce and wipe
out crime. How in the world are we ever going to wipe out crime
when we are compelling mothers with their children to live in the
slum districts, and the mothers are not properly fed? How in
the world can be expect children to come into the world that will
be sound mentally and physically? In other words, we spend billions of dollars trying to keep down crime and enforce the law,
while we are doing practically nothing to eradicate the cause. I
think what Congress ought to do is to pass such legislation as the
Lundeen bill. I think it would go far toward eradicating it.

Mrs. BLOOR. Not only crime but disease; crime and disease. Of course, crime is very often the outcome of disease.

Mr. DUNN. Yes; but as long as we have our slum districts, we are going to have disease and crime. If we should spend a hundred billion dollars to wipe out the slum districts, it would be a very infinitesimal sum compared to the good it would accomplish.

Mrs. BLOOR. If they would spend just half as much money on maternity protection and mothers' pensions that they spend for the scientific improvements with disease, and investigations, and things of that kind, I think it would be a great help to the citizenship of this country and the future citizenship.

It has been said that no country can rise above the level of its motherhood; and as long as we degrade motherhood, we will surely degrade our citizenship.

Mr. DUNN. But we are degrading them when we compel them to live in alleys, slums, and so forth.

Mrs. BLOOR. And then the mental condition of the mother, the fear all of the time of the future, the feeling of insecurity. I think that word " security " is a tremendous one to use in connection with our bill: " social security ". I think we are socially responsible for that social security. That is the way it seems to me, in my investigation among the men and women of this country.

Mr. DUNN. But we Members of Congress have the power to bring about a condition where that misery does not need to exist.

Mrs. BLOOR. I believe that maternity clause in the bill, and the bill altogether, will help greatly in advancing the standards of our citizens.

Mr. DUNN. Then in your opinion, this Lundeen bill will really do a wonderful lot of good work for all classes of people?

Mrs. BLOOR. Yes, sir.

Mr. DUNN. Have you read the other bills?

Mrs. BLOOR. Yes, sir; and I see no other way than to accept this bill. It is short, concrete, and covers many, many phases of the unemployment situation. It puts the burden of paying for the bill upon the class that can afford it. It does not take more from the workers themselves. It does not put them further down. It is distributed, I think, in a very wise way. I have studied it very carefully, and I believe it is the only way that we can better conditions in the immediate future.

Mr. DUNN. I do not hesitate to say the Lundeen bill is what we call a Christian act, and that Congressmen will be better Christians if they enact it into law.

Mrs. BLOOR. You could put it the other way and say that it is quite un-Christian to degrade our motherhood.

Mr. LUNDEEN. You are going to send down a statement with some statistics, I understand?

Mrs. BLOOR. Yes, sir; I will give you a written statement to put in your record, which I have not had time to prepare now, about the actual conditions.

Mr. LUNDEEN. And giving some statistics?

Mrs. BLOOR. Yes, sir; giving you the facts and figures.

Mr. LUNDEEN. Now, do you believe the bill to be extravagant in its terms and the use of money? We meet occasionally someone who objects to it because he says it is impossible, on account of the large sums that will be involved. What do you think about that?

Mrs. BLOOR. It seems to me that it is far from being extravagant, especially when you compare it with the large appropriations for war purposes that are being put over by the Congress, and have been put over in the past, for the destruction of human life, instead of the protection of human life. I think it is very modest in its requirements in comparison with other appropriations which have been made.

Mr. LUNDEEN. I cannot say that I am in favor of the demobilization of our Army and Navy, but is there any necessity for such tremendous war expenditures as we are making now, when we live with one great ocean on each side of us, the great ice cap on the north, and small friendly nations to the south? If we were right across some little river from a hostile country, it would be a different matter. But Nature here has thrown the arm of protection around America, and it seems to me that instead of increasing our war expenditure, we might leave it where it is, or even reduce it.

Mrs. BLOOR. Of course, that opens up a very large subject, and when we have some hearings on it, I expect to take part in them, as I am tremendously interested against war. I returned recently from France where I attended a large international congress against war, held in Paris. I am deeply interested in that subject. In studying that subject, I find that there are extravagant expenditures made by the Congress and authorized by our Government.

Mr. LUNDEEN. It was supposed a while ago that if we disarmed Germany the world would be very peaceful, and that the devil was chained. I was in Congress when we voted on war and I voted against going into that war. They told us on all sides that when the war was over we would have peace, and no more army and navy. It was to be the last war.

Mrs. BLOOR. I think perhaps if we had a more intelligent race of human beings, as we would have if we had some security, at least, and some peace for life itself, I do not believe we could have such insane expenditures as we have today, for things that are not essential to human life and happiness, but certainly the contrary.

Mr. LUNDEEN. As long as we have talked about this, I want to say for the record, that I do not believe the United States is in danger of any invasion from any great power. I want to put that in the record—I have had a good deal of military experience myself, and I do not believe we are in danger of any invasion now. On the other hand, if we build the greatest military establishment, at great cost, that means that we are going to go somewhere and carry war to some other continent; and that I am hostile to, and irrevocably opposed to. I do not believe in carrying war to some other continent, Asia, Africa, or Europe.

Mrs. BLOOR. I was brought up with American traditions, as all of my ancestors were in the early wars of this country, the Revolutionary War and the Civil War. I was brought up with the traditions of life, liberty, and happiness for our citizens, as a bulwark agains all kinds of evil. It seems to me that if we are disintegrating as citizens by not having healthy children, healthy motherhood, we are deliberately and consciously responsible for lowering the standards of living if we do not, as a community, as a state, as a government, as we are all a part of this Federal Government, take some steps to remedy the present conditions. If we want to make a better home, make life better for our citizens, we must first decide what are the essential things, certainly to make better life, and better homes, better motherhood, and better children; and it is our business here, and your business in the Congress, especially the business of this committee, to protect, not those who won't work, but those who want work and cannot get it.

Mr. DUNN. Mrs. Bloor, when you make that statement, "not those who won't work", I would like to say this: I have often been confronted with social workers in my office in Pittsburgh, and they would say, "Well, now, there are men and women who don't want to work."

Well, my answer to their statement is: "All right. Just provide jobs for those who want to work, and those who don't want to work, we can take care of them. It is my candid opinion that men and women who won't work are to be pitied; it is a mental condition.

Mrs. BLOOR. Or physical condition.

Mr. DUNN. Yes; it is a mental or physical condition.

Mrs. BLOOR. It seems to me that when any advertisement put in the papers for work, men or women, we find a great number of people who want those jobs; showing very plainly that they are very anxious to work. I have watched them in the cities, in the buildings, around factory doors, around Philadelphia lately, and I have noticed so many looking for work. So I think that is a very small part of the argument. I think we won't stop employment by giving them help; they will want to work more, and they will be better able to work physically.

Mr. DUNN. And when we do furnish work, we should not only furnish men and women with work, but at a salary which would be adequate.

Mrs. BLOOR. Certainly.

Mr. DUNN. I have often said that if a man has a mule he can make that mule work hard. Now, if he does not feed that mule properly, the mule has enough mule sense to find out where your brains are, if you will pardon the expression, and he does not care where your brains are, he will use his feet. I have often said that if a man had as much sence as a mule has, there would not be any depression

Mrs. BLOOR. Another thing, gentlemen, that I did not mention in the beginning of my remarks, is the increasing high cost of living. I find that many housewives are organizing against the high cost of living, because the high cost of living has a direct effect upon unemployment insurance, for the reason that the amount of insurance is depndent upon it. What good will a little bit of insurance do, if they have to pay 35 cents a pound for meat? Therefore, I say the increasing cost of living must be taken into consideration in this study, it seems to me.

Now, Mr. Chairman, that is all I have to say at this time.

Mr. DUNN. Thank you, Mrs. Bloor. We will now hear from Mr. Robert Mifflin Sentman.

(Supplementary statement of Mrs. Ella Reeve Bloor is as follows:)

SUPPLEMENTARY STATEMENT OF MRS. ELLA REEVE BLOOR

The following is from an article on unemployment and social insurance that I wrote some time ago—A plea for the preservation of the physical and moral standard of the American people:

" Maternal mortality in New York City has increased during the crisis years from a rate of 5.05 per 1,000 births in 1929 to 6.04 in 1931, and 6.41 in 1933 ", as shown in the report of Shirley W. Wynne, former commissioner of health, issued December 30, 1933.

" In the State of Illinois maternal mortality increased by about 22 percent in the first quarter of 1933 as compared with the corresponding period in 1932. This was the more significant because of birth-rate decline in Illinois as in other parts of the country during the economic crisis; fewer working-class families could afford to have children, and as always in times of depression, birth rates declined. But despite the decline of birth rate, more mothers died in childbirth per 1,000 of the population in these two important districts, Illinois and New York City" (Labor Fact Book 11).

The increase in maternal mortality can be explained by the low resistance of the impoverished woman as well as the fact that childbirth is taking place in the poor homes and under the most unsanitary conditions for financial reasons, instead of properly equipped modern maternity hospitals.

The medical profession recognizes the effect of pregnancy and childbirth on the woman's organism. Well-conducted maternity and health clinics are instructing the expectant mothers about their well-balanced and nutritious diets, mental and physical rest, and proper exercise.

Realizing these fundamental principles the Soviet Union has built a network of institutions under the department of the protection of motherhood and childhood which take care of the woman during her pregnancy and for 2 months after childbirth.

The working woman is freed from work 2 months before and 2 months after childbirth while receiving full wages from the social-insurance funds during these 4 months. All medical care is rendered to her free of charge. She is delivered in a well-equipped maternity hospital. Even in the villages, the women of the collective and Soviet farms are being delivered in modern lying-in departments of general hospitals.

Is there any wonder that the rate of maternal mortality which was frightfully high in the czarist time is practically nil now.

EXTRACTS FROM LETTER WRITTEN TO DR. SAMUEL G. PAVLO, MALDEN, MASS.

Need in the United States. Ten thousand mothers in the United States die needlessly each year in childbirth, according to the United States Children's Bureau. Of the 16,000 who die annually in childbirth, over 60 percent might be saved through adequate maternity care. " Maternal deaths are due in large part to controllable causes " is the outstanding conclusion of a committee of the Nation's leading obstetricians following a detailed study made by the United States Children's Bureau in 1933.

Dr. Louis I. Dublin, statistician of the Metropolitan Life Insurance Co., points out that the United States, with its maternal mortality rate of 7 per 1,000 live births in 1929 (last year of " prosperity "), occupies an inenviable position in relation to other nations that keep maternity death records.

The maternal mortality rate in New York City increased from 5.33 in 1921 (per 1,000 live births) to 5.98 in 1932, according to a study of all puerperal deaths made by the New York Academy of Medicine (committee on public health relations), published in 1933.

Latest figures for 1933 from the Metropolitan Life Insurance Co. shown a death rate of mothers in childbirth of 6.2 per 1,000 live births in the United States, 6.2 per 1,000 live births in New York State, and 6.4 per 1,000 live births in New York City.

STATEMENT OF ROBERT MIFFLIN SENTMAN, NATIONAL PRESIDENT OF THE FEDERATION OF ARCHITECTS AND ENGINEERS, CHEMISTS AND TECHNICIANS

Mr. DUNN. The next witness is Mr. Robert Mifflin Sentman. Mr. Sentman, whom do you represent?

Mr. SENTMAN. I am an architect, and I am national president of the Federation of Architects and Engineers, Chemists and Technicians. I live at 1808 Eye Street NW., Washington, D. C.

I am here to speak as the national president of the Federation of Architects and Engineers, Chemists and Technicians, which has a membership of 7,000 professional technicians.

The inception of our organization dates back to the beginning of the National Recovery Act. At that time the protests of technical men and women against the codes proposed by professional societies took the form of organized action. Since that time we have become the recognized spokesmen for technical employees, and have further established the leadership of our organization among professional technical employees through action in their behalf, which has centered on the abuses existing both in private enterprises and Government projects.

The industrial and economic development of the United States is founded on the technical skill and genius of its inhabitants. The technical workers whose achievements have made the development possible, never received the remuneration commensurate with their contribution to this development, despite the popular impression. Our organization, therefore, was founded with the object of securing for all professional and technical workers standards of living and economic security to which their training and achievements justly entitle them.

The existence and growth of our organization is further evidence of the fact that the architects, engineers, and other scientific workers realize that they can no longer remain passive, and that they have accepted collectively the challenge of economic conditions forced upon their recognition.

As a concrete result of the collective conscientiousness and subsequent collective study and investigation, the national convention of our federation in Chicago, December 1934, unanimously endorsed the following resolution on unemployment insurance, which endorsement I should like to read into the record at this time.

Mr. DUNN. You may do so.

Mr. SENTMAN. The resolution on unemployment insurance reads as follows:

Whereas in this, the sixth year of the crisis in the United States, 90 percent of all architects, 85 percent of all engineers, and 65 percent of all chemists have been denied the right to work through no fault of their own, and

Whereas there are some 15,000,000 workers unemployed in these United States, with 15,000,000 dependent on them, where despite enlarged resources, employment is insecure and standards of living have not been raised or maintained according to the increase in production, and

Whereas private enterprise has repeatedly demonstrated its inability to reemploy the unemployed technicians, and

Whereas the report of the Investigations Committee on Economic Security admits that mass unemployment has become a permanent problem, and

Whereas technical employees who are dependent upon salaries, must be safeguarded against loss of income and livelihood because of involuntary unemployment, and

Whereas the Wagner-Lewis bill, the Wisconsin Unemployment Insurance Act, the Townsend plan, all State acts now in existence, and other acts now being proposed and given extensive publicity, specifically do not provide or protect technical men by limiting benefits to those now employed and by limiting benefits to only those employed for long periods, while the majority of technical men are now unemployed and have always had short periods of employment, and by making the insurance contingent upon payments by the employees, when technical men have no control over their means of employment while the means of production are great enough to easily pay for this insurance, and by limiting amount of payments to substandard amounts, these bills actually become a force for reducing work standards and provide private industry with its chief weapon for obtaining cheap labor: Therefore be it

Resolved, That a genuine social insurance bill must comply with the following principles. That compensation be at least equal to the average salaries which technical men earn if permitted to work in their normal professions and localities; and be it further

Resolved, That compensation be provided by and only at the expense of the Government and the employers. That no contribution in any form should be levied upon workers and other low-income groups; and be it further

Resolved, That representatives directly elected by the workers should administer the social insurance system so that it would be operated in accordance with their conditions, interests, and needs; and be it further

Resolved, That the social insurance system does not exclude any category or class of workers from its benefits, and that the Federation of Architects, Engineers, Chemists, and Technicians of America endorse the workers unemployment and social insurance bill which embodies these principles and was introduced in the 73d Congress of the United States as H. R. 7598, now H. R. 2827; and be it further

Resolved, That the national office and all chapters of the Federation of Architects, Engineers, Chemists, and Technicians use all effective means and cooperate with all other organized groups to publicize and work for the enactment of this bill.

Mr. SENTMAN. A recent census reveals that nearly 80 percent of all professional men and women are employees. However, of this group, 90 to 95 percent of architects, 80 to 85 percent of engineers, and more than 65 percent of chemists and other technicians, are unemployed.

These figures are, however, in the absence of official or other authoritative data, based upon the Nation-wide study by the federation of professional and technical unemployment existing today as compared with the 1930 census, allowing for increases resulting from the productivity of our educational institutions. These figures but meagerly indicate the dire needs. The experience of from 2 to 5 years of unemployment still unmitigated, these men and women are facing the fact that they are and shall continue to be professionally and economically helpless, unless real unemployment and social insurance is provided by the Congress compatible with American ideals of adequacy and comfort.

Therefore, just as emphatically as we opposed the administration's inadequate program of $4,000,000,000 for public works and its so-called " benefits " in terms of work relief and a miserable pittance of $50 and less for each person a month, just as emphatically do we oppose any form of so-called " unemployment insurance " which is typified by the Wagner-Lewis bill, which fails to provide adequate relief immediately for all workers at present unemployed, and who shall continue to be unemployed for a long time through no fault of their own.

The Federation of Architects and Engineers, Chemists and Technicians and millions of other workers who have already endorsed the workers' bill H. R. 2827, refuse to face starvation until the time when the improvident terms of a bill such as the Wagner bill may become effective, and on an actual basis. We therefore endorse H. R. 2827 alone as the only real measure for unemployment and social security for the workers of this country.

Furthermore, as architects, engineers, and scientific workers, we believe that no program of public work, with particular emphasis on housing, can be adequately planned to meet the needs of the millions of unemployed or those employed workers in low-wage brackets, unless (1) such projects shall become public as to ownership and finances, (2) unless rental charges shall be based on ability to pay rather than on the cost of construction and operation and use, (3) unless the cost shall be made a general charge on industry and Government without contributions by workers or farmers, and unless there shall be no charge to workers while unemployed or unless they are receiving unemployment compensation such as provided in the workers' bill H. R. 2827.

These two major issues, (1) a true social measure of public works, particularly housing, and (2) unemployment insurance, are integrally related. Regarding both these fundamental necessities, that is, adequate unemployment and an intelligent, adequate housing program, the federation will accept no half-way measures. We repudiate the unscientific, obscure, and totally inadequate program of public works proposed by the administration at the same time that we repudiate the Wagner-Lewis bill. At the same time, the federation definitely commits itself to the Lundeen bill, H. R. 2827, as the only measure now before Congress that will actually provide social and economic security for millions of industrial, professional, agricultural, and all other workers.

Mr. LESINSKI. Did I understand you to say in your original statement that the Federation of Architects and Engineers, Chemists and Technicians does not agree with the National Recovery Act and its codes?

Mr. SENTMAN. We have not agreed to the codes as proposed by the founder society, namely, the American Institute of Architects and American Society of Civil Engineers. At that time no provision was made for professional employees, leaving them the inadequate provision of 40 cents an hour.

Mr. LESINSKI. You are speaking only of the individual code for architects and professional men?

Mr. SENTMAN. I am speaking about technical men employed under the general construction code.

Mr. LESINSKI. Are you in favor of, in sympathy with, the N. R. A. or are you against it?

Mr. SENTMAN. I am in sympathy with those provisions, the provisions allowing collective bargaining and which maintains the rights of the workers organized.

Mr. LESINSKI. That is what the N. R. A. is attempting to do for the first time in the history of this country, under section 7a of the National Recovery Act. If the employees have not regard for their own rights and have allowed the contractors to write in their own codes, it is up to the employees to fight their own battle, which they have a right to do.

Mr. SENTMAN. We learned that. You know that we are a young organization and that we did not understand.

Mr. LESINSKI. And you did not have time. You did not have an organization to back you. Now you have the right to organize, and I am happy to know.

Mr. SENTMAN. Yes, sir.

Mr. LESINSKI. I happen to know that, although many people have written that the manufacturers are against the N. R. A., and I will say yes, that the larger manufacturers are against it, but the smaller manufacturers and small retail merchants want a proper code. They want a code under the N. R. A., because that is the only protection they have. If they do not have that the big men will eat them up, and those smaller men naturally have a right to live.

Mr. SENTMAN. We want the right to fight for our demands.

Mr. LESINSKI. You have that right under the N. R. A., under section 7a, now. I have been at many hearings myself and I realize that there has not been any organization between labor and employees.

Also, I will state that in certain districts the manufacturers will not allow the employees the right of collective bargaining. I think there should be more teeth and sharper teeth put into the law to enforce the collective bargaining principle unmistakably. I believe it is the only protection the laborer has at the present time.

You also spoke of the housing program that the administration is attempting to push through. You said that you are not in sympathy with it. How will we get recovery, effect recovery, unless the administration helps in general and forces private capital to come out?

Mr. SENTMAN. Apparently my point that the present provisions are wholly inadequate if the entire $4,000,000,000 should be spent for salaries next year was missed. That would average only $21 per worker per week. Since that sum will not all be spent for wages, but the larger portion of it will be spent for material, the average pay of workers from the fund will be less than $50 per month per person. That will be compensation for men who are highly skilled in their trades. It will be used to pay men who are skilled technical and professional men.

Mr. LESINSKI. Let us say that the administration, instead of making allotments to the P. W. A., should make them to the Housing Administration, and enable individuals to go through with a contract, plan buildings, and construct them. When an individual is doing that he has to pay the regular wage under the P. W. A. plan, which plan is under Mr. Ickes. I would not like to see any money going to him, because I doubt that he would handle it properly.

Mr. SENTMAN. We believe that the needs for proper housing in this country are so great for the vast number of workers that it becomes incumbent upon the Government to establish housing as a real social utility and to plan such a program on a Nation-wide basis.

Mr. LESINSKI. Is it not true, in connection with this housing, that if the people had money, if private funds were available, industry would move ahead? There is great room in this country, no doubt, for additional buildings, and our people are willing to build if they can receive financial backing.

Would not that put many of our workers in employment? The difficulty today is that people are not able to borrow a dime in connection with their houses; they are not able to get a 40 or 50 percent mortgage on their homes. Nobody wants to loan money nowadays. It seems that practically all our money is tied up in the banks, and they are hanging on to it. They do not want to let loose of it. Is not that true?

Mr. SENTMAN. I am not a banker.

Mr. LESINSKI. Neither am I a banker.

Mr. SENTMAN. If the Government should take the initiative, on a broad basis, perhaps private capital would find its way into channels of business in an attempt to preserve itself.

Mr. LESINSKI. The testimony here yesterday was to the effect that 74 percent of the men engaged in the building industry are out of work, while other craftsmen and laborers are unemployed to the extent of from 24 to 40 percent, they being not engaged in the heavy goods industry. If we could put these building-trade craftsmen to work, naturally heavy-goods industries would move forward and absorb the workers, such as workers in transportation facilities, workers in the woods making lumber, workers in steel mills, and so forth. That would absorb all that labor—the resumption of real activities in the building industry. In short, if the building industry could move forward and become active, it would take care of all other unemployment.

Mr. SENTMAN. We believe that such a step should be taken by the Government on a Nation-wide basis immediately.

Mr. LESINSKI. I believe that everything would go along better if part of this $4,000,000,000 should be allotted to the Housing Administration for this type of work rather than be allotted to P. W. A.

Mr. SENTMAN. That has been recommended, but the sum, as I have suggested, is still totally inadequate.

Mr. LESINSKI. The sum may not be adequate; therefore let the Home Owners Loan Corporation issue some more bonds. The first $2,000,000,000 given to that organization was not sufficient; and we are attempting to get another $2,000,000,000.

Mr. SENTMAN. We believe that the set-up for the administration and the amount for conducting research work is inadequate. No central authority has been properly established wherein the technicians and workers are represented and given a voice in the proper manner of planning in fields in which they are the field men in constructive enterprise.

Mr. LESINSKI. I do not agree with you there. I come from the city of Detroit. I find that the new set-up in the housing administration that they are employing technical and professional men. The Home Owners Loan Corporation is employing architects as field appraisers, and it has taken care of as many such men as it can. I believe that it is true that you will find that such is the case throughout the whole country.

Mr. DUNN. But the percentage has been small.

Mr. LESINSKI. The Government has been doing that. Of course, the Government cannot take care of all those men.

Mr. DUNN. Referring to the housing proposition, I maintain that conditions are not what they should be, because it is an absolute fact that if one cannot prove to the satisfaction of the director of the housing institution in his locality that he has funds to repay a loan he will not get the loan. One must prove to the satisfaction of the director that he has a job, and that he can pay the principal and the interest, and if one cannot give that assurance he cannot be considered for a loan.

How would the unemployed be taken care of? If a man wants a loan of $400 or $500 to do some work on his house, unless he can show that he has an income and ability to repay the loan, he is not considered. What good is it?

Mr. LESINSKI. I recognize that a man who is on welfare relief will not build a house, because he has no funds. The ones who will build houses are those who are at work, and those who have accumulated some money. Most of the people do not have sufficient money to build. A man wants to raise money by mortgaging his home. There is no way to negotiate a mortgage.

I might surprise you by telling you that I have been in the building game for 32 years. I have been in the lumber industry, and I have met this problem. Not long ago a builder came to me and said that if he could get mortgages at the rate of 50 percent of the value of homes he could have 500 houses to build within the next 10 days. Many people are looking for money to build. It is true that we have certain classes of our citizens, such as the workers on the railroad, street-car conductors, and school teachers, who are working, who are being paid, and they want to build.

Mr. DUNN. Is it not a fact that unless they can prove to the Home Owners Loan Corporation that they can repay the loan, that they can meet the payment of principal and interest, they will not be considered for a loan?

Mr. LESINSKI. Yes; as long as they have jobs, they can get loans.

Mr. DUNN. Anybody can go to a bank and get money if he can prove that he will be in position to repay the loan.

Mr. LESINSKI. It so happens that banks do not loan on mortgages, and the same is true of insurance companies now.

Mr. DUNN. The banks in Pittsburgh are willing to advance money for this purpose if the borrowers can show that they will be in position to repay the principal and pay the interest, and, of course, if they furnish security.

Mr. LESINSKI. Under the insurance plan, Government insurance?

Mr. DUNN. Yes. If one can show that he can repay the principal and interest, he can get money from the bank.

Mr. LESINSKI. As I have suggested, a man who is unemployed and who is on welfare relief cannot construct a house because he has no funds. I am talking about those people who are working and who have funds to construct houses.

Until this new Housing Administration gets moving there is not going to be anything done worth mentioning in the building industry, which is the biggest industry in the country. That is the industry we want to get moving.

You might be surprised to know about a conversation I had only last night with a very prominent official of the Housing Administration. He told me their troubles. That concern has not sufficient funds, and has not been allotted certain things. The Government is moving altogether too slowly in that field. It should move faster and start the building industry forward, and that will help very, very materially I assure you.

Mr. DUNN. I cannot see where we will make progress until we find jobs for the unemployed.

Mr. LESINSKI. The way to put people to work is to stimulate and effect a revival in the building industry, and that will stimulate all other industries. If one part of our population is willing and able to build, and does so, that will take care of workers, not only in the building trade industries but in other industries as well.

Dr. DUNN. The $4,000,000,000 that we provided last week is inadequate?

Mr. LESINSKI. Yes; but we can add a considerable amount to that.

Mr. DUNN. As I said at the time, that amount was inadequate, and it should have been $10,000,000,000. The thing to do is to see to it that the Government appropriates sufficient funds for this purpose. That is the basis, but we cannot get the majority of Congressmen to see our point of view.

Mr. LESINSKI. The Government should, I think, print $10,000,-000,000 of Federal notes, and put the money into circulation.

Mr. DUNN. If the witness has nothing further to tell us, and there are no more questions, let us thank him for his interesting statement and hear the next witness.

STATEMENT OF WILLIAM STRONG, REPRESENTING THE UNEMPLOYMENT COUNCIL OF WASHINGTON, D. C.

Mr. DUNN. The next witness is William Strong, 213 T Street NW., Washington, D. C. Proceed.

Mr. STRONG. I am representing the Unemployment Council of Washington, D. C. In the Unemployment Council we have a membership of approximately 415. These members are, of course, unemployed workers, and they have unanimously endorsed Mr. Lundeen's bill, H. R. 2827.

Mr. DUNN. Are the 415 members of your organization all colored people?

Mr. STRONG. No, sir; they are both white and colored. They endorse the Lundeen bill because they have gone through an experience of unemployment for the last 3 years and some of them langer, and they believe that this bill is a proper one. Our members endorsed this bill after having carefully read and considered at our meetings the workers' bill and the Wagner-Lewis bill. They see the workers' bill as the only measure that will take care of their needs and of the other millions that are already unemployed.

I should like to present, further, the conditions of housing that some of the unemployed workers are forced to meet at the present time. I have visited some of the houses and they are literally and absolutely unfit for human habitation. That is a fact. I myself was very much surprised at the conditions revealed during my visits. I do not know whether I would live in those houses even if I was unable to get anything better. I do not know what I might do under such circumstances. Unemployed workers in Washington, as no doubt elsewhere, are on relief and they are forced to live in houses that are insanitary and without heat, light, and so forth. That all comes from the fact that those on relief are budgeted under the present system of relief at an amount that is definitely and unmistakably insufficient to take care of the persons on relief.

The system that the unemployed workers are forced to submit to in order to get the amount of relief given is that when an unemployed person goes to a relief station, no matter what his circumstances might be at home, no matter if his wife may be at the point of death, if he needs something very urgently, he is forced to get a number and wait to try to see the case worker. He does not get to see his case worker. The applicant for relief is told that the case worker will see him at his home. The case worker cannot go in the case of emergency and afford relief right away under the system that is now used. One is supposed to write a message and send it to the case worker and then go home and wait for the coming of the case worker, and the applicant does not know whether the answer will be yes or no. That is a poor system.

I go through the same process. I am a married man with a wife who is unable to work. I am, unfortunately, through no fault of my own, on relief at the present time, and have been there for some months. I am forced to live on $5.20 a week, which is very much short of a sufficient amount necessary to live. I work 2 days a week for that amount, and I am told to go out and get other work for the days I am not working for the relief.

Mr. DUNN. Have you any children?

Mr. STRONG. No.

It is not possible, obviously, to get work enough every week to make up the difference between $5.20 and the amount it takes to live on. If it were, of course, there would not be so many unemployed.

I have been told to get a statement from the doctor that my wife is not able to work. I got that statement and it has been given to the relief authorities; but I am still forced to live on that same $5.20 a week.

This condition does not affect me only but affects many millions who are unemployed. I appreciate that. Therefore the unemployed in Washington heartily endorse H. R. 2827, because they feel that it is the only measure that will meet their actual needs. The matter of comfort is not even thought of.

Also, it is necessary to point out that the unemployed worker who receives this very small amount is supposed to pay just as much as other persons who get, say, $5,000 a year, for groceries or whatever else he may need. Therefore the workers' bill is the only one that we can see that will fill the needs of the unemployed; and it has been, as I have stated, endorsed by the members of the Unemployment Council.

Mr. DUNN. Is your organization confined to the District of Columbia?

Mr. STRONG. Yes.

Mr. DUNN. If there is nothing further from the witness, let us thank him for his statement.

It seems that there is no other witness to be heard this afternoon, let us recess until tomorrow morning at 10 o'clock.

(Thereupon, at 4 p. m., Tuesday, Feb. 5, 1935, the subcommittee adjourned to meet at 10 a. m., tomorrow.)

UNEMPLOYMENT, OLD AGE, AND SOCIAL INSURANCE

WEDNESDAY, FEBRUARY 6, 1935

House of Representatives,
Subcommittee of the Committee on Labor,
Washington, D. C.

The subcommittee met at 10 a. m., in the caucus room, House Office Building, Hon. Matthew A. Dunn (chairman) presiding.

(The subcommittee had under consideration H. R. 2827, H. R. 2859, H. R. 10, and H. R. 185.)

Mr. Dunn. The meeting will come to order, please. The first witness this morning will be Manning Johnson. Mr. Johnson, will you please come forward and give your name and address for the record, and also tell the committee whom you represent, what organizations.

STATEMENT OF MANNING RUDOLPH JOHNSON, REPRESENTING THE NATIONAL EXECUTIVE COUNCIL OF THE LEAGUE OF STRUGGLE FOR NEGRO RIGHTS, 1695 ST. NICHOLAS AVENUE, NEW YORK CITY

Mr. Dunn. Does any gentleman on the committee want to ask the witness any questions before he begins?

Mr. Schneider. I would like to ask Mr. Johnson about his organization.

Mr. Dunn. All right, Mr. Johnson, he wants to get some information about the organization you represent.

Mr. Johnson. I am perfectly willing to answer any questions.

Mr. Schneider. Your organization consists of what percentage of the colored folk in New York City?

Mr. Johnson. Our organization is a national one. We have branches in practically every large city throughout the country. Our organization is based upon membership branches and affiliated organizations. It is more or less built on the basis of a federation. Its structure is based upon first, membership branches, and second, affiliated organizations. These branches are in existence in practically every leading city throughout the Nation. We have quite a number of churches, fraternal organizations, clubs, and other workers' organizations affiliated with it. The membership and the affiliated organizations of the League of Struggle for Negro Rights embraces approximately 136,000 Negro and white members nationally.

Mr. Schneider. Do you have white folk as members of your organization?

Mr. Johnson. White and Negro.

Mr. Schneider. That is all.

145

Mr. DUNN. May I ask, Mr. Johnson, about how many Negroes belong to the organization?

Mr. JOHNSON. Approximately 60 percent are Negroes.

Mr. DUNN. Thank you. Are there any more questions?

Mr. SCHNEIDER. That is all.

Mr. DUNN. Proceed, Mr. Johnson, with your statement.

Mr. JOHNSON. I wish to present to you the position of the League of Struggle for Negro Rights on the question of unemployment and social insurance, which is the main concern of this committee. In putting forth the position of the organization which I represent, I feel it is necessary to state that we have arrived at our conclusions on the basis of a careful and systematic and thorough study of the conditions of the Negro people throughout the United States over a period of years, and particularly in this period of extraordinary and distressing conditions, a situation of prolonged economic crisis. It is our aim to bring the startling facts that our survey has revealed as sharply as possible to the attention of this committee and to the Seventy-fourth Congress, because we feel that extraordinary measures must be taken by this Congress to remedy the awful and despairing situation in which the white workers in general and the Negro people in particular find themselves today.

The economic crisis which began in 1929 and which is now passing into a permanent depression, has robbed the working people in general, and the Negro workers in particular, of every vestige of any kind of security. The Negro people have been the hardest hit of any racial group. Of the 12,000,000 Negro people in the United States, 5,503,535 are workers. They have, as most of you know, been the last hired, have been the first fired, and compelled to do the meanest, hardest, and dirtiest work, at the lowest pay.

Because of conscious and systematic firing of Negro workers from the skilled trades, we have a situation where approximately 50 percent of the Negro workers are unskilled and semiskilled workers engaged permanently in farm and domestic work. When we consider the fact that these are the lowest paid jobs, then we can fully realize the plight of the Negro workers today. During the depression, the employers have very vigorously applied the weapon of mass lay-off, insofar as the Negro workers are concerned, until we have approximately 3,000,000 Negro workers unemployed, according to the most conservative estimate given in 1932. Since that time, this figure has steadily increased, because, when the employers were compelled to pay minimum wages in accordance with the N. R. A. codes, they began to lay off the Negro employees and replace them with white employees.

I wish to cite here that since the N. R. A., 90 percent of the Negro employees have been laid off by many big industrial firms. For example, in large industrial centers like Gary, Chicago, St. Louis, and Cleveland, 50 percent of the total unemployed are Negroes. For example, in Birmingham, 75 percent of the total unemployed are Negroes. In Pittsburgh, over 60 percent. In direct contrast to the low percentage of Negro population, the high unemployment percentage stands out, pointing to the urgent necessity of unemployment and social insurance, as provided by the Lundeen bill which is now being considered by this committee.

I want to give you just one typical example of the rank discrimination against Negroes in the administration of relief. I want to select Pittsburgh as an example. The total Negro population of Pittsburgh is 83,300. Of this number, 36,000 are on relief. The percentage of the Negro population is 6, the white population, 94. The percentage of unemployed among the Negroes is 60 percent. The percentage of unemployment among the whites is 40 percent. The percentage on relief given to the Negroes is only 13 percent, while the percentage on relief given to the white workers, who constitute only 40 percent of the unemployed, is 87 percent.

In Washington, D. C., the capital of the Nation, the seat of our Government, 78 percent of those on relief are Negroes, although they are only 25 percent of the population, which further substantiates the contention of our organization that the Negro people today are the hardest hit of any, insofar as unemployment is concerned.

There is uniform discrimination in the work relief wages that exist in the South. The Negro workers there receive 10 cents an hour less than white workers, for example in Jacksonville, Fla. In Atlanta, Ga., the Negroes receive 50 cents per day less than do the white workers. Jacksonville, Fla., is a typical example of the practice in the South of forcing the Negro population to contribute 50 percent to the meager relief funds, in order to receive relief.

Practically 85 percent of the Negroes in the South are agricultural workers. In Mississippi, 87 percent of the Negroes are agricultural workers, and in Alabama, 83 percent. In South Carolina, they comprise 80 percent, in Louisina 85 percent, and in Arkansas 85 percent.

The Farm Loan Banks, in the Southern States, make loans only to members. Of course, Negroes are refused membership, and consequently are not eligible for Federal loans. Therefore, these Negro farmers and agricultural workers are forced to make individual loans, and methods are used to force them to pay exorbitant interest rates. This accounts in large measure for the fact that 7,000,000 acres of land in Mississippi, in 1930, were sold for taxes and debts. There are other difficulties suffered by the tenants and share croppers, such as overcharging on the part of the commissary stores, raising interest rates, in many cases outright expropriation of their products. Seventy-five percent of the Negro farmers are dependent on cotton. The cotton crisis has drastically affected the livelihood of the Negro farmers. The Roosevelt agricultural program, the plowing under of acreage, has greatly affected the living standards of the Negro share croppers and tenant farmers in the South, leaving them in a predicament of almost starvation.

The large majority of the domestic and personal workers in the United States are Negro women. There are 1,576,205 Negroes employed in this field of work, the number of women, 1,152,560. It is very significant to note that the number of these women who are on relief at the present time is only 18.4 percent, despite the widespread unemployment among these workers as the result of the crisis. The Wagner-Lewis bill excludes entirely these categories of workers, which are mainly Negroes. The domestic and personal servants, agricultural and farm laborers, and also the professionals, under the Wagner-Lewis bill, are ineligible for relief. I want to at this time read to the committee the editorial from the New York Post of Tuesday, February 5, 1935:

WARNING NOTES ON THE WAGNER-LEWIS BILL

Very bad insurance.—Under the Wagner-Lewis bill, a State could provide that a worker should receive benefits only after a 6-month waiting period, that benefits should be only for 2 weeks and that the amount paid during those 2 weeks should be as low as $3 a week.

Very bad procedure.—Strong-arm methods in putting the bill through. The House Labor Committee, which should have been given the bill, was sidetracked in favor of the tightly controlled Ways and Means Committee.

The Labor Committee was sidetracked because both its chairman, Connery, and the chairman of its Subcommittee on Unemployment Insurance, Dunn, favor the Lundeen bill, which would provide real benefits to be financed by taxes on wealth and speculative profit.

Administration spokesmen were given all the time they wanted, while those who came to the hearings to oppose the bill were gagged with the 5-minute rule. One witness, Herbert Benjamin, representing unemployed organizations, was forcibly ejected.

Very bad liberal leadership.—The La Follettes, who aim to succeed the Roosevelt administration with some " genuine liberal " leadership, are supporting the Wagner-Lewis bill because it makes possible continuance of their own " Wisconsin plan " of unemployment reserves.

Under the Wisconsin plan, separate reserves are set up for each plant, a very unsound method. An employer who guarantees his workers employment for 26 weeks out of the 52 need set up no unemployment reserves whatsoever.

Mr. LUNDEEN. The editorial is taken from what paper?

Mr. JOHNSON. This is the New York Post, founded in 1801 by Alexander Hamilton, of date, Tuesday, February 5, 1935. This editorial presents the position of our organization on the Wagner-Lewis bill as clearly and as sharply as I could present it here.

Mr. SCHNEIDER. I might remark at this point, I hope the witness does not base his contention for this bill upon that editorial.

Mr. JOHNSON. No; I am only using that editorial insofar as it concurs with our opinion with regard to the Wagner-Lewis bill, and for that reason, we whole-heartedly endorse and support the Lundeen bill, which provides the only genuine type of social and unemployment insurance, which is so vital today to the masses of white and Negro workers of this country.

We feel that it is the duty of this Congress, in the face of the despairing and distressing situation that prevails, to enact the Lundeen bill, and particularly so because it covers practically every category of workers, which the other bills do not, and precisely because of the many other weaknesses and shortcomings of those bills, which I am certain have been brought to the attention of this committee by other speakers who have come here.

We support the workers' unemployment-insurance bill, H. R. 2827, because we feel that this bill is superior to all other bills presented. We are categorically opposed to the other measures that have been submitted. We are also opposed to the Roosevelt social-security plan as a means of providing relief for the masses of the unemployed, precisely because of the fact that the Roosevelt security plan does not provide genuine unemployment and social insurance; that there are, using conservative figures, 12,000,000 unemployed in these United States, and the Roosevelt security program only provides for the taking care of 3½ million, to be exact, which means that the balance will have to depend upon the local charitable institutions for relief. There are other groups who give a still larger figure than 12,000,000, but we will accept the conservative figure. That means approximately 8½ million workers will not benefit by the Roosevelt security plan. Therefore, we are categorically opposed to it.

We feel that a better system, the system proposed by the Lundeen bill, will take care of the situation. Our organization, together with the following, representing 138,000 organized Negroes in America, is busy explaining and getting endorsements for the workers' bill, in organizations of a similar character, in all the major cities. We have already gotten the endorsement of the Share Croppers Union. It has a membership of approximately 20,000 share croppers in Alabama.

Mr. DUNN. Is that union made up of 20,000 Negro share croppers?

Mr. JOHNSON. Yes, 20,000. Also, there is the Baltimore Urban League, the Y. W. C. A., the New Negro Alliance, the National Urban League, the Warren Urban League, the Federation of Colored Women, the Joint Committee on National Recovery, and a number of church organizations.

Our organization, the League of Struggle for Negro Rights, is carrying on a campaign for the passage of H. R. 2827, and doing all within our power to rally as many of the white and Negro organizations as possible in support of this bill. A basic part of our program is the struggle for genuine and adequate unemployment and social insurance at the expense of the employers and the Government. Therefore, we whole-heartedly endorse H. R. 2827 as the only bill, and urge this committee to do all within its power, to work as hard as possible, with the support that we can rally among the masses of the working people, to get this bill out of the committee and before the House of Representatives, and to get this bill passed as a necessary guarantee of some degree of economic security to the millions of unemployed workers and their families in this Nation.

Mr. DUNN. Mr. Schneider, do you desire to ask Mr. Johnson any further questions?

Mr. SCHNEIDER. The statement by the witness with reference to the share croppers, it appears to me does not set forth the reasons for the destitution of the Negroes as well as the whites. The reason, to a certain extent, is due to the A. A. A. policy in the cotton areas, wherein acreage is taken out of cultivation, largely owned by the land-owning class, who receive from the Government a certain price per acre for taking it out of cultivation. The owner of the land gets from the Government payment for taking it out of production, and the share cropper is put on the street. Is that not the fact?

Mr. JOHNSON. In the great number of cases, it is; yes.

Mr. SCHNEIDER. Principally, where the acreage is reduced?

Mr. JOHNSON. Yes; most of them are compelled to give up farming entirely and go into what they call "tenant farming."

That means to rent the land from the big landowners. Many of them who owned their own individual farms were compelled to give them up as the result of the crisis and the plow-under program, and go to tenant farming or "share cropping", as it is called, primarily, in the South. Quite a number of these former farmers have become more or less agricultural workers, working on an hourly and a daily basis, in the South.

In 1933, there was a surplus of 26,000,000 bales of cotton in the South, and since the amount consumed in America, in 1929, was only 7,000,000 bales, it is evident that the cotton industry cannot support the farmers and tenants any more, hence the sad state of the Negroes in agriculture. The only artificial life that is given to the agricultural regions is through the constant pumping of Federal funds into them, which does not reach basically the Negro share cropper and tenant farmer, but which goes into the pockets of the big landowners and the banks.

Mr. LUNDEEN. Mr. Johnson, you referred to 3½ million that are to be taken care of by the administration bill. Will you state when they will be taken care of—today, or, supposing the bill were to pass today, would they be taken care of today, or next July or next year or 2 years from now, or when?

Mr. JOHNSON. You are speaking of Mr. Roosevelt's social-security plan?

Mr. SCHNEIDER. Yes; the administration bill.

Mr. JOHNSON. This bill, if it were passed, would first apply to the more than 2,000,000 who are at the present time on the C. W. A. projects, the relief workers on the Federal Emergency Relief, employees and workers in the Civilian Conservation Corps. When we subtract the total number of workers employed on these projects from the number that President Roosevelt aims to put to work under this program, we find the following situation: That only a few thousand additional workers will be employed. I think I have in my bag available statistics on this question. If you will pardon me for a moment, I will get them.

Mr. LUNDEEN. But the first question is one of time. What I mean is, if you are going to give unemployment and old-age pensions to people after they have starved to death, that is not going to do them very much good.

Mr. JOHNSON. Of course not.

Mr. LUNDEEN. There is going to be a period of time there when there is nothing done for them.

Mr. DUNN. Do you maintain that in the city of Pittsburgh, of all the cities you have mentioned, there is more discrimination against the Negroes than in any other city?

Mr. JOHNSON. I do not say there is more discrimination, but I used Pittsburgh only as a typical example of discrimination on relief. Of course, there is rank discrimination in practically every city. I do not think we need to stretch our imagination to any great degree on this question. This is a matter that one need only acknowledge, that this has been in existence for a long time, the racial theory of white superiority and black inferiority, and this is expressed in its most concrete form in industry, in agriculture, and, of course, in the administration of relief. In industry it is manifest from the point of view that the Negroes are the last hired, they are the first to be fired. They are given the dirtiest and meanest work. They are not permitted to enter into the skilled trades, and so forth. Not only that, but a number of the labor unions, for example, have colored clauses in their constitutions. Take, for example, the internationals connected with the transportation department of the American Federation of Labor, they have the following clause:

Only sober and industrious white men are eligible for membership.

Then you have some of the national and international unions which do not have colored clauses in the constitutions, but who compel the white members to pledge that they will not propose a Negro for membership in the organization. These methods of discrimination are known to all. I do not think it is necessary for me to dwell at length on the presentation of that. In the South we know there are the infamous " Jim Crow " laws, and the most flagrant discrimination. In the North and East and West, you have the more subtle forms of discrimination, and of course this is carried into full force in the administration of relief, in practically every city throughout the Nation.

Mr. DUNN. Mr. Johnson, I want to say I agree with you. I know that is a fact. The colored people are discriminated against, and it is unfortunate we have not developed to the point that we should look up to men as men. In fact, we should all be brothers, regardless of race, color, or creed, but I want to ask you this: Are you familiar with the Old and New Testaments?

Mr. JOHNSON. I am familiar with the Old and New Testaments. In fact, I studied them quite a bit.

Mr. DUNN. I want to ask you this question: Have you found any place, either in the Old or New Testament, where it says that when the Negro dies he shall be discriminated against in Heaven or Hell?

Mr. JOHNSON. I do not recall such a passage, but you see there are many pulpit orators, who, in line with the policy of the powers that be, try to create the impression that Negroes are supposed to be kept in an inferior category. I recall reading particularly the sermon of one of the great pulpit orators during the days of slavery, who utilized the Biblical story of the three sons of Noah, the one who laughed at his father's nakedness, and the others who covered him; and when they informed Noah that Ham had laughed at him in his debauchery, he cursed Ham and all of his descendants, stating that Ham and his descendants should forever be the servants of Shem and Japheth. Shem and Japheth represented the yellow race and the white race, and therefore, from the divine angle, the Negroes are to be forever the servants of the white and the yellow race. Of course, they used that to justify their course, and to make the question a racial question. It is not a question of color. This is only artificial. It runs deeply in the economic and social system.

The powers that be are utilizing the question of race to cover up a deliberate policy to play black against white and white against black. We have seen it in practice in practically every industrial conflict, where they have used the Negro labor to break the strikes of white labor. They have used white labor to break the struggles of Negro labor, and of course this antagonism created between the white and the Negro workers prevents unity and accrues to the profit of the employers. It is the old principle that has been in existence ever since the Roman Empire divided and ruled.

Mr. DUNN. May I say, Mr. Johnson, that in my opinion the minister who spoke about Noah and his three sons did not know what he was talking about?

Mr. JOHNSON. Of course not.

Mr. SCHNEIDER. You are aware of the fact that the American Federation of Labor does not bar Negroes from membership?

Mr. JOHNSON. I am aware of the fact that during the 54 conventions of the American Federation of Labor many resolutions have been passed on this question, but still we find that in spite of these splendid resolutions this is a practice. As stated before, the national and international unions connected with the transportation department of the America Federation of Labor have flagrantly discriminated. This was made quite an issue in the fifty-fourth convention of the American Federation of Labor. I do not know if you have read the proceedings, and I am sorry that I did not bring a copy of the proceedings here today for your information, and for the information of the entire committee, in fact; that quite a number of resolutions were introduced at this convention on the Negro question, bringing sharply to the attention of the Congress this deplorable situation that existed inside of the American Federation of Labor, and the resolutions committee, in rejecting the resolution, stated that it is not within the jurisdiction of the executive council of the American Federation of Labor to interfere with the decisions of national and international unions; that the question of membership is solely a question to be handled by the international or national union itself.

Mr. LUNDEEN. You mean it is a question for the individual union?

Mr. JOHNSON. Yes. Mr. Furuseth, president of the International Seamen's Union of North America, speaking on this question, stated in essence that while he was not opposed to Negroes having membership in the International Seamen's Union, he had had this experience, that when Negroes were admitted to the union, it was found that the employers would not pay the Negro members the same wages and give them the same conditions that were given to white workers, consequently they found it impossible to find employment for Negro members. Therefore, the Negro members left the International Seamen's Union, and they in other words did not do anything about it. This clearly shows, first, on the part of the national executive council, that they are not taking this question up seriously and squarely, that they are content with just issuing resolutions, and it is obvious that the national executive council of the American Federation of Labor is in a position to speak to these national and international unions and make definite recommendations on questions of policy.

Mr. SCHNEIDER. Regarding that, just let me state to you that the American Federation of Labor cannot interfere with the autonomy of these organizations, and therefore they cannot force them, but you know it to be a fact that there are untold numbers, thousands of colored workers, who are members of the American Federation of Labor.

Mr. JOHNSON. Primarily.

Mr. SCHNEIDER. And you know that there are thousands affiliated directly with the American Federation of Labor, through the Federal Labor Union.

Mr. JOHNSON. The Federal Labor Unions, which were formed only recently.

Mr. SCHNEIDER. And you know that there are thousands of colored workers who are members of the Longshoremen's Union?

Mr. JOHNSON. Longshoremen's and Seamen's.

Mr. SCHNEIDER. And quite a number are members of the Seaman's Union?

Mr. JOHNSON. Yes; quite a number.

Mr. SCHNEIDER. And you know also that these unions that admit colored workers to membership in the Federation do not discriminate against or prevent promotions of colored workers to skilled and higher positions. You understand that, do you not?

Mr. JOHNSON. Yes, but in a number of instances——

Mr. SCHNEIDER. You are leading this committee to believe that there is a rank and unfair discrimination.

Mr. JOHNSON. Particularly in the national and international unions of the transportation department of the American Federation of Labor. Every union connected with that department, without exception, has a color clause; not only that, but the policy of the American Federation of Labor, according to its constitution, is not to organize Negro and white workers into the same unions, but to organize them into separate unions.

Mr. SCHNEIDER. Of course that is not true, except in part.

Mr. JOHNSON. I am sorry I do not have the constitution.

Mr. SCHNEIDER. It is true that they organize them into separate unions, under certain circumstances, where a situation prevails that makes it quite necessary. The union to which I belong has both skilled and unskilled colored workers in it.

Mr. JOHNSON. That is good.

Mr. SCHNEIDER. They have the same rights in every respect.

Mr. JOHNSON. That is good.

Mr. SCHNEIDER. It is true, is it not, that in the codes the colored worker is discriminated against?

Mr. JOHNSON. Exactly—the textile code, the laundry code in the South, and others.

Mr. LUNDEEN. Mr. Chairman, I think this is a very interesting discussion, but I think we ought to get back to the bill, and I would like to ask, Mr. Chairman, if the Congressman has completed——

Mr. SCHNEIDER. Yes.

Mr. LUNDEEN. I would like to ask the speaker, Mr. Johnson, if there is any discrimination against the colored people in this bill?

Mr. JOHNSON. No; there is no discrimination in the Lundeen bill.

Mr. LUNDEEN. And you are satisfied with the bill? The colored people are satisfied with it?

Mr. JOHNSON. I am satisfied with it, and they are satisfied with it, and I want to tell you of an interesting experience that I had in New York Saturday. I am president of the Negro Workers Council. We have representatives of a number of Negro organizations and various trade unions of the American Federation of Labor, and every one of the members at that meeting spoke on the Lundeen bill, and spoke of the tremendous support that this bill is getting among the members of their respective organizations, and they represent the sentiment of thousands of Negro workers in New York, which goes to show that this bill itself, is becoming the bill to the masses of Negro as well as white workers of this country. I am certain that with the work of the various organizations and trade unions of the American Federation of Labor that are pushing this bill to-day, and who will take it to every nook and corner of the country, they will be able to arouse millions of people in support of this bill.

We have not seen yet the broad united-front movements around this bill that will take place in the near future. The Washington Congress will be as nothing compared with the united-front move-ments that will develop on a national scale. There is already, I might say, under way, and I am in a position to know, because I travel quite a bit, a movement in every locality for the gathering to-gether of the trade unions and fraternal organizations and churches to fight for the workers unemployment insurance bill, the Lundeen bill, and it is only a matter of time before these masses who realize the insecurity of their position are going to rally in support of such a Congress, and I feel this, that it is our duty to go forth and push this campaign to the limit, to bring in millions for this fight, and I am certain this bill will come out of this committee and be passed into law by this Congress.

Mr. LUNDEEN. In this connection, I would like the record to show, so far as I am concerned, since the question has been brought up, while I have only four colored precincts in my district, and a rather small population compared with other districts mentioned here today, I certainly want not only a new deal but a thoroughly square deal for the Negro in America, not only in my district, but in every district.

Mr. DUNN. And I agree with you.

Mr. LUNDEEN. I think the entire committee feels that way.

Mr. DUNN. Yes, they are treated worse than animals. I do not hesitate to make that statement.

Mr. JOHNSON. I wish to state in behalf of the organization our appreciation for the splendid work which you gentlemen have done so far, and we hope that you will continue to work and fight for the enactment of this bill. If that is done, I feel that it will be one of the greatest contributions we could make to the American toiling people today, and we are going to rally all we can in support of this fight, to make it a successful one.

Mr. DUNN. We thank you, Mr. Johnson, because your address was splendid. We have learned a great deal from you, and we appreciate your coming before the committee.

Mr. DUNN. Our next witness will be Mr. Benjamin C. Marsh.

STATEMENT OF BENJAMIN C. MARSH, EXECUTIVE SECRETARY, THE PEOPLE'S LOBBY, WASHINGTON, D. C.

Mr. MARSH. My name is Benjamin C. Marsh, executive secretary of the People's Lobby. As I have not been before this special com-mittee before, Mr. Chairman, I would state that the People's Lobby is a volunteer organization, and incorporated, working for legisla-tion and on administrative measures here in Washington. The presi-dent is Prof. John Dewey, formerly of Columbia University. The other members of the board are Mrs. Ethel Clyde, vice president.

who is in several similar organizations; Dr. John H. Grey, former president of the American Economic Association; and Dr. Harry W. Laidler, who was formerly president of the National Bureau of Economic Research and is now director of the League for Industrial Democracy, as executive secretary.

I want first to read a formal statement—it is very brief—if I may, it will outline the position of the lobby, and then I will make my own comment, if I may, Mr. Chairman. I will be brief.

Mr. DUNN. Yes. Proceed.

Mr. MARSH. The People's Lobby advocated Federal unemployment insurance 6 years ago, when it might have been started on an actuarial basis. That is now impossible to meet the present situation, because of the number of unemployed, and the length of time most of them have been unemployed, resulting in almost total exhaustion of savings, if any, and in many cases heavy debt. The Lundeen bill is in fact income insurance, the income to be paid by the Federal Government.

The People's Lobby has not, and does not, advocate unemployment insurance as a solution of the problem of unemployment. It realizes there is no solution for the unemployment of employables, except socialization of ground rent, of all natural resources, and natural monopolies, and of all basic industries to be acquired by the Government for a reasonable minimum payment, and at a minimum rate of interest.

I might state that that is the program of the People's Lobby, and bills along this line will be introduced in Congress.

The great significance of the Lundeen bill, as we view it, is twofold:

First. It compels the Federal Government to meet currently its obligation to maintain on a decent basis, those who cannot obtain employment.

Second. It will compel the Federal Government to expedite the socialization of ground rent, of natural resources, natural monopolies, and basic industries, since not even wealthy America should maintain an army of 11 or 12 million unemployed, in idleness permanently, as people are fed, clothed, sheltered, educated, cultured, and provided for, out of production, not out of distribution of funds, except to the unemployable.

The recent book of the Brookings Institution on "The British Attack on Unemployment", by Messrs. Hill and Lubin—Mr. Lubin is now Commissioner of Labor Statistics—says that the British unemployment benefit fund "in the 14 years ending March 1934, had incurred a deficit of approximately $671,000,000."

It also states:

Of the total cost of $4,486,000,000, employers and workers paid $2,126,000,000 and the national Government $886,000,000 in premiums. The remainder, excepting a $107,000,000 surplus carried over from the earlier fund which had existed since 1911, came from the treasury. In all but 3 of the 14 years, deficits resulted.

This in spite of the fact that reserves had been built up.

The problem of old age must not be confused with the problem of unemployment insurance or relief of the employable unemployed.

We, the People's Lobby, cannot pass on the amount to be paid unemployed under the Lundeen bill, but obviously it must be sufficient to permit a health standard of living and must be paid during the entire time of unemployment, though the cost of this varies in different places.

The administration's so-called "Economic Security bill" is not practical, since no State can be compelled by the Federal Government to start an unemployment insurance system; workers with less than cost-of-living wages or income must not pay for insurance against unemployment by insuring a submarginal standard of living, which would be involved, and the premiums of the unemployed would have to be paid by relief agencies.

We are probably a decade too late for real actuarial unemployment insurance. I am now discussing, and I am going to do it conservatively, where the money can be raised for this.

In 1933, the total net income of the 320,503 persons with incomes over $5,000 was $4,053,653,000, upon which they paid in Federal income taxes and surtaxes $333,267,000; the net income of corporations reporting net income was $2,506,078,000, upon which they paid in income and excess profits taxes $353,916,261; the total net estate reported was $712,588,000, and the total tax liability was $59,429,000. In the same year the total of taxable gifts was $36,025,000, the net only $17,879,000, upon which the tax was $1,111,000.

At the close of 1932 the cash assets of the 392,021 corporations filing balance sheets was $15,917,202,000, and their tax-exempt investments were $11,916,864,000. Both are probably less now. We have got to be fair. They have been paying a lot out in dividends and in interest.

Obviously, $3,000,000,000 to $3,500,000,000 can be obtained by the taxes suggested in the Lundeen bill, if you will add to it a small provision, page 3, to make it read, "Further taxation necessary to provide funds for the purposes of this act shall be levied on inheritances, gifts, and individual and corporation incomes of $5,000 a year and over, and corporation surpluses." They will hang onto those surpluses and pay them out in dividends and interest, unless you apply a direct tax on them.

Mr. SCHNEIDER. They would pay them out as stock dividends?

Mr. LUNDEEN. "And corporation surpluses" are the three words added?

Mr. SCHNEIDER. They will pay them out in stock dividends, which are not subject to a personal income tax.

Mr. MARSH. Yes; but, of course, they paid out a lot directly. I have got some figures on that, but I was not going to encumber the record. As Congressman Schneider says, a lot has gone out in addition to the stock dividends to which he refers, as dividends and as interest.

Mr. LUNDEEN. The words you add there are "and corporation surpluses"?

Mr. MARSH. Yes. You see, the Government cannot compel them to pay out their surpluses in dividends. They may even in some instances reduce possibly their rate of interest. They perhaps could maintain their surpluses to pay their stockholders. The Government has got to decide that the American people who created those profits which are now in corporation control as surpluses, are the ones who are entitled to be maintained.

Mr. SCHNEIDER. Right on that point, may I ask this?

Mr. MARSH. Yes; Congressman.

Mr. SCHNEIDER. The sentence with reference to that tax feature reads: "Further taxation necessary to provide funds for the purposes of this act shall be levied on inheritances, gifts, and individual and corporation incomes." It is not your belief, is it, that this bill could transfer the authority to the Labor Department to increase the income tax, the inheritance tax, or the corporation tax, is it? That provides for transferring the power to increase the taxes.

Mr. MARSH. I was going to come to that. I am glad you raised the point. I will answer it now. I am not sure whether you can give this power to the Labor Department, but you will recall that in section 2, the public works section of the National Industrial Recovery Act, it was stipulated that the carrying charges for all public improvements should be met in a certain way. In other words, the same principle was adopted in that bill as is adopted here. I would not say that the retention of this section is inherent or essential to this bill. If you vote to do something, then you have got to raise money for it. I am not a lawyer. I am enough of a student of the law to know that certain courts will probably hold unconstitutional what has got to be done if we are going to get out of this mess. Therefore, I do not worry over whether a thing is constitutional or not, according to lawyers, because the last resort of a Nation is that whatever has got to be done to save the Nation is constitutional, and you are going to be up against that on this bill. So I do not go into the details of it. You have got your lawyers who will meet that point, but that is the essential thing. People are here to be taken care of.

Mr. Chairman, I do not want you to think that I have told one story to a Ways and Means Committee and another story to this committee. When I appeared, on January 29, before the Ways and Means Committee on the so-called "administration bill for economic security", I told them that the real name for that bill should be "The insecurity bill to evade the responsibility for meeting the unemployment situation." And I think that was really an accurate description of it.

Mr. DUNN. Did you tell that to the Ways and Means Committee?

Mr. MARSH. I told it to the Ways and Means Committee.

Mr. LUNDEEN. You read that from the report, right there, did you not?

Mr. MARSH. This is part of the transcript of my testimony.

Mr. DUNN. Yes; that is what I thought.

Mr. LUNDEEN. Mr. Chairman, he was reading from a report, when he gave that.

Mr. DUNN. Thank you.

Mr. MARSH. And for your information, I closed my testimony to the Committee with the statement, "From your faces I know I have voiced the sentiment of quite a few members of this Committee, which I trust you will express, remembering that we still have the right of freedom of speech, including that of Members of Congress." And I am very glad that there are some members of Congress who have not bowed the knee to Baal, or to the "new deal."

I would like to point out that the report which the President's own Committee on Economics Security made—and I did this to the Ways and Means Committee—is the worst indictment possible of the Administration's own bill, and constitutes a very powerful argument for the fundamental principles of the Lundeen bill which your Committee is now considering, and I would like to read two or three statements from that report of the President's Committee on Economic Security, and call to your attention that a large proportion of the experts of that Committee repudiated the conclusions of the committee, and their recommendations were ignored. They advocated distinctly that unemployment insurance should be on a national basis; in other words, that the Federal Government is the only agency which could conduct an unemployment insurance system effectively. But let me read two or three statements, with your permission, from this report of the Committee on Economics Security, and as some of your members may want to refer to it, I will note the pages from which I quote. This was printed as a Government document, of course.

Page 2: "At least one third of all our people, upon reaching old age, are dependent upon others for support. Less than 10 percent leave an estate upon death of sufficient size to be probated."

That may be rough on the lawyers, but it is rougher still on the people who do not have anything to be probated.

On page 3 of this report is a splendid argument for the Lundeen social insurance bill. I quote:

The one almost all-embracing measure of security is an assured income. A program of economic security, as we vision it, must have as its primary aim the assurance of an adequate income to each human being in childhood, youth, middle age, or old age—in sickness or in health. It must provide safeguards against all of the hazards leading to destitution and dependency.

Well, that sounds fine. In the estimates that were given of the payment under Federal subvention for State unemployment insurance, it was stipulated for the first year, which starts July 1 this year, the Federal Government would appropriate $5,000,000. Well, there are something like 10,000,000 unemployed. Mr. Green, of the American Federation of Labor, recently reported ten million one hundred thirty-odd thousand. I will be conservative, now. After giving voice to this marvelous statement of the responsibility of the Government for security, this Committee on Economic Security—and I am going to tell you, as I said to the Ways and Means Committee, I do not blame them. They were under the thumb. I will not say whose thumb—this committee suggested all of 50 cents a year, a cent a week as the Federal Government's contribution. They raised it ultimately to $5—another $50,000,000, for 10,000,000 unemployed, and I am being conservative on the number of the unemployed. If I were not a preacher's son I would call it a "darned swindle."

Mr. SCHNEIDER. Pardon me. That was not the Ways and Means Committee?

Mr. MARSH. No.

Mr. SCHNEIDER. It was the Committee on Economic Security?

Mr. MARSH. Not the Ways and Means Committee—the Economic Security Committee.

Mr. DUNN. It was 50 cents a year?

Mr. MARSH. Fifty cents a year was the Federal Government's contribution, to provide safeguards against all of the hazards leading to destitution and dependency.

Mr. DUNN. If there were 50 weeks in the year, that would be a penny a week, but since there are 52 weeks in the year, it is not quite a penny a week.

Mr. MARSH. I was using round figures. It would not pay the postage on mailing unemployment benefits.

Mr. DUNN. No; that would not furnish me a good "beef stew" 1 day.

Mr. MARSH. I will say that it would provide all the food that the people who advocate it are entitled to, if you will pardon me for being rather brusque.

Mr. DUNN. I agree with you, those people who advocate that should be compelled to live on 50 cents a year.

Mr. MARSH. Before I get through, with your permission, I am going to suggest some methods of getting this through, because, on the 28th of this month, I will have been over 17 years in Washington, and I have seen Senators, Presidents, and Members of the House of Representatives come and go.

Mr. DUNN. May I say, Mr. Marsh, I know that you are, you are the one man struggling for the unfortunate laboring people.

Mr. MARSH. Mr. Chairman, this summer I visited four Scandinavian countries, and Russia, Poland, Germany, England, and France, and in all those countries they have different forms of unemployment insurance. I made it a point to talk with different types of people, government officials and others, as to unemployment insurance, and none of them would give it up. I noticed a dispatch in this morning's New York Times: "New British dole fails in a month. Labor minister tells House of Commons injustices to the uninsured will end. Payments will be larger. Stanley says rules will be ignored to permit speedy relief to sufferers."

Well, what is good for England, which is a relatively poor country compared to us, is certainly essential in America, because England, with approximately half our wealth and half our income, raises almost twice as much from income taxes, personal and corporation, as we do in the United States. In other words, we could raise easily four times as much as we do, without any injustice.

I went to the inland revenue office in London this summer and asked one of the officials how they did it. "Why", he remarked, "we levy taxes to the extent we need them, and we make our people pay them." I am not suggesting that we import anybody to administer our laws, but it is a suggestion to us, and you are going to have a knock-out fight on this revenue issue. I am speaking 25 minutes, on a coast-to-coast hook-up of the N. B. C., on Saturday of this week, on pending legislation in Congress.

Mr. DUNN. What time?

Mr. MARSH. I start at 1:30 and go to 1:55, when the grand opera comes on.

Mr. LUNDEEN. You will be on from 1:30 to 1:55 in the afternoon?

Mr. MARSH. In the afternoon, yes, on Saturday of this week. I would like to quote some more from this report (page 23):

In 1930 there were 7,500,000 people over 65 years of age in this country, representing 5.4 percent of the entire population. This percentage has been increasing quite rapidly since the turn of the century, and is expected to continue to increase for several decades. It is predicted, on the basis of the present population and trends, that by 1940, 6.3 percent of the population will be 65 years of age; by 1960, 9.3 percent; and by 1975, 10 percent are going to be of that age. All told, the number of old people now in receipt of public charity is probably in excess of 1,000,000.

Also (page 24):

At this time, a conservative estimate is that at least one-half of the approximately 7,500,000 people over 65 years now living are dependent.

Children, friends, and relatives have borne and still carry the major cost of supporting the aged.

That means just what the whole relief program of this administration has meant; and let me assure you, Mr. Chairman, that I am not a partisan. I have been here long enough to know that the way to get action is to hold the party in power responsible, and not the party out of power. That may not sound like good theory, but it is good practice.

Mr. DUNN. And I agree with you.

Mr. MARSH. What we have done is to try to make the poor support the starving, and we have come very close to pushing the poor over the precipice into the ranks of the starving, because the major part of Federal, State, and local government income is derived by taxing people who ought not to pay much if any taxes. They have got to pay some.

I want to read a little further, page 25:

Men who reach 65 still have on the average 11 or 12 years of life before them; women, 15 years. A man of 65, to provide an income of $25 per month for the rest of his life, computing interest at 3 percent, must have accumulated approximately $3,300; a woman, nearly $3,600. If only this amount of income is allowed to all of the people of 65 years and over, the cost of support of the aged would represent a claim upon current national production of $2,000,000,000 per year.

I point out to you that for the total allowance for the five purposes of this economic security, the first year, something under $100,-000,000 is provided, and the maximum is under $220,000,000, which, of course, is utterly ridiculous.

I want to commend those who worked on this bill, and Mr. Lundeen, who introduced it, for the provision at the bottom of page 2, for compensation for disability because of maternity, which it is provided " shall be paid to women during the period of 8 weeks previous and 8 weeks following childbirth." That is a very important provision, because very few people realize what this depression is doing to children, both by the prenatal condition of the mother and the time after birth, and this, so far as I know—I hope someone will correct me if I am in error—I do not want to be in error, but so far as I know, aside from the small provision which is given under the maternity bill, $25,000,000 for children, this is the only provision of this nature to see that children are well born in America, and it is of very vital importance in my judgment.

Now, I have nothing more to say on the merits of this bill. Adjustments may have to be made. That is not the point. The point is that you have two competing measures before the Congress of the United States. One, the administration bill—because they have accepted responsibility for it, and I so designate the Wagner-Lewis-Doughton bill in all fairness—is an absolute evasion of the issue. We have got to come to centralized government. It is a unique thing that the States' Rights party, the Democratic party, is the one party which has passed more centralizing legislation, and practically the only centralizing legislation, the Federal Reserve Act, the Federal Farm Loan Act, the Joint Stock Act, and these various other measures.

Now, there is only one government agency—and I studied this as carefully as I could, the many times I have been abroad—which can meet economic situations within a nation, and that is the national government. It cannot be done by municipalities alone. It cannot be done by states or provinces, whatever it may be. It has got to be done by the central government. The Lundeen bill meets that fact, accepts it, and places the responsibility squarely upon the Federal Government, where it belongs. The Government, which is supposed to provide protection against a foreign foe, is the central government, and that is the only government which can provide protection against the real enemies of any country, which in every country are within that country, and not outside.

You are going to have a fight on this. You will not consider me presumptuous, Mr. Chairman, if, as I have watched a great many fights here in the past 17 years, and used to come down here before that—I say you will not consider me presumptuous if I recall to you that I wrote to every member of both branches of Congress a few days after Congress met, and pointed out that not a thing which the administration had recommended, or which it was contemplated it would recommend, would justify a single one of you in reelection, because the administration has evaded every basic issue, in our judgment. When you come up—and I am practical; I know that the millennium has not arrived in any country I have visited, including Russia—everyone of you men has a right to your own standing. You have a right, in my judgment, to appraise national issues, not according to a very well organized publicity campaign of a central administration; but whether it is going to prevent or produce results for the people in your district or in your State and for the United States; and I submit there is no possibility of getting out of the mess we are in without income insurance, as intimated in this report of the President's Economic Security Committee, and that the immediate step, to achieve that—not the final—the immediate step is the redistribution of the national income through taxation, which only the Federal Government can do. I trust that you will get the more than 50 percent, or the 5 percent of the members of the House needed, to demand that they be given a vote upon this Lundeen insurance bill.

I think you are going to have a lot of support for it. I can see that it is going to be vigorously opposed, judging from my experience with measures in the past, which Republican as well as Democratic administrations have passed. I have clearly stated the position of the People's Lobby, that we do not regard this as a solution, as I know the introducer and the members of this committee do not regard this as a solution, but the first way to change a system is to make the beneficiaries of that system pay for the keep. I remarked a few years ago to Ogden Mills that the way to break capitalism was to make capitalism pay for its keep. He said, " That would finish it."

Mr. DUNN. But did he want that done?

Mr. MARSH. It was a personal conversation, Mr. Chairman, and in 17 years here I never quoted any expression of purpose, so I know you will not press the question.

Mr. DUNN. I will not press the question.

Mr. MARSH. I suggest his record gives you a better indication than any answer I could report, but you have here a very practical step, as I see it, to force the next essential measures, and I can tell you very frankly that, personally, I will give you all the help I can on the radio; and, incidentally, I speak all over the country, as I have spoken in 20 States since the first of last September, from here to the Pacific coast. I hope the principles of this bill will be enacted.

Mr. DUNN. Mr. Marsh, I think so much of this bill that I am going to introduce exactly the same bill, and one of the reasons for doing so is because of the fact that there are so many people demanding copies of this bill, and the way to get more copies is for another Congressman to introduce the bill too.

Mr. MARSH. Maybe you can get 250 Congressmen to introduce the bill, and then I am sure it will pass. [Laughter.]

Mr. LUNDEEN. I will say for Mr. Marsh's information here that 1 year ago 30 Congressmen signed a written motion to discharge a committee and bring the bill on the floor, which was quite a surprising number, I thought. Congressman Celler of New York introduced a duplicate bill; and I join heartily in the idea that other Congressmen introduce similar bills. If we can get half of them to do it, I would only be too happy to see it done.

Mr. LUNDEEN. I am not at liberty to give the name, but one of the most prominent members of the House told me yesterday that he was going to endorse this bill before the entire membership, in a comparatively short time.

Mr. MARSH. May I make one statement in closing, Mr. Chairman?

Mr. DUNN. Yes.

Mr. MARSH. Some years ago, when Professor Dewey, who I have already indicated is our president, and I discussed this—and understand, I campaigned back and forth across the continent four times on it, speaking in most of the large cities from New Orleans to Minneapolis, and from Boston to San Francisco and Seattle—we raised this question, whether giving people a minimum of existence, which even this bill does not do, but much more than that—whether it would put them to sleep, or whether they would go ahead and demand basic economic changes which are essential. Both Dr. Dewey and I had before been in England a good deal, and we commented jointly on the fact that years ago they started this system in Great Britain. Did that put the British labor movement to sleep? No. Of course, it is not as radical as some other movements, but their members are as radical as they can be and get results, probably, in England.

We are confident that we are going to change the system in America either peaceably—which we want—or some other way—which we do not want—as the British Labor Party, have gotten better unemployment-insurance provisions and old-age pensions, and health insurance and so forth—although the Liberal Party was in power, the Labor Party forced it—they have gone ahead to demand one after another of the basic changes which have got to be made, and we are confident that what has worked in that country will work here. I would be opposed to this bill, very frankly, Mr. Lundeen, and Mr. Chairman, if I thought we were going to stop here, but as I stated, we believe it is the first step towards forcing these other essential changes. I thank you very much, Mr. Chairman, and members of the committee, for your courtesy.

Mr. Dunn. We thank you, Mr. Marsh, because your remarks were beneficial.

Mr. Marsh. The fight will start after you get the bill out.

Mr. Dunn. We are going to make a big effort to get it out.

Mr. Lundeen. I want to state that I appreciate very much the statement of Mr. Marsh.

Mr. Dunn. I thank Mr. Marsh for his contribution to the committee and his wonderful address and his splendid remarks. Congressman Moritz wants 5 minutes of our time, gentlemen. He is from Pittsburgh, and he is willing to express himself now.

Mr. Lundeen. Mr. Chairman, I favor giving Congressman Moritz all the time he wants.

Mr. Moritz. Five minutes will be sufficient.

STATEMENT OF CONGRESSMAN THEODORE L. MORITZ, REPRESENTING THE THIRTY-SECOND DISTRICT OF THE STATE OF PENNSYLVANIA (PITTSBURGH)

Mr. Moritz. I happened during the past year to be in close contact with the rank and file of the people, having been the mayor's secretary, and the mayor, being a good Democrat, having kept his door open. As the mayor of Pittsburgh, he kept his door open so that the rank and file could come in and meet him as they wished. On numerous occasions the Unemployed League of Pittsburgh came up to see him, complaining about this and that, about forfeiting their homes and being evicted. Incidentally, Mr. Lundeen addressed the Unemployed League in Pittsburgh, and I happened to be in the outskirts of the audience. I never dreamed that I would meet you here face to face, Congressman Lundeen, talking about your own bill.

I am heartily in sympathy with this bill for this reason, that we must give these people relief. I have seen so many pitiful examples come in, people who did not have anything to live on. I do not see why our Government is so slow in giving them relief. For the life of me, it breaks my heart because the Government is so slow in doing something for these people, as that is a big point. The same number of people that were out of work last year are out of work now, maybe more.

Mr. Lundeen. If you will pardon me, this bill provides for immediate action.

Mr. Moritz. I know it. Let us get it immediately. We are going to hee-haw around on this for a couple of months, and I doubt whether the Senate will go along with us. That is what hurts me. I think it will go through the House. We will go through empty motions and get nowhere, getting the revenue. We are all right, but there are resources that we ought to get hold of. Take for instance absentee landlords, England puts a tax of 50 percent on Mrs. Astor's income over there, and we, like fools, let her take that income out of the country, when we make that income for her, and she does not do a thing for it. Now, that is only theory. It will take 50 years for us to get that income from absentee landlords.

The trouble with things in this country is that it takes too long to get results. That breaks a person's heart. We ought to get those results overnight almost. The Schenleys, in Pittsburgh, take out of the city of Pittsburgh thousands and thousands of dollars, maybe half a million, and we do not get a cent of it in this country. If we tapped some of those resources we would have an easier time to get along with these things that we ought to give to our helpless unemployed brothers and sisters. Those are my sentiments. I have been out of employment; and only those people who have been out of employment know what it means, the economic worry over paying the rent and buying the groceries. It is terrific, because the landlord will not take your excuses. The groceryman will not take your excuses. You have to pay cash, and how are you going to pay cash if you cannot make it? What good is it to refinance a person's home right now, and not give that same person a chance to make some money and work. If he cannot pay the building and loan company on his mortgage, or the banking house, how is he going to pay the United States Government? The next thing, he will be on relief. So, Mr. Lundeen and Mr. Chairman, let us push this along as quickly as we can.

Mr. Dunn. Mr. Moritz, there is one question I desire to ask. Do you believe it is a fact that if the Congressmen and the United States Senators were out of employment today, they would demand immediate consideration of the Lundeen bill? In other words, I do not believe any Congressman, if he were to meet with some misfortune and lose all that he had, would hesitate in supporting this bill. In other words, of all the legislation which has been presented, both to the Senate and to the House, this Lundeen measure is not only the most progressive but the most humanitarian; am I not right?

Mr. Moritz. Mr. Chairman, you put your finger right on the sore spot. There are too many Senators and too many Congressmen who have been here too many years—20 years, 25 years, or 16 years. They have forgotten what it means to be out of employment, and they just consider that people on the outside are living on a different hemisphere, a different earth, and they cannot know the real troubles and difficulties of their own constituents. They have been sitting on Easy Street for so many years that they are out of touch with their constituents.

Mr. Lundeen. I will say that, had the membership of the House and Senate gone through the experiences you have, a majority of them would be militant for the bill.

Mr. Moritz. Oh, they could not help but be that way.

Mr. SCHNEIDER. Do you not think that it should be the duty of the Government, if private industry does not do it, to provide employment for all the employables in productive enterprises?

Mr. MORITZ. Yes.

Mr. SCHNEIDER. Is it your opinion that the matter of unemployment relief can solve this problem?

Mr. MORITZ. Can solve the problem of unemployment?

Mr. SCHNEIDER. Yes.

Mr. MORITZ. It cannot; no. No; that is not the point here.

Mr. SCHNEIDER. Therefore, we must devise some plan by which the unemployed will secure employment, either in private industry or through the Government, by which they will have or be provided a decent living, and at the same time create some wealth for society.

Mr. MORITZ. Yes; that is true, but we are in an ocean. We are all either swimming or sinking, and we must throw a plank out to those who are not able to swim, and that is what this bill does, until the Government can pull them up on the boats and start them to working again.

Mr. SCHNEIDER. Why not pull them up right now?

Mr. MORITZ. That is what I want.

Mr. SCHNEIDER. And you cannot do it by unemployment. It is merely a straw to save them from drowning. You have hundreds, if not thousands, of idle factories in your city, have you not?

Mr. MORITZ. That is right.

Mr. SCHNEIDER. They are built for the purpose of providing things that society needs?

Mr. MORITZ. Yes.

Mr. SCHNEIDER. You have millions of hands unemployed, the labor of whom goes to waste, the greatest waste in all the history of the world, except war, and yet it is not employed in creating the wealth necessary to sustain society.

Mr. MORITZ. In the first place, those mills in Pittsburgh have so many inventions that they knocked out 400 men. Where 400 men used to work they now have a machine to eliminate the men; so even when they are working to capacity they do not hire as many men as they used to.

Mr. SCHNEIDER. If we put them into use right now, a lot of the millions of the unemployed, as well as those employed, might have the things they need along with a few luxuries in life that the genius of man and the construction of all these industries provide.

Mr. MORITZ. How would you do that?

Mr. SCHNEIDER. That is the problem that is confronting us now, as to whether we are going to do that, or whether we are going to just throw a straw to the fellow, to save him for the present.

Mr. MORITZ. Do I understand you to say maybe the Government will take over these mills?

Mr. SCHNEIDER. Of course, if the private industry cannot do it— or will not do it—and if no scheme can be devised by which to do it, why not? Are we going to perish as a race, rather than do the thing that will save us?

Mr. MORITZ. I wish the municipal government would take over some of the utility companies in Pittsburgh, too. We have 8¼ cents carfare, 25 cents bus fare. A taxicab, to go a mile, costs you 65 cents.

There are 65 subsidiary companies owning our Pittsburgh Railways Co., each one of them having to get a profit before the car passenger is thought of. Just think of that. The city of Pittsburgh is just in a nest of extortionists.

Thank you very much.

Mr. DUNN. I want to thank you for your contribution, and may I say in conclusion that we could start the wheels of industry immediately, if we could put money into circulation. Just let us start and tear down the slum districts in every place in the United States, construct roads, build schools, hospitals, and bridges, drain the swamps, and conduct reforestation work. In fact, we could keep on working for the next 500 years and we would not have finished. We could purify our streams, we could construct reservoirs and canals, and so forth.

Mr. MORITZ. I want to say, Mr. Chairman, I gave my maiden speech yesterday in Congress. You will find it in the Record, and in it I said that if the minority party in Congress, the Republicans, stick with the conservative Democrats, there will be a new party called the People's Liberal Party, instead of just having a few liberals in the Democratic party now.

Mr. SCHNEIDER. It might be called the Progressive Party.

Mr. MORITZ. Yes, sure. I love the word "Progressive."

Mr. DUNN. I love the word "Humanitarian."

Mr. MORITZ. Thank you very much for this opportunity.

Mr. LUNDEEN. Before we recess, I would like to ask Congressman Moritz if he desires to insert any data or statement in the record? If so, I think we should give him unanimous consent to do so.

Mr. DUNN. Yes.

Mr. MORITZ. Thank you very much, Mr. Lundeen. I want to get better acquainted with you.

Mr. LUNDEEN. I will be delighted.

Mr. DUNN. We will recess, gentlemen, until 2 o'clock.

(The hour of 12:10 p. m. having arrived, the subcommittee took a recess until 2 o'clock this afternoon.)

AFTER RECESS

The subcommittee reconvened at 2 p. m.

STATEMENT OF MR. HERBERT BENJAMIN

Mr. DUNN. Will you state the organization that you represent, for the benefit of the committee?

Mr. BENJAMIN. I am appearing before this committee as the executive secretary for the National Joint Action Committee for Genuine Social Insurance. This is the continuation committee of the National Congress for Unemployment and Social Insurance which was held in Washington, D. C., on January 5, 6, and 7, 1935.

I should like to say that I am going to confine myself to some very brief preliminary remarks, because I feel that this committee has provided a very ample and adequate opportunity for the presentation of the problems involved, and is making a very serious study of the question. I feel that I would much rather devote myself to answering any of the questions that may have arisen in the minds of the members of this committee in the course of the hearings thus far, rather than to go into a lengthy presentation. I think that this is especially necessary, because while I feel that the movement for genuine unemployment and social insurance has made very great headway in the course of the past 2 years, particularly, and appears at the present time as a very practical issue before the Seventy-fourth Congress, it is nevertheless clear that precisely for this reason there will be developed in the present Congress a much more vigorous opposition to genuine unemployment and social insurance than has been the case in previous instances when it was still possible to practically ignore the question.

I therefore feel that it would be best that we consider at the moment the problem from the point of view of the workers who are most concerned, to arm this committee, if I might put it that way, with the arguments that are being presented in behalf of this measure by the masses who are in need of such security as this measure intends to provide.

Five years of wide-spread and deep-going economic crisis have served to reveal how insecure is the economic position of the overwhelming majority of the population of this, the richest country in the world. As the result of the fact that millions have been expelled from the industries and forced into a huge army of unemployed and as the result of the struggles which the unemployed have been forced to wage in order to establish their right to live, the entire population has become acutely aware of not only the dire distress which prevails for the unemployed, but also for the aged and other victims of what are now recognized as normal hazards of the present social order. The problem of social insecurity has thus compelled the attention and consideration of not only the active radical opponent of the present social order and the academic reformer, but has become an immediate, practical, political issue of first rate importance. Even those who are opposed to the enactment of necessary social insurance legislation are now compelled to give serious consideration to the problem. The issue is coming to a head. The lines are being sharply drawn. The question is no longer: " Shall we have unemployment and social insurance? " The question has become: " What kind? When? " And we must add, for reasons which will be explained later: " For whom? "

It is natural that under present conditions some shall see a threat in the movement for social insurance. The very fact that this movement for a greater measure of social security grows in power and in insistence, makes some feel more insecure.

Let us imagine, for example, that 100 families found themselves on an island where there were only two wells of water. One well, a very shallow one, would be available to 97 of these families. The other, an almost limitless well, would be available to only the 3 remaining families. Furthermore, the 3 families would forbid the 97 to use the water from the limitless well or to deepen the shallow well. Normally, all the families on the island would then be concerned by the shortage of water. But, while the 97 families would be concerned with the problem of how to supply themselves with necessary water, the 3 families would be concerned with how they could continue to enjoy exclusive possession of the limitless well in the face of the growing desperation of the 97.

This homely example can serve to illustrate the difference in the kind of concern that is now manifested in the problem of social insurance. We who represent the 97 percent of the population of the United States for whom insecurity means that we either already suffer or face the danger of loss of livelihood, are seeking for measures to safeguard our livelihood. The 3 percent who claim ownership of the great wealth of this country are just as vigorously seeking measures to assure their exclusive ownership and control of wealth, despite our desperate need and evermore insistent demands.

It is true that after more than 5 years of unparalleled crisis, which has caused and intensified untold and indescribable misery, suffering, and death from want, privation, and hunger, the Congress of the United States is finally giving consideration to the problem of social insurance. But, it is necessary that we examine the measures proposed in Congress with a view to determining whether they are directed toward assuring means of livelihood for the 97 percent, or are merely measures intended to fortify the position of the 3 percent who seek exclusive possession of the wealth of this country despite the growing desperation among the masses.

We intend to show that of the measures now being considered by Congress, one, the Wagner-Lewis bill, which proceeds from the President's social-security program, is deliberately designed to circumvent the demands of the masses for social insurance and thereby safeguard the wealth, profits, and privilege of the few. The other, the Lundeen workers' unemployment, old-age and social-insurance bill, H. R. 2827, is designed to provide a greater measure of social security for the masses, in the only way this can be done—at the expense of the few who now own most of the Nation's wealth.

Now, Mr. Chairman, in this connection, because I use this example, giving this relation of force, I should like, for the information of this committee, to present some facts to indicate that I have not used an exaggerated example. I will turn myself for substantiation in this case to some very respectable ladies and gentlemen who are highly esteemed in the city of Washington, and the United States, by some people, and never get thrown out of committee rooms.

Mr. DUNN. Pardon me. You are not expecting to be thrown out of here this afternoon?

Mr. BENJAMIN. I certainly do not expect to be thrown out of here, because I feel that this committee is very keenly desirous of establishing the needs and establishing also the demands that are being made by those suffering from the crisis.

I am referring to another incident, which I need not go into at the present time.

However, I shall call first upon Secretary Wallace to testify in this connection, and quote from a dispatch, an Associated Press dispatch, published in the New York Times on December 7. Mr. Wallace said that in 1929 the 36,000 families with the greatest incomes received as much as the 11,000,000 families with the least incomes; and then went on to say that the vast majority of the wealth of the 36,000 families acts as an instinctive and almost unanimous unit in opposing relief proposals brought to the front by agriculture or labor.

So that we have at the same time corroboration of the fact that the group which enjoys and monopolizes the wealth of this country is a very minor group numerically; and on the other hand, corroboration of the fact that this group acts as a unit to preserve the special privileges which they now enjoy in the face of the mass destitution that prevails for the great majority of the population.

Now, a further evidence of this is provided also by the very committee which produced a report on which the Wagner-Lewis bill is presumably based; that is, the President's Committee on Economic Security, headed by Dr. Witte, which issued a booklet of charts, which booklet gives us some very interesting information in graphic form. I might say in this connection that I have been doing my very best to help circulate this booklet, but that Dr. Witte has since decided that he is not interested in having it too widely circulated.

This chart which I referred to may, with your permission, be entered in the record.

It shows on the one hand the income group with incomes of $50,000 and over, consisting of a total of 125,000 families; and then indicates that the aggregate savings of this group amount to 6½ thousand million dollars.

On the same chart, as we reach the very bottom of this pyramid, we find, first, a large family group representing 5¾ million families with annual incomes of $1,000 a year or less. This group has no savings whatever.

The second line of this pyramid consists of 10½ million families whose total income annually is under $2,000. These 10½ million families are able to set aside out of their earnings a total between them of three-quarters of a billion dollars, that is, $750,000,000, according to the 1929 figures.

Thus we have the group on top, a little speck on this chart, representing 125,000 families whose average savings amount to $52,000 each family; while down below we have, first, a group with no savings whatever; then a group with average savings of $71 per family.

Now, certainly——

Mr. DUNN. Pardon me. Is that $71 a year?

Mr. BENJAMIN. That means the total savings that they had in 1929. That might have been the accumulation of years of saving, for all we know. That was the accumulation of savings, in the year 1929, which, incidentally, is a prosperity year, the boom year of prosperity.

Now, it is this relation of force that we refer to when we speak of the group that has very good reason to be concerned in the question of unemployment and social insurance, but not in the same terms in which we are concerned with it. They are concerned in terms of "how can they continue to hold on to this immense amount of wealth" in the face of the fact that they are being constantly encircled by a growing army of millions upon millions of destitute families in this country.

Now, the measure that is before this committee represents a measure formulated in behalf of the large masses of the population of this country, and we may safely say that they are 90 percent of the population, because even Madam Perkins in her address on this question, before the President's Conference on Social Security, spoke of the 90 percent. This group is the group in whose behalf we have formulated the workers-unemployment and social-insurance bill which has been introduced by Representative Lundeen and is before this committee for consideration.

I should like to say a few words in regard to this measure, in order to establish something of its character. It is decidedly a different type of measure from those which have come before this or any other Congress in the past, and cannot be treated in the same manner as all the many bills that are being introduced for the sake of the record, for the sake of form. This is truly, in the fullest sense, a sound measure, of and for the workers. It is not the product of some individual's genius. It is a collective product, not the expression of one individual's point of view, nor an accidental formula. It is a formula based on a careful consideration of the need of the workers.

It is mindful of and related to a realistic study of the economic conditions that make such a measure necessary. It is also mindful of the political elements involved in the struggle of the masses for this legislation, the forces that are set in motion by the demand for the enactment for such a measure as this.

It is not only in name but in fact a workers' bill.

I want to say a few words to indicate in what manner it is different from other bills. First of all, why is this measure so brief? When we compare it with the Wagner-Lewis bill, with its 64 pages, the Lundeen bill looks extremely small. But when we read the Wagner-Lewis bill and try to establish what its provisions are, we find ourselves confused by a great deal of verbiage, and find it very difficult to establish just exactly what this bill would provide.

I think that this is not accidental. I think that those who are introducing such measures as these are decidedly interested in having introduced a measure which would be difficult to understand.

We, on the contrary, in formulating a workers-unemployment and social-insurance bill, have been very much concerned with making this measure state in as brief a manner as possible our needs and what our demands are. We have had nothing to conceal, because we set out with an understanding of what force we have to oppose in order that we may secure enactment of our bill, and therefore the bill has been very frank and very direct. Too, we have been mindful of the fact that it would be necessary, in order that this measure might be enacted, to make it just as simple as possible so that the large masses who had to be rallied in order to support this bill could be enlisted fully in support of the measure.

Yet in spite of this bill being so brief, there is not a single necessary safeguard omitted from this measure, with the possible exception of two items which I will deal with later, and suggest amendments to.

In order also to indicate that it is a collective product, I want to point out that this was first presented in draft form to the first national hunger march which took place in December 1931, where there were some 1,600 delegates from all types of unemployed and trade-union organizations, and it was to them that we first submitted this measure; asking them to make such contributions toward improving it as they might suggest.

It was resubmitted for careful examination to the American Federation of Labor rank and file conference which took place simultaneously with the American Federation of Labor convention in Cincinnati in 1932.

Then it was again submitted to the second hunger march, in which some 3,500 delegates participated in December 1932.

Finally it was presented, already then in the form of a congressional draft, to the Third National Convention of Unemployed Councils in February 1934.

The present measure, H. R. 2827, in its present form, was also submitted for consideration to the National Congress for Unemployment and Social Insurance which was held in this city on January 5, 6, and 7. I should like to say that in convening this congress, we did not ask the organizations to send delegates merely to endorse the workers-unemployment and social-insurance bill. We asked them to accept some principles which we considered to be essential to genuine unemployment and social insurance, and then suggested that they send their delegates free to make any contribution toward formulating such a measure as they might find necessary. And yet the congress, consisting as it did of some 3,000 delegates, unanimously endorsed this measure.

I should also like to point out that the bill has already been submitted in, I might say, tens of thousands of mass meetings, lectures, open forums, union local meetings, lodge meetings, veterans' post meetings, professional organizations, farm organizations, church organizations, and also to expert social workers, attorneys, economists, and so forth; and in all these instances there was a very thoroughgoing discussion taking place on the bill, suggestions for amendments were constantly made and being offered from different directions. All these suggestions were being discussed, and it was only on the basis of all such discussions as these that the bill in its present form was finally adopted.

So that here you may say that we have truly a collective product that rises out of the basic needs and demands of large masses of the population of this country.

In addition, and this I would like to say especially because one of the members of this committee, who is not present today, raised the question in the discussion on the first day of this hearing when he suggested that the various organizations that have endorsed this bill did not really know what they were endorsing, that they were simply for out-of-work insurance, and that when somebody came along and offered this bill to them, they accepted it. But I want to point out that this is decidedly inaccurate, on the basis of my own knowledge and experience with this matter.

Personally I have made several tours across the country, in lectures and mass meetings that were organized around this bill. I also know that in every instance where we presented this measure, we have met with very vigorous opposition. We met with this opposition when we first tried to present this measure in the hunger march of 1931, and in the hunger march of 1932. We met with it again in some manner when we appeared before various organizations to submit this measure.

The official leadership of the American Federation of Labor—and here I refer to the executive council and its officers—have on numerous occasions sent out letters to the various locals of the American Federation of Labor, urging them not to support this bill; and when we received the support of over 3,000 locals of the American Federation of Labor, for the bill, it was in spite of these instructions which they had received. If we did not receive the endorsement of a larger number of locals, it is probably due to the fact that we did not have forces in some instances sufficiently well informed to be able to meet the vigorous opposition that was offered against it.

But certainly the endorsements that have been secured have been secured, especially from the American Federation of Labor, in the face of very vigorous opposition.

Mr. DUNN. Pardon me, Mr. Benjamin. Did you say the executive council of the American Federation of Labor?

Mr. BENJAMIN. Yes, sir.

Mr. DUNN. Sent out these notices telling their different organizations not to support this bill? Did they give any reason why?

Mr. BENJAMIN. Yes, sir; and I will deal with those reasons. They gave a number of reasons, and this was incidentally also the kind of reasons that were offered in many other types of organizations where opposition was expressed by the official leadership.

First of all, many of the official leaders of many organizations are very much interested in keeping the good favor, the good will of people who are in power, people who have political influence and power; and when the administration, let us say the Federal administration, was opposed to unemployment and social insurance, they did not wish to put themselves in opposition to these forces by coming out for it.

Thus, for example, in 1930 and 1931, when Mr. Hoover was still President and when he was declaring that unemployment insurance represented a dole which was degrading to the American workers and which would destroy their rugged individualism, Mr. William Green echoed these sentiments, and also said that unemployment insurance is a dole and would degrade American workers. He went even further and stated, as he did in the Vancouver convention, that unemployment insurance would be a death blow to the trade-union movement in the United States.

Again, however, in 1932 and in 1933, after there had developed a considerable sentiment in the American Federation of Labor which crystallized itself in the form of the Rank and File Committee for Unemployment and Social Insurance, and when the pressure generally upon the Government for unemployment insurance grew, Mr. Green also trimmed his sails in this respect. And I use Mr. Green here only as an example, and I will explain why, because he represents the executive council.

But the point I wish to make is that in every instance the opposition came from the leading officials, and was, of course, related to the general policy which they had in relation to their, what I may term, amiable relations with the administration and Government forces.

Then the charges were made that the bill is impracticable, that it attempts to get too much, that it is inconsistent with the views of

certain experts, that it was unpopular in official ranks and did not
have a chance of being passed, that it is unconstitutional, and finally—and this was most frequently the case—that it was simply a
Communist measure and therefore did not merit any consideration
in the first place.

In this connection, too, alternative measures were being offered to
the masses and the organizations, as against this measure. And I
point out these various forms of opposition in order to indicate that
such support as has already been won for the workers' unemployment
and social-insurance bill has been won in the face of all this opposition.

Now, think of this, for example. So much has been said in the
last few weeks about the Townsend plan. I have discussed this
question with a number of Members, and they tell me that, outside
of California, they received not a single postal card on the Townsend
plan, but they received thousands of cards from all over the United
States on the Lundeen bill, asking for the enactment of this bill.
Yet the newspapers, by reason of the fact that they really fear this
measure and do not fear the Townsend plan, knowing that the
Townsend plan can be a very good red herring to draw attention
away from social insurance, have given publicity to the Townsend
plan, and have yet avoided very studiously any attention to the
workers' unemployment and social-insurance measure.

It is a most difficult thing to get any news in connection with the
development of that measure. The example of this committee is
another instance. It is very difficult to get the local press to mention the fact that these hearings are taking place; and yet, in spite
of these obstacles, it has been possible for us to develop such a broad
mass movement in support of this bill, as is indicated by the number
of endorsements which have already been recorded in these hearings,
and indicated also by those present at the congress or participating
in other activities connected with it.

Mr. DUNN. Pardon me. I want to substantiate the statement you
just made about the Townsend bill and about this bill. Now, I represent the Thirty-fourth District in Pennsylvania, which is a very
large district. May I say that I do not believe I have received over
a half dozen letters to support the Townsend bill; however, I have
received quite a number of letters and cards from the State of California. In addition to that, I have received many letters and cards
from all over the country asking me to give my utmost support in
behalf of the Lundeen bill, H. R. 2827. I just want to substantiate
your statement.

Mr. BENJAMIN. I am very glad to have you state that, Mr. Dunn,
because that conforms also to the reports that I have had from quite
a number of Members of Congress in this connection. We know, for
example, that our office publishes—and some remarks were made
today about the many demands being made for copies of this bill—
we published over 1,000,000 copies of the Lundeen bill last year ourselves, printed them and sold them at $2 a thousand. That is, we
had to sell them, because we could not give them away free, but we
sold them to the various organizations throughout the country at $2
a thousand, over a million copies of them, and disposed of them in
that way. In many communities, in many localities, the organizations themselves printed copies of the bill and distributed them.

We published, we know, over 650,000 postal cards and sold them also at $1.50 a thousand, the kind of cards that you refer to, that you have been receiving through the mail calling upon you for the support of this bill. These are issued directly from our office, so that we have a definite record of the extent to which support is being given to the measure, apart from the various independent activities being developed in this way.

And yet it is true that with all this mass support, it is extremely difficult to get any mention of this in the public press.

For example, again, how does it happen that over 60 municipal legislative bodies, that is, the city councils of a large number of cities, 60 of them and more, have endorsed the workers' bill and memorialized Congress for its enactment? This did not come by accident, with a city such as St. Louis, with a city like Milwaukee, Portland, Oreg., and Spokane, Wash., endorsing this bill in their common council or city council, memorializing Congress for its enactment. This does not happen by accident but as a result of the fact that so many organizations in those cities have concerned themselves with this measure and feel so much interest in it. There developed so large and insistent a demand upon their own municipal bodies that those municipal bodies were compelled to act in accordance with the demands made upon them to memorialize Congress for the enactment of this bill. And even that action received very little publicity.

Mr. DUNN. May I say on behalf of the newspapers in Pittsburgh that they have been giving this bill a great deal of publicity, and almost every day since we started these meetings there has been an article in the papers, and also there was publicity before the meetings started. I want to say that much in behalf of the newspapers of the city of Pittsburgh.

Mr. BENJAMIN. Well, I might say that generally there has been a slight improvement in this connection of recent date. It has become increasingly difficult for the newspapers to ignore this demand. You have heard in the statement submitted to you by Mr. Johnson this morning the editorial quoted from the New York Evening Post also lending their support to this bill. There is a development in that direction which is coming in the face of a great deal of difficulty.

But the mass demand for this bill is becoming so great that it becomes increasingly difficult to ignore it.

I know, for example, Mr. Dunn, that in your congressional district, in the town of Glassport, there was a local newspaper that conducted quite a campaign last year in support of this bill. They had coupons published in the paper, which were to be torn out of the paper and then sent to the Congressman calling upon him to support the bill.

Mr. DUNN. That is adjoining my district; it is not in my district.

Mr. BENJAMIN. Pardon me, then. Now, what does this bill propose to provide? I said that this bill based itself first of all on the recognition of the needs of the masses; and that is correct. In this respect we are just as firm, just as unyielding, just as uncompromising, as are the forces opposed to us. We are just as determined to make this bill a benefit for the masses as the opposition is to have a bill that will safeguard them against the danger that they may have to contribute substantial amounts for the support of the unemployed.

We have therefore framed this measure with a view to assuring that it will meet the needs of the present situation. For that reason, therefore, we first of all make provision for compensation against all loss of earnings; and when I say all loss of earnings, I mean by that, losses that are occasioned by loss of employment, by industrial accidents, by illness, by old age, during the period of maternity, for part-time work, and for all types of loss, not merely for certain specified types of loss of earnings.

Secondly, it must be an amount that will maintain living standards.

Now, we have maintained that the productive capacity of this country is such as to be capable of affording to all of the population an adequate standard of existence.

We have maintained that the standard of living of the masses of employed as well as the unemployed has been too low, even in the best times. We have shown this by the figures presented by the National Industrial Conference Board which pointed out that $1,737.32 a year, or $34.56 per week was necessary in order to maintain a family on a basis of health and decency in 1929, and the governmental estimate was even higher; it was $36.85 a week. And yet the very same figures showed that even in the best of years, that is in the decade from 1920 to 1930, the masses of the population of this country were receiving from 12 to 47 percent less in average income than this minimum of health and decency, which, according to the Government and the National Industrial Conference Board, was necessary.

Now, we said that in the face of this kind of situation there is no reason why the masses, who are not responsible for unemployment, shall be obliged to pay any further, to suffer any further losses in consequence of unemployment; that there is no reason why the standard of living of the American population should be reduced during the period of the crisis; and that therefore it is necessary to provide compensation for losses that will be equivalent to the average wages which the workers received or would have received if permitted to work in their own occupation or industry and locality, and in no case less than $10 per week, plus $3 for each dependent.

For the same reason we have also been insistent on the provision that this compensation shall be provided for all workers, and for this reason we, first of all, oppose State unemployment insurance as against national unemployment insurance.

We maintain that an adequate system that can meet the needs of the situation cannot be provided by the States.

We maintain that it is incorrect to ask of the unemployed, who are now suffering, that they shall wait until the various 48 States get around to enacting legislation on this measure.

We maintain that it would be wrong for us to allow the Negro masses of this country to be left to the mercy of the Bourbons in the South who control the State governmental power, in the Southern States where Negroes are Jim Crowed and discriminated against, to allow these States to enact legislation which would undoubtedly increase the discrimination against the Negro population.

We maintain for the same reason that workers should receive this compensation regardless of their nationality; and in this connection we have an amendment to offer, even to H. R. 2827, as it appears now, because it does not conform in this respect to the draft that we originally drew, in that it excludes from its provisions workers who are not citizens of the United States. Now, we believe that the workers, whether they be citizens or not, who are foreign born, have come to this country largely on the invitation and by the persuasion of the industrial powers of this country. They wanted cheap labor; they brought these workers here; they put them to work at dirty work, and hard work, and low wages. Now they are left stranded, after they have helped to contribute to the wealth of this country. Now, it is difficult for many of those to become citizens. The fees in connection with being admitted to citizenship are too high. We feel that they should not be excluded from the benefits of such an act as this, and therefore we propose an amendment that would specify that workers shall be entitled to these benefits regardless of citizenship.

Also, they should be entitled to these benefits regardless of occupation. That is a very important element here, as is indicated already in the reports that so many have made about marginal workers, agricultural workers, servants, domestics, Government employees; all these, who are excluded from benefits of every other act, should be included.

We do so also for another reason, because we recognize that it is not possible to maintain a decent standard of living and existence for one section of the population, that is, for one section of the working population, as long as there will be low standards for other sections of the population. We feel, for example, that as long as there are 12,000,000 Negroes who are subject to discrimination and abuse, and are therefore subjected to being forced to work for lower wages, that the tendency is to reduce the wage level to the levels that are created for the lowest paid, for the masses discriminated against. Therefore we feel that if any group is left out in such a measure, not only this group will suffer but all groups will suffer that depend on wages, salaries, and self-employment for their existence.

Finally, in this connection, we have, guided by the same principles, insisted, as does the Lundeen bill, that such unemployment and social insurance must and can be provided only by the Government, only at the expense of the Government and the employers. It is not possible for such insurance as will really insure to be provided independently by a private employer. We know, for example, of some instances where, by the action of the organized workers, it has been possible to force certain employers to establish an unemployment plan. For example, the furriers industry in New York City, where the furriers union carried through a strike which won this provision from the employers. But only very recently, in a congressional committee, this union was charged with using racketeering methods to compel employers to pay funds into the union treasury, because they were compelling the employers to abide by an agreement that they shall set aside a reserve fund under the control of the workers for this purpose. We know that in any case it would not be possible to provide an adequate amount of compensation to the workers on the basis of the individual-plant-reserve plan.

Especially we want to take this occasion to deal with the Wisconsin plan, which is based upon reserves. I heard the Wisconsin plan very strongly urged in the President's conference. The speaker who spoke on behalf of this plan was the representative of the Allis-Chalmers Motor Co., on the ground that this was an American plan. We know that the people who own the wealth of this country think that America belongs to them; that everything they are for is American, and everything they are against is un-American.

Mr. SCHNEIDER. May I say at this point that the representative of the Allis-Chalmers Co., and practically all other employers in Wisconsin, did not accept the Wisconsin plan of unemployment compensation until they were forced to do it?

Mr. BENJAMIN. I would put it a little differently. I agree with you in part, but I would say, not until they were forced to do it, but until they found it expedient to adopt such a plan, rather than genuine unemployment insurance.

Mr. SCHNEIDER. That came only since they had a change of heart.

Mr. BENJAMIN. It is very interesting to hear you mention that, because it is exactly what is happening in the case of all the employers interested at the present time. They have fought very vigorously against unemployment insurance, against the very thought and the very principle of it in the past. Today, when it is no longer expedient to openly oppose unemployment insurance, they come forward and say, "We are for it, but we are for a practical kind, we are for an American kind." And then they proceed to present such a plan as this.

Now, I referred, when I spoke of the representative of the Allis-Chalmers Motor Co., to H. W. Storey, vice president of the Allis-Chalmers Manufacturing Co., whose speech before that committee I have before me in manuscript form. Now, he urged it as an American plan; and in this connection I want to point out what must be kept in mind in all these connections. Some of you remember the open-shop question. From 1920 to 1923 particularly, when the National Manufacturing Association decided upon this plan, they said, "We are for the open shop, and this is the American plan."

Now, always that plan which will safeguard the profits, their plant, their wealth, is the American plan, and anything which does not is imported from Heaven knows where.

Mr. SCHNEIDER. I just wanted to put that statement in the record at that point. And in addition to that, I would like to say that the working class in Wisconsin were, from the beginning, for a much better plan of compensation than what was secured in that enactment; and they are now for the best possible plan that we can get of unemployment insurance.

Mr. BENJAMIN. I have no doubt of that, and I know they are very strongly opposed to such a plan as this, which we have been discussing; firstly, because that plan, although adopted 3 years ago, has not yet begun to pay a single cent to the unemployed.

Mr. SCHNEIDER. Well, it did not go into effect until last June.

Mr. BENJAMIN. That is true, but it was enacted about 3 years ago.

Mr. SCHNEIDER. But the party in power—not the Progressives—just deferred it for a year.

Mr. BENJAMIN. That is very true. Undoubtedly that is what will happen to the Wagner-Lewis bill if they enact it. They now say that they can collect taxes in January, 1936. They have not taken the trouble to tell us when they will begin to make contributions in the form of benefits and compensation for those who are supposed to be beneficiaries of the plan. That is what has happened to the Wisconsin plan. They adopted the plan as a stop-gap, to say to the masses, " Now, please stop fighting for unemployment insurance. We will give it to you voluntarily." And then they adopted a plan which was to have gone into effect on July 1, 1932. Then they decided to postpone its going into effect for another year, until January 1933, when times would get better and unemployment be less and the unemployed would not need unemployment insurance any more. Then times did not get better. They could not hold it up any longer, and they decided to begin to collect taxes on July 1, 1934. Those benefits will possibly become available on July 1, 1935, perhaps. Well, of course, there is many a slip betwixt the cup and the lip.

Mr. SCHNEIDER. Well, that is true of all legislation. That would apply to this legislation, too.

Mr. BENJAMIN. That is true. There is one thing more. Even if benefits are granted, these are reserve funds which are established in one plant, and consequently they give the employer every opportunity to use this kind of system in order to bring pressure to bear upon the employees. If you join a union, you are misconducting yourself. If you are discharged for misconduct, then you are not entitled to unemployment-insurance benefits. That is clear.

And not only that, but you must have been employed 22 weeks in a given year before you can become entitled to these benefits.

Now, the employer has the reserve fund. He does not want to spend it if he can help it. He finds that a certain employee has worked for him 21 weeks. He cannot use him any longer. He says, " Why should I keep him on, until he works 22 weeks longer? Then I will have to give him unemployment-insurance benefits." He will lay him off in the twenty-first week and he will hire someone else to do the extra work for the last week, to do the job the other man would have done. This worker will be just out of luck.

There are many such jokers in these various measures. I am firmly convinced that we must guard against such dangers, and therefore make provision against them in the bill.

Mr. SCHNEIDER. I think it is a little unfair to make a comparison between the Wisconsin act and this bill. The Wisconsin act was not an act for the purpose of checking and meeting such a crisis as we are now in. It was first introduced in 1921 and enacted in 1931 to met a normal condition, not for insurance, but for compensation, with a view to stabilizing employment and preventing employers from laying off employees, not for a week or a month, and he would have to show a very good reason for discharging an employee, otherwise he would have to pay him just as if he kept him on the pay roll, except at a lower rate of compensation.

Mr. BENJAMIN. Mr. Schneider is quite correct when he says that this bill was not a bill designed to meet the present situation, but was designed in 1921. But that is precisely the trouble with these measures. That is why we must be on guard against having such measures introduced as unemployment- and social-insurance measures, because they are not designed to meet the kind of problem that we are facing today.

Mr. SCHNEIDER. Let me call your attention to the fact that the authors of the Wisconsin bill, the advocates of the Wisconsin legislation, were the pioneers in it, so far as this country is concerned.

Mr. BENJAMIN. I am quite sure, Congressman Schneider, that there is much in what you are saying in this respect; but what is important for us to establish—and this is really a very important point; I do not wish to be unfair to the State of Wisconsin in this connection, because I think they are not the most culpable by any manner of means—but what is important for us to establish is that all these plans, really reserve plans that have been developed and that some organizations and groups still urge today, are absolutely outmoded, and if they were ever any good, they are certainly no good today, because they do not fit the new problems that we face at the present time. Those people who still insist on adhering to principles and to plans that were destined for entirely different conditions and circumstances, are not doing service to us.

Mr. SCHNEIDER. I firmly agree with you, that those who want now to use that plan to stop the enactment of better legislation were the enemies of the enactment of the Wisconsin measure.

Mr. BENJAMIN. That is very true.

Mr. DUNN. May I say right here that the Lundeen bill which is now being discussed before our committee, is a practical and progressive and very humanitarian measure. However, I could still improve upon it, because I maintain that the amount that we ask in this bill is not enough to take care of the unfortunates, although I am for the bill 100 percent.

Mr. BENJAMIN. In my opinion, Mr. Congressman, if we can unite around this measure sufficient force to win it, we will have no difficulty in making improvements toward gaining more when it becomes necessary.

Mr. LUNDEEN. Mr. Chairman, I just came from the floor of the House, where the general membership was attending; and the chairman of the Committee on Patents, Congressman Sirovich, of New York, gave this bill, the Lundeen bill, H. R. 2827, his endorsement before the entire House. So, speaking of endorsements, I thought it would be proper to put that in the record at this point.

Mr. BENJAMIN. I am very glad to hear that.

Mr. DUNN. That is very good.

Mr. BENJAMIN. Now, I should like to hurry on, just to say one more word with regard to the two other particular proposals of this measure which are important to signalize.

The first is the definite assurance provided against requiring that workers shall serve as strike breakers, as a condition for securing the benefits. In this connection I should also like to offer an amendment, that we shall add, in that section where we deal with that question, the word " present ", so that it will cover present as well as past participation in strikes, in that it is my opinion that we should not penalize workers who undertake to organize, and through organized action attempt to secure better standards of living for themselves and better wages. They should not be deprived of benefits during the period when they are making an effort to improve their conditions, and especially when we realize how important is the problem of securing a greater share of the wealth produced in the United States for those who produce it, so as to provide for greater circulation of it; and for this reason I should also like to offer that additional suggestion.

Now, finally, the question of the workers' administration; and in this connection I would like to say that here we have a very new approach which is intended to give guarantees for many of the things that we provide for in the first place. No one will be more certain to assure that workers will have this act administered in conformity with its purposes, than the workers themselves; and to this extent, therefore, providing for workers' administration through their own elected committees—of course, under the rules and regulations that are provided in connection with this measure—is an important provision of this measure which should be signalized.

As to the other social insurance provisions that are embodied in this bill, of course, we are very glad that it was possible for us to place in one measure a complete picture of the kind of security that is required, in order to safeguard the masses against all the hazards inherent in the present economic system.

Now, let me say just a few words in conclusion with regard to the difference in the basic approach as between this measure and others, and answer some of the questions that have already been raised, even in my own remarks, and also with regard to the objections that have been offered to this bill.

First of all, there is a difference that is due to an interpretation of the nature of the present crisis. We recognize that the present crisis is not a transient one. It is not a temporary one. It is not to be classified as similar to the psychical crises that we have known in the past. We know that this crisis has already lasted for 6 years. We have had promises that reemployment will take place next year; that prosperity will turn the corner and come back within 60 days; and all that sort of thing. But the fact remains that we are really now in the sixth year of the crisis, and there is no indication of any change in the situation. This is due to certain fundamental conditions inherent in our present system. That is the basic contradiction between our increasing productive capacity, as against our shrinking market, our shrinking purchasing power, if you put it that way.

This constantly widening gap is responsible in the main for the crisis from which we are suffering at the present time. Manifestly, as long as you have the present economic system of production for profit, as long as the employer can profit more when he is able to get more goods out of the labor of an individual worker by speeding him up, by introducing labor-saving and labor-replacing machinery, that long the employer is going to operate on that basis. He is going to displace labor. He is going to get a larger amount of product with a smaller expenditure in the form of wages.

This, of course, is going to result in increasing productive capacity and in shrinking purchasing power, shrinking markets. There is nothing that has been offered by anyone representing either the present or previous administrations, that would do away with this situation. On the contrary, the opposite has taken place. We know, for example, this—and this is interesting in connection with the early operation of the N. R. A. When the textile code was adopted, the textile employers said, " Very well, we are going to increase the minimum wage "; but they proceeded immediately to discharge workers; and somebody said, " Well, now, gentlemen, what are you doing? Don't you know that this is supposed to result in reemployment?" And they said, " Well, now, we were told to increase the minimum wage. We are increasing it, but we are not going to increase our total pay roll, and the way in which we are going to prevent that is by making fewer workers do as much work as was done by more workers before, while we paid them this higher scale of wages."

I recall that when newspaper men came back to General Johnson at that time and asked him what he thought about it, he said, " Well, gentlemen, these are just some of the eggs that have to be broken when you want to make an omelet. We are making an omelet. We have to break eggs." The workers who are being displaced were the " eggs" Who is going to get the " omelet "? I think that most of us have the facts and figures concerning the increased profits to the manufacturing groups, which indicate the results.

Mr. DUNN. Mr. Benjamin, those eggs were broken. I believe quite a number were rotten eggs, were they not?

Mr. BENJAMIN. Well, unfortunately, the rotten eggs were left to retain their rottenness, and it was the good eggs—that is, the workers—who were being broken in this process, and who were being further pauperized.

Mr. DUNN. But the workers are still being fed the rotten eggs. That is, not the workers—the ones who do not have any work. They do not even get rotten eggs to eat, today.

Mr. BENJAMIN. Well, they are getting them thrown at them occasionally, and that is about all. [Laughter.] Now, that approach that does not see the permanent character of the present crisis; that approach which does not see the permanent character of the problems of mass unemployment, is not able to provide a measure that meets that situation. That is precisely the question of the type of unemployment insurance that was being offered in 1920 and 1921, and the type being offered today. You cannot, when you know there is going to be permanent mass unemployment, provide for the building up of reserves which will benefit the ones who will perhaps become unemployed in the future.

We say in response to those who proposed this, " well, now, Mr. Hoover, when "? And, " Mr. Roosevelt ", for that matter, " when "? And as Presidents have never said to the employers of this country who came to the R. F. C. to ask for loans, " Now, gentlemen, wait; go ahead and take some of your present profits and wealth, and put it into a reserve fund, and let us build up this reserve fund, and when you have done that, if you become destitute, when you are on the verge of bankruptcy, several years hence, then come and we will take out of this reserve fund which you helped to build, up and give you some loans in the form of R. F. C. loans."

This they have not said to the employers, but they are saying it to the workers at this time. They are saying to them, " If you want unemployment insurance, dig down into those meager pay envelopes that you are getting now, that are hardly enough to keep you alive at the present moment; pay this into a reserve fund; wait until that reserve fund builds itself up; and if you are fortunate enough to still have a job after this reserve fund begins to operate, come around, provided that you have waited long enough—4 weeks after you have become unemployed—and maybe we will give you one-half of your average earnings for maybe as much as 15 weeks of the year."

That is actually what the present measures propose, and we say of course that such measures can proceed only upon such a theory as the President expounded when he said in one of his fireside speeches last summer:

I stand or fall by my refusal to accept as a permanent condition of our future an army of unemployed.

Here, we come to this question of employment, these jobs we want, and so on.

Mr. LUNDEEN. Before you go into that, may I inquire the figure that you take for the average earnings? What is the amount?

Mr. BENJAMIN. The average earnings under the " new deal "— that is, since the present administration—are $19.61 per week for workers who are employed. That is 3 percent less than they were getting before the N. R. A. came into effect, on the basis of present purchasing power, in accordance with figures that have been issued by the American Federation of Labor.

Mr. LUNDEEN. Thank you.

Mr. BENJAMIN. This question, first of all, of not accepting that there is due to be a permanent army of unemployed, means of course that you do not accept the responsibility of providing for it. Again, saying that the unemployed do not want insurance but want jobs, is merely another way of evading the question. It is true that they want jobs. They want steady jobs that will insure them a regular, decent, adequate income, so that they will be able to provide for themselves and their families, but the fact remains that 5 years have passed. We are in the sixth year. No jobs have been provided. Mr. Hoover, when he was even Secretary of Commerce, had declared that in the next cyclical crisis we would not have any problem at all. Said he:

We will just release a flood of public works, and everybody is going to have a job, and the crisis will be staved off.

Well, it just did not work that way with Mr. Hoover; and it is not working that way, either with the present administration.

They are not able to provide jobs, and precisely because we know that you cannot provide these jobs, especially if you fail to expand the purchasing power of the masses. We say we must have a system of unemployment compensation, or, as Miss van Kleeck so correctly put it yesterday, " compensation for insecurity ", to pay for those who are deprived of the opportunity to work.

We say, if jobs are the desired objective, please enact the workers' unemployment and social insurance bill. Put the employers of this country into a position where they will have to give proper maintenance to the masses, whether they can give them jobs or not, and I tell you it will not be very long before the employers will try to find some job for these workers in return for their compensation, rather than to keep them supported in idleness. Give them that incentive; and in this connection, let me say one more word about the remarks that have been made in the past about the other bills, and that are being made today, in support of the administration's program. They say, " Please let us experiment with this. Maybe it is not such a good plan. Maybe it won't work so well, but please give us a chance to experiment a little while longer with this. If this fails, maybe we will try something else." But we say, " You have been experimenting for the past 6 years and more. You have been telling us that you could solve the problems by your experiments. These experiments have been at the expense of the masses of the unemployed, and now, please, if you wish to experiment, experiment for a while at the expense of wealth; experiment for a while at the expense of those with large incomes, and do not continue to experiment at the expense of the unemployed and the masses generally by denying them that to which they are entitled."

I think that we have covered most of these arguments with reference to the Lundeen bill and all I want to say now is a few more words with regard to some measures with which this bill has been bracketed, and finally conclude with a few remarks about our prospectives as to the possibilities for getting action on this bill.

In the first place, we have seen that in recent periods the workers' bill has constantly been bracketed with the Townsend plan, and has been denounced as one of these fantastic plans, and therefore I should like to state that which I have already stated before the House Ways and Means Committee, with reference to the Townsend plan:

In this connection, too, it is necessary that we state our position with regard to the Townsend plan with which the workers' bill has been bracketed.

We who fight for genuine unemployment and social insurance have nothing in common with Dr. Townsend or his plan. We do not wish, nor is it necessary, to examine into his motives. We know that many demagogues who seek only personal self-aggrandizement are exploiting or attempting to exploit the dire needs and fervent hopes of the masses. Every city, county, and State boasts of a local Huey Long, Father Coughlin, Upton Sinclair, or Dr. Townsend. Every city, too, has its would-be Roosevelt, Perkins, Ickes, and Hopkins. All of these are trying to channel the discontent of the masses. Each offers a so-called " plan " and " solution " which we are urged to adopt as a painless way of reaching the millenium. The one thing that all of them have in common is that they direct various kinds of verbal attacks against capitalists, even while they bend all their efforts to the task of saving the capitalist system. On examination it is therefore possible to determine that in one respect all of these are at least partly correct. Their plans are painless—for the capitalists whom they pretend to attack.

While, therefore, we may forego consideration of motives, it is nevertheless necessary to establish clearly the objective content of the plans and also to differentiate between the merit of the plan and its sponsor and the movement behind the plan.

Certainly the movement behind the Townsend " OARP ", like the movement behind Huey Long, Father Coughlin, et al. (and we might add, like the recent Democratic landslide), reflects the great but misdirected discontent of the masses who are already in or on the brink of the bottomless abyss of economic ruin. They are not yet aware of the nature of the forces that drive them towards this abyss. They, therefore, cannot clearly understand and determine the way out. They are still subject to exploitation and misleadership by various charlatans and demagogues. For the moment, millions can still be fooled by such slogans as "new deal", "forgotten man", "share wealth", "economic security", "EPIC", and "EPIA", and "OARP." But make no mistake as to what the masses want. They want the right to live. They want to be free of the constant dread of unrelieved destitution. They know that the problem they face is not to be met by individual initiative. They begin to realize that it is a social problem and they look for action by the only body that can enact social measures—the Congress and Government of the United States.

It is true that the old-age revolving fund is a fantastic measure. What is more important is that it is a measure that furthers the purpose of those who seek to put new burdens upon the backs of the masses. While it is clear that a 10 percent sales tax would not provide even on the basis of 1929 sales the sum required to pay $200 a month to one-eight of our population, it is even more true that propaganda for such a tax helps to popularize the program of those who want to direct attention away from demands for higher taxes on large incomes, gifts, and inheritances. That is why, although the Townsend plan is so fantastic and has less organized support than the demand for enactment of the workers' unemployment, old-age, and social-insurance bill, those in control of the press are doing their utmost to popularize it. And that is why administration leaders who studiously avoid mentioning the workers' bill freely discuss the fantastic Townsend plan.

Yes. We are most decidedly opposed to the Townsend plan. But we are opposed to it for quite other reasons than those given by various other opponents. We are opposed to it because we know that social insurance must be provided for all who need it and not only for those who reach the age of 60. We are opposed to it because it is another of those "painless" measures— painless for those who alone can afford to pay for old-age pensions and other forms of social insurance. Therefore, very painful and not at all helpful for the masses.

Mr. LUNDEEN. What document is that from?

Mr. BENJAMIN. I am reading from the statement I submitted to the House Ways and Means Committee in this connection. It is taken from the transcript of the hearing by the Committee on Ways and Means, on H. R. 4120, volume 8, January 31, 1935.

I believe in saying this that I have stated our position, which I feel ought to be stated with regard to this, particularly because attempts have been made to bracket the two measures.

I want lastly to say only a very few words with regard to our prospective on this.

Mr. LESINSKI. May I ask what you mean by "our prospective"?

Mr. BENJAMIN. I mean by "our prospective", what I hope and what our movement hopes will be the action of Congress on this measure.

Mr. LESINSKI. Whose movement?

Mr. BENJAMIN. Representing the joint action committee, and the movement behind it of some several thousand organizations that are supporting the bill before this committee.

Mr. LUNDEEN. You mean the unemployed councils?

Mr. BENJAMIN. I mean not only the unemployed councils, but I mean the National Joint Action Committee, which is the continuation committee that grew out of the congress for unemployment and social insurance, in whose behalf I am appearing here today, and that of course includes many thousands of different types of organizations, apart from the unemployed. It includes the trade unions, the professional organizations, the fraternal organizations, the veterans' organizations, the church organizations, and these various other bodies that were represented in the congress. And I should like to say in their behalf, because we have discussed this question, we are very hopeful that we can make a very marked advance in the fight for genuine unemployment and social insurance during the present session of Congress. We do not base our hopes merely on the fact that we feel that this committee has given consideration to this question and is disposed to do everything possible, at least many members of this committee, to advance the measure, but because we know that there is a growing need, first of all, for unemployment and social insurance. We know that all the other measures that have been proposed thus far to solve the situation have failed and cannot succeed. We known that the masses are becoming more and more cognizant of this. We know that their insistence for action in this matter is growing both in its force and in its numbers, and we know that Congress is decidedly responsive at the present time, recognizing that the masses are becoming more impatient with delay in this connection.

We, of course, have no illusions, however. We know that the forces that are opposed to this measure will do their very utmost to prevent any advance toward enactment of the Lundeen bill. We know that this is already indicated by the administration bill which has been brought in, and by the attempts that will be made to railroad it through, and also by the statement which has been made both by the President and by Mr. Farley, the Postmaster General and chairman of the Democratic Party, who directed Congressmen to pay no attention to the pledges that they made during the recent election campaign, saying to them that if they do, they will be as bad as a juryman who goes into a jury box with his mind made up as to the verdict. This, we know, is going to have its effect. We know that the gag rule which was established in Congress during the present session is going to make for considerable difficulty toward advancing such measures as this. We are not unaware of all these forces that operate to place obstacles in the way of the enactment of such a measure as this. We do not expect of the members of this committee that they shall enact this measure. We know the rules, and that they are but seven Members of a large Congress.

We expect of every Member of Congress who is genuinely concerned with the conditions that face the great masses of population at the present time to prove their ability today to meet the opposition that will be directed against this measure. Here, the masses are becoming somewhat more critical, I must say; and when we are critical we are so because we are fighting for something which is very vital to us. We do not merely want, here and now, good intentions and good wishes. We say to our representatives in Congress, "You have been elected to represent us and to provide for our needs." You must prove capable of defending our needs and our interests. If you do not prove capable, even though you may have good intentions, that still does not help us, and therefore in this respect our movement is becoming a movement of power, because it has a consciousness of the problems that are involved in this situation, and not merely a "wishbone."

We not only wish for unemployment and social insurance. We are organized. We are growing. We are going to fight for unemployment insurance. We believe the fight can be won. We do not believe that it will destroy the capitalist system to establish such unemployment and social insurance as this, although it will make a very considerable dent in the profits of those who now make profits. We do not share any sympathy for those who will have to suffer in their profits. We say that this is not a cure-all, a solution for all the ills that beset the world, but we say that it is a means whereby an immediate amelioration can be provided in the conditions of the masses, that this is something that the masses have a right to expect of the Congress of the United States, that this is something that they have a right to expect from the richest country in the world; and it is something that their representatives should be capable of winning for them or of helping them to secure. In this sense, therefore, we look upon the prospectives for the advancement of our bill very favorably. I am not at all pessimistic. We do not feel that it is impractical and unrealizable. We know that we have advanced it already very considerably in spite of opposition, and we hope and believe that we will be able to do so in the future.

Mr. DUNN. Are there any questions the Congressmen desire to ask, Mr. Lundeen?

Mr. LUNDEEN. You spoke of " incentive " a while ago. We hear a lot about incentive in this day and age, do we not, and you believe that this bill will give an incentive to keep these men on the pay roll?

Mr. BENJAMIN. We believe that it will do precisely that, because, if you have to pay the unemployed compensation in an amount equal to average wages, whether they work or not, it is quite clear that you are going to prefer to give them work. At the present time, there is not that incentive. If they are given work, it is only at forced labor, which does not meet the problems at all, which merely means that they are made to work in return for the relief they are getting, which is nothing more than a subsistence dole; and in this sense we feel that this would make for an incentive in all directions toward providing work.

Mr. LUNDEEN. Are you satisfied that the money can be raised, and that the amount is not greater than can be taken care of by the money that can be raised?

Mr. BENJAMIN. The workers are quite well aware of some of the facts that have been presented before this committee already with regard to the wealth of this country.

Mr. LUNDEEN. You are satisfied, yourself, on it? I mean, are you yourself satisfied?

Mr. BENJAMIN. I share with them their opinion that the wealth is here, that if it is necessary to produce more we are all willing to work and produce more, if they will let us, and that therefore there need be no difficulty in creating the wealth or the means of paying such unemployment social-insurance benefits as we are calling for in this bill.

Mr. LUNDEEN. Your opinion, there, is based on statistics and research?

Mr. BENJAMIN. Yes. All of the informational material which has already been placed before this committee, and much of it which I am sure will be placed before you in the further hearings, we have had occasion to examine into. The reason I have not tried to go into it here is because I felt that there were others much more competent, who could take up there questions which are statistical, and speak not only with the authority of those who know what the masses want and need, but also with the authority of those who are equipped to make a study into the possibilities.

Mr. SCHNEIDER. Mr. Benjamin, you heard the testimony of the representative here of the authors, yesterday, did you?

Mr. BENJAMIN. Yes, sir, Mr. Schneider.

Mr. SCHNEIDER. What is your idea of their possible relief under the act; that is, professional people, authors, and so forth?

Mr. BENJAMIN. Since the act specifically provides that it shall include in its benefits professional people as well as workers in all other industries and occupations, they would be eligible to benefits. The only problem that might be raised in this connection is, in what manner to assure a certain specific amount of benefit, in that, for example, we say, "equal to average wages", and perhaps it would be difficult to compute the average earnings, say, of an author, and on that basis establish what he was to have.

It would also be difficult to determine whether $10 plus $3 would be sufficient for him; so that perhaps in the actual administration and application of the act there would have to be used some discretion, some judgment by the administrative forces; but certainly they would come in under the benefits of the act.

Mr. LUNDEEN. The point that Congressman Schneider brings up will, however, be determined by the machinery of the Labor Department, will it not?

Mr. BENJAMIN. That is right—the administrative force.

Mr. LUNDEEN. And that is the most efficient machinery that we have in the Government now to determine it?

Mr. BENJAMIN. That is correct.

Mr. LUNDEEN. And they have the data and statistics; and why should anyone bother with it when the Labor Department has it all?

Mr. BENJAMIN. That is right.

Mr. SCHNEIDER. When you refer to the $10 and $3 payments for each dependent, do you include the wife? Do you figure the wife in that?

Mr. BENJAMIN. The wife is a dependent. The children are dependents. In other words, a family of five would receive a minimum of $21 under the provisions of this act.

Mr. DUNN. Mr. Benjamin, you said that an amendment ought to be made to this bill to take care of the unfortunate man who was not a citizen. Does not the provision in the bill take care of the unfortunate man or woman who is not a citizen, when it says "from 18 years of age and upwards, shall be included in the benefits of this act"? Would not that take care of it, because we do not specify anything about people who are not citizens in the act?

Mr. BENJAMIN. It is true that the act does not specifically exclude the non-citizen, but it is also true that it does not specifically include him.

Mr. DUNN. Read that part.

Miss McCHESNEY (reading):

SEC. 2. The Secretary of Labor is hereby authorized and directed to provide for the immediate establishment of a system of unemployment insurance for the purpose of providing compensation for all workers and farmers above 18 years of age, unemployed through no fault of their own.

Mr. DUNN. Would that not take care of the man and woman who are not citizens?

Mr. BENJAMIN. I might say in this connection, Mr. Chairman, that this is one difficulty that you have, or one problem that you have, that has always to be kept in mind in connection with groups that are subject to discrimination, such as Negro groups, foreign born, and so forth. Unless you specifically safeguard them against the discrimination to which they are subject, it often occurs. In the formulation of the measure, you do not exclude them. Nevertheless, by virtue of the fact that you do not specifically include them, you will have them open to discrimination; and such groups as are subject to discrimination have need for special protection and special safeguards. It is in this sense, therefore, that we feel so strongly the need for always making very specific safeguards in the interest of the Negro, the foreign born, women, youth groups, any groups that are likely to be subject to discrimination.

Mr. DUNN. In other words, it will make the bill more binding?

Mr. BENJAMIN. That is right.

Mr. SCHNEIDER. When you do that, then, you leave opportunity for exceptions, too?

Mr. LESINSKI. Sure.

Mr. SCHNEIDER. Just as soon as you do not include one class, they are out?

Mr. LESINSKI. You get into class legislation, then.

Mr. SCHNEIDER. If you said, there, " all workers of hand and brain ", you then have all, including the author?

Mr. BENJAMIN (reading) :

The benefits of this act shall be extended to workers, whether they be industrial, agricultural, domestic, office, or professional workers, and to farmers, without discrimination because of age, sex, race, color, religious or political opinion, or affiliation.

Mr. DUNN. Would that not take care of it?

Mr. BENJAMIN. By not including. You see, the first section of the act is inclusive. It includes everybody. The other one is really a safeguard. It is to safeguard certain ones likely to be subject to exclusion, specifically from exclusion. It does not by virtue of that exclude somebody else, but it does make certain that these will be safeguarded, and it is in this sense that we present it. Perhaps there will be some representatives here—I understand there will be, later in the hearings—of organized foreign-born workers, who may be in a position to give you a more detailed statement of exactly why they wish to have this amendment; but I can only say that we fully support them in their view of the matter.

Mr. LUNDEEN. I would like your opinion on this proposition. If we made an amendment to that, reading that those who apply for citizenship shall be included providing they complete their citizenship within the period prescribed by law, what would you think of that?

Mr. LESINSKI. Mr. Lundeen, I do not think that is fair, because I know in my own territory thousands of people who have been in there for 15 or 20 years or 30 years, who are not citizens, and only for one reason. The reason is that they cannot fluently read or write English.

Mr. LUNDEEN. That would be a very good reason, of course.

Mr. LESINSKI. Quite often a man will not learn. A man who is 40, 50, or 60 years of age will not learn to write or read English perfectly.

Mr. LUNDEEN. I would like to have that question gone into, in this committee, and the entire Labor Committee, more fully. That particular class was left out because we thought it would further the passage of the bill, if we ever got to that point. We hope to get to that point, and you know there is a strong sentiment among labor along that line. Perhaps they will be educated out of that soon, but there is a large group that feel that way, and I hope that we will have some foreign-born groups here that will present their side of that question. I want to hear it presented very much.

Mr. BENJAMIN. I am pretty sure we will have such presentation.

Mr. LESINSKI. You take it in our territory up there, we have got thousands upon thousands of people who cannot get their papers, although they are willing to take them, and only for one reason, because we have got a judge up there who does not want them to become citizens unless they are English-speaking people.

Mr. LUNDEEN. I am glad you brought that up.

Mr. LESINSKI. I have been at hearings, and I have heard them. The judge will ask a man, " Why was the United States in the War of 1812? " I doubt whether 2 percent of the people right here, now, could answer that.

Mr. DUNN. Do you believe the judge knew?

Mr. LESINSKI. I do not think he did, but that was the question.

Mr. LUNDEEN. Suppose somebody should ask why we got into the late World War. We might have one hundred answers.

Mr. BENJAMIN. And they might not be correct.

Mr. DUNN. Probably if the real reason were given, the judge would deny the application for citizenship papers.

Mr. LESINSKI. That is right.

Mr. DUNN. We got into the war to make the rich richer and the poor poorer throughout the world.

Mr. BENJAMIN. If you gave that answer you would certainly be excluded from citizenship.

Mr. DUNN. Then I would go to Ireland and get my papers there.

Mr. LUNDEEN. Mr. Chairman, I have had it brought to my attention recently about the cost of becoming a citizen.

Mr. LESINSKI. Those fees were cut, here, last year. We have worked on that, and we have got the cost cut.

Mr. LUNDEEN. What is the cost now?

Mr. LESINSKI. I think instead of $10 it is $5.

Mr. BENJAMIN. Five dollars.

Mr. LUNDEEN. Well, that is that; but do not many noncitizens feel that they must go to an attorney?

Mr. DUNN. Yes; they do.

Mr. LUNDEEN. Then, if they go to an attorney—and some of them feel they must—he might charge them $10, $20, or $25 to advise them, so that the figure might run into larger amounts. Someone brought that to my attention, and I wish to make that point.

Mr. LESINSKI. You take it, up our way, the only place you could get citizen's papers was in the Federal court. We have gone over that bump, and they are allowed now to get their papers in the circuit court, through the county clerk's office, so that has helped some, because the circuit-court judges are not as "hard-boiled."

Mr. BENJAMIN. Might I in this connection, Mr. Chairman, also make another point which I think might strengthen the measure; and I hope that Mr. Lundeen will agree with me on this, too? On the question of old-age benefits, in our opinion there should be a very definite specification that one is entitled to these benefits on reaching the age of 55 years, rather than to permit it, as now, to stand without any definite qualification. It could be done by inserting a clause like this, for example: "Persons reaching the age of 55 shall be entitled to the benefits of this act without being required to work." In this way, we would be indicating specifically that we desire to give old-age benefits to those who reach the age of 55, and I feel that this is especially important, now, in view of the fact that all the various old-age pension measures, or most of them at least, that are popularized, are speaking of persons 65 years or 70 years of age.

Mr. LESINSKI. Mostly 70

Mr. BENJAMIN. Or 70 years of age, you see. Now, today, in industry, as Congressman Lesinski pointed out the other day—and this is of course particularly true in such industries as those in the district from which Congressman Lesinski comes—it is practically impossible for a person 50 years of age, not to speak of 55, to stand the pace.

Mr. LESINSKI. Even 40 years.

Mr. BENJAMIN. Forty years, yes, correct. If you go into the Ford plant, and you want to get a job there, you have got to be in the prime of manhood. You have got to have practically virgin power that has been entirely unused, because otherwise you have not the capacity to "stand the gaff." One of those testifying here the other day said it was merely a matter of "pushing a button" in industry today, and that you could get almost anyone to do that, even aged people; but that is not true. If you go into any industrial plant—and I have been a machinist, and I know—you simply cannot "push a button." You have got to stand there, and you have got to do some mighty hard, breakneck work at a tremendous, terrific, devitalizing speed that takes all the energy out of you within the first hour or two of work, and the rest of the time you are working by sheer force of will.

Mr. LESINSKI. Right.

Mr. BENJAMIN. Many a worker collapses, especially in the Ford plant, right at his work. The Ford plant will examine a worker who comes to apply for a job. They will give him a physical examination. They will determine his blood pressure. They will determine his weight. They will determine just how vigorous he is, and not only his age; but if he does not have any other defect, and conforms to their standards of physical perfection, he cannot get a job. That clearly excludes, immediately, the older worker.

Mr. DUNN. May I say, Mr. Benjamin, a man that goes to a plant, as you have just mentioned, to take a physical examination, I know it is a fact that many a man who may be young, and whose blood pressure may be high, because that particular man may just be in love, you know, and have high-blood pressure. You see, that would prevent his getting a job. (Laughter.)

Mr. BENJAMIN. Well, they may be justified, then, on that basis. It may be he would not be able to give his attention to the work, and therefore would not be entitled to a job.

Mr. DUNN. Therefore, the man that is in love may be discriminated against.

You have been speaking about these bills being introduced to take care of men when they attain the age of 65 and 70. I introduced a bill, making a man old when he was 50. I have a bill in Congress now to give him at least $100 a month and permit him to have an income of $2,400 a year; so I maintain that a man at 50 is old; and I know it is an absolute fact in the city of Pittsburgh, and all through the country, men and women who attain the age of 50 are considered old and are unable to get a job because they are aged. The only industry that I know is making any money today is the industry that is making wigs, because a lot of these bald-headed men, you know, are now getting wigs so they can go into the mill and get a job. [Laughter.]

Mr. LESINSKI. I do not agree with you on the age. I am past 50 and still willing to work.

Mr. DUNN. It is not a question of a man being willing to work at 50. You will find in 90 and 95 percent of the cases they are willing to work but cannot get a job.

Mr. LESINSKI. Oh, I can get a job, yet.

Mr. DUNN. I know—you are a Congressman. [Laughter.]

Mr. LESINSKI. No; I could get a job even if I were not a Congressman.

I want to ask Mr. Benjamin a question to clear up a situation. He has made a statement here that with these organizations are affiliated trade unions of the American Federation of Labor, but he has also stated that the officials of the American Federation of Labor are against this plan. I would like to have that straightened out, because Congressman Wood the other day brought that up, when a statement was made here, and he said that the officials of the American Federation of Labor have been attempting to further similar legislation and that they sponsored a plan as far back as 1931 and 1932. That is in the records here. I doubt that your statement is correct.

Mr. BENJAMIN. I am very glad you asked me the question, Congressman Lesinski.

Mr. LESINSKI. Congressman Wood has defended the American Federation of Labor on that subject saying that they had favored it.

Mr. DUNN. In fact, he had something inserted in the record here to verify his statements about unemployment insurance.

Mr. BENJAMIN. I am also very sorry that Congressman Wood is not here, so I could make my reply to him, right now. I should like first of all, however, to say that when we speak of " unemployment and social insurance ", we mean something else than merely a measure that carries the title " Unemployment and Social Insurance." If we did not do that, then we would have to accept, for example, the Wagner-Lewis bill as an unemployment and social-insurance measure, and that we cannot do; and even Mr. Green, when he appeared before the House Ways and Means Committee and the Finance Committee of the Senate, did not approve of the Wagner-Lewis bill in toto as it stands today.

However, the fact is that Mr. Green and a number of other leading officials of the American Federation of Labor, have expressed themselves very vigorously in opposition to the workers' unemployment and social insurance bill; and the plans that they have brought forward have been very similar to those now being sponsored by the administration.

To give you two examples; first, when we were preparing our present congress, that is, the congress for unemployment and social insurance, last month—Mr. Green sent out a letter to all central labor unions in which he urged them not to participate in this congress for unemployment and social insurance, " because ", he said, " we are cooperating with the administration in framing our own measure."

Mr. LESINSKI. Do you know what was his reason?

Mr. BENJAMIN. His reason for that was that he was opposed to the kind of unemployment and social insurance that the workers' unemployment and social insurance bill proposes to give.

Mr. LESINSKI. Was he opposed to the plan, or was he opposed to the group that was sponsoring it?

Mr. BENJAMIN. He might have been opposed to the plan; he might have been opposed to the group; but the open result was that he made it more difficult to mobilize the larger sections of the American Federation of Labor for unified action to advance unemployment and social insurance. Secondly, the plan which he proposed, being so identical with the administration measure, and it's being today different only, for example, as stated before the House Ways and Means Committee, that, whereas they say $15 a week shall be the maximum for benefits under the unemployment insurance, he proposes that that be the minimum. We must bear in mind that in the N. R. A. codes, too, they set the minimum wage, but that became the maximum; so the mere changing of the word " minimum " to " maximum " will not make for change.

Again, his other difference with the Wagner-Lewis bill was that they propose in some cases to make it permissible for States to tax the worker for part of the payment of the cost of the plan. He differed with that, and proposed only a tax on the employer, although he agreed that the tax on the employer's pay roll will also be transferred to the worker, as a consumer.

Mr. LESINSKI. That would be natural, anyway.

Mr. BENJAMIN. Yes; excepting that if you tax income you avoid that to a very considerable extent, as the Lundeen bill does.

Mr. LESINSKI. Personally, I believe you will have to tax both.

Mr. BENJAMIN. We may come to that; but right now we are still in the position where we can see the possibility of providing the funds through the taxing of income only, without pay rolls which will avoid an indirect tax upon the workers.

Thirdly, he suggested, instead of 15 weeks' minimum-maximum benefits, as the Wagner-Lewis bill would suggest, that it be 26 weeks; but he is still far away from the workers' bill, which provides for all time lost.

The reason why we are so clear and sharp in this matter is we might perhaps come in here and try to get an advantage by saying to you that the American Federation of Labor is in favor of it, you see; but we say that we have reached such a point now in the movement for unemployment and social insurance that it is very important to differentiate between what objectively helps the movement for it and what objectively hurts it; and the fact that 3,000 or more locals of he American Federation of Labor have felt it necessary to take issue with the executive officials of that organization on this question; that five international unions in their conventions have endorsed the Lundee bill, in spite of the opposition of the executive officials, indicates that we cannot say that the position of the American Federation of Labor is correctly represented by a statement of its executive officials; and we try to indicate thereby the fact that the membership of the American Federation of Labor, to an increasing extent, is taking a different attitude on the question.

Finally, in connection with Mr. Wood's statement, it might be well for me to point out that what I have quoted here as being the position of Mr. Green in 1931, is correct; that in the Vancouver convention, the American Federation of Labor, Mr. Green, and the other leaders of the executive bodies, were still opposed in toto to unemployment insurance, stating that it would be a death blow to trade unionism. They have changed their position today, but we should bear in mind that so have also the employers changed their position.

The employers, too, take a different position on this question than they used to. For example, they were all opposed, as they now are, objectively, to unemployment insurance in any fashion, until about 1931, when the following statement was made by the National Industrial Conference Board. Let me see if I can find and quote it for you. The following is the quotation from the National Industrial Conference Board:

The movement for unemployment-insurance legislation has gained great momentum in recent years. It is promoted by well-organized propaganda, greatly aided by distressful unemployment conditions resulting from the prolonged depression. Industry cannot afford to pursue a policy of inaction. Agreement should be reached among employers on the fundamentals of a program of unemployment reserves that might reasonably be offered as a substitute for unemployment insurance.

So you see, at that time, in the face of the growing demand which they described as huge propaganda, and so forth, they found it necessary to change the strategy of their position toward unemployment insurance by offering a plan of reserves in the place of the unemployment insurance plan; and insofar, therefore, as the American Federation of Labor still bases itself upon a reserve plan, we may say that they are against unemployment insurance, although they are for the reserves, which are a substitute for unemployment insurance.

Mr. DUNN. Mr. Benjamin, I appreciate what you have said. There are two other witnesses to be heard this afternoon, one a textile man from North Carolina, and another man from North Dakota. We only have 1 more hour, and we may be called over to the floor of the House.

Mr. BENJAMIN. Mr. Chairman, I appreciate your courtesy.

Mr. LUNDEEN. Mr. Chairman, I have a couple of inquiries to make, which will be very brief. There was a statement made, here, about the president of the American Federation of Labor having said that delegates should not attend the congress, " because ", and then a statement of his reasons. Just what was that phrase? What was it he said in that " because " phrase?

Mr. BENJAMIN. Because they said the American Federation of Labor were not connected with this effort, " since we are engaged in working out a plan together with the Administration."

Mr. LUNDEEN. I am trying to find out if the Administration plan and the American Federation of Labor plan were the identical plans. They are working with them, anyway. Is that what you say?

Mr. BENJAMIN. It is practically identical, in that. first of all, Mr. Green was then a member of the President's Advisory Committee on this plan.

Mr. LUNDEEN. That covers the point I had in mind. There was another point in regard to amendments. I would like to see the bill furthered along the line of its possible enactment, and carefully considered, with regard to amendments, to the end that the amendments may not make impossible the passage of the bill. I know we have the most forward-looking bill, now, that was ever introduced along these lines, and if I saw an amendment or two put on, that might imperil the bill, I should regret that very much, so I think that when we come to amendments we should think them over very carefully. I hope we will get further light on the subject.

Mr. BENJAMIN. Might I say, without taking very much time on it, only this: That our feeling is that the best guarantee that this measure will have favorable action is, if we can mobilize the greatest possible support behind the measure; and, if we make certain that the bill includes provisions for all those whose support of the bill is necessary, we will certainly be in a good way toward achieving its enactment.

Mr. LUNDEEN. Let me illustrate. For instance, the 60 years' provision we were talking about, or 65 or 70, it may well be that some day we will come to the 50 years mentioned by Congressman Dunn; but we cannot get that through the Congress now. You cannot pass a bill with the 50-year provision in it. That is my opinion. I may be wrong in that. I hope I am. I do not believe you can pass it with a 55-year provision in it. I think you will do very well if you are able to pass a bill providing for 60 years. That is just my personal opinion, from my knowledge of Congressmen.

Mr. BENJAMIN. What I have presented to you, of course, represents our view of the matter, and it would be for your committee to act on the matter. I should like to say, Mr. Chairman, I appreciate very much the courtesy that has been extended, not only to myself, but also to all those who have appeared before this committee; and I should also like to say that in my opinion this committee has made a great advance toward giving consideration to those most immediately concerned with the problem on which you are trying to legislate; and in that sense, I think it has set a very good example, which we hope will be followed by other committees. I personally plan to be present during all of the hearings, and therefore if any member of the committee should wish to ask me any additional questions which are not permitted at this time, I shall be very glad to answer them.

Mr. DUNN. All right, Mr. Benjamin. We thank you for your very instructive address.

Mr. DUNN. The next witness is Walter L. Pickard, of Burlington, N. C.

STATEMENT OF WALTER L. PICKARD, UNEMPLOYED TEXTILE WORKER (BURLINGTON, N. C.)

Mr. PICKARD. Mr. Chairman, I represent about 600 unemployed textile workers of North Carolina who are on the relief. I came here as a "blacklist" textile worker. There are several thousand in the same fix as myself.

Mr. DUNN. As a "blacklist" worker?

Mr. PICKARD. Yes.

Mr. DUNN. We are not going to blacklist you.

Mr. PICKARD. All right. The textile workers of Burlington, N. C., scraped up their pennies and dimes to send me here to ask this committee to endorse the workers' unemployment and social insurance bill, H. R. 2827. We know that the Wagner-Lewis bill does not reach our case, for we are already unemployed, and we know that bill only puts more burdens on those that have a job. The majority of textile workers who have jobs work under the constant threat of losing them. They have work today but have nothing promised for tomorrow. When they are given more work under the stretch-out system, the boss tells them that if they do not like it there are plenty of unemployed waiting to take their jobs.

In the same mill in which I worked, before the N. R. A. came into effect, we usually ran 4 looms. They now run 6 and 8 looms for about the same wages they made on 4 looms; and they must get production and quality or they will lose their jobs. This same method applies in other parts of the mill. This kind of weaving is "crepe fancy", and some of the cotton mills have doubled the amount of work; for instance, whereas we ran 16 looms, they now run 28.

As for the houses of the mill companies, they furnish shacks on a red, muddy hill, with red, muddy roads; and in some cases there were cracks in the walls that you could almost throw a cat through. We have to pay an average of 50 cents per week per room for these shacks. Also, we pay for lights and water. In most cases the mills do not have enough shacks to accommodate all their help. There are large families now living in tobacco barns near mill towns, because they cannot pay the high house rent of the private home owners.

The textile workers' food consists mainly of bread, pinto beans, fat-back meat, and Irish potatoes. The same 24-pound sack of flour that cost us 50 cents per sack, less than 2 years ago, now costs us $1.15. Pinto beans sold for 5 cents a pound less than 2 years ago, and now sell for 12 cents a pound. Fat-back meat sold for 6 cents a pound less than 2 years ago. We now pay 22 cents a pound for the same part of the hog. These prices are still going up, according to newspaper reports, but we do not see any reports of our wages going up in North Carolina.

The last raise the mills gave us in Burlington was in the form of a bonus on piecework. Now they go over the goods with a "spyglass"; and if they can find anything wrong with the cloth they take our bonus away from us. The unemployed of North Carolina are not sure about the emergency relief. If we go to the emergency relief office, we are told we must work. I, for one, went to them and told them I had to have some relief, and that I did not have anything to eat at home for my babies, and it was 2 days before she sent the lady out to my home to see about it, and then sent for me to come back to the office and gave me a work card. I reported to the foreman on the road, and he gave me a pick and put me to digging ditches for 30 cents an hour. I got 1 day's work. I went back the next day and he told me that I worked the day before, he had somebody that he had to put to work, and he wanted me to " rest." I learned that by almost putting up a fight with the foreman most of the boys got around 2 days work out of the week. That is 16 hours at 30 cents an hour. Some of them are better scrappers than the rest and they get 3 days swinging a heavy pick, busting rocks on rock piles, so the unemployed textile workers want this committee to recommend this workers' bill, H. R. 2827.

The mill bosses used to tell us, before the N. R. A., if we joined the union we lost our job. They do not tell that since the N. R. A.; but we lose our jobs for joining the union just the same. They find some excuse for firing us, excuses that we cannot hardly believe.

Mr. LUNDEEN. That cannot happen, some day when labor has all the power, and labor controls the situation. Then they will not be able to do that.

Mr. PICKARD. I only know the facts.

Mr. LUNDEEN. As they exist now?

Mr. PICKARD. As they exist now, in my experience.

During the general textile strike they used all kinds of police there to stop us from peacefully picketing. There was a large force of deputy sheriffs with tear-gas bombs, and the National Guard charging us with bayonets. They drove us back. On one morning I remember they drove us back from the public road. The mill fence came right up to the edge. Over on the other side of the road was a track of the Southern Railroad. They drove us back of that, and because some of the boys did not get to going fast enough for them, they struck some of them with bayonets. I saw them knock one girl down on the railroad property, when they had told us we had the right to picket peacefully. They also arrested and fined several workers for not moving on fast enough to suit them. So the textile workers cannot expect any protection of the trade union's standard, or protection of the part-time workers, that the North Carolina State law is supposed to give.

As to old age, the mill bosses tell us that if we have a few gray hairs in our temple we are too old to work in the mill. I would like to tell an experience of my own. About 3 years ago, I was head loom-fixer in the weave room in Burlington, which is kind of a " second boss " of the weaving, and my father was working for me. He was 52 years old at that time and the superintendent came through. I was on the night shift and he called me and said, " Who is that old man working over there? " And I told him he was my father. He says, "He is gray headed." He said, "You know we cannot work gray-headed men." I said, "He is the best warper I have on the job." He said, "I cannot help it. The insurance company does not allow us to work men of that age. Get shut of him."

Mr. DUNN. And he was but 52 years of age?

Mr. PICKARD. Yes, sir; 52 years of age at that time.

Mr. DUNN. In other words, in that plant they would not employ at that time any person past 50?

Mr. PICKARD. That was what the superintendent told me. Of course, I had to carry out his orders.

Mr. DUNN. Can you tell me how many men and women were employed in that plant when it was in full operation?

Mr. PICKARD. Seven hundred.

Mr. DUNN. About 700?

Mr. PICKARD. In that particular plant there are three mills inside of one fence. It is all considered as one unit.

Mr. DUNN. You mean 700 in the three mills?

Mr. PICKARD. Yes.

Mr. DUNN. And that superintendent told you, when a man attained the age of 50, he could not obtain employment, is that it?

Mr. PICKARD. That is it.

Mr. DUNN. Thank you.

Mr. PICKARD. So we are turned out with nothing to turn to but the poorhouse, and these gray hairs appear in textile workers' temples before they are 50 years old. They have already appeared in mine, and I am not 36. We ask for the workers' bill, H. R. 2827, to secure us in old age. That is all.

Mr. DUNN. Thank you very much. We appreciate your statements. They were very valuable, and you have substantiated some remarks that I have made in the past about men attaining the age of 50 being considered "old." I am glad you made that statement. Mr. Lundeen, do you desire to ask any questions?

Mr. LUNDEEN. What State are your textile workers located in?

Mr. PICKARD. North Carolina.

Mr. LUNDEEN. You represent them?

Mr. PICKARD. Yes.

Mr. LUNDEEN. And how many of them, approximately?

Mr. PICKARD. They have about 600 employed on the relief.

Mr. LUNDEEN. Of the group that sent you here, how many are there?

Mr. PICKARD. Six hundred unemployed.

Mr. LUNDEEN. Six hundred unemployed. That is all I want to ask. Thank you.

Mr. DUNN. Do you know how many textile workers there are in the State of North Carolina?

Mr. PICKARD. No; I could not say. I think there are 110,000.

Mr. DUNN. About 110,000?

Mr. PICKARD. That was the statement I saw in the paper during the strike, if I am not mistaken.

Mr. DUNN. All right. Thank you. The next witness will be Mr. Andrew Omholt.

STATEMENT OF MR. ANDREW OMHOLT, MEMBER OF THE UNITED FARMERS LEAGUE (NORTH DAKOTA)

Mr. DUNN. Just tell the gentlemen whom you represent Mr. Omholt?

Mr. OMHOLT. I represent the United Farmers League, a farmers' organization, principally organized in the Northwest. In order to substantiate the question that Mr. Lundeen asked me a moment ago, I want to say this. That I took up a Government homestead of 160 acres in Williams County, N. Dak., in 1905. I lived on and farmed this land for 20 years, raising wheat, before the bankers finally squeezed me out.

Mr. LUNDEEN. Where was this homestead located?

Mr. OMHOLT. In Williams County, N. Dak.

Mr. LUNDEEN. I was born on a homestead near Beresford, S. Dak.

Mr. OMHOLT. I am speaking for the United Farmers League, with national headquarters in Chicago, and State offices in many States in the Middle West. I also feel that I am speaking for the hundreds of thousands of farmers who have gone on record in numberless meetings in favor of unemployment and social insurance, as embodied in the Lundeen bill—H. R. 2827—and for the 2,000,000 farm families living in the drought area, whose crops have dried up, whose herds of livestock have been bought up and slaughtered.

I am speaking for the millions who have lost their farms and equipment, not because of drought but because they have been robbed by bankers, merchants, and grain gamblers through high interest, high prices for machinery, and low prices for what we had to sell, ever since they broke the furrow on those prairies. The drought and a succession of droughts has only aggravated and increased the toll taken by these bankers and business people.

I read in a North Dakota paper an article written by a county agent, which said that much of this land should never have been opened up at all for farming. In his county, Government weather records date back 53 years. He shows that this section of the Middle West is semiarid with a very low average rainfall of 14.8 inches for a year. He says:

> I said it was fortunate that we had this long-time weather chart of the past to guide us in the future; I also say that it was an almost criminal mistake on the part of the Government to parcel out the land in this area in homesteads of only 160 acres when they had before them weather records that clearly showed them that a family could not make a living on such a small farm.
>
> With the information that we have on hand the Government should have allowed homestead entries of 640 acres when they opened up this country, rather than to encourage a land policy which meant failure and heartbreak to three out of every four men who homesteaded here. * * *

The farmers in the drought area are doomed to a subsistence level of farming, loaded down as they are with an unbearable debt burden; short of feed for the starving livestock, the farmers are forced to reduce their amount of livestock to a 10-unit system. This cuts the livestock to approximately 1 horse, 1 cow, 5 hogs, 7 sheep, and 100 chickens, and means a self-sufficing farm, which keeps us out of commercial farming.

It is clear from the above that a large proportion of the farmers in the drought-stricken area are unemployed. That is, they have no crop to sell, no seed or money to put in another crop in the spring—nothing to do except to work for relief.

I want to give the committee an idea of why we are interested in unemployment insurance by giving a few examples of the situation as it exists in a number of counties in the drought area. I have used official F. E. R. A. reports so there can be no question of a biased selection of facts.

Here is Burke County, N. Dak. It is in the northwest part of the State, with a population of 9,998 in 1930.

Mr. LUNDEEN. Is that near Williston?

Mr. OMHOLT. Yes. My home town is Williston. Of these, 7,000 lived in the country. In June 1934, 5,458 individuals, or 54 percent of the population as of 1930, were receiving relief. The county has suffered from a 4-year drought.

Ten banks have failed in the county, and according to the receiver of closed banks for the State of North Dakota these failures tied up $1,670,368. To date of the report but $275,191 had been paid back, the current net loss standing at 83.5 percent of the deposits. This fact undoubtedly explains the presence on the relief rolls of many substantial farm households. Tax delinquencies have risen from 2.4 percent of the levy in 1927 to 77.5 percent in 1933.

Mr. LUNDEEN. Pardon me. That means that the people there just quit paying taxes?

Mr. OMHOLT. Sure.

Mr. LUNDEEN. Or cannot pay them?

Mr. OMHOLT. They cannot pay them.

Mr. DUNN. They have nothing with which to pay taxes?

Mr. LUNDEEN. There is no money there with which to pay them?

Mr. OMHOLT. Twenty-one thousand and ninety-eight head of cattle had been sold. Burke County is typical for the western half of North Dakota. There are thousands and hundreds of thousands of people in the same situation.

Another example is Tripp County in the southern part of South Dakota, with a population of 12,112 in 1930; 25 percent of its people lived in villages, the remainder in the country. In June 1934, 7,461 persons, or 59 percent of the 1930 population, were receiving relief. I now quote from the report of the F. E. R. A.:

The work relief program, while it has provided subsistence, has not kept the people sufficiently employed to save them from despair. * * * Farm families throughout the entire area of Tripp County are almost without exception on relief. * * * Properties have been allowed to deteriorate, livestock has been sold, and feed resources have long since been depleted. * * * Since 1920 there have been 11 bank failures in Tripp County, entailing a loss of $1,105,315.

Mr. LUNDEEN. Can you give me the county seat of Tripp County?

Mr. OMHOLT. Tripp, S. Dak.

Mr. LUNDEEN. Is that anywhere near Yankton?

Mr. OMHOLT. It is north and west of Yankton; approximately 50 miles, I think.

Mr. LUNDEEN. It is a little west of Sioux Falls, then?

Mr. OMHOLT. Yes; it is about northwest of Sioux Falls.

Mr. LUNDEEN. Is it on the James River?

Mr. OMHOLT. Yes; it is near the James River.

Mr. LUNDEEN. I just wanted to locate it in my mind. That used to be a pretty fair county, did it not?

Mr. OMHOLT. Sure; you bet. That is located in the best part of South Dakota; in the eastern half.

Mr. LUNDEEN. It cannot be very far from Huron.

Mr. OMHOLT. No; it is just a little from Huron—about straight south of Huron.

Mr. LUNDEEN. People used to get along fine there.

Mr. OMHOLT. Sure. In the northwest Central States the families on relief received on the average $19.40 for October 1934, whereas in the United States as a whole they received $21.04 in the rural areas. In one of the worst hit States, about 80 percent of the farm families are on relief.

In North Dakota, the decrease in the number of persons receiving relief in December 1934 was 2.8 percent; while the decrease in dollars spent for relief was 14.4 percent, compared to November of the same year. For this period, in South Dakota, there was an increase of 3.3 percent in the number of persons on relief and a decrease of 13.2 percent in dollars spent, cutting the already skimpy rations of these thousands of suffering people.

Figures for October 1934 for the 23 drought States show that 1,153,000 relief families lived outside of the large cities. Two-thirds of all families on relief lived on farms or in small towns, but they received only 54 percent of the relief money.

In December 1934—the latest month for which any relief figures are available—the number of families on relief in these States was approximately 2,000,000, or an increase of 300,000 over the total on relief in October. This is an increase of over 14 percent. Figures for noncity relief families have not yet been released for November or December, but everyone knows that most of this increase is due to the plight of the farmers.

Mr. LUNDEEN. Do you mean to say there was an increase from September to October of 14 percent?

Mr. OMHOLT. Yes.

Mr. LUNDEEN. In 1934; is that it?

Mr. OMHOLT. 1934.

Mr. LUNDEEN. And that was where?

Mr. OMHOLT. In the 23 drought States.

Mr. LUNDEEN. Fourteen percent in 1 month?

Mr. OMHOLT. Yes, sir. That is according to Government figures.

Mr. LUNDEEN. That is tragic.

Mr. DUNN. And I believe I understood you to say one million and how many hundred thousand families were on relief?

Mr. OMHOLT. 1,153,000 families.

Mr. DUNN. About 54 percent lived in the country?

Mr. OMHOLT. No. These 1,153,000 families lived outside the large cities; in the rural areas.

Mr. DUNN. What did you say about 54 percent? Did you mean by that that they received 54 percent of the money for relief?

Mr. OMHOLT. They constitute two-thirds of the families on relief, and receive only 54 percent.

Mr. DUNN. I want to get that clear in my mind.

Mr. OMHOLT. The reduction program of the A. A. A. and the coming squeeze-out in the production credits for the poor farmers indicate that permanent unemployment is to be the lot of many of those now on relief. The Outlook for 1935, published by the Department of Agriculture, announces that:

> The demand for credit will probably exceed that of 1934 since the accumulated needs for equipment and repairs are much greater than in recent years. * * * Even in drought areas, credit should be reasonably ample for those who have security to offer. The number of drought-stricken farmers without security for loans, other than their prospective crops, will doubtless be exceptionally large.

This fits in very nicely with the long-time program of the Department of Agriculture, laid down in the speech of the then Assistant Secretary of Agriculture Tugwell, who said:

> It has been estimated that when lands now unfit to till are removed from cultivation, something around 2,000,000 persons who now farm will have to be absorbed by other occupations.

What other " occupations " does the book-farmer mean? The C. C. C. camps, soup lines, forced-labor projects? These are the only other occupations provided for so far for the rural populations by the farm economists of the Roosevelt administration.

On the basis of these facts showing the conditions as they are, with no relief from existing conditions for poor farmers in sight, with a debt estimated at 15 billions in 1933, with forced sales on the increase, why should not the farmers be interested in unemployment and social insurance? And why should the farmers be particularly interested in the Lundeen bill? Because it is the only bill introduced into Congress offering some measure of security for the rural population. This bill and the farmers emergency relief bill, H. R. 3471, are the only bills that put money now held idle by the rich into circulation, actually placing purchasing power in the hands of both city workers and farmers; enabling them to buy the products of the farms and factory.

The Lundeen bill proposes to tax the rich and the people with big incomes for the provision of this insurance. We farmers see no reason why the paying for relief should not be shifted from the shoulders of the poor where it now is to the shoulders of the rich who can and must carry this responsibility.

We have tried to study the Wagner-Lewis bill now before Congress. It beats around the bush and in the end puts the tax back on the workers, relieving the rich and the Federal Government of responsibility.

In conclusion, I want to say that this Congress is facing a greater responsibility then at any time in its history. This session of Congress in its treatment of these two bills will prove to the people whether it has the common people at heart or the privileged few.

The Lundeen bill is clearly for the workers with no quibbles for the rich; it has been adopted by millions of workers, farmers and professionals. The will of the poor people is expressed in the Lundeen bill as a minimum program to provide some measure for their security. We farmers want to know what Congress is going to do about it.

Mr. LUNDEEN. What was the other bill?

Mr. OMHOLT. H. R. 3471.

Mr. LUNDEEN. Is that the one introduced by Congressman Burdick?

Mr. OMHOLT. Yes, sir.

Mr. LUNDEEN. That is the farmers relief bill?

Mr. OMHOLT. That is the farmers emergency relief bill.

Mr. LUNDEEN. Those are the two that you are interested in?

Mr. OMHOLT. Yes.

Mr. DUNN. Do you want to ask any more questions, Mr. Lundeen?

Mr. LUNDEEN. How many do you represent, in coming down here?

Mr. OMHOLT. I represent, I think, approximately 10,000 farmers organized in the United States.

Mr. LUNDEEN. They sent you here as a delegate?

Mr. OMHOLT. Yes; I am sent here by the executive committee.

Mr. LUNDEEN. To give us this information?

Mr. OMHOLT. Yes.

Mr. DUNN. Are those farmers located in your State?

Mr. OMHOLT. Yes; they are located in South Dakota, North Dakota, Montana, Minnesota, and Wisconsin.

Mr. DUNN. That is an organization to which you belong, and they sent you down here to testify before the subcommittee of the Labor Committee?

Mr. OMHOLT. Yes.

Mr. LUNDEEN. Your facts were very clearly presented, and we appreciate your coming here. I know we all do.

Mr. DUNN. Yes; I do. I am glad to get this information, and I agree with everything you have said. We know that the farmer has not been treated right. He is just like the rest of the people who have to struggle for a measly existence, and I want to say to the gentleman I will do my best as a Congressman toward taking the farmers and all other people that labor out of the rut.

Mr. OMHOLT. I will tell the people of North Dakota that.

Mr. LUNDEEN. You can state to the people of North Dakota that the Chairman of the Labor Committee, Mr. William P. Connery, has come out for this bill as well as, of course, the chairman of our subcommittee, Mr. Matthew A. Dunn, and today the Chairman of the Committee on Patents came out for the bill, so we are getting quite a number of distinguished gentlemen to support the bill.

Mr. OMHOLT. That is good.

Mr. DUNN. I have but very few farmers in my district, but I know this, that if it were not for the good old farmers, I would not be able to get my good old ham and cabbage, or pork and beans, because they produce them for me, and I like them because they produce those things for not only me but for every other person who likes to eat.

Mr. OMHOLT. I have also seen some conditions among the farmers in Pennsylvania that are nothing to brag about.

Mr. DUNN. I know, but I happen to live in the section that is near the city of Pittsburgh. You believe that the Lundeen bill, if it is enacted into law, will do a great deal to benefit the farmer?

Mr. OMHOLT. Absolutely.

Mr. DUNN. I agree with you. We have no more questions. I thank you, and I am glad you came, and glad to get your very valuable information.

(The hour of 5 p. m. having arrived, the subcommittee, in pursuance of its previous order, took a recess until 10 o'clock tomorrow morning.)

UNEMPLOYMENT, OLD AGE, AND SOCIAL INSURANCE

THURSDAY, FEBRUARY 7, 1935

House of Representatives,
Subcommittee of the Committee on Labor,
Washington, D. C.

The subcommittee met at 10 a.m., in the Caucus Room, House Office Building, Hon. Matthew A. Dunn (chairman) presiding.

The subcommittee had under consideration H. R. 2827, H. R. 2859, H. R. 10, and H. R. 185.

Mr. Dunn. The meeting will come to order. The first witness this morning will be Mr. I. Amter, of the National Unemployment Councils.

STATEMENT OF I. AMTER, REPRESENTING THE NATIONAL UNEMPLOYMENT COUNCILS, NEW YORK

Mr. Amter. Mr. Chairman, and members of the committee: We are of opinion that our organization is the best equipped organization to make a full exposition of the unemployed situation in the United States, because our organization is the only national organization of the unemployed in the country. We have a membership and following of about 500,000 unemployed. We have conducted all the major struggles of the unemployed throughout the country, at the relief bureaus, city marches, county marches, States marches, and as it well known, the National Unemployment Council led the two national hunger marches to Washington. We were responsible for the inauguration of the workers' unemployment and social insurance bill more than 4 years ago, and also initiated the call for the congress that was held here in Washington on January 5 and 7.

I would like to enter into the records of the committee the proceedings of the congress, as embodied in the Unemployment Insurance Review.

(The copy of Unemployment Insurance Review, presented to the Committee by the witness, is returned with this transcript, to be placed on file with the subcommittee of the Committee on Labor.)

Mr. Amter. The unemployed in this country are unalterably opposed to the Wagner-Lewis bill. They consider it a betrayal of the promise that was made of unemployment insurance. They consider the Wagner-Lewis bill merely as an embodiment of that betrayal. They just as energetically endorsed, supported, and fought for H. R. 7598 as today for H. R. 2827, since it is the only bill that provides the big army of unemployed with the protection that they demand now in the sixth year of the crisis.

It was the National Unemployment Council that in 1930 initiated the broad movement for the workers' bill. This occurred after the tremendous demonstrations on March 6, 1930, when masses of workers under the impact of the first stage of the crisis came into the streets demanding work or wages, and unemployment insurance. In the 5 years that have passed a tremendous amount of support has been gathered for this bill. Today this bill is supported by fully four to five million people. Twenty-five hundred locals of the American Federation of Labor, 5 international unions of the A. F. of L., 6 State federations of labor——

Mr. Dunn. Pardon me. You say 2,500 locals of the American Federation of Labor?

Mr. Amter. Endorsed the bill.

Mr. Dunn. How many locals are there of the American Federation of Labor?

Mr. Amter. I believe there are over a hundred thousand.

Mr. Dunn. Over a hundred thousand?

Mr. Amter. Yes.

Mr. Dunn. And over 2,500 of them have endorsed this bill?

Mr. Amter. Yes.

Mr. Dunn. Thank you.

Mr. Amter. We must add also to this number of 2,500 the locals of the internationals of the State federations of labor and central labor councils, which automatically have endorsed the bill through the endorsement that has been given by their superior body.

These, and upward of 50 central labor councils, have endorsed the bill in spite of the campaign of misrepresentation, distortion, slander, and terror that has been carried on against us by William Green and other leaders of the American Federation of Labor.

The bill is also endorsed by practically every organization or organized group of the unemployed; by farmers' organizations, fraternal veterans, Negro, youth, church, and professional organizations. The workers' bill has been endorsed by 70 municipal councils and county boards of commissioners, these including such cities as St. Louis, Buffalo, Minneapolis, Milwaukee, Bridgeport, Tacoma, Lynn, Youngstown, and Toledo, Ohio, and so forth. The workers' bill is not only before your committee but has already been introduced in four State legislatures, viz, California, Connecticut, Massachusetts, and Washington, and is about to be introduced in six or seven more State legislatures.

I will state here that we have just been informed that the Rhode Island State Federation of Labor, through its legislative committee, is going to introduce it into the State Legislature of Rhode Island.

The workers' bill is so popular that several spurious bills bearing the same or similar names have been introduced in the United States Congress by Congressmen from New York and Illinois; which shows the growing popularity of the bill and the attempts that are being made to thwart its purpose and divide the support that the workers are giving to H. R. 2827.

It is necessary at this point to remember the attitude that was taken to unemployment insurance by people high in Government office. It was in 1930 that Herbert Hoover refused to recognize the crisis and considered that we are merely in a temporary depression that soon would be overcome. As the crisis deepened and involved more millions of workers the turn against the Republican administration became pronounced and sharp and resulted in the change of administration. It was supposed that Mr. Roosevelt recognized the crisis, since he came forward with a promise of unemployment insurance, and unquestionably this slogan was one of the main bases for his election in 1932. Based upon this recognition also was supposed to be the theory behind the establishment of the N. I. R. A. If Mr. Hoover called unemployment insurance " un-American " and William Green, president of the American Federation of Labor, who in his position and pronouncements adopts the position of the existing administration, also called it " un-American against the interests of the American workers, having as its aim to wreck the trade-union movement in this country * * * " today we can say that every political party and Mr. Green himself are in favor of unemployment insurance. Even the National Manufacturers' Association, the American Bankers' Association, the United States Chamber of Commerce, and the National Retail Dry Goods Association are in favor of unemployment insurance. This shows that the tremendous movement that was initiated by the National Unemployment Council has forced its way into the ranks of the biggest capitalist organizations in this country and has compelled them to pretend, at least, that they support a measure that is in the interest of the working class.

The question is what kind of unemployment insurance do they propose and support?

The position of Mr. Roosevelt is supposed to be expressed in his thesis of building " an economy of plenty." The N. R. A. is alleged to be the embodiment of this. The supposed aim of the " new deal " was to return the millions to work, to increase the buying power of the masses and to provide unemployment insurance. The N. I. R. A. has been in operation now for more than a year and a half. The situation has not perceptibly improved, but on the contrary, in many respects the condition of the masses of the United States is far worse than it was in 1933. The number of unemployed has not diminished, but on the contrary, as most recent reports show, at the end of 1934 there were more unemployed than at the end of 1933. We declare that as long as there is insecurity for the unemployed there can be no security for anybody.

What must be the basis for the provision of security? It must be based upon:

1. A recognition of the capitalist crisis which is not merely a passing episode in the life of capitalism but one that is deep-going and cannot be overcome.

2. A recognition of the tremendous masses which are involved and who these masses are.

3. The continuation and deepening of the crisis which is having a most destructive effect upon all sections of the working population.

4. A recognition of what is termed technological unemployment which together with other causes is producing a permanent army of unemployed—not of bums and hoodlums but of able-bodied men and

women and particularly young workers who find no opportunity to do productive and remunerative work.

In face of this situation can we accept the basis for unemployment insurance as expressed by Mr. Roosevelt in his message to Congress on January 17, viz., " the detailed report of the Committee (National Committee on Economic Security) sets forth a series of proposals that will appeal to the sound sense of the American people. This has not attempted the impossible nor has it failed to exercise sound caution and consideration of all the factors concerned; the national credit, the rights and responsibilities of States, the capacity of industry to assume financial responsibilities, and the fundamental necessity of proceeding in a manner that will merit the enthusiastic support of citizens of all sorts." We declare that we cannot.

However, in the light of the position expressed by Mr. Roosevelt, let us briefly examine the Wagner-Lewis proposals insofar, particularly, as they affect the unemployed.

1. The Wagner-Lewis bill makes absolutely no provision for the unemployed. This means that the millions of unemployed would remain in the very same insecure state in which they are at the present time, facing greater impoverishment and destitutions as the years pass on.

2. But even those workers who are still fortunate enough to have jobs do not receive the protection through the Wagner-Lewis bill that is pretended. The Wagner-Lewis bill as such makes no specifications as to insurance even for those who might be entitled to insurance when the bill goes into effect. The Wagner-Lewis bill merely states how the so-called " unemployment trust fund " is to be created. No doubt the report of the National Committee on Economic Security to the President is the argument for the basis of the insurance for the workers. On this basis the unemployed would receive only 50 percent of their average wage but no more than $15 per week, with no minimum established. They would have to wait 4 weeks after being discharged and then receive benefits for only 15 weeks. Thereupon the worker will have exhausted his insurance benefits and have no claim. The worker who is discharged for misconduct would not be entitled to insurance. Misconduct today has a very definite connotation in the eyes of the employers, namely, the struggle for organization in the shop, or going out on strike. It is obvious, therefore, that a bill of this kind can only have a strike-breaking effect.

In addition, the bill is a State bill and would have to be enacted by each of the 48 States. As a result it could not conceivably go into effect before October 1936, provided every State legislature immediately enacted it. In addition, each State is at liberty to adopt or not to adopt the form of unemployment insurance corresponding to Government recommendation. Therefore, the workers as a whole are left to the mercy of the States.

Finally, the fund is to be created by means of a 3-percent tax upon pay rolls. If, however, the business index does not reach 95 percent of normal, then the pay-roll tax is to be reduced to 2 percent or even as low as 1 percent. This can only have one of two effects: (a) Either to postpone payments of benefits to the workers who are laid off; (b) or to reduce the amount of benefits. In any case the tax would be handed on by the employer to the worker by means of raising the price of his products. In other words, in actuality the worker is to pay his own insurance, even though it is collected under the high-sounding term of " pay-roll tax."

It is obvious that a supposed unemployment insurance scheme of this kind is nothing more than a sham. It would grant a maximum during a year of $225 benefit to a worker in any given year. This is nothing more than a dismissal wage. However, the bill also provides for 50 percent of the average wage with no minimum established. We wish to call attention to the fact that the Federal Government which, in the codes, sharply discriminated against the Negro worker, established minimum wages that are almost incomprehensible. For instance, only recently the N. R. A. established a code of $6 per week for 15,000 pecan-shelling workers for a work week of 35 to 40 hours. The reason that such a shamelessly low wage could be established is because the great, overwhelming majority of these workers are Negro workers. We would ask, therefore, if one of these workers came under the Wagner-Lewis bill and were laid off whether he might get 50 percent of his wage as " compensation ", viz. $3 a week for a maximum of 15 weeks. If this is called " insurance " then there is no wonder that the National Manufacturers Association and the United States Chamber of Commerce support such a proposal.

On June 8 Mr. Roosevelt sent a message to Congress. In this message he promised the American people that he would present to the present session of Congress a full system of social insurance to encompass full security for the whole working population. Mr. Roosevelt appointed the so-called " National Committee on Economic Security " which began the study. When this committee made its report on November 13 and 14, 1934, at a conference in Washington Mr. Roosevelt, to use the popular term, " cracked down " on the committee and declared that " first things come first." He stated that the only proposal that would be made would be for unemployment insurance; that old-age and health insurance would have to be further considered and be matters for future decision.

Since that time, owing to the opposition within the national committee there has been a change in his position: viz, he brings forward the question of old-age pension, old-age annuity, child welfare, public health, and so forth, and so forth, in an attempt to remove from consideration the more basic, pressing, and burning issue of bona fide unemployment insurance. The whole series of old-age pensions, child welfare, maternal care, aid for crippled children, and so forth, will not give the persons involved more than $93,500,000 per year. What is this in face of the fearful problems that face the aged, infirm, and crippled in the year 1935? It is merely a bagatelle and certainly cannot compare with the $180,-000,000 increase in the war budget, which the Government without hesitation and without any considerable opposition will obtain from the United States Congress.

However, it is necessary even to examine the old-age pension plan since it contains provisions directed against certain sections of the population. The bill makes it clear that only United States citizens will get the pension in that it ambiguously states that such assistance shall not be denied to any person who is a United States citizen. In addition, the recipient must have "resided in the State for 5 years or more within the 10 years immediately preceding application for assistance." It is obvious that these are two threats at the American workers as against the foreign-born worker who has not become a citizen but who has given all his strength and vitality in piling up wealth in this country; and secondly, that it requires that a worker must have been resident in the State for this period, which due to the crisis, is almost impossible for the worker. Workers today are forced to move from place to place in search of work. The elderly people move from son to daughter and other relatives in the hope of getting support. Quite clearly this pension bill aims to eliminate the really needy, unemployed age from old-age pensions.

The proposal, however, that the United States Government shall grant a maximum of $15 a month pension for old-age which is to be matched dollar for dollar by the States makes the issue even clearer. Mr. Roosevelt seemed content with the fact that in various States old-age pensions are already in operation. We call attention to the fact that such systems are in operation in various States of the country either in a mandatory or optional form. We quote the situation in various States. In the State of Colorado where one must have been a citizen for 15 years and resided in the State for 15 years, the average compensation per month is $7.69. We wish to emphasize, however, that in the same State it costs the State to maintain an old man or woman in the poorhouse $42.30 a month. In the State of Wyoming the average pension is $11.69 a month. The same conditions for eligibility prevail as in Colorado. But the State has to pay to maintain an old man or woman in the poorhouse $78.74. Even in the State of New York, which Mr. Roosevelt states has a very "liberal" system of pensions, the average pension is $20.58 a month. The recipient must be a citizen and even a resident for 10 years. In the New York poorhouse the inmate costs the State $35.80 a month. In other words, the Federal Government proposes to give the old man and woman even less than it costs the States to maintain them in the poorhouse. This quite clearly is not extending more aid to the aged but on the contrary is a step in economy for the State.

However, what guarantee can the Federal Government give that the State will be even as "liberal" as the Federal Government is; that is, that the States will guarantee $15 a month? There is no assurance whatever. On the contrary, there is every likelihood that many States will either refuse or be unable to grant such pensions altogether. We cannot accept any such position in connection with the men and women of the country who have given all their strength to build this country.

On the contrary, we lay down a certain fundamental basis in our demand for unemployment and social insurance. We declare:

1. That every worker has a right to live.
2. That in order to live a worker must earn his living; in other words, he must have a job.
3. If he is denied the right to earn a living and therefore to maintain himself and his family, then he has the basic right to

demand that the Government, which is supposed to provide for the welfare of the people, shall compensate him or her to the extent of his potential earning power.

Mr. DUNN. An interruption, again. The Constitution of the United States makes that statement you just made.

Mr. AMTER. I agree. I did not state it, because I thought that everybody, in particular the members of this committee, were well aware of that.

Mr. DUNN. I just wanted to emphasize it.

Mr. AMTER. Correct.

These demands are basic. We do not raise the question of how much or how little it will cost. It is a fundamental issue, even more basic than provisions for war. Particularly now in a crisis with millions of people facing hunger and starvation this should and must be the first concern of the Government.

We can accept the statement of the Committee on Economic Security to the President as contained in the report of January 17, viz.:

> The one almost all-embracing measure of security is an assured income. A program of economic security, as we vision it, must have as its primary aim an assurance of an adequate income to each human being in childhood, youth, middle age, or old age—in sickness or in health. It must provide safeguards against all the hazards leading to destitution and dependency.

Based upon this contention we drafted and brought to the masses of the workers the Workers Unemployment, Old Age, and Social Insurance bill. This bill and this bill alone provides genuine unemployment insurance to the masses of unemployed. This bill alone covers all sections of the working population without any discrimination. This bill provides that every worker and farmer in the United States above 18 years of age for the full period of his ability to work, whether it be due to unemployment, part-time, sickness, accident, old age, or maternity, shall receive the average local wage, but at no time less than $10 a week plus $3 for each dependent, which shall be provided by the Government. If funds in the Treasury are not available the Government shall raise such funds by means of taxation on all incomes above $5,000, upon gifts, inheritances, and so forth. The compensation shall be distributed to the recipients without discrimination as to age, sex, race, religious or political affiliation. The unemployment and social-insurance fund is to be controlled and administered by rank-and-file workers and farmers, elected by workers' and farmers' organizations.

The proponents of the workers bill demand that those who now control industry shall be made responsible to provide a decent compensation to those who are denied the right to work. The whole burden of this insurance is placed upon the shoulders of the rich who shall be taxed for the benefit of the poor.

It is not at all astonishing, therefore, why not only the unemployed but the masses of the workers who, once they become acquainted with the workers bill, and contrast it with all other bills, lend immediate and enthusiastic support to the workers bill. This is a basic demand today: The right to protection in every emergency, against every hazard that confronts the worker, whether he is employed or unemployed.

The question will be asked: Is this bill "practical"? We do not base our argument upon the practicability of the bill. We know that in an emergency the Federal Government has raised tens of billions of dollars. We say that there is no greater emergency facing the country than the emergency of the crisis and the situation of the unemployed.

However, this question can also be answered in a different manner. The National Conference on Potential Productive Capacity, which is a semiofficial Government institution, ascertained only recently that if the full productive capacity of industry in 1929 had been utilized, without the addition of a single factory or machine it would have been possible to create in the United States instead of $90,000,000,000 of wealth, $138,000,000,000 of wealth. This would have meant for each family in the United States approximately $5,000 per year. Dr. Ezekiel, economic advisor of the Department of the Interior, stated recently that for a "full, normal life" a family in the United States today requires $2,500 a year. The demand through the workers bill for an unemployed worker with a wife and two children—which is the average family—would mean a minimum of $19 per week or $988 a year.

Mr. LUNDEEN. That is $19 per week for an average family?

Mr. AMTER. Ten dollars for the worker, $3 for each dependent, for three dependents, making $19 a week, or $988 a year.

Mr. LUNDEEN. How many do you take to be an average family?

Mr. AMTER. Four—the man and his wife and 2 children—3 dependents for the man.

This is only one-third of the so-called "full, normal life", and surely could be provided if American industry, instead of closing its doors, if American agriculture, instead of being plowed under, were utilized to the maximum. We demand in a period when millions are hungry and millions are going without clothes and shoes, that the factories be opened and workers be put to work, that the land be tilled and the farmers not be ordered to destroy their crops. This is not laying the basis for the so-called "economy of plenty", but is in reality a campaign of destruction.

However, we urge that certain changes that were made in the bill by Congressman Lundeen be again changed. We demand that unemployment and social insurance be granted to all workers and farmers above 16 years of age. At 16 years of age boys and girls are not only allowed but compelled to work because of the inadequacy of the income of their parents. They therefore should have the same protection as all other workers. Mr. Lundeen eliminated the word "citizenship" from the bill which would allow the Government to discriminate against foreign-born workers who have not become citizens. We demand that workers who have given the best of their strength in building for the rich in the United States shall be entitled to as full protection as native workers. Mr. Lundeen also inserted the words that insurance shall be on the basis of "average local wages" instead of "average local wages in the industry." The latter term has an entirely different meaning and the only real protection for the workers maintaining their previous standards. Mr. Lundeen also abstracted the words "present or" from the connection of past participation in strikes. According to this provision workers who go out on strike would be entitled to no insurance. We must vigorously protest against any such provision in a bill which calls itself a "workers bill" since it would be used as the Wagner-Lewis bill will be used to prevent the workers from organizing and going on strike.

In whose interest do we demand enactment of the workers bill? As representative of the National Unemployment Council, and speaking in behalf of the unemployed in this country we raise first of all the question of the millions of unemployed.

Who are the unemployed? They are not only the manual workers but also the white-collar workers, professionals, and the farmers who have been driven from the land, and so forth. We wish to quote only a few facts. Ninety-five percent of the architects are unemployed. Eighty-five percent of the engineers and technicians are unemployed. They are unemployed because 80 percent of the building-trades workers are unemployed. Five million youths have been unemployed for more than 5 years of the crisis. This is according to Dr. Zook, United States Commissioner of Education, and Newton D. Baker, who declared that of the 7,000,000 boys and girls who have graduated from high schools and colleges during the years of the crisis not more than one-third have found any work, and those only part-time work at very low wages. These include millions of Negro people, who are the most persecuted of all. Not only does unemployment hit them hardest, but they are the last to get jobs and get the least relief.

But not only these people are the ones that are affected by the crisis. Two hundred and fifty thousand school teachers are unemployed. There are hundreds of thousands of doctors, artists, musicians, white-collar workers, actors, people of all professions. Only recently there was a report that there are 20,000 unemployed clergymen. At the present time, however, new sections of the population are being forced to obtain relief. These include principally a middle-class section which has been able to eke out an existence on the basis of some savings, help from relatives, and so forth.

How long have these people been unemployed? We quote from a report of the F. E. R. A. of September. On page 10 the report says:

Nearly one-sixth of all who are seeking work have been unsuccessful in finding it for nearly 4 years.

Another recent investigation shows that 12 percent of the unemployed have been out of a job for a similar period. It is obvious, therefore, that we are now dealing with a phase of unemployment such as this country has never faced, of unemployment that is cutting into the very vitals of each section of the working population.

Mr. DUNN. Pardon the interruption. I understand you to say there are about 20,000 clergymen who are out of jobs?

Mr. AMTER. There was a report in the press of a representative of a group of 20,000 clergymen who came to Washington to consult with President Roosevelt, and to ask him to find some means of remuneration or some form of occupation for these unemployed clergymen.

Mr. DUNN. This delegation that came to see our President, in other words, made that statement, that there are about 20,000?

Mr. AMTER. About 20,000. That statement was made; yes, sir.

Mr. DUNN. I do not know whether you can supply us with this information or not, but the 20,000 represented what denominations?

Mr. AMTER. That was not stated.

Mr. DUNN. It was not stated?

Mr. AMTER. I think we all know there is a crisis in the churches.

Mr. DUNN. I want to say I am convinced now more than I was yesterday that we are in a depression, when 20,000 ministers are out of jobs.

Mr. LUNDEEN. Mr. Chairman, I should like to ask the witness this question: Have you reports showing how many doctors and dentists and lawyers are unemployed? There must be a considerable number of them who are not employed at the present time.

Mr. AMTER. There are plenty of them. I cannot state definitely, but I can give you an intimation.

Mr. LUNDEEN. I know we have some attorneys in the relief lines in Minneapolis.

Mr. AMTER. May I answer Mr. Lundeen, Mr. Chairman?

Mr. DUNN. Yes.

Mr. AMTER. We have no figures on these particular professions, but I can say they are coming up to our office, groups of lawyers, doctors, musicians, people of all professions, asking us to organize them, to help them get some kind of occupation and relief.

Mr. LUNDEEN. That is what the administration wants to do with the soldiers who carried the flag in time of war. They want them to sign a piece of paper saying, " We soldiers are paupers. Give us something! "

Mr. DUNN. It is an outrage, the way the people are being treated. What this gentleman is saying, and in fact, all that the previous witnesses have told us, can be substantiated by Congressmen who are willing to tell the truth.

Mr. LUNDEEN. Of course, Americans resent that sort of thing. They feel they should have these things as a matter of right, and not as a result of signing a piece of paper pauperizing themselves.

Mr. DUNN. May I also make this statement for the record? The gentleman mentioned President Roosevelt's plan for unemployment pension and old-age pensions. The President is getting a lot of criticism that, in my opinion, he does not altogether deserve. We Members of Congress make the laws; and if the President is not satisfied with the laws we make, we can pass them over his veto. Therefore, the Members of Congress should be condemned, not the President.

Mr. AMTER. That is correct, Mr. Dunn. On the other hand, Mr. Roosevelt has been an exponent of unemployment insurance for 2 years. There is no question about this—and I do not think anyone will attempt to deny it—that he was elected in 1932 mainly on that issue. Nevertheless, in spite of all the repetitions of his proposals for unemployment insurance, we have now this fake Wagner-Lewis bill, to which he has not yet specifically given his support, although he did give his support to the Wagner-Lewis bill in the last session; and certainly it was no unemployment insurance, so far as the unemployed were concerned.

Mr. DUNN. I realize that, but is it not a fact that we can take the Wagner-Lewis bill that the President wants and make it into a bill similar to this one?

Mr. AMTER. I would advise rather that you adopt the workers' bill.

Mr. DUNN. I am going to do my utmost to see that it is adopted.

Mr. LUNDEEN. Mr. Chairman, I have just learned that Drs. L. Schwartz and M. Schulte, of Brooklyn, N. Y., appearing on behalf of the Economic Federation of Dentists of New York, and representing 2,000 dentists, have requested of the chairman the privilege of presenting their case. So we will have some professionals.

Mr. DUNN. Yes; I wired to one of the doctors, telling him to come. He is coming tomorrow.

You may proceed, Mr. Amter.

Mr. AMTER. How many unemployed are there in the United States? During the regime of Mr. Hoover there was a continual tendency to play down the number of unemployed. In March 1930 Mr. Hoover declared there were only 3,400,000 unemployed. Miss Frances Perkins, who at that time was industrial commissioner of the State of New York, declared that Mr. Hoover falsified the figures for his own political ends. At the present time Miss Perkins is Secretary of Labor, and we must charge that Miss Perkins is doing the same thing that Mr. Hoover did in his term. Miss Perkins and the Government contend that there are about 9,000,000 unemployed. On the other hand, William Green declares there are more than 11,000,000 unemployed. The Committee on Economic Security, in its report to the President, on page 1 of its report declares that "Approximately 10,000,000 workers have no employment other than relief work." At the time of the last convention of the American Federation of Labor, when William Green contended that there were only a few more than 10,000,000 unemployed, Mr. Robert Watt, of the State Federation of Labor of Massachusetts, at the convention proved that there were at least 16,000,000 unemployed.

We declare that on the basis of a clear examination of the situation in the United States today there are more than 17,000,000 unemployed, and we submit herewith an estimate of the Labor Research Association.

Economic notes—Summary of Labor Research Association's estimate of unemployment in November 1934 (preliminary)

Occupation	Wage earners	Salaried employees, independents, owners	Total
Agriculture	719, 000	[1] 1, 070, 000	1, 789, 000
Forestry and fishing	81, 000	4, 000	85, 000
Extraction of minerals:			
Coal	165, 000	4, 000	169, 000
Metal mining	85, 000	} 9, 000	139, 000
Quarries and nonmetal	45, 000		
Oil and gas wells	30, 000	7, 000	37, 000
Manufacturing and mechanical:			
Building			2, 041, 000
Manufacturing [2]	2, 629, 000	631, 000	3, 260, 000
Transportation and communication:			
Railroads (steam)			621, 000
Telephone, telegraph			182, 000
Postal service			34, 000
All other			612, 000
Trade:			
Wholesale, retail [3]			903, 000
All other			427, 000
Professional service			852, 000
Domestic and personal service:			
Laundries, cleaning, dyeing, etc			60, 000
Hotels, restaurants, etc			276, 000
All other			868, 000
Public service			132, 000
Industry not specified			643, 000
Increase in number of gainful workers since 1930			3, 227, 000
Deficiency in unemployment census, etc			800, 000
Total			17, 157, 000

[1] Includes unemployed family labor and farmers.
[2] Includes auto repair, railroad repair shops, and independent hand trades.
[3] Includes automotive agencies.

In this estimate of unemployment, part-time workers are as usual considered as employed. Persons working on Government relief projects are considered as unemployed. These workers on special Government funds were estimated by United States Bureau of Labor Statistics for October 1934, as follows:

On construction projects financed by P. W. A	508, 000
Emergency work program	1, 950, 000
Emergency conservation work	392, 000
Total	2, 850, 000

Excluding these 2,850,000 on special relief and public works, the total completely unemployed in November 1934 was about 14,307,000.

A separate report giving comparisons with our 1933 revised estimate is available for those subscribers desiring it.

We will never know accurately how many unemployed there are in the United States until we have a full system of social insurance embracing every worker.

The number of unemployed is not declining. On the contrary, except for the month of January there has been almost a consistent monthly increase of the unemployed. In every State there is noted a rise in the number of applicants for relief. They are not people who have been on the relief rolls before. On the contrary, while for instance in New York City, 35,000 people have been removed from the relief rolls during the last few months, the number of new applicants per day has risen to about 2,000. In every city of the country this phenomenon is to be noted.

This shows clearly that hunger, misery, destitution, and the degradation of new sections of the population has taken place. We mean that homes are being broken up. There is an increase in crime, murder, suicide, gangsterism, prostitution. Workers are losing their homes; farmers are losing their land and buildings; professionals are being driven on to the breadline. Millions of the children face a future of broken-down lives. This in a land of endless plenty. Can one wonder if in face of this situation there is a growing radicalization of the masses? We state that 17,000,000 unemployed is not a small army. On the contrary, it is an army of hungry, desperate men, who have resorted and may resort again to the most desperate measures in order to live unless the Government is going to assume as its fundamental duty the provision of "adequate income against every hazard."

In his speech on Labor Day William Green declared that the 10,000,000 unemployed represent "a mass of 40,000,000 people in the United States who are dependent on relief." In other words, nearly one-third of the population of the United States is dependent on relief. Mr. Hopkins, F. E. R. A. director, admits that there are only 20,000,000 persons on relief today, but the number is growing. Obviously, therefore, millions are receiving no relief. This embraces a large section of the Negro and foreign-born workers, young and single workers. How they live cannot be surmised.

In face of this growing situation the unemployed above all demand the fulfillment of the promises that were made more than 2 years ago by Mr. Roosevelt in the election campaign—promises that have been reiterated by him and echoed by politicians and leaders of all shades. We demand genuine unemployment insurance and demand it now.

Let us examine in detail the situation of the unemployed. As a result of the crisis homes have been systematically broken up. The father goes one way, the mother another, the children are shifted into foster homes and orphan asylums. We quote from the Annals of the American Academy of Political and Social Science, issue of November 1934, article by J. Prentiss Murphy, of the Seybert Institution of Philadelphia and member of the Pennsylvania State Welfare Commission. Mr. Seybert says:

What is the situation confronting approximately 400,000 children in the care of 1,900 public and private children's agencies and institutions? What concern should we express for the 200,000 children who annually pass through the juvenile courts, and for the average annual population of 65,000 boys and girls and young men and young women who are in our industrial schools and reformatories?

As a result of the impossibly high rents and the continual evictions that have taken place, families have doubled up. In fact, in some homes there live not simply 2 families but sometimes 3 or more families. This is especially true among the Negro people because of the outrageously high rents in the Negro territory and the continual evictions that are taking place.

The situation of the children, however, should be of the most serious consequence to anyone who earnestly considers providing for the welfare of the working population. According to the report of the United States Department of Labor, 25 percent of the children in the United States are undernourished, in some localities rising as high as 70 percent. In a recent investigation that was made it was found that 75 percent of the children are suffering from defective eyesight, 80 percent have bad teeth. Two and a quarter million children in the United States are getting no education whatever. This is the result of the so-called "economy plans" of both the Federal and the State Governments. This is particularly true in the South and affects the Negro children, who altogether receive a poorer education for a shorter period of the year at the hands of less developed teachers, who likewise are very poorly paid.

This situation, however, is most marked when one considers the milk situation. According to reports of the Consumers' Council of the A. A. A., based upon a national milk survey in 59 cities, it has been ascertained that "1 family in every 7, over 14 percent of the total, bought no fresh milk at all. All of the families surveyed had children." In the city of New York during the month of October 1934, when Governor Lehman, with the publicly expressed support of President Roosevelt, was carrying on a ballyhoo campaign for the alleged purpose of extending the use of milk in the State of New York and helping the farmers, and proclaimed October as a "buy-more milk month", actually in the city of New York the consumption of milk declined 5,000,000 quarts. During this month the price of milk went up 1 cent, and as a natural result the working-class families, and particularly the latter, were the worst sufferers. According to the report of the New York State College of Agriculture, "consumption for October 1934 was the lowest for any October since 1925." This is the manner in which America cherishes and develops the children.

As already stated, the Negroes are the worst sufferers from the crisis. They show a higher percentage of unemployment than any other section of the population. Having been forced to a lower standard of living through the practice of race prejudice, now in the crisis they are on the very verge of starvation. The very establishment of lower minimum wages for Negroes in the codes made it possible for the employers to fire them entirely and put on white workers, or in spite of the code to force the Negro workers to work at even lower wages than provided in the code. We read in the papers only a few days ago that in Puerto Rico women doing home work averaged 1 to 4 cents an hour.

We have already noted the number of unemployed youth in the United States. What has become of this youth, boys and girls? It was reported that millions of these boys and girls have been roaming up and down the country, having left home in search of work and a crust of bread. They have lived and are living in jungles and "Hoovervilles." Using freight trains as their conveyance, they have been killed by railroad guards in the yards, have been arrested by police and either sent to jail, or down in the South put on the chain gang. Many of them have died of exposure; tens of thousands of them through corrupt influences have become degenerate. The Government refuses systematically to provide any relief for the young workers.

Mr. DUNN. May I say that at the last session of Congress, and also at this session of Congress, I introduced a bill to abolish the chain-gang system, but unfortunately my bill has been "pickled." In fact, they put it in the barrel, and jumped on it. They say it is unconstitutional.

Mr. AMTER. I might say a word in connection with that. I think it is your colleagues of the Democratic Party who are mainly responsible for that condition, the Democrats being in control of the South.

Mr. DUNN. You say "my colleagues?"

Mr. AMTER. Are you not a Democrat? I know you dissociate yourself from that kind of a Democrat. I am glad to hear it.

Mr. DUNN. I interpret the word "Democrat" to mean one who is progressive and humane. Of course, I happened to be nominated on both tickets. When I first came down here I was elected on the Independent and Democratic tickets. You cannot condemn a man for having the name "Democratic" or "Republican" attached to him. As I said before, to me the word "Democratic" means a person who is progressive and who stands for humanitarianism; so when you say "my colleagues", of course, we are all brothers—no matter if they are horse thieves and porch climbers; but I am down here, desiring to be known as a representative of the people.

Mr. AMTER. I want to differentiate you from the Democrats of the Democratic Party, and also to make it quite clear that although the word "democratic" may signify the rule of the people, nevertheless it is obvious today that democracy, as represented by the Democratic Party, signifies the rule of Wall Street.

Mr. DUNN. I am not going to dispute you.

Mr. AMTER. It is only under the leadership of the National Unemployment Council, where a struggle has been put up, that young and single workers have obtained relief.

Although there are millions of unemployed women the Government practically does not concern itself at all with the fate of these women. In spite of "cherishing womanhood" in the United States, the best recommendation that both male and female relief directors in the relief bureaus can give to women applicants is, "Why don't you get yourself a boy friend?"

The impoverished workers are compelled to live in the worst kinds of tenements, fire-traps, and condemned buildings. It is stated that "some 9,000,000 families live in homes that conservation investigators call 'substandard'" (Social Questions Bulletin, Methodist Federation for Social Service, November 1934). Federal agencies estimate that 3,000,000 live in "slums unfit for habitation", and the United States Chamber of Commerce estimates that "50,-000,000 persons are housed in unsanitary or other undesirable homes." This is stated by F. J. C. Dresser, Director of Housing in charge of the Chicago C. W. A. project. According to Mr. LaGuardia, mayor of the city of New York, "The lives of at least a million persons living in old-law tenements are endangered night and day." According to the Citizens Family Welfare Committee of New York, 16,000 families of unemployed are living in cellars in New York. One-quarter of the families of Manhattan are slum dwellers, according to Langdon W. Post, chairman of the New York Housing Authority. Mr. Post further states that as a result of the old-law tenements "1,500,000 men, women, and children of the city are living simply in fire traps." This means that one-quarter of the population of New York faces the danger of death through fire hazards. In fact, during the year 1934, 56 persons were burned to death in New York as a result of being compelled to live in old, condemned tenement houses.

We are aware of the fact that the Federal Government pretends to have a big building construction and housing program. We say that this program is totally inadequate. As a result, also of the crisis, millions of home owners are in danger of losing their homes, while hundreds of thousands have already been foreclosed.

Mr. DUNN. Pardon me. I introduced a bill calling for the expenditure of $100,000,000,000 on a 10-year plan. Would you say that my bill was inadequate?

Mr. AMTER. No; I would not say that it was inadequate. In fact, we are even a little more modest in our proposal than you were in yours, and I will bring that before you in just a moment.

Mr. DUNN. I introduced that bill this year.

Mr. AMTER. These home owners are in the main workers and small business men who have put their life savings into homes in order to have a roof over their heads for a rainy day. The rainy day is here but the homes are being lost. The Government declares that it has advanced through the Home Owners' Loan Corporation $2,000,000,-000 in loans to the small home owners. These loans have not reached the home owners, but have gone to the banks and insurance companies that hold the mortgages, thus guaranteeing payment to them. The most needy home owners got no loans whatever because they only had a small equity in their home, but even those that did secure loans are losing their homes because they cannot meet their payments. Similarly, the farmers who also supposedly have received loans.

Mr. DUNN. May I again interrupt? I am glad you are bringing this subject up. I want to substantiate what you are saying now. I have had many unfortunate men and women come to my office to see if I could obtain for them a loan from the Home Owners' Loan Corporation in Pittsburgh, and may I say that unless these men and women could show that they were able to pay the principal and interest on the money which was to be obtained from the Home Owners' Loan Corporation, they would not be considered, and I made an address over in the House this year, stating to the Members of Congress that when that bill was presented, and when it was passed, it was passed as a relief measure, but it could not be called a relief measure as long as it did not take care of the unemployed who were unable to pay any principal or interest. May I say that I am having a bill prepared, instead of asking for $2,000,000,000, I am requesting $5,000,000,000.

Mr. AMTER. But the poorest farmers have been unable to obtain loans. Under the program of "economy of plenty" the farmers have been ordered to cut down production one-quarter. Through the payment of bonuses they supposedly are getting higher prices for their food. It is true some have benefited somewhat, but only a certain group to a small degree, whereas the workers in the city have to pay the price. At the same time the poor farmer, the white and Negro share-cropper and tenant farmer, is no longer able to exist upon the farm. This, together with the drought and the crisis which has endured in the farming industry since 1921, has driven hundreds of thousands of farmers off the farms entirely, and forced others to obtain relief or work relief in order to eke out an existence. Thus, as a result of this program, 300,000 cotton sharecroppers and tenant farmers of Texas alone have been forced off the land, adding 1,500,000 persons to the number of those dependent upon relief.

As a consequence of this situation the price of food has gone sky-high in this " economy of plenty." Food has risen 30 percent in about 16 months, the cost of clothing 27 percent. Secretary of Commerce Roper has warned us that during the present winter, prices will advance still higher. The result of this situation is quite naturally a reduction in the purchase of the necessities of life. We point out that between 1929 and 1933 there was a reduction in wholesale trade of 52.8 percent (from $15,600,000,000 to $7,376,000,000), and retail trade dropped in the same period 47 percent.

This shows clearly that because of the rise in the price of food, because of the tremendous unemployment and the meager relief, because of the actual drop in wages, the working population of the country is unable to buy the necessities of life. Its strength is being reduced, and as a result of this general impoverishment diseases of all kinds are rampant. Thus, we find according to the Annals of the American Academy of Political and Social Science, November 1934, the statement by Edgar Sydenstricker, director of research of the Millbank Memorial Fund, New York City, and chief statistician of the United States Public Health Service, that—

The highest sickness rate in 1933 occurred in families which had suffered the most severe decline in income during the period 1929–32. This group has a disabling and sickness rate over 50 percent higher than that of their more fortunate neighbors * * *. In families with no employed members or only part-time wage earners, the death rate increased 20 percent.

In spite of the assertions of physicians and insurance companies that the people of the United States were never healthier than at the present time, in spite of the most stupid statement by a leading physician of California that " children are healthier now in the crisis because their parents cannot feed them such rich food ", we find that according to the Public Health Service in its Associated Press dispatch of December 10, 1934, dated Washington, in the first half of 1934, there was a high rate of pneumonia and other death rates. Infant mortality was 62 per 1,000 live births as compared to 59 and 58 in the 2 preceding years. According to Dorothy G. Wiehl of the Millbank Memorial Fund, " only in families where the income exceeded $5 a week for every member was the food supply adequate from a dietetic standpoint." Miss Wiehl pointed out that " families with incomes of $1 to $4 per week live on a diet average of 2,400 calories a day, or 600 below the minimum for the maintenance of life."

It is obvious, therefore, that in this situation the working masses are steadily being impoverished and cannot meet their needs. Teachers College of Columbia University, New York City, last year pointed out that a family of five requires for food alone per week $9.45. Nowhere in the country is there this minimum standard of relief. As a result the whole working-class family is slowly sinking in vitality.

There has been current in the United States a theory of high wages. In the report of Mr. Roosevelt, the National Committee on Economic Security declares that in 1929—

Eighteen million gainfully employed persons, constituting 44 percent of those gainfully occupied, exclusive of farmers, had annual earnings of less than $1,000; 28,000,000, or nearly 70 percent, earnings of less than $1,500. * * * The average earnings of all wage earners at work dropped from $1,475 in 1929 to $1,199 in 1932.

This whole theory of high wages which was based upon the idea that workers would be able to save money for an emergency had been painfully blasted. Thus the California State Unemployment Commission, in its report of November 1932, states:

In terms of 1913 dollars, real annual earnings in manufacturing industries averaged $700 in 1923 and $668 in 1928.

It points out that according to a study of Dr. P. H. Nystrom, published in 1929—

Eight million persons in the United States were living on the boundary line; 12,000,000 had enough to maintain a minimum level.

The report summarizes the theory of high wages as follows:

The principle of high wages as a vehicle for national prosperity accepted by many progressive business leaders, although trumpeted throughout the length and breadth of the country, failed of adoption on a large scale. Dogmatic belief that high wages prevailed in the country at large had no basis of fact to substantiate it. The facts indicate that labor not only failed to share in the * * * post-war prosperity but that relatively and absolutely there was an actual decline in the real earnings of wage workers in manufacturing establishments. These facts speak eloquently of the disparity existing between productive capacity and consumptive capacity. While the wealth and income of the country were growing by leaps and bounds the income of the masses failed to keep pace with this movement. The advantages of increased wealth and increased national income failed to accrue to those who contributed their share in bringing about this unprecedented increase of wealth.

This makes it clear that the standard of living of the American workers has never been high. On the contrary, it has been a hoax by which the American workers were fooled into the belief that they were enjoying a high prosperity at times when, as the California report shows, they were being more and more exploited and not receiving any of the advantages of increased production which came about through their own efforts.

As a result of this situation vast numbers of workers have been able to save no money whatever. Thus, in the report prepared by the Committee on Economic Security we find that in the year 1929, the year of prosperity, 11,500,000 families, or 42 percent of the families of the country, were living on a "subsistence and poverty line." On the other hand, 375,000 wealthy families had an income of $25,000 each per year. During the same year 5,750,000 families had no savings whatever, whereas 125,000 wealthy families had savings during that year amounting to $6,500,000,000.

I submit for the record the publication of the Committee on Economic Security, which contains these statements.

(The publication of the Committee on Economic Security, entitled, "The Need for Economic Security in the United States", submitted to the committee by the witness, is returned with this transcript, to be placed on file with the subcommittee of the Comitee on Labor.)

UNEMPLOYMENT, OLD AGE, AND SOCIAL INSURANCE

Mr. AMTER. Mr. Roosevelt on October 1 made the following statement:

I stand or fall by my refusal to accept as a necessary condition of our future a permanent army of unemployed.

Mr. Roosevelt may be convinced of his position in spite of all logic, in face of the statements of even the most conservative economists that there is a permanent army of unemployed and that this army is growing. The Committee on Economic Security in its own document points out that at the height of prosperity in February 1929 there were 2,817,000 unemployed in the United States. Let us quote Mr. Harold B. Butler, director of the International Labor Office, in his speech at the conference on Economic Security held in Washington on November 13. Mr. Butler said:

Whatever the truth may have been before the war, it is quite certain that the incidence of unemployment is very much greater now, and I believe that it is true not only of the last 5 years of the depression, but during the whole post-war period in a somewhat limited degree.

Every technologist, every economist knows that by means of technological improvements, stretch-out devices, speed-up methods, the number of workers required for a particular operation is continually being reduced. In face of the minimum codes the manufacturers have threatened and actually are putting through the introduction of labor-saving machinery to do away with human-labor power. These facts are too well-known to require any discussion. However, we wish to mention merely one fact.

In the November 26 issue of the Blue Eagle News, organ of the N. R. A., dealing with the chemical manufacturing industry, we find that whereas between May and September of 1934 the index of employment remained unchanged, the index of man-hours increased only slightly, pay rolls declined a few points, and the index of production rose 27 percent. The same can be duplicated in any industry. This means the permanent dislodgement of hundreds of thousands of workers from industry who cannot be reemployed. Mr. Roosevelt may not like the facts but the facts are unalterable.

As against the demand that the workers thus dislodged shall be provided with unemployment insurance, the raising of the demand for the 30-hour week is not in place. Every worker is in favor of the 30-hour week with no reduction in pay, and we will fight for its strict enforcement; but a reduction in hours will merely mean a further introduction of new labor-saving machinery which will disemploy more hundreds of thousands of workers who will not be able to obtain work. Therefore, the demand for unemployment insurance remains basic irrespective of the hours of work.

As a contrast with this situation we have merely to regard the profits of the bondholders and manufacturers. In 1930, when wages were beginning to collapse, dividends and total interest payments were larger than in 1929. This continued even through 1931. Thus we find the following figures:

Total interest paid:
1929	$4,109,000,000
1930	4,374,000,000
1931	4,553,000,000

We find during the year 1934 when the real wages of the workers continued to toboggan, corporate interest and dividends, according to the Journal of Commerce, amounted to $6,340,000,000, only $45,000,- 000 less than 1933. However, we call attention to the fact that Mr. Richberg reported to Mr. Roosevelt on the anniversary of the " new deal " that earnings and dividends of the same big corporations had increased up to 600 percent. We find that industrial profits, according to the Federal Reserve Board in 1934 were 70 percent greater in the first 9 months in comparison with the same period in 1933. While the situation of the workers became more destitute, the capitalists were able to report 26 more millionaires in the year 1933 than in 1932. This may be considered an " achievement " for the country, but it is only brought about through the pauperization of greater numbers of workers.

In addition, on the pretense of helping the capitalists to put millions back to work, the Reconstruction Finance Corporation has advanced to the banks, railroads, and other corporations more than $8,350,000,000. This has been used not to put millions back to work—for the millions remain unemployed—but for the purpose of paying out higher dividends.

The Government, which pleads economy in all of its measures and particularly now in connection with unemployment insurance, did not hesitate during the last year to spend nearly $2,000,000,000 for war preparations.

Thus we see the contrast of wealth accumulated on the one hand, with the help of the Government to boost it still more, while the situation of the workers becomes more impoverished. Mr. Roosevelt has declared that recovery depends upon profits. This is the position of the big bankers of the United States who make the same assertion. Thus, we read in the publication of the National City Bank of New York, January 1935, that " profits are the very agency by which recovery will come."

On the other hand, the wages of the workers do not correspond to the tremendous growth in the profits of the capitalists. The unemployed are directly affected by the wages of the workers in the shops. This is all the clearer in view of the recent decision on so-called " prevailing rates." On the other hand, the wages of workers in the shops are also dependent upon relief rates. Thus, in March 1933 when Roosevelt became President the wages in 104 industries amounted to $19.65 per week. By September 1934, taking into account the increase in the cost of living, real wages compared with March 1933 amounted to only $19.05. (Monthly Survey of Business, Nov. 1934, American Federation of Labor.) This shows a decline of 60 cents per week in the real wages of the worker in the first year of the " new deal."

With 2 workers in the United States fully unemployed, with 1 working part-time, and only 2 workers fully employed in the United States, it is obvious that the relation between the employed and unemployed is very direct and close. The codes established minimum wages. Not only were these minimum wages not adhered to, the bosses taking advantage of the unemployment situation to reduce the wages even though this constituted a violation of the code, but at the same time minimum wages became maximum wages. Thus, in the cotton-goods industry, which has a minimum code of $12 per week, the average wage in the industry in August 1934 was only $12.55. In addition, the report of the Winant Textile Board shows clearly that the wages of the textile workers in August 1934 were below those of 1933. In other words, under the "new deal" the actual wages of the workers have been reduced. This has been intensified by the rise in the cost of living, which has wiped out any increase that might have been obtained under the "new deal."

The workers in the shops are afraid to organize because of the fear of their jobs being taken by the unemployed. The National Unemployment Council therefore does everything in its power to mobilize the unemployed for assistance to employed workers when they go out on strike. The insecurity of jobs for the employed workers is outstanding today. No worker knows from day to day whether he will have a job. He does not know whether his boss may not decide to run away from the town where he is located— now with the support of the Government plan for "decentralization of industry"; he does not know whether he may not be laid off or only be given a few hours of work a week. As a result of this situation social insurance becomes of outstanding importance also for the employed workers.

We wish to quote only the statement of Frances Perkins made at the Conference on Economic Security on November 13. Miss Perkins said:

The shadow of insecurity that at all times hangs over the lives of fully 90 percent of the American people threatens at any moment to deprive them of the possessive rights they hold most dear. * * * Provision against unemployment and the distress occasioned by it is obviously, then, the major problem which confronts us in any plan for social security.

That is why, in the present situation, we demand unemployment insurance for everybody and particularly the unemployed. It is a primary demand, especially for the unemployed who face a progressively worsening situation. We are in favor of insurance for the aged and infirm, but we demand adequate insurance. We are in favor of jobs on work projects but not at the rates that are proposed by the Government. It is necessary, therefore, in this situation—when the Government has decided that the 17,000,000 unemployed shall not be covered by unemployment insurance but that they shall first be "reabsorbed in the industry" and then later come within the provisions of the Wagner-Lewis bill—to outline what the Government program is.

In brief, (1) 1,500,000 "unemployables" shall be removed from the Federal relief rolls and transferred to the mercy of the States and municipalities. In his message to Congress on January 4 Mr. Roosevelt said: "The Federal Government shall and must quit this business of relief." This sounded like the words of a tyrant who is cracking the whip of hunger over the backs of a million and a half of his slaves. What did this mean in the sixth year of the crisis with the States and municipalities bankrupt?

And how do these governments propose to meet this obligation? In 41 States there are proposals for sales taxes. In many States sales taxes have already been adopted. New York City gives a good example of how the sales tax operates. It was adopted in such a manner that the shopkeepers were obliged under penalty of the law to hand on the 3-percent sales tax to the consumer. In the State of New Jersey Governor Hoffman proposed a 2-percent sales tax exclusively on food so as to relieve realty taxes. These sales taxes mean that the worker in the shop suffers a direct reduction in his pay, but at the same time the unemployed worker, who is on relief, which is supposed to be raised by means of the sales tax, himself must help pay that tax. The State and municipal governments, like the Federal Government, refuse to put the burden of relief and insurance where it belongs—on the shoulders of the wealthy in behalf of the poor. What does it mean when absolutely no provision was being made to take care of these people at a time when the Federal Government itself admits that the number who were on relief and would have to be placed upon the relief rolls would be higher than ever before in the history of the country?

(2) Three and a half million able-bodied workers are to be given relief jobs. But Mr. Roosevelt had declared in compliance with the demand of the National Manufacturers Association, the American Bankers Association, and the United States Chamber of Commerce, that wages on relief jobs will be lower than the local prevailing rates. The purpose of this is to keep the unemployed on a lower level of existence and to use them as a battering ram against the wage standards in the shops. As a result of this decision which was first put into operation in Georgia, the prevailing rate of 30 cents an hour was discarded and wage workers in Georgia were compelled to work at 15 to 20 cents an hour, and Negro workers at 5, 6, or 7 cents an hour.

The Government promises a wage of $50 a month. To put through this program President Roosevelt has asked for an appropriation of $4,800,000,000 to be used by him within his own discretion. This guarantee of $50 a month is untrue. In the month of October 1934 the Government had on its pay rolls on the Emergency Work Program 1,950,000 workers whose pay roll during the month amounted to $51,000,000. This meant an average of $26.16 per month. The appropriation of $4,800,000,000 plus $1,700,000,000 left from the $3,300,000,000 appropriation of 1933, if used in toto as wages for the 3,500,000 workers, will not average, however, more than $25 a a month. If President Roosevelt speaks of an average of $50 a month then it means he will pay some skilled workers a little more than $50 whereas the great bulk of the unskilled workers will get much less than $50, in both cases close to the hunger line. William Green has already consented to this program. This is a signal for a sharp offensive against the living conditions of the whole working class against which the workers must be warned.

This kind of a program we categorically reject. We demand union wages on jobs. We demand that the jobs be useful projects and not such as were embraced in the previous program of C. W. A.— cleaning parks, gathering leaves, but at the same time building warships, barracks, and so forth. A survey that was made by the National Unemployment Council through the Pen and Hammer organizations discloses that an adequate building program to provide decent housing, hospitals, schools, nurseries, playgrounds, electrification, and so forth, would amount to $67,000,000,000. If this program were put into operation it would afford work for millions of workers over a prolonged period of time.

We demand union wages and conditions on all jobs. We demand further that there be a guaranteed number of hours per week and per month so that a worker will at least have some kind of protection during the period.

(3) *Transient camps.*—These camps are being extended and today embrace more than 200,000 men who are compelled to do forced labor for their food and shelter at 90 cents a week. This smacks of Hitlerism. We demand union wages and conditions for these workers and the abolition of every form of forced labor. We want to call attention to the fact that investigations show that the overwhelming majority of the men in these camps are American born who have been driven from pillar to post in search of work.

(4) The only point on President Roosevelt's program which has the consistent support and approval of the bankers and manufacturers is that of the C. C. C. camps. Already more than 900,000 boys and young men have passed through these camps in three contingents. The proposal is now being made that the camps shall embrace 1,000,000 men and to include also married men. Each boy at the camp costs the Government close to $725 a year. The Government refuses to allow the boy to remain at home under family influence and provide that amount of relief to the family.

The Government did this with the consistent knowledge that the purpose of these camps was, not to help the working-class boy, but on the contrary, to use the words of Harry H. Woodring, Assistant Secretary of War, in Liberty Magazine of January 8, 1934, " The organization of these camps was the first real test of the Army's plans for war mobilization under the National Defense Act." Mr. Woodring also pointed out that these boys could be used in case of " internal disorders." Secretary of War Dern recently pointed out that these camps were the cheapest and best investment of the Government. Into these camps are taken the sturdiest, strongest boys of the country who are given the fundamentals of military training, and can be used in any eventuality, particularly in strike struggles and the battles of the unemployed for decent relief. These camps are semimilitary camps under the jurisdiction of the War Department. The workers cannot but be opposed to these camps.

(5) *Subsistence homesteads.*—Mr. H. M. Wilson, of the Subsistence Homestead Division of the Government, recently said at a conference in New York, " I consider the subsistence homesteads the most important part of the whole ' new-deal ' program." Workers are being bullied into the belief that the Government is trying to do something for them and is making them a gift of a little patch of land and an opportunity to work. The fact of the matter is, according to Mr. Wilson, that a million workers are to be transferred from the industrial centers to the countryside where they will be placed upon a little plot of land on which a home will be erected. This will be no gift from the Government, but the workers will have to repay the Government the cost of the homestead, which ranges from $2,000 to $3,500. In order to meet this obligation, the worker will

have to have an income of from $600 to $1,200 a year. How shall he derive his income? He will raise his own fruit and vegetables on his land. He will work in a factory already established or to be erected. at relief wages. Out of these wages he will have to buy the other necessities of life, pay for clothing, light, coal, and so forth, and at the same time pay off the cost of the homestead.

It is not at all astonishing that Henry Ford, Mr. Harriman, president of the United States Chamber of Commerce, and other leading industrialists are in favor of this plan. They favor the "decentralization of industry." The purpose of this is to isolate small groups of workers, to drive the unemployed out of the cities, and thus make it difficult for them to organize and to carry on a struggle. However, the idiocy of this program is manifest from the following. The cause of the crisis is overproduction, as a result of which the workers, who never could buy back what they produced, are thrown out of the factories. Now the Government proposes to establish a new set of workers thereby depriving many of the present employed of their jobs. The Government declares that the purpose of the ploughing-under program is to restrict the production of foodstuffs. After having driven hundreds of thousands of farmers off the land it is now putting the industrial workers on new pieces of land to produce new food stuffs. This is the greatest achievement of the brain trust. This is the contradiction of the whole system which, with their philosophy and methods, they cannot bridge.

In addition the Government is helping so-called "barter" and "self-help" organizations as a means of ridding itself of the need of providing relief and unemployment insurance.

In connection with relief we must state that it is down to the very hunger level. We quote from the F. E. R. A. report of October 1934. We find that in the States of Kentucky, South Carolina, and North Carolina the average relief per month per family of four was $8.23, $9.06, and $9.92 respectively. This means about $2 per week. This is the standard that is established in many States of the South. If in the North, and particularly the industrial cities, the relief standards have been jerked up, this is not due to any kind-heartedness on the part of the Government but to the struggles of the unemployed that have been led by the National Unemployment Council. However, in the month of September 1934, when the number of unemployed was increasing and a large number of applicants had to be received at relief bureaus, the amount of relief actually decreased $1.74 on the average for the country for the month.

This situation has become even more serious as the months have gone by. In large cities such as Chicago, Cedar Rapids, Wichita, Denver, Los Angeles, Houston, and other smaller towns in all parts of the country, while the number of persons on the relief rolls has increased, the appropriations have declined.

The position of the Government in regard to relief and so-called "adequacy of relief" is expressed in the fact that practically in every State there is a demand for acceptance of a pauper's oath, that is the assertion under oath that the applicant has no possessions, no life-insurance policy, no relative, no friend who can assist him.

This is not only humiliating and a prying into the personal affairs of the unemployed, but has prevented many a worker from asking for relief and has driven him to desperation. All members of your committee are acquainted with the story of the mother and son in Chicago who on January 25 murdered a relief investigator at home, and went to the relief bureau and shot down two others. Then the son turned the gun upon his mother and then killed himself. This son was not a vagabond and ne'er-do-well. He was a college graduate, driven to desperation. You read the story of two old women, spinsters, 72 and 73 years of age, who were found dead in their apartment with nothing to eat.

These stories can be duplicated ten thousands of times because the basis of relief is not the needs of the family, not the assurance of an adequate income to maintain any kind of standard, but is best expressed in the words of Welfare Director Hodson, of New York, who, like all other relief directors from top to bottom, are considered liberal. According to the New York Herald Tribune of December 13, 1934, Mr. Hodson said:

" The obligation of the local administration is to provide families with enough to keep them alive and in a reasonable state of health, but not enough to maintain a decent standard of living." If this is the standpoint of the Government, if this is the so-called " economy of plenty ", then there are no words to express our contempt for it.

The workers demand a decent budget, a budget that will enable them to live, and the workers intend to fight for that budget. Nowhere in the country is sufficient being provided. The whole standard by which it is gauged is stated in Mr. Roosevelt's message to Congress, as already quoted, viz., it is founded on " sound caution and consideration of all the factors concerned, the rights and responsibilities of States, and so forth." This is not the standard that the workers will accept and that is why in all parts of the country the workers are carrying on a fight under the leadership of the unemployment councils. We have compelled the relief authorities to raise the standards. We have compelled them to put hundreds of thousands of applicants whom they have rejected onto the relief rolls. We have prevented evictions. We have forced them to put an end to discrimination against the Negro workers. It is only through the organized efforts of the workers anywhere that we are able to accomplish anything.

In addition we must point out that graft, maladministration, inefficiency, are manifest throughout the relief organization. Only recently the report of the State Relief Administration of Kentucky was published which showed that in Blount County it costs $6,200 in administration expenses to dispense $1,200 in relief. Other counties in Kentucky show a similar situation. This is not confined to Kentucky alone. On the other hand, scandals have broken out in all parts of the country. On January 26 a P. W. A. scandal in Texas involving $4,000,000 was disclosed. In the spring of 1934 in Chicago an investigator was sent from Washington to look into the situation of 2,500 pay checks found in the drawer of a relief official. This investigator resigned on the grounds that his inquiry was being obstructed by " higher-ups."

In the relief administration are all kinds of hangers-on, of politicians and industrial leaders; people who are not interested in the welfare of the unemployed; people who do not need these jobs as a livelihood. The unemployed are making the demand, and a proper demand, that the unemployed shall administer the relief funds, and that the whole personnel shall be selected from among the unemployed.

Mr. LUNDEEN. I want to say at this point that I introduced a bill in the last Congress covering that point.

Mr. AMTER. There are evidences, however, that this is not the only method by which the Government intends to handle the unemployed and all the workers. The use of police, gangsters, and National Guards against workers on strike; the use of police, tear gas, and machine guns against the unemployed, indicate quite clearly what the methods of the Government are.

It is good in this respect to quote a few leading persons. Dr. Virgil Jordan, president of the National Industrial Conference Board, one of the most reactionary organizations in the country, speaking in Philadelphia on December 8, said:

> If we are sincere and in earnest we will round up the hoboes and unemployables, deport with decision and dispatch those who are aliens, and put all the rest to work under a form of military discipline. They are a burden and a danger to the Nation.

That this is not an isolated fascist statement of some perverse individual, we quote Mr. Richberg who, speaking on December 28 in Cleveland, according to the Associated Press, said:

> Perhaps it might be better even in a money sense to find work for these idle hands today, than to support the armies necessary to hold them back, if once these millions of bleeding fingers were turned into threatening claws. We may have some reasonable fears of a foreign foe, but the greatest dangers that threaten America are those of internal dissension.

Mr. Richberg spoke of a "jobless uprising" and perhaps the use of troops against the unemployed.

This is the other side of the demagogic story that is being dinned into the ears of the unemployed. "Economy of plenty", "no starvation", "the Government is doing everything possible", while at the same time there is increasing use of terror against the unemployed. We point to the attacks upon the unemployed that have taken place in all parts of the country. In California, Colorado, Oklahoma, Illinois, Michigan, Pennsylvania, New York; we point to the use of police, machine guns, National Guard, and all kinds of fascist organizations through the direct organization and participation of public officials. Only recently in Sacramento the city manager organized a gang of 600 armed vigilantes for the purpose of smashing a conference of the unemployed to be held in that city. The manager directly participated in the organization of that gang. Vigilantes, crusaders, K. K. K., Silver Shirts, and what not, are being openly organized and are functioning within the knowledge of the Federal and State authorities.

I have here a clipping from the New York Evening Post of last night. (The clerk will here insert the article headed, "Confidential Reports Reveal State of Peonage.")

CONFIDENTIAL REPORTS REVEAL STATE OF PEONAGE—IMPERIAL VALLEY NEST OF
SLAVERY, UNITED STATES BOARDS TOLD—REGIONAL LABOR BOARD COMMISSION
FINDS "UNPARALLELED SQUALOR IN LABORERS' HOMES—PRODUCERS AND
GROWERS THWART ORGANIZATION

[By CHARLES MALCOLMSON, *Staff Correspondent, New York Post*]

WASHINGTON, February 6.—Unretarded spread of "virtual peon labor" in
the rich Imperial Valley of California is revealed in confidential reports to the
National Labor Board and the Secretaries of Labor and Agriculture.

These hitherto unpublished reports by a special commission of the National
Labor Board, supported by later Agriculture and Labor Department investigations, have disclosed almost incredible labor and living conditions among
workers in the largest and most fruitful irrigated area in the world.

The commission, headed by Dr. J. L. Leonard, chairman of the Regional
Labor Board, conducted a week-long investigation in January 1934, holding
both open hearings and private interviews and personally inspecting working
and living conditions in cities and field camps.

Their report, made to Senator Robert F. Wagner, then chairman of the
National Labor Board, on February 11, revealed that:

"(1) The abject poverty and utter squalor in which the Imperial Valley
laborer lives almost defies description;

"(2) The relief load in the valley is extremely heavy and relief has been
inadequate. And resentment still flares high against the relief administration
for having fed strikers;

" (3) The prevailing wage is 22½ cents per hour with a guarantee of at least
5 hours a day employment or pay * * * though the minimum wage and
hour agreement is not always observed;

"(4) The fundamental cause of much of the trouble is the desire of the
workers to organize * * * which has been thwarted by a well-defined
opposition on the part of producers and growers."

This report resulted in an investigation by Gen. Pelham D. Glassford on
behalf of the National Labor Board and the Labor and Agriculture Departments. Glassford's report and those of other special departmental investigators
substantiated the Leonard inquiry in all salient features.

FAMILIES ON RELIEF

The commission found that of the families visited, at least "three-quarters
are on relief, a condition which the relief supervisor maintained was not at all
unusual." At the end of each harvesting season, the investigators found relief
rolls swell with laborers whose work in the fields has brought them just enough
to feed their families during the season but not enough to tide them over the
2 or 3 weeks between seasons.

A State emergency relief administration transient bureau has been established on the outskirts of El Centro, with a small colony of bungalows equipped
with beds, mattresses, water, and electricity, but the commission declared it
"woefully inadequate to cope with the situation."

Last year Imperial Valley lettuce growers agreed to reduce acreage and
curtail shipments. Prices improved only slightly and labor was worse off
than before.

"In October 1933", the commission said, "the Mexican Field Workers' Union
demanded that the wage rate be set at 22½ cents per hour and that growers
guarantee any laborer employed at least 5 hours' work."

"COMMUNIST LEADERSHIP"

The large shipper-growers, who employ 70 percent of the workers in the
valley, agreed to these demands and claim to have abided by them. However,
in November, the union again approached the growers with the complaint that
the agreement was not being kept. From then until February 1934 labor
disturbances became more frequent and better organized. Control of the
Mexican Field Workers' Union fell into the hands of the Cannery and Agricultural Workers' Industrial Union, found by the commission to have
"Communist leadership."

"Meetings were broken up by police with the aid of clubs, tear-gas bombs, and guns", the report stated, "and many innocent people were arrested and induced by promise of release to plead guilty."

It was on behalf of these that the American Civil Liberties Union sent attorneys to the valley, one of them being spirited from his hotel on the evening of a labor meeting, dumped 20 miles out in the desert, and warned not to return.

After careful investigation of this and similar incidents, the commission recommended that "Federal and State Governments exercise every power and authority to maintain in fact the rights of free speech, free press, and free assembly, and that men, either citizens or aliens, shall not be harassed by permanent, temporary amateur, or self-appointed officers of the law."

"THE RIGHT TO STRIKE"

The commission also suggested Federal encouragement of organization by workers "in order that collective bargaining may be effective in matters of wages and conditions, both living and working, and that the right to strike and peacefully to picket shall be maintained."

The commission held producer and cannery groups directly responsible for much of the unrest because they actively opposed all labor agitation.

"Any outside interference in their affairs is bitterly opposed" by Imperial Valley residents, the report said. "Hemmed in from the outside world on three sides by mountains and on the fourth by Mexico, they have acquired a rather grotesque sense of individualism and independence which is tantamount to that existing in frontier towns a century ago."

Very little sympathy is felt for labor, the commission reported, because "the overwhelming numerical majority of laborers constitutes a potential danger in the minds of the local citizenry."

Despite the fact that the Leonard report was made almost a year ago and gave warning that "conditions contributing to labor discontent since 1930 have not been ameliorated", and that "strikes may break out again at the next harvest season", no action has been taken by any Federal Department or agency.

"IT'S OFF THE RECORD"

Department of Agriculture officials explain this situation "off the record" as being "too charged with dynamite for any department to touch."

"The Department of Agriculture cannot, without amendment of the A. A. A., take a hand in the matter", one high official revealed, "unless requested to do so by N. R. A. or the Department of Labor, and there will be no such request until 'pressure' has been exerted by enough interested parties.

"The Imperial Valley workers are in fact industrial workers to a large extent, inasmuch as they follow seasonal occupations between cannery and field, but they are still classed as 'agricultural labor' and thus outside labor provisions of codes."

While doing nothing to help the workers, the Department of Agriculture has recognized and cooperates with the recently formed Associated Farmers, an organization dedicated to suppression of unionism in the valley.

Mr. AMTER. This shows what is taking place in California, or did take place in California during the time of the strike of the agricultural workers. It contains a photograph showing the use of tear gas, and underneath the photograph is this statement:

Upper photograph shows Sacramento police being trained at the State fairgrounds to use tear and nauseating gas bombs as means of repelling unemployed farm workers when they meet in Sacramento March 12. The meeting was originally scheduled for February 2, but was postponed for fear that the vigilantes would commit some overt act that would result in rioting and endanger a fair trial for 18 striking farm workers charged with criminal syndicalism because they demanded higher wages. Lower right shows Sgt. Ray Peart, of the Sacramento police, wearing a gas mask of the type with which the city has equipped 600 vigilantes. The lower photo is City Manager James S. Dean of Sacramento, posing for the photographers in a make-believe effect of the gas bombs. Dean is responsible for the organization of vigilantes to meet the unemployed farm workers.

Mr. DUNN. You mentioned the "K. K. K." Whom do you mean?

Mr. AMTER. The Ku-Klux Klan.

Mr. DUNN. I see. They were after me at one time. I introduced a bill at the last session of Congress to the effect that nobody in the United States should have an income above $36,000, and that all wealth above $600,000 should be transferred to the Government. Somebody wrote me a card telling me I ought to go to Russia. It came from Alliance, Ohio, and was signed "K. K. K."; so when you mentioned the K. K. K. I was wondering if you knew the fellow who sent me that card.

Mr. AMTER. No; I do not know the fellow. I know they were all being attacked by the K. K. K.

Mr. DUNN. Why do you suppose they wanted to send me to Russia?

Mr. AMTER. Because I think Russia is a pretty good country, and they wanted you to live there.

Mr. DUNN. Do you think they wanted me to go there because they thought I was trying to be a "red"?

Mr. AMTER. They undoubtedly believed you were a Communist who had no place here in the United States, following the recommendations of the Dickstein-McCormack committee.

Mr. DUNN. In other words, I am a Bolshevist if I believe that every man and woman who is able and willing to work should be entitled to a job which would enable them to maintain a decent standard of living, and if I believe in old-age pensions, pensions for widows and mothers and all those who are disabled, and because I believe that the natural resources of the country should belong to the people of the Government instead of a privileged few?

Mr. AMTER. No; I would not say you are a Communist. I may say, so far as the Crusaders and the Ku Kluxers and similar organizations are concerned, the Wall Street bankers are responsible for all of them. They are the people who are befuddling the minds of the workers, using them to promote their own ends; that is, the ends of the Wall Street bankers. They are being used particularly against the workers and their families, and specially against the Negro people who are carrying on a program to obtain relief.

Mr. DUNN. And they are the biggest thieves in the world.

Mr. AMTER. Correct. They are the people who are befuddling the minds of the workers, using them to promote their own ends; that is, the ends of the Wall Street bankers. They are being used particularly against the workers and their families, and specially against the Negro people who are carrying on a program to obtain relief.

Mr. AMTER. Such terror will not keep down the struggles of the workers and threats of terror will not abash the workers. Hunger will not be fed with bullets. Already it has become obvious to the workers that in struggling for adequate relief, in struggling for jobs at union wages, in struggling for the enactment of the workers unemployment, old age, and social insurance bill, we have at the same time to fight against the developing fascism here in the United States.

What is the perspective in the United States for 1935? Is it an outlook of increasing prosperity as is being ballyhooed throughout the country, or is it not rather something else? On January 11 William Green declared, " Nothing in the present industrial picture gives hope that private industry will raise production back to normal during the current year." Dr. John T. Madden, president of the Alexander Hamilton Institute, declares that " There is a fair possibility that the total volume of business in 1935 will be smaller than in 1934." The outlook is not one of increasing employment, even though production may rise. The program of the Government is not to raise the buying power of the masses either through increased wages established in the codes or through increased relief and unemployment insurance. The whole program of the Government is to get by as cheaply as it can.

The National Unemployment Council agrees with the statement of Secretary of Commerce Roper, who stated at the November 13 conference:

Has not the day definitely passed when any group, in the long run, can expect to win out by pursuing the policy of getting as much and giving as little as possible?

The definite perspective is that the crisis will be prolonged and will deepen. The attacks upon the living standards and the militant organizations of the workers will intensify. War preparations are going ahead with feverish pace. This is the whole program of the capitalist government. The capitalists of the United States and the Government are trying to give the workers as little as possible. They believe that the unemployed can be driven down still further in their standard of living and thereby drag down the whole working class. They believe that they can harass and terrorize the working class into accepting even a coolie standard of living in the United States.

After 6 years of crisis and after 2 years of the " new deal " the workers of the United States are becoming ever more convinced that there is only one way out of the crisis, and that is by organizing and carrying on a bitter struggle. Our immediate aim in this struggle is the provision of some measure of protection under the present system. This protection for the whole working class, and particularly the unemployed, is embodied in the workers unemployment, old age, and social insurance bill, H. R. 2827. The enactment of this bill by the United States Congress is our immediate aim.

The National Congress for Unemployment and Social Insurance, held in Washington January 5 to 7 on call of the National Unemployed Councils, was a stage in the development of this struggle. Our struggles are not at an end. On the contrary, we are mobilizing more millions of workers, white-collar workers, professionals, in this vast movement. We urge your committee to most seriously consider this situation as not a normal one that requires some attention, but to realize that the workers no longer believe in the N. R. A. Even William Green and Norman Thomas, Socialist leader, both of whom had boasted of the N. R. A. as a " new charter of labor " had to revise their position, not of their own volition, but as a result of the radicalization of the masses.

We urge your committee to report the workers' bill favorably to the House, while we in our turn will do everything possible to exercise that mass pressure which is necessary upon every Congressman in the United States that will compel him to vote aye in favor of the workers' unemployment, old age, and social insurance bill, H. R. 2827. We have marched in the cities, counties, and States and no terror has stopped us. We have marched already to Washington and if need be we will march again. The battle is on and we will not stop until we have won. (Applause.)

Mr. DUNN. I want to thank you for your very interesting address. It has been very instructive.

Mr. LUNDEEN. In view of what was said about the use of troops, there, I want the record to include a very short resolution which I introduced after the Birmingham killings and strike riots in Alabama, forbidding the use of troops against the workers. I would like to have permission to place that in the record.

Mr. DUNN. Absolutely. You can have anything you want inserted into the record, so far as I am concerned, Mr. Lundeen, because I know that you are a real representative of the people.

(The clerk will here insert H. Res. 385.)

[H. Res. 385, 73d Cong., 2d sess.]

Whereas newspaper reports coming from Birmingham, Alabama, state that eight thousand iron-ore miners are striking in the mines controlled by the Tennessee Coal and Iron Corporation, and other large Alabama mining interests; and

Whereas, according to said press reports, police and special-armed deputies and National Guard and other State and National troops are being used against the strikers, depriving them of their rights to strike and peacefully picket; and

Whereas during the past week, according to said reports, many striking miners have been killed, numerous strikers wounded, and the picket lines broken by the extreme terror of the police, Militia, and special-armed deputies; and

Whereas the machinery of the Government should be used to protect the farmers and workers in the natural course of their work and duties, guaranteeing them the right to exercise their inalienable rights as free citizens; and

Whereas it is common practice, and it frequently happens, that force and violence and terror are used against the producers of the Nation's wealth, causing them loss of wages, hunger, and destitution; and

Whereas it is also common practice for employers to retain and hire private armies, armed with powerful and dangerous weapons, and amply financed by big business serving as quasi-government troops; and

Whereas it is often common practice to swear in wholesale numbers of armed deputies to argument all said forces: Therefore be it

Resolved, That the House of Representatives condemns the use of private armies by the money masters of the Nation, and that the Committee on Labor be hereby instructed at once to draw suitable legislation to forever prevent and severely punish the use of such barbarism against labor, against farmers, against workers, and against the producers of the Nation's wealth.

SEC. 2. For the purpose of obtaining information necessary as a basis for legislation, the Committee on Labor, as a whole or by subcommittee, is authorized to proceed to Alabama, and to such other points or places where Government troops and private armies with arms are now being used against labor, to conduct a thorough investigation of the entire strike situation and of the unprecedented and unwarranted attacks on the rights of the workers.

SEC. 3. The committee shall report to the House during the present Congress the results of its investigation, together with such recommendations, including such recommendations for legislation, as it deems advisable.

SEC. 4. For the purposes of this resolution the committee is authorized to sit and act during the present Congress in the District of Columbia or elsewhere, as a whole or by subcommittee, at such times, whether or not the House is sitting, has recessed, or has adjourned, to hold such hearings, to require the attendance of such witnesses and the production of such books, papers, and documents, by subpena or otherwise, to take such testimony, to have such printing and binding done, and to make such expenditures not in excess of amounts made available for the purposes of this resolution, as it deems necessary. Subpenas shall be issued under signature of the chairman and shall be served by any person designated by him. The chairman of the committee, or any member thereof, may administer oaths to witnesses.

Mr. LUNDEEN. And I can say, if it adds to your comfort at all, Mr. Chairman, that practically all the liberals in the last election were called all sorts of radical names.. You, in Pittsburgh, were not alone in that.

(The hour of 11:30 a. m. having arrived, the subcommittee took a recess until 2 o'clock this afternoon.)

AFTERNOON SESSION

The subcommittee reassembled at 3 p. m. at the expiration of the recess.

Mr. DUNN. The committee will be in order, and we will hear Mr. Harry L. Lurie.

STATEMENT OF HARRY L. LURIE, NEW YORK CITY

Mr. DUNN. Mr. Lurie, will you give the reporter your name and the organization you represent.

Mr. LURIE. My name is Harry L. Lurie, New York City.

I should like to preface my remarks by saying that I am appearing at this time in an individual capacity as a social worker whose field of activity is social research. I happen to be chairman of a committee of the American Association of Social Workers, which is a national professional social work organization, called the " Committee to Outline a National Social Welfare Program ", but I am not representing the association or that committee at this hearing, because there is some difference of opinion among the members of the committee. We have not as yet arrived at a definite conclusion.

The general point that I want to make is that the measures proposed by the administration for relief and economic security, so-called, now pending in Congress leave unprovided large masses of the population whose distress and insecurity should be the primary concern of the National Legislature. Other dependent and insecure groups will be provided for so inadequately that without supplementary provisions the welfare of masses of the people will be less satisfactorily achieved than by the present admittedly inadequate relief program which is being financed by the Federal Government. Any improvement in the conditions of a part of the group requiring assistance which may follow from some of the proposed measures is counterbalanced by the less desirable situation in which many now on Federal relief will find themselves. Social-insurance measures introduced by Senator Wagner which are being considered, if enacted, will not begin to function for a number of years and therefore have little bearing on the present problems of need which the country is facing. Furthermore, the insurance measures sponsored by the administration involve a number of dubious social and economic aspects. I am, therefore, urging the need for more comprehensive measures such as the one which is under consideration in this committee.

I should like to consider first the appropriation for relief work amounting to $4,880,000,000 which has recently been passed by the House. Judging by official announcements which have accompanied this measure, these funds aim to provide a maximum public-relief employment for 3,500,000 persons at less than prevailing wages offering them substantially less in the way of regular income than can be obtained by an individual were he able to secure regular employment in private industry.

The report to the President's Committee on Economic Security issued on January 15, 1935, makes this statement (p. 7):

A program of economic security for the Nation that does not include those now unemployed cannot possibly be complete. They, above all, are in need of security. Their tragic situation calls attention not only to their own desperate insecurity but to the lack of security of all those who are dependent upon their own earnings for a livelihood.

It is wholly obvious that the proposed provision for the unemployed in this work-relief measure is designed to furnish relief to approximately not more than one-third of the jobless in the United States who are seeking employment. Is there any justification for attempting only one-third of a problem and leaving two-thirds entirely adrift during this crisis?

It has been suggested that additional indirect employment will be furnished through the expenditure of these funds for materials for the projects and that the expenditure of income received by both groups of employees will furnish employment to an additional number. Our previous experience with public-works projects indicates that while some stimulation in employment accompanies the expenditures for public works, the total result is not overly large and I believe we may conservatively estimate that at least one-half of the present unemployed load will remain without work as a result of the proposed expenditures. I can see no justification for the Federal Government presumably concerned with this problem to take the stand that it can now terminate its responsibility for the bulk of the unemployed. The administration has advanced no specific provisions for this group which remains.

I should like particularly to point out the effect of the work-appropriation measure upon the many millions of families and individuals who are now being aided through the F. E. R. A. From the F. E. R. A. release dated January 17, 1935, referring to conditions in November 1934, and from the testimony of Mr. Hopkins more recently on December experience, we may estimate that there are 4,650,000 families and 1,100,000 single persons at present on Federal relief throughout the United States. This means that there are at least 20,000,000 persons in this country whose sole or chief source of subsistence is obtained through the program of the F. E. R. A. Preliminary figures for November 1934 give 4,233,084 families and 770,601 single persons, with a total of 18,017,815 persons, on Federal relief. Mr. Hopkins announced an increase of 5.8 percent in the number on relief rolls from November to December and local reports testify to a further increase in January.

We are informed by the Research Department of the F. E. R. A. that based on a survey made in 79 cities in 1934, 20 percent of the families contain no employable member between the ages of 16 and 65. This group includes the aged over 65, broken families with no worker and families in which the only adult member is totally or permanently disabled. In additional, approximately one-third of the families in this group of 20 percent consists of women required primarily in the home to care for children.

Because of this study it has been estimated that the total number of the employable unemployed on the relief lists seeking work in the balance of 80 percent of relief cases amounts to approximately 6,500,000 persons. This is based upon information in various local studies which indicates that there are on the average 1.5 employable wage earners per family in the families on relief. We must, therefore, keep in mind that if the expectations of the works appropriation measure are carried out there are only 3,500,000 jobs to be provided for the 6,500,000 jobless now on the relief rolls.

It has been estimated by Mr. Corrington Gill, Research Director of the F. E. R. A. in Midmonthly Survey, January 1935, that 80 percent of the families on Federal relief contain one or more employable members between the ages of 16 and 65. It would seem on the basis of this estimate that approximately 1,000,000 families and 200,000 single persons considered as the unemployable group are not to be covered by the proposed bill and that this residual relief group may safely be thrust back upon State and local responsibility. He, therefore, assumed that if the work-relief measure were to go into effect there would be left only 1,000,000 families, that is 20 percent of the unemployable group, which he believed could be safely thrust back on the States and localities for care, and that the Federal Government would not need to concern itself with any other part of the problem except the work projects for the unemployed. Actually, it seems to me from a careful study of the information he himself has used, that the number of those who are not likely to be absorbed in any type of public-works project is much greater than the 20 percent.

And in connection with that, I think the following facts need to be considered:

The first is that over 25 percent of the individuals considered as within the 80 percent employable group consists of a man or woman between the ages of 45 and 65. Reference is made to Monthly Report of the Federal Emergency Relief Administration, September 1–30, 1934, pages 8–10, Employment and and Employability in the Relief Population. It is extremely doubtful whether projects can be developed which will offer job opportunities for the women in this age group. It is also obvious that many of the men in these age groups will require special projects which, judging from past experience, may be outside of the practical possibilities of the work-relief program.

The second point is that included in what Mr. Gill considers to be the employable group, the study shows an additional 11 percent who are seeking work but have a recognized physical or mental disability. While not all of this group are unplaceable, it is apparent that large public-work projects are frequently unsuitable for persons in this group.

The third point I would like to make is that the percentage of the families that have, as the only employable member, youths between the ages of 16 and 25 years, has also to be considered in the setting up of the works program. Third, the actual percentage has not been published, but in the total group of 4,000,000 persons in urban relief families working or looking for work in 1934, 26 percent were in the age group of 16 to 24 years, inclusive. Many of these youths have little or no work experience or skill and will also require specialized types of employment which may be difficult to achieve in the regular run of work projects.

In the survey article " How many are unemployed? " (Corrington Gill), it is stated that in May 1934 there were in 17 percent of the cases now on relief rolls in 80 cities, one or more members with some private employment. These are earnings so little in part time or even full-time work that relief has been necessary to keep the family from extreme privation. Many of these individuals are working children or women receiving extremely low wages. The proposed measure, that is the $4,000,000,000 works appropriation measure, we may safely assume, does not contemplate shifting these individuals from poorly-paid private employment to the public work-relief system since it is the announced intention of the relief measure not to interfere with private employment.

While the figures given refer to urban population only, the report of the Committee on Economic Security previously referred to states on page 8 that " Public employment is not the final answer to the problem of stranded communities and impoverished farm families." All of these elements are present in the current relief load of the F. E. R. A.

On the basis of these factors, it is unsafe to estimate that more than 60 percent, and probably not more than 50 percent, of the present Federal-relief load can be provided for by the proposed work projects furnishing employment to not more than one worker per family. This would leave between 2,200,000 and 2,725,000 families and single persons from whom Federal relief is to be withdrawn unless further plans are made for their benefit.

There were engaged at work relief during the month of November 1934, 2,154,067 individuals receiving average weekly compensation of approximately $9.50. We cannot conclude that an additional number to complete the total of 3½ million relief workers will be taken from the present relief lists. We know that when such projects go into effect increased applications from unemployed individuals not now on relief are stimulated. These unemployed somehow manage to eke out an existence through their own efforts and fail to apply for relief until it is available to them through work-relief projects. We should also keep in mind that, to some extent, the present measure may replace the program of the regular public works which, according to the American Federation of Labor Monthly Survey of Business, January 1935, estimates 470,000 employed individuals. The C. C. C. camps in the same report employed 359,000 individuals.

If these, too, are to be financed from the same appropriation there will remain less than 1,000,000 additional jobs to be created.

On the basis of these facts, it should be acknowledged that the proposed 4⅘ billions work appropriation is an inadequate measure and will leave unprovided for at least 2½ million families and individuals who are now in receipt of Federal relief.

It has been announced that it is the intention of the Federal Government to shift back to States and local government the residual relief load that will not be absorbed in the employment projects. This move has already been carried forward in recent months. There is ample evidence which should convince us that such a plan is indefensible. It will involve perilous lowering of the standards of living and increased privations to masses of the people whose only safeguard against starvation at the present time is the meager relief allowances made possible in many parts of the country only because of the availability of Federal funds. For the second quarter of the year 1934, Federal-relief funds constituted 73.9 percent of the total expenditures under the Federal Emergency Relief Administration. While this means an average of 26.1 percent of the funds contributed by States and localities, we should recognize that there are considerable variations in the States and that this average cannot, therefore, be applied. For example, the report of the F. E. R. A., January 7, 1935, covering the period January 1933 to September 1934, inclusive, shows 9 States, Alabama, Arkansas, Florida, Georgia, Louisiana, Mississippi, New Mexico, South Carolina, and Tennessee, providing from zero to 5 percent of the funds being expended for F. E. R. A. relief, 5 States, Kentucky, Nevada, North Carolina, Oregon, and West Virginia, providing between 5 percent and 10 percent. The proportion of State and local funds has been diminishing and the number of States carrying a small proportion of the cost has been increasing. In the second quarter of 1934, there were 14 States where the Federal appropriation constituted 95 percent or more of the total expenditures and 9 other States where Federal funds were from 90 percent to 95 percent of the total relief. It is obvious that particularly in these States it is impossible to contemplate assumption of the present Federal-relief burden even if the optimistic estimates that the residual load will amount to only 20 percent should prove to be correct.

It is more conservative to assume that in many States between 40 percent and 60 percent of the relief load will become the responsibility of the State and localities if the plan is carried into effect, and that the outlook in these States at the present time of obtaining sufficient State and local resources to provide for this large group is highly improbable.

In this connection I would like to give some estimates recently made by the American Association of Social Workers on this point. I am quoting from the Compass, which is the publication of the professional social workers, for January 1935:

Consideration should be given to the extent to which States are already providing welfare services not included in Federal figures. Complete estimates of costs are lacking but might be conservatively estimated at 300 million annually. These include State provisions for old age, dependent children, blind pensions, almshouses, poor relief, institutions for care of insane, feeble-minded, etc.

If from 30 to 50 percent of the present cost of relief estimated at the rate of approximately 2 billion a year were to be accepted by the States, it would mean an annual obligation of 600 million to 1 billion in addition to the 300 million mentioned above. If such a situation were forced on the States and local governments, it is doubtful whether it would be possible to expect any improvement over the situation which led in 1933 to a Federal relief policy.

Mr. DUNN. Will you give me the States that gave the $26?

Mr. LURIE. The 26 was the average. All of the States except those mentioned gave over $20 a month, some of them going up as high as $40 to $45 a month in the northeast part of the country.

Mr. DUNN. Thank you.

Mr. LURIE. A further indication of this fact may be derived from the present low standards of relief in many parts of the country. Even with Federal assistance, local conditions and local attitudes, coupled with the pressure which has been exercised from Washington on compelling State and local responsibility, have resulted thus far in very inadequate and niggardly programs. I shall not take the time of the committee to recount the hardships which are being experienced by many families in many parts of the country. It is perhaps sufficient to point out that in October 1934 the average family relief for the whole country was only $26.39 per family per month, and that in Kentucky and Tennessee the average relief was less than $10 a month, and in Virginia, North Carolina, South Carolina, Georgia, Florida, Alabama, Mississippi, and Oklahoma relief was under $15 per month, and that in Missouri, Kansas, Arkansas, New Mexico, Arizona, and Washington relief averaged under $20 per family for the month.

One other effect of throwing back the residual relief problem upon States and localities should be pointed out. At the present time one-sixth of the families on relief have some supplementary income from wages of some member of the family in private industry. The Division of Research of the F. E. R. A. has recently, on February 1, 1935, published a bulletin on "Relief administered to workers in the tobacco industry in Winston-Salem, Durham, and Richmond during November 1934." Of the number studied more than two-thirds of the households had fewer than 20 days' employment during November, and the average earnings were $23.66 for the month and only $21.91 in households with one worker. The median relief—this is Federal relief—given to supplement these wholly inadequate earnings ranged from $9.33 to $20.57 for the month in various groups. The report of the F. E. R. A. concludes that underemployment and low wages provide income insufficient in amount for minimum subsistence, according to the relief standards in the cities in question.

On the basis of information of this character, it is indeed blind and callous to thrust problems of this nature back upon the localities possessing in most instances insufficient legal ability to obtain funds even if taxable resources were available.

The assumption upon which the present relief measures of the administration are based is that the combination of work relief, mothers' aid, and old-age grants in aid and related measures provide a sufficient guarantee of Federal responsibility. This follows the conclusion reached by the President's Committee on Economic Security, which said:

We believe that if these measures are adopted, the residual relief will have diminished to a point where it will be possible to return primary responsibility for the care of people who cannot work to the State and local governments.

Even disregarding the fact that the work measure provides only for a part of the employable group, I believe it can be shown that the additional measures proposed do not provide a coverage for the unemployable groups, the aged, the dependent children, and others.

Insofar as aid to dependent children is concerned, there are mothers' aid laws which constitute a system of poor relief to families without employable adults in 45 States. The most recent report, 1931, United States Children's Bureau, indicates only 93,620 families with 253,298 children being aided by these measures, with an average grant of $21.78 per month. In many parts of the country, however, it is inadequate and amounts to as little as $4.33 per family per month in one State. In some States the legislation is permissive rather than mandatory and only 54 percent of the counties in the United States grant this form of assistance. Only a few States have thus far assisted the local units to administer mothers' aid by aiding with State funds. The Committee on Economic Security reports that—

Due to the present financial difficulty in which many States find themselves far too many of such dependent children are on the relief lists than are in receipt of children's aid benefits—

and estimated 700,000 on the Federal relief lists compared with 250,000 getting mothers' aid assistance in the States.

The proposed measure introduced by Senator Wagner, S. 1130, will make available only $25,000,000 for the fiscal year ending June 30, 1936. It is doubtful whether even with these supplementary funds, States will be able to produce from their own revenues enough resources to absorb the large numbers of families with dependent children now in need of assistance. It is entirely likely that the funds available from both local and Federal sources will permit for little assumption of additional local and State responsibility and that the group of widows, families, and families with incapacitated wage earners will be reduced to extreme privations if direct Federal relief is eliminated. The cost of providing for the 700,000 and more dependent children on relief at present average relief figures amounts to approximately $80,000,000 annually. You want to compare that sum with the $25,000,000 which is being set aside for grants in aid for this purpose in the proposed measure.

The situation confronting the aged in the United States is even more acute. While there are 27 States that have passed old-age relief laws, in only three States, Massachusetts, California, and New York, is there any approximation to comprehensive action. In the report issued by the United States Labor Bureau, Monthly Labor Review, August 1934, it is shown that these three States expended in 1933, 87 percent of all old-age relief funds operating in the United States. The proposed grant of $50,000,000 for the fiscal year ending June 30, 1936, will be insufficient to bring the program for the relief of the aged to the point of adequacy. As pointed out in the report of the President's Committee on Economic Security, page 5, 700,000 dependent aged over 65 were on the Federal relief lists at the time studied in 1934 and derive their support principally from the Federal Government and that many of the States cannot assume the financial burden of compensation unaided.

The report also states that " at this time a conservative estimate is that at least one-half of the approximately 7,500,000 people over 65 years now living are dependent principally on relatives or some form of relief. Even if we reduce this aged group to only 1,500,000 persons who might be considered eligible for relief in the proposed measure and set their average pension at only $20 a month, the sum of at least $360,000,000 annually would be required. Toward this amount the Federal Government is proposing to appropriate only $50,000,000. If the share of the individual States were to be computed at only $10 a month per person, expenditures of $180,000,000 annually coming out of State and local funds are necessary. In 1933 the various States with old-age assistance laws spent $26,000,-000. Nevertheless, the Federal Government is proposing to throw the problem back on the States irrespective of their capacity to finance the additional sums required. We may also question whether the administrative difficulties of passing new State legislation and setting up new State machinery for the care of the aged may not take many years to accomplish.

Before discussing the Wagner unemployment compensation measure, I should like to point out that the various relief measures now before Congress with the exception of the bill being considered by this committee perpetuate essentially the undesirable features of the antiquated poor laws throughout the United States. The essential features of the poor laws under which we operate are meagerness of assistance below a decent standard of living and the withholding of assistance unless need, that is, destitution, can be proved. Adding to the general poor-relief measures, Federal grants in aid to the so-called " mothers' aid " and " old-age assistance plans ", does not materially change the inferior character of poor-law administration even if the State, rather than the county or township, becomes the major unit. Essentially, these measures fail to recognize that the problem to be dealt with is fundamentally the problem of insecurity of labor income in the present industrial system. No measure which disregards this essential can do otherwise than deal with individuals as dependents and paupers and it is this most undesirable status to which many millions of American wage earners are being consigned by these measures.

I come now to the consideration of title 7 of the economic security bill, Senate 1130, introduced by Senator Wagner. There are many inadequacies and objectionable features in the measure—the lack of national uniformity brought about by the fact that action by States is not assured even though the taxing feature of the bill assumes that such action will be stimulated, the probability that State measures will be limited in scope will be haphazard and will rarely exceed the minimum provisions. Obviously, the measure is not immediately applicable to the present situation and makes possible only a future plan of compensation for unemployment to be built up by pay roll and wage earner contributions. This means only 1 percent of pay roll unless industrial conditions materially improve. Even with the maximum of a 3 percent tax, exceedingly limited reserves for payment of unemployment compensation will be available for a great many years to come.

If we want to be overly optimistic and grant that after enactment of the measure all of the States will collect 3 percent of pay rolls and set up unemployment reserves and that 15 weeks of unemployment compensation equal at least to 50 percent of prevailing wages will be paid to the entire group covered by insurance, the application of such a measure to an unemployment situation of a type in which we now find ourselves is negligible and is in fact ludicrous. We can estimate the extent to which a measure of this type would affect an unemployment situation in the year 1940 similar to the unemployment situation of today, or in other words, what it would mean in the present situation if the Wagner unemployment plan had been operating for 4 or 5 years.

In the first place, there are the excluded classes covering most of the agricultural laborers and most of the persons engaged in domestic and personal service—20 percent of the total number of unemployed on urban relief rolls in May 1934 were formerly engaged in domestic and personal service—the self-employed individuals and numerous other vocational groups who would not be eligible to the provisions of an insurance bill of this character.

The value of 15 weeks or even 26 weeks unemployment compensation to an industrial community may be inferred from information on the length of time of unemployment in Dayton, Ohio, according to a study issued February 1, 1935, by the Division of Research of the F. E. R. A. This report is called, "The Occupational Characteristics of the Relief and Nonrelief Populations in Dayton, Ohio." Facts were collected concerning all of the employed and unemployed in Dayton, Ohio, during July 1934. It was found in the unemployed group on relief that 81 percent of the total had been unemployed for 6 months or more. Applying the proposed measure to Dayton, we see that at least 81 percent of the relief groups would have exhausted all insurance benefits from the contemplated insurance measure at that time. When for the remaining 19 percent of the relief group who had been unemployed for less than 6 months we realize that the last previous employment for many consisted of temporary and part-time employment which would have built up little eligibility for insurance for them and that only 60 percent of the total group now on relief would have been eligible for unemployment insurance at any time, the resulting estimate which we can conservatively make is that an unemployment insurance measure of this character would have affected the present relief lists of Dayton, Ohio, in less than 10 percent of the cases. Conditions in other urban localities, we may assume, do not vary greatly from the facts obtained in this detailed study.

In the Dayton study, it was found that the median period of unemployment of the workers on relief was 30 months at that time. Forty-two percent of the total relief unemployed group had been out of work for 3 years or more and 24 percent of the total group had been unemployed for 4 years or more. It is obvious that the proposed unemployment-insurance provision has no real relationship to a period of industrial depression. Its value, if any, consists exclusively in the temporary assistance such a measure may offer to persons out of work for brief periods during conditions of general prosperity. There seems little merit at this time when the outlook for recovery is so dubious to be planning measures which are related only to the minor problems of a prosperity period.

The Wagner measure essentially is a plan for imposing the method of compulsory savings upon wage earners. Contributions from wages and from pay rolls are fundamentally savings by Government compulsion. Part of the funds in this bill are to be derived from wage deductions. The balance is a contribution from pay rolls and has a similar effect upon the effective income of wage earners as actual deductions from pay. This has been admitted by Mr. Edwin Witte, executive secretary of the President's Committee on Economic Security, who stated frankly that the pay-roll contribution will normally be passed on to the consumer in the form of higher prices.

The old-age-insurance measure similarly is a measure which, through compulsory savings of wage earners, attempts to provide funds which may be used for pensions when workers become aged and are unable to find work. The amounts of old-age insurance to be paid are less than the present amounts of old-age relief in many instances.

I come now to some brief conclusions that I should like to draw from this material.

After a careful consideration of the various measures proposed, we are brought face to face with the fact that all of them combined have little merit in providing economic security and that any sincere program for achieving economic security must necessarily follow the principles which the bill being considered by this committee, H. R. 2827, sets forth. While some elaboration and clarification of this bill under discussion may be required before it will be enacted, the principles which it attempts to introduce are essentially sound and applicable to the present conditions of need and distress.

1. Unlike all of the other measures discussed, it asks that all those who are economically insecure and particularly those who are in greatest distress be covered by an organized system of protection.

2. It provides for minimum adequacy of income under a single system to continue as long as there is need instead of setting up haphazard and inadequate measures which present many gaps and uncertainties and diverse administration for those in need.

3. It substitutes a modern decent system of economic compensation instead of perpetuating the centuries-old poor laws which are at the base of American relief systems.

4. It recognizes the need for a continued Federal responsibility, taking into consideration that the experience of the last 5 years amply demonstrates the incapacity of States and localities to provide the necessary funds.

5. It places the burden upon those surpluses of income and production which should be utilized for economic security rather than the make-shift plan of having wage earners themselves share their inadequate incomes with those who are unemployed or economically insecure.

6. And finally in recognition of modern industrial organization, it places administration of economic measures where it properly belongs—as a function of labor organization.

The bill, in my opinion, is practical, realistic, and grows out of a sincere recognition of modern conditions and modern industrial problems. I hope that this committee and Congress will recognize the importance and the validity of this bill.

Mr. DUNN. Does any gentleman here wish to interrogate the witness?

Mr. HARTLEY. I would like to ask an estimate as to the number of those who would come under the direct provisions of the bill; that is, who would receive at least the minimum of $10 per week. Have you estimated the number of unemployed today?

Mr. LURIE. Under your present bill that you are considering?

Mr. HARTLEY. Under the Lundeen bill.

Mr. LURIE. As defined at present, the whole group of unemployed would come under it. I assume that it would mean at present, my guess would be about 10,000,000 families and about 2,000,000 individual persons other than families.

Mr. HARTLEY. Did you not estimate that there were about 20,000,000 who were dependent?

Mr. LURIE. Twenty million persons? No. In the families on Federal relief.

Mr. HARTLEY. The 10,000,000 are to come under the direct provisions of the bill?

Mr. LURIE. Ten million families?

Mr. HARTLEY. Yes.

Mr. LURIE. That would be about 35,000,000 persons. I would say that the difference between those now on relief and those who would come under compensation in this bill is the difference between 20 million and about 30 to 35 million persons. At the present time the Government provides relief for 20 million. Probably there are another 15 million who should be compensated because of unemployment but now receive no compensation whatsoever.

Mr. HARTLEY. Do you fell that the matter of providing this unemployment insurance can be handled better through a Federal agency, possibly through Federal agencies set up in the different States and other political subdivisions than through the States themselves?

Mr. LURIE. I think the question of administration is different than the question of sources of funds. I see no way at present of financing relief or compensation without Federal funds. It is pretty well exclusively Federal funds at the present time for most of the States. As for administration, I think the administration under a national plan would have to be divided on the basis of local and State units in order to be workable.

Mr. HARTLEY. There are other questions that I had in mind asking, Mr. Chairman, but I will withhold them at the moment so that we can go on.

Mr. DUNN. Do any other gentlemen desire to interrogate the witness?

Mr. LUNDEEN. I would like to, but I think we are short of time.

Mr. DUNN. Thank you very much. We appreciate your coming here, and have enjoyed your address.

STATEMENT OF LEO J. LINDER

Mr. LINDER. Mr. Chairman and gentlemen of the committee, I am here to speak to you on the constitutionality of the Lundeen bill. Since I come here before you as an expert, I presume I should, within the limitations of modesty, state my qualifications very briefly.

Mr. DUNN. Yes; we want them.

Mr. LINDER. I shall state briefly that I am a member of the bar of the State of New York, a member of the bar of the United States Supreme Court, that I have practiced, tried cases, and argued appeals before the appellate courts of very many States besides the State of New York, and that I have briefed and argued questions of constitutional law before the highest court of our land, the United States Supreme Court. About 2 months ago the International Juridical Association, an association of lawyers of which I am a member, requested me to make a study of the constitutionality or the constitutional questions involved in the Lundeen bill, H. R. 7598.

Mr. DUNN. That is the old bill.

Mr. LINDER. Yes. The request was also made that if I came to the conclusion that the bill was constitutional, I should then draw a brief establishing the constitutionality of the bill. I made a very careful study of the decisions, the texts, and all of the other authorities to which lawyers resort in determining constitutional questions. At the termination of my study, I became thoroughly and completely convinced that the bill was unquestionably constitutional. Of course, my research with respect to H. R. 7598 is equally and perhaps more applicable to H. R. 2827, because H. R. 2827 is without question an improvement on the other bill, because it simplifies many of the constitutional questions there involved.

The statement that I am going to read you very briefly states the affirmative argument supporting the constitutionality of the bill, and then, after stating that affirmative argument, deals with various objections that might possibly be raised to the constitutionality of the bill, such as the question as to whether the bill involves an unconstitutional delegation of legislative power, the question as to whether it is unconstitutional by reason of the indefiniteness of the appropriation contained in it, the question as to whether the bill involves any violation of due process, and, finally, the question as to whether the bill involves the violation of State rights.

The affirmative argument establishing the constitutionality of this bill is really very simple. This bill provides for the appropriation of Federal moneys out of the Treasury of the United States for the payment of compensation to the unemployed, the sick, the disabled, and the aged. It is thus simply an exercise of the appropriating power; that is, the power of Congress to spend money. The bill does, indeed, do more than provide for appropriations; it provides for the setting up of administrative machinery. But the appropriating power of Congress necessarily carries with it the incidental power to provide administrative machinery for disbursing the moneys appropriated and for insuring their proper application to the purposes sought to be achieved by Congress.[1]

---

[1] The Constitution of the United States, art. I, sec. 8, cls. 1 and 18; Willoughby on the Constitution of the United States, ch. 3, sec. 62, p. 105.

What limitations are there on the power of Congress to appropriate Federal moneys? The Federal Government is a government of
enumerated powers, that is, powers enumerated by the Constitution.
Some constitutional lawyers have, therefore, argued that Congress
may only expend moneys for the execution of the specifically enumerated powers. Upon some such argument, an appropriation for
social insurance would be unconstitutional, since the Constitution
does not enumerate any power to provide social insurance for the
people of the United States. The argument is, however, wholly unsound, for it ignores the fact that one of the enumerated powers set
forth in the Constitution is the power to " lay and collect taxes, pay
debts, and provide for the common defense and the general welfare
of the United States ".[2] To limit this power to spend moneys for
the general welfare, to the power to spend moneys for the execution
of the other specially enumerated powers, is to rob the general welfare clause of its meaning and thus to violate an elementary principle of constitutional construction.[3] Such distinguished constitutional authorities as Washington,[4] Madison,[5] Monroe, [6] Hamilton,[7] Calhoun,[8] and Justice Storey,[9] have definitely repudiated the
conception of an appropriating power limited by the other powers.
Our highest authority, the United States Supreme Court, has in
the famous Sugar Bounty case [10]—I will not here take the time to
read the citations, all of which are set forth in the footnotes to the
brief—definitely upheld appropriations by the Government in payment of purely moral obligations, entirely beyond the scope of the
other specifically enumerated powers and has, indeed, held that an
appropriation even out of " considerations of pure charity " [11]—the
words " considerations of pure charity " are a quotation from a
United States Supreme Court opinion—cannot be reviewed by the
judicial branch of the Government. Congress itself has uniformly
and consistently exercised its appropriating power for any purpose
which it deems for the general welfare and irrespective of whether
the purpose comes within the specifically enumerated powers or not.
    Consider the appropriations which Congress has made. Congress
has spent millions—I should say billions—for the purchase of
Louisiana from France, of Alaska from Russia, of Florida from
Spain; Congress has made outright gifts of millions of dollars to the
individual States; [12] it has appropriated billions of dollars for
agriculture; [13] and for internal improvements; [14] it has appro-

---

[2] Constitution, art. I, sec. 8, ch. 1.
[3] Chief Justice Taney in *Holmes* v. *Jennison*, 14 Pet. 538, 570, 571 ; Story Commentaries
on the Constitution, 5th ed., secs. 812, 913.
[4] Story on the Constitution, 5th ed. note to sec. 978.
[5] The Federalist, p. 41 ; Richardson, Messages and Papers of the President, vol. 2,
485, 568.
[6] Annals of Congress, 17th Cong., 1st sess., vol. 2, p. 1839 ; Richardson, op. cit., vol. 2,
p. 165.
[7] Hamilton's Works, Lodge's edition, vols. 3, 294, 371, 372.
[8] Eliot's Debates, 2d ed., vol. 2, 431, note.
[9] Story on the Constitution, vol. 1, secs. 922 to 924 ; see also Pomeroy Introduction to
Constitutional Law, secs. 274, 275 ; Hare, American Constitutional Law, p. 155 ; Willoughby on the Constitution of the United States, sec. 269 ; Burdick on the American
Constitution, sec. 77.
[10] *United States* v. *Realty Co.*, 164 U. S. 427.
[11] *United States* v. *Realty Co.*, *supra*, p. 441, 4.
[12] In 1837 Congress, finding that there was a surplus, appropriated $20,000,000 to be
paid to the individual States in proportion to their population ; Congress made a second
appropriation of this nature in 1841.
[13] Orfield Federal Land Grants to the States, pp. 37, 41, 48, and 67 : the acts establishing the Bureau of Animal Husbandry, Weather Bureau, Bureau of Plant and Industry,
Forest Service, Bureau of Soils, Bureau of Biological Survey, Bureau of Crop Estimates,
etc., etc.
[14] The Geological Survey, Bureau of Mines, Department of Education, road building.

priated the moneys of the Nation to aid destitute foreigners suffering severe calamities, as in the case of the Santa Domingoes in 1794;[15] and the citizens of Venezuela, who suffered an earthquake in 1812;[16] it has, in the last 2 years, appropriated billions of dollars for emergency relief to " needy and distressed people ";[17] it has appropriated billions for the setting up of a Reconstruction Finance Corporation;[18] Home Owners' Loan Corporation;[19] and the Federal Housing Corporation[20]—not to mention all the other characters of the " alphabet soup."

None of the enumerated powers would justify these expenditures. You can look in vain through the Constitution for any specific enumeration of any power to do any of the things which I have just enumerated. Yet surely no one would presume to say that Congress exceeded its power in making the Louisiana Purchase, or in setting up the Geological Survey, which has increased the natural resources of the Nation, or that Congress should never have contributed to the country's educational needs.

It is thus entirely clear when you consider it that, wholly without regard to the enumerated powers, Congress may use Federal moneys for any purpose whatsoever which it deems will accomplish the general welfare. Surely it could not be said that a bill which will provide a system of unemployment and social insurance for millions of unemployed, sick, disabled, and aged, is less for the general welfare than any of the bills which have just been mentioned. When Congress passes this bill, it will thereby declare that, in its judgment, this bill is for the general welfare and no court has the power to substitute its judgment on that question for that of Congress.

The fact is that the Supreme Court of the United States has itself stated that it has never in its entire existence attemped to set any limitations to the power of Congress to appropriate moneys.[21] On the contrary, the Supreme Court has explicitly declared that the exercise of the appropriating power is not at all a subject for judicial consideration.[22] The Supreme Court has appreciated that if individual taxpayers were permitted to harass and obstruct the Federal Government with questions as to the propriety of national expenditures, that this would render wholly unworkable the whole machinery of the Federal Government. There is a historic case in which a taxpayer tried to stop the Secretary of the Treasury from paying out moneys for the construction of the Panama Canal.[23] Certainly there you have as good an example of an expenditure and an appropriation beyond the enumerated powers of Congress as is possible to find, and solely justified by the general-welfare clause. The United States Supreme Court declared that the taxpayer could not interfere. The Court pointed out that the taxpayer could not show—and this is the technical reason—any " direct injury ", since he could not point to any property belonging to him

---

[15] Act of Feb. 12, 1794, ch. 2.
[16] The act of May 8, 1812, ch. 79 ; 4 Eliot's Debates, 240.
[17] Emergency Relief and Construction Act, 1932, 47 Stat. 709, July 21, 1932. c. 520.
[18] Jan. 22, 1932. c. 8, 47 Stat. 5.
[19] June 13, 1933, c. 64, 48 Stat. 128.
[20] National Housing Act, no. 479, 73d Cong., approved by President June 27, 1934.
[21] *Mass.* v. *Mellon*, 262 U. S. 447, 487–88 ; in *Field* v. *Clark*, 143 U. S. 649, *United States* v. *Realty Co.*, *supra*, and *Mass.* v. *Mellon, supra*, the Supreme Court refused to pass on the question of the propriety of the exercise of the appropriating powers.
[22] *Mass.* v. *Mellon, supra.*
[23] *Wilson* v. *Shaw*, 204 U. S. 24.

which was directly affected by the way the Federal Government spent its money. After all, the money in the United States Treasury appropriated, might very well be interest on the foreign debts or the proceeds of the sale of governmental property and no taxpayer could point to any specific tax or any specific moneys paid by him which was used for the appropriation in question.

As I read this, it comes to my mind that only recently the United States Government made a neat little profit of over $2,000,000,000 on the devaluation of the dollar. That profit constituted part of the funds of the United States. So long as this bill contains simply a general appropriation—and that is all it does contain—because the language of the bill as I have it here is that there is appropriated out of the Treasury of the United States money sufficient to enable the consumption of and the effectuation of this bill—but where you have an act of Congress which appropriates moneys generally out of the Treasury of the United States without any reference to any earmarked moneys, no taxpayer can point to any specific moneys of which he has been deprived by virtue of any tax laid upon him. And since no taxpayer can point to any such specific moneys, he cannot technically, as the United States Supreme Court said, show any direct injury.

The United States Supreme Court, however, went much further than this technical argument with respect to the matter of direct injury. The Court declared explicitly that the question of the purpose for which Congress may use moneys, is a legislative question, not a judicial one.

I would like to read you a few quotations from treatises on constitutional law, which definitely establish, with the aid of the authorities there cited, this proposition. Pomeroy, in his monumental text on constitutional law, declares:

What expenditures will promote the common defense or the general welfare, Congress may alone decide, and its decision is final.

Hare, in his early text on American constitutional law, puts the matter as follows:

The question of for what purpose Congress may use its powers of taxation (and thus ultimately for appropriation) is a legislative question, not a judicial question.

Therefore, I think it is perfectly clear that this bill is not only constitutional as a constitutional exercise of the appropriating power, the power to spend moneys for the general welfare, but there is no legal way by which the propriety of the exercise of this power can be questioned by anybody.

That is the affirmative argument in support of the constitutionality of the bill. It seems to me to be entirely irrefutable.

Mr. DUNN. The word "welfare" there makes it constitutional, does it not?

Mr. LINDER. The words "general welfare" and the fact that Congress has the power to appropriate moneys for anything which Congress regards as for the general welfare. That is right.

Mr. DUNN. Thank you. I wanted to have that statement substantiated.

Mr. LINDER. I proceed now to the negative part of this argument, that is, the answer to objections which have been or can be raised.

The most serious objection which can be raised, it seems to me, is the question with respect to whether this bill involves an unconstitutional delegation of legislative power. While the bill does indeed invest the Secretary of Labor with large discretion, this does not render the bill unconstitutional. The United States Supreme Court has, again and again, sustained delegations of power to the President, Cabinet officers, and Commission. The Court has recognized that Congress might very well find it impossible to do more than to " lay down an intelligible principle to which the person or body administering the bill is directed to conform." [25] The Court has appreciated the practical difficulty of fixing precise and definite standards in advance of the complex contingencies certain to arise and has recognized that Congress might " from the necessities of the case, be compelled to leave to the executive officers the duty of bringing about the result pointed out by the statute." [26] Thus, the Tariff Act of 1922 was held constitutional by the United States Supreme Court, although it vested the President with the power to raise or lower the tariff upon any imported article whenever it found that the American products were at a competitive disadvantage with those imported from abroad.[27] I dare say you can search high and low in an effort to find an example of a broader power of administrative discretion than that which was here regarded as constitutional, lodged in the President. But if that is broad, consider the broad power which was held to have been constitutional, delegated to the Commissioner of Internal Revenue by the Revenue Acts of 1918 and 1921, which authorized the Commissioner to adjust the very rate of excess-profits tax. Again, in another case an act of Congress, which gave the Secretary of the Treasury, on the recommendation of experts, the power to fix and establish standards of purity, quality, and fitness for consumption of certain commodities imported into the United States, was held constitutional.[29]

In the recent " hot oil " case [30], handed down by the United States Supreme Court about the beginning of January this year, the United States Supreme Court declared that the " hot oil " control clause of the N. R. A. was invalid as an unconstitutional delegation of legislative power. But, in that case, no " primary purpose " or " primary standard " whatsoever was clearly stated. The legislation there considered is wholly distinguishable from this bill for here in the Lundeen bill a primary purpose is stated, and it is clear that the Secretary of Labor is not invested by this bill with anything more than a properly constitutional " administrative dis-

[25] *Hampden* v. *United States*, 276 U. S. 394.
[26] *Buttfield* v. *Stranahan*, 192 U. S. 470, 496.
[27] *Hampden* v. *United States*, supra.
[29] *Buttfield* v. *Stranahan*, supra.
[30] The " hot oil " decision, *Panama Refining Co.* v. *Ryan*, 79 L. Ed. Adv. 223, Jan. 7, 1935, Sup. Ct. Rep. —; but see Carpenter on the Constitutionality of the N. R. A., Southern California Law Review, Jan. 1934, p. 125; Cheadle on the Delegation of Legislative Function, 27 Yale Law Journal, 892.

cretion." Indeed, when you consider it, the discretion invested in the Secretary of Labor under the Lundeen bill is narrow, for the beneficiaries who are to receive the compensation are named, the minimum compensation is prescribed, the maximum compensation is ascertainable and the nature of the compensation is fixed. Certainly the discretion here vested in the Secretary of Labor is far less wide than that vested in the Secretary of Agriculture by the Agricultural Adjustment Act of 1933.[31] In the A. A. A. bill, the Secretary of Agriculture was granted the power—and I now quote from the statute—

to provide for rental or benefit payments in connection with crop reduction in such amounts as the Secretary deems fair and reasonable.

Mr. Hartley. On that point, has that question been tested yet?

Mr. Linder. No; not the A. A. A. Of course, I present the A. A. A. only because I am presenting this to a congressional body that found it thoroughly constitutional to pass the A. A. A., which provides for this extravagant area of administrative discretion, should have no difficulty in passing a bill which said that the Secretary of Labor is empowered to pay compensation, the minimum level of which is fixed, the maximum level of which is ascertainable, to persons who are definitely described in the act. Here in the A. A. A. the Secretary of Agriculture is given the power to provide for benefit payments in such amounts as he deems fair and reasonable. The Lundeen bill does not do that. It does not say the Secretary of Labor is given the power to provide for such compensation as he or she deems fair and reasonable at all, because there is a minimum stated. But the A. A. A.—I refer to that only because I am speaking to a congressional body—has this argument: The direct argument is that the area of discretion which is vested in the Secretary of Labor is narrow, and that it is narrower than the area of administrative discretion which was held constitutional in the various cases that I have cited. It would be proper argument, arguing from precedent as one would have to argue before the United States Supreme Court, that you have held the Tariff Act which allowed the President to adjust the very rate of tariff wherever he found that the domestic product was at a competitive disadvantage—you held that constitutionally there is no limitation on the discretion there, except the President must determine whether the domestic product is at a competitive disadvantage. You held it perfectly proper—if you are arguing to the United States Supreme Court—for the Congress to enact a bill by which the Commissioner of Internal Revenue is authorized to adjust the rate of excess-profits tax.

Mr. Dunn. Pardon me; you are referring to the reciprocal tax, are you not, that was passed last year?

Mr. Linder. No, no. This is the 1922 act. I am referring to the tariff bill which came before the United States Supreme Court for consideration in Hampton against United States. In Hampton against United States, the United States Supreme Court said that it was perfectly legitimate for Congress to vest the President with such discretion. When I wrote this brief originally, I inserted in the brief this statement, that the United States Supreme Court has

---

[31] May 12, 1933, c. 25, 48 Stat. 31.

never in its entire history invalidated an act on the ground that it involved unconstitutional delegation of legislative power. But I had to take that sentence out of this brief because lo and behold, to the everlasting astonishment of every constitutional lawyer in this country, without question, the United States Supreme Court in the " hot oil " case a month ago held that section of the N. R. A. which gives the President the power to regulate the production and the distribution of " hot oil " invalid, because that was, as the United States Supreme Court says, an unconstitutional delegation of legislative power. Mr. Joseph Cardozo wrote a brilliant dissent. He was alone in his dissent. In that dissent he pointed out that this decision was a break with the whole line of decisions in which the tariff act and the other acts were considered.

Therefore, it is necessary for us to consider whether this bill is constitutional within the recent decision of the United States Supreme Court in the " hot oil " case. I say that it is on a much different basis because in the " hot oil " decision the United States Supreme Court was considering a clause in a bill which stated that the President might interfere with an prohibit the transportation of " hot oil " products, without in anywise defining under what circumstances he should do it. The Lundeen bill does set definite criteria and standards, because it fixes a minimum, it determines how the maximum shall be ascertained, and it determines to whom the benefits and competition shall be paid. And since it does that, it cannot at all come within the criticism of the United States Supreme Court in the " hot oil " decision.

Mr. HARTLEY. May I ask another question? I do not want to interrupt your testimony here too much.

Mr. LINDER. That is quite all right.

Mr. HARTLEY. But I am very much interested in your argument. Do you not think we can strengthen this bill by further defining the powers of the Secretary of Labor in this bill?

Mr. LINDER. You could strengthen it further, but it would not strengthen the constitutionality of the bill. The bill is perfectly constitutional as it stands, because you do not need to do any more than fix the minimum, state how the maximum shall be ascertained— and when you say " average local wages ", that can be ascertained; there is no difficulty about it, that is purely a matter of statistical determination. A finding can be made as to that, just as in the tariff case it was entirely possible for the President to determine whether the domestic product was at a competitive disadvantage. It is possible to determine it. The criterion is stated and the formula is given on the basis of which the administrator can determine how he should proceed. And insofar as that is done in the Lundeen bill—and it is unquestionably done in the Lundeen bill—the Lundeen bill cannot be attacked on the ground that it involved any delegation of legislative power.

Mr. HARTLEY. Then you do believe that this is as great a delegation of authority and power as was granted in the " hot oil " case?

Mr. LINDER. Not at all, because in the " hot oil " case the President's power to prohibit the transportation of " hot oil " products was not in any wise restricted. He was not told that he could restrict " hot oil " products already brought in, or under what circumstances, or what kind of findings he should make or anything else of the kind.

Mr. LUNDEEN. You might say he was given unlimited power.

Mr. LINDER. Right. Whereas here, the Secretary of Labor is given a limited power.

Mr. LUNDEEN. A restricted power.

Mr. LINDER. Yes.

Mr. HARTLEY. Do you really think the Secretary of Labor is given limited authority in this bill? Do you not think it is rather broad authority?

Mr. LINDER. Do you think it is any broader than the power of the President in the tariff bill to adjust the rate of tariff from nothing to 100 percent, if he so please?

Mr. HARTLEY. No; I agree with you that is a delegation of authority.

Mr. LINDER. Do you think it is any greater than the delegation of power which is involved in the act in which the Commissioner of Internal Revenue is given the power to adjust the rate of excess-profits tax? He is not told whether he is to adjust it at 1 percent or 100 percent. Yet that was held perfectly legitimate. What broader example of administrative discretion could you have than the act which was held constitutional by the United States Supreme Court in which the Secretary of the Treasury was authorized to fix the standards of quality and fitness for consumption of products.

Mr. HARTLEY. May I ask this? Do you think that the decision in the "hot oil" case indicates a possible change in the trend of opinion of the Supreme Court as to the right of Congress to delegate this authority?

Mr. LINDER. I should say that the decision of the United States Supreme Court in the "hot-oil" case indicates that the United States Supreme Court will not hold constitutional any act which delegates an administrative power to an administrator without defining and in some wise, in some intelligible way, limiting and restricting that power. I think that any constitutional lawyer who reads the "hot-oil" decision will have to say now that if this Lundeen bill said that the Secretary of Labor was to pay compensation to the unemployed, periodically, without saying how much, without fixing a maximum or a minimum, then it would be under the "hot-oil" decision and the United States Supreme Court would hold that bill unconstitutional. But I do not think that criticism can be at all urged against this bill in the present form.

Mr. HARTLEY. Do you not agree that that decision was sort of an admonition to the Congress to call a halt?

Mr. LINDER. I have said so.

Mr. HARTLEY. My questions may indicate that I am opposed to a bill of this kind. I am not. I am merely trying to get opinions which will enable this committee to write a bill that is going to stand up after the bill has been put into effect.

Mr. LINDER. I think I would like to extend my remarks on that question a little in this respect: This bill cannot be attacked as unconstitutional delegation of legislative power, from a different aspect. This bill is not one under which the President is given the power to tax anything, or the Secretary of Labor to tax anything, or to forbid something from coming into the United States or to forbid something from being transported in interstate commerce.

In that respect it is wholly different than the "hot-oil" case, it is wholly different from the tariff case and all the others, because this bill rests on a wholly different basis. This bill is a bill by which Congress spends money. So long as this is a bill by which Congress spends money, the power of Congress to spend money being unlimited within the sole limitation that Congress must regard it as being for the general welfare, in that sense no one can intelligently urge for a minute that this involves an unconstitutional delegation of legislative power. The power to spend money, as I stated before, carries with it the power to set up an administrative machinery for the spending of the money. That is perfectly obvious, that it must. If the Congress has the power to spend 100 million dollars, it obviously must have the power to devise the machinery by which the money is to be spent, and to set up the criteria which are to govern and guide the administration of the fund. In that sense, a breath of unconstitutionality cannot be attached to the Lundeen bill.

The other decisions and these other cases involve a wholly different set of situations. The "hot-oil" case involves the power of the President to stop something from going across the State lines, but we are not stopping anything from going across the State lines. All that is being done here is that Congress is spending money and stating how the money is to be spent.

Mr. DUNN. Attorney Linder, I do not like to interrupt, but this is absolutely necessary. There has been a question come before the committee about this section 2, line 7. Will you read that? There are quite a number here who would like to have that explained.

Mr. LINDER. Section 2, line 7: "A system of unemployment insurance"?

Mr. DUNN. Yes.

Mr. LINDER. Section 2 provides:

The Secretary of Labor is hereby authorized and directed to provide for the immediate establishment of a system of unemployment insurance for the purpose of providing compensation for all workers and farmers above 18 years of age, unemployed through no fault of their own.

Mr. DUNN. That is the point I want to make. Would this bill, the way it is written, apply to men who are not citizens? That is what I want to find out. That question has been asked. It came up this morning when one of the witnesses said that they would like to have that question answered.

Mr. LINDER. I should say that this bill in its present form would be applicable to any worker and any farmer in the United States, unless there is something in section 4 which would restrict that interpretation. The only thing in section 4 which might restrict it would be line 9 to the end:

The benefits of this act shall be extended to workers, whether they be industrial, agricultural, domestic, or professional workers, and to farmers, without discrimination because of age, sex, race, color, religious, or political opinion or affiliation. No worker or farmer shall be disqualified from receiving the compensation guaranteed by this act because of past participation in strikes, or refusal to work in place of strikers.

I see nothing in this bill which would make it inapplicable to aliens who are workers and farmers. It seems to me that it would be wholly improper to restrict the interpretation of this to citizens wholly.

Mr. Dunn. Thank you.

Mr. Linder. That is not a constitutional question. It is a question of construction of the bill.

Mr. Dunn. Someone made the statement it would be necessary to insert another section to take care of people who are not citizens.

Mr. Linder. I should state it as my opinion that this bill applies to workers, to anyone who is a worker or a farmer, unless there is some other statute of the Federal Government—it would have to be a Federal statute—which would make it impossible for a person not a citizen to acquire the benefits of any such act. I know of no such statute at the moment. I can say, though, I proceeded to answer the question as best I could because I did not want to appear to refuse or to be unwilling to answer any questions, but that is not a question which comes within the confines of the constitutional questions which I have been here considering.

Mr. Lundeen. And you have not given that any particular study?

Mr. Linder. I have given it no particular study. It is purely an off-hand opinion on my part.

Mr. Dunn. But your interpretation of the act now would be that they would not be discriminated against?

Mr. Linder. I should say not. I would say that my off-hand reaction would be that I see no social reason why an alien worker should not receive the benefits under this act. I should say that if there were any doubts in the minds of any Congressmen or in the minds of the constituents of any Congressmen as to it, it might be a very good idea to bring it home to any reader of this bill that no discrimination is intended by providing in the act a provision that no worker shall be disqualified from receiving the compensation guaranteed by this act by reason of his being an alien or by reason of lack of citizenship. I should say that on the ground that it seems to me that an alien worker who by his work and by his toil and by his lifeblood has contributed to the wealth and the welfare of this country is entitled to as much protection as any citizen is.

Mr. Dunn. Attorney Linder, one of the members of the committee stated yesterday that in his district there were many people wanting to become citizens, but the judge before whom they appeared would not grant them citizenship papers because they could not read or write. It is not because the men do not want to become citizens, but some object.

Mr. Linder. I should say that certainly whether a man can read or write, if he is a worker, if he is a human being, he needs the means whereby to live, and his children need milk just as much as children of a man or woman who can read or write. You are certainly suggesting another reason why it would be outrageous——

Mr. Dunn. I agree with you that we should not discriminate against the unfortunates.

Mr. Linder. Yes.

Mr. Schneider. I would like to have your comment on this, are all the powers delegated in this bill delegated to the Secretary of Labor?

Mr. Linder. Yes.

Mr. SCHNEIDER. On page 3, line 6, where it says, "Further taxation necessary to provide funds for the purposes of this act shall be levied on inheritance, gifts, and individual and corporate incomes", and so forth, would that power be all delegated to the Secretary of Labor?

Mr. LINDER. Oh, no, no. The Secretary of Labor has no power to tax.

Mr. SCHNEIDER. Who has?

Mr. LINDER. Only Congress has.

Mr. SCHNEIDER. But we are delegating the power.

Mr. LINDER. Oh, no, no. The only proper construction of this language would be that when you say "further taxation" you mean further taxation shall be levied by whoever has the power to levy it. The Secretary of Labor has no power to levy taxes, therefore this must mean that Congress would levy the taxes. I should say the spirit of this act and its clear intention is this: Section 4 starts out by saying:

All moneys necessary to pay compensation guaranteed by this act and the cost of establishing and maintaining the administration of this act shall be paid by the Government of the United States. All such moneys are hereby appropriated out of all funds in the Treasury of the United States not otherwise appropriated.

That means if it costs 10 million dollars to pay the compensation under this act, if this act is passed, that 10 million dollars is a charge on the Treasury of the United States just like the President's salary or the cost of maintaining a battleship is a charge on the Treasury of the United States. If there is not enough money in the Treasury of the United States to pay this compensation, Congress in enacting this bill says that further taxation necessary to provide such funds shall be levied in a particular way. That is, if there is not enough money in the Treasury, Congress should put more money in the Treasury by levying taxes of this kind.

Mr. LUNDEEN. That is a declaration of policy?

Mr. LINDER. That is only a declaration of policy. That is what I was going to say. This is not a tax measure. It is absurd to regard this as a tax measure. As a matter of fact, this language, "Further taxation necessary to provide funds" is stated as a declaration of intention on the part of Congress, wholly without meaning and wholly without significance, because Congress does not levy taxes by using such language. When taxes are levied they are levied with reference to the whole body of revenue acts which are in existence. If Congress were levying a tax bill, Congress would, considering the whole body of the revenue acts, amend, repeal, or modify existing revenue legislation. It is ridiculous to think that this sentence, "Further taxation necessary to provide funds for the purposes of this act shall be levied on inheritances, gifts, and individual and corporation incomes of $5,000 a year and over", is language by which the tax is itself levied. The tax is not levied by this. All that Congress is doing here is saying, "If there is not enough money in the Treasury, then we, the present Congress that passed this bill, think, we believe, it is our feeling in the matter, that the way that further money should be provided is by this method." That is all this means, purely a declaration of intention.

Mr. HARTLEY. If this were a tax-raising bill it would not have been referred to this committee, but to the all-important Ways and Means Committee.

Mr. LINDER. That is right.

Mr. HARTLEY. There it would rest in some cubby hole.

Mr. LESINSKY. Absolutely correct.

Mr. LINDER. It is not a taxing measure. If you will bear with me in the course of this argument on the constitutional law, I will cover the whole question of the taxing power and all the rest of it, because I mean to consider all those questions.

I think that the question as to whether this bill involves an unconstitutional delegation of legislative power is pretty much covered, and I think is irrefutably disposed of by the statement that I have made, and the statement that has been elicited by the questions that have been asked.

I want to go on now as to the question as to whether this bill is constitutional or unconstitutional because of the fact that it does not appropriate a specific amount. One might say, looking at this bill, that Congress has not in this bill stated how much is appropriated. Congress does not say that a million or a billion or ten billion is appropriated. Congress says simply, "All monies necessary to pay compensation are appropriated", and that is all. Now, that is not a constitutional objection. No specific amount is appropriated by this bill. But this does not render the bill unconstitutional. For general indefinite appropriations are common. The first of such general indefinite appropriations was passed when the very first Congress, in 1793, directed that all expenses accruing or necessary for the maintenance of lighthouses be paid out of the Treasury of the United States.[32] Congress did not say that they appropriated a dollar or 10 thousand dollars or a million dollars. Congress simply appropriated the money that was necessary to maintain the lighthouses, that is all. Since then hundreds of statutes containing similar indefinite appropriations have been passed.[33]

In the footnote to the brief there are collated some references that, I think, will fully persuade you that when Congress passes a bill of this kind with an indefinite appropriation it is doing the sort of thing that Congress has been doing ever since 1793 and has done hundreds of times.

From the moment the bill is enacted, this general appropriation becomes a charge upon the Treasury of the United States. When it is determined that any individual is entitled to a certain amount of compensation, his claim is a claim on the United States, to be honored by the Treasury just as any matured bond or other obligation of the United States must be honored. In other words, claims for compensation would arise, considering the matter from the standpoint of machinery and mechanics, much in the same way that a claim on a Home Owners' Loan bond would arise. The bond is issued. When it is issued it becomes a claim upon the United States, to be honored out of the Treasury of the United States by the Secretary of the Treasury when the obligation or the bond becomes due.

[32] Act of Aug. 7, 1789. c. 9, 1 Stat. 53.
[33] Introduction to Hearings before the Subcommittee of the House, Committee on Appropriations on H. R. 9410, 73d Cong., 2d sess.

So you would conceive that the Secretary of Labor, through a proper administrative official, would determine that a particular individual was entitled to $12.32 compensation, and if that compensation were, according to the terms of the requisition made by the administrative officer, payable immediately, it would become a charge upon the United States Treasury just the same as a bond which has become due would be a charge. Like all other matured claims on the United States, these claims for compensation when fixed must be provided for as a part of the Budget of the United States. In other words, the administrative officer would determine how much if any compensation would have to be paid, and when he determined it, that would have to be provided for, along with the battleships and the salaries and all the other items of expenditure of the Federal Government. I do not think there is any serious objection that can be raised with respect to the fact that no definite appropriation is made.

I come now to an objection which is the bugaboo of all social legislation. That is the "due process of law" objection. Unlike all other employment and social insurance plans, and also unlike the Wagner-Lewis bill, this bill does not involve the setting up of reserves created by enforced contributions by employers or employees. The only way that any person could regard himself as in any wise deprived of property for the purpose of financing this bill, would be by regarding this bill as a taxing measure.

There is no pay roll tax here. There is no enforced contribution to reserves. The only way in which any human being, any person in the United States, could be regarded as in any wise hurt or interfered with or burdened by this act, would be by the taxes that he might have to pay if Congress thought it necessary to provide further tax or revenue-raising bills.

The bill provides that "it is the sense of Congress that if any further taxation is necessary to provide funds for the purposes of this act, it shall be levied on inheritances, gifts, and individual and corporation incomes of $5,000 a year and over."

Even if it can be argued that this is a taxing measure, and I submit that it cannot intelligently be so argued or so regarded, the bill is a proper exercise of the taxing power of Congress. Congress has the power under the Constitution to lay taxes for the "general welfare", subject only to two limitations.[34] In the case of duties, imports, and excises, "this must be uniform." This is not a duty, import, or excise, so the objection of uniformity is not available here. In the case of direct taxes, they must be apportioned according to the census. Neither limitation, however, applies to incomes, gifts, or inheritances since the sixteenth income-tax amendment.[35] If you regard this bill as a tax measure—and I say you cannot so regard it—it would be a perfectly proper tax measure because it would come within, first, the general welfare clause, and second, the income tax amendment to the Constitution.

Thus, a tax levied by Congress on incomes, inheritances, and gifts is wholly proper so long as Congress deems it to be for the

[34] *Hilton* v. *United States*, 3 Ball. 171; *Pollock* v. *Farm Land & Trust Co.*, 158 U. S. 601.
[35] The Sixteenth amendment reads as follows: "The Congress shall have power to lay and collect taxes on incomes, from whatever source derived, without apportionment among the several States, and without regard to any census or enumeration."

"general welfare." Once Congress has levied such a tax, the tax cannot be assailed by any taxpayer, since the courts will not review the exercise of the congressional discretion involved in income taxation. The decision of Congress is thus final.

The limitation on the taxing power of the States, "that the taxation must be for a public purpose", is not a limitation applicable to the Federal Government.[37] But even if it were, clearly the purposes for which funds are to be raised by taxation and to be spent under this bill, is a "public purpose." The fact that private individuals benefit, does not alter the fact that it is to the public interest that these private individuals receive such public benefit.[38] Finally, what is or is not a "public use" or purpose, has been held by the United States Supreme Court in the famous North Dakota nationalization cases to be a question concerning which the legislative authority is best able to judge.[39] Just as in the case of the exercise of the appropriating power, so in the case of the exercise of the taxing power, where the tax is levied on incomes, inheritances and gifts, the taxpayer is wholly without remedy. When Congress determines that such a tax is for the "general welfare", its decision is final and cannot be constitutionally assailed.

This brings me to the last objection, that is, the objection on the ground that this bill might violate State rights.

It has been argued that this bill is unconstitutional on the ground that it involves an usurpation of the rights of the States. This argument is based upon the proposition that the power of Congress to regulate commerce and industry is limited to the "interstate commerce power" and that any regulation by the Federal Government of intrastate business and of matters "not commerce", is unconstitutional.

This argument is wholly inapplicable to the present bill. For this bill is not an exercise of the interstate commerce power; it is an exercise of the appropriating power.

This bill does not involve any regulation of intrastate commerce or of matters "not commerce." This bill does not tell any merchant or manufacturer how he is to do his business; it does not involve the setting up of reserves; it does not compel any manufacturer to pay contributions to a particular reserve fund. It does not set up such business relationships as might possibly be involved in the creation of special accounts with employers or employees, based on their contributions to a reserve fund.

In the Wagner-Lewis bill the whole concept is that employers shall contribute a pay roll tax to a specific fund. There the machinery that is contemplated by Congress is a machinery which will involve the setting up of reserves, of accounts. It might very well be argued that Congress would be going into the insurance business, would be going into an elaborate set of business relationships, something which only the States should do. But do you not see that that has nothing to do with a bill like this, which does not involve any pay roll tax, does

[36] Pacific Insurance Co. v. Soule, 7 Wall. 433.
[37] Billings v. United States, 232 U. S. 261.
[38] Noble Bank v. Haskell, 219 U. S. 104; Fallbrook Irrigation District v. Bradley, 164 U. S. 112; O'Neill v. Leamer, 239 U. S. 244.
[39] Greene v. Frazier, 253 U. S. 232.
[40] Child Labor case, 247 U. S. 251.
[41] First Employers Liability case, 207 U. S. 462.

not involve any reserves, does not invole any enforced contributions? This bill simply spends money.

Mr. HARTLEY. On that point, does not this bill indirectly call for the setting up of reserves for the payment of unemployment compensation?

Mr. LINDER. No; it does not call for the setting up of one dime of reserve. All this bill does, as you read the bill, is, it spends money. It spends money by way of compensation to the unemployed, just the way the United States Congress spends money when it provides for a battleship. There is no reserve set up for the battleships. There is no reserve set up for the President's salary, or for the salaries of Congressmen. It is there. If it is not there, Congress has to raise the money by levying taxes. There is no reserve at all provided. That is the basic concept of this bill, that the Government has the obligation to provide social security to every human being, every worker and farmer who, through no fault of his own, is unemployed. The basic concept of this bill is that the Government in recognition of that social obligation to every human being who cannot earn a living through no fault of his own should pay directly to that person money; not because any reserve is set up for no reserve is set up. This bill says, " Let Congress pass a tax statute. Let Congress tax inheritances and incomes and gifts, not by way of any reserve but out of the money that the Congress can create." When you consider that Congress can, on occasions, raise billions for specific purposes—I understand that Congress spent about 30 billion dollars to wage the World War for the United States—Congress can create the money, can get the money. How it gets the money is not the purpose of Congress when it passes this bill. All that Congress does when it passes this bill is, it says, " Compensation shall be paid out of the United States Treasury and the compensation shall be a claim against the United States Treasury, and it shall be paid out of the United States Treasury." If the money is not there, Congress should raise the money by taxes.

If you consider the bill fundamentally and basically, therefore, you see that it involves vitally a wholly different social conception of the obligations of government and that which is involved in the Wagner-Lewis bill. In the Wagner-Lewis bill the money is to be created by reserves based upon insurance actuarial principles, reserves that are to be created over a period of time. A small amount of money is to be paid upon the basis of insurance principles to workers and farmers when they lose their employment. That is why the Wagner-Lewis bill does not provide for the present unemployed. The Wagner-Lewis bill deals with those who are employed now. It looks forward to the possibility of creating reserves out of pay roll taxes; it is really gotten out of the pay rolls of the workers and farmers, who would thereby be affected, looking to the creation of those reserves. It does not contemplate the Government spending its own money. The Government is not spending its money in the Wagner-Lewis bill. It is spending the money, it is providing for reserves out of which the insurance should be paid. This bill, however, has nothing to do with the question of reserves. This bill spends money. It spends money the same way that Congress spends money when it provides for the building of a post office or——

Mr. Dunn. Or battleships?

Mr. Linder. Or battleships.

Mr. Lundeen. Only this is for a better purpose.

Mr. Linder. Yes.

Mr. Hartley. Then you say that this bill merely recognizes the obligation that we have to provide unemployment insurance to our unemployed today, and indirectly directs Congress, then, to pass a new tax bill to raise the revenue to pay it.

Mr. Linder. It does not direct Congress to do it. Suppose that Congress were to pass a bill providing for the appropriation of a million dollars for the building of a post office in Kankakee, or somewhere. Congress then would not be concerned with how the million dollars should be raised. That is a job for the Secretary of the Treasury. The Secretary of the Treasury can inform the individual who is responsible for the balancing or for the preparation of the budget, and then the individual who is the Commissioner of the Budget can say whether there is money enough or whether there is not.

Mr. Hartley. Then you say that this directs the Secretary of the Treasury to raise the money to pay unemployment insurance?

Mr. Linder. It does not even do that. I mean, it does a very simple thing. It simply spends money. If the money is not there, then it is for Congress to work out ways and means for getting it there; that is all.

Mr. Hartley. Did you not say it was up to the Secretary of the Treasury to find money if it was not there?

Mr. Linder. If I said that, I spoke a little loosely. I mean the Secretary of the Treasury, of course, could not fill the job of finding the money or of getting money. It is up to Congress to tax and to provide the money.

Mr. Hartley. Then that gets back to my first question, that we are indirectly directing Congress to get the money in the event it is not there.

Mr. Linder. After all, it is conceivable that Congress might authorize the President to sell public lands. It is conceivable that Congress might direct the President to devaluate the dollar further. It is conceivable that Congress could work out one or a hundred different ways in the light of raising money.

Mr. Hartley. In the light of the last few years, it is possible.

Mr. Linder. That is right. But this is not a tax measure. I think it is important that you gentlemen should conceive it simply as an appropriating measure; just as you do not concern yourselves directly with how the money is to be provided when you pass any other appropriating measure, so you must regard this as an appropriating measure. How the money is to be provided is another question that Congress has to determine. That question I am not going into now, because it has nothing to do with the constitutional-law questions with which I have been concerned. Economists and statisticians, financial experts, and experts on the potential capacities of this country and on the earning power of the people of the country can advise you as to how Congress can get the money. I am not here for the purpose of telling you how Congress can get the money. I am here only for the purpose of persuading you, as I think I can—

I hope I can—that this bill is constitutional as an appropriating measure.

Mr. HARTLEY. Then, as I understand you to say, Congress has the right to direct the people of the State of New Jersey and every other State in the Union to pay taxes to provide unemployment insurance in the event there are not funds in the Federal Treasury?

Mr. LINDER. No; I did not say that. I said Congress had the power to spend the Federal moneys——

Mr. HARTLEY. Yes.

Mr. LINDER (continuing). For any purpose that Congress deems to be for the general welfare. If Congress says that it is for the general welfare of the people of the United States that every unemployed person should receive compensation, Congress has the power to provide for the payment of compensation to those persons. How the money is to be raised is a revenue question, it is a question of the budget. Money can be raised by the sale of land. It can be raised by the——

Mr. LUNDEEN. Sale of bonds.

Mr. LINDER. Yes; the sale of bonds. It can be raised by various fiscal and other measures.

Mr. LUNDEEN. They are always oversubscribed about seven times.

Mr. LINDER. Congress can provide for the issuance of a new Liberty bond, of course. Congress can provide for the money. But that is really not germane to the question we are now concerned with. The question that we are concerned with here is this: Has Congress the power as a matter of constitutional law to provide for the payment of compensation to the unemployed? The answer is "yes", because Congress has the power to spend money for any purpose Congress pleases, so long as Congress deems it to be for the general welfare.

Mr. SCHNEIDER. Getting back to that question I asked you some time ago, this bill quite specifically directs the Government to raise the additional money necessary by certain methods, inheritance taxes, income taxes, and so forth; not the selling of bonds, and so forth.

Mr. LINDER. It does not direct, though. As Congressman Lundeen pointed out, it is simply declaring the intention of Congress. It is simply saying that Congress thinks that the best way of raising money would be by income taxation, inheritance, and gift taxation. This is not the act in which it is doing that.

Mr. SCHNEIDER. Yes; I understand that part of it. However, if this has any meaning in its enactment, it means that the Congress is establishing the policy that the raising of additional money for the purpose of meeting this expenditure will be done by these means.

Mr. LINDER. It is a suggestion.

Mr. SCHNEIDER. Taxation of incomes, inheritances, and so forth and so on.

Mr. LINDER. There is no question in your mind, is there, sir, that Congress has the power to pass such taxation legislation?

Mr. SCHNEIDER. Oh, no; they have that, of course.

Mr. LINDER. Very well. If they now tax an income to the extent of so much percent, they can jack up the percentage if Congress so please.

Mr. SCHNEIDER. Yes. Are you familiar with the A. A. A. system of taxation—the processing tax?

Mr. LINDER. Yes. But you see, there you have a wholly different concept, because there you have something which is a little akin to the reserve-fund theory. The Secretary of Agriculture is given the power, as I stated before, to pay benefits to farmers in such amounts as he deems advisable and reasonable.

The Agricultural Adjustment Act also provides that the Secretary of Agriculture has the power to lay a processing tax on the products of agriculture, which come within the sphere of the Secretary of Agriculture's administration under this act. Then the act also goes on to say that the Secretary of the Treasury shall advance money to the Secretary of Agriculture as a sort of an advance to him for the purpose of paying these benefits to the farmers. And then the Secretary of Agriculture is to lay the processing taxes and it is the intention, stated in the act, that the processing taxes are to make up or to create a fund which is sufficient to reimburse the Secretary of the Treasury for the moneys he has advanced to the Secretary of Agriculture for these benefits. In other words, what Congress was there, in the A. A. A. doing, was to pay money to farmers and to provide the money which was being paid to farmers by processing taxes. That in a way is similar to the Wagner-Lewis bill and the conventional unemployment-insurance bills, where you create pay-roll taxes for the purposes of enabling you to pay compensation. A reserve is created. But, you see, the A. A. A. involves some very serious questions of constitutional law, because it does just that. In the case of the Lundeen bill, no taxpayer whose income tax was jacked up 25 percent or so could come into court and say, "I object to this bill. I think this bill interferes with my constitutional rights. I ask that the Secretary of the Treasury be enjoined from paying out the money by way of compensation under this bill, and the Commissioner of Internal Revenue be enjoined from collecting the taxes." He cannot do it, because he cannot point to any specific dollar which he paid which went for this bill. It is just impossible, because the $1,500, let us say, that this man paid might have gone for the battleship. It is impossible.

In the A. A. A. when the processing tax is levied and he pays the processing tax, he can point to specific money. He says, "The Government has levied a processing tax upon me which was used to pay benefits to farmers. I think that scheme is wrong. I think that is an improper method of use of money. I think it is improper to tax me for such a purpose."

But he cannot do that under the Lundeen bill.

There is another aspect, also, in which this bill is strikingly different from the other unemployment-insurance bills and from the other social legislation which involves due-process questions. This bill does not interfere with the conduct of any intrastate business. A farmer who is raising a cash crop, for instance, or who is raising a crop without limitation as to the nature of the crop, and who is taxed by this processing tax, can come into court, and they have come into court, and said, "We object to this processing tax because that is an interference with our business." As a matter of fact, if the sad truth must be broadcast, the A. A. A. has been held unconstitutional on a number of occasions in the last few months, insofar as it provided for the regulation of intrastate businesses. But the beauty of the Lundeen bill is that you cannot touch it on that point, because the Lundeen bill is not interfering with any business. Nobody can come and say, " I am being interfered with, I am not being allowed to run my business in the way I want to, I am being taxed ", because he cannot point to anything—this is not a bill which interferes with business; it just spends money—just as he cannot come in and object to the money that they are using for a post office somewhere, because he cannot say that his money went for that post office; and so he cannot do anything with this, either.

After all, take the taxpayer who so many years back was outraged because Congress was spending money for the building of the Panama Canal. He brought a proceeding, and the United States Supreme Court said, " We are sorry, my dear sir, you just cannot do anything about it, because Congress is just spending money, and Congress can spend money for anything it pleases so long as Congress does this for the general welfare." This is the same situation.

This bill does not prohibit the transportation of any product by interstate commerce. In the *Child Labor Case* the United States Supreme Court said that it was unconstitutional for the Federal Government to forbid the transportation in industry of the products of child labor, because the business in which this child labor was employed was an intrastate business subject only to the management and to the governance of the State; and it was a violation of the rights of the State to prohibit the transportation industry of the products of that child labor.

That argument simply has nothing to do with our present situation, because we are not interfering with the transportation of anything in interstate commerce. We are simply spending money.

A very important decision which has had a tremendous importance in constitutional law affecting social legislation is the employers' liability cases, in which the United States Supreme Court held that it was improper for Congress to regulate the liability of employers to their employees in intrastate business. That may be one of the many Achilles' heels of the Wagner-Lewis bill. These pay-roll taxes may very well be regarded as a regulation of intrastate business. But that does not apply here, because I have said now for the fifteenth or twentieth or one hundredth time you are just spending money here.

The bill simply sets up an obligation of the United States Government to pay out of the United States Treasury compensation. There is a case in the records, in the reports of the decisions of the United States Supreme Court, where a State came in and objected to the spending of money by Congress for a particular purpose, because the State said that was an interference with the proper province of the States. It is the very famous maternity bill. I think it was the Smith-Townsend bill. It is referred to in the footnotes of this brief. Congress there passed a bill appropriating so much money for the creation of a board of maternal and infant health hygiene, and it provided that so much money should be given to the States provided they set up in each State a hygiene board subject to the rules of and pursuant to the provisions and the general plan outlined in the statutes. The State of Massachusetts, in a case which is known as *Massachusetts* v. *Melton*,[42] a very famous case, came in and objected. They said, "When Congress provides for the appropriation of moneys to the particular States, provided they subject themselves to a Federal plan, Congress is interfering with the proper province of the States."

The United States Supreme Court said, "Oh, no; Congress is simply spending money, and in the exercise of appropriating money the power and authority of Congress to spend money cannot be questioned."

I am going to embark upon a line of reasoning here that has certain limitations and certain perils, which I am going to point out, but I would like to present the argument to you because while this argument would not be an argument which I would present to the United States Supreme Court, it is an argument which I have a perfect right to present to a Congressman because it is an argument based upon the sort of bills that Congress has just been passing; although I am not saying that those bills are constitutional.

Even if, however, the exercise of the appropriating power should, by any stretch of the imagination, be regarded as a regulation of matters "not commerce" and of intrastate commerce—I think I have demonstrated that it cannot so be regarded—it does not follow that the plan is beyond the powers of Congress. For it is the present doctrine of the United States Supreme Court that Congress has the power to regulate intrastate commerce and matters that are "not commerce" at all, provided that the burdensome character of these activities on interstate commerce is clear and direct.[43] Thus the United States Supreme Court has held the Packers and Stockyards Act of 1921 constitutional, although that act gave the Secretary of Agriculture supervision over the commission men and livestock dealers in the stockyards of the Nation and thus enabled the Secretary of Agriculture to regulate prices and practices in matters wholly intrastate.[44]

The Court appreciated that the object of the act was to "free and unburden"—this is the language of the Supreme Court—the flow of interstate commerce.

Again, in another case, the passenger rates of the branch line of a railroad, wholly within the boundaries of a single State, were held constitutionally subject to the control of the Interstate Commerce Commission, by reason of the effect of the intrastate rates on interstate rates and interstate business.[45] The Court has again and again regarded similar——

Mr. HARTLEY. Is this a decision of the United States Supreme Court?

Mr. LINDER. Yes, sir. The *Safety Appliance Act Case*, 222 U. S. 20. For further decisions along the same line I refer you to the footnote 43 of the brief.

[42] *Mass.* v. *Mellon,* supra.
[43] Safety Appliance Act case, 222 U. S. 20; *Wisconsin R. R. Com.* v. *C. B. & Q. R. R. Co.*, 257 U. S. 553; *Stafford* v. *Wallace*, 258 U. S. 485; *Board of Trade* v. *Olson*, 262 U. S. 1; *Colorado* v. *U. S.*, 271 U. S. 153.
[44] *Stafford* v. *Wallace*, supra.
Colorado v. *U. S.*, supra.

The Court has again and again regarded similar acts as a proper exercise of the " interstate commerce power."

Certainly, it must be clear—and this is the argument I would like to present as forcibly as I know how to Congressmen—that Congress in 1933 and 1934 has proceeded upon the constitutional theory that it lies within the province of the Federal Government to prevent practices which deter the free flow of interstate commerce and to promote practices which stimulate the free flow of interstate commerce. As a matter of fact, if you will read the preamble to the N. R. A. you will find language in that act which was introduced at the suggestion of a constitutional lawyer, made to Senator Wagner, which he very gratefully adopted, according to the minutes of a hearing on the N. R. A. just before the act was passed.

Mr. SCHNEIDER. A Senate hearing?

Mr. LINDER. A Senate hearing. In that Senator Wagner accepted with great gratitude the suggestion of a constitutional lawyer that they should stick into the N. R. A. some language which should indicate that the purpose of the N. R. A. was to deter practices which interfered with the free flow of interstate commerce, and to encourage practices which would stimulate the free flow of interstate commerce. As a matter of fact the A. A. A. contains language which is even clearer than the National Recovery Act.

The Congress which passed the Agricultural Adjustment Act of 1933 declared that the loss of the purchasing power of the farmers endangered the entire economic structure of the Nation.[48] The mechanism set up by that act was conceived as a device to restore purchasing power. Certainly, if that is the argument for the N. R. A. and the A. A. A. the workers' bill is similarly an effort to remove obstacles to the free flow of interstate commerce. Clearly, it provides for the general welfare much more directly than the N. R. A., the A. A. A., the P. W. A., and the other emergency acts which Congress has enacted during the Roosevelt administration.

This bill is an effort to deal with the same problem—the crisis in the purchasing power of the people of the United States. The basic conception of this bill is that the millions of workers and farmers throughout the United States who are unemployed, sick, disabled, and aged, lack purchasing power and that the soundest and most intelligent way to restore that purchasing power is simply and without further ado to give them money. But not to give them money by way of charity or relief, but to give them money as of right, as a compensation for a disability which they suffer, due to no fault of their own and due to the operation of social forces. The basic idea of this bill is that funds should be given to create purchasing power for the masses who must spend the money for the necessities of life and who, in spending the money for these necessities, for milk and for bread and for rent and for things they need to live, will thereby remove obstructions to the free flow of interstate commerce.

Furthermore, a consideration of the advantages of the Federal as against the State or Federal-State social insurance systems will show what the United States Supreme Court terms the " administrative necessity " of a Federal system.

---

[48] See Declaration of Policy, National Industrial Recovery Act, June 16, 1933, c. 90, 48 Stat. 195.

The vast growth of American industry spanning the entire continent and the development of a national economy that is interconnected and interdependent has completely transformed the Nation which was originally the subject of the Constitution. For most purposes of business and commerce State boundaries have ceased to exist. The existence of 48 governmental systems endeavoring to solve problems, essentially national in scope, in 48 different ways has created stupendous contradictions and difficulties. Of course, it is obvious enough that the Wagner-Lewis bill provides precisely that misfortune, 48 different State bills, all different, as different as the ingenuity and the intelligence—or the unintelligence—of the State legislatures can provide. The lack of purchasing power of the unemployed, sick, disabled, and aged is a national phenomenon, national in scope; its causes are bound up with the causes of the national economic crisis.

The administrative advantages in simplicity and efficiency which in here in a uniform and integrated Federal system, as against the chaos of different plans in different States, are obvious.

The Federal system is the only feasible one, because it is only the Nation which can deal with the problem as it must be dealt with. The problem is a problem of mass unemployment, with millions out of work. The loss in purchasing power runs into billions of dollars. Only the Federal Government, with its vast resources and imponderable taxing power, can provide the funds to meet a problem of such magnitude. Many of the States simply do not have the necessary financial resources or adequate taxing power. Their unemployed, however, need compensation no less than the unemployed of the wealthier States, and it is equitable that the wealthier States should contribute to the support and maintenance of the human beings in the poorer States. The incomes earned from Nation-wide industry are, in a large measure, beyond the taxing power of any but the one State where the income is received. Consider a huge industrial plant in the Middle West owned by a corporation domiciled in New York. Its income, earned in the Middle West, is received in New York. It is New York which can most effectively tax that income. Yet when a depression occurs and the plant in the Middle West is shut down, the human beings whose labor has contributed to the income received in New York are dropped, and the burden of their maintenance lies in the Middle Western States. The surplus, resources, and continuing income of the New York corporation in New York are not adequately available to the taxing power of the Middle Western State. Only the Federal Government can properly distribute the burden, because only it can effectively reach the income and property of a New York corporation. Thus the taxes paid by the New York corporation may, through the instrumentality of the Federal taxing power, be made available to meet the human needs of the unemployed throughout the country. Clearly it is only the long arm of the Federal Government which can reach out and deal with this problem.

The national emergency legislation which has been enacted during the Roosevelt administration involves an understanding of the national character of our economic problems. Furthermore, this legislation indicates a keen appreciation of the inadequacy and cumbersomeness of the Federal subsidy system. This legislation provides for direct aid to persons, firms, and corporations in the States. The A. A. A. provides Federal moneys directly to farmers all over the country. There is no nonsense requiring the Federal Government to grant subsidies to the States and the States to grant the money to the farmer. The Federal Government deals with the farmer directly. It does so in the firm realization that the price of crops grown by a farmer in Iowa determines his purchasing power, and that even if his crops never got beyond the boundaries of his State and even if his purchasing power is exercised for the purchase of products made within the State, his purchasing power is a matter of direct concern to the entire Nation.

Similarly, the Reconstruction Finance Corporation Act created the R. F. C. to supply Federal money direct to bankers throughout the country. The money was not given to the States to parcel out to the bankers. The bankers, whether their business was intrastate or interstate, whether they did a Nation-wide business or a neighborhood business, were the objects of national concern and were dealt with as such. Similarly, the Home Owners' Loan Corporation was organized by the Government to supply money, in theory, to home owners throughout the country; in practice, to mortgagees throughout the country. Thus "farmers' relief", "bankers' relief", and "home owners' relief" have all been envisaged as Federal problems requiring Federal solution.

There is no intelligent reason why the unemployment problem, which is similarly a Federal problem, and which similarly requires national solution, should not be dealt with in the same way.

We must remember that the bill here considered does not depend for its constitutionality on any consideration of the "interstate-commerce power" upon the argument that the regulation of intrastate business is necessary because of its effect on interstate business. Although I have stated the argument by analogy from the R. F. C. and the H. O. L. C. and the A. A. A. and the N. R. A., I do not at all mean to imply that the constitutional argument is based on that analogy, because I could not be sure of that ground. The N. R. A. has been held unconstitutional again and again and again in the inferior courts of the country—and the citations are collated here—on the ground that it involves an interference with intrastate business. And the Wagner-Lewis bill involves a mare's nest, a hornet's nest of constitutional complications because of all the problems of that character that are there involved.

This bill does not have to depend upon any argument that we are trying to deal with the purchasing power of the Nation; we are trying to stimulate the flow of interstate commerce, because, as I said at the outset, and I repeat, much in the form of a musical rondo, in which you start with the theme and come back to it, it is simply an act by which Congress spends money. It rests upon the same constitutional basis as the Reconstruction Finance Corporation Act and the Home Owners' Loan Corporation Act. The Reconstruction Finance Corporation Act is an act by which Congress spends money for the relief of bankers throughout the country. The Home Owners' Loan Corporation Act is an act by which Congress spends money for the relief of mortgagees who cannot get a dime on their mortgages. The A. A. A. is an act for the relief of farmers directly. I want to withdraw the reference to the A. A. A., because the A. A. A. involves the whole complication of difficulties involved in the processing tax, with all the problems of direct injury and all the rest of it, and due process, that are there involved. Here we have something which rests for its constitutional basis upon the same basis that the R. F. C. and the H. O. L. C. have.

The Congress which passed, and this is all that I want to say by way of summary. I trust I have made it clear, as an act it rests on the same constitutional basis as all these other acts, as the R. F. C., which spends money. The Congress which passed the Reconstruction Finance Act apparently was convinced that it was for the general welfare, that the banks in this country should be given money out of the Treasury of the United States so the banks could stay in business. The Congress which passed the H. O. L. C. Act apparently was convinced that it was for the general welfare that individuals and corporations owning mortgages affecting real estate should be given bonds of the United States in payment of their mortgages.

When Congress, and this is my concluding statement, when Congress passes this bill, if, as and when it does, it will at last have realized that it is for the general welfare of the United States, that all human beings in the United States who, through no fault of their own, are unable to earn the necessities of life, should receive money so that they may purchase the necessities of life, of living, and in so doing maintain not only their own very lives, but the economic life of the country.

The CHAIRMAN. On behalf of the committee I want to thank you for the valuable information you have given.

Mr. LINDER. If there are any constitutional law questions, I will be very happy to try to answer them, so far as I can.

I am submitting herewith for your convenience a list of citations and am prepared to submit additional citations if it is desired.

Mr. HARTLEY. Did I understand you to say before that we would be strengthening our case by further defining the powers of the Secretary of Labor?

Mr. LINDER. Well, I should say that you would strengthen the bill by an elaboration of the bill, but I should say that the energies of the House Committee on Labor, if it were determined that this bill were sound, should rather be devoted to the enactment of the bill as it stands than to getting into a lot of arguments that would be aroused, and would be involved in the question of definition. The bill in its present form is, I think, simple and intelligent; so simple that even a lawyer used to complicated and technical language can understand it. This bill is so simple it states its method by which it solves this problem, so simply and intelligently that any further attempt at elaboration here and now would involve a diverting of the energies of the committee into collateral arguments on definitions and that sort of thing. I should say I think it would be laudable and it would be splendid if a formal, technical bill in language which perhaps is more technical than this bill should be drawn, and should set up an elaborate administrative mechanism, and so forth; but it seems to me that the problem of the proponents of this bill in the present Congress is to persuade Congress that this idea is right.

If you persuade Congress that this idea is right, the formulation of the technical bill is simply a matter for experts. I mean, a matter of definition, and that sort of thing; you can state what is said here more technically, but I do not think you could state it much more intelligently. I think that this bill in its present form is intelligent, is clear, is readable, and most important of all, as far as I am concerned, is constitutional.

Mr. LUNDEEN. Would you say it is workable?

Mr. LINDER. It is unquestionably workable as a bill appropriating money for the building of a battleship. If that is workable, this is. It is as workable as the Liberty bonds, as the acts by which Congress threw $30,000,000,000 into the war; just as workable as that. It is as workable as any measure that Congress decides that the income—I will withdraw that, "the income"—that the funds in the Treasury should be used for.

The CHAIRMAN. May I say that the difference between an appropriation for the construction of battleships and appropriations to carry out this bill are that with battleships you destroy life, and by the provisions of this bill you maintain life.

Mr. LINDER. Apparently, you have more trouble getting a bill through for the maintenance of life than for destruction.

Mr. LUNDEEN. I am going to ask one question: You made a statement about getting Congress to pass this bill. Can you suggest any way by which we can get a majority of the Members of Congress to pass this?

Mr. LINDER. I have not come here—that is a question of practical politics, and that question I would like to discuss sometime. I am perfectly prepared to discuss it now, if you wish.

Mr. LUNDEEN. In other words, you say it is practical politics?

Mr. LINDER. It seems to me this bill will be passed if the people in the United States want it.

Mr. LUNDEEN. I am convinced the people want it, if we could only get the bill to them.

Mr. LINDER. I would suggest at the outset that there are not very many people in the United States who know about it.

I will be very happy to give you any more material. You can regard me as subject to your call with respect to the citation of authorities.

The CHAIRMAN. Thank you. I have read the Constitution a number of times, with my fingers. It is in Braile, and the words that appeal to me most are, "life, liberty, and the pursuit of happiness." And I know we cannot continue to have life if we are going to continue to have depressions. We cannot have any liberty. I do not think there is a man living who can say he is happy when he is in need of bread and beans.

Attorney Linder, I want to make a statement here. This gentleman told us this morning there was a committee of ministers sent to see the President to see what he could do about furnishing positions for the 20,000 ministers who are out of jobs. Won't you admit that 20,000 ministers out of jobs in this depression is bad?

Mr. LUNDEEN. Mr. Chairman, I never thought when I was here years ago I would ever live to hear a Congressman from Pittsburgh talk as you do. I am very happy that you are here.

Mr. DUNN. Thank you, Congressman Lundeen.

The CHAIRMAN. Gentlemen, you have heard the motion made and seconded. I am to send a letter to Miss Perkins, the Secretary of Labor, to send an attorney here to give us an opinion as to the constitutionality of the Lundeen bill, 2827.

STATEMENT OF FRED BRIEHL, OF THE EXECUTIVE COMMITTEE OF THE FARMERS NATIONAL COMMITTEE FOR ACTION

Mr. BRIEHL. I am a dairy farmer from Wallkill, N. Y., a member of the executive committee of the Farmers National Committee for Action. As such, my testimony here today is given not only in behalf of 120,000 farmers affiliated with this organization, but we feel in behalf of the entire impoverished portion of our farming population.

The locality in which I live is in nowise exempt from the oppressive economic conditions being suffered throughout the country by the farming element. Personal observation and investigation has shown us that many farm hands are idle because the income of the dairy farmers does not permit the hiring of this idle help. This condition works a two-fold hurt; firstly, it deprives these hired hands from an opportunity to earn a livelihood, meager as it was, and forces them to a pathetically low living standard; secondly, it is an added burden to the hiring farmers themselves by reason of added toil of which the average farmer already had sufficient. In my immediate neighborhood are cases where children had to be supplied with shoes to enable them to go to school. Visiting nurses report malnutrition in an alarming number of cases, proving that relief is inadequate. The cause of all this misery is the lack of a job and income of the breadwinner of the family.

Right within my own locality is the case of a family breadwinner, who I employed during the summertime past through the fall. I have had to lay him off absolutely. No means of income. In years past it always used to be a problem to get help when we had a job such as harvesting ice. The last several years, however, I could have gotten 3 or 4 times as much help as I needed, which shows any number of idle help in rural districts.

Another neighbor of mine, his family broken up, the husband had to go to the city in order to seek work there.

Mr. LUNDEEN. Do you operate a farm yourself?

Mr. BRIEHL. Yes, sir. I am a dairy farmer.

Mr. LUNDEEN. Do you work that farm with your own hands?

Mr. BRIEHL. I do; and with hired hands.

Mr. HARTLEY. What do these hired hands get when they are working steadily, a month, we will say?

Mr. BRIEHL. The wage will vary somewhat. It will vary from as low as board and cigarette money to perhapse $35 a month.

The CHAIRMAN. That includes his board?

Mr. BRIEHL. That would include his board.

Mr. HARTLEY. You mean he would get his board in addition to the $35?

Mr. BRIEHL. Correct. When these conditions exist in my small environment it is but a matter of arithmetic for a statistician to determine on what scale it prevails nationally in this vaunted land of plenty. Lest this last remark be construed as irony, permit me to say that the administration regards production as so over-abundant as to practice programs of crop destruction. Here is the irony, hunger and misery in the face of plenty. What a contradiction!

All sociologists know that social legislation always lags far behind social need. The mere fact that any social and unemployment bill is being considered at this time is in itself sufficient proof of the crying need for the same. It is only when the problem becomes extremely acute that it is given any consideration at all; so in view of what is general knowledge, it would be useless repetition to confront you with a mass of facts and figures to impress you with the need for social insurance. However, it is to the concern of all of us as to just what some of the underlying causes of these circumstances are and to determine quite definitely the course the correction is going to take. The original premise of the need being granted, this latter becomes all important.

For a better understanding of our problem we could with value briefly sketch some of the economic trends of agriculture in recent years. According to Secretary of Agriculture Wallace, we find the following:

Farmers' portion of national income

Year	Gross income	Population on farms
	Percent	*Percent*
1850	35	63
1900	20	36
1920	14	28
1932 (less)	8	25
1934	9½	23 to 25

We find, according to the United States Census, that the gross farm income is divided as follows for the years 1929 and 1930:

Of the farmers, 48.8 percent receive 14.1 percent of the gross farm income; 42.4 percent receive 45.9 percent of the gross farm income; and 8.8 percent receive 40 percent of the gross farm income.

The gross farm income of $6,000,000,000 for 1934 was but a little over half that of 1929.

These figures given by representatives of our Government should be irrefutable proof that the broad lower strata of the farming population have become, year by year, ever more impoverished until now when a goodly portion are absolutely destitute.

What is worthy of note in these tabulations is not only the greatly lessened income of the farmers but also the greatly lessened percentage of the population engaged in agriculture. The members of this "lost battalion" have not all been absorbed in other fields of endeavor; many are idle in rural and farming communities. Due to technological improvement in agriculture fewer hands are needed, thus leaving the long hours of toil and the small monetary returns unchanged for those engaged in farming. Dr. Ladd, dean of Cornell Agricultural College of New York, recently stated that for the past

40 years 100,000 acres have been withheld from production each year in New York State alone. This totals 4,000,000 acres. And of the 18,000,000 acres still in production in New York State, 4,000,000 acres are being considered for further withdrawal. We must realize when these millions of acres are divided by the average number of acres in a farm that tens of thousands of farm families have been separated from their former mode of earning a living.

Mr. LUNDEEN. Pardon me. Where did those people go?

Mr. BRIEHL. Many of them——

Mr. LUNDEEN. I mean from your own personal observation.

Mr. BRIEHL. Some of them are still floating around in the rural sections and comprise this idle farm help.

Mr. LUNDEEN. And go to their relatives, and so on?

Mr. BRIEHL. Go to their relatives; some go to the cities.

The CHAIRMAN. Many are going to the dogs because they cannot find anything to eat; isn't that right?

Mr. BRIEHL. Well, many of them are going there.

Speaking generally, we can safely say that most dropped into a lower strata of which the pauperized group received even more than its proportionate share. And be assured, gentlemen, that all this has taken place in the face of greatly increased national wealth, and that the future trend is far from what Secretary Wallace said:

Farmers will have a fair share of the national income when their share is sufficient (1) to maintain a flow of production in balance with the maximum needs of consumption; (2) to provide for a decent known living; (3) to achieve these ends without impoverishing the soil.

Since it is evident to those masses of farmers that have been ruined and to those still struggling to carry on under the burden of narrowing markets and lower purchasing power that those ends cannot be achieved through an individualistic, competitive system, the purpose of which is profit instead of human welfare, we are compelled to use a safety valve in the form of social and unemployment insurance. Even this cannot be a safety valve unless it is thoroughly adequate.

There is an inseparable connection between cause and effect. In social problems, such as these, people generally concern themselves too much with effects and too little with causes. In the final analysis, we must concede that the need for social insurance is the result of an economic system which benefits the few at the expense of the many; a system quite incapable of social planning for human welfare.

Lincoln must have had this clearly in mind when he said:

Inasmuch as most good things are produced by labor, it follows that all such things ought to belong to those whose labor has produced them. But it has happened in all ages of the world that some have labored and others, without labor, have enjoyed a large proportion of the profits. This is wrong and should not continue. To secure to each laborer the whole product of his labor as nearly as possible is a worthy object of good government.

To my knowledge, I know of no single instance where our Federal Government ever made even a feeble attempt to bring about what Lincoln calls a "worthy object of good government." Passing the Lundeen social-insurance bill would be such an effort.

President Roosevelt remarked in his inaugural address that the masses lacked purchasing power. There was nothing particularly new in this information for it was common knowledge and is most emphatically correct. Little or nothing has been done about it, however, and certainly it is not the fault of the masses that it is so. Since they are unemployed through no fault of their own, what better program has been presented to give them purchasing power other than H. R. 2827? It is exactly in this way that the still "forgotten man" can be remembered. As for the Wagner-Lewis bill doing this—it is not even a farce, but an insult, for it does not even mention farmers or farm hands at all. The impoverished farmer is worse than forgotten: he was never recognized!

As to whether or not the alleviation of mass misery is possible in this land of plenty by the passage of the Lundeen bill, what better proof can be offered than a comparison with another country with considerably less material wealth than our own.

Quoting Prof. R. A. McFarland, from Columbia University, who recently wrote about his investigation of treatment of what he calls "economic neurosis" in Russia, in part:

> In the first place, every person is made to feel that his life counts; that he is wanted and badly needed in the common ideal of building socialism. In the second place, he is guaranteed economic security and a job to which he is well suited. * * * If physically weakened or unstrung they are sent to rest homes for a vacation, or their environment is completely altered. The emphasis is on prevention rather than cures.

If Russia, with less material wealth than the United States, can practice such social insurance, why not the United States? The Lundeen bill would be a start in that direction.

Undoubtedly the main objection to the Lundeen bill will come from certain sources who will claim that it cannot be put into effect because of the great finances involved. To them let it be said that billions of dollars have been spent in wars to kill people, why not billions for people to live? The bill clearly states from where the money is to come; from the rich. Naturally, to this they will object, claiming that the bill is confiscatory. Let them be reminded of an historical event in 1917–18. At that time the United States Government had little hesitancy to draft, confiscate if you please, the very lives of American manhood to protect Wall Street's investments in a commercial war. This Government should now have no hesitancy in taxing some of that wealth to protect the very lives of the millions of unemployed workers and farmers who helped create that wealth.

H. R. 2827 must be passed! We think the Government will be compelled to listen for there are many chapters in history which show that no government can withstand the impact from below of millions of its population, who always, in the end, refuse to starve to death.

Mr. LUNDEEN. Pardon me. Have you made any comparison, or has your organization, any comparison of policy of bills? How do you know this bill is any better than any other, without any study?

Mr. BRIEHL. I have here, Congressman Lundeen, a comparative chart.

Mr. LUNDEEN. Well, all I want to know is that you did compare them?

Mr. BRIEHL. Correct.

Mr. LUNDEEN. That is all I want to know.

The CHAIRMAN. Pardon me. What is the name of the professor that made that statement?

Mr. BRIEHL. Prof. R. A. McFarland, professor of psychology, Columbia University.

The CHAIRMAN. Is the professor, Professor McFarland, still a professor in Columbia University?

Mr. BRIEHL. As far as I know, I think he is.

The CHAIRMAN. How long ago did he make that statement?

Mr. BRIEHL. This is quoted in the February 2 issue of the Literary Digest.

The CHAIRMAN. Of 1935?

Mr. BRIEHL. 1935. Now, this is by way of a slight apology which is self-explanatory. Due to the expense involved and the terroristic methods, including lynchings, practiced against share-cropper negroes active in organizational activities, it was impossible to have a personal representative from that group here to present their case in favor of the Lundeen bill. However, the share-croppers' union with a membership of 10,000 is closely affiliated with the Farmers' National Committee for Action, of which I am a member of the executive committee. As such, I wish to present their problem, their condition and misery is well known throughout. I had a longer statement of their condition than I am going to read. It is very much condensed by an article in today's News. What is said here can be very readily verified by information, voluminous information that we possess. This article goes on to say:

A. A. A. COTTON CONTROL MAKING REFUGEES OF FARM SHARE-CROPPERS

SCENES IN SOUTH LIKE " WAR-TORN BELGIUM " DESCRIBED BY WOMAN INVESTIGATOR AFTER SURVEY

The Agricultural Adjustment Administration, already on edge by wholesale dismissal of left-wing officials, today was presented with a request that its cotton program was bringing scenes like those of war-torn Belgium to southern share-croppers.

The report was filed by Mary Connor Myers, A. A. A. legal official, and former Chicago justice agent, after a survey of cotton regions west of Memphis, Tenn.

Mr. LUNDEEN. Is that published? What paper?

Mr. BRIEHL. The Washington Daily News.

The red-haired woman agent, who aided the Justice Department clean-up of Chicago gangsters, said conditions among poor tenant farmers and share-croppers were beyond words.

She charged wholesale violation of acreage-control provisions, supposed to protect tenants from eviction.

The report of serious difficulties in the cotton program came with the A. A. A. generally upset over the purge effected by Administrator Chester C. Davis. Mrs. Myers made her report to Agriculture Secretary Wallace. It was not expected to be made public.

What action would be taken, if any, was uncertain, and the uncertainty was increased by the shifting emphasis of A. A. A. policies under Davis.

Mrs. Myers made an intensive study of social conditions in five northeastern Arkansas counties.

She reported evicted tenant farmer families struggling along highways, wandering hopelessly in search of shelter and employment. She said hovels were crowded until there was standing room only, because families in slightly better economic circumstances had shared shelter with the evicted.

Some landlord planters, Mrs. Myers charged, have turned out their tenants without warning and influenced local relief officials to refuse them aid.

She exhibited snapshots of rough-boarded shacks in much-mired fields, the gaps in their walls admitting bitter winds; evicted Negroes standing in the road, not knowing where to turn for succor; a truck piled high with bed springs, a stove, and ramshackle ends of the household equipment of a poor family.

Mrs. Myers characterized the scenes as "like those of refugees war-time Belgium."

She blamed the situation on violation of an acreage-control contract clause providing: "The least possible amount of labor, economic, and social disturbance, shall, so far as possible, maintain on this farm the normal number of tenants and other employees."

The causes of eviction are two, Mrs. Myers reported: (1) Reduction in labor requirements produced by reduction in acreage, and (2) ever-increasing unionization of share-croppers to bring pressure on planters for retention of the customary number of tenants and for payment to the tenants of their full share of A. A. A. benefit money.

Now, there is nothing that I could say, gentlemen, that would bring the story home clearer than that, an investigator of the A. A. A. itself, and as to whether they require any social and unemployment insurance personally must be beyond question.

I might conclude with this remark, that a point has been reached in American history where as never before will the broad strata of the people so definitely learn as to whether or not this is a Government of, for, and by the people. What action this Congress takes on the Lundeen bill will determine that, and we farmers who are familiar with the social and economic condition of the United States urge most emphatically that that bill be passed.

Mr. LUNDEEN. Mr. Chairman, this gentleman, and the able gentleman, Mr. Linder, referred to the cost of the World War. Now, I would like the record to show, since that was mentioned, this information, which is overlooked by the American public: On November 11, 1928, the last Armistice Day of Coolidge's administration, the President of the United States made a statement, to be verified in the speech itself, that when the last man of the World War has passed over the horizon the cost of that war will have exceeded the staggering sum of $100,000,000,000. Now, those are not the words of Ernest Lundeen. Those are the words of Calvin Coolidge, and I would like the record to show that Senator Robert M. La Follette and Congressman Charles Lindbergh stood on the floor of Congress and protested entering the war and predicted the many things and the destitute circumstances that would surely result if we did enter into the war, if we made that most colossal blunder.

The CHAIRMAN. Congressman Lundeen, isn't it also a fact that the men who went across the pond to fight to make this world safe for democracy, many thousands who have returned, are now compelled to get on their knees and ask some would-be charitable agency for a crust of bread? And isn't it also a fact that many thousands of these men who went over there to fight to make this world safe for democracy have lost their homes, and are still losing their homes, and are in the ranks of those who are now pleading to Congress to do something for the unfortunate people of the United States?

Mr. Briehl, I want to ask you this question: I heard you quoting good old President Abraham Lincoln. Do you believe if he were alive today and he were our President that he would hesitate in asking us to pass the Lundeen bill?

Mr. BRIEHL. That is rather a prophetic question to ask. I might answer it this way: That if President Lincoln were alive today, and if we can take his word sincerely, which I do——

The CHAIRMAN. And I do, too——

Mr. BRIEHL. I certainly think there would be no hesitancy at all on his part to favor the Lundeen bill; but I might supplement that little remark by saying that if a man such as Lincoln, or any other man, for that matter, were so intensely interested in social welfare, I doubt whether today he would ever reach the point of being President.

Mr. LUNDEEN. Mr. Chairman, there are plenty of brains on the American farms right today.

The CHAIRMAN. It has been demonstrated here this afternoon.

Mr. BRIEHL. I would go to the extent, however, of making this remark: It certainly would be a great deal more satisfactory to the broad mass that are suffering under this economic depression if he would favor the Lundeen bill instead of the Wagner-Lewis bill. That would be immensely more satisfactory to us.

The CHAIRMAN. It is my candid opinion that if we could get the Congress to pass this act, I believe the President would sign it.

Mr. BRIEHL. I hope so.

Mr. HARTLEY. As long as you are just stressing that point, I would like to ask the witness a question. Do you think that the President—if the President favored the Lundeen bill, there would be any fear of its failure to pass?

Mr. BRIEHL. No; I think that it would give the bill tremendous additional push, by reason of the confidence the President has; it certainly would popularize it, and I even would hazard a guess that its chances of going through would be quite good.

Mr. HARTLEY. You don't know of many instances where the House—I am not referring to the Senate now—but you don't know of many instances where the House has failed to listen to the dictates of the President, do you?

Mr. BRIEHL. Well, it is common knowledge or opinion, anyway, that Roosevelt's programs were quite completely accepted.

Mr. HARTLEY. That is the point I am getting at. That is why I ask you if you did not believe that if the President admitted he was for the Lundeen bill, it would go through.

Mr. BRIEHL. That is right.

The CHAIRMAN. May I say this: I wonder if anyone has presented the President with the Lundeen bill to learn whether or not he would give it his utmost support?

Mr. BRIEHL. I would like to have that information myself and know how he would regard it.

The CHAIRMAN. Mr. Briehl, I want to thank you for your address. It was very instructive and to the point.

STATEMENT OF NORRIS WOOD, OF THE UNEMPLOYMENT COUNCIL, PHILADELPHIA

Mr. WOOD. Mr. Chairman, I want to bring to the attention of the members of this committee the peculiar situation involved in the Wagner-Lewis bill. I think that the city of Philadelphia and the unemployed, some number of 3,000 in the organization which I represent there, is a striking illustration of how far we will get with any attempt at separate State bills, or anything of this nature.

For the past 6 years the City Council of Philadelphia has not only failed but has positively refused to appropriate one penny for any kind of relief whatsoever for the unemployed of the city of Philadelphia; and if this is the way we are going to have to continue as unemployed workers depending upon local governments, either State or municipal, to provide for our primary needs, why, then we might as well stop living right now, because we will never get anywhere.

Mr. HARTLEY. On that point, do I understand you to say the city of Philadelphia has not made any appropriation?

Mr. WOOD. Not one penny.

Mr. HARTLEY. For how many years?

Mr. WOOD. For 6 years.

Mr. HARTLEY. Well, during the entire depression?

Mr. WOOD. During the entire depression the city of Philadelphia has not paid one penny for relief.

Mr. HARTLEY. Then you got either State or national funds?

Mr. WOOD. The State has appropriated, or did not appropriate until after the Federal Government, during Mr. Pinchot's administration came down here, and for a long time the State did not even appropriate any funds.

The CHAIRMAN. May I interrupt you? I will explain that. The witness is correct when he makes that statement. There was a law in the State of Pennsylvania; it was a constitutional law that no money could be appropriated by the State of Pennsylvania for benevolent purposes unless the State constitution was amended, and I happened to be in the legislature, as the gentleman states, under Governor Pinchot in 1931, and I was the man who first introduced the bill of $4,000,000 to give relief to the unfortunate people of the State of Pennsylvania, and, of course, I was not authorized to do this. I did not know a great deal about the constitution, but I knew there were many unemployed, so the president of the State Federation of Labor came to me and asked me would I increase that amount to 10 million, so I did, and the State Federation of Labor wanted to have a public hearing; so I contacted the chairman of the appropriations committee of the house and the chairman of the appropriations committee of the senate, and they held a joint session, and they gave us the legislative hall to hold this meeting in. We had men and women from all over the State of Pennsylvania representing various labor organizations to tell the members of both appropriations committees, the senate and the house, and also the people there, the necessity for this $10,000,000.

Now, then, after that committee—after that, why, a man named Mr. Talbott, Representative Talbott, he then introduced a bill for $10,000,000. That came on the floor of the house. My bill did not come up. I was a labor representative and an organization man got the opportunity to present it, and that bill was declared unconstitutional, but it passed the house practically unanimously, and it passed the senate.

Now, at the time the bill was considered unconstitutional, and even constitutional lawyers of the State of Pennsylvania maintained it was; however, Governor Pinchot did not any way veto it. He passed it. And it was brought before the Supreme Court of the State, and they decided it was not unconstitutional, that it was an emergency measure, and that was the year it was declared that any municipality of the State of Pennsylvania would have the right under the law to appropriate money for benevolent purposes.

Now, Philadelphia has that right under that act.

Mr. WOOD. I would like to comment, Mr. Chairman, that despite the fact that Philadelphia has the right, and you have correctly stated the situation, the objections which have constantly confronted the unemployed, have been these constitutional objections with regard to relief. When this was dissipated by the statement of fact that you have just made, however, since that time the city of Philadelphia, despite the fact that they now have a constitutional right, has not appropriated one penny for relief. These are the facts in the case.

I want to say that I am going to confine my remarks largely to illustrative material of the need for the passage of the Lundeen bill. There is a family by the name of Elwell, who lives in that portion of Philadelphia known as "Strawberry Mansion." They had four children, and the father of this family was a painter by occupation, and the building trades have been very largely idle in that city, the same as they have throughout the entire United States. He had followed the advice of William Green, the head of the American Federation of Labor, and considered himself to be too proud to apply for relief. He thought it was an un-American thing to do, to desire any assistance whatsoever, with the result that four children died in 1 year in that family from malnutrition, starved to death, and finally, the unemployed councils convinced this man that they were entitled to relief as a right and not as a gift, and when the relief board, through the pressure brought to bear by the unemployed councils of the city of Philadelphia, finally did get around to give them any relief, the fourth child in the family died 2 weeks prior to the delivery of the first bottle of milk by the county relief board.

The CHAIRMAN. Right there, in other words, you would say that that child was starved to death?

Mr. WOOD. Starved to death. All four of the children were starved to death, and not only a question of starvation, but it is a question of the workers in homes. A family by the name of Diamond——

Mr. HARTLEY. May I ask when that last case took place?

Mr. WOOD. This last case was in the month of October 1934. And the same month, between the dates of October 11 and 15, a case came to the Unemployed Council of a family by the name of Diamond. He was a Greek worker, a stonemason by trade, who had lived in the house and been the breadwinner of the family, and in 5½ years paid a total of $15,750 for rent in that apartment, and despite that fact, the landlord—and he had been out of work for the past 2 years—and despite this fact, that this fellow had been willing to work, and he was on the relief board getting the miserable $4 and something a week, and he had 4 children and himself and wife, $4, a store order to provide food for that sum, for that family of six, 4 children, a man, and his wife, $4.80 was what he got a week in his store order, and he borrowed money and pawned things, and did everything else that he could possibly do and tried to keep up his expenses as far as rent was concerned; and the landlord, who is a wholesale fruit dealer by the name of Glick, who has his place of business at Second and Spruce Streets, in the city of Philadelphia, and for $5 Mr. Glick set the constable on to this man and threatened to throw his family into the street of the city of Philadelphia. It was my task as a member of the Unemployed Council to go with the committee to this landlord, and this Mr. Glick told me and told the members of the committee that if it cost him $500 he would throw that family into the street. But the Unemployed Council saw to it that the family was not thrown into the street, and the family is residing in the house today and Mr. Glick is getting no pay, because there is no provision for any cash relief, even to pay for the rent.

The CHAIRMAN. In other words, had it not been for your organization a man and his wife and children would have been thrown out into the street.

Mr. WOOD. Correctly so. I could go on and take up the time of this committee, which I think it is unnecessary to do; and I know that you have your time limited, I could cite many such cases of this character, not only questions of starvation, not only questions of eviction, but the matter has been ably told by national secretary, Mr. Empter, in his report before the committee this morning, and I am not a financial expert, or a social expert. I am just an unemployed worker that has passed that dead line, and is thrown out on the scrap heap, and that has been cast aside into the ranks of the unemployed. I can neither get relief nor can I get a draft. There is neither a draft nor relief because I am too old, if there were jobs to be had.

The CHAIRMAN. Pardon me. How old a man are you?

Mr. WOOD. I am 50 years of age this month, the 20th.

The CHAIRMAN. You would be eligible then for my pension that I introduced.

Mr. WOOD. I am vitally interested not only for the some other 16 or 17 million other jobless of the United States, for the passage of this Lundeen bill, and I need only speak in the name of the organization which I represent, but I would like very much to have an old-age pension. I think I am entitled to it as a producer, and I would not think that anybody was giving me one red cent because in my lifetime I have produced more than the Government can possibly pay me between now and the time that they cart me away in the box. And I don't see in the Wagner-Lewis bill anything of any hope. And I agree with the farmer, who preceded me in his testimony, that the Wagner-Lewis bill is not an insurance bill; that it is a noninsurance bill; that it is a sheer downright political trick on the part of the President of this United States to make the workers think that they are getting something.

I want to quote what President Roosevelt said when he was campaigning, on October 6, for the Presidency of the United States. In discussing the unemployment situation, he said:

We need for them—that is, the unemployed—a greater assurance of security, old-age, sickness, and unemployment insurance of the minimum requirements in these days.

And 6 days later, on the 12th, he made the statement:

I am utterly unwilling that economy should be practiced at the expense of the starving people.

And, once more, 8 days after that, on October 20, he said:

If starvation and dire need on the part of any of our citizens, any of our citizens—

And he did not exclude anybody in that statement—

make necessary the appropriation of additional funds which would keep the Budget out of balance, I shall not hesitate to tell the American people the truth and recommend the expenditure of this additional amount.

The CHAIRMAN. Stop right there. That is on the 6th and 12th?

Mr. WOOD. On the 6th and on the 12th and on the 20th of October, prior to his election in November.

The CHAIRMAN. They were in his addresses?

Mr. WOOD. They were in his addresses. These are quotations taken from his addresses on those dates, and I want to put these into the record of this committee for the purpose of contrasting these statements of the President and the statement that he made just prior to the great National Congress for Unemployment and Social Insurance that was held in Washington on January 5, 6, and 7, when he said that it is time for us to quit relief. And we replied in that Congress that instead of the time to quit giving relief it was time to begin. And I say that it is time for the Congress of the United States to pass the Lundeen bill and give to the workers of this country what they have a right to expect, and that is life and liberty and the pursuit of happiness.

The CHAIRMAN. Did the President speak before your organization?

Mr. WOOD. The President has not spoken for our organization.

The CHAIRMAN. No; I mean before your organization.

Mr. WOOD. No; the President has not spoken before our organization. Congressman Lundeen spoke before our organization at that time.

Mr. HARTLEY. I think that this presentation, together with the others I have listened to this afternoon, has been very interesting and instructive, and I am glad to hear them. I want to ask one question. Your organization is one that strictly believes in the ideals and the institutions of the Government?

Mr. WOOD. Our organization is not a political organization. Our organization has membership in all, every political persuasion under the sun. And there may be people in our organization that do not believe in government, for all we know. Government, as I conceive it, is something that should govern.

Mr. LUNDEEN. What you mean is, you have Republicans and Democrats.

Mr. WOOD. We have Democrats, Republicans, and everything else.

Mr. LUNDEEN. Socialists?

Mr. WOOD. And every kind of religious faith and no religious faith.

The CHAIRMAN. Nonsectarian?

Mr. WOOD. Nonsectarian.

Mr. HARTLEY. Understand, Mr. Chairman, what I am getting at. I haven't any objection to any fellow's belief or to any fellow belonging to one party or another, and I am not a strict partisan myself. The question that I meant was that your organization believes that in attaining the end that you seek here, that is to obtain unemployment insurance, it should be obtained through the Congress of the United States.

Mr. WOOD. This is the reason for my appearance.

Mr. HARTLEY. Yes. I want to have that reiterated for the purpose of the record.

Mr. WOOD. This is the reason for my appearance.

The CHAIRMAN. May I ask this question: Isn't it a fact that you gentlemen who are fighting for justice, for a square deal, you are classified as Communists? Isn't that a fact?

Mr. WOOD. Well, anybody who is hungry today, and who is willing to put up a fight to get a piece of bread is classed as a Communist.

The CHAIRMAN. May I say to the gentleman, because I have advocated what the Lundeen bill calls for, I have been called a Communist, and I do not hesitate to say right here and I said it before, if believing and favoring adequate old-age pensions, and adequate unemployment insurance, and providing for our widows on the natural resources, and public utilities, and giving men work and women work at a living wage, and taking care of those who are physically incapacitated, I do not hesitate to say if that is communism, then I am willing to be branded as a communist, because I believe that is real Christianity. We hear a lot about Christianity today, but not because I am blind and not able to see Christianity. What we are having today is too much " churchianity ", and not enough Christianity, and I want to say, what the gentleman has said I agree with, not only in Philadelphia but in Pittsburgh, and every city and every town in the United States, and I do not doubt, Mr. Hartley, I know you are very broad-minded and fair, you as a Congressman have had men and women come into your office pleading for help, telling you that they are losing their homes. Am I not right?

Mr. HARTLEY. Oh, absolutely.

The CHAIRMAN. And you receive letters today?

Mr. HARTLEY. Every day of the week.

The CHAIRMAN. And I made a statement on the floor of the House when I said that every Congressman in the United States had men and women come to their offices and tell them that they were losing their homes, and that the Home Owners' Loan Corporation Act was enacted into the law to give relief, and I made the statement on the floor, in my candid opinion, it was not a relief measure unless it would take care of those men and women who were out of work and who could not pay any principal or interest.

I want to say this: Every time you come forth with a proposition that is going to benefit the masses, someone makes the statement it is either unconstitutional, or where are you going to get the money?

Now, I have stated on the floor of the House, especially this last session when it came to reducing the salaries of Federal employees, that in my candid opinion that was not economy. I said we make the statement that we are valuable; our valuation is about $350,000,-000,000, and that is on the surface. I make that statement again, that I made a year ago on the floor of the House, that no man has ever had enough intelligence to be able to estimate the value of our natural resources. They are not worth billions but are worth trillions of dollars.

Now isn't it a fact, if by some freak of nature gold and silver were to evaporate, would that mean good old Mother Nature would refuse to provide for your bread and beans and ham and cabbage? We can do without gold and silver, but we cannot do without foodstuffs to eat and water to drink, but if by some freak of nature water was to evaporate, well there would not be such a thing as life on this planet. Therefore, I say again when anybody tries to come forth with a statement that our natural resources are valued at 400 or 500 or 600 billions of dollars, he does not know what he is talking about, because, in my candid opinion, we are worth trillions of dollars. We could take our rivers and our creeks and turn them right into power-plant systems, and we could produce power so cheap that we could do everything that we want to do. I also know that it is a fact that in the United States we produce more than we can consume in the line of foodstuffs, and this is also true that one-fourth of the United States, if it were put under scientific cultivation, that it would feed 10 times the population. I just wanted to make that statement.

Mr. LUNDEEN. I move that we recess until 10 o'clock tomorrow morning.

Mr. DAVIDOW. Before you recess. I am delegated by the Unemployed Councils of New York. I have a report, but since you won't take it up now, I would like to submit it for the record. It is not typed yet. I would like to have the privilege of sending it in through the mails.

Mr. LUNDEEN. Can't you be here tomorrow?

Mr. DAVIDOW. No; I cannot.

Mr. HARTLEY. I move that the gentleman be permitted to send his report in by mail.

Mr. LUNDEEN. I second the motion. What is it about—the statement of what?

Mr. DAVIDOW. A statement of my organization of the bill.

Mr. LUNDEEN. What organization?

Mr. DAVIDOW. The Unemployed Council of New York City.

The CHAIRMAN. All right. You will be permitted to send it in by mail.

(Whereupon, at 6:53 p. m., Feb. 7, 1935, the committee adjourned until 10 a. m., Feb. 8, 1935.)

Local unions of the American Federation of Labor and various labor bodies in various parts of the country are affiliated to our American Federation of Labor trade union committee for unemployment insurance and relief. Similar committees have been established with the purpose of advocating unemployment and social insurance have been established in the following cities: New York, Boston, Detroit, Minneapolis, Oakland, San Francisco, Los Angeles, Philadelphia, Omaha, Toledo, Kenosha, Racine, and Youngstown. Other cities are Spokane, Wash., and Kansas City.

Mr. Chairman and gentlemen of the committee, I am going to read a prepared statement which I wish to submit on behalf of the American Federation of Labor trade union committee for unemployment insurance and relief.

283

Local unions of the American Federation of Labor and central labor bodies in various parts of the country are affiliated to the American Federation of Labor trade union committee for unemployment insurance and relief. Similar committees have been established for the purpose of advocating unemployment and social insurance within the American Federation of Labor unions in Detroit, Chicago, Cleveland, Boston, Butte, New York, New Haven, Newark, Milwaukee, Minneapolis, Oakland, San Francisco, Los Angeles, Philadelphia, Great Falls, Kenosha, Pittsburgh, Racine, Seattle, Salt Lake City, Spokane, Washington, D. C., Kalamazoo, and Grand Rapids.

The members of these committees are all bona fide members of American Federation of Labor local unions, of district councils, and of central labor bodies. Many are elected by their respective organizations to further the movement for unemployment insurance through affiliation with the American Federation of Labor committee. In some American Federation of Labor organizations, where unemployment insurance is considered foreign to organized labor by the presiding officers, who refuse to entertain the election of delegates to such a committee, those members who are interested in unemployment insurance elect unofficial representatives to the committee.

It is necessary to emphasize at the very outset that statements issued by some international presidents and by some members of the executive council of the American Federation of Labor that the American Federation of Labor committee for unemployment insurance and relief is not a bona fide American Federation of Labor organization, that it does not represent the American Federation of Labor, are untrue. I will elaborate on this question in greater detail later and will prove conclusively that we are the real representatives of the great majority of the American Federation of Labor membership.

Very often my membership in the American Federation of Labor has been questioned by William Green, president of the American Federation of Labor. Without investigating, Mr. Green has issued public statements to the effect that I am not a member of the American Federation of Labor. Had Mr. Green taken the time to look into the matter, he would not have issued such irresponsible and groundless statements. My stubborn fight for unemployment insurance has provided a pretext for the international and some district council officials of my organization (Brotherhood of Painters) to oust me from the union, but they were unsuccessful in their attempts.

Up to this time neither the executive council of the American Federation of Labor nor any of the internationals affiliated with the American Federation of Labor have conducted any sort of referendum on the question of unemployment insurance in order to find out the sentiment of the membership on the Wagner-Lewis bill, on the workers' bill, H. R. 2827, and on other unemployment-insurance proposals.

Mr. Dunn. Pardon me, but did I understand you to say that the American Federation of Labor never conducted a referendum to ascertain anything about unemployment insurance?

Mr. Weinstock. Never.

Mr. Dunn. Thank you.

Mr. WEINSTOCK. The American Federation of Labor trade union committee for unemployment insurance and relief, on the other hand, immediately upon its organization conducted a referendum in the American Federation of Labor organizations and brought the workers' unemployment and social insurance bill in a detailed form with all necessary explanations to the attention of the membership in the American Federation of Labor. In a very short time more than 1,000 local unions adopted the workers' bill and informed the initiators of this referendum of their whole-hearted support of this measure. Since then more than 3,000 local unions have endorsed the workers' bill.

During the 6-year period of economic crisis, a period of the greatest mass unemployment ever experienced in America, every section of the working population has felt the specter of poverty and hunger. Even the more highly paid workers, the organized workers in ·the American Federation of Labor, have not been exempt from the tremendous misery and suffering the horror of insecurity which the working population has had to endure.

The rank and file in the American Federation of Labor have seen their union standards of wages and hours wiped out after years of struggle to raise them during this crisis. They are today side by side with the rest of the working population recipients of charity. They stand in the bread lines, their children are sent to C. C. C. camps, and their meager savings have been consumed. It must be remembered that in 1929, the last year of prosperity, 5,570,000 families had an income of less than $1,000. They saved nothing to protect them against economic insecurity. Receiving between $1,000 and $2,000 in 1929 were 10,500,000 families. For these families savings aggregated $750,000,000, or an average of about $71.43 per family.

Almost 80 percent of the families in the United States in 1929 received an income of $3,000 or less per family. " It is generally conceded ", declared the Committee on Economic Security, "that the families in these categories need some form of protection against loss of income from such hazards as unemployment, old age, destitution, and sickness." A statement recently made by Brookings Institution showed that—

The aggregate income of the 6,000,000 families at the bottom of the scale, even when the negative incomes shown by some families are eliminated, amounted to $2,500,000,000. In other words, about 21 percent of the families received only 4.5 percent of the income. The 11,653,000 families with incomes of less than $1,500 received a total of about $10,000,000,000. At the other extreme, the 36,000 families having incomes in excess of $75,000 possessed an aggregate income of $9,800,000,000. Thus, it appears that 0.1 percent of the families at the top received practically as much as 42 percent of the families at the bottom of the scale.

Today there are over 33 percent of the " gainfully occupied " persons in this country without jobs, a total of more than 17,000,000 men, women, and young workers. These figures include the workers employed temporarily on relief jobs in Federal emergency projects, a total of 2,850,000. Even with this figure subtracted, there remain over 14,300,000 jobless in the United States. The figures show an increase of 800,000 over the revised figure for November 1933. Even the more conservative figures of the American Federation of Labor, as printed in the January issue of the American Federationist, estimate a total of more than 11,000,000 unemployed, and this figure excludes the unemployed on temporary emergency work.

The January issue of the American Federationist says that—

Unemployment is higher than last year's level by more than 400,000 * * *. This rise in unemployment is due largely to the normal increase in population, which yearly adds more than 400,000 to the army of job seekers.

The American Federationist points out that there has been a striking decline in employment on farms, in construction, and on railroads.

We want to point out, further, that in December 1934, 54 percent of the union building-trades' workers in the American Federation of Labor were unemployed and 23 percent were employed on part time; that 27 percent of the union metal workers were totally unemployed and 7 percent on part time; that 16 percent of the union printing workers were totally unemployed with 3 percent on part-time work.

According to the conservative American Federation of Labor figures, 26 percent of the total membership in the American Federation of Labor unions are totally unemployed at the present time.

By cities the unemployed totals are very much higher. For example: In New York City, in December 1934, 73 percent of the union building-trades' workers were unemployed; in Philadelphia, 61 percent; in Pittsburgh, 66 percent; in Chicago, 59 percent. In New York City 36 percent of the total membership of organized labor was unemployed.

Since the crisis unemployment has more than doubled among union members in all trades. From this it is clear that members of organized labor have been extremely hard hit during these 6 years of crises.

Demands for relief on the part of the unemployed have been steadily increasing. The American Federation of Labor survey of employment announced in the New York Times on February 5, 1935, reports that 4 percent more persons were on relief in December than in November in 141 of the largest cities in the country. "This fact", says the report, "points to the exhaustion of resources among the unemployed, many of whom have now been without regular work for 3, 4, or even 5 years."

According to the Federal Emergency Relief Administration, there are over 19,000,000 persons who must depend for their means of subsistence on public relief. There are millions more that are not yet on relief, but for whom the possibilities of employment are so meager that they will be compelled to resort to relief in order to live. Over 15 percent of the entire population of the country must depend for their food, lodging, clothing, and other necessaries of life on the inadequate relief handouts of the existing agencies.

Such large numbers of unemployed dependent on miserable amounts of relief for subsistence has not only meant the plunging of masses of the working population into hitherto unknown hardships but it has served to depress the standard of living of the working class as a whole.

The wage standards of American labor are now so low that even while employed the specter of insecurity without any possibility of savings to cover this period hangs over the head of every employed worker. In 1933 pay rolls showed a drop of 55 percent, as compared with 1929 in the manufacturing industry. At the same time employment showed a drop of 34.3 percent. Wages dropped more rapidly due to wage cuts, part-time employment. As a result of the excessive layoffs, speed-up increased in the shops. Fewer workers are producing more at lower wages. In iron and steel, for example, while employment showed a drop of 33 percent as compared with 1929, pay rolls were 55 percent below the 1929 level; in textile, 1934 figures show a drop of 13 percent in employment as compared with 1929, but pay rolls are 32 percent below that year.

The effect of the N. R. A. codes in establishing minimum wage levels of $12 to $14 a week, which is known to have reduced the wages of the higher paid workers to the minimum, has also had the effect of developing a condition of greater insecurity among the workers. Today it may be confidently stated that not only the unemployed workers but the masses of employed workers who have felt the wage cutting, the speed-up on the job, the effect of the N. R. A. codes on their standards, and the rising cost of living are now clamoring for unemployment insurance as a means of protecting their wage standards, as well as securing them against a future of possible unemployment without the means of setting aside any reserves from their meager earnings.

Membership in the American Federation of Labor has been sharply affected by the unemployment situation. Millions of members of the American Federation of Labor unable to find jobs have been dropped from the rolls of their unions which they had helped to build because of inability to pay dues. Members of organized labor have been compelled to leave their homes to seek employment, break up their families, and uproot their connections. Their unions have been weakened and in many instances demoralized. The most important weapon of the toiling population, the trade union which has aided the workers to maintain their standard of living and to defeat any encroachments on their rights, was in danger of being destroyed.

We have only to quote to you the loss in members of various internationals as recorded in the executive council report to the fifty-fourth convention of the American Federation of Labor to demonstrate the correctness of our statement. In 1929 the United Mine Workers of America had a membership of 400,000. Today, despite a wave of organization since 1933, there are 100,000 fewer members in the miners' organization. In the Painters' Brotherhood—that is my own international—a membership of 110,000 in 1928 was reduced to 57,800 in 1934. The carpenters' union had 332,000 members in 1928, and in 1934, 200,000. The electrical workers 142,000 in 1929, and today 113,500. The Seamen's Union declined from 15,000 members to 5,000. I represent herewith a complete list of the international unions which have declined in membership since 1929:

A list of international unions—American Federation of Labor—showing decline in membership from 1929 to 1934

[Executive council American Federation of Labor report submitted to fifty-fourth annual convention]

	1929	1934
Bricklayers, Masons & Plasterers' International Union Association	90,000	45,800
Carpenters and Joiners, United Brotherhood of	322,000	200,000
Electrical Workers, International Brotherhood	142,000	113,500
Hod Carriers and Common Laborers	91,700	44,200
Painters of America, Brotherhood of	108,100	57,800
Plasterers' Intl. Assn. of U. S. & C. Oper	39,200	18,000
Mine Workers of America, United	400,000	300,000
Printing Pressmen, International	40,000	32,000
Boot and Shoe Workers' Union	32,400	19,200
Carmen of A. Bro. Railway	80,000	55,000
Cigar Makers' Intl. Union	17,000	7,000
Lathers Intl. Union of W. W. of Metal	16,500	8,100
Molders Union of North America	23,700	8,800
Taylors Union of North A. Journeymen	6,800	2,600
Upholsterers, International Union of	10,700	6,500
Actors, Associated and Artists of Art	11,500	3,100

Social insurance is a vital necessity to the toiling population. But it must be the kind of social insurance that will guaranty every man, woman, and child who is today deprived of the necessities of life because he has been denied the right to work, a decent, adequate, standard of living. It must protect the standards of the employed, it must offer security against illness and old age, and against a condition where millions of children are undernourished and starving, where families must live in overcrowded slum firetraps and are faced with evictions and lack of shelter, and where there is misery and grim suffering of millions in the midst of plenty.

It is our opinion that it is possible for the richest country in the world to provide an adequate system of unemployment insurance. We disagree with the President when he maintains that " it is overwhelmingly important to avoid the danger of permanently discrediting the sound and necessary policy of Federal legislation for economic security by attempting to apply it on too ambitious a scale."

This, in our opinion, smacks too much of protection of the rich in the name of caution against an ambitious program. It has been widely publicized in the press that the higher incomes have not suffered seriously during the crisis. The Bureau of Internal Revenue, in a preliminary study, made public in the New York Times of December 10, 1934, showed that the net income of corporations increased $654,502,697, or 35.35 percent, in 1933 over the previous year, while net incomes in the lower brackets dropped. The Times report point out that—

* * * The number of individuals who received incomes of under $25,000 and the total of net income they reported dropped below the 1932 level, while the number and total net income in the classes from $25,000 upward increased. Those receiving incomes of $1,000,000 or more increased from 20 to 46, and the net income they reported rose to $81,558,532, compared with $35,239,556 for 1932. * * *

Furthermore, profits have not suffered. Industrial profits for the first 9 months of 1934 were 70 percent greater than in the corresponding period last year, according to the Federal Reserve Board report. These are but a few indications of the ability of the country to provide a decent and adequate system of unemployment insurance.

We favor the Lundeen bill because it provides for the basic needs of the unemployed more than any other measure thus far presented. First, the Lundeen bill covers all the present unemployed, and does not discriminate against any section of the toiling population. Adequate unemployment insurance for all the present unemployed will assure protection to the millions of starving men, women, and children now living in want. The Lundeen bill provides an adequate amount of weekly compensation to cover the entire period of unemployment. It calls for a Federal plan to go into effect in all States uniformly and immediately. It provides funds out of the income of the wealthy, of those whose millions have increased while millions of men, women, and children have gone without food and shelter. It provides for taxation out of the income of the higher brackets. It provides for the return to the working population of some of the earnings of which they were cheated when employed through low wages and speed-up. We believe this is not only just but that it is the only way in which the expense of unemployment insurance shall be met.

We want to go on record squarely against the Wagner-Lewis bill, which in every one of its measures is directly antagonistic to a real plan for unemployment insurance. President Roosevelt, in his message to Congress on the security program, lays down the principle that the funds must not come from the proceeds of general taxation, but that the system should be "self-sustaining." This means, in simple language, the imposition of the burden of the insurance on those who are to receive it. It means that the workers will be compelled to sustain the system. A tax on pay rolls will be passed off on the consumers who are also the workers. Whether directly or indirectly, the workers will pay through higher prices or wage cuts. It means new and added burdens to those who are employed at wages already cut far below the workers' needs.

Mr. LUNDEEN. At this point I would like to state that Leo J. Linder yesterday in his legal brief on constitutionality cited cases which would indicate that the Wagner-Lewis bill would probably be tied up in the courts on questions of constitutionality for some years, and that it probably is unconstitutional; whereas our bill is constitutional, as shown by the decisions of the courts.

Mr. WEINSTOCK. In addition to this, we believe that, irrespective of the constitutional phase of the bill, if mass pressure from the trade-union organizations and from the unorganized workers is strong enough, the constitutional question will be settled by pressure from the labor organizations, forcing the Congress to act immediately—otherwise millions of people will starve.

Mr. DUNN. May I say right there that even if your bill should be declared unconstitutional by the Supreme Court, the Constitution should not be an obstacle in the path of giving relief to the aged and unemployed.

Mr. LUNDEEN. I agree with you, Mr. Chairman.

Mr. DUNN. We should remove that obstacle, even if it is the Constitution.

Mr. LUNDEEN. But I believe our bill is clear on the point of constitutionality.

Mr. Weinstock. It is significant that big business makes no serious objection to the President's program, because it recognizes that the expense will not come out of their profits but out of the pockets of the middle class and toiling population who form the majority of the consuming public. " The action of the stock markets yesterday ", says the New York Times of January 18, the day following the President's security message, " indicated that Wall Street was not alarmed by the President's message to Congress on social-security legislation * * * the market indicated that Wall Street did not feel that the plan would increase taxation unduly, since it will be largely self-supporting."

We maintain that if it is possible for Congress of the United States to give millions of dollars to moribund banks and collapsing industries, it is equally within their power to provide funds for the millions of unemployed without compelling the workers to bear the costs of unemployment insurance.

We believe that the workers whose labor has built up the power and wealth of this country should be treated at least equally with the banks and industries, and that Congress should appropriate funds based on the taxation of higher incomes of over $5,000 to provide sufficient funds for the maintenance of all unemployed workers in the United States adequately, as provided in the Lundeen bill.

We are opposed to the method of voluntary State insurance plans which is part of the Roosevelt program. We have seen how this has worked out in other legislation affecting the workers. We are for a Federal system of social insurance.

Our experience with so-called " welfare legislation " has taught us that the method of enactment of legislation, State by State, only serves to discriminate against large sections of workers. For example, there is the Workman's Compensation Act. The first State law for workmen's compensation was passed in 1911. It is now more than 25 years that workmen's compensation legislation has been discussed in the United States. In 1934 there were still four States that had no accident compensation laws: Arkansas, Mississippi, Florida, and South Carolina. It would take a half a century before the country as a whole would adopt unemployment-insurance measures. It is estimated that at least 7,000,000 workers are debarred from workmen's compensation because they belong in the categories of railroad workers, farm laborers, and workers in small shops who are excluded from the State laws. The same experience can be recorded in the history of old-age legislation, which was raised in the United States in 1911. In the past 24 years only 24 States have passed this legislation.

What kind of economic security does the Roosevelt program provide? The Wagner-Lewis bill makes no mention of the amount or the period of insurance. The unemployed workers will not be satisfied with the kind of " security " which offers them a small amount of benefit for a short period after which they must be forced on relief rolls again. Government spokesmen frankly admit that the tax on pay rolls will be made with the understanding that a waiting period of 4 weeks will be established before payments begin, that benefits will last for no more than 15 weeks at 50 percent of the normal wage but no more than $15, and that after 15 weeks the workers lose their so-called "security." By no stretch of the imagination would this be considered a bill for "social security." On the contrary, it is an insecurity program.

The Lundeen bill calls for immediate payment of benefits to all unemployed during every week that a worker is jobless and to the extent of his average weekly wages, but no less than $10 a week and $3 for each dependent. This can honestly be called a security standard.

Mr. Green pleads for an increase in the pay-roll tax to increase payments for 26 weeks instead of 15 weeks. In his testimony before the House Ways and Means Committee he signed over the effect of the pay-roll tax on wages and prices. Yet he does not hesitate to recommend an increase in the tax on the pretext that it will extend the benefits for a few more weeks. Whether the benefits are provided for 15 weeks or for 26 weeks, they cannot be said to be benefits providing "security." This kind of talk is construed by the workers as demagogy and insincerity. An unemployed worker and his family is "secure" only when he can be certain that during unemployment which comes through no fault of his own he and his family will have adequate funds to provide a roof over their heads and the necessary food and clothing. The meager amounts to be paid by the administration plan will go to a few small sections of the workers for a limited time, exclude millions, and will not be effective until some period in the distant future. It is a scheme to turn the attention of the masses away from a genuine unemployment-insurance plan.

The American Federation of Labor trade-union committee for unemployment insurance and relief, speaking in behalf of nearly 1,000,-000 workers in the American Federation of Labor, declares that it rejects the Wagner-Lewis bill in toto, and that the only plan worthy of the name of a social-security plan is that embodied in the Lundeen bill, H. R. 2827, which is the only bill that provides for the workers' needs.

While officially organized labor did not take the initiative in forcing the administration, nationally or locally, to provide for the unemployed, other organizations outside of the American Federation of Labor, organizations like the unemployed councils with the active support of members of the American Federation of Labor though without official sanction, carried through demonstrations before city halls, in various parts of the country, and organized huge hunger marches to State capitals and to Washington, D. C.

Mr. Dunn. It is necessary for me to get this information. Can you tell me why the head of the American Federation of Labor has not up to this date taken an active part in bringing about adequate old-age pensions and unemployment insurance?

Mr. Weinstock. The policy of the executive council, until June 1932, was totally against any kind of unemployment insurance.

These actions of the unemployed organizations helped to stimulate a rank-and-file movement for unemployment insurance in the American Federation of Labor and resulted in the establishment of the American Federation of Labor committee for unemployment insurance and relief. Many local unions without waiting for instructions from their international officials took the initiative in setting up official committees to deal with the burning issue of unemployment insurance. They organized conferences in many cities and American Federation of Labor committees came into existence as a result of this. Throughout the country wherever conferences were called the influence of the rank and file grew tremendously. In a book entitled "The American Federation of Labor", by Lewis L. Lorwin, published by the Brookings Institute, we find the following explanation of the position of the executive council of the American Federation of Labor, from which I quote directly as follows:

In the summer of 1930 the demand for compulsory State unemployment insurance was taken up by individuals and organizations interested in social legislation. The executive council opposed the idea, branding unemployment insurance as a "dole", incompatible with American principles. However, at the 1930 convention of the Federation in Boston a number of delegates proposed the issue. The convention evaded commitment by requesting the executive council to make a study of the subject and report to the convention in 1931.

During the year the executive council indicated repeatedly that it would not relinquish its stand against unemployment insurance. In reporting to the 1931 convention in Vancouver, the executive council gave a brief summary of the experience of Great Britain and Germany and concluded that unemployment insurance subsidized idleness, turned the Nation's resources to unproductive ends, and in the long run retarded real progress. (Proceedings of the fifty-first annual convention of the American Federation of Labor, 1931, p. 361.)

Mr. LUNDEEN. But they have reversed themselves since that time, have they not?

Mr. WEINSTOCK. I will come to that right away. (Continuing the quotation:)

The main argument of the executive council was that every system of unemployment insurance contemplates supervision and control by both Federal and State Governments and requires registration of all workers. This, according to the executive council, would subject every worker to undue control by the law and deprive him of the freedom to fight for better conditions. Union men would thus be forced to accept jobs in nonunion plants by the threat that otherwise their unemployment benefits would be withdrawn. The claim was also made that the employer would be in a position to hold the worker to his job by refusing to issue the proper certificate in case of dismissal. Finally it was urged that insurmountable constitutional difficulties would arise regarding methods for obtaining the necessary funds.

These arguments of the executive council, however, were not accepted by large sections of affiliated unions. In the course of 1931 the Brotherhood of Railway Clerks, the International Association of Machinists, the Teamsters' Union, the Molders' Union, some of the printing-trades unions, and a large number of local unions came out for some form of compulsory insurance. The State federations of labor of Illinois, Pennsylvania, and Wisconsin were active in support of proposed legislation on the subject. Many local unions lent their aid to nonlabor bodies and to disguised Communist groups which advocated a Nation-wide system of insurance against unemployment.

The executive council of the Federation thus faced a convention in 1931 which had a strong element favoring a turn in policy. The debate was heated. Many delegates who had stood together on most issues for years parted company. President Green finally swayed the vote in favor of the report of the executive council, rejecting unemployment insurance by promising a vigorous campaign for immediate relief.

Although on July 2, 1932, the American Federation of Labor "Weekly News Letter" still wrote that "labor abhors unemployment insurance", a few days later the executive council, in session at Atlantic City, instructed President Green to draw up an unemployment-insurance bill to be enacted by Congress. The executive council ascribed its change of policy to the prolonged depression, to the distress of the unions, and to growing clamor for action on the part of the workers. The ultimate responsibility for the new turn in policy was placed upon management and the Government which had failed to provide work for all or to give proper relief to the millions of unemployed.

Undoubtedly the Federation gave way on this issue to the combined pressure from its own local unions, from the radical elements in and outside its ranks, and from middle-class organizations.

At first it was announced that the executive council would demand a Federal law on the subject. But to the Cincinnati convention in November 1932 the council recommended compulsory unemployment insurance by States. The committee on resolutions of the convention reported favorably on the recommendations. The delegates in the convention voted overwhelmingly for it, regardless of the fact that a considerable number of them were still skeptical about the desirability of compulsory State insurance. (Proceedings of the fifty-second annual convention of the American Federation of Labor, 1932, pp. 343–360, pp. 442–443). The decision was forced upon the convention by the disturbed state of mind of the country, the exhaustion of union funds, and the distress of workers.

The membership in the American Federation of Labor local unions has shown a real desire for a genuine unemployment-insurance system. They have expressed their opposition to plans such as the Wisconsin act, the Wagner-Lewis bill, and others, which deny real unemployment insurance.

In 1933 the executive council of the American Federation of Labor came out unconditionally in support of the Wagner-Lewis bill and urged all its affiliated organizations to endorse and support this measure. This is the first time that the executive council sent out communications to all central labor bodies, State federations of labor, and local unions, urging the locals to endorse the Wagner-Lewis bill.

Mr. LUNDEEN. So that when they reversed themselves, they endorsed the wrong bill?

Mr. WEINSTOCK. Exactly. We will come to that right away.

Mr. DUNN. Pardon me a moment. I understood you to say they sent out a notice to the local unions to give their support to the Wagner-Lewis bill?

Mr. WEINSTOCK. Right.

Mr. DUNN. Is it not a fact that the American Federation of Labor stated recently that the Wagner-Lewis bill was not adequate?

Mr. WEINSTOCK. Right. This only proves the zig-zag policy of the executive council. If someone would take the trouble to get the official proposals of Mr. William Green, for 1932, since the convention, they would be illuminating. I do not know, Congressman Lundeen, whether you saw this. This is the unemployment insurance proposal, contained in the report of the executive council, adopted by the fifty-second annual convention of the American Federation of Labor, Cincinnati, Ohio, November 21 to December 2, 1932. In this official document, William Green sets forth the present Wagner-Lewis bill, so I could call him the originator of the Wagner-Lewis bill. Today, 1935, he goes to the hearings of the Ways and Means Committee, and he is raising objections against exactly the paragraphs that he put in, in his recommendation in 1932.

Mr. LUNDEEN. Mr. Chairman, I think we should have that in the record. It is only 6 small pages.

Mr. DUNN. I have no objection.

Mr. LUNDEEN. I ask that it be inserted.

Mr. DUNN. All right.

Mr. LUNDEEN. And I have also inserted in the record, here, prior to this, the statement by Mr. Green in which he says that the identical bill which I understand was recommended in this report, is inadequate.

Mr. WEINSTOCK. Exactly. This will show the contradictions in Mr. William Green's statements.

(The matter referred to is as follows:)

UNEMPLOYMENT INSURANCE

REPORT OF THE EXECUTIVE COUNCIL, ADOPTED BY THE FIFTY-SECOND ANNUAL CONVENTION OF THE AMERICAN FEDERATION OF LABOR, CINCINNATI, OHIO, NOVEMBER 21– DECEMBER 2, 1932

Because local conditions of each State vary to such a marked degree that it is impossible to frame a single model bill to be enacted in every State, the report contains basic principles which are recommended for the guidance of our State federations of labor in framing unemployment-insurance measures. The report follows in full:

"In reporting to the last convention of the American Federation of Labor, which was held at Vancouver, British Columbia, beginning October 5 a year ago, the executive council, in dealing with the subject of unemployment insurance, stated:

"'There are just two approaches to this problem—prevention and relief. Either we must make employment secure or provide an income for the unemployed.'

"In another section of its report to the Vancouver convention, the executive council made the following direct and positive reference to this social-justice problem:

"'Workingmen have arrived at the point where they are firmly of the belief that they are as much entitled to work security, to enjoy the opportunity to work, as the owners of capital are to returns from their investments. Labor demands that these principles be recognized and accepted by the employers of labor. Obviously, the owners and management of industry must decide as to whether working men and women shall enjoy the opportunity to work or whether, as a result of the denial of this opportunity to work, industry shall have fastened upon it compulsory unemployment-insurance legislation. It must be work or unemployment insurance. Working people must be privileged to earn a living or be accorded relief. If compulsory unemployment insurance is fastened upon our industrial, political, and economic life, it will be because industrial ownership and management have failed to provide and preserve work opportunities for working men and women.'

"The experience which working men and women have been forced to face and undergo during the past year has been most bitter and disappointing. They cannot be expected to maintain faith in an economic order which has failed them so completely. They charge industrial management with failure to stabilize employment. The facts are that the management of industry has not provided work security or created work opportunities for those who are able, willing, and eager to work. Unemployment has increased; there are more workers idle now than there were 1 year ago; approximately 11,000,000 are out of work, seeking employment, unable to find it.

"The American Federation of Labor has always emphasized both the necessity and importance of supplying work for all. Working people and their families depend upon wages earned for a livelihood. Life and living, in the full meaning of that term, are inseparably associated with employment, wages, work security, the possession of a job, and the exercise of the right to work.

"The executive council has given most careful, painstaking, and serious consideration to the problem of unemployment and to the application of the principle of unemployment insurance. The council would much prefer that working people be privileged to work and be accorded job security than to see them forced to accept relief because of unemployment. The extension and enjoyment of the opportunity to work at decent wages, so that working men and women may earn a decent living, is the real objective of the American Federation of Labor. The executive council urges work first and relief second, but it must be clear that working people must be permitted to earn a living or be supplied relief. They must earn their living or be supported. They cannot earn their living unless jobs are provided and work opportunities accorded them.

" Obviously, the owners and management of industry have failed to provide work for all and thus make it possible for all to earn a livelihood. Their failure is reflected in the fact that during the past 3 years unemployment has steadily increased and that at the present time about 11,000,000 people are idle. The executive council believes that the owners of industry and industrial management must have known that the creation of an army of 11,000,000 unemployed, forced to shift for themselves, to become dependent upon local, State, and Federal relief agencies, would create an intolerable economic situation fraught with most serious consequences.

" The economic facts arising out of the unemployment situation, the continued displacement of millions of workingmen through the mechanization of industry, and the substitution of power for human service make it absolutely necessary, in the opinion of the executive council, to develop and put into operation, through the enactment of appropriate legislation, an unemployment-insurance plan which will provide for the payment of weekly benefits to working men and women who are forced to suffer from unemployment.

" The council holds that because the ownership and management of industry have failed to provide and maintain work opportunities for working men and women unemployment-insurance legislation is made imperatively necessary. The responsibility for this state of affairs rests squarely upon industry and industrial management. They control industry ; consequently they control jobs. Labor cannot wait longer ; it must now act. Industry must be compelled to do what it has thus far failed to do. Work or relief must be provided. If industrial management fails to provide work, it must be compelled to assume the burden of supplying relief.

" Having all these facts in mind, the executive council, at a meeting held July 12–22, 1932, directed the president of the American Federation of Labor to draft and present to a subsequent meeting a plan of unemployment-insurance legislation. These instructions were complied with. As a result of a detailed survey and careful study of the subject, the president of the American Federation of Labor submitted to a meeting of the executive council, held October 18–27, 1932, a report which embodied within it a plan of unemployment-insurance legislation.

" The executive council has always endeavored to guard jealously the organization structure of the American Federation of Labor. For that reason, the council was apprehensive over the effect which compulsory unemployment-insurance legislation might have upon the exercise of the right of working men and women not only to join but to maintain membership in trade unions. In the drafting of an unemployment-insurance measure, the council has constantly kept three very distinct fundamental principles in mind.

" First, it has endeavored to provide in the plan which it submits to the convention a full measure of protection to the membership of the American Federation of Labor, and the preservation of the right to become a member and to continue membership in a trade union.

" Second, that the payment of relief shall be made a fixed charge upon industry. Relief funds should be created out of the earnings of industry. The council does not believe it is fair or just that any part of the money out of which relief would be paid during periods of unemployment should be collected from employees.

" Third, that unemployment insurance should be compulsory and that the execution and administration of unemployment insurance laws should come wholly within the control and administration of Federal and State governments.

" The executive council submits the following plan for the consideration and approval of the convention. This plan embodies within it the fundamental principles just enunciated and represents the best thought and judgment of the members of the executive council and of the trained experts upon social justice legislation who rendered valuable assistance in the preparation of the plan. The council recommends this plan of unemployment insurance legislation for the favorable consideration and acceptance of the officers and members in attendance at the convention.

" *Principles recommended for unemployment-insurance measures.*—It would be desirable, where it possible, to press for the enactment of one uniform measure for unemployment insurance applicable throughout the United States. But, due to the provisions and limitations of the United States Constitution as interpreted by the courts, since the regulation of manufacture and industry lies primarily within the province of State rather than Federal activity, it is practically impossible to enact constitutional Federal legislation adequately providing for unemployment insurance covering employees engaged in work in the different States. The American Federation of Labor therefore advocates the passage of unemployment-insurance legislation in each separate State, and the supplementing of such State legislation by Federal enactments; such for instance, as bills covering employees engaged in interstate commerce or employed in the District of Columbia or in Federal territories, or such as the bill recently introduced into Congress by Senator Wagner, allowing corporations substantial income-tax credit on their Federal income taxes for such payments as they have made under State laws toward the creation of unemployment reserves.

" It is evident that the local conditions of each State vary to such a marked degree that it would be unwise, even were it possible at the present time, to frame a single model bill to be enacted in every State. It is possible, nevertheless, to set forth certain general fundamental principles and standards to which such State legislation should conform. The American Federation of Labor, after mature consideration and discussion, has formulated the following principles which should guide in the framing of State unemployment-insurance bills:

" 1. *Protection of union standards.*—Every unemployment-insurance act should contain specific provisions to protect union members from being obliged to accept work contrary to the rules and regulations of their organizations or employment under conditions such as tend to depress wages or working conditions.

" 2. *Underlying object of unemployment insurance.*—Unemployment-insurance legislation in this country should be carefully devised to promote its two primary objectives: (*a*) The stimulation of more regular employment, insofar as possible, and (*b*) the payment of unemployment compensation to those who are temporarily out of work through industry's failure to provide steady employment for its working forces.

" 3. *Voluntary* v. *compulsory schemes of insurance.*—The American Federation of Labor advocates a scheme of unemployment compensation made compulsory by law. Voluntary schemes are unlikely to pervade industry generally, and are frequently open to other serious objections. Only by compulsory legislation can workers be adequately protected.

" 4. *How and from whom contributions should be made.*—Since unemployment is, to a certain extent, one of the inevitable incidents of production and must, therefore, be regarded as part of the inescapable cost of industry, it, like other costs of industry, should be paid by industry itself. It, therefore, follows that, as a matter of principle, no part of the contributions to support unemployment insurance should be paid out of the wages of labor, but the whole should be paid by management as part of the cost of production. The necessary funds should be raised as a charge on industry.

" The amount of such contribution must depend upon the local conditions in each State. A minimum contribution must be required sufficient to cover (*a*) the building up of adequate reserves, (*b*) the cost of the benefits to be paid under the act, and (*c*) the costs of administration. To cover these costs the American Federation of Labor believes that the contribution rate should be not less than 3 percent of the total pay roll. The exact percentage, however, must vary in different States, and will come to depend upon various actuarial data, which must be carefully collected as a basis for such determination from the experience gained both before and after the passage of the act. The absence of complete data should not, however, prevent the passage of a law, since the liability of the fund is limited to the amount of the income provided by law. As experience is accumulated it will be possible to determine the income necessary to provide the benefits decided upon in the law.

" 5. *Reserve* v. *insurance systems.*—At this time the American Federation of Labor deems it inadvisable to take an irrevocable stand as between the plant reserves system or unemployment insurance embodied in the Wisconsin law and an insurance system such as is under consideration in Ohio and in operation in many European countries. Whatever plan is adopted, whether based on plant reserves or on a broader basis, we believe that it should be administered by the State and all reserve funds held and invested by the State. We are unalterably opposed to company-controlled unemployment reserves and believe that without State administration plant reserves will prove but another ' company-union ' device. We are also of the opinion that, at least at the outset, it is advisable to have but a single unemployment insurance fund (with, if a plant-reserve system is adopted, separate accounts for separate employers) and a flat rate of contributions by employers regardless of the industry in which they may be engaged. Later on, after more accurate data are obtained, the contributions in each industry, occupation, or enterprise may be scaled according to the hazard of unemployment, but sufficient data are not now available to warrant such classifications at this time.

"6. *Exclusion of private insurance companies.*—Sound public policy requires that no insurance company in this country be allowed to invade this new field of unemployment compensation. No insurance company is allowed under present State laws to write this class of insurance. The Federation believes that this policy is wise and should in no case be abandoned.

"7. *Investment of funds.*—All funds should be invested in Federal securities or in the bonds of States or municipalities such as have never defaulted in payment of principal or interest.

"8. *Eligibility for benefits.*—Insurance in general should cover temporary and involuntary unemployment. Unemployment means the conditions caused by the inability of an employee who is capable of and available for employment to obtain work in his usual employment or in another for which he is reasonably fitted. Nothing in the unemployment compensation act should require an employee to accept employment, nor should any employee forfeit his right to benefits under the act by refusing to accept employment under any or all of the following conditions:

"(*a*) In a situation vacant directly in consequence of a stoppage of work due to a trade dispute;

"(*b*) If the wages, hours, and conditions offered are less favorable to the employee than those prevailing for similar work in the locality, or are such as tend to depress wages and working conditions;

"(*c*) If acceptance of such employment would abridge or limit the right of the employee either (1) to refrain from joining a labor organization or association of workmen, or (2) to retain membership in and observe the rules of any such organization or association.

"(*d*) Workers who quit work without good cause or who are discharged for misconduct shall not thereby forfeit benefits beyond a reasonable period.

"9. *Scope or coverage.*—The coverage should be as wide as possible. It should include clerical as well as manual workers. There are, however, certain classes of employment which it may be necessary to exclude from the general operation of the act, and these classes will vary according to local conditions. It would seems that the legislation should approximate, insofar as practicable, the coverage of State workmen's compensation acts. As time goes on the scope or coverage of the act may well be broadened.

"10. *Payment of benefits.*—The claim of employees to receive unemployment compensation as provided under the act should be clearly recognized as a legal right earned by previous employment within the State. Receipt of unemployment benefits shall in no way entail loss of suffrage or other civil rights. Persons not legal residents of the State and those not citizens of the United States shall not by reason of that fact be disqualified from receiving benefits.

"The amount of benefits to be paid and the number of weeks during which they shall be paid must depend upon the local conditions in each State and upon the amount of contributions paid unto the fund. We are informed, for instance, that under the conditions prevailing in Ohio, a contribution of 3 percent of the total pay roll makes it possible after a waiting period of 3 weeks per year to pay benefits for a maximum period of 16 weeks in a year based upon 50 percent of the normal weekly wages, but not to exceed $15 a week.

"It seems advisable to restrict the payment of benefits to unemployment occurring after a specified waiting period. The length of this waiting period will materially affect the amount of the benefits which can be paid and the length of time during which they can be paid.

"Workers who are partially unemployed should receive unemployment compensation at a reduced rate. The exact amount of the reduction will presumably vary, in different States. We suggest that a fair principle would be to pay for partial unemployment the amount of the benefit which would be payable in case of total unemployment reduced by subtracting one-half of the amount of the wages actually received.

"11. *Administration.*—(*a*) Nature of commission.

"The administration of the scheme of unemployment compensation and the responsibility for the keeping and investment of the unemployment funds should be in the hands of a State commission. This should be either a special commission created for the specific purpose, or an already existing State commission or department of labor.

"(b) Both labor and management should have a voice in the administration of unemployment insurance. Advisory committees composed of an equal number of representatives of labor and management will prove very useful and, in some States, local appeal boards similarly constituted will be found desirable. It should be recognized, however, that workingmen can have genuine representation only through labor organizations. Unless labor can, in effect, through its organization select its own representatives, pretended representation is but a farce.

"(c) Cost of administration.

"The cost of the administration of unemployment compensation should be met out of the unemployment fund itself.

"(d) Employment exchanges.

"The operation of employment exchanges is closely and vitally connected with the administration of unemployment insurance. The commission should take over, supervise, and expand public-employment exchanges in States where these already exist, or in States where none exists should create and operate such exchanges.

"(e) Procedure for obtaining benefits.

"The administration regulating the payment of benefits should be decentralized as far as possible. Payments should be made upon claims presented through local agencies, established and supervised by the commission and acting in close cooperation with the public employment offices. Appeals should be allowed to a central authority.

"12. *Regularization of employment.*—The whole scheme should be so construed as to induce and stimulate so far as possible the regularization and stabilization of employment. This may be affected in various possible ways; as for instance, by basing the amount of contributions payable upon some merit-rating scheme, or in States not adopting an exclusive State fund, by the establishment of separate industry or separate plant funds.

"This statement embodies within it certain standards and principles that we believe should be incorporated in unemployment-insurance legislation. We suggest, however, that a flexible policy be pursued in all the States, and that unemployment-insurance legislation be secured which will maintain the above standards, so far as possible, and yet which will accommodate itself to the varying circumstances and conditions in each State. It is essential that the protection of the rights of citizenship and of union membership be maintained in all acts.

"Pending the adoption of compulsory State insurance, voluntary unemployment compensation schemes should be subject to State regulation. We, therefore, believe it vital that suitable legislation be enacted to provide for State supervision of all such plans, including as a minimum the deposit of benefit funds in separate trust accounts, whether or not such funds include payments made from employees."

Mr. WEINSTOCK. The rank-and-file members in the American Federation of Labor unions, in spite of definite instructions received from the top officials to endorse the Wagner-Lewis bill, were not ready to follow without analyzing the measure proposed. Wherever they had an opportunity to compare the workers' bill and the Wagner-Lewis bill, the result showed that they favored the workers' bill and rejected the Wagner-Lewis bill. As outstanding examples of this fact, we will point to:

1. The convention of the Amalgamated Association of Iron, Steel, and Tin Workers of America held in April 1934 in Pittsburgh, Pa., attended by delegates from all steel mills in the country. At present this organization has a membership of over 100,000. The workers' bill was unanimously endorsed by the delegates present, who rejected the Wagner-Lewis bill, and instructed their officials to support the workers' bill at the American Federation of Labor convention in San Francisco. I would like to state right here that in many local unions I personally had occasion to listen to discussions from

the floor, and both bills were presented. Not only were we waiting for William Green to send these bills down but we ourselves brought to the attention of the members the two bills, and requested a comparison of them, and as the result of these comparisons, and as a result of the discussion, the rank-and-file members decided in favor of the Lundeen bill and against the Wagner-Lewis bill.

Mr. DUNN. May I say right here that if every laboring man and woman in the United States, and the lawyers and professional men who are out of employment, would have the opportunity to read both bills, I will venture to say 100 percent would give their endorsement to the Lundeen bill, H. R. 2827.

Mr. WEINSTOCK. That is it, exactly.

Mr. DUNN. That is my candid opinion.

Mr. WEINSTOCK. Mr. Chairman, I think what I have just read regarding the convention of the Amalgamated Association of Iron, Steel, and Tin Workers of America, held in Pittsburgh, Pa., in April 1934, proves your statement.

Mr. DUNN. In other words, Mr. Lundeen, at a convention held in Pittsburgh, representing 100,000 people, your bill was unanimously endorsed; so you see there are some good things that can be said even for Pittsburgh!

Mr. WEINSTOCK. And I might state for Congressman Lundeen's city of Minneapolis that organized labor almost unanimously endorsed the workers' unemployment insurance bill; so you are even on that question.

This international, organized into districts, immediately after the convention, sent communications to the lodges affiliated with the respective districts to take up the question of the workers' bill and to vote for or against it. Those locals which received this communication, without exception, voted favorably on the workers' bill.

2. The convention of the United Textile Workers, an organization with hundreds of locals all over the country, held August 1934, in New York City, went on record for the workers' bill by a great majority. The delegates gave similar instructions to its officials to support the bill at the American Federation of Labor convention in San Francisco.

3. The International Molders' Union at its convention held on August 27, 1934, in Chicago, Ill., passed the workers bill and rejected the Wagner-Lewis bill. The proceedings of this convention show that considerable discussion developed around the workers bill. The Molders' delegation to the American Federation of Labor convention was also instructed to vote for the bill when brought up on the floor of the convention.

4. Mine, Mill, and Smelter Workers' Union, a militant organization in the Northwest, at its convention in August 1934 held in Salt Lake City, Utah, and attended by delegates from 30 States unanimously endorsed the workers bill, decided to notify every local of this action, and ask for their approval of the convention decision. This was done and the locals gave full support to the action of the convention decision.

Scores of central labor bodies, district councils, State federations of labor and other bodies have also endorsed the workers bill. I will have for the records of the committee a partial list of those American Federation of Labor organizations which have voted for the workers bill. This list is by no means complete, as endorsements are coming in to our office daily. In addition a number of local unions have endorsed the bill but failed to notify our national office. Many of the locals write directly to their respective Senators and Congressmen notifying them of their action and urging them to support this measure.

Mr. LUNDEEN. These are all American Federation of Labor unions, am I correct?

Mr. WEINSTOCK. Right.

Mr. LUNDEEN. I believe that this list ought to go into the record. There has been considerable controversy as to the position of certain leaders in the Federation of Labor. A letter has been referred to supporting the opposition, and that letter has been talked about here. This list is concrete evidence on the question of whether the American Federation of Labor favors this bill or whether it is opposed to it. This is a list, as I understand it, of those who favor the bill?

Mr. WEINSTOCK. Right. And supported by these signatures of local officials and district council officials, although I cannot leave these here.

Mr. LUNDEEN. What are these papers which you submit to the committee?

Mr. WEINSTOCK. These are stubs returned to us from the local unions, informing the American Federation of Labor committee that they have discussed the unemployment-insurance bill and have voted favorably upon it.

Mr. LUNDEEN. And the sealed stubs are here presented as evidence that these are bona fide endorsements.

Mr. WEINSTOCK. Right.

(The list presented by the witness is as follows:)

International unions of the American Federation of Labor.—Amalgamated Association of Iron, Steel, and Tin Workers of America; United Textile Workers of America; International Molders' Union; Mine, Mill, and Smelter Workers Union; Full Fashioned Hosiery Workers of America.

State federations of labor of American Federation of Labor.—State Federations of Labor of Arkansas, Iowa, Montana, Colorado, Rhode Island, Wisconsin, and Nebraska.

Central labor unions.—Kalamazoo Federation of Labor, Kalamazoo, Mich.; Trades and Labor Assembly, Sioux City, Iowa; Central Labor Union, Lincoln, Nebr.; Schenectady Trades Assembly, Schenectady, N. Y.; Trades Assembly, Bradford, Pa.; New Kensington Central Labor Council, New Kensington, Pa.; Central Labor Council, Jeanette, Pa.; Federation of Labor, Pittsburgh (Hazelwood), Pa.; Federated Trades Council, Reading, Pa.; Jamestown Central Labor Council, Jamestown, N. Y.; Central Trades Council, Spokane, Wash.; Central Labor Union, Essex County, Newark, N. J.; Central Body, Clifton, N. J.; Central Body, Linden, N. J.; Great Falls Central Trades Council, Great Falls, Mont.; Central Labor Union, Danbury, Conn.; Salt Lake City Federation, Salt Lake City, Utah; City Central Body, Providence, R. I.; Federated Trades and Labor Council, San Diego, Calif.; Central Labor Council, St. Louis, Mo.; Trades Labor Council, Racine, Wis.; Central Labor Union, Atlantic City, N. J.

District councils.—Painters District Council, Newark, N. J.; Painters District Council, 36, Los Angeles, Calif.; Carpenters (Hudson County), Jersey City, N. J.; Painters District Council, Kansas City, Mo.; Carpenters District Council, Kansas City, Mo.; Painters District Council, 21, Philadelphia, Pa.; Painters District Council, 28, Jamaica, N. Y.; Full Fashioned Hosiery Workers, New York and New Jersey.

International Association of Heat and Frost Insulators and Asbestos Workers, Local 31, Providence, R. I.; Local 25, Detroit, Mich.

Aeronautical Workers, Federal Labor Local 18286, Buffalo, N. Y.

Automobile Workers, Federal Labor Local 18614, Cleveland, Ohio; Buick Local, Flint, Mich.; Hudson Local 18312, Detroit, Mich.; Ternstead Local, Detroit, Mich.

Brotherhood of Railway Clerks, Local 611, Columbus, Ohio; Local 257, St. Paul, Mich.

Damp and Waterproof Workers Association, United Slate, Tile, and Composition Roofers, Local 80, Great Falls, Mont.; Local 4, Newark, N. J.; Local 55, Denver, Colo.

Railwaymen's Union Local 823, New York, N. Y.

Riggers, Machine Movers Local 170, New York, N. Y.

Umbrella Makers Union Local, Rand School, New York, N. Y.

Dyers and Mercerizers Local 702, Philadelphia, Pa.

Boot and Shoe Workers Union Local 613, Huntington, W. Va.

Bartenders Union Local 485, Spokane, Wash.

Brewery Workers Union Local, Tacoma, Wash.

Longshoremen's Union Locals 38 and 12, Seattle, Wash.

Paper Plate and Bag Makers Union Local 107, New York, N. Y.

Pocketbook Workers Union Local, New York, N. Y.

Druggists Union Local, Philadelphia, Pa.

Full Fashioned Hosiery Workers Local 4, Langhorn, Pa.

Knit Goods Workers Union Local, Philadelphia, Pa.

Suit Case, Bag and Portfolio Workers Local 52, Philadelphia, Pa.

Taxi Drivers Union Local, Philadelphia, Pa.

Window Washers Local 125, Providence, R. I.

Hotel and Restaurant Employees and Beverage Dispensers' International Alliance, Local 271, Petaluma, Calif.; Local 781, Washington, D. C.; Local 733, Detroit, Mich.; Local 34, Minneapolis, Minn.; Local 109, Newark, N. J.; Local 508, Atlantic City, N. J.; Local 2, Brooklyn, N. Y.; Local 72, Cincinnati, Ohio; Local 659, Dallas, Utah; Local 237, Pittsburgh, Pa.

United Hatters, Cap and Millinery Workers International Union, Local 10, Danbury, Conn.; Local 8, New York, N. Y.

Milwaukee Coke and Gas Workers Union, Federal labor, Local 18546, Milwaukee, Wis.

Brotherhood of Painters, Decorators, and Paperhangers of America; Locals 531, 50, Cincinnati, Ohio; Local 639, Cleveland, Ohio.

Federal Labor Union, Local 19155, Breckenridge, Tex.

International Moulders Union of North America, local, Spokane, Wash.

Ice and Cold Storage Workers, Local 16918, Centralia, Ill.

Oil Field, Gas Well, and Refinery Workers of America, Local 210, Hammond, Ind.

Order of Railway Conductors of America, Local 69, El Paso, Tex.; Local 1, Oak Park, Ill.

International Association, Protective, Retail Clerks, local, Butte, Mont.

Bakery and Confectionery Workers International Union of America, Local 125, Berkeley, Calif.; Local 43, Fresno, Calif.; Local 24, San Francisco, Calif.; Locals 62, 237, 2, 49, Chicago, Ill.; Local 190, Metuchen, N. J.; Locals 79, 164, 507, New York, N. Y.; Local 14, Rochester, N. Y.; Locals 39, 334, Cleveland, Ohio; Local 177, Youngstown, Ohio; Local 45, Boston, Mass.; Local 204, Pittsburgh, Pa.; Local 122, Providence, R. I.; Local 473, Bellingham, Wash.

Bakers Union, Local 26, Denver, Colo.

Journeymen Barbers International Union, Local 175, Danbury, Conn.; Local 72, Norwalk, Conn.; Local, Belleville, Ill.; Local 182, Boston, Mass.; Local 913, Brooklyn, N. Y.; Local 164, New York City; Local 2, Philadelphia, Pa.; Local, Salt Lake City, Utah.

International Alliance of Bill Posters and Billers of America, Local 49, Seattle, Wash.

International Brotherhood of Blacksmiths, Drop Forgers and Helpers, Local 303, Butte, Mont.; Local 77, Milwaukee, Wis.

International Brotherhood of Boiler Makers, Iron Ship Builders, and Helpers of America, Local 244, Sioux City, Iowa; Local 81, Readville, Mass.; Local 104, Seattle, Wash.; Local 249, Huntington, W. Va.; Local 281, Boston, Mass.

Bridge and Structural Iron Workers International Association, Local 420, Reading, Pa.; Local 2416, Portland, Oreg.; Local 350, Atlantic City, N. J.

Bricklayers, Masons, and Plasterers International Union of America, Local, Baltimore, Md.; Local 2, Detroit, Mich.; Local 1, Brooklyn, N. Y.; Local 37, New York, N. Y.; Local 18, Cincinnati, Ohio; Local 1, Providence, R. I.; Local 9, Oshkosh, Wis.; Local 5, Huntington, W. Va.; Local 8, Milwaukee, Wis.

Brotherhood Railway Carmen of America, Locals 227 and 210, Chicago, Ill.; Local 13, Princeton, Ind.; Locals 2031 and 266, Sioux City, Iowa; Local 56, Atchison, Kans.; Local 431, Bay City, Mich.; Local 641, Port Huron, Mich.; Local 299 Minneapolis, Minn.; Local 618, Providence, R. I.; Local 1085, New York, N. Y.; Local 815, Philadelphia, Pa.; Local 235, Milwaukee, Wis.; Local 1054, Detroit, Mich.; Local 698, Spokane, Wash.

United Brotherhood of Carpenters and Joiners of America, Local 1687, Montgomery, Ala.; Local 1089, Phoenix, Ariz.; Local 891, Hot Springs, Ark.; Local 210, Stamford, Conn.; Local 132, District of Columbia; Local 352, Anderson, Ind.; Local 1953, Greencastle, Ind.; Local 487, Linton, Ind.; Local 523, Keokuk, Iowa; Local 948, Sioux City, Iowa; Locals 1784, 416, 419, 13, 58, 62, 181, 504, Chicago, Ill.; Local 896, Crystal Lake, Ill.; Local 1366, Quincy, Ill.; Local 16, Springfield, Ill.; Local 720, Auburn, Mass.; Locals 11, 56, 157, Boston, Mass.; Local 296, Brockton, Mass.; Local 116, Bay City, Mich.; Local 337, Detroit, Mich.; Local 1299, Iron River, Mich.; Local 1199, Pontiac, Mich.; Local 361, Duluth, Minn.; Local 7. Minneapolis, Minn.; Local 87, St. Paul, Minn.; Local 1329, Independence, Mo.; Local 286, Great Falls, Mont.; Local 2237, Bayonne, N. J.; Local 349, East Orange, N. J.; Locals 119, 1782, Newark, N. J.; Local 299, Union City, N. J.; Local 2717, Brooklyn, N. Y.; Local 2372, Garnersville, N. Y.; Local 66, Jamestown, N. Y.; Locals 2090, 2163, New York City, N. Y.; Local 163, Peekskill, N. Y.; Local 1115, Pleasantville, N. Y.; Local 203, Poughkeepsie, N. Y.; Local 1660, Raymondsville, N. Y.; Local 188, Yonkers, N. Y.; Local 224, Cincinnati, Ohio; Locals 1180, 2159, Cleveland, Ohio; Local 735, Mansfield, Ohio; Local 186, Steubenville, Ohio; Locals 226, 2218, 2154, Portland. Oreg.; Local 1065, Salem, Oreg.; Local 59, Lancaster, Pa.; Local 207, Chester, Pa.; Locals 1050, 1051, 1073, 1856, 2194, Philadelphia, Pa.; Local 1695, Cranston, R. I.; Local 810, Kingston, R. I.; Local 2016, Eastland, Tex.; Local 1666, Kingsville, Tex.; Local 1984, Magna, Utah; Local 317, Aberdeen, Wash.; Local 562, Everett, Wash.; Locals 1184, 1335, Seattle, Wash.; Locals 84, 98, Spokane, Wash.; Local, Tacoma, Wash.; Local 161, Kenosha, Wis.; Local 2244. Little Chuta, Wis.; Local 849, Manitowoc, Wis.; Locals 1053, 2073, Milwaukee, Wis.; Local 460, Wausau, Wis.; Local 1620, Rock Springs, Wyo.; Local 1241, Thermopolis, Wyo.; Locals 277, 102, 122, Philadelphia, Pa.

International Association of Fire Fighters, Local 37, Chicago, Ill.; Local 301, Burlington, Iowa; Local 96, Butte, Mont.; Local 287, Long Beach, Long Island, N. Y.

International Fur Workers' Union of United States and Canada, Local 3, Brooklyn, N. Y.

International Brotherhood of Firemen and Oilers, Local 32, Detroit, Mich.

Granite Cutters' International Association of America, Local, Concord, N. H.; Local Penacook, N. H.; Local, Baree, Vt.

International Jewelry Workers' Union, Local 19253, Great Falls, Mont.; Local 2, Newark, N. J.; Local 1, New York, N. Y.; Local 21, New York, N. Y.

Paving Cutters' Union of the United States of America and Canada, Local, Clark Island, Me.; Local 108, Tenants Harbor, Me.; Local 9, Thomaston, Me.; Local 43, Woodstock, Md.; Local 53, Rockport, Mass.; Local, Concord, N. H.

Printing Pressmen's and Assistants' Union of North America, Local 140, San Diego, Calif.; Local 147. Wichita. Kans.; Local 3, Chicago, Ill.; Local 4, Chicago, Ill.; Local 196, New Brunswick, N. J.; Local 23, New York City, N. Y.; Local 315, San Mateo, Calif.; Local 81, Spokane, Wash.

United Association of Plumbers and Steam Fitters of the United States and Canada, Local 230, San Diego, Calif.; Local 18, Sioux City, Iowa; Local 64, Northampton, Mass.; Local 98, Detroit, Mich.; Local 41, Butte, Mont.; Local 139, Great Falls, Mont.; Local 1, Brooklyn, N. Y.; Local 206, Elmira, N. Y.; Local 98, Cleveland, Ohio; Local 108, Hamilton, Ohio; Local 42, Reading, Pa.; Local 28, Providence, R. I.; Local 504, Beaumont, Tex.; Local 608, West Allis, Wis.

American Federation of Musicians: Local 403, Willimantic, Conn.; 219, Stanton, Ill.; 24, Akron, Ohio; 362, Huntington, W. Va.

Musicians Protective Union: 346, Santa Cruz, Calif.; 661, Atlantic City, N. J.

Amalgamated Meat Cutters and Butcher Workmen of North America: 333, Butte, Mont.; 545, St. Louis, Mo.; 18, New York, N. Y.; 174, New York, N. Y.

International Hod Carriers, Building and Common Laborers' Union of America: Local 591, Santa Barbara, Calif.; Local 270, San Jose, Calif.; Local 524, Norwich, Conn.; Local 499, Stamford, Conn.; Local ——, Belleville, Ill.; Local ——, Centralia, Ill.; Local 608, Zeigler, Ill.; Local ——, Princeton, Ind.; Local ——, Waltham, Mass.; Local 210, Worcester, Mass.; Local 563, Minneapolis, Minn.; Local 150, Butte, Mont.; Local 278, Great Falls, Mont.; Local 187, Missoula, Mont.; Local 690, Newark, N. J.; Local 31, Union City, N. J.; Local 141, Port Chester, N. Y.; Local 435, Rochester, N. Y.; Local 173, Pittsburgh, Pa.; Local 271, Providence, R. I.; Local 242, Seattle, Wash.; Local ——, Spokane, Wash.

International Ladies' Garment Workers' Union: Local 65, Los Angeles, Calif.; 84, Los Angeles, Calif.; 54, Chicago, Ill.; 20, New York, N. Y.; 22, New York, N. Y.; 66, New York, N. Y.

United Garment Workers of America: Local 75, Philadelphia, Pa.; 27, Minneapolis, Minn.

International Association of Machinists: Local 84, Berwyn, Ill.; Local 234, Chicago, Ill.; Local 83, Chicago, Ill.; Local 337, Chicago, Ill.; Local 915, Chicago, Ill.; Local 390, Park Ridge, Ill.; Local 178, Sioux City, Iowa; Local 404, Baltimore, Md.; Local 64, Massachusetts and Rhode Island; Local 1122, Detroit, Mich.; Local 459, St. Paul, Minn.; Local ——, Concord, N. H.; Local 816, Hoboken, N. J.; Local 402, New York, N. Y.; Local 226, New York, N. Y.; Local 417, Staten Island, N. Y.; Local 162, Cincinnati, Ohio; Local 729, Cincinnati, Ohio; Local 439, Cleveland, Ohio; Local 203, Akron, Ohio; Local 404, Youngstown, Ohio; Local 187, Sharpsville, Pa.; Local 79, Seattle, Wash.; Local 57, Huntington, W. Va.; Local 119, Newport, R. I.; Local 110, Newport, R. I.; Local 86, Spokane, Wash.

International Union of Mine, Mill, and Smelter Workers: Local ——, Eveleth, Minn.; Local 3, Bingham, Utah; Local 61, Spelter, W. Va.; Local 125, Iron River, Mich.; Fairmont Local 82, East St. Louis, Ill.; Local 56, Midvale, Utah; Local 16, Great Falls, Mont.; Local 126, Crystal Falls, Mich.

International Molders' Union of North America: Local 161, Stamford, Conn.; Local 182, Belleville, Ill.; Local 275, Chicago, Ill.; Local 153, Hazelcrest, Ill.; Local 24, Baltimore, Md.; Local 388, Kalamazoo, Mich.; Local ——, Anaconda, Mont.; Local 84, Buffalo, N. Y.; Local 78, Watertown, N. Y.; Local 27, Cleveland, Ohio; Local ——, Cheltersham, Pa.; Local ——, Philadelphia, Pa.; Local 111, Philadelphia, Pa.; Local 348, Reading, Pa.; Local 171, Port Orchard, Wash.; Local 158, Seattle, Wash.; Local 338, Spokane, Wash.

United Mine Workers of America: Local 3664, Auburn, Ill.; Local 3543, Benton, Ill.; Local 52, Centralia, Ill.; Local 1397, Centralia, Ill.; Local 3464, Gillespie, Ill.; Local 2840, Middlegrove, Ill.; Local 2109, Nashville, Ill.; Local 721, Pana, Ill.; Local 2403, Springfield, Ill.; Local 720, Staunton, Ill.; Local 691, Troy, Ill.; Local 5509, Westville, Ill.; Local 6803, Bicknell, Ind.; Local 5584, Princeton, Ind.; Local 916, Hitema, Iowa; Local 191, South Hibbing, Minn.; Local 4472, Glen Robins, Ohio; Local 1451, Connerton, Pa.; Local 2399, Daisytown, Pa.; Local 4439, Fayette, Pa.; Local 494, Homer City, Pa.; Local 1560, Lost Creek, Pa.; Local 807, Maple Hill, Pa.; Local 2587, Raven Tun, Pa.; Local 1545, Torty Fort, Pa.; Locals 5383, 3506, Renton, Pa.; Local 1398, Shaft, Pa.; Locals 2011, 113, 2346, 1509, 1414, 1443, 1685, 1467, Shenandoah, Pa.; Local 4439, South Brownsville, Pa.; Local 458, Swoyersville, Pa.; Local 6147, Besoco, W. Va.; Local 6107, Killarney, W. Va.; Local 6106, Mead, W. Va.; Local 2980, Pimberton, W. Va.; Local 1, Butte, Mont.; Local 456, Creighton, Pa.; Local 762, Pittsburgh, Pa.; Local 920, Pottsville, Pa.; Local 4426, Harmonville, Pa.; Local 4963, Sarver, Pa.; Local ——, Glen Ridge, Ill.; Local 6109, ——, Pa.

Brotherhood of Painters, Decorators, and Paperhangers of America: Locals 713, 449, Glendale, Calif.; Locals 235, 5, Hollywood, Calif.; Local 1346, Inglewood, Calif.; Local 256, Long Beach, Calif.; Locals 1065, 92, 1345, 1348, 51, 202, 1345, 51, 831, 792, 644, 511, 636, 1348, 1063, Los Angeles, Calif.; Local 92, Montrose, Calif.; Local 1147, Roseville, Calif.; Local 315, San Jose, Calif.; Local 821, Venice, Calif.; Local 441, Whittier, Calif.; Local 949, Wilmington, Calif.; Local, 930, Denver, Colo.; Local 190, Bridgeport, Conn.; Local 1276, Westport, Conn.; Local 368, Washington, D. C.; Local 1088, Dayton Beach, Fla.; Local 1321, Clearwater, Fla.; Local 1175, Coral Gables, Fla.; Local 193, Atlanta, Ga.; Local ——, Belleville, Ill.; Locals 637, 275, 194, 637, Chicago, Ill.; Local 863, Lake Forest, Ill.; Local 460, Hammond, Ill.; Local 1215, Boone, Iowa; Local 460, Hammond, Ind.; Local 277, Atlantic City, N. J.; Local 653, East Rutherford, N. J.; Local 997, 426, Haddon Heights, N. J.; Local 705, Irvington,

N. J.; Local 777, Newark, N. J.; Local 174, 140, Passaic, N. J.; Local 144, Perth Amboy, N. J.; Local 442, Brooklyn, N. Y.; Local 504, Flushing, Long Island, N. Y.; Local 822, Glen Cove, Long Island, N. Y.; Local 721, Islip, N. Y.
Local 498, Jamestown, N. Y.; Local 121, Long Island City, N. Y.; Locals 848, 892, 499, 997, 1101, 905, and 261, New York, N. Y.; Local 707, Oneida, N. Y.; Local 1035, Richmond Hill, Long Island, N. Y.; Local 795, Rockaway Beach, Long Island, N. Y.; Local 1134, Rockville Center, N. Y.; Local 229, Kansas City, Kans.; Local 1244, New Orleans, La.; Local 623, Chelsea, Mass.; Local 258, Boston, Mass.; Local 675, Dearborn, Mich.; Locals 42, 357, 591, 37, and 552, Detroit, Mich.; Local 9, Kansas City, Mo.; Local 386, Minneapolis, Minn.; Local 681, Rochester, Minn.; Local 540, Winona, Minn.; Local 720, Butte, Mont.; Local 260, Great Falls, Mont.; Locals 50, 308, and 866, Cincinnati, Ohio; Locals 765, 867, and 128, Cleveland, Ohio; Local 1103, Mentor, Ohio; Local 546, Toledo, Ohio; Local 443, Okmulgee, Okla.; Local 935, Tulsa, Okla.; Local 788, Sandusky, Ohio; Local 438, Steubenville, Ohio; Local 476, Youngstown, Ohio; Local 751, Gibsonia, Pa.; Local 380, Lancaster, Pa.; Local 887, Oil City, Pa.; Locals 21, 306, 997, 703, and 632, Philadelphia, Pa.; Locals 479, 282, 6, and 84, Pittsburgh, Pa.; Local 15, Central Falls, R. I.; Locals 195 and 692, Providence, R. I.; Local 586, Spartanburg, S. C.; Local 965, Jackson City, Tenn.; Local 123, Gilman, Vt.; Local 743, Olympia, Wash.; Local 1220, Tacoma, Wash.; Local 1114, Janesville, Wash.; Locals 201 and 300, Albany, N. Y.
Federal Labor Union, Local 19128, Lincoln, Nebr.
Federal Labor Radio Workers, Local 18832, Philadelphia, Pa.
Federal Labor, Local, Providence, R. I.
Midvale Steel Federal Union, Local, Philadelphia, Pa.
Federal Labor, 18546, Milwaukee, Wis.
Chemical Workers, 18634, Huntington, W. Va.
Casket Makers, 19306, Chicago, Ill.
United Association of Plasterers International Association of the United States and Canada, Local 343, Long Beach, Calif.; Local, 460, San Francisco, Calif.; Local 32, Denver, Colo.; Local, Bloomington, Ill.; Local, Omaha, Nebr.; Local 60, New York, N. Y.; Local 1, Cincinnati, Ohio; Local 7, Toledo, Ohio; Local 179, Youngstown, Ohio; Local 40, Providence, R. I.; Local 182, Franklin, Pa.; Local 31, Pittsburgh, Pa.; Local 746, Mount Vernon, Wash.; Local 77, Seattle, Wash.; Local 110, Great Falls, Mont.; Local 428, Racine, Wis.
Amalgamated Clothing Workers of America, Local 1, Boston Mass.; Local 4, New York, N. Y.; Local 75, Philadelphia, Pa.; Local 38, Chicago, Ill.; Joint Council, St. Louis, Mo.; Local 110, Philadelphia, Pa.
Retail Clerks' International Protective Association, Local 753, Philadelphia, Pa.
Retail Food and Employees Clerks, Local 770 of R. C. I. P. A., Los Angeles, Calif.
Cigarmakers' International Union of America, Local 225, Salt Lake City, Utah; Local 14, Chicago, Ill.
Coopers' International Union of North America, Local 9, Philadelphia, Pa.; Local 54, Detroit, Mich.
International Union of Operating Engineers, Local 835, Philadelphia, Pa.; Local 3, Brooklyn, N. Y.; Local 48, Los Angeles, Calif.; Local 5, Detroit, Mich.; Local 506, Philadelphia, Pa.; Local 37, Providence, R. I.
International Brotherhood of Electrical Workers of America, Local 83, Los Angeles, Calif.; Local 31, Brooklyn, N. Y.; Local 122, Great Falls, Mont.; Local 292, Minneapolis, Minn.; Local 623, New York, N. Y.; Local 58, Detroit, Mich.; Local 3, New York City, N. Y.
International Typographical Union, Local 231, San Jose, Calif.; Local 899, Whittier, Calif.; Local 221, San Diego, Calif.; Local 21, San Diego, Calif.; Local 491, Pocatello, Idaho; Local 241, Turvi Falls, Idaho; Local 330, Berwyn, Ill.; Local 215, Decatur, Ill.; Local 306, Alton, Ill.; Local 192, Cedar Rapids, Iowa; Local 590, Hobart, Ind.; Local 41, Atlanta, Ga.; Local 727, Hibbing, Minn.; Local 131, Elmhurst, Long Island, N. Y.; Local No. 6, New York, N. Y.; Local 499, Okmulgee, Okla.; Local 63, Toledo, Ohio; local, Cleveland, Ohio; Local 242, York, Pa.; Local 43, Charlestown, S. C.; Local 195, Paterson, N. J.; Daily News Chapel, New York, N. Y.; Local 10, Indianapolis, Ind.
Journeymen Tailors Union of America, local, Youngstown, Ohio; Local 46, Buffalo, N. Y.; Local 131, Pittsburgh, Pa.; Local 323, Bethlehem, Pa.; Local 106, Spokane, Wash.; Local 86, Milawukee, Wis.; Local 282, Green Bay, Wis.

United Textile Workers of America, Local 1733, Paterson, N. J.; Local 2030, Philadelphia, Pa.; Local 1789, Birmingham, Ala.; Local 1766, Birmingham, Ala.; Weavers Local, Fall River, Mass.; Local 2052, Union City, N. J.

International Brotherhood of Teamsters, Chauffeurs, Stablemen, and Helpers of America, Local 429, Reading, Pa.; local, Los Angeles, Calif.; local, Atlantic City, N. J.

International Association of Marble, Slate, and Stone Polishers, Rubbers and Sawyers, Tile and Marble Setters, Helpers, and Terrazzo Helpers, Local 62, Philadelphia, Pa.; Local 8, Providence, R. I.; Local 47, Milwaukee, Wis.

International Federation of Technical Engineers, Architects, and Craftsmen's Unions, Local 54, Milwaukee, Wis.

American Federation of Teachers, Local 256, Grand Rapids, Mich.; Local 194, Mena, Ark.; Local 340, Baltimore, Md.

Sheet Metal Workers' International Association, Local 2, Stockton, Calif.; Local 615, Buffalo, N. Y.; Local 137, New York, N. Y.; Local 329, Salisbury, N. C.; Local 37, Providence, R. I.; Local 446, Great Falls, Mont.

International Stereotypers' and Electrotypers' Union of North America, Local 8, East St. Louis, Ill.; Local 15, Dayton, Ohio.

Switchmen's Union of North America, Local 240, Libera, Kans.; Local 291, Paducah, Ky.

Simmons Bed Federated Union, Local 18456, Kenosha, Wis.

Journeymen Stonecutters' Association of North America, local, Akron, Ohio; local, Concord, N. H.

Suitcase Workers, Local 52, Philadelhia, Pa.

International Watch Makers of Jewelry Workers' Union, Local 21, New York, N. Y.; Local 421, New York, N. Y.

United Plush Weave Textile Workers of America, Local 471, Philadelphia, Pa.

United Association of Plumbers and Steam Fitters of the United States and Canada, Local 476, Providence, R. I.

International Brotherhood of Pulp, Sulphite, and Paper Mill Workers of the United States and Canada, Local 37, East Millinocket, Maine; Local 27, Woodland, Maine.

Metal Polishers International Union Local 6, Chicago, Ill.; Local 277, Chicago, Ill.

Brotherhood of Maintenance of Way Employees Local 1077, New York, N. Y.; Local, Sioux City, Iowa.

International Union of Mine, Mill, and Smelter Workers Local, Salt Lake City, Utah; Local 1635, Kansas City, Mo.

Operative Plasterers' International Association of the United States and Canada Local 65, Minneapolis, Minn.; Local 87, Montgomery, Ala.

Ornamental Structural Iron, Brass, Bronze, and Wire Workers Local 19103, Chicago, Ill.

International Union of Operating Engineers Local, Sioux City, Iowa.

International Union of North America Quarry Workers Local 82, Rockport, Mass.; Local 81, Lanesville, Mass.

International Association of Machinists Local 234, Milwaukee, Wis.; Local 915, Chicago, Ill.; Local 119, Newport, R. I.; Local 110, Newport, R. I.; Local 68, San Francisco, Calif.

United States Tile and Composition Roofers, Damp and Waterproof Workers' Association Local 4, Newark, N. J.; Local 80, Great Falls, Mont.

Order of Sleeping Car Conductors Local 15, Chicago, Ill.

Order of Railway Conductors of America Local 52, Port Jarvis, N. Y.; Division 1, Chicago, Ill.

Brotherhood of Railroad Trainmen Local, Milwaukee, Wis.

Brotherhood of Locomotive Engineers Local 405, Milwaukee, Wis.; Local 54, Milwaukee, Wis.

International Alliance of Theatrical Stage Employees and Moving Picture Machine Operators of the United States and Canada Local 130, Altoona, Pa.; Local 361, Kenosha, Wis.; Local 475, Eau Clair, Wis.; Local 598, Marion, Ohio; Local 644, New York, N. Y.; Local, Sioux City, Iowa; Local 306, New York, N. Y.; Local 223, Providence, R. I.

Motion Picture Projectionists 150, Los Angeles, Calif.

United Mine Workers of America Local 13, Des Moines, Iowa; Local, Shenandoah, Pa.; Local 1, Butte, Mont.; Local 5497, Powhatan, Ohio; Local, Six Mine Run, Pa.

Window Glass Cutters' League of America Local 528, New York, N. Y.

Flint Glass Workers Local 93, Chicago, Ill.

International Hod Carriers, Building and Common Laborers' Union of America Local, Belleville, Ill.; Local, Bridgeport, Conn.

United Textile Workers of America Local 1759, Philadelphia, Pa.; Local 2052, Union City, N. J.; Local 702, Philadelphia, Pa.; Local 1586, Philadelphia, Pa.; Local 1733, Paterson, N. J.; Local 2030, Philadelphia, Pa.; Local 2053, Philadelphia, Pa.; Local 471, Philadelphia, Pa.

Brass Bobbin Winders Local 14659, Philadelphia, Pa.

Upholsterers' International Union of North America Local 75, Baltimore, Md.; Local 77, Philadelphia, Pa.

Federal Labor (Vincent McCall) Local 18846, Kenosha, Wis.

International Wood Carvers' Association of North America Local, Philadelphia, Pa.; Local, New York, N. Y.

International Jewelry Workers' Union Local 421, New York, N. Y.; Local 87, Newark, N. J.; Local, New York City.

Hotel and Restaurant Employees and Beverage Dispensers' International Alliance Local 659, Dallas, Tex.

Asbestos Workers International Association of Heat and Frost Insulators Local 31, Providence, R. I.

Federal Labor Aeronautical Workers Local 18286, Buffalo, N. Y.

United Federal Labor Automobile Workers Local 18614, Cleveland, Ohio; Local 18677, Detroit, Mich.

Dental Laboratory Technicians Local 18405, St. Louis, Mo.

Amalgamated Association of Iron, Steel, and Tin Workers Local 149, Clairton, Pa.; Local Sparrows Point, Md.; Local 37, Providence, R. I.; Local, Ellwood City, Pa.; Local 410, Great Falls, Mont.; Local 184, Sioux City, Iowa; Local 1, Follassbee, W. Va.; Local 709, New Britain, Conn.; Local 169, Pa.; Local 195, Ellwood City, Pa.; Local 162, Versailles, Pa.

International Union of Wood, Wire, and Metal Lathers Local 305, Great Falls, Mont.; Local 113, Sioux Falls, Iowa; Local 455, Lake Worth, Fla.

United Leather Workers International Union Local, New York, N. Y.; Local, Chelsea, Mass.

Laundry Workers' International Union Local 108, St. Louis, Mo.

Brotherhood of Locomotive Firemen and Engineers Local 13, Jersey City, N. J.; Local 183, Cleveland, Ohio; Local, Montevideo, Minn.; Local 1, Port Jervis, N. Y.

Lithographers' International Protective and Beneficial Association of the United States and Canada Local 5, St. Louis, Mo.

Building Service Employes' International Union Local 1077, New York, N. Y.; Local 125, Providence, R. I.

Bricklayers, Masons, and Plasterers International Union of America Local 8, Milwaukee, Wis.; Local 19, St. Louis, Mo.; Local 3, Philadelphia, Pa.

Automobile Mechanics Lodge Local 447, New York, N. Y.

International Union of Teamsters and Dairy Drivers Local, Birmingham, Ala.

Hobson Walker Brickyard Federation Local 18434, Bessemer, Ala.

Alabama Clay Products Co. Federation Local 18435, Bessemer, Ala.

Cooks Union Local 44, San Francisco, Calif.

Cabinet Makers Local, Belleville, Ill.

Cement Finishers Local, Belleville, Ill.

Metal Polishers Union Locals 6 and 277, Chicago, Ill.

Mailers Union 10, Indianapolis, Ind.

Patternmakers Association, Detroit, Mich.

Package Freight Handlers Union, Duluth, Minn.

Millmens Local 1635, Kansas City, Mo.

Flour and Cereal Workers of America Local 19253, Great Falls, Mont.

Mr. WEINSTOCK. Mr. Chairman, I had occasion to visit the executive council of the American Federation of Labor twice on this subject. I visited them a year ago with a delegation of about 25 people, and when we confronted the executive council with the bill they had no excuse, but instead of putting up an argument against the bill they said the executive council would consider the workers' unemployment-insurance bill and inform us later of their decision. They have never informed us.

Again, during the unemployment congress in January we had a delegation of people who went up to the executive council of the American Federation of Labor, but the legislative agent, whose name, I believe, was Mr. Roberts, listened for about 2 hours or more to about seven or eight representatives of various organizations on this workers' unemployment-insurance bill, who asked that it be endorsed by the executive council. The gentleman was unable to answer a single question put to him, and his only statement was, " I will bring the whole statement and the bill to the next meeting of the executive council, and the executive council will decide." The executive council is in session right now, and our members of the various organizations will go up again and see Mr. Green to find out what is their decision.

Every indication points to the workers' bill as the bill which the membership in the American Federation of Labor organizations want, as the only measure which can answer their immediate needs.

The question of authority I wish to raise here, because it was raised at other committee hearings; that is, whether the rank and file in the American Federation of Labor must be represented by international officials or whether they can be represented by rank-and-file delegates, which was raised previously by some Congressmen, becomes to me only an academic question.

If we wish to go into details and examine the authority and rights of certain international presidents and of some of the members of the executive council of the American Federation of Labor, we will find that their authority to speak in the name of the membership exists only on paper. Actually these officials have very little connections with the members of the organizations which they are supposed to represent. I also wish to point out that, although the constitution of these American Federation of Labor organizations calls for conventions of the internationals to be held every 2 years, and some every 4 years, the officials of many of the internationals have completely ignored this part of the constitution and have failed to call conventions and postponed them for an indefinite period. The membership is thus given no opportunity to express its opinion or grievances. Very often we find that repressive measures are taken against the rank-and-file members in the local unions who are dissatisfied with such practices. When members of local unions protest against the undemocratic methods used by some of the international officials, instead of attempting to remedy the evil they institute a reign of terror and expulsions against individual members and whole locals by revocation of their charters.

This is by no means a criticism against our organization as a whole. The rank and file in the organization will remedy this situation without any outside interference. I have raised this point for the sake of answering the doubting Thomases, who cannot conceive of the idea that labor can represent itself rather than be represented by some self-appointed politicians, as is usually the case.

In conclusion, I wish to emphasize that the executive council of the American Federation of Labor, due to its zigzag policies, is now faced with a very serious situation. Their opposition to a genuine unemployment-insurance system, their approval of all kinds of schemes which would not benefit the workers, have created a real gap between the membership and leadership of the American Federation of Labor.

The rank and file very often have had to take matters into their own hands in order to correct and remedy the situation they faced. The general strike in San Francisco was a warning to the executive council and to the employers, and it demonstrated that the workers will not stand by passively and permit their standards of living to be lowered, their wages cut, and conditions reduced. The general strike in textile and hundreds of other strikes, none of them approved or endorsed by the executive council or by the international officials, indicates the brewing revolt of the membership and the deep dissatisfaction with the present administration and with the policies of the N. R. A.

The recent extension of the auto code and the dissatisfaction among the auto workers is enough proof of the coming struggles in the industry. The opposition to the Winant report in the textile industry indicates that a larger strike is looming than ever the last one. The public works appropriation bill passed by the House with the indication that a maximum of $50 will be the monthly wage on these projects has resulted in a Nation-wide protest. The building-trades workers especially, whose weekly earnings when employed amount to $50 per week, have been greatly aroused against this proposal. This is an open invitation to the employers in the industry to cut down the wages and to force down the living standard of the building-trades workers to that of a starvation level.

The general dissatisfaction with the steel labor board also points to the fact that the steel workers will have to take the path of struggle.

In all these industries we find that the rank and file are going over the heads of the executive council of the American Federation of Labor. We are warning the administration, as well as the executive council, that the rank-and-file workers in the American Federation of Labor are ready to struggle for improving their working conditions, as they have demonstrated again and again, for higher wages and for uniting with all other working-class organizations, social, and fraternal organizations, in the fight for a genuine unemployment-insurance system as embodied in H. R. 2827.

After 6 years of unemployment, misery, and starvation, the workers in this country will not stand idly by while their children and their families are starving. Organized labor has other means besides petitioning Congress or State legislatures to force the administration to adopt an adequate system of social and unemployment insurance. This is not a threat, but it is a warning. We are tired of waiting and are fed up with promises. The responsibility rests upon the administration and upon the owners of wealth and industry. Labor will not starve. We will fight. Organized labor will join together with the millions of unorganized, with the impoverished farmers, with white-collar workers, and all others who believe in the right to live like decent human beings.

We earnestly request the Subcommittee on Labor to bring a favorable report to the Congress and to impress upon the other Members of the Congress the need for passing this measure. Thank you, Mr. Chairman.

Mr. DUNN. Thank you for your intelligent discussion.

Mr. LUNDEEN. Reference has been made to a letter which was sent by the officials of the American Federation of Labor in opposition to the Lundeen bill. I would like to have that in the record, to show the American Federation of Labor's complete record and attitude toward the bill, whether they are opposed to it or whether they are for it. Do I understand from you that their attitude in the letter referred to is one of hostility?

Mr. WEINSTOCK. Yes; that is true.

Mr. LUNDEEN. We want to know just what the letter states. As I remember it, from the previous statement here, it was to the effect that the Lundeen bill was unconstitutional, and also I believe the term "communistic" was used in connection with this bill.

Mr. WEINSTOCK. Something like that.

Mr. LUNDEEN. I am not sure about that, but if it is an attitude of hostility or of opposition or of "sabotage", or whatever you might call it, I would like to know it.

Mr. WEINSTOCK. The letter is self-explanatory, and as soon as I can get it here, I will supply it for the record. I will mail it.

Mr. LUNDEEN. In other words, I would like to have the record show the complete attitude of the American Federation of Labor, before 1931 as well as after that time, and when the change was made, what bill they endorsed, and their present attitude. Then we will have the whole story.

Mr. WEINSTOCK. Congressman Lundeen, I do not know how much space you have, but, if you are interested, I have here records of the American Federation of Labor conventions consecutively from 1913 to 1934 dealing with nothing else but social and unemployment insurance. These are quotations from the proceedings of the conventions.

Mr. LUNDEEN. You have checked those quotations and you know them to be correct?

Mr. WEINSTOCK. They have been checked. They are from the proceedings. For example, it is cited in this matter, "Proceedings, 1922, pages 72-78." These are all correct quotations.

Mr. LUNDEEN. Mr. Chairman, do you not think those should be included in the record? That is the largest labor organization in the country. Let us find out where they stand on this thing.

Mr. DUNN. As far as I am concerned, these witnesses can put everything they have in the record.

Mr. LUNDEEN. How many pages are there?

Mr. WEINSTOCK. Perhaps you would want to take it only from 1930 to 1934. That would reduce it considerably. It would mean only about 5 or 6 pages, but here you will have the exact statements made by the various committees.

Mr. LUNDEEN. I would like to have it in the record in a way that will make a fair presentation of their attitude. I know you would do that. I do not want a biased presentation. I want a correct one.

Mr. WEINSTOCK. This statement was prepared by a research association and checked, every single statement.

Mr. LUNDEEN. What I mean is if you were to take out some of them and leave others, would that present a complete picture?

Mr. WEINSTOCK. No. This begins with 1913, so, instead of beginning with 1913, we would begin at 1929.

Mr. LUNDEEN. Mr. Chairman, these quotations do not take up very much space in the record and I would like to have them all in the record.

310   UNEMPLOYMENT, OLD AGE, AND SOCIAL INSURANCE

Mr. Dunn. You want them in the record, Mr. Lundeen?
Mr. Lundeen. Yes. They will not take up very much space.
Mr. Dunn. All right. We will place them in the record.
(The excerpts from convention proceedings of the American Federation of Labor, presented by the witness, are as follows:)

AMERICAN FEDERATION OF LABOR SOCIAL SECURITY COMMITMENTS, 1904–34

Presidents of American Federation of Labor; Samuel Gompers, 1904–25;
William Green, 1926–

PROCEEDINGS, 1904–5

Resolution no. 130, proceedings 1904–5, page 156, by Delegate Victor L. Berger,
International Typographical Union

Whereas the present insurance system is notorious as a method of exploitation and graft and has simply become an adjunct to Wall Street, New York, and

Whereas in spite of the tremendous wealth being accumulated by insurance corporations, the life and property of wage workers finds little or no protection in insurance. It is now exceedingly costly and the workmen are often, by all kinds of legal tricks, defrauded by insurance companies: Therefore be it

Resolved, That the twenty-fifth convention of the American Federation of Labor endorse the general principle of State insurance now in operation in Germany, in which the expense is met by the Government, the employer, and the working people, each paying one-third of the premiums; * * *

(Advocates the adoption of such a plan— "only on a much larger and more effective scale—for the United States of America." Referred to committee on resolutions.)

Committee report on Resolution No. 130, proceedings 1904–5, pages 179–80

The committee recommended that last two "resolves" be stricken out and following substituted:

"*Resolved*, That in accordance with same, and as the recent investigations have shown unparalleled corruption and mismanagement of insurance companies, we endorse the principle of Government insurance of a voluntary nature, and that our executive council be authorized to favor legislation to that end."

Treasurer Lennon offered a substitute for the report asking that the principle of insurance by trade unions for the working people of this country be adopted.

The report of the committee was accepted.

NOTE.—Rejects trade-union plan.

PROCEEDINGS, 1906

For compulsory life and other insurance by the State. Report November 12 to
24, 1906, page 117, Resolution No. 58

After declaring that the wage workers receive scant protection, the following resolve was made:

"*Resolved*, That we demand that some plan of compulsory life and other insurance be enacted, either by the States or by the Nation, in such a manner as to give adequate security to the toiling masses of the people."

Referred to committee.

NOTE.—Made by Victor L. Berger—left indefinite as to type of form.

Committee recommended nonconcurrence to Resolution 58, page 160.

Old-age pension report.   November 12 to 24, 1906, page 148, Resolution No. 132, by Victor L. Berger

Whereas labor creates all values and makes them useful and accessible to mankind, but the present economic system is such that it is impossible for great mass of wage earners to save up a sufficient amount of money or property to secure them against want and misery, and indignities of capitalistic charity in their old age; and

Whereas it is the prime object of the trade-union movement to improve and elevate the standard of living of the working class everywhere, and in every possible way: Therefore be it

Resolved, That the executive council of the American Federation of Labor be instructed to use its best efforts to induce the Congress of the United States to pass a bill which will secure to every wage worker in the United States who has earned no more than $1,000 average wages per year, a pension of not less than $12 per month at the age of 60, and thereafter for the rest of his or her natural life: *Provided, however,* That such wage earner is a citizen of the United States, and has lived in this country for at least 21 years continuously at the time application is made.

Referred to the committee on resolutions. Rejected after long discourse by Berger, page 235.

PROCEEDINGS, 1907

Compulsory insurance for workers by the States or Nation.   Report, 1907, pages 167–168, Resolution No. 131

Proposing that the convention favor some plan of compulsory life and other insurance for workers by States or Nation.

The committee concurred in the resolution. It was adopted by the convention, pages 333–334.

Old-age pension.   Report, 1907, page 158, resolution 104 by Victor L. Berger

Resolution asking that convention favor old-age pensions. (Same as resolution 132, p. 148, in 1906 convention.)

The resolution was again rejected. However, after considerable discussion the following action was adopted by the convention:

"Delegate Kennedy (W. E.) moved as an amendment that the entire subject matter be referred to the executive council, with instructions to investigate and report to the next convention."

PROCEEDINGS, 1908

Old-age pension.   Report, 1908, pages 99–102

In accordance with resolution no. 104 of the convention at Norfolk in 1907, President Gompers made a summary report of the administration of old-age pension in the following countries: Austria, Belgium, Denmark, Iceland, France, Germany, New Zealand, New South Wales, Victoria, and England.

Mr. Gompers believed that it would be quite some time before old-age pension can even get a hearing in the United States. Such questions as that of Federal and State jurisdiction would have to be settled before any progress could be made on the problem. Further, some definite understanding of what constitutes "bad conduct" would have to be defined. (In most countries persons are disqualified from receiving aid when found guilty of "bad conduct.")

Old-age pension.   Report, 1908, page 260

The resolution committee after reviewing the reports of the president and the executive council made the following recommendation on old-age pension:

"We would therefore recommend that the executive council be authorized to secure the assistance of such competent legal advice as will enable them to prepare the draft of a bill providing for old-age pensions, and that such bill be introduced either in the legislatures of the States or in Congress, their action in this being governed by their decision as to whether this legislation is to be most readily secured and applied through the individual action of the several States or by Federal legislation, or by both."

On motion, the convention adopted the report.

PROCEEDINGS, 1909

Old-age pension. Report, 1909, pages 97–101. "The old-age home guard of the United States Army"

A proposed draft of a bill on old-age pension drawn up by order of the convention of 1908. Among other things, it provided that—

An old-age home guard of the United States Army shall be composed of persons not less than 65 years of age. The pay would be $120 per annum, with reductions for persons having property in excess of $300.

A brief in support of the proposed bill was presented—both were drawn by Congressman W. B. Wilson from Pennsylvania.

The bill was approved as submitted on motion of the resolution committee. (Text, pp. 330–331.)

PROCEEDINGS, 1910

Old-age pension. Resolution no. 34 by E. William Carr. Report, 1910, pages 157–158

Resolution proposing that old-age pension be extended to all citizens 60 years or over who would receive $30 per month from the Government.

The committee recommended nonconcurrence in the resolution, at the same time reaffirming the action on the subject the year before in Toronto.

Committee's report was adopted.

PROCEEDINGS, 1911

Old-age pension. Report, 1911, pages 268–269, resolutions 2, 4, and 57

No. 4 contained the endorsement of the Massachusetts State branch of the American Federation of Labor on old-age pension.

Nos. 2 and 57 referred to pensions for Federal employees. All were referred to the executive council.

PROCEEDINGS, 1912

Old-age pension. Report, 1912, pages 52 and 347

On the question of old-age pension, the following report was adopted:

"We reaffirm our former action on this question and regret that no further progress has been made than as indicated by the report.

"We recommend that the efforts for the establishment of a general old-age pension be continued."

PROCEEDINGS, 1913

Industrial insurance by unions. Report, 1913, pages 251–252

After noting the progress of industrial insurance in other countries, Resolution No. 162 provided that—

"Whereas we, as heretofore, are now in favor of all national and international unions paying strike, unemployment, old-age, partial disability, sick, and death, and other benefits:

"*Resolved,* That the executive council of the American Federation of Labor make an exhaustive investigation and study and report to the next convention."

It was also suggested that the American Federation of Labor consider the advisability of establishing an insurance department.

Referred to committee on education.

Federal pension. Report, 1913, page 259

Resolution favoring pension for civil-service employees adopted.

Old-age pensions. Report of proceedings, 1914, pages 87–88

After referring to a number of old-age pension bills which had been introduced into Congress, the executive council recommended that a general campaign of education in behalf of an old-age pension law would meet with a general response by the people.

The recommendation was adopted by the convention, page 327.

Union social insurance. Pages 219–224

Charts showing the cost of social insurance to the international unions for 5 years, included in report of the executive council for 1914 on social insurance.

Union social insurance. Pages 66–68

Report of the executive council on the question of social insurance made in accordance with resolutions (nos. 44 and 162) which authorized an exhaustive investigation and study of the whole problem.

The council reported that the scope of the resolution required a force of experts far beyond the means of the federation, although it endorsed the general principle of the resolution.

Report of committee on report of executive council recommended that the council continue its study so that the federation would be able to decide on a definite policy, page 361.

Old-age pension for Government employees. Proceedings, 1915, page 111

A number of conferences have been held on old-age pensions for government employees. However, the employees differ greatly on plans and method, thus not much progress has been made.

*   *   *   *   *   *   *

Progress reported in 1916 convention. See proceedings, 1916, page 265.

*   *   *   *   *   *   *

1917 proceedings carries note that no plan suggested to date has met with the full approval of all the employees, pages 116–117.

Social insurance. Proceedings, 1915, page 164

The executive council reports that among the subjects upon which no substantial progress can be reported are: Social insurance and the world congress of unemployment.

Old-age pension. Proceedings, 1916, pages 295–296

After reviewing the general problem of old age, the following resolution was made, Resolution No. 25:

Resolved, That the executive council of the American Federation of Labor is hereby instructed to present to the thirty-seventh annual convention of this body a review of the old-age pension systems of Great Britain and Germany, together with such other information on this subject as may be helpful in determining the action necessary and desirable in forming suitable legislation looking to the establishment of a universal old-age pension system by the Government of the United States of America. Resolution committee reported that the war made compliance with the resolution almost impossible. However, it recommended that the matter be left to the executive council. Report adopted.

PROCEEDINGS, 1918

Health insurance—Insurance against unemployment. Proceedings, 1918, pages 282–283

Resolution 101 viewed with alarm the " great efforts " which have been made to obtain the approval and support of organized labor to a scheme for social health insurance by persons outside the labor movement. It resolved among other things that " the executive council are hereby instructed to make an immediate investigation of this question and to point out its dangers or benefits with their recommendations thereon as soon as possible, * * * ascertain. if possible, what are the financial resources of the persons and organizations promoting this scheme and what relation they may have with those interests who are opposed to the best interests of the labor movement. * * * "

Resolution No. 135, introduced by members of the International Ladies' Garment Workers' Union, advocated the adoption by the Government of a comprehensive national system of social insurance. Resolution No. 135 was defeated. No. 101 accepted and a special committee was appointed.

PROCEEDINGS, 1919

Health insurance. Proceedings, 1919, pages 378–379

"It must be apparent to all who have given this subject serious attention that it is one possessed of great good and at the same time fraught with much danger. Your committee regrets that time did not permit the executive council to give this subject that consideration so essential to a fair and intelligent determination of the principles involved, as well as to the methods of application and procedure necessarily entailed. Because of the importance of this subject, and by reason of the vast consequences involved, your committee recommends concurrence in the request for further investigation and consideration of this matter by the executive council. * * * "

NOTE.—Final action was to be taken at the next convention.

Report of committee unanimously adopted.

Maternity aid. Page 439

Resolution No. 89, directing Federal cooperation with the States in providing funds for necessary medical and nursing care, was adopted.

PROCEEDINGS, 1920

Health insurance. Proceedings 1920, page 176

" The executive council finds itself unable to reach a unanimous agreement upon the subject of voluntary health insurance and trade-union health insurance on the one hand as against compulsory State or industrial health insurance on the other. Therefore, because of our inability to agree, we recommend to the convention that the entire subject matter be referred to a committee to be selected by the executive council.

The recommendation was approved, page 387.

PROCEEDINGS, 1921

Health insurance. Proceedings, 1921, pages 310–311

The executive council announced the appointment of a special committee to study health insurance under the authorization given by the Montreal convention. The committee is requested to make its report in full at the next convention.

PROCEEDINGS, 1922

Old-age pension. Proceedings, 1922, page 472

Resolution No. 19, asking that "The American Federation of Labor endorse the old-age pension system of providing for those who have grown old in honest toil without being able to lay by for themselves" was referred to the executive council to take whatever action possible, page 272.

Old age. Proceedings, 1922, pages 141–144

By action of the Denver convention, the proposal to have introduced into the Congress of the United States a bill for the payment of old-age pensions in the interest of and embracing all the citizens of the United States, was referred to the executive council for investigation and such action as might be deemed proper and necessary. The principle of the bill advocating the establishment of an "old-age home guard of the United States Army" is again reaffirmed and suggest that this bill be introduced in the next Congress.

This report was approved by the convention, page 360.

Unemployment. Proceedings, 1922, pages 72–78

The committee on unemployment authorized by the Denver convention was appointed after the President's conference on unemployment. After reviewing the work of the conference, the committee recommended that findings of the conference be approved along with the following procedure:

1. That the president of the American Federation of Labor arrange for the continuous study of the unemployment problem either through a committee or a designated agency or executive secretary.

2. That this official agency made continuously available to trade unions information that concerns regularization of industry and that relations be established so far as practicable with studies and efforts to develop such information.

3. That the labor movement make special effort to secure the enactment of legislation providing for an adequate Federal employment service and for the extension of public credit for the purpose above enumerated.

This report was adopted, page 263.

PROCEEDINGS, 1923

Unemployment—The Business Cycle and Unemployment. Pages 40–42

The business cycle is a constant recurrence of irregularly separated booms and slumps. Organized labor was in hearty accord with the findings of the Unemployment Conference in 1921, which placed squarely upon industries the responsibility of eliminating preventable unemployment.

"That disastrous slumps in American business are not unavoidable, and that they man in a measure be prevented or at least discounted by prudent timely foresight during periods of expansion, was the conclusion reached by the Committee on Unemployment and Business Cycles, appointed by Secretary of Commerce, H. Hoover."

The general recommendation of these conferences approved and—

"In addition we have no hesitancy in emphasizing the fact that the most potential factor against unemployment is the resistance against wage reduction."

Unanimously adopted by the convention, page 208.

PROCEEDINGS, 1924

Old Age. Resolution No. 15. Pages 293–294

" Whereas individual workers suffer from many ills during the active period of their lives which quickly sap their vitality and render them physically unfit at a comparatively early age to earn a livelihood for their families and themselves. * * *

" Whereas this is an intolerable situation and a disgrace to our boasted civilization, and we are unworthy if, in the name of humanity, we are unable in this enlightened age to correct this grievous wrong * * *."

The resolution committee revised the whole resolution leaving all of the " whereas " out and changing the wording of the " resolves " to a much milder tone.

The substituted proposal was adopted.

Insurance. Proceedings, 1924. Pages 266–268

The Portland convention of the American Federation of Labor, 1923, adopted a resolution, no. 83, authorizing the President of the American Federation of Labor to investigate or cause to be investigated the amount and kind of death benefit insurance paid by national and international unions, group insurance, and other forms of insurance.

The income and the administration of American insurance companies were examined. Special attention was given to the report of Mr. Nesbit and that of Mr. L. D. Wood. Both were favored by the committee, which concluded with the following statement:

" Your committee makes no definite recommendations as to the form our insurance enterprise shall assume. We have been convinced and fully persuaded that it is not only advisable and safe but almost the duty of the unions jointly to adopt some form of proper insurance. However, we are opposed to have the American Federation of Labor as such actually engage in the insurance business."

Report of the committee was adopted, pages 266–268.

NOTE.—Vice President Green was very skeptical about the whole thing.

Old Age. Proceedings, 1924. Pages 33–34 (from executive council report)

" The old-age pension in principle attempts to do the same thing as the policies insurance companies are writing for " assured " incomes. In essence, all forms of life insurance are a method of prolonging the income-producing capacity of the individual—whether during old age or after death.

" * * * We, therefore, deem it advisable that the problem of old-age pension be made part of the larger problem of labor insurance, upon which initial report is made to this convention. In order to give unity to our determination of policies it is necessary that we first decide upon the fundamental issue and make decisions upon related problems harmonize with our general plan of procedure * * *."

The view expressed in the report was accepted by the convention, page 251.

PROCEEDINGS, 1925

Unemployment benefits and old-age pensions. Proceedings, 1925, page 260

The executive council reports that "A considerable amount of information upon these important subjects has been secured and will be compiled and published at the earliest possible date."

Unanimously adopted by the convention.

PROCEEDINGS, 1926

Mothers' pension plan. Proceedings, 1926, page 66

" This act appropriates a sum of $100,000 to be used to provide home care for dependent children in the District of Columbia. The Commissioners of the District are authorized to appoint a supervisor to administer the act."

Unanimously approved, page 212.

Mothers' pensions. Report on States legislation, proceedings, 1927, page 77

Illinois—Mothers' pensions were increased; pension laws for policemen, library employees, teachers, and other county employees were amended beneficially.

Maryland—Enacted old-age pension law.

Old age. Proceedings, 1927, pages 258–260

Resolution no. 14. After a series of whereas it was resolved:

" * * * We direct the executive council to make, cause to be made, or support, if conducted by other competent authority, public or private, a thorough investigation and study for the establishment of an American system of invalidity and old-age pensions, to assist in the preparation of suitable legislation for the accomplishment of such purpose, and to promote its enactment by the creation and development of an earnest and enduring public opinion in favor thereof, to the end that the poorhouse may be abolished as an American institution and there be provided in its stead a system founded upon a higher conception of public welfare and regard for human and social progress."

Resolution no. 97 embodied the same scheme. Both resolutions were recommended to be referred to the executive council. Report of the committee unanimously adopted.

Old age. Proceedings, 1928, pages 96–107

Under the caption "Old-age pension" (pp. 96–107) the executive council presents the results of a comprehensive study which the council has made on the subject of old-age pensions. It is pointed out that old-age pension bills have been passed by the legislatures of 11 States and 1 Territory. In 2 States the acts were declared unconstitutional, and in 3 States were vetoed by the Governors, thus leaving the laws on the statute books at present in 6 States and in the Territory of Alaska. In 18 other States, during the past 10 years, the report says, commissions have been appointed to study old-age dependency, poor relief, and, in most cases, old-age pensions. Canada has enacted old-age pension legislation.

The report of the committee on the executive council report was adopted unanimously, pages 249–250.

Old age. Proceedings, 1929, pages 257–263

The executive council made the following recommendations on old-age pension:

1. That laws be enacted requiring a pension commission for every county, pensions to be at least $300 annually, and that 65 be set as the age for applicants.

2. That a model compulsory old-age pension bill be drafted by the Federation and recommended to State federations of labor, and that an active campaign be inaugurated for the enactment of such laws in every State.

3. That the general problem of old-age retirement for employees in private industry be given careful study, and that an effort be made to secure the counsel and cooperation of sympathetic individuals and groups in an effort to work out constructive plans on this subject during the coming year.

Original report on pages 48–57.

A debate followed recommendations—finally adopted by the convention.

Old age. Proceedings, 1929, pages 258–263. Debate on question

Delegate FREY. I am not in accord with the recommendations made on old-age pension. (See summary of executive council report, 1929, pp. 257–263.)

The most important thing which the American trade unions " can do is to center all of their efforts upon one thing—the establishing of our rights so that our trade unions can function as successfully as a trade association can function." * * *

* * * * * * *

President GREEN. And you are opposed to old-age pension legislation?
Delegate FREY. At this time, sir, I am.

* * * * * * *

Vice President Woll, Delegates Walker, Madsen, and Olander agreed and defended the report of the council.
Delegate Furuseth supported the position taken by Frey. Olander agreed that the " injunction " was perhaps most important.
The report of the committee was adopted.

Old age. Proceedings, 1929, page 264

Resolution No. 3, urging State federations of labor to use all possible efforts to cooperate with all other agencies or fraternal organizations not having old-age pensions to work for its enactment, " with compulsory provisions that will not leave its application optional with boards of county commissioners " * * * in any State.

PROCEEDINGS, 1930

Unemployment insurance. Remarks of Delegate Zuritsky during debate on resolutions favoring unemployment insurance which had been attacked. Proceedings, 1930, pages 317–319

" * * * Today, when a cap maker is out of work, he receives unemployment insurance, not a dole, to the amount of $13 a week from his own organization, but the contributions come from the employers direct." * * *
" I propose that we do not lay it at the door of industry, but make industry accept it. Industry alone is responsible for the curse of unemployment, and if in England the unemployment worker has to contribute one-third toward this fund, the American worker contributes 100 percent toward it. Today the burden of unemployment in America is entirely upon the shoulders of the unemployed workers, and in England only one-third of the burden is on them. I prefer that system to the system of irresponsible starvation of the unemployed workers in this country."

Unemployment insurance. Proceedings, 1930, pages 371–398

The committee on resolutions recommended no concurrence with the following resolves :
Resolution No. 32. * * * " Resolved, That this convention of the American Federation of Labor go on record as favoring a system of unemployment insurance, inaugurated and controlled by the States and subsidized by the Federal Government."
Resolution No. 43, favoring the unemployment insurance bill introduced by Senator Wagner.
Resolution No. 72. * * * Resolved by the Fifty-first Convention of the American Federation of Labor that we record ourselves as favoring a system of Federal unemployment insurance * * *."
NOTE.—These resolutions started a debate which lasted for almost two sessions. The report of the committee was adopted.

Unemployment insurance. Proceedings, 1930, pages 309–319

A series of resolutions were presented on unemployment. Resolutions nos. 16, 51, 76, and 92 favored unemployment insurance ; resolution no 17 favored unemployment and social insurance ; and resolution no. 32 proposed that the American Federation of Labor should study remedial legislation to relieve unemployment.
A stiff debate followed the report of the resolution committee recommending that all of the resolutions be referred to the executive council.
The report was adopted.

Unemployment insurance. Remarks of Delegate Ohl after resolution committee had made a bitter attack on a series of resolutions proposing unemployment insurance. Proceedings, 1930, pages 312–313

" I do not oppose the committee's report referring these resolutions and the
subject matter to the executive council. I do not, however, agree with all that
has been said on the question of unemployment compensation by the committee. * * * I say that a fund to compensate the unemployed because of their
unemployment is not in all cases a dole, any more than the payment of a stipulated sum to those who become old in industry is a dole."

Unemployment insurance. Remarks of Delegate Slavens after resolution committee had attacked a series of resolutions on unemployment insurance.
Proceedings, 1930, pages 313–314

" I cannot seem to agree with the recommendation of the committee. In fact,
I am greatly disappointed in it. This recommendation will undoubtedly be interpreted as placing the American Federation of Labor against unemployment
insurance. It will greatly retard the work of the State federations that have
already gone on record for the adoption of unemployment insurance."
Rhode Island labor had two objects for their resolution:
1. Convention to add the principle of unemployment insurance to other schemes
proposed. 2. Hope that from the delegates assembled ideas would come which
would make unemployment insurance sounder for good of all. * * * "I go
into the mill villages, only a stone's throw from Newport, and see the misery
which is driving our mill workers to desperation. I know if those people who
live in Newport, who live in luxury on Bellevue Avenue—leaders of industry
want to protect their wealth—must realize that we live in a new age and that
poverty and starvation must be abolished."

Unemployment insurance. The attitude of the resolution committee, which
considered a number of resolutions on the subject. Proceedings, 1930, pages
311–312

" Every system of unemployment insurance advanced here contemplates supervision and control by both Federal and State Governments and will require
registration not only of the aliens among the workers but of all workers.
* * * Shall we discard the system under which we move freely from one end
of our great country to the other, crossing State lines, stopping where we please,
leaving when we choose, living where we will, without ever undergoing the
scrutiny of a Government official or reporting to Government officers? * * *
"Are we to join in the fallacious argument now being offered in some quarters
that the laws proposed for unemployment insurance are on a par with workmen's compensation acts? Is it not true that unemployment schemes of the sort
advocated in the resolutions before this convention will tend to prevent the
workers from joining in movements to increase wages * * * ? "
Report of the committee was adopted.

Old age. From executive council report. Proceedings, 1930, pages 115–116

"Agitation for the protection of those who are unable to take care of themselves after they have reached the retirement age spread throughout the Nation
during the past year. The demand for old-age security reached Congress and
for the first time in the history of that body an extensive hearing was held at
the request of the American Federation of Labor on the question of old-age
pensions.
" Experts from many organizations appeared and gave conclusive evidence
that those who are unable to care for themselves after reaching old age should
be protected. Already 10 States and 1 Territory have enacted old-age pension
laws, but none of them is of such a practical character that the American
Federation of Labor can unequivocally endorse them as model laws. The States
leave it to the counties to determine whether they shall pay the pension provided for in the acts, and many of the counties take no action." Federal aid
was advocated. American Federation of Labor will draft a bill.

Unemployment-insurance remarks of President Green during debate over report of the resolution committee, which attacked a series of resolutions on unemployment insurance. (Several members had opposed the report.) Proceedings, 1930, pages 314–317

" Some are sponsoring a more ambitious program than that of England, who has had unemployment insurance for a quarter of a century.

" If I believed that we could require industry to care for the idle worker, perhaps I would be for it. I am not sure that I would be for it, if I thought such a thing was possible; but I am talking to hard-headed men. I am hard headed myself, and I am not going to appeal to their passions; I am going to talk to them in practical terms. * * *

" No man is touched by human suffering more than I am. This tragedy of unemployment stalking throughout the land must touch the heart of every worker; but, if we are to find a remedy, if we are to provide help, let us do it in a way so that the one we help may maintaing his manhood and self-respect."

Unemployment. From remarks of President Green. Proceedings, 1930, page 308

" The Chair desires to just make a brief statement. * * * Unemployment is the outstanding economic fact at the present time. To me it is a tragedy. The suffering and distress which follow unemployment are in a way indescribable. * * *

" I believe there is a remedy for unemployment, and I believe we can seek and apply that remedy if the people of the country will become sufficiently aroused so that they will demand that industry itself shall put its house in order and it shall discontinue these periodic conditions in the cycle of employment. * * *

" I maintain that it is a reflection upon our civilization to have here in America 3,000,000 people unemployed seeking work and wanting work. It is indefensible, it is economically wrong, it is morally wrong, socially it is a disgrace, and the American Federation of Labor must press forward until we find a solution."

Maternity and infancy. Proceedings, 1930, page 105. From executive council report

" The maternity and infancy act came to an end June 30, 1929. Before that time, however, bills were introduced to extend the life of the law. In December 1929, President Hoover made a recommendation that the maternity and infancy act be restored, but that part of its provisions come under the control and supervision of the Public Health Service. Bills to that effect were reported in February 1930, but there was such opposition that nothing was done. It was contended that maternity and infancy laws should be administered by the Children's Bureau of the Department of Labor."

Note.—Indicates how often social necessities are sidetracked.

PROCEEDINGS, 1931

Unemployment insurance—debate. Proceedings, 1931, pages 374–393

Chairman Woll reading from a statement submitted to the royal commission of unemployment insurance by the Trade Union Congress and General Council. Chairman Woll attempted to show that the proposals before the convention were " doles " and not what should be called " unemployment insurance." " It is true we have a body here and there that has declared in favor of unemployment insurance. That does not say they have given the thoughtful study and consideration required before taking our Nation into an adventure of this kind. I think we should be commended for pointing out the dangerous features of a system of this kind."

Pages 372–398: Delegate Duncan, Seattle * * * " You did not hear the British fraternal delegates referring to unemployment insurance as a ' dole ', did you? No. They told you that unemployment insurance has done more to maintain the standards of the workers in Great Britain than any other agency in this crisis. Instead of degrading man, it has given a man a chance to stand up and say, ' No; I will not go in and work for less than my fellows get. I at least will not starve to death.' Oh, they may paint a very fine picture in this report, but I hope we will not have to go back to our constituency and say, ' Read that, it is good soothing sirup.' "

Pages 376–377: Delegate Hoffman, meat cutters. " There may be danger in unemployment insurance, call it what you will; you can call a horse a cow, but that does not necessarily make a horse a cow. So I say relief ought to be given to this unemployed situation in the United States and it ought to be given at once. I am for anything that is going to help the unemployed."

Pages 377–379: Delegate Trotter. Suggested that the fraternal delegates be permitted to make corrections on the bitter attack made by Chairman Woll. President Green felt that the visitors did not want to inject themselves into the internal affairs of the American Federation of Labor.

Delegate Furuseth, seaman, declared his sympathy with remarks favoring unemployment insurance made by Delegate Duncan, Seattle, as far as it afforded bread for the unemployed. In floor discussion with Delegate Tobin he claimed that neither the executive council nor the committee told what workers must do for bread. Meanwhile, he perhaps did not favor unemployment insurance.

Unemployment insurance. Proceedings, 1931, pages 148–165

The executive council presented an extensive review of unemployment insurance in Great Britain and Germany. Finally offering the following proposals:

" First, we propose that a national conference of employers and labor be called by the President of the United States to deal directly and constructively with the unemployment problem and to devise ways and means by which and through which all working people may be accorded an opportunity to share in all work available.

" Second, in order to accomplish this purpose, we propose the immediate inauguration of the 5-day work week and the shorter workday in all public and private industry.

" Third, the maintenance of the wage structure and wage standards.

" Fourth, work assurance. A guaranty to all those workers who are employed that they are secure in their positions and that through the application of the shorter work day and the shorter work week all would be accorded an opportunity to share equitably in all work available.

" Fifth the prohibition of child labor and the employment of adults in order that the slack of unemployment may be taken up.

" Sixth, the stabilization of industry with particular reference to those industries which are classified as seasonal in character. This would contemplate the application of a plan whereby improvements could be carried on during periods of seasonal recession when because of the season character of the industry the demands for goods has substantially declined.

" Seventh, the application of more scientific plan of industrial production so that a stable balance may be maintained in order that production may be carried on systematically over longer periods of time."

Maternity and infancy. Proceedings 1931, page 347

" Your committee expresses very great gratification in the work done to protect the Children's Bureau in the Department of Labor in its function of caring for maternity cases.

" It recommends that every effort be made to secure the passage of a maternity and infancy act that will enable the Children's Bureau to function as formerly in the care of maternity cases."

Unanimously adopted.

Unemployment. Pages 354–368

A series of resolutions suggesting many remedies short of unemployment insurance. The principle ones were public works programs and long-range planning.

Unemployment insurance. Pages 334–360. A series of resolutions were presented on unemployment insurance.

Resolution no. 8, proposed that Congress be petitioned to pass a law creating unemployment insurance.

Resolution no. 13, presented a resolution adopted by the thirty-second regular convention of the United Mine Workers of America calling for a study of the subject to the end that "unemployment insurance or some plan equally as good or better be worked out and presented in the legislative halls of the State and Nation"—and is accompanied by a comprehensive report which is submitted as the work of the international officers of the United Mine Workers of America, favoring the enactment of laws to establish unemployment insurance or unemployment reserves.

Not accepted.

Pages 335–360. Resolution no. 29 urged the enactment of compulsory unemployment insurance at the expense of the State and the employers.

Resolution no. 39 proposed "a system of unemployment insurance inaugurated and controlled by the States and supervised by the Federal Government" and "to be a charge on industry in the same way as workmen's compensation for accident."

Resolution no. 59 declared for unemployment insurance by State and Federal enactment.

The report of the executive council recommending enactment of unemployment insurance, the contributions to which "should be paid by management as a part of the cost of production—was adopted after an extended debate.

NOTE.—This is their "most definite swing before 1934 toward social insurance."

Pages 358–360: Delegate Donnelly, representing the Ohio Federation of Labor, and a member of the Ohio Commission on Unemployment Insurance, wanted the American Federation of Labor to take a definite stand on unemployment insurance. He concluded as follows: " *   *   * So I say, and this commission says (the Ohio commission) that even during periods of prosperity we have unemployment that affects great groups of people and we could relieve the situation. Even if we had to face such a situation as we have had in the past 3 years we would have had at least $184,000,000 in Ohio to reimburse the workers of the State, and we would not have been losing the homes of the State."

Old age. Page 362

The executive council's report contains references to certain bills on old-age pensions pending before Congress.

"We express the hope that legislation on this subject will be forthcoming in the near future. Steady progress is being made in the promotion of State legislation providing for old-age pension systems. Further efforts of the American Federation of Labor and the various State branches was advocated."

Report was unanimously adopted.

Old age. Page 526

Resolution No. 13, with the following resolve, was unanimously adopted:

"Resolved, That the American Federation of Labor, in its fifty-third annual convention held at Washington, D. C., beginning October 2, 1933, request every serious effort possible to find ways and means to force the next session of the Congress of the United States to enact a compulsory old-age pension as Federal and State laws."

Unemployment insurance. Page 461, from Resolution No. 14

The following resolution was adopted after the committee on resolutions had noted the executive council report of the year before which had pointed out the constitutional limitations preventing enactment of a compulsory unemployment-insurance law applicable to all workers.

"*Resolved*, That the American Federation of Labor * * * beginning October 2, 1933, urges every possible means and power available to make the necessary arrangements to fight during the next session of the Congress of the United States for the enactment of such compulsory unemployment insurance legislation as may be permissible under the Constitution, including provisions for Federal aid to the States, and to urge the enactment of compulsory unemployment insurance laws in every State in the Union."

PROCEEDINGS, 1934

Old age. Page 551

The executive council report called attention to the fact that 20 States are still lacking old-age security laws. Attention was also directed to the failure of Congress in enacting an old-age security law for the District of Columbia. "It is to be gretter that our National, as well as so many of our State Governments, have failed this far to respond to this great and humane requirement. We direct every possible effort be made to remedy this grevious situation and recommend approval of this section of the report of the executive council."

After a brief discussion, it was unanimously adopted. Page 553.

Social insurance. Proceedings, pages 598–603

Resolutions Nos. 10, 20, 32, 38, 57, 76, 91, 101, 124, 126, and 186 dealt with the question of social insurance. They were reported upon in a group, as follows in part:

"The Cincinnati convention in 1932, by unanimous action, placed the American Federation of Labor on record in favor of compulsory employment insurance. Three years before, the Toronto convention gave an equally effective expression to the conviction on the part of this Federation that the time had arrived in American industry when it was in the interest of general welfare that provision should be made for old-age pensions. Taken together with workmen's compensation this provides for the major hazards of industry. The experience of the passing months has confirmed your committee in the soundness of their declaration in favor of social insurance. Your committee therefore recommends concurrence with the intent of these several resolutions looking toward the endorsement of this proposal." * * *

"Your committee recommends the whole-hearted endorsement by this convention of the general proposals for social insurance, in line with action which has already been taken by previous conventions, and of study of those other phases of social insurance upon which previous conventions have not already acted. We concur with those proposals for support of social insurance that have been set forth in the legislative program of the Federation and nonconcur with methods that have been advanced which are at variance with this sound and established policy."

Report unanimously adopted.

Mr. LUNDEEN. What organization made the foregoing research?

Mr. WEINSTOCK. It was given to me by a research worker, but I would not be able to say which one it was.

Mr. LUNDEEN. It has been inserted as part of your remarks.

Mr. WEINSTOCK. Yes. Anyone could check them with the proceedings of the conventions, year by year. I am sure that is the source from which they were taken, from the proceedings.

Mr. DUNN. May I say that Congressman Wood, who is the president of the State Federation of Labor for the State of Missouri, stated here the other day that the American Federation of Labor was not opposed to unemployment insurance and old-age pensions. In fact, he presented some statistics for the record, and I believe he stated that in 1930 or 1931 the American Federation of Labor was on record favoring unemployment insurance.

Mr. WEINSTOCK. May I answer this, Mr. Chairman?

Mr. DUNN. Yes.

Mr. WEINSTOCK. I prepared for his questions. I expected that Congressman Wood would be here, because I wanted to take up many other questions concerning the organization. Here is my answer, which is the answer of Mr. William Green, and I will also leave this for the record. At the Vancouver convention, 1931, Mr. William Green said the following—and I am quoting word for word what Mr. Green said, now, as it appears at page 369 of the convention proceedings:

Acceptance of compulsory unemployment insurance, therefore, from the point of view of American workers, having in mind actual industrial conditions as they prevail in the United States, would in a large measure amount to a virtual surrender on the part of the workers in the battles they are now waging in many industries for recognition of their right to organize.

That is the answer, given in the words of Mr. William Green.

Mr. DUNN. In what year was that?

Mr. WEINSTOCK. That was at the Vancouver convention in 1931. Not only was he opposed to unemployment insurance, but he said unemployment insurance would weaken the trade-union movement, and that therefore the executive council was opposed to unemployment insurance.

Mr. DUNN. You have given the quotation of his remarks?

Mr. WEINSTOCK. Word by word.

Mr. DUNN. The statement has been made that the reason why the American Federation of Labor is opposed to this bill is because it is "communistic." The fact that the witness has presented evidence of favorable action by a number of organizations that are affiliated with the American Federation of Labor would signify that it is not a communistic piece of legislation; that it is humanistic; and may I ask the witness whether these labor organizations are affiliated with the American Federation of Labor?

Mr. WEINSTOCK. Absolutely.

Mr. DUNN. They do not brand themselves as "communistic" organizations, do they?

Mr. WEINSTOCK. No. They are units of the American Federation of Labor.

Mr. LUNDEEN. As far as that is concerned, Mr. Chairman, we, of Minnesota, are not worried by that term, because every candidate, from the Governor and United States Senator, down to the last man on our Farmer-Labor ticket, in the last election, was called a "communist" from one end of the State to the other; and we all received a bigger average vote than ever before.

Mr. DUNN. I am not taking exception, Congressman Lundeen, to the use of that term "communistic", because I have been branded as such. As you have heard, I make this statement, that if favoring adequate old-age pensions, unemployment insurance, pensions for widows, and legislation providing jobs at adequate wages is "communistic", I am willing to be branded as a "communist."

Mr. LUNDEEN. We were denounced, and especially the Governor of our State was put under terrific fire.

Mr. DUNN. Is it not a fact that the President of the United States, on account of what he has already advocated, has been classified as a communist on the floor of the House?

Mr. Lundeen. And the first lady of the land has also been referred to as a "dangerous radical" by Republican Members of Congress—not by Socialists or Farmer-Laborites, but by the Republicans.

Mr. Dunn. I made a statement a few days ago when the $4,800,000,000 bill was being considered that it would not solve the economic problem because the amount specified was inadequate.

Mr. Weinstock. I might say this for the sake of the record. I am sure the gentlemen here are familiar with the local union proceedings. The procedure is that we receive a communication from an organization, informing us that they are interested in social insurance. On the basis of the communication, a discussion takes place in the local union, and as a result of the discussion a vote is taken, and the majority of the workers vote in favor of the Lundeen bill. That is the way our committees are organized all over the country. There are no questions asked of the delegates as to whether they are Republicans, Socialists, Democrats, or Communists. They are asked whether they were sent officially by the local union, whether they represent the local union, whether they favor the unemployment insurance, or are opposed to it. On this basis we have elected delegates all over the country. I present my credentials from a local union of 1,100 members, good trade-unionists. I believe some of them have been members for 35 or 40 years, and I am sure every one of them is willing to go to all the locals of the city and support and vote for the workers' unemployment-insurance bill.

Mr. Dunn. In fact, Mr. Weinstock, the members who belong to your organizations may be Democrats, Republicans, Socialists, Catholics, and Protestants?

Mr. Weinstock. Absolutely.

Mr. Lundeen. White or black?

Mr. Weinstock. It makes no difference. We ask one question, Are they affiliated with the American Federation of Labor? If they are, then we ask them to support this workers' unemployment-insurance bill. If they have any objections, they raise the objections, and we endeavor to convince them in the local unions, if there are people who need to be convinced that this workers' insurance bill is the only bill which will provide for the unemployed at the present time.

(The credentials letter presented by the witness is as follows:)

BROTHERHOOD OF PAINTERS, DECORATORS, AND
PAPERHANGERS OF AMERICA,
LOCAL UNION NO. 848,
New York City, N. Y., December 22, 1934.

Mr. HERBERT BENJAMIN,
Secretary National Congress Unemployment Insurance.

DEAR SIR: This credential is to certify that the bearer, Mr. Louis Weinstock, was duly elected a delegate to the unemployment congress, to be held in Washington, D. C., January 5, 6, 7, 1935, from this organization, local union no. 848.

Yours truly,
[SEAL.]
THOMAS A. JONES,
Secretary, Local Union No. 848.

Mr. Dunn. The next witness is Mr. T. Arnold Hill.

STATEMENT OF T. ARNOLD HILL, EXECUTIVE SECRETARY OF THE NATIONAL URBAN LEAGUE

Mr. HILL. Mr. Chairman, and members of the Committee: I am here to advocate the passage of bill H. R. 2827, introduced in the House of Representatives on January 3, 1935, by Mr. Lundeen, and known as " The Workers' Unemployment, Old Age, and Social Insurance Act."

This bill seeks to establish an insurance system to provide, among other things, for:

1. Compensation for all workers and farmers above 18 years of age, unemployed through no fault of their own;

2. Compensation of not less than $10 per month, plus $3 for each dependent, but a minimum in conformity with rises in the cost of living;

3. Compensation for all workers and farmers who are unable to work because of sickness, old age, maternity, industrial injury, or any other disability;

4. Payment of all costs by the Government of the United States from taxes levied on inheritances, gifts, and individual and corporation incomes of $5,000 a year and over;

5. Benefits to industrial, agricultural, domestic, office, or professional workers, and farmers.

6. No discrimination because of age, sex, race, color, religious or political opinion or affiliation; and

7. Protection of standards and labor-union rights of all workers who refuse to work in place of strikers, or at less than average local or trade-union wages, or under unsafe or unsanitary conditions, or where hours are longer than the prevailing union standards of a particular trade or locality, or at an unreasonable distance from home.

These are the essential provisions of the bill, and they represent principles that are sound, safe, and necessary.

I am in favor of the bill, first, because it includes farmers and domestic and personal-service workers. These two groups are the most insecure of all American workers. For them there are no codes of fair competition, no labor unions, and no unemployment benefits contemplated, except those this bill sets forth.

There is a prevalent assumption that if manufacturing can be revived to the 1928 level farming would automatically reflect the revival to a like degree. Assuming that this is the normal or usual reaction to industrial improvement, one is compelled to conclude that such a favorable balance between farm revival and industrial revival is not likely to occur at any time in the near future. I say this because of the very definite movement of people to the country from the cities—estimated at from 1,000,000 to 2,000,000 a year; also because of the Government program to rebuild stranded rural and semirural populations; and also because young men are not moving from the country to the cities to work in the industries because the industries are not active, and they are being discouraged from settling in the cities where relief loads are heaviest.

The effect of this growth in rural population will be felt in decreasing markets in cities for farm products. In other words, the farmers will produce less for shipment to the cities and more for their own use. But with the improved methods of producing farm goods, agricultural workers will not employ all of their time farming for their own use. Thus we shall have a decreased production per worker, with a consequent lowering of standards of living. There is great danger that the movement from the cities to the farms will constitute exploitation of the entire agricultural population. Unemployment will be transferred from the cities to the country on the theory that the farmer can live through producing his own food necessities. This is erroneous and fallacious under the constantly developing improvements now going on in farming. It is, therefore, absolutely necessary that the farmers be protected, and that standards of living be assured through compensation for them during periods of idleness.

The Negro working population is largely agricultural and unskilled. A little more than 65 percent of all Negroes who were engaged in 1930 labored as farmers and domestic and personal servants. Shutting off benefits to farmers and domestic and personal-service workers would immediately exclude almost two-thirds of all Negro workers.

While I am concerned with the security of all workers, I am close to the interests of some 5,500,000 Negro workers who labor in despair on the insecure fringe of our modern industrial employment system. These workers, by the very nature of their employment, are the first sufferers when a financial depression or technological innovation causes considerable displacement of labor.

The unemployment-relief census of October 1933 showed that 16.7 percent of the recipients of relief were Negroes, whereas they constitute only 9.7 percent of the total population of the country. Stated in another way, almost 18 percent of the entire Negro population was receiving relief; whereas only 9.5 percent of whites were receiving relief. In the District of Columbia, where Negroes have only a relatively few professional jobs, 21.8 percent of the Negro population was on relief as compared with 2.4 percent of the white population. The economics of this is that so many Negroes in the District of Columbia (51.6 percent of all Negro workers in the District) are in the field of domestic and personal service, and thus have been dislocated by unemployment. Unless, therefore, unemployment insurance covers such type of work, it will be of little help to the vast majority of Negroes who labor in the country.

I favor this bill for another very significant reason—because it upholds the right of workers to organize unions for their own welfare, and protects them when they refuse to work below the average local or trade-union wages, or under unsafe or unsanitary conditions, or where hours are longer than the prevalent union standards of a particular trade locality. Furthermore, no worker or farmer shall be disqualified from receiving compensation because of past participation in strikes. Heretofore workers have had no support of their contention that they ought not to be forced to labor where conditions are not conducive to good health, and wages not sufficient to support minimum standards of living. This bill makes possible the elimination of bad working conditions, which would tend to be corrected under pressure of the Government as unemployment benefits began to mount because workers refused to labor under unsatisfactory working conditions.

So far as Negroes are concerned, this bill takes the profits out of strike-breaking. Negro workers have broken strikes because it was frequently the one way they had of making a living. Denied the opportunity to join unions and thus work at union wages, they have felt called upon to go into a plan to work at any wage they could receive. Now with the security of unemployment benefits, they will not be forced to break down the standards of organized labor by going in to work at wages that are lower than the average local or trade-union wage.

I favor this bill also because it provides for administration of this act by the Government of the United States. The experiences of Negroes with State Governments has not been satisfactory. In one-fourth of the country today, the precious heritage of education is withheld from black citizens by State governments. In 18 Southern States, including the District of Columbia, the average expenditure for public schools per child of school age is $45.63 for a white child, as against $14.95 for a Negro child. In South Carolina the average for a white child is $52.89 and for the Negro child $5.20; in Louisiana, $40.64 for the white child, as against $7.84 for the Negro child; and in Georgia, $31.52 for the white child, as against $6.98 for the Negro child. If we leave the administration of unemployment-insurance benefits to the States, it is a safe guess that the Negro, the most insecure worker of all, will not profit fairly. It has not been possible to insure adequate handling of relief funds, even when appropriated by the Federal Government, because the administration of these funds has been delegated to State authorities.

This bill has one further benefit in its favor, namely, it benefits all workers irrespective of race, color, religion, or political affiliation. The wisdom of this clause needs no argument to one who is familiar, and certainly we all are, with the differences so often practiced because of race, nationality, and politics.

If unemployment insurance is to guarantee security to workers, then it ought to guarantee security to those who are the least secure. The group in this country whose earning is the lowest, whose working conditions are usually the poorest, and whose employment status is the most uncertain should have the first call upon the benefits of this act. Such a group is composed of 5,500,000 workers who labor in various parts of the country; and while I plead for the passage of the bill for all workers, I make a special plea on behalf of these.

Mr. DUNN. We will include in the record at this time the statement of Mr. David Drummon, representing the Waterfront Unemployed Council.

STATEMENT OF DAVID DRUMMOND REPRESENTING THE WATERFRONT UNEMPLOYED COUNCIL (BALTIMORE, MD.)

Mr. DRUMMOND. Mr. Chairman and members of the committee, the unemployed seamen of Baltimore wholeheartedly endorse the unemployment and social insurance bill (H. R. 2827) as presented to the Seventy-fourth Congress of the United States by Congressman Lundeen. We believe that this is the only bill that will adequately provide for a decent living for the unemployed in the United States, including the seamen.

At the present time the unemployed seamen on relief are forced to work 30 hours a week for the sum of $1 and their meager meals and lodging. This forced work done by the seamen deprives workers in various trades of legitimate employment at regular trade-union scales of wages. At the same time it deprives the seamen of the opportunity of finding employment at their own occupation because they are forced to work at places of employment that are removed from their own sources of work. The present system of relief ruins the health and morale of the unemployed by congregating them in unhealthy common lodging places where they are subjected to the discrimination of bureaucratic officialdom and are liable to be cut off relief whenever these officials so desire.

Unemployment insurance, as provided for in the Lundeen bill (H. R. 2827), would provide a minimum amount that could take care of the unemployed seamen during the period of their unemployment. It would also give them the opportunity of looking for proper employment, and maintain their physical and moral fitness for service at sea.

While the Government gives millions of dollars to the shipowners in the form of subsidies, the shipowners are cutting the wages of the seamen, utilizing the unemployed who are forced to accept employment at low wages, thus cutting the wages of those that are employed.

We believe that the funds which the unemployed would receive in the form of unemployment insurance would greatly cut down the number of unemployed by bringing this money back into circulation, by the unemployed buying the many things that they need and of which they have been deprived in the course of the 5 years of economic crisis. The increased number of buyers would greatly increase the number of those employed in producing the necessities of life for the workers.

This statement has been drawn up after careful examination of the other bills (Wagner-Lewis) before Congress. We believe that the Wagner-Lewis bill does not provide any form of security for the millions of unemployed. The Wagner-Lewis bill would serve as a weapon to break the strikes of the workers for higher wages and better working conditions. The Wagner-Lewis bill would place the burden of paying for unemployment insurance on the back of the workers instead of the Government, whose first duty, in our opinion, should be to secure the welfare of the people of the United States.

A ballot conducted by the Waterfront Unemployed Council in Baltimore proved conclusively that the seamen almost unanimously want the Lundeen bill to be enacted. This ballot, in the course of 2 weeks, had the votes of 765 seamen for the Lundeen bill and 11 for the Wagner-Lewis bill. This bill was also endorsed by hundreds of seamen at indoor and outdoor meetings.

The seamen are becoming discontented and disillusioned with the policies of the Roosevelt administration of empty promises, while millions of workers are forced to exist without the elementary necessities of life.

We request the immediate enactment of the workers' unemployment and social insurance bill (H. R. 2827).

Mr. LUNDEEN (acting chairman). I believe the next speaker is Maxwell S. Stewart, associate editor of The Nation.

STATEMENT OF MAXWELL S. STEWART, ASSOCIATE EDITOR THE NATION: "WHAT RECOVERY HAS MEANT TO THE WORKING CLASS"

Mr. STEWART. Mr. Chairman and members of the committee, during the past 2 years the United States, in common with most of the other leading countries of the world, has enjoyed a substantial measure of business recovery. The extent of the upturn is a matter of some dispute, but that there has been improvement is beyond question. We find, for example, that the Federal Reserve Board's index of industrial production for November 1934, the latest month for which complete figures are available, was approximately 15 percent above the level of 1932 and 3 percent above that of November 1933. Commodity prices have risen 20 percent in the 2-year interval, half of this gain having occurred in the past 12 months. Other indices vary widely but without exception show at least slight improvement over the 2-year period.

If we analyze the current statistics in some detail, however, we shall discover that the fruits of recovery have by no means been distributed evenly over the whole population, and that those groups which suffered the most from the depression have in many cases enjoyed little or no benefit from the upturn. The most remarkable gain has been in corporation profits. According to the report of the Bureau of Internal Revenue, the net income of all manufacturing corporations in 1933 rose $550,000,000 above the total for 1932—an increase of over 80 percent. In the first 9 months of 1934 the net profits of 290 of our largest industrial and mercantile concerns, as analyzed by the Federal Reserve Bank of New York, increased from $202,800,000 to $430,500,000, a gain of 112 percent, while the dividend declarations of 675 companies for the first 11 months of the year were more than $350,000,000 above the corresponding period of the previous year.

This phenomenal rise in business profits has been reflected in the growth of income among the wealthier groups in our population. The number of individuals reporting incomes of over $25,000 increased from 25,089 in 1932 to 26,142 in 1933, a rise of 4 percent, while the total income of this group advanced from $1,350,000,000 to $1,480,000,000, or 10 percent. This disparity becomes more pronounced as we ascend the income scale. No less than 46 individuals obtained an income of more than a million dollars in 1933, as against only 20 such individuals in 1932, while the total income reported by this group in 1933 was $81,558,000 as compared with $35,240,000 in the previous year, a rise of 130 percent! Every income group above $25,000 enjoyed an improved status for the year, and every group receiving an income below that figure suffered losses for the period, with the largest decline occurring among those receiving less than $5,000.

Mr. LUNDEEN. Pardon me. What are your authorities for those figures?

Mr. STEWART. Those are the figures of the Revenue Department.

Mr. LUNDEEN. They are Federal Government statistics?

Mr. STEWART. Yes; they are Federal Government statistics, Mr. Chairman.

Mr. DUNN. Do you know how many men who are writers and newspapermen at the present time are out of employment?

Mr. STEWART. I do not have the figures. Of course, I know it is very large, but I do not have the figures.

Mr. DUNN. There are many newspapermen, magazine writers, and so forth, who are very much in need of relief?

Mr. STEWART. I know there is a very large number, but I do not have any idea how many.

Mr. DUNN. And would you say that those newspapermen who are in need of the necessities of life would favor the Lundeen bill (H. R. 2827)?

Mr. STEWART. I am sure that a very large number do, and I am sure a very much larger number would be if they knew its provisions.

Mr. DUNN. Yes; I agree with you. But it is a fact many newspapermen are out of employment today because of the consolidation of newspapers, magazines, and so forth?

Mr. STEWART. Yes.

Mr. LUNDEEN. Mr. Chairman, I am informed that the American Newspaper Guild has endorsed the bill.

Mr. STEWART. I believe the president of that guild is going to testify here on this, is he not?

Mr. DUNN. He may.

Mr. LUNDEEN. Someone representing them will be here, I understand.

Mr. DUNN. Heywood Broun was supposed to testify, and he may come down next week before the committee to give us information pertaining to the many thousands of newspapermen and writers who are out of employment. I am willing to do what I can do, all that I possibly can to bring about a condition where newspapermen and every other class of the people who are out of employment will get a job at a living wage and those that are physically incapacitated will be provided for adequately by the Federal Government.

Mr. STEWART. Of course, the Lundeen bill is the only bill before Congress now that proposes to do that.

Mr. DUNN. Yes. I agree with you.

Mr. STEWART. Next to business corporations and those in the high-income groups, the farmers as a whole have probably obtained the greatest benefits from the upturn of the last 2 years. Farm income for 1934, despite greatly reduced production, is estimated to have been approximately one-fifth above 1933. This was partly offset by the increased price of the articles which the farmer must buy, but after making all allowances agriculture has unquestionably obtained a larger aggregate purchasing power. But as the farmers have suffered more acutely from the depression than any other group, such improvement as has taken place has left them with a deficiency of at least 20 percent in real buying power as compared with 1929.

Mr. LUNDEEN. Does that take into consideration the drought also? We have higher prices in Minnesota, in places where the drought wiped out everything, but the farmers have nothing to sell.

Mr. STEWART. I am sure that is true.

Taken as a whole, labor has also enjoyed a rise in money income, though on a much more moderate scale. An increase in dollar income does not, however, necessarily indicate an improved economic status. The true position of any group can only be measured by real wages and comparative living standards, which take into consideration cultural and recreational opportunities as well, as the essentials of livelihood. If we take all factors into consideration, it is doubtful whether employed labor has made any substantial gain. It is true that as compared with 2 years ago, employment in manufacturing industries has risen approximately 20 percent and pay rolls nearly 40 percent. But all this gain was achieved by midfall of 1933. In the past 12 months labor has not been able even to hold its own. We find, for example, that the number of persons estimated to have been employed in manufacturing industries in October 1934 was 6,585,800, as compared with 6,671,500 in the corresponding month of 1933, a decline of 1.5 percent. Total weekly pay rolls for this group was $123,527,000 in October 1934, as against $120,930,000 in 1933, while the average weekly income of factory workers rose from $18.60 to $18.90, a net gain of 1.5 percent in money income.

This apparent gain is soon turned into a loss, however, when account is taken of rising prices. During the same interval retail food prices, which represent about 45 percent of expenditures of the lowest income group, increased 8 percent, while the United States Bureau of Labor Statistics index of the cost of living advanced 3 percent. Nor was October an exceptionally unfavorable month. If we had taken September as a basis for comparison, we would have found that between 1933 and 1934 employment had declined 5 percent, pay rolls had fallen 2 percent, and that average weekly wages had remained virtually unchanged in face of an increase of 8.8 percent in retail food prices. In November both employment and pay rolls declined sharply, but the comparison with the previous year was slightly more favorable. Thus, while no sweeping generalization is possible regarding the relative status of the working class as a whole, it is evident that the average employed worker was worse off at the end of 1934 than at the end of 1933.

That business recovery has resulted in a lower rather than higher standard of living is indicated, moreover, by the New York Federal Reserve Bank's index of department-store sales. Despite the marked rise in prices, the dollar volume of transactions in 1934 was approximately the same as in 1932, which means a reduction in actual purchases. Chain-store sales throughout the country were about 6 percent higher than 2 years ago, but this again is less than the increase in prices. The total sales of chain groceries in 1934 was only 0.1 percent above those of 1933.

Additional evidence of the reduction in living standards is to be found in the cultural field. Although shorter working hours and the elimination of child labor have brought an increased demand for cultural opportunities, public expenditures for education and recreation have continued to decline. In the rural districts some 2,000 schools have closed their doors, while in 18,000 other schools a total of 900,000 children received less than 6 months' schooling during the past school year. Despite an increase in school enrollment, 40,000 fewer teachers were employed in 1933–34 than in the previous year. Libraries have suffered even more severely. Although attendance has shown a marked rise in recent years, the appropriation for books has been cut on an average of more than one-third.

Labor's failure to profit by business recovery stands out more sharply by virtue of the fact that the wage-earning portion of the population bore a disproportionate share of the burden of the depression. Between 1920 and 1932 the income of workers in the manufacturing industries dropped approximately 60 percent, while the return to property fell only about 30 percent. The middle class who obtain their income chiefly from fees, salaries, and the profits of small enterprises, likewise suffered a loss of approximately 30 percent, or a little more than the decline in the cost of living.

Studies of the utilization of income show rather conclusively, moreover, that the lower income groups have suffered much more serious deprivation from the reduction of their incomes than has any other group. This is due to the fact that the lower-income groups must employ a much larger proportion of their expenditures than others for the purchase of the basic essentials of life—food, clothing, and shelter. As we ascend the income scale, we find an increasingly large percentage of the total expenditures being utilized for cultural, educational, and recreational purposes as well as a larger proportion being set aside for savings.

The precarious position in which the working class finds itself is perhaps best illustrated by a recent survey conducted by the Department of Labor into the effects of the depression on the living standards of 1,000 railway employees. Even in this relatively favored group which had not suffered from unemployment we find that 44 of 370 families, (1 out of every 8) who owned or were buying homes in 1929, had lost them either through foreclosure or forfeiture.

Two hundred and seventy-two of the eight hundred and forty-eight (1 out of every 3) who had savings accumulated prior to the depression, had spent all of their savings to provide for their daily necessities.

Two hundred and ninety-five of the nine hundred and thirty-nine workers (1 out of every 3) who carried life insurance either dropped or cashed in their policies.

Seventy-four of the three hundred and five workers (1 out of every 4) who carried accident insurance were obliged to drop it; and these were railway workers.

Five hundred and twenty-four families (more than half) had incurred debts running from $50 to $1,000 per family.

One hundred and fifty-seven boys and girls either had dropped out of school or college or had deferred entrance.

Two hundred and twenty-five families had moved at least once within the last 4 years, mainly to reduce rent costs.

Most of the families reported no purchases of clothes since 1930 or 1931.

In nearly 30 percent of the families, one or more members required medical attention which they could not afford; while more than half of the families reported need of dental care.

These, I repeat, were employed workers who had not suffered from complete unemployment, but they were all railway workers who had regular jobs and who had suffered from partial unemployment and part-time work.

I cite this as evidence of the appalling insecurity of American labor, even when employed. But these problems, serious though they are, dwindle into insignificance before the plight of the Nation's great army of unemployed. The most crying indictment of the business recovery thus far achieved is not that it has brought lower living standards to the employed worker—that possibly was to be expected in a transitional period—but the fact that practically no progress has been made in reducing the volume of unemployment. I shall not attempt a new estimate of the number of men and women in this country who are still without jobs. I have seen guesses which vary all of the way from 9,600,000 and 17,150,000. But taking the figures which have gained the most wide-spread acceptance, the monthly estimates of the American Federation of Labor, we find that the total number of jobless in November 1934—11,459,000—is almost identical with the average for 1932, under the Hoover administration, and 429,000 higher than for 1933. That one fact alone should be enough to make us realize that drastic action is necessary. It is obvious that this vast group of men and women has been deprived of their income through no fault of their own; they have been the hapless victims of defects in our political and economic system for which we, if anyone, are responsible. To my mind no recovery program is worthy of the name which does not restore to this great army—nearly one-quarter of our working-class population—the essentials of life of which they have been robbed by society.

It should be obvious, moreover, that the needs of these millions who have borne the brunt of the depression is not even being touched by existing programs of relief and public works. And if we are honest with ourselves we shall have to admit that we cannot discharge society's responsibility to this group by any scheme of unemployment reserves. Nor can any program of actuarial unemployment insurance such as in conceived in the Wagner-Lewis bill meet the challenge of future insecurity. In foreign countries where actuarial schemes have been tried they have almost invariably been abandoned in favor of a program based on the principles of caring for all of the jobless, regardless of the amount they may or may not have contributed to an insurance fund. Moreover, it is apparent that no scheme which limits payments to 15 weeks, or even 50 weeks, would have been adequate in this depression. In a survey made in Buffalo in November 1933 it was found that 71 percent of the jobless had already been without work for more than 40 weeks, while 60 percent had been unemployed for more than a year.

Others have doubtless made a comprehensive analysis of the fundamental shortcomings of the administration's security program. I merely wish to point out in passing that I consider its defects to be those of principle rather than of detail. The administration plan in frankly based on the assumption that the hazards of life can be adequately distributed by the application of actuarial principles. This I deny. The risks of industrial unemployment are so wholly unpredictable that they cannot be reduced to mathematical formulas. The basic weakness in the actuarial approach lies in the fact that it treats money as an end in itself, as if it could actually be stored up to meet future contingencies. Yet money is only valuable as a claim on current production. Consequently, it is evident that the problem is one of equalizing the burdens of the day rather than that of saving for future hazards.

In principle I fully endorse the Lundeen bill. It seems to me to represent the only sound approach to the problem of industrial insecurity in its entirety. It would protect the worker who is on part time as well as those who are wholly unemployed. You have heard others sketch in some detail what the advantages of this bill are in comparison, say, to the Wagner-Lewis bill. I should like in closing merely to answer some of the criticisms which have been made of the bill. In the first place, you have doubtless heard it said that the bill is loosely drawn. There are advantages as well as disadvantages in that fact, but it seems to me that before this committee reports the bill out on the floor of the House it should endeavor to meet these objections by a careful reworking which will retain all of the essential features of the bill, yet make it explicit enough so as to avoid future misinterpretation.

It is my impression, however, that the rewording of the bill will not reduce the opposition of certain groups who are inimical to any form of real security for the working class. They will continue to assert, as you have no doubt already heard, that the bill would be too expensive. This I would dispute. What the bill would actually cost is problematical. At the outset it would probably be greater than any other of the proposed security measures. But, as Miss van Kleeck has pointed out, it would cost precisely what is now being paid by the working class as a result of the depression and other social hazards. To say that this is more than the Nation can bear is saying in effect that the United States does not possess the human and physical resources necessary to give every individual the equivalent of the prevailing wage. This is disproved by the fact that there have been numerous periods in our history when we did just that. The World War is, perhaps, the best example. Between 1917 and 1919, despite the huge wastes of war and profiteering, virtually our entire adult population was employed at reasonably good wages. In peace time the task should be infinitely easier.

Opponents of the Lundeen bill have alleged that under prevailing conditions it would cost between 12 and 20 billion dollars annually. I think that this is an overestimate. But assuming for the moment the higher figure to be correct, what would be the effect of this huge expenditure upon business conditions? Obviously not all of the money obtained from the income tax would represent new purchasing power. At least $1,000,000,000 is now being distributed in relief, which could be dispensed with, while a considerable portion of the remainder would otherwise be spent for luxury goods. But we know that nearly 40 percent of the total income of families receiving over $5,000 a year is not expended for consumers' goods, and but a fraction of this is now being invested in capital goods. We may assume, therefore, an immediate increase in effective purchasing power of at least $7,000,000,000. This would suffice, accepting Keynes' estimate that each dollar is utilized at least twice, and probably three times, under the present conditions, to put at least 10,000,000 persons back to work, thus saving 12 to 14 billion in insurance payments. In other words, I believe that we could expect that the Lundeen bill, if enacted, would restore normal economic conditions in the United States. It would not, perhaps, bring back the halcyon days of 1929 on Wall Street, but it would do something far more important—it would guarantee every man that protection which is available only to a favored few under present-day conditions.

Mr. LUNDEEN (acting chairman). We thank you for your very able statement. Have you any other data which you wish to submit for the record?

Mr. STEWART. No; I do not believe I have. Are there further questions?

Mr. LUNDEEN. There has been some debate about the age at which old-age pensions should begin, whether 60, 65, 50, or 55 years. What would be your opinion on that?

Mr. STEWART. My opinion is that you cannot place an arbitrary figure as to the age at which it would begin. That, after all, would differ with every individual. It would be the time at which he could not get a job.

Mr. LUNDEEN. I mean, there is an old-age provision in the bill.

Mr. STEWART. It seems to me that is covered in the Lundeen bill.

Mr. LUNDEEN. You mean that as long as he is taken care of, that is sufficient?

Mr. STEWART. When he cannot get a job.

Mr. LUNDEEN. Therefore we do not need to put that provision in the bill.

Mr. STEWART. Therefore, you do not need to put that provision in the bill.

Mr. LUNDEEN. I am glad you brought that out. That is your opinion. Is there any other point? Have you looked into the constitutionality of the bill at all?

Mr. STEWART. I am not a lawyer, but I have talked to a number of lawyers on the subject, and the impression that I get every place is that the bill is constitutional, and that it is based on much sounder constitutional principles than the Wagner-Lewis bill. I have heard that a number of times from lawyers.

Mr. LUNDEEN. From lawyers in good standing?

Mr. STEWART. From lawyers in good standing; yes.

Mr. LUNDEEN. From a number of them?

Mr. STEWART. Yes.

Mr. LUNDEEN. Lawyers at the New York Bar?

Mr. STEWART. Yes; that is right.

Mr. LUNDEEN. And you are satisfied on that point, yourself, as a layman?

Mr. STEWART. Yes, as far as I know. I am not, of course, a lawyer.

Mr. LUNDEEN. Have you made a study of economic questions and social security for some time?

Mr. STEWART. Yes. I am an economist.

Mr. LUNDEEN. Your magazine deals with those questions a great deal, so that you are familiar with them?

Mr. STEWART. As a matter of fact, I am primarily an economist, and I have just completed a study of the American national income, its distribution, and so forth, so I feel particularly competent to deal with this question at present.

Mr. LUNDEEN. I am glad to get that information, because we want authoritative statements, and you have the information from the Government records and have made a survey yourself?

Mr. STEWART. That is right.

Mr. LUNDEEN. Thank you very much.

We could probably hear a short statement at this time.

STATEMENT OF JACK RAND, REPRESENTING THE METAL TRADES UNIONS (NEW YORK CITY)

Mr. RAND. I represent an organization of metal workers who are not in the American Federation of Labor, due to various causes, namely, that they are opposed to the form of the organization; they have had experience with the bureaucrats of the American Federation of Labor; and in the past they have been directly organized into their own unions, to better their conditions and wages. Nevertheless, these workers are cooperating with local labor unions of the American Federation of Labor, wherever these local organizations have workers in the same shops, large or small, that are under the control of the Metal Workers' Industrial Union, or where, in the process of organization, we seek a form of unity in the interests of the workers in the shop, regardless of what organization they belong to.

The organization has locals and members in Chicago, Cleveland, Connecticut, Massachusetts, New Jersey, and other districts of the country, and they are vitally interested in measures concerning workers, who through no fault of their own are incapacitated to work, by old age or sickness, or who are thrown out of employment, or who are working part time, thereby further lowering the standard of living for these workers. The promises of the N. R. A. to place more men at work have not taken effect. Those metal workers who received jobs during the first boom of the enactment of the N. R. A. are now again walking the streets.

The terrific speed-up imposed upon the employed workers has increased the production, with even a less number of workers employed. Instead of jobs, additional thousands of skilled mechanics and production workers have been thrown on the street. Today, 60 to 75 percent of the metal workers are without jobs. The cost of living is rising sky-high. On the other hand, the manufacturers have increased their profits by millions at the expense of a terrific speed-up of those workers who are employed. The codes for the different branches of the metal industry, with the 40-cent minimum provision for all workers, serve as encouragement to the employers to maintain low wages, and even to cut the wages of thousands of unorganized skilled and unskilled metal workers in the open shops.

Only in those shops that were unionized were there any efforts made to maintain or to raise wages to a more decent standard of living. Therefore, we of the Metal Workers Industrial Union are in favor of the workers' social insurance and unemployment bill, H. R. 2827, because it gives the unemployed metal workers, first, the benefit of payment equal at least to the local average wages and in no case falls below a standard of health and decency. Second, full costs for such insurance to be a general charge upon industry and Government, and no contributions by the workers and farmers. Third, all workers, regardless of age, occupation, color, sex, nationality, citizenship, religious or political belief, must be assured unemployment-insurance benefits. Fourth, that the workers form their own administration for these funds.

We feel that the Wagner bill and the other bills, with the exception of H. R. 2827, do not adequately take care of workers over the

age of 45. Especially in the metal industry is the vicious practice
of firing workers over 40 years of age practiced, to get younger
men and women to keep up the intense speed-up that drives workers
prematurely old.

Our organization of Metal Workers' Industrial Union has initiated
a conference with other allied independent unions in the metal industry, and at a conference held January 19, representing 25,000
workers, these delegates unanimously endorsed H. R. 2827. I say
this, especially in view of the fact that earlier today one of the.
members of the American Federation of Labor spoke in the interest
of the American Federation of Labor locals, and I am speaking in
the name of independent locals in the metal industry who are also
in favor of this bill.

Mr. DUNN. How many?

Mr. RAND. This conference representing 11 organizations of metal
workers and allied trades has a total membership of 24,750 organized.

Mr. DUNN. And they are affiliated with the American Federation
of Labor?

Mr. RAND. No; they are not affiliated. They are independent
organizations, such as the Radio and Metal Workers of Newark;
the Independent Radio and Metal Workers Industrial Union of New
York; the Tool and Die Makers Local, Philadelphia.

Mr. DUNN. They are all union organizations?

Mr. RAND. They are all union organizations, but not affiliated
with the American Federation of Labor. The Radio and Metal
Workers Union of Camden; the National Die Casting Workers
League; the Tool and Die Makers Club of Newark; and, interesting
to say, we had representatives of the Federation of Architects, Engineers, Chemists, and Technicians, who feel they are a part of the
metal industry or allied; also the Mechanics Educational Society
(these two locals in the vicinity of New York were present), the
Aircraftsmen's Federation, the Electrical Industry Employees Union
of Schenectady, and the Independent Sheet Metal Workers Union
of New York.

These delegates fully endorse H. R. 2827, and call upon all the
local unions to do the best they can to push this bill among their
Senators and Congressmen, and also to take any steps necessary when
any hearings are being held to push this bill, since they feel that
they are linked up with the other organized workers—the American
Federation of Labor as well—for this bill; that there is no difference of opinion, when it comes to this bill, in securing the rights of
workers, when unemployed, to unemployment insurance.

Mr. LUNDEEN. You have come here with credentials from your
union?

Mr. RAND. Yes. That is, the Metal Workers Industrial Union.

Mr. LUNDEEN. That is unaffiliated?

Mr. RAND. Unaffiliated with the American Federation of Labor.

Mr. LUNDEEN. But you cooperate with them?

Mr. RAND. We cooperate as far as possible. In fact, we are now
going through a campaign for "one union" in the industry, making
various proposals to the American Federation of Labor locals, most
of them being craft organizations, to cooperate even closer than ever

before; and eventually we hope we will be able to have one union in the industry. Whether it happens to be in the American Federation of Labor or independent depends upon the various conferences and conventions that will be held among these workers.

Mr. LUNDEEN. And how many men were you sent here to represent?

Mr. RAND. Twenty-four thousand seven hundred and fifty organized workers.

Mr. DUNN. Where are the most of those men located; in what State?

Mr. RAND. Within New York. Most of them are within the vicinity of New York—that is, Connecticut, New Jersey, and New York State.

Mr. DUNN. Can you tell me why the various union organizations are not affiliated with the American Federation of Labor?

Mr. RAND. Very briefly, I think it was pointed out by the delegate representing the American Federation of Labor committee that there are instances of bureaucracy, of gangster control, of lack of democracy within the union, racketeering, denial of the rights of the workers to conduct their own strikes and to make their own settlements, where these bureaucrats of the American Federation of Labor want to have a one-man organization—all these things accumulate to such an extent that workers are either fired out of the union—that is, expelled—or whole locals are expelled, or the workers themselves in disgust have walked out of the American Federation of Labor; and yet they see the necessity of organizing to protect themselves, and they form independent organizations.

Mr. DUNN. Have you any idea about how many union organizations in the country are not affiliated with the American Federation of Labor?

Mr. RAND. I could not tell you exactly, but I feel that there probably are about 150,000 to 200,000 of the workers organized. That is not a definite figure. I mean organized into independent organizations.

Mr. DUNN. That is what I meant. Would you say there are approximately 150,000 independent local union organizations?

Mr. RAND. No; 150,000 workers, members of these independent organizations throughout the country.

Mr. DUNN. Could you tell me about how many organizations that 150,000 would represent? Would it represent 25,000?

Mr. RAND. You mean locals?

Mr. DUNN. Yes; that would not be affiliated with the American Federation of Labor.

Mr. RAND. That I could not tell you.

Mr. DUNN. I would like to get that information.

Mr. LUNDEEN. Where could we get that information?

Mr. RAND. I would not be surprised but what the brother who is present from the American Federation of Labor committee, Mr. Weinstock, probably could give you more information, because I remember reading that he made a tour throughout the country, and he probably could give you better information than I can.

Mr. LUNDEEN. Probably he could supply that for the record. He says he will.

Mr. RAND. I want to bring out one further fact. We have no quarrel with the workers' locals of the American Federation of Labor. We hope that the workers of the American Federation of Labor locals will see their way clear to conduct their organizations in a rank-and-file manner, to push aside any official who dares to stand in the way of the interests of the workers in that particular union. I know many organizations where the workers have risen up and dethroned czars in their organizations, the racketeers, and brought the organization of the union back into the control of the rank and file; and, naturally, as this tendency increases, as it is increasing within the American Federation of Labor, we can see a tendency toward forming one organization again and not being split up into various locals outside the American Federation of Labor, or in the American Federation of Labor, or independently of both organizations. We can see the tendency of unification of all these organizations of the workers into one organization again, as the workers demand their right of democratic, rank-and-file control, electing their own officials, having full rights to conduct their own strikes and union activities, not in the hands of a few; and I am confident that the day is coming when we will have only one federation of workers throughout the entire country.

Mr. DUNN. It would be a wonderful thing if there could be such a thing as an organization representing all tradesmen and men who labor and having a platform. In fact, I made that statement to some of the officials of the American Federation of Labor who were testifying before the Labor Committee at the last session of Congress.

Mr. RAND. A political platform?

Mr. DUNN. I would not just call it a " political platform ", yet it would be, for instance, just like what the Lundeen bill now calls for.
Do you want to ask any more questions, Mr. Lundeen?

Mr. LUNDEEN. No.

Mr. DUNN. I have no more questions. We will now recess until 2 o'clock. Thank you, Mr. Rand.

(Thereupon, at 12:15 p. m., the subcommittee took a recess until 2 o'clock this afternoon.)

AFTERNOON SESSION

STATEMENT OF L. B. SANDBLAST

Mr. LUNDEEN. What is your name?

Mr. SANDBLAST. L. B. Sandblast, of Portland, Oreg.; lawyer.

Mr. LUNDEEN. Please give us your connections.

Mr. SANDBLAST. I do not represent any particular group at all at this time.

Mr. LUNDEEN. Please give your profession, your work, what you do.

Mr. SANDBLAST. I am a lawyer, and have been all my life. I represent here in a business way some organizations and counties out in western Oregon and Washington.

What I have to say today is a matter of showing a means of providing funds to a certain class who can repay the money which they may receive through unemployment insurance or otherwise from any fund that might be made available to them. The abstract

statement of what I have in mind might be expressed also as one
plan or outline that would summon the middle classes or those who
are self-sustaining to a large extent, and have the real get-ahead
American spirit, who are propertied to some extent or have the
primary means of life but are without the liquid assets that they
need temporarily, and starting from the premise of those whom one
would think of immediately as good, moral, character risks.

Summoning the middle classes to create or formulate a fund
would necessarily carry with it the assumption, the fundamental
background, that the fund which is created will belong to those
who are summoned and who will respond to create and build it
up. I think that it would tend to reduce the number that would
be on direct pay. It might tend to keep a great number from becoming entitled to draw from this fund or desiring to draw from it.
The creation of a fund like this will belong to those who have created it; and, as near as I can find here, there is no possibility of a
fund being created without cost to anyone except those who participate, and they would only pay the reasonable cost of what they
might draw from the fund by a method of contributing 10 percent
of their income in the future to pay out what they owe—the tithing
system.

Mr. LUNDEEN. You mean a reserve fund?

Mr. SANDBLAST. Yes. They will create a reserve fund.

Mr. LESINSKI. Whom do you mean by "belonging to the people
who put up the money"?

Mr. SANDBLAST. Every person. Now, take any unemployed person
or any person out of business or any person that may not right now
have the liquid assets, but is a propertied individual or one of good
moral character, which anyone of us will say he will take care of it
when he becomes able, when his property becomes valuable or reasonably valuable—say, he has as much property as he ever had, but the
banks would not extend him anything, although they know that if
he were given a reasonable line of credit or some method whereby he
can obtain the other primary necessities of life, owning a home, and
the average comforts that every family has—but to keep him from
actually drawing on a fund as in this bill, he would have the option
of entering into a contract; only four documents necessary to carry
this out as we have computed it. He would qualify by showing his
resources and liabilities, make certain covenants as to his willing-
ness to make an accounting of what he may earn, and that he will
not sell anything that he owns without obtaining a release, in order
to reasonably assure that there will be a 10 percent payment on the
obligation which he has incurred under such an agreement.

Mr. LUNDEEN. That would necessitate a change in the bill, would
it not, an amendment or something? I am asking your opinion.

Mr. SANDBLAST. I might say that they could create it; but there
would be an agreement among them all—between, say, this fund,
the appraiser department or the organization, the commission that
would handle the disbursements of the fund, which will be paid directly out of the Treasury by your bill—some method or by some
amendment whereby these people with the get-ahead spirit, the
American spirit—they will not take it if it partakes of a gift, but
at the same time they really want it and need it and it would save

them from embarrassing despair—that they would just have the temporary permission to enter into a proposal whereby they will contribute toward this particular fund out of which this particular money will be drawn.

Mr. Lundeen. That is the idea you want to present?

Mr. Sandblast. Yes.

Mr. Lundeen. That is covered in your brief there?

Mr. Sandblast. No; it is not. It is not really covered in it.

Mr. Lesinski. From what I can gather of your statement, you would expect the unemployed to share, also, and donate to this fund?

Mr. Sandblast. They will be privileged to do so if they desire.

Mr. Lundeen. And are able.

Mr. Sandblast. If they are able. They will contribute only in this way.

When I was in the Indian Service I found when I purchased rations for the unallotted and allotted Indians on the public domain in Oregon that the merchants would discount about 20 percent of anything that was sold in bulk upward of about $50 or so, because it did not involve any credit risk or any expense in merchandising it, and they would still make 10 percent. If those who qualified under this here who are to participate would forego the margin between retail and wholesale purchasing and contribute that 20 percent, say, 20 percent into this fund as a validation of their requisition, their certificate which they obtained, they would be getting $120 worth of commodities at retail prices, because this would enable them to purchase in wholesale, and that 20 percent should not go to them; it should not go to the merchant. So if they would contribute 20 percent to this found it would represent one-fifth of the amount of the indebtedness on the $100; they would still owe the $100, but the $20 validation would be the amount saved by the purchase in bulk. If it were a million dollars, that would be $200,000 paid in as soon as the requisitions had been cashed or turned in later on. It would require something like the H. O. L. C., that the bonds would be guaranteed. But immediately there would be a fund before the million dollars had been expended of one-fifth, or $200,000, in reserve, which would not cost the purchaser anything, because he, buying at wholesale, or akin to wholesale, bulk purchases, would save that $20 on the transaction, and he would also help create this reserve fund which would partly belong to him. He could draw, say, $100 for 2 or 3 months out of this until he had become restored to business, until he had become reemployed, and these requisitions would act to give him this credit for any primary needs or clothing within reason, as he might qualify in his station in life. When he sells anything or when he becomes reemployed or comes into funds he agrees then to contribute 10 percent of his income toward the liquidation of the obligation that he has incurred under his contract or covenant with the commission that you may create under your bill here.

Mr. Lesinski. If I understand you correctly, this legislation here is for the benefit of the unemployed. Your theory is that in paying the benefits of this type of legislation a man can draw against this account until such time as he receives employment. Is that it?

Mr. Sandblast. Yes.

Mr. Lesinski. Then after he has employment, he is to pay 10 percent of the wages he receives back into the fund; is that your theory?

Mr. SANDBLAST. If he is within that division, should you have two divisions in your commission here which you set up, or your provision for unemployment. Those who enter this contract have the option of drawing this $10 a week, or they can join the other, which is more independent, and creates a reserve and a permanent annuity for them from the very beginning. They would join together the same as summoning the get-ahead spirited people, the independent people, the middle class, the creators, builders, those who have made our Nation what it is today, who are temporarily embarrassed. They can say, "I will not because I am temporarily unemployed take this $10 a week. I can provide this validation expense of everything I buy of 20 percent if I get the requisition certificate which will give me any kind of commodities I want." So that would be an opportunity provided by the commission which a great number would prefer who want to be interested in a fund that is created by those who voluntarily desire to become a member of an annuity plan that would be self-sustaining, which would not charge them at all but having been given anything whasoever.

Mr. LUNDEEN. My dear sir, would not that fit in with the Wagner-Lewis plan better than with this plan? We are trying to keep things as simple here as possible, because if we put in a lot of amendments and changes we are going to run into difficulties.

Mr. SANDBLAST. It seems to me that there were so many who, under your bill there, would be glad to say, "Well, I am perfectly willing; I can always provide 20 percent if I can get $100 worth and $120 worth of provisions, and I would rather be on an independent basis and draw on that fund as I reasonably need it until I am restored or until recovery is brought about or hastened in some manner or another. I will pay 10 percent, or all, or whatever might be owing. I can sell my crop or my automobile or my library or anything else. I may want to change my business, and I will unload, and when I do I will pay up."

Mr. LESINSKI. Your theory would change the face of this bill and probably make it an insurance plan or an endowment fund of some type, that a person who wanted to join could join if he wished.

Mr. SANDBLAST. Yes.

Mr. LESINSKI. That is your theory?

Mr. SANDBLAST. Every person who qualifies under this would automatically be insured under a group or blanket-life insurance, that would be paid out of this 20 percent 5 years in advance, to guarantee the fund against loss on account of the bread winner being taken away from the family suddenly, and a few provisions like that. But all the property which he has will be impressed with a lien, just a friendly contract lien, nothing of record especially would be required for that case, I think, but to show his liabilities and his assets on a contract in triplicate or duplicate. And these purchases which he obtains he would agree that the title should remain probably in the Government until it has been consumed or worn out, so as to prevent anyone from taking advantage of it. Also, before he changes his place of residence, he would notify the mail carrier, and if he shows any indication of having attempted to defraud this fund in any way on maturity of the obligation it may be recovered immediately and the fund can be protected in that manner—or if he should be an absconding debtor.

UNEMPLOYMENT, OLD AGE, AND SOCIAL INSURANCE

The life-insurance protection, it is a group life insurance for 5 years, 25,000 mortality; quite low for a brief insurance policy which might be continued.

Mr. LUNDEEN. Do you not think that would be rather complicated?

Mr. SANDBLAST. I think it would be very simple. There would be very little bookkeeping in it. I think four forms would do it. One would be this contract containing these covenants. I remember when I was in the Postal Savings Department here, when it was inaugurated in 1912, every postmaster was made a banker overnight. I had supervision over distribution of the blank forms at First and K at that time, in 1914 and 1915, when I was studying law. There was a lot of objection to the postmasters taking this obligation upon them, and that it assumed a lot of work, but it worked out nicely.

One set of contracts cover everybody. Say, a mail carrier carries 10 with him every morning. If he met a man that he knew qualified, he could give him one and have him turn it back, give them to the collector of internal revenue to look over. Ordinarily he could tell whether anybody qualified under that by looking over this blank. He would have property, liabilities, and assets set out there. Have one form signed by the adult members of the family—they might be fingerprinted if necessary—and that form would be the basis of the agreement upon which the requisition for credit certificates could be issued. The mail carrier now takes up deposits from the people on his route. When he returns he would give this certificate to the person who has executed this contract, say, for $100. He would validate it by purchasing an N. R. A. stamp for $20, and then it could be cashed at any N. R. A. store. Then he would have that just the same as money. That then removes the money one step from the person who gets the cash. The merchant the first of the month would take all of these and go to the post office and get the bonds or the certificates the same as the H. O. L. C.—whatever he wanted, the bonds or the money. There it would involve only the contract and the requisition blank, and the stamp that he would have to purchase to cancel on it to prevent any overlapping duplication of bookkeeping, because the stamp cancelation on his record would always tally. All of the requisitions would tally with the amount of bonds issued or the obligation against the fund. But there would be this 20-percent reserve surplus and the 100 percent would still be owing.

Only those three blanks would be necessary, that I can see, and there would not be any duplication.

The mail carriers, now having certain authority to collect for postal savings, could deliver these to homes, and when they change their residence, so as to know where they may be all the time, they would notify the mail carrier, and the mail carrier can even execute a waiver if he wanted to sell something, if he should say, "I need it for the education of my children, and I will pay the interest a small amount, say 10 percent."

They should be liberal in the administration of this language if they felt reasonably secure.

Mr. LUNDEEN. You have presented your plan, have you not?

Mr. SANDBLAST. I probably have, partly.

Mr. DUNN. It will go in the record.

Mr. LESINSKI. You have your plan in writing, have you not?

Mr. SANDBLAST. I have it outlined some here, but this is written out rather rapidly. I could leave this here.

Mr. LUNDEEN. That is very interesting.

Mr. DUNN. Thank you for the information.

STATEMENT OF DR. L. L. SCHWARTZ, REPRESENTING THE ECONOMIC FEDERATION OF DENTISTS OF GREATER NEW YORK

Dr. SCHWARTZ. Mr. Chairman and gentlemen of the committee:

At this hearing today all sections of our working population are attesting to their need for an adequate system of unemployment insurance. Many of these people are supporting the Workers Unemployment and Social Insurance bill (H. R. 2827), because they have asked themselves the question, "Will it immediately take care of our needs?" and have found the answer to be "Yes."

We dentists have also evaluated this bill from this point of view. We, too, answer in the affirmative. But, in considering the bill now before your committee, we professionals who have as our job the maintenance and restoration of health—we have asked ourselves another question, "Will it enable us to function efficiently in our professional capacity?"

We possess certain knowledge, training, abilities. And we are vitally concerned that they be made available to all our people who need them.

For example, we dentists have the job of preserving health through the care of the mouth. In spite of the fact that the particular disease with which we are most concerned—the decay of teeth—affects nearly all people, of all ages, at all times, and never cures itself, we nevertheless possess methods of treatment, which, if instituted in time, are simple, inexpensive, effective.

Therefore, if we dentists were really taking care of all the dental needs of our population, we would be very busy indeed.

But, gentlemen, we are not so busy. And why not?

The report of the Committee on the Costs of Medical Care, contributed an important fact; the fact that in 1929 only 20 percent of our people received dental care. Is this because the other 80 percent were negligent, too lazy to take care of their teeth? This is not the reason.

The factors which determined which people received dental care that they all needed were not personal but rather economic. This is verified again by the Wilbur report which pointed out that that section of the population whose incomes were over $10,000 per year received 62 percent of full dental care. At the same time that section of the population whose incomes were under $1,200 per year received only 11 percent of adequate dental care.

It is therefore clear, that those who did without dental care were those whose incomes were below $1,200—those who could not afford it.

But, gentlemen, in 1929 those whose incomes were less than $1,200 per year made up 61 percent of our population. In 1932 this group made up 75 percent of our population. In other words, most of our working people are doing without vitally necessary care simply because they cannot afford it.

But let me not leave you with the impression that workers are only doing without dental care. In 1929, 46 percent of our population went without any medical, dental, or eye care and today, with workers' incomes reduced by 45 percent since 1929, our working people are depriving themselves of necessary medical care, depriving themselves of this care when even it is a matter of life and death.

Dr. Thomas Parran, Health Commissioner of the State of New York, stated that in this State 50,000 people die every year for lack of medical care. The stern facts are, that today millions of our working people have less chance of remaining healthy than ever before; that millions have less chance of recovering from illness than ever before.

In the face of such a situation, anything short of immediate enactment of adequate legislation on the part of our Government can be interpreted in no other way than as expression of callous indifference.

What can be done?

The immediate enactment of an adequate system of unemployment and social insurance. But, gentlemen, it must be adequate. The name " social insurance " alone cannot be used as magic words to solve a problem of such magnitude.

A bill of the type of the Wagner-Lewis bill can obviously not do it. This bill proposes to force contributions from employed workers, so that if and when the individual States pass similar laws, the workers of that State may be eligible for small benefits for future unemployment. Such a bill is useless.

Only a bill of the type of the Lundeen bill can be of any value for it is a national measure, immediately providing the equivalent of wages to all workers who are unemployed through no fault of their own.

But, the enactment of such a measure has a significance to health workers in addition to the fact that it will also take care of their needs.

Its significance lies in the fact that only this measure will assure our working population of the necessities of life. And gentlemen, unless they are assured of this, the best medical and dental care is of no avail.

You cannot maintain the health of a people who are underfed, without adequate clothing, poorly housed, and distraught by the worry of economic insecurity.

The Milbank Foundation reports in a study of the health of families that disabling illness was 39 percent higher in families of the unemployed than in those of the employed. Can medical care by itself prevent this greater incidence of disease in the families of the unemployed? Certainly not.

Only an adequate system of unemployment and social insurance can do this. Only the workers' bill, H. R. 2827, can do this.

Therefore, we dentists, and we believe we express the sentiments of physicians, pharmacists, nurses, and other health workers, ask you to report favorably on this bill and to work for its enactment in Congress.

The passage of this bill will be the first great step towards liberating the vast material health resources and medical and dental knowledge that exist in our country—liberated for the benefit of our working people.

Mr. DUNN. Thank you, doctor. That is a wonderful contribution. Gentlemen, do you wish to ask any questions?

Mr. LUNDEEN. Your percentage of people getting dental service was for the State of New York only 20 percent?

Dr. SCHWARTZ. That was for the United States.

Mr. LUNDEEN. If we had a socialized health service for the Nation, would that cure the condition?

Dr. SCHWARTZ. It all depends on what you mean by "socialization." If you had a health service that at the expense of the Government would take care of all the needs of the people and at the same time guarantee a decent standard of livelihood to the professional practitioners, this would solve the condition.

Mr. LUNDEEN. I cannot conceive of anything more important than health service for all, even if the individual has no money to pay for the service.

Dr. SCHWARTZ. Correct.

Mr. LUNDEEN. For the reason—and this applies especially to the medical profession in addition to dentistry, because it is all the same in a way—that anyone in this room that has a contagious disease that can be communicated through the air or by contact will imperil the rest, and it is the duty of society to see that society as a whole is protected from these dangers, is it not?

Dr. SCHWARTZ. Yes; but heretofore we have been sorrowfully neglectful in this responsibility that you mention.

The additional point that I would like to bring out is that the workers' bill will be the first step in the creation of this adequate system of health service. It is true that complete medical and dental care cannot be realized just so long as the cost of this care must come out of the wages of the people who receive it. For this purpose, an additional measure, a health insurance feature of adequate appropriations is necessary to provide this medical, dental, and other care, also at the expense of the Government and employers. The two bills are interdependent and interrelated. That is, one supplies the basis for the maintenance of health, the other provides the means for the restoration of health when sickness appears.

Mr. LUNDEEN. Is there anything in government that can possibly be more important than health service? You cannot exist without life and health. You must have health to be useful, and life to even exist. Here is the first thing to aid. I am vitally interested in the health service of America for the American people.

Dr. SCHWARTZ. May I point out just one thing, that when it comes to tribute in the form of words, the Government heretofore has not been lacking. If I recall correctly, a bulletin of the Federal Emergency Relief Administration states that the preservation and conservation of the health of our people is a primary function of our Government; but it is one thing to have this statement and another thing to translate it into law. That which we are asking here is to translate these statements into life, so that a situation as drastic as that which I have pointed out to you shall no longer continue in the United States.

Mr. LUNDEEN. That is a very important point, to translate it into statutes and into action. I know that many members, perhaps all

348 UNEMPLOYMENT, OLD AGE, AND SOCIAL INSURANCE

members of our committee, are just as much interested in this as I am.

Dr. SCHWARTZ. I am certainly glad to hear that.

Mr. LUNDEEN. Of course, there is already, as you know, a feeble beginning in the examination of the teeth of children in the schools and a little medical examination; just a faint glimmering of a beginning. I have sometimes wondered how far that would expand, and if I would live to see complete health service. I would hope to see that.

That is all, Mr. Chairman.

STATMENT OF DR. MAURICE V. SCHULTE, REPRESENTING THE ECONOMIC FEDERATION OF DENTISTS

Mr. SCHULTE. My name is Dr. Maurice V. Schulte. I represent the American Federation of Dentists.

Mr. DUNN. Is that a State organization, or national?

Dr. SCHULTE. City, with affiliates in different cities in the United States.

Mr. LUNDEEN. Are you a regular physician?

Dr. SCHULTE. A dentist.

Mr. LUNDEEN. You are a dentist?

Dr. SCHULTE. Yes.

Mr. LUNDEEN. Please give us your qualifications. What school did you attend?

Dr. SCHULTE. Columbia University.

Mr. LUNDEEN. We want to know something about you. People will say, "Who was that man; what was his training; what was his experience?" This is a big country, you know.

Dr. SCHULTE. All right. I am chairman of the educational committee of this organization, and editor of their publication. They have sent me down to present their point of view. Dr. Schwartz has given it to you from the point of view of maintaining the health of the working people. I will present to you what is the actual economic condition of the physician and dentist, that is, how they are faring and what this bill means to them.

Mr. LUNDEEN. Thank you.

Dr. SCHULTE. The question must arise in the minds of the committee: What are dentists doing at a hearing on the workers' unemployment and social insurance bill? Or even: What have dentists got to do with unemployment insurance at all?

After all, you undoubtedly are thinking, dentists are professional people. They are not workers. They do not become unemployed. They are not in want. Why dentists are doctors; substantial, comfortable, middle-class doctors.

We can understand why you may think this way. It was not so long ago that our opinions were the same. We once thought that we were a privileged section of the population. We once thought, as you may now, that we were secure in the dignity of our title; that with our professional degree, we could know no economic want.

Yes, gentlemen, we once held those beliefs. Not that they were in any way justified. Not that they were based on fact. Yes, we once cherished such belief despite the fact that, as revealed by the Wilbur report, they were entirely untrue.

According to the Wilbur report the median net income of physicians in 1929, in that banner year of prosperity, was $3,800, or $75 per week. Furthermore, in the same year, one-third of all private practitioners had an income of less than $2,500 a year, less than $48 per week. Yes; approximately the same figures hold true for dentists in the height of our prosperity, 1 out of every 3 doctors was earning less than $48. It is true that many doctors earned over $200 per week. But for every one who earned $200 per week there were two who earned less than $50 per week.

Well, then, gentlemen, from where then did these illusions of grandeur arise? They arose from the fact that we were comparatively better off than the worker doing the type of work that we liked and that we commanded respect on the basis of this illusory economic security and the fine type of medical and dental service we were rendering.

But what is the situation today? Today, gentlemen, we suffer no illusions. Today we do not need Government-collected statistics to prove that we do not have economic security. Today our own bitter experience tells us how insecure we are.

Today from all over the country we get reports of physicians and dentists being compelled to give up their practices and become house-to-house salesmen, of being evicted from their offices, of even being forced to suicide.

Mr. DUNN. May I interrupt?

Dr. SCHULTE. Yes.

Mr. DUNN. With reference to the statement you just made about dentists and doctors being evicted from their homes, I received a letter recently from a doctor in the district which I represent. He resides in Clairton, Allegheny County, Pa. This doctor, who is married—and, by the way, he is an ex-service man—last week wrote me a letter and asked me to do something for him in the way of obtaining a loan, in order to save his home because it was going to be sold by the sheriff. I did what I possibly could to get this man help.

May I also make this statement, that one of the reasons why this man is losing his home is not because he did not work, but because he was unable to collect money from the poor people whom he attended. That is the reason why that man is up against it. That is the reason why many dentists and many doctors today are losing their homes. They are really doing Government work and not receiving one cent of compensation.

Mr. LUNDEEN. I want to say as an attorney that what is said here about doctors and dentists applies equally to the attorneys.

Mr. DUNN. I know that, Mr. Lundeen.

Mr. LUNDEEN. Eviction, loss of home, and all that sort of thing.

Dr. SCHULTE. In New York City it has been estimated that 60 percent of the dentists cannot be considered to be making a living. In New York City there are 140 dentists working for the Federal Government at $18 per week, with 400 on the waiting list, and with 400 more who have inquired about the position. Of the 7,000 dentists in New York City, almost 1,000 have indicated an interest in $18-a-week jobs.

These F. E. R. A. dentists are so pressed that they have been seeking for months a $3-a-week increase in salary. They have had, as yet, no success.

Today, gentlemen, the profession no longer seeks for statistics as to its economic security. Nor do we look to our professional degrees as a source of solace. Today, the profession faces want—yes, want.

The question soon formulated itself in the minds of the profession. What was wrong?

We turned our attention to the clinics where there were so many patients; where the doctor was giving so much of his time without compensation. We thought of ideas of restricting the number of patients in these clinics.

And we thought of other things, too. We thought of conducting intensive radio campaigns to sell the people medical and dental care. We even thought of politics and lobbies.

It soon became apparent that from these methods we could gain nothing. We very soon learned that before we could arrive at any solution we would have to seek the basic cause of our ills.

Dr. Schartz showed you that millions of people are seeking the services of physicians and dentists. I have pointed out that thousands of physicians and dentists are seeking patients to treat. What was keeping the patient from the doctor?

The answer was simple and clear: The potential patient cannot pay for medical and dental care, because he is unemployed.

We are all suffering from the effects of unemployment; those without jobs, those part time employed, small shopkeepers.

It is obvious that we can gain no economic security for ourselves; that there can be no solution of our problem, which is not a solution of our patient's problem. It becomes clear to us that so long as patients must pay for medical care, unless our patients had an income, we will have no income; that our economic welfare is inextricably bound up with that of our patients.

Here, gentlemen, is the answer to your question: What are dentists doing at an unemployment-insurance hearing?

Our patients must have an income. If they cannot get jobs—and it is admitted that they cannot—then they must be given an income equivalent to a job—they must be given unemployment insurance.

But there are so many unemployment-insurance bills. What type do we favor?

We have only one formula for an unemployment-insurance bill. It must do the unemployed some good. It must give him a decent income, as soon as he becomes unemployed, for as long as he is unemployed. It must take effect at once. It must be paid for at the expense of that section of the population which can afford to pay—upper-income brackets. It must be controlled by the workers themselves.

There is only one bill that supplies such insurance, the workers' unemployment- and social-insurance bill, H. R. 2827, known as the "Lundeen bill." There is no other.

In the name of our organization, in the name of physicians and dentists everywhere, we ask you to report favorably on this bill.

Mr. Dunn. That is a wonderful contribution, and we thank you for the information you have given the committee.

Mr. LUNDEEN. Are you and Dr. Schwartz both Columbia University men?

Dr. SCHULTE. Yes.

Mr. DUNN. Doctor, did I understand you to say that 60 percent of the dentists——

Dr. SCHULTE. In New York City.

Mr. DUNN. Do not have anything to do?

Dr. SCHULTE. No, no; I said are not considered to be making a living.

Mr. DUNN. How many dentists are there in New York City?

Dr. SCHULTE. Seven thousand, approximately.

Mr. DUNN. If it is 60 percent in New York City, it would be a bigger percentage, or as large, in other towns, would it not?

Dr. SCHULTE. It has been shown by the Wilbur report of the committee which President Hoover appointed that the practitioners in rural sections, both medical and dental, usually make about one-half the income of the city practitioners, and therefore rural practitioners, both medical and dental, are undoubtedly twice as bad off as city practitioners.

Mr. DUNN. Can you give me any information pertaining to medical doctors, regarding their position today on the unemployment list?

Dr. SCHULTE. Yes. There has been some sentiment—I cannot tell you precisely—but I do know that some medical organizations send down delegates in support of this bill. I do not know if they testified here, but I do know that they have sent delegates in support of the Lundeen bill.

Mr. DUNN. We had two doctors here. Were they medical doctors? Besides, we had doctors of philosophy. One of them was Dr. Mitchell, from Johns Hopkins University.

Mr. LUNDEEN. Dr. Mitchell? No; he is a professor, an economist from Johns Hopkins University. Dr. Gillman was from the City College of New York.

Mr. DUNN. Have we any medical doctors on our list?

Mr. LUNDEEN. I understand next week we are to have a physician, a lawyer, and possibly clergymen.

Mr. DUNN. I have no doubt that we could get many lawyers, physicians, and ministers here if we could prolong the meeting.

Mr. LUNDEEN. We want an authoritative, brief, condensed statement. Some of the statements that have come in have been pretty long. But they can be put in in just a few minutes, as these gentlemen here did. They had some very good statements, and made them briefly.

Mr. DUNN. We had, of course, a constitutional lawyer here yesterday who maintained the bill is constitutional in every respect. That was Attorney Linder, from New York, a constitutional lawyer? Are there any more questions anyone desires to ask the doctor?

We thank you, Doctor.

STATEMENT OF WILLIAM M. LEADER, REPRESENTING THE AMERICAN FEDERATION OF HOSIERY WORKERS

Mr. LEADER. My name is William Leader. As a representative of branch 1 of the American Federation of Hosiery Workers, which includes 12,000 members, and of which I am the president, I am here today to speak for the enactment of the Lundeen bill.

For the benefit of the record, our organization has been affiliated with the A. F. L. for the past 25 years.

With the huge rolls of the unemployed of this country, with the ever-growing threat to trade-union standards that exists when many thousands of workers are given civic works and other jobs at far less than union rates, it becomes imperative for organized labor to act on a satisfactory form of unemployment insurance.

Any form of unemployment insurance that takes a year to go into effect once it is passed, that includes only special groups of workers, that makes no provision for the protection of trade-union standards, such as the Wagner-Lewis bill which is under consideration, is of little value to us. Such bills are absolutely dangerous. Unless the gains that organized labor has made through long years of development and effort are thoroughly protected, progress in this country will be arrested, and labor will be set back 50 years. Low-paying jobs for 3,500,000 people, a national campaign of company unionism, inadequate relief—these are the things that bring Local 1 of the American Federation of Hosiery Workers to the support of the Lundeen bill.

We shall back this bill to the utmost, since we are convinced, after a careful analysis of all offered alternatives, that this is the only measure that decently takes care of the unemployed and gives full protection to trade-union standards at the expense of those who can best afford it.

We further believe that the funds to support this bill, loosened from long-stagnant accumulations of wealth in the hands of a few, will serve to stimulate industry to the point where unemployment will soon become a thing of the past.

That is the statement which I want to present. In addition to that, I want to add that, as the statement says, our organization has backed this bill to the limit. I introduced a resolution in favor of this bill at the Central Labor Union of Philadelphia.

Mr. DUNN. Do you have the resolution here?

Mr. LEADER. I could get a copy of the resolution and send it to you.

Mr. DUNN. Is it very long?

Mr. LEADER. It is not; no.

Mr. DUNN. We can put that in the record.

Mr. LEADER. This resolution passed the C. L. U. of Philadelphia. Introduced the same resolution at the United Textile Workers Convention in New York last summer, and it was passed unanimously by the U. T. W., which, as you know, is an affiliated organization.

Mr. DUNN. Is that the same kind of resolution?

Mr. LEADER. The same resolution, backing this bill.

Mr. DUNN. That was a resolution, I believe, presented here from some labor organization. Probably that is the same resolution. Do you have the resolution with you?

Mr. LEADER. I could get copies of both resolutions and send them for the benefit of the record.

Mr. DUNN. That is up to the members of the committee.

Mr. Lesinski. I do not think it is necessary to have those resolutions. The statement was made that they passed the resolution. I believe that will cover it.

Mr. Dunn. There was a resolution presented here yesterday, similar to the one that you are talking about.

Mr. Lesinski. There was one; yes.

Mr. Leader. The only two points which I believe have hindered the acceptance of this bill by the entire working classes of the country who learn about it, are, first, that there are definite claims that it is unconstitutional—of which I have never had any proof sent to me—which was the cause of the C. L. U. of Philadelphia retracting its motion some weeks later, due to the fact that it was explained by the executive council of the A. F. L. that the bill was unconstitutional.

Mr. Dunn. Let me interrupt, please. You can go back and tell those people that we had a constitutional lawyer here, a recognized lawyer who practices before the United States Supreme Court and who is affiliated with the Bar Association of New York, and he testified for one hour and a half. He went into every detail on this bill, and he said it is absolutely constitutional in every respect. In fact, he said the Wagner-Lewis bill was not constitutional. Your organization will get a copy of this attorney's report as soon as the testimony is printed, and you will be able to read it.

Mr. Leader. I will be glad of that information, because with that information I believe I can go back to Philadelphia and get the endorsement of the C. L. U., with information, if it is correct, to that point. That is the one reason that they rescinded their motion.

That is about all I have to say, except that I believe the reason the bill appeals to the workingman or the workingwoman is, it is simple. You can read the bill over and understand it. You know that it means something. It is not full of complications. I think the reason the working class in general is not perhaps in back of it the way it should be is because it has not had the advertisement of the Wagner-Lewis bill in the public press. I would suggest to the committee that if there is any way it can get this bill in the public press, they will find thousands of supporters in the A. F. L. unions. I believe that in time the A. F. L. itself will certainly back the bill. If I do not agree with an organization, I do not believe in getting out of it. I have been in it for 18 years and I intend to stay in it. But I do think that the A. F. L. and every other organization in the country will back the bill if those two points are advertised substantially throughout the country.

I hope the bill passes. The statement says our organization will certainly back it to the limit. As its president, I assure you that I hope it passes, and I will do my part to help it along.

I thank you.

Mr. Dunn. Thank you for your contribution.

Mr. Lesinski. When you go back you can assure your people that the statement made here by a constitutional lawyer was that this bill is absolutely constitutional. There is not a thing in the bill that they can distort. The Supreme Court could not rule against this bill. He made that definite yesterday, so you can be sure.

Mr. Leader. I certainly appreciate that.

Mr. LUNDEEN. The New York Herald Tribune today, February 8, has an article in it that I would like to read:

Tax on pay roll in security bill called illegal.
Contention to reveal United States is already worried about that phase of it.
" Not levy for Treasury, but a lever to get State legislation on subject."

That is the very point that was brought up yesterday by Attorney Linder, verifying that there is grave doubt in the minds of good lawyers whether the Wagner-Lewis bill will stand up. Those who have objected to the constitutionality of H. R. 2827 have made the statement, but they have never produced any arguments.

[By the Associated Press]

WASHINGTON, February 7.—A contention that the pay-roll tax in the administration's social security bill is unconstitutional brought the disclosure today that the Justice Department is studying that phase of the measure.

The argument was advanced by James A. Emery, general counsel for the National Association of Manufacturers, one of the last witnesses before the House Ways and Means Committee. The bill will be considered for possible amendments next week in secret session.

Mr. Emery did not use the word " unconstitutional ", but expressed the view of the unemployment-insurance tax of 3 percent on pay rolls in this language:
" The tax here imposed we believe to be injurious instead of beneficial, and when we examine it closely we believe it is not a legal tax at all."

Representative Robert L. Doughton, of North Carolina, chairman of the committee, subsequently informed reporters that he had asked Attorney General Homer S. Cummings to assign an assistant to consider the constitutionality of the bill.

Mr. Emery's argument was that a tax to be legal should be purely for the purpose of raising revenue for the Federal Treasury. " This legislation upon its face," he told the committee, " is pointed to one result—that is to secure State legislation upon a subject on which the States have not legislated."

He was referring to provisions in the bill under which the Federal Government would collect the 3 percent pay-roll tax, but credit to any employer against that charge 90 percent of what he had paid into a State job insurance fund provided it had the approval of the Federal Government.

Mr. Emery said also that the 3-percent tax would pyramid, being collected on every pay roll from raw material to finished goods; was not levied in accord with ability to pay, and would tend to make machines replace men because machines draw no salaries and hence do not add to the pay rolls.

Mr. Doughton said the bill was so voluminous that the committee would have to pass tomorrow, Saturday, and Sunday absorbing it. " Then next week we can start talking about amendments ", he said.

Before the Senate Finance Committee, meanwhile, Abraham Epstein, spokesman for the American Association for Social Security, said he felt the $30-a-month old-age pension proposed in the administration bill was " ample."

STATEMENT OF EARL PAYNE, REPRESENTING THE MARINE WORKERS' INDUSTRIAL UNION

Mr. PAYNE. My name is Earl Payne. I represent the Marine Workers' Industrial Union and the Waterfront Unemployed Councils of all the ports of the United States.

Mr. LESINSKI. Is your organization affiliated with the American Organization of Labor?

Mr. PAYNE. It is not.

Mr. LESINSKI. Is it a communistic organization?

Mr. PAYNE. It is not. It is a trade union.

Mr. LESINSKI. A trade-union organization?

Mr. PAYNE. It is a trade-union organization. The Waterfront Unemployed Council is an unemployed council organization for seamen mainly. The Marine Workers' Industrial Union is a trade union for seamen. The Waterfront Unemployed Council has as its main purpose the organizing of unemployed seamen for the bettering of their relief and their conditions while unemployed.

The Marine Workers' Industrial Union has a membership of about 10,000, nationally. The Waterfront Unemployed Council have a very fluctuating membership, but it runs between five and ten thousand.

The statement I wish to make is that unemployed seamen get one of the lowest forms of relief. They are forced to live in rotten hotels, such as the hotels in the Bowery in New York, or in such places like the Seamen's Institute in New York, and places of this type in other ports throughout the Nation, which places seamen decidedly do not like. In these places, such as the Seamen's Institute, the seamen are terrorized by hired thugs. They are forced to sleep in dormitories with consumptives and others of this ilk. If they open the windows in order to have fresh air in these places, they will freeze for lack of heat and blankets. Therefore, in order to keep warm it is necessary that they sleep in a place with polluted air, where there is hacking and coughing and spitting all night long by these people who are very sick, but do not know it, usually.

The food which unemployed seamen staying on relief are forced to eat is of the lowest quality, and the quality is merely on a subsistence level. Many of the restaurants which seamen on relief eat in would not pass an honest board of health test. In these restaurants, seamen have found in the food pieces of wood, nails, hairs, and so forth.

Mr. LUNDEEN. Pardon me, Mr. Chairman; that is almost as bad as the food that was dished out to the Spanish-American War veterans, the embalmed beef.

Mr. DUNN. Yes.

Mr. PAYNE. There is one case of a seaman eating in a restaurant on the Bowery in New York that bit into a piece of food and had a nail run through his gums. Things like this happen every day in these restaurants. They are open 24 hours a day and never take time out to clean up.

Mr. SCHNEIDER. I want to know whether this relief administered to a citizen who is a seaman is different than it is to any other working person.

Mr. PAYNE. Decidedly so.

Mr. SCHNEIDER. Why?

Mr. PAYNE. Because of the nature of seamen. They are migratory. Teherefore, for a certain length of time seamen were given a certain category of relief on an occupational basis, but I think the beginning of this year the Federal Relief Bureau put in a policy that seamen would no longer be given relief on an occupational basis, but merely on the basis that they are transients. Therefore they receive transient relief, whereas other workers who are not of a migratory nature receive so-called " home relief ", which, though very poor, is still of a much better nature than that which seamen receive.

Mr. SCHNEIDER. In that respect, seamen are the same as all other itinerants?

Mr. PAYNE. No. There is a different question, for the simple reason that the Government has pursued and still pursues the policy of segregation for seamen; that is, putting seamen in houses specifically for seamen.

Mr. SCHNEIDER. Are you a seaman?

Mr. PAYNE. I am.

Mr. SCHNEIDER. Do you have any credentials?

Mr. PAYNE. I have. I have discharges dating from February 1930 up until the last ship I paid off of was May 22 last year.

Mr. LUNDEEN. Do you have them with you?

Mr. PAYNE. I have.

Mr. LUNDEEN. Did you ever belong to the Seamen's Union?

Mr. PAYNE. The International Seamen's Union? I joined the International Seamen's Union twice.

Mr. LUNDEEN. Do you know Mr. Furuset?

Mr. PAYNE. Yes. I met Mr. Furuset personally in New York here in January.

Mr. LUNDEEN. Would you think that he was in sympathy with your statement?

Mr. PAYNE. I did not think of the matter. I was assured by Mr. Furuset himself that he was not in favor of the statements that I made to Mr. Furuset and with some other seamen.

Mr. SCHNEIDER. Is that a statement you made here?

Mr. PAYNE. No. That was a statement on union problems.

Mr. LUNDEEN. Oh, no; I do not mean that; I mean in regard to relief.

Mr. PAYNE. The International Seamen's Union insofar as seamen are concerned have refused the Waterfront Unemployed Council offer of a united front on the basis of bettering the present relief standards of seamen, and also have refused to back the workers' unemployment-insurance bill, H. R. 2827, which has been proposed to them.

Mr. LUNDEEN. Does that include Mr. Furuset?

Mr. PAYNE. That includes, from what we can understand, the whole executive board of the International Seamen's Union.

Mr. LUNDEEN. Of which he is one?

Mr. PAYNE. Of which he is the president.

Mr. LUNDEEN. I have always held a very high opinion of Mr. Furuset. He was a very close friend of old Bob La Follette.

Mr. SCHNEIDER. Is it not true that the Seamen's Union regards your organization as a communistic organization?

Mr. PAYNE. What the International Seamen's Union's opinion of our organization is is really not of any material value, for the simple reason that there can be no such thing as a communistic union unless all the members of the trade union are Communists, and this is not true of our union. We do not ask a man coming into our union or organization what political body he belongs to, what religion he believes in, or what he looks like, or what race he is.

Mr. DUNN. May I interrupt? In other words, Mr. Witness, you have in your organization men who are Protestants, Catholics, Hebrews, and all other denominations, have you not?

Mr. PAYNE. We have everything.

Mr. DUNN. And of every political party?

Mr. PAYNE. We have.

Mr. DUNN. I just wanted that to go in the record.

Mr. PAYNE. In order to illustrate this political-party basis, during October of last year, before the marine strike on the East coast, the strike of seamen, we had a mass meeting in the Manhattan Lyceum in New York, and a fellow who works in the steward's department on board ships got up on the platform of this hall in front of about 700 seamen and absolutely stated that he was a follower of Tammany Hall. And yet he is today an active member in our union.

Mr. SCHNEIDER. As I understand it, then, you do not require a statement from prospective members that they must believe in communism to get in your organization?

Mr. PAYNE. Absolutely not.

For these reasons and many others, seamen throughout the Nation demand a genuine unemployment-insurance bill. In the workers' unemployment, old-age, and social-insurance bill, seamen find what they want in the way of unemployment insurance.

On the question of old age, the only provisions for seamen when they reach an age when they can no longer work at this hardy trade there is only one place open to them, that is Snug Harbor, in New York. This place can take care of very few men and has strict rules on the acceptance of seamen and on their life while staying in this institution. Therefore, it is mandatory that real old-age insurance be enacted at this Congress, particularly so as in the last few years many steamship companies have put age limits into effect. In fact, the Standard Oil Co. has put an age limit of 45 years into effect.

Since 1928 thousands of ships have been laid up, throwing tens of thousands of seamen out of work; until these ships are put into operation again there will be tens of thousands of seamen unemployed, and, naturally, these men will demand that the shipowners or the Government, or both, give them the wherewithal to live.

One of the main reasons that there are a large number of unemployed seamen today is that the shipping companies deliberately underman their ships, thereby cutting down the amount of possibilities for seamen to get jobs. In this undermanning there is a grave danger to the general public who travel on ships. This has been proven by the recent disasters on the Atlantic seaboard, especially the ships of the Ward-Agwi lines, such as the *Morro Castle*, the *Havana*, and the *Mohawk*. Seamen would gladly take these jobs if the shipping companies were forced to hire full crews; that is, sufficient men to adequately man the ship, in calm and in storm.

The National Recovery Act and other measures under the "new deal" have not in the least helped seamen. In fact, many of these new measures have in effect made his lot worse. There is no code for seamen, because the shipowners killed the only proposed code.

When the country went off the gold standard the seaman who sails to foreign ports took a virtual 50-percent wage deduction. Then, the policy of inflation has given him another cut as his wages have not risen, but clothing prices and other prices have risen.

Very recently the shipowners, with the aid of the National Labor Relations Board, came to an agreement with the International Seamen's Union. The seamen in and those of this union had no say in the negotiations. The wage scale agreed upon is much lower than that which the seamen were demanding. There is no provision for overtime work, no bettering of the food, and no bettering of the miserable living conditions on board the ships.

Seamen today are being forced to join the International Seamen's Union at a minimum cost of $6. This is true of unemployed seamen, as well as employed. If one cannot get the money to join the union he is out of luck for a job. This also causes continued unemployment.

Mr. SCHNEIDER. Right there, I would like to ask you, how does that cause unemployment?

Mr. PAYNE. It does not cause unemployment, but it causes continued unemployment, in this, that if I am on what the seamen call the beach, or unemployed, for a certain length of time, I have no money; in order to get a job I must pay $6 into a union before I can even get one ship or make one trip in order to make money. How am I going to be able to get a job?

Mr. SCHNEIDER. The ships that are union shop jobs, you always have the right to go on if you meet all requirements of the union, whether you have paid or not.

Mr. PAYNE. This is supposed to be the policy, that you could make one trip and pay at the first port that you got a draw on your wages. But I do not think that this is quite true. The seamen have been going up to the International Seamen's Hall and asking to take out a pledge card, that they had the possibility of a job, and the secretary and the delegates of this union have absolutely refused to O. K. them for this job, even though the seamen have promised to join in the next port.

Mr. SCHNEIDER. Why?

Mr. PAYNE. Why? There is no reason given except that they must lay the $6 on the table before they get O. K.'d for a job.

Mr. SCHNEIDER. Is it not true that they bar fellows from your union for going onto ships of that kind?

Mr. PAYNE. In the first place, I have a great many workers who do not belong to the Marine Workers' Industrial Union, and many who have never been to our hall before, but because of the policy this International Seamen's Union is pursuing, forcing unemployed seamen to dig up some place $6 before they can make a ship, they have come around to our hall and told us about this. In the second place, why should any seaman be discriminated against because he belongs to one union or another? The policy of unionism is the same throughout. It is to organize the workers in order that they might win better conditions through organized power.

Mr. SCHNEIDER. That is the contention of all dual organizations, and particularly the Communists. The reason why the seamen demand the closed shop is that only members of the American Federation of Labor will be employed on those ships, and therefore those who belong to your organization are barred from those ships. On the other hand, the unemployed man, of course, cannot go on the job if he is not a member of the union, so long as there are men who belong to the union there to take the jobs.

Mr. PAYNE. What are we going to do with these men that are being fired off the jobs because they do not desire to join the union? What are we going to do with honest seamen who have worked at sea for years and years and have not the money to pay $6 to join this union? Yet the company that hires them says that this is a good seaman, his discharges are O. K.; it shows that his ability is good, his character is good, on his discharge signed by the United States shipping commissioner. Yet the International Seamen's Union looks at him and says, "Have you got $6?" and he says, "No." He says, "Well, you cannot sail on this ship." I think that this is a very incorrect policy.

Mr. DUNN. May I interrupt you? Suppose the shipowners are willing to give him a job, does the International Seamen's Union prevent him from taking that job?

Mr. PAYNE. The International Seamen's Union will prevent him from taking this job.

Mr. DUNN. How would they prevent him if the owners of the ship want to give him the job?

Mr. PAYNE. The seamen are hired mainly through a system of what they call shipping crimps. These people run stores or rooming houses, bootlegging places—well, not bootlegging any more; barrooms, now—and the like. If a seaman contributes in one way or another to the financial betterment of this crimp, then this crimp ships him out. There are crimps for certain definite lines. But now the International Seamen's Union have approached the shipping crimps, and the like, and told them that before they ship any man this man has to belong to the International Seamen's Union.

Mr. DUNN. I see. I just wanted to get that straight in my mind.

Mr. SCHNEIDER. It is true that the crimps bring down all classes of people for signing on those ships, whereas the union ship does not permit that. The Seamen's Union will decide who is going to go on that ship, and the decision as to "Is he a member of the Seamen's Union, or one desirable to belong to that union?" That is the crux of this proposition.

Mr. PAYNE. The whole thing is this: First, that this is mainly today a hearing on unemployment insurance; secondly, that the fact that no matter who the man is, if he has worked at the trade for a number of years, if his ability and his character have been good, no matter what his union affiliations have been, I do not think any union or anybody—outside the shipowner, who might not want to hire him because his ability is not good—should have the right to say that this man cannot have a job because he does not have $6 to pay. I think this is against all American principles, against the American principles allowing a man the right to pursue happiness in the way that he sees fit, not the way that union officials see fit.

Next is this, that the seamen, that is, the rank and file of the seamen, the huge mass of them, are unorganized as yet. They belong to no union. Therefore, when we say that the seamen will decide this, this is not true, because the seamen really did not have any voice in this agreement. They did not vote whether they did not want to accept this agreement, this wage scale, or whether they wanted a closed shop or wanted an open shop. They had no vote on it when this agreement was made. Therefore, I think this policy is incorrect.

Mr. LESINSKY. You in one breath talk for organized labor and in another breath entirely against organized labor organizations. What type of an organization is correct, then, for labor?

Mr. PAYNE. The type of organization I believe in for labor is one where the rank and file, that is, the members of that organization have the right to vote and do vote on any agreement made by the union officials, because the union officials are the representatives, and only representatives insomuch as they are spokesmen, just like when a representative is elected to Congress he is elected on a certain platform. If he does not follow out that platform, the next election he does not get elected. This is the principle here. But in the International Seamen's Union it has been so many years since there has been a good honest election that they no longer represent them. At the time that this agreement was signed by these union officials, the vast majority of seamen going to sea on the ships and unemployed were absolutely not in any union.

I would like to continue on the question of unemployment insurance.

As to other unemployment-insurance bills that have been presented to this Congress and through the press to the people of the Nation, we seamen find that they do not cover our needs. Because of the nature of this occupation men do not stick to one job for long periods. They do not even stay with one company for long periods. Therefore, any money they would have paid into any insurance plan would be a loss to them and a profit to the shipowner. Then, the Wagner-Lewis bill, which is so greatly publicized in the press, does not provide for seamen as seamen in the pursuit of their work leave the continent, and shipping companies do not operate within any one State. Therefore this bill is out of the picture insofar as seamen are concerned. Insurance plans of many natures have been tried in many steamship companies, and in all of these the seamen have been the losers, that is, in these plans where the seamen have donated along with the company.

The seamen want work at a living wage, but cannot get it because of the reasons I have stated. Therefore, if the shipowners or the Government cannot provide the seamen with regular jobs, they should pay them unemployment insurance, and not the seamen. The speaker a few speakers ago proposed a plan of the unemployed paying back at 10 percent, or something of that nature. This would be impossible for seamen, because they do not make much money in the first place, being the lowest paid of workers, and not staying in one company for a long time they would never be able to pay back for any fund. They go to sea and make one or two trips, they get off, they are unemployed awhile until they make another ship. By the time they got through they would be making no wages but paying back the money they had gotten on unemployment insurance. Therefore, I state again, in the name of the organization, we demand that the shipowners or the Government, or both, pay for unemployment insurance.

Then under most of the unemployment-insurance bills proposed there is no provision for the present unemployed tens of thousands of unemployed seamen. In the Workers' Unemployment bill (H. R. 2827) these things are provided for.

Among seamen throughout the Nation there is a mass desire for the Workers' bill (H. R. 2827). In January of this year seamen in every port on the Atlantic and Gulf of Mexico elected and supported delegates to the National Congress for Unemployment Insurance held in Washington, D. C. Tens of thousands of seamen have signed ballots and petitions signifying their desire and need for the

Workers' bill (H. R. 2827). Seamen have demonstrated their demands, which is real unemployment insurance, and they demand the immediate enactment of the Workers' Unemployment, Old Age, and Social Insurance bill (H. R. 2827).

Mr. Schneider. I would like to ask if it is not true that a large number of seamen on the United States lines or American merchant-marine ships are aliens, many of whom have their domicile in Germany or Great Britain; that is, their families live there; and they work on these boats?

Mr. Payne. Today, among the seamen in the American merchant marine, there is a very small percentage of foreign born. Before 1929 the percentage was much greater, simply because of the fact that when there were plenty of jobs ashore, American men would not sail the sea, would not go to sea, on a mass scale, for the reason that the conditions were so miserable that they were much better off making half that money ashore. Therefore, the shipowners had to go and find men to sail ships, and they found them among the Latin American, among the Spanish, among the German, the English, and the Scandinavian nationalities.

Mr. Schneider. What would you do about it?

Mr. Payne. The point is this: That these seamen who are foreign born, most of whom have taken out their papers, although some have not, they still have homes on the other side—these seamen helped to build up the American merchant marine to what it is today—or to what it was before they started laying up all these ships. Therefore, I do not think, at this period when the American merchant marine is not in as good condition as it was, that these men who helped to build up the American merchant marine should be thrown on the scrap heap.

Mr. Schneider. Just how would you arrange the bill to pay them? They are unemployed, and their families live in Germany. Under those conditions, would you have this bill fixed so that they could have unemployment insurance?

Mr. Payne. If they have sailed in American ships for a certain length of time, in order to make them bona fide seamen, and if the shipowner has hired them when he found use for them, I think that the shipowner, through his share of unemployment, and the Government, for whom the American merchant marine has been a benefit, should pay for these seamen when they are unemployed. These men worked on these American ships, and while there was work for them, the Government and the shipowner found use for them; but when they no longer need them, is it fair to throw them on the scrap heap? We do not even do this with old horses; we farm them out.

Mr. Schneider. Yes; but I am making the point with the idea of getting this cleared up in the bill—not necessarily in the bill, but sooner or later it has got to be settled. What about the seamen on these American ships who live in Germany, and whose money practically all is spent in Germany, or in England, France, or Belgium? When they are out of work they naturally would not remain here; they would naturally go to their homes in Germany. Do you think it would be right that he should be sustained in his unemployment in Germany or Great Britain at the expense of a tax on the American people?

Mr. PAYNE. Oh, no, that would not be true. But if the ship-owner lays up his ship here, in the United States, or finds a reason to cut down the crew here, in a port in the United States; and among those seamen laid off are foreign-born seamen, some of whom may not be citizens; if they are laid off in an American port by an American shipping company, I think then that those seamen are entitled to unemployment insurance so long as they stay within the boundaries of this country. The Government already has laws and regulations whereby foreign-born, or foreign seamen, those not having citizenship papers, are only allowed to stay in this country a certain length of time between ships. These same seamen are not allowed to run coastwise—that is, between American ports—they have to run to foreign ports. So there are already laws covering these men, so that they will not be a long period in the United States. While these men are unemployed in the United States, not through their fault but through the fault of the shipowner, I think they should get unemployment insurance.

Mr. SCHNEIDER. Then they would have to go to Germany, if they were unemployed?

Mr. PAYNE. No; they would not have to go to Germany immediately. They are given a certain length of time in order to find another ship.

Mr. SCHNEIDER. Yes; but they would not find another ship if their family lived in Germany, and under my supposition, naturally they would go to their home. Now, of course, if we paid them, they would remain here; and if we did not pay them, the chances are that they would go home.

Mr. PAYNE. No; this is untrue, Congressman, for very specific reasons. First, the seaman makes very little wages; and if he is supporting a family in any country today, he finds it very hard, very difficult, to do it on his own wages. Do you see the point? So, therefore, if he became unemployed in the United States, I am sure he would not have the wherewithal to take himself back home to Germany. I do not know how he would do it, unless he got a job. So this is the case, whether he is paid or not.

Mr. SCHNEIDER. Maybe he would get a job working himself back. That is often done, you know.

Mr. PAYNE. Well, seamen's unions of all natures are against work-aways on ships. So they would be against a man working his passage, because that is in the nature of forced labor; and we are against any type of forced labor.

Mr. SCHNEIDER. I am not saying that I am in favor of it either, but I am saying that that has been done; it is done now, and I imagine it will be done in the future.

Now, you spoke about the fact that when we went off the gold standard, the wages of the seamen were reduced practically 50 percent. How do you figure that?

Mr. PAYNE. I figure that by the actual facts of what seamen running to foreign ports experienced after we went off the gold standard, that the exchange was not worth as much in these foreign countries. The exchange rate was not so high, so therefore when they got paid in these foreign countries, for instance, for $5 they did not get as many marks, or pounds, or francs, or whatever it might be, wherever they may have been; and in that way it is a wage cut.

Mr. SCHNEIDER. Seamen on American ships get paid in American money, do they not?

Mr. PAYNE. No; for this reason, that in foreign ports, whether the captain gives them American money or not, they go ashore to the money changers; and sometimes the captain himself pays them in foreign money on the ship.

Mr. SCHNEIDER. But the American seamen do not spend so much of their money in those foreign ports?

Mr. PAYNE. Well, there is a large number of seamen running between American and foreign ports. Some of the seamen are not steadily on these lines year in and year out, such as the American-France line, running to France, and the International Mercantile Marine boats, the *Roosevelt*, and those big boats, running into Germany. These seamen are not on the boats year in and year out; and after they are paid they spend their money for whatever they buy; they have about as much time in one port as they do in another.

Mr. SCHNEIDER. Well, under those circumstances, when our dollar was on the old standard, he had a lot of money, that is, he could buy a lot in the other countries; while now, when the exchange is the other way, he cannot buy as much in the other countries.

Mr. PAYNE. I think the point you are driving at, if I understand you, is that therefore he spends his money in America. But that is not the question. It is a question of the seamen going ashore, when they go to get a meal, or go to a dance; their money is gone much more quickly than it used to go. It does not go as far, and therefore it is a cut, it is a wage cut; no matter what he spends it for, it is a wage cut. He spends half of his shore time across there.

Mr. SCHNEIDER. That is all, Mr. Chairman.

Mr. LESINSKI. Are there any other questions? If not, that will be all, sir.

STATEMENT OF THOMAS JEFFERSON CRAWFORD, GLASSBORO, N. J.

Mr. LESINSKI. Will you state your name for the record?

Mr. CRAWFORD. Thomas Jefferson Crawford, Glassboro, N. J., R. F. D. No. 1.

Mr. LESINSKI. And what do you represent?

Mr. CRAWFORD. I am representing the Agricultural and Cannery Workers' Industrial Union of New Jersey—South Jersey. I have been working, doing agricultural work, ever since 1927, employed principally by Seabrook Farms, and am representing the Agricultural and Cannery Workers' Industrial Union of New Jersey. Before the "new deal" policies the condition of the agricultural workers was 75 percent better than since the N. R. A. After the N. R. A. the small farmer could not compete with the big farmer, who could afford to get lower prices for his products because of his better equipment and his ability to hire more workers. As a result the small farmer had to leave his farm and go to work for wages. This increased and is continually increasing the number of unemployed wageworkers in this region. Since the "new deal" policy about 75 percent of the agricultural workers in New Jersey are unemployed.

Before the depression on the big farms the agricultural workers were getting from $2 to $3 a day on the average for all of Jersey. At that time the workers would be employed a good 6 or 7 months out of the year. Since the depression on the big farms the biggest season for the agricultural workers is from 3½ to 5 months, with no chance of work out of the season at all. Wages fell from $3 to as low as 75 cents a day, and the highest was $1.50 a day.

Mr. SCHNEIDER. You are not really making a comparison between the wages before the N. R. A. was enacted and since, but rather between the wages before the depression and since that time; is that it?

Mr. CRAWFORD. Yes, sir. Before the depression the agricultural workers could make better than what they can make at the present time, because the prices were not as high as they are at the present time under the N. R. A.

Mr. LESINSKI . What prices are you talking about?

Mr. CRAWFORD. Prices of food, especially, and clothes.

Mr. LESINSKI. Well, clothes and food are cheaper now than they were in 1929. You can buy a good suit for $25 now that you paid $50 or $60 for then.

Mr. CRAWFORD. Well, I never paid that much for a suit of clothes in my life, because I never made that kind of money, not in agricultural work.

Mr. LESINSKI. What has the N. R. A. to do with those prices?

Mr. CRAWFORD. Well, you take the N. R. A.; in buying food and clothes, they have taxes on the food, and naturally you cannot go in there and buy it with the money that you make out in the agricultural fields.

Mr. LESINSKI. But is it not a fact that your prices today, in spite of what you have said, are cheaper than in 1929?

Mr. CRAWFORD. Well, maybe the prices are cheaper, but at the same time the wages are cheaper than what they were at that time.

Mr. LESINSKI. All right. Proceed with your statement.

Mr. CRAWFORD. As I say, since the depression wages have fallen. Farm workers could not afford to send their children to school and could not make enough to support their families. Nearly all the agricultural workers, everyone on the fields, were forced onto relief. Even the relief given the agricultural workers was not anywhere near adequate. My family of five received at the most for relief, up until 1934, $1.40, and that had to last 2 weeks. Then that $1.40, when it was given me, was given to last 2 weeks, but they did not give me an order and tell me that I could get what I wanted to get. What they did was this: They would put it down, like so many pounds of beans, or so many pounds of flour, and things like that; and naturally a person could not live off of it. If he would turn around and say, " I will eat the beans today ", if he did that, he had to save the soup for tomorrow.

Mr. SCHNEIDER. You know that is true pretty much all over the country. It is largely due to the local management of the relief. There are always people among the workers discriminated against, and every community has a different standard by which they are going to take care of the unemployed, at the present time and in the past.

Mr. CRAWFORD. Yes; but not only certain kinds of people are discriminated against, but you take the whole entire field, the people that are doing agricultural work, I don't care what complexion they are, what color, what nationality, that is all they receive.

Now, the head man of the relief administration was the big farmer. In Deerfield Township, the head of the relief administration was Mr. Seabrook, who is the biggest farmer-owner in the East. He had complete power over relief and could give and deny to anybody he chose. And as everywhere, the Negro worker was the last to get relief, even though he was the first to be fired and unemployed. He was the last to be hired and the first to be fired. Therefore the Negro people in the agricultural regions are the very most oppressed. When the C. W. A. was started in 1933, in Cumberland County, Mr. Seabrook, who was overseer of roads during the winter months gave the jobs to the people on his own farm instead of to the workers who were unemployed and living only on the small amounts they could get from the relief. He gave the jobs, too, to the small farmers that were close to his farm, in order to keep the agricultural worker down at the point of starvation. This was so that he could then hire them at very low wages when the season started. That is the way it is done all over south Jersey, and not only south Jersey but the whole entire Jersey. During the winter months, if there is any kind of work, naturally the big farmers will get together and set the prices that they are going to give the people, in order to keep the farm workers down. Then they cut them off the relief, right around the last of January, or the last part of February, so that they will be hard up against it, in order to force them back to work for the very lowest-paid wages.

Mr. LESINSKI. Whose fault would you say it would be that that discrimination has been made?

Mr. CRAWFORD. The discrimination against the workers?

Mr. LESINSKI. Yes.

Mr. CRAWFORD. Well, I would say the " new deal " policy, Mr. Congressman, because if the " new deal " policy would keep up the rate of the laborer, naturally the farmer would have to pay the price, but instead of that, they cooperate with the big farmer, and the big farmer can turn around and say, " They don't need this." That is just the same as the big farmers have done in South Jersey. When anything has been sent down, they send it back to the Government and say, " They are well taken care of here."

Mr. LESINSKI. Is it not a fact that the Government has allowed all the States to take care of their own relief administration? What does the " new deal " have to do with it?

Mr. CRAWFORD. Well, they give them power.

Mr. LESINSKI. I do not agree with you. Right in my own town all the administration of relief was done by Republicans, and I am a Democrat. I would not object to it, and neither did they. They just went there and did the work. The " new deal " has nothing to do with local administration. It is your local administration you can kick at, but the " new deal " has not anything to do with it.

Mr. CRAWFORD. Well, you take the " new deal ", if they would continue to keep up the rates that they promised, that they started to pay the people working on the C. W. A., instead of letting the big farmers say, " This is too much to give them ", in order that when they start to work, they can say to the agricultural workers, " We cannot pay you what you ask."

Mr. LESINSKI. Then it is the fault of your local administration that they have not paid the prices that they should have paid. There was no agreement, no restriction put on any local administration, no requirement to pay a living wage. Right down in my town of Dearborn, I know there were painters who ordinarily earned 40 cents an hour, and when they went to work on C. W. A. work, they got $1.40 an hour. If your local administration has done something wrong, you cannot blame the national administration.

Mr. CRAWFORD. Well, but how about a situation where they complain, if they do like we did, what will be done? We brought a complaint to Washington, and what was done about it? They did not do anything about it.

Mr. LESINSKI. Of course, I do not know the details of that, and I cannot answer it.

Mr. CRAWFORD. Mr. Seabrook even sent clothes, which had been sent by the relief, back to the Government, forcing the workers to stay there and work for him. At these low wages, from 50 cents to 75 cents a day, with the highest being $1.50 a day, with children from 7 years of age working to help keep the family from starvation, Mr. Seabrook could hire all the workers he could use. He was hiring everybody he could get, working them from 10 to 16 hours, knocking off work in the fields and going right into the cannery to work during the night. They had to do this to get enough to buy food at the high " new-deal " prices.

Now, as to the situation after the strike: The strike forced Mr. Seabrook to pay higher wages. To get rid of these higher wages and to kill the union, Mr. Seabrook cut down on his labor staff, firing the Negro workers and union workers first. He did this by changing his crops and getting more machinery on the farm.

In conclusion, even when the workers are employed, the rates are so low they can barely live. When they fight to get better wages, the big farmers try to kill their organization by firing them. The only solution is a good social-insurance bill that will be on a high enough standard to keep wages up during employment, and that will prevent the terrible misery of unemployment.

The Wagner-Lewis bill does not give any security at all to agricultural workers, especially those working on small farms. It leaves insurance to the States, and no State yet has made any arrangement for insurance for agricultural workers.

Only the Lundeen bill, which provides that if the agricultural worker is unemployed he will get $10 a week, plus $3 for every dependent, especially for the agricultural worker, due to his extremely low wages and his partial employment, takes care of his situation. The Lundeen bill also provides that he shall receive the difference between what he actually earns while working and what he would receive as a totally unemployed worker.

Mr. LESINSKI. Any questions? Do you want to make any other statement, or is that all you want to say? Does that complete your statement?

Mr. CRAWFORD. Yes, sir.

Mr. LESINSKI. That will be all, then, Mr. Crawford.

(Thereupon, at 4:25 p. m., the subcommittee adjourned until Monday, Feb. 11, 1935, at 10 a. m.)

UNEMPLOYMENT, OLD AGE, AND SOCIAL INSURANCE

MONDAY, FEBRUARY 11, 1935

House of Representatives,
Subcommittee of the Committee on Labor,
Washington, D. C.

The subcommittee met at 10 a. m., in the caucus room, House Office Building, Hon. Ernest Lundeen (acting chairman) presiding.

(The subcommittee had under consideration H. R. 2827, H. R. 2859, H. R. 10, and H. R. 185.)

Mr. Lundeen. The committee will to come to order. First, we will hear Mr. Kade.

STATEMENT OF WILLIAM KADE, REPRESENTING THE NATIONAL EXECUTIVE WORKMEN'S SICK AND DEATH BENEFIT, TOWNSHEND, MD.

Mr. Lundeen. Your name is William Kade?

Mr. Kade. Yes, sir.

Mr. Lundeen. And your address is 413 Virginia Avenue, Townshend, Md.?

Mr. Kade. That is my address.

Mr. Lundeen. You represent the National Executive Workmen's Sick and Death Benefit Fund?

Mr. Kade. I am representing the national office.

Mr. Lundeen. You are sent here as their delegate?

Mr. Kade. As their delegate, yes; to represent the national office.

Mr. Lundeen. How many do you represent here?

Mr. Kade. I am supposed to represent the whole organization.

Mr. Lundeen. How many are they?

Mr. Kade. The membership of the Workmen's Sick and Death Benefit today is about 50,000. It used to be 61,000, but according to the last report, at the end of December, we had lost approximately over 10,000 members, on account of this depression.

Mr. Lundeen. You mean on account of their being unable to pay dues?

Mr. Kade. On account of their being unable to pay dues, although we have made a great effort to save our members, by paying the dues out of the national office funds.

Mr. Lundeen. All right, then, go ahead with your statement. If you have a brief, here, you may file the brief.

Mr. Kade. No, I haven't brought anything like that.

Mr. Lundeen. All right, then, go ahead with your statement.

Mr. Kade. I just thought all that was necessary was to state the position.

Mr. LUNDEEN. Well, proceed and state your position.

Mr. KADE. Our organization, you know, is composed of working-men, all working people. They work in all different industries. We have machinists, we have stevedores, we have cabinetmakers, we have laborers, we have clerks, and so on. We have practically all kinds of working people in our organization. When the unemployment set in, in 1929, the membership of our organization was hit rather hard, especially those members that have worked on the waterfront, you know; the trade has come to practically a standstill, and from the branch that I am secretary of, branch 169, we have approximately about 36 percent of the membership, working as stevedores, and there were none among them that made more than a day or a day and a half a week, so it was a pretty tough struggle. We have tried our utmost to save the members, and we have, for instance, in our local treasury, $600 less than we had at the end of 1929.

We had in the local treasury over $600 at the end of 1929. That is absolutely wiped out now. We have paid dues for the men in order to keep them from losing their membership and their benefits in case of sickness. The same thing holds true for all the rest of the members of the organization. Unemployment is very great amongst the membership, very great. There are some of them that have been out for years, and very likely will be unable to get back, especially those that are over 50 years of age. As a matter of fact, it seems like all a man over 50 years of age is able to pick up is a job here and there, occasionally, you know—odds and ends. I have gone through the same experience. That is how I know. I consider myself physically fit and able to work, and yet I have been laid off. I was laid off in 1932, and since that time I probably have not earned over $600. I have always tried to hustle and to find odds and ends. The same holds true with the organization. The best proof is that we have lost such an immense number from our membership, although we have tried to do for them all we could. Take, for instance, the last month's statement. We have paid dues out of the treasury, again, for 256 members, so that is always running like that, between 250 and 300 every month. Each time the dues are paid for a member it is paid for 3 months.

Mr. LUNDEEN. Are conditions getting better?

Mr. KADE. I do not think so, Mr. Chairman. I do not think so.

Mr. LUNDEEN. You think they are getting worse?

Mr. KADE. They are about stationary.

Mr. LUNDEEN. How long have they been stationary?

Mr. KADE. The way I consider it, they have been stationary since probably last fall a year ago, or since the fall of 1933. Men have found work occasionally, here and there, and then lost out again, and others, again, have lost their jobs entirely since then.

Mr. LUNDEEN. Mr. Kade, you have stated the conditions there, quite in detail. Now, what about this bill?

Mr. KADE. Well, we are in favor of that bill, because we think that something should be done for the workingman, giving him some kind of protection.

Mr. LUNDEEN. The administration has a bill which they claim is going to do something for him. Mr. Townsend has a bill, and he is going to do something for him.

Mr. KADE. I do not consider the administration bill sufficient, and I think that the Townsend bill is probably excessive.

Mr. LUNDEEN. You believe this bill, however, is the golden mean, and the road between the two extremes?

Mr. KADE. That is what I think. That is what I think.

Mr. LUNDEEN. Do you think the bill is practical, and one that can be carried out?

Mr. KADE. I think so.

Mr. LUNDEEN. Has your organization studied it?

Mr. KADE. Yes, sir.

Mr. LUNDEEN. You know the provisions of it?

Mr. KADE. Yes; I know the provisions, as far as the benefits that are supposed to be paid are concerned. I consider them, at least, sufficient means to keep people living, while I consider some of the things in the Government measure as insufficient and as permitting starvation.

Mr. LUNDEEN. Have you discussed H. R. 2827, or, during the session of the Seventy-third Congress, H. R. 7598, in open session, in your organization?

Mr. KADE. Oh, yes. Oh, yes.

Mr. LUNDEEN. Did they take any vote on it?

Mr. KADE. Oh, yes.

Mr. LUNDEEN. What was the vote?

Mr. KADE. They were in favor of it, always, practically unanimously.

Mr. LUNDEEN. Is there anything else you want to state?

Mr. KADE. No.

Mr. LUNDEEN. I think that is a very good statement, and I thank you very much. Are there any other questions?

Mr. LUNDEEN. The next witness is Mr. Frank McCulloch, of Chicago, representing the workers' committee on unemployment.

STATEMENT OF FRANK W. McCULLOCH, CHAIRMAN OF THE CHICAGO WORKERS COMMITTEE ON UNEMPLOYMENT

Mr. LUNDEEN. Will you state your name and address?

Mr. McCULLOCH. I am Frank W. McCulloch, chairman of the Chicago Workers Committee on Unemployment, whose main offices are at 20 West Jackson Boulevard, Chicago, Ill. The organization is an organization of unemployed and part-time workers, centered in the city of Chicago, probably the oldest unemployed organization in that city. It, at present, consists of some 3,500 locals, numbering about 7,500 paid-up members. It is affiliated with the Illinois Workers Alliance, of which it is a branch member, which numbers some 235 locals throughout the State of Illinois, and is the largest organization representing the unemployed in the State of Illinois. I would estimate that the number of members in the Illinois Workers Alliance is in excess of 50,000, and they are active in all parts of the State. The Chicago Workers Committee, itself, with a history going back over 3½ years, has been pressing the struggle of the unemployed in that city, not only for the jobs which they all so much desire, but also for an improved measure of unemployment relief, and for the State responsibility for the handling of the relief burden, principally by means of an unemployment-insurance system.

The insistence of our members throughout has been, in the first instance, for jobs, and if you can get a riot on any one thing, about as easily as any other, it is over the effort of the unemployed, themselves, to take advantage of opportunities that are thrown out, to get jobs. Chicago has probably seen plenty of riots, people standing in line, attempting to get the few jobs that were offered, just as they have those people protesting against the unjust distribution of relief. The Chicago Workers Committee has endorsed the present Lundeen bill, H. R. 2827. It considered the bill, introduced in the previous session of Congress, and endorsed that bill, and has thoroughly studied the provisions of those legislative measures for dealing with the unemployment problem.

For several reasons the bill of the present session seems to us to be absolutely essential of passage, if the workers are going to get any adequate provision for their needs. In the first place, it recognizes the primary responsibility of the Federal Government for caring for needs. It does not depend upon possible but somewhat doubtful State cooperation, in order to insure workers in any State protection. I consider this point, because a great many States may not have, first, an appreciation of the necessity for such support of workers; and, second, may not have the financial credit necessary to carry on an adequate system, such as that proposed in this bill.

Mr. LUNDEEN. In that connection, may I state that it is reported in the press that several States have already announced they will be unable to meet even the provisions of the administration bill.

Mr. McCULLOCH. I think that is very important. It reinforces the necessity of the Federal Government taking a lead with its resources of credit and its appreciation, or at least partial appreciation, of the enormity of the task that is to be achieved.

In the second place, the bill appeals to the unemployed workers, because it permits a system of compensation providing for immediate payments, and does not depend upon some remote, future time, when, through a contributory system, a substantial fund has been built up.

If all of the American workers were presently employed, a contributory system might have some real meaning in this country. With over 11,000,000 workers out of jobs, any system which substantially depends upon contributions from wage pay rolls for the payment of benefits has no present meaning to the masses who are out of work. The bill that we are now discussing makes provision for those groups, and is to that extent the only bill which holds out any real hope to the unemployed workers in the country.

Mr. LUNDEEN. In that connection, contributions mean that you will have to wait a year or two before any benefits can be had, as I understand it.

Mr. McCULLOCH. Yes; and I think the workers are perfectly willing to bear their fair share of the cost, when they have jobs out of which they can bear that cost; but when they do not have jobs, it seems a heartless and a cruel thing to make any payment of compensation to them conditioned only upon payments out of wages which they do not receive.

Mr. LUNDEEN. In other words, the administration bill does not touch the center of the problem?

Mr. McCULLOCH. That is it; exactly.

Mr. LUNDEEN. They do not get down to bedrock?

Mr. McCULLOCH. And it deals with future unemployment, not with the unemployment which we have with us, which is bad enough to require immediate attention.

Mr. LUNDEEN. Might I say it probably would attempt to deal with the next panic? It is no solution for present problems.

Mr. McCULLOCH. That is it.

Mr. LUNDEEN. But it does not take care of the one we are in today?

Mr. McCULLOCH. So it seems to us in Chicago, at any event. The bill also appeals to the workers in Chicago, because it seems the most realistic attempt to pay this compensation to workers for unemployment—which is no fault of their own—from sources which can best afford to meet that cost.

Considerable talk is made about the prospective cost of this bill, but as we compare it with some of the other expenditures of the administration, for war preparations and the like, the cost likely to be entailed by this bill seems in no way to be exhorbitant. The war against the suffering of the unemployed in this country ought to be carried on with as much vigor and as much sincerity as the preparation of our armaments for the carrying on of wars against foreign nations.

I may say, with further reference to the sources from which the money for these compensations are to be derived, that according to the bill, that it is to come from the Treasury, and such surplus as is needed is to come from increased gift, inheritance, individual, and corporate income taxes.

That seems to our organization to attack the present depression at the point where it most clearly needs attack, and, unlike the Townsend plan, which provides for the payment of benefits out of a sales tax, and which in effect taxes workers in order to pay benefits to workers, this attempts to supply the Government with resources that are available, namely, resources accumulated from incomes of over $5,000, and the recent statistics published by the Bureau of Internal Revenue, as to the large increases, even within the last year, in incomes of both corporations and private individuals, indicates that there has been a far greater measure of recovery in that field, and that the Government, if it is going to tax for the support of this bill, where the money is, will tax those high incomes, and will not tax the pay envelopes of the workers by using such measures as increased sales taxes.

I will not go into detail about the other provisions of the bill, such as the administration by commissions set up by the workers' and farmers' organizations, themselves, but we are heartily in accord with that principle, as being one which recognizes the primary interest of these groups in the administration of this whole matter of an unemployed indemnity.

In conclusion, I may just say that the unemployed workers have been patient for a long time. Their patience has been from time to time completely worn out, and riots have been the result. In no sense expressing a threat, but indicating for the record the increasing tension which exists in my own city of Chicago, I think the committee and the House should appreciate that only by some such provision as this, which in a sensible way attempts to meet the needs of the workers, can they avoid more violent efforts to achieve the same results.

Mr. LUNDEEN. You believe, then, that some bill, along the line of this bill, is necessary in order to preserve the peace of the country?

Mr. McCULLOCH. I think it is quite essential.

Mr. LUNDEEN. And the safety of the Nation, itself?

Mr. McCULLOCH. I do. There is increasing tension and sullenness among the unemployed, and while I think their patience, great as it is, will continue for sometime, I do not think that the Nation or its Representatives ought to continue to impose upon that patience, and expect them to sit quietly, in utter need and privation.

Mr. LUNDEEN. If the administration proposes to put across an administration measure now, which permits or requires the localities to take care of themselves, how is Chicago going to take care of herself, and Illinois, when, just recently, the city came here and received a loan of some $25,000,000 to pay their teachers, and are continually getting funds—how are they going to take care of the local situation, or can they take care of the local situation?

Mr. McCULLOCH. I do not see that they will be able to do so. The Governor, himself, in conferences with representatives of our group, has asserted that the State has no further resources from which to draw funds, and his representatives must have asserted the same thing when they received loans here in Washington.

Any such system as requires the cooperation of the States would therefore be practically impossible for Illinois to come in on—unless the State representatives have been fooling with the unemployed before. We have recommended in Illinois, I may say, the adoption of a necessary constitutional amendment, which would also permit income taxes with higher rates, on high incomes. If that were adopted, it might be possible for Illinois to raise some money, but that would be a long process, probably not completed for at least several years, and in the meantime we have hundreds of thousands, and with their dependents, millions of people in Illinois dependent upon a very inadequate relief.

Mr. LUNDEEN. You mean to say that the State of Illinois has millions depending upon relief?

Mr. McCULLOCH. That is right. There are 300,000 heads of families on the relief rolls. They estimate the average families at about four and a few tenths individuals per family; so that the State itself has well over a million persons now dependent upon relief.

Mr. LUNDEEN. We thank you for your statement. Are there any further statements?

The next witness is Prof. Horace Davis, of Bradford College.

STATEMENT OF HORACE B. DAVIS, COLUMBIA PH. D., BRADFORD COLLEGE, BRADFORD, MASS.

Mr. DAVIS. Mr. Chairman, I think that the big advantage the Lundeen bill has over the administration social security bill is its simplicity and its inclusiveness. The experience of other countries has shown that different kinds of payments for risks tend to run into each other. For instance, in England where I was a few years ago, we found that in one of those towns, Middlesbrough, which was very badly hit by the chronic crisis in England after the war, the poor relief and the unemployment payments had tended to amalgamate, so that the poor relief payments, which were set on a local basis, had been made exactly the same in amount, and were paid to exactly the same classes of people, as the unemployment payments; but, furthermore, the British experience was—and this has been repeated in other countries, too—that unemployment payments were far superior to poor relief payments from the point of view of maintaining the morale and the self-respect of the recipients.

The experience went to this extent that at times, when the unemployment insurance funds were not adequate to meet the payments to the unemployed, they were even paying poor relief through the unemployment insurance offices, by a special administrative arrangement in order to maintain self-respect.

Now, if that expedient was resorted to, would it not be far better to make an unemployment insurance scheme adequate and self-supporting from the beginning, and maintain self-respect and morale that much more? The administration bill, of course, does no such thing. It is not even pretended that the Wagner-Lewis bill will take care of any major depression such as the present one, or even such as that of 1921.

Mr. LUNDEEN. Would it be fair to say that the administration measure is aimed at future depressions?

Mr. DAVIS. The administration measure does not pretend to take care of future depressions, if they are on anything like the scale of the present one. Admittedly, it does nothing for the people who are unemployed at present, but further, it does not even pretend to take care of the unemployed in a future depression.

Mr. LUNDEEN. That is, adequately?

Mr. DAVIS. Well, it does not undertake to take care of them at all, after the first 10 or 15 weeks, after the waiting period.

Mr. LUNDEEN. In other words, it would be inadequate?

Mr. DAVIS. Absolutely, absolutely inadequate; any kind of unemployment that lasts more than 19 weeks will not be taken care of under the administration bill.

Mr. LUNDEEN. Is it fair to say that it means nothing for the present crisis, and is inadequate for a future crisis?

Mr. DAVIS. Absolutely fair. There is one particular kind of unemployment that is likely to escape attention, because it is one that crops up in particular parts of the country. Take, for instance, the situation in New England, where there are several industries that are moving either to other parts of the country, or else moving out of the large centers and into the small centers. Now, in a town like Haverhill, Mass., for example, I am informed that there were 20,000 shoe workers as recently as 1929, and at the present time there are less than 10,000, and the number of jobs for the shoe workers that are there is below 8,000, and still going down.

I have here an official report from the Department of Labor and Industries, of the Commonwealth of Massachusetts, which shows that in 1933 there were listed in Massachusetts 368 shoe-manufacturing establishments, and during 1933, 30 removed from their former locations in Massachusetts to other cities and towns in Massachusetts, and 31 moved to other States; making a total of 61 which removed from their former locations; and 53, which were in operation sometime during the year 1933, went out of business, making a total of 114 establishments whose workers were thrown on the community, and the only thing to balance that in the way of new employment was that some few establishments were started up fresh, or moved into the State; but during the whole of 1934, it was reported that only 14 establishments had been newly organized in Massachusetts, and only 7, which went out of business, had reorganized as new companies; so it is perfectly evident that there develop pools of unemployed workers in particular places, for whom the present social security bill has nothing whatever to offer, until the workers would be old enough to be able to apply for an old-age pension.

It is my contention that all relief to workers who are out of a job or disabled, for any reason, should come to them as of right, not as of charity, but there is another point of view that we have to consider on this question of social security, and that is the effect on the national economy.

I made a computation, one time, of the consumption in Germany, shortly after it had adopted unemployment insurance, and it was very striking to find, even in a period when employment was fluctuating very greatly, both seasonally and cyclically, that unemployment did not cause, apparently, any immediate falling off in consumption. Consumption remained quite steady, and I attributed that, at least in part, to the effects of the unemployment insurance. A really adequate program of social insurance, which kept the consumption steady, would undoubtedly maintain the markets to some extent.

In this present depression we find that the income of workers has fallen off in the same proportion as the national income has fallen off. It has been calculated that labor income is about two-thirds of the national income. That is putting it a little high, perhaps, but let us assume that is correct.. I think that is the Department of Commerce calculation. The decline in labor, anyhow, has been in the same proportion as the decline in national income.

Now, that would obviously not have been so if there had been an adequate system of social insurance, and the internal market would have been to some extent maintained. It is perfectly ridiculous to enter on a system of different State schemes of unemployment insurance, after our experience with workmen's compensation. The effect of leaving it up to each State to enact its own law on unemployment insurance, is to make a competition between the States as to which one will enact the worst law. Even today, 25 years after the States began adopting workmen's compensation laws, we find there are two States that do not have workmen's compensation laws, and, of those that do, there are some that might just as well not.

Even when experience has shown the desirability, from the social point of view and the point of view of the workers, of the exclusive State-fund system of workmen's compensation, or risk insurance, there are only two of the big industrial States that have such a system, and even the great State of New York, although it has been invited to enact such law, and the Governor has recommended the enactment of such a law, has recently reported unfavorably out of a Senate committee on the establishment of such an exclusive State fund.

In other words, in a system where business is run on a national scale, any social-insurance legislation that is going to be adequate must be run also on a national scale. The forces of national business can bring very intensive pressure to bear on State legislatures to prevent their enactment of adequate laws.

Mr. LUNDEEN. I was about to ask you if you thought that, in these days when the Federal Government, through the R. F. C. and other agencies, finances big business, banks, railways, war contractors, great refunding operation of taxes, and so forth, perhaps it might be well also, on a national scale, to let the Federal Government take care of the producers of wealth. That would be the import of what you are saying, would it not?

Mr. DAVIS. I think your contention is absolutely correct. If business is worth aiding on a national scale, then labor is at least as much worth aiding on a national scale.

I pass to my second point, which has to do with the administration of the bill. Your bill, Congressman Lundeen, provides for administration by elective committees of workers and farmers, and some have been inclined to think that this provision was something rather new—at any rate, new in our experience. I shall try to show that this provision is not a new experience for western countries, and that, where the experiment has been made, it has been entirely successful. I return to the experience of England, with which I am a little familiar. The British health-insurance system has been administered for many years, now, by committees on which the insured workers were represented by people of their own choosing. When I was in Middlesbrough, some years ago, I had occasion to talk to one of these workers' representatives, and he told me that, on this committee, where he sat along with certain professional people and Government bureau representatives, he, the workers' representative, had always taken the lead; he had made all the important motions that were made since he started serving on that committee some 10 years before. The committee had functioned successfully within the terms of its reference; the workers were doing the administering, in effect.

Mr. LUNDEEN. You mean to say there are nations that are really concerned with health service?

Mr. DAVIS. I mean to say that, in England, they have gone far.

Mr. LUNDEEN. Are there such nations?

Mr. DAVIS. There are.

Mr. LUNDEEN. In this country, if you declare for a national health service, you immediately become a Bolshevik, or a " red ", or at least a " pink."

Mr. DAVIS. I think, Congressman, the time is past when we need to be afraid of being labeled with such designations. Although, as you say, I shall undoubtedly be known as a Bolshevik, because I favor the Lundeen bill, I am content to try to carry that appellation with such honor as I may.

Mr. LUNDEEN. I had no reference to you, but they certainly put plenty of labels on " yours truly."

Mr. DAVIS. As far as sickness insurance is concerned, I noticed the only provision that is made in the Government bill is for a commission to study the subject. That subject has been studied by public bodies at least 16 years in this country, and for far longer in other countries. In England the health insurance has been well established for nearly a generation, and has been partially successful.

Mr. LUNDEEN. I would say, if a nation does not have national health service, it is guilty of barbarism. The health of the people should come first. Is that a fair statement to make?

Mr. DAVIS. I think a system of health insurance is fundamental to any adequate system of provision for workers, and the experience of England and Germany has proven thoroughly satisfactory with them, so that other countries have absolutely no excuse for not adopting such a system, even if they did not care to go as far as Soviet Russia, which has probably the best system in the world.

But, to return to this point of administration, the German health-insurance system is also administered by committees on which the workers hold, I think, two-thirds, or did, before the present regime came to power in Germany. Workers take these elections for the sickness bodies seriously. They choose their best men, and their best men are good men. They are competent administrators. It is my belief that there is a wealth of unused administrative ability in the working class, which is quite competent to administer far more than the health-insurance system.

Mr. LUNDEEN. Is it not the proud boast of this country that almost every man of prominence came from the farm and the log cabin? So your statement would be borne out by that.

Mr. DAVIS. I should be ashamed to think that the American workers were not at least as good administrators as the British and German and Russian, and inasfar as we have had any experience in this country, it has been favorable. I simply call your attention to the experience of the Baltimore waterfront, where committees of workers ran the relief for a period of some months, practically single-handed, before they were displaced, and they received a tribute from the Government Administrator at the time that he took over the job. He said, "Yes, you did a good job when you were running things here." And furthermore, this system of administration by the workers and farmers would have the inestimable advantage of avoiding bureaucracy in this country, and the creation of a staff of Government officials who were inclined to look down on the people that were entitled to aid, or treat them with the distance that is characteristic of bureaucrats.

Mr. LUNDEEN. What would you say as to the maternity-benefit clause in H. R. 2827?

Mr. DAVIS. I think the maternity-benefit clause in the Lundeen bill is one of its strongest points. "Eight weeks previous to and 8 weeks following childbirth" is not a bit too long for a woman to be off, and to give them full pay is the greatest protection that the child can receive. A woman ought to nurse her child, for its own good, and the effect of the present inhuman wage system is to drive working women back to work before they have a chance to get their children through the first dangerous period. I should not be at all surprised to see the period of 8 weeks after childbirth extended.

Mr. LUNDEEN. What about the accident and old-age and part-time provisions, and so forth? Do these clauses meet with your approval?

Mr. DAVIS. I, myself, have been a victim of an industrial accident, and I have never received any compensation, and I never could see why a victim of an industrial accident was any less entitled to receive compensation than a man who kept right on the job. I think that full wages for the period of disability is not a bit too much, and as for the old-age provisions, I am thoroughly in favor of them, too.

With your permission, I want to say just a word about the possibility of raising the money, which is one of the points on which your bill is sure to be attacked.

Mr. LUNDEEN. Before you go into that, what about the part-time provision, where men work just part time? Say I work 1 day a week, and I have a family; I have dependents. I cannot support those dependents, working 1 day a week, or 1 week a month, or 2 or 3 days a month, yet in many places, if a man works at all, he does not qualify for aid. This bill attempts, and I wonder if you feel that it achieves the point of raising the part-time man's wages up to full-time wages?

Mr. DAVIS. Well, Congressman, I have made a study of the steel industry in this country, and I have found that there are communities in which it has been not at all unusual for the steel workers to work, on the average, 1 day a month, and, from the money they made in that 1 day, was deducted the premiums for the company's group-insurance plan. On the remaining money, they were supposed to support a family, and if they applied for relief at the local agency they were then expected to surrender their employment check, which none of them wanted to do, because that would have prevented them from getting back to employment, if and when employment picked up.

Now, that was the system the steel companies attempted to impose in some communities, and I consider that such a system is absolutely inhuman, and, as a matter of fact, it could not be maintained. A man who is employed only part time is just as much entitled to relief, in my view, as the man who is altogether out of work, and possibly even more so.

Mr. LUNDEEN. You are the author of Labor and Steel?

Mr. DAVIS. That is right.

Mr. LUNDEEN. Where is your college located?

Mr. DAVIS. Bradford, Mass.

Mr. LUNDEEN. What is the name of it?

Mr. DAVIS. Bradford Junior College.

Mr. LUNDEEN. You are an economist?

Mr. DAVIS. Yes, sir; " social economist ", I call myself.

Mr. LUNDEEN. Did you state that the part-time employment clause meets with your approval, then? You think that accomplishes the end sought?

Mr. DAVIS. Perhaps you can point out to me just where this is.

Mr. LUNDEEN. It attempts to raise a part-time man to full-time wages.

Mr. DAVIS. Yes; I think that is what should be done. I think that one or two of the terms in this bill will have to be more definite,

Congressman, if you do not mind my saying so. I think you will have to be a little more definite on the "average local wages", and on your definition of worker.

Mr. LUNDEEN. What would you say should be stated as to the "average local wages"? We attempt to regulate that through the Department of Labor. Is that not definite enough?

Mr. DAVIS. That is all right with me, providing you specify whether you mean that skilled workers should receive the full wages that they were earning, or whether you mean average, local, unskilled wages. I think that is a point that needs to be cleared up.

Mr. LUNDEEN. You mean the average of their own craft?

Mr. DAVIS. The average of their own craft; yes, sir.

Mr. LUNDEEN. Or the average of all?

Mr. DAVIS. I think that point should be cleared up. I think that is a point that cannot safely be left to the administrative discussion of any Secretary of Labor. The "average local wages" might be interpreted to mean the average local unskilled wages, and the skilled worker, who was getting average local unskilled wages,, would, obviously, not be receiving the full wages of which you speak. On the other hand, if you undertook to pay average wages to all salaried people, including the presidents of companies and big corporations, you would find yourself in an impossible situation, and I, for one, should not be in favor of any bill that paid average local wages to corporation presidents at the scale of corporation presidents today.

Mr. LUNDEEN. Do you favor making this the average wage of all workers?

Mr. DAVIS. I think you might have some categories of workers; classify the workers into, say, five or six categories, according to their usual earnings, and pay unemployment insurance to them in the category in which they were accustomed to be.

Mr. LUNDEEN. Do you not think that is dangerous ground to get on?

Mr. DAVIS. I would like to have the intention of the bill, as it is, a little clearer in mind before I criticize it, really, to make sure just what you are intending to do when you speak of "average local wage." Did you mean average local wages of all crafts?

Mr. LUNDEEN. I think that is the only construction you can put on it, unless there are amendments made. We can amend the bill in the subcommittee or in the general committee. Many amendments have been suggested.

Mr. DAVIS. I personally do not feel that this is dangerous ground, necessarily.

Mr. LUNDEEN. You are going to set up a lot of classes—here is a group, and here is a group, and here is a group.

Mr. DAVIS. Of course, that is the thing that has been done in all the European unemployment-insurance schemes.

Mr. LUNDEEN. You feel that that works out there, and it should work out here?

Mr. DAVIS. I do not see why it cannot.

Mr. LUNDEEN. Well, perhaps that is a defect. I am glad you mentioned it.

Now, will you proceed, about the raising of the funds?

Mr. DAVIS. With regard to the question of raising money, my contention is that the great reservoir of untaxed wealth which can be

used for your purposes, is one of these which you quite correctly
mentioned, namely, inheritances. I do not mean to say that this
is the exclusive thing we ought to be taxed on, but it is the biggest
unused reservoir, and the best one to use. It has been calculated by
Dr. William J. Shultz, the author of a book on the taxation of inheritances, that the total amount of property passing at death, per
year, is, on the average, more valuable than the total amount of
taxes, national, State, and local.

The inheritance tax is, according to all theories, capitalistic and
communistic, the ideal tax; it is easy; it is plainless; it cannot be
evaded. It hinders the solidifying of class lines. It eliminates the
rule by the "dead hand of antiquity", and, when combined with
social insurance, it stimulates saving on the part of the broad masses
of the population.

Now, just a word on this "dead hand of antiquity." My college
happens to be Harvard, and not long ago, maybe 15 or 20 years ago,
a large bequest was received by Harvard for the purpose of establishing an engineering school. At about the same time the Massachusetts Institute of Technology, located in the same town, was
greatly expanding its facilities and establishing one of the finest
engineering schools in the country. Harvard wanted to turn over
the money that it had received to establish an engineering school, to
Massachusetts Institute of Technology, on condition that students,
registered at the Harvard engineering school, should be allowed to
go down and take some or most of their courses at Massachusetts
Tech, and an arrangement on that basis was actually completed
to the satisfaction of both institutions. But some disgruntled party
undertook to prove in the courts that this was contrary to the terms
of the will. The man who had made the will was presumably of
sound mind when he made it; at any rate, his will was never chal-
lenged in the courts by any disgruntled relative who wanted to prove
that he was insane. He would presumably have been open to conviction on the subject; he would presumably have seen the reason;
but, being dead, he could not be appealed to, and so the money was
taken back from Massachusetts Tech and turned over to Harvard,
which was then obliged by the will of this dead man to establish
its own engineering school. A friend of mine, who visited this school
afterwards and who is competent to form an opinion, reported that
the equipment they had been able to put in there was sadly antiquated and wholly inadequate.

I cannot go into all the details that I should like to on the other
advantages of the inheritance tax. Suffice it to say that the only
serious argument which has been presented against it by economists
is that it might interfere with saving, and it is my contention that,
on the contrary, a system of inheritance taxation, combined with a
system of social insurance, would stimulate saving among the very
people who are really the ones who should do the saving, namely, the
working people. The workers are now in a state of profound dis-
couragement, because they have seen their savings swept away by
bank failures or used for current living expenses and they are
beginning to say, "What is the use?"

Saving has been the exclusive privilege of the rich or the mod-
erately well to do, and it is not safe, it is not desirable to leave it up
to those people. In Soviet Russia, which has heretofore been known

as a country of low living standards, although perhaps not at the present time, or in the near future, it has been reported that there are no less than 1,600,000,000 rubles on deposit in the state savings banks. I say, when the working class can save like that, it is an indication of sound economy, and it is a thing that we ought by all means to encourage. Ultimately, I am in favor of a 100-percent inheritance tax.

Mr. LUNDEEN. However, our banks, here, are bursting with money, are they not? So people must be saving here, according to that; or, whose money is it?

Mr. DAVIS. I think you will find there are a lot of people that have more money than they know what to do with, who, when the depression began, took their money out of common stocks, or whatever it was, and put it into savings accounts, and the great inflation of savings accounts since the depression has largely been from exactly those people who had excessively large incomes. The problem of what to do with excess savings is not one which is likely to bother a country with a really well-balanced economy. It is only when the savings are in the hands of people who have far too much money, that savings are at all a problem from the economic point of view, as I could demonstrate to you if time permitted.

Mr. LUNDEEN. Did you say a moment ago that there is some doubt in your mind as to how the word "worker" should be defined, or that there is some uncertainty in the bill?

Mr. DAVIS. It is perfectly possible that you have in mind the current common definition of "worker"; that is, "wage earner." If that is so, then I would have no objection to the use of that term.

Mr. LUNDEEN. You consider yourself a worker, do you not?

Mr. DAVIS. I consider myself a worker.

Mr. LUNDEEN. You are an educational worker?

Mr. DAVIS. I am an educational worker, and yet I receive a salary. The question would arise, would I be entitled to unemployment insurance? I think you should define "worker" so as to include not only wage earners, but at least the lower salaried workers. I should be sorry to think that all salaried workers were included at their present salaries.

Mr. LUNDEEN. You have some documents that you are going to file, there?

Mr. DAVIS. I will file this summary.

Mr. LUNDEEN. Have you completed your statement?

Mr. DAVIS. I have completed the points that I wanted to make.

Mr. LUNDEEN. We have been very pleased to hear from you, Dr. Davis. Thank you for your statement.

Mr. DAVIS. You are very welcome, I am sure.

(Professor Davis presented for the record the following summary:)

SUMMARY, PRESENTED BY HORACE B. DAVIS, PH. D., COLUMBIA

Simplicity and inclusiveness are two big advantages which the Lundeen bill has over the administration social security bill. It is admitted that the administration bill will not provide for unemployment in such major depressions as the present one, or even that of 1921. In such depressions men will exhaust their unemployment benefit and go on to relief, with consequent loss of self-respect and morale. The experience of England, with which I am familiar, shows that from the social as well as the administrative point of view, it is far better to plan on a comprehensive unemployment-insurance plan from the beginning. England even came to the point of paying poor relief through the employment exchanges in order to preserve the self-respect of the recipients.

Administration of the social-insurance plan by committees of workers and farmers is not at all a new experiment in the history of western countries. For more than a generation now the social insurance of Germany has been administered by committees composed chiefly of elected representatives of the workers, while the British health insurance has also been on a similar basis from the beginning. The elected representatives of the workers have shown themselves competent administrators familiar with local problems and responsive to the opinion of the committee, and they in all respects proved themselves fully capable of the job. In the United States workers have made good in the only opportunity afforded them of a similar nature, namely, the administration of relief on the Baltimore waterfront by committees of workers.

Taxation on inheritances is the great reservoir which should be tapped in order to provide the extensive funds required for the purposes of the Lundeen bill. It has been calculated by Dr. William J. Shultz that the total amount of property passing at death per year is on the average more valuable than the total amount of taxes, national, State, and local. The inheritance tax is, according to all theories, capitalistic and communistic, the ideal tax. It is easy, just, and painless; it cannot be evaded; it hinders solidfying of class lines; it eliminates rule by the dead hand of antiquity; and when combined with social insurance, it stimulates saving on the part of the broad masses of the population.

Saving is now a privilege of the rich, but it can also be a widely distributed custom of the less-well-paid workers. Even in the Soviet Union, which has heretofore been known as a country of low living standards, the Finance Commissar has recently been quoted as saying that there were 1,600,000,000 rubles on deposit in the state savings banks, and one-third of the accounts had more than 1,000 rubles. Saving in a country which is afflicted by periodic depressions, and which has no adequate social insurance provision is apt to be discouraging. The chief difference between the man who saves and the man who spends as he gets is likely to be that the former goes on relief a little later. If he does not find his savings swept away in some bank crash, they are all exhausted on current living expenses, and he is no better off. Many thousands of wage earners are today asking, "What's the use?" With their living guaranteed by an adequate system of social insurance, such as is provided only by the Lundeen bill, such workers would take renewed hope. Saving would become a widespread custom in the bulk of the population. This indeed is the only safe and proper way for such an important function to be performed. We cannot afford to intrust it to an extremely small group of very rich people as we have in the past. The part of the inheritance tax in stimulating saving has been widely misunderstood. It is one of the most important recommendations of this fundamentally important tax.

There is really no reason why an inheritance tax should not be levied up to 100 percent. In fact, the only reason that I do not recommend a 100-percent inheritance tax at this time is that to levy a tax on this scale at once would mean abandoning certain other forms of taxation which are useful and should be retained for the present. Ultimately, I am strongly in favor of the 100 percent inheritance tax. Inheritance has always been a privilege and not a right, both in law and in morals. It is time to put an end to this pernicious and iniquitious institution.

Mr. LUNDEEN (acting chairman). The next witness is Mr. John Lyding.

STATEMENT OF JOHN LYDING, REPRESENTING LOCAL 1733, DYE WORKERS FEDERATION, UNITED TEXTILE WORKERS OF AMERICA, PATERSON, N. J.

Mr. LYDING. My name is John Lyding, and I represent the Dyers' and Finishers' Union of Paterson, with a membership of 6,000, affiliated with the American Federation of Labor. We have taken up

your bill in our membership meetings, and have explained it to the
workers. We have studied it at different meetings. In a general
membership meeting your bill was approved, and delegates were sent
down here to speak in favor of the Lundeen bill.

The workers in Passaic Valley—that is, Paterson, Passaic, and
vicinity—feel that, under this bill, we will really have adequate
protection in times of unemployment.

Mr. LUNDEEN. You find that the American Federation of Labor
unions support this bill?

Mr. LYDING. I may say that the United Textile Workers of America
comprises 240,000 members, all over the United States. We had
a convention last August in New York, at which a motion was passed
in favor of the Lundeen bill. Two hundred and forty thousand
workers voted in favor of this bill in New York.

Mr. LUNDEEN. That union is affiliated with the American Federation of Labor?

Mr. LYDING. That union is affiliated with the American Federation
of Labor; yes. We also sent a resolution to the convention in San
Francisco, urging the adoption of the Lundeen bill.

Mr. LUNDEEN. Are you familiar with the letter that was sent out,
or which is supposed to have been sent out, by officials of the American Federation of Labor, stating that this bill is unconstitutional,
and, I believe, stating that it is "communistic"?

Br. LYDING. Yes; I have seen the letter, and I know that the
higher-ups in the American Federation of Labor are actually in
favor of the Wagner-Lewis bill, although the militant membership
itself, the rank-and-file workers, are absolutely opposed to the
Wagner-Lewis bill, for we find it totally inadequate to take care of
the unemployed workers. We favor the Lundeen bill.

Mr. LUNDEEN. Do you think a letter like that was fair to be sent
out?

Mr. LYDING. Absolutely not. We tried to pass a resolution in our
convention in New York criticizing Mr. Green, but the resolution
was not passed, due probably to the presence of so many paid
organizers of the U. T. W. Our resolution endorsing the Lundeen
bill was passed. The resolution criticizing Mr. Green was not
passed. It lost by a vote of 96 to 150.

Mr. LUNDEEN. Proceed with your statement.

Mr. LYDING. The workers in Paterson and the Passaic Valley feel
that, since they have created the wealth of this country through years
of labor in dye houses and workshops, endangering their health, and,
after creating the wealth, through no fault of their own, they are
thrown out of employment and have to rely solely on relief agencies
and poor-masters; the best they get is a basket of groceries, forced
to live in hovels, and unable to pay rent, with about a half a ton of
coal through the winter; they feel they are entitled to have some
insurance to enable them to maintain their self-respect—insurance
such as workers have in other countries.

I formerly was a citizen of Holland. In that country we have an
unemployment insurance bill which is working very well. Our people in Paterson work an average of 30 weeks in the year, with an
average income of about $11 for a man and $8 for a woman. Under
the N. R. A. many of our mills are now moving out of Paterson,

because, under the N. R. A., we have two codes, the rayon code and the silk code, and the rayon comes under the cotton code. Our mills formerly were all silk mills but at present about 75 percent of our work is on rayons, and under provisions of the cotton code, the rayon factories and workers can go under the cotton code, working in the vicinity for as low as 30 cents an hour. This makes too great a differential, and the work is actually going out. Only in the last 5 months, five or six plants have totally closed down in Paterson, throwing another 1,500 workers on relief. Those mills have moved to New England, to Pennsylvania, and some to the South.

Mr. LUNDEEN. Let me ask you there: Has there been any endorsement of the administration bill by the unions?

Mr. LYDING. Absolutely not.

Mr. LUNDEEN. Has there been any reversal of their endorsement of the Lundeen bill, H. R. 2827, the so-called "workers' bill"?

Mr. LYDING. Our union voted twice in favor of the Lundeen bill; once, as the bill was known before, and now, as the bill is today.

Mr. LUNDEEN. There does not seem to be any great tidal wave of appreciation and support for the administration bill among the American Federation of Labor members, does there?

Mr. LYDING. Absolutely not. In the rank and file, there is much grumbling.

Mr. LUNDEEN. Have you heard of a single union endorsing it?

Mr. LYDING. No. It should never have been endorsed. You mean the Wagner-Lewis bill?

Mr. LUNDEEN. Yes.

Mr. LYDING. No; I have not, and I go around the country quite a bit. I feel that the sentiment is absolutely opposed to it, and I might add that the patience of the unemployed has been stretched to the breaking point, especially in our vicinity. We feel that something must be done to finally take care of those people. Today, they must go and beg for something they have a right to demand. We feel that they created this wealth: why should they not take part of it? And here in Washington, if the right people were in command, and if they actually had the best interests of the people at heart, they could do something immediately to relieve us, and something must be done, otherwise chaos will come. That is the feeling in Paterson, and I feel it is that way all over the country.

Mr. LUNDEEN. I think you are right, and if we wish to keep calm and quiet in the country, this is about the least we must do.

Mr. LYDING. Absolutely. That is how the workers feel about this, and I feel it will be no hardship to the Government. If, tomorrow, war broke out, and the workers of this country were called upon to go and slaughter and kill off the workers in another country, 10 or 15 billions of dollars could be appropriated immediately, as we ourselves saw in the World War; so we know the money can be brought forth. The money is at present in hiding, in the hands of a few multimillionaires, and it is to me a wonder how the workers have stood for this, when it is theirs. "God gave the country to the people", the old song says, and the people take no part in it. We have nothing to say. All we do is to beg for something, when we have a right to demand it, of course.

Mr. LUNDEEN. You say we can raise 10 or 15 billions for war?

Mr. Lyding. Absolutely; I have seen it.

Mr. Lundeen. And people would go and die in that war?

Mr. Lyding. Yes, sir.

Mr. Lundeen. Just think how glorious it would be to make the world safe for democracy.

Mr. Lyding. Of course, we at present are fighting for democracy ourselves, in our country. I feel, and many of the workers feel, that our country is slowly drifting toward Fascism, but I am sure that the workers in America will never stand for any dictatorships, and that is why we appreciate the effort now brought to bear by you, and by Congressmen like you, Mr. Lundeen, and by some of the other Farmer-Laborites; and, of course, I might add to this that, in our vicinity, we are now engaged in organizing a real party, not Communist, not Socialist, but a real progressive labor party, and we feel that it is to be a live power in America, and we will learn more about this as the year goes on; I am sure of that.

Mr. Lundeen. I will shake your hand on that. I am glad to hear you say it. I have been advocating a labor party since I was a very young man.

Mr. Lyding. And it is going to come. I have worked on it, and it is going to come; I am sure of that. What we do not like in the Wagner-Lewis bill is this: That the workers now employed receive less wages and the workers receiving these low wages will be obliged to pay out of them 2 or 3 percent, to help pay for the insurance on people who are now unemployed. It really means the poor taking care of the poor, and I would suggest that one way of raising this money by the Government is, of course, the inheritance tax. We have heard of that and also of the tax-exempt bonds. Take a man like Andrew Mellon: He has an income of millions—God knows how many millions—he lives like a king, and he does not pay a cent of taxes.

Mr. Lundeen. But think of all the crumbs that fall from his rich table upon the people below.

Mr. Lyding. Sure. If this were 300 years ago, when people were totally uneducated and could not read or listen to the radio, you would expect them to be like that, but the people's patience is now at an end, and I think they are now beginning to realize that they have a right to a better living. I think Mr. Mellon and those other millionaires who now have tax-exempt bonds should know that such bonds will be taxed, and that they will be made to pay as they do in other countries.

Mr. Lundeen. I agree with you.

Mr. Lyding. Mr. Mellon should be made to pay.

Mr. Lundeen. I agree with you, but we have not much more time. Will you proceed with your statement?

Mr. Lyding. Yes. This is on what I said before, that the workers in Paterson are losing much time, due to the N. R. A. That is about all I want to say, unless there are questions.

Mr. Lundeen. General Johnson says the N. R. A. is "as dead as the Dodo bird." Do you agree with him on that, or how does it work out there?

Mr. Lyding. Well, the N. R. A. is still working wonderfully for the "upper crust"—for the manufacturers and industrialists, for under it it is shown they actually gained 76 percent in dividends and profits, while the workers actually, in real wages, lost money. We can prove by the statistics of our union that real wages went down, and, of course, we are glad that Mr. Johnson—with whom I had personal contact—is out of the N. R. A.; however, the replacement is very poor; Donald Richberg today being looked upon as a traitor to the labor movement, of course. If real men were in charge of the N. R. A. and, as I told General Johnson at one time, if we had been given a place on the National Industrial Recovery Board, to formulate these codes, starvation wages would never have been put in, and I just want to say this: I regret to say I read this morning that the President approved the code of 25 cents an hour for the tobacco industry which, of course, is really a blot on civilization, that a man who is himself used to living on thousands a week should approve a code of 25 cents an hour for the workers.

Mr. Lundeen. And I would say, for your information, that when the Labor Committee of this House was meeting a year or so ago the great industrialists came before us; men of great wealth came before our committee, and, without exception, they were delighted with the N. R. A., and strongly favored it, with eulogistic praise. I was wondering if their optimism and joy about the N. R. A., would coincide with the same sort of good will on the part of labor and how long that would last. You think that is over now?

Mr. Lyding. The bosses still favor the N. R. A., some of them, because they are still left in every locality; Mr. Williams, of the tobacco industry; Mr. Whiteside, of the cotton industry—those men have the say. They sit around the table and make codes. The worker has no say at all, and when we make a complaint there is nothing done about it, of course.

Mr. Lundeen. Your opinion, then, is that the N. R. A. is not saving us, and that the crisis is such that we must have a social-insurance bill of some kind?

Mr. Lyding. Absolutely. That must be done, and the sooner the better; and I hope that it is put through in this session of Congress so the workers, in the coming winter, will be absolutely provided for; and I must say that something is required to be done before a tidal wave actually sweeps the country and the workers take things into their own hands, which I would rather not see happen. I would rather see things begin at Washington, because, eventually, the workers would have to take things into their own hands. Your bill provides adequate insurance for the workers. It is a step in the right direction, and I certainly hope it will be passed.

Mr. Lundeen. If this bill is passed, it will avoid violence and trouble in the country?

Mr. Lyding. Absolutely. I believe this surely, in all sincerity. I have seen the spirit of the people. I am speaking tonight at a meeting in Paterson; my colleagues, there, are speaking at a rally of the unemployed, and we know how those people feel.

Mr. Lundeen. Does that complete your statement?

Mr. Lyding. Yes, sir.

Mr. Lundeen. Thank you very much.

Mr. Lundeen (acting chairman). The next speaker is Mrs. Frieda Pearl, speaking on behalf of the United Council of Working Class Women.

STATEMENT OF MRS. FRIEDA PEARL, ON BEHALF OF THE UNITED COUNCIL OF WORKING-CLASS WOMEN, NEW YORK CITY

Mr. LUNDEEN. You may proceed.

Mrs. PEARL. The United Council of Working Class Women is an organization representing thousands of women throughout the country, including women at home and in the factory.

The purpose of this organization is the improvement of the conditions of the working woman and her family.

In the course of our activities, we find that the conditions of women in the United States today are most deplorable. During a survey taken on one night at the Salvation Army, Y. W. C. A., Red Cross, municipal lodging houses, and so forth, more than 12,680 women reported for shelter.

Mr. LUNDEEN. Where was this—what city?

Mrs. PEARL. No specific city, any one particular city. This is quoted from Grace Hutchins' work, Women Who Work. She gets all her data from the labor research bureaus, from the United States Bureau for Women, and so forth.

Mr. LUNDEEN. We are glad to get this, because we have so much talk about unemployed men. We do not hear much about the women.

Mrs. PEARL. I know that. They always forget about the women.

On that same night, a survey was made in 800 cities; 1,956 women were found sleeping in hobo camps beside railroad tracks.

To really estimate the total of homeless women, one would have to multiply the number by at least five, since it is a known fact that women and girls apply for shelter only as a last resort.

Many girls have left their home towns because, in most sections of the country, there is no relief provision at all for single women. It is estimated that of the more than 16,000,000 unemployed workers in the country, about 22 percent are women; in other words, about 3,500,000 girls and women want jobs and cannot find them.

Many women are faced with the double burden of caring for the home and at the same time being forced to work for a living. In order to do this, many women work at home for rates as low as 2 cents to 10 cents per hour, and so forth, with children as young as 4 and 5 years assisting, earning the paltry sum of $8 or $10 per month. Mrs. Elinor Herrick, of the New York Regional Labor Board, stated on October 24, 1934:

Home work is the most pressing industrial issue before this State this winter.

Maternity is another grave problem facing the working woman today. According to the United States Children's Bureau, 16,000 mothers die needlessly each year in childbirth, and over 60 percent, or 10,000, might have been saved through adequate medical and maternity care.

Mr. LUNDEEN. Are you familiar with statistics showing that this country has one of the highest mortality rates of any nation of the world, on that point?

Mrs. PEARL. Yes; I am.

H. R. 2827 is the only bill which provides for this; containing a maternity clause granting insurance for 8 weeks before and 8 weeks after the birth of the child. With no funds to meet the exorbitant prices of " bootleg " birth-control information, these mothers add to their already large families more mouths to feed and clothe. According to the Children's Bureau, 9,000,000 children are suffering from malnutrition. Because of this, they are susceptible to all types of disease and cannot be given proper medical care. These children are our future citizens; on them depends the future of the country.

The United Council of Working Class Women has endorsed the unemployment, old-age, and social-insurance bill, H. R. 2827, because, after a thorough study of all the unemployment-insurance bills presented to Congress, we find that H. R. 2827 is the only bill which will adequately take care of the workers. It is also the only bill which provides maternity insurance and includes all workers unemployed at this time. Other bills, such as the Wagner-Lewis bill, do not begin paying benefits until 12 months after enactment; leaving the present unemployed, whom industry cannot absorb, without any means of assistance.

Mr. LUNDEEN. And when they do begin payments it is only for a few weeks?

Mrs. PEARL. It is only for a few weeks; that is all.

Mr. LUNDEEN. Leaving the workers to starve to death thereafter?

Mrs. PEARL. That is just what it amounts to.

H. R. 2827 calls for immediate payments after the bill is enacted, and does not discriminate between any types of workers, whether industrial, farmer, professional, Negro or white, native or foreign-born.

In view of all the facts here presented, we, the United Council of Working Class Women, urge that this, the workers' unemployment, old-age, and social-insurance bill, H. R. 2827, be taken out of committee and presented to Congress for immediate enactment.

Mr. LUNDEEN. Just what are your qualifications for testifying? What experience have you had with the social problem?

Mrs. PEARL. Well, working in this organization, coming in contact with so many workers' wives and working girls, learning of their experiences, how they have been living and existing; and, as a matter of fact, I have to go no further than myself. I have been unemployed for a year and a half.

Mr. LUNDEEN. What is your work?

Mrs. PEARL. I do either bookkeeping or selling. I have been trying to do both. I have been trying to get any kind of a job.

Mr. LUNDEEN. You have had business experience and a great deal of contact with working women?

Mrs. PEARL. Yes.

Mr. LUNDEEN. And with these social problems?

Mrs. PEARL. Exactly.

Mr. LUNDEEN. I am just trying to lay a foundation for your testimony.

Mrs. PEARL. In regard to relief, even the present relief system, I will say, I have a husband who is working at the " large " sum of $12 a week. We have a child. Owing to the fact that my husband is already working and earning $12 a week, we cannot obtain relief. Surely, a family of three cannot live on $12 a week, and we are not entitled to unemployment relief, or any of the relief which is being doled out with the attitude of "aiding" these workers, when these workers, themselves, have contributed to the wealth of the country.

The workers are put in the position of being just beggars, that they should be thankful for the piece of bread they get, but that is not the case. The workers produce everything and are entitled to the benefits of the country. The Constitution provides itself that if Congress finds the people are not being supplied with the proper things and receiving proper care, the Congress itself has the power to administer this in the right way; and, therefore, we find that your bill is the only one which will give us any adequate relief. That is all I have to say.

Mr. LUNDEEN. How many members has this organization that you represent?

Mrs. PEARL. We have 5,000 members in New York City alone; 10,000 throughout the country.

Mr. LUNDEEN. You live in New York?

Mrs. PEARL. Yes, sir.

Mr. LUNDEEN. And you were sent here as a delegate or representative?

Mrs. PEARL. As a representative of the entire Council of Working Class Women.

Mr. LUNDEEN. That is your statement? You have concluded?

Mrs. PEARL. Yes.

Mr. LUNDEEN. We thank you very much. We are glad you came. Is there anyone else present that wants to be heard?

STATEMENT OF DR. REUBEN S. YOUNG, PHYSICIAN AND SURGEON, REPRESENTING THE INTERPROFESSIONAL ASSOCIATION, NEW YORK CITY

Dr. YOUNG. I would like to say something on maternity care. It has been found by studies in New York City that, at the present time, mothers who are admitted to the hospitals are in very low physical condition, due to improper feeding. In some cases it has been found that their blood count is sometimes below 50 percent of normal. In a recent study, made in the western part of the country, it was found that mothers who had no vitamin B during their pregnancy had a very high mortality rate, and also the children. It was found that mothers who had a large amount of vitamin B—that is, milk and eggs in large amount—had a low mortality rate, both mothers and children.

It has been found also that among the Negroes in this country the mortality rate for mothers—and the same for the infants—is almost twice as great as that of the whites, showing that the economic condition of the mothers has much to do with the mortality rate of both mothers and children.

It, therefore, becomes necessary that any unemployment insurance take into consideration the care of mothers during pregnancy. In a study of maternity insurance in different countries, I found that in England they have a maternity insurance that provides $10 a week for the mothers, from about 2 or 3 months beforehand up to delivery. In France there is a maternity insurance in which the mother receives one-half of her salary 6 weeks before and 6 weeks after delivery.

Mr. LUNDEEN. Are not maternity benefits quite general in Europe?

Dr. YOUNG. Yes. I found, in England, France, Austria, Germany, and in all the countries I went to, they had maternity insurance.

Mr. LUNDEEN. You have traveled over there?

Dr. YOUNG. Oh, yes.

Mr. LUNDEEN. And you are familiar with the situation?

Dr. YOUNG. Yes.

Mr. LUNDEEN. Then why should we not have it here?

Dr. YOUNG. Well, that is what I want to see.

Mr. LUNDEEN. You favor it?

Dr. YOUNG. Yes; I favor that. The condition among physicians, especially in New York and in Harlem, today, I think, is deplorable.

Mr. LUNDEEN. You have knowledge of the general physicians of New York, both white and colored?

Dr. YOUNG. But I am specially concerned with Harlem and with the Negroes. I think the condition is deplorable in Harlem especially. Only about 10 percent of the physicians there today are able to make a decent living. Twenty percent are practically destitute. Most of them have lost their homes, or are about to lose their homes and all their investments over a period of 10 or 15 years.

Mr. LUNDEEN. What is the colored population of Harlem, by the way?

Dr. YOUNG. About 327,000, and we have 150 physicians. Health insurance, therefore, would help to alleviate this condition. I found that in England, before the health-insurance law was passed, conditions there were similar to the conditions in America today, but since the passage of their health-insurance bill the doctors have been pretty well protected. For instance, I found that among the doctors in England, under the panel system, there are some who make as high as £100—that is $500 in American money—and with that as a basis or as a minimum to live on, plus their private practice, they are able to make a fair living.

Mr. SCHNEIDER. I would like to ask the witness if the mortality is greater or less in England than it is in the United States, according to statistics?

Dr. YOUNG. I have not the statistics for England available, but I think it is not very much different from America.

Mr. LUNDEEN. Are you engaged in the active practice in Harlem now?

Dr. YOUNG. Yes, sir.

Mr. LUNDEEN. How many years have you practiced?

Dr. YOUNG. Seven.

Mr. LUNDEEN. What is your university?

Dr. YOUNG. Howard University.

Mr. LUNDEEN. Of Washington?

Dr. YOUNG. Yes; and extra work in England and Vienna. I would like to state also that among the Negroes, due to their low economic standard, it has been found, in Harlem especially, that there is a very high death rate, the figures showing that the death rate per 100,000 population in Harlem is 212, and for the rest of the city 55.

Mr. SCHNEIDER. What year was that?

Dr. YOUNG. 1933.

Mr. SCHNEIDER. What was it in 1927 and 1928? Have you those figures?

Dr. YOUNG. I can give you the figures. This is not New York. This gives the Southern States. In 1928, all cases, 1,631; negroes 160, whites 61. Tuberculosis, negroes 160, whites 59.2.

Mr. LUNDEEN. That was for the Southern States?

Dr. YOUNG. That was for the Southern States.

Mr. LUNDEEN. And not for Harlem?

Dr. YOUNG. Not for Harlem.

Mr. SCHNEIDER. Now, let me ask you how the death rate of colored folks compared as between those living in Harlem and those living in the Southern States?

Dr. YOUNG. Well, I will give you all cases in the Southern States in 1932: Whites, 909; Negroes, 1,368. In New York the death rate per 100,000 population in Harlem, 212; in the city, 55.

Mr. SCHNEIDER. I did not get the comparison.

Mr. LUNDEEN. What is the proportion—greater or less?

Dr. YOUNG. It is less in New York than it is in the South.

Mr. LUNDEEN. Is that due to a better health service there?

Dr. YOUNG. Yes; better health service. The same is true of the tuberculosis rate in New York. In a 10 years' study it was found that 10 years ago the death rate was something like 450 for Negroes, 150 for whites. In 1933 the death rate jumped to 150 for Negroes, 50 for whites—one-third.

Mr. LUNDEEN. Can we conclude that the health of the Negro of the North is better?

Dr. YOUNG. It has improved in the last 10 years.

Mr. LUNDEEN. Is that due to climate or to service?

Dr. YOUNG. No—to better health service.

I was trying to prove here, however, that the lower economic standard of the Negro always causes a higher death rate. That is what I was trying to prove when I gave the figures on Negroes and whites. The same is true of the cases of tuberculosis in New York, where the figures are segregated into homes that are congested and in which the care is not as great as in the other sections, and we had a death rate on tuberculosis in 1933 in Harlem of 458, and for the rest of the city 136. I am trying to show also that with a low economic condition the death rate of a people is higher than the death rate with a better economic condition, and that if America continues to drift downward economically, then I guess that in the future the death rate, both among whites and Negroes, will go upward, even though it has not taken the upward trend as yet.

Mr. LUNDEEN. You would not agree with the statements you see in the press that the health of the people is improving because the times are bad?

Dr. YOUNG. No; I would not.

Mr. LUNDEEN. That statement has appeared in a number of papers.

Mr. SCHNEIDER. And the death rate generally is not increasing, is it, in the country?

Dr. YOUNG. Well, it has not. The point is, you see, people have a certain amount of resistance, and when that resistance is lessened they become more susceptible to disease.

Mr. LUNDEEN. No; but we mean the actual figures.

We do not want to theorize on it. We want the figures. In our home city I think the death rate is about stationary.

Dr. YOUNG. Yes; and it is stationary in New York, up to the present time.

Mr. LUNDEEN. I think there is a good deal of suffering there; nevertheless, the death rate is about the same, I think.

Dr. YOUNG. Yes. Last week there was a report in the paper, giving the death rate in Manhattan, showing 15, which was just about the same as for the previous year. I would like to file a statement here.

Mr. LUNDEEN. If there is no objection on the part of the committee, you may file it. You have no objection, Congressman Schneider, to the witness filing two pages?

Mr. SCHNEIDER. No; I do not object, but I think it is for the chairman to discourage a repetition of material that is already in the record.

Mr. LUNDEEN. Yes; indeed.

Mr. SCHNEIDER. If there is anything new, we are glad to have it.

Dr. YOUNG. I have here also a statement on malnutrition, a report by the Association for Improving the Condition of the Poor, and that is in my statement.

Mr. LUNDEEN. Then we do not need to go into that now.

Dr. YOUNG. That is something new.

Mr. LUNDEEN. We thank you very much.

(The statement presented for the record by Dr. Reuben S. Young is as follows:)

NEED FOR MATERNITY INSURANCE

The findings of the committee on maternity mortality of the New York Academy of Medicine reveal that the economic status of the mother has much to do with the risk of maternity. In a study of 341,879 births that occured in 1930, 1931, and 1932, it was found that there were 49 deaths per 10,000 live births for the slum population; 42 in the artisan group; 46 in the white-collar class; and 39 among the wealthier class; a difference of over 20 percent between the two extremes.

Since a large majority belong to the class of the poor, it is necessary that special attention should be given to their needs. The ineffectiveness of the present economic order to provide a decent standard of living for the majority of people not only effects the risk of motherhood but endangers the life of the child. In a study made recently in the Western States, it was found by statistical evidence that there is a connection between infant mortality and the lack of vitamin B, that is mothers who were unable to supply themselves with sufficient milk, eggs, and fresh meats during pregnancy showed a higher infant-mortality rate than those who were able to secure these necessities.

Where there is a high death rate under 1 month of age and also high premature birth rate, the mothers were found to be on a diet deficient in vitamins, especially B. With high vitamin consumption the death rate and premature-birth rate are low. A broad view of maternal welfare involves not only hospital and medical care, but other causes such as poverty, unemployment, poor housing, and malnutrition. The present insecurity of a large proportion of our people is prejudicial to healthy motherhood.

MALNUTRITION

In a recent report in the New York Times by Miss Frances Perkins, she said: "According to the United States Department of Labor, one-fifth of all preschool children are below par of health. Malnutrition has increased from 13 percent in 1929 to 23 percent in 1932.

The Association for Improving the Conditions of the Poor reported that less than 25 percent of the children examined in the summer of 1932 could be classified as properly nourished. It has been found also in many New York hospitals that at the present time a large number of mothers show a low-blood count, less than half the normal, that is that the large proportion are suffering from anemia attributed to malnutrition.

At the prevailing rate of relief it is impossible for pregnant mothers to obtain the essential food with the result that anemia tends to increase and with the increase in anemia will follow an increased mortality rate among mothers and an increased infant mortality.

SICKNESS

According to the Milbank Fund report 50 percent more illness occurred in families whose incomes dropped than those not much affected by the depression. This is corroborated by the American Association of Hospital Social Workers. In Dr. Wilbur's report it was found that between 1928 and 1931 only 68 percent of those ill received medical care. In 1933 it was found that only 52 percent received medical care, a reduction of 23 percent.

CONDITION AMONG NEGROES

It has been found, according to the United States census, that the mortality rate among Negro mothers is almost twice as great as of the white; the same holds true of the infant mortality rate. In New York City the maternal mortality is for Harlem 11.5 and for whites 6.41. Infant mortality rate for Negroes 89 and for the whites 53 per 1,000. (NOTE.—this is due to the low economic standard of the Negroes and to the differentials existing throughout the country.)

In New York it has also been found that the death rate per 100,000 population is Harlem 212, whites 55; for tuberculosis: Harlem 458; whites 136.

In a recent study of the Southern Conference Area for 1930–32, the average mortality from all causes among the Negroes constituted 39 percent of the mortality of the entire population; that from tuberculosis 53 percent of the total tuberculosis mortality in the entire population. This shows readily how disproportionate is the mortality among the Negroes since the Negroes constituted only 28.5 percent of the total populatoin. (United States census.)

PROFESSIONALS

It was found that 80 percent of graduates of high education institutions were unemployed in 1933: 10 percent of the private schools in the South were closed; 50 percent of those opened were on the brink of being closed. A large number of teachers are being thrown out of jobs and the rest are all underpaid. In Alabama Negro teachers were receiving $44 per month.

Physicians: A recent study of the Negro physicians in Harlem showed that the depression has affected them very severely. Not more than 20 percent of them are making a decent living, and about 20 percent are absolutely destitute. Since there are over 65 percent of the workers unemployed who cannot afford to pay for medical care, it becomes quite impossible for the medical man to exist on private practice.

Mr. LUNDEEN (acting chairman). The next witness is Joseph Howard.

STATEMENT OF JOSEPH HOWARD, REPRESENTING LOCAL 23, WOODLAWN, AMALGAMATED ASSOCIATION OF STEEL, IRON, AND TIN WORKERS, AFFILIATED WITH THE AMERICAN FEDERATION OF LABOR, BIRMINGHAM, ALA.

Mr. HOWARD. My name is Joseph Howard, Birmingham, Ala.

Mr. LUNDEEN. Are you a steel worker?

Mr. HOWARD. Yes, sir.

Mr. LUNDEEN. Just what is your work in the steel mill? What do you do there?

Mr. HOWARD. I am a galvanizer.

Mr. LUNDEEN. You do galvanizing?

Mr. HOWARD. Yes.

Mr. LUNDEEN. I have a picture in my office of a steel worker, denominated a "steel soaker." Do you know what that is?

Mr. HOWARD. Well, a "steel soaker"—there are different ways, because we call them "soakers" in the galvanizing department, the worker who soaks the steel in the acid. They call him a "soaker", too, so I do not know whether there is another "soaker" or not.

Mr. LUNDEEN. I am not familiar with that. I was interested. Make your statement as briefly as you can.

Mr. HOWARD. I am representing the Amalgamated Association of Steel, Iron, and Tin Workers, Local 23, Woodlawn.

Mr. LUNDEEN. What local? American Federation of Labor, or affiliated with it, or what?

Mr. HOWARD. Affiliated. Affiliated with the American Federation of Labor.

Mr. LUNDEEN. You belong to the American Federation of Labor?

Mr. HOWARD. I do.

Mr. LUNDEEN. Have you got their card?

Mr. HOWARD. I have got it, but I have not got it out here with me. Sure, I have got their card.

Our local fully endorses the workers' bill. I want to speak of the condition of the union people there in the industry that I worked in. There are 300 workers; 285 are members of the union. Two hundred of the union men have been laid off, unemployed, while the rest are piddling around there, working part time. This not only goes for this local, but there are two locals of the Amalgamated Association of Steel, Iron, and Tin Workers, in Birmingham. One is in the Connell Mill and one is in the Tennessee Coal, Iron & Railroad. We had a joint meeting with the Tennessee Coal, Iron & Railroad Co. workers, and they authorized me; I am representing them all. There is a membership of 2,000. The 2,000 workers are totally unemployed now because of the fact that they have shut down the whole plant, and the workers have no way to exist.

When the company shut the plant down for a period of 2 months, they placed the workers on the relief rolls. Afterward, through somebody connected with the company and the welfare department, the workers were dropped from the relief roll. Therefore, they have no way to exist. So, this also links up with the population of Birmingham as a whole. Out of 250,000 population 72,000 families are on the relief roll.

Mr. LUNDEEN. What is that? How much population?

Mr. HOWARD. The figures show 250,000.

Mr. LUNDEEN. And how many families are on the relief?

Mr. HOWARD. Seventy-two thousand.

Mr. LUNDEEN. That cannot be possible.

Mr. HOWARD. That is their statement, their figures, not mine.

Mr. LUNDEEN. That is more people than Birmingham has.

Mr. SCHNEIDER. I think 50 percent of the people in Birmingham are on the relief rolls; so your Congressman has told me.

Mr. LUNDEEN. Congressman Huddleston?

Mr. SCHNEIDER. Yes.

Mr. HOWARD. It is more than 50.

Mr. Schneider. More than 50 percent?

Mr. Howard. Yes, sir. It is more than 50 percent.

Mr. Lundeen. I wish you would check up on that 72,000 families. That cannot be possible.

Mr. Schneider. There would not be 72,000 families in the city—hardly 52,000 families in the city, all told. You have confused the number. You use the number, in one case, and the families in another. Of course, the family is supposed to represent four or five.

Mr. Howard. Well, they said " families."

Mr. Lundeen. Who said that?

Mr. Howard. The Birmingham Post reported " families." That is the report from the paper.

Mr. Lundeen. Well, it must be a misprint there.

Mr. Howard. It could have been, but it was there.

Mr. Lundeen. I wish you would check up on it.

Mr. Howard. Now, in the relief situation there, a family of two, who are working on the project, get the amount of $2.45 per week. The family has to buy the fuel and clothes and pay the rent out of the $2.45, and live.

A family of eight gets $5.95, either on direct relief or on work.

Mr. Lundeen. What is your authority for those figures?

Mr. Howard. My authority is because I, myself, am on the direct relief.

Mr. Lundeen. You are basing it on your own experience?

Mr. Howard. My own experience; yes, sir. I am not going to say what someone else says, now. I have, in the family, eight. I get $5.95 per week—no fuel and no clothes. These, I have to get out the best I can.

Mr. Schneider. You get that for work relief?

Mr. Howard. That is work relief.

Mr. Schneider. You get the same amount, whether you work or not?

Mr. Howard. Whether I work or not. I get the $5.95. On direct relief I get $5.95 worth, and on the work project I get $5.95 in money, so that is that. Now, the members of the locals there endorse the Lundeen bill.

Mr. Lundeen. You say the " members of the locals." Now, that is a broad statement. You mean the Federation of Labor locals?

Mr. Howard. That is exactly what I mean.

Mr. Lundeen. How many of them? How many locals?

Mr. Howard. Four locals endorsed the bill; 2 locals of the Mill, Mine, and Smelter Union; 1 local of the A. A.; 1 Federal local endorsed the bill. That was the first bill. Since it was newly numbered, we have the fifth local to endorse the bill, which is the Switchmen's Local of North America, No. 46; so that, now, makes five locals that have endorsed the bill, speaking of the new bill.

Mr. Lundeen. They are all Federation of Labor locals?

Mr. Howard. All are Federation of Labor locals. One of these locals was one of the strongholds of Congressman Huddleston's voters, when he was running for Congress. That was the Switchmen's Local of North America, which consists of all white workers.

Now, the workers endorsed the bill, first of all, because they see the need for some adequate relief, some bill that would give a substantial relief that they themselves could live on. And I want to state here something with which we are all familiar, that Negroes make up the overwhelming majority of the population in Birmingham.

Mr. LUNDEN. What is the percentage of Negroes?

Mr. HOWARD. Around 60 percent.

Mr. SCHNEIDER. Do you have any mixed locals, white and colored?

Mr. HOWARD. We have some mixed locals.

Mr. SCHNEIDER. There is no discrimination against the colored workers with reference to becoming members of the union, is there, of the American Federation of Labor?

Mr. HOWARD. In some locals, there is.

Mr. SCHNEIDER. But in the Steel Workers Union?

Mr. HOWARD. In the metal.

Mr. SCHNEIDER. But I am speaking of the Amalgamated Association of Steel Workers.

Mr. HOWARD. Yes, it is.

Mr. SCHNEIDER. Where is the discrimination?

Mr. HOWARD. In the T. C. I.

Mr. SCHNEIDER. What is that? What kind of a local—mixed?

Mr. HOWARD. No, it is not mixed.

Mr. SCHNEIDER. Is it colored?

Mr. HOWARD. There is a Negro local and a white local.

Mr. SCHNEIDER. Two locals?

Mr. HOWARD. Two locals.

Mr. SCHNEIDER. Where is the discrimination?

Mr. HOWARD. Some of the Negro and white workers wanted to meet together; so the field organizer, who is Mr. Crawford, said it was better for the white workers to meet in one local and the Negro workers in another. He did not state why, but he, himself, refused to let the Negro and white workers meet together.

Mr. SCHNEIDER. Well, that was no discrimination?

Mr. HOWARD. That was a segregation.

Mr. SCHNEIDER. That was the order; that was the decision, that they should organize; and they organized a colored local, and they organized a white man's local, and therefore all colored men should go into the colored men's local, and the whites, into the white workers' local?

Mr. HOWARD. But they see it somewhat as I see it. A lot of my local members see it this way: So long as they are in separate locals, there is no possibility of strength, because of the fact that the Negro does not know what is going on among the whites, and the whites do not know what is going on among the Negroes; therefore, in order that they be able to know these things, the minority of the white workers, with the majority of the Negro workers, put the question to Mr. Crawford, that they should meet together, so they would have the same thing.

Mr. SCHNEIDER. But that is more a matter of opinion. It is true that there are a number of local unions in many of the steel towns, where there are no colored people at all, where they are all white; and still there is a number of local unions, and they get along.

Mr. HOWARD. In other words, in local 23, the field organizer, it may have been the national organizers, too—I do not see why that was, because the president of the local, with the secretary and the vice president, had been writing for a communication, and they failed. Now, here is what happened: They allowed the company to take our

Negro job, a Negro union man's job and give it to the white worker, and they both were union men, so what was this? They did not say anything about it. The local president " raised sand ", but the field organizer did not say one word about it, so what is this?

Mr. SCHNEIDER. That often happens where there are all white workers; one white worker is laid off, for a reason, and another white worker takes his place.

Mr. HOWARD. No; this is a Negro job.

Mr. SCHNEIDER. I understand, but I am telling you; I am pointing out that that takes place where the workers are all white workers, or they may be all colored workers. Of course, that is not a subject to come up here. That is a difficulty you have within your union.

Mr. HOWARD. Yes; I understand.

Mr. SCHNEIDER. But what I was trying to bring out was that the colored worker had the right to membership in the Amalgamated Steel Workers, in the American Federation of Labor. That has been disputed here, and you are the witness to prove the fact that they do have access to membership in these unions.

Mr. HOWARD. Oh, yes; they have membership in the union, but there are separate locals. The main feature that was discussed, and that is discussed mostly, especially among the Negro and the poor white workers, which we can see that we all understand, is that the condition of both is going down rapidly, and it is going down on certain points. One of the main points is because of the Federal Relief Administrator uses lots of discretion, in order to hold back giving the relief to a big percentage of the workers. We see in this bill that it provides for workers, " regardless of age, sex, race, color, religion, or political belief."

We know, in our locality, that there are four families of white workers who have only been there for a short time, probably 2 months now, but they have been living there before now. These workers were refused relief on account of being out of the city for a while, so this bill shows that, regardless of where we are, we are entitled to relief.

Mr. LUNDEEN. In general, you have discussed the bill and agreed with the provisions of it?

Mr. HOWARD. We agree with the provisions; and the main thought of the union members is that the bill does not discriminate against workers who have been on strike. Also, it provides for average, local, trade-union wages, and this is something that all workers, especially in the South, and throughout America, actually need. We know that with the rising prices of food, and with the rising prices in the whole living standard, $2 and $3 and $4 a week do not provide for a family. Therefore we fully endorse the Lundeen bill. That is about all.

Mr. LUNDEEN. Is there any sentiment for the administration bill down there?

Mr. HOWARD. Not a bit.

Mr. LUNDEEN. Have they discussed it? Do they know about it?

Mr. HOWARD. The four bills have been discussed in mass meetings, but the endorsement of this bill, at the time that the workers held their congress here, was given.

Mr. LUNDEEN. You mean to say no unions have endorsed the administration bill?

Mr. HOWARD. I have not heard of a single union endorsing a bill in our city, except this bill. I have not heard of it.

Mr. LUNDEEN. That is your complete statement, then?

Mr. HOWARD. That is my statement.

Mr. LUNDEEN. Thank you very much.

(The hour of half past 12 having arrived, the subcommittee took a recess until 2 o'clock this afternoon.)

AFTERNOON SESSION

Mr. LUNDEEN. The committee will come to order, please.

STATEMENT OF MISS MILDRED FAIRCHILD

Miss FAIRCHILD. I am assistant professor of social economy at Bryn Mawr College. I am a member, perhaps you would like to know, of the Interprofessional Association, which is very much interested in Congressmen Lundeen's bill. I am a member of the national council of that organization. I am a member of the American Federation of Teachers; vice president of local 192, which is the Philadelphia local. I am a member of the American Association of University Professors, American Economics Association, and American Sociological Society, but I do not represent those organizations here.

Mr. LUNDEEN. Is the American Federation of Teachers affiliated with the American Federation of Labor?

Miss FAIRCHILD. Yes. The American Federation of Teachers is affiliated with the American Federation of Labor.

I want particularly to discuss the needs of women for unemployment insurance, especially. It is the section on unemployment insurance in your bill, Mr. Congressman, that I think I am most qualified about, though I am interested in the other sections. But as you said this morning, we do sometimes forget the needs of women. There is a common assumption apparently in this country and others that women do not suffer as much from unemployment as men, and that if they do suffer from unemployment, they do not have dependents, they are working rather for pin money, which is an old idea, and therefore it is not as serious and important that they should be taken care of.

We have quite a bit of data in this country from various well-recognized reports, and I would like to bring some of it in, if I may, in connection with H. R. 2827.

As you know, of course, to sum it up there are in the country, according to the 1930 census, 22 per cent women of the gainfully occupied people. But in industrial cities the tendency seems to be for the proportion of women to be rather higher than that. In Philadelphia, according to the State emergency relief board survey in February of 1934, among 876,000 employable persons, 68.8 percent were males, and 31.2 percent were females. Even in Pittsburgh and its vicinity, with its great preponderance of heavy industry, we find in the same State emergency relief board survey that out of 544,187 employable persons 25.3 percent were women. So that so far as industrial communities are concerned—I am using them just as an example, because I have recent figures—the figures of 22 percent are probably low, inasmuch as they include also agricultural areas where naturally the number of gainfully occupied women is not quite so large.

As to the question of unemployment among women, the statistics would seem to show that it is nearly as great as among men. In recent statistics, and for certain industries it tends to be greater than among men. It is interesting to see that if one compares it from 1930 up to the present time, the unemployment of women has increased and has come closer to the unemployment of men, and the two are much more in the same position than they were in 1930.

According to the unemployment census of 1930, taken by the United States Bureau of the Census, the unemployed women in all seven classes into which that was divided; that is, the total number, were 6.2 percent of the women ordinarily employed, whereas the unemployed men amounted to 8.5 percent. In classes A and B of the 1930 census; that is, the two classes that were ordinarily used throughout that census, the proportion of women was listed as 4.7 percent and the proportion of men as 8.5 percent.

We recognize, of course, that the census of 1930 has been charged by a great many very competent authorities as being a very definite understatement of the unemployment at the time. I am quoting these figures rather as comparison between the men and women than for the figures themselves.

In the industrial States the proportion of women unemployed tended to be higher, ranging from 11.3 percent in Rhode Island, as compared to 12.5 percent of the men, to 5 percent in Connecticut, as compared to 8.4 percent among the men. In my brief which I will submit to you, I will have more details than that.

Taking the census of 1931 made by the United States Bureau of the Census, in some 19 selected cities, in January of 1931, it showed that 23.6 percent of the women were normally employed in gainful occupations, and it revealed that 18.9 percent of these women were then unemployed. The proportion among men at the same time was 26.2 percent. That varied. In three boroughs of New York that were covered, it was for women 15.9 percent as compared to 21.6 percent for men. I think the proportions run very nearly the same all the way through. In some it is higher than that, in some lower.

Later figures show similar tendencies. Not only did the number of unemployed women increase, but their proportion of the total increased. As it happens, no unemployment survey on a national scale, as you know, has been undertaken since 1931. We have two important surveys, however, that are very indicative at the present time. A census of unemployment in Massachusetts as of January 2, 1934, was carried on as a civil-works project, under the direction of the State department of labor and industries. Last year also we had a study of Pennsylvania of unemployment, undertaken as a project under the State emergency relief board, in the spring of 1934. We have preliminary data from both of these surveys.

In the case of Massachusetts we find out of a total listed of 1,808,-804 employable persons, 522,616 were women and 1,286,224 were men. Of these, 18.9 percent of the men were unemployed and 19.6

percent of the women—a larger percentage of inactive women than men. Also, as one goes through their figures on Government projects, one finds 7.3 percent of the men employed and only 1.4 percent of the women. In work of a temporary nature, one found 0.2 percent of the men employed and only 0.1 percent of the women. So that the ability to take care of the women in any way was apparently in Massachusetts definitely less even though the unemployment was larger.

Taking the Pennsylvania study, in Philadelphia County there were 876,236 employable persons last spring. Of these, 32 percent of the men were unemployed and 33.9 percent of the women. In Allegheny County of Pennsylvania, which is in that same survey, we see a similar tendency. Out of 544,000 employable persons, 32 percent were out of work; 31.2 percent of the men were unemployed, and 35.8 percent of the women.

Mr. LUNDEEN. How do you account for the larger figures in Pennsylvania, or is there any reason?

Miss FAIRCHILD. Both of these, as it happens, of Massachusetts and Pennsylvania that I have taken—and I have taken them simply because they were the two that I could get—are States in which we have women employed; that is, both of them have textile industries; Massachusetts, of course, considerable textile, Pennsylvania some textile. The extraordinary thing is that we also have in Pennsylvania, of course, a great deal of metal industries, electrical trades, and women are employed in those trades. We have also iron and steel and coal. Women are not employed in those trades. I think the figures from Pittsburgh and Allegheny County very surprising, because there supposedly we have the heavy industries concentrated largely; still, we show a very large percentage of women unemployed last spring.

Women, of course, are used in clothing trades, as well as the textiles, and we have a great deal in the way of clothing trades in Pennsylvania. I can account for it only by the type of industry.

If I could go on and select at random, I would show in Carbon County and in Clearfield County, the same thing, although I was not particularly picking out the counties at all where the percentage of women was greater than of men. York County, one that I picked out, has 16.2 percent of the men unemployed and 16.1 percent of the women. But in every county as you go through there is a tendency for the percentage of the women to be very nearly the same as the men, or larger. Apparently at the present time the women are suffering unemployment very much. That is, those figures were as of last year.

A recent report of the Federal Emergency Relief Administration shows the occupational status of women on the relief rolls of 79 cities surveyed in that year. During this last year 7 percent were engaged in some relief work but had to have their wages supplemented by relief; 34 percent were looking for work but were unable to find it. In other words, a total of 41 percent of the women of employable age on relief were seeking full-time work. The other percent, the 59 percent, did not consider themselves gainful workers. They considered themselves housekeepers or homemakers, or occupied at home. But 41 percent were actually seeking gainful employment.

The report goes on to say, incidentally, that—

The 9 percent of both sexes who are employed are proving their capacity to work, but are unable to earn wages sufficient to support their dependents. Two-fifths of those working are women whose wages are traditionally low.

A bit on the subject of the duration of employment. I think that is extremely important now, because in the States where unemployment insurance bills are up, and in the Wagner bill, which is up at the present time, the assumption of the duration of unemployment is either that if it is wrong it can be disregarded, or we may expect that it is not extremely long.

Data on the duration of women's unemployment shows how extremely serious it has proven to be. Even in 1931, at least one-fifth of the unemployed women had been out of work over 6 months. And 26 weeks is the longest time in any of the State bills. New York State has a bill before it at the present time which allows for 26 weeks. But 6 months is a long time for most of the State bills to allow unemployment compensation to run.

I have here a report taken from the Women's Bureau Bulletin No. 113, on the subject of "Women's unemployment", which shows that in considerable detail. I will not go into that data except to say that those were the total over-all figures I gave.

The findings of the Massachusetts census of unemployment, which were for 1934, show that over 44 percent of the women wholly unemployed had been unemployed 1 year or longer. Of a total of over 45,000 out of 102,000 women wholly unemployed, over 25,000 of them had been unemployed 2 years or more and 18,000 had been unemployed 3 years or more.

The Federal Emergency Relief Administration, in its monthly report for September 1934, states that nearly one-sixth of all those who are seeking work have been unsuccessful in finding it for nearly 4 years.

We have had in Philadelphia, in 1933, a study of the unemployed by the industrial research department of the Wharton School of the University of Pennsylvania. An analysis of those figures shows that of the men, 59 percent have been unemployed more than a year, and of the women, 40.8 percent have been without work more than 1 year. Indeed, of the women, only 18 percent have been unemployed less than 3 months. I mention that because that 3-month figure, of 12 weeks, is again an important figure in the legislation that is being presented at the time in the various States and in the Wagner bill. Only 18 percent have been less than 3 months, and 40 percent have been without work more than a year. At the same time, the number that have been without work more than 4 years was extremely small, less than 2 percent, showing that there is a turnover, that there is a tendency again to get work, but not in a short time.

As to the responsibilities of these unemployed women—because, as I said, it is assumed possibly that women are working for pin money, or at least only for their own support—the Unemployment Census of 1930, showed only 9.7 percent of the unemployed women were heads of families, but it did show that 9.7 percent were heads of families; that is, they had the entire family resting upon them.

According to the Women's Bureau Report, No. 113, of 1931, " If information could be obtained for a later date, almost certainly it would show this proportion of 9.7 percent to be enlarged." The Women's Bureau report gathers data together from a selected list of 21 special studies that have been made. It found that over one-half of the unemployed women had others dependent upon them, though not all of them were responsible for the complete support of the others besides themselves.

In Pennsylvania 2 years ago the department of labor and industry made a study of a shut-down of two silk plants in Philadelphia and Bethlehem. That study was reported by the Philadelphia Bureau of Women and Children. It States that, practically two-fifths of the women who were turned out of those shut-down mills were or had been married; that all of the married women were accustomed to considering their earnings as part of the family income; and that three-fourths of the single women living with their families turned their earnings entirely over to the head of the family.

There is some interesting material in that same connection which has been gotten from the summer schools of women workers. I do not know whether you are familiar or not, Mr. Chairman, with the fact that at Bryn Mawr College for 10 years we have had a summer school for women workers. Following that, also, and affiliated with it have grown up a group of summer schools.

An analysis has been made of the responsibility of those women at the summer schools, of their relation to the family income, and that has been published by the Federal Women's Bureau. Of the women in summer schools, 459 reported on contributions to the family; that is, nine-tenths of all women in our summer schools. Those also, incidentally, were young women, because those were the type of young women who were in the summer schools. Just over half gave 50 percent or more of their earnings to the family, about one-fifth giving their entire wage.

The Massachusetts census of unemployment in 1934 likewise offers some figures on the employment status on heads of households. It shows at that time that 11 percent of the women were definitely heads of households.

As to the industries which are affected, it is quite usual for most of the bills for unemployment insurance to assume that if we take care of wage earners in the manufacturing industries we have taken care of the problem. The figures do not support that, Mr. Congressman. The 1930 census of unemployment does show the largest proportion of women unemployed in the manufacturing and mechanical industries, particularly in woolen or worsted mills, in electrical machinery, in cigars and tobacco, cotton, fabrics, and certain food industries. But while that census of 1930 shows 7.7 percent of the women in manufacturing industries unemployed, it shows 4.6 percent of the women in domestic service unemployed, and even 2.4 percent of the women in professional service.

Domestic and personal services were second to manufacturing. Figures in that census were not obtainable for the clerical group.

In the Census of 1931 the figures are larger. It shows again clothing industries, cotton, woolen, food, electrical machinery—much the same list—having a large percentage of women unemployed. By that time it had gone up from 10 to 22 percent. Taking the figures of this 1931 census, unemployment in the manufacturing industries was shown to reach 30.3 percent of the employed group of women.

But the so-called "white-collar" occupations, such as clerical, had a high proportion also, of 13 percent unemployed. Trade showed 19.4 percent and professional service, which includes public-school teachers, 4.8 percent.

"In every city the professional group had the smallest proportion of unemployment," so says the Government report, "but it must be remembered that in many cases women so trained are likely to go into other than professional work rather than remain wholly unemployed."

Again, it should be noted that next to manufacturing, domestic and personal services shows the highest rate of unemployment. Domestic service is a little hard for the census to define very definitely, because there will be people employed in personal service by large households who do not call themselves domestic servants, and yet they are personal servants, and therefore are listed together.

I said manufacturing was 30.3 percent of the women unemployed. The second group was domestic and personal, with 24.2 percent unemployed. Clerical occupations showed 13 percent, as I said, trade 19 percent and professional service 4.8 percent.

The later data that we can get on that are fragmentary, but the same University of Pennsylvania study that I referred to shows an equally interesting analysis in 1933. There, out of the total number studied—and this was merely a sample survey, covering 22,500 men and 7,900 women—the largest single group of unemployed persons in Philadelphia in 1933 was the domestic and personal-service group, making up 29.4 percent. The next group was the skilled and semi-skilled mechanical trades, where the women made up 28.2 percent. The clerical group made up 14 percent. Those figures are not very different from the others, with the exception of the fact that the domestic service has come around now in Philadelphia to head the list, instead of being second. In every case it has been quite close, you will remember, to the number for manufacturing industries.

It seems to me obvious from those figures that domestic workers ought to be included in any plan for unemployment insurance, and so ought clerical workers as such. That is, they should not be excluded.

In regard to employment among professions, general information is lacking. The Philadelphia survey to which I have referred shows them as 3.2 percent of the unemployed sample taken in Philadelphia. There is some information on the subject of unemployment among teachers, but not very much, I am afraid. The F. E. R. A., as you know, has recognized that there were a good many unemployed teachers and has made a very specific allowance, amounting to $2,000,000 a month, to the States, to provide at least part-time employment to the unemployed teachers and persons qualified to teach. They have had a quota of some 40,000 teachers. All of the States, I believe, except Oklahoma and Delaware, have had programs financed under that.

According to a recent statement from the Bureau of Education, apparently there are no accurate figures on the number of unemployed teachers. The outside estimate they say is 200,000, and the inside estimate, 100,000.

The National Educational Association estimates 200,000. But that figure may include young graduates from normal schools and colleges who have not actually taught.

I think that in this connection it is interesting to see a report from the National Educational Association as to teachers' salary. It is not right to assume that teachers could be left out. This report shows that fully one-half of the rural teachers in this country are receiving less than $750 a year. That is less than N. R. A. code wages. If, therefore, we have teachers out of the unemployment-insurance scheme, we are going to leave out a body of workers who are certainly no better off than the manufacturing industry workers whom we are including. So that they are not in a distinct economic class in anything like the way that is ordinarily assumed.

The F. E. R. A. report for January 1934 shows approximately 10 percent of the persons employed on works projects are classified in the professional and clerical group. And then it cites data on employment and employability in the relief population, showing that some 16 percent of the total number on the relief rolls belong to the white-collar anad professional groups.

A word about unemployment among Negroes, because your bill, Mr. Congressman, has very wisely, I think, a very definite clause prohibiting discrimination because of race. According to the 1931 census in the group of 19 cities, native white women unemployed constituted 16.9 percent of the white women ordinarily employed, and foreign unemployed women were 12.4 percent, while Negro women were 42 percent. In some cities it was as high as 58 percent. Those figures are borne out by the study in Pennsylvania this year, in both Philadelphia and Allegheny Counties, where the proportion of Negroes in most cases is considerably higher than the proportion of white, either native or foreign born. The Negroes in every case suffer first.

All of the evidence available seems to me to show that women workers are in practically as great need in the country as are men. It shows that the women are carrying much responsibility for dependents, whether as heads of the family or as contributors to the family income. Moreover, women are extremely difficult to care for by such things as Government works projects. How under the sun the Federal Government plans to handle the half of our unemployed women on relief in Philadelphia who are domestic servants, I do not know. It is difficult to bring that group into works projects.

To conclude, it seems to me that only the principles of H. R. 2827 provide any solution for unemployment compensation in this country. A Federal system providing uniformity and wide coverage, and a method giving compensation for the unemployed as one group, seems to me to be essential. Finally, what is perhaps most important of all, the burden of expense involved in this problem will never be carried systematically and adequately without Government participation, if not without the Government carrying it as the sole or major responsibility.

Mr. LUNDEEN. By "Government" you mean the National Government?

Miss FAIRCHILD. I think it has to be the National Government, because I think it has to be uniform from State to State, and I know of no way by which you can get it uniform from State to State except by having the Federal Government do it.

It seems to me that there is a tendency among experts at the present time to underestimate the cost of this thing which we are facing. We must do it. But it is going to be expensive. It cannot be done from State to State. Moreover, I do not think it can be done by a tax on pay rolls, which then will be transferred into prices, whether that tax is paid by employers or employees, and it seems to me obviously unjust and impossible to get it from employees.

Mr. LUNDEEN. Pardon me; will this bill cost any more than the relief we are going through now?

Miss FAIRCHILD. Yes; I think it will, if we follow out the provisions of your bill, Mr. Congressman, because I think you are going to do a better job than we are doing with relief at the present time, most decidedly. I think we must do a better job.

Mr. LUNDEEN. I mean the Government expenses in general, such as financing through the R. F. C., various banks, railroads, and so forth. That is supposed to be included in the mass of contributions now made for recovery, because that is supposed to spill a little of the prosperity on the lower grades from the abundance of the table.

Miss FAIRCHILD. They suppose that some of it will seep through?

Mr. LUNDEEN. Yes.

Miss FAIRCHILD. I do not myself have the figures as to the total amount being spent by the Government.

Mr. LUNDEEN. I do not mean the amount going to plain relief, I mean all of them piled together would not be very far different from this figure here, would they?

Miss FAIRCHILD. It is hard to estimate exactly. I think one has, however, to take into consideration the amount of unemployment that we are likely to have. In the first place, I am convinced myself that your bill in itself is going to help to reduce unemployment, because it will increase purchasing power, because a great deal of that money does not filter through that is not spent for relief one way or another. But I think the tendency we have at the present time to assume that unemployment is going to drop back again to our 1921–31 level, which is the figure that is being taken by many of our experts at the present time, assuming that we will have, say, an average unemployment in the next decade of 13 percent—if our average unemployment now, and we do not know what it is, but if it is 26 percent or above, we have to take it away down to something like 6 percent in order to get an average in the decade of 13 percent. I do not for a moment think that that is going to happen. I think we have to assume a higher unemployment coming. There is no use in our shutting our eyes to that fact and assuming that we can put a little tax of, say, 3 percent on pay rolls and do anything worth while about it; because we are going to make identically the same mistakes as the British before us have made, which they made in 1921 and have made repeatedly. I think it is useful to look at British experience in that connection.

The report of the Royal Commission on Unemployment Insurance, published in 1932, with which you are doubtless familiar, shows very definitely that the British made two very great mistakes in

1921. Aside from the fact that the system which was set up was not adequate in its coverage, they estimated their volume of unemployment on the decade before 1921, which they assumed was going to be 8 percent, because that had been the volume before, 8 percent of their normal employment. As a matter of fact, they were up against 13 percent of normal employment for the decade 1921 to 1931. The British had some excuse for that in the decade 1921 to 1931. I think there is absolutely no excuse for our making the same mistake in 1935, because we have had very much more time to see the trends of this post-war period than the British had in 1921. Moreover, the British raised the necessary funds by means of a tax on pay roll. Even though they did get part of it from employers and part of it from employees—I do not know from this point of view that it would make any difference if they got it all from employers—it was perfectly impossible, at least, politically it was impossible, to raise the necessary amount from a tax on pay rolls. In other words, as the Royal Commission puts it, the insurance principle broke down completely. It is interesting to see that the report of the British Trade Union Congress recognized this difficulty, and the recommendations of the minority, with which you may be familiar, the minority report of the Royal Commission on Unemployment Insurance supported the trade unions' point of view, and both are rather in line with the principles of your bill, Mr. Congressman, as regards unemployment insurance.

May I quote from that statement of the minority report of the Royal Commission?

The scheme for the payment of unemployment benefit as set forth in this chapter follows in many respects the same lines as the scheme which was placed before the commission by the representatives of the Trade Union Congress General Council. We agree with them in thinking that the insurance principle has broken down, that unemployment should be a national responsibility; that the scope of the scheme should be widely extended; and that benefits should be payable as long as unavoidable unemployment lasts. At the same time, there are certain other matters on which our proposals are a modification or variation of those put forward by the general council.

We wish at the outset to make clear four general considerations which in our view are essential.

(1) The cost should be a national burden.
(2) The scheme should be inclusive of all occupations.
(3) There should be no limit to the duration of benefit to the genuinely unemployed.
(4) Provision should be made for maintaining the employability of beneficiaries and for reinstating them in industry.

Mr. LUNDEEN. That is absolutely an argument for our bill here, is it not?

Miss FAIRCHILD. Yes. I am saying that the British Trade Union Congress and the minority report of the Royal Commission are putting forth principles which, so far as unemployment insurance is concerned in their report—and it is primarily on unemployment insurance—are very much in line with the principles of your bill.

Mr. LUNDEEN. That is, after the British have gone through the fire.

Miss FAIRCHILD. That is after having gone through 10 years of experience with unemployment insurance. In other words, they are discarding in their recommendations the very things which in our tendency in this country in the administration bill and in our

State bills we are trying to put in. I think it is worth while for us to realize what the experience of the British is in this connection, and not just assume that we are sailing on a completely unchartered sea. We are not. There is that experience there.

In my own opinion—I do not know—I do not think this bill was designed, and I am certain it is not likely, as has been charged, to break the economic system. I think it is a possible bill, a practical bill, not a dreamer's bill; a practical bill for us to absorb. I think it is simply drawn in some cases, Mr. Congressman, and I think there are certain ambiguities which need to be worked out, straightened out. But I think those defects could be easily remedied. The principles of the bill seem to be absolutely sound, and the only sound ones that I know of in this country.

Mr. LUNDEEN. Do you wish to point out the ambiguities there?

Miss FAIRCHILD. It seems to me that the question of the definition of who would be included in the bill is not clear.

Mr. LUNDEEN. You mean the definition of who are workers?

Miss FAIRCHILD. Yes; who are workers. I am assuming that the intention of the bill is not simply manual workers, but clerical workers, white-collar workers, every kind that you wish. And yet there are certain of the large groups who have a very much higher wage or salary than others, and it seems to me there might be an upper limit very well in this.

Mr. LUNDEEN. I do not know how the law might look at it if it is enacted, that is, how the courts would look at it. My own conception has been that, for instance, you are an educational worker——

Miss FAIRCHILD. Yes; and I am a worker.

Mr. LUNDEEN. I am an office worker myself, as a lawyer and as a Member here.

Miss FAIRCHILD. I consider myself absolutely a worker.

Mr. LUNDEEN. A Federal employee, or whatever it may be.

Miss FAIRCHILD. And I do not consider my salary high enough but what I might be grateful for unemployment insurance if I became unemployed. But I do think there are, if it is constitutional to do it, within the range of salaried workers persons whose salaries not only are high enough so that it ought to be possible for them to save, but also persons whose salaries are so high that it would be a considerable burden for the National Government to attempt to pay them compensation. I think the question as to the amount that would be paid is not entirely clear. I should suppose from the bill that you mean the average local wages would mean the average for a locality, not necessarily the average that a person receives. But I am not sure what the intention is.

Mr. LUNDEEN. Would you say that there should be a provision, too, covering the average of the craft in which the person works, or the average of all crafts?

Miss FAIRCHILD. I think that is a problem that one needs to think about, Mr. Congressman. I do not know that I want to answer definitely at once. I do think, if we are going to be thoroughly practical, that the experience of every country is that one wants to pay for unemployment insurance not more than a person can earn by his wage, otherwise it becomes the man's duty to his family to stay unemployed in order to provide shoes for his children. Obviously, you and I know that wages are very low. They do not provide an adequate living. And yet I do not think we can put upon unemployment insurance the task of lifting those wages. That has to be done, I think, in other ways. I am trying to be practical about it, you see.

Mr. LUNDEEN. There was no such intention, of course. I fear that the Congress in enacting a bill of this kind may reduce by a certain percentage the amount below the average wage. As far as I am concerned, I am willing to let it stand, but I know the disposition of many Members. I do not know what Congressman Lesinski might think of that, but I have heard Members state that perhaps if the bill were enacted it might be 90 percent or 85 percent or 75 percent of the average wage.

Miss FAIRCHILD. Of the average wage? For each group of workers?

Mr. LUNDEEN. That has not been clear in their own minds.

Miss FAIRCHILD. I think it should be. It is perfectly possible to think that out, but it needs to be done, I think, in a group. I would rather not state definitely at the moment what it seems to me is the desirable thing to do. I think heads need to be put together on that subject. Germany, of course, has tried it by dividing into categories. England pays a flat benefit.

Mr. LUNDEEN. For all workers?

Miss FAIRCHILD. For all workers, with an addition for dependents. This would do that as a minimum, would it not? In Soviet Russia when they had unemployment up to 1930, as I remember, it was a flat rate that was paid.

Mr. LUNDEEN. For all workers?

Miss FAIRCHILD. For all workers; and in line with the minimum with which there was a minimum wage law, a national minimum.

Mr. LUNDEEN. It has always seemed to me that if you are going to begin to divide them into categories, you are going to get into a lot of difficulties.

Miss FAIRCHILD. That is an administrative problem.

Mr. LUNDEEN. Did Germany find any difficulties there?

Miss FAIRCHILD. It is a difficult administrative problem; yes.

Mr. LUNDEEN. So the British and the Soviet systems were simpler?

Miss FAIRCHILD. Yes.

Mr. LUNDEEN. The British and the Soviet systems were alike in that respect, were they not?

Miss FAIRCHILD. My impression is that they were. Yes; I am quite sure of that. I was in Soviet Russia in 1929 and 1930 for nearly a year, just studying. That was before the unemployment was over.

Mr. LUNDEEN. I preceded you by a couple of years. That was one of eight countries that I traveled through at that time.

Miss FAIRCHILD. It was simply one of a number. I did not spend my entire time in Soviet Russia.

Mr. LESINSKI. I believe the madam has given us some valuable information regarding the percentage of unemployment for both men and women. There is only one thing that strikes me now. If you take, for instance, a family of 4—a husband and wife and 2 children of medium age or middle age—who are all employed, or in other words, they all had gainful occupations, how would you list that family against another family where the husband is the only provider, with a wife and 6, 7, or 8 children?

Miss FAIRCHILD. I think there is no question but under this bill, or probably under any bill that you can set up, that family will have a higher return than the family with one wage earner and 6, 7, or 8 children. On the other hand, when you have an allowance for dependents, you do give to that one wage earner some chance to lift the amount that he has for his dependents. Again, my answer would be, you are not trying by unemployment insurance to iron out some of the inequalities that already exist. After all, the family with four wage earners has a very much higher standard of living to maintain than the family with one wage earner. I may say that any family with 1 wage earner of an unskilled type that has 6, 7, or 8 children has absolutely not enough earnings to live on by any standard of living that has been set up in this country.

Mr. LESINSKI. There is still an education to give to the children.

Miss FAIRCHILD. He is suffering the entire time from inability to provide for the children at that rate.

Mr. LESINSKI. Of course, you get into another category where the husband is the wage earner and the wife is a teacher, both employed.

Miss FAIRCHILD. Yes.

Mr. LESINSKI. Then, in another instance, you will find where the husband is unemployed, but the wife is still a teacher, she is gainfully employed and gets a salary. Is that man entitled to unemployment insurance?

Miss FAIRCHILD. I should suppose that unemployment insurance in the countries where it is set up, as far as I know—and I may be subject to correction on this—is on the basis of the person who is employed. Therefore, if he becomes unemployed he has a right given to him as a self-respecting person to compensation for his unemployment, whether or not there is someone else in the family earning, who customarily does earn and therefore customarily contributes to the family expense.

Mr. LESINSKI. Then, that would be unfair to the big families who have only one wage earner.

Miss FAIRCHILD. No more unfair than our whole wage system is, Mr. Congressman. We are not attempting, it seems to me, and we cannot attempt by an unemployment insurance scheme, to provide an equality in the economic level between families. We do not have that. We are not trying to argue one way or the other as to whether that is desirable. By this scheme, it seems to me, a perfectly practical problem, we are trying to compensate for unemployment.

Mr. LUNDEEN. In the British system they made no exceptions, did they?

Miss FAIRCHILD. So long as the British system was operating—well, while the labor government was in and the system was operating on the basis of unemployment benefits for the unemployed person, as I understand it, that rule was followed and the unemployed person had it. Under the National Government the unemployment scheme has been changed in Great Britain and the means test has been introduced. As I understand it now, where there is no evidence of need there may be denial of the right. But that is the very thing which the British Trade Union Congress protest very sharply.

Mr. LUNDEEN. By that you mean a pauper clause?

Miss FAIRCHILD. The present law, I believe, stops the unemployment benefits after 26 weeks and throws the unemployed back on to public assistance.

Mr. LUNDEEN. I mean, the means clause; is that a pauper clause?

Miss FAIRCHILD. It amounts very nearly to that. It is a means of giving assistance to the person who actually shows necessity.

Mr. LUNDEEN. Even now for soldiers in this country we are drifting into the proposition where a soldier must state that he is pauper before he gets so and so.

Miss FAIRCHILD. Yes.

Mr. LUNDEEN. That has been the tendency. I do not say that it is so in every case, but it has been the tendency since the economy act.

Miss FAIRCHILD. It has been the tendency for 300 years in the past, Mr. Congressman, and I think it is time we changed it.

Mr. LUNDEEN. I just had those words in my mind.

Miss FAIRCHILD. It is the old English poor law, which assumes that there should be deterrents; in order to keep people working they have to be given a certain disgrace, or otherwise they will not work. We know better than that now, and we do know, I think, that people want to work.

Mr. LUNDEEN. I think the pauper clause is a piece of barbarism.

Miss FAIRCHILD. I agree with you, Mr. Congressman.

Are there other questions that I may answer?

Mr. LESINSKI. I have none. I think it was a wonderful statement. It was very clear.

Mr. LUNDEEN. We thank you very much for giving us this very able and fine statement.

STATEMENT OF JOHN McDONOUGH, PITTSBURGH, PA.

Mr. LUNDEEN. May I ask what you intend to cover? The conditions and the need for the bill, is that the point?

Mr. McDONOUGH. That is correct.

Mr. LUNDEEN. If so, then we have had a great deal of testimony on that, and we would appreciate your making it as brief as you can. Whom do you represent?

Mr. McDONOUGH. I represent the Pittsburgh Water Heater Co. Independent Union, also the Western Pennsylvania Committee for Social and Unemployment Insurance.

I wish to state right now that I feel rather ill at ease, being that I am only a worker. I work in the factory. But, nevertheless, I realize how acute this situation is. Day by day I am in daily contact with poverty and with unemployment and distress. I am not an economist. I am not highly educated enough to be one. But I feel the unemployment situation is such at this time that it does not require statistics nor a very diligent study. Since 1929 the bill has been studied all over the United States by economists, social workers, and others. My constituents have asked that when I come here I demand action. That is what we want—action. We do not want any more study of this bill.

Mr. LUNDEEN. Pardon me; you come from Mr. Dunn's district?

Mr. McDONOUGH. Yes; that is right; Matthew A. Dunn.

Mr. LUNDEEN. How many Congressmen do you have there?

Mr. McDonough. Just one.

Mr. Lundeen. There is more than one there, is there not?

Mr. McDonough. Matthew A. Dunn is from our district.

We feel right now there is a very drastic need for this unemployment insurance, because in our factory in particular some men are working part time; therefore, they cannot meet their needs through this relief. I know that these people who have studied out the relief have figured it right down to where a person is supposed to exist on that amount of money which they dole out in order to buy food, but that is impossible. I not only know from the experience of others but from my own personal experience. I do not work every day. I am working part time right now; although I do not receive any assistance at this time, I have in the past few years. Right now I am more or less independent.

We feel that the Lundeen bill, H. R. 2827, should be passed, because, once it is really passed, it will provide this unemployment insurance for the people instead of the relief which is being doled out now. The relief, I believe, causes people to lose their self-respect. It is not very respectable for someone to apply for relief. Whereas if the Government were to give people so much money per week to get their necessities of life, it would be much better.

Now, I have covered that much, I feel that I have impressed upon the assembly here the need in my vicinity for this unemployment insurance. Now I want to contrast it to the present administration bill.

Mr. Lundeen. Before you go into that, are conditions better or worse or stationary in your district as compared with a year ago?

Mr. McDonough. Compared with a year ago they are far worse.

Mr. Lundeen. Is that based on an opinion or experience or statistics?

Mr. McDonough. It is not only based on statistics—I do not have them on hand, but another member of our delegation has—but it is based on personal experience. I can see in my own neighborhood the changed condition from 1 year ago.

We disapprove of the Roosevelt security bill, or the program rather, which advocates the Wagner-Lewis unemployment-insurance bill, because under this bill we would have to wait 1 year before we could receive any unemployment insurance, and, if I am not mistaken, one is not eligible to receive anything at all from this bill unless he has been employed 10 weeks previous to its passage, at some time within 10 weeks previous to its passage.

Mr. Lesinski. In other words, the mass of the unemployed today are not eligible to any insurance at all.

Mr. McDonough. That is correct.

Mr. Lesinski. Except those that are working.

Mr. McDonough. That is absolutely correct.

Another feature about this Wagner-Lewis unemployment-insurance bill is that once one does receive it, it is only received for 26 weeks. That is the maximum length of time, I believe, 26 weeks. Twenty-six weeks of unemployment insurance would be just a little better than nothing at all, because, after all, when one is unemployed he is going to be unemployed for some time, and it is not just a temporary situation, and he has to have a permanent way of taking care of his needs.

Mr. Lesinski. Then your understanding is that under the Wagner-Lewis bill the greatest unemployment today exists among the older men. That is a fact, is it not?

Mr. McDonough. Yes.

Mr. Lesinski. Mostly 40 and over. There is more unemployment among that type than among the younger men. This older man who has raised a family and owns a house will have to lose it because he is not eligible to any compensation under that bill.

Mr. McDonough. That is true. I would like to be asked a few questions before I leave here.

Mr. Lesinski. You stated that the unemployment today is larger than a year ago. A year ago there were a lot of C. W. A. and P. W. A. works going on. That, of course, has taken up part of the unemployment. At the present time there is none of that type of work going on. Is there any other reason why in your district there is more unemployment now than a year ago?

Mr. McDonough. There is more unemployment in our district now than there was a year ago because the factories 1 year ago today were operating to greater capacity. Right now they are slow. Most of them are not moving at all. The L. W. D., that is, the Government relief work, is hardly operating at all in our district. Very few men are placed on these projects, and what few who are must be receiving money from the relief in order to get this job.

Mr. Lesinski. A year ago there were many projects going on in your district which took up a lot of this unemployment. Is that the way I should understand it?

Mr. McDonough. That is right.

Mr. Lesinski. And this year they are not operating?

Mr. McDonough. That is correct.

Mr. Lesinski. What I want to compare is the manufacturing employment of a year ago and today. Is it about the same or is it less in the manufacturing district—in the factories?

Mr. McDonough. It is less. They are not operating now as they were 1 year ago.

Mr. Lesinski. What types of plants are there in your district?

Mr. McDonough. Steel mills, metal shops, the Water Heater Co.; that is where I am employed.

Mr. Lesinski. That will be all.

Mr. McDonough. Rather as a conclusion, I want to say if this Lundeen bill is not passed in Congress, we do not intend in our vicinity to give up the fight. The fact is, we are going to carry on such an active campaign that we will be so strong before this next Congress goes that maybe we will not be satisfied to stop at an unemployment insurance bill. That is all.

Mr. Lundeen. Thank you very much.

STATEMENT OF C. H. BUSH

Mr. Lundeen. State your name and your connections.

Mr. Bush. I am speaking here for the textile workers in Massachusetts, through the State action committee on unemployment insurance in the State of Massachusetts. I am also here as the regularly elected representative from my trade union, branch 21 of the

American Federation of Full Fashioned Hosiery Workers in the city of Holyoke, Mass., which is an A. F. of L. affiliate.

The union workers in our trade union, local no. 110, have for 2 years now endorsed the Lundeen bill; that is, last year's number and this year's number. Also, in the hosiery workers' convention, taking in the membership of the whole federation, the bill was endorsed last June. I was the delegate from my local to the United Textile Workers of America convention, held in New York in September, which also endorsed the Lundeen bill—all A. F. of L.

As far as the hosiery workers are concerned, and it holds true to a greater extent among the textile workers in the State of Massachusetts, there is no question but what the question of the need of unemployment insurance is all over with. We believe and they believe that after 6 years, 5½ years of this depression, or call it what you will, the economic conditions of the textile workers in Massachusetts, including the hosiery workers, are such that there is no question in their minds but that what is immediately needed is something in the hand that can be transferred into the necessaries of life, either scrip or United States currency or whatever will procure for them——

Mr. LESINSKI. Or Federal notes.

Mr. BUSH. Anything at all; a green sheet, if it does the trick. The unemployment in textiles in Massachusetts since this codification of industry and workers, and whatnot, has increased.

Mr. LESINSKI. May I stop you right there? Have the wages increased since the codes?

Mr. BUSH. Generally speaking?

Mr. LESINSKI. I mean per person.

Mr. BUSH. If they have, it has been slightly.

Mr. LESINSKI. What is the reason, then, for unemployment?

Mr. BUSH. The reason for unemployment is, as they say, the stretch-out. I have talked, in the last 5 days, personally with textile workers from Fall River, New Bedford, from Salem, from Holyoke, Chicopee Falls, and Ludlow. The Johnson & Johnson Manufacturing Co., employing between five and seven hundred——

Mr. LESINSKI. Then, in other words, it is not the N. R. A., but it is the manufacturers who have conceived the stretch-out system?

Mr. BUSH. It is not the manufacturers, but the manufacturers working under the N. R. A.; that is, the N. R. A. The codification of the textile industry along with economic conditions practically compelled the manufacturers to stretch out. Here are a couple of specific examples: In Chicopee Falls, the workers tell me—this is not picking on any workers, just meaning the first 10 or 12 I came in contact with—I put the question to them, "Are you getting more money; are you doing more work for the same money as you were getting?" And they said, "Well, we are doing a lot more work." Very, very few will say that they are actually getting a few cents more in their pay envelop. The majority will say they are doing considerably more work for the same amount of money that they were getting before for a less amount of work.

In Johnson & Johnson—this is pretty well established in my mind simply from talking with the workers and their representatives—two workers are doing the work of three workers today, with not one penny increase in the pay envelop for when they were doing the work prior to this stretch-out.

In Holyoke, in Skinner's, the company has proposed to the spokesman for the workers, the union representative, the business agent, that they take 8 looms instead of 6, and that the basis of payment on that unit of work, namely, 100 picks, be reduced from $2, somewhere between $2.03 and $2.07, to between 95 and 98 cents.

Mr. LUNDEEN. How would 30 hours do, if you threw that bill in?

Mr. BUSH. If the textile code included the 30-hour clause, if the textile manufacturers are not allowed more than two 30-hour shifts, or a 30-hour shift for one worker? It would have a tendency to reemploy some textile workers. However, as I understand that with the technical development in the type of machinery that the textile industry uses, it would be much over a year before that gain would be canceled, and the workers would be unemployed again through the introduction of machinery that I understand is all ready, just waiting for someone to pick up. The same holds true in the hosiery industry.

Mr. LESINSKI. Let me put it to you this way:

If the Government, when they started the N. R. A., had provided all these codes and had given the first thought to the worker, and had said, " Here, Mr. Manufacturer, this worker can produce only so much and work so much on their machine ", and did not allow the manufacturer to make the worker work two or three machines when he is supposed to work only one, and cut the speed to a certain speed where the worker would not be a slave of the machine, would we not now have been farther along?

Mr. BUSH. I do not think that the worker as such—myself, anyway—is interested in so-called " laying down " on the job. I myself am willing to produce 10 times what I am producing now, provided I do not come home at night like—well, so the wife hates to see me come home, and I cannot sleep, and I am all played out.

Mr. LESINSKI. But that is the reason they have speeded up these machines, so that you are a slave of the machine.

Mr. BUSH. Yes; but the point I want to make is, I do not believe that we as workers—I would just as soon make 10 times more, provided it was not taking so much out of my physical self.

Mr. LESINSKI. What was the speed on their looms in 1929?

Mr. BUSH. I cannot speak of the technicalities in the whole textile industry. I can speak of the technicalities in quite minute detail so far as full-fashioned hosiery is concerned. However, from talking with hundreds, if not thousands, of textile workers, the speed has been considerably increased. Up in Adams and North Adams, I have friends and relatives that work up there. One of my relatives up there is a machinist. He was compelled at night to come back into the works and put larger pulleys on either the motors or the machines to change the ratio, to increase the speed, and attempt to do it so that the workers would not find it out.

Mr. LESINSKI. If the law were written in such a way that no machine could operate any faster than it operated in 1920, what would that do?

Mr. BUSH. That would have about the same effect as shortening the hours.

Mr. LESINSKI. I think it would have a better effect.

Mr. BUSH. Slowing down the machines? But is not that counter to a historic trend? You get more production so that humanity can be better off.

Mr. LESINSKI. I know, but we do not want to stop the minds of our people who have a genius for new machinery.

Mr. BUSH. Oh, no.

Mr. LESINSKI. We do not want to stop that.

Mr. BUSH. No.

Mr. LESINSKI. But what we want to do is to see that this new machinery is for the benefit of man.

Mr. BUSH. Yes.

Mr. LESINSKI. In speaking of your 1929 production, that was the peak of your production. If in that time a man operated 4 looms, in 1935 he should not operate any more than 4 looms, at 6 hours, at the same pay he was getting then for 8.

Mr. BUSH. You say 1929 was the peak of production? For industry, but not for the worker.

Mr. LESINSKI. I know it was the peak of production for the industry.

Mr. BUSH. For industry, yes. However, the peak production for a worker rises from day to day.

As far as the N. R. A., there is no question in my mind from talking with workers, white-collar workers, manual workers, and whatnot, that by and large, the N. R. A. was not a device, primarily—I call it a device, a plan, or scheme—it was not primarily in the interest of the worker. That is becoming more and more strong in the opposition to section 7 (a) as day by day goes by, just on such a simple thing as that. Section 7 (a) is written in about as clear language as I have ever seen in any sort of a legal document. It is quite clear. However, in the last analysis, we as workers look at the pay envelop, and look at our physical selves at the end of the day or the week.

Mr. LESINSKI. You say you are an operator on a loom machine for the stocking industry?

Mr. BUSH. Full-fashioned hosiery.

Mr. LESINSKI. How many pieces per hour can you produce in that time?

Mr. BUSH. In full-fashioned hosiery there are so many different gages, so many different sizes of machines; at present I am running a 54-gage. There is only one gage finer in America, with the exception of some experimental machines that are 60—54, 57, and 60. It is a 16-section machine. Our employer, when he put those machines in back in 1928, thought we could make 20 dozen, and would have been perfectly satisfied with that.

Mr. LESINSKI. That is the point I wanted to get to. You have to produce 20 dozen?

Mr. BUSH. Twenty dozen in a 48-hour week.

Mr. LESINSKI. In a 48-hour week. All right. What are you doing today?

Mr. BUSH. Today, when I work, due to certain modifications in the style of stockings—styles vary on the same machine, of course, depending on what the orders call for—I have produced quite consistently for over a period of 3 or 4 weeks that I happened to work. just prior to the Christmas holiday season, 30 to 32 dozen in a 40-hour week.

Mr. LESINSKI. Then if the law were written in such a way that the speed and production should not be any larger than it was in 1928 or 1929, and the hours were shortened, would not that have a tendency to reemploy double the amount of people?

Mr. BUSH. I am not so strong on the speed of the production equipment. I do not believe that the workers are so much as they are on the hours of work, because it will even up. It is either work more hours on a slower speed machine, and you feel about the same at night or at the end of the week physically.

Mr. LESINSKI. I know, but if you cut the hours on the slow-speed machine, not on the high-speed machine—I am talking of the slow-speed machine—would that reemploy more people?

Mr. BUSH. That is what I say. Instead of having a small percentage of the employable workers employed today, why not spread the available amount of work over all the employable people? You see what I mean?

Mr. LESINSKI. Yes.

Mr. BUSH. Rather than have some working night and day and killing themselves, and thousands and millions of others walking the streets without an hour's work a month. It is irrational; there is no point to it.

Mr. LESINSKI. I am still getting back to the 1929 speed, and saying if those machines were operated at the speed of 1929, if, in other words, you are producing 20 dozen pairs per week in 48 hours, and you now cut down to 6 hours a day, 5 days a week, but still with the speed of 1929, you would probably produce only 12 or 13 dozen on the average.

Mr. BUSH. The full-fashioned hosiery machines cannot be speeded up like that. We run them as fast as it is mechanically possible to run them almost from the day that they are set up.

Mr. LESINSKI. But still continuing, trying to get back to the slowing up of the system of speed, because your stretch-out system today has caused more unemployment than anything else——

Mr. BUSH. That stretch-out is not primarily machine speed. The stretch-out is calling upon one human being to operate more machines.

Mr. LESINSKI. Correct.

Mr. BUSH. In some cases these machines are speeded up.

Mr. LESINSKI. If we get back to 1929, and employ the man 6 hours a day on the speed of 1929, would we double the employment and in some cases triple the employment, but still paying a man the same wage he was getting for 8 hours?

Mr. BUSH. The important thing for the whole economic set-up is purchasing power, consumption power, which is reflected only in the worker's income. If the workers can work 2 hours a month, it is what they get in their pay envelops that keeps the economic system going; that is, the wages, employment system, and all the rest of it going. There is no question in anyone's mind that there is a lack of productive facilities and possibilities here in America, of all countries. But still we have what? We have on the one hand millions of us that barely know where our next meal is coming from, or our next piece of clothing. And here we have clothing workers and food workers unemployed in mass.

Mr. LESINSKI. If, for instance, you were getting 24 hours a week for 48 hours work, and then were reemployed on 30 hours a week, you are still drawing $24 per week for the 30 hours and the other 18 hours went to another worker, would not that help things along?

Mr. BUSH. Certainly, certainly.

Mr. LESINSKI. And then with that cut your speed of the machine so that the fellow who worked 18 hours would have to get 30 to keep that same ratio of the amount of material produced?

Mr. BUSH. What you mean simply carries out my contention, that we must increase purchasing power. We continue to maintain my purchasing power as one worker, $24. But by this extra 18 hours, or whatever hours they will be, we are putting that much smaller purchasing power into a worker who has had no purchasing power for some time. And so we are increasing the total purchasing power by the amount that this other worker besides myself gets. Yes; that is a step in the right direction.

Mr. LESINSKI. Does that conclude your statement?

Mr. BUSH. No. The workers for whom I speak are agreed—there were a few questions as to whether or not the Wagner-Lewis bill in view of all the publicity that it received in the press, and in view of the fact that it is a bill that the administration is backing—they said, "Well, surely that must be the better bill."

However, after getting a copy of it—of course, it is in flux as yet, they are still making changes and modifications one way or another—but as we got it at the time from the New York Times, we went over it item for item, and as far as we could figure out the Wagner-Lewis bill, it was impossible. We could not expect to receive a nickel before 1938. We interpret the Wagner-Lewis bill this way: Reserves will begin to be collected in 1938. At the rate of collection, provided the business index is at such a figure, it will be years before enough reserves from employer and employee—and then the State and Federal Government will contribute—are created so that there will be a fund large enough to begin payments on unemployment insurance.

Mr. LUNDEEN. That covers only those who are working. It does not cover those unemployed.

Mr. BUSH. We are aware of the clauses of that.

Mr. LUNDEEN. Is that your statement?

Mr. BUSH. Yes.

Mr. LUNDEEN. I mean, are you through now?

Mr. BUSH. No, no.

Mr. LUNDEEN. Have you finished your statement? Your time has expired, unless you have something else.

Mr. BUSH. It is simply that we are 100 percent in favor of the Lundeen bill and that our activities as individuals and as organized groups in Massachusetts in behalf of the unemployment bill are being reflected at this moment here in Washington, I believe.

Mr. LESINSKI. You are a member of the A. F. of L.?

Mr. BUSH. The American Federation of Hosiery Workers.

Mr. LESINSKI. Are they affiliated with the A. F. of L.?

Mr. BUSH. We are affiliated with the American Federation of Labor through the United Textile Workers. It is a branch of the American Textile Workers.

Mr. LESINSKI. There was a statement made here last week that the A. F. of L. would be against this bill.

Mr. BUSH. I understand from a recent article in the official organ of the United Textile Workers, the Textile Worker, that William Green, of the powers that be, condemned it. A congress was held here the first part of January. These delegates assembled were discussing this particular bill—the Lundeen bill—of which Mr. Lundeen spoke. It was branded as a sort of a rallying point for A. F. of L. members, so that the Communist element could capitalize that thing, the fact that the A. F. of L. was subscribing to this. I might say that the American Federation of Labor—that is, all the members for whom I speak—we feel that regardless of William Green—he is not suffering from unemployment, and therefore, he can make whatever statements he feels like—we as members, even though we are members of the A. F. of L., are suffering from unemployment. Therefore, we feel that what he says is his saying. He has not consulted us when he makes those statements.

I thank you.

STATEMENT OF ROY HALLAS, OF CLAIRTON, PA.

Mr. HALLAS. Before I commence to talk of H. R. 7598 formerly— today H. R. 2827—I want to say whom I represent and how I got here. Primarily I am one of a committee of six who are here on a little internal trouble of our own with the A. F. of L. We were elected at a conference on February 3 of 78 locals of the Amalgamated Association of Iron, Steel, and Tin Workers.

Mr. LUNDEEN. You say " we " were elected. Who is the " we "?

Mr. HALLAS. The six. I will bring myself into this later on if you will let me continue for a moment. Also, this committee was instructed to testify on this bill. The committee itself has elected me to come here and testify in behalf of the workers bill, H. R. 2827.

First, I want to state that I happened to be the delegate at the fifty-ninth convention of the Amalgamated Association that unanimously endorsed this bill. I introduced the bill and the convention unanimously endorsed the bill. I am also president of my local, Revival Lodge 169, which endorsed it. Also the first district of the association endorsed it. I want to state here we are for the bill. I want to speak mainly of the unemployment in the Pittsburgh district, the heart of the steel industry, where permanent unemployment in the steel mills existed even in 1929. We had a very large number of men in our district who were unemployed even at the height of steel.

Mr. LUNDEEN. Is this also from Congressman Dunn's district?

Mr. HALLAS. Yes. I am from Congressman Dunn's district.

I can cite my own case up there, we will say, in Clairton, where I work in the open hearth. Out of the year I probably worked not more than 8 months—out of that total year. During that length of time they introduced new machinery there that, in one little department where 30 men were employed on one small job, today 7 men do that amount of work; and even if they were to put these men on 6 hours a day, it would not put all of those men back to work.

Mr. Lundeen. You would not say that this was all caused by machinery, however, would you?

Mr. Hallas. This was caused by new machinery in the steel industry.

Mr. Lundeen. Do you think that this panic or depression is all caused by that?

Mr. Hallas. No, no, no. I want to point out, where are these men out of the steel industry going to? Where are they going to be employed? What work are they going to get? They have to go into some other industry, and every other industry is in the same condition as the steel industry.

Take in Homestead, where they put in a new strip mill or a new continuous mill, where the ingot goes in there from the open hearth and comes out the finished product, where they have done away with several hundred men. You take throughout the tin mills where they have put in the " knee-high-" mills, the new strip mills that have done away with thousands of workers. These mills will never, under any conditions, be able to put the number of men back to work that they formerly employed. Take the open-hearth departments, where they have enlarged the furnaces. In the mill I worked in, furnaces that were formerly 50-ton furnaces which are today 100-ton furnaces. This means that heated steel is just twice as large as it was before. The same crew of men produces that amount of steel. This proves to us that even with increased production, with a pick up in steel, they will never be able to put the steel workers back to work.

Take back in 1929. Throughout the United States we had 7,000,-000 men then unemployed in this country. I would like to cite an instance in Duquesne last year where the president of the local in Duquesne compiled statistics of the average earnings of those men in that plant, of several hundred men. Their wages for the entire year of 1933 were $330, an average of $6 a week. These men, many of them, are in debt to the corporation, the United States Steel Corporation, for rent. It will probably take some of them 10 or 12 years to pay this back rent. How they are going to pay it nobody knows. They do not know. Pays that I have seen—just the last pay they drew in the last month, I saw the pay of one man who earned $38. From his pay they took $28 and left him $10 to support himself and his family on. They took that for rent. I myself am a blacklisted member, blacklisted in the Clairton plant due to strike activities, organization activities. I am one of about 1,100 up there. Today I owe the corporation $1,040.30 back rent, and probably—I do not know—my family may be on the street now; they are liable to be evicted at any time.

Mr. Lundeen. If this panic continues, these men will be practically steel-mill serfs.

Mr. Hallas. They will not practically be; they are practically steel-mill serfs today, right now, at the present time.

Mr. Lundeen. They will never be able to emancipate themselves under the present conditions because of the debts that they owe?

Mr. Hallas. Correct. Take for instance the grocery bills. Many of these men owe $250. I, myself, owe today $238 to one groceryman. This man happened to be a particular friend of mine and carried me over until he could not carry me any longer. I do not know whether I will ever be able to pay that man. If something is not done so that this man gets his money back, probably he will be looking for some unemployment insurance, too.

Mr. LUNDEEN. It might be a good case for the R. F. C. to finance that grocery instead of all these banks and railroads.

Mr. HALLAS. The R. F. C. does not finance our class of people. They finance the bankers, the railroad companies, the big industrials. They are not interested in us.

I would like to mention one thing in particular of this relief work.

Mr. LUNDEEN. Perhaps after a while the R. F. C. will be taught to be interested in you folks.

Mr. HALLAS. By the masses of people only. They are the people that will have to teach them. We have all decided that. A large majority of the workers have decided that that is the only way that it can be done. Unemployment insurance will help that a whole lot, but unemployment insurance will not solve the problem altogether.

Mr. LUNDEEN. That is granted.

Mr. HALLAS. I would like to mention this thing of relief work. Take a single man who has no home. He gets $4.75 a week in our county, Alleghany County. Out of this amount of money he must pay room rent, he must buy his clothing, he must feed himself—out of $4.75. If he is fortunate enough to get a job in Alleghany County— and we have 287,000 people on relief out of a million——

Mr. LUNDEEN. Two hundred and eighty-seven thousand?

Mr. HALLAS. Two hundred and eighty-seven thousand out of a million, and I think probably we may have 7,000 on relief work.

Mr. LUNDEEN. Are those 287,000 giving any thought to organizing a labor party in America, or are they content to go along with these old parties that are putting this deal on their necks like a yoke from year to year? How much longer will it take to teach them that they must have their own party?

Mr. HALLAS. A large number of them are thinking of their own party; yes. And a lot of them, had they known what the " new deal " was going to do for them, there may not have been the kind of a " new deal " that we are getting. This has taught them a little bit of a lesson.

Mr. LUNDEEN. You think the " new deal " is the " old deal " in a different coat?

Mr. HALLAS. It is the same deal out of a marked deck; a " new deal " out of a marked deck, that is what it is. A good gambler, when he sits down to gamble, if he is an honest gambler, asks for a new deck, one that the cards have never been broke. But the cards in this deal were stacked on the workers when they were dealt.

Today beeksteak is 30 cents a pound. Wages did not go up. The amount of relief did not go up. In fact, we got a cut back there when we got cash relief. I have a family of nine children, myself, and my wife. I have to live on $18 a week, buy food, buy clothing, pay my gas bill, my electric bill, pay $22.50 a month out of that amount, buy milk—and I am unable to buy milk for children that ought to have milk. I cite my case because I have a big family, and I know others that have bigger families. I can cite my own troubles better than somebody else's. But I realize that there are many in a worse condition than I am, because I realize that there are many do not have a wife who can manage as well as some other man's wife can. This helps out a little bit in some cases.

I would like to say another thing on this bill, the workers' bill. I would like to compare it with the Wagner bill.

Mr. LUNDEEN. Make that as brief as you can.

Mr. HALLAS. The workers are unable to pay for their own insurance. They cannot do it. It just simply cannot be done. We take the case of these men in Duquesne. They pay for that, and they receive what? $3.30. A man that has nine children to keep, and just because his earnings are $6.50 a week, if I understand rightly, the Wagner bill will pay only 50 percent of his wages, and not more than $15 a week; but specifically 50 percent of his wages.

Mr. LUNDEEN. You do not mean $15 a week.

Mr. HALLAS. Not more. At the most, no matter how much he is making, he will not be paid more than $15 a week. And no matter how large his family is; take the man who makes $6 a week; he will receive $3 a week. If he has nine children, he has $3 a week to live on. We compare that with the workers' bill. What a difference. The workers' bill says $15 a week, plus $3 a week for each dependent; and that will not give them one cent more than they have to have, not one cent more than they can barely live on.

The next point in the Wagner bill is the raising of the funds to pay this bill. The worker will be taxed a certain percentage of his wages, and it will have to be paid, or they will take it off of him, take it out of his envelop. The rest is supposed to be taken from the employers. But how is it taken from the employers? Is it taken from the employers' profits? No. It will be added to the cost of production, and the worker pays the whole bill. He pays the employer's share and his own share. It will not be taken from the profit. The workers' bill says that these funds will be raised by taxing all incomes over $5,000 a year, corporation surpluses, and so on. I would like to be making $5,000 a year; I would not mind being taxed; $5,000 a year is more than I have made, that is more than I have made in the last 7 or 8 years combined. In the year of 1932 my wages were $360 for the entire year. The last pay that I drew was $6.80.

Mr. LUNDEEN. Is your case typical of the rest of them?

Mr. HALLAS. That is typical of the rest of the men; and I was one of the skilled men in that plant—one of the men of higher brackets of wages. Many men made only $4 for a pay. Even today when there is supposed to be a pick-up in the steel industry, how is it picked up? How many men has it put back to work? They have not put one man back to work in our part of the country. All they have done is, the man who has a job is getting maybe 1 day more in a pay, and they mostly are getting 3 and 4 days in a pay. Even though these men cannot get relief, they cannot get on relief.

Mr. LUNDEEN. You really think there will be a labor party in Pennsylvania and Pittsburgh some day?

Mr. HALLAS. Some day; yes.

Mr. LUNDEEN. Before we are all dead? Some day soon?

Mr. HALLAS. That is a pretty hard thing to say, absolutely how soon, but these things can happen quick. Unless there is something done it may happen much quicker than we think it will. We do not know how quick these things are going to happen. The steel workers are much dissatisfied with the conditions in the mill. They are very much dissatisfied with the whole set-up. The miners are very much dissatisfied with their conditions. They are not living—well, take Fayette County, where miners are living in coke ovens.

Mr. Lundeen. You are an American Federation of Labor man, are you not?

Mr. Hallas. Yes, sir.

Mr. Lundeen. Why is it that your federation of labor opposes a labor party?

Mr. Hallas. Maybe our national officials oppose such things. They do not speak for all the workers.

Mr. Lundeen. The officials were elected by the workers.

Mr. Hallas. Oh, yes; some of them; some of them. Some of them we doubt that a little bit, too.

Here is the McKeesport Central Labor Union, which endorsed the Lundeen bill. William Green has not endorsed it but the central labor union has endorsed it.

Mr. Lundeen. How many members are there in that union?

Mr. Hallas. There is the Barbers, No. 522; Billposters, No. 3; Building Laborers, No. 136; Carpenters, No. 1048; Electrical Workers, No. 5; Flint Glass Workers, No. 2; Painters, No. 417; Picture Operators, No. 566; Pittsburgh Musical Society, No. 60; Plumbers, No. 27; Typographical Union, No. 225; Sheet Metal Workers, No. 261; Stage Hands, No. 161; Street Car Men, Division No. 85; International Fire Fighter Association, No. 10. United Mine Workers of America: Blythedale local; Elizabeth local; Ocean, No. 5. Amalgamated Association of Iron, Steel and Tin Workers: Pioneer Lodge, No. 158; McKee Lodge, No. 161, Versailles Lodge, No. 162; Tube-E-Co., No. 163; Revival Lodge, No. 169; Sterling Lodge, No. 181; Fort Duquesne Lodge, No. 187. Teamsters, Stablemen and Helpers Union, No. 47; Junk Dealers Union, No. 18642; International Brotherhood of Foundry Employees, No. 79; Glassport Union, No. 18948; Bartenders, No. 163.

These are all unions of the central labor body.

Mr. Lundeen. Have all of those unions endorsed the bill?

Mr. Hallas. Their delegates, their members, and the central labor body have endorsed this bill. The central labor body is made up of delegates of five members from each one of these locals, elected by their own local and sent to this convention; that makes up its membership.

Mr. Lundeen. Do you know of any unions that have endorsed the administration bill?

Mr. Hallas. I do not.

Mr. Lundeen. When you hear of one, send me a card, will you?

Mr. Hallas. I will.

There is one other thing in the Wagner bill that does not in any way—and it was mentioned here a little while ago, but I do not think it was raised, I do not think it was pointed out strong enough— we will take the unemployed workers. If that bill is passed, I would like somebody to point out to me where it would benefit the unemployed worker. You actually must be on the pay rolls in an industry, you must be on the pay roll for so many weeks; and there are hundreds of thousands of us that I doubt whether we will be on the pay rolls in the next 2 or 3 years. What is to become of us in the meantime, while we are waiting on this? If as a steel worker I was to leave Clairton and go to Detroit, then that puts me out.

Mr. LUNDEEN. Do the workers realize that this bill could be passed? It has some imperfections that might be corrected, but it could be passed at noon or shortly after noon tomorrow when the House meets. It could shortly thereafter be passed in the Senate, and the same day be signed by the President. Do they realize that?

Mr. HALLAS. I do not think the majority of them realize that. I know what you mean.

Mr. LUNDEEN. And immediately the funds in the Treasury of the United States would be available to take care of the situation. This bill has no more ambiguities or contradictions than a lot of the alphabetical category have that we have already seen pass in parade.

Mr. HALLAS. Still there is a weakness in this bill to which we are opposed.

Mr. LUNDEEN. What is that?

Mr. HALLAS. Take line 16 on page 3, " because of participation in strike." " No worker or farmer shall be disqualified from receiving the compensation guaranteed by this act because of past participation in strikes."

Mr. LUNDEEN. Does not that suit you?

Mr. HALLAS. No, sir; absolutely it does not. It does not suit any man who belongs to any union. What about present strikes? This is going to be used as a weapon against us. This is in this bill.

Mr. LUNDEEN. Is there any bill before Congress at the present time that even goes as far as that bill on the strike question?

Mr. HALLAS. No, no. I will say there is not; but this one can go further, and this is what the workers want, too.

Mr. LUNDEEN. If you go a little bit further you will not get any bill at all, probably, unless you get a new Congress, and that will take two years. Do you not think this bill is progressive enough and liberal enough, forward-looking enough to be satisfactory as it is written now with a few minor changes? I admit there should, perhaps, be some changes.

Mr. HALLAS. That is one particular place where it should be changed.

Mr. LUNDEEN. What about the provision that is in there now? Everybody that has been connected with a strike is not barred.

Mr. HALLAS. Do you think there are not going to be any more strikes? There is apt to be a real strike in the very near future; nobody knows. How does labor ever get anything if they do not strike? The only weapon that the laboring man has is through a strike.

Mr. LUNDEEN. No; I would not agree with you there. He has other weapons, but he does not use them.

Mr. HALLAS. I do not know. I have been working for a long time. I have put about 17 years in the coal mines and 19 years in the mills.

Mr. LUNDEEN. If labor controlled the Government, that would be weapon enough, would it not? And they have the votes; the farmers and laboring men have the votes to control this Government, have they not? They have the votes. That is undeniable. What I cannot understand is why they do not use them to put the men they want in Congress. If they do not want their present Member.in Congress, why do they not take a man out of their own ranks and put him in there and get what they want?

Mr. HALLAS. And probably after they take a man out of their own ranks, how long is he one of their kind?

Mr. LUNDEEN. You do not mean to say that the entire membership of the unions is unworthy of trust?

Mr. HALLAS. But under the system I do not think it can possibly be done. Under the system it cannot be done.

Mr. LUNDEEN. I see what you mean.

Mr. HALLAS. It cannot be done.

Mr. LUNDEEN. Have you any further statement to make now?

Mr. HALLAS. I think I have said about enough. I think I have said plenty, only that I want to add that this conference, the February 3 conference, represented approximately 50,000 workers, and this is their voice. This is the bill that they asked for.

Mr. LUNDEEN. You mean the January conference?

Mr. HALLAS. The February conference.

Mr. LUNDEEN. What conference is that; the February conference?

Mr. HALLAS. The February conference is the joint district conference of the steel workers.

Mr. LUNDEEN. Pardon me; I confused it with the congress that was held here.

Mr. HALLAS. The conference, the February 3 conference, and this bill was brought forth in the conference and endorsed, and it was written into the minutes that this committee should send somebody here to testify for this bill. This is the will of the workers, what they want done.

Mr. LUNDEEN. I appreciate your statement. But suppose that you carry back to the workers that you represent this, that bills such as the administration bill on some technicality or other do not come to our Labor Committee but are diverted into the Ways and Means Committee, and that your folks in Pittsburgh, Philadelphia, and New York had better give a little attention to the Ways and Means Committee, which is a committee of considerable importance here. I do not think you have very much to fear from the Labor Committee or this subcommittee, which is rather friendly. I hope to see the bill reported out in the subcommittee and perhaps the general Labor Committee; I cannot be sure, but I hope so. But the Ways and Means Committee is another proposition. That is where the administration bill is being cradled now for the floor of the House. I wonder if you realize that?

Mr. HALLAS. Yes.

Mr. LUNDEEN. Thank you very much.

STATEMENT OF L. H. WITTNER

Mr. WITTNER. I represent the National Equal Wealth Society. It is a society that we organized in September under the District code, chapter 18, subchapter 3, to fight the influence of the American Liberty Union.

Mr. LUNDEEN. Are you fighting the American Liberty League?

Mr. WITTNER. Absolutely.

Mr. LUNDEEN. Let me shake hands with you. I wish you would also fight the Economy League.

Mr. WITTNER. Yes, sir; I do.

Mr. LUNDEEN. It is about the same thing, I think.

Mr. WITTNER. I represent a veterans' group, too. I give you this for your own reference [handing document to Mr. Lundeen].

I have quite a brief here, Mr. Lundeen. Will it be all right for me to submit that later?

Mr. LUNDEEN. You have it fairly well condensed, have you not?

Mr. WITTNER. Yes, I have it condensed; yes.

Mr. LUNDEEN. I wish you would make your statement as brief as possible, and leave the brief with the secretary here.

Mr. WITTNER. First of all, I want to say that we like your bill, but we have certain amendments to suggest.

Mr. LUNDEEN. I wish you would suggest them so we will know.

Mr. WITTNER. I have them set down here. I think on page 1, at line 8, the words " male and female " should be inserted before the word " workers ".

Mr. LUNDEEN. Before " all workers and farmers ".

Mr. WITTNER. "All male and female workers." I want to take in the wives.

Mr. LUNDEEN. Do you not think " all workers " means all workers?

Mr. WITTNER. No, sir. Insofar as you have used the word " domestic " over here, it seems to me that of itself means some menial that is employed in the home and I think the wife earns just as much as the husband. I think that we will never have an organization that will represent the Americans unless we get the women to the point where they can have their own income or a proportionate amount of income.

Mr. LUNDEEN. I think the housewife would be very much in accord with your ideas. Do you think that would cover the housewife?

Mr. WITTNER. No, sir; I do not.

Mr. LUNDEEN. I do not quite get your idea.

Mr. WITTNER. What I would take in would be all of the citizens of the United States. Instead of saying, " Compensation for all workers and farmers above 18 years of age, unemployed through no fault of their own ", I would say, "All of the citizens of the United States." Our charter provisions provide that——

Mr. LUNDEEN. Some folks want us to include aliens.

Mr. WITTNER. No; citizens; because they would have to be treated in a different category. They ought to have a good living as long as they are here, because we were all aliens at one time or another unless we were born here—our ancestors were.

The charter of this society provides:

> The particular business and objects of such corporation shall be to promote and secure, by any and all constitutional means, the mutual improvement of all of the citizens of the United States, through the permanent and perpetual equal distribution and equal utilization of the entire natural resources of the United States.

Mr. LUNDEEN. You want this to read " all citizens "?

Mr. WITTNER. Yes; all of the citizens of the United States, irrespective of age.

Now, I could give you that. This is a different recommendation that we have here. I was just trying to clarify and to explain some of the provisions in the first, and then I would come to this second. Would that be all right with you?

Mr. LUNDEEN. Yes; go ahead.

Mr. WITTNER. On page 2, line 1, insert " twelve " instead of " ten " dollars. Fifty dollars is recommended as being——

Mr. LUNDEEN. Twelve instead of ten?

Mr. WITTNER. Yes, sir. They want to pay $50 under this work bill. I think $50 would perhaps be better than $40. This would bring $520, and the $12 would bring $624.

Then insert in line 2, " $6 per week " in place of " $3."

Mr. LUNDEEN. I will say to the gentleman, I would just as soon do that, but there are some citizens who fear that the expense will be too great.

Mr. WITTNER. Yes, sir; I realize that; and I doubt very much whether your bill will be passed, but I think that here we have some sounding board where we can get the thinking people of the United States, and if we could get them to think more like they do in Minnesota and in some of the Northwestern States where I have campaigned, it would be a whole lot better for the people. If we can waken them, we have got to waken the whole group of those that may be exploited at the present time.

Mr. LUNDEEN. It would be very difficult to make the Congress raise those figures, I am afraid.

Mr. WITTNER. I realize that, and you probably would not report this out of committee.

Mr. LUNDEEN. I am not so sure. We may report it out of the committee; out of this committee or the next one, I am not so sure.

Mr. WITTNER. May I submit these amendments?

Mr. LUNDEEN. Yes, indeed. I want to hear all of them.

Mr. WITTNER. Insert after the word " dependent ", before the period, in line 2 on page 2, the words, " child, under 18 years of age." That would make this read, " But shall in no case be less than $12 per week plus $6 per week for each dependent child under 18 years of age." Sixteen I would like better, but since we have used 18 on the other side, we have to make it conform.

Mr. LUNDEEN. Their dependents are not children, however.

Mr. WITTNER. Oh, yes; but we will come on down to that. But I would not make the wife a dependent. I would not make the wife in any instance dependent on the man.

Mr. LUNDEEN. No; but there might be some other person there.

Mr. WITTNER. I think it is well taken care of in section 3.

Mr. LUNDEEN. Yes; I see.

Mr. WITTNER. I was just trying to follow out your terminology.

In line 3, after the word " employment " insert a comma, and the following, " and workers working full time but receiving less than the minimum wage herein provided." That is, this bill provides that " workers willing and able to do full-time work but enable to secure full-time employment shall be entitled to receive the difference." Now, I maintain that if they are working for $6 a week, working full time, they ought to be compensated as to the difference then. That would bring up this average that we are speaking of. The average is all right as to the crafts, but when you come down to the average in the farm communities, especially in the South and in the West, where they get them for $15 and $25 a month, I say that the people that are working on the farms as tenant farmers and employees ought to be entitled to the full benefit of this act. What do you think of it?

Mr. LUNDEEN. Well, it is something to think about.

Mr. WITTNER. In line 14, page 2, insert after " elected " the words " from and " and strike out " members of " and the apostrophes after the word " workers " and " farmers ", and strike out " organizations " making that read:

In conformity with the purposes and provisions of this act through unemployment insurance commissions directly elected from and by workers and farmers.

Most of our workers and farmers in the United States are unorganized at the present time. I think that we could not force them into organizations. I think then we would take the viewpoint of speaking for the unorganized at the present moment.

I would strike out the last sentence in section 3, lines 23, 24, and 25, following the words " in like manner ":

Compensation for disability because of maternity shall be paid to women during the period of 8 weeks previous and 8 weeks following childbirth.

I say they are entitled to it all the time.

On page 3, line 8, after the words " act shall be levied ", strike out the rest of the sentence and after the word " levied " insert:

and assessed upon all capital wealth of the United States.

The following is another sentence:

Commencing on the immediate establishment of this act there shall be levied and assessed upon all property in the United States a direct capital wealth excise tax, to be collected from and paid by every owner of an equity in private property in the United States. The tax shall be at the annual rate of 5 percent of the entire capital wealth to insure the collection of funds to meet the social security purposes of this act.

We will never be able to redistribute wealth by having a tax on income, because the income is just that little part that is exploited from the worker annually. The distribution of wealth being more than 90 percent concentrated in the hands of a few of the plutocrats, who are the real exploiters, makes it so that it is impossible for us to get any redistribution of wealth through—well, of course, we do get some in inheritance and gifts, but we do not get it on incomes.

In line 11, page 3, or line 10, rather, add " all " before " workers ", and the words " and dependents " after " workers " before the comma.

Line 11, strike out " domestic " and " or."

Line 12, add the word " domestic " and the words " or nonproductive service " before " workers." That would take in those that take care of filling stations and work that is really not productive, and cleaning establishments, and stuff like that, which I think is not covered in industrial, agricultural, domestic, office, or professional workers.

In line 12, add " all " before " farmers " and " or dependents " after " farmers " before the comma. And then I would put in a clarifying provision as to separability. I recommend that. I will just turn this over to you and not take your time on that.

Our organization believes in the equal distribution of wealth. That is arbitrary, but I think it is no more arbitrary than the unequal distribution of wealth that is the basis of our predatory capitalism. We can have capitalism without that predatory influence.

I have here a recommendation: On line 7, page 1, strike out all of section 2 after the words "a system of" and insert the following, which would make it read:

The Secretary of Labor is hereby authorized and directed to provide for the immediate establishment of a system of social security for the purpose of providing economic security of all of the citizens of the United States. Such economic security shall be equal to the equal average distribution of capital wealth to all of the citizens of the United States, based on the equal average distribution of wealth as of 1929, but shall in no case be less than $3,000 capital, free of debt.

Three hundred and sixty billion dollars are supposed to be the wealth. It has been as high as $487,000,000,000, estimated by the so-called "laissez faire" economists. The $360,000,000,000 should allow a capital of $3,000 to all, counting from Rockefeller, Ford, and Mellon, right on down.

The second sentence of that would read:

The Secretary of Labor is hereby authorized and directed to provide for the immediate establishment of a system of secured equal social income to provide an equal economic income to all of the citizens of the United States. Such equal economic income shall be equal to the average distribution of all usable income to all of the citizens of the United States, based on the estimated average income for the year 1929, but shall in no case be less than $750 annually.

That would take care of the objection that the Honorable Mr. Lesinski made, that is, that a family that is large and has only one wage earner would receive only $10 a week under your bill provided they were unemployed; but this would give the same income to each individual from the baby that is just a day old right on up to old age.

I just wanted to give you that idea on that.

Then on line 8, section 4, page 3, strike out all after the words "act shall be levied" and insert, "on all capital wealth at the rate of 100 per centum." It taxes all capital wealth. Of course, there could be a provision that it would not be taxable if it were less than $3,000, because we are trying to establish a $3,000 equal wealth distribution.

I would like to leave this brief with you.

Mr. LUNDEEN. All right. Does that complete your statement?

Mr. WITTNER. Yes, sir.

STATEMENT OF JOSEPH FINAN

Mr. FINAN. I am from the mining district of southwestern Pennsylvania. Last Saturday the United Mine Workers of America Convention was held in Uniontown, Pa. Represented there were 77 local unions, with 3 delegates from each local union, which is about 97 percent of all the United Mine Workers in that district.

Mr. LUNDEEN. How many workers would that represent?

Mr. FINAN. Twenty-eight thousand in the one district, no. 4 district.

Mr. LUNDEEN. Twenty-eight thousand?

Mr. FINAN. Twenty-eight thousand miners; yes.

At that convention our State senator who was elected and went into office January 18—he is a member of our organization—Mr. Cavelcante—made a motion on the floor that this bill, the Lundeen workers' bill, should be endorsed by the workers. It was unanimously adopted.

At that convention I was also chosen as the scale committee, a member of the scale committee. Two men were elected there to make a new contract on the 1st of April, or try to make one, with the coal operators, on the 18th of January.

I wish to state in passing that in southwestern Pennsylvania where it is the stronghold of the United States Steel Corporation and its subsidiary, the Frick Co., they rule in that district with an iron hand. They are the government. They are the " works." They control everything, those two counties, Greene and Fayette, in southwestern Pennsylvania, there are no industries except mines. After a man is 45 years old it is impossible or practically impossible for him to get a job. They tell him he is too old to work any more.

There are in Fayette County 15,000 persons on relief rolls, and I venture to say that 80 percent of those are miners. The conditions in reference to a year ago in our part of the State are much worse, very much worse today than a year ago. They use up there their relief rolls as the barometer of work. In other words, if they have 15,000 on relief this month, and there are only 12,000 or 13,000 on relief next month, the press comes out with the spiel that conditions have so much improved, while the contrary is true. They take them off the relief rolls to rid the Government of the burden and they allow them to shift for themselves. They take them off and they get a job in the mines. They go back to work in the mines. Instead of getting $8 or $10 a week like they get off the relief, they cannot make $8 or $10 in a month in lots of these mines.

Mr. LUNDEEN. You mean it is not the " new deal ", it is the " worse deal "?

Mr. FINAN. Oh, absolutely. As far as the " new deal " is concerned, it certainly is a rotten deal for us, because we are in worse shape now—I am positive of this—worse shape than we were a year ago. To convince the public that conditions under the " new deal " are doing the world and all for the workers, the press uses the relief statistics, the relief figures. What is the use of taking a man off of the relief and putting him on a job where he cannot make anything but practically nothing? I know a man at home who showed me a statement. He made $18.19 in 2 weeks' time. He did not buy 1 cent's worth of food out of that $18. He did not buy 1 cent's worth of food. He paid the company for the powder that he used, the caps that he used, the pick sharpener, his check-off for his dues, and so forth, and he had 19 cents left. He bought himself not a dime's worth of bread out of the whole pay. Those are the things that mislead people in regard to this bill.

In our section of the country until 3 or 4 months ago this bill was not known of or heard of, because if anybody would come into the State and advocate and talk and try to propose or support the contents of this bill, they would be run out of there by the Frick deputies and yellow dogs and all that kind of thing; run out of the State.

They put you in jail for advertising that thing where I come from. Oh, the company is boss. You are put in jail if you advocate the workers ought to try to organize. They have no hearing for you, ask you no questions. They just take you deliberately in there and put you in jail. When they are through with you they turn you loose.

There was a case of that kind just last month. The workers decided at one of their meetings that they would have a certain man, just as the honorable chairman suggested here, that they had the power to vote. I want to show you where they do not have the power to vote in some parts of the country. Those brothers had this legal meeting of theirs and suggested that they would go in a body to the polls, and that they would all vote for this particular man. The particular man that I speak about is the man that endorsed this bill, Senator Cavelcante. The miners elected him. This fellow suggested at the meeting that we go in a body to the polls to try to make an impression, to try to break down some of the injustice against the workers in that part of the State, to try to show the people that we were solidly together, and to try to run out these ward heelers and politicians that hang around with dollars and pints of whiskey in their hands to buy the workers over to them. The same day that the motion was made and carried there were three of our workers deliberately taken out of our town and taken into the jail at Uniontown and locked up for 15 days, and turned loose with $8 expenses. Automobiles were sent up there to take them in, without any charge being brought against them. This is your freedom, the freedom up in the coal fields.

Speaking about machinery, gentlemen, I am positively for machinery. I do not think that whether it throws men out of work or not the abolition of or wiping out the machine is going to cure this at all. I think this, we ought to advocate more machinery in all industries but use this machinery for the benefit of everybody, not for the benefit of the fellow who now possesses it, who controls it, who puts it in there, or the fellow who got the patent on it.

I believe this, that if a machine is installed in a mine, a mill, a factory, or wherever it is put in, if that machine is going to displace 100 men, that work should be cut down so that all these men will be kept at work, and the work should be reduced to such a point that it would protect the output or the product that this machine would do by such installation. That is the theory that I work on.

Furthermore, in our country we have got what? Perhaps the Honorable Chairman does not know what they are, but we have what we call a " coke oven." It is built out of brick. We put coal in there to manufacture coke. In 1918 practically all of the coke ovens in Fayette County were abolished. They tore them down and so forth. They used the byproduct-system coke thereafter. Still there are a few small plants which make coke in the district. But that one thing, moving the coke industry out of the county, threw thousands of men out of work. That was in 1918. In 1922 the national strike of the United Mine Workers came off. They went down in the cotton fields of Alabama, Tennessee, and all through there and brought up thousands of Negroes. I suppose they were making a decent living down there, or they were getting along all right, at least.

But they took these men and they dumped them in there. They were not practical men, not used to mining. Hundreds upon thousands of them were injured and maimed for lack of experience.

At our conference last week we presented a bill to our State legislature that from henceforth in the State of Pennsylvania—we are going to try to get it through if we can, and I believe we can—that a man must be certified, or he must serve at least a 2-year apprenticeship in the mines before he is permitted to go in there, and not commit suicide, for the coal companies care nothing about him. They will put him in this, immaterial of whether he is capable of doing the job or not, provided he is not a member of any labor organization.

Mr. LUNDEEN. Do you not know, now, that you are placing yourself in opposition to the divine right of money?

Mr. FINAN. Yes; I realize that.

Mr. LUNDEEN. We used to have the divine right of kings in some countries. Now this is the aristocracy of wealth. Only by labor uniting can they ever meet the power of that united-money aristocracy.

Mr. FINAN. I realize that.

Mr. LUNDEEN. The farmers and the laboring men have the numbers to acquire political and economic power if they wish to do so. In your region there, has there been any labor party at all?

Mr. FINAN. Never; no.

Mr. LUNDEEN. In other words they are satisfied with the rule of the parties you have?

Mr. FINAN. They are not satisfied, Mr. Chairman. They are not satisfied by any means, but the methods that the courts and the powers that be, the coal companies——

Mr. LUNDEEN. But you elect your judges?

Mr. FINAN. I doubt it. I doubt it very sincerely. I doubt if we elect the judges. We have no possible chance of defeating the judges, because our people are controlled, as I told you, by the bosses, and they are forced into doing those things. The polls at those election precincts are surrounded with the tools of these companies. And if they know or if they can find out or if they even suspect that you are against their man, you are discharged, you lose your job, you are fired, you are blacklisted.

Mr. LUNDEEN. You mean they control the elections?

Mr. FINAN. Absolutely, beyond any question of doubt. They control them absolutely.

Mr. LUNDEEN. Through the press first?

Mr. FINAN. Yes, sir; through the press, through the company, and through the stool pigeons that get into our organization for no other purpose than to draw a salary off of the company and to serve them, serve the companies; get on the inside of your organization and then report everything that is going on.

Mr. LUNDEEN. How long will that continue?

Mr. FINAN. I do not think that is going to continue very much longer. I hope it gets worse. That is what I am interested in. If the thing is going to come to a head in the near future, they have just got to keep going the way they are going now. If they just keep up the way they are going now there will be a decision made pretty shortly. That is my opinion about it from watching——

Mr. LUNDEEN. You are not in the Pittsburgh district?

Mr. FINAN. In southwestern Pennsylvania, around Uniontown, Fayette County, Greene County, Westmoreland, and that section.

Mr. LUNDEEN. I have driven through there.

Mr. FINAN. Yes; the National Highway goes right through there. Perhaps you remember Summit Mountain.

Mr. LUNDEEN. Yes; I do, and Washington, Pa., is right near there.

Mr. FINAN. Yes; little Washington is right close, about 24 miles from my home. There is nothing there but mines.

There is one point I wanted to bring up about these coke ovens. We have today in Fayette County 500 men under 30 years of age living in coke ovens, living there with no beds, no sanitary accommodations, no nothing, in frost and snow and everything else. There is no way—the relief association will tell you that there is no way that they can take care of them. At the same time, there are hundreds upon hundreds of empty houses in our neighborhood, falling down, where the coal companies have finished the coal that they had there and pulled away and left their people there, too. Those of them that were able to get moved out of there and get away left, but their houses are there. We made the proposition to the relief association that they repair these houses and move those men into it. They said, "We cannot do anything of the kind. The coal companies will not permit us to do this." They leave the houses fall down, the windows and roofs fall off of them, but they will not allow the relief and will not allow the workers to use them to shelter themselves and their families.

Those are the conditions that are existing, and they are intolerable. They are intolerable, absolutely intolerable. That is only one reason why this bill is endorsed in Fayette County. I submit that statement, that the only reason this bill is endorsed in Fayette County is because of the misery and the way the people have to live there. They are not going to tolerate it much longer.

Mr. LUNDEEN. Coal is a public utility, is it not?

Mr. FINAN. Yes, sir.

Mr. LUNDEEN. Like electric light or anything else. Is there any reason why the Government should not own the public utilities? Why should a millionaire or a billionaire own the public utilities?

Mr. FINAN. I fail to see, Mr. Chairman, where——

Mr. LUNDEEN. I have reference to Niagara Falls. There is a plunging cataract of tremendous power. Part of that power runs into the turbines that turn the light and power into Canadian channels. The Ontario people have the good common sense to own their own light and power. On the New York side they do not know quite so much, and there the millionaire and the billionaire own the light and power that comes out of this cataract. The result is that the electric light and power in New York costs the consumer nearly three times as much as it does in Ontario where the people own it.

Do your people study that problem?

Mr. FINAN. Oh, yes, yes; they study it.

Mr. LUNDEEN. Do they have meetings and discuss those things?

Mr. FINAN. Yes, sir. Yes; they have meetings and they discuss those problems. Many times their meetings are broken up and a lot of fellows go away with battered heads.

In answer to your question, I do not think that under the present set-up the ownership of public utilities is going to solve, even in a small way, our problem in this respect. For instance, we would be Federal employees in the coal mine under such a condition; is that what you mean? If the coal was then a public utility and the United States Government owned it, we would be Federal employees. I am positively sure that the workers' condition would not be one bit better under the Federal jurisdiction than what they are under the big corporations today.

Mr. LUNDEEN. Why are you convinced?

Mr. FINAN. I will point to the Federal workers here in Washington, D. C., for instance, where they are working under the Government. I was here in 1931——

Mr. LUNDEEN. You mean to say that the workers who work for the Government here are not any better off than the people who are starving to death somewhere else?

Mr. FINAN. If there be only a certain amount of workers to be taken care of, I would say yes; I would be in favor of your point. But the fact that the Government would operate the coal mines, that is not going to solve my problem in any way. I do not think from the standpoint that even if we go back to war times when the Government took over——

Mr. LUNDEEN. What would you do?

Mr. FINAN. My opinion is this: That when the natural resources of this country become the property of everybody, when it becomes public property——

Mr. LUNDEEN. If it belongs to the Government it is the property of everybody, isn't it?

Mr. FINAN. Not under this set-up. I cannot say that. I do not think it is the property of everybody under this system, because you notice that even in the Government today—we do not want to accuse them of it—but in your system that you have got here in Washington, for instance, you will agree that you have a friend in Wisconsin, or Buell Snyder has got one up in Pennsylvania, if he recommends that fellow for some big job around Washington here that fellow would get it. I may be far more competent than he. I may be more qualified to fill this job, but through this political influence that he has he is able to get somewhere. There is no equality. There is no chance open there for competition.

Mr. LUNDEEN. My dear friend, that occurs in all governments.

Mr. FINAN. I realize that. I realize that, with the possible exception of one country.

Mr. LUNDEEN. Oh, I do not except that. There is difficulty there even there.

Mr. FINAN. Oh, yes. Yes, but it is not as——

Mr. LUNDEEN. There is favoritism, there is difficulty, but probably not so much. You cannot do away with human nature.

Mr. FINAN. No. The question that arises in my mind is this: Even after this bill, if it would pass, as you stated it would pass, tomorrow, if that bill would pass it is a far cry from even solving—it may solve in a small way. You take for instance myself. I have seven children. I am the father of seven children. I have got my wife and myself. That makes nine in the family. I get $8.25 a week to live on, relief. Now, that is Federal control. That is handled by the Government. Now, as you said, if they go to work and handle the mines like they are handling this relief, I do not want to work with that kind of a system. That is my contention.

Mr. LUNDEEN. You prefer to leave it as it is?

Mr. FINAN. I prefer to leave it as it is and let the thing come to a head and let nature take its course rather than accept the decision like we are accepting this today, pushed down our throat that we have a "new deal", we have new conditions, we are 100 percent better off than we were a year or 2 years ago, when we know actually in our hearts that we are not blind, we are wide awake to the fact that conditions are actually worse and that they will continue to get worse because they have not even made an effort.

This "new deal", when it was originated, the R. F. C. was not intended to cure these evils. It is just a fake move. It is not right to compare a human being to a dog, but if you have a dog and if you starve it 3 or 4 days and then throw him a beefsteak, he will not bother howling so much for 3 or 4 days, and will quit and cool down. That is what we are. They are giving us this relief, just enough to keep our mouths shut, to keep us calmed down. Personally, I would be glad to see them take the relief away. It is just the thing that would suit me, because the people have to be crucified more than what they have been crucified before they will realize exactly what the trouble is with the whole matter.

Mr. LUNDEEN. Did the people of your region vote for Wilson, to keep us out of war?

Mr. FINAN. They were all for Wilson.

Mr. LUNDEEN. They were all for saving the world for democracy?

Mr. FINAN. Yes.

Mr. LUNDEEN. Financing Europe and ruining our own Treasury, to the starvation of our own people? And I want you to know that I voted against entering that war and against conscription for foreign service, and I will do so again should the occasion require.

Mr. FINAN. Yes; I realize that. I realize that thoroughly.

That is all I have to say. Thank you very much, Mr. Chairman, for listening.

Mr. LUNDEEN. We thank you for your appearance and the information you have given the committee.

If there is no one else to be heard the committee stands in recess until 10 o'clock tomorrow morning.

(Whereupon, at 5 p. m., a recess was taken until 10 o'clock tomorrow morning, Tuesday, Feb. 12, 1935.)

UNEMPLOYMENT, OLD AGE, AND SOCIAL INSURANCE

TUESDAY, FEBRUARY 12, 1935

House of Representatives,
Subcommittee of the Committee on Labor,
Washington, D. C.

The subcommittee met at 10 a. m., Hon. Matthew A. Dunn (chairman) presiding.

Mr. Dunn. The committee will be in order. The first witness on our calendar this morning is Theodore Mischell. Mr. Mischell, if you will come forward, we shall be glad to hear you.

STATEMENT OF THEODORE MISCHELL, EXECUTIVE SECRETARY OF THE NATIONAL FRATERNAL ADVISORY COMMITTEE FOR UNEMPLOYMENT AND SOCIAL INSURANCE, NEW YORK CITY

Mr. Mischell. Mr. Chairman and gentlemen of the committee: My name is Theodore Mischell. As executive secretary of the National Fraternal Advisory Committee for Unemployment and Social Insurance and organizer of the Fraternal Federation for Social Insurance, I come here representing over a million workers organized in fraternal orders and mutual-aid societies. We members of fraternal organizations know of the crying need for unemployment and social insurance.

Mr. Lesinski. Before the gentleman goes any further, I should like to ask him whether his statement that he represents over a million workers is not an exaggeration. I think a witness should tell exactly whom he represents.

Mr. Mischell. I will be able to show you, as soon as I proceed further with my statement. I represent locals of various national organizations.

Mr. Dunn. You may proceed.

Mr. Mischell. It is now established beyond doubt that millions are doomed to remain part of a great army of permanently unemployed. Unable to pay dues to their organizations, many members of fraternal organizations are being dropped from the rolls and hence face the bleak prospect of losing valuable assistance and protection that their fraternal societies afford them. The very life of fraternal organizations is bound up with this problem, as the loss of many thousands of our members has done much to harm their financial security. Old age has become a crime, and its penalty starvation. Accidents, unsanitary working conditions, and the lack of proper safety devices form a cruel threat to the health and life of the worker.

435

Social remedies are necessary to cope with these conditions. Yet we have no laws in the United States which protect, to any great measure, the lives and health of the American people.

We members of fraternal organizations have tried through our organizations to meet the failure of the Government to provide social insurance. But aside from the fact that this mutual aid was necessarily inadequate and that it could not meet the greatest threat to the workers' existence, unemployment, and old age, it also put the burden of the insurance on the workers themselves. But when the need of the worker for protection increases, his ability to pay for it decreases. Exactly where the jobs are most dangerous and the security least, there the need for insurance is greatest.

We, in the fraternal field, heartily endorse the workers' bill as against the measure put forth by the Federal administration, the Wagner-Lewis bill. This bill is utterly inadequate to serve the unemployed and employed workers, farmers, professionals, and other workers in the United States. The Wagner bill gives no compensation to those unemployed to date. It calls for the accumulation of reserves by pay-roll taxes which are necessarily passed on to the consumer. The bill when enacted in the House of Representatives and the Senate is then sent to the States for their approval and enactment.

The bill calls for a maximum of 15 weeks of compensation and at the maximum of $15 per week. The States that do enact this bill are given the opportunity of cutting the compensation to approximately $8 per week for 7 weeks. This is possible, since there is no set minimum. Yet, even if the $15 and 15-week rates were upheld, what are the workers to do for the remaining 37 weeks? Are they to get the miserable relief such as is doled out in the various States in the Union, such as in the State of Kentucky, with the "magnificent" sum of $8.23 a month for a family of four? What about the transients? What about the medical profession which is dependent upon the worker in the factory and mine for its livelihood? Indirectly, the Wagner bill excludes the Negroes, who are the most oppressed, starved, and maltreated workers of this country, since it is known that 666 out of every 1,000 Negroes who are employed are employed in domestic and farm occupations.

Secondly, the old-age plan as set forth in the Wagner bill is nothing but a cruel jest to the working people of this country. It is generally known that workers are not employed in industry after they have passed the 50-year mark. How are these workers to get old-age insurance, since they will no longer be able to pay the compulsory taxes as specified in the Wagner bill, which calls for insurance after a worker reaches the age of 65, and at that how many workers in the mines, mills, and factories live to be 65 years of age?

No; this is not the insurance for the membership of fraternal organizations in this country. This is the protection of the interests of the finance class of America. We members of fraternal organizations endorse the Workers' Unemployment and Social Insurance Act, and we will rally all members of fraternal organizations to fight for its enactment. It is the only bill that states that there shall be no limitation of the period of compensation and that a worker shall receive insurance for the entire period of his inability to work. It states that there shall be no discrimination against any worker because of race, nationality, color, creed, age, or sex. It definitely states that unemployment and social insurance shall be paid by the Government and the employers without cost to the workers, who are barely able to maintain themselves and their dependents. It calls for the management and the administration of the funds by those for whom this protection is created, namely, commissions of workers and farmers. It states that no workers shall be disqualified from benefits because of refusal to work in place of strikers or at less than normal trade-union rates. We endorse this bill. We will fight for its enactment until it becomes the law of the land.

However, gentlemen, until the workers' bill is passed, we wish to bring forth proposals for the protection of the members of fraternal organizations. The Government of the United States is protecting and subsidizing the loans and investments of the banks, railroad trusts, insurance companies, etc., through the Reconstruction Finance Corporation and other governmental agencies. The bank deposits and investments of fraternal and mutual aid societies are in constant danger of losing value, wholly or in part, due to bank failures, devaluation of bonds, mortgages, and real estate, and to inflation. The bank depositories and allowable investments of fraternal organizations are strictly controlled by the State and National Governments. Therefore we propose that the Government guarantee the funds and investments of fraternal organizations from any loss due to bank failures, devaluations, and inflation.

Our second proposal is that the Federal Government instruct the various local relief administrations, through the P. W. A. or the Federal relief administrating body, to pay the membership dues of the unemployed members of fraternal organizations, since a great number of members of fraternal orders and societies are dropped from the rolls of their organizations because of their inability to pay their dues and are therefore unable to receive the meager amounts of compensation that their fraternal orders can give them.

We call upon you to endorse the workers' bill, to fight for its enactment, and to pass on our proposals. The workers' bill to date has received the endorsement of over 4,000,000 people throughout the United States. It is the only bill that guarantees some security to workers of this country. We members of such national fraternal orders as the Workmen's Sick and Death Benefit Fund, National Slovak Society, Independent Order of the Sons of Italy, Hungarian Aid Association of America, Slovak Evangelical Union A. C. of America, International Workers Order, Russian National Mutual Aid Society, Rackocsi Hungarian Sick Benefit Society, Association of Lithuanian Workers, and from hundreds of local lodges from such organizations as the Foresters of America, Independent Order of Odd Fellows, Loyal Order of the Moose, Workmen's Circle, Masonic lodges, etc., pledge that we will rally and organize the millions of workers who are members of fraternal organizations in this country behind the movement to secure the enactment of a genuine Federal system of unemployment and social insurance as proposed in the Workers' Unemployment and Social Insurance Act, H. R. 2827.

Mr. LESINSKI. These various orders or mutual aid societies that you have mentioned, you actually represent them?

Mr. MISCHELL. That is correct.

Mr. LESINSKI. In what way?

Mr. MISCHELL. They are members of our national committee.

Mr. LESINSKI. They are members?

Mr. MISCHELL. Yes.

Mr. LESINSKI. I happen to know that the Hungarian Society have endorsed the plan, because I have had some letters from them.

Mr. MISCHELL. Yes.

Mr. LESINSKI. I did not know that the Odd Fellows and the Moose and organizations like that had taken action.

Mr. MISCHELL. I was not referring to the national organizations but to local lodges of the Odd Fellows, for instance. There are in New York alone over 65,000 to 75,000 members of fraternal organizations who are represented in the fraternal federation that has endorsed the bill. There are about 15 or 18 courts of the Foresters of America and the Odd Fellows——

Mr. LESINSKI. What I am trying to guard against is a statement by a witness which would not be absolutely correct, and therefore would tend to have his whole statement misinterpreted.

Mr. MISCHELL. I see. If necessary, I could bring you the exact figures. I could show you that we have over a million members of national organizations and local lodges of national organizations.

Mr. LESINSKI. Local lodges of national organizations is what you mean?

Mr. MISCHELL. These are national organizations that I mentioned, about nine or 10 of them. The rest are local lodges.

Mr. DUNN. May I say, Congressman, that some of the organizations the witness has mentioned are located in and around Pittsburgh. I know that they have endorsed this bill, because I have in my office letters from them stating that they are back of H. R. 2827.

Mr. LESINSKI. I know that. I have letters of the same kind. I just wanted to make sure that the witness' statement of the number of people represented was an accurate statement.

Mr. DUNN. Did I understand you to say that the Odd Fellows have endorsed this bill?

Mr. MISCHELL. Local lodges of the Odd Fellows; yes. You see, I sent a letter to the State lodge, and the State lodge necessarily sends it to the grand sire who, in turn, must pass upon it. Otherwise, they will be expelled or something of that sort.

Mr. LUNDEEN. You know of the meeting of this organization at the Engineers Hall in New York?

Mr. MISCHELL. Yes.

Mr. LUNDEEN. Mr. Chairman, that was one of the most impressive meetings I ever attended. There were present a large number of teachers and engineers, architects, business and professional men of all classes. There were also workers there from various trades. It was a very representative group of trades and professions, but mostly the professions, I believe.

Mr. DUNN. There are no further questions, and we thank you for your contribution, Mr. Mischell.

STATEMENT OF MRS. THERESA E. GOLD, REPRESENTING THE BROTHERHOOD OF SHOE AND ALLIED CRAFTSMEN, BROCKTON, MASS.

Mr. DUNN. Will you please proceed?

Mrs. GOLD. My name is Theresa E. Gold. I represent the Brotherhood of Shoe and Allied Craftsmen, Brockton, Mass.

I have been delegated to appear at this hearing in behalf of the Brotherhood of Shoe and Allied Craftsmen, a rank and file organization truly representing approximately 13,000 shoe and allied workers.

This organization represents a unit of the shoe and allied workers located in the Brockton, Mass., district. That district is an area in southeastern Massachusetts, comprising one industrial city, Brockton, and about 12 shoe manufacturing towns located within a radius of about 15 miles of Brockton.

The general and control boards and 16 local unions have gone on record endorsing the Lundeen bill, H. R. 2827. There is an active committee made up of delegates from all the locals and several fraternal organizations working for the passage of this bill. Their representatives in Congress have been requested by fraternal and control boards, by each local, and by individuals, and both members and nonmembers of the organization, to work and vote for the Lundeen bill.

The bill has been carefully studied by the committee and explained to the rank and file at local meetings. The bill has received the whole-hearted and enthusiastic support of the shoe workers for many reasons. I might outline only a few of them here.

First, over 3,000 shoe workers in the Brockton district are now unemployed with almost no hope of ever again being employed in their trade. Many are employed in the shoe industry now as only temporary workers; that is, they are only able to secure a few weeks' work out of each 52 weeks in peak seasons. Third, the shoe industry is tending to move from the centers in Massachusetts, where the trade unions have been able to exact relatively higher wages and better working conditions from the employer, to the smaller towns, and to other States where the code minimum wages have become the maximum, and where no union can gain a foothold. When these factories move these workers are thrown on the E. R. A. and relief agencies.

Single men and women are not able to get either jobs or relief. The relief possible to the married man, either from public or private charity, or from these E. R. A. jobs is absolutely inadequate to provide even for the barest standard of living.

I wish to emphasize that this group of workers has the reputation of being the best, most highly skilled shoe workers in the country. The district is known as the center of the high-grade men's shoe industry.

Further, this group of workers is known as a conservative, intelligent group. They have been union-conscious for over 40 years.

They have now arrived at a point in their thinking where their patience is sorely tried. The shoe code is an absolute failure from the workers' point of view. Instead of employing more workers the opposite has been the case, with a minimum wage of $12 for women and $13.50 for men, a population differential between cities and towns, a lack of enforcement of either of these very poor provisions of the code, so that the temper of these workers, both of the employed and the unemployed, is quickening. They demand action from those in Washington who are elected to Congress to represent all the people, not the privileged few.

Five shoe workers' unions have demanded that the code of fair competition for the shoe industry be reopened, and that drastic changes, including shorter hours and a graded minimum wage, providing for skilled, semiskilled, and unskilled workers be stipulated; labor representation on the code authority and local compliance board, and that other changes be written into the new code.

However, even a good code does not take care of those now unemployed, nor does it take care of the people who are thrown out of employment every time a new labor-saving machine is introduced. Neither have the shoe workers any assurance that the shoe code will be reopened or modified.

My organization is not interested in the Wagner-Lewis bill, H. R. 4142, because it does not provide any relief for those now unemployed and the provisions for future economic tragedies are too inadequate. It does not include any provisions for the masses of unemployed white-collar, professional, clerical, and domestic workers.

Mr. LUNDEEN. And may I say that the provisions for relief are too remote.

Mrs. GOLD. I agree with you; they are too remote.

Mr. LUNDEEN. They are not only inadequate but they are too remote, too far distant in the future.

Mrs. GOLD. That is true. It transfers the initiative to the several States instead of setting up a Federal system. This would put a premium on the States that accepted the challenge and there would be a wholesale exodus by industries to States where no such additional tax was levied.

We favor the Lundeen bill over any other bill for its other social provisions; old age, maternity, industrial injury, or any other disability.

We are heartily in accord with the method of raising the funds to administer this bill and the method of administration.

In closing I would like to leave this impression with you. I am typical of and represent a group of workers and their families who are conservative, intelligent, alert American citizens, who have assisted in creating the wealth of this Nation, who know that Rome was not built in a day, but who also know that millions of workers are never again going to be gainfully employed. The Lundeen bill attempts to relieve some of these injustices.

Mr. DUNN. May I interrupt you? Did I understand you to say that millions will never be gainfully employed again?

Mrs. GOLD. Yes.

Mr. DUNN. What do you mean by saying that they will never again be gainfully employed?

Mrs. GOLD. I mean that industry with the introduction of labor-saving machinery, as it is now set up, is throwing millions of workers out of employment, and they are not going again to be gainfully employed in industry.

Mr. DUNN. You mean under this kind of a system.

Mrs. GOLD. Yes.

Mr. DUNN. But under a different system, do you not think that could be changed?

Mrs. GOLD. That is possible. The 13,000 members of the Brotherhood of Shoe and Allied Craftsmen intend to use all their influence to get this bill through this session of Congress. The temper of the workers is significant. They no longer accept promises nor excuses for delay. They placed their faith in the N. R. A. They expected a code of fair competition offering them certain safeguards. They thought they would be written into the code and enforced. They feel that the N. R. A. has been tried and found wanting. They have delegated me to say to this committee that they are endorsing the Lundeen bill without reservations.

It must receive your support, gentlemen, and must be passed at this session of Congress.

Mr. LUNDEEN. You are located not very far from Congressman Connery's district?

Mrs. GOLD. Not very far. We are 20 miles south of Boston.

Mr. LUNDEEN. You have a good deal the same type of district that he has?

Mrs. GOLD. Only that his is a women's shoe district and we are a district that makes a specialty of men's shoes. But we have the same problems, perhaps not to the same extent that he has in his district; that is, manufacturers moving out of the cities into the smaller towns and up into Maine and New Hampshire where they can get a lower minimum wage, and where the minimum tends to become the maximum, because they have no unions to safeguard the workers.

Mr. LUNDEEN. Suppose this bill were passed and in addition a 30-hour week bill. What do you think would happen then?

Mrs. GOLD. We are asking for a 30-hour week to be provided in the new shoe code. We think that a 30-hour week would keep the shoe workers employed.

Mr. LUNDEEN. All of them?

Mrs. GOLD. No; not all of them, 52 weeks in the year. It would keep all of them employed in peak seasons and part of them employed all seasons, all year.

Mr. LUNDEEN. It would help greatly?

Mrs. GOLD. Yes; it would. Under the code we are allowed a 40-hour week with 48 hours, 8 weeks out of each 6-month period. In many places, of course, they are running their maximum hours, 45 hours for 8 weeks out of each 6-month period.

Mr. LUNDEEN. These workers who are out of work; what kind of health service does your community give them, any?

Mrs. GOLD. Yes; some, but very inadequate. Just what is provided under the relief, either private or public relief. The city, of course, has a board of health and they have a few physicians at their call. But the service is very bad.

Mr. LUNDEEN. Have you any maternity benefits there?

Mrs. GOLD. No; none at all.

Mr. LUNDEEN. That is all.

Mr. LESINSKI. Are these factories producing as much in these years as they were in 1928 and 1929?

Mrs. GOLD. No; they are not.

Mr. LESINSKI. They are not producing as much?

Mrs. GOLD. No.

Mr. LESINSKI. Do you employ in the peak seasons approximately the same number of people, or less?

Mrs. GOLD. As in 1928 and 1929?

Mr. LESINSKI. Yes.

Mrs. GOLD. Very many less.

Mr. LESINSKI. What is the reason they do not produce as many shoes now as they did in 1928 and 1929?

Mrs. Gold. More machines have been introduced, and they have taken away jobs; also, the speed-up system.

Mr. Lesinski. If a 30-hour week bill were passed, which was mentioned a moment ago, and more teeth were put into the N. R. A. codes so that the speed-up system in force now were curtailed to where it was in 1928 or 1929, would that help any?

Mrs. Gold. Some; but it would not be adequate.

Mr. Lesinski. If it was adequate in 1928 or 1929——

Mrs. Gold. It was not adequate in 1928 or 1929—far from it.

Mr. Lesinski. They worked at high speed at that time, then?

Mrs. Gold. Yes.

Mr. Lesinski. What was the average speed in the years before that?

Mrs. Gold. I am not prepared to make any statement on the average speed.

Mr. Lesinski. The biggest trouble in this country is the speed-up system, is it not?

Mrs. Gold. Yes. In our case we work on piecework.

Mr. Lesinski. If the speed-up system were curtailed and each worker would produce only a minimum amount instead of a maximum, and we had shorter hours per week with the same pay as is being paid today with a 45-hour week, that would be of great help, would it not?

Mrs. Gold. It would help, naturally.

Mr. Lesinski. Personally, I am convinced that it would eliminate all unemployment.

Mrs. Gold. I am afraid not—not by any stretch of the imagination.

Mr. Lesinski. Well, what is the average number of pairs of shoes today turned out by a shoemaker now?

Mrs. Gold. I am sorry, but I have not that information at hand either. I do not know whether anyone could make such a statement.

Mr. Lesinski. There must be an average number of shoes turned out per day.

Mrs. Gold. There may be an average for a district, but I do not know whether there has been an average arrived at throughout the country. Those statistics would be available somewhere, I suppose.

Mr. Lesinski. You state that your people work piecework?

Mrs. Gold. Yes.

Mr. Lesinski. They must average a certain number of pairs of shoes per day.

Mrs. Gold. Yes.

Mr. Lesinski. Then there is an average.

Mrs. Gold. I presume that information is available, but I do not have it.

Mr. Lundeen. Can you tell us the minimum and maximum that they will make in a day?

Mrs. Gold. No, I could not tell you that. You see, it would vary according to the operation that is performed.

Mr. Lesinski. And the type of shoe, I suppose.

Mrs. Gold. Yes. Let us take an operator who might work on 8 to 10 dozen pairs of shoes a day, which would be a maximum day's work on that particular operation, but on another operation a man may handle 150 dozen pairs of shoes a day.

Mr. Lesinski. Which is actually too much to handle, is it not?

Mrs. GOLD. Yes, of course it is. It would be too much in either case. But you have to do that in order to make anywhere near a day's pay, because the rates per unit have been reduced.

Mr. LESINSKI. In other words, the manufacturers have distorted the provisions of the N. R. A., and the provisions of section 7 (a), so that instead of giving the benefits to the workers, they have taken the benefits themselves.

Mrs. GOLD. I would say so. I would agree with you.

Mr. LESINSKI. The only thing I can see to do is to put more teeth into the N. R. A. and make it a Government control, so far as the amount of production is concerned; and that is something which the manufacturers and the newspapers are fighting against.

Mr. DUNN. Mrs. Gold, how many women workers do you have in the shoe factories in your district?

Mrs. GOLD. I should say about 3,000.

Mr. DUNN. How many men?

Mrs. GOLD. At the present time, probably around 5,000.

Mr. DUNN. Do you know if those factories have an age limit?

Mrs. GOLD. They do not have an age limit. I presume you mean in taking on people?

Mr. DUNN. Yes. Suppose a person applies for a job, do they take into consideration his age or her age?

Mrs. GOLD. If you are applying for a position to learn a job, yes; they take into consideration your age. If you are applying for a job at which you are already skilled, then they do not consider your age but rather your ability to perform the job.

Mr. DUNN. It depends on your ability, in other words.

Mrs. GOLD. Yes.

Mr. DUNN. There are no further questions. Thank you for your contribution, Mrs. Gold.

The next witness is John J. Vanecek, Cleveland, Ohio.

STATEMENT OF JOHN J. VANECEK, REPRESENTING THE OHIO ASSOCIATION FOR UNEMPLOYMENT RELIEF, CZECHOSLOVAK BRANCH

Mr. VANECEK. My name is John J. Vanecek, Cleveland, Ohio. I represent the Ohio Association for Unemployment Relief, Czechoslovak Branch, which numbers 145 lodges and has about 45,000 members. Our lodges have combined with the Catholic, Protestant, Evangelical organizations, gymnastic unions, and also sporting clubs.

Mr. DUNN. Would you mind stating what organizations you represent?

Mr. VANECEK. This organization of lodges belonging to this association is composed of Catholic, Protestant, Evangelical organizations, and gymnastic, and sport organizations, and also Democratic, Republican, and even Socialist groups. They all belong to this branch of the Ohio Association for Unemployment.

Mr. LESINSKI. What do you mean by gymnastic organizations, sokols?

Mr. VANECEK. Yes; sokols. One is a sokol and one is a workers' gymnastic organization. They all belong to this united organization.

Besides that, I represent individual business men's organizations, an association of which I am president.

We have studied these bills very carefully, and they have decided to send me here as their representative, and ask you Congressmen to endorse the Lundeen bill.

We have had a meeting and we feel that it is necessary to pass the Lundeen bill. They have read the other bills and the business men's association decided a few weeks ago to endorse the Lundeen bill.

We believe the Lundeen bill is the only bill that will help the poor, common people, at the same time as it helps the professional people. We believe it is the only bill that will bring this country to a better situation than we are in at the present time.

Mr. LESINSKI. You do not favor the Wagner-Lewis bill?

Mr. VANECEK. We do not favor it, because the Wagner-Lewis bill provides only for 16 weeks of assistance during the year. In the meantime, we feel that that bill may be good 2 or 3 or 4 years from now, but we need help right now. We do not want to wait 2 or 3 years. We believe the Lundeen bill is much better because it provides insurance through the year. Of course, we hope that we will not need insurance always. People will sometimes ask, "How can we pay for this insurance; how can it be done?" But if our situation gets better, as we hope it does in this country—and the country is rich enough and there is plenty of everything here—we may not need unemployment insurance always. If we can bring about a better system we will not need any insurance a few years later.

Mr. LESINSKI. The organizations that you represent are in favor of the Lundeen bill?

Mr. VENECEK. Absolutely; 100 percent.

Mr. LESINSKI. You state you come from Cleveland?

Mr. VANECEK. Yes.

Mr. LESINSKI. You actually represent the Czechoslovak clubs, as I understand?

Mr. VANECEK. Yes. I also represent the Ohio Business Men's Association. I am president of that organization. That is composed of individual business men, small business men.

I lost my business 3 years ago. I had a jewelry business. But other small business men, my brother-in-law and hundreds of others, who sell groceries and meats, when hard times come and people come to their stores for things, they have no money and naturally, as they are their friends, and they know that they have children to support, they trust them and some of them have lost as much as three and four and five thousand dollars. Then, at the last moment they have to close up their stores because they cannot support these people any more, and they cannot get any money from those people because those people have not any work.

Mr. LESINSKI. In other words, the retail merchant finds himself in the same position.

Mr. VANECEK. Absolutely.

Mr. LESINSKI. After he takes care of his customers and friends he finds himself in a position where he cannot go on with his own business.

Mr. VANECEK. That is right.

Mr. LESINSKI. Do you know anything about conditions in the retail business? Have the N. R. A. codes, as we enacted them, helped the retail trade?

Mr. VANECEK. I am afraid they have not helped us. The codes have not helped. I believe the codes that they have now hurt the small business man.

Mr. LESINSKI. Do you know the reason for that?

Mr. VANECEK. The small business man needs help. He is not able to hire people like the big business man is. Let us say that a girl 16 years of age, who has just come from high school, wants a job. She may not be able or ready to accept a job for $18 or $20 a week, but she is willing to help a few hours a day for maybe $10 a week, a sort of a temporary job. According to the code, the small business man cannot hire a girl on such a basis. So that it does not help the small business man. But it is different with the big business man.

Mr. LESINSKI. The codes were designed to help the small business man.

Mr. VANECEK. So far we do not see that it has.

Mr. LESINSKI. And to cut off the competition of the big chain stores. The chain stores were stopped in their practices of cut-throat prices, which was an attempt to allow the small man to exist.

Mr. VANECEK. I was in a business in my city for 20 years. I am in this country for 28 years. I know how they are doing. We have in Ohio a sales tax. These chain stores would sell books in advance, for $5 a book. Naturally, the rich people can go and pay $5 a book, and any time they want 2 pounds of coffee or sugar, they just punch the ticket or the slip. There is a 3-percent sales tax. The poor people are not able to buy a $5 book at one time, and go to the chain store and save the tax. They cannot do that. The poor people hardly get enough to be able to spend 50 cents or $1. I know for myself, I have not worked for 3 years already, and since I lost my business I know how hard it is for me to go in and buy $3 or $4 worth of food. I cannot do that. I go in and spend 50 cents or 30 cents. That is the way it goes.

Mr. LESINSKI. Would a large tax on the chain stores help the retail merchants any?

Mr. VANECEK. I believe it would help. But at the same time the big stores in Ohio make business. You have one grocery company that has 480 stores in Cleveland.

Mr. LESINSKI. The A. & P.

Mr. VANECEK. Yes. They buy stamps for a couple of thousand dollars and pay a tax of 3 percent. They make money. But the poor man cannot do that because he has got to go and pay $5 for a book and spend 25 cents for a street car or automobile to get that stamp from the main office.

Mr. LESINSKI. Have they a stamp system of taxation there?

Mr. VANECEK. Yes, sir.

Mr. LESINSKI. That tax should have been passed on to the manufacturer instead of the retail stores. That is the asinine provision in that kind of a tax. We have that in Michigan. The stores have to collect it at the source, from the people directly. In our State, under 10 or 15 cents you pay no tax. Starting from 18 cents you pay a 1 cent tax.

Mr. VANECEK. With us below 9 cents there is no tax. Above 9 cents you pay 1 cent. Above 40 cents you pay 2 cents.

Mr. LESINSKI. Our taxing system is slightly different. We pay nothing below 17 cents and it is a 3 percent tax above that.

Mr. VANECEK. Ours start from 8 cents.

Mr. LESINSKI. In other words, if you buy for 40 cents, you still pay only 1 cent. When you get above 50, then you pay 2 cents.

Mr. VANECEK. Our State taxes 2 cents on 40-cent purchases and above.

Mr. LESINSKI. That type of taxing system is all wrong.

Mr. DUNN. If there are no further questions, we thank you for your contribution.

Mr. VANECEK. Thank you very much, gentlemen.

Mr. DUNN. Mr. Greenfield will be the next witness.

STATEMENT OF E. C. GREENFIELD, EXECUTIVE CHAIRMAN OF THE SMALL HOME AND LAND OWNERS FEDERATION OF OHIO, CLEVELAND, OHIO

Mr. GREENFIELD. There are only a few points that I want to cover, and that I suppose would interest the committee most—why home owners need unemployment insurance, what the condition of the small owners is, why the other bills and schemes are more or less inadequate, and why they support H. R. 2827.

In the first place, let me say something about the organization. The Small Home and Land Owners Federation is an organization throughout the State of Ohio, approximating some 20,000 persons in membership, not all of whom are paying dues, by any means, because they are unemployed. Perhaps 70 percent of them are unemployed, and are carried on the books as unemployed, paying no dues. Included within its membership are people of all shades of political opinions, embracing all religious opinions and groups, containing many of the various language groups. They comprise a small property-owning class of people who have acquired from two to three thousand dollars, up to $12,000.

The program, objectively, is to stop foreclosures and evictions during the period of the crisis, or until means and ways of paying mortgages and taxes have been restored to them. The economic conditions of the small home owners is far worse than what might be imagined from a purely surface observation. Sixty-five to seventy percent of the membership is entirely unemployed, or working part time, 1 to 2 days a week. Fifty percent have been declared delinquent in taxes. Thirty percent are already behind over 1 year in taxes. The rest have received home loans, but, already, half of these that have applied for extensions have missed their last payments.

There are two reasons for the great percentage of unemployment among small-home owners. First, of course, is the condition of widespread unemployment; second, the majority of the small-home owners in our organization are workers who have spent their lives trying to accumulate enough money to buy a home. They are people who are nearing the age of 40, or who are over that age, and who will be the last taken back into industry. Among those members who have double houses, or more than one house, their tenants are mostly charity tenants, who pay no rent. It is a well-known fact, especially in Cleveland, that the small-home owner is carrying the burden of housing the unemployed.

This category of thrifty workers is rapidly disappearing as one of the main props of the American institution. Their bank savings have been lost, either in closed or liquidated banks, or they have been forced to draw them out, in order to weather the storm, and they now have no means of replacing them. They are the last to be placed upon the relief rolls, because they are termed "property owners," although what equity they may have has already been lost in the falling real-estate values.

How rapidly these home owners are disappearing, as home owners, can be better understood if we study the following figures. Over $30,000,000 worth of property, averaging from five to six thousand dollars in value, has gone to sheriff's sale in the 2 years, 1933–34, in Cleveland. This is at the present low real-estate appraisal. January 1, 1935, shows 5,100 pending foreclosures—nearly a 100 percent increase over January 1, 1934, in Cleveland.

What happens to these small-home owners when they are evicted? They are thrown out in the street, onto the relief rolls, and the relief administration absolutely refuses to pay over 1 month's rent, and from then on it is a case of one eviction following another eviction. I want to say that life is very unbearable for them. In Cleveland, last year, the bailiff's office issued 10,000 eviction writs, and the sheriff's office over 500. This has resulted in establishing the doubling up of families that were once prosperous home owners. They are now actually living in slum and crowded conditions.

I think these brief facts and figures show quite clearly why every branch of our organization has voted to support the workers' unemployment and social insurance bill, H. R. 2827. I want to say here, also, that this is not the only bill that has been brought before the organization for consideration. H. R. 2827 was endorsed after discussions on many other schemes of social security. First, our organization is opposed to all bills for unemployment insurance that increase the tax burdens that are already excessive. Second, they are opposed to bills that do not provide benefits for the millions already unemployed, or that do not take care of workers in all relations of life, such as farm workers, professional workers, domestics, or servants.

As to the question of who is to pay for such unemployment insurance, they are agreed it must be borne by those who are best able to pay it. They are impatient with broken promises of legislative bodies, who now, instead of decreasing taxes upon the working class of people, are absolutely trying new schemes of taxation which increase it. In Ohio, they are now faced with the 3- to 10-percent sales tax, and are passing a 4½ million dollar levy on the people as a property tax this month. That is an increase on property values.

Mr. Dunn. May I interrupt you? Do you know Congressman Sweeney, from Ohio?

Mr. Greenfield. Yes.

Mr. Dunn. He has introduced a resolution to bring about an investigation of the Home Owners' Loan Corporation, and he and Congressmen Truax and Prosser, and other men from Ohio, are doing their bit to bring about a condition in the State of Ohio that will prevent anyone from losing his home.

Mr. GREENFIELD. I have only this to say, if I may make some remarks upon that——

Mr. DUNN. Yes.

Mr. GREENFIELD. And it is not the first time that the Government has proposed that no home owner should lose his home. The Home Loan Act of 1933 specifically stated that it was a 3-year moratorium, although it was disguised in fake terms by which they have been able to avoid it, and the best they can get now is a 6 months' extension, if they can prove absolutely that they have not a penny in their pocket.

Another thing is that even the Home Loan Act, which was inadequate to start with, as far as furnishing enough money to take care of $21,000,000,000 worth of mortgages in the country, is still inadequate.

Mr. GREENFIELD. Yes, very much; but that is not the worst of it. Even though these bills may start out with some favorable intentions, amendments after amendments are piled onto them until they become useless, and only become a means of furthering the interests of the big fellow. For instance, take the institutional amendment to the Home Loan Act, which virtually made it impossible for a home owner to get a loan unless his mortgage was being held by some liquidating bank. We have very much evidence on hand, in the office in Cleveland, of people who have applied for home loans, and, because their mortgage was not held by some liquidating bank, they did not get it; and also there are other people who are not in distress at all who have received refinancing from banks, merely because their mortgages were in the hands of liquidating banks. For instance, Judge Wannamaker, of Akron, a $12,000-a-year man, I think, had his home refinanced through the Home Loan Corporation. Stephen Young, I think, here the other day, mentioned an individual in Cleveland who had a $25,000-a-year income, whose home was refinanced through the Home Loan Corporation, and at the same time the small-home owner, the fellow who actually needs this relief, is being foreclosed and thrown into the street continuously. We have case after case—so many of them it would take too much time to state them all.

Mr. LESINSKI. We have the same condition in Detroit and the same trouble.

Mr. DUNN. But your organization maintains that the Lundeen bill will benefit the men and women who are losing their homes?

Mr. GREENFIELD. Absolutely. I will tell you why. For instance, in our organization, 80 percent of them are in basic industries. They are either in a basic industry or the building trades, and their whole livelihood depends, of course, the same as that of any other worker, on ability to get a job and to receive wages. If that is shut off, there is no other means except the relief rolls, which have proven entirely inadequate. I do not think we need discuss that. I think we are pretty well convinced that the proportion of relief that is given is not enough to maintain a good standard of health and morale among the unemployed.

Mr. LESINSKI. Is not the largest unemployment today in the trades organizations?

Mr. GREENFIELD. In trades organizations?

Mr. LESINSKI. I mean, in different types of trades. Is not that where most of the unemployment is today?

Mr. GREENFIELD. The percentage of people that are unemployed? Well, I would not be able to answer that offhand, but I would say this, that we certainly know that a slump in the building trades has not been taken up, to any great degree, and certainly unemployment does not decrease under conditions of that kind. I imagine that the building trades, if we were just to take that category of workers, would probably show a greater percentage of unemployment than perhaps other industries.

Mr. LESINSKI. If the building trades and that type of industries were to start moving again, then the basic industries would be taken up?

Mr. GREENFIELD. I do not know. I could not say as to that. I hardly believe so. I do not see how we can have very solid advancement in building construction, unless we have the basic industries picking up.

Mr. LESINSKI. I know; but the basic industry would pick up, itself, if the building trades were to start moving. That would follow naturally, would it not?

Mr. GREENFIELD. Why not put the horse before the cart?

Mr. LESINSKI. You cannot produce lumber without building houses. You have got to build a house, or have a contract for a house first before you produce the lumber; and the same is true with respect to brick and other building materials.

Mr. GREENFIELD. I am not prepared to go into all of these things. I am merely stating the position of the home owners on this question, and why they themselves favor this bill.

To continue: They are also very impatient with the Government's continually promising them a return to prosperity. That is in line with the Congressman's remark here about what Congressman Sweeney is going to do. They have had so much experience with these things that they have very little faith now that any of them will be carried out in the way that they are talked about sometimes in the public press.

Mr. DUNN. But on the other hand you cannot take exception to the Congressman, though?

Mr. GREENFIELD. No; I am not taking exception to the Congressman. I am just merely talking about the more or less vague demagoguery that is released through the public press and also through official statements of the Government; not alone the Federal Government, but local and State governments as well. It all seems to be the same. The people hate to be told that they are better off than they were a year ago and at the same time have to be digging down into their pockets and finding out that they have got less money and less ability to purchase things, and that as far as their homes are concerned they are in a more dangerous position than they were a year ago.

In conclusion of these remarks, my constituents have instructed me to emphatically state that no other employment bill than H. R. 2827 is acceptable to them, and they have also asked me to say here— although Charles V. Truax is not present—that the small-home owners of Ohio are looking to Charles V. Truax to bring his official position as one of the members of this committee, to bear upon this situation, inasmuch as he gave our committee an indication that he was sympathetic toward the bill and that he would probably endorse the bill; but so far we understand that his position now is somewhat reversed, and they are wondering why he has changed his attitude.

Mr. DUNN. You mean that Congressman Truax has intimated that he is not favoring the bill?

Mr. GREENFIELD. That is what I understand. That is the understanding that has been given to our organization.

Mr. LESINSKI. Have you communicated with Mr. Truax?

Mr. GREENFIELD. We have tried to communicate with him, to verify it.

Mr. LESINSKI. You can get him very easily in the office building.

Mr. GREENFIELD. No; he is in Ohio.

Mr. LESINSKI. Is he in Ohio now?

Mr. GREENFIELD. Yes. His father died, and he is at home in Ohio. He will probably be back sometime today, and, if possible, I will see him.

Mr. DUNN. The reason I made that statement is because I know Congressman Truax is very progressive, and I would not want a false statement made, because I believe if he told you he was for a bill, he would be for that bill.

Mr. GREENFIELD. There are ways and means of being for a bill, and not for a bill, you know. You can be sympathetic to any number of things and still find reasons why you cannot support them.

Mr. DUNN. Not me!

Mr. GREENFIELD. Well, I am not talking particularly about individuals.

Mr. DUNN. But before broadcasting a statement that Congressman Traux is not for the bill: I would learn from him what his reasons are, and so forth, and give him an opportunity to explain.

Mr. GREENFIELD. I am preparing a statement and expect to do that.

Mr. LESINSKI. Mr. Truax has been one of the most progressive men on the floor that we have had here in the last 2 years. He is one of the few that has been "sore" at the administration. Charley has been one of them.

Mr. DUNN. Yes. That is the reason I made that statement about Mr. Truax, because I know how he has fought the banks. In fact, just recently on the floor he spoke in behalf of the ex-service men. He was telling what bills should be reported from the committee.

Mr. GREENFIELD. I will be very glad to report to my organization any indication on the part of any Congressman or Senator that he endorses this bill. I think that when we get right down to brass tacks the greatest indication that a man can give that he is for the interests of the working class of people in the lower brackets and categories of the middle class is to actually come right out in the open and endorse H. R. 2827, and let everybody know about it.

Mr. DUNN. May I make this statement in behalf of all the Congressmen? You know there are many bills introduced. I think it has reached the 6,000 mark at this session. In fact, as I said here this morning, I introduced an exact duplicate of this bill, H. R. 2827, to show the people that I am for it, and also to satisfy the demands that are made upon me for copies of the bill.

The statement you made leads me to defend all the Congressmen. For instance, they are criticized for not coming out for a certain bill. Well, I am here to tell you that the average Congressman does not know what kind of bills have been introduced, and yet the statement is made that he is not supporting such and such a bill. It may be a bill that he did not even know had been introduced. That criticism was leveled at me once. I made an investigation to find out what kind of a bill it was. The man who criticized me condemned me for not making some statement about it. So you see the Congressman may not know that those bills have been introduced until their attention is called to it. In the case I mention, my attention had not been called to the introduction of such a bill. There was no man on the floor of Congress last year that stood by the soldier and his dependents more than I did. Of course, there were other men who fought just as hard, and I did not want to be second to any man in the United States in behalf of the ex-service man, and I do not want to be second now to any man in the United States in behalf of the unemployed or the ex-service man; still I received nasty letters from ex-service men, criticizing me for not supporting such and such bills, and yet I had introduced many of the bills. I was being " bawled out " by the soldiers. That is the reason I wanted to make a statement in behalf of Congressman Truax and others, because oftentimes you are misled, and the man who is being criticized severely is really innocent and has been doing his utmost in behalf of his people, but he does not get publicity.

There are a few men who can get publicity in the papers. They do very little, but when they endeavor to do something, they make a mountain out of it. Then, there are other men who are down here, struggling and fighting, and doing whatever they possibly can to take the people out of the rut, and you never read anything about them in the paper. Well, I am not a man of means, neither am I a mean man, only when somebody attacks me. However, I am down here struggling as hard as other Congressmen.

I just wanted to make that statement in defense of Congressman Truax, and other Congressmen who might be down here working hard, and yet the people back home may not know about it.

Mr. GREENFIELD. All right. I will be glad to take your statement back to Cleveland.

Mr. DUNN. Let me say, in conclusion, that I was over at the White House last week, and I went over there with a delegation in connection with this unemployment-insurance and old-age pension bill, the administration measure. There were, I believe, about 15 of us, and we talked to the President, I presume, for an hour and 15 minutes, and I told him about the Lundeen bill, and I told him about the Townsend plan, and the bill embodying it. Most of the Congressmen were from the West, and they informed the President they were receiving thousands of letters, demanding that they do their utmost to report out the Townsend bill, and they appealed to the President to modify his bill and make the pension larger.

I told the President if I received five letters to support the Townsend plan it was a large number from my district in Pennsylvania. I said, however, " I have received letters from all over the country, from various organizations ", and I also told the President that, at the present time, a subcommittee is holding a public hearing on the Lundeen bill, H. R. 2827, and I said, " Up to date, we have had very intelligent men and women, both colored and white, professional and nonprofessional, tradesmen, and so forth, who have appeared before us, and these people represent every type of organization, and come from every part of the country, endorsing the Lundeen bill." I said to him, "Therefore, in my candid opinion, the Lundeen bill is the bill that the people want. In fact", I said, "I think so much of it that I introduced it." Mr. Lundeen wanted me to do that, and I did it because there was such a demand made on me for copies of the bill.

When he asked me about how the money was going to be obtained, I said, "Well, in my candid opinion, the Lundeen bill is the most practical and the soundest way of obtaining money," and I told him that nobody would be taxed except those who could well afford to pay it, people with incomes of $5,000 and over, and that we had a gift-tax—an inheritance-tax—clause in the bill.

Do you want to say anything more, Mr. Lesinski?

Mr. LESINSKI. No. That is all.

Mr. DUNN. I thank you, Mr. Greenfield.

The next witness is Mr. Earl Browder.

STATEMENT OF EARL BROWDER, GENERAL SECRETARY OF THE COMMUNIST PARTY OF THE UNITED STATES, NEW YORK CITY

Mr. BROWDER. Mr. Chairman, I would like to present this prepared statement and then answer any questions that anyone may wish to ask. The bill under consideration, H. R. 2827, has the unqualified support of the Communist Party. This bill embodies the principles which alone can provide any measure of "social security" for the workers and, thereby, also alleviate the condition of impoverished farmers, professional, and middle-class people.

It is noteworthy that among all political parties, the Communist Party alone has a clear, definite, unequivocal position on this question.

Enemies of the workers' bill have failed to present their arguments against it, relying rather upon an attempt to smother it with silence. To make this more plausible, there has been trotted out, as the main alternative to the administration program, the utopian Townsend plan, which provides an ideal straw man for administration supporters to knock down. But, as many workers have told this committee, the only real alternative to the administration's Wagner-Lewis bill is H. R. 2827, the workers' bill.

The enemies of real unemployment insurance have, however, prepared carefully to attack this bill should it come up for a vote in the Congress. They would be acting more in good faith if they presented their arguments to this committee. Their absence, thus far, makes it necessary to answer them without having in hand the definitive text of their arguments.

It is known that the main argument against the workers' bill is that it costs too much, that the country cannot afford to pay such a tremendous sum as would be called for. This argument ignores the fact that the country must pay the full cost of unemployment, that there is no way to avoid it; the only question is, what part of the population shall pay? Those who now pay with the lives of their women and children the price of degredation and misery, or the rich who still evade payment, whose profits are going up while mass starvation increases, the rich who alone can pay in any currency except the life-blood of the country.

We Communists are accused of being the enemies of our country, of being a menace that demands, in the language of Hearst and Liberty magazine, unceremonious hanging—as they express it, " shoot first, and investigate afterward."

Mr. DUNN. Pardon me. Do I understand you to say that the magazine called " Liberty " made that statement?

Mr. BROWDER. Yes.

Mr. DUNN. Shoot first and investigate afterwards?

Mr. BROWDER. Yes. I would be glad to submit a copy of that to the committee, if you are interested.

Mr. DUNN. Oh, absolutely. I do not want to see anybody " shot first ", you know.

Mr. BROWDER. Or, in the more decorous proposals of the spokesmen for the McCormick-Dickstein committee, the legal prohibition of the Communist Party after their investigation which refused to hear the official spokesmen of the Communist Party.

Allow me to denounce all these current slanders against the Communist Party.

Mr. DUNN. One more interruption, please. It is necessary for me to interrupt. Did I understand you to say that the Dickstein committee refused to permit one of the men, representing the Communist Party, to appear before it?

Mr. BROWDER. Yes.

Mr. DUNN. How long ago was that?

Mr. BROWDER. That was in November and December.

Mr. DUNN. 1934?

Mr. BROWDER. 1934. I made several attempts.

Mr. DUNN. I am glad to get that information, because I want to say that when Congress appropriates money to make investigations, and if they mention the word " Communist ", it is their duty to let a representative of the Communist Party, being investigated, to appear before the committee and testify. That is a right that every man should have.

Mr. BROWDER. I was summoned by this committee, myself, to appear before it in a closed meeting in September, but was not allowed an opportunity to present any evidence, except to answer two or three limited questions which they asked me, and I was not allowed to enlarge upon that; and later, demanding a hearing, we were refused.

Mr. DUNN. Would you mind, at sometime in the near future, putting that in writing, just as you have told it to me, and send it to me?

Mr. BROWDER. I would be glad to.

Mr. DUNN. Even if I do not believe in another man's party, when I attack his party, or am setting out to investigate it, it is undemocratic for me not to give that man an opportunity to defend himself, and it is very un-American, I would say, and very undemocratic to refuse him such an opportunity.

Mr. BROWDER. We agree with you on that, and it is for that reason that I shall take the advantage, in just a moment, to state before this committee our position on this question of the charges against us.

We Communists yield to no one in our love for our country. It is because we love our country that we fight for the workers' bill, which alone can save millions of our men, women, and children from utter degradation. When we declare our love for our country, we mean our love for these millions of people who are being reduced to an Asiatic standard of living.

Mr. DUNN. And yet, there were charges being preferred against the Communist Party and the Fascist Party and the Nazi Party, but your organization was not considered, or permitted to testify before the Dickstein committee. Is that right?

Mr. BROWDER. That is correct.

Mr. DUNN. Well, I believe that every person should give the other man an opportunity to explain himself, whether he believes in his policy, or whether he does not believe in it.

Mr. BROWDER. We Communists must seriously doubt the quality of that love for country which says that profits must be maintained even though these millions starve.

This country has half the accumulated wealth and productive forces of the entire world, with much less than 10 percent of the population. Yet we are told that "the country cannot afford" to guarantee its workers a minimum standard of decent living! It is clear that this phrase, "cannot afford", has a special meaning. It does not mean that the country has not the necessary resources; it means that those who rule the country, that small, infinitesimal fraction of the population which owns all the chief stores of wealth and means of production, considers it contrary to their selfish class interests.

This ruling class, the monopolists, the Wall Street financiers, have dictated the administration program. They do not hesitate to condemn tens of millions to a degraded standard of life, just too much to die on but not enough to live on. These are the real enemies of America; here is the real menace faced by our country.

If revolution, or the threat of revolution, has become a major problem of this country, this is only secondarily the result of the work of the Communist Party. In the first place, it is because millions have lost their last hopes of relief, after being disillusioned with all promises, one after another, based upon the present system. Communism, and the threat of revolution, will not be crushed by outlawing the Communist Party; it will grow in spite of everything, unless the conditions of life of the masses are improved, unless real social security is provided.

Mr. DUNN. May I interrupt. Did I understand you to say that unless the conditions are made better for the people, the Communist Party will grow in the country.

Mr. BROWDER. That communism and the threat of revolution will grow.

Mr. DUNN. In other words, you are making the statement, now, that communism will grow unless adequate provision is made for the people. In other words, if adequate provision, is provided for unemployment, or rather for employment at adequate wages, and unemployment insurance, and adequate old-age pensions are brought about, then do you think communism would become the predominant organization in the United States?

Mr. BROWDER. Communism would grow much more slowly, and the opinion of our party is that communism will inevitably grow, under any conditions conceivable, under the present system.

Mr. DUNN. In other words, you believe it is evolution?

Mr. BROWDER. Yes.

Mr. DUNN. May I make this statement? You are familiar with the teachings of communism?

Mr. BROWDER. Yes.

Mr. DUNN. According to the knowledge that you have of it, is communism fundamentally a dictatorial form of government?

Mr. BROWDER. Perhaps you would permit me to answer that after I have finished this statement? I think it would come better at the close of this statement, and be better understood.

Mr. DUNN. Proceed.

Mr. BROWDER. Precisely, because those who rule are determined not to grant any real measure of social security, is the reason for the attacks upon the Communist Party. These attacks are designed to prepare for a rejection of any real unemployment insurance; when the ridiculous charge is made that the Communists are " plotting to kidnap the President "—which you have read about in the papers. It was in the Washington papers, and in the papers throughout the country.

When the ridiculous charge is made that the Communists are " plotting to kidnap the President ", that is only a cover for the real charge, that the Communists are arousing a great mass demand for the workers bill, H. R. 2827. It is only a cover for the " open-shop " and company-union drive, exhibited in the renewal of the automobile code and the Wolman "Anti-Labor Board ", which threatens destruction to the American Federation of Labor. Even those staunch servants of the President, the executive council of the American Federation of Labor, have been forced to recognize in these events the beginnings of fascism in the United States. Germany taught the whole world to understand the fascism, which beginning with the demand to crush the " Communist menace ", ends with the crushing of all trade unions, all civil rights, even all religious liberties. Fascism can only be halted if determined resistance is made to its first steps. That holds good for the United States of America as well as it did for Germany.

The demand for enactment of the workers' bill, H. R. 2827, the fight for the only proposal of real social security is the front-line trench today in the battle for preserving a measure of life, liberty, and the pursuit of happiness in this country.

Mr. DUNN. Do you believe in the Constitution?

Mr. BROWDER. I do believe in the Declaration of Independence, which I quote.

It is the essential foundation for preservation of a measure of civil liberties, for resistance to fascism and war. It is the fight for all those good things of life, which the masses of the people, as distinguished from the professional patriots, mean when they speak of "Americanism."

If real unemployment insurance is denied, this will only add fuel to the fire of discontent, sweeping through the working population today, rising into waves of struggle and radicalization. The American masses are approaching that mood and temper, in which our ancestors penned those immortal words of the Declaration of Independence. These words have been outlawed in many States of this country, but I hope that it is still possible to quote them before a subcommittee of Congress.

Mr. DUNN. Proceed.

Mr. BROWDER. The Declaration contains the following words:

Whenever any form of government becomes destructive of these ends (that is, life, liberty, and the pursuit of happiness), it is the right of the people to alter or abolish it, and to institute a new government, laying its foundations on such principles, and organizing its powers in such forms, as to them shall seem most likely to effect their safety and happiness.

And it continues:

It is their right, it is their duty, to throw off such a government, and to provide new guards for their future security.

This fundamental right of revolution, inherent in the masses of the toiling population and represented today by the Communist Party and its program, is the ultimate guarantee that the principles of the workers' bill, H. R. 2827, will finally prevail. If not enacted into law by the present Congress, or if refused entirely by the rulers of the present system, these principles appear again and again, and finally will be enforced by a new government representing a new social-economic system, that of socialism.

That is my prepared statement. I would be glad to answer questions.

Mr. DUNN. What you just read was from the Declaration of Independence?

Mr. BROWDER. Yes.

Mr. DUNN. Written by one of the outstanding Americans, Thomas Jefferson, was it not?

Mr. BROWDER. There is some dispute as to the exact personal authorship, but Jefferson was at least one of the outstanding sponsors of it.

Mr. DUNN. Nevertheless, it is an American document?

Mr. BROWDER. Yes; that was truly an American document. At the same time, it was an international document. It is generally recognized that that document was the spark which lit the flames of revolution in Europe, also, and at that time, they said that revolution was imported from America, just as today they say revolution is imported from Moscow.

Mr. DUNN. I know when revolution started—when Eve got Adam up the tree to bring down a couple of apples. That is when it started! [Laughter.] Nobody knows when it is going to end.

Mr. BROWDER. The Communist Party believes that all forms of government are dictatorships, as against some classes, and democracies, for others. We believe the present form of government in the United States is, in substance, a dictatorhip of the big property owners, a democracy for those who have property; because the effective use of this " democracy " depends upon the possession of property. As against this form, we stand for a rule by the masses of the people, directed againt those who own property, to take this property away from them and make it the common property, all property in the means of production, all property which is necessary for the life of the people. That is the form of Government we propose—a dictatorship as against those who now rule; a democracy—the only real, broad democracy for the masses. I should qualify that slightly by saying that there are various forms of dictatorship by the property classes. At the present time, the form of this dictatorship in the United States is the form of a democracy, but such a form of democracy that the masses who have no property cannot make any effective use of it to defend their own interests. It serves the interests of those with property.

Mr. DUNN. How many men and women in the United States belong to the Communist Party, that are registered Communists? Have you any idea?

Mr. BROWDER. Approximately. I could say almost the exact membership of the Communist Party is between 30,000 and 31,000.

Mr. DUNN. That is, registered Communist?

Mr. BROWDER. Yes. That is, members who pay dues to the party every week.

Mr. DUNN. I have noticed in some elections, like Presidential elections, the vote runs up close to 200,000.

Mr. BROWDER. I think the largest vote we have polled nationally, which has been accorded to us in the national return, is about 225,000. Of course, we know that perhaps as many more votes were not registered, although cast. If you want a gage on the mass following of the Communist Party, a better gage would be the membership of organizations which endorse the various proposals of the party, which number about 600,000. We believe that the social and economic system must be so organized as to take care of those hazards of life which cannot be met by individual or volunteer effort.

Mr. DUNN. Proceed, Mr. Lesinski.

Mr. LESINSKI. That is all. The gentleman made himself clear.

Mr. DUNN. Thank you, Mr. Browder. I am glad you came.

We will recess, now, until 2 o'clock, ladies and gentlemen, and we will do our best to hear everybody. We want to give everybody an opportunity to express themselves, so at 2 o'clock, if you come back, we will be glad to see you and to hear you.

(The hour of 12:15 o'clock having arrived, the subcommittee took a recess until 2 o'clock this afternoon.)

AFTER RECESS

(The subcommittee met at 2:15 p. m., pursuant to the taking of recess.)

Mr. DUNN. Is Mr. Rothstein in the room?

Mr. ROTHSTEIN. Yes.

STATEMENT OF DAVE ROTHSTEIN, CLEVELAND, OHIO, REPRESENTING LOCAL 765 OF THE BROTHERHOOD OF PAINTERS, DECORATORS, AND PAPER HANGERS OF AMERICA

Mr. DUNN. Mr. Rothstein, will you please tell whom you represent?

Mr. ROTHSTEIN. I was officially elected and delegated to represent my organization, Local No. 765 of the Brotherhood of Painters, Decorators, and Paper Hangers of America, affiliated with the American Federation of Labor. That has a membership of 800.

114096—35——30

Also, Local No. 867, which has a membership of 1,000, voted in favor of the Lundeen bill, and it is the largest in the country. They endorse this bill.

I also represent the rank and file of the building trades in the city of Cleveland.

My organization, Local No. 765, had formerly elected two delegates to attend the National Congress of Unemployment Insurance, which was held here in Washington in January, but upon receiving a communication from President Green of the American Federation of Labor these two delegates were recalled. However, the rank and file of Cleveland elected a delegation to represent them at the National Congress for Unemployment and Social Insurance held at Washington in January. In spite of that, my organization saw fit at this time to send me to bring to you the greetings of that organization and to state that they were heart and soul in favor of the Lundeen bill, which is otherwise known as H. R. 2827.

We also endorsed the bill in January, the Lundeen bill, otherwise known as "House Bill No. 7598." My organization was the first to present a resolution at the Vancouver convention of the American Federation of Labor, introducing an unemployment-insurance bill, held there in 1930, but it was rejected. After pressure was brought upon him from the rank and file on the proposition of unemployment insurance, it changed the mind of President Green, and at that time he showed a tendency in favor of unemployment insurance.

We have in Cleveland an unemployment-insurance organization of A. F. of L. members. This organization, with the aid of the rank and file, also contributed toward forcing the issue upon President Green. We have read other unemployment-insurance bills presented at our meetings, but none have met favor as the Lundeen bill did.

The reasons for endorsing the Lundeen bill are as follows: Because a painter's work is of a seasonal nature.

Secondly, because we have small contractors not employing men continuously.

Thirdly, because we workers do not contribute anything toward the levying of a tax that would fall upon the workers.

Fourthly, the cost of extending the payment of insurance, whereas the other plans failed to take that under consideration. Also a continual-payment plan, whereas the others do not cover this question of continual employment.

Fifthly, that old age is a matter that we have to contend with as a trade where production is the main objective. Men above 45 years of age are considered nonproductive in our trade. Therefore, we see in the matter of old age a matter of vital importance. Then, there is the question of disability. The painters' trade carries with it many changes of conditions that sometimes cause disability on the part of the injured, primarily because of faulty scaffolding, and the speed-up system under which we labor. There is another question with which we are confronted, and that is the question of occupational diseases. This is also of vital importance to us in our trade. I may say that I could go on and speak further of the conditions of our trade, but I do not think it necessary to enlarge on this question at this time.

I was instructed to ask the Congressmen in our district, and also our organization has sent out communications to all Congressmen and Senators throughout the United States and received favorable responses on those communications, and we ask at this time that all Congressmen vote in favor of this Lundeen unemployment bill, known as the workers' bill, or H. R. 2827.

It has also been brought to my attention to ask Congressman Truax his position in relation to the workers' bill number 2827, as it has been assumed that he has displayed little interest after showing more at the beginning of the introduction of this bill.

Mr. DUNN. You just mentioned the fact that you have been requested to get information concerning Congressman Truax's attitude regarding H. R. 2827, or the Lundeen bill?

Mr. ROTHSTEIN. Yes, sir.

Mr. DUNN. Another gentleman from Ohio made a similar statement, and in view of that I wish to ask you this question: Have you contacted Congressman Truax?

Mr. ROTHSTEIN. I had intended to attend to that matter. I was up to his office, and I was told that he would not be in for a day or two because of a death in the family. I was told to stay here to see about that, and to spend a large part of my time to get that information for my organization. I will try to get in touch with Congressman Truax and endeavor to ascertain his position with relation to this bill.

Mr. DUNN. May I ask you this question: What has given you the impression that Congressman Truax is opposed to this legislation? The reason I am putting these questions to you, and I put them to one of the previous speakers, is because I know that Congressman Truax is considered very liberal, and also an excellent fighter down here, and I cannot understand why he would oppose this legislation.

Mr. ROTHSTEIN. I came personally to inquire, and inasmuch as I have not met Congressman Truax I am only speaking as to information that I have not succeeded in receiving.

Mr. DUNN. What about the other Congressmen from the State of Ohio, have you contacted them regarding this bill, H. R. 2827?

Mr. ROTHSTEIN. I have visited with other delegates from Cleveland, but we were not successful in meeting any of the other Congressmen up to the present time.

Mr. DUNN. You make the statement that you have not been successful in contacting any of the Congressmen. I cannot understand why you single out this man, Congressman Truax. The reason I make this statement is because I know that he has been, and on the floor of this session he has demonstrated to me that up to date he is for the underdog. Why do you single out Mr. Truax, and yet you have not mentioned other Congressmen's names?

Mr. ROTHSTEIN. Yes, sir. As I understand it I am here bringing my report, and I cannot answer for someone that I have not been able to ask the question. Therefore, the reason for my asking—or for being instructed to visit Congressman Truax was similar to the other Congressmen, and because of the fact that Congressman Sweeney was in favor of this bill I did not find it necessary to place it upon him.

Mr. LUNDEEN. Has he made that statement in writing or by a speech?

Mr. ROTHSTEIN. As I have stated formerly we have sent out questionnaires about his position on unemployment insurance, or, I should say the organization did.

Mr. DUNN. But that does not establish the fact that they are in favor of the Lundeen bill, does it, according to you?

Mr. LUNDEEN. Pardon me, Mr. Chairman, that might mean that they favor the administration bill. That is also unemployment insurance of a certain kind or type.

Mr. DUNN. That is the information I am trying to get from this man. There were two other witnesses here this morning who singled out Congressman Truax.

Mr. LUNDEEN. Mr. Chairman, I have not contacted nor asked Congressman Truax about where he stands on the bill, but I had supposed that he would be one of the first to support the bill.

Mr. DUNN. You have the same opinion I have.

Mr. LUNDEEN. I may be mistaken about it, but that was my supposition that he would be one of the first for our bill.

Mr. DUNN. The question I want to put to you, my friend, is this: As to these letters that you sent out to your Congressmen, how many from Ohio responded that they were in favor of the Lundeen bill, H. R. 2827?

Mr. ROTHSTEIN. I cannot speak officially because of the fact that these letters were written from one week to another. Those letters accumulated from one meeting to another, and you could not really keep count of them, but according to the correspondence itself a number of those were favorable to the Lundeen bill.

Mr. DUNN. Congressman Sweeney is a very progressive man and he has demonstrated to me that he stands for the people, and do a number of other Congressmen from Ohio.

There will be another gentleman here who will give me that information?

Mr. ROTHSTEIN. Yes.

Mr. DUNN. All right, Mr. Rothstein, I want to thank you for your address. Your organization has endorsed the Lundeen bill, H. R. 2827, on the belief that that is the bill which will provide for old age, unemployment, and so forth, do you?

Mr. ROTHSTEIN. Yes.

Mr. DUNN. Thank you very much, Mr. Rothstein.

Is Mr. Jackson in the room, please?

Mr. JACKSON. Yes, sir.

STATEMENT OF JAMES C. JACKSON, REPRESENTING THE NATIONAL STUDENT LEAGUE, EXECUTIVE COMMITTEE, NEW YORK CITY

Mr. DUNN. Give the reporter your name and the name of the organization you represent.

Mr. JACKSON. James C. Jackson, the National Student League, executive committee, 257 Seventh Avenue, New York City.

The National Student League is a national organization of students with chapters in more than 150 colleges and high schools throughout the United States. All of our chapters have gone on record as supporting the workers' unemployment, old-age, and social-insurance bill, H. R. 2827, also known as the "Lundeen bill."

The program of the National Student League calls for an organized struggle, first, in support of working-class demands; second, for adequate social insurance; third, against retrenchment in education and for free city colleges in all cities of a population of 100,000 and over; fourth, against racial and political discrimination, both in the schools and outside of school, and specifically for equal rights for Negroes; fifth, for academic freedom for students and teachers; sixth, against the militarization of high-school and college students through the Reserve Officers Training Corps and other military and semimilitary organizations, such as the citizens' military training camps and the Civilian Conservation Corps; against war and fascism.

In keeping with this program, we are in favor of this bill both in our capacity as students, that is as sons and daughters of workers, and in our capacity as potential workers, that is as young men and young women who, within a short time, will be out there competing against our jobless elders.

As a member of the national executive committee of the National Student League, I submit to you the following statement as the reasons in support of the workers' unemployment-insurance bill, H. R. 2827.

We were unable to find reliable data on the cost of elementary or high-school education, but, according to the Office of Education of the United States Department of Interior, the minimum cost of one year in a State-controlled college is $475. Even if the average worker were employed full time it would be practically impossible for him to provide his children with a higher education. But we know of course that very few workers have full-time, steady jobs. For instance, according to the December Monthly Labor Review of the United States Department of Labor, the average annual earnings of leather workers in Ohio was less than $1,100 even in the good years of 1928 and 1929. According to the United States Census of Manufactures these figures are typical of workers in manufacturing industries in the whole country. During 1932 these earnings dropped to as little as $690 due to unemployment and wage cuts. It is almost unbelievable that with this income anyone can maintain a family on even a subsistence level and send children to elementary school, let alone high school and college.

It was not until the fifth year of the depression that Federal funds became available to destitute college students who had somehow found their way into the colleges. This aid is so small that it can hardly be said to constitute relief. According to the monthly reports of the Federal Emergency Relief Administration, 96,000 college students, or less than 10 percent of the total, are now being permitted to earn less than $13 a month on jobs financed by Federal funds.

Mr. DUNN. Did you say 10 percent?

Mr. JACKSON. Yes; something less than 10 percent.

Mr. DUNN. I should like the total figures you gave in that last statement.

Mr. JACKSON. According to the monthly reports of the Federal Emergency Relief Administration, 96,000 college students, or less than 10 percent of the total are now being permitted to earn less than $13 a month on jobs financed by Federal funds.

Mr. DUNN. Thank you. Proceed.

Mr. JACKSON. Many of these students work for less than 20 cents an hour.

While students in the colleges and high schools, we are receiving an excellent training course in starvation and low wages in preparation for what awaits us when we leave school and attempt to find jobs.

Mr. DUNN. Did you say an excellent training in " starvation "?

Mr. JACKSON. Yes.

Mr. DUNN. Thank you. I just wanted to get that statement.

Mr. JACKSON. I can clarify that by a statement.

Mr. DUNN. Do you have to be trained to starve?

Mr. JACKSON. I can clarify that by a statement that I said just before, working at as little as 20 cents an hour, and some students are in college at great sacrifice to health and even to efficient work.

We have rapidly been made aware of the fact that there are no jobs for us. The American Federation of Labor says there are more than 11 million unemployed; other estimates run as high as 15 million and 16 million. According to an official unemployment census of the State of Massachusetts, taken in January 1934, as shown in the December Monthly Labor Review of the United States Department of Labor, almost half, or 47.6 percent, of all the employable persons under 20 years of age were unemployed. Of the students in Massachusetts who left school during 1932 and 1933, more than 30,000 had no jobs. In this State alone there were 17,000 vocationally trained persons who had never even had a chance to work in the occupation for which they trained. Of these 17,000, almost 14,000 were clerical and professional people. If the Massachusetts data are typical of the country as a whole, there are in the United States approximately one-half million trained clerical and professional people who have never had a chance to use their training.

The same census shows that more than 35 percent of all the employable people are either wholly or partially unemployed. Of those wholly unemployed about 25 percent had had no job at all for 3 years or more. All of these conditions although acute among white workers are even more so among Negro workers. Even in Massachusetts, where discrimination against Negroes is less vicious than in the South, fully one-half of all employable Negroes were unemployed as compared with only one-third of the whites.

Because of the limitation of time and because other speakers have already adequately covered other phases of the unemployment problem, we are not presenting any data to this committee bearing on the problems of old age, sickness, maternity, and other phases covered by the Lundeen bill.

In conclusion, the National Student League wishes me to impress this committee with the necessity of reporting the workers' bill favorably to the floor of the Congress both because of the facts presented to the committee and because the Lundeen bill or workers' unemployment, old-age, and social insurance bill is the only bill before this Congress which, first, covers all of the unemployed without discrimination because of race, color, or political opinion or affiliation; second, provides for full compensations for all wages lost because of unemployment, sickness, old age, maternity, industrial injury, or any other disability; third, because it is the only bill which includes the domestic workers, migratory workers, and agricultural workers. Inasmuch as most of the negro workers are to be found in these categories, the workers' bill is the only bill which provides social insurance for them. Fourth, because the workers' bill is the only bill which provides us students with a measure of security, both because it affords security for our parents, and because it holds forth the hope of security to us when we enter the labor market.

Mr. DUNN. Do you desire to interrogate the gentleman?

Mr. LUNDEEN. No; I have no questions, Mr. Chairman.

Mr. DUNN. I want to ask you one question, Mr. Jackson. Do you know how many colored college students there are in the United States today?

Mr. JACKSON. How many college students?

Mr. DUNN. Colored boys and girls in the United States in colleges?

Mr. JACKSON. No; I do not have that available. I do not know that, Mr. Chairman.

Mr. DUNN. I wish to thank you for your excellent address.

Is Mr. Bedacht in the room?

Mr. BEDACHT. Yes, Mr. Chairman.

STATEMENT OF MAX BEDACHT, GENERAL SECRETARY INTERNATIONAL WORKERS UNION, BROOKLYN, N. Y.

Mr. DUNN. Will you give your name and address, and the organization you represent?

Mr. BEDACHT. My Name is Max Bedacht, residing at 2042 East Thirty-seventh Street, Brooklyn, N. Y., and I am representing the International Workers Order.

The International Workers Order is a mutual benefit society, a fraternal organization with over 62,000 members. It is organized on a national scale, and chartered in the city of New York. I am speaking in the name of this organization, and both in convention, and on a referendum vote they have unanimously endorsed the unemployment social insurance bill now before Congress as House bill no. 2827, and in their name I am submitting to this committee an urgent request for the passage of the bill, and in their name I am giving the reasons for our request.

The masses of members in our organization are workers. These workers seek in the fraternal organizations a measure of economic security. They know from experience that their only income is the wages they may be able to earn. If they are unemployed and cannot find jobs, they cannot earn wages. If they get sick and cannot work, they cannot earn wages. If they are old and are refused jobs because of age, they cannot earn wages. When they stop earning wages their economic source of life stops flowing.

The workers join fraternal organizations as an effort of establishing a continuous flow of their economic source of life. Through sick benefits and similar mutual aid features, they want to tide themselves over interruptions in their flow of earnings. But such efforts can at best only serve emergencies. They cannot solve the problem. In the first place all help supplied by the fraternal organization is limited by the limited ability of the workers to pay dues. The lower the worker's income, the less able he is to pay dues, but the more frequent and the more intense is his need for help.

In the second place, fraternal and mutual help can be organized by the workers only for a limited number of categories of emergencies, for sickness, disability, cases of accident, and so forth. It cannot be organized for old age and unemployment. The workers never clearly saw these limitations until the present crisis arose. Up to 1929 they thought it within their power to provide against all their economic emergencies. They believed it when they were told that it was up to them to put aside reserves during days of prosperity and to prepare for a rainy day of depression. They did prepare for a rainy day. They put money in the banks. They bought homes. But when the rainy day did come the workers found to their astonishment that their carefully provided-for umbrella had mysteriously disappeared. The banks had closed their doors. Their own homes were turned from places of shelter into unbearable and foreclosed mortgage burdens. It was then that the workers found that they were facing a social problem. Theirs was not a problem faced only by individual workers, to be solved by those workers individually.

Mr. LUNDEEN. The panic has been a great teacher.

Mr. BEDACHT. Yes, you bet it was; and a teacher that will have to be obeyed. Other teachers may be disobeyed, but not the panic.

It was a social problem that the workers depend on wages for a living. It was a social problem that the workers did not have control over their jobs and over their wages. It was a social problem that the workers do not control the economic sources of their lives.

We who are working in the fraternal organizations are daily faced with the limitations of our fraternal help. On the one hand we see the needs of workers who are victims of incurable diseases and hear their pitiful demands for help. Their need for help goes far beyond the reserves established by the collective effort of the workers in the fraternal organization; on the other hand we see in our ranks the workers who thought they had established for themselves a certain measure of security by membership in the fraternal organization; they became unemployed for months at a stretch and can no longer maintain their membership in the fraternal organization. They ask help so they may maintain at least the limited aid which membership in the fraternal order does secure for them. But no matter what we do—and we do a great deal—we cannot come within any reasonable distance of a solution of the problem.

That is why we in the International Workers' Order come to the conclusion that only a measure of adequate social insurance can help. Only a united social effort can hope to solve the problem. We are of the conviction that House bill 2827 is the only measure yet proposed that attacks the problem.

This bill puts no limitation to the period in which help or insurance is supplied. This is fundamental. Without such a provision in a social insurance measure all talk of social security is a cruel deception.

All other proposals submitted to Congress heretofore, like the Wagner-Lewis bill, insofar as they provide any insurance at all, provides for serious limitations in the periods for which insurance is supplied. They all start with an inadequate and fundamentally wrong method of raising funds for the insurance; then they make actuarial deductions as to how far those inadequate funds will go. Since very little can be collected from the workers because they do not have anything, and since the capitalists refuse to have much collected from them, the funds upon which the actuarial figures are based must of necessity be totally inadequate. The result is that all these schemes provide help only to some workers in some distant future, and then only for a miserably few weeks. The rest of the workers or all of the workers the rest of the time are doomed to misery and starvation.

Such insurance is no help at all. When in connection with this you consider that the establishment of such a measure of insurance will seriously cut down and even eliminate other forms of public and private relief, you can readily imagine that this kind of social insurance will make matters worse for the workers instead of better.

The problem of unemployment, old age, and disability of the workers must be approached like the Government approached the problem of the war. The question then was not how many cannons can be buy for the money we have. The question was how many cannons do we need; then the necessary money was gotten by loans and by taxation to buy the necessary cannons. Is the need of the masses of workers and their dependents less important than the needs of a war? Evidently the prevailing opinion in the circles of capitalists and the war profiteers considers these needs less important. Well, the masses of workers do not. They say, "When it was a question of providing billions to kill and to destroy these billions were provided. No one called in an actuary to cut down on the expenditures for war materials because of lack of funds. At this moment it is not a question of killing people and destroying property as it was in the war. Now the question is to feed and to maintain the masses. That is more important. Against this need all other needs must stand aside. If the prevailing national economy cannot provide the necessities to feed and maintain the masses of workers, then it is hopelessly bankrupt. It should acknowledge this bankruptcy and go into a receivership. I am sure that the workers are ready to take over the receivership. If, however, the existing national economy refuses to declare its bankruptcy, it must stop acting the bankrupt and must meet its obligations. The first and foremost obligation is to feed, to house, and to clothe all of the people. These obligations demand of them the maintenance of the working masses. The masses are entitled to this maintenance.

Congress must recognize that the masses of workers have only the proceeds of their labor power to live on. Whenever through no fault of their own they are unable to turn their labor power into an income, when unemployment deprives them of jobs, when sickness or disability disables them, when old age disqualifies them, it must provide for them an income other than wages. This income must be social insurance. House bill 2827 provides this income for the masses.

The purpose of social insurance is the establishment of a continuous guaranty of existence for the worker. As long as the worker himself can guarantee his existence and the existence of his dependents by working, well and good. But when for social reasons beyond his control he can no longer provide the means of his and his dependents' existence the Government has to provide these means.

It is clear that the masses of workers cannot be the source of funds for such insurance. The national wealth must provide this source. The workers with their labor produce the national wealth. Those who control that national wealth must be made to contribute the necessary share to the maintenance of the workers. The rich, the capitalists, must pay for this social insurance.

We in the fraternal movement are particularly anxious to get an unemployment and social insurance that will really insure the existence of the worker and his dependents against the insecurity of his existence. We know how inadequate and how pitifully insufficient an insurance must of needs be that bases itself upon funds accumulated out of the workers' contributions. We want no such social insurance. Such social insurance would make matters worse for the workers. While it would eliminate public and private relief, it would hardly improve the actual insurance that the worker does get today from his fraternal organization. Besides, it would deprive him of the right of management and administration of his own insurance funds.

In this respect none of the existing proposals, aside from House bill 2827, contributes one iota to the improvement of the workers' position. A much better result could be obtained by Government subsidies to the fraternal organizations. Such subsidies would eat less money than insurance provisions for the workers.

But neither such a measure nor all other existing unemployment insurance, old-age pension, and so forth, will solve the problem. House bill 2827 will.

That is why we support it. That is why we ask this committee to report it out favorably. That is why we demand of Congress to pass it.

Mr. DUNN. Congressman Lundeen, do you wish to interrogate the witness?

Mr. LUNDEEN. I am afraid, Mr. Chairman, that the gentleman knows more about unemployment and old-age pensions than I do. I want to say that he supplied a direct, able, and searching statement, and I think his analysis of the Wagner-Lewis bill supplied a knock-out, solar-plexus punch, which was very well stated in a few words.

Mr. DUNN. I agree with Congressman Lundeen. Your address was very constructive and impressive.

Is Frank De Rosa in the room?

Mr. DE ROSA. Yes, sir.

Mr. DUNN. Please give your name to the reporter?

STATEMENT OF FRANK DE ROSA, PRESIDENT OF THE ORGANIZATION OF ITALIAN-AMERICAN DESCENDANTS, CLEVELAND, OHIO

Mr. DE ROSA. Frand De Rosa, 2191 East 38th Street, Cleveland.

Mr. DUNN. Proceed, Mr. De Rosa.

Mr. DE ROSA. This demand will come to you as one from a united organization composed from Mutual Lodge, Order Sons of Italy; Independent Order Sons of Italy; International Order; Democratic and Republican independent clubs, and also juvenile clubs from different types.

The sentiment of 10,000 members request me to address to your honors about something which I hope will receive a favorable influence. On the course of life, we have run, for the past years, on this rich country of America; day by day the good citizens of this great land have disapproved of this charity and dole. The mothers and fathers have been very unhappy to see their children go without clothes and shoes.

It is discomforting for our youth to be out of school because they do not have the necessary equipment for their class. Therefore, we demand that the workers' bill H. R. 2827 be recommended by this respectful body as one to have the urgent support of they people of the United States, without discrimination. Furthermore, we demand that the bill will meet your consent to be an enactment to our Constitution for security of livelihood as our President stated on June 8, 1934.

At the present time, we have no liberty under the charity system, because we must eat what the grocer gives us whether we like it or not.

Humanity is worthy to be applied on our conscience, and the Government shall see if the people get the necessary care to live as humans. On this question I might say that the charity has no conscience when it refuses to give our children shoes, and tells the parents to keep their children home because they do not have money in the budget.

Justice is the principle of the right, and this right has been opposed under the same system. So let us retain the word " glory " for the ornament and quality for our justice.

Mr. DUNN. That is a very splendid address, and I want to say to the gentlemen that I agree with you; that many times people of my district and other districts around my congressional district have written to me for the purpose of obtaining food, clothing, and other necessities, and time and time again they have written and come to see me and said that they were unable to get it, I have any number of men of all nationalities, of all religious creeds and color, who have told me that they cannot get anything.

Mr. DE ROSA. Yes, sir.

Mr. DUNN. I want to say to the gentleman that the statements you have made are correct. Before you conclude I want to ask you how many Italian organizations you represent?

Mr. DE ROSA. Sixty organizations.

Mr. DUNN. Sixty Italian organizations?

Mr. DE ROSA. Yes.

Mr. LUNDEEN. In Ohio?

Mr. De Rosa. In Ohio; yes. Of course, there are more than that number. I just represent 60.

Mr. Dunn. Are those 60 in the State of Ohio?

Mr. De Rosa. Yes, sir; the 60 are in the State of Ohio, and most of them are in Cleveland, Ohio.

Mr. Lundeen. How many members are there?

Mr. De Rosa. Ten thousand.

Mr. Lundeen. Ten thousand?

Mr. De Rosa. Yes.

Mr. Lundeen. And you represent them here?

Mr. De Rosa. Yes; I represent them all.

Mr. Dunn. Can you not get in touch with all of the Italian organizations and tell them to send somebody down here to support this bill? If you do that, I will get in touch with all of the Irish organizations.

Mr. De Rosa. That will be fine.

Mr. Lundeen. I am very happy to hear your statement that you come here representing so many people. Have you contacted your Congressman back home?

Mr. De Rosa. Yes, sir; we have.

Mr. Lundeen. How about Congressman Crosser?

Mr. De Rosa. Congressman Crosser; yes, sir; we have a letter, and he said he was in favor of that.

Mr. Lundeen. In favor of this particular bill?

Mr. De Rosa. Congressman Crosser and Congressman Sweeney; I talked to both of them personally; and then we have a letter from him.

Mr. Lundeen. Did they tell you that they were in favor of unemployment insurance?

Mr. De Rosa. Yes.

Mr. Lundeen. I know; but we also have the Wagner-Lewis bill.

Mr. De Rosa. I understand that.

Mr. Lundeen. And then we have this bill.

Mr. De Rosa. Yes.

Mr. Lundeen. And then we have bills such as the Townsend bill.

Mr. De Rosa. Yes.

Mr. Lundeen. And many other bills?

Mr. De Rosa. Yes.

Mr. Lundeen. Did they specify they would support this particular bill?

Mr. De Rosa. Yes; everywhere when I present this bill I ask them to support this bill, no. 2827, and 7598.

Mr. Lundeen. Did you write letters to them asking them to support this measure?

Mr. De Rosa. Yes; I wrote letters, and I also saw them personally.

Mr. Lundeen. Did they reply to those letters?

Mr. De Rosa. He replied and said he would support it.

Mr. Dunn. Did these men from Ohio tell you they were in favor of the Lundeen bill?

Mr. De Rosa. I will tell you the truth, Mr. Chairman, as to the answer I had. When this movement started we understood the President of the United States had a bill himself, and he said if the President's bill is better than yours, we will support the President's bill. If your bill is better than the President's, we will support your bill.

Mr. Dunn. In other words, they said if the President's bill is better than the bill you were writing to them about that they would support the President's bill; is that your statement?

Mr. De Rosa. Yes.

Mr. Dunn. And, on the other hand, if this bill is better than the President's bill, they will support this bill?

Mr. De Rosa. Yes; if this bill is better than the President's bill, correct.

Mr. Dunn. Do you recall if they mentioned the word "Lundeen" bill?

Mr. De Rosa. The Lundeen bill?

Mr. Dunn. Yes.

Mr. De Rosa. Yes.

Mr. Dunn. In their letters they said they would support the Lundeen bill if they were convinced it was better than the other?

Mr. De Rosa. Yes.

Mr. Dunn. Is that the information you want?

Mr. Lundeen. Yes. You understand that under the administration's bill it would be very difficult for you to get any money before 1938?

Mr. De Rosa. Yes; we all understand that.

Mr. Lundeen. What a beautiful picture for these 15 million unemployed that makes in the next 3 or 4 years! What are they going to do to be sustained during that time? My point is that something must be done now.

Mr. De Rosa. Immediately.

Mr. Lundeen. Yes. Right now, in 1935, in February, March, and April of 1935, this late winter and spring something must be done before it is too late. Our point is that this bill will safeguard the stability and security not only of the worker but of the Government itself.

Mr. De Rosa. Yes. On this question Mr. Lundeen, the very last time I was here, I went over to see Mr. Young, I had talked to him personally in Cleveland, and he gave me the same answer, but when I got here and went to talk to him, he said, "Well, I will tell you, as to the Lundeen bill, I do not think I will support it for one reason."

Mr. Lundeen. Who said that?

Mr. De Rosa. Mr. Young, Stephen M. Young, Congressman at large, and I said, "Why do you think you are not going to support this bill?" He said, "Because this bill is being sponsored by the Farmer-Laborites, a Congressman from the Farmer-Laborites." I said, "What is the difference to you?" I said, "When you were running your campaign in the State of Ohio you did not qualify yourself that you would serve one party or another party. You qualified yourself by saying that you would serve the people of the State of Ohio." I said, "If you think you are not going to use or adopt this just because it comes from Mr. Lundeen or somebody else, it does not make any difference to me. If you want to put your name on it I will support your name as long as the bill contains the same provisions that that contains." I said, "You are elected by the people. You are going to lose after another two years." He said, "I do not want you to feel that way, because I am going to support the bill." But I do not believe it.

Mr. LUNDEEN. He said he would support it?

Mr. DE ROSA. Yes.

Mr. LUNDEEN. As far as I am concerned, I would be willing to step out of the picture. If the name Farmer-Labor is going to prejudice the bill, I would step out of the picture, providing these other honorable gentlemen of the House and Senate will see that it becomes a law. I will step out of the picture if I am going to hurt the bill, if they will see that this bill becomes a law.

Mr. DUNN. If anyone advances the argument that it was a Farmer-Laborite who presented the bill, and that for that reason they hesitate to support it, you can say that Congressman Dunn, from Pennsylvania, is not a Farmer-Laborite, and he introduced the same bill. Mr. Lundeen is entitled to all the credit he can get, because he is the man who has been fighting for it.

Mr. LUNDEEN. Mr. Chairman, I would like to say to the gentleman, since he is going back to Cleveland, are you?

Mr. DE ROSA. Yes; I am.

Mr. LUNDEEN. I should like to say to him that not only is the honorable subchairman of this committee in favor of this bill, Congressman Dunn, but the Chairman of the great Labor Committee, Mr. William P. Connery, of Massachusetts, himself a prominent labor leader of the House and Democratic leader, has declared himself for the bill and will support it. He stated that over his signature, in the committee and on the floor.

Mr. DUNN. And he told me in person, because I had sent out what they call a release, and I asked the Congressman if it was all right to quote him, and he said, "Absolutely, Congressmen Connery, Lundeen, and Dunn", and that went out over the country, that the Chairman of the Labor Committee had endorsed it and the chairman of the subcommittee endorsed it, and included Congressman Lundeen.

Mr. LUNDEEN. And then Congressman Moritz, of Pittsburgh, came in and testified for the bill.

Mr. DUNN. Yes.

Mr. LUNDEEN. And the Chairman of the Committee on Patents, Mr. Sirovich, said on the floor of the House of Representatives the other day, in the presence of not less than 150 Congressmen, that this bill, in his opinion, was the only bill that would solve social security that had thus far been presented in Congress this year; and it was the only bill that would do that, in his opinion, in the last Congress, and for that reason he signed the petition on the Speaker's desk 2 years ago. Many other Congressmen have made similar statements. So that we are not alone here on this. We are not as lonesome this year as we were 2 years ago.

Mr. DE ROSA. If the Congressmen and Senators from the State of Ohio do not support this bill they are not going to be elected in the next election. We will work, and we will work hard on this thing. We are not saying they have to be in favor of Mr. Lundeen or anybody else. We want them to be in favor of the bill. The funds in the benefit associations for sick benefits are gone. The men who were members have dropped out because they cannot pay their dues.

Mr. DUNN. Thank you, Mr. De Rosa. Mr. Jackson, did you get that information for me on the number of students?

Mr. JACKSON. About 300,000.

Mr. DUNN. Who are now in the colleges of the United States, that is, colored boys and girls?

Mr. JACKSON. There are about 6,000,000 college students in the United States. The Negro population is about 12 percent of the population of the United States. Therefore, a proportionate Negro college population would be about 500,000. Subtracting a conservative 200,000 for difference in opportunity, a good guess would be about 300,000 Negro college students.

Mr. DUNN. Thank you very much for that information, Mr. Jackson.

The next witness is Mr. Frank Rogers.

STATEMENT OF FRANK ROGERS, REPRESENTING THE CLEVELAND COMMITTEE FOR UNEMPLOYMENT INSURANCE

Mr. DUNN. Tell the Congressmen your name, address, and the organization you represent.

Mr. ROGERS. My name is Frank Rogers, and I represent the Cleveland Committee for Unemployment Insurance. This is a committee and a movement that has grown out of the campaign for genuine unemployment insurance which started about 2 years ago in the city of Cleveland. This organization or movement—that is, and the various organizations affiliated to it—is also at the present time extending its activities outside of the city of Cleveland and is working for a State measure for the enactment of a State bill in the State of Ohio.

To give you an idea of the extent of the support for the Lundeen bill and the organizations that have endorsed this bill and are affiliated to our movement in Cleveland, I want to call your attention to the following character of the organizations and to give you some sort of an estimate of the membership of these organizations.

First of all, as far as religious organizations are concerned, we have the endorsement of the Polish Catholic Church, of Cleveland, Ohio, with a membership of 10,000. That is the largest Polish church in the United States. This church conducted an open hearing on the Washington Congress, where delegates reported to the congregation. We also have the endorsement of a large Hungarian Baptist church that elected delegates to the Washington Congress for unemployment insurance. As to the men engaged in the campaign, we have the endorsement of the Cleveland Community Religious Hour, a large church association in Cleveland, that has on its advisory board such prominent individuals as Rabbi Silver and Rabbi Bruckner, of Cleveland. That is an indication of the support that is coming from the religious organizations for the movement for the Lundeen bill in Cleveland.

Now, as far as some public officials are concerned. In the city of Cleveland we are working to have the city council of Cleveland go on record for the Lundeen bill and to memorialize Congress accordingly. Thus far we have the written endorsement of four councilmen. These four have sent out calls to convene all of the city councilmen in Cleveland into a special meeting, there to take up the question of endorsing the bill in the city council and thus have the endorsement of the city council. We have the written endorsement of two State representatives of the Ohio General Assembly. We have the written endorsement of one Congressman in Ohio. That is Congressman Sweeney.

The question has been raised here as to the attitude of Congressman Truax. Many here have introduced this question, and I would like to clear it up. When we were here for the Washington Congress, the committee visited Congressman Truax. At that time we did not know whether he was a member of the Labor Committee or not. Congressman Truax at that time told the committee that he had a general idea as to the principles of the Lundeen bill and he felt that as far as he understood the bill it was a good bill and he would support it. With this impression in the minds of the committee we went back to Cleveland, Ohio, and in our literature and publicity we have gotten out we have stated that Congressman Truax is a supporter of the Lundeen bill.

Mr. DUNN. That is what I want.

Mr. ROGERS. We then wanted to get his signature on a letter, a letter from him stating his position. However, his letter to our committee was of such a general character that it created the impression that he was not altogether convinced. Since Congressman Truax is the only member of the Labor Committee from Ohio, that is the reason we have started a sort of a special campaign in Ohio, and also since we know something of his liberal inclinations, to have his endorsement for the bill officially, and his vote is of great importance. That is why Congressman Truax's name has been brought up here so often, because we just conducted sort of a special campaign to get his official endorsement.

Mr. LUNDEEN. You are not attacking him in that campaign?

Mr. ROGERS. Not at all.

Mr. LUNDEEN. You are merely seeking his endorsement?

Mr. ROGERS. We are merely seeking his endorsement, yes.

Mr. LUNDEEN. I do not think he should be attacked until you know where he stands.

Mr. ROGERS. Yes.

Mr. LUNDEEN. I do not think you should attack him until you know where he stands, and you should give him fair play in that connection.

Mr. ROGERS. Yes. In our letter we said the committee visited him and at that time he gave a sort of an official reply. At this time we want a sort of official endorsement as to his position.

Mr. LUNDEEN. I do not believe we should attack any Congressman until we know where he stands.

Mr. ROGERS. As far as labor endorsement is concerned and their support, the committee is familiar with the attitude of the officialdom and of the top leadership of the American Federation of Labor, who have circulated a letter against supporting the Lundeen bill.

Mr. DUNN. Let me get this clear. Did I understand you to say the American Federation of Labor circulated a letter opposing the Lundeen bill?

Mr. ROGERS. Yes.

Mr. DUNN. How long ago was that?

Mr. ROGERS. This was about 3 weeks prior to the Washington Congress, I believe the first part of the year, the 1st of January.

Mr. DUNN. This year?

Mr. ROGERS. Yes.

Mr. LUNDEEN. I have requested that a copy of that letter be inserted in the record.

Mr. ROGERS. In Cleveland, as the result of this letter they instructed the business agents of the union there that they must stand guard at the doors of labor-union meetings and prevent anyone from taking the floor in support of the Lundeen bill.

Mr. DUNN. They did that?

Mr. ROGERS. They did, yes; that is in the city of Cleveland. Despite this fact, we have the endorsement of the Ohio district of the Amalgamated Association of Iron, Steel, and Tin Workers, including the entire State of Ohio. We also have the endorsement of the Cleveland American Federation of Labor Automobile Council, which has affiliated with it 11 local unions. We have the endorsement of 11 locals of the United Mine Workers of America, that is in the eastern part of the State. In spite of this we have the endorsement of Federal locals from certain shops, and we have the Boot and Shoe Union of the A. F. of L., and the Journeymen Tailors' Union also, which are isolated unions, rather than large sections of the organization.

We also have the indorsement of the Cleveland Newspaper Guild, which is the newspaper union. We also have the indorsement of the Mechanics Educational Society of America, which includes the entire district 16. This is an indication of the support of labor unions for the Lundeen bill.

A representative just spoke here elected by the Painters' Union, of the American Federation of Labor. Prior to the Washington Congress they were opposed to sending anyone to Washington to support the Lundeen bill, and they used the excuse that that money could be used to much better advantage for feeding the unemployed union painters. Today the number in support of the Lundeen bill is more in that particular local, and many of the building trades joined with them and instructed this particular delegate to stay here as long as it is necessary to stay to campaign for the Lundeen bill, and the American Federation of Labor Painters' Union would be responsible for any expenses incurred in staying here. That is an indication of the support as far as the American Federation of Labor is concerned.

As to the fraternal unemployed organizations two representatives have already spoken here. The Ohio Association for Unemployment Insurance has a membership in excess of 40,000 with 155 branches, mostly of Czechoslovak and Bohemian people. We have the Italian United Front fraternal movement of some 60 lodges, and the Independent Sons of Italy, and the American-Russian clubs with a membership of some 10,000. And we have the Lemke Association. That includes all the Croatian fraternal societies.

Mr. LUNDEEN. These are all in Ohio?

Mr. ROGERS. All in Ohio, and in the city of Cleveland the Croatian and fraternal unions and its branches have given their indorsement.

As far as the unemployment organizations are concerned, we have the Unemployed Council of Ohio and Unemployed Leagues fully endorsing the bill. Then, there is the Small Businessman's Association of Cleveland that has somewhere around 150 or so business establishments connected with it, and they are also on record in favor of the Lundeen bill. That is an indication of the fraternal following in support of the bill.

As far as the city councils and municipalities are concerned, as stated before, we are getting the endorsement of these bodies. Thus far, in Ohio, we have succeeded in getting the endorsement of the City Council of Bedford, Ohio; of the City Council of Brookline Village; of the City Council of Lawndale, Ohio; of the City Council of Canton, Ohio; and of the City Council of Toledo, Ohio. All of these municipalities and their governing bodies have gone on record as in favor of the Lundeen bill, and have memorialized Congress accordingly.

Mr. DUNN. You mean those municipalities you have just mentioned have endorsed this bill?

Mr. ROGERS. Yes; they have endorsed this bill, five of them in Ohio.

Mr. DUNN. I see.

Mr. ROGERS. We are hopeful to have the City Council of Cleveland go on record in that regard also.

In addition to this, support has grown throughout the State for the Lundeen bill to such an extent, and the campaign has affected State officials in such a way, that we introduced a bill into the Ohio General Assembly on February 4 as a State measure, an exact duplicate of the Lundeen bill, with provision that it should be in effect in the State of Ohio until such time as Congress would enact a Federal system of unemployment insurance. So, we have sort of a State Lundeen bill in addition to the Federal bill in the State of Ohio.

Our records indicate that we have in excess of 200,000 supporters in the State of Ohio for the Lundeen bill actively engaged in the campaign.

Now, a couple of remarks to indicate the attitude of these people toward our bill, and toward other measures, such as the Lewis-Wagner bill. It is very difficult to convince people in meetings and in other places that the Lewis-Wagner bill actually contains the provisions that we know that it contains. For instance, you go to a group of workers, and you tell them that the Lewis-Wagner bill does not include the present unemployed, and you will get a statement from them that they must be crazy in Washington to draw up such a measure. They cannot understand that anyone would consider unemployment insurance which would exclude the present unemployed. The question of taxes immediately arouses opposition among the laboring people, particularly the home owners. Now that the sales tax of 3 percent is in effect in Ohio the workers categorically state that they are against any additional taxation burdens. As far as administration of funds are concerned, this they can understand, because they have had some local examples of the money used that has been allotted for relief purposes that is used and squandered in the process of administration.

As far as the Townsend plan is concerned, there is already a decline. For instance, in Cleveland at a meeting there were some 800, at which this Captain Hawks of some national fame as an aviator was speaking. That attracted a crowd of 800, and in the process of the workers asking questions as to the provisions of the bill and questioning its feasibility, and so forth, the chairman yelled out, " Well, if you do not believe us, do not support us, do not come to our meetings ", or some such remark, and as a result of that the majority of the 800 just walked out of the Townsend meeting. This Utopian idea is very appealing; nevertheless, when they come to study the situation, they realize it is not practical, and it is used for the purpose, really, of blocking and covering up a campaign for real unemployment insurance.

As to the situation in Cleveland the figures indicate that there are about 200,000 jobless in Cleveland.

Mr. DUNN. Pardon the interruption. You say there are 200,000 jobless in Cleveland?

Mr. ROGERS. Yes.

Mr. DUNN. What is the population of Cleveland?

Mr. ROGERS. It is better than a million.

Mr. DUNN. In other words, practically one-fifth of the population is unemployed?

Mr. ROGERS. About one-fifth of the population is unemployed.

Mr. DUNN. Thank you.

Mr. ROGERS. The unemployment of the entire State is in excess of a million and a half, through the State of Ohio.

These workers are today on Government relief, and efforts are being made to put them on these F. E. R. A. projects. Various compromises have been made as to wages and the workers think that they are going to get the same wages as during the C. W. A., which amounted to something around the figure of $1 per day, more or less, but to give you an idea of what they are actually going to pay and intend to pay there, a small group of seamen, lake seamen, were put to work at relief wages plus $1 cash. They authorized a strike already against these wages, and the entire thing is up in the air now awaiting some final action by the administration in Washington.

The effect of this unemployment on youth can be pictured in the increase in juvenile crimes. In Cleveland, for instance, 2 weeks ago, there was an outrageous crime committeed by a gang assault of some 25 or 30 youths on a woman in one of the working-class districts. Now, this can be attributed directly to the fact that these youths, whose ages were from 18 to 25 years, had nothing else to do except hang around pool rooms, as they were jobless.

Mr. LUNDEEN. And got into bad company.

Mr. ROGERS. Yes; and got into bad company, and they were being denied the right of marriage and to set up a home and to work.

Mr. DUNN. And not fed properly.

Mr. ROGERS. That is true. Those things result in such criminal activities as this.

Mr. DUNN. You say there were about twenty-five?

Mr. ROGERS. Twenty-five, yes.

Mr. DUNN. Twenty-five boys and young men were arrested?

Mr. ROGERS. Twenty-five were arrested; yes.

Mr. DUNN. For attacking this one woman?

Mr. ROGERS. Yes.

Mr. DUNN. Proceed.

Mr. ROGERS. As far as ages are concerned, most of these men are housed in the jail, and they also have what is known as a " municipal lodging house " or " wood yard ", where, regardless of your age, either 16, 45, or 70 years old, they are all packed, some 2,000 of them in this sort of a lodging place, there to get a cup of coffee and some soup, and must work 1 hour on the wood yard. That is the character of the relief conditions there as far as age is concerned.

Of course, in Ohio we have the old-age pension there which officially calls for a figure of $25 for those over the age of 65. However, due to the funds being exhausted that has been cut to $18, and the latest report is they cannot pay anything today.

This is a report that I want to make here. The main thing that they told us to emphasize down here was that the Government, let us say, warns the workers against counterfeit currency. Well, they want to warn the Government not to establish any counterfeit unemployment-insurance schemes which will not guarantee security, but we wish to insist that the members of the committee and other Congressmen give every support to genuine unemployment insurance and the Lundeen bill.

Mr. DUNN. Congressman, do you wish to interrogate the witness?

Mr. LUNDEEN. No; thank you very much.

Mr. DUNN. I enjoyed what you said and thank you, Mr. Rogers, for the information you have given us.

The next speaker is Mr. Waldo McNutt.

STATEMENT OF WALDO McNUTT, NEW YORK CITY, REPRESENTING THE AMERICAN YOUTH CONGRESS, NATIONAL CONTINUATIONS COMMITTEE

State your name and the organization you represent.

Mr. McNUTT. Waldo McNutt. I represent the American Youth Congress. My local residence is in Topeka, Kans., but my office headquarters is 112 East Nineteenth Street, New York City.

Mr. LUNDEEN. What is your business?

Mr. McNUTT. I was graduated from law school last year. I am full-time secretary now for the American Youth Congress.

Mr. DUNN. How many members belong to the American Youth Congress?

Mr. McNUTT. I come to that in my speech. Gentlemen of the committee, I appear before you today on behalf of the youth of America, the citizen of tomorrow. The American Youth Congress national continuations committee has delegated me as their chairman to appear before you to put forward our position on unemployment and social insurance.

For the committee's information, the American Youth Congress now comprises over 150 organizations from coast to coast and in the Territories, including Hawaii, representing over two and a quarter million youths. This body is a united front. Youth has succeeded in building a united front where our elders have failed. The organization includes student workers, black and white, of all political complexions except Republicans. The ages range from 15 to 30 years.

The program of this organization is a minimum one. We do not go in for politics as a new party, leaving the strictly political actions to organizations in that field; but we do set forth a program on which we can all agree.

I quote first from the program adopted at New York University, August 15 to 17, 1934.

Unemployment is the most burning problem before America's youth. Seven million young people under the age of 25 are jobless. A large proportion of these have never had the opportunity of employment, having been graduated from school directly into the army of unemployed. This, coupled with increased destitution at home, has resulted in close to 1 million homeless youths, aimless wanderers of American highways.

We disagree with the proposals to place the million of jobless and homeless youths into C. C. C. or transient camps. Such proposals are identical to the steps taken by Fascist Germany, Poland, and Italy to militarize the young generation. The military character of our C. C. C. camps was admitted by Assistant Secretary of War Harry Woodring when he wrote:

"In 2 months last spring the Army recruited, conditioned, equipped, and mobilized more men than we recruited in the Spanish-American War, and we did it so quietly and efficiently that few people in the country realized what was happening. This achievement, the organization of over 300,000 men in more than 1,500 Civilian Conservation Camps was the first real test of the Army's plans for war mobilization." (From Liberty of Jan. 7, 1934.)

This Congress goes on record as favoring:

1. The replacement of all existing C. C. C. and transient camps with jobs at regular wages and with a system of unemployment and social insurance such as contained in the Lundeen bill, to provide for those who are unemployed through no fault of their own. Such social insurance should include the paying of workers and farmers, insurance for loss of wages because of part-time work, sickness, accident, old age, or maternity. We disagree with the premise of the city, State, and national governments that no funds are available for jobs and insurance should be derived from increased graduated taxation of all incomes of $5,000 a year or over.

2. Such insurance to apply without discrimination to all unemployed, regardless of nativity, age, sex, color, or creed, or former employment.

The Lundeen bill was the one measure on which there was the greatest unanimity of opinion. We have only one suggested change that we want to submit to this committee, and that is that the age limit should be lowered from 18 to 16 years, so as to include the youth coming out of high schools, who cannot have the opportunity to go to college, and who are unable to find employment; but since this bill is the only one that makes any provisions for the youth, at all, we are giving it our whole-hearted support, on the following specific points, which may draw for you the difference between H. R. 2827 and the so-called "Wagner-Lewis unemployment and social insurance bill."

Point 1. The H. R. 2827 measure calls for relief to all unemployed workers from date of unemployment, and for the whole period. The Wagner-Lewis bill calls for relief only to those who have been unemployed for a period of 12 months, a maximum of 15 weeks' relief per year. The masses of the youth who have left school the last 5 years are excluded from any benefit under the Wagner-Lewis bill. It is estimated that 7,000,000 young people are thus excluded.

Point 2. H. R. 2827 provides relief to all workers, youth included, as well as domestic, agricultural workers, Government employees, teachers, and other professions, whereas the Wagner-Lewis bill excludes the agricultural workers, the domestic workers, the Government employees, teachers, and other professionals.

Point 3. H. R. 2827 provides a minimum of $10 a week and $3 additional for each dependent. The Wagner-Lewis bill provides only $7 minimum, no provision for dependents of those provided for, and compensation to be limited to the funds collected.

Point 4. H. R. 2827 provides for funds to be raised by those able to pay, and the Wagner-Lewis provides funds to be raised by the workers; which means that the costs will be passed on to them by the manufacturers, and the people that should pay for the social and unemployment insurance escape taxation.

Point 5: H. R. 2827 provides for immediate payment, and the Wagner-Lewis bill provides that we must wait for a full year. On this particular point, the American Youth Congress wants to be placed on record as being strongly opposed to any further delay; that immediate payment is the thing that is needed.

Point 6: Funds to be administered by workers and farmers; and, under the Wagner-Lewis bill it keeps it in the hands of the petty politicians, and the distribution of funds falls into the hands of many of our State politicians who in the past have been known to graft on such measures.

That is the report of the American Youth Congress, representing 2¼ million American youth, stretching from coast to coast, including the Territory of Hawaii.

Mr. DUNN. Thank you very, very much.

Mr. LUNDEEN. I want to thank you for your statement. I did not hear quite all of it, but such a report from an organization representing so many of the youth of America is encouraging. You have credentials showing that you represent these organizations?

Mr. McNUTT. Yes, sir; yes, sir. I might say that the Farmer-Labor Political Federation is one of the organizations that came into the American Youth Congress in New York, last August, and Mr. Alfred Bingham has sat in on our national continuance committee, when he has been in New York.

Mr. LUNDEEN. Are you the national secretary or local secretary?

Mr. McNUTT. I am the national chairman of the continuance committee. Our second American Youth Congress will be held in Detroit the last part of June, and they are expecting to have at least 5,000 delegates there.

Mr. LUNDEEN. Nation-wide?

Mr. McNUTT. Nation-wide.

Mr. DUNN. If I come, will you let me come in?

Mr. McNUTT. Sure; we will be glad to put you on the program.

Mr. LUNDEEN. I hope you do a better job than your elders have done, in government.

Mr. McNUTT. Well, at least, we have effected a united front where the elders have failed.

Mr. DUNN. I want to say that I am mighty, mighty glad to have heard what you had to say here today, and I do not doubt it is up to the young men and young women to step right into this fight and demand that your Government provide jobs at adequate salaries and, until your Government does that, that you see to it that they give you the necessary amount of money to provide you with the necessities of life. I know that the young people in the United States do not want to be idle. They are not demanding unemployment insurance; they are demanding jobs; but, since your Government will not give you a job, then you have the right to ask for unemployment insurance.

Mr. McNUTT. We have to have something.

Mr. DUNN. Absolutely; in fact, I feel elated that the young people of our country are taking an active interest in the affairs of their Government.

Mr. McNUTT. I want to say, for the benefit of the committee, and for the record, too, that in the State of Michigan, the Michigan Youth Congress has collected some 10,000 signatures, and has taken them to the State legislature, trying to get them to endorse H. R.

2827; and pressure is being brought to bear throughout the country, where we have representatives, on particular Representatives in Congress, to see that they familiarize themselves with H. R. 2827.

STATEMENT OF JAMES ASHFORD, REPRESENTING THE NATIONAL COMMITTEE OF YOUNG COMMUNISTS LEAGUE, NEW YORK CITY

Mr. ASHFORD. As a representative of the national committee of the Young Communists League of the United States of America I want to make clear to this committee the position of my organization on unemployment and social insurance.

Being a political youth organization which actively, day in and day out, defends the economic, political, and social needs of the youth, the Young Communist League is very much concerned over these problems. According to the Baltimore Sun of January 2, 1935, there are about 7,000,000 unemployed youth in the United States of America between the ages of 16 and 25. After 5 chaotic years of crisis the American youth see no future. For the American youth, therefore, unemployment and social insurance is a life-and-death question.

My organization and its national committee have seriously studied the various bills before this session of Congress dealing with unemployed and social insurance. Two bills are most prominent in the deliberations before this committee: One bill is the Lundeen unemployment, old-age, and social-insurance bill, H. R. 2827; the other is the Wagner-Lewis social-security bill, which has the support of the Roosevelt administration.

After a thorough study of both bills we, the Young Communist League, are convinced that the bill which best protects and serves the needs of the 7,000,000 jobless youth is the workers' bill, H. R. 2827.

We are equally convinced that the Wagner-Lewis bill is entirely inadequate. The national committee of the Young Communist League has decided to thoroughly oppose the Wagner-Lewis bill for the following reasons:

1. It calls for relief only to those who are employed and for a maximum of 15 weeks' relief per year. This means that those masses of youth who have not been employed since they left school during the past 5 years of crisis are not provided for.

2. It excludes agricultural workers, domestic workers, sharecroppers, tenant farmers (many of whom are Negroes), professional workers, and Government employees, and so forth.

3. It provides for 50 percent of weekly wages but not to exceed a wage of $15. There is no minimum relief. This is most inadequate. Even this miserly sum is to be given for only 15 weeks per year. What will the unemployed do the rest of the year? To go to Florida or Bermuda? They have to eat even there.

4. Under the Wagner-Lewis bill the burden of the funds is to be placed precisely upon those who can least afford it. It calls for a 3-percent pay-roll tax, which even Miss Perkins, speaking before the Senate Finance Committee, admitted would be passed on to the consumer.

5. Even if the Wagner-Lewis bill is passed in Washington, it would not be obligatory for the States to carry it out. It requires the ratification of this bill by the State legislatures. In addition to this long delay, even those who are adjudged eligible for relief will have to wait at least a year until sufficient reserves are accumulated.

We approve the workers' bill, H. R. 2827, on the other hand, because it does not suffer from any of these serious inadequacies.

1. It fully and adequately provides for all unemployed workers, 18 years of age and above, from the date of unemployment and for the whole period of unemployment.

2. It calls for compensation to all unemployed workers, youth as well as adults, without discrimination because of sex, race, color, religious or political opinions, whether they be agricultural, domestic, white-collar, or professional workers.

3. It provides for at least $10 per week with $3 for each dependent.

4. It calls for funds to be raised by the Federal Government at the expense of employers and corporations, through taxes on inheritances, gifts, and incomes of individuals and firms $5,000 per year and over.

5. This bill also provides for old-age pensions, maternity benefits, and other social-insurance protection.

This workers bill, H. R. 2827, is the only bill which answers the needs of the 7,000,000 jobless youth and masses of unemployed in general.

I also want to raise very sharply here the question of relief and unemployment and social insurance for the Negro people. Sinse the N. R. A. 90 percent of the Negro employees have been laid off by big industrial firms. In large industrial centers like Gary, St. Louis, Cleveland, Chicago, 50 percent of the total unemployed are Negroes. For example, in Birmingham, Ala., 75 percent of the total unemployed are Negroes; in Pittsburgh, over 60 percent. These figures are from the Urban League.

In direct contrast to the low percentage of the population, the high unemployment percentage stands out, pointing to the urgent necessities of adequate relief. Guaranties must be made in the administration of any system of unemployment and social insurance against " Jim Crow " practices and for equal treatment for Negroes. Especially in the South, what assurances do the Negroes have that they will be given this insurance when millions of them are not even permitted to vote?

As a typical example of crass " Jim Crow " discrimination against Negroes, let me give you the case of Pittsburgh. The total Negro population in Pittsburgh is 83,000, of whom 36,000 are on relief. More figures on Pittsburgh:

Percentage of population:

Negro	6
White	94

Percentage of unemployed:

Negro	60
White	40

Percentage on relief:

Negro	13
White	87

Mr. LUNDEEN. You say that 87 percent of those on relief are whites, in Pittsburgh?

Mr. ASHFORD. Yes; 87 percent. That is in proportion to the ones that are unemployed, see, and the percentage among Negroes is 13 percent. That brings out the example of discriminating in giving out relief, and so forth, in this place.

Mr. DUNN. Those figures you have just given are from the city of Pittsburgh?

Mr. ASHFORD. Yes.

Mr. LUNDEEN. You reside there?

Mr. ASHFORD. I beg your pardon?

Mr. LUNDEEN. You live there?

Mr. ASHFORD. I am from New York.

Mr. LUNDEEN. But you are giving Pittsburgh as an example.

Mr. ASHFORD. I am giving Pittsburgh as an example.

Mr. LUNDEEN. Do you live in Harlem?

Mr. ASHFORD. Yes.

Mr. LUNDEEN. You are familiar with conditions there; are they about the same?

Mr. ASHFORD. In Harlem, I would state that about 85 percent of the total population among the Negroes are unemployed. Getting relief is a very difficult proposition, discrimination is even worse there than in any other portions of the country, I can assure you.

Mr. DUNN. What would be the percentage, in New York City, of the Negroes obtaining relief?

Mr. ASHFORD. Getting relief? I do not know. In Harlem, the Negroes get more relief than in any other place. Of course, that is the most densely populated section among the Negro people. In other portions of the city, they practically receive no relief. I was talking with a fellow a few days ago, and he was telling me how some Negro fellows went down to get relief, on the east side of town, and they were told they should move up into Harlem, and they did not give them relief up in that part of the city.

Mr. LUNDEEN. What is the population of the Negro sections of Chicago and Baltimore, do you know, approximately?

Mr. ASHFORD. I am not familiar with the general populations of Baltimore and Chicago. I know that as far as the unemployment is concerned in Chicago or Baltimore, also, it stands more or less the same. Generally, you find since the introduction of the N. R. A. codes in most places, many of the Negro workers have been excluded from the jobs, and white workers have been placed in their jobs at these places.

Mr. LUNDEEN. Let me ask you this: There is a new administration in New York now. Has that improved conditions any for you?

Mr. ASHFORD. Not any whatsoever. They are just as bad, or worse.

Mr. LUNDEEN. You mean as it was before the new mayor came in?

Mr. ASHFORD. Yes; before the new mayor came in. Relief stations at the present time are controlled by the police, more or less; and when people go down to get relief they are more or less clubbed instead of anything else. There is more vicious terror against the workers now than there was before the LaGuardia administration.

Mr. DUNN. Do you blame LaGuardia for that?

Mr. ASHFORD. Well, LaGuardia is partially responsible, of course, together with the whole administration. You see, this is a part of the whole system. We cannot blame one fellow, but we have to blame the whole administration; and he is a part of the administration.

Mr. LUNDEEN. Well, he is accounted a liberal and a progressive, is he not?

Mr. ASHFORD. Well, he is one of these demagogic fellows, as I call them—liberals, you know, that tell you one thing and shoot you in the back at the same time that he is telling you that. That is what is actually taking place in New York.

Mr. LUNDEEN. Has there been any real terrorism in New York in the last few months?

Mr. ASHFORD. Well, yes, there has been plenty of terror.

Mr. LUNDEEN. You have held meetings, have you not?

Mr. ASHFORD. There has been plenty of terror; workers arrested walking down the streets. A few months ago I knew of a Negro young fellow that, due to unemployment, had no money. He went to one place and took a loaf of bread. He was shot down in the streets. I know of many cases of Negro fellows that are cold-bloodedly shot down on the streets, without any words whatsoever, and there is big terror against the Negro and white worker, in New York also.

Mr. LUNDEEN. I had special reference to your meetings. You are allowed to hold your meetings, are you not?

Mr. ASHFORD. There is terror.

Mr. LUNDEEN. But you are allowed to hold your meetings?

Mr. ASHFORD. In some places you can hold meetings, in certain instances. Meetings are also broken up.

Mr. LUNDEEN. Within the last few months?

Mr. ASHFORD. Within the last few months.

Mr. LUNDEEN. Upon what ground are they broken up?

Mr. ASHFORD. Well, they never give the grounds of breaking up the meetings. They just come down on you and break them up.

Mr. LUNDEEN. Were these white meetings or colored meetings, or both?

Mr. ASHFORD. Well, in our organization we just do not have white meetings and colored meetings.

Mr. LUNDEEN. They were mixed? They were workers' meetings?

Mr. ASHFORD. Yes. We have meetings of the working-class people, and this more or less puts fear into the administration, and they want to break these meetings up, because they see the unity of the Negro and white workers there and they know that where there is unity we mean business.

Mr. LUNDEEN. Are you allowed to meet in the central parks, say, Washington Square?

Mr. ASHFORD. Washington Square? Madison Square? The last time we were supposed to have a meeting there they did not allow us to hold it. They put a statue out in the square there to keep us from holding our open demonstration on the inside of the place and refused to let us have the place there. That is the part of " liberal " LaGuardia.

Mr. DUNN. Did a delegation of your organization ever undertake to interview Mayor LaGuardia?

Mr. Ashford. Yes; many times.

Mr. Ashford. Eighty-five percent of the agricultural workers in the South are Negroes. Federal loan banks in Southern States make loans only to members—Negroes are refused membership.

According to various authorities, like the New York Times, there are about a million and a half homeless boys and girls roaming aimless around the country, without relief, food, or shelter. Because they are not provided with adequate relief or any relief at all, these boys and girls are compelled by poverty to leave their parents.

Mr. Lundeen. When you make that statement about the number of those, that is only a guess, is it not?

Mr. Ashford. A guess?

Mr. Lundeen. You have no census figures on that?

Mr. Ashford. No; there is no census on it, but it is approximately that amount.

Mr. Lundeen. How do you arrive at that?

Mr. Ashford. Well, we got these figures here—at least I got these figures here from the New York Times.

Mr. Lundeen. Well, that answers my question. Proceed.

Mr. Ashford. The workers bill, H. R. 2827, is the only bill before Congress which provides for these legions of homeless youth.

There are millions of unemployed boys and girls who are staying at home, a heavy burden upon their parents. In New York City, for example, there are about a million and a quarter unemployed, of whom many thousands are youth. These youth have no provisions whatsoever. They must live on the family relief allowances. No provision is made for their own personal needs, like clothes, medical, and dental attention, and so forth. Here, too, the workers bill, H. R. 2827, is the only bill which meets the needs of the youth.

The single unattached youth in the cities are also not provided for. Most of them never get on relief. Those that do receive from $1 to $2.50 per week for their living expenses (food, clothes, incidental expenses, and so forth). The workers bill, H. R. 2827, does provide for these youth, too.

According to Government figures, more than a million boys have already passed through the C. C. C. camps. At present there are about one hundred and fifteen thousand boys in these camps. President Roosevelt and General MacArthur, according to the press, plan to extend these camps to at least twice the present number.

These boys in the C. C. C. camps are living under primitive, backwoods conditions. They are paid a dollar a day, of which they actually get only $5 monthly. These boys thus take jobs away from professional forest workers who were formerly paid 5 and 6 times the amount paid to C. C. C. boys.

Mr. Dunn. It is necessary to interrupt you. You said they were getting a dollar a day, when in reality they received but $5.

Mr. Ashford. Yes.

Mr. Dunn. Explain where the balance goes, will you, please?

Mr. Ashford. This money is sent to their parents, or is sent to some other people at their homes. They only receive $5, for tobacco, and this, that, and the other.

Mr. Dunn. Out of their $30?

Mr. Ashford. Out of their $30.

Mr. Dunn. And the remainder?

Mr. Ashford. They have nothing to say about the rest of it.

Mr. Dunn. You mean it is taken right out of their pay?

Mr. Ashford. Yes.

Mr. Lundeen. You should also state in fairness that they receive their food and their shelter. Do they not receive clothing?

Mr. Ashford. Yes; they receive it; but what kind is it? They have a right to administer what they are supposed to get.

Mr. Lundeen. Well, let us have the whole story.

Mr. Ashford. Well, let me get through.

Mr. Lundeen. You did not state that they get medical attention?

Mr. Ashford. Yes; they get medical attention.

Mr. Lundeen. We should have the whole story and not a portion of it.

Mr. Ashford. But the kind of attention that these fellows get in these places is inadequate. I have here, if you wish to see it, a bulletin that is issued by the fellows on the inside of the C. C. C. camps, and that is a bulletin that gives the information that I am conveying here, and it is the voice inside of the C. C. C. camps.

Mr. Lundeen. I voted for higher pay than $1 a day for them, and I was not satisfied, but I do think that when you say their pay is so and so, you should tell the whole story.

Mr. Ashford. In the C. C. C. camps the boys are subjected to various militarization schemes, like military formations, drilling, use of military phrases and terms, and so forth. Actually training in the use of arms is being given in some camps under the guise of " rifle clubs."

In the C. C. C. camps, too, " Jim Crow " discrimination is rampant. The Government is segregating Negro boys into separate Negro camps. In these Negro " Jim Crow " camps conditions are characteristically worse than white camps. An example of a Negro " Jim Crow " C. C. C. camp is camp no. 41, company 1251, in New Jersey.

In many camps these C. C. C. boys are subjected to rigid military discipline. Not only are they fined $2 and $3 for minor violations for rules, but often are sentenced to confinement in guardhouse on bread and water.

According to the Wagner-Lewis bill, 50 percent of the weekly wages are to be allotted for relief, but never to exceed a wage of $15 per week. The overwhelming majority of juvenile workers are not even receiving the N. R. A. minimum wages; in textile mills, for example, they receive an average of $8 to $10 per week. In the field of agriculture and domestic service, much less. This means that young workers in textile towns will never receive more than $5 per week relief, the others mentioned, nothing, and this only for a period of 15 weeks per year.

All these facts show that the American youth are living under desperate conditions. For them unemployment and social insurance is a burning need of today. My organization, the Young Communist League, will energetically and ceaselessly work for the passage of the Lundeen workers bill, H. R. 2827, into law.

Mr. Lundeen. I am interested in your statement. I take it that, as a Communist, you are opposed to military training of workers in this country?

Mr. Ashford. Being forced into military training camps for militarization, for the purpose of new imperialist wars.

Mr. Lundeen. But your party, in the Soviet Union, believes in training youth in the use of arms?

Mr. Ashford. Yes; but in the Soviet Union, you have a workers' form of government, and there they are not trained for imperialist purposes; that is, for plundering and attacking.

Mr. Lundeen. They are trained for defense, you mean?

Mr. Ashford. Yes; for the defense of the workers within the Soviet Union, but not for new imperialistic, plunderous wars; that is, suppression of more masses of people, plundering colonies, and so forth.

Mr. Dunn. This is a friendly question: How do you know that the United States Government is taking these youths into these camps and training them for imperialistic purposes? Why can it not be for defensive purposes, the same as it is in Russia? That is just a fair question.

Mr. Ashford. Well, under capitalism, or any imperialistic form of government, there is no such thing as "defensive" wars. All wars are fought for the profit of imperialists because, under imperialism, you only have the question of fighting for new markets, the fighting for the domination of certain other countries, and so forth, and so on, the suppression of national minorities and national countries, and so forth; but in the Soviet Union you do not have this. You do not have to fight for the suppression of national minorities. There, they have liberty; all the national minorities have equality in the Soviet Union. They are not fighting there for profit, and so forth, but for the benefit of the people, as such, for the masses of the people, and not for a small minority of rich rulers who suppress the masses of the people, as they do in America.

Mr. Dunn. Do you believe that the United States Government has any designs on any other territory?

Mr. Ashford. Any designs?

Mr. Dunn. Yes.

Mr. Ashford. Well, of course. What do you mean?

Mr. Dunn. When you speak of our Army, or of our men being trained for imperialistic purposes, I judge by your statement that they are being trained for the purpose of going out and declaring war on some other nation, and probably confiscating from a weaker nation what that weaker nation possesses. Is that what you mean?

Mr. Ashford. That is right.

Mr. Dunn. Tell me, what nation do you think we want to go after, just now, to confiscate what they have?

Mr. Ashford. Well, I can state a number. At the present time, we know that between America and Japan there is a big conflict brewing. This is for spheres of influence in the East, in China, and so forth.

Well, even in South America, between Paraguay and what is the other place?

Mr. Dunn. Uruguay and Paraguay?

Mr. Ashford. Yes. There is war going on at the present time, between American imperialism, between the Standard Oil Co., as you know, the big concerns in America, and the British oil concerns. These are wars that are financed and backed more or less by American imperialism, and at the present time, in China, American imperialism is backing Chiang Kai-shek, against the Chinese masses that are fighting for liberation in China, and in many other places, the American imperialists would like to stretch their hands out, in order to be able to get more profits for the Rockefellers, for the Morgans, and for the rulers.

Mr. LUNDEEN. What information have you along that line? What aid are they lending Chiang Kai-shek's armies there?

Mr. ASHFORD. What aid?

Mr. LUNDEEN. Yes.

Mr. ASHFORD. Well, if you will notice the recent columns of the Daily Worker, you can see a lot of these answers to these questions.

Mr. LUNDEEN. I did not ask for that. I asked for your information.

Mr. ASHFORD. What is your question?

Mr. LUNDEEN. What aid is the United States Government lending, or what aid are the United States imperialists lending, to the Chiang Kai-shek armies, led by the Fascist general, over there?

Mr. ASHFORD. Well, I gave my opinion on the whole question. I think you know it is a question concerning unemployed insurance, and it does not involve that.

Mr. LUNDEEN. You did not tell me that any battleships or any money went in there, did you?

Mr. ASHFORD. No; I did not tell you any money went there.

Mr. LUNDEEN. I am interested, because I opposed America's entry into the World War. I denounced it as a commercial war; and in that respect I would agree with you, that these wars are commercial wars. Even Wilson, at St. Louis, in a speech after the World War was over, termed that war a "commercial war." What we are trying to get from you is this information: You made a statement we were aiding in the war to crush the Chinese.

Mr. ASHFORD. No; you asked me a question. You asked me about the intentions of certain American imperialists. I gave you the facts in connection with what was going on in South America and in Japan.

Mr. LUNDEEN. Yes; but you said the imperialists were aiding the suppression of the Chinese masses. Now, what aid are they giving?

Mr. ASHFORD. Well, sending ammunition, selling ammunition to Japan, and so forth.

Mr. LUNDEEN. I believe that. I believe that absolutely.

Mr. ASHFORD. Well, that is an aid, is it not?

Mr. LUNDEEN. Well, I wanted you to name it. I do not want you to make a statement without supporting it.

Mr. ASHFORD. O. K. Then, I gave you the explanation.

Mr. DUNN. You said something about Japan. Now, I am not against any race of people, because of color.

Mr. ASHFORD. Neither am I.

Mr. DUNN. But when you make a statement about Japan and the United States, what do you believe Japan's purpose is in building up a big navy?

Mr. ASHFORD. The same purpose that the American imperialists have.

Mr. DUNN. Do you not think it is necessary for the United States, at the present time, to defend herself against what she feels is going to happen the near future; that Japan has designs on some of our possessions?

Mr. ASHFORD. Well, I told you before, there is no such thing, under imperialism, as " defensive " wars—there are only wars for profits, and so forth. As between Japan and the United States, also, it is a question of fighting for profit.

Mr. DUNN. The point I want to make: It is a known fact that the Japanese have made the statement they no longer want to be the slaves of the white race, that the time has come when they must rise, and their statesmen have gone into China, and are educating the Chinese that they are their brothers and that it is necessary for them to combine, and so forth, because the time is going to come, and it is not far distant, when there will be a war between the white man and the yellow man. I have had that statement read to me, and, judging from what has transpired recently, Japan is building up her navy and army and unquestionably expects to tie up with somebody. I know she is not going to declare war on the man in the moon, because the man in the moon is too far away, so, for that purpose, do you not think it is necessary for the United States to be prepared, not for aggression—I do not believe in it at all—but for defensive purposes?

Mr. ASHFORD. We do not support—at least, I would not, and my organization would not support a national war, in that sense, for profit, for domination, as to the question you are asking.

Mr. DUNN. I am against wars. I am for bills to abolish wars, to take the profits out of war; no indemnities or annexations. Russia has a wonderful army; not such a wonderful navy; but she has a wonderful air corps, and it is for defensive purposes.

Mr. ASHFORD. Yes, it is for defensive purposes.

Mr. LUNDEEN. In other words, Congressman Dunn, you would support a war to defend the soil of the United States?

Mr. DUNN. Yes, to repel an invader.

Mr. LUNDEEN. So would I.

Mr. ASHFORD. To defend the people of the United States—yes.

Mr. LUNDEEN. But I would not vote for an attack on Africa, or Asia, or Europe, or Timbuktu; and I would not spill one drop of red American blood to retain the Philippine Islands. I was in the Spanish-American War, and I would not want to spill one drop of an American soldier's blood to retain the Philippine Islands.

Mr. DUNN. And you know what you are talking about, because you are a Spanish-American War veteran.

One more question. How many young men and women belong to your communistic organization?

Mr. ASHFORD. About 8,000.

Mr. DUNN. Are they mostly in New York State?

Mr. ASHFORD. About 3,000 in New York.

Mr. DUNN. In New York City?

Mr. ASHFORD. Yes.

Mr. LUNDEEN. How old are you?

Mr. ASHFORD. Twenty-four.

Mr. LUNDEEN. What schooling have you had?

Mr. ASHFORD. College graduate; finished at Northwestern University.

Mr. LUNDEEN. I can tell you are well read, and well posted on international affairs. I am very much interested in your views.

Mr. DUNN. Yes, so am I. In other words, young man, you want to see that the young men and young women in this country are provided with adequate wages, and if the United States Government does not provide them, you feel they should give you adequate insurance; and you believe in adequate old-age pensions—in other words, that is what you want, is it not?

Mr. ASHFORD. That is correct.

Mr. DUNN. That is what your organization is fighting for?

Mr. ASHFORD. Yes, sir.

Mr. DUNN. And therefore you believe the Lundeen bill is the best bill for that purpose?

Mr. ASHFORD. Yes, sir.

Mr. DUNN. Thank you for appearing before the committee.

Mr. DUNN. The next witness is Mr. Roy Mizara.

STATEMENT OF ROY MIZARA, REPRESENTING THE ASSOCIATION OF LITHUANIAN WORKERS, INC., NEW YORK CITY

Mr. MIZARA. Mr. Chairman and gentlemen: My name is Roy Mizara. I represent the Association of Lithunian Workers with a membership of over 6,000 and about 170 branches spread throughout the country, a fraternal body, incorporated in the State of New York. This organization endorsed the Workers Unemployment, Old Age, and Social Insurance Act, H. R. 2827, and is pledged to do everything to have this bill adopted by the United States Congress.

Besides, over 50 Lithuanian delegates to the National Workers' Congress, which took place in Washington, January 5–7, 1935, representing between 35 to 40 thousand organized Lithuanians, unanimously endorsed this workers bill as the only genuine means for the establishment of unemployment and social insurance in the United States.

A great majority of the Lithunanian workers in the United States are in the basic industries—steel, coal mining, automobile, textile—therefore, the present depression affected them in an appalling manner. Thousands of them have been thrown out of their jobs and find themselves with their families today in poverty and semi-starvation situation.

We feel and maintain that this mass starvation and suffering of men, women, and children is unnecessary. Our country, with its wonderful technical equipment and practically inexhaustible natural resources is able to provide all its people with a decent living. The responsibility for this plight of the great masses must be placed upon the shoulders of the Government and the employers.

Secondly, as a representative of a fraternal organization, I wish to point out that thousands of Lithuanian workers have been members of all sorts of sick- and death-benefit societies or lodges. Today, as a result of the depression, these people are compelled to leave these organizations.

Lithuanian fraternal organizations are losing their members by thousands and many local sick and death benefit societies have been liquidated or are near liquidation because of the inability of their members to pay their dues. The meager relief that is now being paid to the unemployed and the future plans of the Government do not take into consideration the problem that these workers have carried death and disability insurance for years, skimped to pay their premiums and now, because of unemployment, have to give up this insurance, lose all money paid into these organizations and companies, as well as their meager security against sickness and other misfortunes of our industrial life.

We believe that H. R. 2827, if adopted by the United States Congress, would bring about a necessary relief for the masses of the unemployed workers, as well as those who are unable to work on account of old age.

The H. R. 2827 provides a substantial unemployment insurance to all unemployed workers, immediately after its enactment. It provides for caring of all unemployed at the expense of the rich.

Furthermore, and which is very important, this workers' bill provides that the administration of the funds of the insurance should be controlled by the workers themselves through their organizations.

In conclusion, Mr. Chairman, I want to express the emphatic opposition of my organization to the Wagner-Lewis bill, H. R. 4120. We believe that this bill, sponsored by the Roosevelt administration, is meant to prevent the establishment of a real unemployment and social insurance in the United States.

Mr. DUNN. Thank you.

Congressman Lundeen, do you wish to interrogate him?

Mr. LUNDEEN. Referring to your last statement, is that because they fail to appreciate the crisis we are in?

Mr. MIZARA. I beg your pardon.

Mr. LUNDEEN. Your last sentence was, that the bill of the administration was designed, as I understand it, to stop real social insurance.

Mr. MIZARA. Real social insurance.

Mr. LUNDEEN. You do not believe they would have any such malicious purpose as that, do you? Or, is it because they fail to appreciate the crisis we are in?

Mr. MIZARA. It is unintentional, perhaps, but that is what we consider.

Mr. LUNDEEN. But that is what it amounts to?

Mr. MIZARA. That is it.

Mr. LUNDEEN. That is all.

Mr. DUNN. I just want to ask one question: Supposing, now, that this bill comes out on the floor of the Congress within a week or so. I presume it will.

Mr. MIZARA. This bill? Our bill?

Mr. DUNN. The Wagner-Lewis bill. Now, there are many people throughout the country who want that supported, although they are in favor of the Lundeen measure, but they maintain that it is a foundation. Now, do you think it would be right for the Congressmen, although they favor this bill, to vote for the Wagner-Lewis bill?

Mr. MIZARA. I think it would not be right.

Mr. DUNN. Supposing demands are made by people from your district, stating, " We cannot get the Lundeen bill, but we can get this, and it means something to us; it is a foundation." They are making those demands.

Mr. MIZARA. That is true, but that will prevent the movement from growing, for H. R. 2827.

Mr. DUNN. You think it would prevent that movement?

Mr. MIZARA. That would prevent it, to an extent.

Mr. DUNN. In what respect would it prevent it?

Mr. MIZARA. Because some people would wait, perhaps, until the Wagner-Lewis bill comes into existence, and then they would say, "Why should they pass this one"?

Mr. DUNN. The people would not be satisfied, still, could they not insist on having it amended, to bring about what the people really need? For example, I have talked on this bill, and I am for it, 100 percent, and yet I have talked to many who have also read the bill, who are for the Lundeen bill. They are for it, 100 percent, like I am; nevertheless, they still maintain that if the bill comes up, it should be voted for, because it means a help to some people. It is not very much, but it is a little help; but you do not feel that way about it?

Mr. MIZARA. We feel that that would pacify those people that are very active now for this bill.

Mr. DUNN. I do not think it would, if you people just keep on persisting in the fight for a better pension bill. It is like the fight we had in the State of Pennsylvania. We fought hard to bring about an old-age pension bill, and the kind of a bill which was finally passed is not the kind of a bill in which I was interested; nevertheless, we have got the foundation laid, the bill has been passed; and now, the members of the Legislature of Pennsylvania are going to change that bill and make it a real old-age pension.

I also was instrumental in getting a bill creating a pension for the blind, through the State of Pennsylvania Legislature. We wanted at least $50 a month, and we had no " whereases " to the effect that if you have a grandfather or a grandmother living in some country town you could not get the pension, but it was a straight pension for the blind. Of course, the welfare agencies worked and reduced it, putting it down to $30, and including the word " maximum ", which means that they can give you $2 a month; but the foundation is laid. We are making an effort to change it. We feel that, when the foundation is laid, you can come to Congress and amend it, whereas if you do not put through some kind of a bill it would be harder in the future to lay this foundation on which you can build and get an adequate pension.

Mr. MIZARA. We think that if H. R. 2827, the Lundeen bill, is not enacted, the mass pressure will compel many Congressmen to vote for it at the next session of the Congress.

Mr. DUNN. Then you think it would be more of a detriment, even to enact the Wagner-Lewis bill, than a benefit to the people?

Mr. MIZARA. I do.

Mr. DUNN. In fact, some of the poor old men and women today think the bill is already enacted into law, and they are coming to me for their pensions. In other words, the impression I want to give is that the $30 which would be given, although it is insufficient, nevertheless it is $30 which they would be getting, if the bill were enacted into law, that they are not getting now. That is a point I want to make, just as it was in the State of Pennsylvania, as I said before; we did not get the kind of a bill we wanted, but we put the bill through, and there are many hundreds now that are getting the $30 a month pension in the State of Pennsylvania; and they are pleased that they got it.

Mr. MIZARA. I do not know about Pennsylvania.

Mr. LUNDEEN. Mr. Chairman, if I may supplement your questions, there—are you familiar with the bonus situation in Congress? I want to illustrate what we mean there, and what Congressman Dunn has spoken of.

Mr. MIZARA. Well, not very extensively.

Mr. LUNDEEN. We have a Patman bonus bill, which provides that the soldiers shall be paid $2,000,000,000 in currency. A majority of the Congress today believe in that, and passed the bill by a vote of 295, in the Seventy-third Congress. I might say that 308 votes were cast in favor of placing it before the Congress. On the Lundeen motion in writing Congressman Dunn here was one of the very first to sign the petition and bring it before the House. However, here comes the Legion now with the Vinson bill, wanting to pay the soldiers that $2,000,000,000 in bonds, with interest on the bonds. Congressman Dunn and myself will have to face the guns on that, and are we going home and tell the soldiers we voted against the bonus because there were bonds in there, when we actually tried to get currency in the Patman measure? Suppose we defeated the Patman measure, then could we not vote for the Vinson bill?

Here, the problem we will have to meet is, we will try to get H. R. 2827 through, and if we are defeated on it, what are we going to do then? Will you give us some thought on that, if you have it prepared, or will you send it in? That is the problem, is it not, Congressman Dunn?

Mr. DUNN. Absolutely. You see, that is what we have to face, today. Those of us who are progressive want to get the best kind of legislation we can get, but nevertheless, if our opponents, who are after us, could get the newspapers against us, saying we voted against an old-age-pension bill, they would not explain in their talks or in the papers why we did it.

Mr. MIZARA. Yes; I understand.

Mr. LUNDEEN. And our friends might turn in and help destroy our ability to aid you, whatever aid we have been able to give you here. We have tried to do the best we could, but our own friends might be misled by statements that we voted against these bills.

Mr. MIZARA. But, Mr. Chairman, if you will fight for the enactment of this bill, you will get still wider support from the working people.

Mr. DUNN. We are glad that you came to give us your views.

STATEMENT OF CHARLES C. MAYER, REPRESENTING THE EPIC SOCIETY, "END POVERTY IN CIVILIZATION", WASHINGTON, D. C.

Mr. DUNN. You were not on the schedule but you may speak.

Mr. MAYER. Thank you.

Mr. DUNN. We close here at 5 o'clock. It is 5 minutes of 5.

Mr. MAYER. Do I have the privilege of extending my remarks?

Mr. DUNN. Yes.

Mr. MAYER. I can supply you with all the ammunition that you want.

Mr. DUNN. I will tell you, my friend, as far as being supplied with ammunition, the transcript of these hearings, when it is published in book form, will furnish more ammunition than all the countries in the world could muster together. You have heard this afternoon what is going on here, and the same thing happened last week. I do not want to be misunderstood. I doubt whether you can add one iota to what has already been said, and to that which has already gone into this record, from representatives all over the United States. We have had representatives from the Interprofessional Association, and also from the rank-and-file workers. I am willing to give you an opportunity.

Mr. MAYER. I will undertake to dispel your doubts, by supplying you with economic information that nobody has supplied you, covering a long period of years.

Mr. DUNN. For your information, my friend, we have had economists, statisticians that have gone back 10 and 15 years, and that information has already been placed in the record. We have had witnesses here from Johns Hopkins University and from universities in New York City. If you can furnish this committee with any information that we have not already had, we would like to hear it.

Mr. MAYER. I will do it.

I represent the Epic Society, "End Poverty in Civilization", with headquarters in Washington. I have been a publisher and newspaperman, in all the departments.

Mr. DUNN. When you speak about "End Poverty in Civilization", you are not ahead of me. I introduced a bill here, going even beyond the radicals, asking for $100,000,0000,000 to end it in the United States.

Mr. MAYER. We have $250,000,000,000 of debt, so your $100,000,-000,000 would be only two-fifths of the total debt.

Mr. DUNN. But I am not going to put that into operation right away. When you say $250,000,000,000, you are wrong. That is the estimate that is supposed to have been given, but when it comes down to the real value of our property, it is at least $300,000,000,000; and no man ever had enough intelligence to be able to estimate the value of the natural resources. They are not worth billions, but trillions of dollars.

Mr. MAYER. But I mean the debt.

Mr. DUNN. Yes.

Mr. MAYER. The interest-bearing debt.

Mr. DUNN. Now, are you in support of the unemployment measure?

Mr. MAYER. Yes, sir.

Mr. DUNN. All right. Proceed, Mr. Mayer.

Mr. MAYER. Mr. Chairman, slavery in these United States is more wide-spread, virulent, destructive, dangerous, and deadly than ever chattel human slavery was.

Mr. LUNDEEN. How much do you wish to place in the record?

Mr. MAYER. Whatever you consider pertinent to the subject. I will give you some economics that deal with finances, from the Civil War period, when the Government paid in bonds, $2 for $1 of bankers' money, and then gave the bankers the privilege of issuing 100 cents on the dollar for their Government-bought paper, and put the Government " in hock " to them; and that has been increasing ever since to an unbearable amount, from which we can hardly get free today.

Mr. LUNDEEN. Are you with the Epic group of California?

Mr. MAYER. Yes, sir.

Mr. LUNDEEN. That is the Sinclair group, there?

Mr. MAYER. He started it; yes.

Mr. LUNDEEN. And you wish to present the ideas of that group?

Mr. MAYER. And the general economic necessity of 125,000,000 people, as we see them.

Mr. LUNDEEN. But that, in general, is the program of Sinclair?

Mr. MAYER. Primarily, a program of unemployment and employment—profitable employment, putting everybody to work.

Mr. LUNDEEN. But I mean, the people in general would say it is the program of Sinclair?

Mr. MAYER. On the contrary, if they will read my argument, they will see that we propose only an expansion of what President Roosevelt has already started.

Mr. LUNDEEN. Yes; but if you are here for the Epic Society, naturally you present their views and ideas, do you not?

Mr. MAYER. Which coincide with and dovetail into the Lundeen bill 100 percent.

Mr. LUNDEEN. I do not dispute that.

Mr. MAYER. We present their views.

Mr. LUNDEEN. But those are the issues, are they not, of the campaign which was recently conducted in California?

Mr. MAYER. Yes, sir; amplified to fit this proposal, now.

Mr. LUNDEEN. And they are well known in the literature of California politics of last fall?

Mr. MAYER. Yes, sir.

Mr. LUNDEEN. That is probably one reason why the statement could be fairly well condensed, could it not, because it is known now?

Mr. MAYER. No; not if we are going to undertake to employ 10,000,000 or 11,000,000 idle workers on a money basis. The Epic Society of California, perhaps, should take the first step that it can possibly take to put people on a self-sustaining basis, the same as you would turn horses loose from a stable, where you had quartered them, to eat their heads off; you had no more grain or forage, and you permitted them to shift for themselves.

Mr. LUNDEEN. Your contention is, then, that your group favor H. R. 2827?

Mr. MAYER. Yes, sir.

Mr. LUNDEEN. For enactment, now?

Mr. MAYER. Yes, sir.

Mr. LUNDEEN. And your argument is in behalf of the bill?

Mr. MAYER. Yes, sir.

Mr. LUNDEEN. That is all, Mr. Chairman.

Mr. DUNN. Before you conclude, I do not know how much material the gentleman has. As far as I am concerned, I would like to see everything go into the record that every witness presents. We will continue these meetings until and including next Friday, and all that was said last week and this week, and all that has been presented to the reporter, go into book form, and there might be some objection.

Mr. MAYER. Is this all on the record, that we have been discussing?

Mr. DUNN. Yes. Everything you say, the reporter takes down, unless you say it is " off the record."

Mr. MAYER. That might save an excessively large volume, to discuss the preliminaries " off the record."

Mr. LUNDEEN. I presume we were a little alarmed by the large mass of papers you have.

Mr. MAYER. Yes; a few words here, and a few words there.

Mr. LUNDEEN. I see. Perhaps our alarm was not justified.

Mr. MAYER. And then, in type, I would like to submit my extended remarks, for your approval.

Mr. LUNDEEN. All right. Go ahead.

Mr. DUNN. Proceed, now.

Mr. MAYER. Slavery in these United States today is more widespread, virulent, destructive, dangerous, and deadly than chattel human slavery ever was. This Lundeen bill contains measures to stop strangling, choking, subjugating, and enslaving humanity. No one would deliberately or carelessly choke you to death, Mr. Chairman, by taking advantage of your blindness. If anyone in Congress wants to enslave or choke to death millions of Americans, economically, then Congress must and will do its duty to put these millions of workers back to a profitable employment at a living wage.

Mr. DUNN. Pardon me for interrupting you. Now that there has gone into the record a statement about " choking the chairman because of his blindness ", let me make a statement, my friend. You do not know what they are liable to do to me, because of certain bills I have introduced into Congress, here. I have been told to " get out of the country ", so undoubtedly I would have somebody who would be willing to choke me for my views.

Mr. MAYER. We must all hang together.

Mr. DUNN. But I do not want to hang. Proceed.

Mr. MAYER. I would like to offer a plea for the unemployed, and I offer four lines, paraphrasing Flanders' Fields:

> We are ditched! Short days ago
> We lived, felt dawn, saw sunset glow,
> Loved and were loved; and now we lie
> In fallow fields, cast out to die.

I shall hand the reporter 12 lines, entitled, " Profits! Profits! Profits! " in the holy name of trade:

> Can you tell me, O you workers, why the money-demon gloats,
> Why the rulers never stop you when you tear each other's throats?
> Can you tell me, O you toilers, why the young are born to poverty,
> Why so many work ahungered when the land is filled with plenty?
> Yes! For profit, profit, profit, all these broken hearts are made—
> In the holy name of trade. In the holy name of trade!

Mr. Chairman, this bill deals with the fundamental rights of humanity, deals with fundamental, equal rights guaranteed by the Declaration of Independence, and the equal rights guaranteed by our Constitution. This bill aims to correct wrong policies, pursued more than a hundred years. According to President Roosevelt and

Secretary Wallace, the most vital constitutional powers, the money powers, in control of wildcat banking since our Constitution was originally adopted, have been used as if the Constitution were a mere scrap of paper. Control of the money power, of Congress, of the Army and Navy and Department of Justice, police power, control of the entire Government, has been in the hands of or under the domination of autocrats, who have progressively confiscated our national wealth throughout our constitutional history, since 1789.

Autocrats have dictated and ruled the power of the purse and of the sword in these United States almost continuously. Autocrats have built a solid stone wall to stop human progressive. They have taken their confiscated wealth and entrenched themselves in their strongholds of financial power, behind all the safeguards and protection that special laws, special rules, and special legislation can give them. A few of them have usurped financial and economic control over 126,000,000 people. They have seized the greatest and most vital power, granted exclusively to Congress by the Constitution, and they are now given every protection that can possibly be provided without Congress surrendering the actual legislative direction of Government to their exclusive management under their specially chosen dictators.

An editorial in the Hearst papers, entitled, "A National Disgrace", refers to article I, section 1, of the Constitution, which provides:

All legislative powers herein granted shall be vested in a Congress of the United States, which shall consist of a Senate and House of Representatives. These powers cannot be delegated to any other branch of the Government.

If the President does not agree with the majority of Congress, two-thirds can compel legislation. Congress is all paramount in legislative matters—

The men who fashioned the Constitution feared the usurpation of Executive authority.

Congress must be the guardian of our liberties—

Is our Constitution only a scrap of paper?

That is the end of the editorial.

I have made a little study of the President's economic security bill. Titles III and VI undertake to provide unemployment insurance. There is no comparison of the value of the proposals made by college professors, who are responsible for the economic security proposals in this bill, that compares in the least degree with the provisions of H. R. 2827.

Autocrats, in control of the wealth of the American people, compel Congress to adopt new legislation, such as is proposed in this bill. They have built barricades and barriers so strong and so high that there is no hope for humanity unless the Lundeen bill is adopted, or an improvement of the Lundeen bill.

President Roosevelt and Secretary Wallace proved these statements. They proved the necessity for this bill. The President has declared the United States was fast drifting into an oligarchy.

In Secretary Wallace's book, New Freedom, he declared private interests took over control of the Government at the beginning, and he says, "private control continued."

Private interests have always regulated Government revenues. Private interests have always regulated financial authority over the purse, over the power to issue money, to expand or inflate, and to deflate currency and money tokens, and over the tariff.

Through private control over money, a power which the Constitution says belongs only to Congress, a small class of men hold the power of life and death, economically, over all the people. Through this exclusive power, privately operated, a few men have pyramided scores and scores of unfathomable thousands of millions (billions) of dollars of back-breaking debt upon the people, to impoverish, "povertize", or pauperize most of them so completely that their only hope to avoid economic destruction or extinction depends upon the enactment of the Lundeen bill, or a better bill.

Mr. Chairman, my primary purpose now is to expose the reasons why we are hopelessly lost without a bill of this nature. I aim to point out the necessity for such a bill. The merits of the bill are amply understood. The benefits of the bill are most eloquently covered by many witnesses.

Because a few men are "gorged and glutted with riches", with their millions piled into the hundreds to make them masters of the revenues of empires, while tens of millions of their fellow men beg for bread, the legislation now proposed is unavoidable, if these United States are to continue as a democracy.

Some poorly informed people, and the few autocrats who now control the wealth and economic life of all our cities, make many wild claims about the dangers of socialism and communism.

The advocates of this bill want only their constitutional rights. They want only Americanism. They do not want fascism, nazism, or dishonest capitalism. They want real democracy. They want what the American people once enjoyed for only a few years in the 146 years of their history. They want the honest democracy that was established under Andrew Jackson, America's most courageous, greatest Democrat.

Mr. LUNDEEN. He was a great man and a courageous man, a real genuine American.

Mr. MAYER. Unquestionably—the only man who had the nerve to suppress the money changers when the control of money by private banks was abolished. At that time nearly all dishonestly piled-up debts were wiped out, when President Jackson charged the dishonest "money changers" with being "vipers" and drove them from the temples of our civilization.

Mr. DUNN. When President Abraham Lincoln said this should be "a Government of the people, for the people, and by the people", do you not think he really meant that the people of our country should be provided with jobs and a living wage, and that we should take care of the old and the physically incapacitated?

Mr. MAYER. President Lincoln made several statements that glorified and exalted labor, crediting labor with producing the wealth, and spoke of the robbery of the man who earned his bread by the sweat of his brow, while the racketeers, profiteers, and extortioners of humanity ate the bread. I would like to quote Lincoln in several respects, briefly.

Mr. Dunn. Pardon me, my friend. How much more time would you like to have? It is almost half past 5, and I am beyond my time, now.

Mr. Mayer. I will leave these quotations. I will leave these three quotations from Mr. Lincoln.

Mr. Dunn. Put them in the record. You can have a few more minutes.

Mr. Mayer. I would like to insert here some remarks regarding the number of people on or below the subsistence level, on the border line of poverty. Senator Borah says there are 80 percent on the border line of poverty. Brookings Institute gives a total of 50,-000,000 people now having a "subsistence or poverty" standard of living. These are the people with less than $1,500 for a family, or $750 annual income for an individual. The well-to-do make up less than 2 percent of the population, according to Brookings Institute. Those in moderate circumstances make up 13.7 percent of the people.

Mr. Lewis Corey, in his latest book, Decline of American Capitalism, recites: "Standards of living among wage workers, clerical employees, and farmers, roughly, below subsistence levels, 10,000,000; subsistence levels, 20,000,000; comfort levels, 6,500,000", in the golden age of American capitalism, the period that crashed in 1929.

Robert R. Doane, in his book entitled "The Measurement of American Wealth", estimates that in 1929 the workers' share—farmers, clerical employees, and wage workers—in all expenditures, including services and finances, was 31 percent; the agricultural share, 10 percent.

Now I thank you for your attention.

Mr. Dunn. That is all right. We appreciate the information you have given us, and I would not mind staying longer, but as I said, we usually adjourn at 5 o'clock.

Mr. Lundeen, do you wish to interrogate the witness upon anything?

Mr. Lundeen. Is the witness through?

Mr. Dunn. Yes.

Mr. Mayer. I wanted the privilege of extending my remarks, so as to give you a brief survey of the depth of degradation, financially, into which the country has been driven.

Mr. Lundeen. The question was whether we should permit that.

Mr. Dunn. We would have to see what the other members of the committee say about it, if it is a long statement, because we have had certain statistics before.

Mr. Lundeen. I would be in favor of that, provided we have the opportunity of looking it over and revising it with you.

Mr. Mayer. Yes, sir.

Mr. Lundeen. Because, if it were too long, we would want to condense it, you know.

Mr. Mayer. I want to give you a financial sketch of our history that you will find nowhere else.

Mr. Lundeen. How many pages do you have? How many pages do you think that would take of an ordinary book?

Mr. Mayer. Of the printed record?

Mr. Lundeen. A book such as this. How many pages of a book like this would that take?

Mr. Mayer. A dozen.

Mr. LUNDEEN. Oh, I do not see any objection to that, Mr. Chairman—a dozen pages.

Mr. DUNN. All right, about a dozen pages. Then you will submit that, will you?

Mr. MAYER. Thank you, sir.

Mr. DUNN. Do you want to ask any more questions, Congressman Lundeen?

Mr. LUNDEEN. That will include the balance of your statement?

Mr. MAYER. Yes, sir.

Mr. LUNDEEN. I am very much interested in what you are saying, and I know that there have been some wonderful people out there in California. Are you a Californian?

Mr. MAYER. No, sir.

Mr. LUNDEEN. And there have been some very able people working along these lines, who have made some very fine speeches and written articles along these lines, and I think this is a proper committee before whom to appear and give expression to your views.

Mr. MAYER. This is a book by former Senator Henry C. Hansbrough. You know him?

Mr. LUNDEEN. I knew him.

Mr. MAYER. No one undertakes to give the information that he even dares to supply in that little volume.

Mr. LUNDEEN. Did you give us your address, where you can be reached?

Mr. MAYER. 2015 Taylor Street NE., Washington.

Mr. DUNN. Is there an organization in Washington called the "Epic Society"?

Mr. MAYER. I represent it here in Washington.

Mr. LUNDEEN. Is that in the telephone book, under your name?

Mr. MAYER. No.

Mr. LUNDEEN. What number is it under?

Mr. MAYER. It has no telephone number.

Mr. DUNN. Too poor to have one?

Mr. MAYER. Too poor; yes, sir. We are devoting our efforts without pay, almost without invitation. The only way we are going to get any liberty is to fight for it, or else be ground to dust under the heel of tyranny.

Mr. LUNDEEN. Well, the soldiers at Valley Forge left their bloody footprints in the snow.

Mr. MAYER. I would like to read you what the soldiers at Valley Forge had to say. I can give you in a few words the reaction of the soldiers at Valley Forge.

Mr. LUNDEEN. Possibly you could include that in the statement.

Mr. MAYER. All right, sir.

Mr. LUNDEEN. You may include certain quotations in there, if they are not too long.

Mr. MAYER. The Saturday Evening Post gave a diary of C. W. Barron, Wall Street publisher.

Mr. LUNDEEN. Colliers?

Mr. MAYER. No, sir; Boston News Bureau, and another Wall Street publication, published in New York City. The Post quotes Barron, July 25, 1931:

Morgan did not put up any money—

To float $1,400,000,000 of steel paper, with which to steal money from the public, floating it in the stock market at over $5, up to 260 in 1929. Intrinsically, it is not worth its present price, some $30.

Mr. LUNDEEN. What do you think of Morgan's disposition of billions of dollars of foreign bonds, which they immediately proceeded to repudiate, to our cost and grief, over here?

Mr. MAYER. Senator Fletcher's Senate committee on Wall Street practices and Wall Street frauds has proven conclusively that Morgan is as big a thief as there is in the country.

Mr. LUNDEEN. I would like to refer to my speech on April 6, 1917, when I referred to Mr. Morgan as one of the chief causes for our entry into the World War, and referred to the $400,000,000 which was owing to the Morgan firm by the British Government, and which they repudiated and stated they would not pay; and which $400,000,-000 burden, due to Morgan by the British Government, was transferred, made a public debt, and put on the backs of the American taxpayers—where it rests to this day—on the day we entered the war.

Mr. MAYER. We were driven into the war to save the British financial monarchy and the House of Morgan jointly.

Mr. LUNDEEN. You forgot to say, we went into the war " to save the world for democracy."

Mr. MAYER. Morgan did not put up any money. He simply made trust notes, and the banks and corporations did his bidding.

Quoting C. W. Barron:

Willie K. Vanderbilt gave him his box, and John D. Rockefeller sent him a big part of his securities. John D. Rockefeller is worth a billion. He can make his money by simply tipping out securities; then the market goes down, and he can take them back at his leisure. Of course, the market cannot stand the weight of his selling—

The Saturday Evening Post commented in its foreword:

February 13, 1935
The tone of business, as reflected in the conversations of C. W. Barron's visitors, is distinctly higher in the later years than in the earlier years. We find in the record of the post-war years no such bitter personal antagonisms, no such callous disregard of public interests or investors' rights, as appear in the revelations of the nineties. To the editors who have studied all the notes the evidence to this effect is unmistakably clear, and we think even the casual reader will be struck by this change for the better. American industry rose on the foundations laid in the nineties, but in its progress it has sloughed off many of the practices than in vogue, and gives unmistakable signs of having acquired a more ethical point of view.

To offset that statement, the record of Wall Street, in the post-war period, shows they have nearly subjugated all the American people. Senator Glass, in 1927, wrote an eulogistic book praising security credit inflations under his Federal Reserve System, a privately operated scheme of inflation and deflation, used fraudulently. In 1927 the president of the American Bankers Association chanted, " Panic times will never return ", as reported in the New York Herald Tribune, October 10, 1927.

Mr. LUNDEEN. May I ask if you are familiar with the financial philosophy of Charles A. Lindbergh, Sr.?

Mr. MAYER. Yes, sir; I am.

Mr. LUNDEEN. He was a Congressman here for 10 years, and the most distinguished Member of Congress, in House or Senate, ever sent here by the State of Minnesota.

Mr. MAYER. Yes, sir; and the ablest American on money matters that ever sat in Congress.

Mr. LUNDEEN. I thank you for that statement; and, by the way, founder of the Farmer-Labor Party.

Mr. MAYER. In my extended remarks I should like to have the rare privilege of paraphrasing the Declaration of Independence.

Mr. DUNN. Pardon my interruption. In other words, Congressman Lundeen, if we had more men like Congressman Lindbergh, undoubtedly we would get this bill of yours into operation in the very near future?

Mr. LUNDEEN. Oh, absolutely.

Mr. DUNN. He was a very progressive, humanitarian gentleman, was he not?

Mr. LUNDEEN. He was a battler for human rights; and whenever dollar rights or property rights conflicted with human rights, he was always the defender of human rights, and placed them in first position.

Mr. DUNN. That is the way it should be—above property rights— all the time. You could not have property rights if you did not have human rights.

Mr. LUNDEEN. We are ready to recess?

Mr. DUNN. We will recess until tomorrow at 10 o'clock.

Mr. LUNDEEN. With the statement to be prepared by the witness and submitted to the committee?

Mr. DUNN. Very well.

Mr. MAYER. Thank you, sir.

(The hour of half past five having arrived, the subcommittee, in pursuance of its previous order, took a recess until 10 o'clock tomorrow morning.)

(The extended remarks, submitted by the witness, Mayer, are as follows:)

The Soviet Government of Russia has not begun to prove itself a historical success or even a practical experiment as a dictatorship.

Our American democracy undoubtedly is the greatest form of government ever conceived. It should be allowed to function for all our citizens.

Operation of our democracy up to now has been a dismal failure for the majority. It has failed to provide equal economic rights leading to liberty and the pursuit of happiness for the masses of men. A true, honest democracy has been denied the overwhelming masses of our citizens.

The Lundeen bill's principles must be adopted if we are once again to live under a truly democratic government that approaches the truly democratic conditions established under Andrew Jackson. Our Government then got out of debt. It accumulated so much surplus cash that a distribution of many millions of dollars was made to a number of States.

President Roosevelt today cannot do what Andrew Jackson did without a Nation-wide unsettlement. He cannot count on the Seventy-fourth Congress immediately canceling the money-issuing privileges and prerogatives of national banks and Federal Reserve banks. But the President may do much by insisting upon the Lundeen bill's humanitarian provisions rather than the "brain trust's" provisions contained in H. R. 4120.

Mr. Chairman, most of our countrymen are in shackles and chains. Economically they are enslaved. Enslavement is eternally wrong and cannot last.

Chains and shackles that bind the limbs of productive labor—farmers, clerical workers, wage earners—must be broken.

Economic slaves must be freed.

Liberty dwells only where men are free. What crimes have been committed in the name of liberty!

"The general welfare, inalienable (equal) rights, justice, domestic tranquillity, the pursuit of happiness," are all denied to the tens of millions of economically disfranchised, dispossessed, economic slaves throughout our 48 States today.

Idle men become economically disfranchised citizens and serfs. Boys without marbles lose their mutuality, their cooperating activities, and languish just as men without money income must also languish.

Congress must provide work. There is no equal alternative.

For 73 years Congress has allowed private brokers and bankers to control the circulation and issuance of money, an abrogated constitutional power.

For 73 years, since legal-tender dollars were demonetized and discontinued, Congress has allowed the British-Rothschild gold monopolists to gold-brick the American people in alliance with Wall Street's money masters and money conspiracies. They have gouged the Government with high interest charges for letting the Government use its own money. They have printed or ordered money printed by the Government's own printing presses. They have paid from 29 cents to 40 cents for each $1,000 of this printed money we now use as dollar bills for pocket use. They have had the exclusive right to deal in this money. They buy it cheap as the cost of paper, ink, and printing costs. They sell it dear (exchange it) for Government bonds, paying the bankers interest in the hundreds of millions of dollars annually.

For generations the Wall Street-British Rothschild allied gold monopoly bankers have collected billions of dollars tribute from all our citizens for the bankers' unconstitutional, exclusive power to issue or deal in money. They still continue to get all the Government printed money they want, printed at their direction, at cost of printing, for their exclusive use, for them to lend back to the Government or to hire out to the public and corporations at their price and profit.

For the past 73 years all money deals and all debts have been based on a minimum supply of monopoly-controlled gold and a multiplying supply of debts. Due to the control of gold by a few money jugglers the American people have been put through the wringer and drained of their wealth periodically in nearly a dozen deliberately-managed panics, depressions, and Wall Street stock market squeezes, gold corners, etc.

" Gold ", said the famous Senator John J. Ingalls, " is the money of monarchs, and was in open alliance with our enemies in the Civil War."

Congress is now obligated to adopt an honest money system by beginning to assume its sacred constitutional power " to coin money, regulate the value thereof ", so as to put everybody on a work basis or a security basis under the Lundeen bill (H. R. 2827).

A few billion dollars of actual gold or other cash cannot by any possibility be stretched to pay 250 bililons of existing debts. Must 50 millions of citizens driven to poverty be sacrificed or driver to death to suffer or pay this impossible debt? In his inaugural address President Roosevelt promised to drive from the temples the "money changers" who have piled up our enormous, unbearable debts through their private control of money-issuing privileges.

Railroads, cities, corporations, and farmers have been favored with legislation by Congress to repudiate impossible-to-pay debts. Hundreds of thousands of farm and home owners have lost their homes through foreclosure of imposible-to-pay debts. Nearly a million other home owners have been saved from foreclosures by recent legislation. Fifty million povertized citizens must have the help and humanity offered by the Lundeen bill.

Many millions of families, workers, and producers of wealth have been impoverished through no fault of their own.

The same thing that happened to destroy Rome is now happening here to disrupt the United States. Wealth was absorbed and seized by autocrats and "money changers."

The poor were dispossessed and pauperized.

Fifteen years ago in an early Outline of History, H. G. Wells wrote regarding Rome, "money was young in human experience. It was now abundant and now scarce. Men made sly and crude schemes to corner it, to hoard it, to send up prices by releasing hoarded metals. A small body of very shrewd men was growing immensely rich. Many patricians (people of the better classes) were growing poor, unscrupulous. The growing mass of the expropriated (the masses of humanity) was permeated by that vague, baffled, and hopeless sense of being bested, which is the preparatory condition for all great revolutionary movements."

Since Wells wrote that the American people have been going through the same experience 1,500 years after Rome's civilization vanished. Then followed the Dark and Middle Ages of stagnation and human suffering.

"For a thousand years the policy of European States was vitiated by the crudest and silliest fallacies concerning the nature of money. * * * Money, like dynamite and other tools used by men, can very greatly damage, as well as very greatly serve his society."

"The failure of the Romans to manage the money mechanism * * * was due, in part, to the absence of paper, printing, and a convenient numerical system." Two quotations from Norman Angell's book on Money, pages 107, 151.

"Accumulated wealth was hoarded; general decay ensued," says Prof. W. Cunningham.

"Cato Major took pains to point out that the usurer ("money changers" interest-exacting tribute was branded by the Roman law as a greater evil than the common thief. Indeed, Cicero makes him avow that 'usury is a form of homicide'." Quoted from N. Angell, who further says, "some profound students are convinced some ancient peoples decided the value of money should be controlled in quantity, a means of social bookkeeping, a piece of money being evidence that its holder is entitled to a certain amount of goods."

A. Del Mar, a British authority, in 1886 wrote: "Metalic money seems like one of the machines designed by illiterate mechanics for perpetual motion; it carries with it its own negation * * * it has begun to fail from the very instant when it was first set in motion * * *. The civilizations of India, of Egypt, of Greece, and of Rome have all moved toward a vanishing point, and that is where gold and silver mining ceased to be sufficiently productive; and unless proper measures to avert it are adopted in time, it would seem that that of the modern world must move in the same direction."

Del Mar points out the great variance in people's conception of money. Rome fell under the hypnotism of gold, the lure of spoil. A system and law of numerical, quantitative money used as symbols and tokens (numerata) it became a thing, gold and for a while silver, radiant and glistening (moneta). Then it took another step toward materialism according to weight (fonderata). When "the weights were degraded—the thing fell to barter", says Del Mar. He says the renaissance reestablished weights first and then "pounds, shillings, and pennies, dennies, or denarii, which passed by tale."

Regarding Rome's money troubles, "money got out of hand", says H. G. Wells.

"The fall of the Roman Empire was in reality brought about by a decline in the silver and gold mines of Spain and Greece", says the English historian, Sir Archibald Alison.

The feudal conception of money was something to be privately controlled, an actual thing (a coin or coins) apart from any social convention or contract (the Rothschild theory of control through gold deposited with goldsmiths who issued their credit notes or bills of exchange repeatedly against one identical supply of metal, gold).

History is strewn with the wrecks of governments and civilizations. The greed of "money changers" has ruined many.

All Europe has been shaken by money disturbances. Austria was completely despoiled.

Canada's Minister of Trade and Commerce, Harry Stevens, says "big business", made up of "unscrupulous financiers and business men", exploited Canada's consuming public, starved her producers, sweated her workmen, gouged her industries, and left her a choice of reform, dictatorship or revolution.

Harper's Magazine of February 1929, recites " Rome's rampant materialism ", comparing it to our recent conditions.

The February Forum, 1935, recites that Tiberius, of the highest nobility of Rome, and his brother Gaius, pursued public-works policies and " production-for-use " policies.

" Because the ruling classes failed to continue to solve the problems of the poor, says the writer, J. Blake Lowe, " there came the epoch of the decline and fall of the Roman Empire."

Shall denials, depressions and destruction of our surpluses prevent a bountiful life and sink our civilization?

Assurance of guaranteed work at nominal pay must be provided henceforth if our Nation is to march forward in the scale of civilization to keep abreast or ahead of Japan and other nations.

Japan, Mr. Chairman, threatens our white and mixed-race civilization. Shall our white people survive? Shall we yield to Japanese just as the poorer civilization of Indians were unable to compete with the Nordic races that built these United States?

Is our American civilization worth saving, Mr. Chairman?

Are 50 to 100 million people, driven and being driven to poverty, worth rescuing—saving? Shall the 70 million people of Japan continue their march up and up in the economic scale while we go down and down?

Japan buys all surplus crops of food, cotton, and especially scrap iron. We junk or sell as junk, or burn and destroy the natural wealth that Japan buys. Japan's commerce grows all over the world. Ours decays.

The glory that once was the United States fades. Our people grow constantly poorer, subjugated by monopoly master kings of coin who control our wealth and our machinery, and who refuse to let 100 million people produce their necessities. Natural wealth is destroyed, not distributed. Prices are increased artificially. Scarcity is increased. Poverty is increased. This is the picture that America faces. With Japan the picture is entirely reversed. And Japan conquers the trade of the world while the " glorious " United States declines and fades away.

The Lundeen bill or a better bill must save America.

One dead Lindbergh baby, Mr. Chairman, seems more important than 50 million American citizens cast out to die, cast adrift to die economically.

Tens of thousands of words a day, day after day, week after week, for several months in all, have been printed by many metropolitan newspapers concerning one infantile dead life. Fifty million Americans, driven to poverty, to become paupers and to be blotted out of our civilization, are largely ignored. One dead baby is given more public consideration than 50,000,000 live Americans destined to die as paupers unless Congress passes the Lundeen bill or a better bill.

One baby, born while its mother was at work earning pennies for its clothes in a Michigan automobile shop, unable to give up her job a single day, as reported in these hearings, is of more value to the world than the dead Lindbergh baby. When 50,000,000 Americans are wiped out of consideration economically, one new baby born while its mother toiled in a shop, don't matter— except to its mother. Who else cares?

When one Austrian archduke was killed in 1914 all the autocrats of wealth and " kings of coin " in Europe and the United States got ready and made haste to slaughter millions of men, to maim, murder, to gas or to blind millions upon millions of men in a commercial war of greed and murder. Which of these three lives was most important—the Lindbergh baby, the automobile baby, or the Austrian archduke?

United States Senate records contain evidence that 38 newspapers accepted pay to support and print propaganda to drive America into the great war. Congressman Lundeen at that time told Congress the purpose of the war was to save J. P. Morgan's investments—to save Morgan from bankruptcy, and England.

Producing food and materials to kill men for profits, then, was more important than producing food and materials to save men from poverty and death today. Profiteers only count in a land of limitless wealth and boundless resources.

Congress must pass the Lundeen bill or a better bill to save the United States.

Mr. Chairman, the necessity for this bill cannot be denied. Contrast the conditions that exist today when there are 50 million poverty-stricken citizens in distress, with earlier disruptions in our history. Today's conditions are the worst we have ever had.

The King of England who tried to burden our early colonists with a few stamp taxes was rated as a bitter tyrant. Today we are far worse off. Then we had a virgin continent of unfathomable wealth to develop. Today we have a subjugated continent developed by the now enslaved masses of mankind—a continent confiscated and owned by the supreme kings of finance.

Instead of one British monarch trying to subjugate a few million frontiersmen, scattered peasants and farmers in a dozen loosely held colonies, today we are actually subjugated by dozens of financial money monarchies, corporation monopolies, and individual money kings, all closely knit together and allied with more than one European master gold-money combine. Collectively the Wall Street-British-Rothschild financial autocracy, built up on a gold-brick basis, tyrannously dominates and dictates the destiny and economic enslavement of 126,000,000 people.

Early Americans demanded and got equal rights.

Americans today, Mr. Chairman, demand equal rights in the bounties of nature and in the collective achievements of all their fellows who built our Republic since earliest colonial times. The independence principles then, of alert, illiterate free men without highways, railroads, a daily press, and radios, are the unyielding economic principles demanded today. Mankind will no longer be denied its free and equal economic rights to life, liberty, and happiness that belong to free men.

Tom Paine's " times that try men's souls " are here again.

Europe's thousands of millions payable-in-gold contracts, due all the American people for peace-time materials, goods, services, and cash, today are repudiated. Not so with our early American forefathers. They redeemed their " cross of gold ", though they had no gold mines. They became saddled with Europe's gold-brick standard of fraud money in the beginning. Because of this debt-burdening, civilization-wrecking, monopoly controlled system of cruel financial slavery, over 10,000,000 unemployed men in our Nation today are wearing " crowns of thorns " pressed down on the brows of economically disfranchised labor. These men have grown tired of raw deals from their industrial masters.

Economic slavery is as intolerable as political slavery and financial slavery, or chattel slavery.

Untold millions of men are held in debt slavery today. Many of them live in corporation owned houses and cannot hope to pay their back rents. They are held bound to their masters in bondage.

Living wages for all the unemployed to pay their way, or cancelation, or repudiation must be arranged. Men must have money to pay debts. Without work they are without money.

A " new deal " bill of rights is the Lundeen bill. This is a life and death necessity. The exploited masses of American workers demand its passage.

Exploitation of the many by the few has been the one fixed policy that has dominated the American people in all financial boom periods of their history.

Exploitation is more flagrant and violent today than ever before. It is intolerable.

Exploitation of labor and confiscation of the fruits, of the products, wealth and profits produced by labor, are not only unjust and dishonest. They are also tyrannous as well as intolerable.

Policies that delay and refuse justice are a complete negation and denial of justice, of equal and inalienable rights.

Wealth, fraudulent wealth always has violated the law at its will.

Courts, judges, and the law they interpret, are all the outgrowth of autocratic power built up, directed, and exercised by agents of wealth who have evolved our present financial dictatorship of property control, acquired through unconstitutional money-manipulating powers on a monopoly basis.

Railroad and other receivership rackets, upheld and directed by the courts, as disclosed by the Congress committee on receiverships under Congressman A. J. Sabath of Illinois, have swindled the thriftiest investors in America out of thousands of millions of dollars (billions). This is a conclusive evidence of the monumental miscarriage of justice.

Improved machinery and increased profits always sacrifice the earnings of the producers of wealth, the workers.

Poverty increases as profits increase.

The more profits, the more poverty. The poor increase in numbers as wealth becomes more concentrated. Profits always monopolize the robbers' share. New interest-bearing debts constantly are created to exact new tolls and taxes and tribute from workers and consumers both. More profits bring increased debts, less consumption, and more poverty.

Democracy has grown too indifferent, if not misguided and misdirected.

If Congress produces no substantial remedies humanity will find other means. The Declaration of Independence provides and urges revolutionary methods to get results, if necessary.

Despotism sometimes rules under democratic institutions, as it did in Rome, where for centuries the absolute master of the Roman world pretended to rule only under the decrees of a senate which dared not disobey his desires.

Congress is on trial in the pending unemployment legislation.

Congress must justify its right to act as agents of the people and agents of the Constitution.

Congress must choose on the one hand either to recognize or ignore the fundamental rights of mankind through fundamental legislation. These rights are based on the primary independence and constitutional rights of all citizens; based on citizens' rights to justice, to tranquillity; their general welfare, and their inalienable heritage to the peaceful pursuit of life, liberty, and the pursuit of happiness, as proposed to a limited extent by H. R. 2827. Otherwise Congress will obey the masters of unconstitutionally pyramided wealth.

The greatest danger lies in ignoring demands of the masses of men who actually produce our life-sustaining economic wealth. These men now know who get the doles in unlimited supplies. They know from Government records that thousands of millions of dollars of specially printed money have been poured into railroads, insurance companies, banks, and other institutions to prevent their decay and the wiping out of billions upon billions of dollars of piled up debt represented by bonds, stocks, receivership certificates, and " cats-and-dogs " securities. These billions have been poured in at the top to nourish economic effervescences piled sky high upon the solid wealth produced by over 90 percent of humanity that struggles, sweats, and actually labors for a living. Very little of all these billions have trickled down to save from decay the solid masses of human life whose backs and vitality grow weaker and weaker, steadily, under compulsion to carry the gargantuan towers and superstructures of superwealth as represented by tribute-exacting, financial holding companies and other excrescences. Congress must not listen too attentively to hot-house theorists and high-brow professors schooled in the exotic and rarified atmosphere of cloistered halls, built and endowed by questionable wealth, nearly all of whom bow down and worship at the altar of the great god of greed.

H. R. 2827 or a better bill must be enacted. A bureaucratic nightmare of unemployment inconsistencies cannot be tolerated. Nothing can be tolerated that is designed to still further restrict and hobble humanity by letting " the 80 percent on the border line of poverty ", quoting Senator Borah, continue in a hopeless devil's brew of economic futility and slavery. No deadly broth of unemployment debt-shackling proposals, no narcotic broth brewed from witches' dreams, lacking all-essential, remedial elements of recovery nourishment, can possibly be of any value to 50 million people at present steeped in poverty.

Until the pits of distress and despair into which tens of millions of our citizens have been sunk, are made to give up their trapped victims for rehabilitation under enlightened economic policies, under policies far removed from the feudalistic, financial, monarchical, and oligargical conceptions of robber-baron policies of the middle ages, there can be no real progress to justify the purposes of the founders of our great, misguidedly or wrongly developed democracy of these United States.

The principles of 1776 are as vibrant with life and as vital today as then. " In Congress, July 4, 1776, the unanimous declaration of the thirteen United States of America ", starting with the words, " when in the course of human events, it becomes necessary," was made to mean what it recited by the blood of many patriots. The principles that declaration espoused must once more be galvanized into life and vibrant action without delay to save our civilization.

We quote and paraphrase the immortal declaration, in part, below.

If men " are endowed by their Creator with certain [equal] unalienable Rights, that among these are life, liberty, and the pursuit of happiness: " if " to secure these rights, Governments are instituted among Men, deriving their just powers from the consent of the governed—That whenever any form of Government becomes destructive of these ends, it is the Right of the People to alter or to abolish it, and to institute new Government," then it is supremely advisable that this Seventy-fourth Congress take time to exhaustively consider the best possible unemployment legislation. The " general welfare " of 50 million povertyized citizens is of prime importance to halt the surging foment of revolt, of mounting, unrelieved discontent that, if inadequately treated, will sweep this present Seventy-fourth Congress into oblivion as surely and swiftly as the financial autocracy of Great Britain, its colonial governors, officers and guards were swept out of their then direct power over the American people.

" When a long train of abuses and usurpations evinces a design to reduce them [the people] under absolute despotism, [now existing economically] it is their right, it is their duty, to throw off such Government."

" The history of the " present dictators of the existing financial-economic control of the United States is " a history of repeated injuries and usurpations, all having in direct object the establishment of an absolute [financial] Tyranny over these States. To prove this, let Facts be submitted to a candid world."

For decades the masters of finance and their agents have refused " assent to laws, the most wholesome and necessary for the public good." They have objected to public works, " Laws for the accommodation of large districts of people." They have objected to and refused " to promote the general welfare " through legislation valiently fought for by our greatest patriots who have " opposed with manly firmness invasions on the rights of the people," invasions that have exposed our entire Nation to terrible distress and unwarranted convulsions. They have " obstructed the administration of justice, by refusing assent to laws for establishing " equal justice according to constitutional law. They have given judges injunction, veto, and receivership power over the rights of the multitude, over all valid principles of fairness and Equity. They have promoted the erection of swarms of swindling stock promoting corporations " to harass our people, and eat out their substance." They have " combined with others to subject us to a jurisdiction " of money controls " foreign to our Constitution and unacknowledged by our laws, giving assent to acts of " subversive legislation, " for cutting off our trade with all parts of the world " because the honorable masses of men abroad were tricked by the gold-fraud system of financial settlements whereby thousands of millions of foreign debts became repudiated when the fictitious supply of payable-in-gold money was found out to be an impossible swindling device of financial tyrants, " for imposing taxes on us without our consent " in the many hundreds of millions of dollars annually through holding company superstructures and other usury devices, " for taking away our constitutional charter rights 'to coin money, regulate the value thereof ' " an exclusive right granted only to Congress to protect the public with legal tender, honest money, abrogating our most valuable safeguards for protection of property and savings of all the people.

To justify and protect their subversive policies they have abdicated Government at times by declaring us out of their protection and waging war against us in foreclosing properties and confiscating the people's wealth. To meet their program they have plundered our lands, ravaged our homes, destroyed or plowed under our crops, destroyed our cattle and destroyed the welfare of millions of our people. They have excited domestic insurrection amongst us, and have endeavored to accentuate the ravages of poverty, the merciless annihilation of worry and want, whose known effects are " as undistinguished destruction of all ages, sexes, and conditions. In every stage of these oppressions we have petitioned for redress in the most humble terms. Our repeated petitions have been answered only by repeated injury." Financial masters " whose characters (are) thus marked by every act which may define tyrants, are unfit to be the rulers (masters) of a free people.

" We, therefore, the people of the United States of America, appealing to the Supreme Judge of the world for the rectitude of our intentions, do, in the Name, and by Authority of the good people of these United States, solemnly publish and declare. That these States are, and of right ought to be free and Independent from control of Financial Tyrants; that they are absolved from the rule of Financial Tyrants, that we have full power to establish Commerce without scuttling or plowing under our Merchant Marine, to Coin Money as provided in the Constitution, restore the wealth taken from Each and All of our Inhabitants, and to do all other Acts and Things which Independent States may of right do.—And for the support of this Declaration, with a firm reliance on the protection of divine Providence, we mutually pledge to each other our Lives, our Fortunes and our sacred Honor." Done at the instance of agents of the dispossessed and financially disfranchised, representing from 50 to 100 million of loyal citizens of these United States.

The Lundeen bill, Mr. Chairman, is merely an unavoidable, modern bill of rights. It is just as much a bill of rights as was the Magna Carta rights won by Nordic white races seven centuries ago.

H. R. 2827 is just as much a necessary bill of rights as the American colonists demanded and got from Britain's monarchs 160 years ago.

King George III was less ridiculous in regard to the American people than are the present economic rulers of the United States today.

George III prevented only a couple million colonies to from coining money and raising revenue for their needs, from promoting their own local commerce and trade. He denied their economic freedom. He denied their right to circulate their own sovereign, legal tender, self-taxing money mediums of exchange in 13 separate colonies. King George III demanded his own revenue-money policies.

The rulers of the United States today, the money-coinage rulers, demand abject surrender of their vassals represented by over 80 percent of all the people. The masses of men today are vassals and slaves of the masters of finance who monopolize and dictate the economic control of this Nation more completely than the governors of the Kings of England ever dominated any one of our original 13 Colonies.

Our financial and economic rulers today, through their tory agents who so completely intimidate all the people, do not intend to surrender their control of the public purse and money coinage privileges. They will not consent to the agents of citizens of all 48 States in Congress to collectively take over and exercise the sovereign right of all States "to coin money, regulate the value thereof," as provided and decreed in the Constitution.

Unless Congress recovers its constitutional right to tax and its right to "coin money" for all the people, there can be no social security for the 50 million citizens now economically disfranchised, unemployed without income and now living in poverty.

England's kings disregarded the Commons (the Congress of agents of the people) and listened to the nobles and lords, the heirs, and agents of the feudalistic aristocracy (represented today by our money master, monopoly aristocrats, and their tory allies or agents, college professors and brain trusters).

England's kings' council of nobles were called the "Council of Wise Men." The nobles and aristocrats of Rome destroyed Rome. The same class in the United States today destroy human values, natural wealth and human welfare. They operate to destroy wealth, create scarcity, increase prices, increase want, poverty, distress, bureaucracy. "Smart-aleck" stupidity arrogantly refuses necessary State relief to many States. Nor do they provide any adequate alternatives.

Unpopular measures, prepared by college professors and bureaucrats (the "wise men") are given to Congress as mandates. They are violent and arbitrary measures. They do not provide social security or adequate relief demanded by H. R. 2827 or H. R. 5228. The money nobles and "wise men" consider our honorable Congress as a body of political menials.

Rights and demands of the American people today are treated as the demands of the English people were treated in the Middle Ages.

The tactics of England's King John I are followed against Congress at the present time. This monarch 700 years ago, renounced the constitutional or Magna Carta rights of the people's agents (or Congress). He renounced their self-government tax rights.

King John failed even after getting Pope Innocent III to annul the Great Charter and excommunicate the Barons (Congress).

The American people are thrown back to Thirteenth Century rule when the childish King Henry III annuled all the charters forcibly renewed before his manhood. But civil war restored those charters. Then King Edward I ignored the people's rights and commanded control as Roosevelt now does, until his follies failed. And until he needed further guidance and support of the baronials and commons (Congress). Necessarily, King Edward convoked a parliament (Congress) in the year 1300 and restored the rights of the people's houses of representatives to coin money, to raise revenue, to promote commerce, economic freedom, etc.

The fatuous follies and ruinous policies of England's monarchs seven centuries ago, of Rome's aristocracy, and of the French nobility, cannot be tolerated as now duplicated in these United States. America's financial autocrats and aristocrats must admit failure. They must return to the people's Houses of Congress their long abrogated Constitutional power "to coin money, regulate the value thereof", very ably discussed by Senator Austin, pages 1326 and 7322 of the 1934 Congressional Record.

The "coin money" power is the all-important, vital, essential power that rules the lives of all the people. This power Congress must begin at once to use for all the people.

The private bosses of the money coinage power in England and France have invariably used it to enrich silk-stockinged parasites who have persistently denied economic equality or freedom to, and have impoverished the masses of humanity. This power and its dominating taxation policies became intolerable to the spirit of American Independence and provoked the Colonial Revolution just as it now provokes a nation-wide revolution.

The continued denial, even temporarily of the economic liberties and welfare of the people exceeds the wanton disruption of the slowly won rights of the Anglo-Saxon-Norman freemen under Henry VIII, 400 years ago.

Tyrants and their tyrannies still submerge mankind.

The subjugation of the Commons (Congress) and oppression under the Plantagenet Kings of England became prolonged under the Tudors with more absolute authority exercised by Henry VII and Henry VIII.

Six centuries ago, under Edward III, our existing Anglo-Saxon form of Government had restored vital, fundamental rights, today shamelessly flaunted and denied. Today's finance rulers of men and their lords, then "openly sworn to observe the laws of the land and Magna Carta", ignore and subjugate mankind.

Half a century after Edward III the levying of taxes (identical with the coining of money) was definitely lodged with the Commons (Congress). At the same time the King (President) was foresworn from meddling with legislative deliberations. Liberty of speech was granted.

Fundamental rights, established early in the Middle Ages, were usurped by some British Kings.

Above all other obligations Congress must resume its coin money taxation rights, surrendered continuously the past three-fourths of a century. And Congress oaths, "openly sworn to observe the laws of the land and Magna Carta" (Constitution), demanded and granted as essential among Anglo-Saxons the past 600 years, must be once more respected and rigidly adhered to.

Retrogression behind or beyond the dawn of the dark or Middle Ages is impossible for compliance with the demands of America's 1776 Revolution, and a modern 1935 American civilization's new revolution to at least establish the 1776 aims for liberty, equality, independence, economic freedom.

Ferment in Europe along the same lines grows.

Rights demanded by the subjugated citizens of France preceding their eighteenth century, revolution, are also revivified in the United States today.

When Hamilton's clique in emulation of British royalty, usurped the fruits of the American Colonists' Revolution and appropriated the most vital powers, the finance and taxation rights of our Constitution, newly instituted in 1789, in this identical year liberal leaders of the determined masses of France gathered in their National Assembly to halt the King's royal doctrine, "I am the State," and to promulgate the "Declaration of the Rights of Man," Tom Paine's litany and religion.

French revolutionists declared as had our Colonists, "sovereignty resides essentially in the Nation." Not in monarchs, usurpers, dictators.

Equal freedom, "the law should be the same for all", equal rights, and "the right to establish for themselves" equal coin-money-taxation privileges, were the basis of the French Revolution, as they had been of our revolution. And as written into the Constituition of the United States.

Betrayal for generations of the fundamental rights of all the American people must now necessarily and unavoidably be reversed. The same problems, especially gold-money control, agitate the aroused masses abroad.

Senate and House Members and committees have disclosed overwhelming evidence of the same shortcomings the French people warned against in 1789: "Ignorance, forgetfulness, and contempt of the rights of man are the sole causes of public misfortunes and of the corruption of governments."

Concurrent "preferred" cliques privately and collusively operated a robbery bank system, begun and intrenched first under the first Secretary of the United States Treasury, the half-British Alexander Hamilton. "Private control of government has continued since Hamilton," says Henry Wallace.

The American Colonists' War of Independence that won this country's wealth for all the people immediately became subjected public wealth for private privilege.

Control through private privilege has continued by private use of the public domain and resources under private control of Congress' sacred constitutional power "to coin money, regulate the value thereof."

The unearned increment inhering in the public domain and in the "sovereignty (which) resides essentially in the Nation," has been continuously usurped and distributed by private thieves in control of the Government and the Constitution's money functions. By private "coin money", usury-collecting, annihilating taxation gougers.

UNEMPLOYMENT, OLD AGE, AND SOCIAL INSURANCE

WEDNESDAY, FEBRUARY 13, 1935

House of Representatives,
Subcommittee of the Committee on Labor,
Washington, D. C.

The subcommittee met at 10 a. m., in the caucus room, House Office Building, Hon. Matthew A. Dunn (chairman) presiding.

(The subcommittee had under consideration H. R. 2827, H. R. 2859, H. R. 10, and H. R. 185.)

Mr. Dunn. The meeting will come to order.

STATEMENT OF JAMES HANNON, REPRESENTING UNEMPLOYED MINERS OF THE RANK AND FILE UNEMPLOYED LEAGUE AND UNEMPLOYED COUNCIL, WILKES-BARRE, PA.

Mr. Hannon. I represent 20,000 unemployed miners of the Rank and File Unemployed League and Unemployed Council. They have endorsed, and whole-heartedly support, the Lundeen bill, H. R. 2827. After a thorough investigation by the National Industrial Recovery Board, it has been agreed that 32,000 miners, in district no. 1 alone, including Luzerne and Lackawanna Counties, will never again be given jobs in the mines, not to mention the miners in districts 7 and 9. There are 14,000 miners in 7 and 9 working out of 48,000.

Conditions at the present time warrant our supporting social and unemployed insurance. We are living on relief, $4 for two adults and one child, which is a total of $1.30 a week for each. We are only fighting for a just cause—to uphold our just and right principles.

The United Mine Workers and the coal companies, assisted by the local and city police and the State constabulary, are determined to crush the people in those two counties. The contract with the United Mine Workers of America has been openly and flagrantly violated. I have a duebill here at the present time to show that on March 15, 1932, the contract with the United Mine Workers of America gave the miner for his work a consideration of $6.92. February 28, 1933, it had been cut down to $5.60, which is over $1.40 reduction.

Also, since the N. R. A. became effective, they have cut down the size of the envelope, or the size of the duebill. They have refused to put a name of it at the John Collin Coal Co. James A. Gorman, of the fact-finding commission, the investigating commission in the hard-coal region, admitted on the stand that it was a direct violation of the United Mine Workers' contract, but, up until today, nothing has been done.

We believe unemployment insurance must be passed to protect the rights of the individuals in Luzerne County and Lackawanna County.

Mr. DUNN. And in every other county in the Nation?

Mr. HANNON. And in every other county; yes. Hatred and bitterness are growing in the hearts of the people. It appears that they are forced into slavery at starvation wages in this Nation, in the midst of plenty. The mechanical system in the mines today has been sanctioned by the United Mine Workers thus depriving the men of an honest day's work.

Mr. DUNN. Who do you say are the ones who are against you, or who work with the coal operators? You say these union leaders work with the coal operators?

Mr. HANNON. Yes.

Mr. DUNN. In other words, they are against you, in your opinion?

Mr. HANNON. They are against the upholding of the contract. They have alined themselves with the coal operators and the city, local, and State constabulary. We are fighting the miners' battle.

Mr. DUNN. You mean these supposed union officials are doing that?

Mr. HANNON. Yes, sir. Here is their contract.

Mr. DUNN. Can you give us the proof of that statement?

Mr. HANNON. Back in there, there is a powerful organization, which is known as the "Anthracite Miners of Pennsylvania." They are organized to uphold the contract, and because they are fighting to uphold the contract the United Mine Workers, with the assistance of the coal operators and the State police, have created a situation of terror. There is terrorism. At the present time there is a strike.

Mr. DUNN. Another interruption: Are these union officials that you have named cooperating with the police to crush you fellows?

Mr. HANNON. Yes, sir.

Mr. DUNN. They are?

Mr. HANNON. Yes, sir.

Mr. DUNN. All right. Proceed. Thank you.

Mr. HANNON. We had a strike in November 1933. We received a telegram from Senator Wagner saying that there would be no discrimination and that no one would lose his job through affiliation with the new union. The telegram, in its effect, was not carried out. Men lost their jobs. Discrimination became rampant, and today there is terrorism, conflict, starvation, and no work; and the United Mine Workers are familiar with it all. They openly uphold the coal operators.

In Luzerne County it is claimed 25 percent of the children are undernourished and underclothed. The Government has a few projects there. There is one project that I work on. I received $47 a month for myself and two children, and that is only a typical case. There are other cases there, where the families, with from 5 to 12 children, receive wages in comparison, the highest being $21 a week for that large number of children. We cannot live on such relief. Over 3,000 homes have been confiscated, the mortgages foreclosed, and sold by the sheriff in Luzerne County.

Mr. DUNN. And within the last year or 2 years?

Mr. HANNON. The last 2 years.

Mr. DUNN. Thank you.

Mr. HANNON. And therefore we asked our Representatives in the United States Congress to give us unemployment insurance, which means at least $10 a week and $3 for each dependent, that we may not be reduced to servitude, destitution, and, finally, to destruction. The people of Luzerne and Lackawanna Counties are fair-minded citizens. They believe in upholding the principles and righteousness of the common citizens, and they do not want to be reduced any further into unbearable and deplorable conditions. Therefore, we want the Government to immediately pass this bill, H. R. 2827, that we may again live according to the American standard of decency and righteousness.

Mr. DUNN. What is the name of the organization you represent, Mr. Hannon?

Mr. HANNON The Unemployed Council, the Unemployed Insurance Council. I am the county chairman, you see, for the Unemployed Insurance Council in the County of Luzerne.

Mr. DUNN. For the County of Luzerne?

Mr. HANNON. Yes.

Mr. DUNN. You spoke of both counties. Are any of the members belonging to your organization in Lackawanna County?

Mr. HANNON. Yes.

Mr. DUNN. And Luzerne?

Mr. HANNON. Yes.

Mr. DUNN. Combined?

Mr. HANNON. Yes.

Mr. DUNN. And you are the chairman?

Mr. HANNON. Yes.

Mr. DUNN. Chairman in Luzerne County?

Mr. HANNON. Yes.

Mr. DUNN. In addition to that, I want to ask you another question: The members of your organization are not restricted by party, religion, color, or creed?

Mr. HANNON. Absolutely not.

Mr. DUNN. In your organization, that is supporting the Lundeen bill, H. R. 2827, you have men who are Protestants, Hebrews, Catholics, Polish, Slavish, and all nationalities?

Mr. HANNON. Yes, sir; and colored.

Mr. DUNN. Colored?

Mr. HANNON. Yes, sir.

Mr. DUNN. And all races and political parties?

Mr. HANNON. Yes, sir.

Mr. DUNN. And you say there are about 30,000 miners?

Mr. HANNON. There are 32,000 miners. The investigating committee of the National Industrial Recovery Board agreed that 32,000 miners, in district no. 1 alone, that will never again be returned to work.

Mr. DUNN. In what county?

Mr. HANNON. Luzerne and Lackawanna Counties.

Mr. DUNN. Thirty-two thousand?

Mr. HANNON. Thirty-two thousand.

Mr. DUNN. Then your organization, or the people you are representing here this morning, believe that the Lundeen bill will take care of those people?

Mr. HANNON. Yes, sir.

Mr. DUNN. Thank you.

Mr. DUNN. The next witness is Brown Squire.

STATEMENT OF BROWN SQUIRE, REPRESENTING POST NO. 197, AMERICAN LEAGUE OF EX-SERVICE MEN, CHICAGO, ILL.

Mr. DUNN. You are a World War veteran?

Mr. SQUIRE. Yes, sir.

Mr. DUNN. Were you across the water?

Mr. SQUIRE. No, sir.

Mr. DUNN. You were in the Army?

Mr. SQUIRE. In the Army; enlisted in 1917.

Mr. DUNN. How long were you in the Army?

Mr. SQUIRE. I was in the Army from August 17, 1917, up until 1918.

Mr. DUNN. How many members belong to the organization you are now representing?

Mr. SQUIRE. Five hundred, in the city central committee of Cook County.

Mr. DUNN. Cook County, Chicago?

Mr. SQUIRE. Yes, sir; Chicago, Ill. I will read now:

Brown Squire, member Post No. 197, American League of Ex-Service Men, Chicago, Ill.; member of the rank and file veterans' organization, representing the veterans, who have gone on record in this city at their national convention, for immediate payment of the soldiers' bonus, repeal of the economy act, and as a major point the support of the Lundeen bill, H. R. 2827.

I want to ask, as a matter of a little information, whether or not it was at that time H. R. 7598, and whether the number of the bill was changed?

Mr. DUNN. Yes; it is now H. R. 2827.

Mr. SQUIRE. Yes.

Mr. DUNN. That is what you are supporting?

Mr. SQUIRE. Yes; H. R. 2827. (Reading:)

At the Union Stockyards in the city of Chicago we veterans who would offer our discharge as reference, were vigorously turned aside with the words, "You veterans are not able to give us a good day's work, especially you oversea veterans. Because you're shell shocked, wounded, and half illiterate."

So we were not hired. Many of us have been discriminated against because we were veterans. The average veteran is older than 40 now and men over 40 are not hired at the Union Stockyards.

They are too old.

Mr. DUNN. Is there an age limit in that organization, the Union Stockyards?

Mr. SQUIRE. Yes.

Mr. DUNN. If you are over 40 probably you do not stand a chance of getting a job; is that it?

Mr. SQUIRE. Yes, sir.

Mr. DUNN. All right, proceed.

Mr. SQUIRE (reading):

We are the most exploited section of the working class. We are exploited as a worker and again as veterans. The bonus is our back wages. We paid for that out of our $30 wages as a soldier, $6.50 per month. Many of us took out Liberty bonds and war stamps. This means that we protected ourselves at our expense. The finance which was raised from our Liberty bonds and war stamps to help to pay for the war.

We were given many promises when we enlisted in the service that if the heroes of America would bring back the bacon, nothing would be too good for us. That meant, to make the world safe for democracy. We thought in terms to make the world safe for the people to have democracy and at least the American people. But we veterans and workers since the crisis came find that we are met with autocracy. What more could be autocracy than veterans sleeping in flop houses?

Mr. DUNN. I want to interrupt you to ask a question. When you speak of "flop houses" please describe what a "flop house" is, for the benefit of myself and others who probably would like to know something about them.

Mr. SQUIRE. In the "flop houses" in the city of Chicago, the veterans are sleeping in cots, and in these cots, which are not even 40 inches apart, as required by the board of health, they are sleeping, many of them, with their faces close together; I mean, breathing and contracting germs from each other; not head to foot, but many of them sleep head to head.

Mr. DUNN. You mean that the cots are about 40 inches apart?

Mr. SQUIRE. Not 40 inches, but closer than that.

Mr. DUNN. About how close would you say?

Mr. SQUIRE. I would say it is not over 30, if that.

Mr. DUNN. And what did you say is the board of health's ruling?

Mr. SQUIRE. The board of health's ruling is that in a shelter house of this sort, the cots should be not closer than 40 inches apart.

Mr. DUNN. That is their ruling?

Mr. SQUIRE. It is.

Mr. DUNN. And you say they are about half of that; is that it?

Mr. SQUIRE. It is about half of it.

Mr. DUNN. All right. Proceed.

Mr. SQUIRE. And then, many of those, particularly in these crowded shelter houses, had to be shoved close together, in order to make room. Through our investigation, we learned that many of them went into the shelter houses, and many of them are sleeping, sometimes, on the floors. We learned that through the veterans investigating committee.

Mr. DUNN. And may I also ask this question? Would you say that oftentimes there are too many in one room?

Mr. SQUIRE. Too many in one room.

Mr. DUNN. And the sanitary condition is what?

Mr. SQUIRE. There are at least over 500 veterans in the city of Chicago that are sleeping in these shelter houses.

Mr. DUNN. These veterans who are compelled to sleep in "flop houses", many of them have been in actual battle across the seas?

Mr. SQUIRE. Many of them have been overseas veterans.

Mr. DUNN. And would you say that many of them who are compelled to sleep in these "flop houses" are disabled men?

Mr. SQUIRE. Yes, sir.

Mr. DUNN. Proceed.

Mr. SQUIRE. I wanted to give you an incident that happened in the fall of last year. On account of the food that had been given to these veterans in the shelter house at Twenty-ninth and Wabash, 250 were poisoned.

Mr. DUNN. Two hundred and fifty men?

Mr. SQUIRE. Two hundred and fifty were sick from eating bad food.

Mr. DUNN. All 250 men who were compelled to reside in these "flop houses" were poisoned through bad food?

Mr. SQUIRE. Bad food.

Mr. DUNN. Did any of them go to the hospital?

Mr. SQUIRE. Many of them had medical attention on account of their having eaten this bad food and becoming sick from it. They required and received medical attention.

Mr. DUNN. Proceed.

Mr. SQUIRE. What could be more autocratic than veterans sleeping in the shelter houses, dying for the want of attention? I might cite one case, that of Sherwood Wilson, a Negro World War veteran, living at 4033 South Dearborn Street, an overseas veteran, Chicago, Ill. He laid at home. We tried to make every effort in order to get him into the Hines Hospital, and only 2 days before his death he was taken from his house. After reaching the hospital he only stayed there approximately a day and a night, when we got word he was dead. For at least 3 months we tried to get him into a hospital. Later his wife died.

Mr. DUNN. Was he a World War veteran?

Mr. SQUIRE. Yes, sir; an overseas veteran.

Mr. DUNN. Proceed.

Mr. SQUIRE. About 2 months after that his wife died. Five children survived him. We have tried, through our organization, to get their allowances started, but we have been unsuccessful.

Mr. DUNN. Can you give me any figures regarding the number of people in the city of Chicago or in the State of Illinois that have died of malnutrition or for the want of sufficient nourishing food? Have you those statistics?

Mr. SQUIRE. No; I do not have those statistics.

Mr. DUNN. The reason I asked you Mr. Johnson, from New York, stated here before the committee that last year 50,000 people died in New York because of malnutrition.

Mr. SQUIRE. With veterans dying from want of attention, the mothers of veterans stand in bread lines waiting for a stale loaf of bread; the veterans and their dependents are being evicted, and many of them denied relief. John Butler, living at 4045 South Federal Street, has been denied relief on account of the fact that he received his first 50 percent of his adjusted-compensation certificate, and since then he could not give an adequate account of what he had bought with it; and he has been, until now, totally denied the right to get relief.

Mr. DUNN. That condition has prevailed not only in Chicago, but I have no doubt it has prevailed in every large city in the United States. I have men coming to my office in Pittsburgh who have been denied relief, and——

Mr. SQUIRE. To cite a case or two: In my own case, I was put on work of the Civil Works Administration, the municipal airport. I have a family of 10.

Mr. DUNN. You have a family of 10?

Mr. SQUIRE. Mother and father and eight children. I was given 62 cents an hour, 8 hours work. Taking this up with the Relief Administration, being a skilled-labor worker, I asked for such jobs.

Mr. DUNN. Pardon me. On this 62 cents an hour for you and your wife and 8 children, you were not able to live in the big, swell hotels of Chicago, were you?

Mr. SQUIRE. No, sir. We were living at that time in a condemned house, which later was torn down. I have taken this up with the

Relief Administration, the employer of labor for the Civil Works Administration, stating that this salary would be too small in order to take care of a family of 10. Figuring out a budget, we found that they had to supplement the amount which was paid in salary, working only 14 days; after asking which, we were discriminated against in the skilled-labor jobs.

Negroes were not allowed to have such jobs paying $1.20 but worked on Public Works Administration projects at that time, such as school buildings, hod carrying, laying brick, and as carpenters.

Then I was withdrawn from this Civil Works Administration job and placed back on the relief roll. Since then I have not obtained any more project employment.

Mr. DUNN. May I ask whether you are now on the relief roll?

Mr. SQUIRE. I am on the relief roll.

Mr. DUNN. About how much money are you getting now to maintain your family, since you have been placed on the relief roll?

Mr. SQUIRE. $22 per month, for 10, in a grocery order.

Mr. DUNN. And you are compelled to pay rent?

Mr. SQUIRE. They pay the rent.

Mr. DUNN. They give you $22 worth of food slips a month?

Mr. SQUIRE. In grocery orders.

Mr. DUNN. To maintain your wife and eight children?

Mr. SQUIRE. My wife and eight children.

Mr. DUNN. Proceed.

Mr. SQUIRE. And they give three boxes. I do not know positively what the value of the boxes is, but they give that, from the Sprague & Warner Co.

Mr. DUNN. What is in those boxes?

Mr. SQUIRE. Things such as canned goods.

Mr. DUNN. That means your groceries?

Mr. SQUIRE. They give you two separate allowances. They give you one in a grocery order, to go to the neighborhood stores and take up the things such as green stuffs and vegetables.

Mr. DUNN. Is that included in your $22 a month?

Mr. SQUIRE. That is not included in the $22. The three boxes that they give you are extra.

Mr. DUNN. In addition to the $22?

Mr. SQUIRE. Yes.

Mr. DUNN. What would you say that that would amount to in dollars?

Mr. SQUIRE. It seems to me that they would amount to at least $13.

Mr. DUNN. That is, $13 in addition to the $22?

Mr. SQUIRE. Yes.

Mr. DUNN. That would be about $35, then, a month?

Mr. SQUIRE. Per month.

Mr. DUNN. With that you are supposed to maintain your wife and eight children?

Mr. SQUIRE. That is the food. So far as clothing is concerned, I have not received anything but underwear, top shirts, and things such as pajamas since I have been on the relief roll, and that is 4 years in a stretch. I received one pair of cotton pants.

Now, to cite one or two more cases: Here is a case that happened at Chicago, at Fiftieth and State Streets. An overseas veteran named Lee Ford, with his wife and five kids, were living in a basement with water continually running on the floors. The wife developed pleurisy, which later developed into pneumonia, of which she died. Two months later Lee Ford and his five children were evicted on the streets. This is an overseas veteran. We forced the relief, through our veterans' committee continually hammering and fighting.

Mr. DUNN. Was he a colored man?

Mr. SQUIRE. Yes, sir; a Negro veteran. By having several fights to place him on the relief roll, finally he was put on the relief and moved. Then the relief began paying his rent.

Another case, from Wheaton, Ill.: A month ago Frank Florido's house was burned down and he was forced to collect three old, demolished box cars in order to have a shelter for him and his family. He is living in box cars now that were condemned for use on the railroad. He has put them together, and he and his family are living in them.

Another case: Tennis L. Pope. I got this through our veterans' Rank and File, the official organ. It is the rank-and-file's paper. In Atlanta, Ga., he was sentenced to the chain gang for 6 months for organizing the rank-and-file veterans to fight for their 3-point program, including their major point of attack, the Lundeen bill, H. R. 2827. He is now serving that time.

There have been large appropriations for the Army and Navy, for national defense, but not one dime for the men who fought to make the world safe for democracy. In return our disability allowance has been reduced. Many disabled veterans have been cut off. Then the economy act was passed against the veterans as a whole. Interest has been placed on the 50 percent we got. The remaining 50 percent which the veterans should obtain will almost be eaten up by the interest, if it remains until 1945.

The veterans whom I represent have pledged themselves to carry on a relentless fight until we are able to force through the Lundeen bill, H. R. 2827, with the cooperation of the rest of the workers, farmers, intellectual, professional, and industrial workers.

The veterans' delegation will go on record before this hearing as being in favor of even all war funds, if possible, being turned into unemployment and social insurance. We have fought one war for democracy, and we have got unemployment, starvation, misery, and deprivation of all kinds; so it will be our ultimate aim to fight against war, and for the right to live.

Mr. DUNN. What is the name of the gentleman that you said was put in the chain gang, and who is now in prison, because he tried to organize this movement?

Mr. SQUIRE. Tennis L. Pope, Atlanta, Ga.

Mr. DUNN. And he was put in prison, why? Give us that statement again.

Mr. SQUIRE. Tennis L. Pope, of Atlanta, Ga., was sentenced to the chain gang for organizing the rank and file veterans to fight for the three-point program, including this bill, the Lundeen bill, as the major point.

Mr. DUNN. And he is now in the chain gang?

Mr. SQUIRE. Yes, sir; serving a 6-month sentence.

Mr. DUNN. How long ago was he sent there?

Mr. SQUIRE. Hand me that Rank and File right there.

Mr. DUNN. Just about how many months has he been in the chain gang now?

Mr. SQUIRE. He has been in about 2 months now.

Mr. DUNN. That is what I wanted to know. Thank you for your information.

Mr. SQUIRE. Yes, sir.

STATEMENT OF PAUL P. CROSBIE, REPRESENTING THE AMERICAN LEAGUE OF EX-SERVICE MEN, NATIONAL HEADQUARTERS, NEW YORK CITY

Mr. CROSBIE. Mr. Chairman, my name is Paul P. Crosbie, of New York City, representing the American League of Ex-Service Men, national headquarters. I would like, for the record, to identify myself as an American citizen of Revolutionary descent; an officer in the Three Hundred and Thirteenth Field Artillery in the last war; member of the American Legion; and a member of the American League of Ex-Service Men.

Mr. DUNN. You say you were an officer in the World War?

Mr. CROSBIE. Yes.

Mr. DUNN. What were you?

Mr. CROSBIE. I was first lieutenant of the Field Artillery.

Mr. DUNN. You were across the seas?

Mr. CROSBIE. I was across for more than 12 months. We were in action at St. Mihiel and throughout the Meuse-Argonne.

I have, in the last few days, received a letter from one of your citizens in Pennsylvania—Batista Passera—at Clairton, Pa.

Mr. DUNN. That is in Allegheny County.

Mr. CROSBIE. The situation in regard to Batista is that he was one of my drivers. The horse that he was standing beside was killed by a shell. The horse fell on him and knocked him unconscious. He recovered from that, and the case was not reported to the hospital. Batista finds, now, that for years he has been suffering with pains in the back of his head and neck. I have a letter from him, written the other day, saying he had been in the hospital for 4 months. He is unable to get disability allowance because there is no medical record of his war-connected disability. I have recently sent him an affidavit of my recollection of the circumstances under which he was injured, in the hope that he could get something from it.

Mr. DUNN. Would you have the man contact me as soon as possible?

Mr. CROSBIE. When I get back to New York I will.

Mr. DUNN. Because I make it my business to take care of such unfortunates.

Mr. CROSBIE. I will send you his full name and address and a copy of the affidavit.

Mr. DUNN. I know there are many who have written to me, and I have gone to the Department and fought hard; but there is a ruling, you see, that unless a man can prove that he met with his misfortune while in the line of duty, he is unable to get anything. Of course, the economy bill, as you know, stripped many of these unfortunates from what little compensation they were receiving.

Mr. CROSBIE. I know it only too well.

In my capacity as representative of the American League of Ex-Service Men, I speak in behalf of the three-point program adopted by this organization at its national convention in Chicago in December 1934. This program demands:

1. Full and immediate cash payment of the bonus.
2. Repeal of the Economy Act.
3. The enactment of the workers' unemployment and social-insurance act—H. R. 2827.

The veteran represents an important part of the population. He, and she, because I include the thousands of American women who were with us in the war, is in every rank of society from multimillionaire Frank N. Belgrano, of the American Legion, down to the dying and destitute victim of the crisis, but statistics show that he is the greatest victim of unemployment. Today the average age of the veteran over 42 is above the age when reemployment in industry is likely. According to a statement of James Van Zandt, national commander of the Veterans of Foreign Wars, over 62 percent of the veterans of the latest war are unemployed, and I, as an agent for group insurance in industry, have learned that employers will not take on employees for whom the insurance rate is high.

Mr. Dunn. Are you now an agent for that company?

Mr. Crosbie. I am an insurance broker. I handle all kinds of insurance, including group insurance, of which I have always disapproved.

Mr. Dunn. And you are in a position to know that these insurance companies, these corporations, will not give a man or woman employment after attaining the age of probably 40?

Mr. Crosbie. Absolutely. That is a known fact in the insurance field. We teach the employer that if he takes the employees above 35 he is going to have to pay more for his insurance.

Mr. Dunn. And you presume that is one of the reasons why?

Mr. Crosbie. That is one of the reasons why.

Mr. Dunn. Because the corporations probably will be compelled to give to the insurance companies a little more money if they take a person beyond 40?

Mr. Crosbie. And we know, also, that when they come to lay off men, they lay off those for whom they are paying the higher rates of premium.

Mr. Dunn. Proceed.

Mr. Crosbie. Besides, these veterans have reached the age when they cannot stand the speed-up of the present day factory system in America, and 1,000,000 of them are suffering with disabilities incurred during their services in armed forces.

We veterans are unyielding in our demand that our Government should pay now the back wages that were due 15 years ago, and we are likewise insistent in our demand that the economy act, a measure enacted in favor of the rich at the expense of the poor, be repealed, but we are not deceived into thinking that these demands that represent the special needs of the veterans will solve their greatest problem, which is the problem of economic security.

In pressing our own immediate demands, we support the demands of the whole American working class. We demand for ourselves, as veterans' the full and immediate cash payment of the so-called " bonus " as a payment of a debt long past due, but on behalf of the veterans' the full and immediate cash payment of the so-called enactment of unemployment and social insurance, as represented by H. R. 2827, with the full cost to be borne by the Government and the employer.

Mr. DUNN. To be borne by the employer and the Government?

Mr. CROSBIE. Yes.

Mr. DUNN. I believe the Lundeen bill, H. R. 2827, provides for the money that is to take care of the aged and the unemployed, the mothers, and so forth, by a tax on people who have salaries over $5,000, a gift tax and an inheritance tax.

Mr. CROSBIE. Yes.

Mr. DUNN. I just wanted to make that statement.

Mr. CROSBIE. Yes. That is clear. I did not elaborate on it in the statement.

The Wagner-Lewis bill is not only a fake in that it gives no relief to the millions now unemployed but it is a fraud on all those who are employed and expect through it to gain economic security against disability and old age. The cost of this bill is to be borne not by the rich, out of their swollen profits, but by the wage earner in the form of wage cuts and by the consumer in the form of higher prices. This Wagner-Lewis bill is all a part of the " new deal ", Roosevelt, big business' attempt to solve the capitalist crisis at the expense of the toiling masses.

Real unemployment and social insurance as represented by H. R. 2827, which we endorse, will not solve the contradictions of capitalism but it will give to the American worker some of the security to which his magnificent productive labor in the past so well entitles him. Of real wealth, America has an abundance. Our fields and factories stand ready to produce the goods that we require; our trained workers are idle. It is imperative to put into the hands of the sick, the aged, and the unemployed the means to buy, without taking, as the Wagner-Lewis fake does, the means away from other workers.

Gentlemen, forget for a moment the importunities of monopoly capital, of chambers of commerce, of self-appointed committees for the Nation, and remember that you are the representatives of 120,-000,000 Americans. These Americans have elected you to represent them, not to represent the profits of monopoly capital. If you refuse to represent them, if you are guided not by their needs but by the pressure of profit makers, you have betrayed them. Support the American people by reporting out this bill, H. R. 2827, and fighting for its enactment by Congress.

In conclusion I would like to state that I appear not as a person suffering from lack of employment, not as a person who expects to gain from such legislation, but as an American citizen who is deeply concerned with enabling his fellow citizens to enjoy the real wealth that our country has in such abundance. I thank you.

Mr. DUNN. I appreciate all that you have said. If we would have more men who are getting along to come before this committee and state that they are interested, not selfishly but in behalf of the other poor unfortunates of our country, the depression would soon end.

Mr. DUNN. Thank you.

114096—35——34

STATEMENT OF ELMER JOHNSON, REPRESENTING THE CHICAGO BRANCH OF THE AMERICAN FEDERATION OF LABOR, TRADE UNION COMMITTEE FOR UNEMPLOYMENT INSURANCE

Mr. JOHNSON. Mr. Chairman, and members of the House Labor Subcommittee, my name is Elmer Johnson. I represent the Chicago branch of the American Federation of Labor Trade Union Committee for Unemployment Insurance, with offices at 160 North Wells Street, Chicago, Ill., of which I am secretary.

Mr. DUNN. May I ask you a question here? How many are there in your organization?

Mr. JOHNSON. About 20,000. This committee is a bona fide organization, set up by 27 local unions of the American Federation of Labor, whose delegates met at a conference July 1, 1934, and after a full and free discussion of the various bills, unanimously endorsed the principles contained in the workers unemployment, old-age and social insurance bill, H. R. 7598, now known as " H. R. 2827."

I am also a member and secretary of Painters Local Union No. 637, which sent me here to support H. R. 2827. The organizations I represent support the workers' unemployment insurance bill because they consider it is the only measure before Congress that provides adequate unemployment benefits for all workers who are unemployed through no fault of their own, regardless of whether they are industrial, agricultural, transportation, or domestic workers, and for the entire period of unemployment. Additional reasons for our support of H. R. 2827, are:

This bill, if enacted, would be a safeguard for the economic conditions won by organized labor through years of struggle, whose standard of living must be maintained; that the unemployed workers must be given benefits equal to average wages, not less than $10 per week, $3 for each dependent.

If this bill were enacted, the unemployed workers would not be disqualified from benefits because of past participation in strikes or refusal to work in the place of strikers.

The bill, if enacted, would help to safeguard the employed workers' hard-won conditions. We are for this bill because it provides for the participation of trade unions in the administration of unemployment insurance.

Finally, the bill puts the financial burden, not upon the underpaid workers, but upon those who are able to pay. The Chicago Federation of Labor's executive committee has endorsed the Wagner-Lewis reserves bill. The organizations I represent sent me here to oppose the Wagner-Lewis bill, and I will tell you in a few words why we reject the Wagner-Lewis bill and other similar bills introduced in the Congress.

The official unemployment report for January 1935, submitted by the executive council of the American Federation of Labor, which gives a very conservative estimate of the situation of unemployment, states that 61 percent of the building-trades workers in Chicago are unemployed. The rest of those who are working are employed only part time. I am giving figures on the building trades because very large numbers of the locals I represent are in the building trades. Other trades, which are included in this report, show a large section of their members unemployed. The printing trades were least affected, showing 17 percent total unemployed, and 35 percent working part time, less than 50 percent working full time.

The Wagner-Lewis reserves bill, and other bills, were rejected and opposed by the organizations I represent, because those bills, particularly the Wagner-Lewis bill, exclude from unemployment insurance all those who are at present unemployed. The benefits only apply to certain sections of the workers who have steady employment and who will have contributed to the reserve fund; but even these workers, in the event they lose their jobs, would only be entitled to a very limited amount of weekly benefits.

The workers of Chicago have gone through 5 years of economic crisis. Many of them, for several years, have been forced to depend for their existence upon the rations given out by the relief stations. Many workers have even been denied this help.

In many of the local unions I represent, a relief committee has been organized, which committee takes up the cases of our members who are unemployed and in need of food, clothing, and so forth, but who have been denied relief by the station on certain technical grounds, through the red-tape procedure and so forth. Hundreds of members are denied even this small, miserable allowance handed out by the relief station.

Mr. LUNDEEN. Will you state what unions you represent, then?

Mr. JOHNSON. I will give you a statement. I represent 27 local unions of the American Federation of Labor. Shall I name them?

Mr. LUNDEEN. American Federation of Labor?

Mr. JOHNSON. Yes; with a membership of approximately 20,000.

Mr. LUNDEEN. You bear credentials? Were you elected to come here, or how did you come down here?

Mr. JOHNSON. I was elected by these organizations to come down here to represent them at this hearing.

Mr. LUNDEEN. Through their central body, or how was that done?

Mr. JOHNSON. I explained in the beginning of my testimony that on July 1, 1934, 27 local unions of the American Federation of Labor sent delegates who met and discussed the various unemployment-insurance bills, and after a full and free discussion of these bills, they unanimously endorsed the workers unemployment insurance bill and set up this committee for the purpose of continuing the work of organizing the rest of the American Federation of Labor workers behind this bill. This committee is still in existence, and we are getting more and more endorsements for the bill right along.

Mr. LUNDEEN. What I am trying to find out is, was this committee authorized by these unions?

Mr. JOHNSON. They were authorized by these unions.

Mr. LUNDEEN. And they were all American Federation of Labor people?

Mr. JOHNSON. Absolutely.

Mr. LUNDEEN. They were not a self-constituted committee of a few individuals?

Mr. JOHNSON. They were duly elected delegates from their own local unions.

Mr. LUNDEEN. Proceed.

Mr. SCHNEIDER. What trades are included in this union that you represent?

Mr. JOHNSON. It is made up of painters, carpenters, molders, metal polishers, bakers, coopers, cigarmakers, the building-service employees, the Chicago wood-carvers' locals, upholsterers, and carpetmakers.

Mr. SCHNEIDER. Can you say whether that question was ever brought before the Chicago Federation of Labor; and if so, what disposition was made of it?

Mr. JOHNSON. The Chicago Federation of Labor executive committee is very much opposed to this organization set up independently by these local unions. The Chicago Federation of Labor executive committee is doing everything it can to undermine the influence of this organization in the eyes of the local unions and the American Federation of Labor.

Mr. SCHNEIDER. The question I was trying to have you answer is whether or not the question of the Lundeen bill ever had been discussed in the meetings of the Chicago Federation of Labor; and if so, what the decision was?

Mr. JOHNSON. I am also a delegate of the Chicago Federation of Labor. I have brought this bill up to the Federation of Labor a number of times. They refused to take it up in the Federation of Labor. It was ruled out of order, and the executive council of our organization, the American Federation of Labor trade-union committee, has sent delegates, too, for the purpose of requesting the right to bring this bill up, but we have been refused the right to bring up this question in the Chicago Federation of Labor proper.

Mr. SCHNEIDER. Could you say whether the Chicago federation has endorsed any other unemployment bill?

Mr. JOHNSON. The Chicago Federation of Labor has endorsed the Wagner-Lewis bill.

Mr. SCHNEIDER. Has the group that you speak for here any other reason for existence than this unemployment insurance?

Mr. JOHNSON. I will answer this way: Our group realizes that in the fight for unemployment insurance it is also necessary to fight for democracy in the unions and for other issues, such as the fight against gangsterism, because, if we have no democracy in the unions, you cannot raise the question of unemployment insurance.

In some of the locals, which are controlled by gangster elements, it is there impossible also to raise this question.

Mr. LUNDEEN. Have you any political-party affiliations of any kind?

Mr. JOHNSON. In our committee there is no restriction as to the party you may belong to.

Mr. LUNDEEN. It is a nonpartisan committee; is that it?

Mr. JOHNSON. Absolutely.

Mr. LUNDEEN. You are not organized for the purpose of advancing any political party?

Mr. JOHNSON. We are organized for the purpose of getting the American Federation of Labor locals behind this bill and to have Congress enact it.

Mr. LUNDEEN. You say that is the first and main purpose of the organization?

Mr. JOHNSON. That is the first and the main purpose of this committee.

Mr. LUNDEEN. But you have never been able to convince the central authorities and the highest authorities in the American Federation of Labor in Chicago that they should take this action?

Mr. JOHNSON. No; we have not as yet; but we believe that this is a question not of convincing them but of organizing the local unions. We believe that after a larger number have endorsed it the Chicago Federation of Labor officials will then approve of it, not because they like it but because of the pressure that will be put upon them. That is the way we look upon the question.

Mr. SCHNEIDER. Do you feel you are doing justice to the Chicago Federation of Labor in saying that? Do you think they understand the bill?

Mr. JOHNSON. I do not mean the Chicago Federation of Labor as a whole. There are many sincere and honest people in the Chicago Federation of Labor. The major part of the delegates, I believe, are very honest and sincere people, but the executive committee is not working in the interests of the local unions they represent when they call for local unions to endorse the Wagner-Lewis bill.

Mr. LUNDEEN. As I understand it, they have had no other bill presented to them, have they, but the Wagner-Lewis bill?

Mr. JOHNSON. There have been a number of others. We have forced the question of the workers' unemployment insurance upon the floor.

Mr. LUNDEEN. But it has never been discussed?

Mr. JOHNSON. We have forced the question upon it until it was finally ruled out of order. Although there have been a number of resolutions introduced into the Federation of Labor calling for a referendum vote on this question, these resolutions are ruled out of order because they claim this question was decided on April 1, 1934, when an economic conference was held, at which, under the protest of a large number of delegates, the Wagner-Lewis bill was endorsed.

Mr. LUNDEEN. They got a majority vote for it then, did they not?

Mr. JOHNSON. There was no count of the vote. The chairman called for ayes and nays, and there was a doubt raised as to the number of votes registered, and the workers' bill was not known at that time to the majority of the delegates and to the local unions.

Mr. SCHNEIDER. Are you employed in the building trades?

Mr. JOHNSON. At present I am not working. I am secretary of the largest local of the Brotherhood of Painters.

Mr. SCHNEIDER. What percentage of the building-trades men in Chicago are now unemployed, so far as you know?

Mr. JOHNSON. The building-trades men at the present time, according to the official report of "Bill" Green, are 61 percent totally unemployed. That is a very conservative estimate.

Mr. LUNDEEN. I was going to say I would imagine it would be 80 percent.

Mr. JOHNSON. You see, there are many workers who because of unemployment have been forced to drop out of the union. They could not pay their dues, and this figure does not take in these workers at all, but only those workers who are at present in the union.

Shall I proceed?

Mr. LUNDEEN. Yes; unless Congressman Schneider has further questions at this time.

Mr. Schneider. No; that is all.

Mr. Johnson. The workers of Chicago have gone through 5 years of economic crisis. The relief committees that have been organized in many of the locals to take up the cases of our members who are unemployed and in need of food and clothing realize that it is not the needy condition of the client that determines whether or not he shall get relief, but the membership is beginning to see that it is necessary to organize and to bring pressure to bear upon the relief authorities; for in many cases, in our experience, this has been the determining factor which got the relief; and that is the thing which counts; and this is the way we look upon the movement for the workers' unemployment insurance bill. We believe that it is not so much a matter of convincing Congress by arguments of the necessity for enacting this bill into law, but we believe that it is necessary to organize the unified support of all workers and farmers behind this bill and to demand that Congress enact this measure. I may say we believe that this kind of a movement will help to change, perhaps not the minds of many of the Congressmen, but their votes.

Mr. Lundeen. Just what do you mean by that?

Mr. Johnson. Well, I mean that many of the Congressmen who are at present opposed to this bill today or who are not in favor of it can be brought to vote favorably upon the bill if sufficient pressure from organizations is put upon them. Even though they do not like the bill, they will vote for it, depending upon the pressure that is brought to bear upon them. That is the way the organizations I represent look upon the question.

In conclusion, Mr. Chairman, and in the name of the organizations I represent, I ask that this committee report the bill out favorably.

Mr. Lundeen. Are you the only man from Chicago here today?

Mr. Johnson. We have Lockner, who will speak on the unemployed.

Mr. Lundeen. Lockner? Is that the man who used to be secretary for Senator Lane?

Mr. Johnson. He is the secretary of the Unemployed Councils in Chicago.

Mr. Lundeen. I knew a man named Lockner years ago who was secretary for United States Senator Lane. That is not the man?

Mr. Johnson. No; that is not the man.

Mr. Lundeen (acting chairman). Are there any questions, Congressman Schneider?

Mr. Schneider. No.

STATEMENT OF KARL LOCKNER, REPRESENTING THE UNEMPLOYMENT COUNCIL OF COOK COUNTY, CHICAGO, ILL.

Mr. Lockner. My name is Karl Lockner. I live at 2923 Armitage Avenue, Chicago. I represent the Unemployment Council of Cook County, whose office is at 1611 North Artesian Avenue. Our council is made up of delegates from 33 local unemployed organizations in Chicago and 10 such organizations in 10 suburban towns around Chicago. We have a total membership of 5,500. I also represent the Illinois Unemployment Council, with locals in 60 villages and towns outside of Cook County.

We, of the Unemployed Council, are for the workers' unemployment, old-age, and social-insurance bill, because we need it. This has been a very bitter winter in Chicago. I should like to give examples of what is happening among the unemployed of Chicago.

A schoolboy from the Anderson School came to us a week ago. He told us of 2 weeks' happenings in his class. First the children of Joseph Mitchell, 1739 Division Street, reported that their father had hung himself. Then the children of Majercak, 1027 North Hermitage Avenue, reported that their father had slashed his wrists and killed himself. Both families were unemployed and on relief. The fathers had just given up.

Then, a classmate of this little boy, named Gladys Vendrine, 1252 North Lincoln Street, died. At the inquest, the doctor testified she died from exposure. The family had been 6 days without coal. These facts were brought out at the inquest. An 11-year-old boy saw this happen to his classmates within a period of less than 2 weeks, the time from January 10 to January 23, 1935.

During that same time the Tomsic family, living in another part of the city of Chicago, 2652 South Sacramento, were benefited by the fact that in December the father had the good fortune of finding a job. He had six children. His job was for 3 weeks, at $14 a week. He was taken off the relief rolls. When he finished his work, he reapplied for relief. It took a week, 10 days, 2 weeks. Father went to the relief station day after day, became discouraged; on the last day he got unruly and the police put him out. George Tomsic shot his wife and himself, leaving the children for the city to take care of.

Then, on January 25, the Arden family, 1718 Sedgwick, shot their overworked case worker, the station supervisor, and themselves. The Ardens had been on relief for 1 year. Mrs. Arden had been on work relief part of that time, earning $40.50 a month. When winter came, the relief authorities told the Ardens they had been getting too much, they should only have been given $35.75, according to the budget. The relief stated they were going to make an adjustment, so in January the family was given $6.45. The rent was unpaid, the electricity was shut off, they had little food. They complained to the station, but in Chicago relief complaints are often not taken up for a month, because of overworked case workers. The case worker has to go through a lot of red-tape investigations. They cannot cover all their cases; secondly, the relief authorities do not want the case workers to take care of all the complaints—which saves more money for them.

On January 24 Mrs. Arden telephoned her complaint. After telephoning, she went to the home of a neighbor and cried because the relief station had asked her where she got the nickel to telephone with. The relief told her she could not be so bad off if she could waste money telephoning. On January 25 the tragic shooting took place.

This has been a horrible winter in Chicago. Our organization realized that the Ardens were driven by desperation to such actions. Our organization does not approve but disapproves of individual violence, because such things only give the relief authorities an excuse for further repressive measures.

The Arden tragedy has not led to an improvement in the handling of relief cases in Chicago. On the contrary, more police have been placed in the relief station, to suppress any protests the relief clients may make.   In Chicago, police are placed in every relief station and are on duty at all times.   In some stations machine guns have been part of the regular equipment of the relief station—machine guns. At no. 505 Fiftieth Court there was a time when some 12 to 15 police were stationed in the relief station at all times, literally to prevent the unemployed from getting much-needed food and clothing.

Our organization believes that these facts are the best arguments we know for the workers' bill, H. R. 2827.   We are against the Wagner-Lewis so-called "security bill", first, because it gives nothing to the millions now unemployed; second, at best, from what we understand, it would protect a limited number of the present employed, for a very short period of time.   Other arguments have been very well presented here to this committee by such witnesses as Herbert Benjamin and Mary van Kleeck.

I want to say that we demand favorable action from Congress, but our experience with public officials has taught us that they will do nothing unless they are forced to.   We have many examples to prove this.

There was a time, for example, when rent was not paid to Chicago's unemployed.   Evictions were as many as 50 a day.   Our committees went to the relief stations, to Mayor Cermak, and to high relief authorities to demand the payment of rents.   Families would be sitting in the street.   We would ask the relief to pay rent, but they would refuse.   We had to take things into our own hands. Neighbors of unemployed families, organized by unemployment councils, got together.   We broke down the doors of the homes where these workers had been evicted, and set back the furniture. Chicago's unemployment councils have done that for more than 3,000 families.

Mayor Cermak ordered his police to stop this, and so on August 3, 1931, three of our Negro comrades were murdered when they attempted to set back the furniture of an evicted 72-year-old woman. An aroused working class forced Cermak to stop evictions for 4 months.   The relief began to pay some rents, but even today municipal court records show thousands of rental cases and more than 1,200 actual evictions for the first 6 months of 1934.   Rent was paid in Chicago for only 35,000 Chicago families.   That is stated approximately in round figures for October 1934; though there are 135,000 on relief.   We organized for a demonstration in November, and then the rent payments jumped up to 55,000.

Mr. LUNDEEN. What is your authority for those figures?

Mr. LOCKNER. I am using figures where they state how much money they spent for the relief.

Mr. LUNDEEN. From their own documents?

Mr. LOCKNER. From their own documents, and they do not give exactly how much rent, but they give the total amount of money spent for rent, and the average rental ranges between $12 and $15, and it is very simple to calculate in round figures what the rents were per family.

At the present time rent payments have again dropped.   Down State in Illinois, only 2.9 percent of relief moneys go for rent payment.   It is estimated that less than 5,000 of the 165,000 families on relief get their rents paid.   I think, for accuracy, though, we should state that some of these may own their own little cottages, but there are no figures available to my knowledge that would give these rents.

Similarly, on gas and light, Chicago in the last 8 months has developed this situation: If a building is condemned, within 24 hours that building will be wrecked and taken apart—the neighbors need the wood. They need the fuel. In the last 8 months three such buildings tumbled down, and the result was hospital cases; in one case death ensued.

Our unemployment local councils have been forced, in many cases, to turn on the gas and light. We openly state that we have our own gas committees, we have our own electric-light committes. First, they try to get the relief to pay the gas and light, and second, they take the relief into their own hands and turn the gas on, posting a little sticker, " Turned on by order of the Unemployment Council—collect from the relief."

Mr. SCHNEIDER. Does the relief pay it?

Mr. LOCKNER. Does the relief pay it? I do not know. I do not care.

Mr. BENJAMIN. The people get their lights, though.

Mr. LOCKNER. Yes.

Mr. SCHNEIDER. That is the important thing.

Mr. LOCKNER. To get food and clothing, you cannot go into the stores and take it, just like that. There, our organization sends committees, and in Chicago, in the last 3 years, we must state the public officials have carried on a reign of terror against the neighbors of unemployed families. They do not allow a neighbor or a committee of neighbors to go in and speak for some unemployed worker in need of food. Such committees are arrested. The number of arrests of unemployed workers would amount to somewhere between three and five thousand in the last 2 or 3 years.

Mr. SCHNEIDER. You are speaking now about the neighbors being prohibited from appearing before the relief committees?

Mr. LOCKNER. At the relief stations.

Mr. SCHNEIDER. What about the city council? Do they have any control over that? Do they give any assistance in securing relief for the unemployed?

Mr. LOCKNER. There are aldermen in Chicago that have driven committees of the unemployed from their offices. In the Tomsic case that I spoke about, the alderman just ignored their appeals. I will name him. He was Alderman Sonneschein, from the twenty-second ward. He refused to help the Tomsic family. After they killed themselves he paid for the funeral and got himself in too good with the voters again, but the aldermen do not bother very much about relief. The aldermen have never made any protest against the use of force in the relief stations, and that force is used primarily to keep us from getting the things that we need.

Mr. SCHNEIDER. You brought out, there, that the neighbors of the suffering people were arrested because of their interceding on behalf of the unemployed. Who causes those arrests?

Mr. LOCKNER. The police, under Mayor Kelly, or Mayor Cermak—it matters not what politics they are.

Mr. SCHNEIDER. What position does the relief administration take in connection with that?

Mr. LOCKNER. I am very sorry to have to say this about the Illinois Emergency Relief Commission, but they help in such arrests. They even furnish prosecuting attorneys. The Illinois Emergency Relief Commission has a very sorry record. I know of towns in Illinois, like Hillsboro, where they gave relief to tombstones. Their agent, Mr. Denton—I would like to have the name on the record, please—of Hillsboro, Ill., at one time gave relief orders to tombstones, to vacant lots, and he is still in charge of relief in that city.

Mr. SCHNEIDER. You mean that he put on the roll the name of some person who was dead?

Mr. LOCKNER. I do not know that he did, but I mean, under his administration. And to this day no prosecutions have been made, but all the Unemployed Council leaders of Montgomery County were arrested and held in prison on high bail for as much as 2 and 3 months last summer.

Mr. SCHNEIDER. Do you mean that the poor-relief money was given for the purchase of tombstones?

Mr. LOCKNER. No; no. I mean the names of people who had gravestones in the graveyards were forged and used on the roll.

Mr. SCHNEIDER. The names of dead people were on the poor rolls, and the relief money was paid out to those names, somebody receiving the money?

Mr. LOCKNER. Yes.

Mr. SCHNEIDER. Do you know who it was?

Mr. LOCKNER. I know who the officials were in charge of relief. I do not know who got it. I could not investigate, and the State's attorney there refused to investigate because he said prominent people of that county were involved; and Governor Horner, though these facts were brought to his attention, never has even answered registered letters to that effect. Wilford Reynolds waved those things aside, but at the same time the relief has furnished attorneys to prosecute members of the unemployed council who have gone to bat for relief for some of their neighbors.

Mr. SCHNEIDER. Then the charge you make is that, at certain relief stations, people are receiving money in the name of somebody else who does not exist; is that it?

Mr. LOCKNER. I did not say that. I said that in Hillsboro, Ill.—I gave the name of the town—one time the administrators of relief issued relief to people who had no existence and forged the orders and took the money. The orders were cashed in Mezerek Bros.' store in Hillsboro, Ill., and the orders were cashed presumably by people who were administering relief, and nothing was ever done about it. I bring these out in contrast. They would not prosecute, in this instance, but they prosecuted leaders of the unemployed councils on framed-up charges—I think "attempting to overthrow the Government", or something like that.

Mr. SCHNEIDER. Is Hillsboro a mining town?

Mr. LOCKNER. It is.

Mr. SCHNEIDER. Do you live there?

Mr. LOCKNER. I do not; but I am an official of the Illinois Unemployment Council, and we have a local there, and it was our comrades that were arrested there.

Mr. SCHNEIDER. And what do you do for a living?

Mr. LOCKNER. I am a chemist, unemployed at the present time.

Mr. SCHNEIDER. A chemist?

Mr. LOCKNER. Yes.

Mr. SCHNEIDER. Your home is in Chicago?

Mr. LOCKNER. Yes.

Mr. LUNDEEN. Pardon me. You speak of relief being paid to people that were dead. That reminds me of the Congressmen who voted against war being voted out of office largely by people who were in the cemetery, their names being used on the voting lists. People walked in and voted the names of the dead men. That, too, is an interesting story. It is an old game.

Mr. LOCKNER. If I may continue, our whole experience has been that where the unemployed have been organized, and in masses have taken protest action, the relief has been forced, not because they wanted to, but has been forced to improve conditions, partially. I could cite a number of instances to that effect—some down-State counties of Illinois, Calhoun County, for instance. The relief in that county during the month of September 1934, had 253 people on relief. They spent $2,214, or on an average, $8.75 per person, in that county. That is a western agricultural community. In the city of Chicago, or in Cook County, at that time there were 131,610 families on relief. They spent $5,021,430.88, or an average of $38.15, for the average family. In Cook County the workers have organized. In Calhoun County, there are few unemployed there. They are unorganized and they get less relief. Our organization believes in organizing and will continue to organize the unemployed and the working class to support the workers' bill and bring pressure on public officials and on Congress, and in that way to force its enactment.

We ask that the Labor Committee act favorably on H. R. 2827 and report this bill out of committee immediately; further, if the Rules Committee attempts to delay the vote or limit the debate on this bill, we ask the members of this committee to do everything possible to expose such delays or manipulations.

(The hour of 12:10 o'clock having arrived, the subcommittee took a recess until 2 o'clock this afternoon.)

AFTERNOON SESSION

The recess having expired, the subcommittee reconvened at 2 p. m., and was called to order by Mr. Dunn as chairman.

Mr. DUNN. Will you give the reporter your name, address, and the organization you represent?

STATEMENT OF FRANK N. TRAGER, CHAIRMAN OF THE PEOPLE'S UNEMPLOYMENT LEAGUE OF MARYLAND, AND REPRESENTING THE NATIONAL PROVISIONAL COMMITTEE OF THE ORGANIZED UNEMPLOYED

Mr. TRAGER. My name is Frank N. Trager, representing the People's Unemployment League of Maryland, and the National Provisional Committee of the Organized Unemployed.

Mr. DUNN. Mr. Trager, will you tell us something about your qualifications?

Mr. TRAGER. I am former instructor of philosophy in the Johns Hopkins University, and a member of the American Federation of Teachers Union in Baltimore.

Mr. DUNN. Are you a teacher there now?

Mr. TRAGER. I am not teaching now; I am doing other things. I am a free lance, as a matter of fact I have taught at Johns Hopkins for 6 years. Do you want any other information as to that?

Mr. DUNN. Whatever you want to give us about yourself. We like to get all the information we can about a man.

Mr. TRAGER. I told you about Johns Hopkins and the American Federation of Teachers Union.

Over 2 years ago I was one of the organizers of the People's Unemployment League of Maryland, a group representing some 6 percent of the total relief population in the State, attempting to raise standards of relief and to work for special legislation. This is a non-partisan group.

Likewise, I have been party to a group who have been attempting to form a national union of organized unemployed, who have been consistently at all times for the Lundeen unemployment insurance bill, and who plan to hold a convention on March 2, 3, and 4, this coming month. I think that is enough for a beginning.

We are sure that many groups of organized unemployed workers have appeared before this committee in order to support H. R. 2827, otherwise known as the "Lundeen workers' unemployment old age and social insurance act." In speaking for the organized unemployed, as represented by the People's Unemployment League of Maryland and the Provisional National Committee of Organized Unemployed, I want to point out that we have a special concern for this bill because it is the only legislative measure, other than the Black-Connery 30-hour week bill which, if passed, will provide something approximating security, not only for the now employed but also for the unemployed. It is clearly demonstrable that the Wagner-Lewis bill, H. R. 4120, and the administration $4,000,000,000 works-relief program will fail lamentably in accomplishing this avowed purpose.

In view of the closing of these valuable hearings—hearings which unfortunately have not received a press commensurate with their importance—it might be profitable if we attempted to summarize some of the main arguments in support of the House bill 2827. In so doing it will be useful and necessary to compare it with the Wagner-Lewis bill.

First, opponents of House bill 2827 come from two main sources: Those who claim that this bill is "ideal", strives to bring in the "millenium", or is not practicable; and those who claim that this bill has been supported by "radical" groups. The unemployed assert that the support of a legislative measure by radicals is no evidence against the value of the measure supported. Every radical in the country has been supporting unemployment insurance and old-age pensions since the days before the Great War, when the Socialist Congressman, Victor Berger, introduced such measures in the House of Representatives.

Mr. DUNN. In 1927, when I was a member of the Legislature of Pennsylvania, I introduced an unemployment bill, so it is not a recent matter has come up in the last year. And when I did it I was considered a radical.

Mr. DUNN. Yes.

Mr. TRAGER. It is a testimony to their persistence that the administration is now preoccupied with such measures.

With respect to the first statement that this bill is an " ideal " or " impractical " or will bring about a " millenium ", we maintain that House bill 2827 is a more realistic, more practicable, legislative measure than House bill 4120, the Wagner-Lewis bill, or whatever name the Wagner bill is going to have, and in fact can accomplish more of its expressed aim than the verbally similarly expressed aim of House bill 4120.

I have before me copies of both bills. One reads in its initial statement:

To alleviate the hazards of old age, unemployment, illness, and dependency, to establish a social insurance board in the Department of Labor, to raise revenue, and for other purposes.

The other reads:

To provide for the establishment of unemployment, old-age, and social insurance, and for other purposes.

The committee cannot help but notice the verbal similarities in the expressed aims of these two bills, but there ends the similarity.

House bill 2827 can achieve its goal by virtue of the following facts: Whereas House bill 4120 seems to wish to be doomed to failure, we say House bill 2827 can achieve its goal by virtue of the following facts: First, it is a form of compulsory Federal or National scheme of insurance as distinguished from the hybrid Wagner-Lewis variety, which would in effect create 49 systems of insurance. States' rights may be of importance, but human rights must come first. Our disastrous experience with 49 systems of banking in the United States, or, to pick another instance, our experience with the discrimination in various States under similar arrangements practiced by the Federal Emergency Relief Administration seem to us to indicate that where States retain control the results are unfortunate for the persons thereby affected. If there were more time, I should like to expand upon the virtue of this uniform compulsory Federal insurance scheme of House bill 2827 as distinguished from the other.

But let me give you just one illustration. Yesterday I testified before the Committee on Unemployment Insurance of my State, Maryland, the Governor's committee. I heard there members of the association of commerce coming in somewhat unprepared for the hearing, but raising these difficulties: " The canning industry in our State," it was said, " cannot possibly operate under a 3 percent payroll tax. We have special conditions in our particular industry." Up piped another member of the association of commerce representing the retail merchants, saying that " we have special conditions in our industry." I am sure that those experiences are typical in most States of the Union, where it will be left, as it will be under the jurisdiction of the Wagner-Lewis bill, to the States to set up State programs.

Therefore, our first major point is that the Workers' Unemployment Insurance Act, the Workers' Old-Age and Social-Insurance Act, is superior to the major point in the Wagner-Lewis bill by virtue of the fact that it will set up one uniform Federal compulsory system as distinguished from 49—I say 49; there would be one for each State, and then the Federal policy superimposed on them.

The second point is that the Workers' Old-Age and Social-Insurance Act extends coverage and benefits, not to some industrial workers, excluding some 50 percent of the working population of America, as would the Wagner-Lewis bill, but extends coverage and benefits to all workers throughout the whole period of unemployment, and also including those now unemployed. That point cannot be stressed too much as a prime recommendation for the Workers' Unemployment-Insurance Act as distinguished from the other. In support of this principle of universal coverage, during the whole period of involuntary unemployment, we should like to cite this fact: That the experience of other countries tends to prove that where social insurance is established on an actuarial basis, presumably the basis for the Wagner-Lewis bill, and as now contemplated by the present administration, such insurance may be on an actuarial basis, but it is hardly social insurance. The hazards of society, which these bills aim to alleviate, or to insure against, cannot be alleviated nor insured against, if we deliberately allow half of our working population to remain uninsured, as would happen under the Wagner-Lewis bill, if we allowed insurance for the others for only an insignificant period of from 10 to 20 weeks, as the case may be, nor is it satisfactory to say that insurance must be on an actuarial basis, or else it should be called something else. As the Secretary of Labor has told us, we do not care what the thing is called. We wish, however, very emphatically, to point out that adherence to an administrative measure useful perhaps 25 years ago is fatal today, because it cannot be made to work. No State will add to the 3-percent pay-roll tax except by demanding employee contributions.

This, in effect, will mean that the owners of industry will pass on the cost of their pay-roll tax to the consumer—to the employee. The employee will thus be making a threefold contribution. He will contribute in labor power; he will contribute to his tax on wages; and he will be contributing through additional costs for the commodities that he needs. The net result of the Wagner-Lewis bill of setting up presumably some 49 systems of social insurance will be to impose, in fact if not in name, a sales tax on the working population. These workers will be asked to pay for the stupidities and mismanagement of an industrial machine which otherwise ignores them.

My third point is that the workers' unemployment insurance act avoids the fiscal inequities of the Wagner-Lewis bill by arrangement whereby the cost of insurance or insuring against the hazards of society will be borne by society through the only just way to collect such costs, namely, by progressive taxation on capacity to pay; in other words, through income and inheritance taxes.

Our fourth point is that the workers' unemployment, old-age, and social-insurance act calls for an administration of its provisions by technical experts and representatives of those directly involved; that is the working population. This appears to us to be the only sound and democratic way of administering so important an act.

In conclusion, we should like to restate what seems to be the crucial point. The Wagner-Lewis bill provides a minimum security for a minority of our population during an insignificant period. It allows so much State action as to insure discrimination against workers as we now see discrimination practiced under the F. E. R. A. It imposes the cost of this minimum insurance upon the very people who are innocent of its causation. It necessitates both by Federal and State Government other and duplicative agencies to repair (*a*) its own ineffectualities, and (*b*) its indifference to literally millions of unemployed and employed workers excluded from its meager benefits.

In contract H. R. 2827 sets up one uniform Federal system of social insurance which avoids all these errors, both of omission and commission. It sets up one Federal agency, financed by those able to pay, to care for all the hazards of those who create the wealth of the country throughout their whole period of need. Duplication, discrimination, and inequalities are eliminated.

We believe, if this bill succeeds in passing, we are given the chance to inaugurate such a system which from every point of view will go further to realize its expressed aim than any other measure now before tion, and inequities are eliminated.

That completes the statement. I should be perfectly willing to answer any questions, but before I do may I direct your attention to Mr. Blackwell, who would like to say a few words?

Mr. DUNN. Very well. We allow anybody and everybody to say anything they want to about this bill and the other bills pertaining to unemployment insurance, and if anybody in the auditorium wants to get up here and tell us that this bill is not a practical bill, we will listen to him or her. We have Mr. Blackwell on the list. We have made arrangements to hear him.

Mr. TRAGER. Mr. Blackwell is now chairman of the Eastern Federation of the Organized Unemployed. It is a subgroup which is attempting to organize this national movement.

Mr. DUNN. Mr. Trager, I desire to ask you a few questions. You spoke about a sales tax?

Mr. TRAGER. Yes.

Mr. DUNN. In other words, you do not believe that a sales tax, a tax put on the people for food and clothing, is a proper way to obtain money to help the unemployed?

Mr. TRAGER. No, sir; nor the employed.

Mr. DUNN. No. A tax which the unemployed, the laboring man has to submit to, would be in your opinion an obnoxious tax, would it not?

Mr. TRAGER. That is right, sir.

Mr. DUNN. I agree with you.

Mr. TRAGER. And our point is that inevitably the effect of the Wagner-Lewis fiscal arrangements, putting a 3 percent national tax on pay rolls for the employer, and leaving it up to the State whether or not it would ask further contributions from employees, our point is the effect of such a pay-roll tax would be immediately to transpose that to the cost to the consumer, and thereby actually charge the employee who has really not brought about the debacle we have now to pay for.

Mr. DUNN. Can you tell me this: I have not had anybody prove to me that the people who are now unemployed are going to pay any taxes, or are able to pay any taxes to take care of the Wagner-Lewis bill. Can you in any way show me how the unemployed are going to pay any taxes?

Mr. TRAGER. The unemployed would be contributing in the increased cost of commodities for the support of people, and in turn receiving no support themselves.

Mr. TRAGER. I should like to show you, and I am sure you understand it already as to this point, under the administration's plan there would be the Wagner-Lewis bill, which would operate only in a limited way. I understand from reports, which Director Witte did not make public, indicated that the coverage of the Wagner-Lewis bill would be approximately 50 percent. Now, there would be the arrangements under the Wagner-Lewis bill, and such arrangements insofar as they took care, even on a minimum basis, of only a portion of the workers, would still make it necessary to have some sort of relief agency to mop up those who became unemployed but do not fit into the peculiar language of the Wagner-Lewis bill, knows who are now unemployed, and could not fit into those particular bills; and you would have to have the Wagner set-up, the relief set-up, and perhaps a forced labor set-up; and under the legislation which they are now trying to put through they will have to have three set-ups, each with a separate administration, each with separate fiscal arrangements; duplicating and wasting, so far as I can see. The Lundeen bill, on the other hand, creates one Federal agency with one source of funds, with uniform application to all workers now employed or unemployed. That seems to me to be incontrovertible.

Mr. DUNN. I want to say, when you are speaking about the set-up, that in my candid opinion if we do not do something in this Congress—that is, enact legislation that is going to take care of the unemployed and the aged and others, the people are not going to be able to sit up, but will have to lie down and die. That is my opinion.

Mr. TRAGER. I think there is going to be a small portion, Congressman Dunn, who will not take it lying down.

Mr. DUNN. Many unfortunates have already been compelled to go on their backs and die.

Mr. TRAGER. That is so.

Mr. DUNN. Because of malnutrition.

Mr. TRAGER. Yes.

Mr. DUNN. I do not think we are able to get an estimate of the number of people right now in this country who are starving to death. I think the number is large. That is my opinion.

Mr. TRAGER. I would not doubt it for a moment.

Mr. DUNN. Have you finished?

Mr. TRAGER. Yes, sir. Thank you for the opportunity of presenting my remarks.

Mr. DUNN. We appreciate your remarks.

The next witness is Mr. James Blackwell.

STATEMENT OF JAMES BLACKWELL, REPRESENTING THE PEOPLE'S UNEMPLOYMENT LEAGUE, CHAIRMAN OF THE EASTERN FEDERATION OF THE UNEMPLOYED ORGANIZATIONS, BALTIMORE, MD.

Mr. DUNN. Give the reporter your name, address, and who you represent.

Mr. BLACKWELL. James Blackwell, 713 North Calvert Street, Baltimore, Md.; I am an officer of the People's Unemployment League, chairman of the Eastern Federation of the Unemployed Organizations.

Congressman Dunn and members of this committee, I appreciate the opportunity very much to say these few words. I will not detain you very long.

Mr. Trager has, I believe, presented a very excellent case for the Lundeen bill, a case which has been thoroughly discussed by the organized unemployed of this Nation.

I would like to call to your attention that last November 24 the organized unemployed of the United States demonstrated in hundreds of cities throughout this country in support of the Lundeen bill. I want to say that the Lundeen bill is not something new to the organized unemployed nor are the provisions of the Wagner-Lewis bill by any means strange to them. They are fully aware that under the Wagner-Lewis bill there is no provision made whatsoever for those who are now the victims of the depression of the economic system.

We further wish to state to you, and perhaps this may be interesting to you in view of your previous remarks to Mr. Trager, that the unemployed are taking further steps to see that certain legislation is enacted. On March 2, 3, and 4, nonpartisan organizations of unemployed, including people of all affiliations, will appear in Washington to perfect a national organization, the creation of jobs, the public-works system, and the public-works plan of paying $30 a week as the minimum for a 30-hour week are the chief points of their demands. The Lundeen bill and its passage also figures largely in their program.

Speaking as chairman of the Eastern Federation, I want to say to Congressman Dunn that I, at least, do feel that he is sympathetically inclined toward the Lundeen bill and its provisions.

Mr. BLACKWELL. Yes, sir.

Mr. DUNN. You may proceed.

Mr. BLACKWELL. In view of your statement, Congressman Dunn, as just made, I am sure that the national convention of the unemployed, which will be here March 2, 3, and 4, will greet this announcement with the greatest satisfaction.

We hope that the labors of the House labor subcommittee will make all possible efforts to have the Lundeen bill enacted.

That is all that I wish to say, Congressman Dunn. I am sure that we do appreciate the knowledge that there are some individuals on the committee who do realize that the Lundeen bill, or the provisions which are equal to the Lundeen bill are all that will meet the present needs of those who are unemployed.

Mr. DUNN. Mr. Blackwell, we appreciate your intelligent remarks. Is Mr. Kroon present?

STATEMENT OF RICHARD M. KROON, REPRESENTING LOCAL UNION 37, DETROIT, MICH., BROTHERHOOD OF PAINTERS, DECORATORS, AND PAPER HANGERS OF AMERICA.

Mr. DUNN. Tell the reporter your name, address, and the organizations you represent.

Mr. KROON. My name is Richard Kroon; my address is 8350 Carbondale Avenue, Detroit, Mich.

Mr. Chairman, first of all I would like to indicate to you the organizations I am representing directly and those in Michigan who have endorsed and are whole-heartedly supporting this bill. I am a member of Local Union 37, Detroit, Mich., Brotherhood of Painters, Decorators, and Paper Hangers of America, affiliated with the American Federation of Labor, and have been for the last 11 years. My local union has supported the Lundeen bill since it was introduced on February 2 in the Seventy-third Congress.

The Michigan State Painters' Conference, American Federation of Labor, met in Lansing, Mich., Sunday and went on record to whole-heartedly support this bill. I was requested by the secretary to represent the conference at this hearing. I have credentials here from two organizations, representing approximately 75,000 members through the various affiliated organizations. They are as follows:

DETROIT CONFERENCE FOR UNEMPLOYMENT RELIEF AND INSURANCE,
Detroit, Mich., February 8, 1935.

Chairman DUNN,
    Subcommittee on H. R. 2827, House Labor Committee.

DEAR SIR: This is to certify that R. M. Kroon has been designated to represent our conference at the hearings being held on H. R. 2827 in Washington. Any courtesy extended him will be appreciated.

With best wishes, yours truly,

JOSEPH FREEDMAN, *President.*

A. F. OF L. TRADE UNION CONFERENCE FOR
UNEMPLOYMENT INSURANCE OF DETROIT,
Detroit, Mich., February 9, 1935.

Chairman DUNN,
    Subcommittee on H. R. 2827 of the House Labor Committee.

DEAR SIR: This is to certify that R. M. Kroon was officially designated to represent our conference in Washington on this bill. Any courtesy extended him will be appreciated.

With best wishes, yours truly,

R. M. KROON,
*Secretary, A. F. of L. Trade Union Conference
for Unemployment Insurance and Relief.*

These are all urging the immediate adoption of H. R. 2827 as a bill which will alleviate the plight of the unemployed, the aged, and the sick. The support for the bill throughout the State of Michigan is tremendous. Practically all independent trade unions, such as the Mechanics Educational Society of America; architects, engineers, and chemists; Federation of Workers; opticians, sheet-metal workers, and many others have endorsed it. The American Federation of Labor unions, including organizations of Italians and Hungarians, many factory organizations in Detroit, the International Coopers' Union, the Tailors' Union, and all the painters' locals in the State of Michigan, the Forgotten Man's Clubs, many fraternal organizations, and many others, almost too numerous to mention, endorsed this bill.

Mr. DUNN. All the painters' locals in the State of Michigan have endorsed this Lundeen bill, H. R. 2827?

Mr. KROON. Yes, sir; last Sunday, February 10.

Mr. DUNN. You may proceed.

Mr. KROON. I also wish to mention that through the Detroit Conference for Unemployment Relief and Insurance, from which I have a credential, 45,000 members from various Italian organizations in Detroit are represented in this hearing.

Mr. DUNN. Do you mean 45,000 in the city of Detroit?

Mr. KROON. Yes, sir.

Mr. DUNN. Do you mean Italian organizations?

Mr. KROON. No; Italian members of organizations.

Mr. DUNN. I thought you said there were 45,000 Italian organizations in Detroit. I thought there were more Irish in Detroit than there were Italians, and I could not understand that.

Mr. KROON. No. These represent approximately 51 organizations in Detroit.

Mr. DUNN. All right. Proceed.

Mr. KROON. These organizations are whole-heartedly supporting this bill.

I wish also to state that division 106 of the Forgotten Man's Club of Detroit, Mich., has through its chairman instructed me to represent it at this hearing.

In regard to the Lundeen bill, it is the only bill that provides unemployment insurance for all the unemployed. Also no waiting period is required. It stands to reason that those in the greatest need of unemployment insurance are those workers who have experienced the longest period of unemployment. Doles, charity hand-outs, and work-relief jobs are not unemployment insurance; they are but schemes and palliatives to keep the unemployed on the edge of destitution.

Another very important point: The Lundeen bill is the only bill that will take social insurance out of the hands of the politicians. The bill provides that such unemployment insurance shall be administered and controlled and the minimum compensation shall be adjusted by workers and farmers through unemployment-insurance commissions directly elected by members of workers' and farmers' organizations.

With these few general remarks, let us turn our attention to the Roosevelt social-security plan, which he submitted to Congress on January 17. The press gave the widest publicity to the plan, stressing above all the need for immediate adoption of the new Wagner-Lewis bill, which was introduced almost simultaneously with Roosevelt's message. On January 15 in New York City the National Retail Dry Goods Association, at its convention, adopted practically the complete Roosevelt social-security plan, although the plan was presumably not known to the general public. I have here a complete copy of their plan as it appeared in the New York Times on January 16, and, in examining it, find it almost an exact replica of the Roosevelt plan.

Senator Wagner, of New York, one of President Roosevelt's wheel-horses, has been quoted in the press to the effect that the wishes and desires of the employers have been fully considered in the drafting of his bill. It is rather superfluous of Senator Wagner to inform us of this fact. The evidence is quite complete. Because he was so rash and clumsy as to attempt to deny the need for unemployment and social insurance Herbert Hoover ceased to be of use to the masters of finance and industry who rule this country. The up-to-date guardian of wealth and privilege follows a more clever policy. He admits the facts, but denies, disputes, and opposes the conclusions.

We ask the simple question, Why the haste to adopt a social-security plan, whose effective date is placed in the distant future and is primarily dependent upon individual State adoption? While it is true that the President urges haste in order that the individual States may act on his plan, we must consider that the reintroduction of the Lundeen bill, the tremendous support it is receiving throughout the country, its obvious concreteness in dealing with the problem of unemployment and social insurance has forced the employers to exert all the power at their disposal to combat the workers' unemployment and social insurance bill. Very cleverly the President " plays " with this burning problem, laying down the dictum of " no taxation " for social insurance, but a pay-roll tax, which means that indirectly the working and professional people will have to pay for their own insurance, so to speak, instead of the possessors of wealth and special privilege who are directly responsible for the prevailing conditions which result in economic insecurity, destitution, and poverty.

Very generously, the administration in Washington will hand over to the politicians in the 48 States, beginning in 1936, $215,000,000 for administration expenses. A schoolboy will have no difficulty in figuring what part of this will eventually reach the unemployed, the aged, the sick, and the widows and orphans, all of whom are supposed to share this tremendous sum.

When we compare this sum with the $1,000,000,000 being spent annually for the Army and Navy by our Government, the slogan of a " new deal " for the people becomes ridiculous, if it did not involve such tragic conclusions. The new Wagner-Lewis bill can without contradiction be labeled a fake unemployment insurance bill, primarily because it does not insure these now unemployed, and exempts large sections of workers who are fortunate in having jobs at the present moment, or will have in the immediate future.

In passing, I wish to state or, rather, I wish to say a few words relative to the relief-work program recently adopted by Congress and involving an expenditure of almost $5,000,000,000. Too much confidence should not be placed in a Public Works program directed toward these ends since experience shows that it tends to be directed toward unproductive tasks and to be wasted in the processes of making contracts with private contractors, to such a degree that the actual public works put into operation fall far short of the appropriations made by Congress, and the actual employment provided and the compensation for it are quite out of proportion to the appropriation.

Mr. DUNN. Out of this $4,850,000,000, $850,000,000 is for immediate relief; and $4,000,000,000, of course, was to create employment for public works.

Mr. KROON. Yes.

Mr. DUNN. Approximately two billion and a half would be paid out in salaries, and about a billion and a half would be for transportation and material.

Mr. KROON. Yes.

Mr. DUNN. Do you believe that amount of money is insufficient to take care of the unemployed?
unemployed?

Mr. KROON. Absolutely.

Mr. DUNN. I spoke on that bill. I supported the bill. I stated it was insufficient, that it should be at least $10,000,000,000. Do you agree with me that that amount of money would have been much better to appropriate to take care of the unemployed than the $4,000,-000,000?

Mr. KROON. I have had some experience with relief, as I happen to be a relief worker myself.

Mr. DUNN. Do not misunderstand me. My idea of helping the unemployed is to give them work, as I introduced a bill and put in my bill 5 days a week and 6 hours a day at $1 an hour. Would you favor a proposition of that kind?

Mr. KROON. Well, partially. It is a rather complicated question. I only wish to touch upon it to indicate that the present proposed set-up in regard to work relief is entirely inadequate, and there are some very vicious and bad features involved, particularly in the question of the present wage rate. Now, in the statements at our State painters' conference in Lansing on Sunday, the delegates spoke very sharply against the attempt of the Roosevelt administration to do away with the prevailing wage rate as far as this $4,000,000,000 program is concerned. You will note from today's press that the American Federation of Labor has gone over to the Senate committee that is holding hearings on this bill to protest very vehemently against the abolition from the P. W. A. of the prevailing wage rate. In other words, we are faced with the probability that in this $4,000,000,000 bill we are seeing an attempt by the administration, backed up by the employers, to lower the standard of living, not only of the unemployed, but also of the employed worker. In what way? In this way, that the prevailing rate on the relief jobs and in this building program will be lowered, with the result that the employers will also be able to lower their rate, instead of acknowledging and subscribing to the principle that is involved, which is through the Government's efforts to raise the standard of living of the working people to increased wages.

Mr. DUNN. Again, I want to interrupt you. The organizations which you represent would not say that 5 days a week and $6 a day, with a minimum wage of $1 an hour, which would be $6 a day, would be inadequate, would they?

Mr. KROON. As far as our own individual organization is concerned in the State of Michigan, our rate on an average is around 80 cents per hour. Our working week is 40 hours. So, therefore, it stands to reason we would not object to a 30-hour week at a rate of $1 an hour.

I think I left off that too much confidence should not be placed in a Public Works program directed toward these ends since experience shows that it tends to be directed toward unproductive works and be wasted in the processes of making contracts with private contractors to such a degree that the acual public works put into operation fall far short of the appropriation made by Congress and the actual employment provided, and the compensation for it are quite out of proportion to the appropriation.

We are informed that the average wage on these relief projects will be $50 a month. This is approximately the present wage, and we certainly cannot disagree with the workers on these jobs at present that this is an adequate compensation and conforms even with what the social worker terms " minimum relief requirements." This lower standard has also the direct effect of keeping the wages of those employed in private industry down to a mere subsistence level.

Mr. DUNN. The social workers maintain that $50 is sufficient for a family to live on. In your opinion, is it not a fact that that is what the average social worker, who holds a pretty good position, thinks is necessary to maintain the average family?

Mr. KROON. Yes.

Mr. DUNN. You may proceed.

Mr. KROON. With the result of insuring larger profits for the employers, while causing an ever decreasing ability of the workers to buy back the products they produce. The " new deal " then can be summed up as being the same old deal for both the employers and the workers—the rich grow richer and the poor poorer.

One question that some supporters and most of the opponents of the workers' bill raise is it will never get passed. This is always the first objection raised by opponents of adequate social legislation. But those same opponents, together with the faint-hearted, whom they frighten by their specious warnings, fail to recognize the tremendous force of mass pressure in getting legislative results. No effective legislation for any social end that costs money will get passed until there is mass pressure behind it. It is the only force powerful enough to defeat the highly organized groups of employers in opposition. The working and professional people must begin to recognize this great potential force of mass pressure to have confidence in it, to see that only by coordinating this mass pressure and expending its energy in the direction of effective action will their objective be achieved.

Now, as to the auto industry in particular, as I come from an auto-manufacturing State, Michigan, the largest in the Union: In no industry in the country is unemployment insurance needed so badly as in the auto industry. Here unemployment is most destructive to a normal life. The continuous introduction of new machinery and increased speed-up in the auto plants narrows the opportunity for work for the auto workers. In Wayne County, in which Detroit is located, we are confronted with the glaring fact that while employment was at its peak in the 1934–35 production season, the number of unemployed on the welfare rolls was higher than at any time in the history of the city. The same is true in the city of Flint, the second largest auto center in the State.

Such a situation makes the need for unemployment insurance in Michigan greater than anywhere else in the country. The auto workers also suffer from the evils of seasonal and part-time work. Talk of increasing the number of working weeks per year is a fantasy, and such talk will not solve the needs of the automobile workers.

I wish here to quote from the press under date of February 9, the Detroit News, the following in regard to this question [reading] :

In the instance of Studebaker, the closing of the plant all last week was due to its policy of running at high capacity for the purpose of greater efficiency, which caused a lay off of a temporary nature. Shortage of bodies is reported to be responsible for Hupmobile's halt of its assembly lines.

I read this to indicate the cooperation the automobile manufacturers in the State can be expected to give to that spread the work as far as the automobile season is concerned. I wish to point out also that in the automobile industry in order to make profits there must be intensified speed-up, there must be short periods of employment. This is the nature of the industry itself because of the factor of competition which enters into the industry. In other words, when the industry is at its peak employers are making their largest profits. When production is at its lowest point that is when employers lose money, practically lose money in the automobile industry.

Unemployment insurance is needed, not only to take care of those workers who are permanently unemployed but it is needed also by those who work part time. The testimony given before the Henderson committee when it was in the auto centers showed that the average yearly wage of the automobile worker ranged from $300 to $500. Surely, you will admit that such a wage is inadequate and far below the needs for maintaining a family at a decent living standard.

The auto workers are revolting against this and are striving to increase their wages. But, even with what increase they can win, their total yearly wage will be below the $1,850 which the United States Department of Labor has set as a minimum yearly wage needed to maintain a family in the State of Michigan. The workers' unemployment-insurance bill, H. R. 2827, contains provisions which will supplement the meager earnings of the workers and give them this minimum wage which the United States Department of Labor says they must have.

The workers' unemployment-insurance bill, therefore, is a vital need for every employed worker as well as unemployed worker in the auto industry. The bill is also needed because of the numerous accidents which take place in the auto plants due to the hellish speed-up. The State compensation law is worded in such a way as to prevent payment for lost time in a majority of accidents, and even the payments allowed are inadequate to maintain a family during this trying period. The workers' unemployment-insurance bill which provides insurance against accidents is also a protection to the thousands of workers who are hurt in the auto plants.

H. R. 2827 would be of special aid to the thousands of women workers who are employed in the large auto plants. You gentlemen may have heard of a case where a young woman gave birth to a child while at work in the L. A. Young factory last year, being forced to work up to the last minute in order to get the few more dollars which she needed to keep her body and soul together. The workers' unemployment-insurance bill provides for maternity insurance and thereby fills a great need for the masses of women in the State who work for a living.

In conclusion, it is important to point out that the adoption by Congress of a system of unemployment and social insurance at this time cannot hope to do more than compensate for unemployment, old age, and so forth. It cannot constitute unemployment insurance, nor establish economic security. Security which would eliminate the ups and downs of business traceable to the anarchy of production under private ownership can be established only by the substitution of social economic planning for the ownership which by its results has tragically proven its inability to maintain security. However, it is possible that through the unifying of our forces in the process of security the adoption of a program of unemployment and social insurance a definite contribution will have been made to the well-being of the working people. Out of this experience and the developed united action will emerge the power for economic and political action to deal with the more fundamental problems which the enactment of the program would tend to clarify.

Mr. DUNN. The organizations you are representing here today are composed of Protestants, Catholics, Hebrews, and people of all nationalities?

Mr. KROON. Just about.

Mr. DUNN. Yes; and also Democrats and Republicans?

Mr. KROON. Yes.

Mr. DUNN. And other party affiliations?

Mr. KROON. Yes.

Mr. DUNN. Congressman Lundeen, do you have any questions?

Mr. LUNDEEN. You seem to believe in intelligent national planning?

Mr. KROON. Yes.

Mr. LUNDEEN. I am interested. Many people do not seem to know what you are talking about when you mention that, and I want to commend you for what you said about that.

Mr. DUNN. Any other questions?

Mr. LUNDEEN. That is all.

Mr. DUNN. I wish to thank you for your splendid address.

The next witness is Mr. J. E. McDonald.

STATEMENT OF J. E. McDONALD, CHAIRMAN OF THE NATIONAL COMMITTEE OF THE RAILROAD BROTHERHOODS, UNITY MOVEMENT, CHICAGO, ILL.

Mr. DUNN. Give your name, address, and the organization you represent to the reporter, if any.

Mr. McDONALD. My name is J. E. McDonald, chairman of the National Committee of the Railroad Brotherhoods, unity movement, room 309–11, 208 North Wells Street, Chicago, Ill.

I am a railroad worker, train dispatcher by occupation. I am a member of the American Train Dispatchers Association and also of the Order of Railroad Telegraphers.

As an introductory remark, permit me to state that the Railroad Brotherhoods unity movement, which I serve as chairman of the national committee, is an association for the purpose of uniting the members, lodges, and brotherhoods of the 21 recognized standard railroad labor unions into common action for the benefit of all. It is confined to members of those unions.

I speak in the interest of and shall try to express the viewpoint of that large army of railroad labor which is at present unemployed as a result of an unparalleled campaign for technical development and speed-up that has been carried out by the roads since 1926, and also those additional thousands who face unemployment in the near future as the roads push this campaign more ruthlessly than ever and undertake to tap new lay-off possibilities through mergers, consolidation of facilities, pooling of equipment, and so forth, of the properties heretofore operated separately by the different companies.

More than 500 railroad brotherhood lodges have directly or through their elected representatives already endorsed unemployment, old-age, and social insurance, specifically naming this bill, H. R. 2827 of the Seventy-fourth Congress or H. R. 7598 of the Seventy-third Congress. This includes the midwest and the western conferences of the Brotherhood of Locomotive Engineers.

Mr. DUNN. Did I understand you to say 500 brotherhoods.

Mr. McDONALD. More than 500 of our brotherhood lodges have directly or through their elected representatives already endorsed the unemployment, old-age, and social-insurance bill, specifically naming this bill, H. R. 2827 of the Seventy-fourth Congress.

Mr. LUNDEEN. Are those the lodges that support the paper Labor?

Mr. McDONALD. Yes, sir; those lodges are affiliated or a part of the international brotherhood for whom Labor is the official organ; yes.

Mr. LUNDEEN. This paper is a block from the House Office Building?

Mr. McDONALD. Yes, sir; these are the same.

Mr. LUNDEEN. And more than 500 of their organizations endorsed this bill?

Mr. McDONALD. Yes; and there is more yet in addition to that. This includes the midwest and the western conferences of the Brotherhood of the Locomotive Engineers.

Mr. LUNDEEN. Have you ever heard of an organization of laboring people, the American Federation of Labor, or anyone else, that ever endorsed the administration's bill?

Mr. McDONALD. No; I have not.

Mr. LUNDEEN. If you do, will you kindly send me a postcard. I would like to hear it.

Mr. McDONALD. I can state positively that none of the brotherhood organizations have endorsed that bill.

Mr. LUNDEEN. I have asked a number of labor representatives here to advise me, but I am still waiting for the first postcard.

Mr. McDONALD. I have here a list of those lodges that I will be glad to file, if the committee so desires it.

Mr. DUNN. Is there any objection, Mr. Lundeen?

Mr. LUNDEEN. I would be delighted to have them in the record.

Mr. DUNN. I have no objection.

Mr. LUNDEEN. About how many thousand in numbers, do you think that covers?

Mr. McDONALD. Upward to 100,000.

Mr. LUNDEEN. One hundred thousand in those organizations that endorsed the bill?

Mr. McDONALD. Yes, sir.

Mr. DUNN. We are glad to have that in the record.

Mr. LUNDEEN. Send that to the White House.

(The list referred to is as follows:)

Local 611, W. M. Toole, 619 East Newton Avenue, Eldon, Mo.; local 578, B. B. Erdson, box 316, Sapulpa, Okla.; local 151, H. C. Seeber, 1101 South Tenth Street, Burlington, Iowa; local 860, John Lehe, 1531 Second Street, Boone, Iowa; local 159, O. E. Cress, 1905 Park Avenue SE., Cedar Rapids, Iowa; local 677, John Harwood, box 38, Hopper, Minn.; local 88, H. N. Getty, 317 West Fifth Street, North Platte, Nebr.; Local 98, F. R. Rider, Orlo Apartments, B–3, Lincoln, Nebr.; local 344, J. C. Landreth, 1010 East Eighth Street, Wellington, Kans.; local 364, G. E. Bloyer, 1744 Fairview Avenue, Wichita, Kans.; local 462, Lloyd P. Duncan, 410 East Madison, Arkansas City, Kans.; local 164, O. F. Dale, 119 North Fourteenth Street, Atchison, Kans.; local 141, Tom E. McMahon, 202 East Williams Street, Ellis, Kans.; local 349, H. J. Schreer, 1079 De Sota Street, St. Paul, Minn.; local 146, Roy Graft, 701 North E Street, Ottumwa, Iowa; local 150, A. N. Baldwin, 3424 Forty-sixth Street, Minneapolis, Minn.; local 144, D. R. Bryson, 421 Seventh Street SW., Staples, Minn.; local 413, Chas. M. Hudson, 335 Nineteenth and One-half Avenue N., St. Cloud, Minn.; local 474, C. A. Green, 3919 Aldrich Avenue N., St. Paul, Minn.; local 768, J. W. Anderson, 1209 La Bee Avenue N., Route No. 2, Three River Falls, Minn.; local 802, Otto Morhen, 507 Lincoln Avenue, Bemidji, Minn.; local 180, J. R Tatam, 3041 James Avenue, Minneapolis, Minn.; local 357, O. G. Oeltjendier, 3043 Thirty-second Avenue, Minneapolis, Minn.; local 625, A. G. Stewart, 1825 Taylor Street NE., Minneapolis, Minn.; local 559, Allen Clausson, 68 East Third Street, Proctor, Minn.; local 494, Ira N. Morrill, 2509 Pierce Street NE., Minneapolis, Minn.; local 9, Fred Wolcott, Waseca, Minn.; local 102, Fred B. Higbee, 311 West Oakland Avenue, Austin, Minn

Local 202, O. C. Thompson, Dilworth, Minn.; local 356, James W. Wilson, 304 North Seventh Street, Breckinridge, Minn.; local 614, Gus Moks, 619 East Lincoln Street, Austin, Minn.; local 395, V. E. Seashore, 1925 West Third Street, Duluth, Minn.; local 470, F. R. Thomas, 407 North Third Street., East Grand Forks, Minn., local 570, John M. Luth, 16 East Oak Street, Gnelwood, Minn.; local 114, Wm. H. Boylar, 525 Logan Avenue, Waterloo, Iowa; local 82, C. R. Bishop, 510 Virginia Street, Sioux City, Iowa; local 601, Amos Kirby, 601 South Cecilia Street, Sioux City, Iowa; local 555, John Donie, 1812 Summit Street, Sioux City, Iowa; local 687, R. Campbell, 2759 Court Street, Sioux City, Iowa; local 670, C. L. Clark, 120 Second Avenue NW., Oelwein, Iowa; local 313, W. S. Haslean, 521 North Sixth Street, Montevido, Minn.; local 130, A. L. Burrell, 513 Neosho Street, Emporia, Kans.; local 369, George Lowe, 993 Payne Avenue, St. Paul, Minn.; local 420, A. T. Betzler, 602 Eighth Avenue, Two Harbors, Minn.; local 214, J. W Henamen, 415 South Highland, Cleonute, Kans.; local 675, Jay Rose, 308 South Fourth Street, Council Grove, Kans.; local 333, H. M. Brown, 571 State Street, St. Paul, Minn.; local 549, L. H. Wetherby, 603 East Third Street, Willmar, Minn.; local 912, Carl Leigh, 3147 South Fourteenth Avenue, Minneapolis, Minn.; local 504, J. E. Peterson, 924 Second Avenue NW., Great Falls, Mont.; Local 392, W. R. White, 1405 Fifth Street, Havre, Mont.; local 870, B. C. Proctor, box 51, Lema, Mont.; local 232, William Dean, 414 South Yellowstone Avenue, Livingston, Mont.; local 835, A. W. Cooper, General Delivery, Mineola, Tex.; local 219, A. L. Smith, 708 East Burleson Street, Marshall, Tex.; local 620, P. E. Druer, Mart, Tex.; local 834, George E. Davis, 2301 Ashland Avenue, Fort Worth, Tex.; local 194, William Milton, 922 North Sycamore Street, Palestine, Tex.; local 789, A. H. Stejer, 523 West Avenue D, San Angelo, Tex.; local 197, N. G. Leap, 523 Mason Street, San Antonio, Tex.; local 736, H. E. Bradley, 1316 Sixteenth Street, Wichita Falls, Tex.

Local 835, R. F. Shields, 1804 Collins Street, Wichita Falls, Tex.; local 500, Paul Kinbro, 610 North Main Street, Cleburne, Tex.; local 530, L. C. Fain, 1614 Bois d'Arc Street, Commerce Tex.; local 592, H. V. Payne, 414 Conlon Street, Dalhart, Tex.; local 566, Thomas Kent, Del Rio, Tex.; local 725, R. N. Hill, box 414, De Leon, Tex.; local 568, R. M. Doak, 118 East Hull Street, Dennison, Tex.; local 591, Frank Meyers, 610 North Stanton Street, El Paso, Tex.; local 573, B. F. Smith, 2215 King Street, Greenville, Tex.; local 139, H. N. Wilder, 1904 Decatur Avenue, Houston, Tex.; local 366, T. Kreft, route, box 394, Houston, Tex.; local 680, C. K. Dobbins, 221 Devereux Street, Jacksonville, Tex.; local 731, F. R. Kirk, box 785, Kingsville, Tex.; local 438, John Maher, 601

Market Street, Laredo, Tex.; local 487, O. E. Runnels, 901 North First Street, Lufkin, Tex.; local 523, J. L. Ainsworth, 1120 South Hoff Street, El Reno, Okla.; local 630, Edward Earley, 314 North Monroe Street, Enid, Okla.; local 763, R. P. Peter, Fairview, Okla.; local 539, George H. Green, box 278, Haileyville, Okla.; local 569, T. R. Olliver, Burns Hall, Heavener, Okla.; local 638, A. E. Hood, 603 North Second Street, Hugo, Okla.; local 711, W. E. Lamson, 710 South Third Street, Muskogee, Okla.; local 853, H. Russel, box 44, route 2, Muskogee, Okla.; local 721, G. A. Walker, 1628 Fourteenth Street NW., Oklahoma City, Okla.; local 879, D. B. Ambrose, 312 East Franklin Street, Clinton, Mo.

B. J. Buhl, secretary, Harmon-on-the-Hudson. N. Y. Meets at 110 East One Hundred and Twenty-fifth Street, New York City.

BROTHERHOOD OF RAILWAY CONDUCTORS

Local 52, Charles F. Carley, 6 Brooklyn Street, Port Jervis, N. Y. (61 members); local 266, J. B. Bougher, 4429 Iybr, Sioux City, Iowa (106 members); local 13, H. Harvey, 618 East Water Street, Princeton, Ind. (155 members); local 611, Thomas G. Penington, 362 Woodrow Avenue, Columbus, Ohio (104 members); local 618, Providence, R. I.; local 235, Milwaukee, Wis.; local 815, Philadelphia, Pa.; local 227, Chicago, Ill.; local 1085, New York City, N. Y.; local 823, New York City, N. Y.; local 815, Liberty Bell Lodge; local 1, Oak Park, Ill.; local 69, El Paso, Tex.; local 698, Chicago, Ill.; local 431, Joseph M. Janowitz, 900 South Madison Avenue, Bay City, Mich. (43 members); local 1054, H. E. Gerhold, 1932–6 Gallegher, Detroit, Mich. (53 members); local 641, J. D. Morash, 824 Ontario Street, Port Huron, Mich. (390 members); local 210, B. W. Tabor, 13256 Baltimore Avenue, Chicago, Ill. (350 members); local 56, F. H. Giddings, 1726 Main Street, Atchison, Kans. (7 members); local 2031, W. H. Radochley, 3101 Jackson Street, Sioux City, Iowa (74 members).

BROTHERHOOD OF RAILROAD TRAINMEN

Local 191, W. A. Gardner, Milwaukee, Wis.

BROTHERHOOD OF LOCOMOTIVE FIREMEN AND ENGINEMEN

Thomas Bradley, 17841 Grovewood Avenue, Cleveland, Ohio, belongs to local 183; local 579, Montevideo, Minn.; local 13, Jersey City, N. J.; local 183, Cleveland, Ohio; local 1, Port Jervis, N. Y..
Arthur S. Lee, 32 Elm Place, Glenbrook, Conn. (contact).

BROTHERHOOD OF MAINTENANCE-OF-WAY EMPLOYEES

Local 1855, Joseph Klinkiewitz, 32 Broadway, Jersey City, N. J.; local 1077, New York City, N. Y.; New York City division, local 1048, Sixty-fourth Street, Brooklyn, N. Y.

UNITED BROTHERHOOD OF MAINTENANCE-OF-WAY EMPLOYEES

J. F. Fisher, 1001 Whitcher Avenue, Sioux City, Iowa (80 members).

SLEEPING-CAR CONDUCTORS

Local 15, room 811 Capitol Building, Chicago, Ill. Secretary's name not given.

SWITCHMEN'S UNION OF NORTH AMERICA

Local 240, R. N. Martin, 505 West Second Street, Liberal, Kans. (22 members); local 291, H. C. Small, 2700 Clark Street, Paducah, Ky. (12 members).

INTERNATIONAL ASSOCIATION OF MACHINISTS

Local 79, R. E. Squire, 107 Labor Temple, Sixth Avenue and University Street, Seattle, Wash. (250 members); local 64, J. E. Sullivan, 28 Barnaby Street, Fall River, Mass., district lodge for Massachusetts and Rhode Island; local 439, C. Nuly, 4289 East One Hundred and Thirty-seventh Street, Cleveland, Ohio (36 members); local 119, 5 Channing Place, Newport, R. I. (912 members); local 86, Thom. Goddard, Spokane, Wash.; local 459, Arthur Schultz, 1034 Edmund

Street, St. Paul, Minn. (165 members); local 417, Felix Hall, Staten Island, N. Y.; local 226, President Rogers, 110 East One Hundred and Twenty-fifth Street, New York City, N. Y.; local 402, 243 East Eighty-fourth Street, New York City, N. Y.; local 390, Henry W. Higge, 314 Knight Avenue, Park Ridge, Ill. (400 members). Meets at 3257 Sheffield Avenue, Chicago, Ill.; local 915, 4122 West Lake Street, Chicago, Ill.; local 83, 113 South Ashland Boulevard, Chicago, Ill.; local 178, Allen Holloway, 2315 East Tenth Street, Sioux City, Iowa (20 members); local 1122, A. Rumpf, room 1, 4864 Woodward Avenue, Detroit, Mich. (53 members); 68, William F. Hennebury, 1744 Sanchey Street, San Francisco, Calif. (1,375 members); local 337, Henry Reichelt, 1630 North Harding Avenue, Chicago, Ill. Meets at 1638 North Halsted Street; local 84, meets at 2619 South Lawndale Avenue, Chicago, Ill.; Louis Tomsovic, secretary, 1505 South Grove Street, Chicago, Ill. (175 members); local 68, San Francisco, Calif.; local 83, Chicago, Ill.; local 234, Milwaukee, Wis. (on Chicago, Milwaukee & St. Paul R. R.); also women's auxiliary; local 390, Park Ridge, Ill.; local 337, Chicago, Ill.; local 84, Berwyn, Ill.; local 404, Baltimore, Md.; local 178, Sioux City, Iowa; local 57, Huntington, W. Va.; local 1122, Detroit, Mich.; local 459, St. Paul, Minn.; local 816, Hoboken, N. J.; local 417, Staten Island, N. Y.; local 402, New York City, N. Y.; local 203, Akron, Ohio; local 404, Youngstown, Ohio; local 729, Cincinnati, Ohio; local 162, Cincinnati, Ohio; local 110, Newport, R. I.; local 226, New York City, N. Y.; local 491, Hazelwood, Pa.; local 52, Pittsburgh, Pa.

Also convention of all machinists of New England held at Boston, Mass.

RAILROAD MACHINISTS' HELPERS

Local 915, Chicago, Ill.

Mr. McDONALD. In addition to this, the principles contained in this bill and not contained in any other have been endorsed by many other of the brotherhood lodges and by the national convention of the Brotherhood of Locomotive Engineers.

Mr. DUNN. At a national convention?

Mr. McDONALD. At a national convention, without specifically naming the bill by number, they endorsed the principles contained therein.

Mr. DUNN. In the Lundeen bill?

Mr. McDONALD. The principles of the Lundeen bill; yes, sir.

Mr. DUNN. And when did they endorse it?

Mr. McDONALD. Last July.

Mr. DUNN. July. That is what date?

Mr. McDONALD. In 1934.

Mr. DUNN. What date in July, do you remember?

Mr. McDONALD. I do not know just exactly the date of the convention itself, as it was several weeks in length; I do not know the date.

Mr. LUNDEEN. I would like to discover your thought in regard to the bill along this line. The administration's bill does not take any account of the unemployed of today, probably around 15 million, it takes no account of them, but it is going to supply unemployment insurance for the ranks in the future out of the ranks now unemployed, and at small rates. I want you to get my point. There is one bill which is inadequate, as William Green himself says in a statement published in Labor recently, a very inadequate bill. Then here come utopian bills that are impossible of performance, many of them. Does not this bill that we are considering now go right down the main street of possibility and is it not one that can be enacted into law and made to operate, and one which embodies common sense?

Mr. McDonald. I believe that the Lundeen bill is the only solution of unemployment as applied to railroad labor, and I believe that the Wagner-Lewis bill is really preposterous, as I hope to show in this report here, as applied to the railroad industry.

Mr. Lundeen. My point is, does not this occupy the middle ground between the extreme misery on the one side and utopia on the other side that is impossible of achievement?

Mr. McDonald. Yes.

Mr. Lundeen. It takes the middle road?

Mr. McDonald. I would not say it was taking a middle road. I believe it is taking the only course that offers security to the unemployed.

Mr. Lundeen. Then put it that way.

Mr. Dunn. I would say, Congressman Lundeen, it is taking the main road, and the road that should be taken.

Mr. Lundeen. Very well. That is well stated.

Mr. McDonald. Associations of the lodges and members of the 21 railroad unions have been established around this and other issues of common interest to rail employees and new associations are springing up every day. Associations of this kind that have already endorsed H. R. 2827 are located in Chicago, Ill., Bloomington, Ill., Gary and Evansville, Ind., Eldon and Kansas City, Mo., and Seattle, Wash. There is a growing sentiment among organized railroad workers for demanding enactment of H. R. 2827.

The attitude prevails among the leaders of our 21 organizations that unemployment of railroad workers will be solved by a retirement pension system and the adoption of a 6-hour day without reduction in pay. Certain measures intended to partially control speed-up have also been proposed.

Certainly if rail workers would get in behind these measures with the vigor and in the same manner that they went after the 8-hour-day law and force their immediate adoption these measures would go a long way toward stopping layoffs now taking place at the rate of about 20,000 per month.

Mr. Dunn. Pardon the interruption. Can you in any way contact these various organizations that you are respresenting here today to help us Congressmen who want to see this bill enacted into law at this session of Congress?

Mr. McDonald. Through our unity committees we have groups in 118 railroad centers, and we are, since Congress convened and these hearings began, bringing this matter especially to the attention of our groups, and each day we are receiving information of new lodges that passed the bill. Generally these lodges when they pass the bill send copies of their resolution to the President, their Senators, and to Congress, and all down the line.

You can rest assured that Congressmen from all the districts wherein these lodges are located have heard or are hearing from their constituents.

Mr. McDonald. They have written in specifying they want it in general at the expense of the employers and in general not specifying the number of the bills but just outlining the features of them. This would especially be true if the control of speed-up should be extended to all departments. Partial control has been proposed for train and engine road service in the form of full crews and limitation of train length.

Although there is a decided movement developing among the rank and file to lift the campaign for adoption of the measures mentioned out of the agitational and propaganda stage where leaders appear determined to hold them, there are many obstacles to be overcome before this is accomplished. Immediate realization is uncertain and even if adopted at once would not solve the problem for the hundreds of thousands already idle, the thousands being dropped daily under present conditions, and those additional thousands slated for dismissal through consolidations as I shall show.

The average number of employees for roads having annual operating revenues above $1,000,000 as compiled by the I. C. C. for 1926 was 1,779,275. In 1929 this number had been reduced to 1,487,839, although the total net ton-miles reported were 3½ billion greater than in 1926. Nearly 300,000 less employees produced 3½ billion more ton-miles. This shows the inroads made upon railroad labor through technical and speed-up means even before the economic collapse.

This process was very greatly accelerated after 1929, and in May 1933 the low point of 932,000 was reached; more than 850,000 less than the peak month of 1926.

From 1929 on layoffs, through technical and speed-up measures, are combined with reduction in forces due to loss of business and are difficult to separate, but studies conducted by the Department of Labor reveal that productivity of the basic groups has increased by 121 percent, while hours have been reduced 51 percent. For example, with the same number of workers employed in 1934 as in 1932 the roads were able to handle a 9.2-percent increase in car loadings.

Numerous examples could be given of the measures taken to reduce this great army of men to the status of objects of charity. I shall mention only a few.

Since 1922 average freight-train speed has been increased by 41 percent, locomotive tractive power by 40 percent, with corresponding increases in trainload, while fuel consumption has been reduced by 26 percent in freight and 15 percent in passenger service. Along with this the production tasks of employees have been greatly increased. Men are cut off and their duties assigned to other employees, one employee being required to perform the work previously done by two or three. Service to the public has been curtailed. Manual block systems and even automatic block systems have been abolished.

Dispatching territories, track-maintenance sections have been doubled and tripled, piecework forms of production placed on tasks in repair departments, and employees generally speeded up to the limit of human endurance. Highest authorities state that one of the new light-weight, high-speed, stream-lined trains can replace two steam trains. This gives us a glimpse into future possibilities of railroad employment.

This great exploitation of labor and technical development has not resulted in higher earnings for those remaining in the service; on the contrary, their earnings have been greatly reduced through elimination of overtime, demotions, reclassification, as, for instance, mechanics being required to perform the same duties at helper's rates, station agents reduced to the status of caretakers, and so forth, and through a wage deduction. Twenty percent of rail workers now employed earn less than $600 per year each and all classes, excluding only executives, earn less than $100 per month.

Mr. Lundeen. When you mention " executives ", what about the salaries of executives?

Mr. McDonald. They are excluded from these figures, which give the average earnings of railroad employees. These figures, however, include all officers except executives, meaning general managers and superintendents and higher-paid staff officers.

Mr. Lundeen. It would be very instructive to have those huge executive salaries listed here.

Mr. McDonald. Yes.

Mr. Lundeen. But you do not have them, do you?

Mr. McDonald. No; I do not have those average salaries. They run all the way from $25,000 to $125,000 a year.

Mr. Lundeen. Do you believe that any man in the United States in this panic, in all this misery and destitution and poverty should receive a salary higher than that of the President of the United States?

Mr. McDonald. No; I do not, and especially, I think, it is interesting to note that those roads which were placed in the hands of receivers, the receivers appointed, usually, too, receiver higher salaries than the single president received before their bankruptcy. For instance, the president of the Seaboard Air Line, before it went into receivership, received $40,000 a year. After the receivership two receivers were appointed who received $50,000 a year each.

Mr. Lundeen. Mr. Chairman, don't you think that we, the Government of the United States, the Congress and the Senate and the President ought to take up the proposition of these enormous, huge, swollen salaries that are paid to executives, some of whom work an hour or two a day and play golf the rest of the time, and if they would pass out of existence the vice president would run the company better than they, and the folks would not even know they were gone?

Mr. Dunn. I agree with you.

Mr. McDonald. And those are just the fellows who cut these section men down to 35 cents an hour and less and expect them to live on 2 and 4 days' work per week at that earnings. Twenty percent of rail workers now employed earn less than $600 a year.

I took that statement from the Coordinator of Railroads, Mr. Eastman, who in his report gives that figure.

Mr. McDonald. He was not making it, however, to prove the need for House bill 2827 but to establish some other points rather contrary to that.

Mr. Dunn. But in my opinion the fact that that statement has been made convinces me, and ought to convince everybody else of average intelligence, that this bill which is now being discussed before the committee, the Lundeen bill, H. R. 2827, should immediately go into operation.

Mr. McDonald. Yes.

Mr. Lundeen. Now, you are speaking for conductors, engineers, and firemen?

Mr. McDonald. Yes, sir; all classes of organized labor who have endorsed specifically the principle of the workers' unemployment-insurance bill.

Mr. Lundeen. Does it include railway-maintenance and shop workers?

Mr. McDonald. Yes, sir; all of the 21 craft unions.

You perhaps know that the executives of these unions have not committed themselves to any form of insurance, either the Wagner-Lewis bill, or the Lundeen bill. They have, as I stated here, taken the attitude and instructed and advised members and lodges who have written to them for advice that the problem could be solved, and ought to be solved, through the shorter workday, for which they have proposed legislation.

Mr. Lundeen. There is nothing to prevent both remedies, is there?

Mr. McDonald. No. I think like I pointed out there that as to those measures if the railroad workers get in behind them without fail and they endorse them in the same way that they did the 8-hour bill, that that is the only chance in my opinion that they have to secure them, by similar action, and that it would go a long ways toward alleviating, but would not still solve the problem. Nor has the saving effected gone to provide lower freight rates to lower the cost of living. During 1932 the roads secured an increase in rates on heavy commodities. Freight rates are 37 percent above the pre-war average. Who, then, received the benefits of these huge savings, this fierce exploitation, and these rate increases?

From 1926 to 1933, inclusive, the roads paid out in the form of interest and dividends $8,357,377,000 in direct payments and $103,-000,000 in the form of stock dividends, mostly noncarrier securities.

From the Government they have received cancelation of the $400,-000,000 debt accrued under the recapture clause, the setting aside of the antitrust laws, and loans of upward of a half billion dollars. These Federal Government grants are being used to further reduce labor; through mergers and the purchase of more efficient equipment.

Spreading the work plans under which those who still hold jobs are compelled to divide up their work with others have been introduced in all departments.

Trackmen and mechanical department employees have been reduced to from 2 to 5 days' work per week. A number of roads required employees to donate days of work without pay. Many earned less than the unemployed received at relief stations. Limits have been placed upon the mileage run per month by train and engine men and yard crews have been limited to a maximum number of hours per month.

Basic wage rates were established in times of generally complete employment and on the assumption that they would be supplemented by overtime, by commissions, or by additional minimum days being worked within the calendar month and since these sources of income have been wiped out a general lowering of living standards has resulted which has been greatly aggravated by compelling the man who has a job to divide up with the man who has none.

In addition to the great number of railroad workers at present unemployed it is well known that the roads are about to tap new lay-off possibilities.

I refer to the consolidation of facilities and pooling of equipment plans advanced first through Mr. Prince and later through Coordinator of Railroads, Mr. Eastman.

To use the words of Mr. Eastman, these economies will be largely at the expense of labor. Additional thousands of railroad jobs will be abolished when these mergers get under way.

To expect railroad workers to remain passive under these circumstances indicates an ignorance of the traditions of these men.

Perhaps Mr. Eastman sensed this spirit when, in addressing the conference of general chairmen in Chicago on January 12, he said:

It has often seemed to me that while the leaders are in the front rank, they do not always lead, but at times are driven; they are dealing with elemental forces which now and then get out of hand. On such occasions it may be possible to stay in front but not to lead.

As may be expected the economy drive of the roads has resulted in a sharp increase in the number of accidents.

Railroad workers are excluded from the protection of the workmen's compensation laws of all States and remain the one large industrial group having no protection under compensation laws.

Such hospitalization facilities as exist for railroad workers are maintained by deductions from their own pay. They have no voice in the management of this service and the rates are fixed and the funds are handled by the roads. Millions of these funds have been lost through unsound investment or speculation.

To sum up: The rank and file of railroad labor demand a form of unemployment, old-age, and social insurance that will place the responsibility for giving each and every worker either a job or direct relief, exactly where it belongs—upon those who own and operate industry and who reap the profits therefrom.

They demand a law that will become operative immediately to provide for those hundreds of thousands already out and those who will be dismissed in the months to come.

They demand a law that will remove the burden of caring for the unemployed from those who remain in service and that will retain the accustomed living standards.

They demand a law that will assure wages during time of sickness or in case of accident.

Only the enactment of H. R. 2827 into law will solve the problem of unemployment and social insurance for railroad workers.

We know that substitute bills are being offered for H. R. 2827, but there is no substitute for food to an empty stomach.

Mr. DUNN. Have you concluded, Mr. McDonald?

Mr. McDONALD. Yes, sir.

Mr. DUNN. The only substitute that I know of for empty stomachs is to die; then there will be no more pain. Of course, that all depends on where you are going when you leave this world.

Mr. McDONALD. I do not think the workmen class are ready to fold up and die.

Now, I have a more comprehensive statement here that deals with the whole railroad problem, the problem of unemployment, and the problem of the railroad unions, and so on. It explains the move for unity among the brotherhoods, and so on.

Mr. LUNDEEN. It deals with unemployment insurance, too, doesn't it?

Mr. McDonald. Yes, sir. And you can see that the question of unemployment is the major and most burning issue of the railroad workers at this time.

Mr. Lundeen. Is this your own document?

Mr. McDonald. Yes, sir. There was a brother that was supposed to come with me today. I happened to come alone. I have a telegram from him saying that he had to go to the Missouri Legislature. He is of the B. of L. E., the Brotherhood of Locomotive Engineers, and they more than any other group have been active for the Lundeen bill.

Mr. Lundeen. Do you think it should be in the record?

Mr. McDonald. I think it should be, in view of this fact, that the railroad organization employees have not come to any understanding as to the position they should take one way or the other in unemployment insurance, and therefore it is not likely that there will be any other representatives from the railroad industry appear before either committee, except myself, and in order that it clear up the entire situation I think you should know what it contains.

Mr. Lundeen. And your first statement here today will not duplicate this, but the two should go together?

Mr. McDonald. No; but it rather more or less supplements it. It is rather along the same general line, except that it goes into details, you understand, and all of the figures that you will find in here are taken from the Interstate Commerce Commission report, and statistics, and so on.

Mr. Lundeen. I have no objection to it.

Mr. Dunn. All right. I have no objection.

Mr. McDonald. This is as to the revolt in the railroad unions, as to the railroad brotherhoods' unity movement; the history of railroad unionism is filled with instances where union officials have surrendered the interests of the membership to those of the railroad bankers, but one would have to look far to find anything rivalling the wage cut of 1932.

After months of informal conferences, laying the basis for a 10-percent cut, official negotiations began at the Palmer House in Chicago, January 15. In 2 weeks the roads had everything they wanted. At one stroke of the pen the railroad labor executives, with the approval of their 1,500 general chairmen, gave away $200,000,000 in railroad workers' wages and prepared the ground to continue this cut for 3 years. All the demands of the men were refused—the 6-hour day; stabilization of employment; limitation of train lengths; protection of the interests of those laid off.

When the men began to take stock of their shrunken pay envelops, a wave of resentment swept the lodges. For the most part protests were stifled. But in the Bensenville yards of the Chicago, Milwaukee & St. Paul Railroad in Chicago a number of workers got together to discuss some method of uniting the rank and file to prevent a repetition of such sell-outs. This was how the railroad brotherhoods' unity movement started.

This is not a new union. Realizing that most of their trade journals would be closed to their opinions, and handicapped because the movement lacked influence outside its immediate circle, the men decided to raise enough money to issue their own paper. The first number appeared in March 1932 under the name "The Chisler." This was changed to R. R. Unity News.

Those responsible for the development of the unity movement were not led astray by the lure for a new union. They had learned that to attempt to abolish craft unionism, clean out reactionary leaders, or change their servile policies by uniting railroad labor outside the standard unions was incorrect. Many of them had been members of the American Railway Union under Debs. They had seen the most advanced section of railroad labor, 150,000 strong, walk out of the unions, leaving the bulk of the membership under the influence of reactionary officials. They now understood that such a policy isolates the more progressive workers from the majority, and so defeats their own cause.

In the switchmen's strike of 1920 they had seen the strike outlawed by the grand lodge, brother members used as strike breakers under the direction of union officials, and members of other lodges kept from joining the strike. At that time there was no rallying center to unite the men against their strike-breaking officials.

The shopmen's strike of 1922 exposed even more clearly how the grand lodge played one craft against another, prevented united action, and so brought about the defeat of the strike.

It showed that the union officials would call a strike if and when they could no longer hold back the membership, but that they would do this only to maintain their leadership, weaken the struggle, and sacrifice the interests of the men to those in the lodges to guarantee against treachery from within as well as for a movement to unite and give leadership to such groups.

The Railroad Brotherhoods' unity movement grew out of that need. It helped break down the barriers of craft unionism by giving members an opportunity of meeting, discussing, and fighting together against the attacks of the roads and the misleadership of reactionary union officials.

Those who took the lead in forming the policies of the unity movement understood that mere physical amalgamation of the 21 railroad unions would not of itself solve the problem. As one worker put it:

A leader like Al Whitney, of the trainmen, or Al Johnston, of the engineers, as head of one amalgamated railroad union could do even more harm than as head of only one of our craft unions.

They felt that it was better to work for united action on the basis of issues which the men were demanding: The restoration of the 1931 wage scale, the 6-hour day, adequate retirement pensions, a minimum wage, and relief for the unemployed. At the same time, they knew they must clean house and establish rank-and-file control within their own unions.

By March 1933, 1 year after the first issue of the Chisler was off the press, a conference of 22 delegates from unity-movement groups was held in Chicago to take stock of policies and make plans for carrying the work forward on a wider scale.

Engineers, firemen, trainmen, machinists, electricians, boilermakers, and maintenance men were present. There were also two Negro delegates, a Pullman porter and a dining-car cook.

A national committee was elected. It was decided to rally the workers to fight for the return of the 10-percent cut, oppose the pending coordinator bill, and support movements for retirement pensions, unemployment insurance, and the 6-hour day. At the same time, emphasis was placed on union action to redress grievances without waiting for endless boards and committees of adjustment and mediation.

The conference discussed finances, not to pay high salaries but to ensure regular publication of R. R. Unity News and to assist local groups in their struggles.

By January 1935 the paper was circulating in 118 cities and 34 States. Unity committees were functioning in many lodges and in most of the important railroad centers. The Railroad Brotherhoods Unity Movement had become a factor in all major issues affecting railroad labor.

As to the railroad unions' organized strength, railroad labor during the past decade was potentially the best organized and without doubt the most strategic section of the American working class. Yet the railroad labor executives have led their members from one defeat to another.

There are today (Jan. 1935) over 400,000 members of the 21 standard railway unions. This is in spite of withdrawals due to unemployment, inability to pay high dues and assessments (because of wage cuts and part-time work), and a general disgust with the failure of the union leaders to protect the interests of the members.

The membership of the four transportation brotherhoods (engineers, firemen, trainmen, and conductors), even after a loss of 33 percent between 1931 and 1933, still totals a quarter of a million. These unions hold agreements on every class I road in the country. They are in a position to immediately tie up the entire transportation system. To a lesser extent the other 17 craft unions, some independent of the American Federation of Labor, others affiliated to it, have agreements with most of the roads.

Even the 50 open-shop systems have been forced to recognize one or more of the standard unions in addition to the transportation brotherhoods. Despite terror and intimidation, 200,000 railroad workers have in the past 2 years rejected the company unions and joined the standard union of their craft. Where the standard unions have failed to profit by this wave of organization, it is not because the workers do not want to rid themselves of the company unions. It is because they have no faith in those leaders who so shamefully betrayed them in 1920 and 1922 and whose weak organizational campaigns are based on dues collections and initiation fees rather than on the grievances which are agitating the men.

Over three-quarters of a million workers went on strike in the first 10 months of the Roosevelt administration. Of this number close to half a million won wage increases and an additional 70,000 gained other substantial concessions. Railroad labor, through abandonment of strike action, received a wage-cut extension of some $200,000,000, followed by further extensions up to April 1, 1935.

During the past few years workers in two important industries, Federal employees and longshoremen, not yet covered by compensation, succeeded in getting through Congress Federal compensation laws for accidents and occupational diseases fully financed by the employers. Railway workers remain the only body of organized workers excluded from workmen's compensation. And railway accidents are increasing to an alarming extent.

Longshoremen on the West coast, members of the International Longshoremen's Association, as a result of a heroic strike, supported by other organized trades, particularly in the general strike in San Francisco, won within a few months the 6-hour day, together with a net wage increase. The railroad unions, who made history for the 8-hour day when they forced Congress to pass the Adamson Act through strike preparations, have now abandoned this method and rely on legislative persuasion to win the 6-hour day.

A relatively unimportant group of workers, the furriers section of the Needle Trades Workers Industrial Union, with not nearly the organized strength or power of one of the transportation brotherhoods, have gotten their employers to completely finance a system of unemployment insurance for the men laid off, with a committee of union members in control of the fund.

In the railroad industry, 800,000 men are out of work while the union leaders stand supine before a Federal Coordinator whose job is to throw more thousands of railroad workers on the street and who has the effrontery to call these workers "pawns in a game of chess to be sacrificed" for the good of the industry. The railway labor executives are taking no steps to unite the lodges to prevent this dismemberment of the ranks of railroad labor. They obstruct the national campaign carried on by the workers of the country for a Federal unemployment insurance bill financed by the Government and the employers, although such a bill has been introduced in the Seventy-third and Seventy-fourth Congresses and has the support of hundreds of railroad lodges; they take no part in winning immediate assistance for the men laid off from the roads and local relief bureaus. In spite of speeches rejecting the proposals of Mr. Eastman for unrestricted lay-offs to "save the roads", they are actually sanctioning these lay-offs by accepting a "dismissal wage" for those deprived of their jobs. An agreement was made between the brotherhoods and the Baltimore & Ohio, Pittsburgh & Lake Erie case, and with the Staten Island Railroad in the transfer of their traffic to the Jersey Central January 1935.

Of the entire set of counterdemands put forward by the labor executives in return for the 10-percent cut in 1932—6-hour day, unemployment relief and stabilization, Federal bond issue for grade-crossing elimination, protection of employee interests in railroad consolidations, Federal legislation to provide retirement insurance and elective workmen's compensation, coordination between train crews and train lengths—only one accomplishment in favor of the men can be recorded. This is the passage of the Railroad Retirement Act in the Seventy-third Congress.

Yet the pressure which forced the passage of this measure came from outside the standard unions in an organization of rank and filers called the "Railroad Employees' National Pension Association." The brotherhoods first opposed any retirement-pension bill and so notified legislators. When mass pressure reached a point where adoption of some retirement pension seemed certain, the labor executives came with a counter bill much more favorable to the railroad interests.

The Retirement Pension Act, as finally passed, is far from adequate. It is based on a system of employee contributions, a dangerous feature which the employers and the Government have already embodied in other proposed " security " legislation; and there is every reason to believe that unless a much more aggressive fight is carried on to save the pension the roads will amend the act reducing even the meager benefits which have so far been salvaged.

The question is, Who is to blame? Some railroad workers place the blame for what has taken place on individual grand-lodge officials. They feel that if these leaders were replaced things would be all right. They overlook the fact that the disease which has the railroad unions in its grip runs right through the grand-lodge apparatus and centers around policies, not individuals.

Other brothers feel that if the unions would liquidate their banking ventures all other problems would be solved. They forget that most of the organizations have no banking ventures and are no better off than the unions that have them. They lose sight of the fact that while Brotherhood of Locomotive Engineers members lost $17,000,-000 through their financial investments, these very members lost close to $50,000,000 in wage cuts in the past 2½ years—three times the amount of their banking losses.

It would take volumes to record the numerous weaknesses and misdeeds of the railroad union leaders, but the great majority of them spring from one source—the basic distortion of the role of trade-unionism—the theory that the interests of workers and employers are identical, or, as W. W. Atterbury, president of the open-shop Pennsylvania Railroad expressed it, "We are all one happy family."

A brief review of the past 10 years will prove that it was the policy of union-management cooperation which brought about the present deplorable condition of railroad labor and made the most powerful unions in the country the most ineffective.

Let us consider before and after the Railway Labor Act. From 1914 to 1921 railway labor unions grew in number and strength. By the end of the World War nearly all the 1,800,000 workers in the industry were organized. Machinery for united action of the 21 crafts was being forged through federations on a terminal system and national basis. The workers were learning how to consolidate and use their organized power.

In 1917 (check date) railroad labor prepared to strike for the 8-hour basic day with time and a half for overtime. The demand was won in 24 hours.

Immediately afterwards, sentiment ran righ for wage increases and an onsweeping, powerful, united labor movement demanded and won better wages and conditions. For the first time railroad workers negotiated one national agreement for the entire industry.

To stop this victorious march and keep railroad labor " in hand " a plan was worked out through which trade union submitted to a policy of " impartial " mediation and arbitration. This plan was embodied in the Transportation Act of 1920.

In accepting the Transportation Act the railroad union leaders changed the whole course of the organizations and paved the way for the events which followed: The scrapping of the national agreement, wage cuts, and reestablishment of piecework.

That the men were against this policy of retreat was proven by the insurgent "outlaw strike" of 1920, lost because the officials of the Brotherhood of Railroad Trainmen refused to support the demands of the strikers for wage increases and saw to it that switching was performed by members of the organization not on strike. It was proven by the 1922 shopmen's strike against a ruling of the Labor Board under the Transportation Act, sustaining the roads in cutting wages of shopmen and maintenance workers.

By 1926 the railroad magnates felt the time ripe for fresh attacks on railroad labor. Remembering the militant struggles of 1920 and 1922, which the Transportation Act failed to prevent, they proposed to substitute more effective machinery. The brotherhood chiefs gladly cooperated in this plan. The result was the Railway Labor Act with its boards of adjustment, mediation, and arbitration, and emergency boards, aimed to stall off strikes. The bill was written jointly by the railroad magnates and the officials of the 21 railway unions.

With what abandon the roads used the Railway Labor Act to throw to the winds agreements and working schedules was only fully revealed with the publication of the grievances listed in the strike ballots of 1933 and 1934.

Although thousands of accumulated grievances were listed in the strike ballots of 1933–34 (dating from the very passage of the Railway Labor Act), it was not these accumulated grievances which finally determined the strike votes authorized by the grand lodge officials. It was the fact that roads encouraged by the failure of these grand lodge officials to call strikes, were confident that they could go still further under the protection of the Railway Labor Act, even to the point of ignoring the unions altogether. It was only when the very existence of the unions were at stake, when the jobs of the union officials were in danger and the bankruptcy of their antiunion policies exposed, that strike ballots were resorted to.

The first grievance on the Southern-Pacific strike ballot (lines west), dates from January 31, 1925. It involved the abolition of the mileage basis of pay for conductors and trainmen in freight service from Bakersfield, through Mojave, to Los Angeles and vice versa, a trip of 100 miles. But the strike ballot did not question the abolition of this division point (Mojave) since 1925. With reduced pay for conductors and trainmen, it questioned only the right of the carrier to " change working rules and conditions without first serving notice as provided for in agreements." Two thousand grievances had accumulated on the Texas & New Orleans (Atlantic lines of the Southern Pacific), before a strike vote was taken on that line.

Having saved its face with the membership by authorizing this strike ballot, the union officials on the Southern-Pacific went back to the "safe" machinery of the Railway Labor Act accepting the appointment of a presidential board who ruled that "no strike was justified, because the grievances could be amicably settled."

On the Mobile & Ohio the national wage agreement had been violated for 2 years before the grand lodge officials found it expedient to take a strike ballot. But instead of calling the strike they accepted an emergency board decision allowing a road to keep 6½ percent of all back wages and extending a 3½ percent cut in addition to the 10 percent prevailing on all other roads.

On the Chicago & Northwestern, President Sargent was authorizing basic changes in working rules, contending that these were "managerial questions" outside the province of union interference, before the rank and file finally forced the union officials to take a strike ballot. The ballot cited 512 grievances dating from 1926 awaiting action by the board of adjustment to which they had been referred.

The new schedules introduced on the Louisiana, Arkansas & Texas, previous to the strike ballot, cut wages of engineers to 70 and 76 cents an hour; firemen to 53 and 57 cents; conductors, 66 cents; brakemen, 50 and 60 cents. This road also put over an 8-hour minimum in place of an hour-hour maximum basic day and abolished time and a half for overtime. The road is still continuing these depredations (February 1935) because the Emergency Board has failed to reach a decision.

As regards the D. & H. and K. C. S. offensive: Under cover of the wage-cutting negotiations of 1932, Leonor F. Loree, open-shop president of the Delaware & Hudson, sent an ultimatum to the engineers, firemen, trainmen, and conductors on his road, abolishing the mileage basis of pay, punitive overtime, and certain other working rules. The Locomotive Engineer's Journal stated at the time that cuts up to 32 percent could be made under this plan. Nevertheless it was accepted "for a period of 1 year."

When the 1-year contract ended, August 1, 1933, Loree refused to withdraw his plan. In place of the union he set up his own hand-picked board of disciplining officers through which he proposed to deal with the men. Seven months later the union officials took a strike vote. The men were determined to strike and even the emergency boards could not swallow Loree's board of disciplining officers. The mileage basis of pay was restored and plans to extend its abolition to the Kansas City Southern, Loree-owned, were also defeated because of militant strike preparations.

Thus we see how the roads tried to use the Railway Labor Act to rid themselves of all union interference and to throw overboard such restrictions on their profits as punitive overtime and the mileage basis of pay. They were thwarted in these attempts by the overwhelming strike sentiment of the men.

The Railway Labor Act has proven itself effective up to a certain point. If the roads were to go ahead with their plans, which involved intensifying their attacks against the workers, the compulsory arbitration features of the act had to be strengthened.

The amendments which they succeeded in having passed for this purpose abolish the National Mediation Board of 5 Presidential appointees and substitute a board of 3, more dictorial in power and easier for the roads to control. Through national adjustment boards, it provides for the compulsory arbitration of the very disputes which brought on the strike ballots of 1933 and 1934.

Where disputes have not been settled in the usual manner and where after submission to the proper division its members "fail to agree upon an award", then such division shall select a "referee" to sit as a member and "make an award." Where a division fails to select a referee the National Mediation Board is authorized to name one. In other words, after the workers have gone through all the long-drawn-out procedure set up to postpone strike action, and are still determined to fight, compulsory arbitration is injected to force an arbitrary upon them.

Now, the wage cuts by proclamation. In the 10 years 1920–30, class I railroads paid out in dividends almost $5,000,000,000 in addition to some three quarters of a billion a year in interest on fixed charges. During this same period half a million workers were thrown out of the industry, another half million were reduced to part-time work, and other " economies " at the expense of labor were netting the roads annual savings of more than a billion dollars. This was the situation when the roads proposed a national wage slash, in the summer of 1931.

The members of the railroad unions were never given a chance to vote on this cut. Up until 3 days before the agreement was signed, press notices were being sent out to the effect that " the unions will not stand for wage cut being jammed down their throats " and that they " are going to fight to a finish."

But behind the scenes the brotherhood leaders had already decided just how much of a fight would be made. A letter produced at the 1933 convention of the Brotherhood of Locomotive Engineers implicates both the engineers' and the conductors' organizations although an affidavit attempting to clear Alvanley Johnston, grand president of the B. of L. E. was read at the convention. The letter in question was signed by C. Stirling Smith, at that time president of the B. of L. E. bank, and reads as follows:

Mr. H. L. VAN KLEECK,
  Vice President Chase National Bank, New York City.

I have been spending a great deal of time with Mr. Johnston on the voluntary wage cut which he is endeavoring to put through, but he is meeting with such opposition from other brotherhoods that it is going to be an awful lot of effort on his part to put it over.

He is, however, being supported 100 percent by the conductors' organization, and the engineers and conductors have finally decided that they are going to put through a voluntary cut whether the others go along or not.

Mr. Johnston carries a lot of influence with the other organizations, so they will probably go along in the end. He fully appreciates what it means to the country and particularly to the holders of railroad bonds, and with this in view he is doing everything he possibly can to bring about the necessary reduction.

I can scarcely believe that the Chase would want to ruin the Engineers Bank when they are trying to do so much to bring about more satisfactory conditions and increase the value of railroad securities.

Smith's prediction that the other organizations " will probably go along in the end " was, of course, correct. Wall Street was quite satisfied with the results and the labor chiefs wallowed in its praise. In the February 9 issue of Labor the Wall Street Journal is quoted as follows:

In common fairness it should be acknowledged that railroad labor might have resisted wage reductions for many months; it might even have yielded to the temptation to play the political game in a Presidential campaign year. Its leaders, fortunately, are bigger men than that.

The most disgusting scenes ever witnessed at a supposed battle between capital and labor took place at the Palmer House when the 10-percent sell-out was completed. The union chiefs and the railroad magnates congratulated one another that an agreement had been reached without recourse to force. The railway labor executives presented Daniel Willard, chairman of the Railway Employers Association, with a basket of flowers and had themselves photographed with him. They deluded the membership that " by their noble sacrifice " the unemployed would be put to work. " Thousands of men will be employed in the next 12 months who would not have been employed if railway labor had not agreed to the 10-percent deductions."

But in practice 145,000 more railroad workers lost their jobs during the first wage-cut year. These layoffs, plus the wage cut, enabled the railroads to enrich their stock and bondholders by the payment of $1,026,000,000 in 1932. Nor was the B. of L. E. bank in Cleveland saved! It crashed, and with it went the savings of thousands of members of that organization. President Johnston was indicted for grand larceny, but it is said that his " good friends " will be able to keep him from serving his jail sentence and so preserve him for further services to the railroad bankers.

At this time the Government stepped in. It was now necessary to call in the Government to extend the 10-percent cut which the men had been led to believe was only for 1 year. Under plea of " loyalty to the country in the serious financial crisis ", President Hoover urged a 9-months' extension of the cut. The labor chiefs quickly agreed.

A second extension was engineered by the new railroad coordinator, Joseph B. Eastman, whose appointment followed the passage of the Emergency Transportation Act, June 16, 1933.

In 1934 the cut was again extended, although conditions at this time were such that a united struggle could have forced complete and immediate restoration of the 10-percent cut and an increase in wages! Even the capitalist press admitted the injustice of a further cut at this time. " No better argument against the demands of the railroads for another wage sacrifice by their workers has been presented than the railroads' own figures on income ", stated the New York Herald-Tribune, March 7, 1934.

Freight-car loadings had been steadily rising since the summer of 1933. Railroad profits were soaring. Strike votes had just won certain concessions on several roads, and on the D. & H. and K. C. S. the possibility of immediate strikes threatened at the very time of the wage negotiations. A general strike move was gripping the country. Even the possibility of a strike on the railroads would have seriously embarrassed the administration, forcing them to concede a wage increase.

Yet so strongly did the roads count on the acquiescence of the railroad labor executive that President Roosevelt demanded that the unions accept the full 10-percent extension. To Coordinator Eastman was assigned the task of putting over this cut!

THE RANK AND FILE TAKES A HAND

At the time of the first wage cut, February 1932, there was no organized opposition in the ranks of the railroad brotherhoods. By the spring of 1934, however, thousands of railroad workers were supporting the unity movement, building groups in their lodges, opposing any extension of the 10-percent cut, demanding an increase in wages to meet higher living costs, and proposing strike action to back up their demands. Floods of resolutions, protesting any extension of the cut began pouring into the offices of the grand chiefs, to coordinator Eastman, and to Roosevelt himself. Many lodges demanded a 10-percent increase in wages. It looked as if the grand lodge officers might this time be forced to make good their strike talk, as had been the case with reactionary union officials in other industries. A decisive victory lay within reach.

But the rank and file were not organized to move beyond the stage of resolutions. They hesitated, once more misled by the fighting words of the Whitneys and Robertsons. This hesitation was fatal. It gave the labor executives the breathing spell they were waiting for. During this lull in activity, this uncertainly as to the next step, this refinance on the effectiveness of negotiations as the only logical procedure, the 2½-percent compromise was put over.

To the militancy of the rank and file, to their rallying to the call of the unity movement, was due this partial victory. But the organizational weaknesses of the unity movement, the fact that it was no more firmly grounded in the lodges, the fatal reliance of many of its followers on agitation in place of uniting the lodges for action, turned what might have been a complete victory into a poor compromise.

The New York Times frankly stated:

The " deduction " from each week's pay envelop has been extended long beyond the 12 months for which it was originally intended to remain in force. The transportation companies are assured that they will have to face no labor difficulties during the next 14 months * * * this is a distinct gain over the " 6-months' truce " as first proposed.

During the very month that the wage negotiations were going on, 40 railroads reported profits of $31,500,000, six times their profits for 1933.

IDENTICAL INTERESTS

The theory that the interests of labor and capital are identical was accepted by railroad labor executives as far back as 1907. At this time Warren Stone, of the engineers; Garretson, of the contractors; and Morrissey, of the trainmen, launched their American Employers and Investors Association, the purpose of which was—

To cultivate and maintain between its members such a mutual spirit of interest and concern for the welfare and prosperity of the American railroads as will promote their successful and profitable operation. (From constitution.)

This scheme received its death blow at the 1900 convention of the Brotherhood of Railway Trainmen when Morrissey was kicked out of office for his services to the railroads. But the general principles on which it was built continued to flourish.

In 1920, Grand President Prenter, of the Brotherhood of Locomotive Engineers, made the statement that—

In America there is no such thing as a working class as distinguished from a capitalist class. It is the brotherhood's aim in its financial enterprises to show its members and workers generally how to become capitalists as well as workers. We have demonstrated American labor's answer to the theories of Marx and Lenin, to the theories of the class struggle.

These ideas were being fostered by leading economists of the time. " The saving power of the American workingmen is so great ", said Professor Garver, of Harvard University, a man paid by the powerful monied interests which control this institution and who won large blocks of railroad stock, " that if they would save and carefully invest their savings, in 10 years they would be one of the dominating financial powers of the world."

With such hypnotics the unions were being turned away from successful struggles for higher wages and better working conditions into the morass of banking and real estate ventures.

In less than the 10 years in which they were to " dominate the financial world ", railroad labor awoke from its dream of world power to find the entire financial superstructure erected by the Prenters crashing down over their heads. The labor banks were bankrupt; the real-estate ventures foreclosed or wiped out; and many of the union officials stood convicted of grand larceny for trying to salvage their personal investments and those of their relatives and friends. The union treasuries were gutted. The savings of the members were gone. Even the insurance departments had been wrecked. Moreover, the roads had taken advantage of the peaceful business absorption of the unions to scrap agreements and wipe out many of the gains won in early struggles.

Let us give the B. & O. plan. During the time that the financial enterprises of the unions were at their height, the roads went in for a new form of production drive which they sold to the labor executives under the label: " Union-Management-Cooperation." This plan was officially accepted as trade union doctrine at the 1925 convention of the American Federation of Labor, at the request of the railroad department. The B. & O. shop crafts were the first to adopt the plan and it became known as the " B. & O. plan."

The B. & O. plan is a scheme through which the unions " cooperate " with the companies to speed up and cheapen production. By its very nature it necessitates the abandonment of all real struggles against the companies. The unions change their aims from winning concessions to increasing production; thus degenerating into part of the employers' productive machinery.

Before 1923, when the B. & O. plan was introduced an average of 25,000 workers were employed in the B. & O. repair shops. In the period following employment " stabilization ", 5,000 shop workers were permanently laid off. Drives to get the men to " cooperate " with the roads by doing more and better work and getting more business through cheapening production are continuously carried on by the road. The net result of one of these recent drives (spring of 1934) was another lay off of 1,500 men.

The essence of the B. & O. plan was soon adopted by the Chicago & Northwestern, the Milwaukee, the Canadian National, and other important systems. It was found to be a very effective substitute for getting around union agreements. On the Grand Trunk it is used, according to one of the workers—

First, as a propaganda bureau for the dire needs of the roads; second, as a meeting point where petty union officials can outdo one another in proposing ways to eliminate waste; third, as a place to settle certain troublesome questions without rank and file discussion in the lodge room. Union meetings thereby become mere rubber stamps for decisions of the company.

The poison of union-management-cooperation has pretty well percolated through the entire trade-union apparatus. In 1934 the grand lodge officers of the Brotherhood of Maintenance of Way Employees, steam-rollered a reendorsement of this idea through their national convention in place of a rank-and-file resolution for union committees to stop speed-up and strike action where agreements were being violated.

Likewise, the fourth annual conference on organization of the Brotherhood of Railway Clerks (December 1934) stated that, " we, the railroad workers, are not merely employees; we are a part of an industry upon which the public depends." Because it is our industry, the brotherhood felt it should demand a greater voice in management.

It is interesting to note that of the 13,307 railroad workers laid off between August 15, 1934, and September 15, of the same year, 10,307 were clerks and maintenance-of-way employees. In this way the mutual interests of the railway employees are being served by our industry and the nonstruggle policies of the grand lodge officials.

" Recognizing the mutual relations of the employers and the employees has, to a great extent, removed the need for ' unionism ' ", stated a bulletin of the New York Trust Co. as far back as 1934.

Between 1926, when the Railway Labor Act became law, and 1932 the heart of the wage-cutting campaign, the railroads were able to reduce working forces from 1,821,804 to 1,030,000—that is, by over 800,000. During this same period pay rolls were cut more drastically—from $3,001,803,606 to $1,500,000,000. This difference between wages saved through actual lay-offs and the 1932 pay-roll figure represents the more intense drive by the roads against these workers left on the jobs. It is accounted for by changes in rates of pay— demotions and reclassifications—by cutting down the number of days and hours worked, by installing labor-saving machinery, and efficiency methods. In comparison with 1926, hours of railway workers had dropped 51 percent by 1932, while productivity per worker rose 121 percent.

Probably the most intense exploitation took place in the maintenance-of-way departments. Over 1,000,000,000 man-hours were eliminated in this section of the industry between 1921 and 1932. The Lehigh Valley Railroad boasts that it was able to cut costs in its maintenance department from $12,000,000 to $3,000,000 in 6 years. Employment was cut 66 percent but pay rolls 75 percent.

"About 3 years ago ", writes a worker from Philadelphia, " clerks on the Pennsylvania were treated to a new form of speed-up. At that time all stations were doing their own rating, billing, sorting, mailing, and accounting. Enter the new system ! Billers were all brought to one point. Two Ford trucks were put on time schedules, allowing 2 to 3 minutes between stations. All records, correspondence, and accounting have been centralized. The work is now being done with one-tenth of the former forces."

" Formerly a train of 50 cars carrying 2,000 tons was considered a heavily loaded train, while nowadays a train of more than 100 cars carrying 6 or 7 thousand tons is not uncommon ", comes a report from the Boston & Maine. A brother in St. Louis counted 163 cars in a Missouri Pacific train moving 40 miles an hour. The average length of freight cars increased 21 percent between 1922 and 1933.

In 1922 the average speed of freight trains was 11.1 miles per hour. In 1934 the New York Central's merchandise freight from New York to Buffalo averages 43 miles per hour on its 438-mile run, including setting out and picking up cars at four intermediate points. Many freight trains were run at 60 miles an hour. The average for the country was 16 miles per hour in 1934, an increase in 10 years of 38.3 percent.

"Speed, and still more speed" was the railway's slogan in 1934. Record-breaking runs averaging a mile a minute have been introduced on all major roads utilizing new stream-lined locomotives and trains, high-powered motors, and lighter equipment.

Hundreds of millions of dollars in Government loans make it possible for the roads to allow old locomotives and freight cars to go without repairs in the expectation that these can be scrapped and new equipment of greater speed capacity substituted. Expenses for maintenance of roadways and structures were cut almost 10 percent between 1932 and 1933, from $351,179,041 to $322,355,022. In 1931 they were over half a billion. The roads spent $20,000,000 less on maintenance of equipment in 1933 over 1932. They hope to permanently reduce working forces engaged in these departments and so keep for their stock and bond holders the full fruits of these payroll savings.

Class I railroads were able to increase their net operating income $144,000,000 in 1933 over 1932. They did this by moving 8 percent more freight with 60,000 fewer workers. In 1934 they paid $104,-876,721 in dividends compared with $81,410,363 in 1933, an increase of 29 percent. "The ability of the railroads to handle more freight without increasing yard service and freight-car tonnage was perhaps the most important factor in their increased income", frankly comments Ernest K. Lindley in the January 13, 1934, issue of Today.

This is where union-management cooperation has led.

DEATH RIDES THE RAILS

The increased speed at which the roads are running both freight and passenger trains, coupled with a glaring cut in maintenance forces, was bound to result in an increase in railroad accidents. Already in 1932 a marked rise was recorded.

While in 1931 one worker was killed in road service for every 1,907 employed, in 1932 one was killed for every 1,829 employed. In train service the rate rose from 1 killed for every 810 employed in 1929 to 1 killed for every 736 employed in 1932.

Deaths to brakemen rose from 1.95 to 2.37 per 1,000.

In the month of September 1933 at least 25 persons were killed and scores more injured in serious railroad wrecks. Referring to wrecks on the Southern and Southern Pacific, where main-line bridges were washed away, a worker asks: "Why weren't these bridges patrolled when it was realized that an unusually heavy rainfall would certainly cause damage? * * * Simply because the carriers had probably taken off a $50 a month trackwalker or watchman for the sake of false economy. It was only a miracle that the loss of life

wasn't greater. In both instances the engine crews were killed."
(Footnote: J. F. Ashmore, in a letter to the New York World-
Telegram, Sept. 14, 1933.)

For the first 3 months of 1934 deaths of "employees on duty"
rose 89.66 percent and injuries rose 28.86 percent. In the 10 months'
period, January to October, deaths rose from 403 to 434 over 1933
and injuries increased from 4,591 to 5,231.

In the fall of 1934 a series of derailments due to bad track and
defective equipment killed more than 18 persons and injured more
than 100 others.

"Under the spurs of foremen and yardmasters", writes a Chicago switchman, "speed-up in the yards has reached a point where
all hands are afraid to live up to the 15 miles an hour rule for
switch engines, as well as any of the other safety rules. Switch
engines are running up and down the yards at 40 and 45 miles an
hour. To actually live up to the safety rules would place a limit
on speed. These rules are not made to be lived up to, but only so
that the blame can be placed on the men in case of accident."

"The yardmaster", says another switchman, "removes every foreman who doesn't 'hit the ball' and the men fight for the few jobs
that are left. Profit at the expense of the men is the goal of the
roads."

Union committees to control speed-up; union safety committees to
enforce rules to protect life and limb, and a Federal compensation
law with benefits entirely financed by the roads are concrete methods
for reducing railroad accidents.

A quarter of a million starve! The myth of high railroad wages
has now been publicly exploded by no less an authority than Joseph
Eastman himself. His statement is based on studies of employment
and wages on seven important roads. "In 1933", he says, "the
average annual earnings of 98 percent of all railroad employees
amounted to a little more than $100 per month. Furthermore, from
15 to 20 percent of all railroad employees in 1933 were earning less
than $600 yearly." (Labor, issue of Feb. 5.)

Comparing earnings of railroad workers in April 1933 with those
of July 1929, an official Government report states that 7 out of
every 10 were living on 20 percent less wages; 3 out of 10 had been
cut 40 percent, and 1 out of 10 had a wage loss of 60 percent or more.

Twenty-eight percent of those classed as "employed" lost from
5 to 12 months' earning time in 1933.

"Most of the freight handlers were working part time and many
are on the spare list" writes a "mule." "We all have to report
every day * * * the majority have to go home empty handed.
Some are asked to wait until afternoon to see if anything shows
up. We are not paid street car fare or for the hours spent waiting
for call."

"Outside the crew dispatcher's office", writes another worker,
"every day there are scores of spare workers waiting patiently for
any vacancy left by a 'regular.' On special occasions like football
games we may get a chance. Generally we are turned down by the
dispatcher with a 'not today brother; come again tomorrow.' and
a railroad man, if he wants to keep his place on the roster, must be
available for duty at any hour."

In September 1933, the firemen's roster for one division on the New Haven called for 14 regular jobs and 15 spare jobs.

SPREAD THE WORK

The union policy for retaining jobs when lay-offs threaten is to spread the work. By reducing the number of days or hours for all the roads are able to make a substantial pay-roll saving and the workers are forced to adapt themselves to a lower standard of living, which makes future direct wage cuts easier to put over.

The most dramatic example of " voluntary starvation " comes from the B. & O. shops (Glenwood) in the summer of 1932. Here union members cut their working time from 4 days a week to 8 days a month under threat of a lay-off. Calling shopmen in for 3 or 4 days' work a week is quite general on the railroads.

For train- and engine-service employees " spread the work " involves cutting mileage. Passenger runs for trainmen have been cut to a maximum of 5,500 miles and freight runs to 3,500 miles. Earnings have been cut in this way from $40 to $80 a month.

The schedule for yardmen on the Chicago, Burlington & Quincy, effective January 1932, cut hours from 240 to 208 a month and wages proportionately.

The grand lodge officers of the B. of L. F. & E. were very active in a campaign to reduce the men to 26 days a month and cut road mileage. " The grand lodge wants to place the burden of the depression on the shoulders of the workers so that the big railroad bankers and bondholders can receive bigger dividends and the stockholders can make larger profits out of the workers' misery. The grand chiefs are drawing full pay at high salaries and expenses paid. They are not staggered. They have full bellies ", writes a fireman on the C. & E. I. Too few workers understand the purpose of the stagger system as does this brother.

But in train and engine service as well as in the shop crafts, the pressure of low wages is forcing a reversal of the policy of sharing work. The men want to lengthen runs and hours so they can make both ends meet. To do this they are willing to allow those low on the seniority list to be squeezed out of the industry altogether.

The alternative is to reduce hours and mileage but increase the basic rate sufficiently to maintain earnings at the level prevailing before the cut. This is the essence of the demand for the 6-hour day without reduction in earnings.

Resentment of the men in road service to restrictions on mileage cannot be understood without a knowledge of how the basic rates were established. With the passage of the Adamson Law in 1918, 100 miles was established as the basic day with time and a half for overtime after 8 hours work. But it was assumed that upward of 50 of these minimum days would be worked in each calendar month. Thus the low basic rate was overcome by long hours of overtime.

With the advent of the crisis, overtime has been largely eliminated by increasing average train speed and this, plus limitation of mileage makes a huge wage cut.

AT THE BOTTOM OF THE HEAP

The largest proportion of underpaid workers in the railroad industry are in the maintenance-of-way department. Wages as low as 7 cents an hour are paid section men in some parts of the country, living standards for thousands of maintenance workers are down to the level of Chinese coolies and actual starvation faces their families. The seasonal nature of maintenance work leaves men in this department without any source of income whatever during much of the year.

All roads hire extra gangs for regular maintenance work at rates far below the union standard. A rate of 25 cents an hour for this class of work is quite common. Out of this the roads deduct for meals, lodging in road camps, and insurance. Conditions are so intolerable that spontaneous strikes have broken out among section crews in Bellingham, Wash., and Pippen, Wis., this last year.

Official studies of maintenance workers have repeatedly exposed the plight of these workers and President Roosevelt, confronted with these facts during the last wage negotiations recommended that a minimum equal to the 31½ cents per hour for N. R. A. codes be set for railroad workers " at the bottom of the heap." To make the 1934 wage cut extension sound less brazen a clause was inserted allowing the unions to reopen negotiations on this matter road by road.

Officials of the Brotherhood of Maintenance of Way Employees, at their 1934 convention, admitted that they had not taken advantage of this clause and that in their eagerness " to cooperate with the President of the United States, the railroad managements, and other standard railway labor organizations " they had accepted a settlement that did not provide for " correction of the totally inadequate minimum rates of pay " for maintenance men.

Although a program was presented to the convention calling for a minimum hourly rate of 50 cents, a daily $4 minimum wage, a guaranty of not less than 208 days work a year, and immediate negotiations road by road to win these demands, " inauguration of a movement providing for general wage increases " was postponed until the 1935 negotiations.

As against proposals for a membership to strengthen the union, lowering of dues, and allowing the unemployed all privileges of membership, the convention, composed largely of section foremen, confirmed its contempt for the lower paid and unemployed by refusing to reduce dues and by actually raising assessments of unemployed members to $16 a year. Yet it was reported that only 52,000 of the 350,000 workers eligible to join the union were members.

The convention likewise ignored the demands of Negro members to stop the policy of establishing separate lodges for Negro workers and the rule that Negro lodges could only be represented in negotiations by delegates of white lodges. No action was taken on the request that Negro lodges be allowed representation in conventions.

But the grand-lodge officers took occasion to strike back at all those who might oppose their union's wrecking policies by authorizing the expulsion of all militants.

114096—35——37

NEGROES IN THE INDUSTRY

The caste system practiced by the railroad brotherhoods has kept the Negroes out of the skilled railroad crafts except in certain parts of the South, where they hold jobs as firemen, trainmen, and conductors. Nine American Federation of Labor unions, with jurisdiction over the railroad industry, specifically bar Negroes from membership, as is also the case with the four transportation brotherhoods. This policy is, of course, to the advantage of the roads, giving them a potential force of strike breakers and a club for reducing wages.

The 1930 census listed 118,908 Negroes employed on class I railroads, 10.4 percent of the total number of railroad employees at that time. Since unemployment has increased up to one-third of the working force and Negro workers dare not claim a job that a white man wants, there are probably no more than 90,000 Negroes working on the roads today (January 1935). This includes 20,000 Pullman porters and 15,000 dining-car service employees. The overwhelming proportion of Negro railroaders are shop and track laborers. In the entire country in 1930 there were only 4,642 Negro locomotive firemen, 3,813 boilermakers and engine hostlers, 3,347 brakemen, and 2,571 switchmen and flagmen.

Fierce competition for jobs during the crisis years has unleashed a terrific rein of terror against these Negroes whose seniority keeps them in service when lay-offs take place. When the Illinois Central shortened its run between Vicksburg and New Orleans there was a corresponding cut in jobs on the old route through Baton Rouge. Negro firemen retained their seniority, while white firemen with shorter service records lost out. This fight for bread fanned into flame the whole rotten lynch spirit of the southern ruling class. More than a dozen Negro firemen have been shot while on duty in an attempt to get the Negro firemen on the system to give up their claims to their jobs, that is to reduce the proportion of Negro jobs to white to 40 percent.

An agreement recently signed by the Brotherhood of Locomotive Firemen and Enginemen with the Atlantic Coast Line states that "at least 51 percent of the firemen on this line must be white." This road also agreed "not to employ Negro firemen, and in the future all vacancies will be filled by white firemen."

Race hatreds such as those which inspire the shooting of I. C. firemen, agreements such as those used by white firemen on the Atlantic Coast Line to deprive Negroes of their jobs, may temporarily benefit white railroad workers. But, in the long run, the employers are the ones to profit, because by this division of ranks united action of Negro and white railroad workers against wage cuts and broken agreements is prevented.

By excluding Negroes from the standard railway unions they are forced into dual unions such as those for Negro firemen and brakemen in the South, or into company unions which flourish on such soil in the shops and yards, both North and South.

A Negro trackman writes from Norfolk:

To meet the coming conflict between capital and labor the workers must be organized into one powerful union if possible, and if such an organization is impossible, then into independent unions. The crying need of the hour is organization, but when it comes to the Negro maintenance-of-way workers I am confronted with this situation. We have maintenance-of-way foremen willing to take Negroes into the brotherhood, but upon equal standing with the white. Others are unwilling to accept them on any terms * * * although they are willing to help them form an independent union. A third group don't want them organized at all.

There are growing numbers of white railroad workers who understand the serious consequences of dual unions and divided struggles. These workers have come forward in many lodges for the admission of Negroes with the same privileges as white members. On the other hand, it is possible to organize into separate lodges, where this is the only way open, and to make the lodge so much a part of the general struggles of railroad labor as to demonstrate its value to the white lodges. We know of one instance where a Negro maintenance lodge in the South paved the way for organizing white women car cleaners and took them into their union, because there was no other union for these women to join.

Similar departures from Jim Crow practices doubtless exist in many parts of the country. Outstanding is the case of Local No. 351, A. F. of L. union of Dining Car Stewards, Cooks, and Waiters. This lodge takes in all employees in dining-car service on New York Central Lines west of Buffalo, including the Michigan Central and the Big Four.

This was done on the strength of the slogan— writes a member—

you work together for the New York Central; you eat together for the New York Central; you sleep together for the New York Central. Why not band together for your own benefit?

This union has already won a number of concessions for its members. Recently 40 men who had been demoted with consequent reduction in wages had their seniority rights restored. In two cases alone increases amounted to $360 per man per year. At the same time it has extended its organization to other roads and increased its membership to upward of 400.

The lesson that "labor in the white skin can never be free while labor in the black skin is branded" has been brought home with all the force of economic necessity to members of the Order of Sleeping Car Conductors, a white A. F. of L. union.

Pullman porters, all Negro, working alongside the conductors, have their own A. F. of L. union, although they have never been given recognition in wage negotiations. In 1932 a $5-a-month wage cut was given the porters, making their average wage $68.11 a month. Out of this, $33.52 a month goes for uniforms and other occupational expenses—shoe blacking, laundry, and so forth. Tips which are supposed to supplement wages have fallen off 75 percent during the crisis. Porters are required to work many hours before and after runs without pay. Average hours are 77 a week, without punitive overtime. In a 4 nights' run one porter reported that he got 5 hours' sleep.

Pullman conductors had taken no interest in the miserable wages and conditions of their black brothers. But when the Pullman Co. began taking advantage of these low wages to ease the Pullman conductor out of his job, that was a different story. The Order of Sleeping Car Conductors decided to absorb the Brotherhood of Pullman

Porters, and their application was granted by the 1934 convention of the A. F. of L.

The Brotherhood of Pullman Porters are fighting this ruling, determined to maintain a separate organization, a policy so profitable to the roads. A much more correct attitude is taken by a group of furloughed Pullman porters, who write:

Our attitude is that the question of the Pullman porters and conductors cannot be settled by the porters and maids being taken over by the conductors.

We feel that the most logical way to go about the affair is to call a conference with conductors, porters, and maids and form one organization with equal rights to all members, regardless of race or color. If this cannot be done, then to form a united front and work for the interest of all.

Experience has taught us all that to struggle together is more effective than being divided. We are therefore proposing what we consider the necessary steps to establish the unification of our efforts.

The words of these five Pullman porters can well stand as a lesson for the entire railroad industry.

THE DRIVE ON JOBS

In the boom period of railway expansion, when Government grants of rich timber and valuable right-of-way padded the bankrolls of the Goulds and Vanderbilts, railway labor looked forward to limitless opportunities for work and wages. After the fortunes from this source had been salted away the roads were busy meeting increased demands for goods shipments, war orders, and the replenishing of depleted markets. This was a period of huge increases in railroad investments, financed by stock and bond issues sold to the public and stock dividends pocketed by the railroad bankers.

It was during this time that the Van Sweringens built their railroad empire under the protecting shadow of J. P. Morgan, and railroad financiers laid the basis for the bankruptcies which took effect when "hard times" came. It was at this time that the now bankrupt Missouri Pacific bought the Union Terminal Railroad, a 9-mile line with 3 locomotives, for $4,300,000, paying $920 a share for stock worth at the most $100.

The crisis years following the high employment level of 1929 found the roads totally unprepared. To cover fixed charges on their huge overcapitalization they would have required increases in gross operating revenues absolutely impossible of realization. For example the Atlantic Coast Line would require a 72-percent increase in gross revenue; the Wabash, a 45-percent increase; the C. & N. W., a 43-percent increase, and so on.

The roads were maintaining a system of cut-throat competition, artificial in many cases, leasing lines to themselves at high rentals, and so juggling their books as to make them appear at grave disadvantage with competing types of transportation—buses and trucks, oil and pipe lines, water carriers, and airways.

Income which should have been used to replace outworn equipment and maintain right-of-way and rolling stock had been poured into the pockets of stock and bondholders. Unwilling to deprive the Vanderbilts and Morgans of their million-dollar incomes the roads turned to the workers to get them "out of the red."

By May 1933 railroad employment had struck bottom, averaging 932,406 for the month compared with a yearly average of 1,660,850 for 1929. But pay rolls had been cut in 1933 to $1,424,391,647, as against almost $3,000,000,000 in 1929. The drive against wages, hours, and working capacity was carried on road by road during the crisis with the results already described in this report. However, although the roads were able to move 9.2 percent more traffic in 1934 than they did in 1932, with the same number of workers, they were unable to drive employment below the May 1933 figure, through individual economics.

THE EMERGENCY TRANSPORTATION ACT

The Federal Government has always liberally assisted the building of railroad fortunes since the heyday of Southern Pacific land grants. This policy is being continued in other forms. A $400,000,-000 debt owed the Government by the roads since the passage of the recapture clause of the Interstate Commerce Act was still outstanding in the spring of 1933, except for repayment of $13,000,000.

When Roosevelt took office the Reconstruction Finance Corporation had already authorized railroad loans totaling $339,700,000 to relieve the roads from obstructions and burdens resulting from the present acute economic emergency, the Emergency Transportation Act was passed June 16, 1933.

Concretely the act sets aside the Sherman antitrust law as applied to railroads. It wiped out the $400,000,000 " recapture " debt and actually returned to the roads the $13,000,000 already repaid, with interest. It laid the basis for unified control of the railroads in line with the growing centralization of power in Washington. It provided machinery for speeding up consolidations which had been gradually going on with the approval of the Interstate Commerce Commission. Finally, it put Government pressure behind wholesale " economies " providing for continued profits through greater exploitation of railroad labor. A Railroad Coordinator, appointed by and directly responsible to the President of the United States, was authorized to administer the act.

The passage of the Emergency Transportation Act followed a period of agitation for unification of all railroads in the country into seven huge systems, a scheme known as the " Prince plan ", after the Boston financier who backed it. This financial transportation monopoly was far beyond the realms of possibility at that time because it involved wiping out competing railroad empires still exceedingly profitable to their owners. Nevertheless plenty of publicity was given the plan, particularly its labor features, under which Prince proposed to abolish some 300,000 railroad jobs.

This gave the railroad labor executives a chance to support the emergency act as the lesser evil, which they did on three grounds:

1. The bill gave railroad labor the right to organize.

2. The resentment of railroad labor against further lay-offs was so intense that it forced an amendment through which rail jobs were " frozen " at the May 1933 level, as effected by consolidations, and limited other reduction in forces to 5 percent annually.

3. There was no use opposing the bill as the Government was behind it.

Let us examine these arguments in the light of the serious menace which this law has become to railroad labor.

THE RIGHT TO ORGANIZE

In 1926 the Railway Labor Act was hailed by the railroad labor executives as a weapon for abolishing company unions because it provided for representation and collective action without interference, coercion, or influence exercised by either party over the self-organization or representation by the other. Yet every railroad worker knows that company unions continued to flourish after the passage of the Railway Labor Act. In fact the open-shop roads quoted this very clause in justification of the company unions. "We see that the existence of independent organizations has been safeguarded" stated the Union Pacific Co. Union Bulletin.

Neither did the company unions melt out of existence after the Emergency Transportation Act was passed in 1933. In fact, soon after the act was passed, Railroad Coordinator Eastman called a conference of representatives of company union roads to see how these roads could adapt their unions to the new law. The Pennsylvania did this very effectively.

On the other hand, where workers tried to get out of the company unions and organize into the Federated Shop Crafts, the roads resorted to every known method of intimidation, bribery, dismissals, blacklisting, and general terror. Plain-clothes men and police attended the meeting of the Rock Island Association in Blue Island, Ill., at which workers discussed withdrawing from this company union and establishing their own union. On the Erie Railroad freight handlers were told that if they did not allow a check-off of 25 cents a month for company union dues they could look elsewhere for jobs.

On the Delaware, Lackawanna & Western, where the A. F. of L. had already organized the clerks and carmen, the road continued its old organization, at the same time deducting company union dues from the pay checks of A. F. of L. members. On the western roads, the newly organized Shop Crafts Association was pushed as having—

All the legal standing that any other labor union has in the United States—

And it is—

so recognized by all boards established by the United States Government and also with the Federal Coordinator of Transportation. (Leaflet of Southern Pacific.)

Railroad workers do not need a law giving them the right to organize. Where they are too weak, no amount of Government sanction will either secure this right or retain it. Railroad labor has lost this right completely in all fascist countries of Europe through the very policies of employer cooperation and abandonment of struggle pursued by the brotherhood leaders in the United States.

THE CHALLENGE

The first year following the passage of the emergency act was one of preparation. There were numerous railroad interests to reconcile, each reluctant to give up any advantages of trackage or terminal facilities. The regional coordinating committees were slow to get into action. Studies with specific recommendations for reducing costs through pooling of equipment, consolidating facilities, and laying off workers were not yet completed. Carloadings showed considerable pick-up, making it possible to greatly increase net operating income by keeping employment around the low level of May 1933. No objection came from the labor executives when the emergency act was extended for another year.

By the summer of 1934 the railroad coordinator was ready for action. In a speech in Kansas City he proposed concentration of all traffic facilities in one terminal to save $2,000,000 annually at that point. " The savings would be largely at the expense of labor ", said Eastman. " This is typical of what can be done all over the country."

In October Eastman issued his report on the pooling of empty box cars to save another $100,000,000 a year. The roads carried this proposal further through their newly organized Association of American Railways, headed by the former open-shop president of the New York, New Haven & Hartford Railroad, J. J. Pelley. In an interview with F. E. Williamson, president of the New York Central, a plan was revealed for the repair of all freight cars in a pool, foreshadowing the abandonment of all local points. In New England the regional coordinating committee announced that they had already approved unification of freight and passenger facilities in small eastern towns, estimated to save the roads $400,000 annually.

In November Eastman made his infamous " Birmingham speech ", in which he said:

The railroad industry is in no position to furnish unnecessary or wasteful employment.

If you have ever played chess, you know that often the way to victory is opened up by making an initial sacrifice of a piece.

Railroad jobs were the pieces which Eastman proposed to sacrifice. Between July and January 93,000 railroad jobs had been cut off. It was at this point that an agreement was reached with the Association of Railway Labor Executives to have Eastman present his lay-off program to a conference of the 1,500 general chairmen for their endorsement.

MOVE TO PROTECT JOBS

The labor executives have accepted without effective protest every contrivance of the roads to increase production and eliminate man power. They have directed the fight for jobs, not against the speed-up and sharp practices of the roads, but against other crafts in the industry. Less brutally on the Illinois Central in Mississippi, but with the job as their goal, switchman and trainman and conductor, engineer and fireman, machinist and sheet-metal worker, outbid one another for the benefit of the roads.

The roads are able to abolish telegraph stations and discharge telegraphers because they can get conductors to take over the work of the telegrapher, receiving train orders direct from the dispatcher by phone.

Engineers on the Pennsylvania, in the Chicago terminal, knowing that a consolidation of service was under way, pooled seniority lists on two divisions. When the lay-off came, only members of the firemen's organization lost their jobs.

These temporary victories for one union or another weaken the organizations as a whole and pave the way for more ruthless consolidations in which all crafts will be trapped.

A better method of fighting lay-offs was started in the Chicago shops of the C. & N. W. Following announcement of a proposed lay-off, committees representing the shop crafts were called together. After much quibbling a representative of Lodge No. 227, B. of R. C. of A., acting on a previous suggestion of a representative of the road, suggested that it would be best to divide up all available work and go on a 3-day week. To which the spokesman for the road replied: " O. K. with me. Go back and fight it out among yourselves."

But the membership, looking behind the lay-off to the economy and production drives of the road, thought otherwise. In the machinist helpers' lodge a motion was made to hold a mass meeting and dramatize the plight of the unemployed. Another lodge proposed a protest parade. These general proposals gave way to a specific program presented by the very lodge whose representative previously suggested the 3-day week starvation rate. The program called for: A 30-hour 5-day week, without reduction in present weekly earnings; establishment of relief committees in all C. & N. W. lodges to represent needy members at relief stations; control of production and distribution of work through union committees to reduce speed up; endorsement and support of an adequate Federal unemployment-insurance bill.

Although handicapped by grand lodge opposition, which temporarily delayed joint-lodge action on the system, the four-point program, as it was called, soon spread to other systems and lodges. It formed the basis of the rank-and-file program presented at the maintenance-of-way convention. It served as a model for resolutions adopted by the 21 organizations in many terminals against consolidations and lay-offs.

The logic of empty stomachs has forced the lodges into the fight for relief and insurance for the unemployed, as the logic of lay-offs is forcing them into uniting to prevent speed up, consolidations, and the cutting off of more jobs.

Efforts of the grand lodge to obstruct support of the workers' unemployment and social insurance bill by railroad lodges has not succeeded. Endorsed in principle at the 1933 convention of the engineers, it was endorsed specifically by both the midwest and northwest conferences of that brotherhood in 1934. In Gary, Ind., the entire Shop Crafts Federation on the E. J. & E. pledged support for this bill, and it was also endorsed by organizations of the 21 brotherhoods in Gary, Eldon, Mo., and Bloomington. In New Orleans and Bloomington railroad lodges took an active part in meetings to support this measure. Altogether 500 railroad lodges are on record for House bill 2827, under which number the bill has been introduced in the Seventy-fourth Congress.

THE MEMBERSHIP UNITES

When Railroad Coordinator Eastman arrived in Chicago on January 12 to win the 1,500 general chairmen of the 21 railroad brotherhoods to his program of railroad profits at the expense of jobs and conditions, he became aware of a new force standing back of the railroad labor executives.

Although scarcely 3 weeks had elapsed between the time the conference was announced and when it took place, this short space of time was sufficient to crystallize into action the smouldering anger of railroad labor. From all over the country came resolutions of protest, instructing the general chairmen to reject Eastman's proposals point-blank. More than that, the membership realized that the time had come to go beyond mere talk to prevent lay-offs and to win the 6-hour day, limitation of train lengths, a workmen's compensation law for railroad men, and unemployment insurance. Recognizing in the conference of their 1,500 general chairmen an instrument to unite for immediate action the entire trade-union apparatus of their brotherhoods, they demanded that following the rejection of Eastman's proposals the chairmen go into executive session to take strike action, if necessary.

1. To prevent the roads from putting into effect, at any one point, their program of consolidations.

2. To control the elimination of jobs now taking place through reclassifications, increasing production tasks, doubling of work, lengthening of runs, trains and sections, increasing length and speed of trains by winning the 6-hour day without reduction in earnings, a minimum living wage for the industry, union committees to control speed-up and production tasks, enactment of the workers' social- and unemployment-insurance bill, no. 2827, and an adequate retirement pension law.

The unity movement had drafted the basis for this resolution and sent it out in the hope that some lodges meeting in those remaining 2 weeks would light the spark and fan into flame the demands of the men. Whole systems took up the challenge.

A short time ago—

Writes an engineer on the New Haven—

I attended a meeting of progressive members from various lodges. * * * These men were instructed to bring up the Eastman proposals at their lodge meetings and pass on a set of resolutions. * * * I understand these resolutions were put through in the trainmen's, signalmen's, firemen's, clerks', and engineers' in a number of lodges all over the New Haven system. In the engineers' copies were made and sent to all lodges on the New Haven and action taken on same.

Only the skillful maneuvering of the railway labor executives prevented the force of this rank and file sentiment from uniting the general chairmen to back up the demands of the men back home. Eastman himself was well aware of the shift in policy when he stated in his talk:

It has often seemed to me that while the leaders are in the front rank, they do not always lead, but at times are driven. They are able, longheaded, forceful men, but they are dealing with elemental forces which now and then get out of hand. On such occasions it may be possible to stay in front but not to lead.

The labor executives took Mr. Eastman's suggestion. They stayed in front by abruptly adjourning the conference without working out plans to put into effect their statement of opposition to consolidations, nor their legislative program of 5 years' standing. Once more craft divisions were utilized to block united action. The general chairmen were disbanded and instructed to meet craft by craft; then to go home and carry out the purposes of the conference.

UNITY FOR ACTION

Many months before the general chairmen's conference lodges of the 21 railway unions had developed the beginnings of united action to prevent consolidations and lay-offs. While much of the activity of these bodies had been taken up with passing resolutions in support or against legislation, the value of meeting together, burying craft differences, and discussing common grievances, were being demonstrated.

The failure of the labor executives to carry out the wishes of the members nationally, turned back to the lodges in the terminals responsibility for preventing further raids on jobs and working conditions. The fight for the 6-hour day, for unemployment insurance, to stop speed-up became the fight of the 21 organizations on the systems and terminals.

Joint meetings between the various crafts—

writes one correspondent—

appear to be the need of the hour and these meetings should stress the fact that concerted action is imperative. Since, in my opinion, organized railroad labor has been the greatest if not the only force that has stood between the workers and conditions bordering on peonage, it is fitting that organized railroad labor be the first to unify itself and be in position to resist the attempts now being made to impose such conditions upon us.

The power of the grand lodge officials to carry through their policy of working with the roads instead of struggling against them is not almighty. To maintain it thus far the chiefs have resorted to gag rule and expulsions of individuals and lodges. In the face of such terror, which also means loss of jobs as the roads and the chiefs work together against the militants, a surprising amount of revolt exists in the lodges of the 21 organizations. This revolt has in recent years broken through in the building of the railroad brotherhoods unity movement, in the organization of the Railroad Employees National Pension Association, in the strike ballots of 1933 and 1934, and finally in refusal to accept the layoff proposals of the railroad financiers, even though the full pressure of the National Government has been swung against the men.

At the same time lodges in a given system are pooling their efforts against violations of agreements, speed-up, and for the relief of their unemployed members as in the case of the C. & N. W.

The understanding that a successful fight against the roads cannot be separated from a fight against the grand-lodge policies of pitting craft against craft and substituting union management cooperation for action is developing wide interest in the movement for amalgamation of the various railroad craft unions.

"At the 1930 convention of the B. of L. E.", writes an officer of that brotherhood, " a resolution favoring amalgamation with the firemen was submitted."

No action was taken on this matter, however, until the 1933 convention, where a committee was appointed to meet with a similar committee already authorized by the firemen.

Meetings have been held at intervals, and at great expense the two committees have haggled over finances, always arriving at a deadlock. Never once has the order of the convention been carried out to make an offer of unconditional amalgamation by either side.

At their 1931 convention at Houston, the B. of R. T. sent a committee to the O. R. C., also in convention at Kansas City, and made a flat and unqualified offer of unconditional amalgamation, which was as flatly rejected.

At the present time the most deadly warfare is being carried on between competing organizations in the same branch of service. The engineers are pulling members away from the firemen and vice versa. The O. R. C. is carrying on a national campaign of villification against the B. of R. T., assisted by the Brotherhood of Railway and Steamship Clerks. The switchmen's union, where it is still sufficiently alive, injects itself into this turmoil on its own right, pot calling kettle black, all for the benefit of the roads and the confusion of and division of the membership.

The first step in uniting two or more organizations is to get the members to work together against the attacks of the roads. When such unified action with a common purpose is achieved, physical barriers in the organizations will fall apart of themselves. This seems to be clearly understood by a member of a well-functioning local of the switchmen's union, who writes:

First we want to end this fight between Whitney and Cashen. Then we want to put control of the brotherhoods into the members' hands. We want action on the 6-hour day. We want an answer to the consolidation plans of Eastman and unemployment and old-age protection. We have endorsed H. R. 2827.

In order to make these things possible we want to call a special convention of the switchmen and if possible of the Big Four, jointly to discuss our problems and wipe out internecine warfare.

We are hoping to build in this terminal a local conference of the 21 organizations to build local unity.

Similar moves exist in others of the 21 brotherhoods. They were expressed in the resolutions and activities of the progressive group at the 1933 B. of L. E. convention; in the resolutions against gag rules and for union action to right grievances circulated by the rank-and-file convention committee of the B. of R. T. in 1934–35.

If within each of these organizations at each division point and on each road these various rank-and-file movements work together on all issues which affect them jointly; if these groups become the pivot around which the members in the lodges fight to protect their wages, their contracts, and their jobs, then the day is not far off when the dream of every honest railroad worker for one organization in the industry will be realized.

It was toward this end that the railroad brotherhoods unity movement was organized.

In this direction it has carried on its work. It can claim some credit for the defeat of the last 10-percent wage-cut extension; for the unification of a wider support for an adequate pension bill; for the movement among the railroad unions in favor of the workers' unemployment and social insurance bill (2827); for making concrete proposals to prevent the realization of the lay-off policies of the roads; and, finally, for stimulating organizations of the 21 railroad unions to unify their forces to stop these plans from being put into effect.

In conclusion, the following is from a letter from Brother James Miller, legislative representative, division 611, Eldon, Mo.:

The problems which confront railroad labor today cannot be solved through the use of methods which rapidly changing industrial conditions make obsolete. Our craft organizations which came into being as the result of necessity must for the same reason give place to a higher form of organization.

Having played their part—and a magnificent part it has been—in promoting the interests and advancing the well-being of their members, it is the right of the majority of the members to whom the brotherhoods belong to propose and execute such changes as seem to them necessary in safeguarding and promoting their interests.

Are you willing to cooperate with your fellow worker in what has to be done? If so, talk the matter over in the engine cab, in the caboose, switch shanty, offices, and shops, and help bring about that degree of unity which is essential to success.

Mr. DUNN. I also wish to thank you for your very excellent address.

Mr. McDONALD. For my part, I assure you the efforts of yourself and Mr. Lundeen and the others which are being made in behalf of this bill are very fully appreciated by the railroad workers, especially the rank and file generally, and I am glad to have this opportunity to thank you.

Mr. LUNDEEN. Will the organizations and those you represent continue to communicate with your servants in Washington?

Mr. McDONALD. Most assuredly. We expect to be able to build a fire under them.

Mr. LUNDEEN. Mr. Chairman, if there is nothing further, I move we adjourn until 10 o'clock tomorrow morning.

Mr. DUNN. We will adjourn.

(Whereupon the committee was adjourned at 4:45 p. m. until tomorrow, Thursday, Feb. 14, 1935, at 10 a. m.)

The CHAIRMAN. Before you proceed, I should like to state that the
chairman of the Interprofessional Association for Social Insurance is
Dr. Joseph M. Gillman, an economist of New York, and professor in
the College of the City of New York, who has already appeared before
the subcommittee and has given very valuable testimony.

Mr. HARTWELL (reading) —

UNEMPLOYMENT, OLD-AGE, AND SOCIAL INSURANCE

THURSDAY, FEBRUARY 14, 1935

HOUSE OF REPRESENTATIVES,
SUBCOMMITTEE OF THE COMMITTEE ON LABOR,
Washington, D. C.

The subcommittee met at 10 a. m., in the caucus room, House
Office Building, Hon. Matthew A. Dunn (chairman) presiding.

Mr. DUNN. We are to hear, this morning, from Mr. Albion A.
Hartwell.

STATEMENT OF ALBION A. HARTWELL, EXECUTIVE SECRETARY OF THE INTERPROFESSIONAL ASSOCIATION FOR SOCIAL INSURANCE, NEW YORK CITY, N. Y.

Mr. DUNN. Mr. Hartwell, tell the reporter the organization you
represent.

Mr. HARTWELL. Mr. Chairman, my name is Albion A. Hartwell,
executive secretary of the Interprofessional Association for Social
Insurance. The material which I have here has been prepared by the
research division of the Interprofessional Association for Social Insurance under the direction of Dr. Joseph M. Gillman, economist and
lecturer, of New York, chairman, and he has already appeared here
previously, so you are familiar with his testimony.

Mr. LUNDEEN. He is also connected with the College of the City
of New York?

Mr. HARTWELL. That is right. However, before I begin, I should
like to ask, Mr. Chairman, if there can be included in the record a
telegram which I received this morning from a group of actors in
New York City? They have sent me two telegrams, one asking that
it be read into the record, the other a statement which they would
like to have read into the record. In view of the fact that no actors
have appeared here, and if it is agreeable, I would like to present that
for the record.

Mr. LUNDEEN. Mr. Chairman, I ask that it be included.

Mr. HARTWELL. Would you like it read? It is short.

Mr. LUNDEEN. Certainly.

Mr. HARTWELL (reading).

As actors, we the undersigned wish to record our enthusiastic endorsement of
H. R. 2827, the only unemployment-insurance bill which affords adequate protection to members of our profession.

That is signed by Sam Jaffe, J. Edward Bromberg, Eileen Douglas,
John Brown, and Lionel J. Stander. I might add a further note there,
that this group represents a group in Actors Equity, which is affiliated
with the American Federation of Labor; and because, on his own
statement, Mr. Frank Gilmore, who is president of Actors Equity,

581

will only support a bill which Mr. William Green supports, Actors Equity has not gone on record. However, a group of the rank and file within Actors Equity, represented by these gentlemen here, are going on record in support of the workers bill.

Mr. LUNDEEN. Can you tell me what bill Mr. William Green is supporting? He has declared the administration bill inadequate.

Mr. HARTWELL. Yes. Well, up to the last time I heard from one of these men in Actors Equity, Mr. Green was supporting the administration bill.

Mr. LUNDEEN. In spite of its being inadequate?

Mr. HARTWELL. Apparently.

Mr. LUNDEEN. I had hoped that he would not do that.

Mr. HARTWELL. This is only second-hand testimony that I am giving you on that.

The statement prepared by the research division of the Interprofessional Association for Social Insurance is as follows:

To determine the cost of the social insurance which would be provided in H. R. 2827, requires several estimates, which should be used with caution. In the first place, the United States has no current basis for ascertaining accurately the number of the unemployed. This point is discussed and amplified both in Dr. Gillman's testimony just cited and in the testimony filed by the national chairman of the Interprofessional Association for Social Insurance (Mary van Kleeck) with the House Committee on Labor on February 5, 1935. In lieu of exact data, the best possible estimate has been made, but it should be pointed out that it is the procedure of making the estimate which should be studied, rather than the exact figures. The extent of unemployment changes from time to time, and therefore the figures used today might not be true a month later.

The second and more important point requiring caution relates to the estimate of the effect of social insurance upon purchasing power, and its consequent results in decreasing the amount of unemployment. This point will be discussed more fully later in this foreword, but it should be clear at once that no experience in this country is available to indicate the extent to which an increase in consumers' purchasing power for those in the lower income groups would stimulate production and increase employment.

Having in mind these cautions, it may be said at once that if there be 10,000,000 unemployed the annual gross cost, after taking care otherwise of those who should receive old-age pensions and those who are unemployed because of sickness or disability, and eliminating those under 18 years of age, to whom the workers bill does not apply, would be $8,235,000,000. Deducting from this the estimated decrease in the cost of unemployment insurance on account of the reemployment of workers following the establishment of a social insurance program ($6,090,000,000) and adding to it the cost of old-age pensions, sickness, disability, and accident insurance and maternity insurance, and deducting present annual expenditures for relief amounting to $3,875,000,000, we would have a net annual increase for the Federal Government imposed by the provisions of the workers bill, amounting to $4,060,000,000.

That is on the basis, of course, of 10,000,000 unemployed.

Mr. LUNDEEN. You would say that comes well within the range of our Treasury to handle, would you not?

Mr. HARTWELL. Very much so, I would say. That is, on the basis of Dr. Gillman's statement on February 4 here before this committee.

If the number of unemployed be equal to the average number estimated by us as unemployed in 1934 as 14,021,000, then the annual net increase in cost, after deducting present expenditures for relief and estimating the reemployment which would follow adequate social insurance, would be $5,800,000,000.

If for safety's sake no estimate be made of decrease of cost through reemployment, there would have to be added to this net cost the sum of $8,699,000 if there be 14,000,000 unemployed, or $6,090,000,000 if there be 10,000,000 unemployed.

In all these figures it is necessary to point out that the estimates of cost are merely an indication of the present annual loss suffered by the workers of America through unemployment for the various hazards covered by the workers bill.

It should be pointed out that for any given number of unemployed it is necessary to go through the process of calculation followed in these two estimates. It is not possible merely to divide costs per million, since, for example, the cost of old-age pensions would not be proportionate to the total number of the unemployed. What has been done in these estimates is to attempt to show what factors enter in, always with the understanding that much of the data must represent a guess without adequate statistical basis. There is urgent need for the taking of a current census of the unemployed.

It has already been pointed out that the great unknown is the effect which a social-insurance program would have upon reemployment.

Mr. DUNN. May I interrupt you?

Mr. HARTWELL. Surely.

Mr. DUNN. You said something about its being necessary to take the current census of the unemployed. I might say that I have prepared a bill, now, to take care of that.

Mr. HARTWELL. I had the experience a few weeks ago of going to the Labor Department and trying to find statistics on professional workers, for example, and they had absolutely nothing.

In making the estimates which follow, it is assumed that the entire amount of benefits paid under the workers bill would appear in the market as new purchasing power. Of this total, 60 percent, according to the calculation shown, would become available as wages and salaries. On the basis of given average wages and salaries it can be estimated how many persons could be reemployed, and this would result in a corresponding decrease in the number of unemployed eligible for benefits and therefore in a reduction of costs.

Thus we arrive at the following figures:

On the basis of 14,000,000 as the number of unemployed, the annual gross cost of the workers bill would amount to $18,374,000,000. From this sum should be deducted the $3,875,000,000 currently spent by various governmental agencies to relieve unemployment and in payment of old-age and other benefits to the dependent classes. That leaves a total of $14,499,000,000 as the net benefits under the workers bill. This sum, as new purchasing power, would provide $8,699,000,000 as new pay rolls and reemployment (60 percent of $12,590,000,000). This leaves a balance of $5,800,000,000 as the sum that would have to be provided in addition to current expenditures for relief to meet the cost of unemployment insurance, old-age pensions, and so forth, counting 14,000,000 as the number of unemployed today.

On a basis of 10,000,000 unemployed, the sum would be $4,060,000,000, which, together with present expenditures for relief, would add up to $7,935,-000,000 as the total cost of the program called for under H. R. 2827.

Once more, however, note should be taken of the uncertainty in the allowance made for the amount of reemployment that might follow the adoption of the workers bill. The allowance made assumes an amount of reemployment in proportion to the amount of new purchasing power thus made available. Thus it is assumed that every dollar paid as benefits under the workers bill would go wholly to the market as new purchasing power for consumers' goods. But it is conceivable that a goodly portion of these sums might go to pay debts, and some smaller fractions might go into hiding for a "rainy day." Again, it is calculated that for every dollar paid out in benefits 60 cents would turn up in the form of new wages and salaries. Only to the extent that this may be true, may we expect the return to work of a proportionate number of the unemployed.

Mr. LUNDEEN. That is the statement of an economist.

Mr. HARTWELL. It is the statement of the research group in the Interprofessional Association. It is a group, not only one, you see.

Mr. LUNDEEN. A group of economists and research workers?

Mr. HARTWELL. That is right.

But there is no way of telling whether reemployment to this extent may be expected under present-day circumstances. In the first place, we have not taken into account the amount of commodity stocks on hand and how rapidly they would be used up and how soon workers would have to be put back to work to increase and replenish them.

In the second place, there is no way of estimating with any degree of accuracy the extent of industrial rationalization and technological advance that have taken place in this country in the course of the past 6 years of depression. According to recent findings of the National Industrial Conference Board (Bulletin of Dec. 10, 1934), compared to the 1923–25 average, current pay rolls stood in October last, at 60 percent; employment, at 78.6 percent; and output per man-hour, at 129.5 percent. This means that for the sampling industries covered in the National Industrial Conference Board's survey, 77 workers can now produce as much as 100 did 10 years ago. Twenty-three percent of the workers must now remain unemployed or find employment in new occupations. A similarly distressing situation was recently reported by the Division of Research and Planning of the National Recovery Administration as existing in the automobile industry.

Our estimates of the amount of reemployment, therefore, must be taken as purely mathematical, and should be considered mainly as illustrations of possibilities rather than as probabilities.

Finally, our estimate of total costs of the program for social insurance under the workers' bill should be compared with the amount the workers have lost in wages and salaries since the beginning of the depression. According to stimates published in the Survey of Current Business for January 1935, page 17, total income paid out to labor since 1929 was as follows: 1929, $52,700,000,000; 1930, $48,000,000,000; 1931, $40,700,000,000; 1932, $31,500,000,000; 1933, $29,300,000,000; loss from 1929: 1930, $4,300,000,000; 1931, $12,000,000,000; 1932, $21,200,000,000; 1933, $23,400,000,000.

Mr. DUNN. The comparison between 1932 and 1933, when prosperity started to come from around its corner, shows that instead of more wages being paid, less wages were paid?

Mr. HARTWELL. That is right.

Mr. DUNN. The figures show quite a reduction, is that not true?

Mr. HARTWELL. It represents a loss of $2,200,000,000.

Mr. DUNN. Would you say that, according to those figures, this "prosperity" we have been talking about, in 1933, is mythical?

Mr. HARTWELL. No; I would not. It certainly was prosperity for one group, but nothing accrued to labor during that prosperity.

Mr. DUNN. I am talking about the laboring masses of the people.

Mr. HARTWELL. Certainly there is a definite downward trend shown in those figures as far as labor was concerned in that period.

Mr. DUNN. I notice, while you were reading, that you do not have a comparison for the year 1934.

Mr. HARTWELL. 1934 is not yet available.

"And the total loss in the first 4 years of the depression"—and, that is, the loss to labor, in income paid—"has amounted to $60,900,000,000." That is, adding the year-by-year difference as represented by the figures, there, compared to the 1929 figure.

It is with these huge losses sustained by American workers during these 4 years that the costs of security provided by the workers' bill, H. R. 2827, should be compared.

That is the end of this prepared statement.

The statistical material upon which it is based follows:

ESTIMATES OF COST OF WORKERS' UNEMPLOYMENT, OLD AGE, AND SOCIAL INSURANCE BILL

(Prepared by research section of Interprofessional Association for Social Insurance for hearings before House Committee on Labor with reference to workers' unemployment, old age, and social insurance bill, H. R. 2827, February 1935.)

[NOTE.—Two estimates have been prepared: "A" relates to a hypothetical unit of 10,000,000 unemployed; "B" is calculated for the current estimate of average unemployment in 1934, namely, 14,021,000, the details of which were entered into the record of proceedings before the House Committee on Labor, Feb. 4, 1935, by Joseph M. Gillman, economist, on behalf of the Interprofessional Association for Social Insurance.]

Estimate A

Number of persons unemployed (hypothetical)_____	10, 000, 000

Deductions:

1. Estimated number of unemployed under 18 years of age (basis 1930 Census)_____ — 320, 000
2. Estimated number of unemployed who will replace workers 65 years of age and over retiring on old-age pensions_____ — 2, 250, 000
3. Estimated number unemployed because of sickness or disability_____ — 250, 000

Balance of unemployed_____ 7, 180, 000

I. Annual cost of unemployment insurance (7,180,000 by $1, 147)_____ $8, 235, 000, 000
II. Estimated decrease on account of reemployment of workers, following establishment of social-insurance program_____ 6, 090, 000, 000

III. Annual net cost of unemployment insurance_____ 2, 145, 000, 000
IV. Annual cost of old-age pensions_____ 4, 535, 000, 000
V. Annual cost of sickness, disability, and accident insurance_____ 1, 200, 000, 000
VI. Annual cost of maternity insurance_____ 55, 000, 000

VII. Total annual cost_____ 7, 935, 000, 000
VIII. Present annual expenditures_____ 3, 875, 000, 000

IX. Annual net increase in cost_____ 4, 060, 000, 000

Estimate B

Average number of persons unemployed in 1934, all ages_____	14, 021, 000

Deductions:

1. Estimated number of unemployed under 18 years of age (basis: 1930 Census)_____ 550, 000
2. Estimated number of unemployed who will replace workers 65 years of age and over retiring on old-age pensions (see above)_____ 2, 250, 000
3. Estimated number unemployed because of sickness or disability (see above)_____ 250, 000

Balance of unemployed_____ 10, 971, 000

I. Annual cost of unemployment insurance (10,971,000 by $1, 147) (see p. 586)_____ $12,584,000,000
II. Estimated decrease on account of reemployment of workers, following establishment of social-insurance program (see p. 589)_____ 8, 699, 000, 000

III. Annual net cost of unemployment insurance_____ 3, 885, 000, 000
IV. Annual cost of old-age pensions (see p. 586)_____ 4, 535, 000, 000
V. Annual cost of sickness, disability and accident insurance (see p. 588)_____ 1, 200, 000, 000
VI. Annual cost of maternity insurance (see p. 588)_____ 55, 000, 000

VII. Total annual cost_____ 9, 675, 000, 000
VIII. Present annual expenditures (see p. 589)_____ 3, 875, 000, 000

IX. Annual net increase in cost_____ 5, 800, 000, 000

Estimated annual wage loss of unemployed in 1934

[Based on average annual wage and salary rates for 1932 in National Income Report [1]]

Industry	Unemployed (in thousands)			Annual wage or salary			Loss of earnings (in millions)		
	Wage earners	Salary earners	Not classified	Wage earners	Salary earners	Not classified	Wage earners	Salary earners	Not classified
Agriculture	1,847			[2]$648			$1,196.9		
Mines and quarries	231	18		909	$2,210		210.0	$39.8	
Electric light and power and manufactured gas			73			$1,339			97.7
Manufacturing	2,345	643		876	2,241		2,054.2	1,441.0	
Construction	959	108		1,151	2,297		1,103.8	248.1	
Transportation			1,409			1,409			1,985.3
Communication			253			1,320			334.0
Wholesale and retail		2,200			1,245			2,739.0	
Finance		427			1,958			836.1	
Government:									
(a) Excluding public education		99			1,477			146.2	
(b) Public education		185			1,400			259.0	
Service:									
(a) Recreation			208			1,382			$287.5
(b) Personal			460			1,045			480.7
(c) Domestic			1,123			670			752.4
(d) Professional			373			1,416			528.2
(e) Miscellaneous			79			1,105			87.3
Miscellaneous industries			871			1,285			1,119.2
Total	5,382	3,680	4,849				4,564.9	5,709.2	5,672.3

Total wage and salary loss _____ $15,996,400,000
Unemployed entrepreneurs (110 at annual average loss, $973) _____ 126,200,000

Total _____ 16,072,600,000
Average loss _____ 1,147

[1] 73d Cong., 2d sess., S. Doc. No. 124, National Income, 1929–32.
[2] 1929 rate; 1932 rate only $352.

Cost of old-age pensions

I. (a) Number of persons aged 65 and over (1930 Census) _____ 6,634,000
   (b) Estimated number of persons aged 65 and over in 1934 (President's Committee on Economic Security Report, p. 24) _____ 7,500,000

II. (a) Number of persons aged 65 and over, gainfully occupied (1930) _____ 2,205,000
   (b) Estimated number of persons aged 65 and over who were gainfully occupied in 1934 (average) _____ 2,500,000
      NOTE.—II (b) to II (a) in same ratio as I (b) to I (a).

III. (a) Estimated number of gainfully occupied persons who would be eligible to retire upon enactment of the Workers' Bill___ 2,250,000
      NOTE.—10 percent allowance for entrepreneurs of substantial means (U. S. Census estimate, letter to Committee, IPA, Dec. 3, 1934).

IV. (a) Nongainfully occupied persons aged 65 and over (I (b)– II (b)) _____ 5,000,000
   (b) Estimated number eligible for old-age pensions (males, 1,422,000; females, 3,078,000) _____ 4,500,000
      NOTE.—10 percent allowance for those of substantial means.

Cost of old-age pensions—Continued

V. (a) Number of gainfully occupied persons in III (a) (2,250,000) plus husbands or wives aged 65 and over (777,000, or V (e) + V (g)) or (V (b) + V (c) + V (e) + V (g)) [1] _____ 3, 027, 000

(b) Gainfully occupied males (less entrepreneurs) _____ 1, 950, 000

(c) Gainfully occupied females _____ 300, 000

(d) Gainfully occupied males, married _____ 1, 242, 000

(e) Gainfully occupied males, married, whose wives are 65 and over (assumed not gainfully occupied) _____ 673, 000

(f) Gainfully occupied females, married ___ 104, 000

(g) Gainfully occupied females, married, whose husbands are 65 and over (assumed not gainfully occupied) _____ 104, 000

VI. (a) Balance of married persons among nongainfully occupied ((d) + (e)) _____ 1, 237, 000

(b) Balance of males (1,422,000 − 104,000) (IV (b) − V (g)) _____ 1, 318, 000

(c) Balance of females (3,078,000 − 673,000) (IV − V (a)) _____ 2, 405, 000

(d) Married males in VI (b) ⎫ whose ⎫ = 1,237,000 above _____ { 802, 000
(e) Married males in VI (b) ⎬ ⎬ { 435, 000
wives are 65 and over _____ ⎭ ⎭

Of the 4,500,000 in IV (b), these have been accounted for:

(1) Wives, 65 and over, of gainfully occupied males (assumed not gainfully occupied) (V (e)) _____ 673, 000

(2) Husbands, 65 and over, of gainfully occupied females (assumed not gainfully occupied) (V (g)) _____ 104, 000

(3) Balance nongainfully occupied males 65 and over, married (VI (d)) _____ 802, 000

(4) Balance nongainfully occupied females 65 and over, married (VI (e)) _____ 435, 000

Not yet accounted for:

(5) Nongainfully occupied widows, widowers, divorced, single persons, aged 65 and over _____ 2, 486, 000

Annual cost of old-age pensions

A. Number of gainfully occupied workers aged 65 and over, eligible for old-age pensions at annual average rate of $1,200 per annum ($1,199 average annual rate, 1932, 1929–32 National Income Report) _____ 2, 250, 000

B. Number of married couples nongainfully occupied, husband or both 65 or over _____ 802, 000
Annual pension, $676 ($10 plus $3 per week).

C. Number of unmarried persons 65 or over _____ 2, 486, 000
Annual pension, $520 ($10 per week).

Cost of A _____ $2, 700, 000, 000

Cost of B _____ 542, 000, 000

Cost of C _____ 1, 293, 000, 000

Total _____ 4, 535, 000, 000

[1] All figures in V and VI are estimated from ratios derived from 1930 Census.

Cost of Sickness, Accident, Disability Insurance

Class C, 1930 Unemployment Census (persons out of a job and
unable to work on account of sickness or disability)_____   172, 661

NOTE.—Would assume 250,000, since census figures are out
of line with other experience.

Class D, 1930 Unemployment Census (persons having jobs, but
idle on account of sickness or disability)_____   273, 588

Total_____   446, 249

NOTE.—According to Report of President's Committee on
Economic Security, which states that 2.25 percent of all industrial workers are at all times incapacitated, it would seem that
the total of 446,249 badly underestimates the amount of sickness and disability.

Would assume—
    Class C type_____   250, 000
    Class D type_____   750, 000

                                                          1, 000, 000

Cost of sickness, accident and disability insurance (1,000,000×
$1,200)_____ $1, 200, 000, 000

NOTE.—$1,199 average annual wage or salary in 1932
(National Income Report 1929–32).

Cost of Maternity Insurance

Number of gainfully occupied married women between ages 15 and
  44 (1930 Census)_____   2, 425, 000
Number of married women between ages 15 and 44 (1930 Census)_ 17, 836, 000
Birth rate per 1,000 population (1930)_____   18. 9
Birth rate per 1,000 married women (above)_____   137. 0
Number of births per annum to gainfully occupied married women
  (on above basis)_____   332, 000
Probable number of births_____   150, 000

Annual cost for 16-week benefit (150,000×$369) ($369 = $\frac{16}{52}$×$1,200) $55, 000, 000

NOTE.—$1,199 average annual wage, 1932, National Income Report 1929–32.

---

*Present annual expenditures for unemployment, old age, sickness relief, public
and private*

A. UNEMPLOYMENT

I. Federal Government (source of statistics: General Budget
    Summary, Treasury Department, estimated expendi-
    tures for year ending June 30, 1935, schedule 3):
        (1) Federal Emergency Relief Administration_____ $1, 733, 208, 700
        (2) Civil Works Administration_____   13, 842, 100
        (3) Emergency conservation_____   402, 363, 000
        (4) Relief of unemployment_____   100, 000, 000

    Public Works:
        (3) Loans and grants to municipalities_____ [1] 166, 300, 000
        (5) Public highways_____ [1] 428, 600, 000

        Total expenditures of a relief character_____   2, 844, 313, 800
II. State and city (basis: Federal Emergency Relief Adminis-
    tration reports)_____   400, 000, 000

        Total unemployment relief_____   3, 250, 000, 000

[1] Eliminated from employed, hence deduct as funds to provide employment.

Present annual expenditures for unemployment, old age, sickness relief, public and private—Continued

B. OLD AGE

1. Federal Government to veterans and widows (report of Administrator of Veterans' Affairs, 1933)_____ $235,000,000
2. State old age assistance (President's Committee on Economic Security)_____ 43,000,000
3. Industrial and trade union pensions (President's Committee on Economic Security)_____ 100,000,000
4. All other (rough estimate)_____ 50,000,000

Total_____ 428,000,000

C. SICKNESS, DISABILITY, ACCIDENT (TO GAINFULLY OCCUPIED PERSONS)

NOTE.—National Safety Council estimates for 1932 that wage loss from occupational disabilities was $370,000,000. Compensation probably did not exceed $200,000,000. Practically no other sickness or weekly accident benefits were paid in the United States by governmental agencies.

Total annual expenditures for relief of old age, unemployment, and sickness at present time_____ $3,875,000,000

Estimate of dimunition in cost of unemployment insurance on account of reemployment following passage of workers' bill

Year	National income (excluding Government)[1]	Salaries and wages (excluding Government)[1]
1929	$76,500,000,000	$45,300,000,000
1930	63,500,000,000	40,600,000,000
1931	47,800,000,000	32,900,000,000
1932	34,000,000,000	23,700,000,000
1933	36,300,000,000	21,900,000,000

[1] National Income, 1929–32; National Income, 1933; Survey Current Business, January 1935.

Ratio of salaries and wages to income produced

1929 _____ 0.592
1930 _____ .639
1931 _____ .688
1932 _____ .679
1933 _____ .603
1934 (estimate) _____ .600

Total insurance benefits payable (annually) under workers' bill (p. 585, I+IV+V+VI)_____ $18,374,000,000
Present expenditures for relief, old age, etc_____ 3,875,000,000
Increase in purchasing power of lower income classes upon passage of workers' bill_____ 14,499,000,000
Increase in annual demand for consumers' goods (100 percent assumed) (see Brookings Institute, "America's Capacity to Consume", p. 84)_____ 14,499,000,000
Increase in annual wages and salaries to meet increased demand for goods (decrease in cost of unemployment insurance) (60 percent of $12,590,000,000) (ratio of salaries and wages to income produced, 1934, above)_____ 8,699,000,000

Mr. LUNDEEN. I would like to have the contrasting statements, as to the tremendous increase in a few great fortunes and great incomes. Have you that?

Mr. HARTWELL. I do not have that, but I have the increase in profits, the comparison of jobs, wages, and profits, which was submitted to the research division of the Interprofessional Association by the Labor Research Association.

Mr. LUNDEEN. That might serve somewhat the same purpose?

Mr. HARTWELL. That is right, and this is in statistical form. I submit it for the record, showing a comparison of profits and wages according to industries.

Mr. LUNDEEN. It is not a long document?

Mr. HARTWELL. No.

Mr. LUNDEEN. I ask that it be inserted.

Mr. DUNN. All right.

Mr. LUNDEEN. Are you going to review it?

Mr. HARTWELL. I shall not, unless you request me to.

Mr. LUNDEEN. All right, then, I ask that it be inserted. For the purpose of the record, I would like to have that same information. I do not care what source you have it from, except that it must be from some accepted source, relating to that ever-decreasing number of great fortunes that are piling skyward.

Mr. HARTWELL. Those figures have been published, and we will prepare them for you and submit them for the record, if you wish.

Mr. LUNDEEN. Will you do that?

Mr. HARTWELL. I will.

Mr. LUNDEEN. I would like that in this record, because this hearing, though many people do not realize it, is going to be a textbook for a great many discussions in the next 10 years.

Mr. HARTWELL. That is right. As one man remarked the other day, it will save the historians a great deal of time and trouble some day.

Mr. DUNN. May I also suggest that you get those figures, because tomorrow we discontinue, and we want this to go to press as soon as possible.

Mr. HARTWELL. I cannot promise that immediately, Mr. Dunn.

Mr. DUNN. You cannot?

Mr. HARTWELL. I can only promise it within the next 3 or 4 days. I will read you a statement here which has been prepared by the Labor Research Association:

INCREASED PROFITS OF CORPORATIONS AND INCREASED INCOME FOR THE RICH; LESS FOR THE WORKERS

That the "new deal" has increased the income of the rich at the expense of the workers and lower middle-class groups is clearly shown by the figures on Federal income taxes in 1933, recently made public by the Bureau of Internal Revenue. While the number of million-dollar incomes more than doubled in the year between 1932 and 1933, incomes of less than $5,000 were sharply cut.

Corporations reporting net income in 1933 showed a gain of 35 percent in their earnings for the year. Individuals with net income of $25,000 or more enjoyed an increase of almost 10 percent in total income reported. On the other hand, those receiving less than $25,000 a year suffered a decline of about 4 percent in total income reported during that "recovery" year.

The largest decrease in income was suffered by the lowest income group, those earning less than $5,000, whose total income dropped by $320,000,000. The number of returns in this group was more than 2 percent lower than in 1932, since fewer had that much income to report and the aggregate net income shown was down well over 4 percent.

In the very high income brackets, on the other hand, there were spectacular increases for individuals in 1933. Where in 1932 there were 20 persons who reported incomes of over a million, in 1933 there were 46 reporting such incomes.

One of these drew more than $5,000,000 (probably John D. Rockefeller, Jr.), corresponding to the total relief income of about 20,000 unemployed families, or some 80,000 persons.

The little group at the top of 46 million-dollar-income persons got $81,558,981 in 1933 as compared with $35,239,556 that went to the million-dollar group in 1932. Thus while the number of these richest individuals doubled in the year, the amount they took increased by more than 130 percent.

Sharp increases were shown for 1933 in profits from sales of real estate, stocks, and bonds.

But during the same period, total wages and salaries on which income taxes were paid decreased by about $567,600,000 from $7,764,393,347 in 1932 to $7,198,828,256 in 1933—a drop of almost 8 percent.

Large numbers of salaried and professional persons, as well as small business men, failed to enjoy any increase in income in 1933 as compared with 1932. Commenting editorially on these facts, the Journal of Commerce (Dec. 11, 1934), admits that the situation was even worse for the lower-income groups than the figures would indicate, because of the increased cost of living.

"In fact, their position changed for the worse last year even more than the income-tax returns would indicate, for they faced a period of rising living costs and taxation with smaller incomes."

Back of these figures on the larger incomes for the rich and the smaller incomes for the poorer groups are the facts on increased profits of corporations, represent ing increased exploitation of the workers. Profits have increased greatly in 1934 as compared with 1933. For 392 firms, as reported by Standard Statistics Co., net profits after all deductions aggregated $335,870,000 during the first 6 months of 1934, an increase of 609 percent over the corresponding period of last year. For 166 of the larger industrial firms, net income aggregated $175,000,000 in the first three-quarters of 1933 and $300,000,000 in the first three-quarters of 1934. (For further information on profits, see Labor Research Association, Economic Notes, August, September, November, 1934.)

Is that sufficient?

Mr. LUNDEEN. Yes, we want facts and authorities.

Mr. HARTWELL. You would like a list of these?

Mr. LUNDEEN. I would like to have it detailed a little more than that. The statement in itself, of course, is a good statement, but if we could get a little more detailed information in the record there for reference, I should be glad to have it.

Mr. HARTWELL. Do you want us to prepare a more detailed statement?

Mr. LUNDEEN. I would like to have that.

The statement requested by Mr. Lundeen follows:

Comparison of net income returns for 1932 and 1933 [1]

Net income classes	Number of returns	
	1932	1933
Up to $5,000	3,420,995	[2] 3,339,602
$5,000 to $10,000	237,273	[2] 219,735
$10,000 to $25,000	77,045	[2] 74,626
$25,000 to $50,000	17,658	18,168
$50,000 to $100,000	5,644	5,927
$100,000 to $150,000	962	1,085
$150,000 to $300,000	589	693
$300,000 to $500,000	136	139
$500,000 to $1,000,000	80	84
Over $1,000,000	20	46
Total returns filed to Aug. 31, 1932	3,760,402	
Total returns filed to Aug. 31, 1933		3,660,105

[1] Prepared by the research division of the Interprofessional Association for Social Insurance on the basis of the preliminary report entitled "Statistics of Income for 1933", submitted to the Hon. H. Morgenthau, Jr., Secretary of the Treasury, on Dec. 3, 1934.
[2] Incomes of less than $25,000 declined in number of returns from 1932 to 1933. All income classes above $25,000 increased in number of returns. Net incomes of $1,000,000 or over increased 130 percent in number of returns.

Mr. LUNDEEN. In the midst of this poverty, destitution, and hunger, we should have a detailed statement as to the increase in wealth on the part of the multimillionaires and billionaires of this country, the profits of the great corporations, and how they are increasing their wealth in the midst of this destitution and poverty, clearly set forth.

Mr. DUNN. Congressman Lundeen, is it not a fact that we tried to obtain that information on the floor of the House, to get the incomes of those who were not paying any taxes?

Mr. LUNDEEN. Indeed, Mr. Chairman, and it was overwhelmingly defeated. We rallied 108 Congressmen who wanted that information, to something like 242 Congressmen who preferred to let the veil of secrecy remain.

Mr. DUNN. But is it not a fact that both of us were willing to get that information?

Mr. LUNDEEN. Indeed.

Mr. DUNN. We voted to get it, so that the people of the United States would know.

Mr. LUNDEEN. I will say, Mr. Chairman, you have always supported measures of that kind, to give information to the public.

Mr. DUNN. You have done likewise. The reason I know that you have is because I can always tell your voice when you vote.

Do you want to interrogate the witness any more, Congressman Lundeen?

Mr. LUNDEEN. That is all.

(The statement presented for the record by the Witness Hartwell, Entitled, "Jobs, Wages, and Profits During the Crisis Years", is as follows:)

JOBS, WAGES, AND PROFITS DURING THE CRISIS YEARS

Prepared by Labor Research Association

The data which follows are presented for the purpose of showing certain trends in employment and earnings of workers and the profits made by corporations during recent years. The figures speak for themselves, showing the contrast between the amounts received by the wage-earning class—due to unemployment, part-time unemployment, and wage cuts—and the amounts which were reported as profits during the same period by leading corporations in various industries.

These figures show very clearly the way in which the position of the workers has become less and less secure, and, in the absence of unemployment insurance, they show just what it has cost the working class to carry the crisis on their shoulders while corporations were reporting substantial profits which in a large number of cases were translated into dividends for the investing class.

EMPLOYMENT, PAY ROLLS, AND ANNUAL EARNINGS

Severity of the decline in employment in manufacturing industries in the United States between 1929 and 1933 is clearly indicated by table I which shows the percentage declines, industry by industry. In some instances the decline was as much as 50 or 60 percent. The greatest declines are noted in such producers' goods industries as electric manufacturing, lumber, and foundry and machine shop products.

The list of selected manufacturing industries given in tables II and III includes all industries which employed over a hundred thousand wage earners in 1933 with the exception of the motor vehicles industry, which covered about 98,000 wage earners in 1933. Table I shows that out of every 100 wage earners employed in 1929 only 40 were employed in the electrical industry in 1933, only 43 in the motor vehicle industry, only 45 in lumber and timber products, and so on.

This sharp decline in employment between 1929 and 1933 was accompanied by an even sharper decline in pay rolls or the total amount of wages paid to the workers who were still employed. As indicated by table I, pay rolls dropped as much as 74.6 percent in the electrical machinery industry, 73.2 percent in lumber and 71.7 percent in the motor vehicle industry. This greater decline in the pay-roll column was of course due to the wage cuts forced upon the workers as well as the part-time work prevalent under the stagger or share-the-work system, under which the workers actually shared their misery with one another.

The effect on individual workers of the relatively greater decline in pay rolls than in employment may be better observed from table II, which shows the decline in average yearly earnings from 1929, 1931, and 1933, industry by industry. Here we find that average yearly earnings of workers in some industries dropped as much as 46.4 percent, for example in steel works and rolling mills. It should be noted also that some industries that showed relatively smaller declines in average yearly earnings were those that showed a very low average to begin with in 1929. The lowest in 1929 was cotton goods which declined to $570 in 1933.

Compared with the drop in the cost of living, as measured by the budgets of the United States Bureau of Labor Statistics—a drop which amounted, even according to their figures, to only 23 percent between 1929 and 1933—we find that the decline in average yearly wages in most industries was far greater. In one of them—steel works and rolling mills—the wage drop actually doubled the drop in the cost of living.

The data on separate industries as given in table III shows the extent of the actual decline in various manufacturing industries from 1929 to 1933. It will be seen that even those industries such as meat packing and steel that showed some increase in employment between 1931 and 1933, registered at the same time a still further drop in annual earnings.

TABLE I.—*Decline in employment and pay rolls in selected manufacturing industries in the United States from 1929 to 1933* [1]

Industry	Percentage decline, 1929 to 1933	
	Employ- ment	Pay rolls
All food industries	−11. 6	−31. 2
Bread and bakery products	−9. 2	−28. 4
Boots and shoes, other than rubber	−7. 2	−36. 1
Electrical machinery, apparatus and supplies	−60. 2	−74. 6
Foundry and machine shop products	−52. 4	−71. 0
Furniture, including store and office equipment	−45. 5	−68. 6
Lumber and timber products	−54. 8	−73. 2
Meat packing, wholesale	−7. 6	−32. 3
Motor vehicle bodies and parts	−34. 2	−59. 5
Motor vehicles	−56. 7	−71. 7
Nonferrous metals and their products	−40. 2	−62. 4
Printing and publishing	−24. 0	−42. 2
Steel works and rolling mill products	−29. 8	−62. 4
Textiles and their products	−13. 7	−41. 3
Clothing, women's	−14. 8	−47. 7
Cotton goods	−10. 7	−33. 3
Knit goods	−9. 0	−37. 3
Silk and rayon goods	−15. 4	−46. 1

[1] Based on U. S. Census of Manufactures. With the exception of motor vehicles industry, all industries covered had 100,000 or more wage earners in 1933. All 1933 figures used for this table are preliminary. Slight corrections may be made in the final census tabulations.

TABLE II.—*Average yearly earnings and percentage decline from 1929 to 1933 in selected manufacturing industries in the United States* [1]

Industry	Average yearly earnings			Percentage decline from 1929–33
	1929	1931	1933	
All food industries	$1,198	$1,142	$931	−22.3
Bread and bakery products	1,367	1,307	1,078	−21.1
Boots and shoes, other than rubber	1,082	900	744	−31.2
Electrical machinery, apparatus and supplies	1,388	1,135	885	−36.2
Foundry and machine shop products	1,535	1,153	933	−39.2
Furniture, including store and office equipment	1,256	987	724	−42.4
Lumber and timber products	1,006	793	598	−40.6
Meat packing, wholesale	1,354	1,261	992	−26.7
Motor vehicle bodies and parts	1,656	1,286	1,018	−38.5
Motor vehicles	1,621	1,162	1,060	−34.6
Nonferrous metals and their products	1,409	1,150	886	−37.1
Printing and publishing	1,801	1,717	1,368	−24.0
Steel works and rolling mill products	1,746	1,279	935	−46.4
Textiles and their products	1,015	871	690	−32.0
Clothing, women's	1,301	1,088	797	−38.7
Cotton goods	763	666	570	−25.3
Knit goods	1,011	840	696	−31.2
Silk and rayon goods	1,054	892	672	−36.2

[1] Same source as table I.

TABLE III [1]

ALL FOOD INDUSTRIES

Year	Wage earners	Wages	Average yearly earnings
1929	753,247	$902,143,000	$1,198
1931	635,359	725,669,000	1,142
1933	666,237	620,558,000	931

BREAD AND BAKERY PRODUCTS

Year	Wage earners	Wages	Average yearly earnings
1929	200,841	$274,562,000	$1,367
1931	183,161	239,331,000	1,307
1933	182,382	196,672,000	1,078

BOOTS AND SHOES (OTHER THAN RUBBER)

Year	Wage earners	Wages	Average yearly earnings
1929	205,640	$222,408,000	$1,082
1931	181,374	163,271,000	900
1933	190,914	142,054,000	744

ELECTRICAL MACHINERY, APPARATUS, AND SUPPLIES

Year	Wage earners	Wages	Average yearly earnings
1929	328,722	$456,378,000	$1,388
1931	180,106	204,488,000	1,135
1933	130,857	115,750,000	885

FOUNDRY AND MACHINE SHOP PRODUCTS

Year	Wage earners	Wages	Average yearly earnings
1929	454,441	$697,509,000	$1,535
1931	284,900	328,459,000	1,153
1933	216,439	201,940,000	933

FURNITURE, INCLUDING STORE AND OFFICE EQUIPMENT

Year	Wage earners	Wages	Average yearly earnings
1929	193,399	$242,832,000	$1,256
1931	127,605	125,972,000	987
1933	105,488	76,346,000	724

[1] Source: Same as tables I and II. The third column is obtained by dividing the second column by the first.

LUMBER AND TIMBER PRODUCTS

Year	Wage earners	Wages	Average yearly earnings
1929	419,084	$421,585,000	$1,006
1931	196,647	155,870,000	793
1933	189,367	113,183,000	598

MEAT PACKING, WHOLESALE

1929	122,505	$165,867,000	$1,354
1931	106,707	134,530,000	1,261
1933	113,193	112,266,000	992

MOTOR VEHICLES

1929	226,116	$366,579,000	$1,621
1931	134,866	156,756,000	1,162
1933	97,869	103,785,000	1,060

MOTOR-VEHICLE BODIES AND PARTS

1929	221,332	$366,503,000	$1,656
1931	150,649	193,770,000	1,286
1933	145,745	148,322,000	1,018

NONFERROUS METALS AND THEIR PRODUCTS

1929	314,741	$443,467,000	$1,409
1931	208,855	240,177,000	1,150
1933	188,271	166,722,000	886

PRINTING AND PUBLISHING

1929	281,119	$506,290,000	$1,801
1931	255,480	438,630,000	1,717
1933	213,786	292,472,000	1,368

STEEL WORKS AND ROLLING MILL PRODUCTS

1929	394,574	$689,016,000	$1,746
1931	264,634	338,387,000	1,279
1933	276,847	258,803,000	935

TEXTILES AND THEIR PRODUCTS

1929	1,707,798	$1,733,031,000	$1,015
1931	1,420,808	1,238,179,000	871
1933	1,474,325	1,017,301,000	690

WOMEN'S CLOTHING

1929	187,500	$243,851,000	$1,301
1931	173,890	189,187,000	1,088
1933	159,832	127,418,000	797

COTTON GOODS

1929	424,916	$324,289,000	$763
1931	329,962	219,680,000	666
1933	379,445	216,384,000	570

KNIT GOODS

Year	Wage earners	Wages	Average yearly earnings
1929	208, 488	$210, 714, 000	$1, 011
1931	178, 011	149, 589, 000	840
1933	189, 698	132, 030, 000	696

SILK AND RAYON GOODS

1929	130, 467	$137, 547, 000	$1, 054
1931	109, 225	97, 409, 000	892
1933	110, 322	74, 110, 000	672

SPECIAL MEMO ON COAL MINING

The problem of the coal industry is not simply a result of the present great depression. Progressive unemployment and decline in wages began in the years preceding 1929. The data given below show that coal miners in the bituminous and also in the anthracite fields have been exposed to severe unemployment and wage cutting for an even longer period of time than workers in other industries.

In all, about 325,000 miners were dropped by the coal industry in the 10 years between 1923 and 1933, according to figures from the United States Bureau of Mines, shown in table IV. In 1923 the soft coal industry employed 704,793 workers, while in 1929 the figure was 502,993. In 1932 the number employed in soft coal mines was 406,380. In 1933 total employment was still only 418,703 in the bituminous industry. In other words, 286,000 men who had jobs in this industry in 1923 were out of the industry in 1933. Nor do preliminary figures for 1934 indicate much improvement in employment.

TABLE IV.—*Bituminous coal industry*

Average number of men employed at mines in operation—

1923	704, 793
1929	502, 993
1930	493, 202
1931	450, 213
1932	406, 380
1933	418, 703

Anthracite mining dropped about 40,000 men between 1923 and 1932. From 157,743 workers employed in 1923, the number fell to 151,501 in 1929, to 139,431 in 1931, and then to only 121,243 in 1932. The index of employment in anthracite mining in November 1934, as given by the United States Bureau of Labor Statistics in Trend of Employment, shows employment in anthracite mining standing at only 60.7 percent of the 1929 level.

About 325,000 mine workers, including 286,000 from the bituminous industry and about 40,000 from the anthracite industry, are the jobless mine workers who cannot find work in or around the coal mines of the United States.

A report just issued by the U. S. Bureau of Labor Statistics under the title "Wages and hours of labor in bituminous coal mining: 1933." shows how wages of soft coal miners have fallen since 1922.

Here is the summary conclusion of this Government Bureau in reporting the earnings of miners, loaders, and other wage earners in all occupations in the industry, during the early part of 1933:

"The various studies made by the Bureau of Labor Statistics of wages and hours of labor of wage earners in the bituminous-coal industry in the United States show that there has been a continuous decrease in average earnings in the industry from 1922 to 1933.

"The amount earned per hour averaged 85.3 cents in 1922; 78.8 cents in 1924, 76.3 cents in 1926; 65.9 cents in 1929; 59.8 cents in 1931, and 41 cents per hour in 1933. *The decrease between 1922 and 1933 was 52 percent and between 1929 and 1933 was 38 percent.*" (Our italic—L. R. A.)

For miners and loaders, representing nearly two-thirds (63.3 percent) of all the mine workers, the drop in average hourly earnings was even greater. Where miners and loaders averaged 91.5 cents an hour in 1922, they averaged only 39.5

cents an hour in 1933. The report points out that this average per hour in 1933 is 57 percent less than the 1922 average and 34 percent less than the 1931 average.

Miners and loaders averaged $7.03 a day in 1922. By 1931 average earnings per day had dropped to $4.82, and by 1933 to $3.18.

Yet while wages fell, the average time per day spent in the mine increased from 8.3 hours in 1922 to 8.9 hours in 1933. Miners must now spend more time in traveling to get from the mine mouth to the working face and back, as the mines in the United States are gradually worked out. Here are a few figures that show how earnings fell, while hours increased, for miners and loaders:

TABLE V.—*Bituminous coal mining—Average hours and earnings of miners and loaders, 1922–33*

	Average hours (time in mine)	Average earnings	
		Half month	Per day
1922	8.3	$62.30	$7.03
1924	8.5	54.44	6.60
1926	8.6	61.61	6.46
1929	8.8	49.85	5.50
1931	8.8	33.82	4.82
1933	8.9	22.59	3.18

But this Government report just issued does not point out that N. R. A. code wages for miners in 8 of the 17 districts have now been set at a rate lower than the average for all miners in 1931. Where the general average 4 years ago was $4.82 a day, the N. R. A. basic day rate is $4.60 in district C, and only $3.80 in Alabama, Georgia, and southern Tennessee.

In November 1934, according to the Trend of Employment issued by the United States Bureau of Labor Statistics, the total pay roll in bituminous mining was still only 58.3 percent of the 1929 level.

In anthracite mining the same Federal bureau shows total pay rolls in November 1934 as only 51.2 percent of the 1929 level.

It should always be kept in mind, in connection with these tables, that "net income" or "net profits", as shown in a corporation report, do not adequately reflect the real earnings of the corporation. This is because of the many ways that can be used to hide the real profits made during a given period. Excessive reserves for bad debts, inventory losses, contingencies, depreciation, and depletion, and income charges to write-down patents, trade marks, and goodwill, are among the widely used methods to scale down the published profit figures.

Furthermore, many unproductive expenditures are made. These include large advertising appropriations, large salaries and bonuses to executives, large outlays for rent and other office expenditures, charges and fees for services—as for example in the utility industry—excessive interest payments and commissions to bankers and bondholders and other similar items. Such expenditures, from the workers' point of view, are so much waste and are wholly unnecessary for the maintenance of production.

It should also be noted that a "deficit" shown by a corporation does not mean that it is any poorer at the end of a given period. For example, many instances of increased cash resources and greater financial strength are revealed even after a year when large "losses" were made public.

TABLE VI.—*Net profit of certain representative companies in tobacco, food, automobiles, tires, meat-packing, and shoe and leather industries*

TOBACCO

Company	1934	1933	1932	1931	1930
American Cigar Co		$2,666,628	$2,711,963		
Consolidated Cigar Co	$778,217	497,779	935,858	$2,122,173	$2,372,535
General Cigar	2,333,545	721,520	2,058,370	2,720,667	3,201,522
American Tobacco Co.[1]		17,401,208	43,267,084	46,189,741	43,294,669
Liggett & Meyers Tobacco Co	20,086,690	16,731,175	23,075,213	23,121,382	24,002,315
R. J. Reynolds Tobacco Co.[1]	21,536,894	21,153,722	33,674,800	36,396,817	34,250,665
U. S. Tobacco Co.[1]		3,396,484	3,534,934	3,020,779	2,950,818

[1] In 1934, 1 of 49 industrial companies paying dividends as high or higher than in 1929.

FOOD [2]

Company	1934	1933	1932	1931	3930
Continental Baking	$2,004,672	$2,788,430	$2,781,938	$4,273,193	$6,149,144
General Baking	1,941,371	2,035,649	3,789,625	4,838,123	5,165,982
California Packing Co		4,131,863		4,877,595	91,180
Borden Co		4,646,444	7,524,489	16,812,269	21,681,214
National Dairy	[3] 4,009,388	7,051,872	12,537,380	22,547,974	26,254,326
National Biscuit	[4] 8,931,969	14,995,305	17,104,125	19,739,491	22,879,898
Great Atlantic & Pacific		22,732,772	29,792,974	30,742,776	26,219,631
Kroger Grocery & Baking		4,546,203	2,740,867	2,731,128	2,168,247
National Tea Co	[5] 327,632	1,180,390	899,504	716,279	1,239,926
Safeway Stores	[3] 1,781,692	4,289,635	4,390,227	5,415,590	3,749,901

[2] Note the specially strong profits of these food companies. It should be noted also that their declines from 1933 to 1934, in spite of the increase in prices, indicates the decline in purchasing power of the masses under the "New Deal" and consequent decrease in food consumption.

Source.—Company reports and Moody's Industrials. Blank spaces indicate either "deficits" or no reports yet available.

MOTOR VEHICLES AND TIRES [6]

Cord Corporation	$75,320	$1,380,007	$1,523,503	$582,788	$1,477,477
Chrysler Corporation	[4] 9,422,826	12,129,120		1,468,935	234,155
General Motors	94,769,000	83,213,676	230,599	96,770,407	153,766,247
Motor Products Co	[4] 252,103	[4] 169,027			487,140
Motor Wheel Corporation	[4] 613,909	[4] 313,293			1,096,751
Briggs Manufacturing Co	[4] 4,825,576	1,591,425		688,932	4,035,913
General Tire & Rubber	679,199	414,912	202,354		542,579
Goodrich (B. F.) Co	[3] 1,486,956	2,272,514			
Goodyear Tire & Rubber	[3] 2,617,197	4,134,006		5,454,047	9,912,233

MEAT PACKING

Armour & Co	$8,235,835	$8,121,641			$4,741,027
Cudahy Packing Co	1,986,262	1,813,766	$905,985	$2,009,991	2,930,318
Swift & Co	11,602,156	10,297,378		676,993	12,491,189
Wilson & Co	3,840,923	3,055,925	51,336		2,542,656

SHOE AND LEATHER

Endicott-Johnson Co	$2,167,678	$2,154,941	$1,188,241	$2,580,566	$765,268
International Shoe Co	8,967,024	9,090,567	6,647,527	9,744,815	12,874,104
Melville Shoe Corporation	[3] 1,074,402	1,355,517	721,644	945,993	

[3] 6 months.
[4] 9 months.
[5] 40 weeks.
[6] A few companies in auto parts and tractor field are given in this table.

TABLE VII.—*Net profits of certain steel, metal, and allied products companies* [1]

Company	1934	1933	1932	1931	1930
Acme Steel Co	$1,031,116	$941,794	$21,340	$372,027	$940,949
Allegheny Steel Co	[2] 626,000	292,017		50,228	1,610,293
American Rolling Mill Co	[2] 1,454,000				251,886
American Smelting & Refining Co	[3] 4,263,577	6,010,384		874,976	11,098,751
Atlantic Steel Co	116,720	54,274			
Bendix Aviation Corporation	[2] 1,742,000	1,242,891		1,555,479	1,183,860
Bethlehem Steel Corporation	550,571			115,745	23,843,406
Bohn Aluminum & Brass Corporation	[2] 1,263,456	1,494,552		295,333	725,596
Bridgeport Brass Co	[2] 392,944	314,582			
Buckeye Steel Castings Co	181,198				854,236
A. M. Castle & Co. (iron and steel products)	304,308	102,824			365,105
Caterpillar Tractor Co	3,651,190	302,717		1,361,200	8,714,801
Chicago Pneumatic Tool Co	[2] 291,211	93,091			209,839
Compo Shoe Machinery Corporation	[2] 204,003	184,219	124,341		
Continental Can Co	10,707,122	7,547,401	4,819,323	5,670,699	8,738,094
Corrigan, McKinney Steel Co	729,050				
Crucible Steel Co. of America	[3] 712,034				4,045,122
Deere & Co. (tractors)	379,734			406,554	8,299,112
Electric Auto-Lite Co	[2] 1,421,000	684,372	1,364,059	3,913,833	5,024,477
Food Machinery Corporation	485,412			446,597	

See footnotes at end of table.

TABLE VII.—*Net profits of certain steel, metal, and allied products companies* [1]—Continued

Company	1934	1933	1932	1931	1930
Fostoria Pressed Steel Corporation	$11,664	$914	$8,353		
Granite City Steel Co.[2]	[2] 154,000	506,652	13,827	$332,319	
Gulf States Steel Co	[3] 191,803	193,041			
Hercules Motors Corporation	[2] 144,722	76,515		324,861	
Inland Steel Co	3,730,332	166,693		1,263,599	$6,498,967
International Business Machines Corporation	[4] 5,611,702	6,725,342	7,642,877	8,707,131	8,340,426
Iron Fireman Manufacturing Co	521,708	330,784			
Ludlum Steel Co	[2] 442,436	161,063			
McKeesport Tin Plate Co	[3] 833,407	1,888,417	1,503,088	1,952,029	2,503,897
Midland Steel Products Co	[2] 374,000	672,729		775,744	1,271,968
Moto Meter Gauge & Equipment Corporation	[2] 438,629	150,666			
F. E. Myers & Bro. Co. (pumps)	567,744	242,776	197,116	643,250	
National-Standard Co. (wire cables)	388,123	359,654	256,033	621,867	
National Steel Corporation	6,050,724	2,812,407	1,662,920	4,443,324	8,415,822
New Jersey Zinc Co	[2] 2,833,149	3,994,073	2,013,120	3,051,589	5,013,403
Otis Steel Co	[2] 732,211				868,730
Remington Rand Inc	[3] 389,000	554,307			
Republic Steel Corporation	[3] 805,443				
Jos. T. Ryerson & Son (steel products)	1,380,897	301,490			
Sharon Steel Hoop Co	[3] 436,671	105,719			
Spang, Chalfant & Co	[2] 621,912				3,414,214
Sperry Corporation	[3] 874,745	455,818			
U. S. Pipe & Foundry Co	818,068			1,012,216	2,881,046
U. S. Smelting, Refining & Mining Co	[5] 5,711,746	5,169,875	1,995,232	2,504,759	3,699,656
Warren Foundry & Pipe Co	818,068			294,188	417,143
Wheeling Steel Corporation	[2] 145,390				2,697,103

[1] Compiled from Moody's Industrials.   [2] 9 months.   [3] 6 months.   [4] 10 months.   [5] 11 months.

Mr. LUNDEEN. Mr. Chairman, I think at this time we should hear some of the telegrams, at least, that have been received. I do not know whether the letters are too long to be read or not, but the telegrams at least should be read, and possibly some of the briefer, shorter letters that have been sent in to your office should likewise be read, Mr. Chairman, letters that have come from all over the United States, from very important organizations. As I understand it, there are many hundreds, and even thousands of communications besides these, but I understand that you bring these in as samples of the communications that are being received in your office.

Mr. DUNN. As I stated, I have received many communications from various organizations and individuals, supporting the Lundeen bill, H. R. 2827.

Mr. LUNDEEN. I could bring in, Mr. Chairman, stacks of communications which I have received, but I prefer that you, as chairman of the committee, present such communications as you care to present.

Mr. DUNN. I think it would be good material for the record to give the people who are going to read it an idea of the many organizations that have supported the bill. I maintain it is worth while to read some of these telegrams that I have received. Proceed to read them, Miss McChesney.

Miss McCHESNEY (secretary). With the exception of one or two telegrams, the following telegrams are all addressed to the chairman of the subcommittee, Mr. Dunn.

The first telegram is from Philadelphia, Pa., dated January 26, 1935, and reads as follows:

We, the undersigned, do heartily endorse the bill H. R. 2827, and also ask your endorsement.

That is signed, Susquehanna Branch Unemployment Council, Cora Danridge, secretary.

The next telegram is from Philadelphia, Pa., dated February 6, 1935, and reads as follows:

Support workers' unemployment, old-age, and social insurance bill, H. R. 2827.

It is signed, N. Sanick, secretary, U. T. Organization in Philadelphia, Pa.

The next telegram is from Pittsburgh, Pa., dated February 7, 1935, and reads as follows:

We, the members of Branch No. 2, Lithuanian Supreme Lodge of America, held meeting February 3, 1935, at 2 p. m., McKees Rocks Borough, representing membership of 200, overwhelmingly endorsed the Lundeen bill, H. R 2827. Since you are a chairman of this important subcommittee we have faith in you to get this bill in act. Yours sincerely.

It is signed, president of Lithuanian Supreme Lodge of America, Joseph Marazowski, 24 Locust St., McKees Rocks, Pa.

The next telegram is from New Brunswick, N. J., and is dated February 7, 1935, and reads as follows:

We urgently request your support of workers' insurance bill, H. R. 2837, introduced by Representative Lundeen by unanimous resolution of mass meeting of North Stelton Citizens League.

It is signed, H. Luderer, secretary.

The next telegram is from New York, N. Y., dated February 8, 1935, and reads as follows:

Be advised that the 2,000 members of Pharmacists Union of Greater New York support and urge the immediate passage of H. R. 2827, the workers' unemployment old-age and social insurance bill which we, with millions of others, recognize the only measure that makes the necessary provision for genuine social insurance. We absolutely oppose the Wagner-Lewis bill as entirely inadequate.

It is signed, Benjamin M. Barish, president Pharmacists Union of Greater New York, 55 West 42.

The next telegram is from Philadelphia, Pa., dated February 8, 1935, and reads as follows:

Be it resolved that we, the members of the Association of White Collar Workers, in meeting assembled on Thursday February 7, 1935, do hereby demand that the Workers Unemployment, Old Age, and Social Insurance Act, H. R. 2827, be voted out of the House Committee on Labor to the floor of the House of Representatives of the Congress of the United States for favorable action and be it further resolved that a copy of this resolution be forwarded to Mr. Mathew A. Dunn, chairman of the subcommittee holding public meeting on Act H. R. 2827. And be it further resolved that the contents of this resolution be written into the minutes of the subcommittee.

It is signed, Association of White Collar Workers, Frank J. Goodwin.

The next telegram is from New York, N. Y., dated February 8, 1935, and reads as follows:

Dear sir: The Textile Trimming Workers Union, with a membership of over 2,000, many of whom are unemployed, are opposed to the Wagner-Lewis bill because it does not provide the necessary means for the unemployed. We demand immediate favorable action on the workers unemployment insurance bill, H. R. 2827, introduced by Representative Lundeen. We favor this bill because it is the only bill which provides a measure of relief for the unemployed.

It is signed, R. Zucker, secretary, Textile Trimming Workers Union, 5 East Nineteenth Street, New York City.

The next telegram is from New York, N. Y., dated February 8, 1935, and reads as follows:

The full membership of the Writers Union equivocally endorses and pledges its support of the Lundeen unemployment and social insurance bill, H. R. 2827, and repudiates the Wagner-Lewis bill as grossly made "to meet the social and economic needs of the masses of the people."

It is signed, Writers Union.

The next telegram is from New York, N. Y., dated February 12, 1935, and reads as follows:

We, thousands of workers, demand that you immediately act on the workers bill, H. R. 2827, and bring it out for immediate vote on the floor of Congress, this bill is the only genuine social unemployment insurance bill, pass this bill at once.

It is signed Rutger Square Local of Unemployment Council, Madison Street, New York.

The next telegram is from Philadelphia, Pa., dated February 11, 1935, and reads as follows:

Societa M. S. Montorioal Al Vomanto insists you support H. R. 2827. Our organization 90. Reply your stand requested to read before membership.

It is signed Vincent Minervini, 1224½ Dickinson Street, Philadelphia, Pa.

The next telegram is from Detroit, Mich., dated February 12, 1935, and reads as follows:

Appreciate your effort in behalf bill H. R. 2827. Best wishes for success.

It is signed Branch 274 Pennsylvania Slovak Roman and Catholic Union, Michael Benkovic, chairman, 5015 Cecil Street.

The next telegram is from Detroit, Mich., dated February 12, 1935, and reads as follows:

Appreciate your effort in behalf bill H. R. 2827. Best wishes for success.

Assembly 716 National Slovak Society, Joseph Melotic, chairman, 8100 Wheeler Avenue.

The next telegram is from New York, N. Y., dated February 12, 1935, and reads as follows:

Recreational Leaders Association, an organization 700 relief workers, wholeheartedly endorses the workers unemployment and social insurance bill, H. R. 2827, the only genuine unemployment insurance bill now before Congress. We urge your committee report favorably on this bill on the floor of Congress.

It is signed, Recreational Leaders Association, ex-Chairman H. D. Bearman.

The next telegram is from Philadelphia, Pa., dated February 12, 1935, and reads as follows:

The Orsaresi Society of Philadelphia insists you support H. R. 2827. Our organization 100. Reply your stand requested to read before membership.

It is signed, M. Campanella, secretary, 2647 South Eleventh Street.

The next telegram is from New York, N. Y., dated February 13, 1935, reads as follows:

Local 802 American Federation of Musicians voted unanimously to support Lundeen bill at membership meeting February 11. Local has 15,000 members. Please record.

It is signed, Jacob Rosenberg, secretary Local 802.

114096—35——39

The next telegram is from Boston, Mass., dated February 13, 1935, and reads as follows:

Massachusetts State Unemployment Insurance Committee representing 255,000 affiliated workers demands from your entire committee to report H. R. 2827 favorable and bring it on floor of House. Lack of finances deprives our representatives to appear before committee to testify. We are 100 percent behind bill. Read this before your committee into the record.

It is signed, S. Winn, Secretary.

The next telegram is from New York, N. Y., dated February 14, 1935, and reads as follows:

The workers bill, H. R. 2827, is the only bill that makes provisions for the social security of professional men and we strongly urge favorable action upon it.

It is signed, Walter S. Percivil, president, United Scenic Artists Local Union 829.

The next telegram, addressed to the House labor subcommittee, is from Thief River Falls, Minn., dated February 8, 1935, and reading as follows:

Whereas the employed and unemployed workers of the unemployment council of Thief River Falls regular meeting assembled demand that the workers unemployment old age and social insurance bill, H. R. 2827, be voted out of the committee onto the floor of Congress for vote. We further demand that a copy of this telegram be read into the records.

It is signed, Earl Elofson, secretary.

Mr. DUNN. At this time, I desire to state that I dictated a letter to Miss Frances Perkins, Secretary of Labor, on January 29, 1935, to which I received no reply. I again wrote Miss Perkins under date of February 7, 1935, and to that I received a letter under date of February 11, 1935.

Mr. LUNDEEN. Mr. Chairman, I request that the two letters referred to, to Miss Perkins, together with her answer to one of them, and a notation that there was no reply to the other, be included in the record.

(The motion was agreed to. The three letters referred to are as follows:)

JANUARY 29, 1935.

Hon. FRANCES PERKINS,
    Secretary of Labor, Washington, D. C.

MY DEAR MADAM SECRETARY: Hearings on H. R. 2827, introduced by Congressman Ernest Lundeen, "To provide for the establishment of unemployment, old-age, and social insurance, and for other purposes," will begin on Monday, February 4, at 10 a. m., in the caucus room, House Office Building. The hearings will continue daily for approximately 10 days.

You are cordially invited to appear before the subcommittee of the Labor Committee which will have charge of the hearings, to discuss the above-mentioned bill.

With best wishes, I am,
    Very truly yours,

————— —————,
Chairman House Labor Subcommittee.

(No reply.)

FEBRUARY 7, 1935.

Hon. FRANCES PERKINS,
    Secretary of Labor, Washington, D. C.

MY DEAR MISS PERKINS: Under date of January 29, I sent you an invitation to appear before the subcommittee of the House Labor Committee, who were to conduct public hearings on the Lundeen old-age, unemployment, and social insurance bill.

Today a motion was made by a member of the subcommittee which was unanimously adopted to "request the Secretary of Labor to furnish counsel to give an opinion as to the constitutionality of this bill", (H. R. 2827).

The public hearings on the said bill will continue until Wednesday, February 13.

With best wishes, I am,

Very truly yours,

————— —————,
Chairman Subcommittee of the House Labor Committee.

———

DEPARTMENT OF LABOR,
OFFICE OF THE SECRETARY,
Washington, February 11, 1935.

Hon. MATTHEW A. DUNN,
House of Representatives, Washington, D. C.

MY DEAR MR. DUNN: I have your letter of February 7 informing me that the subcommittee of the House Labor Committee has unanimously adopted a motion to "request the Secretary of Labor to furnish counsel to give an opinion as to the constitutionality of this bill", (H. R. 2827).

As you are undoubtedly aware, the Department of Labor, while charged with fostering the interests of working persons, has no authority to give opinions of law to Congress, particularly on questions of constitutional importance. I assume that the Congress itself has certain advisers who are able to pass upon questions of law; but if in addition to those advisers other counsel is sought, it seems to me that the only executive department which might possibly be authorized and competent to give the opinion that you seek, is the Department of Justice.

Very truly yours,

(Signed) FRANCES PERKINS.

Mr. LUNDEEN. Mr. Chairman, in view of the answer now read, I hope that we will hear nothing further from the Department of Labor, or persons associated with that Department, about the constitutionality or unconstitutionality of any bill.

Mr. DUNN. I might also say that I addressed a similar letter to Mr. William Green, president of the American Federation of Labor, on January 29, 1935.

Mr. LUNDEEN. Mr. Chairman, I think the letter referred to, to Mr. Green, should be included along with the other correspondence there.

Mr. DUNN. You make that as a motion?

Mr. LUNDEEN. Yes.

(The motion was agreed to unanimously. The letter referred to, addressed to William Green, president of the American Federation of Labor, under date of Jan. 29, 1935, is as follows:)

JANUARY 25, 1935.

Mr. WILLIAM GREEN,
President American Federation of Labor,
901 Massachusetts Avenue NW., Washington, D. C.

DEAR MR. GREEN: Hearings on H. R. 2827, introduced by Congressman Ernest Lundeen, "To provide for the establishment of unemployment, old-age, and social insurance, and for other purposes", will begin on Monday, February 4, at 10 a. m., in the Caucus Room, House Office Building. The hearings will continue daily for approximately 10 days.

You are cordially invited to appear before the Subcommittee of the Labor Committee, which will have charge of the hearings, to discuss the above-mentioned bill.

With best wishes, I am,

Very truly yours,

————— —————,
Chairman House Labor Committee.

(No reply.)

STATEMENT OF MRS. EDWARD BELLAMY, CHICOPEE, SPRING-FIELD, MASS.

Mrs. BELLAMY. Mr. Chairman, ladies and gentlemen, it is becoming more and more apparent that the unemployment problem bids fair to become a permanent problem. Its causes lie deep in the bedrock of our industrial system and it can never be permanently solved until different arrangements can be worked out which will be in accord with the changing conditions brought about by the machine age. Meanwhile, it is our solemn duty to provide for the human needs of those of our countrymen who have been so mercilessly thrown upon the dust heap. For that reason I am glad to be here today to endorse the workers' bill.

It is the most inclusive of all bills aimed to provide social security; in fact, it is the only one which makes any adequate provision for all the millions of men, women, and children in this country who, through no fault of their own, are suffering from the inestimable ills arising from the defects in our present unplanned economy.

First of all, we must heed the cry of the children, such an astounding number of whose lives, from the very start, are blighted irreparably by the shadows of hunger, cold, and disjointed family life, arising from actual want and the constant menace of destitution. We owe them at least some measure of decent food, housing, and healthful environment. They hold in their hands the future destiny of our race.

To the youth, the restless flaming youth, whose bright hopes of accomplishment are blighted before they have even begun to be realized by the deadening weight of the knowledge, so soon forced upon them, that there is no place for them in the workaday world; many of whose energies are turned into channels of crime, where they taste the bitterness of jail and prison, or sink into an apathy of inaction, from which many of them can never be wakened.

To the adult, unemployed, unmarried, or the father or mother of a family, who day after day makes the weary rounds of seeking work and finding none, applies at length to the welfare and eats thereafter the bitter, insufficient crusts of charity.

To the man or woman on part-time employment, whose wage is far below subsistence level, to the sick poor who have no hope, the pitiful poverty-stricken aged, the mother whose sacred function of maternity, because of the interruption in her earning power, brings suffering and privation to the family.

To all of these the workers' bill holds out a definite measure of security.

If there is any dignity in a human being, it is worth preserving at any cost; and we are not doing it now. With our present policies of relief we are insulting the unhappy army of men and women whose birthright is equality, liberty, and happiness. Only by insuring to the citizens of our land an adequate scale of living can we hope as a Nation for any real progress or prosperity. Nor indeed do we deserve any.

Aside from the ethics of the matter, which unfortunately leave many business men and politicians stone cold, from the practical view of plain dollars and cents, our case is as sound. It is coming to be a generally recognized fact that only by placing adequate buying power in the hands of the masses of our people can any measure of permanent prosperity be achieved and maintained.

In the workers' bill this principle is recognized in the provision that "compensation shall be equal to average local wages, but shall in no case be less than $10 a week plus $3 for each dependent, and that workers unable to secure but part-time employment shall receive the difference between their earnings and the average local wages for full-time employment", and furthermore that the minimum compensation in all cases shall be increased in conformity with rises in cost of living. In this wise provision is assured a nonfluctuating buying power, which is a necessity to any stable pr)sperity.

Another virtue of the workers' bill is the plan of placing the maintenance and administration of this fund for security under the direct control of the Government of the United States, thus assuring the equitable carrying out of its provisions, which would be impossible if attempted by the separate States.

Furthermore, the method of taxation required to raise the necessary funds is wholly right and just, as it recognizes the axiom of true service, "from each according to his ability, to each according to his needs." In levying taxes upon individual and corporation incomes in excess of $5,000 and upon inheritances and gifts, no hardship or privation is incurred, and also the purchasing power of the mass of our people is not reduced.

Further evidence of the humanitarian provisions of this bill is found in section 4, where full protection is accorded workers and farmers "against discrimination because of age, sex, race, color, religion, or political opinion or affiliation, in the true spirit of the bill of rights." Also, and what is further to be commended by all lovers of justice, "no worker shall be disqualified because of past participation in strikes or refusal to work in the place of strikers."

Among the many who have protested against the iniquities of a system which through the years has piled accumulative misery upon the heads of a majority of the world, no one group stands out more prominently than the strikers. Although probably they have had no idea that they have been striking at the present economic set-up as such, all the same they have been pioneers in the revolt against this barbarous system and all it stands for. With their continual striking, they will never let us forget that there is an industrial problem, until their wrongs, which are the wrongs of all the world, shall be righted. They stand for a type of devotion far deeper than that of soldiers; for in the face of certain revilement and public scorn, of hunger and often of death, they are protesting in the only way they can while others stand by, against the economic system which has the world by the throat. It is a tribute to the understanding of the writer of the workers' bill that such shall in no way be discriminated against.

When the fact is universally recognized, as in this bill, that the workers of this country, to whose labor and skill we are indebted for every necessity and comfort of life, shall not only be considered worthy of the care and respect of this Nation, but also, that as a Nation we prosper or fail in direct proportion to their well-being, we shall have traveled far toward the solution of our economic problems.

Ladies and gentlemen, I, Mrs. Edward Bellamy, ask that you give the workers' bill your support.

Mr. DUNN. Mrs. Bellamy, on behalf of the committee, I want to thank you for your very instructive address and remarks.

Mr. LUNDEEN. I want to thank you, Mrs. Bellamy for your inspiring address.

Mrs. BELLAMY. It has been a pleasure to do my bit.

Mr. DUNN. You have done it, and we are going to ask you a few questions. I am sure you will not have any objections.

Mrs. BELLAMY. I will ask my daughter, Mrs. Earnshaw, to help you out on that, because she has made a study particularly of all these things, and she is far better able to answer questions about it than I am.

Mr. DUNN. They will not be hard questions.

Mrs. BELLAMY. Any questions that you would like to ask, I think she will be able to answer them.

ANSWERS TO QUESTIONS, BY MRS. MARION BELLAMY EARNSHAW, SPRINGFIELD, MASS.

Mr. DUNN. Congressman Lundeen, do you wish to ask any questions?

Mr. LUNDEEN. Mr. Chairman, as I understand it, Mrs. Bellamy favors a national act, rather than 48 different acts.

Mrs. EARNSHAW. She certainly does.

Mr. LUNDEEN. And that is very important; and that the funds to carry through this measure shall come from the Federal Treasury, through taxation upon those best able to bear the burden?

Mrs. EARNSHAW. That is the idea.

Mr. LUNDEEN. The great fortunes and the great inheritances; and where they seek to escape the tax upon gifts, as the fortunes are given away. I understand that to be her position.

Mrs. EARNSHAW. That is our position.

Mr. LUNDEEN. You believe the bill to be entirely adequate and in line with common sense; you believe that it can be carried out, and that it is practical?

Mrs. EARNSHAW. I think it is not only practicable, but I think it is necessary.

Mr. LUNDEEN. It is necessary, and it can be carried out?

Mrs. EARNSHAW. It can be.

Mr. LUNDEEN. There is nothing impossible about the bill?

Mrs. EARNSHAW. It is very practical, and necessary at the same time.

Mr. LUNDEEN. It is my belief that here we have the administration bill, with no provision for the unemployed of today, and only a very limited care for the unemployed of the future who are now working; and with that picture of destitution and misery and poverty the Administration bill on one side, and then some fantastic schemes on the other. Our bill has taken the main road between them, the golden mean, and you think it is possible of performance?

Mrs. EARNSHAW. That is my impression, yes; and it is also Mrs. Bellamy's conviction, her absolute conviction that your bill is the only bill which covers the situation.

Mr. LUNDEEN. We want to keep peace and calm and quiet and good order within our domain, do we not?

Mrs. EARNSHAW. Absolutely.

Mr. LUNDEEN. We want this country to be free from riots and troubles?

Mrs. EARNSHAW. Absolutely.

Mr. LUNDEEN. There are those in the country who fear that the flag will be torn down, the Constitution ripped up, and all that. If we want to preserve American institutions as founded by the fathers, we had better put through a social-security bill, had we not?

Mrs. EARNSHAW. That seems to be the crying need of the moment.

Mr. LUNDEEN. I believe that it is in the interest of Government security as well as in the interest of social security that this bill be passed; not that there should be no changes, of course, in our Constitution and Government, as needed from time to time.

Mrs. EARNSHAW. Those were all provided for in the preamble to the Constitution.

Mr. LUNDEEN. True; and I am delighted to know that students of economic and social questions come here as you have come here, and as Dorothy Douglas will come here from Smith College, and Miss Fairchild, of Bryn Mawr, and the many economists who have come here and testified, as you have. It strengthens and fortifies our spirit in the battle.

Mrs. EARNSHAW. Well, you deserve support from every thinking person in the country, because you have taken the position, you have recognized the need in all its details, and you, to my way of thinking, have supplied it in your bill.

Mr. LUNDEEN. Thank you.

Mr. DUNN. Mrs. Earnshaw, is it not a fact that in every town and city in the United States large sums of money are being donated to various charitable agencies for the purpose of giving relief to the unfortunates?

Mrs. EARNSHAW. It is true.

Mr. DUNN. You believe that if Lundeen bill, H. R. 2827, is enacted into law, it would no longer be necessary for these welfare agencies to be calling upon you and your mother and other generous-hearted people throughout the United States for donations for the purpose of taking care of the people who are in need of relief?

Mrs. EARNSHAW. I do. There would be no further need for it anywhere in the country.

Mr. DUNN. It is my candid opinion, and I have some knowledge of charitable agencies—in fact, I have referred to them many times as "would-be charitable agencies"——

Mrs. EARNSHAW. Yes; that is it.

Mr. DUNN. That hundreds of millions of dollars—and I am not exaggerating when I make this statement——

Mrs. EARNSHAW. Oh, no.

Mr. DUNN. Hundreds of millions of dollars are being collected annually for the purpose of taking care of people who are physically and mentally incapacitated, and of the unemployed; and according to information which I have received, 80 percent of most of the money which is donated to take care of the unfortunates in society goes in the form of salaries and for overhead expenses.

Mrs. EARNSHAW. Yes; not only that, but people are not taken care of.

Mr. DUNN. Also, I maintain that if the Lundeen bill, H. R. 2827, becomes law, it will no longer be necessary for charitable agencies to be in existence.

Mrs. EARNSHAW. Oh, no.

Mr. DUNN. Because the Government then will be taking care of them.

Mrs. EARNSHAW. They can shut up their doors and depart.

Mr. DUNN. In other words, this bill, if enacted into law, would eventually save the taxpayers millions of dollars.

Mrs. EARNSHAW. Absolutely.

Mr. DUNN. No longer would there be any need for poorhouses.

Mrs. EARNSHAW. Not only that, but think how it would save the self-respect of people, who sometimes suffer the pangs of hunger before they will even apply to a welfare agency.

Mr. DUNN. In fact, I have had many men and women come into my office in Pittsburgh who were doctors and lawyers and nurses and musicians. They would say to me: "Congressman, I do not like to call upon you for assistance. I see you are handicapped yourself. We do not like to think that we have got to come to a man who cannot see and ask him to get us a job." The unfortunate thing about the relief bill which Congress put through in 1933 and 1934 was that in order to obtain a job a person had to go on the relief roll.

Mrs. EARNSHAW. We feel so definitely that there is a dignity in every human being, just as my mother said, which should be preserved at all costs; because once it is gone, it is like a person without a soul, almost.

Mr. LUNDEEN. That is a beautiful statement, and her statement was wonderful about preserving the dignity of the human being at all costs.

Mrs. EARNSHAW. Preserving the dignity of human beings.

Mr. DUNN. In fact, it is my opinion that the amount of money which would be required in this bill to take care of the people would be an infinitesimal sum compared to the amount of good it would do.

Mrs. EARNSHAW. I am sure of it. I am sure of that; and it is not as though we did not have the money to do it with. If we did not, we would have to accept conditions as they are and make the most of them, but we have the means to do it.

Congressman Lundeen, do you have any more questions?

Mr. LUNDEEN. Mr. Chairman, I just want to say this, that just before you good people testified here in behalf of the bill, we had a very able statement here as to the costs of the bill, and I want to say that economists and research workers have given us statistics and data.

Mrs. EARNSHAW. Yes; I am sure of that.

Mr. LUNDEEN. And that data shows that the bill is entirely practical, is fully within the limits of the Treasury, and can be carried out without disturbing the finances of this country in the slightest; so I want you to carry that assurance with you.

Mrs. EARNSHAW. I already know that, because I have talked with statisticians myself.

Mr. LUNDEEN. I am delighted to know that.

Mrs. EARNSHAW. Mary van Kleeck, you know, is a statistician.

Mr. LUNDEEN. Yes.

Mr. Dunn. She appeared before our committee here.

Mrs. Earnshaw. We had luncheon with her in New York.

Mr. Lundeen. She is a very able woman.

Mrs. Earnshaw. Yes; she is.

Mr. Dunn. And may I also say, Congressman Lundeen, we had a very brilliant attorney here from New York, Leo Linder, a constitutional lawyer, who sat here for at least an hour and forty-five minutes, explaining the constitutionality of the bill; and he said, from beginning to end, it is constitutional.

Mrs. Earnshaw. I would make one suggestion, however, in the rewording of it, if I may.

Mr. Lundeen. Indeed, we would be very happy to have your suggestion.

Mrs. Earnshaw. It is that you make it clear that it applies to all workers. It has not seemed clear to some people to whom I have shown the bill that your definition of "workers" means everyone who is working for a living. According to the dictionary, and according to the general impression, a "worker" is a person who works for wages in some industrial capacity, a miner or a person of that sort. We know, of course, you mean that everyone in the country who wants work and cannot get it is included.

Mr. Lundeen. May I say in that connection, we take rather the European definition, which is my definition. I am an office worker.

Mrs. Earnshaw. Yes, surely.

Mr. Lundeen. As a Member of Congress, I am nothing but an office worker or a Government worker, a Government employee.

Mrs. Earnshaw. It seems to me that if, at the beginning of the bill, it is made apparent that that is the meaning of the word "worker" it would perhaps get you a larger staff of adherents.

Mr. Lundeen. For instance, we said to some famous economists and professors who came here, "We take it that you call yourselves educational workers?"

Mrs. Earnshaw. That is so.

Mr. Lundeen. And if Americans have not been educated to that, they soon will be.

Mrs. Earnshaw. Yes.

Mr. Lundeen. But I think your suggestion is well taken, and we may take some steps to clarify it.

Mrs. Earnshaw. At the beginning of the bill, make evident what it means. I have noticed in some of the other bills I have been reading lately that the terms are defined at the beginning of the bill. Definitions are made of certain expressions so that it will be quite clear in reading the bill what is referred to when that term is mentioned. That is all.

Mr. Lundeen. We had a bill here at the beginning of the last Congress, called the "economy bill", and it had some beautiful statements at the beginning of it, stating that it was for the "preservation of the Government"; and the way we proceeded to preserve the Government was to cut the wages of the little fellow to pieces and take everything away from the soldiers who had defended the country; but in our bill we could well define these things as being in the interest of real social justice.

I think, Mr. Chairman, that is all.

Mr. Chairman, with regard to the letters which you have received, relating to the subject matter of this hearing, I move that they be incorporated in the record.

Mr. DUNN. Very well.

(The motion was agreed to. A list of the letters received in support of H. R. 2827, together with information as to the organizations, etc., is on file with the committee.)

(Mrs. Marion Bellamy Earnshaw thereupon requested and was granted the privilege of extending her remarks in the record.)

(The hour of 12:30 having arrived, the subcommittee took a recess until 2 o'clock this afternoon.)

AFTERNOON SESSION

(The recess having expired, the subcommittee reassembled at 2 p. m., and was called to order by Mr. Dunn, as chairman of the Subcommittee on Labor.)

Mr. DUNN. The first witness this afternoon will be Mr. Reginald A. Johnson.

STATEMENT OF REGINALD A. JOHNSON, GRADUATE OF THE UNIVERSITY OF MINNESOTA, SOCIAL WORKER, EXECUTIVE SECRETARY OF THE ATLANTA URBAN LEAGUE

Mr. JOHNSON. Mr. Chairman, and members of the committee, when we consider provisions for the protection of the unemployed and old age, we are constantly mindful of the extent of protection given those who are earning a living and are dependent upon their wages as a means of providing food and shelter and other minimum necessities of life. When we observe the Lundeen bill (H. R. 2827) and compare it with the Wagner-Lewis bill (S. 2616) it is necessary for us to turn our attention to the consideration these bills give to the 48,829,920 people who are gainfully employed in all occupations as reported by the 1930 census.

We find that the Wagner-Lewis bill, among other exclusions, eliminates from its provisional features the 4,962,451 domestics which comprise 11 percent of all occupations and 4,392,764 farm laborers who comprise 9 percent of all occupations. In these exclusions, we find that according to the 1930 census, 1,600,000 Negro domestics, comprising 20.4 percent of all gainfully employed Negroes and 31.8 percent of all gainfully employed domestics, white and colored; together with the 2,000,000 farm laborers, which is 43.9 percent of all Negroes gainfully employed or 19 percent of all farm laborers employed, totaling 64.3 percent of all Negroes employed and 20 percent of all white and colored employed as farm laborers and domestics are excluded from the benefits and protection of social insurance. We feel that if a measure for unemployment and old age is to mean anything to the social security of the working man, it should include all gainfully employed persons, without exclusion whatsoever. Most certainly, such a measure should include those who are in the lowest income brackets and consequently those who are subject to the greatest amount of economic insecurity.

During normal times of employment, there are gainfully employed 5,503,535 Negro wage earners, of which 64.3 percent, unfortunately, are in the brackets of the lowest incomes and belong to two of the groups that would be eliminated by the Wagner-Lewis bill. It is generally estimated that today some 40 percent or 2,225,000 of this group, is unemployed, with well over 700,000 Negro families on relief. In a survey made by the Department of Labor and issued in Bulletin 113, entitled "Employment Fluctuations and Unemployment of Women", and covering 1928 to 1931, it was found that as far back as that date, 42 percent of Negro women in the eight cities covered by this survey were unemployed.

In considering the fact and consequences of unemployment to a group of people, let us take for example a survey that was recently completed in the city of Atlanta which is a sampling of unemployment in one city, but illustrates just what is happening to many unemployed Negroes throughout the country, but would be benefited by the Lundeen bill. Under the Federal Emergency Relief Administration, in the tentative findings of a test-study sample of unemployment and of white-collared and skilled Negroes, we found according to this test sample, 45 percent of the Negroes in the community were unemployed. Sixty-seven and seven-tenths of these unemployed were domestics; 19.5 percent were unskilled; 5.9 percent were skilled and 3.4 percent were in the white-collared group. In comparing what has happened to the white-collared and skilled in Atlanta from 1929 to 1934, we found that in 1929, of a test sample of 594 white-collared and skilled men and women, 4.5 percent had held the job they were in less than 1 year. In 1934, 15.4 percent of this same group had held their present jobs less than 1 year. In 1929, we found that 4.17 percent had been at their job less than 10 years and in 1934, we found that 66.3 percent had been at their job less than 10 years. This gives an idea of the extent to which insecurity has affected the group which comprises only 3.4 percent of those unemployed in the community. In this white-collared and skilled group, 94 percent had no other regular income than their immediate salary or wage and 42 percent were forced to supplement this salary income through loans, mortgages, and other means of making enough for a living.

Of the 14,110,652 listed in the 1930 census as gainfully employed in manufacturing, we find that 37 percent or, 5,271,909, are employed with companies that have products that are valued under $20,000. Though the number in such plants would vary, depending upon the items manufactured, this data shows that 37 percent of those employed in manufacturing are working in plants where there are few workers and many would be excluded from the benefits of social insurance in case of the elimination of plants employing 10 or less.

To carry the picture of the relative instability of the Negro further: In the effort of the Government, through the N. R. A., to decrease unemployment and raise wages, we find that though there were many Negroes who received increased wages, decreased hours, and improved working conditions, there were large numbers who were employed in marginal occupations, such as porters, helpers around filling stations, as well as many who were employed in other occupations, lost their employment, due to the fact that N. R. A. regulations, when fully complied with, eliminated to a large degree the marginal job. Under the Civilian Conservation Corps, of the 6,000 quota allotted for Georgia, only 600 Negroes were permitted to go to camp and in many communities throughout the South, there was an absolute refusal to accept Negroes for these camps, with the excuse that no provision was made for including them. In relief, in rural sections particularly, there was marked indifference on the part of local officials to give full and adequate consideration to the relief needs of colored and under the Civil Works Administration, there were throughout the South, many instances of refusal to permit Negroes to work under the C. W. A., because of the more favorable income received through C. W. A. in contrast to those who were on relief.

In observing the sources from which funds are raised, we find that in the Wagner-Lewis bill and other unemployment insurance bills that have either at the present time been enacted by a State or are being considered, the employee must contribute to the fund that is to provide for his security. We find that the average wage per day as secured from the Monthly Labor Review, September 1929, was $1.55 for the 10 Southeastern States—South Carolina, Georgia, Alabama, Louisiana, Mississippi, Tennessee, Arkansas, Florida, North Carolina, and Virginia—as contrasted with an average of $3.25 for the remaining States, showing that at that period of security and prosperity, a few weeks before the stock market crash, the average wage for labor in these 10 States was 47.7 percent of the average wage for the rest of the States. In a summary trend of skilled and unskilled labor from 1928 to 1935, made by the Atlanta Urban League, we found that in 1933, an average low of $2.34 per week was struck, with $4.58 a week as an average for the highest wages paid to Negroes in that city and that in 1935, an average low of $2.96 per week in contrast to an average of $4.62 for the highest brackets was paid. An average of the highest wages paid from 1928 to 1935 to domestics, factory workers, skilled and unskilled labor, gives only $6.24, with the average low wage for these occupations being $3.50, striking a general average of $4.87 for wages during the 7-year period, dating from 1928. Any kind of tax exacted from the wages of these people, would therefore be a definite hardship and an unfortunate sacrifice of their meager earnings.

On the other hand, in any enactment of social legislation, we must consider the economic conditions in the State concerned. In the income-tax returns made in 1926, which is known as an average income year, California averaged the highest percentage of any State filing returns with 7.31 percent and South Carolina carried the lowest, with 0.76 percent. The five Southern States had the following percentages: Georgia, 1.17; Alabama, 1.13; Arkansas, 1.02; Mississippi, 0.96, and South Carolina, 0.76. The average for the 10 Southeastern States—South Carolina, Georgia, Alabama, Louisiana, Mississippi, Tennessee, Arkansas, Florida, North Carolina, and Virginia—which are in the lowest brackets—is 1.43 percent, while the average for the rest of the country is 4.01. In 1927, the average wage for the 10 Southeastern States was $828, as supplied by the census of manufacturers in monograph no. 10, entitled "Earnings of Factory Workers from 1849 to 1927", in contrast to $828 for these 10 States, in the South, the remainder of the United States averaged $1,366, showing that the percent in the South was 60.6 of the remainder of the country.

In addition to this, we find that the amount of money issued for relief in Georgia from November 1933 to November 1934, was in excess of $32,000,000, to which the State of Georgia made no contribution in the second quarter of 1934 and only 4.2 percent was contributed through other local funds. In other words, 95.8 percent of the contributions to Georgia in the second quarter of 1934 came through the Federal Government. Of the $32,000,000 that went into relief during these 12 months, we find that it exceeded the value of the cotton crop for Georgia for 1932, which was $29,900,000. We are only using Georgia as an example because it is typical of what is happening in many States of the South, and knowing the importance of the cotton crop to the prosperity of the State, it would be difficult to find much of a matching of funds from this State and others that are in a similar financial condition, or have low income.

As to the enactment of legislation among the States to supervise and arrange for unemployment insurance, matching similar legislation by the Government, we are met with the problem of a dire lack of social legislation in many of the States. Unfortunate as it may-be, there are many States that have shown little disposition to enact laws and legislation for the protection of minors and women as to the limitation of hours of work, days of rest, prohibition of night work, and minimum wages. With this indisposition on the part of these States to protect and provide for the labor of those who contribute to the State's welfare and income, it would be indeed unfortunate for an unemployment insurance bill not to be enacted by Congress under the complete and full administration of the Federal Government.

The best example we have of the effects of Federal regulations and Federal supervision is that of the Relief Administration. Before the Federal Relief Administration was created, relief was administered by the States as they saw fit. As a result, the funds were poorly administered and noneffectual as far as sane relief programs were concerned, and included distinct discriminations because of race, color, and political affiliations. To secure a program of adequate unemployment insurance, it will be necessary that the Federal Government have sole and full authority for its administration, that the employee be exempt from contribution and that there be no exclusion because of occupation or race.

Mr. DUNN. I want to ask you a few questions, Mr. Johnson. How many colored people are there in the United States?

Mr. JOHNSON. There are approximately 12,000,000.

Mr. DUNN. What percentage of that number would you say are now out of employment?

Mr. JOHNSON. We have estimated that possibly 2,225,000 Negroes are utterly unemployed.

Mr. DUNN. Other witnesses testified before this committee as to the discrimination of Negroes.

Mr. JOHNSON. I know there is considerable going on.

Mr. DUNN. Do you believe the Lundeen bill (H. R. 2827) if enacted into law, will not only benefit the whites but will benefit the colored people?

Mr. JOHNSON. It will benefit the Negro, more so than any other bill that is before Congress at the present time.

Mr. DUNN. On behalf of the committee, I wish to say that we appreciate the statements you have made.

Mr. JOHNSON. If it is possible, I should like to obtain a copy of the printed proceedings of this subcommittee. My address is 250 Auburn Avenue, Atlanta, Ga.

Mr. DUNN. The next witness will be Mrs. Ida Evans.

STATEMENT OF MRS. IDA M. EVANS, REPRESENTING 8,000 WORKERS OF THE NATIONAL COUNCIL OF RADIO AND METAL WORKERS INDUSTRIAL UNION (CAMDEN, N. J.)

Mr. DUNN. You may proceed.

Mrs. EVANS. I just want to read this outline I have here. I am here to represent 8,000 members, directly affiliated with the National Council of the Radio and Metal Workers Industrial Union. At the national convention of the union, the workers' unemployment bill, H. R. 2827, was endorsed unanimously. Indirectly, I represent many other thousands of workers from other organizations. I have their permission to speak—construction workers, marine workers' industrial union, the canners' industrial union, and quite a few other organizations. I have been given permission to speak in their behalf. They represent many other thousands of workers.

Our membership is spread throughout the States of New Jersey, Pennsylvania, and New York. The reason we are for unemployment insurance is that the radio and metal workers industry is highly seasonal. By that I mean that even in the prosperous days, thousands of radio workers throughout the country are laid off regularly around Christmas time. Today, many departments in the radio industry work an average of only 5 and 6 months a year. The rest of the year the workers either have to starve or be content with the miserable relief orders that are now the order of the day, and which are totally inadequate. Some of the workers are refused relief because they own a home, and naturally we know that they cannot eat a home.

Mr. DUNN. Pardon an interruption. I will substantiate the statement you have made. That condition prevails all over the United States; if you have a home, you are not considered to be in need.

Mrs. EVANS. Yes; that is right. I have one case, here, that I have taken up with the relief people, one of our members who is unemployed; and because he owned a home, he was refused relief. I believe they are taking that matter up at the present time. Workers that are not laid off entirely also suffer in these slack periods. Some of these so-called "employed" workers have shown checks for a period of 3 and 4 weeks, ranging from $3 to $9 per week. Many of these workers have families of 6 and 7, 8, and 9 children. I would like to know whether the Congressmen that are representing these people feel that that wage is adequate to maintain a family in a decent, self-respecting American fashion.

Mr. DUNN. I will say that it is not.

Mrs. EVANS. No; it is not. Everyone knows that. Owing to the fact that our living expenses have gone up in the past year, alone, 78 percent, it is clear why we are in favor of unemployment insurance. However, many people claim to be for unemployment insurance.

We, the Radio Metal Workers Industrial Union and affiliates, are in favor of H. R. 2827 and opposed to other so-called "unemployment insurance" bills. They are totally inadequate for the worker, in that the worker has to pay for that unemployment and social insurance from his own pocket; and I feel, now that we are so thoroughly taxed and overburdened with taxes, we cannot afford to pay any more.

The Radio Corporation of America, by whom many of our workers are employed, has shown a profit of over $8,000,000 for the year 1933, and for the year 1934. over $11,000,000; and under these circumstances we feel we are not expecting too much when we ask these companies to assume a larger burden of this unemployment insurance.

Our membership has again demonstrated the support of this bill, and thousands of post cards, requests, and practically pleas to our Congressmen to stand behind this bill and vote for it when it comes out in committee have been sent. We feel it is the only bill for the workingman.

I myself am a worker. I am here speaking for thousands upon thousands of workers. I am a mother of four children. I have to keep my home and work in a factory because my husband is not able to make enough money to keep his family, and I feel that such a condition in this country is intolerable, and I do not see why it is too much to ask that our Congressmen stand behind us in this matter, and vote "yes" on this matter, insofar as we look upon them as our friends and servants; in fact, they have promised to be our friends and servants and to represent us in all matters pertaining to the public good— meaning the workers, because 94 percent of the people in the United States are workers; and, as you and everyone else know, the workers are the backbone of the Nation. We are willing to work to make the wealth; in fact we have made wealth, which is adequately demonstrated by my statement of the profits of our concern alone. These figures were not printed in the American papers in the United States, but they were printed in the press of England, the Times, I believe. It is plain to be seen why they are not printed in these papers. They do not want us to know how much they are making and how much wealth we are creating for them without getting any adequate return.

We feel that we are working hard, we are helping to create wealth for these people, and we want them to at least give us some share of this money, so that we can live and raise our families. I myself am working to help give my children the comforts and necessities of life. I want to give my children an education, which I have not, so far, been able to gather for myself without a great deal of trouble. I do not mean it is trouble, but when you consider a woman with a family, having to go to night school to help educate herself so she can help educate her children, I think it is high time that we have some form of legislation that will support relief conditions, as this bill will most certainly do.

This is the only bill for unemployment and social insurance possible for the worker today, and I earnestly hope that our Congressmen will not let us down on this question. I ask and plead with them to vote "yes" on this question when it comes up in committee. I do not know whether any of our Congressmen are represented here; I know that you, Mr. Chairman, are from Pennsylvania, and a great many of our workers are from Pennsylvania, as you know, and I had hoped to see Congressman Wolverton here. He is a representative of the First Congressional District, of which I am a unit.

Mr. DUNN. May I interrupt you there? You see, Congressman Wolverton is not a member of this committee. There are seven Congressmen on this subcommittee. We are a Subcommittee of the Committee on Labor which consists of 22 members. He is not on the Labor Committee. However, your Congressman probably is at other meetings. We are holding this public hearing on the Lundeen bill and other social insurance measures; so that it is not any fault of his that he is not here. He will have an opportunity to read the testimony, and you will have an opportunity to contact him about this bill.

May I say it is my opinion that the Congressmen are willing to do what is right. Their hearts are in the right place, but you know how it is, that pressure is brought to bear here and there, and I would suggest that one of the best ways to get your representative to support this legislation—and we are public servants; that is what we are supposed to be—is to contact him by mail and ask him to read the bill, and if he believes it is a bill which is going to give the benefits which you are interested in, and in which everybody else is interested, to give it his utmost support. Now, that is the way that we will be able to get action on this measure. Of course, I have announced many times that I am for the bill 100 percent.

(The pamphlet presented for the record by the witness, Mrs. Evans, is as follows:)

To all members of the Radio and Metal Workers' Industrial Union:
To all radio and metal workers:
To their families and friends:

Today unemployment has become a permanent problem in the United States. Everybody, therefore, talks about unemployment and social insurance. However, the proposals vary from miserable starvation allotments to a real system of unemployment and social insurance as provided by bill H. R. 2827. This bill was introduced by Congressman Lundeen, from Minnesota, and was endorsed by our union—the Radio and Metal Workers' Industrial Union.

The only way the proposed bill H. R. 2827 can become a law, is through mass pressure. We have, therefore, reprinted bill H. R. 2827, as well as the comparison of this bill with other proposed measures.

We urge you, your families and friends, to read, study it, and then pass judgment. If you agree that bill H. R. 2827 is the only bill meeting the needs of the workers, then we urge you to sign the attached post card, and return it to your shop steward, or directly to the Union office, 216 Federal Street, Camden, N. J. Your opinion will be forwarded to the respective Congressman.

RADIO AND METAL WORKERS' INDUSTRIAL UNION—LOCAL NO. 1,
216 Federal Street, Camden, N. J.

Comparison of bill H. R. 2827 and other proposed measures

	Workers' unemployment, old-age, and social-insurance bill H. R. 2827 (introduced by Congressman Lundeen), Federal funds	President Roosevelt's security program (introduced by Senator Wagner), State reserves	Proposed plan of William Green, president of the American Federation of Labor, reserves
Beneficiaries	Includes all occupations—industrial, agricultural, domestic, and professional workers; benefits cover all time lost.	Industrial workers only; excludes domestic workers, agricultural workers, professional workers, and Government employees; excludes over 15,000,000 already unemployed now.	Same as President Roosevelt's.
Protection against discrimination.	Full protection; trade-union standards protected; part-time workers covered; provides insurance for industrial accidents, sickness, old-age, and maternity.	Does not protect trade-union standard; provides no discrimination of strike participation.	Denies benefits for unstated periods to workers who "quit work without good cause" or "who are discharged because of misconduct."
Length of benefit periods.	Throughout unemployment.	No term set; State law to specify. (President Roosevelt's committee proposed for not more than 16 weeks per year.)	26 weeks per year.
Amount of benefits	Equal to average local wages; in no case less than $10 a week plus $3 for each dependent; as prices rise, rates to be increased.	50 percent of workers' average weekly wage, but not to exceed $15 per week.	50 percent of normal weekly wages; $15 minimum.
Sources and security of funds.	The Federal Government, by taxation of incomes over $5,000, inheritance, and gifts.	Wage taxes under approved State plans; workers to contribute 50 percent of all taxes.	5-percent tax on pay rolls.

Congressman _____

DEAR SIR: Having read and studied bill H. R. 2827, the workers' bill for social and unemployment insurance, introduced by Congressman Lundeen, as well as the comparison with other measures proposed, I am firmly convinced that only H. R. 2827 really meets the need for social and unemployment insurance.

As a resident in your congressional district, I therefore urge you to support bill H. R. 2827, and vote and fight for it on the floor.

Name_____

Address_____

City_____ State_____

Congressional district_____

The Radio and Metal Workers' Industrial Union is an industrial union controlled by the rank and file.

It fights in the shop daily to adjust grievances, improve working conditions, and to get higher wages.

Realizing that the radio industry in particular is a seasonal industry, we take an active part to help the unemployed and are participating actively in the campaign for the establishment of a real system of unemployment and social insurance.

We stand for the unity of the employed and unemployed workers in the effort to get better conditions for all workers.

The more members we have the stronger is our fight, the better is the chance to win these improved conditions, both for the employed and unemployed workers.

Will you do your bit in this undertaking?

Join the Radio and Metal Workers' Industrial Union now by apllying for membership to your shop or department representative, or by coming up to the union office, 216 Federal Street, Camden, N. J.

If you are a member, get another member.

Mrs. EVANS. I would like also to say one more word on this question. I would like to impress on everyone's mind that anyone over 18 years of age unemployed through no fault of his own is eligible for this insurance; also, that the compensations shall be equal to the average wage, the local wage, but not less than $10 a week for every unemployed man and $3 for each dependent; and the same, of course, goes for women that are supporting themselves and families, as dependents. It is to be administered by the workers and farmers through an unemployed insurance committee directly elected by the workers, farmers, and people concerned, ruled and regulated by the Secretary of Labor. That is one of the provisions of the bill.

The compensation for maternity is also a very important part of this bill. The mother is to be paid compensation 8 weeks before her child is born and 8 weeks afterward, and I would like to say here that if you are not poor the way we are—we are all poor; we are workers, and I am one of them—if you are not poor and expecting to have a child when you have no wherewithal to take care of the child, you cannot appreciate how wonderful this would be for the mother to have medical care and attention 8 weeks before the child is born and 8 weeks afterward. That is a wonderful provision in this bill.

Mr. DUNN. Is it not a fact that today children are being born into the world that cannot grow up as men and women, physically and mentally sound, because the mothers are not receiving sufficient food, and so forth?

Mrs. EVANS. I stand as a living example of that truth. I do not mean that I had to go as far as some of them had to go, because, just by luck and Providence, I happened to have a good mother that was willing to share with me and help me; but I was on relief for a period of 2 months and had to live on $4.50 a week for myself and husband and four children, and if anyone here can consider that adequate for a wife and husband and four children I do not see how. When I asked for coal, I was told they had none. They did not have even wood with which to keep the house warm.

I would like to impress on the mind of everyone that it touches me when I think of some of these people, the heartaches that the mothers endure when they think of what their children are losing in the way of nutrition and their very life's blood, because everyone knows that if a child is not properly nourished he cannot grow up to be a healthy, sound citizen, and if he is not going to be a healthy, strong citizen it stands to reason that diseases come into the mind, through malnutrition and the effects of poverty; they are going to take hold of him, and therefore his mind is not going to be what it should be on civic matters. What is he interested in regarding civic matters, when his stomach is empty and his shoes are out and he is cold and sick and cannot even spend money for a doctor? I have had to be Doctor Evans and Barber Evans and everything else in my family. I have never had the money to take care of my own family or have someone else take care of my family properly. It has all fallen on my shoulders, I have not admitted that I am licked, as yet, and I do not intend to admit it now. That is why I am fighting and that is why I am appealing to everyone now to get behind this employment and social insurance bill.

Mr. DUNN. May I ask, would you be in favor of a bill providing that dentists and doctors were to take care of men and women and children who cannot pay for dental and medical assistance? Would you be in favor of that kind of legislation?

Mrs. EVANS. Yes, sir. That is also included in this bill.

Mr. DUNN. Well, I introduced such a bill last week.

Mrs. EVANS. It is a wonderful thing.

Mr. DUNN. It is a supplement to this bill, that every child in the United States, every mother and father out of work will, under this bill which I introduced, which is also considered a workers' bill, receive medical and surgical assistance when they are in need of it. In addition, it is a wonderful bill for the dentist and doctors because there are many doctors today and many dentists who are really doing Government work and not receiving 1 cent of compensation. In fact, I know many of them who have gone out and given their service, and these men are not able to collect any money and are completely down and out, and this bill which I introduced, of course, will see to it that the doctors are compensated for the services they render.

What you have told me here this afternoon is true. I know that every word you have said is true. In fact, when I made the statement to you to say whatever you wanted to, I meant that and in my opinion you did not go far enough.

Mrs. EVANS. Well, I have been a little conservative, because it is hard to sit and think of the hardships you have been through. After all, there is an old saying, "Laugh and the world laughs with you; weep and you weep alone"; and I have found that to be true in a great number of cases, especially among men and women who have rather a "soft living," as the saying is, and they cannot appreciate the hardships that we have to go through. I have tried to bring this up, not to bring my own poverty before you and throw it in anyone's face, but for the masses that have put their confidence in me and sent me here to speak for them. I can mention thousands of cases right now that are receiving wages that are not even to be mentioned in the same breath with an adequate living wage—as I mentioned here, $3 to $9 for a week's check for a man with a family. Now, there are any number of those cases. I can get the records of the Radio Corporation of America, the manufacturing company. You can look them up, yourselves. I am not afraid of being unable to substantiate everything I have said.

Mr. DUNN. I know what you are saying is the truth. I also want to make this statement: Of course, I am unable to see, but I have been informed many times that the expressions on the faces of men and women walking around on the streets of the city of Pittsburgh indicate there is something radically wrong. In fact I have talked to many who have come into my office. I could tell by the tone of their voice just how they felt and how they looked; in other words, they do not have anything to smile about.

Mrs. EVANS. Not much.

Mr. DUNN. Men and women come to my office and tell me that their homes are going to be taken from them, they want jobs—not men who have worked in coal mines and mills and factories, and poor women that wash for a living, not those at all, but lawyers, doctors, school teachers, men of all trades, professional men of all kinds. You see, this depression has not affected just the laboring man, but it has affected every type of man and woman. They are completely down and out, and I know that our abominable system here in this country of having a man go on the relief in order to get work under the Emergency Relief Administration should not be tolerated. They have to get on their knees and ask some would-be charitable agency for assistance before they can get a job.

Many Congressmen this year have made the statement on the floor that in their congressional districts people by the hundreds are writing to them to save their homes, to do something for them; so in what you have said you did not exaggerate. The people that sent you up here are to be congratulated. I do not hesitate to say that you have made an excellent representative and an excellent witness before the committee. All you have said, will be put into book form and sent all over the country.

Mrs. EVANS. Many of my personal friends have lost their homes. There are a few that managed to save them, but they are put in such a precarious position with this Home Loan that I suppose eventually they will lose their homes anyway. One man, in particular, a very good friend of mine, has six children. He has been out of work for 2 consecutive years. I myself have been trying for the last year and a half to get him work, but owing to the fact that I do not seem to carry very much weight with the Radio Corporation of America, the manufacturing company—in fact, my checks are mostly $3.50 a week—I do not seem to be able to get anywhere in getting this man a job. Naturally, I cannot go before the city fathers and ask them for work, because they do not like it when you get up and say that you are not getting what you should get; and owing to this fact, I feel that this bill for unemployment and social insurance is the best bill so far introduced, although I will say this: It is not good enough, but as I understand, there have been quite a number of wonderful provisions taken out of this bill as it was introduced in this session of Congress; but we hope that, as it stands, it will be passed.

Mr. DUNN. May I say this in behalf of Congressman Lundeen: The provisions to which you refer were not taken out except for one purpose. I believe the purpose in taking them out was so no one could say the bill was unconstitutional.

Mrs. EVANS. I see.

Mrs. EVANS. In this pamphlet that we have drawn up for our members, to be distributed among their families and friends. We have sent out 11,000 copies of these pamphlets, also 5,000 postcards, for which we have stood the expense ourselves, and we have given these different organizations, a few of which I have mentioned to you, these pamphlets, asking them to get behind this thing, and they have promised now to take care of the financial part, as far as they are concerned, because we have given them quite a few thousand of these pamphlets and we feel as though they should do their share in the financial responsibility. Of course, we are a very poor organization as it stands now. We are practically in our infancy, but we hope to be able to do a lot for our fellow men through this bill and through measures that I hope will be introduced in time.

Mr. DUNN. Congressman Schneider, do you wish to interrogate the witness?

Mr. SCHNEIDER. I do not know that I care to, excepting I might ask, Is the union affiliated with the American Federation of Labor?

Mrs. EVANS. No; it is not. We are an independent union, sir.

Mr. SCHNEIDER. Independent of all other affiliations?

Mrs. EVANS. Independent of all other affiliations outside of our own organization; yes, sir. It is nonpolitical.

Mr. SCHNEIDER. Purely economic?

Mrs. EVANS. Yes; it is purely an industrial union of the workers in the States of New Jersey, Pennsylvania, and New York. Our members are scattered over that territory.

Mr. SCHNEIDER. You are in favor of this bill?

Mrs. EVANS. I am; and the thousands of people that have asked me to come and speak for them are also in favor of it.

Mr. SCHNEIDER. They have endorsed it?

Mrs. EVANS. Yes. This is something new for me. It is the first time in my life I have had to make a speech, especially in Washington. I believe the only speech I ever made was at night school, year before last, to my class. I was made the speaker of my class. That was my first speech and this is my second.

Mr. DUNN. You are doing very well.

Mrs. EVANS. Thank you.

In connection with these pamphlets, we ask our friends to fill out the facsimile with their name and address, the name of their Congressman and the congressional district, and send it in to the Congressman as an indication of what we ask for—"Please vote 'yes' on this bill."

That is what we ask you to do.

Mr. SCHNEIDER. That is all, Mr. Chairman.

Mr. DUNN. We thank you very much for your instructive and intelligent address.

Mrs. EVANS. Thank you for your kind attention.

Mr. DUNN. We have sent for Mr. Gebhardt, transient director of the District of Columbia. I understand that Mr. Gebhardt is present at this time, together with two of his assistants, Miss Agnes Hill, director of the Emergency Relief, and Mr. David Linden.

STATEMENT OF RICHARD GEBHARDT, TRANSIENT DIRECTOR FOR THE DISTRICT OF COLUMBIA, WASHINGTON, D. C.

Mr. DUNN. Mr. Gebhardt, do you have any prepared statement that you want to present?

Mr. GEBHARDT. No.

Mr. DUNN. You are just up here more for the purpose of being interrogated?

Mr. GEBHARDT. Yes; I understood that that was your purpose.

Mr. DUNN. Mr. Schneider, were you here the day that the Congressmen requested that I send a letter to Mr. Gebhardt?

Mr. SCHNEIDER. I was here that day, but I do not recall so much of the testimony that was given that really caused the members to feel that somebody representing the transient department should come before the committee and state the condition of the institution and something about its operation, with reference to the number of people, and how much they paid out, the number of employees, and so forth.

Mr. DUNN. Mr. Gebhardt, you may proceed and tell us how many men you have there and how much compensation they receive, and something about their living quarters; and if you will tell us that, we will be able to ask you a few questions.

Mr. GEBHARDT. The transient bureau is a department of the Emergency Relief. Each State and the District of Columbia were asked to set up accommodations for the transients who had left their homes in search of employment. A Federal ruling went into effect that these men were to be given food and maintenance and paid at the rates of $1, $2, and $3 a week plus maintenance.

Mr. DUNN. Interrogation, please: You say they get as much as $3 a week?

Mr. GEBHARDT. Some of them, depending entirely upon the type of work done. The skilled people are paid more, naturally, than the unskilled.

Mr. DUNN. If I recollect rightly, the gentleman who appeared before us mentioned a dollar a week for 24 hours' work.

Mr. GEBHARDT. A week?

Mr. DUNN. Yes. You say some get as much as $3?

Mr. GEBHARDT. Depending entirely upon the kind of work done.

Mr. DUNN. He did not state that. He just said they received $1 a week for 24 hours a week.

Mr. GEBHARDT. There are those three rates which were put into effect by the Federal Government.

Mr. SCHNEIDER. Do all those transients do some work each week?

Mr. GEBHARDT. Yes; unless they have permission to not work. I mean, there are some that are on sick leave.

Mr. SCHNEIDER. What is the nature of the work they do?

Mr. GEBHARDT. In the District of Columbia there is a pest squad that do some work. Some of them are sent on the wood yard, on cleaning details in the various lodges, clerical jobs, and so forth.

Mr. SCHNEIDER. Do they do the work in connection with the maintenance of all of the transients—waiters, cooks, and cleaning, and so forth?

Mr. GEBHARDT. That is right.

Mr. SCHNEIDER. And all of that?

Mr. GEBHARDT. Yes.

Mr. SCHNEIDER. You do not have any laundry there, do you?

Mr. GEBHARDT. No; there is no laundry in the District of Columbia. I mean, there is none in connection with our organization.

Mr. SCHNEIDER. Where is the laundry work of these folks done, individually and collectively?

Mr. GEBHARDT. It is done under contract, let by the District of Columbia to a laundry company.

Mr. SCHNEIDER. About how much does the weekly or monthly laundry bill amount to under that contract?

Mr. GEBHARDT. I am afraid that I do not know.

Mr. SCHNEIDER. Approximately? Just approximately?

Mr. GEBHARDT. I would not even have an approximate idea.

Mr. SCHNEIDER. Does it run a thousand dollars a month?

Mr. GEBHARDT. Do you have any idea, Miss Hill?

Miss HILL. The bills are paid in the District Office Building. They do not come through us. The bills are simply audited by us.

Mr. SCHNEIDER. You mean they are paid by the District government, and charged up to the Federal Emergency Relief Administration?

Miss HILL. Yes.

Mr. DUNN. Would you please give the reporter your name?

Miss HILL. Yes; my name is Miss Agnes Hill.

Mr. GEBHARDT. I have been in the District just a month. Miss Hill is director of the Emergency Relief, so that some of your questions naturally can be answered better by her.

Miss HILL. May I make a suggestion there?

Mr. DUNN. Yes.

Miss HILL. I think there is a confusion here as to whether we are talking about laundry work that is done for the lodges, the bedding and linen and things of that kind, or whether we are talking about the individual laundry for the transients, is there not? Are you sending the individual laundry of transients out on contract, too?

Mr. GEBHARDT. No, no.

Miss HILL. I thought they were doing that themselves with the facilities within the lodge.

Mr. GEBHARDT. Yes; that is right. It was the bedding and things of that sort I mentioned.

Mr. SCHNEIDER. And the transient, himself, must pay for his own personal laundry?

Miss HILL. There are some facilities for him to do his own laundry work in the lodges, rather small facilities for that work.

Mr. SCHNEIDER. No particular facilities other than the usual living facilities?

Mr. GEBHARDT. That is right.

Miss HILL. You have a laundry in the Canal Street lodge?

Mr. GEBHARDT. In the new lodge that has just been opened.

Mr. SCHNEIDER. You say that the laundry bill for this "relief station," as you might call it, is sent to the District government?

Miss HILL. The bill?

Mr. GEBHARDT. The bill is sent to the District Building to be paid.

Mr. SCHNEIDER. But does the payment of it come out of the Federal Emergency Relief Administration fund?

Miss HILL. Yes.

Mr. GEBHARDT. You see, the F. E. R. A. funds are allotted to the District, and the District in turn appropriates it to the various divisions in the District.

Miss HILL. That is right.

Mr. SCHNEIDER. Is that true of all the other expenses you have in this organization?

Mr. GEBHARDT. Yes, sir.

Miss HILL. All subject to the procedure of the District of Columbia.

Mr. SCHNEIDER. But do they give you any amounts in a lump sum which you yourself pay out?

Mr. GEBHARDT. No.

Miss HILL. Yes; you have a petty cash account.

Mr. GEBHARDT. We have a petty cash, but I mean, no large amount.

Mr. SCHNEIDER. That is all.

Mr. DUNN. Mr. Gebhardt, how many men sleep in a room?

Mr. GEBHARDT. It would depend pretty much on the capacity of the lodge. We opened a new lodge, or at least a new lodge has been opened, within the past 2 months, that was taken over with an idea of housing between 700 and 800 men on three floors, with a capacity for that number.

Miss HILL. It is a dormitory proposition.

Mr. GEBHARDT. Yes.

Mr. DUNN. Would you say that these rooms are crowded?

Mr. GEBHARDT. Yes. I think that all of our rooms are crowded, but simply as they are or would be any place else, where the registration is beyond the capacity that you would ever imagine, where you were constantly getting an influx of people that you have not accounted to yourself for.

Mr. DUNN. That is not your fault?

Mr. GEBHARDT. Well, not exactly. I mean, if you accommodate your quarters for a thousand men, and day after tomorrow you have 250 bonus marchers arrive, you have not fitted your quarters to accommodate that number.

Mr. DUNN. Congressman Schneider, my secretary has the statement which was made by the gentleman who came here that day, and we will have her read it and then make comparisons. Any objection?

Mr. SCHNEIDER. No objection to bringing out those facts.

Mr. DUNN. Proceed.

Mr. SCHNEIDER. We want to get the facts.

Miss McCHESNEY (secretary). You want me to read his testimony in regard to H. R. 2827, or just about the conditions down there?

Mr. DUNN. No; not H. R. 2827—just the statement made by this man who was representing the men from the transient bureau.

(The testimony of Joseph Murray, given before the Subcommittee of the Committee on Labor, Feb. 5, 1935, supra, was thereupon read by the secretary.)

Mr. DUNN. Now, Mr. Gebhardt, you heard what my secretary just read. Take the first statement there, pertaining to the dollar a week. Well, you answered that question about the dollar a week. You say some receive $3 a week?

Mr. GEBHARDT. That is right—which is not only true in the District of Columbia but pretty true nationally. I mean, there have always been three rates since the beginning of the transient program, $1, $2, and $3.

Mr. Dunn. That answers that question. What is the next question?

Miss McChesney (reading):

The conditions that exist in the transient camps relative to sanitation, housing, and sustenance, are such as to keep the transients migrating from city to city, seeking employment and decent living conditions, which they never find.

Mr. Dunn. You mentioned something about the unsanitary condition. Can you give us a statement about the sanitation?

Mr. Gebhardt. Yes. I think that is a criticism that everybody recognizes, and everything possible is done constantly to remedy it. It is a matter of finding facilities that are adequate rather than have a man sleep out of doors. It means putting in extra cots, and if you have set up a lodge for 50 men and you have 25 extra with no place to send them, your sanitary facilities which have been set up to accommodate 25 men must accommodate 75. I mean, it is just one of the things that you have to recognize because of the great influx of people into the District for various and sundry reasons, and always groups that you have not anticipated or prepared for.

Mr. Dunn. You have answered that question. Did you want to ask any questions pertaining to that, Mr. Schneider? He just stated about the conditions; in other words, that they are doing the best they can, but they are not responsible.

Mr. Schneider. You have five buildings, as I understand it.

Miss Hill. We have more than that.

Mr. Gebhardt. We have about 17.

Mr. Schneider. Seventeen buildings in which these transients live?

Mr. Gebhardt. To which they are sent.

Mr. Schneider. They are leased or rented by the Government?

Mr. Gebhardt. That is right.

Mr. Schneider. From private interests?

Mr. Gebhardt. Not always. Some of it is Government property. I think that is true.

Mr. Schneider. Now, are there any bathing facilities for these transients?

Mr. Gebhardt. Yes. In many instances it is a matter of moving men in and getting the sanitary conditions arranged after they have moved in; but there are some facilities for bathing.

Mr. Schneider. You say "some." What do you mean by "some"?

Mr. Gebhardt. I mean as many facilities as it is possible to get. Just recently, for instance, we have had orders that we should have a bath for every 10 men. That happens to be not one of the bases on which we have worked in the past, but sufficient facilities to take a bath were provided. If a man wants a bath he may have to wait.

Mr. Schneider. In other words, you mean there are facilities there?

Mr. Gebhardt. There are facilities.

Mr. Schneider. There are facilities they furnish the transients, to enable them to take baths if they desire them?

Mr. Gebhardt. That is right.

Miss Hill. You have showers in all the lodges, have you not?

Mr. Gebhardt. Yes.

Miss Hill. It is just a question of whether you have enough for the number of men?

Mr. Gebhardt. That is it.

Miss HILL. In other words, if you build a lodge to accommodate 50 and then you get 100 men who are put in there in double-decker beds, for example, you do not have as many shower baths for the 100, per man, as you do for the 50.

Mr. SCHNEIDER. What about the medical facilities? It has been said by witnesses here that you had no accredited physician to examine and give treatment to these transients.

Mr. GEBHARDT. Of course, it just happens that in the District any physicians that we have must be licensed. While we may not have enough physicians or nurses on the job—which is again a question of not enough—any that are there are accredited. They must necessarily be, by the laws of the District of Columbia.

Mr. SCHNEIDER. How many do you have for these 1,600 or 1,800 men?

Mr. GEBHARDT. Up to rather recently, I think it was a matter of about nine.

Mr. SCHNEIDER. You have nine?

Mr. GEBHARDT. Yes.

Mr. SCHNEIDER. Are they regularly employed in this work?

Mr. GEBHARDT. Yes.

Miss HILL. Not full time.

Mr. GEBHARDT. No; on an hourly basis.

Miss HILL. Giving certain hours of the day.

Mr. GEBHARDT. I mean, giving certain hours of the day, when these people, for example, go to our infirmaries for examination. I mean, each man does not get a physical examination, but a man who needs medical attention is sent to the infirmary and examined by our physicians on duty.

Mr. SCHNEIDER. It has been said that he is not examined by an accredited physician.

Mr. GEBHARDT. And I am saying that all the physicians who are on the staff are licensed, because they must necessarily be so.

Mr. SCHNEIDER. Are they there, I am asking you, to give this examination?

Mr. GEBHARDT. Yes; they are at the infirmary.

Mr. SCHNEIDER. Or is some interne or orderly there?

Mr. GEBHARDT. The physicians themselves are there on the job, both in the infirmaries and going into our lodges.

Miss. HILL. That is at certain hours, is it not?

Mr. GEBHARDT. Yes.

Miss HILL. It is not a 24-hour service.

Mr. GEBHARDT. And the hours are posted on the bulletin board.

Mr. DUNN. You say they are posted?

Mr. GEBHARDT. Yes.

Mr. DUNN. Are these physicians there every day?

Mr. GEBHARDT. Yes.

Mr. DUNN. Certain hours every day?

Mr. GEBHARDT. That is right.

Miss HILL. Do you not want to give them a picture of what that medical program is that you have going right now?

Mr. GEBHARDT. I presume you are all familiar with the fact there is an epidemic of meningitis in the District, and at present we have full-time physicians and nurses in all of our lodges.

Mr. Schneider. As I recall it, this witness testified that there was a serious, dangerous condition, and that there was going to be a situation just as it developed the next day.

Mr. Gebhardt. That was almost prophecy, was it not?

Mr. Schneider. It was a good prophecy, I declare, because what he prophesied took place the next day. That is why we are asking whether the physicians are on the job.

Mr. Gebhardt. Yes; 24 hours, both physicians, and nurses.

Mr. Dunn. May I say that the day that Mr. Murray testified I happened to tune in the radio and a man by the name of Murphy, a newspaperman, stated that spinal meningitis had broken out in the District.

Mr. Gebhardt. Actually, when Mr. Murray was here, the lodges were under quarantine.

Mr. Dunn. That is what I wanted to know. Excuse me, Mr. Schneider. I want to ask this question now. When Mr. Murray came up here and testified, were the lodges under quarantine?

Mr. Gebhardt. That is right.

Mr. Dunn. In other words, he knew the lodges were quarantined?

Mr. Gebhardt. That is right.

Mr. Dunn. I mean, on his first appearance.

Mr. Gebhardt. That is right. The day that I had the call from your office.

Mr. Dunn. Oh, was that the first day?

Mr. Gebhardt. I assume that it was.

Mr. Dunn. But he had been here previously.

Mr. Gebhardt. Well, of course, I did not know that.

Mr. Dunn. In other words, he came here, I believe, last Tuesday, a week ago. I believe it was the second day; but the day I was talking to you, was that the day it was declared?

Mr. Gebhardt. That is right.

Miss Hill. That was a week ago Monday. Was it not a week ago Monday night we put in the quarantine?

Mr. Gebhardt. I think that is right.

Miss Hill. That is right.

Mr. Dunn. I may be mistaken, but the same day that Mr. Murray testified, I heard Mr. Murphy over the radio say that the institution down there was quarantined. He said this over the radio that night, the night of the first day on which Murray made his first appearance; and the day I was talking to you—is that the day the rule went into effect that no person was to leave the institution?

Mr. Gebhardt. The day that you talked to me over the phone was the day following the quarantine, and Mr. Murray had escaped quarantine.

Mr. Dunn. In other words, Murray knew about the institution being quarantined, yet he left the building?

Mr. Gebhardt. That is right.

Mr. Dunn. And is that the reason he was arrested?

Mr. Gebhardt. One of the reasons.

Mr. Dunn. He came here and said there was a warrant out for him, and there were some other men here with him.

Mr. Gebhardt. There was a warrant for everybody who escaped, because immediately a man escapes quarantine his name is turned over to the police. It was a matter between the District of Columbia board of health and the police department.

Mr. DUNN. That law exists, I believe, in every city of the United States.

Mr. GEBHARDT. Yes.

Mr. DUNN. That when the board of health puts up a sign, if you leave the property without permission you are fined.

Mr. GEBHARDT. Yes.

Mr. DUNN. Laws like that exist everywhere. I told Murray that, the day he appeared here. I said, "Was a quarantine sign up"? He said, "No." I said, "If so, you violated the law. But if it was not, of course, you did not violate the law," and he said he did not violate the quarantine; but I learned after you talked to me that the quarantine sign had been put up. Of course, when he left here he was arrested.

You probably do not know this, Mr. Schneider. They called me. The police picked him up here, and I went to see the police, and Mr. Lineberg said, "All I know, Congressman, is we were told to pick him up. I do not know whether he is guilty or not. If he is guilty he must stand trial, but he is now back in the building." I believe he had his trial yesterday, and the evidence was against him. I do not know what they have done with him since, but I told him, "If you left after you were quarantined, that was a violation of law, and the supervisors of your institution are not responsible for that, because that is the law in every State in the Union." However, you say that the quarantine sign was up when he left the building?

Mr. GEBHARDT. I am saying that the day you talked to me was the day following the time that the quarantine had been placed on our lodges by the board of health, but whether he had appeared previously or not, I, of course, do not know.

Mr. DUNN. Yes; he appeared.

Mr. GEBHARDT. But if it was that day that he predicted that this thing would happen, it was the day after the quarantine had been effected.

Mr. DUNN. Well, when he made his first appearance we did not hear anything about this epidemic of spinal meningitis. I heard it that night over the radio, and then when I was talking to you that day, I would say it was the next day, the signs were put up, after you were talking to me, or was it that day?

Mr. GEBHARDT. No; the quarantine was put into effect the night previously.

Mr. DUNN. Oh, the night previously to the day I was talking to you?

Mr. GEBHARDT. Yes.

Mr. DUNN. I see. Well, in other words, then, he was down here, right here in the room, when I was talking to you, so you say the night before, the signs had been put up?

Mr. GEBHARDT. That is right. I did not say the signs had been put up.

Miss HILL. No.

Mr. GEBHARDT. I said the quarantine was effective.

Mr. DUNN. Well, did they know about it?

Miss HILL. Yes.

Mr. GEBHARDT. Did the men know about it? Yes. We made a tour of all the lodges and explained it, and the board of health rather hoped it would not be necessary to put up signs. It seems that frequently signs are not put up for an epidemic of meningitis; and it was not until the board of health realized that the men were not taking the quarantine seriously that they decided to put up the sign, because I recall rather distinctly my conversation with you, in which you asked whether or not Mr. Murray would be treated kindly if he came down there, and I assured you that no other treatment would be given him, but that either he must return to the lodge or he would be arrested; and my reason for that statement was that the quarantine was effective and that if he did not return to the lodge from which he had escaped he would have to be arrested. I mean, I think I went into that over the phone, at the time.

Mr. DUNN. Yes; you did. I will tell you, he came back the second time and told us that a warrant was out for him and that they were singling him out because he came before this committee and testified.

Mr. GEBHARDT. Well, was not that really sort of silly?

Mr. DUNN. I could not see why they arrested him. When you told me to send him down he left this building and was arrested.

Mr. GEBHARDT. That is right.

Mr. DUNN. But the other men who were with him were not arrested, and I had gone down to the police station, and Mr. Lineberg, the head of the crime-prevention department, I believe, stated that he was told to pick him up, and of course he did not know anything about it, but they would investigate that, and of course if he was guilty he would have to stand trial. According to information I received, he had his trial yesterday.

Mr. GEBHARDT. If this is to be a matter of explaining Mr. Murray, I might tell you that story, if this will help clear up any matter pertaining to any of the statements that Mr. Murray has made.

After talking with you, instructions were left at the office that Murray was either to return to the lodge or he would be arrested. He was picked up by a policeman and returned to the lodge, so that it was not an arrest but rather a return to the lodge.

His trial came up for again escaping.

Mr. DUNN. Oh, did he escape again?

Mr. GEBHARDT. That is right.

Mr. DUNN. I did not know that.

Mr. GEBHARDT. And also for inciting a riot on Government property. It happens that the lodge in which he was located is not one rented from private individuals, but is Government property.

Mr. DUNN. You say he incited a riot?

Mr. GEBHARDT. Yes, sir; an attempted riot.

Mr. DUNN. What was the cause?

Mr. GEBHARDT. Well, simply a matter of the quarantine not being official, and that they were being held in this lodge not because of an official quarantine but rather that it was just a matter of vengance on them as individuals; and it was necessary to call the head of the board of health to persuade these men that the quarantine was actually official.

Miss HILL. Mr. Gebhardt, would it help any to have Mr. Linden give you any information on that? He says the charge was a disorderly-conduct charge, but that was what was in the disorderly-conduct charge. The official charge was that.

Mr. GEBHARDT. Of disorderly conduct?

Mr. DUNN. This is the point I want to get clear: After he was arrested he was taken back to the lodge?

Mr. GEBHARDT. That is right.

Mr. DUNN. And it was then, of course, under quarantine. Did I understand you to say he again left?

Mr. GEBHARDT. I think that is right; is it not, Mr. Linden? Did he not leave the second time?

Miss HILL. Two or three times.

Mr. LINDEN. He threatened to leave, and in fact he claimed, in explaining his previous leaving the lodge during the time it was under quarantine, in telling the police, as I understand, or as I received it from Mr. Lineberg, that he had had special permission from Congressman Dunn and Congressman Lundeen to leave the lodge.

Mr. DUNN. What did he say? Speak a little louder, please. He had special permission from Congressmen Dunn and Lundeen?

Mr. LINDEN. I was told by the police department he claimed to have had special permission from Congressmen Dunn and Lundeen to leave the lodge, because he was here to testify to this committee; which I questioned, and I only received that over the phone from Lieutenant Lineberg. He was replaced in the lodge and since that time we have used a staggering system for getting the work done that is necessary to be done, so that one man will not be doing all that, but that they will all take part; and in doing this particular thing he refused and immediately tried to antagonize everyone and to make remarks about the various officials of the whole organization, so that he was brought into court yesterday, charged with disorderly conduct and violating the quarantine, and was sentenced on those two charges.

Mr. DUNN. But you said that he said Congressmen Dunn and Lundeen gave him permission.

Mr. LINDEN. Yes.

Mr. GEBHARDT. He said that at this meeting immediately following his appearance here, after talking with you over the phone, that it was by your permission. I mean, the conversation I had with you, which was very clear in my mind, was very much distorted by him in telling it to these 200 men, or whatever the number was.

Mr. DUNN. I do not think you will find that in the record. I plainly said to Mr. Murray on the second day of his appearance, what I have repeated here. He did not testify the second day. He was just talking, and I said this to him: "Is the institution under quarantine?" He said, "It has gone into effect." I said, "Were you notified it was quarantined, and after you were notified did you leave?" And he said, "No." "Well", I said, "if you did they can hold you; there is a charge; it is not only a District charge but that law exists throughout the land." But I did not hear him make any statement like that and Congressman Lundeen did not.

Mr. GEBHARDT. Of course, all I know about that is what I have told you.

Mr. DUNN. When he called up he said he was arrested. He told us he was arrested because he testified. We contacted the police department. In fact, I made a special trip to the police station to see that he was going to get justice, but Mr. Lineberg told me that he was authorized and picked him up because he had violated the quarantine.

Mr. GEBHARDT. Correct.

Mr. DUNN. And I know that is a violation of the law.

Mr. GEBHARDT. Well, as I say, my understanding of my being called here was to answer the charges of Mr. Murray, as a personal matter, a thing I would be very glad to talk with you about any time you choose.

Miss HILL. But I do not think it ought to be a part of this hearing, do you?

Mr. DUNN. No; it does not need to be, but I am just telling you what he said.

Mr. SCHNEIDER. This is for the record. I am not sure yet in my own mind whether what Murray said here was a prophecy or a fact.

Mr. GEBHARDT. It was a fact, sir. A quarantine had become effective the night previous to the time that he was here—just what I told Congressman Dunn over the telephone when Mr. Murray was in his presence, that the quarantine had become effective the previous night; that Mr. Murray would have to return to the lodge from which he had escaped or would be arrested. That was my conversation with Congressman Dunn, because the quarantine was effective. That is the truth, is it not?

Mr. DUNN. Yes. But, Mr. Schneider, the day I was talking to Mr. Gebhardt was the day that Mr. Murray made his second appearance. Maybe you were not here. Were you?

Mr. SCHNEIDER. I was not here. Was it the day after he first appeared, or on another day?

Mr. DUNN. My secretary went down to get the data. The first day he was here, I believe, was on a Tuesday. It was not that day. I believe I was talking to you, Mr. Gebhardt, on Tuesday, or was it on a Wednesday?

Mr. GEBHARDT. I would not recall, excepting that a letter I have from you might indicate the date.

Mr. SCHNEIDER. Did you write that letter, Mr. Chairman?

Mr. DUNN. Yes. I was requested by the committee to write it.

Mr. SCHNEIDER. Did you write it that night or the next day?

Mr. DUNN. I believe I called him first.

Mr. GEBHARDT. On Tuesday, February 5, the transient worker appeared before a subcommittee. Now, that would have been a week ago day before yesterday. This is the 14th.

Miss HILL. Quarantine went into effect the night before, Monday night.

Mr. GEBHARDT. Quarantine went into effect Monday night.

Mr. DUNN. The day before that?

Mr. GEBHARDT. Yes.

Miss HILL. Then he came back to supper.

Mr. DUNN. Then it was quarantined when he was here?

Mr. SCHNEIDER. We did not know anything about that.

Miss HILL. I think the fact you need to consider is, there was a group in the transient bureau that did not feel that the quarantine was legal. You see, they did not have the sign on the house, and they could only take our interpretation, or the staff present in the lodge, who told them those were our instructions from the health department. They resented it. They did not feel it was fair, and they protested it was not legal because the sign was not on the building, and that was the difficulty that we had from that quarantine.

Mr. SCHNEIDER. What I am trying to get clear in the record is simply this: Of course, I do not care so much about it. I recall that there were several other transients came here, the day he appeared, on

Tuesday, when Mr. Murray appeared, and, of course, all that we have talked about here, we knew nothing about. We were simply taking the testimony as he presented it, and as I said before, it was to clear any indictment of your institution, and the object in asking you to come here was to state to the committee the actual condition that exists in the institution. Now, what happened after that, of course, I am not concerned about.

Miss HILL. If we only had a report of the condition of "an" institution, it would be simple; but it is 12 to 16, and some are much better than others, and we know they are; we wish they were all good, but we do not get quite the same conditions in any two of them, as you can imagine.

Mr. SCHNEIDER. That is the condition with all the human race— there are none of us alike; and when you are dealing with transients, of course, you are dealing with that element.

Miss HILL. You see, you must build lodges here for colored men and for white men; you must have infirmaries, you must have mess halls; it is a very complicated program, with as many as about 2,200 men a night staying in our city.

Mr. SCHNEIDER. What about this charge of bad food? The charge was made here that the food was very poor, and I believe the charge was made that many of the people from your institution go down to the Volunteers of America or some other relief station to get sufficient to satisfy their hunger.

Mr. GEBHARDT. I think the answer to that is, the quality of the food is something that we are constantly striving to improve. The quantity may not be sufficient; but again the answer would be that if you prepare for 75 and suddenly have an addition of 25 or 50, rather than have that 25 or 50 go hungry, your quantity is kept down. I question whether any man applying at any of our lodges for food at any time really goes hungry. He may not have as much food as he thinks he is entitled to, but he has sufficient, or at least enough to carry on. I mean you cannot just prepare food and then have an influx, and your intake is something that governs the capacity of both your dining rooms and your lodges.

Mr. LUNDEEN. This committee is not instituted for the purpose of investigating anything or anybody. It is here to find out who is for H. R. 2827.

Mr. DUNN. I know; but you see, Congressman Lundeen, this matter came up before the committee. Were you here when a motion was made that I send a letter to Mr. Gebhardt, to have him appear before the committee, because Mr. Murray, one of the men from the institution, appeared before the committee, and of course he told us how the men were being treated there. Were you not here that day?

Mr. LUNDEEN. I believe I was.

Mr. DUNN. I believe you voted for the motion to have him come up here, did you not?

Mr. LUNDEEN. It is all right to have him come up here, but I am interested in knowing whether Mr. Gebhardt and these other witnesses who come here are for H. R. 2827. I have my hands full with this bill, and I cannot investigate the hospitals and transient camps, and so forth, in addition.

Mr. DUNN. Now, Congressman, let me tell you this, in addition: In my candid opinion, this is going to do something for your bill, because Mr. Gebhardt is telling about the conditions, and so far he has given us a lot of valuable information. He has not exaggerated anything he said.

Mr. LUNDEEN. Well, that is fine.

Mr. DUNN. Therefore, it goes right in with your bill. In other words, if your bill were enacted into law, all these transient bureaus would be eliminated in the United States.

Mr. LUNDEEN. Well, will Mr. Gebhardt say that to us?

Mr. DUNN. Are you asking me that or asking Mr. Gebhardt that question? You see, all he is testifying is in answer to certain questions. The members of the committee made a motion to have me write him a letter requesting him to come here, and he has come here to answer charges that have been preferred against the institution of which he is the director or supervisor.

Mr. LUNDEEN. Mr. Chairman, I think that is all right, but I do not think we ought to let ourselves be drawn off into something that is foreign to the purpose of the committee. It is all right to have Mr. Gebhardt meet the charges that were made, if he can, but I do not think that we should go into days and afternoons of investigating anything.

Mr. DUNN. We are not going into days and afternoons, but I still disagree with you, while we are the best of friends. I can make this statement, that this man Murray came up and testified before this committee and told about the conditions down there; and he maintained that the organization, or those men down there who had read the bill and knew about the bill, were in favor of it. In fact, he said in his testimony that they held a meeting; and I think he said there were about 400 men attended, and they were on record endorsing the Lundeen bill, which in their opinion, if enacted into law, would prevent this condition. Murray, I think, made that statement.

Mr. LUNDEEN. That part is fine.

Mr. DUNN. Of course, Mr. Gebhardt is up here; charges were preferred against him; and the committee members made that motion, and I had to do my duty, when I was told to do those things. In other words, I would like to ask one more question, and then if the Congressman does not have any desire to interrogate Mr. Gebhardt, we will conclude the discussion.

Mr. LUNDEEN. I have no objection to a statement being made. If they want to clear up any charges that have been made, that is all very well; and only that, but I do not think we ought to be led off the track too far.

Mr. DUNN. Oh, no. I have excellent sight and will see that the engine stays right on the main track.

Mr. LUNDEEN. All right. Thanks. That is fine.

Mr. DUNN. One more question I would like to ask: Mr. Murray made this statement; for about 6 transients there is at least an official who receives a salary from the Government or from the District. In other words, I think he maintained there are about 1,800. Am I right?

Mr. GEBHARDT. There are in the neighborhood of 3,000 transients under guard now.

Mr. DUNN. Three thousand?

Mr. GEBHARDT. Yes.

Mr. DUNN. He said 1,600 men and 200 women—1,800.

Mr. GEBHARDT. That is my recollection.

Mr. LUNDEEN. Now, you say 3,000?

Mr. GEBHARDT. We just happen to have records and statistical information, which is something which we can show.

Mr. LUNDEEN. You mean you can back up your statement with statistics and records?

Mr. GEBHARDT. Yes.

Mr. DUNN. Now, in regard to the number of officials employed, what would you say, Mr. Gebhardt?

Mr. GEBHARDT. I have just said the number of transients under care is in the neighborhood of 3,000. As of January 1, the staff consisted of 45 people. Much of the clerical work was done by transients themselves, who hire on this $3 rate now.

Mr. DUNN. Are they included in the 45 you just mentioned?

Miss HILL. No.

Mr. GEBHARDT. No; they are not.

Mr. DUNN. The 45 are paid a salary?

Mr. GEBHARDT. That is right.

Mr. DUNN. And you have about 3,000?

Mr. GEBHARDT. That is right.

Miss HILL. Administrative employees are running about 8 percent of what your expenditures are for the men.

Mr. DUNN. Let that go in the record. That is important. That answers my question.

Does anybody else wish to ask Mr. Gebhardt any questions, or Miss Hill, or Mr. Linden?

Mr. LUNDEEN. May I say, as long as we are drawn into this, that I should like to ask if the Government is doing everything in its power to help these men down there?

Mr. GEBHARDT. If by "everything in its power" you mean——

Mr. LUNDEEN. Well, everything—all the facilities at its disposal.

Mr. GEBHARDT. All the facilities we can lay our hands on; all the energy and brains that people who have an interest in these people are trying to use. I mean, if that answers your question, that is the answer.

Mr. LUNDEEN. We have an impression here that there was much crowding.

Mr. GEBHARDT. Very true.

Mr. LUNDEEN. Unsanitary conditions that had led to disease and dangerous epidemics, and all that sort of thing.

Miss HILL. That is our most serious problem, without any question, our overcrowding.

Mr. GEBHARDT. We are overcrowded.

Mr. LUNDEEN. That, of course, is a tragedy.

Miss HILL. It is.

Mr. DUNN. He answered my question. He maintained that was true.

Miss HILL. One of the things that has created our difficulty is quarantines at just such places as Eustis, where we were sending our men regularly, and that backed up everything into our own lodges, and overcrowded us, you see, because we could not send them day after day, there, which was our one outlet for people here.

Mr. GEBHARDT. And I think the answer to your question as to whether our professional workers or our paid staff are doing everything possible, is that when this quarantine was effective men left their own families and homes and went into quarantine to keep up the spirits of these men, and they have been in quarantine the entire period of time. I think that answers the question as to whether or not everything possible is being done for them.

Miss HILL. People who are not doctors or nurses, but staff members who were not medical people.

Mr. LUNDEEN. Mr. Chairman, this is only one small part of the national picture. If we appropriate money under this bill, or some other bill, sufficient to raise the income tax and inheritance tax rate, even up to the British rates, we could have habitations, clean and sanitary, and with proper food and equipment to make these folks happy. Yet we refused to raise those taxes on incomes and inheritances, even up to the British rate, and that sum in itself, in my humble opinion, would be sufficient to cure all these difficulties we are having, not only in Washington but in other cities throughout the United States; and, as long as this matter is brought up, I want the record to show that I am in favor of higher taxes upon the big fortunes and inheritances of this country, to meet this emergency and to meet it with the cash that they have, that the people have produced, that these very men who are in these camps have produced with their own hands.

Mr. DUNN. In other words, Congressman Lundeen, these camps are unnecessary. As we have stated before, if our Government would make it possible to provide jobs at a living wage for men and women who are physically able to work, and provide an adequate compensation or pension for the aged and those who are incapacitated, there would not be any necessity for poorhouses or transient bureaus at all, and the Government can do it. We have the wealth, but unfortunately it is in the hands of a few. I want to go on record by making this statement. I was in the White House for about an hour and fifteen minutes last Friday, and the President of the United States made a similar statement that the industries, the wealth of the country, was in the hands of a few, and we must as soon as possible legislate to bring about a condition whereby the wealth will be more equally distributed, and as long as we Congressmen will not legislate to bring about such conditions—that is, conditions whereby the men and women who are able to work shall have jobs at a living wage—and as long as we are going to permit people to work and compel them to accept small wages, we are going to have sweatshops, and as long as we have sweatshops we are going to have poorhouses; and as long as we have poorhouses and sweatshops we are going to have slum districts, and as long as we have slum districts we are going to have criminals; and as long as we have criminals, the Federal Government is going to be compelled to pay out gigantic sums of money to keep down crime.

Mr. LUNDEEN. Judging from your statement, Mr. Chairman, the President is in favor of the provisions of the Lundeen bill, H. R. 2827. I hope he will come through on it.

Mr. DUNN. May I make this statement? There were about 15 Congressmen there. Many, of course, were there from the West, and they were telling the President they were receiving thousands of letters. In fact, I was talking to one of the Congressmen the other night, who received 8,000 letters supporting the Townsend plan, and they went to the President to see if he would not increase the amount of pensions and unemployment insurance, and he was willing to do it. He made the statement that he believed in better pensions, but where were we going to get the money? He said experts came to him and told him the amount of money which was to be obtained was all that he could get at the present time, and he would always ask the question, "Where were we going to get the money?"

Mr. Schneider, do you have any questions?

Mr. SCHNEIDER. I have no more questions.

Mr. DUNN. Mr. Gebhardt?

Mr. DUNN. I have no more questions. Thank you for making your appearance.

Mr. DUNN. The next witness Rosa Rayside.

STATEMENT OF ROSA RAYSIDE, REPRESENTING DOMESTIC WORKERS UNION, NEW YORK CITY

Mr. DUNN. You may proceed.

Miss RAYSIDE. As a representative of the Domestic Workers' Union, I wish to state the reasons why my organization endorses the unemployment and social insurance bill, H. R. 2827.

It is the only unemployment insurance bill which does not exclude domestic workers from the categories of workers entitled to receive benefits under the act.

According to the United States census of 1930 there was a total of 4,952,451 domestic workers, of which number 1,772,200 were men and 3,180,251 were women. This is a total increase of 1,572,556 workers in the domestic field in 10 years, as shown by comparison with the census statistics for 1920. With the continuance of the crisis, many workers have been forced into the domestic line who cannot find employment as stenographers, teachers, and so forth, as well as housewives whose husbands are no longer able to support them.

The section in the bill (H. R. 2827) which provides for the extension of the benefits of the act to workers and farmers without discrimination because of sex, race, or color is of utmost importance to domestic workers. The Urban League gives the number of Negro women employed in domestic and personal service as 1,152,560. This is nearly three-fourths or 72 percent of all Negro women gainfully employed. (Y. M. C. A. report 1932.) Negro women represent nearly one-third of all women employed as domestics. In the Southern States 86 percent of the women working in laundries are Negroes. (U. S. Women's Bu. Bul. 78.)

"Depression Ends Servant Problem—Magazine Finds that Untrained Maids Can Be Hired as Low as For $4 a Month." This is the heading of an item in the New York Times for November 25, 1932, in which it quotes an article from Fortune magazine. According to Fortune the "servant problem is solved." Yes, it is solved for the employers, but not for the workers. The article goes on to state that the wage for domestic workers in Virginia is $8 a month and $5 a week in the North.

The employers have taken advantage of the crisis to force wages of domestic help below a subsistence level. Many of them, posing as philanthropists, offer "opportunity" homes, that is, they contract for the full-time work of a houseworker in exchange for a "good" home. In many cases the accommodations consist of a folding cot in the hallway or the kitchen and the poorest sort of food. According to a Federated Press correspondence in the spring of 1933 the Cleveland (Ohio) papers carried advertisements offering a good home in exchange for a full week's work.

In 1933 the New York State Labor Department reported that 15- and 16-year-old girls were working from 6:30 in the morning to 10 in the evening for $10 and $15 a month.

The Domestic Workers' Union has found cases in which houseworkers received $4.50 a week for a 65-hour week. Out of this money they were required to pay 70 cents a week carfare as well as their complete maintenance. In Sunnyside, Long Island, there were many instances of young girls who had been brought from other States to work for $15 a month on a 10- and 11-hour day with one afternoon off a week. Twenty-five dollars a month is a usual wage for a 70-hour week in New York City.

A woman working in the Bronx, New York, received 50 cents for 6 hours' work. Another woman was sent on a job from a charity agency in New York City and she received 50 cents as complete payment for 2 full days' work. Another houseworker worked regularly once a week for $1.25 for 8 hours.

The State agency at 200 West One Hundred Thirty-fifth Street sends houseworkers out for as low as 25 cents an hour (the regular was in 1929 was 50 cents). Another agency was found sending out cards to employers advertising experienced workers for $2.50 a day.

We have found no complete figures on unemployment for domestic workers but the statistics on wages and the information on conditions given above indicates in a measure the number of unemployed domestics who are competing for jobs. The employment agencies in every city are crowded with workers seeking jobs. In certain sections of New York and Brooklyn women stand on the streets in a modern form of slave market waiting for employers to offer them a few hours of work. The wages on the corners vary from 10 to 25 cents an hour.

The Urban League which conducts an employment agency in Harlem gives the following figures for the month of February 1935. Two hundred women registered for domestic work. There were 90 openings of which only 55 actually provided jobs for domestic workers.

Figures on unemployment among women and Negroes may give some indication of conditions in domestic work because of the numbers of these groups in the domestic field. The United States Women's Bureau reports in a study of 19 cities made in 1933, one-fifth of the working women were unemployed. In Buffalo, N. Y., according to a report made by that city in 1933, 56.2 percent of the women workers were unemployed and 27 percent of the workers were on part time. In Pittsburgh, in 1933, 60 percent of the Negroes were unemployed.

It has been my purpose in presenting these facts to show the miserable conditions which unemployment has forced upon the domestic workers. Wages have dropped below subsistence level but even these starvation jobs make the workers ineligible for relief. For example, the Home Relief Administration in New York City has just instituted the practice of requesting former employers to rehire the workers and no matter what wage is offered the worker is forced to accept.

Domestic workers are the first group to suffer when an employer receives the least reduction in income. It is an excuse for a drastic cut or in many cases firing of the workers. It is essential that any bill designed honestly to give security to the workers against unemployment should include domestic workers. That is why the Domestic Workers' Union endorses without reservation the unemployment and social insurance bill, H. R. 2827.

Mr. DUNN. You believe that the Lundeen bill (H. R. 2827) if enacted into law, will be very beneficial to the colored as well as the white people?

Miss RAYSIDE. Yes. I do believe that.

Mr. DUNN. And the organization which you represent here today has gone on record endorsing this bill, H. R. 2827?

Miss RAYSIDE. Yes.

Mr. DUNN. Thank you very much.

Mr. DUNN. We will now hear from Mr. James Eaton.

STATEMENT OF JAMES O. EATON, REHABILITATION OFFICER, VETERANS NATIONAL RANK AND FILE COMMITTEE, WASHINGTON, D. C.

Mr. DUNN. You are the rehabilitation officer?

Mr. EATON. Yes, sir.

Mr. DUNN. How many men belong to your organization?

Mr. EATON. There are, by paid-up membership, 5,000.

Mr. DUNN. Five thousand?

Mr. EATON. Yes.

Mr. DUNN. In the District of Columbia?

Mr. EATON. No. That is in the United States.

Mr. DUNN. This is your headquarters?

Mr. EATON. This is the national office, here. I am from the national office.

Mr. DUNN. You said "paid-up members, about 5,000"?

Mr. EATON. About 5,000, yes.

Mr. DUNN. Have you any idea of the number that would be in your organization if they had sufficient funds to pay their dues?

Mr. EATON. That is problematical, but we have reason to believe that it would be equal to the American Legion. I think they claim 750,000 membership at the present time.

Mr. DUNN. You are here to testify in behalf of the Lundeen bill, H. R. 2827?

Mr. EATON. I am. I have a statement prepared for that purpose.

Mr. DUNN. All right. Proceed.

Mr. EATON. I am here representing the veterans' national rank and file committee elected at Fort Hunt, Va., in May 1934, by 1,500 veterans from 48 States, many of them showing membership in the American Legion, the Veterans of Foreign Wars, the Disabled American Veterans, local rank and file committees, Workers Ex-Servicemen's League, and so forth.

These veterans, representing practically every occupational group, had come to Washington to attend the rank and file convention in answer to a call sent out by the veterans' national rank and file committee, which was elected at Fort Hunt, in May 1934, by 3,300 veterans. That convention in turn had been called by the veterans' national liaison committee, elected by 600 veterans in Washington in December 1932.

In all cases, a three-point program was adopted. In December 1932 the program was:

1. Immediate payment of the balance due on the adjusted-compensation certificates;
2. No cuts in compensation or allowances;
3. Relief for the unemployed and farmers.

In 1933 the second and third points of the program were changed to meet the changing conditions, to repeal the economy act, and adequate remedial relief for the unemployed and farmers. At the last convention, which elected the present committee, the third point became workers unemployment and social insurance, H. R. 7598, now H. R. 2827, introduced by Mr. Ernest Lundeen of Minnestoa.

Thus this committee, under one name or another, has maintained headquarters in Washington for almost 2½ years. It was the first nationally organized group of veterans, with one exception (the American League of Ex-Servicemen), to identify itself concretely with the masses of workers, farmers and professionals in their struggle for relief from the ravages of the crisis, now in its sixth year.

In addition, the influence of the three-point program among veterans has spread beyond the rank-and-file groups throughout the country directly affiliated with our committee. The Army and Navy Union, at its last convention, held at Atlantic City, N. J., August 1934, adopted as the third point of its program unemployment insurance, although not specifying what form or type of insurance was preferred. Recently, however, in the State of California, the veterans affiliated with the End Poverty in California groups, endorsed workers, unemployment and social insurance, H. R. 2827. Though the V. F. W. has made no official statement on this question, certain local committees of that organization have come out in favor of enactment into legislation of unemployment and social insurance. This is also true of a number of posts of the American Legion.

In a comparatively brief period of time, since December 1932, the objections then being raised on all sides to social insurance, unemployment insurance, and so forth, as "doles", have subsided considerably, with the question now being, What form shall the unemployment and social insurance take? Though the necessity existed then as well as now for such legislation, the bitter experiences and the accompanying awakening of the masses have developed a mass demand as evidenced by the hearings conducted by your committee, growing steadily stronger for the right kind of relief from unemployment, hazards encountered in industry, as well as from the insecurity of old age, sickness, and maternity.

The veterans, in growing numbers, realizing that their problems are basically the same as those of the rest of the people, are joining in the fight for enactment of Federal legislation for workers' unemployment and social insurance.

Therefore, I am here for my organization, to join with the 3,000 A. F. of L. locals, the 5 State federations of labor, the 5 international unions, the 50 central labor bodies, the farmers and unemployed groups, the fraternal, and professional groups, with the knowledge that I am voicing the sentiments of tens of thousands of World War veterans, Spanish-American War veterans, and ex-service men, in support of H. R. 2827.

It is not strange that veterans in increasing numbers should support the bill under consideration. One of the fundamental principles embodied in this bill and distinguishing it from other bills and plans of unemployment and social insurance, is that it places the responsibility for the unemployed, the care of the aged and the sick directly at the door where the responsibility belongs, the Federal Government and the employers. This principle of national and employer responsibility already exists in the veterans' legislation pertaining to pensions, hospital and domiciliary care, and so forth, though these benefits are entirely inadequate at the present time. But it is now generally accepted that the Federal Government as employer should assume the responsibility for the care of those who have participated in the most hazardous and the most poorly paid of all industries— war. Only those who benefit from wars, the bankers and industrialists, oppose this responsibility. In the case of unemployment and social insurance for all workers, the same bankers and industrialists who profit most from industry oppose genuine relief from the misery attending involuntary unemployment, and so forth. This similarity of responsibilities is more clearly revealed when we consider that the youth of 1917 were not consulted as to their desire in the matter of entering the war to "make the world safe for democracy" any more than the 16,000,000 unemployed are responsible for their present predicament.

Furthermore, we World War veterans also realize that even if our back wages are paid, though this is far from being a certainty, due to the conflict now raging in the Ways and Means Committee and the opposition of the administration to payment, such payment would not eliminate the need of veterans as workers and farmers and so forth for unemployment and social insurance. Further, the attempt in administration circles to introduce a compromise calling for payment to needy veterans is at once an evasion of the principle of adjusted compensation embodied in the act of 1924 and of the problem of relief for the unemployed.

The question logically arises how many World War veterans, veterans of other wars and campaigns, and peace-time ex-service men are among the ranks of the unemployed. There are close to 4,000,000 World War veterans. Veterans' Administration figures disclose 5 percent of all World War veterans are unemployable, 21 percent of employable World War veterans are unemployed. This means that approximately one-quarter of World War veterans are either unemployed or unemployable, or close to 1,000,000 World War veterans. There are at least 3,500,000 other veterans and ex-service men of all campaigns and service. Applying the same percentages to this other group, we obtain a figure close to 2,000,000. This is a conservative estimate, for it does not take into consideration the greater age of the large Spanish-American War, Boxer Rebellion, and Philippine Insurrection group.

Even this conservative figure shows to what extent the blows of the crisis have fallen upon the veteran population, as the total number of veterans drawing compensation and pensions from the Federal Government was 581,225 in 1934 (Veterans' Administration figures). This leaves approximately 1,500,000 not receiving any aid from the Federal Government under veterans' laws. This proves still further the common need and interest of veterans and nonveterans and the extent to which the veterans will be benefited along with the non-veteran workers, farmers, professionals, and so forth by the passage of H. R. 2827.

In joining with others in the demand for workers unemployment and social insurance, the veterans national bank and file committee wishes to make it clear that it will not relinquish its demand for the immediate payment of the balance due on the adjusted compensation certificates and the repeal of the economy act, because the veterans have their own special claims upon the Federal Government for services rendered.

However, we unequivocally endorse H. R. 2827 because among its provisions (1) it prescribes Federal and employer responsibility; (2) it eliminates no category of the unemployed; above the age of 18; (3) it provides compensation equal to average local wages; (4) it provides compensation covering the difference between wages received on part-time jobs and the average local wages for full-time employment; (5) it provides for the administration and control by those affected, the workers and the farmers; and lastly, provides the most logical method of financing genuine unemployment and social insurance, namely, taxation upon inheritances, gifts, and individual and corporation incomes of $5,000 a year and over; in other words, those most able to assume the burden.

We are opposed to any plan or bill which shirks Federal and employer responsibility, which taxes workers' pay rolls, which excludes those now unemployed or any section of the unemployed or category of workers, which discriminates because of race or creed, which does not provide for rank-and-file administration and control.

Mr. DUNN. Mr. Eaton, then of course your organization believes that if this bill is enacted into law it will be very beneficial to the ex-servicemen?

Mr. EATON. Absolutely.

Mr. DUNN. And to every person who today is out of employment?

Mr. EATON. Yes. Might I enumerate some of the things that have been discovered in the last 6 months, from my rehabilitation work among veterans?

Mr. DUNN. Yes. Is it a big list?

Mr. EATON. No; I am just going to give you a few things.

Mr. DUNN. Proceed.

Mr. EATON. Out of 226 cases for rehabilitation purposes that have reached our office, 198 have been a demand for repeal of the economy act, and 210 have been in the form of an appeal of cases cut off by the economy act, of presumptives and service connected, above 10 percent and below 50 percent. We have been able to find that in the South the Negro veterans, as a whole, have been discriminated against. There are instances standing today in the United States Veterans' Administration where cases are on file there, and have been so for 6 months, and have not been acted upon. The same condition prevails in the regional office or the adjudication office in the South, namely, Georgia, Alabama, Florida, and Mississippi.

We have recently been able to establish a committee at Biloxi, Miss., that is doing some work in getting things going there. We find that 9 out of every 10 letters want to know "Where we can get a position or a job." I would like to know, myself, because I have been unemployed—in fact, I am unemployable—for 4 years. I am a disabled veteran, formerly a member of the Disabled Veterans of America; very poorly compensated for the loss of an eye in France, and four other disabilities that were aggravated by service not sufficient to be service connected. Yet they disable me 100 percent, which is recognized by the Veterans' Administration as preventing any gainful employment.

I cite this case of my own in the District of Columbia. My last job here was as janitor in a school, for 2 years, at a salary of $1,200 per year. I have a wife and six children. I resigned on the orders of a physician. That was in August 1930, and since that time I have been unable to earn a dollar. My family is on relief, and has been for a number of years, and the relief conditions have gotten so bad—I wanted to have a chance to say this before Miss Hill and Mr. Gebhardt left—that since last Thursday two of my boys who are in junior high school have been without food except one meal per day, consisting of rice and condensed milk. When we go to Miss Hall or to the relief department, they tell us that "budgets are too big." We are receiving the sum of $48 a month, to feed a family of eight. I get $30 a month from the Government in compensation, and pay $30.50 for a house to live in. I am 50 cents in the red when the rent is paid; that, of course, has to clothe and feed and buy the necessary medicine—if there is any, and there is not—and that gives you a picture of the things that are coming to us through the mails all over this country, especially the Negro veterans in the South. They are suffering greater than their white comrades. In the West, the Southwest, men and women are suffering. We have information that they are riding in box cars and asking, "What is next?" We do not know what is next, but we believe that the passage of H. R. 2827 will not completely eliminate these conditions. We know it will not, but it will greatly alleviate the intense suffering that confronts the people of America today.

Mr. DUNN. We thank you for that information, and I agree with you that the unfortunate soldier is certainly up against it, because I have had many of them come into my office, asking me to see if I cannot get them something to do, and unfortunately many of the poor wounded fellows who were overseas, are able to get but very little compensation from the Government because they could not prove they met with misfortune while in the line of duty, and I believe you will agree with me when I say the information I have received is that many of these soldiers did not want to have on their discharge that they were injured, because they felt that when they came back to the United States they would not be able to get a job.

Mr. EATON. That is correct.

Mr. DUNN. And when they came back, they found there was no work, and now, because they are unable to show that they met with misfortune while in the line of duty, they are not considered eligible for compensation.

Mr. EATON. On that, Mr. Chairman, I do not know whether you are acquainted with our three-point program, or not. The present three-point program is as follows:

No. 1, immediate cash payment of adjusted certificates.

Mr. DUNN. In which I concur. I am in favor of that.

Mr. EATON. No. 2, the repeal of the economy act, that will put the veterans back in hospitals and back in their homes, where half of the beds are vacant at the present time, and take them off of the streets and away from the charity organizations in their communities.

No. 3, H. R. 2827.

Mr. DUNN. That is your three-point program?

Mr. EATON. That is our three-point program.

Mr. DUNN. Well, that is all right in my opinion, and I want to say that I am more than willing to support it.

Thank you very much, Mr. Eaton. We appreciate your coming before the committee and giving us this information.

(The hour of 5 o'clock having arrived, the subcommittee, in pursuance of its order, took a recess until 10 o'clock tomorrow morning.)

UNEMPLOYMENT, OLD-AGE, AND SOCIAL INSURANCE

FRIDAY, FEBRUARY 15, 1935

House of Representatives,
Subcommittee of the Committee on Labor,
Washington, D. C.

The subcommittee met at 10 o'clock a. m., in the Caucus Room, House Office Building, Hon. Matthew A. Dunn (chairman) presiding.

Mr. DUNN. I have received a statement from Michael Davidow, which he mailed in and which he requests be included in the record. That will be done.

(The statement of Michael Davidow is as follows:)

STATEMENT OF MR. MICHAEL DAVIDOW, REPRESENTING THE UNEMPLOYMENT COUNCILS OF GREATER NEW YORK

I represent 10,000 members of the Unemployment Councils of Greater New York, chartered by the National Unemployment Councils, who, for over 5 years, have been fighting for the workers' bill, now known as "H. R. 2827" and who are firmly determined to intensify the struggle for its enactment. The demonstrations of May 26, when hundreds of unemployed and relief workers protested the lay-offs and the stoppage of relief, despite the brutal attack of the police, the Albany hunger march which had as one of its main demands the enactment of the workers' bill, the numerous demonstrations at the home relief bureaus, the strikes on relief jobs, all show that the unemployed are increasingly struggling against the policy of hunger which the Roosevelt administration is attempting to carry out.

What are the conditions of the unemployed of New York City which makes the passage of this bill an immediate necessity? The key to the explanation of the misery of the unemployed is contained in Commissioner McGoldrick's statement, "The bankers have the last say in the giving of relief." Mayor LaGuardia agrees with him when he says, "I have to go hat-in-hand to the bankers." Let us contrast: According to Commissioner Hodson, there are 215,000 on direct relief and 115,000 on work relief. For these 300,000 families the city government provides a yearly sum of approximately $50,000,000. For a handful of bankers, however, they can afford to set aside a sum three and a half times as large, $180,000,000 for interest on debt service. The whole relief program of the city government is dictated by this policy of providing for the bankers at the expense of the unemployed.

What are some of the facts? While the food allowance for an adult remains at $1.65 a week, the price of food has been increasing by leaps and bounds. The same bread that a year ago was 4 cents a pound now sells for 8 cents a pound. All in all the increase in the cost of food in the last year has arisen approximately 30 percent. While prices soar the LaGuardia administration gives them an additional boost by introducing a sales tax which places the burden of providing for relief upon the backs of the unemployed, workers, and small businessmen while the bankers are not at all touched. To those on relief these cold figures become translated into a thick slice off the thin crust of bread. As for the allowance for rent, it is from $12 to $18. For New York City, which is notorious for its high rents, this leads to but one situation; it has forced the unemployed to move into old, filthy fire traps. The outbreak of fires in the tenement areas of New York and the toll of lives they have taken fills the newspapers daily. The LaGuardia administration and the Roosevelt government which sets the general policy stand condemned of causing hundreds of New York's unemployed families to be wiped out in flames. Especially does this apply to Negro workers, who are segregated and condemned to live in uninhabitable condemned fire traps at exhorbitant rentals. On Bristol Street, in the Brownsville section, several months ago, 11 Negroes were burned to death in a literal tinder box. Only crocodile tears and fake investigations have been the reply.

I want to deal briefly with the policy of the Home Relief Bureaus. The entire approach of the Home Relief Bureau is "How little can you be made to starve on and how long can you be kept from getting that little?" Hence the red tape that permeates the Home Relief Bureaus—the weeks of waiting, questioning, forcing unemployed workers who skimped for years in order to get insurance policies to sell them for whatever they can get, the systematic cutting off of thousands (11,000 in December) from the relief rolls upon the flimsiest excuse. In one of the coldest winters that New York has experienced since the 1888 blizzard, no clothing was given those on relief. Only in extreme emergencies was the royal sum of $15 a month given to a family regardless of its size, and the unemployment councils by its struggles forced them to give even this amount. What clothing can any of you buy for your family with $15? The single unattached who are given the starvation sum of $2.55 a week are now being threatened with being sent to Camp Greycourt, a former prison where they will be forced to work for 50 cents a day. When the unemployed, led by the unemployment councils, replied to these miserable conditions by demonstrations at relief bureaus and at City Hall, and strikes on relief jobs, they were met with brutal police attacks and insults hurled by Mayor LaGuardia, Park Commissioner Moses, and Welfare Commissioner Hodson who called the unemployed "yellow dogs," "loafers," and "chisellers," respectively. The present policy of the city government is to destroy the Unemployment Councils in order to carry out its policy of economizing at the expense of the unemployed. In the Bronx, Brownsville, East Side, the police have beaten and jailed delegations of unemployed who demanded food and clothing. There is a refusal to meet with the elected committees of the unemployed in an attempt to prevent organization among the unemployed. All of you probably know that the unemployed of New York City are not and will not take these attacks lying down. The Unemployment Councils are mobilizing larger and larger masses against these miserable conditions and for H. R. 2827.

How do the proposed measures other than H. R. 2827 aim to meet the needs of the unemployed? The most popular is the Wagner-Lewis bill, which we flatly reject. Why?

1. It does not include the present unemployed.
2. Relief will be started 1 year after the bill is passed.
3. It starts 4 weeks after you become unemployed.
4. It gives relief only for a maximum of 15 weeks at a maximum of $15 a week.
5. It is not a Federal measure.
6. The money derived from a 3 percent tax on pay rolls is transferred to the consumer.
7. It excludes agricultural, domestic, and governmental employees.

We demand the passage of H. R. 2827 because it is the only measure which provides for some security for all unemployed and at the same time places the expense where it belongs, upon the employers and the Government. It answers the problems constantly facing the unemployed:

1. When am I going to get relief?
2. Will I get enough to at least keep body and soul together and care for my family?
3. How long will it continue? Will it suddenly be stopped?
4. Will I or my fellow-workers be forced to bear the burden through sales tax, fare tax, or tax upon pay roll?
5. Will I be discriminated against because I am a Negro, foreign-born, a young worker, or if I am an agricultural, domestic, or professional worker?
6. Will I be compelled to scab in order to get relief?
7. Will a lot of red tape prevent or forestall my getting relief?
8. Will part of my benefits be grabbed away by political favoritism?

H. R. 2827 answers these vital questions satisfactorily. For over 5 years our organization has been in the forefront of the right to live, even if unemployed, We are proud of the leading part we have taken in the struggle for the enactment of H. R. 2827.

Gentlemen, we wish to inform you briefly of some of the support that H. R. 2827 enjoys among New York workers. You are all probably acquainted with the broad mass support behind H. R. 2827. It is no secret that that is the reason that many of you have decided to support it in Congress. Over 100,000 have filled out ballots voting for the bill. On the very day that the National Congress for Social and Unemployment Insurance opened in Washington, over 5,000 workers demonstrated at city hall in support of the bill. In the send-off for the delegates to the Congress, of whom there were over 900 from New York, representing hundreds of thousands, St. Nicholas Arena was jammed with supporters. Not a day goes by but that the demand for the endorsement of the bill is presented by unemployed delegations and demonstrations at the Home Relief Bureaus. There has been a wave of picketings of the homes of Congressmen and alderman for the support of the bill. The conditions I so briefly and sketchily presented indicate the reason for the support of H. R. 2827 and likewise shows why the workers will not cease their struggle for its adoption. We are here to tell you that we are sick and tired of waiting, of being given promises and such insults as the Wagner-Lewis bill and the President's forced labor program at "wages below prevailing rates". We want H. R. 2827, and we want it in a hurry, and if necessary we will come in a mass hunger march together with the rest of the unemployed in the United States to get it.

Mr. DUNN. We are now to have the pleasure of hearing from Dorothy W. Douglas, of Smith College.

STATEMENT OF DOROTHY W. DOUGLAS, ASSISTANT PROFESSOR OF ECONOMICS, SMITH COLLEGE, NORTHAMPTON, MASS.

Mr. DUNN. You may proceed.

Mrs. DOUGLAS. Any unemployment insurance scheme to be worth its salt today must take account of the fact of mass unemployment. Not only for the immediate crisis in which we find ourselves, but for an indefinite future. Any scheme that is modeled upon the conditions of relatively slight unemployment obtaining 15, 20, 30 years ago is out of date. Today technology has so improved that even if we went back to 1929 levels of production many millions of workers could be "dispensed" with.

Unemployment insurance is only one branch, a late branch, of general social insurance. Social insurance is a broad term used to cover various types of regular, standardized payments, under Government auspices, to persons who for one reason or another have met with a loss of wage earning. Its primary purpose is to maintain living standards that would otherwise fall. It differs from commercial insurance in that it is governmentally initiated, is intended as a welfare measure, and does not necessarily presuppose a prior accumulation of payments on behalf of the beneficiary. Any talk of a social insurance measure being, or not being, "actuarially sound" is therefore beside the point. It is not the way the fund is accumulated, but the way it is disbursed, that makes it social insurance.

Social insurance differs from relief on the other hand in that the benefits are received as of right when the emergency for which they were intended occurs, and in that the payments are supposed to be entirely regular and assured. Both mothers' pensions and old-age pensions (to which neither worker nor employer contribute anything) are a form of social insurance; so is accident compensation (where the employer pays all).

Unemployment insurance was first introduced in Great Britain in 1911. At that time the more advanced wing of the labor movement was demanding "the right to work or the right to maintenance." The Lloyd George government sidetracked this demand for full unemployment insurance, by a hybrid scheme, financed only in part by government, chiefly by small weekly contributions exacted from employers and workers, and yielding only a fraction of the funds that would have been necessary, even in that day, for care of all the unemployed.

As unemployed mounted during the 1920's, a smaller proportion of the unemployed workers became eligible for the so-called "standard" benefit since it could only be "earned" by a long period of regular prior employment. Moreover, an increasing proportion of those who did qualify failed to find new employment when their benefit period (6 months) was up. For a time such workers were cared for by so-called "extended" benefit payments paid for entirely out of borrowings from the Exchequer.

Today, with the Conservatives in power, the borrowing powers of the fund have been stopped, and all workers who run out of benefit, as well as those who were unable to qualify in the first place, have to go onto a centralized system of poor relief with a severe "means" test. Bitter complaint has been made by British workers, and there is at present talk of some reform of the scheme. The latest British figures show over twice as many insured unemployed on the poor relief as on unemployment benefit.

However, inadequate as the British scheme is, it should be noted that it is not nearly so bad as what the administration is proposing for this country. Even today the British Government is still paying one-third of the total cost of insurance (for a time it paid about two-thirds), and it is paying it as an integral part of the fund.

Turning to Germany, we find there a vain attempt to build up an insurance fund from employers and workers alone, without direct Government contributions at all; that is, with the Government merely standing in the background to catch the workers who fell out of the insurance net, with some form of emergency relief. The German scheme did not begin until 1927, and it remained solvent for less than a year. Rates were successively raised and benefits lowered, until by the end of 1932 the rates were 6½ percent of pay roll for employers and workers, and unemployed workers even though they had paid their contributions regularly were still unable to draw benefit until they had first passed a "means" test, proving themselves and their families destitute. Today, with the National Socialists in power, the greater part of the unemployed workers have been declared ineligible altogether.

Mr. DUNN. May I interrupt you there?

Mrs. DOUGLAS. Yes.

Mr. DUNN. Do I understand you to say that the National Socialists are in power in Germany?

Mrs. DOUGLAS. The Nazis. They call themselves the "National Socialist Party." It just means the Nazis, the Hitler group.

Mr. DUNN. I am glad to get that information. That is the first time I had heard of it. I thought that they were opposed to socialism.

Mrs. DOUGLAS. They are. They are opposed to genuine workers' socialism, and the name "National Socialist," as with so many names in political life, was used as a bait to make the workers of Germany satisfied with what has turned out to be a dictatorship of finance and capital.

Mr. WOOD. In other words, they just assumed the name as a matter of convenience?

Mrs. DOUGLAS. Yes, sir; but they have used it.

Mr. Wood. The fact of the matter is, there is nothing approaching socialism in the Hitler regime, at all.

Mrs. Douglas. No.

Mr. Wood. It is as far removed from it as Czarist Russia is from the real socialist philosophy.

Mrs. Douglas. It is probably the most undemocratic country in the world today.

Mr. Wood. Yes; just so; just the reverse of the Social Democrat Party in Germany, which was the socialist party.

Mrs. Douglas. And the Social Democrat Party in Germany was completely suppressed and its leaders driven out of the country.

Mr. Wood. They never called that the "National Socialist Party."

Mr. Dunn. For your information, Mrs. Douglas, Mr. Wood is the president of the State Federation of Labor in Missouri.

Mr. Wood. I am a Member of Congress, now, Mr. Chairman.

Mr. Dunn. And a good Member, too.

Mrs. Douglas. The trade-unionists in Germany, of course, as you very well know, sir, were thrown out of office and had their funds commandeered when the present government came in. They were suppressed.

Mr. Wood. Oh, yes; there is not any labor movement there at all. They simply quashed the movement. There is no progressive movement in Germany at all.

Mr. Dunn. Do they not have any labor organizations there any more?

Mr. Wood. No.

Mrs. Douglas. They have no independent organizations in Germany, do they, Mr. Wood?

Mr. Wood. No independent labor organizations in Germany.

Mrs. Douglas. All they have are unions under the control of the Fascist organization.

Mr. Wood. It is similar to these company unions; not so much in force and effect, as far as the worker is concerned, as the company union is here; not as representative as the company union.

Mrs. Douglas. And the government gives its official stamp of approval to the company union, thereby, you see, in those systems.

Mr. Wood. Oh, yes.

Mrs. Douglas. What then of the lessons of Germany and England for us? They are that no contributory scheme, even with a very high rate of contributions—twice as high as any proposed by the Roosevelt Administration—can take care of the bulk of the unemployed during the bulk of their unemployment. Even England, where the government pays one third outright, cares for only a fraction of her unemployed workers out of the unemployed insurance fund. And, a point that should perhaps have been stressed earlier, the benefits in both England and Germany, have been totally inadequate for maintenance even during the period when the insurance was running.

In the words of a conservative British authority—

Let it be stated here once and for all that the rates of insurance benefit (as paid in Great Britain) have nothing to do with guaranteed maintenance * * * What will determine the amounts and duration of benefit * * * will be the contributory income of the insurance fund.

That is quoted from Ronald C. Davidson, "The New British Unemployment Act", in the Social Service Review, December 1934, page 606.

The British Ministry of Health states—

It seems unnecessary to say that where unemployment has been prolonged and no other resources exist, unemployment benefit is not sufficient to pay the rent and provide clothing and necessities for a household of any size after food has been paid for (Great Britain Ministry of Health, report on an investigation in the coal fields, February 1929, p. 8).

The shortcomings of the British and German systems are indicated further by the following statements from authoritative sources:

At the present time (in Germany) insured persons who become unemployed and qualify receive the ordinary benefit for 14 weeks, but a "means test" is applied during this period (that is, after 5 weeks). The test is very strict and an applicant must prove that he has no other means of support, no one to help him financially, no one to take care of him or his family, and that his relatives, if any, are not in a position to support him (U. S. Bureau of Labor Statistics, Monthly Labor Review, August 1934, pp. 304–305).

For those outside insurance and those who have exhausted their statutory right to benefit, it (the present British law) offers a harsh poor law system entrenched and strengthened and removed from democratic control (Arthur Greenwood, former Secretary of Labor, in the 1929–31 Labor Government, quoted in the Social Service Review, December 1934, p. 708).

The question arises whether the worker compelled to insure against unemployment can feel that he thereby makes himself safe against the loss of income that unemployment entails. Under a scheme which limits his benefit to a short period he certainly cannot.

Mr. DUNN. That is exactly what the Wagner-Lewis measure proposes.

Mrs. DOUGLAS. To limit it to a short period.

He has no security at all against the type of unemployment which he most dreads, that which is prolonged beyond weeks into many months (from the royal commission on unemployment insurance, final report (minority), November 1932, p. 397).

And the British trade-union movement states to the royal commission on unemployment insurance in 1931:

* * * The Unemployment Insurance Scheme as such, could not cater and never has catered for the unemployed * * * Unemployment is a national and international problem resulting from the industrial system under which we live. The workers are not the authors of the system but the victims of it, and unless the community so organizes its resources as to provide work for every willing worker, the unemployed, as the reserves of industry, are entitled to maintenance (memorandum from the British trades-union congress general council to the royal commission on unemployment insurance, May 4, 1931. Quoted in Social Service Review, June 1934, pp. 346–347).

From all these statements it would appear that the contributory systems of England and Germany have operated largely, not as an expression of, but as a defense against, the workers' claim to a right to maintenance.

The same would apply with even greater force to the proposed Roosevelt administration legislation for America. Taking the latest figures from my own State of Massachusetts, the State unemployment survey of January 2, 1934, we find that for the leading industrial cities of the State, two-thirds of the unemployed workers had been unemployed for a year or more, four-fifths for over 6 months. Yet the administration (Wagner-Lewis) proposal for a contributory scheme would limit the longest possible benefits to 15 or 16 weeks, and then only after a waiting period of a month. In Massachusetts, even if the bulk of the unemployed had been able to qualify for insurance in the first place (which of course they could not have), only 14 percent of them would have fallen within the prescribed benefit period. The other 86 percent would have fallen outside. They would have received no advantages from the Wagner-Lewis bill whatsoever.

There is only one way to take care adequately of the bulk of the unemployed, and that is by full insurance out of Federal funds raised by taxation of the higher income groups. This is provided by the workers bill, H. R. 2827, and by no other.

Mr. DUNN. In other words, you maintain that the Lundeen bill really will bring about the necessary assistance to the people who are now unemployed, and the aged, and so forth?

Mrs. DOUGLAS. The Lundeen bill is the only bill that will do so, and it will do so adequately. It will maintain the standard of life of the present unemployed, of the aged, and other classes whose wage-earning capacity has failed.

Mr. DUNN. Thank you.

Mrs. DOUGLAS. I have some additional material here I would like to call to your attention, if you would care to have it.

Mr. DUNN. Yes, we will be glad to have you present that. The members of the committee will interrogate you after you are through reading.

Mr. LUNDEEN. You have made quite a study of this subject, have you not?

Mrs. DOUGLAS. I have been teaching social legislation for a number of years, and have made studies myself in the field.

Mr. LUNDEEN. And you are quite familiar with methods of unemployment insurance?

Mrs. DOUGLAS. Yes, sir.

Mr. LUNDEEN. Methods for taking care of unemployment, all over the world?

Mrs. DOUGLAS. Yes, sir.

Mr. LUNDEEN. You spoke a while ago about Germany. You refer to the present Germany. Under old Germany, they had some unemployment insurance, did they not?

Mrs. DOUGLAS. Yes, sir.

Mr. LUNDEEN. It was a different form?

Mrs. DOUGLAS. The original, the beginning of social insurance in Germany was back in the time of Bismarck. At that time, the social Democrats and the trade unionists of Germany were demanding something not so different from what we are demanding here today. They were demanding the right of maintenance for those who were incapacitated, and the Bismarck government was anxious to prevent organized labor and to prevent the Social Democrat Party of Germany from gaining adherents.

It therefore took occasion to do two things: It outlawed the socialist party of Germany, the Social Democrat Party, and at the same time the Bismarck government brought in its own bill for a contributory system of social insurance—not unemployment insurance—at that time. That had not become a leading problem in the minds of statesmen, but the system of insurance against sickness and accident, and that contributory scheme was brought in not by labor members at all. It was brought in, just as I maintain the present Wagner-Lewis bill is being brought in, to sidetrack the demand for maintenance by·

a scheme which only gives assistance up to the amount of contributions that shall have previously been paid in; and the worse the times, the less contributions, naturally.

Mr. LUNDEEN. And it is a bill which meets with the approval of financiers and big business?

Mrs. DOUGLAS. Quite so; yes.

Mr. LUNDEEN. And capital, as we might say?

Mrs. DOUGLAS. Yes.

Mr. LUNDEEN. Sickness and accident insurance in Germany was the first system in existence in Europe?

Mrs. DOUGLAS. The first anywhere in Europe. Germany led the way in making national provision against these ills, but it made the national provision by making the worker and the employer bear the burden, instead of having the State assume it.

Mr. LUNDEEN. And Germany led the way because the rank and file compelled action, as I would take it.

Mrs. DOUGLAS. Quite so; yes.

Mr. LUNDEEN. I think we should remember that.

Mrs. DOUGLAS. Yes, sir; but it was a misfortune for the rank and file that the action taken was able to take this form of fastening permanently the burden of contributory insurance upon the German people. Had the Social-Democrat Party that day not been outlawed, it would probably have been able to prevent any such scheme from going through.

Mr. LUNDEEN. And if they had had their way, they would have inaugurated a system something like this H. R. 2827.

Mrs. DOUGLAS. Yes; maintenance out of national funds. Now, the next important step in social insurance was when England, under Lloyd George, again under the pressure of the Labor government, mind you, initiated a series of acts to protect workers, and the first of those was an act much more nearly along the line of what the workers wanted, because at that time, when the Lloyd George government first came in, you remember, in 1905–6, there was a great deal of very heavy labor pressure put upon it. They had the so-called "Liberal-Labor" combination. The Liberals only stayed in power because of their being able to work for labor support, and at that time various measures were passed that were distinctly in the interest of labor.

In 1908, the British passed their old-age pension scheme, which was not a contributory scheme. It was a scheme whereby the government assumed support of the aged. Of course, the pensions granted were very small, but it was a definite assumption of responsibility by the national government. The business interests of the country were never satisfied with that. They fought against it, and finally in 1924 or 1925 they succeeded in having substituted for that old-age pension scheme, a scheme of contributory insurance for the aged, which is in force in England now, and is very much objected to, indeed.

The unemployment insurance scheme in Great Britain, as I pointed out, started in 1911 and was on a contributory basis, but the state contributed one-third of the total, and through various so-called "borrowings" later on it got so that by the late 1920's you had the state contributing what amounted to practically two-thirds of the total expenses; so that, although it was nominally still a contributory scheme, you can see for yourself that the employer and the worker were not the chief contributors, by any manner of means.

Lately, with the labor party out and the conservatives substantially in, the business interests have once more been able to dictate an increasing restriction of funds, and the latest slogan is to make the insurance system what they call "self-supporting", "self-sufficient", which means no contribution from the national government aside from that one-third contribution which they make by law, anyhow; no more borrowings, no more help. Consequently, the British workers are much worse off today than they were at the beginning of the depression, so far as government aid is concerned.

Mr. LUNDEEN. So far as Europe is concerned, where does the best system obtain—in what country?

Mrs. DOUGLAS. If you are speaking about the capitalistic western countries of Europe, the English system is the best, because it has the Government pay one-third of the total.

Mr. LUNDEEN. That admits the principle of government responsibility?

Mrs. DOUGLAS. That admits the principle of government responsibility to some extent, but they have tried to restrict that principle of government responsibility by saying the scheme must be self-supporting and that the government's responsibility shall be limited to the one-third which it makes as a contribution and not as a grant. You see the difference?

Mr. LUNDEEN. Yes.

Mrs. DOUGLAS. A contribution limits you to the specific amount that is written down in the law; a grant makes you give according to the need.

Mr. LUNDEEN. Would you tell us briefly something about Holland and the Scandinavian countires? What are they doing?

Mrs. DOUGLAS. I cannot tell you about Holland and the Scandinavian countries. The British and the German schemes are the most important ones in Europe today, and other countries have not adopted schemes that differ materially from them.

Mr. LUNDEEN. That answers that question.

Mrs. DOUGLAS. With your permission, I would be glad to go on and say something about the administration proposals.

Mr. DUNN. Yes; we would be glad to have you say anything that you desire to, because it is helpful.

Mrs. DOUGLAS. Thank you. I would like to underscore the fact that the present administration proposals for America would give us the worst type, the German type of European proposals, you see; and that, far from being a first step or an entering wedge to the Government really assuming responsibility for the unemployed, they are a definite dike against this mass demand which is rising all over the country.

Mr. DUNN. Doctor, I would like to interrupt you there to ask this: If the Wagner-Lewis bill is enacted into law, would you say it is the best form of pension in the world?

Mrs. DOUGLAS. It is the worst.

Mr. DUNN. The worst?

Mrs. DOUGLAS. Yes, sir.

Mr. DUNN. The reason I ask that question is this: I was down at the President's house last week for about an hour and fifteen minutes.

There was a delegation that went down to see if they could not do something about making it a better pension bill, and one man made the statement—

We will be the laughing stock of the world if we go through with this Wagner-Lewis bill—

to which someone replied—

It is the best pension bill in the world if we enact it into law even in its present form.

So of course I had the Lundeen bill with me, and I had introduced the same bill, because I was so interested, and so many people were demanding copies of the bill from me that I had to get a supply for myself, and I made the statement to the President that I thought this was the solution; and of course every Congressman who made a statement about a better pension bill would meet the response from the President, "Where are you going to get the money?" And he maintained it was the best that he could do; he believed in better pensions and more adequate pensions and more adequate unemployment insurance.

Mrs. DOUGLAS. I say it is not half a loaf, but "stones in place of bread", as the Bible says.

Mr. DUNN. One more question I would like to ask: What is your opinion regarding the bill? For instance, when it comes out on the floor, which it may, there will be men who firmly believe in adequate old-age pensions and unemployment insurance, who have been advocating it and want the best that Congress can give; nevertheless there are thousands of people who are making demands upon them to support the Wagner-Lewis bill. Would you say that if a person had in mind, "Well, it is not the bill that I want, but I believe that if some sort of a pension bill is passed the seed is planted and then future Congresses can change it"; do you think it would be better for a person to vote against that measure or vote for it—a man who was extremely conscientious, and especially, as you know something about politics, will a man who wants to do what is right and is doing what is right, they could use that as a weapon against him the fact that he did not support an old-age pension bill.

For example, the Wagner-Lewis bill is getting a great deal of publicity throughout the country. The Lundeen "progressive, humanitarian measure", as I call it, is getting but very little publicity. If a man would not vote, we will say, for the Wagner-Lewis bill, they would use that as a weapon against him to keep him from coming back here in the future. Would you maintain that it would be wrong to vote for it?

Mrs. DOUGLAS. Yes, sir.

Mr. DUNN. You do?

Mrs. DOUGLAS. I should say that anybody who supported the Wagner-Lewis bill at this time is thereby giving the Federal Government an opportunity to evade its plain obligations. It is not a case of helping the Federal Government to begin to meet its obligations which it would then later on meet more fully; it is the direct opposite of that. It is permitting the Federal Government to say like Pilate in the Bible story, "I wash my hands of national responsibility for the unemployed. I will shut up the unemployed to stew in their own misery, with no help save what can be got for them by this accumulation of petty contributions."

And as for the aged, it similarly says, instead of a Federal grant for a real, permanent responsibility for the aged of this country, it on the contrary says the aged and their employers must all their life long pay these petty contributions so that at the end they may have a tiny dole.

The whole principle of the thing is one which it seems to me should be shown up for what it is, namely, not a support, not an entering wedge for increased standards of living for labor, but on the contrary what I call a "dike" to prevent the labor forces from securing that to which they are entitled. I truly think so, sir.

Mr. DUNN. In other words, you believe that this measure would prevent in the future real progressive and humanitarian legislation being enacted into law?

Mrs. DOUGLAS. I think that it would serve to help prevent it. I do not think it would prevent it permanently, because I think the same forces that are pushing their way against it now will triumph in the end, but I think it will give them a set-back.

Mr. DUNN. You think, in other words, it would retard the progress toward a real piece of legislation?

Mrs. DOUGLAS. Yes, sir; because it is trying to sluice off those forces in a false direction. It is very difficult for you Congressmen, I appreciate fully, on the political side, extremely difficult.

Mr. DUNN. It is not difficult for me.

Mrs. DOUGLAS. The end result would be disastrous for the workers.

Mr. DUNN. It would not be difficult for me, because I want to get it clear in mind, as an individual, and it is immaterial to me whether I ever come back here or not; and as I have often said, I am going to do what my conscience tells me to do, and if somebody can convince me that voting for this bill will prevent or retard the progress of real humanitarian legislation I will vote against it.

The reason I am asking these questions is because you are an expert. In other words, I want to do what I possibly can for the short time I am going to be on this planet, to help alleviate the suffering of humanity. I may live until tomorrow or for 50 years, but I want it said about me when I die—"Here lies a blind man. He did not do very much while he was living, but one thing he did—he made a big effort to help his fellow men." I would rather have that said about me than to accumulate a fortune or to have the most perfect sight in the world. That is what I want to make clear. Is it any help at all? Would this bill be of any advantage to the aged?

Mrs. DOUGLAS. I think it would be a definite hindrance all along the line. That is my reasoned judgment on the matter.

Mr. DUNN. In other words, you are convinced that it would retard the progress of real humanitarian legislation?

Mrs. DOUGLAS. Yes, sir.

Mr. DUNN. Thank you very much.

Mr. WOOD. Mr. Chairman, if you are through questioning the witness, I would like to ask one or two questions.

Mr. DUNN. Yes. Proceed, Mr. Wood.

Mr. WOOD. You made the statement just now that if the Wagner-Lewis bill were passed it would be a detriment?

Mrs. DOUGLAS. Yes, sir.

Mr. Wood. And that the Members of Congress should not vote for that bill?

Mrs. Douglas. Yes, sir.

Mr. Wood. Have you had much actual experience in securing legislation?

Mrs. Douglas. I have had a good deal of rather sad experience in working with reform organizations.

Mr. Wood. Before what assemblies—the State legislatures, or where?

Mrs. Douglas. I had experience in the Pennsylvania State Legislature, which is a very conservative one, as you know, and I have found that the reform organizations with which I was associated, which I will be glad to go into detail on if you would like me to, later——

Mr. Wood. Well, I would just like to get your viewpoint on this.

Mrs. Douglas. It is that they have continually sacrificed their opportunities by being ready to compromise, which amounted to being ready to be licked before they began to fight.

Mr. Wood. You do not believe in compromises, then?

Mrs. Douglas. I do not believe in compromising on those principles which are absolutely essential. I believe very much in compromising on detail, but not on compromising principle.

Mr. Wood. If you compromise the main principle of the Wagner-Lewis bill, and the principle of this bill, are they not designed for the same purpose, the principle of unemployment insurance?

Mrs. Douglas. That is where I would differ with you.

Mr. Wood. They are both based on the principle of insurance for unemployed?

Mrs. Douglas. The name of "insurance" as applied to these two schemes is as different as the name of "socialism" applied to National Socialism and as applied to the socialism of the social democratic parties of Europe.

Mr. Wood. Your position is, then, that the Wagner-Lewis bill is not unemployment insurance?

Mrs. Douglas. It is not unemployment insurance for the worker, employed or unemployed. It is unemployment insurance for the Government insofar as the Government is insured against having to do much for the unemployed.

Mr. Wood. Your theory is, then, that the Wagner-Lewis bill would not be of much benefit to the unemployed?

Mrs. Douglas. No, sir; I think not.

Mr. Wood. Did you ever know of a piece of initial legislation being perfect?

Mrs. Douglas. I have known of pieces of initial legislation sacrificing their opportunities for future usefulness by compromising away their basic principles to begin with. It is not a case of perfection, it is a case of the initial direction in which you are going. You can go one step in a direction in which you later want to go to, but if you go one step in a direction which is at cross purposes with your final step you are not helping yourself.

Mr. Wood. Well, I would just draw what I think is a parallel of this bill—another social legislation. When they first attempted to pass a child-labor law, did the pioneers in the movement insist that we secure the passage by the State legislatures, where the movement first started, of laws prohibiting the employment of children under 14 years of age, or none at all? Is it not a fact that every State which has pioneered in child-labor legislation has first attempted to prohibit the employment of children in industry below the ages of 16 and 18, as a beginning, and then eventually the States, a great many of them, after establishing the principle or the public policy that they were opposed to child labor in industry, then subsequently have continued improving upon their child-labor laws until many States have very good child-labor laws? My own State of Missouri has a very good child-labor law that in a great many instances prohibits children working in industry under the age of 14. When the child-labor law was first passed it prohibited children working in industry under the ages of 16 and 18. Do you not think we have made some progress?

Mrs. DOUGLAS. I think, sir, that you would not have made very much progress if your original child-labor law had said that the children of certain parents only should be prevented from working, or the children on whose behalf certain payments would previously have been made by employers, or some other arbitrary distinction like that which failed to draw a line as to the actual needs and ages of those children. The trouble with the contributory insurance fund is not that it says the Government will provide something for all the unemployed, and later will provide something more. It says the Government does not need to provide for the unemployed, but instead of that will have the employer and maybe the employed themselves gradually build up reserves, and beyond those reserves the unemployed have no claim upon the Treasury of the United States.

Mr. WOOD. I will draw another comparison with reference to workmen's compensation legislation. The first law was passed, I think, in 1911. I believe the New Jersey law was the first law. The New Jersey law was a very loosely-drawn piece of legislation. It did not mean a great deal. It had a great many exceptions and applied only to employees in certain industries; it had a very low minimum weekly compensation for personal injury; and they administered that law through the circuit courts. In other words, the first workmen's compensation law that was passed did not abolish the old common law defenses. They abolished, in a way, comparative negligence, contributory negligence, the assumption of risk, the fellow-servant rule, but on the other hand they provided for the administration of these laws by the circuit courts, and naturally the lawyers and the courts involved the law in much litigation and great costs for attorneys' fees, so that the New Jersey law just about defeated itself, on account of its features of administration more than anything else.

Of course, the initial legislation was very poor, but it was a beginning. Now, since that time laws have been passed by various States. About every State in the Union now except three has workmen's compensation laws. Since that time Ohio, California, New York, and some 15 other States have adopted monopolistic State insurance and competitive State insurance. They have raised their rates of compensation. They have eliminated the common-law defenses, and they have administered the law by a commission, which has proven to be logically in the interest of the worker. Now, do you suppose that if we had waited until we could have gotten a law like California, Missouri, New York, or Ohio before we accepted any legislation we would have gotten very far with workmen's compensation?

That effort has been over a period of many years, so I think your theory that we must pass carte blanche this bill or any other bill with specific provisions, or we should not vote for any, is not taking the right position. The theory of legislation is and always has been, as established by experience and practice, that it is first very important to establish the principle. Now, when we established the principle of workmen's compensation, first in New Jersey and then in Massachusetts, that was the beginning, but it grew and developed and spread. It expanded throughout the United States, and at that time we had to take the experiences of European countries before we started. In our beginning, we had to take the experiences of Germany, England, Finland, and several other countries that had some system of workmen's compensation. It was new. We were planning in a new field, just as in this unemployment insurance we are indeed launching out, as it were, on uncharted seas, and we are going to run into a good many squalls or storms before we get through with it, before we get a law of perfection.

Mr. WELCH. Congressman Wood, did I understand you to say that New Jersey was the first State to enact the workmen's compensation law?

Mr. WOOD. Either New Jersey or Massachusetts in 1911.

Mr. WELCH. In what year?

Mr. WOOD. 1911. In 1911, the first workmen's compensation law was passed in the United States. I think that was in New Jersey, I am not just sure.

Mr. WELCH. California enacted a workmen's compensation law in 1911.

Mr. WOOD. No, in 1913 or 1915, I think it was, Mr. Welch.

Mr. WELCH. It was 1911. In 1909 I was a member of the State Senate of the State of California and was the author of a constitutional amendment for the workmen's compensation law. That was submitted to the people, and passed by an overwhelming vote in 1910.

Mr. WOOD. Well, that is to your everlasting credit, Mr. Welch. I compliment you.

Mr. WELCH. That year, Senator Johnson was elected Governor of the State of California, in the fall of 1910, and in 1911 under his administration the law, pursuant to the constitutional amendment to which I have just referred, which was mine, was enacted. I think that Wisconsin enacted a law about the same time, 1911.

Mr. WOOD. Probably that is true.

Mr. WELCH. I know you are pretty clear on those things, as a rule, but my impression is that California and Wisconsin are the first two States that enacted workmen's compensation laws.

Mr. WOOD. I do not know what kind of law you had in California. All the rest of the States were taking New Jersey's law as a pattern. It was assumed at that time that the New Jersey law was the first law on that subject. Of course, that same year California may have passed the law, I do not know.

Mr. WELCH. It did, absolutely.

Mr. WOOD. I just wanted to get through.

Mr. DUNN. Congressman Wood, are you through with your statement? If so, Dr. Douglas can have an opportunity to answer you?

Mr. WOOD. No, I am not through.

Mr. DUNN. Do you want to proceed further?

Mr. WOOD. She can answer me now.

Mr. Lundeen. After Congressman Wood finishes, I would like to make a short statement.

Mr. Dunn. All right. Congressman Wood, proceed now with your argument.

Mr. Wood. There is just one other matter I want to talk about, and I raised this question the other day when I was here.

Mr. Lundeen. Pardon me, Congressman Wood; are you leaving the question of workmen's compensation law now?

Mr. Wood. Yes.

Mr. Lundeen. May I ask your permission to make a brief statement here?

Mr. Wood. All right, I will be glad to have you do so.

Mr. Lundeen. Minnesota enacted a workmen's compensation law in 1913. That, I know. I served in the legislature at that time, and I just wanted that statement made in connection with Wisconsin.

Mr. Wood. Minnesota has a very fair law, too; not as good as New York or Missouri, but it is a very good law.

Mr. Lundeen. Pardon the interruption.

Mr. Dunn. Not to be outdone by the Congressmen from other States, I should like to say at this time that Pennsylvania also has a fairly good law—not quite fair enough for me.

Mr. Wood. Yes, Mr. Dunn, your State passed a law early—I think it was 1915 or 1917—but they had a very, very low maximum and a very low minimum, but Pennsylvania has very greatly improved her conpensation law since.

Mr. Dunn. Yes; I happened to be a member of the legislature that helped increase the compensation.

Mr. Wood. The fact of the matter is, when Pennsylvania first passed the law, it was willing to take a law similar to that of New Jersey, but now they have since improved upon it and strengthened the law until it is a very good law.

I would just like to see a bill like this passed. I was instrumental in having introduced into the Missouri Legislature at the sessions of 1927, 1929, and 1931, an unemployment insurance bill.

Mr. Dunn. Congressman Wood, pardon me for this interruption, but so that I understand it correctly, did I understand you to say just now that you would like to see a bill of this kind passed; that is, the Lundeen bill?

Mr. Wood. Certainly.

Mr. Dunn. You would?

Mr. Wood. Yes.

Mr. Dunn. I wanted to get that clear in my mind; proceed, Congressman.

Mr. Wood. The question is the feasibility of the law, and the question arises in my mind as to the manner in which we are going to finance this law if it is passed. If we pay an average of $50 a month out-of-work insurance, with a minimum of $10 a week—it is not quite $50 a month, but it would average $50 a month—striking that as an average—there are 10,000,000 unemployed now. There are, I assume, approximately five or six million wage earners working part time, and probably more. I would not be surprised if there were 10 or 11 million more people that are working now, part time. No one knows. There is no way to get statistics on that until we have a a real adequate unemployment insurance law, and then we can get some real actual statistics, but I do not know. When a law is passed, the first thought in my mind is whether it is actuarially sound or not, and I have not been able to ascertain how we are going to get the money, how we are going to raise the finances; and the $50 a month, if there are 10,000,000 unemployed, at $600 a year, that would take $6,000,000,000 a year. Then, assume that there are five or six million that are employed part time. That would probably require another three or four billion. You have to make arrangements.

Now, you would be required to raise 9 or 10 billion dollars to finance this bill with reference to unemployment insurance, let alone the old-age pension that is included in here. It also includes the farmers, the wage earners on the farm. I assume that on the farms there are probably 10 or 12 million employees, and, needless to say, about half or two-thirds of them are unemployed.

Of course, we have not any real statistics on that, either, but we will have to make arrangements to finance the paying of these farm employees. We know there are millions of them, and at $50 a month, it would take several other billions of dollars, so when you analyze the cost of the bill it would probably take 10 or 12 or 14 billions of dollars annually to finance it. The question in my mind is how we are going to raise that money.

Mr. DUNN. Congressman, I am just going to ask one question, Do you not think if we would appropriate some of the money that we are now appropriating for the construction of battleships and other unnecessary things, that money could be taken and appropriated to alleviate the suffering of the people?

Mr. WOOD. Now, Mr. Chairman, I am considerable of a pacifist, but I am not going to be foolish enough to stick my head into the sand like an ostrich and think that I am safe. It is not what we think ought to be. You have to meet a situation that confronts you. The world is armed. The European nations are a veritable arsenal. The people in the Balkan States and some of those other countries, instead of having beautiful pictures on the wall for scenery, have a general or an adjutant or an army officer, or they have a big howitzer up there, some of these big guns. They decorate the walls with war pictures.

Europe is war torn, but they are warring nations. They are armed to the teeth. Almost the whole of the national income, or from two-thirds to eight-tenths of the national income of nearly every European nation is devoted to armaments, and they are building armaments in the air, on the ground, in the sea, and under the sea, and we cannot just sit idly by and say, "Well, we do not believe in building these things."

I do not, but if you have an adversary that is going to attack you, you naturally have to arm for defense. I wish it were so we would not have to build any battleships.

Mr. DUNN. I want to give Dr. Douglas, now, an opportunity to answer you, and probably she will be able to tell you something about where we can obtain this money. I know I am convinced beyond doubt, when you speak of the 10 or 12 or 14 billions of dollars that would be necessary to carry out the provisions of this act, it can be obtained if we Congressmen will enact the kind of legislation to obtain it, so I will let Dr. Douglas answer your questions, now, pertaining to these matters you have brought up.

Mr. Wood. Mr. Chairman, I just want to finish my statement in reply to your remark about the battleships, because I do not think it is well to let a question like that go over.

Mr. Dunn. I would like to have that rest where it is for a moment. I believe in self-defense, but it is still my candid opinion that a great deal of the money we are appropriating for battleships and other armaments of war could be appropriated to relieve human misery.

Mr. Wood. Mr. Chairman, but now as to the building of battleships, the question arises as to whether they are necessary for defense or not; battleships and armaments.   If armament is necessary for defence, and we do not make provision for it, then if by our negligence in preparing to defend ourselves some nation should invade our shores and subjugate this Nation—and that is not impossible at all—what we do here in legislation would not be very substantial.

Mr. Lundeen. Mr. Chairman, I would like to ask the Congressman what he thinks of the intelligence of preparedness patriots in this country who take the *George Washington* that cost $40,000,000, and sink it, for the scrapping of a British plan that was just in the drawings?

Mr. Wood. Well, of course, I was not in Congress then, Mr. Lundeen, when they passed the law to scrap many of our good battleships.

Mr. Lundeen. And that was only one phase of the situation. Then, of course, in 1917 I sat on the floor of Congress and heard very wise Members of the House and Senate state that if we disarmed the German "War Devil" everybody else in the world would be peaceful.   Now it appears that that was all erroneous, that there are other warlike nations in the world.

Mr. Wood. That just gets back to the question of building battleships.   This Nation, after the World War, in the armament conference we held, agreed to disarm.   This Nation destroyed scores and scores of fine cruisers and battleships, and the other nations destroyed them—on paper.   The European nations destroyed them on paper, but they have never destroyed a single battleship that was worth anything.

Mr. Welch. They destroyed the blueprints.

Mr. Wood. They destroyed some old battleship that was not fit to use 40 years ago.

Mr. Welch. Our good friend, the chairman of this committee, should keep in mind the fact that Japan has withdrawn from the League of Nations.   Subsequently, she gave notice to the nations of world that she would disregard the 5–5–3 treaty drawn and signed in the city of Washington.   Japan is going ahead and building such a navy as she considers adequate for her interests.   If our friend can prevail on the other nations of the world to disarm or cease building battleships, then we may well carry the argument to Congress and elsewhere that we should cease building battleships.

Mr. Dunn. I believe in self-defense.

Mr. Welch. Because the United States had sufficient evidence which was adduced at the last session of Congress, when we appropriated sufficient money to bring this country up to treaty strength. We had not built up to treaty strength.

Mr. Wood. Let us get back to the employment insurance.

Mr. Dunn. Mr. Wood, have you finished?

Mr. Wood. Yes, I have finished.

Mr. Dunn. We want to give Dr. Douglas an opportunity to answer your very intelligent questions, and I would like to hear her answer them.

Mr. Lundeen. Mr. Chairman, I do not want to start another "war" or anything like that, but I want to say this, referring to the statement about large sums needed for this bill. That may not be entirely correct. We have had very complete statistics given here by Dr. Gillman.

Mr. Dunn. Yes, Dr. Gillman, of New York.

Mr. Lundeen. Of the College of the City of New York. He placed the figures far below any such estimate as that given by Congressman Wood, and I think Congressman Wood, who is a very able student of labor affairs, when he examines those figures will be quite interested in them. He placed one estimate of cost at $3,561,000,000.

Mr. Wood. I thank you for the compliment, but I am not an actuary. I am not a statistician, and I do not know what it is going to cost, and nobody else knows, whether he be a college professor, or whoever he may be. There is no man can tell now authentically what this unemployment insurance bill is going to cost. We can just make estimates. Of course, we can make estimates that come pretty close to it.

Mr. Lundeen. I want to say to the Congressman, I think you will join in with me on this, that we must take care of these 12 or 15 million people referred to, even if we have to tax the rich "until it hurts".

Mr. Wood. Certainly, there is no question about that.

Mr. Lundeen. In 1917 they talked about paying for war "until it hurts". Now, we will take care of the unemployed that the war brought to this country, even if it hurts the pocketbooks of the super-rich. That can go into the record and stand there.

Mr. Wood. I agree with you, very, very heartily, and I want to say further that while I am very strongly in favor of an adequate out-of-work insurance bill, I do not agree with this Wagner-Lewis bill, but if that is the only thing I have an opportunity to vote on, I am going to vote for that bill for the purpose of establishing the principle.

Mr. Dunn. Now, Doctor, would you answer Congressman Wood from Missouri regarding his idea of supporting legislation, although it does not mean anything when it is first introduced, but, as he maintains, after it is once presented it becomes a seed. Will you answer Mr. Wood?

Mrs. Douglas. Congressman Wood, I think that we could answer your remarks on two scores. In the first place, in regard to what you were saying about the battleships, suppose for argument's sake that you and I were preparedness advocates—which I am not—would you and I seriously propose that the funds for building necessary battleships during a war emergency should be raised exclusively by a series of petty contributions gathered bit by bit over a period of years from the pay rolls of those men that were fortunate enough to have full employment?

Mr. Wood. Well, of course, we would both be in favor of any kind of legislation that would enable us to build a battleship quickly, if we were preparing.

Mrs. Douglas. Yes, sir.

Mr. Wood. And we are also in favor of that, now, but the question now is as to the mechanics of the thing.

Mrs. Douglas. Similarly, with the unemployed—if you regard unemployment as a minor catastrophe and one which you do not need to take immediate and serious steps to remedy——

Mr. Wood. Well, just pardon me there.

Mrs. Douglas. Yes, sir.

Mr. Wood. There is no doubt we are all advocates of unemployment insurance, and there is no one but what believes we ought to take immediate and serious steps to secure that legislation. There is no question about that.

Mrs. Douglas. I merely was putting a hypothetical case. Let me put it negatively: I would say that the only person today who has a right to support on the floor of Congress or elsewhere such a bill as the Wagner-Lewis bill must be a man who has a fair-weather view of the unemployment problem. By a "fair-weather view" I mean a view that after the present depression we are going to have a small amount of unemployment hereafter. Everything that any statistician in this country can tell you indicates that we are going to be faced not with a fair-weather but with a black-weather condition of continued heavy unemployment for many years to come. We cannot meet that out of petty contributions any more than you can build battleships on them. It is an expensive proposition, just as you said. The funds will require a lot of money. It will hurt the people from whose pockets it comes. Those people will pay. The only pockets that are sufficiently deep and wide today to hold necessary funds are the pockets where the stored wealth of the country today lies, the sources where income is still large. There is no use going for large funds to petty pay-roll contributions from employers, who are just keeping their heads above water, and from workers whose heads are not even above water.

Mr. Wood. Doctor, you made a statement that anyone that would support this Wagner-Lewis bill if it came on the floor of the House, you think has a fair-weather view of unemployment insurance. I had just previously stated I would vote for the Wagner-Lewis bill if I could not get anything better. I would just like to ask you, in view of the statement you have made, if we cannot get this bill, or similar legislation, you think then it would be better to vote against the Wagner-Lewis bill and wait another 2 years before we do anything, do you? Is that your theory of legislation, that if it comes to the last step, where the Wagner-Lewis bill is reported out of committee and that is the only thing we have the privilege of voting upon, and it comes before the House as the only thing we will have an opportunity to vote upon, your theory is, or your idea is that we should vote against the Wagner-Lewis bill, knowing when we did so that if we defeated that bill we would get no unemployment insurance at this session—just to vote against that and then wait 2 years until we could get our model bill passed. Is that your theory of legislation?

Mrs. Douglas. My theory of legislation is to vote down the Wagner-Lewis bill if it is the only bill that comes before Congress at this session, and to vote it down with the assurance that if the energy which you would be giving to the Wagner-Lewis bill you instead give in your respective States for the enactment of adequate unemployment insurance laws in those States, you will be doing a greater service to the cause of labor than you are by supporting the Wagner-Lewis bill, which does not of itself enforce any standards of unemployment insurance legislation in any one of the 48 States, but merely attempts to encourage the States to set up laws which shall have maximums but not minimums. The Wagner-Lewis bill proposes that States shall enact laws which shall be water-tight, which shall not call upon State or Federal funds but only upon the employers and workers, and that those funds shall not provide for more than a very short period of benefits, at best. It does not say any State law which is passed must come up to certain minimums. It is a negative bill all along the line.

With your permission, I would be glad to read you an analysis I have of the Wagner-Lewis bill, which would answer you.

Mr. WOOD. I have made quite an analysis of it myself. Being a Member of Congress I usually take quite an interest in legislation on which I may be called upon to cast my vote. You have not answered my question, though. I asked you, do you think it would be the better part of valor, if the Wagner-Lewis bill is the only thing we have to vote upon, to vote for it?

Mrs. DOUGLAS. I would vote it down on the floor of the House.

Mr. WOOD. You think we ought to just vote it down and wait 2 years until we get a model law?

Mrs. DOUGLAS. But I would not wait 2 years. I would go to work in my own State at once, and see that the pressure of labor throughout the country was sufficient to call a special session of Congress, which may be easily done if conditions keep getting worse.

Mr. WOOD. Whether you happen to know it or not, about two-thirds of the State legislatures are now meeting, and when this Congress is over those legislatures will be over, so in two-thirds of the States there will be no action whatever for 2 years. You cannot depend upon the States taking the lead. If you have had any experience in legislation I think you will agree with me that you cannot depend upon the States in this. Now, they did in workmen compensation, but there is the experience. It has taken 23 to 24 years of untiring effort in every State of the Union to get a universal workmen's compensation law, and there are 3 or 4 States yet that have not the law.

Now, how far do you suppose England would have gotten if, when it passed the first law—which I think was in 1911, was it not, or 1915?

Mr. DUNN. 1911, Dr. Douglas said.

Mr. WOOD. When England passed the first law, it covered but a few thousand workers. It was very inadequate. It was very loosely drawn. It did not meet the situation at all, but since that time Great Britain has improved upon its unemployment-insurance law. It has made many changes, until it now is very workable, and it has been England's salvation in the past 5 or 6 or 8 or 10 years, since the war. How far do you suppose England would have gotten, if they had waited until they got a model piece of legislation passed?

Mrs. DOUGLAS. May I say two things about the English system? One is, that the English system has not been improved or altered in any respect since its origin, except that——

Mr. WOOD. Oh, yes; it has.

Mrs. DOUGLAS. ——it has applied to a great many more individuals.

Mr. WOOD. Well, certainly, and they have given a greater weekly compensation.

Mrs. DOUGLAS. The weekly compensation today in England is $4.25 for a man and only $1.25 a week for a girl under 18 who works. For the man's wife it is now $2.50, and for each of his children, 50 cents a week.

Mr. WOOD. Yes.

Mrs. DOUGLAS. That would make for the man, wife, and three children $8 a week.

Mr. WOOD. Yes; and it started with a maximum of $1.75 a week.

Mrs. DOUGLAS. It started with a great deal less, and the cost of living was less, although not proportionately less.

Mr. WOOD. It was $1.75 a week, American money.

Mrs. DOUGLAS. But the English system, from the outset, provided that the national Government must pay one-fifth of the total contributions to that fund. It was subsequently changed to one-third, and it has been one-third ever since. That feature distinguishes it absolutely from the present Wagner-Lewis proposal. Moreover, the English system from the outset was a Nation-wide law. It did not say to each county in England as the President said— and I am quoting the words of the President himself—"those States which are now ready to take this progressive step may be encouraged by this bill to pass their own laws." I quote his exact words. That is not the way England proceeded. We have taken the worst features of the English system.

May I make my other point, sir, in regard to what you originally said about the workmen's compensation, about the principle starting in a small way and then developing? You will find that the workmen's compensation started in 1911 was the same basic principle which it has today, namely, that the burden of accidents is a social burden, not one to which the individual can be asked to contribute; that the burden of accidents must not be rewarded only where negligence or fault on the part of the employer or a fellow worker can be proved.

Mr. WOOD. Of course, the workmen's compensation law is based upon that principle, that industry shall bear the burden of its own accidents. That is true.

Mrs. DOUGLAS. Quite so.

Now, suppose you had started your accident legislation by saying, "For the present we will be satisfied with the outworn principle of employers' liability, and we will model the American legislation upon an advanced form of employers' liability." Would you be where you are today? You would not. We say that in the field of unemployment insurance there are two principles involved, two possible ways, and you have to choose between them. You cannot have both.

Mr. WOOD. This Federal Government started with an employers' liability law for the railroad men. Now, we have an employees' workmen's compensation commission. We started, and the first law this Government passed that had to do with the compensating of injured workers was a railroad man's employers' liability law, and they were for it. Now, we did not have to stick to that, and now we have an employees' workmen's compensation commission, but we are continually broadening and improving upon our present laws through experience.

Mrs. DOUGLAS. In the case of unemployment insurance, we have a great deal of experience, and the American use of that experience seems to be moving backward as far as possible down the scale, to pick out the poorest features of various laws.

Mr. Wood. You said that the compensation laws were based upon the principle—of course it was—that industry should bear the burden of its accidents.

Mrs. Douglas. Yes, sir.

Mr. Wood. But in the early history of the effort for the enactment workmens' compensation laws, these early laws were very loosely drawn, and they did not remove all the defenses. The employers still held the defenses of contributory negligence, and the employee contributing to his injury, for example, by intoxication, and the first law did not compel the employer to provide safety appliances. The present-day workmen's compensation law that was passed within the last 10 years is vastly different. We have changed the structure entirely. The mechanics of it have been changed just as much as the change in the mode of production between now and 25 years ago when the effort first started.

Mr. Dunn. Congressman, we will interrogate Dr. Douglas later. We want her to continue her statement, if you please.

Mr. Wood. All right. I was just answering the Doctor's questions that she asked me.

Mr. Dunn. It is very interesting and I have been enjoying it.

Mr. Wood. I would be very glad to do that, of course.

Mr. Dunn. I have been doing all I possibly could to keep myself quiet. I wanted to get into the debate. So do the other Congressmen.

Mr. Wood. Well, the Congressman does not talk very much. That is one good thing about this hearing.

Mr. Dunn. Proceed, Doctor.

Mrs. Douglas. With your permission, I will read some sections from an article that I have written, which has appeared in a magazine called "Social Work Today", and which describes the Roosevelt program. As I am reading excerpts they may be a little disconnected, and please feel free to interrupt.

In President Roosevelt's and his committee's own words, the "system adopted should be self-sustaining", "on a contractual basis and without governmental subsidies."

That is the basis of the thing, and that is the basis which I think is fundamentally wrong for the people.

Mr. Wood. Mr. Chairman, if you will pardon me, if the Doctor will just submit that for the record I think we can get along. It is a quarter to 12 now, and we have not but a few minutes longer.

Mr. Dunn. May I say, Doctor, the House is going to be called at 12, and I think what the gentlemen on the committee wanted was to ask some more questions.

Mr. Lundeen. I think it is a very good suggestion, Mr. Chairman, that the article be incorporated in the record.

Mr. Wood. There is no use spending time on it.

Mrs. Douglas. The whole article?

Mr. Dunn. Give it to the reporter, and anything else you have there, because this record is going to be published in book form and you can get a copy when it is printed. It goes all over the country. What you have said here and what you submit to the reporter will be put in print.   The Congressmen want to interrogate you.

Mr. LUNDEEN. But, Mr. Chairman, would we not have time to have the doctor state just the salient points?

Mr. DUNN. Yes.

Mr. LUNDEEN. The central points of the article could be stated in just a few minutes.

Mr. DUNN. Could you do that, Doctor?

Mr. LUNDEEN. Could you state them briefly?

Mrs. DOUGLAS. Yes, sir.   The central point is, as I said, that the Roosevelt program calls for no Federal contributions.   It calls for a pay roll tax.   "Funds for the payment of insurance benefits should not come from the proceeds of general taxation."   This, I maintain, prevents the owners of concentrated wealth in the higher income brackets from being reached effectively.

The beauty of such a scheme is, that any appeals for further funds when the system breaks down, can be met with the statement that that was not part of the "contract"—the worker "contracted" to have certain payments made on his behalf into the fund, and naturally he cannot ask to take out more than had been put in.   If he and millions of his fellows have the ill luck to fall upon hard times and lose their work, the fund automatically ceases to be replenished and presently runs dry—the worse the times, the less and shorter the benefit.

In the words of Mr. Hoar, of the Wisconsin Manufacturers' Association, quoted in the American Labor Legislation Review, December 1934:

Experience has shown that there is never any difficulty in getting employees to understand that a fund contributed by their employers at a fixed percentage of pay roll will not be able to stand unlimited drains, and that it is not fair to expect that it should do so.   But if the State contributes there can be no acceptable excuse for shortages.   Hence the problem is to be solved by the State not contributing, so that the shortages may go on.

Mr. LUNDEEN. Is there any provision in this administration bill for the present unemployed?

Mrs. DOUGLAS. None.

Mr. LUNDEEN. Is not that the problem with which we dealing now, to find out what to do about those who are now unemployed?

Mrs. DOUGLAS. Yes, sir; and those who will be unemployed in the near future.

Mr. LUNDEEN. And it does not reach them at all?

Mrs. DOUGLAS. Not at all; nor does it reach those who will be unemployed in the next couple of years.   The first benefits that are paid under this scheme could not be paid until the 1st of January 1938 at the earliest.

Mr. DUNN. I am going to permit the Congressmen now to ask questions.

Mr. LUNDEEN. We want in this country to preserve calm and quiet and the safety of the Government.   Will the safety of the Government be promoted by absolutely ignoring the 15,000,000 who have absolutely exhausted all their reserves and who are right up against the most terrible conditions?   The picture that has been painted here is the worst I have ever heard of in modern history of any civilized nation.   I have never heard anything like it, yet nothing is being done for them in the administration bill and they propose to let that state of affairs continue for 3 more years.

Mrs. Douglas. The administration's committee says, in its own words:

This bill will not directly benefit those now unemployed until they are reabsorbed in industry.

Mr. Dunn. And there is no provision whatever for the farmers?

Mrs. Douglas. No.

Mr. Dunn. Congressman Schneider, do you wish to interrogate the witness?

Mr. Schneider. No. I have no particular questions; but in the interpretation of the administration's position on the unemployment situation, of course, the President recommends, however, that the States do something to take care of the unemployables, that the Federal Government hopes to take care of the employables through the $4,000,000,000 act. I think it is only fair to state that that is the position of the President. Now, whether that can be worked out or not is a different matter.

Mrs. Douglas. May I point out that to attempt to take care of the many millions of unemployed through public works means that you assume a very optimistic attitude as to the extent to which public works can be expanded to take in all the ages and conditions of workers, all the women workers, all the professional workers, all the agricultural workers. What are you going to set them to work at on even a $4,000,000,000-work program that will really provide for them not only one day in the year but every day in the year?

Mr. Lundeen. Right there, Mr. Chairman, may I ask the witness this question: Have you any statistics, Dr. Douglas, as to how many people the Public Works Administration has employed in the last 2 years? That would be a kind of gage.

Mrs. Douglas. I have not the figures on that.

Mr. Lundeen. I think they are not very large.

Mrs. Douglas. No.

Mr. Lundeen. The numbers are very small.

Mrs. Douglas. They are very, very small compared with the total of unemployed.

Mr. Schneider. I think we are all agreed on the fact that the unemployment program of the administration will not take care of the present employables unemployed.

Mrs. Douglas. That is it.

Mr. Schneider. If there were $10,000,000,000 or $15,000,000,000 to start off with, of course then we might hope something could be done for the employables, but it cannot be done with the sum of money that is appropriated; and then comes the question of the States taking care of the unemployables.

Mrs. Douglas. And may I say this, sir: If you had the Federal Government attempting to put through a public works program large enough to take care of this great mass of millions it could not help interfering with private business. You simply cannot set all those millions to work doing fancy work. They have got to do something that has commercail value, naturally.

Mr. Schneider. Is it your position that in case private industry does not do something to reemploy or to employ the unemployed, the Federal Government should take over the factories and start them in operation?

Mrs. DOUGLAS. No, sir; I do not think that with the present competitive system running as it is you can or you will get the Government to run the factories. You would have an outcry against that, beside which the outcry against higher taxation is a mere nothing. If you were asked to suppose for one moment that the employers of this country are going to let the Government take over a large proportion of the factories and run them, it is ridiculous to think of such a thing.

Mr. SCHNEIDER. You take the position that private interests will not let the Government do that. Is that the idea?

Mrs. DOUGLAS. And the Government has no such intention. It has disavowed any such intention. Harry Hopkins, head of the Federal Relief Administration, has said repeatedly, and he said it a short while ago before our New England council, which is the manufacturers' body in my State, that the Federal Government would not dream of doing any such thing; it would not interfere with private business.

Mr. SCHNEIDER. Are you in favor of the public ownership of railroads?

Mrs. DOUGLAS. I am not interested at this moment in discussing the railroad problem. I am worrying about the unemployed, whether they are on the railroads or anywhere else.

Mr. SCHNEIDER. That is why I asked that question. If the Government took over the railroads right now there would be a place for the employment of probably millions, to put them back into shape so that they could be operated efficiently and at rates so that people could ship the goods they are producing.

Mrs. DOUGLAS. May I say this in regard to unemployment insurance for the unemployed: If you have the Federal Government having to pay large sums for the support of the present unemployed, it is my prophecy that you will have a great many schemes devised rapidly for reabsorbing those unemployed either into private industry or into some form of Government works. There is nothing like financial pressure to make people aware of the seriousness of a problem, and to say, as Congressman Wood was suggesting, that the United States could not afford to have $50 a month spent on its unemployed workers——

Mr. WOOD. I beg your pardon, I did not say that. I did not say the United States could not afford it.

Mrs. DOUGLAS. You said it would be very expensive. I agree with you, and I think we must be ready to bear the expense.

Mr. WOOD. I did not say the United States could not afford to pay $50 a month to its unemployed workers. I said a huge amount of money would be necessary and I was interested in knowing how to get it, that is all. There are two sources from which we can get it, all right.

Mrs. DOUGLAS. From the higher incomes in this country?

Mr. WOOD. Certainly—income taxes, corporation franchise taxes, excess profits taxes, and income taxes.

Mrs. DOUGLAS. Yes, sir.

Mr. WOOD. But I did not say we could not afford to pay $50 a month. I just want to get that straight in the record, Mr. Dunn.

Mr. DUNN. I understood you probably as the Doctor did, when you spoke of each person receiving $50 a month, which means $6,000,000,000, together with the farmers. In other words, you said it would require 12 or 14 or 15 billion dollars to put this bill into effect, and you asked, "Where are we going to get the money?"

Mr. Wood. That is what I am interested in, Mr. Chairman.

I did not say we could not afford to pay it. I just want to have it straight in the record. I did not say this Government could not afford to pay unemployed workers $50 a month, but it is necessary for us to find out where we are going to get the money.

Mr. Dunn. You have a bill in, now, I believe, asking for more than that, have you not?

Mr. Wood. I have a bill asking for $300,000,000 for the tenant farmers.

Mr. Dunn. No; I mean for old-age pensions.

Mr. Wood. Yes; I have an old-age pension bill in.

Mr. Dunn. For $50 a month?

Mr. Wood. Fifty dollars a month, 60 years of age.

Mr. Dunn. And I have one in for $100 a month, for 50 years of age.

Mr. Wood. I am asking for an appropriation of $60,000,000 to pay for that.

Mr. Dunn. Now, Congressman Lundeen, do you wish to interrogate the doctor?

Mr. Lundeen. I think not. I prefer to have the able doctor make her own statement.

Mrs. Douglas. I think I have said the substance of all you would be interested in, gentlemen. It is just that I seriously feel that if at this time, as a stopgap, those of us who are interested in real unemployment insurance for the unemployed let ourselves be diverted into the channel of supporting the Wagner-Lewis bill, we will be doing the unemployed a disservice rather than a service.

Mr. Dunn. In other words, Doctor, you believe that the Lundeen bill, H. R. 2827, is a practical bill and that it could be worked out successfully?

Mrs. Douglas. Yes, sir.

Mr. Dunn. If we Congressmen wanted to work it out?

Mrs. Douglas. Yes, sir. It would be very, very expensive, but it is an expense which is being borne now by the employed and the unemployed workers of this country and by all those from whom they have to buy goods. I think it is an expense that should be turned over to the sources of wealth.

Mr. Dunn. Congressman Wood, do you have any more questions you desire to ask the witness?

Mr. Wood. No more questions.

Mr. Dunn. Any more questions, Mr. Schneider?

Mr. Schneider. No more.

Mr. Dunn. Mr. Lundeen?

Mr. Lundeen. You spoke of the factories and the outcry in case anyone should talk about taking over the factories. You remember one or two factories were taken over?

Mrs. Douglas. Little mattress factories.

Mr. Lundeen. Yes.

Mrs. Douglas. Look at the howl you had about it.

Mr. Lundeen. And in Minnesota we had in our platform something about taking over factories that were idle, "when necessary", and there were certain limits set to it and there was no proposition of completely taking over all factories. It was very circumscribed, and yet the Farmer-Labor Party in the State of Minnesota, because we made that slight reference to the use of idle factories for starving and hungry people, was branded as "Red", "Bolshevik", "Communistic", and "terrible", but I am glad to say the people gave us an average vote higher than we had ever received before, and all this noise just because the word "factory" was mentioned. We did not propose to take over all factories but only certain ones "when necessary" to save human life and do away with misery.

Mr. DUNN. Is that all Congressman?

Mr. LUNDEEN. That is all.

Mr. DUNN. Doctor, in behalf of our committee, I wish to say that I know that every Congressman was mighty glad to have you come and give us the benefit of this discussion with the committee. Your intelligent address made a wonderful impression on me, as it did no doubt on the rest of the members of the committee, and I want to thank you for coming here. You have contributed a lot.

Mrs. DOUGLAS. I thank you very much, and I have thoroughly enjoyed it.

Mr. DUNN. Not only has it been profitable to the committee, but may I say that what you have said here today is of significance both nationally and internationally, because I think a person's remarks pertaining to the unfortunates travel around the world.

Mr. LUNDEEN. Mr. Chairman, it is understood that this article is to be inserted in the record on the request of Congressman Wood?

Mr. DUNN. Yes.

Mr. LUNDEEN. So we will have the benefit of that.

Mr. DUNN. Yes; you will have that.

Doctor, what other things would you like to put into the record?

Mrs. DOUGLAS. That is all.

Mr. LUNDEEN. That states the case on the President's bill?

Mrs. DOUGLAS. Yes; that states the case on the President's bill.

Mr. LUNDEEN. I want to read that very carefully. I know it is of great value.

(The article from Social Work Today, entitled "Unemployment Insurance—For Whom?" presented for the record by the witness, Douglas, is as follows:)

UNEMPLOYMENT INSURANCE—FOR WHOM?

By Dorothy Douglas

For many months American workers have been told to wait and hold their peace until they should see what the President and his Economic Security Committee should bring forth for them in the way of a well-rounded, satisfying social-insurance program, more particularly for the aged and the unemployed. The result is before us today. If it were not for the cynicism of its terms, the deliberate playing upon the workers' critical need for security, one could almost smile. All this mountainous preparation and publicity, and then a bill evading all the main issues at stake.

The general tone and tenor of the new legislation is unmistakable throughout the phrases used by the President in introducing it. It will appeal, he says, to the "sound sense" of the American people. It "has not attempted the impossible." It has exercised "sound caution and consideration" of "all the factors,"—i. e. "national credit," "State responsibility," "the capacity of industry" to pay. We must avoid "any danger permanently discrediting" the policy by "extravagant action."

To attain this desirable and inexpensive end, the Federal Government is to contribute nothing. There is to be "no increase in general taxation." "Funds for the payment of insurance benefits should not come from the proceeds of general taxation." This safety takes care of the owners of concentrated wealth in the higher income brackets, whom the Federal Government alone can reach effectively. Instead, whatever funds are to be raised are to come from pay-roll contributions—i. e., from the workers themselves either directly or indirectly: directly if they themselves compulsorily have their pay docked for half the sum as is contemplated in the old-age scheme; indirectly, if the pay roll contribution is paid in the first instance by the employer, as is contemplated primarily in the unemployment-insurance scheme, since, as Mr. Witte, Executive Secretary of the President's Committee, frankly states, "Such a tax will normally be passed on to the consumer in the form of higher prices." In President Roosevelt's and his committee's own words, the "system adopted should be *self-sustaining*," "on a *contractual* basis and *without governmental subsidies*." (Italics mine— D. D.)

The beauty of such a scheme is that any appeal for further funds when the system breaks down can be met with the statement that that was not part of the "contract"—the worker "contracted" to have certain payments made on his behalf into the fund, and naturally he cannot ask to take out more than had been put in. If he and millions of his fellows have the ill luck to fall upon hard times and lose their work, the fund automatically ceases to be replenished and presently runs dry—the worse the times, the less and shorter the benefit, but

WORKERS OF OTHER COUNTRIES & U. S. PROTECTED BY UNEMPLOYMENT INSURANCE

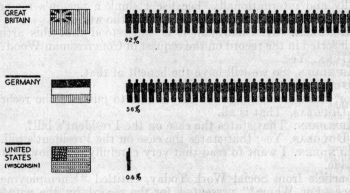

that will be nobody's fault, and the Federal Government—the wealthy taxpayer—will be under no obligation to come to the rescue. In the words of Mr. Hoar of the Wisconsin Manufacturers' Association (American Labor Legislation Review, December 1934): "Experience has shown that there is never any difficulty in getting employees to understand that a fund contributed by their employers at a fixed percentage of pay roll will not be able to stand unlimited drains, and that it is not fair to expect that it should do so. But if the State contributes, there can be no acceptable excuse for shortages * * *." Hence the problem is to be solved by the State not contributing, so that the shortages may go on—Q. E. D.

The old-age provisions of the law come as a reversal of the administration policy since November 14. At that time the President declared, "I do not know whether the time is yet ripe for old-age security legislation." Evidently the Townsend plan publicity, the threat of the workers' bill, and the general public clamor that "something be done" for the older unemployed man necessitated a change of front.

The provisions of the Wagner-Lewis-Doughton bill, however, are neatly turned away from the immediate industrial issue that is at stake; namely, what to do with the industrially superannuated? With the man of 55, or 60, or any age, who can no longer be hired in competition with younger men? This man is the crux of the old-age problem as it actually presents itself to the American people today—a mass problem that will continue increasingly to present itself so long as the present competitive order is allowed to persist. But to handle such a mass problem would require correspondingly large funds, which, to avoid an impossible burden upon the already low wages of the younger worker, would have to be raised, as under the workers' bill, by direct Federal taxation of the higher incomes.

This the Roosevelt program would naturally be unwilling to face. Instead, it calls for the cessation of the care of the aged by direct Federal relief, and, in its place, it proposes first a temporary and then a permanent scheme. The temporary scheme is to give Federal aid to those States that have set up systems of outright pensions for their needy aged. (Or rather, for those of their needy aged who have "good" characters, are citizens, have been long resident in the one State, etc.) The aid is to match dollar for dollar of State or local expenditures, but in no case is it to be over $3.50 a week!—(Result—a maximum total of $7 for any aged person?)

But this munificence is to be only temporary. The permanent system for the aged in the United States is to be not pensions but compulsory contributory insurance, with the cost borne by weekly payments from the worker and his employer, all his life long, and the amount of the benefit dependent upon the steadiness with which the aging worker has or has not had the good fortune to be employed. Actuaries assure us that the costs, as calculated, will soon outrun the contributions. (And the layman may well shudder at the bookkeeping involved—let alone the possible blacklisting involved in keeping track of an American worker all his life long for these petty payments.) Even so, the maximum benefits that would finally be received are absurdly low. A worker employed without interruption at code minimum wages of $13 a week throughout his life from 20 to 65 (and paying contributions all that time) would be entitled at the age of 65 to an annuity of less than $5 a week.

Turning now to unemployment, the Security Committee's report underwrites the present administration's latest policy of shifting all responsibility for the present unemployed to a program of public works and "local responsibility", and it describes that program with all the vagueness of rhetoric which the President himself has used. We are told gravely that "it would be advantageous to include in the program many types of public employment other than those necessary for the regular operations of government." (Distinctly "advantageous" when there are perhaps 12 million to be thus provided for.) We are told further that this "would include appropriate work to employ usefully the professional and self-employed groups of our population." (We are interested to hear that the work is to be "appropriate" as well as "useful", and we think regretfully of the mattress factories of sainted memory.) Finally, we are once more offered the old Hoover device of "loans at a low rate of interest to State and localities * * * such loans * * * should be self-liquidating." [1]

As for the unemployment-insurance feature proper of the new legislation, it is frankly stated by the committee that it makes no provision for the present unemployed. For them it is to be public works or nothing. In the committee's own words, "It will not directly benefit those now unemployed until they are reabsorbed in industry."

So much then for the unemployed who were, after all, the center of the problem and on whose account the whole agitation was started. They are out of the picture. Let "reabsorption" do its work. But what of those who are as yet employed? To what extent will the proposed legislation provide security for them in case later on they lose their work?

In the first place, will it cover all of them? Will it cover them uniformly? Will it cover them soon? Next, what amount of protection, both in size and duration of benefits, does it promise? And lastly, what administrative provisions does it make to insure that the benefits promised shall actually be paid without discrimination to those in need of them?

All these questions are answered, and necessarily answered, in a negative sense, by the very form in which the Roosevelt committee's proposal is cast. The committee is not proposing any national unemployment-insurance law at all. This was made certain from the outset in each of the President's statements on the subject. The States are to be left free to set up, or not to set up, their own laws on the subject. All the Federal Government is going to do is to "encourage" them by taxing employers in those States that do not set up their own laws. In fact, the President and his committee propose nothing more nor less than a revised form of the Wagner Federal tax bill of last year.

This bill as now amended would affect all employers of four or more persons, and it does not exclude agricultural and domestic workers by name. However, it has a seasonal qualification that would exclude most of the workers in large-scale agriculture (as well as industrial workers in seasonal occupations such as canning); and its "four or more employees" limit would pretty well dispose of all the small-scale agricultural workers as well as substantially all of the domestic workers. (And anyone in any sense self-employed, however dependent his economic status— as for instance the share-cropper—would of course be excluded categorically.)

This bill, as I have said, would leave the 48 different State legislatures free to enact (or not to enact) their own 48 different State laws. And it contemplates for them 48 different State funds, each with its own eligibility requirements and its own different actuarial rates of "risk" and "benefit." (For instance, the incidence of unemployment in Michigan in 1930 was four or five times as high as it was in some of the less-hard-hit States. Picture, then, an insured worker traveling from one State to another . . .)

But the real effect, of course, would be not to have any 48 State laws passed in the near future, unless the effective pressure of the initial Federal Wagner bill were very great. Let us see then how it proposes to operate.

Last year, it may be recalled, Senator Wagner, who had for years been trying to pass a Federal act of one kind or another to "encourage" State unemploy-

THE EXTENT OF NEED AMONG THE AGED, 1934

ESTIMATED
POPULATION
65 & OVER

ESTIMATED
AGED IN NEED

EACH FIGURE REPRESENTS A HALF MILLION PERSONS OVER 65

ment-insurance legislation, came out with a new device that was designed especially to avoid the business man's bogey of "interstate competition." (The old bogey: If you "burden" me, I will leave the State.) That device was a Federal pay-roll tax of 5 percent upon employers, against which tax the employer in any State that had an "approved" unemployment-insurance system could credit his State contributions. The device was supposed to be clever in two ways. By its size it might be expected to force recalcitrant employers to turn from opponents to advocates of an insurance system in their own States (since if they had to pay in any case, they would prefer to have something to show for their money, instead of having it stay in distant Washington to be lost in the general National Budget). And by its formula of "approved" laws, the device would certainly force employers to embody in their laws whatever minimum benefit standards the Federal-tax measure insisted upon.

Now a 5-percent tax, such as last year's law set, would avowedly be insufficient to set up an unemployment-insurance fund sufficiently large to take care of all the unemployed all the time; nevertheless, it was a larger sum than had been suggested in employer-dominated schemes such as that of the present Wisconsin act. Hence it was at once seized upon and singled out for criticism by the employers' body of the N. R. A. (the Industrial Advisory Board) in its report to the President of as long ago as last June: They recommended a flat 3 percent. It was therefore to be expected that 3 percent it would be this year. But the

President and his Economic Security Committee can do even better than that. The new bill provides for an ultimate 3 percent, but an actual initial 1 percent only. The method is simple.

The nominal 3-percent tax shall not go into effect in either 1936 or 1937 unless industrial production meanwhile shall have risen from its present low estate to 95 percent or more of the 1923–25 "normal." If it is between 85 and 95 percent, the tax is to be 2 percent; if it remains—as everyone in America knows it will— at less than 85 percent, that is proof positive that business cannot stand further "burdens", and so the tax is to be only 1 percent. (In other words, the more unemployment, the less we are going to do about it.)

Moreover, just to make assurance doubly sure that nothing will be done too hastily (*vide* the President's words about perhaps "permanently discrediting" the idea by "extravagant action"), this year's bill provides that the 48 States, whenever they do pass their own laws and start collecting contributions, may have "2 years after contributions are first made" (instead of 1 year as in last year's bill) before they need begin to pay anything out in benefits. In other words—if a State were sufficiently "encouraged" this winter to pass a "1-percent- and-up" law for itself, it would begin its 1-percent collections in 1936 and 1937 and begin paying the commensurate benefits (save the mark!) in 1938.

So much for the vaunted "pressure" that is to be put upon States to make them speed their legislation. Now for the matter of Federal standard setting in the content of the proposed laws. In the President's own words, "actual manage- ment should be left to the States, subject to standards established by the Federal Government." What are those standards, and are they designed to safeguard the insured worker?

Once more, let us compare this year's with last year's bill. Under last year's Wagner bill, a State, in order to be "approved" for tax-remission purposes, would have had to come up to a series of Federal minimums as regards amount of benefit, duration of benefit, eligibility requirements, etc. These minimums, to be sure, were absurdly low. In fact, they raised a storm of protest. But this year's bill (perhaps to "solve" that very dilemma?) sets no minimums whatso- ever! Each State is left free to offer to its unemployed workers just as little benefits and for as short a time as its own business interests may suggest. Further than this, the only warning which the committee itself in its report gives to State legislators is against promising their prospective beneficiaries too much! They advise that with a 3-percent contribution (which is obviously all that even the ultimate 3-percent Federal tax would ever "encourage" a State to set up), it would be "unsafe" to pay benefits until after a waiting period of 4 weeks, or to pay them on a scale ranging above a maximum of 50 percent of wages or for longer than a maximum period of 15 or 16 weeks a year. (For the other 36 or 37 weeks the worker would have to shift for himself. And of course he would not reach the "maximum" benefit period unless he had been long and steadily employed.) As for minimum benefits, the committee says outright that, assuming the above scale, the setting of any minimum would be unsafe. "In the basic calculations of our actuaries—no minimum was assumed." Of course, this may be hard on the beneficiary, but it will be splendid for the fund, which is after all the main thing. "We suggest caution to the States lest they insert in their laws benefit provisions in excess of collection."

And to make assurance doubly sure, the bill itself provides specifically that each State must be ready if necessary to alter or abrogate its benefit provisions at any time. In order to be "approved" every State law must "include provi- sions which prevent the creation of vested rights against modification or repeal of such law at any time."

Finally, as to the control of the scheme, the degree of worker participation, protection against discrimination—once more we have nothing to count on.

There is to be one more board, a social-insurance board in the Department of Labor, appointed by the President for long terms at high salaries, to "study and make recommendations", to "administer" the old-age annuities, and to "cooper- ate" with the States in their unemployment insurance. But actual administra- tion of the unemployed rests solely with the States, through their State employ- ment offices, with all their freedom to discriminate between Negro and white (as has been done so long in education and now in relief), between politically "desir- able" and "undesirable", between native and foreign born, between "good" and "bad" employees. Compulsory registration at these offices will furnish an extraordinary strong club to the local business communities, which there is nothing in the present law to counteract.

Moreover, employers under the law who so desire may set up their own schemes of separate plant or industry reserves or "guaranteed employment" plans. In these the check-up and control would be even more remote, the employer's hand obviously even more heavy. Strikingly enough, a great many sections of the report and of the new bill are taken up with provisions for this sort of special privilege.

Taking a backward glance now over the whole field, it is easy to see the direction in which the committee, the President, and their bill have been traveling. At every step the supposed object of the bill has increasingly been ignored. At every step each real safeguard for the "security" of the workers has cynically been thrust aside, at every step increasing concern has been shown for each new device for the employers' immediate interests, at every step there has been more effective insistence upon saving the wealthy taxpayer at all costs.

The result is so preposterous that even the original friends of the legislation are at a loss now where to begin in their "constructive" tinkering.

For the professional and industrial worker the conclusion is plain, and it finds its clear expression in the other social insurance bill, the workers' bill, introduced again into this Congress by Mr. Lundeen, of Minnesota, and pressed for so strongly by rank and file labor that it has secured the pledged support of the Chairman of the House Committee on Labor. In contrast to a "security" proposal that spends all its energies upon "ensuring" the funds and the taxpayers, the workers' bill takes its stand upon the basic needs of the workers; it reaches out to mass unemployment, begins here and now, is Nation-wide, adequate, and provides for worker control of the insurance. The issue could not be more strongly drawn.

Mr. Dunn. Gentlemen, it is now about 12 o'clock. The public hearing on H. R. 2827 will conclude today. Of course, there are some other bills here, but nobody has brought them up or said anything about them during the 2 weeks that the hearings have been running. I believe there is one other witness who said he would like to make a few more remarks.

Mr. Wood. What bills are they, Mr. Chairman, beside H. R. 2827?

Mr. Dunn. H. R. 2859, H. R. 10, and H. R. 185.

(The hour of 12 o'clock having arrived, the subcommittee took a recess until 2 p. m.)

AFTERNOON SESSION

(The recess having expired, the subcommittee reassembled at 2 p. m., and was called to order by Mr. Dunn as chairman of the subcommittee of the Committee on Labor.)

STATEMENT OF BELLAMY EARNSHAW, SPRINGFIELD, MASS.

Mr. Dunn. You have given your name and address to the reporter?

Mr. Earnshaw. I have.

Mr. Dunn. Will you be good enough to make a preliminary statement of your training and qualifications?

Mr. Earnshaw. My previous training was in a technical line and not along economic lines, but due to my associations with my family, who have always been interested in forward-looking ideas in the economic field, I naturally imbibed those at a rather early age, the age when most boys are not interested in that sort of thing.

Mr. Dunn. Your grandfather was Mr. Edward Bellamy, the author of Looking Backward?

Mr. Earnshaw. Yes; Looking Backward and Equality, which I consider the greater of the two books.

Mr. DUNN. Are there any other books that you know of that he wrote?

Mr. EARNSHAW. You mean in the economic field?

Mr. DUNN. On any subject.

Mr. EARNSHAW. Some time before he wrote Looking Backward he was a journalist, as my grandmother mentioned when she spoke. He went into journalism at the early age of 18, on the New York Evening Post, and naturally he was affiliated with the Springfield Union for several years, during which he turned out a number of short stories and novels, most of which dealt with the psychic field. Then, around 1880, he wrote several full-length novels, Miss Ludington's Sister, and Dr. Heidenhoff's Process, both of which were novels dealing with psychic phenomena, in which he had always been very much interested. He also wrote Nantucket Idyll, and Duke of Stockbridge, which was an economic novel based on Shay's Rebellion.

Mr. DUNN. What was your grandfather's full name?

Mr. EARNSHAW. Edward Bellamy; no middle name.

Mr. DUNN. And where was he born?

Mr. EARNSHAW. He was born in Chicopee Falls, in 1850.

Mr. DUNN. That is in what State?

Mr. EARNSHAW. Massachusetts.

Mr. DUNN. Proceed.

Mr. EARNSHAW. I want to testify in behalf of Congressman Lundeen's workers' bill, H. R. 2827, because I believe that it is the only bill before Congress at the present time which considers in any real, efficient way the needs of the great mass of the unemployed workers of this country. It is the only bill which provides for it a sufficient amount of money with which to keep up the American standard of living of which the administration representatives are so fond of talking. It is the only bill that will administer relief without the added sting of the workers' having to take that relief in the form of charity.

Many people who oppose this bill oppose it on the ground of its costliness. What can we call "costly" when the real needs of the American people are at stake? Is anything too costly that will save their self-respect and oftentimes even the lives and sanity of the millions of unemployed American workers? Do the people who talk so glibly of "We cannot afford", "It is too expensive", and other like terms, find themselves able to picture the misery, the hopelessness, and the degradation of the lives of most of the American unemployed under our present haphazard no-way system of administering relief?

Even the Public Works and the Emergency Relief Administration have this same degrading aspect in their administration. It is time that we got away from that kind of relief and began to look upon the relief problem not so much as an evil necessity that has to be paid for grudgingly out of the taxes, but as the real due of the people of the United States who deserve the best treatment available.

It is the Government's duty to look after its citizens. If the Government is to be called truly representative of the people of this country it must really represent them and minister to their needs to the fullest extent, and not in a grudging, niggardly manner which leaves them unsatisfied and rebellious.

Many people in opposing this bill have called it "revolutionary." I, on the other hand, say that it is one of the best preventers of possible revolution that has ever come before Congress. Revolution does not come when people's stomachs are full. It comes when their stomachs are empty and their souls rebel against the treatment accorded them, and they cannot but squirm and wiggle under the burden of their miserable existence; and when these squirmings and wrigglings begin to take on a definite harmony of purpose, then is the time when the institutions of our country, of which the opponents of this bill are so fond of talking, really are endangered, and they are not endangered when this bill is passed.

For these reasons and many others which I will not take time to talk of now, I believe that those who really have the welfare of the American people at heart, and even those, I say, of all mankind, should support the Lundeen bill, H. R. 2827, because America will serve again as in 1776 as a model for the rest of the world to follow.

Mr. DUNN. Very good, Bellamy. I want to thank you for your instructive address, and I believe I can see in you that you have inherited not only from your wonderful mother but also from your grandmother and your grandfather those progressive and humane traits.

Mr. EARNSHAW. I am glad you think so.

Mr. DUNN. Congressman Schneider, do you wish to interrogate the young gentleman?

Mr. SCHNEIDER. I did not hear much of his testimony, but what I heard was rather interesting. I am wondering now whether there is any responsibility rests, in your assumption, on the individual citizen, with reference to running the Government in such a way that the terrible conditions that all witnesses picture before this committee will be obviated?

Mr. EARNSHAW. I think the great problem there is one of education. The average person does not realize the extent of the depression, I do not believe. You talk with the average man from the small city, or the small townsman who has very little contact with the outside world and whose reading in the newspapers consists mostly of head-lines, the sports page, and the funny papers; they think quite frequently that the country as a whole is not in a bad mess, that their town is probably worse off than any other, and the problem is to educate them to see that there is a really world-wide depression, and that this world-wide depression is caused by certain factors which they can control if they only know about them.

Then, to educate these people into voting intelligently for intelligent measures that would alleviate the distress—that, as I see it, is the problem.

Mr. SCHNEIDER. Can it be said that the people of the large industrial and financial centers are better educated to cope with this problem than are the people in the rural districts?

Mr. EARNSHAW. Certain kinds of education, I think, especially those found to a greater degree in industrial sections, do not tend to make thinkers of the kind necessary for a radical, social reform. They are more along financial and business lines, and a business education is more an education for getting along under our present way of doing things than for inaugurating new methods.

I think the school of experience is one of the greatest educators, and if we can bring to other people the results of our experience, that will be the best education they can have.

Mr. SCHNEIDER. Do you think that such legislation as this, to take care of everybody so they would have all the things that give pleasure and security in life without any particular effort on their part, would have a tendency to cause them to become educated to cope with their problems?

Mr. EARNSHAW. In a way. I see your point, all right, but look at it this way: The reason why people work is to provide security for themselves and for their children. If they have the opportunity to do so they will work, but under our present system they have not got the opportunity, but their rights as citizens of the United States to life, liberty, and happiness should not be affected merely by the fact that owing to conditions beyond their control they are unable to contribute to their own support. Their rights as citizens are just as good, just as valid—in fact, more so, because they are in need.

Mr. SCHNEIDER. But are they entitled to that?

Mr. EARNSHAW. Yes.

Mr. SCHNEIDER. Without an effort on their part to correct the evil of which we complain?

Mr. EARNSHAW. The effort on their part will have to be made through legislation.

Mr. SCHNEIDER. Is it not true that the situation in which we are is largely due to the fact that the great mass of people in America have made no constructive effort to keep us out of just such a depression as we are in, by permitting the financial interests and big industrial interests to run the Government as they see fit and in their interest, and we find ourselves now at this point, and we are going to get out of this by taking care of everybody and making them happy?

Mr. EARNSHAW. We want to get out of it, but before we make the attempt to get out of it, first we have got to care for the victims, just as during the last World War we had a lot of wounded, casualties of the war. We did not say, "We have got to get out of this war; after the war is over we will take care of these wounded men." We called in the Red Cross and these other organizations and took care of them before the war was over, and then when their wounds were healed we began to reconstruct from the war.

At present, we have got a war on. It may not be a battle with swords or daggers or pistols, but it is a worse war. It is an economic war and the victims of the economic war are the unemployed and underprivileged, and they are just as much casualties as the wounded soldier, and as such I think deserve the same treatment—care for their needs, and food and clothing until such time as they are recovered and the system is changed sufficiently to admit them into their usual place in society.

Mr. SCHNEIDER. I am not disputing that, sir, and if you will recall, the first question I asked you was whether or not this method was going to remedy future evils, similar to this one, by taking care of everybody, realizing of course as I do the necessity of taking care of the casualties of this depression, and being in favor of any legislation that will help to do that, but what is going to be the result of this? Are we going to reestablish a real republic, a republican democracy, with an education and understanding on the part of the people that they are not going to permit this to reoccur?

Mr. EARNSHAW. That is one of my greatest hopes, that we will learn from this depression the lesson on that "United we stand, divided we fall." Our present way of economic rule is really the private-initiative way, which is one of divided effort, each man fighting for himself and oftentimes against the common weal; and until we begin to learn to fight together, using the slogan that practically every person uses to call out united effort, of "Fight together!" and they keep saying, "We must pull together!" and "Put your shoulder to the wheel!" and so on—if we really use those terms and mean them we will have a united effort on the part of the people to pull into economic prosperity again. It will be a cooperative effort, I believe.

We cannot long go on in our present way of doing things. These bills that have come up now, like the Lundeen bill, are primarily bills that are to alleviate the suffering of the people permanently while the depression lasts, and also to be kept on file to be used on future occasions when the necessity arises, because while we have our present scheme of things there will always be unemployed. We have got to look upon it as a permanent problem and therefore provide a measure that will take care of them as long as they exist.

Mr. SCHNEIDER. In view of what you might call "indifference" on the part of the people to participate in government in the past and at the present, can it be assumed that they are going to do it after this is over, or that they will lapse into a state of lethargy, the same as they have after each depression of the past?

Mr. EARNSHAW. Well, as I said, that is a matter of education, and I think this: This depression is proving a much greater educator than other ones, because unlike other depressions this depression has come because out technology has overreached our political methods. We are still using the political machinery that worked perfectly well, in fact was the best method, while we had an age of scarcity. The other depressions up to around the 1880's and 1890's were really merely halting places for the economic machine to gather its forces again. They were not caused so much by actual glut on the market, but now, due to advanced technology, we have come to the point where a depression is caused by overproduction. The irony of it! We cannot eat, we cannot buy and use things because there are too many of them. It is now a problem of distribution, and we have got to set up now an economic system which is based primarily on distribution and not as before primarily on production.

Mr. SCHNEIDER. But it is not true that this period is not due to overproduction but directly due to an underconsumption and inability to purchase, due to the capitalistic profit system?

Mr. EARNSHAW. Sure.

Mr. SCHNEIDER. That takes from those who produce such a portion that they cannot buy it back?

Mr. EARNSHAW. Certainly that is so.

Mr. SCHNEIDER. Now, we ought to understand that.

Mr. EARNSHAW. I know.

Mr. SCHNEIDER. And if we are not going to apply a remedy to overcome that, we are not going to get out of this depression, except to put a few patches on the pants and go along for a while and get back into it the same as we have in the past.

Mr. EARNSHAW. Of course not. That is why I said we have got to create an economic system that is based upon the principle of consumption, which means that we have got to devise a means, and that rapidly, to base our economics upon consumption rather than production.   Raise the ability of the people to consume; not merely the financial ability but their real basic needs.

Mr. SCHNEIDER. We were not in the past in the business of production for consumption.

Mr. EARNSHAW. No; we were not.

Mr. SCHNEIDER. We were in the business of production for profit.

Mr. EARNSHAW. For profit; absolutely.

Mr. SCHNEIDER. And we need to change our system to one of production in the interest of the welfare of the people of the Nation and of the world.

Mr. EARNSHAW. Absolutely.

Mr. SCHNEIDER. And until that time we are not going to get out of these depressions.

Mr. EARNSHAW. No; and it is until that time that such bills as Congressman Lundeen's will do a great job in alleviating the suffering caused by the instability of our present system.   We are now entering—in fact, we are well into—a transition period, as I see it, from the system we have now into a much finer, nobler system where the needs of human beings are taken into account.   At present, we have a system based upon the economics of material things.   Our next system, I believe, will be the economics of human beings where human beings count instead of money and mere things, where the rights of the individual are considered much greater than the rights of mere capital and industry.

Mr. SCHNEIDER. Is it your opinion that in this Congress or in our present set-up we could vote through legislation that would do these things?

Mr. EARNSHAW. I do not know.   I am not a Congressman.

Mr. SCHNEIDER. Well, that of course is the thing that is bothering many of us, our desire to do something, and yet we know the tremendous obstacles that stand in our way from the fact that often in the great financial and industrial centers the workers elect to public office and to Congress men who are opposed to giving the relief necessary to prevent revolution in this country.

Mr. EARNSHAW. Certainly.   Part of that is that under our present system we do not really, in most cases, have true representation.   In some cases, of course, men are elected to public office who are the real servants of the people, but in many cases, especially in the large financial, industrial centers, the people who are elected to public office do not so much represent the real people of the country as the people in power in that particular region, the owners of industry, and they of course are opposed to any measure, even though it may relieve the suffering of the people, that takes money out of their own pockets; but representatives from many other regions are really elected by the working people and farmers of the region and are naturally in favor of methods that will alleviate the sufferings of the people they are representing.   You see each group tries to alleviate the suffering of the group they are representing.   If a man is representing a group of bankers and industrialists—well, if the bankers and industrialists suffer from pains in the region of the pocketbook, caused by taxes to take care of a relief load, naturally their idea is to lighten that load, but if a man comes from a district where he has been elected by the real working people of that district, naturally his desire in life is to alleviate the suffering and misery of those people which of course means he has to tax the wealthy, those who can afford it, which is really the only sensible thing to do.

The real way is, as an old saying goes, "to each according to his need, from each according to his ability." That should be applied in Government as well as in religion. Following out that principle, "To each according to his need", the Lundeen bill, H. R. 2827, is the outstanding bill that takes care of the problem. "From each according to his ability", the taxation of the wealthy who can afford it, is a necessary concomitant.

Mr. SCHNEIDER. Yes; I understand that principle, and I have tried to apply it for a good many years in my home State. We do apply that method of placing the burden of taxation upon those best able to pay.

Mr. LUNDEEN. Mr. Chairman, your secretary has an article there from The Nation, of February 20, just a few lines bearing on what the gentleman has just said. I would like to have it read, and I would also like to insert an article from The Nation of February 27, 1935.

Mr. DUNN. You would like it to go into the record?

Mr. LUNDEEN. Yes.

Mr. DUNN. All right.

Miss MCCHESNEY (secretary). This is from The Nation, Wednesday, February 20, 1935:

As a counter-attraction to the hearings of the Ways and Means Committee on the administration security program, the Labor Committee has been staging hearings on the Lundeen bill. Thanks to the proponents of the Townsend plan, the Ways and Means Committee has had a slight advantage as far as entertainment is concerned. But for a comprehensive view of the plight of America's millions of underprivileged, the testimony on the Lundeen bill cannot be paralleled. Among those appearing before the committee were a blacklisted textile worker from North Carolina, a member of the United Farmers League of North Dakota, representatives of a rank-and-file committee of the American Federation of Labor and of independent metal trades unions, transients, Negroes, seamen, architects, dramatists, and the unemployed. In addition, economists, lawyers, and social workers testified on the technical aspects of the bill. An entire session was devoted to listening to the problems of insecurity as they relate to women. Thus far the testimony has been so overwhelmingly favorable to the Lundeen bill that observers are beginning to speculate on what will happen if each of the two bills is reported out on the floor of the House. Such action would prove extremely embarrassing to the administration in its efforts to portray the Wagner-Lewis bill as a "security" measure.

[From The Nation, Feb. 27, 1935]

CONGRESS DISCOVERS THE CLASS STRUGGLE

(By Maxwell S. Stewart)

WASHINGTON, February 13.—Although the President's security program is still in the early stages of legislative consideration, it has already become apparent that the principal opposition will not come from embittered diehards who fear lest the idle become "demoralized." Many who took this position a few years ago are now pleading for a genuine national plan of unemployment insurance as a means of guaranteeing business stability; the remainder are strangely inarticulate. To judge by developments thus far, the attack will be almost exclusively from the left, from the ranks of the common people who have been angered or bewildered by the chasm which exists between the President's words and his deeds.

The press has played up the rather pathetic but significant efforts of the supporters of the Townsend plan to substitute their pet nostrum for the old-age provisions in the Wagner-Lewis bill. While they appear to have been laughed out of court on this particular occasion, every Congressman fervently prays that their plan may never reach the floor of the House.   If it does, only a brand-new set of Congressional spinal columns can prevent its passage.

On the real threat from the left, however, the press has been strangely silent. During the past week Washington has been treated to the unique spectacle of two Congressional committees conducting hearings on what are essentially rival measures.   For strategic reasons the Wagner-Lewis bill was not referred to the Labor Committee of the House, as was normally expected, but was intrusted to the powerful and conservative Ways and Means Committee.   The hearings of this Committee have been well covered.   But when the Labor Committee, irritated to the point of filing a unanimous protest against the administration's steam-roller tactics, instituted counterhearings on Representative Lundeen's workers' unemployment and social insurance bill, the press exercised its traditional freedom by ignoring it.   And in so doing it has overlooked one of the most remarkable social developments of recent years.

Beyond the general subject of inquiry the two hearings have had little in common.   Even the setting has seemed to accentuate the basic differences between the conflicting security proposals.   As befited its rank, the Ways and Means Committee conducted its hearings in the caucus room of the New House Office Building, where the members of the committee were ensconced on a semi-circular platform, aloof and remote from the crowd.   Witnesses were at a physical disadvantage, standing below the committee with their backs to the audience. Though there was little pretense at dignity, the atmosphere was heavy.   In the caucus room of the old House Office Building, where the Subcommittee on Labor is conducting the hearings on the Lundeen bill, far greater informality, even friendliness, was displayed.   Members of the committee, secretaries, witnesses, reporters, and interested spectators were seated rather indiscriminately around a table, yet there was an earnestness that contrasted with the cut-and-dried proceedings of the other hearing.

These distinctions were particularly evident in the testimony.   The Ways and Means Committee began by hearing various members of the Administration—Dr. Edwin Witte of the President's Committee on Economic Security, Secretary Perkins, and Harry Hopkins.   It also heard Samuel W. Reyburn and Albert D. Hutzler, appearing for the National Retail Dry Goods Association, together with representatives of various civic organizations, proponents of the Townsend plan, and several advocates of the Lundeen bill.   Herbert Benjamin, one of the spokesmen of the latter group, was forcibly rejected when he sought to speak more than 10 minutes.   Much of the testimony was excellent, but it was contradictory and confusing.   Across the street, at the other hearing, the witnesses were chiefly workers, farmers, transients, and representatives of the unemployed, with a sprinkling of experts to analyze the technical aspects of the Lundeen bill.   Probably never in American history have the underprivileged had a better opportunity to present their case before Congress.

Among the witnesses was a young textile worker from North Carolina who had been blacklisted for union activity.   His trip to Washington had been paid for by a collection of pennies, nickels, and dimes from employees in the textile mills. He appeared before the committee without having prepared a written statement, and vanished as suddenly as he had appeared before anyone could discover whether he had funds for the return journey.   Though he spoke in the low monotone characteristic of the "poor white" of the South, his voice carried conviction as he described the plight of the textile workers under the "new deal":

"In the mill I worked in before the N. R. A. came into effect the weavers ran four looms.   Now they run 6 and 8 looms for about the same wages they made on the 4 looms, and they must get production and quality or they will lose their jobs.   * * *   And as for the houses the mill company furnishes—just shacks built on a red mud hill, with red mud roads, and in many cases cracks you could throw a cat through.   We have to pay an average of 50 cents a week a room for these shacks.   * * *   In most cases the mills don't have shacks enough to accommodate all their help.   There are large families now living in tobacco barns near the mill town because they can't pay the high rent of the private home-owners.   * * *

"The same 24-pound sack of flour that cost us 50 cents per sack less than 2 years ago now costs us $1.15.   Pinto beans sold at 5 cents a pound less than 2 years ago; now they sell for 12 cents a pound.   Fatback meat was 6 cents a pound   * * *   now we pay 22 cents a pound.   These prices are still going up   * * *   but we don't see any reports of our wages going up here in North Carolina.   * * *

"The unemployed in North Carolina are not assured of emergency relief. If we are, we have to dig ditches and bust rocks with a heavy hammer for 8 hours a day. We get 30 cents an hour and either we work or we don't get anything to eat. We almost have to fight the gang foreman to get 1 day's work a week. * * *

"The mill bosses don't tell us now that if we join a union they will fire us. But they are firing all the union members they can find out about, for some reasons that would be hard to see with the eye. But they get away with it."

Another representative of the South was Broadus Mitchell, son of one of its best-known educators and himself associate professor of political economy at Johns Hopkins University, who delivered a scorching indictment of the Wagner-Lewis bill as a grudging "compomise with poverty," dominated by "the idea of dearth and the menace of scarcity."

A picture of life in the transients' camps was presented by Joseph Murray, representing the transients' rank-and-file committee. He asserted that the quarters were unsanitary, overcrowded, improperly heated and ventilated, that the food was consistently of poor quality, and the medical service inadequate. He spoke bitterly of cash wages of a dollar a week for 30 hours' work, and declared that thousands of transients were kept perpetually on the move in the vain hope of finding better conditons or paying jobs. Three days after his testimony was given, his charges were tragically confirmed by an outbreak of spinal meningitis which claimed eight victims in the Washington transients' camp. The lot of the unemployed seamen as described by Earle Payne of the Marine Workers' Industrial Union is equally desperate. When they are temporarily or permanently out of a job, their only resort is to soup kitchens and flop-houses of the lowest type, where they are frequently terrorized by hired thugs. Payne pointed out that by the very nature of their occupation few seamen would be benefited by a contributory unemployment-insurance system such as is proposed in the Wagner-Lewis bill.

So it went through the list of occupations and professions. The problems of the farmer were graphically portrayed by Andrew Omholt, a member of the United Farmers' League, who showed that an adequate system of social insurance meant a vast increase in the consumption of farm products. Louis Weinstock, speaking for the more than 2,500 A. F. of L. locals which have endorsed the Lundeen bill, declared that the majority of the rank-and-file members of the federation support it despite the opposition of the officials. Elmer Rice, playwright, told the committee that the Lundeen measure is the only one of the pending bills which offers any real protection for authors and writers, and R. M. Sentman made a similar assertion with regard to architects and engineers. Several Negroes testified concerning the discrimination against their race, pointing out not only that their ratio of unemployment was much higher than that of whites, but that the relief given them was consistently lower.

There was no mistaking the bitterness of these witnesses toward the Wagner-Lewis bill. The principal complaint was that it fails to provide for those now in need. Nor was there any faith that the Government works program now under consideration would care adequately for this group. In addition, many of the witnesses opposed the Federal-State scheme on the grounds that migratory labor would be severely penalized and that State legislation would almost certainly lack uniformity. Other criticisms centered about the limited scope of the bill and the meagerness of its benefits. The tax on pay rolls was opposed, both because it would be passed on to the public in higher prices, and because of its dubious constitutionality.

The question of the constitutionality of the rival measures seemed particularly to interest the committee. It appeared to accept the view contained in the brief submitted by Leo J. Linder, which upheld the soundness of the Lundeen bill on the grounds that (1) it represents a proper exercise of the appropriating power of Congress; (2) it involves no unconstitutional delegation of legislative power; and (3) since it is to be financed by a tax on income, it cannot be said to deprive persons of their property without due process of law. The Wagner-Lewis bill was held to be much more open to attack because its pay-roll tax might be construed as an invastion of the field of intrastate commerce.

In analyzing possible sources of funds to finance the workers' bill, Dr. Joseph Gilman of the City College of New York declared that if the tax rate used in England had been in operation here in 1928, the Federal Government would have collected five times as much in income tax as was actually obtained. This would have given an additional $4,250,000,000 to devote to social purposes. Even on the basis of the much lower income of 1933 the increase would have been $1,129,000,000. A flat 25-percent tax on corporation profits over $5,000 would have yielded $2,600,000,000 in 1928. A similar tax on inheritances would have yielded $888,000,000 instead of the $42,000,000 which was actually collected. In 1933 this tax would have amounted to more than a half-billion dollars. While considerably larger sums could be obtained by increasing the rates in the high brackets in each instance, Dr. Gilman felt that a flat tax on corporation surpluses would be socially more desirable. At 25 percent such a tax would have yielded nearly 10 billion dollars in 1933.

The one-sided nature of the hearings on the workers' bill does not necessarily mean, of course, that the Labor Committee will report it favorably to the House. But if the hearings have no other effect, they should at least reveal to Congress the essential difference in viewpoint between the business executive and technical economist on one side and the rank-and-file worker on the other. Comparatively few of the workers, it is true, are articulate on the question of security. The testimony revealed that American Federation of Labor officials have frequently gone to great extremes to prevent adequate discussion of this basic issue within the organization. But where such discussion has occurred, labor has almost invariably endorsed the Lundeen bill.

It is difficult to see how anyone could read the testimony which has been given without being convinced of the inadequacy of the administration's security program. The Wagner-Lewis bill may be actuarially sound and it may represent a great advance over the chaotic measures of relief which have been adopted in the present crisis, but it is a far cry from the security for the men, women, and children of the Nation which the President declared last June to be the primary objective of his administration. The Lundeen bill, on the other hand, may have all the defects which its critics allege, but it has come to symbolize for the underprivileged workers of the country that protection against the vicissitudes of modern life which Mr. Roosevelt declared to be essential. Encouraged by the President's words, the fundamental urge for security, long repressed as radical or un-American, has emerged as one of the most powerful forces of present-day political life. Congress, like the press, can ignore it, but only at the risk of political suicide.

Mr. LUNDEEN. I just wanted those lines read here because it is right in line with your statement upon that subject, and it bears you out in your very able statement, which I certainly appreciate very much. I must say that while other States have spoken, Massachusetts is able to take care of herself.

Mr. DUNN. Do you want to ask any more questions, Congressman Schneider?

Mr. SCHNEIDER. No.

Mr. DUNN. Congressman Lundeen?

Mr. LUNDEEN. No; that is all.

Mr. DUNN. I am going to ask a couple of questions now. I noticed in your remarks you said that many people criticized the Lundeen bill because it is alleged to be revolutionary. You made the statement, "In fact, it is just the opposite." If such a piece of legislation were enacted into law it would prevent a revolution?

Mr. EARNSHAW. Yes.

Mr. DUNN. That is what you believe?

Mr. EARNSHAW. Yes.

Mr. DUNN. In other words, you would say that this bill instead of being revolutionary is evolutionary?

Mr. EARNSHAW. Yes; I would.

Mr. DUNN. As a young man, you do not believe it is absolutely essential to have such a thing as unemployment in the United States?

Mr. EARNSHAW. Under our present system it is a part of the system, but we can create a system in which it does not exist.

Mr. DUNN. You mean in which it would not have to exist?

Mr. EARNSHAW. It would not.

Mr. Dunn. In other words, you believe that this kind of legislation is absolutely essential under our present system of government?

Mr. Earnshaw. Yes.

Mr. Dunn. When our Government does not make any provision to take care of its aged or its unemployed, or those who are physically incapacitated; in other words, this kind of a bill would go far toward alleviating the suffering of our people?

Mr. Earnshaw. Yes. It would be the greatest step taken, I think, in the history of the United States.

Mr. Dunn. Do you believe the majority of people who are out of work today would rather have work and be paid adequate compensation for their services than to obtain a pension or insurance of this kind?

Mr. Earnshaw. I am sure that they would rather have work if they can get it, but since they cannot have work, and they have got to live and bring up their families and do it on a standard of life that will not make brutes out of them, then this piece of legislation is absolutely necessary, and the Wagner-Lewis labor bill does not even attempt to do that. In fact, it is really, I think, an insult to an intelligent people.

Mr. Dunn. I desire to ask you another question which you reminded me of when you used the word "charity." I am glad you used that word, because I believe you are the first of all the witnesses who appeared here who made that reference. Is it not a fact that in every State and in every large municipality of every State throughout the Nation there are what we call "welfare agencies"?

Mr. Earnshaw. Yes.

Mr. Dunn. And is it not also true that they have these community chests and these agencies that are constantly asking for donations?

Mr. Earnshaw. Yes; it is.

Mr. Dunn. And according to reports, is it not also a fact that of the money received by many of these agencies a great portion of it is used for overhead expenses and is not actually applied for the relief of the people for whom it is intended and for whom it is collected?

Mr. Earnshaw. Well, that is of course inherent in the system. Wherever you have a large number of bodies administering the same system, you have a large overhead expense.

Mr. Dunn. If the Lundeen bill is enacted into law will it not automatically wipe out of existence all these would-be charitable agencies?

Mr. Earnshaw. It will.

Mr. Dunn. Will it not also eradicate the poorhouses?

Mr. Earnshaw. It would eradicate all present forms of caring for the poor and the aged.

Mr. Dunn. And would it not also do this greatest thing of all—wipe out the slum districts?

Mr. Earnshaw. Naturally. If you give the American people a decent standard of living, they will not stand for the housing conditions in our big city slums. At present, they have to, because they have not the means to get others.

Mr. Dunn. It has been said here before this committee that there is some question where we are going to get the money to carry out the provisions of this act. Is it not a fact that the Federal Government today is spending hundreds of millions of dollars to keep down crime? Is it not also a fact that there is a way to reduce crime, and that way is to wipe out the slum districts, and the way to wipe out the slum districts is to wipe out the sweatshops—and the way to wipe out the sweatshops is to provide jobs for the people who are able to work and pay them adequate compensation for their services and also to provide adequate old-age pensions and adequate pensions for the disabled? Would not the slum districts disappear, then? And if the slum districts disappeared, would not crime be reduced considerably?

Mr. EARNSHAW. In my opinion the whole basis of crime is economic.

Mr. DUNN. I am glad to hear you make that statement. I agree with it.

Mr. EARNSHAW. Money is behind every crime practically, except the few crimes of passion that occur. A man does not go into stealing because he likes to, but you take the average evolution of a gangster: He lives in the city's slums; he sees around him in the city, wealth, and he sees around himself, individually, poverty; he wants things that other boys have but has not the means to get them. If he is brave enough to attempt to steal, he will do it to gratify his desires. Then gradually he comes to stealing greater things. His mind is now incapable of distinguishing between "mine" and "thine", and so he evolves into a gangster or thief of some sort or other. Under a system that provided sufficient money for him to have a decent standard of living, that tendency would be greatly reduced if not eliminated altogether.

Mr. DUNN. I agree with you.

Mr. LUNDEEN. Mr. Chairman, if I may, I should say the gentleman has very ably stated what this bill would accomplish, but it does not propose to accomplish these things by the use of any fantastic amounts.

Mr. EARNSHAW. No.

Mr. LUNDEEN. All amounts proposed in this bill, I think you will agree with me, come within the limits of common sense. The minimum is just a bare minimum, and the maximum never exceeds the average wage in the community in which the individual lives. There are no hundreds of dollars for this or that or the other thing proposed, no fantastic schemes or allowances impossible of achievement, but everything in this bill is practical, in line with common sense, and can be carried through as stated at this hearing by Dr. Gillman in his analysis of what the bill will cost, and entirely within the limits of the Treasury of the United States.

Mr. EARNSHAW. Absolutely.

Mr. LUNDEEN. With perhaps the tax rates of the British Empire added?

Mr. EARNSHAW. I was going to say that just without needing to be a real statistician, a simple knowledge of figures can show that this unemployment insurance really will not cost anything; that is, considering what the administration is already expending. For example, take in the city of Springfield, 150,000 people, the expenses of caring for the poor, counting poor relief and the charity institutions and the welfare agency, I believe the figure approaches $5,000,000 a year. Taking that as an average of the whole country—and I believe that according to statistics Springfield is pretty well up as far as prosperity is concerned—that would mean over $3,000,000,000 is now being expended by local agencies for relief.

Mr. LUNDEEN. Pardon me; you have a Government arsenal there, have you not?

Mr. EARNSHAW. Yes.

Mr. LUNDEEN. That may be one reason for your apparent prosperity.

Mr. EARNSHAW. Let us say there are 15,000,000 people who will need this relief under the Lundeen bill. Their average monthly compensation will be around $50, which is $600 a year, or a total of $9,000,000,000. Subtract present local relief expenses from that, and you get $6,000,000,000, which is the excess amount over that now being spent for relief; but now the administration has just passed or is passing a work-relief bill of nearly $5,000,000,000. Subtract that amount from your $6,000,000,000 necessary and you find $1,000,000,000 additional needed to administer the Lundeen bill. A great deal of that will be saved by the relief given real estate in cities from the taxation that is now necessary to support our present system of relief, and the rest can be raised by the excess income taxes on incomes of the rich; and surely this added amount is a small sum to pay for the increased well-being of the great mass of unemployed in this country.

Mr. DUNN. I think you are somewhat of a statistician. Figuring it from that point of view, you reach practically the same conclusion that Dr. Gillman reached, and your statement I believe is practically the same as his—almost a duplicate of it—so you are a statistician at that, only you do not know it.

Mr. LUNDEEN. I would like to say that I hope you will continue your studies along these lines.

Mr. EARNSHAW. I intend to.

Mr. LUNDEEN. I believe you have a future. If we continue to study there is much before us.

Mr. EARNSHAW. A person is never too old to learn, and when he stops learning he really dies as far as his usefulness to the world is concerned.

Mr. DUNN. Do you have any more questions, Congressman Lundeen?

Mr. LUNDEEN. No.

Mr. DUNN. I believe we have asked you enough questions, and I want to say you answered every one of them very intelligently. In behalf of this committee, I appreciate your testifying, because you gave a wonderfully instructive address and your answers to the questions were to the point and were very instructive.

Mr. EARNSHAW. I am very glad to be able to add my bit to the weight of testimony that has been given at this committee hearing.

STATEMENT OF GEORGE REID ANDREWS, EXECUTIVE SECRETARY OF THE AMERICAN EUGENICS SOCIETY

Mr. ANDREWS. Mr. Chairman, I am representing the American Eugenics Society, being its executive secretary.

We are interested in the contents of H. R. 2827, which provides among other things for compensation to mothers in childbirth, "to be paid to women during the period of 8 weeks before and following childbirth." This is a generous proposal in behalf of motherhood and we are in favor of it.

SUPPLEMENTARY STATEMENT BY HERBERT BENJAMIN: SUMMARY, EXECUTIVE SECRETARY, NATIONAL JOINT ACTION COMMITTEE FOR GENUINE SOCIAL INSURANCE, NEW YORK CITY, N. Y.

Mr. BENJAMIN. I wish to make a few remarks which are by way of a summary expressing the point of view, I believe, of the organized forces that have been most effective in advancing the workers' unemployment and social-insurance bill during the past several years.

I believe that it is well that we draw some conclusions from the hearings that have been conducted here during these past 2 weeks. The hearings on H. R. 2827 have served to corroborate and sustain every claim that has been made in behalf of this, the workers' unemployment, old-age, and social-insurance bill. In this, as in many other noteworthy respects, these hearings stand out uniquely in congressional history. The hearings, as well as the bill itself, afford striking proof of the fact that the masses of workers and farmers whom the self-annointed leaders and so-called statesmen regard and treat with contempt, can, when permitted to do so, devise the measures that are essential to their welfare, and can marshall the facts, figures, and arguments as well as the forces needed for support of their measures. This, it seems to me, is the most significant and outstanding conclusion that can be drawn from these hearings.

Those who aspire to real democracy, those who take pride in what is the real American; namely, the genius, resourcefulness, intelligence, perserverance, and courage of the American masses, will find in the record of these hearings on H. R. 2827, a source of real hope for our future. These records establish the fact that the masses of producers, the workers, farmers, and professionals are rapidly graduating from a condition of mere discontent and becoming intelligently aware of the causes for these conditions. They prove also that on at least one remedial measure a high degree of unity has already been achieved. That measure is the workers' unemployment, old-age, and social-insurance bill, H. R. 2827.

We consider it necessary to emphasize this at the present time because this is the most decisive test of the practicability and realizability of H. R. 2827. The eighty-odd witnesses who have testified in these hearings have presented indisputable evidence of the need for immediate establishment of genuine unemployment and social insurance. Together with the experts among them, the workers have presented equally uncontestable proof of the possibility of providing such social insurance by the means outlined in the workers' bill. The representative character of the qualities displayed by these witnesses is the best proof and guaranty that forces are rapidly maturing that can and will secure the enactment and establishment of such a system of unemployment and social insurance as is called for in H. R. 2827.

The record of these hearings present for the first time through an official committee of the Government a full and authentic picture of the kind of conditions against which a social-insurance program must be directed if it is to be worthy of such a designation. For the first time in the history of Congress, a congressional committee opened its doors not only to a few more or less representative leaders of the workers but to the workers themselves. As a result, it became possible, as never before, to record the real needs, hopes, aspirations, and demands of those whom Congress is supposed to represent and in whose behalf Government is supposed to operate.

For those who have attended these hearings and for those who read this record there can be no question as to whether those who appeared here have a right to speak for the masses. It was the masses themselves who spoke here. They spoke through workers, farmers, veterans, professionals—who are true spokesmen because they come from the very midst and depths of our toiling population. They came from the chief industrial centers and from the rural sections. They came from the West as well as from the East, from the South as well as from the North. They represented the most skilled and talented as well as the most impoverished and underprivileged of the producers. They represented every type of organization, every type of political opinion, every type of religious affiliation.

They, each one of them, displayed earnestness, sincerity, and a serious attempt to inform themselves and others such as is seldom encountered in a legislative hearing. They demonstrated that each had arrived to his conclusions in consequence of a searching study and analysis of his own peculiar experiences. And all of them, unanimously, came to the same firm conclusion—the workers' unemployment and social-insurance bill is the one measure all need and demand as the means of meeting the vital problem of existence under present-day conditions.

The testimony that has been recorded in these hearings also served to answer clearly those who think or profess to believe that the masses who endorsed H. R. 2827 did so simply because they favor "some kind of out-of-work insurance" and not because they understand the difference between this and other measures and plans. Certainly even the most simple and apparently untutored worker who has appeared in these hearings has shown a greater awareness of differences as between genuine and spurious social-insurance plans than most of the Members of either House of this Congress or any other legislative body in this country can show. Even when unable to phrase their views perfectly, they have each one displayed an unerring estimate of such spurious measures as the administration's so-called "social-security" bill. In a similar measure they have displayed a sometimes conscious and sometimes instinctive capacity to differentiate as between genuine and merely formal support of their program. Members of Congress will do well to realize that the masses are rapidly arriving to a state of political maturity which makes possible such a critical attitude. They are no longer satisfied with blandishment, with political diplomatizing which substitutes as far as most politicians are concerned for earnest service.

It is especially necessary to call attention to this because even in this committee it has been made apparent that even those Congressmen who are ready to endorse and support this vital need of the masses are by no means as firm, as unyielding, and as determined as they must be if they are to be effective supporters of such measures as the workers' bill. We for whom this issue is a life-and-death question are not willing to accept any excuse for compromise on this issue. We are not concerned with the amenities of parliamentary conduct when we know that these amenities are but part of the whole system of parliamentary trickery whereby our enemies hide their acts upon our interests. We want no friendly relations with our enemies and we are distrustful of those professed friends of ours who find it possible to be also friendly with our mortal enemies.

Similarly, we cannot have a high regard for those who, while sincerely in agreement with our demands and program, prove incapable of the kind of action and struggle that is required in order to advance our program and defeat its enemies. We who must fight every day for the right to live must meet and defeat very powerful enemies and opponents in the course of these struggles. We know the power of our opponents, we know that they are fighting for high stakes. We know that they spare no effort in order to defeat and outmaneuver us. We know that they are resourceful and clever as well as possessed of power. But we are learning how to fight against and defeat them. We, too, are becoming resourceful. We expect those who must carry on our fight in Congress to do likewise. If our professed friends in Congress do not want to fight for us, they are not of any help to us. Even if they want to fight for us, but don't know how, they are still of little help, and we cannot afford to depend on them. We must then look for an place in Congress those who wish to and can fight rather than those who merely have good intentions.

The administration is using within Congress and in the country at large two tactics for imposing the Wall Street hunger program upon the masses. Physical repression and suppression is the one tactic. Against the workers this takes the form of police, military, and extra-legal fascist terror. In Congress it takes the form of gag rule, bribery, and so forth. The other is the less crude but no less effective method of chicanery and demagogy. Here it is for the masses false promises, deception, and so forth, and for Congress, parliamentary trickery and maneuvers.

In relation to the life-and-death question of social insurance, those in power are at present employing the latter method in order to defeat our fight for social insurance. Concretely they bring forward the Wagner-Lewis supurious social-security bill. In these hearings and elsewhere we workers have made clear that we are not to be fooled and defeated by this device any more than by any other method that may be employed to deprive us of social insurance. We expect those Members of Congress who aline themselves with us in the demand for genuine social insurance to fight as consistently and as resourcefully as we do against those who are opposed to us. We say if you are for the Wagner-Lewis bill then, regardless of the reasons you may give for this, you are objectively and actually supporting the effort of the ruling to defeat our demand for genuine unemployment and social insurance. If you are with us you must stand as we do, firmly and uncompromisingly, militantly and consistently opposed to the fraudulent Wagner-Lewis bill. You must help us expose this scheme. You must help us discredit it. You must help us convince ever larger masses that only a bill based on the principles of H. R. 2827 can comply with the need and demand of the masses for a system of social insurance that will provide safeguards against hunger, misery, and want in a land of plenty.

I have concluded my prepared statement, Mr. Chairman, although I have a few other points that I have taken notes of since I prepared the statement last night, that came up in discussion this morning, and on which I want to make a few remarks. Also, I have a little material that I want to enter in the record, so at this point you may interrogate me without disturbing me, even now.

Mr. DUNN. To the last statement you made, I want to say that the Wagner-Lewis bill in its present form will not begin to provide the relief that is now needed in the United States.

Mr. LUNDEEN. Mr. Chairman, it does not provide a thing, not a red sou, for the present unemployment.

Mr. DUNN. I know. That is a fact.

Mr. LUNDEEN. Not a thing.

Mr. DUNN. Practically nothing.

Mr. LUNDEEN. I do not believe the word "practically" is apropos, because it does not provide a thing for the unemployed of today; is that correct?

Mr. BENJAMIN. We believe that the Wagner-Lewis bill represents merely another way for the administration to say "no" to our demand for unemployment and social insurance.

Mr. LUNDEEN. Before you leave that, is it your understanding that the Wagner-Lewis bill provides anything for the unemployed of today?

Mr. BENJAMIN. The Wagner-Lewis bill makes absolutely no provision for any of those who are now unemployed.

Mr. LUNDEEN. That is the point I was trying to make.

Mr. BENJAMIN. It makes absolutely no provision for those who will become unemployed in the course of the next 2 years.

Mr. LUNDEEN. Even though they are employed now?

Mr. BENJAMIN. Even though they may be employed now, if they become unemployed within the next 2 years; that is, during a period while the reserve fund is presumably being accumulated; there will be no provision, they will not be benefited when they have become unemployed. It is only after some 2 years have passed that a certain limited section of the unemployed, which would represent at the very most, according to Dr. Witte, the head of the President's Committee on Social Security, less than 3 percent of the eligible population would be subject to any benefits under that plan.

Mr. LUNDEEN. And then only for brief periods of time?

Mr. BENJAMIN. For a period of the maximum, according to the advice of the President's Committee on Economic Security, of 15 weeks. That is what they advise, after a waiting period of 4 weeks.

At the same time they point out that if it is suggested to extend the period of benefit, then they advise another waiting period, which means that actually the coverage will be just as limited, and it is simply a question of whether you wish to wait a longer period of time before you get it, and then get it for a longer period of time following this, or you shall have a shorter—that is, 4-week—waiting period, and get it for 15 weeks.

Mr. LUNDEEN. Is it not a fact also that a number of the President's committee do not favor the Wagner-Lewis bill?

Mr. BENJAMIN. It is true that a number of the members of the Advisory Committee that helped to draft this measure are opposed to it; that is, opposed either in part or in whole. In the main, they are opposed only in one part. That is, they offer certain amendments; that is, such people as Mr. William Green and Helen Hall, of the Henry Street Settlement, and a number of the members of that committee are opposed and took issue with the Wagner-Lewis bill both in the Advisory Committee and in the hearings that have taken place since then in the committees of the Congress.

Mr. LUNDEEN. Do you mean the Ways and Means Committee?

Mr. BENJAMIN. The Ways and Means Committee and the Senate Finance Committee. The testimony which has been given in these committees has, it seems to me—and I have had an opportunity to study it only very cursorily—been the most ample indictment of the Wagner-Lewis bill itself, more so than anything we could say.

For example, Madam Perkins, in testifying before the Senate Finance Committee to a question of Senator Black, who asked:

Is it not true that the money you propose to raise through the Wagner-Lewis bill, this excise tax measure, will go into the General Treasury of the Government, that it need not of necessity be spent on unemployment insurance or any other form of social insurance; that as a matter of fact it may be spent on battleships?

And Madam Perkins said, "Yes; that is quite true." The funds to be raised by the Wagner-Lewis bill may be expended on battleships, may be expended for any other purpose the Government may determine; "But," said Madam Perkins, "certainly the members of Congress have no objections to finding new sources of revenue." So that we say that the Wagner-Lewis bill is really a revenue measure, in that it proposes to impose a tax, but it is in no sense a measure that proposes to give anything to the masses, and there is not a single thing that is given to the masses through the Wagner-Lewis bill, anywhere in the United States—and that includes employed, unemployed, aged, and anyone else—not a single thing, unless the States, in the course of their legislative sessions, enact measures which are suggested by the Wagner-Lewis bill.

Mr. LUNDEEN. This is the 15th of February, and those sessions are rapidly coming to a close. They will come to a close within the next 30 to 60 days. In view of the fact that several States have already served notice that they cannot even meet the proposition of the Government under the bill as proposed, because they have no funds, cannot even meet this remote relief, and then, added to that, the fact that many sessions of the legislatures will come to a close without any action being taken at all, even where they may be able to do something, certainly that leaves a very incomplete picture.

Mr. BENJAMIN. It leaves not only an incomplete picture, but it will leave a very small speck, hardly a discernible speck of actual benefit—hardly discernible. But I might say in this connection that perhaps the best description I could give of that bill is one that I gave the House Ways and Means Committee when I pointed out that it was similar to the type of insurance scheme which was being sold among illiterate people by high-pressure salesmen some time ago. They used to go around and sell it as an accident policy which would carry benefits of $2,000 for a $2 premium. Now, the only hitch in this thing was this, that they had a very lengthy contract form which illiterate people could not read, and it said you would get a $2,000 benefit provided you were hit by a Mack truck; and another, providing you were thrown 200 feet and no less; providing that you hit a fence that was painted with Sherwin-Williams paint, and provided that you broke the small finger of your right hand, and no other. Then, in the event that all these circumstances were combined, you would perhaps get the $2,000.

Mr. LUNDEEN. Will you specify where that was? In what State was that?

Mr. BENJAMIN. They were selling this kind of insurance against accidents, I am told—and it is a good story whether it is true or not. I mean, it is primarily used by way of allegory and illustration—selling these in the Southern States particularly amongst illiterate people.

Mr. LUNDEEN. You mean policies of that type and nature?

Mr. BENJAMIN. Policies of that type. I think the Wagner-Lewis bill certainly conforms to that type of insurance.

Mr. LUNDEEN. Do you agree with Dr. Dorothy Douglas, of Smith College, who spoke here today, that this is the worst of all forms of social insurance?

Mr. BENJAMIN. I absolutely do, for the reason that it does not even agree. It calls itself a "social security bill", and taking on such a very ambitious title, it does not provide even a minimum, the barest minimum of real benefit in the form of insurance. As I say, unless the States enact something this bill does nothing else but collect revenue—nothing else. But I should like to emphasize this point, which seems to me requires the utmost of emphasis: It is not so important for us to establish for our record that the Wagner-Lewis bill does not provide these things. I think almost every intelligent person who reads this understands that, but to me the Wagner-Lewis bill represents that form of parliamentary maneuver which I refer to in my statement here, and is most dangerous by reason of that. It is not merely a negative measure, in that it does not provide certain things: It is a positive measure, in that it definitely directs itself and becomes strictly an instrument for defeating those who are seeking some form of genuine social insurance, that it seems to me has been indicated—perhaps at this point I can answer the question that was suggested by our chairman—that even in these committee hearings it was indicated that the Wagner-Lewis bill is managing to succeed in its purpose as a parliamentary maneuver.

First of all, this is an omnibus bill. It carries everything on the omnibus, with the consequence that you are not in position to differentiate certain changes; and why is that? Is that an accident? No; it was so definitely drawn as it was in order to put Congressmen on the spot and put them in a very difficult position for voting against it, because when you come before the Ways and Means Committee, they say to you, "Are you against the child-welfare measures?" You say, "No". "Well", they say, "the Wagner-Lewis bill is a child-welfare measure. Are you against social insurance?" "No". "Well, the Wagner-Lewis bill calls itself a social security bill". This, of course, is really a very crude type of political maneuver, and yet I cannot understand for the life of me how it is possible that very earnest members of this Congress who recognize the need, who are ready to be responsive to the demand which comes to them from their constituents, are willing themselves to fall into this trap, and feel that they must vote for the Wagner-Lewis bill in order to square with their constituents, so that their constituents may not say that they voted against a social security measure; but that is precisely the purpose of those who framed the measure.

We must learn to avoid that kind of a trap, and we must not fall into it, and therefore we must be very vigorous in exposing the

Wagner-Lewis bill as such a trap, as having nothing to do with social insurance but as being a mere parliamentary maneuver for defeating the movement for social insurance.

Mr. DUNN. For real social insurance.

Mr. BENJAMIN. For real social insurance, and we must therefore be prepared to say very emphatically, "Yes, I shall most absolutely vote against the Wagner-Lewis bill, because I do not propose to lend my support to the administration's effort to circumvent and defeat the demand for unemployment and social insurance", and if you vote for it then you have supported it. Actually you have supported the administration in that purpose.

Mr. LUNDEEN. What would you say to the people, for instance, of my State, who sent be a box about the size of a steamer trunk, full of signatures for an old-age pension plan termed the "Townsend plan", and in those petitions they state repeatedly that "If Congress does not vote for this plan, there will not be social security, or, that is, real old-age pensions." I have that large box and I would be very glad to show it to you.

Mr. BENJAMIN. I would say this, Congressman Lundeen: It seems to me the Members of Congress today have a very much more difficult job than they used to have before. I think that what I have suggested in my statement was intended to indicate that the masses are becoming discontented. The masses are beginning to make demands. Some of them are becoming conscious as to the nature of the problem and the program that must needs solve it. Some are not quite so.

Congressmen today have the obligation of helping to educate, to enlighten their constituency on these questions, but you cannot oppose the Townsend plan by saying, "I am against it because it provides too much." You can only oppose the Townsend plan by showing that it is not a measure which meets the problem that they have, and that you are in a position to help them secure a better measure; and if you come to them with the workers' unemployment and social insurance bill you are certainly doing so, and the fact is that in these hearings you have had sixty-odd witnesses, and you have had people who came from every part of the country, and you have had people who came right out of the depths of the population. You knew that they were in touch with the needs and the feelings and the aspirations of these people. You did not have a single person come here to speak for the Townsend plan, not a single one.

Mr. DUNN. No; nor did a single person come here to oppose this plan.

Mr. BENJAMIN. That is right.

Mr. DUNN. And yet we sent out letters to the American Federation of Labor, and to Miss Perkins, the Secretary of Labor, and to many organizations. We were willing to give anybody the opportunity to speak and prove to us that the Lundeen bill, H. R. 2827, is impractical. Every person who came here spoke in its behalf and maintained it is the only bill that would solve this unemployment situation.

Mr. LUNDEEN. Mr. Chairman, I would like to hand the witness a copy of the Texas Legion News for February 1935. It contains a few lines on unemployment insurance.

Mr. Benjamin. I have just now for the first time seen this statement. It reads as follows:

Unemployment insurance and old-age pensions are talked of daily here. Those who are interested in the subject will not allow themselves to be switched from the real theme to that advanced by the Communists. The issue before Congress calls for a method of raising the money by percentage taken from the pay rolls of the Nation. Communists want the money but want the Government to take care of the cost directly. Why? Because the Communists do not want work. Unemployment insurance based on pay rolls means the recipients must give value received to their employers, assist pay rolls to carry the load. Do not be deceived by false propaganda, your Congressmen will be glad to forward you the correct information on all subjects coming before Congress.

Mr. Lundeen. I want to state that articles of this sort are being sent all over the country.

Mr. Benjamin. Exactly so.

Mr. Lundeen. I ran across it today, and I offer that as a type of article we find everywhere.

Mr. Benjamin. I think that should be considered in the light of these facts: First, the opposition did not come here to speak against this bill. Second, the press had deliberately suppressed word of these very important hearings taking place upon such a very important subject, and from the point of view of news value, presenting very dramatic news elements, because when you can bring ordinary rank-and-file workers right out of their industries and put them on the witness stand and have them speak to you in simple, plain language as they did here, showing such a grasp of the problems that they have, certainly there is a dramatic quality in this thing itself, which makes for news, if they wished for news, yet they have deliberately suppressed this.

On top of that, there are such types of editorials as this to be found in the press throughout the entire Nation, when they choose to mention anything with reference to genuine social insurance at all, and yet is it possible for any member of Congress, for any committee of this Congress, to point to any measure before Congress at the present time that can demonstrate such a widespread movement of support behind it as is to be found behind H. R. 2827, the Lundeen bill?

Was there ever a bill which evoked so much interest amongst the masses everywhere that they were willing to make sacrifices involved in traveling to Washington, which meant to gather up nickels and pennies which they can poorly spare, in order to send their representative here, in order to come and plead before these committees? Certainly, such a manifestation of interest as this could not come from anything but a deep, firm conviction, and certainly the witnesses who appeared here have reflected the firmness of their interest in this matter. It is not a fly-by-night idea they have got.

Mr. Lundeen. But you noted in the article they said: "We must not be deceived by this sort of a bill."

Mr. Benjamin. Yes.

Mr. Lundeen. Now, your argument is that the other bill is deceptive. Now, why are these charges hurled back and forth?

Mr. Benjamin. Of course, the mere hurling back and forth of charges does not answer things. It is possible to speak of a question in terms of denunication, which we do also in relation to the Wagner-

Lewis bill, but it is necessary also to be prepared to back up the denunciation with facts, to back them up with proof. In this instance, if we analyze this editorial briefly, we see what? The argument made is that the reason why Communists—meaning those who are in favor of genuine unemployment and social insurance—are opposed to a pay-roll tax is because they do not want to work, and since they do not want to work they will not be in a position to provide for a pay-roll tax, therefore they say they want it to come directly from the Government.

Now, two things are set up which are manifestly untrue. The first, that we who are fighting for genuine unemployment and social insurance do not want to work. The fact of the matter is that any of the witnesses you have heard here would have told you differently, and understand, even Mr. Roosevelt in his book Looking Forward, I think is the title, stated that any person of those who are unemployed wants to work. That is perfectly true, of course, and they want to work. They do not know how to do anything with their time if they do not work. They have worked all their lives. They are eager to be useful. These are people who by training and by tradition and by inheritance and by everything that is part of their being, have been workers, have sought to be useful people in society at all times. Certainly to say they do not want to work is an untruth. But the other point that they deliberately seek to conceal is, they say we want this money to come from the Government, but they very carefully avoid saying that we want it to come from the high incomes of the wealthy class of this country and not from the pockets of the workers through direct or indirect taxation.

Mr. LUNDEEN. That is the very point I wanted you to bring out. If I may, Mr. Chairman, with the permission of the committee, I would like to call attention to the fact that having introduced H. R. 7598—this bill—in the former Congress, I was confronted in the campaign, first, by a man named William Gallagher, former president of the City and County Employees Joint Council of Hennepin County, Minn., a very great county with much industry and a very large population. He had been president of the City and County Employees' Union of that whole county. He confronted me in a meeting. I spoke about the bill. He said, "But the bill you introduced was a Communist bill, was it not?" And I asked him if he was not a member of the Central Labor Union of Minneapolis, and if it was not a fact that that central labor union had endorsed the bill, and I asked him if they were all Communists. They were American Federation of Labor people, representing 35,000 union people in Minneapolis, and I cited many other large, powerful organizations that had endorsed this bill in Minnesota. A day or two ago I received in the mails a signed and sealed endorsement for this bill from the City and County Employees Joint Council of Hennepin County, the very organization of which this gentleman was president, and I am wondering what he is going to tell me next on that proposition.

Mr. BENJAMIN. That is a very interesting point, Mr. Lundeen.

Mr. LUNDEEN. And I would like to have permission, if the Committee will grant it, to insert that endorsements in the record, because it is very brief, just a few lines.

Mr. DUNN. All right.

(The endorsement referred to by Congressman Lundeen is as follows:)

CITY AND COUNTY EMPLOYEES JOINT COUNCIL,
Minneapolis, Minn., February 9, 1935.

Hon. ERNEST LUNDEEN,
Member of Congress, Washington, D. C.

DEAR SIR: We are on record for H. R. 2827, by Congressman Ernest Lundeen, introduced in the Seventy-fourth Congress, and respectfully urge its immediate passage to become operative July 1, 1935, which commences the new national fiscal year.

H. R. 2827, a bill to provide for the establishment of unemployment, old-age, and social insurance, and for other purposes, is the most necessary legislation since Lincoln's time.   This bill would completely abolish all relief rackets—a relief which does not adequately care for the needs of the unemployed.   The Lundeen bill, H. R. 2827, does, however.

Sincerely yours,

C. W. ANDERSON,
Recording Secretary.

Mr. BENJAMIN. I wanted to point out something which I did not point out in my original presentation.   Within the labor movement there is a great deal of internal conflict, dispute, and disagreement. Particularly is this true in regard to the left- and the right-wing sections of the labor movement.   In the unemployed field, for example, this is also true.   There are unemployment organizations which are called "Communist" organizations, of which, of course, I am not, but the largest national unemployment movement—that is, the National Unemployment Council—are alongside these other unemployed organizations that have grown up and originated primarily because they are in opposition to what we call "Communist unemployed organizations", yet with all this opposition, with all this conflict between these two organizations, insofar as their own internal questions are concerned, they have been here, the representatives of all the unemployed organizations have been here, and that included for example the Socialist-controlled organization, such as the Baltimore (Md.) Peoples' Unemployed League, such as the Workers' Committee on Unemployment in Chicago, and a number of others whom I do not recall at the present moment, but these are the spokesmen for the opposing unemployed organizations and the unemployed councils, yet all of them are united on the question of this one bill, specifically, and no other.   Now, this is not an accident.   This is a testimonial to the quality of this measure, in that it has been able to act as unifying force that even broke down the obstacles and the hostilities that exist as between organizations, and that is a very significant matter.   Your statement regarding the Hennepin County organization is an example of that.

The same thing is true, for example, and we might put that in the record at this moment, with regard to the St. Paul Central Trades and Labor Union.   That body, as Mr. Lundeen probably knows, includes in its ranks as delegates the major leaders of the Farmer-Labor Party of Minnesota, who are not altogether in agreement, I understand, with your point of view on this unemployment and social insurance, and on many others.

Mr. LUNDEEN. I would say a good many of them are.

Mr. BENJAMIN. Yes; a good many of them are, but not all of them; yet at any rate Governor Olson, as you know, is sponsoring another type of unemployment insurance legislation.

Mr. LUNDEEN. I must say I do not know that.

Mr. BENJAMIN. Yes. I happen to know that so I am saying so. When the question came up in the St. Paul Central Trades and Labor body, there was a very strong opposition to an endorsement of the Lundeen bill. They had two meetings on the question before they could finally come to a vote, and when the final vote was taken, it was 26 in favor of the Lundeen bill and 25 opposed. That is an extreme example of an instance where people who are themselves involved in the political life of the State and have political responsibility and have therefore the obligation of trying to use the support of the organizations behind their political program are termed a part of this body, and even there the discussion resulted in endorsement of the Lundeen bill.

Mr. LUNDEEN. Have you the date of that?

Mr. BENJAMIN. The date of that I do not recall exactly.

Mr. LUNDEEN. You may supply it.

Mr. BENJAMIN. But it was in the neighborhood of the period when we were preparing for the National Congress, which means maybe in December.

Mr. LUNDEEN. Last December?

Mr. BENJAMIN. Yes. In this connection, too, I should like to point out how all of the support which you have seen revealed and reflected in these hearings for the workers' bill has come about in spite of a great deal of strong opposition in the ranks, where we are most anxious to win support, and we have referred to the letter of the American Federation of Labor executive council with regard to the National Congress for Unemployment and Social Insurance which we held here on the 5th, 6th, and 7th of January, in Washington. As I pointed out in my statement then, the American Federation of Labor council did its very utmost to induce the organizations affiliated with it not to participate in the congress. I should like to file this copy of the letter as it appears in the Union Advocate of St. Paul, Minn., under the date of January 10, 1935, and also as it appears in the official organ of the United Brotherhood of Carpenters and Joiners of America, The Carpenter, in its issue of February 1935, in both of which instances there are more or less complete citations of this letter.

Mr. LUNDEEN. What letter?

Mr. BENJAMIN. The letter of the executive council of the American Federation of Labor, in which they used their influence to induce organizations not to participate in the congress which was held to support the Lundeen bill.

Mr. LUNDEEN. How do you reconcile that with President Green's stand now that the Wagnes-Lewis bill is inadequate, which I would take as a friendly gesture toward our bill.

Mr. BENJAMIN. I should have been very happy to have seen Mr. Green come to this committee hearing and testify both as to his points of agreement and points of disagreement with regard to the Lundeen bill.

Mr. LUNDEEN. Well, he received a very courteous invitation from our chairman.

Mr. BENJAMIN. And I certainly regret, as I believe all members of this committee and everyone else interested in this measure regret the fact that Mr. Green did not come here. The reason I mentioned these questions—perhaps it might be much better if we were to forget about the fact that we have opposition in very high powerful circles, which we know have a strong influence upon Congress and upon other legislative bodies.

Mr. DUNN. In connection with the statement that I invited Mr. Green, president of the American Federation of Labor, to come before our committee, which is a fact, and the fact that I did not receive a reply and the fact that he did not come as a witness, would you say that he was opposed to this Lundeen bill, H. R. 2827?

Mr. BENJAMIN. My frank opinion of the matter, Mr. Chairman, is that Mr. Green does not wish to be put into the position of having to make a statement where he will be subject to criticism on this question. That is, he makes his statements in this matter in such manner that you cannot then call him to task, so to speak. If you could debate it with him, then of course he would be at a very considerable disadvantage in the matter. My feeling is that he will not discuss the genuine unemployment and social insurance as represented by the Lundeen bill. Also, Madam Perkins, for example, who was likewise invited to be a witness here, along with other representatives of other such organizations and administrative departments of the Government, who did not appear, in my opinion did not appear because they do not dare to face a critical examination of their reasons for opposing the Lundeen bill. That is my interpretation.

Mr. LUNDEEN. Mr. Chairman, I do not think we would have a right to construe their absence necessarily in that way. The fact that they were invited to attend here and did not come must speak for itself. They may have had other reasons.

Mr. BENJAMIN. I am quite willing, of course, to let this stand as my personal opinion, which is all that it can be.

Mr. DUNN. Would it be possible that Mr. Green did not receive my letter? A Congressman's letter is usually returned, is it not, if it is not delivered?

Mr. BENJAMIN. I, of course, cannot express an opinion on that. I know, for example, that Mr. McMahon, of the United Textile Workers of America, was invited by you, through communications from you; that Mr. McMahon received the letter and acknowledged it and stated that surely either Vice President Gorman or Mr. Kelly would appear in his place.

Mr. DUNN. Neither of them appeared?

Mr. BENJAMIN. No; neither one has appeared.

Mr. LUNDEEN. Now, Mr. Chairman, about the sending of the letter that was referred to, I have never seen that letter. I know nothing about it.

Mr. BENJAMIN. It was signed by Mr. William Green as president of the American Federation of Labor.

Mr. LUNDEEN. Was that a letter broadcast to all the locals or to just a few?

Mr. BENJAMIN. It was sent to every central labor union in the United States.

Mr. LUNDEEN. How do you know that? Now, you say that, but how do you know it?

Mr. BENJAMIN. It happened that I came in contact with this letter in a very peculiar manner. I was in Omaha, Nebr., on a speaking tour at the time, and was invited by some of the delegates of the

Central Labor Union in Omaha to attend their meeting and speak about the congress.   When I arrived, I sat down and the secretary was reading communications, and he read a letter, of which I later secured a textual copy, which was addressed "to all international unions and to all central labor bodies and all State federations of labor" in which we had statements which substantiated almost completely what was repeated and quoted in this material which I am submitting to this committee.

Mr. LUNDEEN. Has that letter gone into this record?

Mr. BENJAMIN. I think this is the nearest approach to that letter which has come here.

Mr. LUNDEEN. Well, have you a copy of that letter?

Mr. BENJAMIN. I have been looking for a copy for quite some time, but when I was in New York last I was not able to locate it.   I will try again to locate the letter, but you have almost a complete copy of it in this magazine which I am submitting to you here.   I am also submitting correspondence which is self-explanatory.

PHILADELPHIA, PA., *August 27, 1934.*

Mr. WILLIAM GREEN.

DEAR SIR AND BROTHER: Due to the fact that over 2,400 local unions and numerous State federations of labor are solidly supporting and in favor of H. R. 7598, an unemployment and social insurance bill, we stand solidly by a unanimous vote taken at our last meeting of Local 252, Oil Field, Gas Well, and Refinery Workers of America, and want it to be put on record that we are solidly behind this bill.   Half-way measures which are advocated by your leadership, like the worthless Wagner insurance bill, are as good as none; this worthless Wagner insurance bill is not an insurance it's a joke.

Fraternally yours,

GEO. W. BUTLER.

AMERICAN FEDERATION OF LABOR,
Washington, D. C., September 4, 1934.

Mr. GEORGE W. BUTLER,
Philadelphia, Pa.

DEAR SIR AND BROTHER: I am in receipt of your letter of August 30 in which you state that Local Union No. 252 of the International Association of Oil Field, Gas Well and Refinery Workers of America has endorsed H. R. 7598, which is thought to be an unemployment insurance bill.

I presume you are not aware of the motive behind the circulation of this bill among the labor organizations of the country.   The bill was prepared by Communists, who, as it is well known, are opposed to unemployment insurance. They simply had introduced an impossible bill in order that the real bill would be defeated.

In 1931 Senator Wagner was appointed chairman of a committee to investigate the unemployment insurance systems in private industry and also those in force in foreign nations.   The committee reported as follows:

"The subject of unemployment insurance is not within the sphere of congressional action."

In the next session of Congress this subject will receive great attention.   There is some talk of establishing a Federal unemployment insurance corporation which will insure the wage-earners.   There are a number of other plans that will be considered.

However, until some bill that will hasten unemployment insurance is submitted, we will support the Wagner-Lewis measure.

With best wishes and kindest regards, I am,

Fraternally yours,

WILLIAM GREEN,
President American Federation of Labor.

PHILADELPHIA, PA., *September —, 1934.*

Mr. WILLIAM GREEN,
     Washington, D. C.

DEAR SIR: Received your letter of September 4 stating that H. R. 7598 is thought to be an unemployment bill. We of local 252 don't understand your motive by branding this bill as being prepared by Communists. We read both bills before the body and H. R. 7598 is a thousand times better suited to American labor than the half-baked Wagner-Lewis bill which saddles the bill on the worker's pay envelop.

Your offices compile a vast amount of statistical reports. One reads that 10,000,000 workers are without jobs, out of 40,000,000 gainful workers. These figures alone would dig deep into the pay envelops of the American worker. If the Wagner-Lewis bill is finally passed, in round numbers it figures 25 percent more taken from the workers of the country to support the 10,000,000 unemployed.

Is it any wonder that big business, industrial barons, and high finance, big fortunes shudder when they think of footing the bill, for 10,000,000 that are unemployed through no cause of their own, due to speed-up, greed, lust, and avarice for more profit?

You also state the subject of unemployment insurance is not within the sphere of congressional action.

Was there any cry from the American worker of communism when high finance, big business, industry, railroads, banks, who received a governmental dole of not $10 a week, but millions upon millions, poured into their businesses to stabilize itself, through the R. F. C.? And many banks failed to open after the bank holiday, after receiving the governmental dole.

If that condition can come under the sphere of congressional action, anything can happen, and the bill H. R. 7598 is far from being impossible, as you call the bill.

Let's take the other side of the picture. If H. R. 7598 could marshal enough strength with your leadership and the support of the whole American Federation of Labor movement, together with public opinion, instead of your being antagonistic toward the bill unemployment would be a thing of the past. Rather than pay this insurance to workers for not working, jobs would be created overnight, and men put back to work.

How can we expect to have a better bill of insurance, when your leadership advocates a half-baked bill like the Wagner-Lewis bill?

As you say, half a loaf is better than none. We have been getting less than that long enough; it's high time we start getting our just share. Take off that plug hat of reactionism and get into overalls, and give us the leadership that the American laborer justly deserves.

We will quote the obligation that we members took when we joined this Union.

An obligation is required, but let me assure you that in this obligation, there is nothing contrary to your civil or religious duties.

"The union principle which regards capital as the product of the past labor of all toilers of the human race, and that wages can never be regarded as the full equivalent for labor performed; to protect wage earners against oppression and fully secure the toilers disenthralment from every species of injustice."

We hope you haven't forgotten that obligation.

We are not going to beg your leadership to change your opinion of H. R. 7598, bill which is a just bill for the American laborer but demand you to support this bill which is not impossible but just.

Fraternally yours,

GEORGE W. BUTLER.

LOCAL UNION NO. 1856,
UNITED BROTHERHOOD OF CARPENTERS AND JOINERS OF AMERICA,
Philadelphia, February 18, 1935.

Mr. FRANK MOSER,
     Philadelphia, Pa.

DEAR SIR AND BROTHER: Concerning your request for information about our disposition of the matter of the Lundeen bill on unemployment insurance, I offer you the following information:

About the beginning of 1934, we became interested in Mr. Lundeen's bill for unemployment insurance, H. R. 7598. Local Union No. 1856 endorsed this bill and it is still supported by us, our correspondence concerning this bill was quite lengthy, and our records show that about the early part of February 1934, it was the contention of Mr. William Green, president of the American Federation of Labor that the Lundeen bill is unconstitutional, a contention that we questioned at the time. We distributed literature advocating the endorsement of the bill H. R. 7598, and discussed it in the meetings. It is not at all unlikely that the bill might have had even more vigorous support with us had we not received Mr. Green's opinion on the constitutionality of this bill.

Trusting that this is the information you desire, I am,

Fraternally yours,

JOHN HUDSON, *Recording Secretary,*

Haddon Heights, N. J.

(The witness submits the following clipping from "Union Advocate, St. Paul, Minn, Jan. 10, 1935:)

Social-insurance congress is not labor project.

American Federation of Labor warns unions that "national congress for social insurance" is communistic movement to confuse real issues.

Washington.—The American Federation of Labor has dispatched a special communication to all national and international unions, State federations of labor, and city central bodies, warning all to be on their guard against attempts to create the impression that the A. F. of L. is in any way connected with the so-called "National Congress for Unemployment and Social Insurance."

This "congress", with headquarters in New York, has scheduled a meeting in the Washington, D. C., auditorium for January 5, 6, and 7. It is emphasized that this alleged congress is in no way connected with or representative of the American Federation of Labor.

A Communist paper reports that arrangements have been made to visit all locals of the A. F. of L. to get endorsement and urge election of delegates. In issuing the warning, President Green stated:

"The American Federation of Labor has declared its own policy for unemployment insurance and has been participating in the development of an economic security program for the administration. A program for action on unemployment insurance soon will be sent for guidance in securing State legislation. Local unions, central labor unions, and State federations should be warned against believing that in giving support to the 'National Congress or Unemployment and Social Insurance' they are endorsing and supporting the program of the American Federation of Labor."

Mr. LUNDEEN. But the important part is where you state it was addressed to all these unions, which does not appear here, does it?

Mr. BENJAMIN. No; it does not appear here, but it says; "Emphatic denial that the American Federation of Labor has any connection with 'The National Congress for Unemployment and Social Insurance' held in Washington, D. C., in January was made by that body in a special communication to all national and international unions, State federations of labor, and city central bodies, warning all to be on their guard against attempts to create the impression that the A. F. of L. is in any way connected with those who called the meeting."

Mr. LUNDEEN. I would like to see the text. I have heard a great deal about the letter, but I have never seen that letter. I have great respect for the members of the American Federation of Labor, and I have always tried to work with them as much as I could, and I am interested in knowing why that letter was sent out.

Mr. BENJAMIN. I can say to you, Mr. Lundeen, you are working with more members of the A. F. of L. right now, today, and you are in the minds of and supported by more members of the A. F. of L. than any one individual who professes to speak in the name of the A. F. of L. The best proof of this, Mr. Lundeen, has already been submitted in the hearings before this committee, in the records which will be found here listing the names of several thousand locals of the A. F. of L., many central labor bodies, six State federations of labor, six international unions affiliated with A. F. of L., all of whom have endorsed the Lundeen bill, and who have done so in spite of and in the face of such "sabotage" as I might call it, on the part of the leaders of the A. F. of L., as is represented by this letter and so many other actions that they have taken in connection with their whole problem of geniune unemployment and social insurance, so I feel you may probably boast that you have worked, and that you are still working with what is really the A. F. of L., namely, the membership of the A. F. of L., and in their behalf; and I say that as one who has been a member of the A. F. of L. for a good many years.

Mr. LUNDEEN. Our masters should be the mass of the people and the rank and file. Is not that so?

Mr. BENJAMIN. That is correct.

Mr. LUNDEEN. We are servants here in Washington, or ought to be, of the great invisible majority that cannot come here, whom we are supposed to represent.

Mr. BENJAMIN. That is correct.

Mr. LUNDEEN. And we should react to their wishes so far as we are able to ascertain them, within the range of possibility of enacting such measures into law, and I feel that this bill is within the range of possibility. When I spoke of that letter of endorsement, I also spoke of the endorsement of the Central Labor Union, and one or two other endorsements, which is there is no objection I would like to insert in the record.

Mr. DUNN. I have no objection.

(The letters of endorsement referred to by Congressman Lundeen are as follows:)

MINNEAPOLIS CENTRAL LABOR UNION,
Minneapolis, Minn., February 19, 1934.

Hon. ERNEST LUNDEEN,
United States Congressman, House Office Building,
Washington, D. C.

DEAR SIR: This is to inform you that at the last regular meeting of the Minneapolis Central Labor Union, held on February 14, 1934, a motion was unanimously adopted endorsing unemployment insurance bill H. R. 7598 and requesting your support of this measure.

We believe the enactment into law of this bill will solve the unemployment problem in a highly satisfactory manner and adequately care for those who are thrown out of work through no fault of their own.

Trusting that we may have your support, we remain,

Respectfully yours,

MINNEAPOLIS CENTRAL LABOR UNION,
EMERY C. NELSON, *Recording Secretary.*

————

CITY OF MINNEAPOLIS,
OFFICE OF CITY CLERK,
February 1, 1934.

Representative ERNEST LUNDEEN,
House of Representatives, Washington, D. C.

DEAR SIR: Attached hereto is copy of the action of the city council of the city of Minneapolis, Minn., at the regular meeting thereof held January 26, 1934, on the following matter:

Approving the workers' unemployment insurance bill, now being presented to Congress.

Respectfully yours,

CHAS. C. SWANSON, *City Clerk.*

NEW YORK DAILY NEWS
AMERICAN LEGION POST 1234,
October 2, 1934.

Hon. ERNEST LUNDEEN,
  Member of Congress, Washington, D. C.

DEAR COMRADE LUNDEEN: It is a pleasure for me to inform you that Daily News Post 1234, the American Legion, in regular meeting assembled on Friday, September 28, unanimously passed a motion to endorse a bill to provide for the establishment of unemployment and social insurance and for other purposes which we understand will be introduced in the next session of Congress under your sponsorship.

We consider the proposed legislation a step in the right direction for progressive social service, and trust that you and your supporters meet with a greater measure of success in your endeavors for legislation of this type than in the past.   We are familiar with your record on veterans' legislation and take this opportunity to thank you for your whole-hearted support of measures designed to alleviate suffering among our former comrades in arms.

You may use these expressions of our sentiments, if you so desire, among the veterans' organizations in the Third Congressional District of Minnesota, to the end that your campaign for reelection to Congress will meet with the success your record deserves.

  Sincerely yours,

J. J. ANGEHRN, *Post Adjutant.*

EVELETH JUNIOR CHAMBER OF COMMERCE, INC.,
Eveleth, Minn.

Whereas the situation of the workers throughout the country is approaching a starvation point; and

Whereas the relief and work that have been available in the past are no longer to be had; due to a curtailment of the same; and

Whereas the workers' unemployment and social insurance bill provides for immediate relief and is now in the Committee on Labor in the House of Representatives; therefore be it hereby

Resolved; That we, the Eveleth members of the Junior Chamber of Commerce, whole-heartedly endorse the above-mentioned bill and desire immediate favorable action thereon.

Adopted this 28th day of March 1934.

TOM SHEA, *Chairman.*
CARL A. STRAND, *Secretary.*

HENNEPIN COUNTY CENTRAL COMMITTEE,
OF FARMER-LABOR ASSOCIATION,
Minneapolis, Minn., February 26, 1934.

Hon. ERNEST LUNDEEN,
  Congressman-at-Large, State of Minnesota, Washington, D. C.

MY DEAR CONGRESSMAN LUNDEEN: At a meeting of the Hennepin County Central Committee of the Farmer-Labor Association held February 21, 1934, the matter of your unemployment insurance bill was brought up for discussion. Motion was made, seconded, and unanimously passed that the Hennepin County Farmer-Labor Association go on record favoring your bill and commending your efforts in its behalf.

With best wishes for success to your efforts in this connection, I am,
  Yours very truly,

STANLEY B. NEWHALL, *Secretary.*
HENNEPIN COUNTY CENTRAL COMMITTEE.

Mr. BENJAMIN. Mr. Chairman, if there are no other questions, there are a few more points on which I will touch slightly before I conclude.   I should like to say this for the record, if I may.

Mr. DUNN. Proceed.

Mr. BENJAMIN. The movement that has been developed around this bill, known as the "workers unemployment and insurance bill", is the best proof of the power that can be developed by a minority when it works properly, when it adheres to correct principles, and when it understands the forces against whom it must oppose itself, and when it knows how to oppose them. I think the workers in the course of these 5 years, in the struggles that they have waged for the right to lead in the day-to-day battles for more relief, have proven that even without a majority, if they conduct their fight properly they can get results and they can force the majority to give them results. My feeling is that the best thing that the Members of Congress who want to advance genuine social legislation can do is to follow the example of their humble constituents, organize themselves well, take a firm position on principle on important questions, and conduct a fight, and you will see that the majority will proceed to give way, inch by inch, in the face of a well-organized attack.

Mr. DUNN. I agree with you.

Mr. BENJAMIN. I think I have already indicated, in the earlier part of my remarks how unique the hearings before this committee have been. I say again that without a question of doubt, this is the first instance where a committee of Congress has opened the door to those who really make up America, to those who are really the population of the United States, opening the door wide open to those who are the real America, the masses of workers, the farmers, professionals, veterans, to those who are suffering as a consequence of the crisis, to those who individually have very little power and very little influence and enjoy very little respect and consideration ordinarily, but they have been given before this committee the utmost consideration, the fullest opportunity of expressing themselves, the most courteous treatment, and in my mind, therefore, we have had an example in this committee of something of that type of genuine democracy which we are looking for, a democracy that really provides an opportunity of expression to the masses who constitute our population. Such an opportunity is very rare in this country, very rate in congressional hearings, as has been afforded in this committee, and therefore in that sense I think the record of this committee's hearings on this bill will go down as an instance of an unusual, a very splendid consideration of that greater consideration which Congress must increasingly give to those who heretofore have been neglected.

I want to thank the chairman of this committee, Mr. Dunn, who in the conduct of these hearings has helped to make them what they have been, to do everything that I have described them to be, and certainly Mr. Lundeen who has been the pioneer in Congress in presenting this measure, that grows right out of the ranks of the workers; that Mr. Lundeen has worked at all times for what is not merely his own bill, but which is a bill that millions want, that they themselves have developed, and that he has introduced in their behalf; that these have contributed very valuable testimony to those who have appeared before the committee, enabling them to present more effectively their material. Since the other members of the committee are not present here, I should also like to say for the record of this hearing that while we believe that these hearings still were not altogether free from some of the bad habits which Congress has gotten into over many, many decades of bad practice, while they were not altogether free from this, nevertheless they manifested the beginning of a departure in a new and better direction.

Mr. DUNN. Thank you, Mr. Benjamin, for your very instructive summary and for your enlightening remarks and discussion. You have helped us considerably in your remarks and in your discussion of the Lundeen bill, H. R. 2827, the bill of that outstanding man, Congressman Lundeen, the Farmer-Laborite from Minnesota, who in my candid opinion, is one of the most progressive and humane men in Congress.

I want to thank all of the witnesses who testified. I believe there were about 75 of them. As it has been said, we have had men and women from North, South, East, and West, who have appeared before the subcommittee of the Committee on Labor and testified that in their opinion the Lundeen bill, H. R. 2827, is the only measure in Congress today that will give adequate old-age pensions, unemployment insurance, and so forth.

Of the 75 persons who testified there were but two who claimed they represented communistic organizations, and I want to say in behalf of those two that in their discussion before the committee they maintained that the Lundeen bill was an outstanding piece of legislation and if enacted into law would wipe out much of the human misery prevailing in the United States.

In conclusion may I say that I have never attended a meeting that I was able to grasp and learn so much from as I have at this hearing concerning the many millions of professional and laboring people who are in need of the necessities of life. In other words, had it not been for this public hearing I would not be in possession of the facts that I now have, and it has been a tremendous help to me and to every other member of this committee.

I want to say that the Chairman of the Labor Committee of the House, Mr. William P. Connery, who is also a progressive and a very great humanitarian, is to be commended for the wonderful and valuable assistance that he rendered this subcommittee.

I do hope that H. R. 2827 will be enacted into law this session of Congress, because it will make adequate provisions for the aged, farmers, widows, the unemployed, and all those who are physically incapacitated. It will undoubtedly eradicate the slum districts of our country—the breeding place for criminals. If this bill will eradicate the slum district, which in my opinion it will do if enacted into law, it would save the Government billions of dollars; in other words, if it would take $15,000,000,000 annually to put into effect H. R. 2827, known as "the Workers' Unemployment, Old Age, and Social Insurance Act", that would be an infinitesimal sum compared to the gigantic amount of money which we are now spending to keep down crime and for the construction and maintenance of prisons, poorhouses, and so forth.

Mr. LUNDEEN. Mr. Chairman, I desire to add my individual thanks to the Chairman of the Committee on Labor and to the chairman of our subcommittee, to our members of the subcommittee, and to all the witnessss who have furnished us with this very valuable information. I hope this subcommittee will report out H. R. 2827 unanimously.

Mr. Chairman, I move that the subcommittee do now adjourn.

(The motion was agreed to; accordingly, at 5 p. m., the subcommittee adjourned the public hearings on H. R. 2827, H. R. 2859, H. R. 10, and H. R. 185.)

ENDORSEMENTS OF H. R. 2827 RECEIVED BY THE SUBCOMMITTEE ON LABOR

PITTSBURGH LODGE No. 52,
INTERNATIONAL ASSOCIATION OF MACHINISTS,
Pittsburgh, Pa., February 4, 1935.

Hon. MATTHEW DUNN,
Washington, D. C.

DEAR SIR: Our membership has endorsed bill H. R. No. 2827 and urge you to vote for its passage if and when it is reported.

Sincerely yours,

WM. J. TYGARD,
Secretary pro tempore.

GMINA 38, ZWIAZKU NAR. POL.,
Pittsburgh, Pa., January 11, 1935.

Hon. MATTHEW A. DUNN, *Congressman,*
Washington, D. C.

SIR: Whereas district no. 38, consisting of 26 branches, represents a membership of 4,000 members of the Polish National Alliance, resident in Allegheny County, Pa.; and

Whereas nearly all said members are active participants in the industrial life of that State, as workers, artisans, small merchants, and professional people, and nearly all of them of modest economic circumstances; and

Whereas the viccisitudes of the last 5 years of the so-called "depression" has spread unemployment and economic insecurity broadcast among said members; and

Whereas there have been brought to the attention of that membership and of each of the constituent branches thereof for their study and consideration H. R. 7598, sponsored and introduced by Mr. Lundeen, February 2, 1934, entitled "A bill to provide for the establishment of unemployment and social insurance, and for other purposes"; and

Whereas said bill, its contents and purposes, have received the closest and most earnest scrutiny and analysis by all the constituent branches of district no. 38, resulting in their unanimous approbation of an an indorsement thereof; and

Whereas on December 23, 1934, a regular meeting of the delegates of said 26 branches constituting District No. 38 of the Polish National Alliance, after due notice of the time and purpose thereof was held, and at which meeting said H. R. 7598 and its endorsements by constituent branches was considered: It was

Resolved unanimously by the delegates of the District No. 38 Polish National Alliance, That H. R. 7598, introduced by Mr. Lundeen, be approved and endorsed by said district as necessary and indispensable social legislation; and that said formal approval and endorsement be notified officially on behalf of district no. 38 to each and every Senator and Representative in Congress of the county of Allegheny, State of Pennsylvania, to the end of requesting the vote and approval and effort of said Senators and Representatives in behalf of said bill and its early passage and enactment into law of the United States.

Very truly yours,

POLISH NATIONAL ALLIANCE, DISTRICT No. 38.
M. ROZYCKI, *President.*
W. A. SIEROCKI, *Secretary.*

FOND DU LAC, WIS., *January 18, 1935.*

Hon. MATTHEW A. DUNN,
House Labor Committee, Washington, D. C.

Whereas the homes, the families, and the basis for the very existence of the millions of workers have already been destroyed or are seriously menaced as the result of mass unemployment; and

Whereas this condition has become a permanent standing menace to the security of all categories of wageworkers in consequence of the rapid introduction of labor-displacing machinery, of speed-up methods, and other means whereby productivity per workers is increased while domestic as well as foreign markets shrink; and

Whereas prevailing relief provisions in no way meets the needs of those unemployed and threatened with unemployment through no fault of their own, but on the contrary serve to subject the victims of mass unemployment to abuse, humiliation, and oppression; and

Whereas the Roosevelt security measure, "the Wagner-Lewis bill", is totally inadequate and does not provide any security for 17,000,000 unemployed and their families; and

Whereas the right of those who have produced the wealth of this Nation to the essentials of decent existence should have first claim upon the Government and employers who possess and control this wealth: Now, therefore, be it

Resolved, That we, the Labor and Relief Workers Union, assembled in a general meeting on this 18th day of January 1935, at 138 Doty Street, city of Fond du Lac, county of Fond du Lac, State of Wisconsin, and endorsed H. R. 2827 known as "The Workers' Unemployment, Old Age, and Insurance Act", and we therefore respectfully demand that you, Matthew A. Dunn, member of the House Labor Committee, immediately endorse and support H. R. 2827, and also give a recommendation to Congress approving the bill and demand quick action.

LABOR AND RELIEF WORKERS UNION,
WILLIAM CAREY, *Secretary.*

TRADE UNION UNITY COUNCIL OF GREATER NEW YORK,
January 22, 1935.

Hon MATTHEW A. DUNN,
House of Representatives, Washington, D. C.

DEAR SIR: The Trade Union Unity Council, representing 45,000 organized workers of New York City, is vitally concerned with the problem of unemployment insurance, since thousands of our members are unemployed.

Our council has gone on record endorsing the workers' unemployment insurance bill, H. R. 2827. Our council has also discussed the Wagner-Lewis bill endorsed by Congress, and considers this bill absolutely inadequate to meet the needs of the millions of unemployed workers.

We have decided to communicate our decisions to you, and call on you to support the workers' bill, H. R. 2827, and work for its enactment.

Fraternally yours,

TRADE UNION UNITY COUNCIL,
ROSE WORTIS, *Secretary.*

COMITATO ESECUTIVO DEL FRONTE UNICO DELLE
ORGANIZZAZIONI ITALIANE PRO ASSICURAZIONE SOCIALE,
Cleveland, Ohio, January 23, 1935.

Hon. MATTHEW A. DUNN,
Labor Committee, House of Representatives,
Washington, D. C.

DEAR SIR: We have been informed that you have endorsed the Workers' Unemployment, Old Age, and Social Insurance Act (H. R. 2827), introduced into the Seventy-fourth Congress by Congressman Lundeen. Welcome your endorsement and call upon you to give your utmost support for this act and its enactment by Congress.

This act (H. R. 2827) is the only genuine unemployment insurance now before Congress and it has the support of over 2,000,000 workers and their families in the United States.

We herewith inform you of the endorsement of the workers' unemployment, old age, and social insurance act (H. R. 2827) by our organization at its regular meeting on May 20, 1934.

G. R. VENDITTI.

INDEPENDENT ORDER SONS OF ITALY,
Cleveland, Ohio, January 23, 1935.

Hon. MATTHEW A. DUNN,
Congressional Office Building,
Washington, D. C.

DEAR SIR: The Workers' Unemployment, Old Age, and Social Insurance Act (H. R. 2827) has been introduced into the Seventy-fourth Congress by Congressman Lundeen. This act is the only genuine unemployment insurance now before Congress and it has the support and endorsement of over 2,000,000 workers and their families in the United States.

In order that our future and the future of all workers, farmers, professionals, and other unemployed and their dependents may be more secure we demand the enactment of a Federal system of genuine unemployment insurance as contained in the Workers' Act, H. R. 2827.

You must cease delaying the enactment of unemployment insurance and we call upon you, in the name of those who have put you into office and thousands of others, to do your utmost to support our bill and to sign the "round-robin" petition circulated in Congress in support of the Workers Unemployment, Old Age, and Social Insurance Act.

We expect you to vote for the Workers Unemployment, Old Age, and Social Insurance Act, H. R. 2827 and ask that you shall reply to us on your position regarding the enactment of Federal unemployment insurance during the present session of Congress.

G. R. VENDITTI, *Secretary*.

SLOVENIAN NATIONAL BENEFIT SOCIETY (S. N. P. J.) LODGE No. 386,
Library, Pa.

Whereas the Slovenian National Benefit Society regularly met this 20th day of January 1935 for the transaction of business, reaffirms that it is a nonpolitical and nonpartisan organization, and

Whereas the present economic depression has seriously lessened or entirely done away with the incomes of our citizens, creating want and destitutions, and

Whereas the present social legislation has proven inadequate to keep the people of Pennsylvania from want and destitution and in the event of another depression will be even more inadequate, and

Whereas the people of Pennsylvania are aware of these deplorable conditions and want a revision and change in our Constitution; Therefore be it

Resolved, That the Slovenian National Benefit Society urge you to introduce or support all measures and bills, insuring adequate protection from want of our people in abnormal times; be it further

Resolved, That among these measures and bills special consideration be given (1) old-age pensions; (2) unemployment insurance; (3) 6-hour day and similar labor bills; be it further

Resolved, That copies of this resolution be sent to our various representatives in the United States Congress.

MORTT DERMOTTER, *President*.
NICK TRILLER, *Secretary*.

THIEF RIVER FALLS, MINN.,
January 25, 1935.

To the members of the Ways and Means and Labor Committees:

The following resolution was adopted by the resolutions committee of the Unemployment Council of Thief River Falls, Minn., Wednesday, January 23, 1935:

Resolved, That we the members of the Unemployment Council of Thief River Falls, in meeting assembled on this 23d day of January 1935, demand the immediate passage of the workers' insurance bill, H. R. 2827; and be it further

Resolved, That a copy of this resolution be sent to President Franklin D. Roosevelt, and to each of the members of the Committees of Labor and of Ways and Means of the House of Representatives of the United States Congress at Washington.

THE COMMITTEE OF ACTION,
H. S. VANPELT,
TOLLEF AUSTAD,
A. JOHNSON,
CHAS. SCHULTZ,
DR. P. L. VISTAUNET,
EARL ELLOFSON, *Secretary*.

JANUARY 27, 1935.
Hon. MATTHEW A. DUNN,
    House of Representatives, Washington, D. C.
    We, the National Unemployment Council of Payne County, Okla., demand
the immediate enactment of the workers bill, H. R. 2827.
                                                MILDRED GAGE,
        Secretary of Payne County Unemployment Council of Cushing, Okla.

_____

JANUARY 27, 1935.
Hon. MATTHEW A. DUNN,
    DEAR SIR: The Lithuanian organizations have at meeting of delegates on
January 17, 1935, at Lithuanian Music Hall, 2715 East Allegheny Avenue,
Philadelphia, Pa., adopted the following resolution:
    "Whereas at the present there are more than 16,000,000 workers out of work,
totaling over 40,000,000 persons who are facing starvation. These millions of
unemployed are unable to find or obtain employment and have no means of
sustaining their families, and
    "Whereas in the factories and mines systems of speeding up and increasing
production have been established. This modernized and more efficient machinery
has resulted in displacement of millions of workers, and
    "Whereas the workers who have reached the age of 45, or over, the doors of
all factories and mines are closed to them.
    "Therefore we endorse the social and unemployment insurance bill (H. R.
2827) as the only means for the future of all workers, professionals, and self-
employed persons and their dependents to protect their lives.
    "Further, we demand that you as representative of labor Committee from
Pennsylvania to endorse workers social insurance bill (H. R. 2827) and enact
upon it until become as a law based on the principles set forth in the workers bill
H. R. 2827."
    Names of the organizations:
    Lithuanian National Perresh.
    American Lithuanian Citizens Benefishal Club.
    Lithuanian Brothers Benefishal Club.
    St. George Association.
    American Lithuanian Workers Literature Association, branch 149.
    American Lithuanian Workers Literature Association, branch 142.
    American Lithuanian Republican Benefishal Club.
    American Lithuanian Workers Literature Association, branch 30.
    Lithuanian National Benefishal Club.
    American Lithuanian Workers Literature Association, branch 10.
    Lithuanian Wytauts Club.
    American Lithuanian Workers Literature Association, branch 141.
    Corporation of the Lithuanian Music Hall.
    Gedemin Benefishal Club.
                                                M. ZALD,
            Secretary of the Executive Committee of the Organizations.

_____

                                SOCIETA M. S. NORD ITALIA,
                                        DI EAST LIBERTY,
                                Pittsburgh, Pa., January 28, 1935.
Hon. MATTHEW A. DUNN,
    Member of Committee on Labor.
    We demand immediate enactment of the workers' bill, H. R. 2827.
                                        DAN CALABRESE, Secretary.
                                        B. MONGIOT, President.

_____

        AXMINSTER CARPET WORKERS UNION, LOCAL No. 2053,
                                Philadelphia, Pa., January 29, 1935.
Hon. MATTHEW A. DUNN,
    Washington, D. C.
    DEAR SIR: This organization, by a unanimous vote in regular meeting, endorse
the workers' unemployment and social insurance bill (H. R. 2827) presented by
Congressman Lundeen and now in the House Committee on Labor.

Our membership of 500 workers demands that the members of this Committee on Labor report the bill on the floor of the House for vote, and that our local representatives sign the petition now being circulated by Representative Lundeen, to bring the bill out of committee and vote favorably on it.

We further condemn the Roosevelt bill for unemployment insurance presented by Wagner and Lewis as inadequate and even farcical.

Sincerely yours,

THOMAS DICKSON, *Secretary.*

EQUITY LOCAL 100,
BROTHERHOOD OF UTILITY EMPLOYEES OF AMERICA,
New York City, January 30, 1935.

Representative MATTHEW A. DUNN,
House of Representatives, Washington, D. C.

DEAR REPRESENTATIVE DUNN: I wish to inform you that this organization has gone on record in favor of the Lundeen workers' unemployment, old-age, and social-insurance bill, H. R. 2827.

Equity Local 100 has jurisdiction over the New York Edison, United Electric Light & Power Co. employees.

In behalf of these utility workers, I urge you to support this legislation.

Sincerely yours,

JAMES D. SPENCE, *Secretary.*

FEDERATION OF ARCHITECTS, ENGINEERS, CHEMISTS, AND TECHNICIANS,
Hon. MATTHEW A. DUNN,
Philadelphia, Pa., January 31, 1935.
House of Representatives, Washington, D. C.

DEAR SIR: The Philadelphia chapter of the Federation of Architects, Engineers, Chemists, and Technicians, at a general meeting of its membership held January 24, 1935, at 1206 Walnut Street, Philadelphia, Pa., unanimously endorsed H. R. 2827, in the House of Representatives, Washington, D. C., the workers bill for unemployment and social insurance.

As a representative of the Commonwealth of Pennsylvania, we call upon you to actively support the workers bill (H. R. 2827) as the only bill which truly represents the needs of the vast majority of the residents of Pennsylvania.

Very truly yours,

MAXWELL LEVINSON,
Executive Secretary.

VERHOVAY AID ASSOCIATION,
VERHOVAY SEGELY EGYLET
(a Hungarian fraternal benefit society),
Pittsburgh, Pa., February 4, 1935.

Hon. JOHN J. McGRATH,
Washington, D. C.

DEAR CONGRESSMAN: At a meeting of the board of directors, held on the 23d day of January 1935, a resolution was adopted concerning bills introduced in the Congress of the United States providing for unemployment insurance, old-age insurance, and sick-benefit insurance and for legislation abolishing sweatshops and child labor. Copy of said resolution is herewith enclosed.

May we humbly request your support?

Yours respectfully,

VERHOVAY AID ASSOCIATION,
By JOSEPH D. ECRAGO,
Supreme President.

RESOLUTION

Whereas the Verhovay Aid Association is a fraternal beneficial organization having branches in different parts of the United States; and

Whereas most of its members are employed with coal companies, iron, steel, and other industrial corporations; and

Whereas it is the desire of the board of directors of the Verhovay Aid Association to aid in every possible way, the working people who are citizens or residents of the United States to earn a decent living wage; and

Whereas it is the opinion of the board of directors of the Verhovay Aid Association that the existence of "sweatshops" and the employment of child labor, are detrimental to the welfare of the people of the United States; and

Whereas there are, at the present time, several bills pending in the Congress of the United States, providing for unemployment insurance, old-age insurance, and sick-benefit insurance: Now, therefore, be it

Resolved by the board of directors of the Verhovay Aid Association, That in behalf of its 25,000 members, it request each and every Member of the House of Representatives and each and every Member of the Senate of the United States, to vote in favor of any of the bills now pending before the Congress of the United States providing for legislation for unemployment insurance, old-age insurance, and sick-benefit insurance, and to introduce and support bills providing for the abolition of sweatshops and child labor; and be it further

Resolved, That a copy of this resolution be sent to each and every Member of the House of Representatives and to each and every Member of the Senate of the United States.

FEDERATION OF CARPET AND RUG WORKERS OF AMERICA,
Philadelphia, Pa., February 4, 1935.

Hon. MATTHEW A. DUNN,
House Labor Committee, Washington, D. C.

DEAR SIR: This federation representing many locals in the United States, and with a membership of approximately 15,000 workers, by a unanimous vote at regular meeting endorsed the workers unemployment and social insurance bill (H. R. 2827) presented by Congressman Lundeen and now in the House Committee on Labor.

We therefore demand that the members of this House Committee on Labor report the bill on the floor of the House for vote and that our local representatives sign the petition now being circulated by Representative Lundeen to bring the bill out of committee and vote favorably on it.

We further condemn the Roosevelt bill for unemployment insurance presented by Wagner and Lewis as preposterous. It is our desire that delegates from this federation be invited by the Ways and Means Committee to the hearings on the Wagner and Lewis bill to present our opposition.

Sincerely yours,

ROLLA L. WALLACE, *Secretary.*

THE ITALIAN WORKERS' SOCIETY
FOR MUTUAL BENEFIT OF THE WEST SIDE,
Cleveland, Ohio, February 6, 1935.

Hon. MATTHEW A. DUNN,
Committeeman of Labor Committee,
House of Representatives, Washington, D. C.

DEAR MR. DUNN: We demand quick action, endorsement, and recommendation to Congress approving the workers' unemployment and social insurance bill H. R. 2827.

LOUIS DIRRILD, *Chairman.*
ORESTE LISI, *Secretary.*

CAR AND FOUNDRY WORKERS' UNION,
CHARTIERS VALLEY LOCAL NO. 1,
McKees Rocks, Pa., February 6, 1935.

MATTHEW A. DUNN,
Congressman, Thirty-fourth District Pennsylvania.

DEAR MR. DUNN: The Car and Foundry Workers' Union, Chartiers Valley Local No. 1, wishes to congratulate you upon being made chairman of the Lundeen bill.

This letter is to inform you that our union is 100 percent for the bill.

Yours very truly,

ANDREW G. BARATKA,
Recording Secretary.

FEDERATION OF ARCHITECTS, ENGINEERS, CHEMISTS, AND TECHNICIANS,
Pittsburgh, Pa., February 1935.

Congressman MATTHEW DUNN,
House of Representatives, Washington, D. C.

DEAR CONGRESSMAN BROOKS: At a regularly scheduled meeting of the Federation of Architects, Engineers, Chemists, and Technicians, held at the Seventh Avenue Hotel, January 25, we unanimously endorsed and supported the workers, unemployment and social insurance bill, H. R. 2827. We further endorsed the demand that you as one of our Representatives in Washington give full support to this bill and seek its immediate passage.

The above endorsement came about only after careful reading of this bill where it was found that it is the only bill that will adequately and correctly supply the needs of the people.

An immediate answer is requested wherein you will state definitely your support of H. R. 2827.

Very truly yours,

MAX ABER,
Chairman of the F. A. E. C. T.

MATTHEW A. DUNN,
Chairman Subcommittee on Labor,
House of Representatives, Washington, D. C.

DEAR SIR: We, the undersigned, have endorsed the workers' unemployment, old-age, and social-insurance bill, known as "H. R. 2827 ", and ask that your committee recommend this bill favorably to the House and support its adoption.

RUSSIAN NATIONAL MUTUAL AID SOCIETY,
P. KUSHINSKI, *Secretary.*

1382 CALIFORNIA AVENUE, *Akron, Ohio.*

SLOVAK EVANGELICAL UNION,
N. S. Pittsburgh, Pa., February 7, 1935.

Hon. MATTHEW A. DUNN,
Chairman Subcommittee, House Labor Committee,
House of Representatives, Washington, D. C.

DEAR SIR: I am in receipt of your notice relative H. R. 2827 introduced by Congressman Lundeen and now before your committee for hearing.

Twelve thousand members of the above Union, over one-half of them in Pennsylvania, will be grateful to you for a favorable action on this bill.

Very respectfully yours,

PAUL STURMAN, Jr.,
Supr. Rec. Secretary.

TAYLOR SPRINGS, ILL.,
February 10, 1935.

RESOLUTION

Whereas the Workers Unemployment, Old Age, and Social Insurance Act, H. R. 2827, is the only measure that will provide immediate benefits for all those now unemployed; and

Whereas this bill provides adequate benefits equal to average wages and no less than $10 a week plus $3 for each dependent; and

Whereas this bill provides Federal instead of State insurance with money to be raised through an income tax with no contributions from workers; and

Whereas the Wagner-Lewis bill makes no provision whatever for those now unemployed, provides no immediate benefits for anyone, with future benefits for only limited groups, and with workers making direct and indirect contributions; and

Whereas this bill does not meet the needs and was only designed to defeat the movement for genuine social insurance as provided by the workers bill, H. R. 2827: Therefore be it hereby

Resolved, That we demand of our Congressman that he support H. R. 2827 and vote against the Wagner-Lewis bill; and be it further

Resolved, That we demand of the Senate Finance Committee and the House Ways and Means Committee that they reject the Wagner-Lewis bill in favor of the workers bill, H. R. 2827; and be it further

Resolved, That we demand of the House Labor Committee that H. R. 2827 be reported out of committee immediately for a vote; and be it further

Resolved, That copies of this resolution be sent to the above-named committees in Washington, D. C., to Congressman Matthew A. Dunn, Chairman of House Labor Subcommittee, and to the press.

Read and adopted at a meeting of the First Catholic Union, Taylor Springs, Ill., on February 10, 1935.

JOSEPH HOVANEC, *Secretary.*

RESOLUTION

Whereas the Workers Unemployment, Old Age, and Social Insurance Act, H. R. 2827, is the only measure that will provide immediate benefits for all those now unemployed; and

Whereas this bill provides Federal instead of State insurance with money to be raised through an income tax with no contributions from workers; and

Whereas the Wagner-Lewis bill makes no provision whatever for these new unemployed, provides no immediate benefits for anyone, with future benefits for only limited groups, and with workers making direct and indirect contributions; and

Whereas this bill does not meet the needs and was only designed to defeat the movement for genuine social insurance as provided by the workers' bill, H. R. 2827: Therefore be it hereby

Resolved, That we demand of our Congressman that he support H. R. 2827 and vote against the Wagner-Lewis bill; and be it further

Resolved, That we demand of the Senate Finance Committee and the House Ways and Means Committee that they reject the Wagner-Lewis bill in favor of the workers' bill, H. R. 2827; and be if further

Resolved, That we demand of the House Committee that H. R. 2827 be reported out of committee immediately for a vote; and be it further

Resolved, That copies of this resolution be sent to the above-named committees in Washington, D. C., to Congressman ————, and the press.

Read and adopted at a meeting of the Yugoslav Klub on February 11, 1935.

JOSEPH MILOVATS, *Secretary.*

YUKON, PA.

RESOLUTION ON UNEMPLOYMENT INSURANCE

Whereas President Roosevelt's report of January 17, 1935, on social security in no way takes care of the 16,000,000 persons now unemployed and so far as unemployment insurance is concerned affects only those now employed; and

Whereas the funds to finance his unemployment insurance plan are to be raised through a 3 percent pay-roll tax which will no doubt be passed on to the workers in the form of increased prices on commodities manufactured by these companies; and

Whereas the recommended benefit period is to be 15 weeks plus a 10-week additional period if employer has a long service record; and

Whereas this insurance is not to take effect until some time in 1936: Be it

Resolved, That we the unemployed and citizens of Chalfont Boro, Pa., in mass meeting assembled, consider the recommendations of the President totally inadequate and will only continue the pauperization of the American workers and that we reiterate our endorsement of workers' unemployment and social insurance bill, H. R. 2827; and be it further

Resolved, That copies of this resolution be sent to President Roosevelt, our Congressmen, and the press.

ST. MARYS CITY, MD.,
February 9, 1935.

DEAR SIRS: The members of the Slovak Farmers Assembly 699 would like for the insurance bill of H. R. 2827 to be passed.

ANDREW GRESKO, *President.*
JOHN BARONIAK, *Financial Secretary.*

LANSFORD, PA., *February 10, 1935.*
Hon. MATTHEW A. DUNN,
Chairman of House Labor Subcommittee:

We have taken action in our lodge on the Lundeen bill under H. R. 2827. We have studied it carefully and explained it to our members and they are satisfied and pleased, and they have passed a motion which was voted unanimously for you to support this bill.

Yours truly,
OFFICERS OF ST. PETER ASSEMBLY 176, LANSFORD, PA.
ANDREW CHUCHRAN, *Financial Secretary,*
ANDEW HAVRAN, *President.*

MATTHEW A. DUNN,
Chairman Subcommittee on Labor,
House of Representatives, Washington, D. C.

DEAR SIR: We the undersigned have endorsed the workers unemployment, old age, and social insurance bill, known as "H. R. 2827", and ask that your committee recommend this bill favorably to the House and support its adoption.

LEMKO ASSOCIATION,
SIMEON A. HOWE, *Secretary.*
1018 PARDEE AVENUE, *Akron, Ohio.*

FEDERATION OF SLAVONIC SOCIETIES,
Lansford, Pa., February 11, 1935.
Hon. MATTHEW A. DUNN,
Congressman, Washington, D. C.

DEAR SIR: Federation of Slavonic Societies representing throusands of American citizens of Slavonic descent at its public assembly in Lansford, Pa., decided to ask you for your support to the bill, H. R. 2827, introduced by Congressman Lundeen.

Administration at Washington must show to American workingman that his trust put into Democratic Party was not in vain.

ANDREW CHUCHRAN, *President.*
MARTIN KOPUNCK, *Secretary.*

NEW YORK CITY, *February 11, 1935.*
Hon. MATTHEW A. DUNN,
House Labor Subcommittee, Washington, D. C.

DEAR SIR: In behalf of thousands of Italian-American citizens of New York, I request that bill H. R. 2827 be reported back at once.

Respectfully,
MARK DORIS.

BENLD, ILL., *February 11, 1935.*
Mr. MATTHEW A. DUNN,
Chairman House Labor Subcommittee, Washington, D. C.

DEAR MR. DUNN: We, the officers of the Sv. Josef Pestun Assembly 598 of the National Slovak Society of the United States of America, hereby solicitate, in behalf of ourselves and 133 local members, your favorable adherence and recommendation of bill H. R. 2827 pending.

SV. JOSEF PESTUN,
GEORGE DOBOO, *President.*
JAN NOVOTNV, *Recording Secretary.*
JOSEPH J. KOŽAK, *Finance Secretary.*
JOHN HLBOCAN, *Treasurer.*

BATTERY WORKERS FEDERAL LABOR UNION NO. 18551,
Philadelphia, Pa., February 11, 1935.

Hon. WM. P. CONNERY, JR.
Care of House of Representatives, Washington, D. C.

MY DEAR MR. CONNERY: We understand that the subcommittee of the House Labor Committee, which is now conducting hearings on H. R. 2827, will complete these hearings by Thursday of this week.

In order that there may be no misunderstanding in your own mind and those of the other members of your committee concerning the position of Battery Workers No. 18551 Federal Union, American Federation of Labor, our entire membership of 1,800 is signing this letter in support of the above-mentioned bill.

We further wish to call to your attention that we are not alone in the ranks of the American Federation of Labor in support of this bill. Neither are we alone in our opposition to the utopian schemes which are also being considered. We refer specifically to the Townsend proposal, and the unquestionably impossible Wagner-Lewis fraud.

Very sincerely yours,

BATTERY WORKERS FEDERAL LABOR UNION NO. 18551.

PHILADELPHIA, PA., *February 11, 1935.*

Hon. MATTHEW A. DUNN,
Care House of Representatives, Washington, D. C.

DEAR MR. DUNN: You will find enclosed a copy of a letter which has been signed by the entire membership of our union and sent to Hon. William P. Connery, Jr., chairman of the House of Labor Committee.

The copy of this letter is self-explanatory and requires no further explanation on our part.

Sincerely yours,

JAMES PRICE, *Financial Secretary.*

BEDFORD, OHIO, *February 11, 1935.*

Hon. MATTHEW A. DUNN,
Chairman Subcommittee of the
Labor Committee of the House of Representatives,
Washington, D. C.

DEAR SIR: We have been informed that you have endorsed the Workers' Unemployment, Old Age, and Social Insurance Act, H. R. 2827, introduced into the Seventy-fourth Congress by Congressman Lundeen. We welcome your endorsement and call upon you to give your utmost support for this act and its enactment by Congress.

This act, H. R. 2827, is the only genuine unemployment insurance now before Congress and it has the support of over 2,000,000 workers and their families in the United States.

We herewith inform you of the endorsement of the Workers Unemployment, Old Age, and Social Insurance Act, H. R. 2827, by our organization at its regular meeting of the above date.

CLUB RIVISONDOLESI,
C. ROMITO

COURT PLZEN, NO. 115, FORESTERS OF AMERICA,
Lansing, Ohio, February 11, 1935.

Hon. MATTHEW A. DUNN,
Chairman House Labor Committee,
House Office Building, Washington, D. C.

DEAR SIR: We, the members of Court Plzen, No. 15, Foresters of America, in special session assembled discussed the various economic security bills and resolved to request you to favorably report the Lundeen unemployment insurance bill.

Thanking you in advance for said favor, we are

Respectfully yours,

ANDY LEV, *Chief Ranger,*
STEPHEN HERINK, *Financial Secretary,*
MATHEW KREN, *Recording Secretary.*

716 UNEMPLOYMENT, OLD AGE, AND SOCIAL INSURANCE

Z URADOVNY, RADU "VACLAV SNAJDR",
CISLO 251, CZECHOSLOVAK SOCIETIES OF AMERICA,
Bridgeport, Ohio, February 11, 1935.
Hon. MATTHEW A. DUNN,
Chairman House Labor Committee,
House of Representatives, Washington, D. C.

DEAR SIR: The membership of Lodge Vaclav Snajdr No. 251 of the Czecho-slovak Societies of America, in regular meeting assembled, instructed us, below-signed officers, to petition you to recommend favorably the Lundeen unemploy-ment-insurance bill.

Our membership is very much pleased with your sympathetic feeling toward a proper economic security for the as yet forgotten men and women of this Republic of ours.

Respectfully yours,

FRANK MERTT, *President.*
LOUIS BEZNOSKA, *Secretary.*

BELMONT COUNTY EDUCATIONAL AND POLITICAL ASSOCIATION,
Bridgeport, Ohio, February 11, 1935.
Hon. MATTHEW A. DUNN,
Chairman House Labor Committee, Washington, D. C.

HONORABLE SIR: The membership of the Belmont County Educational and Political Association very kindly request you to report favorably the Lundeen unemployment-insurance bill.

Our membership recognizes in the Lundeen bill the only new deal for the forgotten man.

Thanking you in advance for said favor, I am, in behalf of our association,

Yours very truly,

FRANK LEDNIECKA.

Blaine, Ohio, February 11, 1935.
Hon. MATTHEW A. DUNN,
Chairman House Labor Committee,
House Office Building, Washington, D. C.

DEAR SIR: In behalf of Commune No. 50, Polish National Alliance, represent-ing 26 affiliated lodges in Belmont and Jefferson Counties, of the State of Ohio, I very kindly appeal to you to report favorably the Lundeen unemployment-insurance bill.

Very truly yours,

MIKE GRABECKI,
President Commune No. 60, Polish National Alliance.

OBDOR 56, SLOV. ROB. SPOLKU,
Braddock, Pa., February 12, 1935.
Mr. MATTHEW A. DUNN,
Chairman of House Labor Subcommittee,
Washington, D. C.

Resolution of Assembly 2056 of the I. S. W. Society of Braddock, Pa., repre-senting total number of 250 members, ask your full support of H. R. 2827, bill of social insurance.

Fraternally yours,

JOHN BODROG,
JOSEPH SOBEK,
ANDREW JACOBS,
JOHN VERBA,
GEORGE J. BUTCHA.

STATEMENT OF THE SOCIALIST PARTY OF AMERICA, ENDORSING H. R. 2827 FOR THE SUBCOMMITTEE OF THE HOUSE LABOR COMMITTEE, FEBRUARY 15, 1935

(Represented by Prof. Broadus Mitchell, professor of economics, Johns Hopkins University, and recent gubernatorial candidate of the Socialist Party in Mary-land; Dr. S. M. Neistadt, State secretary of the Socialist Party in Maryland; Frank N. Trager, secretary, labor committee, Socialist Party in Maryland)

The Socialist Party of America appears before this committee to offer its endorsement of H. R. 2827, the Workers' Unemployment, Old Age, and Social Insurance Act, known popularly as the "Lundeen bill." It endorses this bill in full awareness that other measures, presumably designed for the same general purpose, are currently before the Congress of the United States. The Socialist Party is firmly convinced that this is the best available bill for social insurance; and that in line with its historic policy, the party joins forces with those workers from 6 State federations of labor, 2,400 American Federation of Labor locals, 65 city labor councils, and most of the workers now organized in various nonpartisan unemployed groups who are suporting H. R. 2827.

At this point the Socialist Party of America is proud to recall its continuous struggle in behalf of enlightened social legislation which would directly benefit the great mass of American workers. Ever since the party was formally organized its declarations of principles registered restored is advocacy of such legislation in general and social insurance in particular. When the people of America elected Socialists to the Congress of the United States, among the first official acts of these elected Representatives were the introduction of bills providing for unemployment insurance and old-age pensions—this almost 25 years ago. There can be no doubt that the Socialist Party has long recognized and fought for a social order which would insure to all individuals the human requirements of security and stability.

The Socialist Party of America endorses H. R. 2827 for the following reasons:

(1) It sets up a single unified system of Federal compulsory social insurance, thereby avoiding the indubitable discriminations and disadvantages which would arise if such legislation should be left to the States.

(2) It is the only measure designed to extend benefits not on subsistence levels but rather on American living-standard levels to all workers who are now unemployed or who become unemployed throughout the whole period of involuntary unemployment, thereby recognizing society's obligations to those who are deprived through no fault of their own of adequate living conditions. The hazards and risks of unemployment, sickness, old age, and the like are derivative from the present conditions of our economic order. It therefore follows that the economic order itself shall provide for the security of its liabilities.

(3) It rightfully recognizes that both experience and theory no longer make it possible to achieve social security by means of actuarial insurance. It therefore provides for the cost of such insurance through the only just method, namely, taxation on incomes and inheritances; or in other words, taxation according to capacity to pay.

(4) It provides for the administration of such social insurance by the exigencies of modern economic society. In this connection the Socialist Party wishes to call to the attention of this committee that under section 2 of H. R. 2827 present phrasing and definition place almost unlimited authority in the Secretary of Labor, with potential direful results whenever such a member of the Cabinet chooses to be irresponsible with respect to his or her proper loyalties. The Socialist Party therefore recommends that this section be rewritten so as to provide for technical experts under the jurisdiction of representatives from labor.

These are the major reasons for the support of H. R. 2827. The Socialist Party is convinced that only through a bill embodying these principles and practices can something approximating social security be achieved for the great mass of employed and unemployed American workers.

The party wishes to record its unalterable opposition to the wholly inadequate and unsatisfactory provisions of the administration measure known as the "Wagner-Lewis bill", H. R. 4120. This bill makes a mockery of social insurance and is in fact thoroughly incapable of accomplishing its expressed aim. Its provisions exclude all those who are now unemployed and all those who work in establishments whose number of employees is less than four. It has been estimated that this administrational short-sightedness deliberately ignores some 50 to 54 percent of the working population of America except insofar as some few of those people may be eligible for the degraded wage levels under an insufficient works-relief program. In addition, the Wagner-Lewis bill estimates that for those whom it might cover security is equivalent to a subsistence level on an average of somewhere between seven and twelve dollars a week and, what is more, this insufficient amount for a minority of the working population will be available only for a limited period of involuntary unemployment. The maximum duration of weekly benefits under the Wagner-Lewis bill falls short of the difference between the actual average number of work weeks and the full year. In other words, minimum or inadequate code wages for a period between 25 and 30 weeks a year, a subsistence pittance for some 15 to 18 weeks after that, and potential charity lists for the balance of the year—this is to be the lot of American workers, a minority of whom will be covered by the provisions of the Wagner-Lewis bill for social security.   The irony of the situation is further deepened when it is recalled that the Wagner-Lewis bill will permit States to set up individual State provisions.   Surely the experience of the Federal Emergency Relief Administration with State policies for average monthly relief showing disparities between $9 and $10 per family per month is a sufficient indication of the futility and unwisdom of leaving the principles of social-insurance legislation to the States.

To the imperfections in coverage and amounts and duration of benefits, to the inevitable State inequalities, the Wagner-Lewis bill adds this further injustice to its caricature of social security; namely, it imposes the cost of such insurance on those who have already borne not only the blight of unemployment but also depreciation in wage levels.   For the fiscal policy of the Wagner-Lewis bill, a 3-percent pay-roll tax will not be a charge against industry and industrial profit but will be passed on to the worker and farmer consumer in the form of increased prices.   A pay-roll tax becomes in effect the most vicious form of taxation, a sales tax.

Thus far the Socialist Party has registered its main objections to the Wagner-Lewis bill in terms of the unemployment-insurance provisions.   With respect to old age the party declares that the age limits are too high, the amount of benefits too low, and the same general objections to the fiscal policy apply.   The public-health and maternity provisions are insignificantly writing into Federal law what most of the enlightened States have already practiced.   There is a sickening absence of national leadership in rounding out a full program for adequate social insurance.

The Socialist Party of America appreciates the opportunity to lay before this committee this general statement.   It wishes to compliment the committee for its independence and courage in holding these hearings.   If the representatives of millions of workers and farmers who have here registered their opinion as favoring H. R. 2827 find that they and their constituents are ignored by the passage of that delusion about security called "H. R. 4120", known as the "Wagner-Lewis or administration" bill, then these workers shall have the opportunity in the not-distant future of electing representatives of their own choosing from and for the working class and the farmers to fight for what they want.

[Telegrams]

MARCH 12, 1935.

CLARENCE SENIOR,
    Socialist Party, National Headquarters, Chicago, Ill.:

Committee on Labor has received for inclusion in hearings on workers' bill, H. R. 2827, statement of endorsement of the bill by the Socialist Party of America, represented by Broadus Mitchell and Neistadt and Trager of Maryland.   Kindly telegraph and confirm by mail for inclusion in record party's official confirmation of this endorsement through these representatives.

ERNEST LUNDEEN, *M. C.*

CHICAGO, ILL.,
March 12, 1935.

ERNEST LUNDEEN, M. C.,
    Washington, D. C.:

Socialist Party national organization committee which was empowered to act endorsed your bill with qualifications incorporated in statement presented, and Mitchell, Trager, Neistadt authorized to represent party at hearings.   Meeting took place mayor's office Milwaukee, February 11.

CLARENCE SENIOR, *Executive Secretary,*
    Socialist Party, United States of America.

STATEMENT OF THE YOUNG PEOPLE'S SOCIALIST LEAGUE ON THE LUNDEEN BILL

The Young People's Socialist League of America has always upheld the principle of social security. It believes that never before has the need for a comprehensive program of social security been so urgent as at present. It is convinced that no such program can be considered either complete or adequate without provision being made for a system of unemployment insurance. The Young People's Socialist League believes that the above ideas are generally accepted in principle by the great majority of American people. Their elected representatives in Congress also profess to accept in principle unemployment insurance. But between acceptance in principle and acceptance in actuality there stretches a vast gulf. It is just such a difference which distinguishes H. R. 2827, popularly known as the Lundeen bill, from all other measures now before the United States Congress, the professed purposes of which are also the establishment of a system of social insurance.

The Lundeen bill, by establishing a unified system of Federal compulsory social insurance, avoids the chaos which would be the inevitable result of leaving such legislation in the hands of the separate States.

The Lundeen bill alone recognizes the necessity of extending benefits not on mere subsistence levels, but rather in accordance with prevailing wages with a fixed minimum.

The Lundeen bill correctly provides for the administration and control of unemployment insurance and the adjustment of minimum compensation through commissions directly elected by members of workers' and farmers' organizations. It is, however, the hope of the Young People's Socialist League that the present phrasing with regard to the administration of the measure may be amended to avoid the placing of practically unlimited authority in the hands of the Secretary of Labor. We should recommend the amendment of this section to provide for technical experts under the jurisdiction of labor organizations.

As an organization of the working class the Young People's Socialist League finds grounds for its support of H. R. 2827 in the fact that this bill provides that the cost of such insurance as it establishes shall be met through taxation on incomes and inheritances. That is, through taxation levied in accordance with ability to pay.

As an organization of and for youth the Young People's Socialist League finds its greatest grounds for support of the Lundeen bill in the fact that according to the most conservative of estimates there are 3,500,000 American young people under 21 alone who are unemployed. Since the present economic order has deprived the great majority of these young people of every opportunity to secure employment, since the great majority of them have never been gainfully employed, it is obvious that any system of social insurance based upon strict actuarial principles, such as the Wagner-Lewis bill, H. R. 4120, would utterly fail to provide any relief whatsoever for this great group.

It is particularly in the interests of the great mass of unemployed youth in America that the Young People's Socialist League expresses its uncompromising opposition to the Wagner-Lewis bill, the financial set up of which, in addition to placing a tax not upon profits but upon pay rolls, provides only mere subsistence benefits for a strictly limited period of time, and fails completely to make any provision for those who have never been gainfully employed. In this manner it fails to recognize society's obligation to a large group of citizens who find themselves suffering from economic distress which has its origin not in any failure or fault of theirs, but which is a direct derivative of the present economic and social order.

The Young People's Socialist League considers H. R. 2827 to be the only measure now before the United States Congress which accepts and provides for a system of unemployment insurance in fact as well as in principle. It regards H. R. 2827 as the only measure which will at all adequately meet the needs of the American young people, which recognizes their numbers, and their distress. Thus, in accordance with its principles and aims, the Young People's Socialist League heartily endorses H. R. 2827, recommends its earnest support by all who seek to ameliorate the present wide-spread distress, and urges its enactment.

INDEX

O